Guide to
First Edition Prices
2004/5

Also Edited by R.B. Russell

Aklo: A Volume of the Fantastic
(with Mark Valentine and Roger Dobson)

Tartarus Press Guide to First Edition Prices, 2002/3

Tartarus Press Guide to First Edition Prices, 2000/1

Tartarus Press Guide to First Edition Prices, 1998/9

Tartarus Press Guide to First Edition Prices, 1997

The Secret of the Sangraal and Other Writings by Arthur Machen

Tales From Tartarus: Collected Stories
(with Rosalie Parker)

Ritual and Other Stories by Arthur Machen

Translation

Le Grand Meaulnes by Alain-Fournier

Guide to
First Edition
Prices
2004/5

Edited by
R.B. Russell

Tartarus Press

Guide to First Edition Prices, 2004/5, edited by R.B. Russell
Published by The Tartarus Press, November 2003, at:
Coverley House, Carlton, Leyburn, North Yorkshire, DL8 4AY. UK.
Book printed and bound by the Bath Press.

ISBN 1 872621 78 3

Wherever possible each value in this *Guide* has been checked against copies of the book offered for sale in the last year. The greatest care has been taken to ensure that the information included in the guide is accurate, but the editor cannot be held accountable for any losses that may occur as a result of the information contained herein. The prices represent the perceived average prices as contained in advertisements of bookdealers, prices paid at auction for books, and with reference to reputable guides credited in Appendix II.

Introduction ... v
Index of authors ... x

Guide to First Edition Prices ... 1

Appendices:
I. Single Title Entries ... 491
II. References and Individual Author Bibliographies ... 496
III. Pseudonyms ... 512
IV. 100 Classic First Editions of the Twentieth Century ... 514
V. The Nobel Prize for Literature ... 515
VI. The Booker Prize ... 516
VII. The Pulitzer Prize ... 516

INTRODUCTION

This is the fifth edition of the Tartarus Press *Guide to First Edition Prices*. Once again, it has been completely revised and updated, and now contains suggested values for more than 33,000 sought-after books by over 600 authors. Wherever possible, author entries include a complete bibliography of their works.

What is a First Edition?

The term 'First Edition' is usually applied to the first ever appearance in print of a particular work in book format. A First Edition is valuable to collectors because it is the form in which the work was first published, despite the fact that later editions of the work may have been corrected, expanded, illustrated, or by other means improved upon.

The value of a First Edition will be determined primarily by the law of supply and demand: in other words, by how many collectors are interested in obtaining a copy, compared with the numbers of copies in existence.

In general, this *Guide* gives a suggested retail value for collectable books in their first British and American editions. Books are not always published simultaneously on both sides of the Atlantic and wherever possible the edition which enjoys chronological precedence is listed first. However, the 'follow the flag' principle means that even though a book has been published after an edition in another country, its desirability is not necessarily reduced: collectors will often favour the First Edition published in their own country, or be guided by the nationality of the author. Really serious collectors will, of course, seek both editions!

Identifying a First Edition

Not all First Editions identify themselves as such. The most obvious sign that a book is not a First Edition is a note, usually on the copyright page, alluding to previous editions or printings. Simple detective work can identify reprints: if the book or its dust wrapper contains a list of works by the same author that post-date the first publication of the book, then it must be a later edition. Quite often, the reproduction of reviews of the book suggests that it is a later edition. One must be careful to verify, though, that the book has its original wrapper.

It is also vital to check that the publisher of the book is the same as the one stated in this *Guide*: reprints undertaken by book clubs quite regularly omit previous publication histories and may look like First Editions to the over-eager collector.

For books published before 1900, the most common means of identification is the date printed on the title page. In the years between 1850-1900 this date will typically be found on the back of the title page along with copyright information. After 1900, publishers did not necessarily date books, although many identified First Editions as such on the copyright page. The various other terms discussed elsewhere in this introduction may also be used: First 'Edition', 'Printing', 'Impression' etc.

In more recent years, many publishers have taken to printing a row of numbers on the copyright page. Even if the book claims to be a First Edition, the important thing to look for is the lowest value number present in this row. It is usually the case that the lowest number given is the number of the printing, so the presence of such rows as '1 2 3 4 5 6 7 8 9 10', '10 9 8 7 6 5 4 3 2 1' or '1 3 5 7 9 10 8 6 4 2' denote a First Edition because the number '1' is present. If, for example, the row is printed '2 3 4 5 6 7 8 9 10', then the book is likely to be a second edition.

The methods discussed above should help you to ascertain whether most books are First Editions or not, but for some books the collector will need to refer to points identified by individual bibliographers, such as the exact binding style, the colouring of the edges of the pages, or some typographical point. In this *Guide* we give, wherever possible, an indication of such points, but please remember that this is only a brief guide. Limitations of space make it impossible to comment adequately on the complexities of different 'states', variant bindings, etc. If you are in any doubt, and especially if you are about to make an expensive purchase, please consult an author-specific bibliography, which may give much more detailed information. We include as an appendix to this volume a list of published bibliographies which often give more detailed information. If in doubt, ask a reputable book-dealer for help in tracking them down.

Values

A rare book will have little value if it is not sought by collectors, and conversely, a book printed in a run of several thousands can still be worth a great deal if there are more collectors eager to acquire a copy than there are copies available. There will always be exceptions, of course, but the fact that a famous author's piece of embarrassing juvenilia may be worth a great deal more than their classic works of more mature years is usually because their first efforts were printed in small runs, i.e. in editions of only a few hundreds or thousands. It is a fact of life that publishers have always been less willing to invest heavily in a young, unknown first-time author than a proven literary heavy-weight. And true collectors will want to own a copy of every book by an author, regardless of literary merit.

Just as important for the value of any book is the condition in which it has survived. Even the smallest of faults can affect the value of an otherwise collectable book. If you are not able to inspect the book yourself before you purchase it; if, for example, you are buying the book by mail order from a printed catalogue or Internet listing; then you will need to pay careful attention to the dealer's description of its condition.

This *Guide* represents the prices that a book dealer might charge a collector, and not the price at which the dealer would necessarily buy books for his or her own stock. My own experience is that a dealer will offer the vendor a quarter of the re-sale value of an ordinary book. For a large number of less desirable titles, the offer will be considerably lower. However, a very collectable and expensive book might command a price much closer to its eventual re-sale value. When offering a book for sale, you should remember that there is nothing wrong with a dealer attempting to make an honest profit. Most dealers choose their profession out of a love of books, but they would not be there to sell you books if they could not make a living out of it. A private sale to another collector would, of course, expect to realise an amount more akin to the full retail value of the book.

The rate of appreciation in the value of collectable First Editions is impossible to predict, but it would be wise to remember that copies in poor condition, acquired for little, will almost always have a similarly low re-sale value. If you can afford it, it is always a better investment to buy a fine copy. John Ruskin (1819-1900), in the following excerpt, was writing about wine, but the advice it contains also applies to book collecting:
'It is unwise to pay too much, but it's worse to pay too little. When you pay too much, you lose a little money—that's all. When you pay too little you sometimes lose everything, because the thing you bought is incapable of doing the thing it was bought to do. The common law of business balance prohibits paying a little and getting a lot—it can't be done. If you deal with the lowest bidder, it is well to add something for the risk you run. And if you do that, you will have enough to pay for something better.'

Advertisements for investment opportunities always carry the caveat (usually in smaller print than this) that prices may go down as well as up. Books, along with much else in life, go in and out of fashion. A well-received film of a book, or media hype of a title can cause the price to soar, but it will always be more risky to buy at the top end of the market. It has been noted, however, that the values of books that go out of fashion rarely drop too much, as the collector or dealer who has paid a high price for a book will probably keep it on their shelf indefinitely rather than sell it at a loss.

Recent Trends in Book Values

The prices asked for First Editions seem to have risen inexorably over the last few years, and the advent of the Internet appears to have only increased the trend. The world of book collecting has changed significantly from the days when most book collectors relied on browsing the shelves of any bookshops they had access to, and waiting for catalogues to arrive through the post. Serious collectors will still keep up a correspondence with dealers and those offering booksearch services, but in the last few years millions of books have suddenly become available to anyone who can switch on and operate a personal computer with access to the Internet. There are a number of Internet websites where you can search the stock of thousands of book dealers and be offered a hitherto unimagined range of titles. And those book dealers who advertise their stock on the Internet now find they have many hundreds of thousands of potential new customers.

The result is that both the supply and the demand sides of the value equation have grown, and the laws of basic economics have gradually come into play. The result for the most common books is that the values have been levelled downwards. However, for the middle rank of books, there is no reason why a small provincial dealer with a limited number of customers should not now ask as much as a well-known specialist dealer with access to the wealthiest collectors. In theory, the Internet gives all dealers access to all collectors.

The most significant increases, though, have been at the top end of the market. Those 'blue chip', famous books by well-known authors that have always been highly sought-after have increased in value many times over in the last few years. Some very rare books that collectors will probably have never seen in a lifetime of searching are now becoming available. And when a dealer has found a rare book in hitherto unknown fine condition, some mind-boggling prices are being asked for it.

There are a few bargains to be found on the Internet, but not many. There is no longer any reason why a bookseller should be ignorant of a book's value, and should not charge accordingly. And if a gem has been offered at a ludicrously low price there are plenty of people who will pounce on it. Those bargains that it is possible to find are among the little-known, speciality and genre books, but you need the specific knowledge to find them.

Condition
The condition of a book can cause widely-varying prices to be asked. Simply put, collectors prefer to have their books in a state as close as possible to when they were first published. Any signs of wear or damage, such as bumps to the corners or creasing to the spine from opening the book roughly or too often will decrease its value. Inscriptions by previous owners, notes in margins, bookplates, etc, will also seriously affect the value of a book, unless the author or some famous person made them. And even then a mint copy of a fragile book may have more value than a scruffy copy inscribed by the author.

The level of wear or damage that can be tolerated will depend upon the age and/or scarcity of the book, but, in general, minor defects such as ripped pages will devalue the book to some extent. Major defects, such as missing pages, will render most books worthless.

Remainder marks, even the most discreet ones, indicating discounting by the publisher when the book was first for sale, will also have an effect on the value. Some publishers, such as Random House, will stamp their logo on books that they are disposing of through remainder outlets, but others may simply put a small line or dot in pen on the underside of the book. The book may be a First Edition, and the mark very small, but some collectors will still reject it out of hand.

The importance of the dust wrapper cannot be over-emphasised, as the most extreme variations in the price of modern First Editions occur between books offered with dust wrappers in varying states of preservation. For some books, dust wrappers almost never survive in a mint state, so when they do a premium can be asked by a dealer. It may be hard to believe, but small nicks or creases in dust wrappers can halve the value of some books. Even an otherwise perfectly-preserved wrapper is devalued if an owner or purchaser has clipped the price from the front flap. So take care of your books and treat them kindly!

Terminology
The term 'First Printing' is often synonymous with 'First Edition', though it is a description employed more by publishers than book collectors or dealers. It refers specifically to the printing of the pages, some of which may have been bound at a later date (a later 'issue'), and therefore does not constitute the first form in which the book was published. Other terms must also be considered with care, for if a book was reprinted from the original printers' plates without alterations being made to the text then this will not technically constitute a new edition. This is a new 'impression' which will still generally be less desirable than the first. Different 'states' refer to various alterations made to the book by the publisher, and over the years collectors and dealers have gauged which 'variants' are considered the more or less desirable.

Other publishing and collecting terms can mislead the unwary. 'First published edition', for example, implies that the work may have been printed previously for a restricted circulation, although it can be assumed that it was probably never offered for sale to the public at large. 'First separate edition' usually implies that the material in the book had been previously published, albeit with other matter. 'First thus' is a term that should be treated with great caution as it usually denotes a reprint, although it will be the first time that the material has been presented in that particular format.

Books that may have appeared in print *before* the publication of the First Edition include 'copyright editions', produced in the 19th and early 20th centuries. These were typically bound up in small numbers, of which only one copy might have been sold so as to establish copyright. If the author is collectable, these copyright editions can be very valuable indeed. Even today, books can appear in various forms before publication, usually as 'proof' copies, and more recently as 'Advance Reading Copies' for publicity purposes. While these may have some value they are not considered true First Editions. The practice of some modern publishers in issuing signed, numbered proof or advance copies does seem an unnecessary affectation to this collector!

Reprints

Not all of the collectable books listed in this *Guide* are First Editions. It may be the case that the First Edition is so rare and expensive that realistic collectors are happy to pay for a later edition, especially if it is similar to the first. Some reprints may contain important new matter not included in the First Edition, and the value of such reprints is once again determined primarily by supply and demand.

The *Guide* also lists 'special editions' of books. These take a variety of forms and are often published in limited numbers, with something extra to appeal to the collector, such as fine quality paper or bindings, the author's signature or even the addition of further material that does not appear in the ordinary 'trade' edition. Although the limited nature of such editions may add to their value, it must be remembered that they are usually recognised as something special by even the most disinterested of owners and may therefore survive in greater numbers than the dowdier, ordinary edition.

How to use this *Guide*

Entries are listed alphabetically by author, then chronologically by publication, within subject classifications such as 'Fiction' and 'Non Fiction.' Where two values are given for a book the first is for an example with a dust wrapper (d/w) and the second for a copy without. If only one price is quoted, it is for a book without a dust wrapper. The term 'wraps' denotes paper covers, usually a paperback: these are not usually produced with a dust wrapper, though there are exceptions.

All books valued in the *Guide* are assumed to be in very good condition for their age. Books published before 1920 are given a single value because the survival of dust wrappers earlier than this date is so rare. If an early wrapper does survive, then it is almost impossible to gauge the value this will add to the book. Books are expected to be in their original bindings, although those published before 1800 are valued assuming that they will have been rebound in the 19th century (a common practice): original bindings will greatly increase their value, whereas recent re-binding will decrease the value enormously.

The known limitation of a First Edition is noted simply as *x* copies. If a book is 'signed', it is assumed that it was the author who did the signing, unless specified otherwise. If a book was re-issued later under a new title, then it is listed under the original title but noted thus:

ditto, as **Starship**, Criterion (U.S.), 1959 . £70/£20

If a book was issued pseudonymously then a note follows the date, i.e. '(pseud. 'Fred Smith')'. A list of authors' pseudonyms is printed in Appendix III to this volume.

Any information provided in the *Guide* listing that does not appear in the book is given in square brackets: [Such as the date of publication].

Acknowledgements

I am grateful to the many people who have helped me to compile this *Guide*, but as editor I must assume all responsibility for any errors which, inevitably, may have crept in. I welcome any suggestions, corrections, etc. at the publisher's address. A criticism of previous editions of the *Guide* has been the omission of certain authors.

We will never be able to do justice to every collectable author, but a number of new entries suggested by dealers and collectors are again included in this edition. As ever, suggestions for new entries for future editions of the *Guide* are welcomed.

No one can learn the tricks of the book trade overnight. This *Guide* does not explain how to become a book dealer, or how to get one step ahead of the trade. It is unlikely that it will help anyone make their fortune, and no one person can be an expert on all of the titles listed here. It is simply a 'guide', and we hope that it is of use to collectors and dealers alike.

I have only been able to compile this *Guide*, however, thanks to the countless book dealers who have advertised books for sale over the last few years, and the bibliographers who have hunted down and published their research. I would like to acknowledge the specific help of A. Osinga and Rosalie Parker in the preparation of this edition, and also the following: John Abrahamson, Donn Albright, Douglas Anderson, The Margery Allingham Society, Mike Ashley, Phil Baker, Mike Berro, Karen Busby, Dr Glen Cavaliero, Shelley Cox, Clarissa Cridland, Richard Dalby, David Downes, Nicholas Granger-Taylor, Norman Gates, Michael Gauntlett, James Goddard, Clive Harper, Hunter Hayes, Malcolm Henderson, Susan Hill, Richard Humphries, Lawrence Knapp, Rick Loomis, Edward Mendelson, Gary Morris & the Compton-Burnett Cabal, CeCe Motz, Timothy Parker Russell, Barry Pike, Ryan Roberts, Colin Smythe, Colin Scott-Sutherland, Ed Seiler, David Tibbetts, David Tibet and Mark Valentine.

INDEX OF AUTHORS

ANTHONY ABBOT
PETER ABRAHAMS
J.R. ACKERLEY
PETER ACKROYD
DOUGLAS ADAMS
RICHARD ADAMS
CHAS ADDAMS
JAMES AGEE
ROBERT AICKMAN
CONRAD AIKEN
JOAN AIKEN
ALAIN-FOURNIER
ALASTAIR
CECIL ALDIN
RICHARD
  ALDINGTON
BRIAN ALDISS
MARGERY
  ALLINGHAM
ERIC AMBLER
KINGSLEY AMIS
MARTIN AMIS
SHERWOOD
  ANDERSON
MAYA ANGELOU
EDWARD ARDIZZONE
MICHAEL ARLEN
DAISY ASHFORD
ISAAC ASIMOV
MABEL LUCIE
  ATTWELL
MARGARET ATWOOD
W.H. AUDEN
JANE AUSTEN
REV. W. AWDRY
CHRISTOPHER
  AWDRY
ALAN AYCKBOURN
H.C. BAILEY
BERYL BAINBRIDGE
R.M. BALLANTYNE
J. G. BALLARD
IAIN BANKS
HELEN BANNERMAN
JOHN BANVILLE
CLIVE BARKER
PAT BARKER
ROBERT BARNARD
DJUNA BARNES
JULIAN BARNES
J.M. BARRIE
H.E. BATES
L. FRANK BAUM
'BB'
THE BEANO
AUBREY BEARDSLEY
SAMUEL BECKETT
FRANCIS BEEDING
MAX BEERBOHM

BRENDAN BEHAN
HILAIRE BELLOC
SAUL BELLOW
LUDWIG
  BEMELMANS
ALAN BENNETT
ARNOLD BENNETT
E.F. BENSON
E.C. BENTLEY
LORD BERNERS
JOHN BETJEMAN
ALGERNON
  BLACKWOOD
NICHOLAS BLAKE see
  C. Day Lewis
KAREN BLIXEN see
  Isaac Dinesen
ROBERT BLOCH
EDMUND BLUNDEN
ENID BLYTON
LUCY M. BOSTON
ELIZABETH BOWEN
PAUL BOWLES
WILLIAM BOYD
KAY BOYLE
MALCOLM
  BRADBURY
RAY BRADBURY
JOHN BRAINE
ERNEST BRAMAH
ANGELA BRAZIL
ELINOR BRENT-DYER
ANNE BRONTË
CHARLOTTE BRONTË
EMILY BRONTË
JOCELYN BROOKE
RUPERT BROOKE
ANITA BROOKNER
FREDRIC BROWN
JEAN de BRUNHOFF
JOHN BUCHAN
ANTHONY
  BUCKERIDGE
ANTHONY BURGESS
JAMES LEE BURKE
W.J. BURLEY
FRANCES HODGSON
  BURNETT
ROBERT BURNS
EDGAR RICE
  BURROUGHS
WILLIAM S.
  BURROUGHS
ROBERT BURTON
A.S. BYATT
RANDOLPH
  CALDECOTT
ALBERT CAMUS
TRUMAN CAPOTE
PETER CAREY
CAROL CARNAC see
  E C.R Lorac
JOHN DICKSON CARR

LEWIS CARROLL
ANGELA CARTER
RAYMOND CARVER
JOYCE CARY
WILLA CATHER
RAYMOND
  CHANDLER
LESLIE CHARTERIS
BRUCE CHATWIN
GEOFFREY CHAUCER
JOHN CHEEVER
G.K. CHESTERTON
PETER CHEYNEY
AGATHA CHRISTIE
TOM CLANCY
JOHN CLARE
ARTHUR C. CLARKE
HARRY CLARKE
WILLIAM COBBETT
LIZA CODY
JOHN COLLIER
WILKIE COLLINS
IVY COMPTON-
  BURNETT
CYRIL CONNOLLY
JOSEPH CONRAD
A.E. COPPARD
BERNARD
  CORNWELL
PATRICIA CORNWELL
HUBERT
  CRACKANTHORPE
WALTER CRANE
JOHN CREASEY
MICHAEL CRICHTON
EDMUND CRISPIN
FREEMAN WILLS
  CROFTS
RICHMAL CROMPTON
HARRY CROSBY
ALEISTER CROWLEY
E.E. CUMMINGS
ROALD DAHL
THE DANDY
LINDSEY DAVIS
C. DAY LEWIS
LOUIS DE BERNIERES
DANIEL DEFOE
LEN DEIGHTON
WALTER DE LA MARE
MAURICE AND
  EDWARD DETMOLD
COLIN DEXTER
MICHAEL DIBDIN
PHILIP K. DICK
CHARLES DICKENS
ISAK DINESEN
BENJAMIN DISRAELI
J.P. DONLEAVY
LORD ALFRED
  DOUGLAS
NORMAN DOUGLAS
ERNEST DOWSON

SIR ARTHUR CONAN
  DOYLE
RODDY DOYLE
MARGARET
  DRABBLE
THEODORE DREISER
EDMUND DULAC
DAPHNE DU
  MAURIER
GEORGE DU
  MAURIER
DOUGLAS DUNN
LORD DUNSANY
FRANCIS DURBRIDGE
GERALD DURRELL
LAWRENCE DURRELL
UMBERTO ECO
BERESFORD EGAN
GEORGE ELIOT
T.S. ELIOT
ALICE THOMAS ELLIS
BRET EASTON ELLIS
JOHN MEADE
  FALKNER
G.E. FARROW
WILLIAM FAULKNER
SEBASTIAN FAULKS
HENRY FIELDING
RONALD FIRBANK
F. SCOTT
  FITZGERALD
PENELOPE
  FITZGERALD
JAMES ELROY
  FLECKER
IAN FLEMING
W. RUSSELL FLINT
FORD MADDOX FORD
C.S. FORESTER
E.M. FORSTER
FREDERICK FORSYTH
DION FORTUNE
JOHN FOWLES
DICK FRANCIS
GEORGE
  MACDONALD
  FRASER
R. AUSTIN FREEMAN
ROBERT FROST
GABRIEL GARCÍA
  MÁRQUEZ
ALAN GARNER
DAVID GARNETT
EVE GARNETT
JONATHAN GASH
ELIZABETH GASKELL
LEWIS GRASSIC
  GIBBON
STELLA GIBBONS
GILES' ANNUALS
WARWICK GOBLE
SIR WILLIAM
  GOLDING

SUE GRAFTON
KENNETH GRAHAME
ROBERT GRAVES
ALASDAIR GRAY
HENRY GREEN
KATE GREENAWAY
GRAHAM GREENE
JOHN GRISHAM
GEORGE and WEEDON
  GROSSMITH
THOM GUNN
H. RIDER HAGGARD
KATHLEEN HALE
RADCLYFFE HALL
PATRICK HAMILTON
DASHIELL HAMMETT
THOMAS HARDY
CYRIL HARE
ROBERT HARRIS
THOMAS HARRIS
L.P. HARTLEY
NATHANIEL
  HAWTHORNE
SEAMUS HEANEY
ROBERT A. HEINLEIN
JOSEPH HELLER
ERNEST HEMINGWAY
G.A. HENTY
JAMES HERBERT
EDWARD HERON-
  ALLEN
HERMANN HESSE
PATRICIA HIGHSMITH
REGINALD HILL
WILLIAM HOPE
  HODGSON
NICK HORNBY
GEOFFREY
  HOUSEHOLD
A.E. HOUSMAN
ELIZABETH JANE
  HOWARD
ROBERT E. HOWARD
L. RON HUBBARD
RICHARD HUGHES
TED HUGHES
ALDOUS HUXLEY
J. K. HUYSMANS
HAMMOND INNES
MICHAEL INNES
CHRISTOPHER
  ISHERWOOD
KAZUO ISHIGURO
HENRY JAMES
M.R. JAMES
P.D. JAMES
RICHARD JEFFERIES
JEROME K. JEROME
RUTH PRAWER
  JHABVALA
CAPTAIN W.E. JOHNS
B.S. JOHNSON
JAMES JOYCE

FRANZ KAFKA
ERICH KÄSTNER
JOHN KEATS
THOMAS KENEALLY
JACK KEROUAC
KEN KESEY
KEYNOTES
FRANCIS KILVERT
C. DALY KING
STEPHEN KING
RUDYARD KIPLING
C.H.B. KITCHIN
ARTHUR KOESTLER
DEAN KOONTZ
PHILIP LARKIN
D.H. LAWRENCE
T.E. LAWRENCE
EDWARD LEAR
JOHN LE CARRÉ
HARPER LEE
LAURIE LEE
J. SHERIDAN LE FANU
RICHARD LE
  GALLIENNE
URSULA LE GUIN
ROSAMOND
  LEHMANN
ELMORE LEONARD
GASTON LEROUX
DORIS LESSING
C.S. LEWIS
NORMAN LEWIS
WYNDHAM LEWIS
DAVID LINDSAY
DAVID LODGE
JACK LONDON
E.C.R. LORAC
H.P. LOVECRAFT
PETER LOVESEY
MALCOLM LOWRY
ROSE MACAULAY
GEORGE
  MACDONALD
PHILIP MACDONALD
ROSS MACDONALD
IAN McEWAN
JOHN McGAHERN
ARTHUR MACHEN
COLIN MACINNES
ALISTAIR MACLEAN
LOUIS MACNEICE
NORMAN MAILER
THOMAS MANN
KATHERINE
  MANSFIELD
GABRIEL GARCÍA
  MÁRQUEZ *see under*
  García Márquez
CAPTAIN FREDERICK
  MARRYAT
NGAIO MARSH
W. SOMERSET
  MAUGHAM

ABRAHAM MERRITT
ARTHUR MILLER
HENRY MILLER
A.A. MILNE
GLADYS MITCHELL
MARGARET
  MITCHELL
NAOMI MITCHISON
MARY RUSSELL
  MITFORD
NANCY MITFORD
NICHOLAS
  MONSARRAT
MICHAEL
  MOORCOCK
BRIAN MOORE
WILLIAM MORRIS
TONI MORRISON
JOHN MORTIMER
IRIS MURDOCH
VLADIMIR NABOKOV
SHIVA NAIPAUL
V.S. NAIPAUL
VIOLET NEEDHAM
KAY NIELSEN
PATRICK O'BRIAN
EDNA O'BRIEN
FLANN O'BRIEN
LIAM O'FLAHERTY
JOHN O'HARA
EUGENE O'NEILL
JOE ORTON
GEORGE ORWELL
JOHN OSBORNE
WILFRED OWEN
DOROTHY PARKER
THOMAS LOVE
  PEACOCK
MERVYN PEAKE
ELLIS PETERS
HAROLD PINTER
SYLVIA PLATH
EDGAR ALLAN POE
WILLY POGÁNY
BEATRIX POTTER
EZRA POUND
ANTHONY POWELL
JOHN COWPER
  POWYS
LLEWELYN POWYS
T.F. POWYS
TERRY PRATCHETT
ANTHONY PRICE
J.B. PRIESTLEY
V. S. PRITCHETT
MARCEL PROUST
PHILIP PULLMAN
BARBARA PYM
ELLERY QUEEN
JONATHAN RABAN
ARTHUR RACKHAM
ANN RADCLIFFE
IAN RANKIN

ARTHUR RANSOME
FORREST REID
RUTH RENDELL
JEAN RHYS
ANNE RICE
FRANK RICHARDS
W. HEATH ROBINSON
SAX ROHMER
FREDERICK ROLFE
  (BARON CORVO)
J.K. ROWLING
RUPERT *see Mary*
  Tourtel
SALMAN RUSHDIE
VITA SACKVILLE-
  WEST
SAKI
J.D. SALINGER
SAPPER
SARBAN
SIEGFRIED SASSOON
HILARY SAUNDERS
  see Francis Beeding
THE SAVOY
DOROTHY L. SAYERS
JACK SCHAEFER
PAUL SCOTT
ANNA SEWELL
TOM SHARPE
GEORGE BERNARD
  SHAW
MARY SHELLEY
M.P. SHIEL
NEVIL SHUTE
ALAN SILLITOE
GEORGES SIMENON
EDITH SITWELL
OSBERT SITWELL
SACHEVERELL
  SITWELL
CLARK ASHTON
  SMITH
STEVIE SMITH
C.P. SNOW
ALEXANDER
  SOLZHENITSYN
MURIEL SPARK
STEPHEN SPENDER
MICKEY SPILLANE
GERTRUDE STEIN
JOHN STEINBECK
COUNT ERIC
  STENBOCK
LAURENCE STERNE
ROBERT LOUIS
  STEVENSON
BRAM STOKER
TOM STOPPARD
DAVID STOREY
GILES LYTTON
  STRACHEY
MONTAGUE
  SUMMERS

R.S. SURTEES
GRAHAM SWIFT
A.J.A. SYMONS
JULIAN SYMONS
JOSEPHINE TEY
W.M. THACKERAY
PAUL THEROUX
DYLAN THOMAS
EDWARD THOMAS
FLORA THOMPSON
HENRY THOREAU
COLIN THUBRON
JAMES THURBER
WILLIAM M. TIMLIN
J. R. R. TOLKIEN
MARY TOURTEL
WILLIAM TREVOR
ANTHONY TROLLOPE
MARK TWAIN
BARRY UNSWORTH
JOHN UPDIKE
FLORENCE UPTON
ALISON UTTLEY
LAURENS VAN DER
  POST
JULES VERNE
GORE VIDAL
KURT VONNEGUT
LOUIS WAIN
ALFRED
  WAINWRIGHT
A.E. WAITE
ALICE WALKER
EDGAR WALLACE
HORACE WALPOLE
HUGH WALPOLE
MINETTE WALTERS
REX WARNER
SYLVIA TOWNSEND
  WARNER
EVELYN WAUGH
MARY WEBB
DENTON WELCH
FAY WELDON
H.G. WELLS
PATRICIA
  WENTWORTH
MARY WESLEY
REBECCA WEST
EDITH WHARTON
DENNIS WHEATLEY
E.B. WHITE
ETHEL LINA WHITE
PATRICK WHITE
T.H. WHITE
WALT WHITMAN
OSCAR WILDE
CHARLES WILLIAMS
TENNESSEE
  WILLIAMS
HENRY WILLIAMSON
A.N. WILSON
ANGUS WILSON

R.D. WINGFIELD
JEANETTE
  WINTERSON
WISDEN
CRICKETERS'
  ALMANACKS
P.G. WODEHOUSE
TOM WOLFE
VIRGINIA WOOLF
CORNELL WOOLRICH
S. FOWLER WRIGHT
JOHN WYNDHAM
WILLIAM BUTLER
  YEATS
THE YELLOW BOOK

APPENDIX I
EDWARD ABBEY
CHINUA ACHEBE
W. HARRISON
  AINSWORTH
EDWARD ALBEE
LOUISA MAY ALCOTT
NELSON ALGREN
JAMES BALDWIN
RICHARD HARRIS
  BARHAM
STAN BARSTOW
WILLIAM BECKFORD
THOMAS BEWICK
R.D. BLACKMORE
WILLIAM BLAKE
ROLF BOLDREWOOD
GEORGE BORROW
JAMES BOSWELL
E.R. BRAITHWAITE
RICHARD
  BRAUTIGAN
PEARL BUCK
JOHN BUNYAN
W.R. BURNETT
FANNY BURNEY
SAMUEL BUTLER
JAMES M. CAIN
ERSKINE CALDWELL
LOUIS-FERDINAND
  CÉLINE
ERSKINE CHILDERS
SAMUEL TAYLOR
  COLERIDGE
RICHARD CONDON
WILLIAM CONGREVE
PAT CONROY
STEPHEN CRANE
W.H. DAVIES
THOMAS DE
  QUINCEY
JOHN DOS PASSOS
CHARLES M.
  DOUGHTY
RALPH ELLISON

EDWARD
  FITZGERALD
JOHN GAY
OLIVER GOLDSMITH
NADINE GORDIMER
GÜNTER GRASS
JOHN GRAY
ZANE GREY
SUSAN HILL
TONY HILLERMAN
E.T.A. HOFFMANN
HEINRICH
  HOFFMANN
ANTHONY HOPE
L. RON HUBBARD
W.H. HUDSON
LANGSTON HUGHES
THOMAS HUGHES
SHIRLEY JACKSON
LIONEL JOHNSON
SAMUEL JOHNSON
BEN JONSON
NIKOS KAZANTZAKIS
CHARLES KINGSLEY
CHARLES LAMB
MATTHEW GREGORY
  LEWIS
SINCLAIR LEWIS
ANITA LOOS
EDWARD BULWER
  LYTTON
RICHARD MARSH
Rev. C.R. MATURIN
HERMAN MELVILLE
JAMES A MICHENER
JOHN MILTON
BILL NAUGHTON
TIM O'BRIEN
BARONESS ORCZY
WALKER PERCY
JOHN POLIDORI
ALEXANDER POPE
COLE PORTER
ELEANOR H. PORTER
MARIO PUZO
THOMAS PYNCHON
AYN RAND
CHARLES READE
SAMUEL
  RICHARDSON
CHRISTINA ROSSETTI
DANTE GABRIEL
  ROSSETTI
HENRY ROTH
PHILIP ROTH
ANTOINE DE SAINT-
  EXUPÉRY
SIR WALTER SCOTT
RONALD SEARLE
DR SEUSS
PETER SHAFFER
PERCY BYSSHE
  SHELLEY

EDMUND SPENSER
WALLACE STEVENS
REX STOUT
HARRIET BEECHER
  STOWE
WILLIAM STYRON
PATRICK SUSKIND
ELIZABETH TAYLOR
B. TRAVEN
ANNE TYLER
S.S. VAN DINE
ROBERT PENN
  WARREN
NATHANIEL WEST
GILBERT WHITE
LAURA INGALLS
  WILDER
COLIN WILSON
LEONARD WOOLF

ANTHONY ABBOT
(b.1893 d.1952)

The pseudonym of Fulton Oursler, whose Thatcher Colt novels are examples of the Golden Age of detective fiction. He wrote many other books under his own name.

'Thatcher Colt' Novels

About the Murder of Geraldine Foster, Covici Friede (U.S.), 1930 . . . . £250/£75
ditto, as *The Murder of Geraldine Foster*, Collins Crime Club, 1931 . . . . £30/£10
About the Murder of the Clergyman's Mistress, Covici Friede (U.S.), 1931 . . . . . £200/£30
ditto, as *The Crime of the Century*, Collins Crime Club, 1931 . . . . £30/£10
About the Murder of the Night Club Lady, Covici Friede (U.S.), 1931 . . . . £200/£25
ditto, as *The Murder of the Night Club Lady*, Collins Crime Club, 1932 . . . . £30/£10
About the Murder of the Circus Queen, Covici Friede (U.S.), 1932 . . . . £200/£25
ditto, as *The Murder of the Circus Queen*, Collins Crime Club, 1933 . . . . . . £30/£10
About the Murder of a Startled Lady, Farrar & Rinehart (U.S.), 1935 . . . . . . £200/£25
ditto, as *Murder of a Startled Lady*, Collins Crime Club, 1936 . . . . £30/£10
About the Murder of a Man Afraid of Women, Farrar & Rinehart (U.S.), 1937 . . . . . £200/£25
ditto, as *Murder of a Man Afraid of Women*, Collins Crime Club, 1937 . . . . . . £30/£10
The Creeps, Farrar & Rinehart (U.S.), 1939 £125/£20
ditto, as *Murder at Buzzards Bay*, Collins Crime Club, 1940 . . . . £75/£15
The Shudders, Farrar & Rinehart (U.S.), 1943 .
. . . . £125/£20
ditto, as *Deadly Secret*, Collins Crime Club, 1943 . .
. . . . £50/£10

PETER ABRAHAMS
(b.1919)

Abrahams left South Africa in 1939 aged twenty, but the impact of the South African system upon him has meant that the majority of his work has been set in Africa and deals with racial conflict, oppression and economic injustice.

Novels

Song of the City, Crisp, 1945. . . . . £75/£20
Mine Boy, Crisp, [1946] . . . . . £50/£15
ditto, Knopf (U.S.), 1955 (wraps) £15
The Path of Thunder, Harper (U.S.), 1948 . £35/£10
ditto, Faber, 1952 . . . . £35/£10

Wild Conquest, Harper (U.S.), 1950 . . £35/£10
ditto, Faber, 1951 . . . . £35/£10
A Wreath for Udomo, Knopf (U.S.), 1956 . £25/£10
ditto, Faber, 1956 . . . . £25/£10
A Night of Their Own, Knopf (U.S.), 1965 . £25/£10
ditto, Faber, 1965 . . . . £25/£10
This Island Now, Faber, 1966 . . . . £25/£10
ditto, Knopf (U.S.), 1967 . . . . . . £25/£10

Short Stories

Dark Testament, Allen & Unwin, 1942 . . £150/£40

Poetry

A Blackman Speaks of Freedom, Durban, 1942 (wraps) £250

Others

Return to Goli, Faber, 1953 . . . . . £35/£10
Tell Freedom: Memories of Africa, Knopf (U.S.), 1954 . . . . £35/£10
ditto, Faber, 1954 . . . . £35/£10
Jamaica: An Island Mosaic, Her Majesty's Stationery Office, 1957 . . . . . £40/£15

J.R. ACKERLEY
(b.1896 d.1967)

For many years Ackerley was literary editor of *The Listener*. *My Father and Myself* is considered by many to be his masterpiece.

Novel

We Think the World of You, Bodley Head, 1960 . .
. . . . £125/£25
ditto, Ivan Obolensky (U.S.), 1961 . . . £100/£20

Poetry

Cambridge Poets 1914-1920, Heffers, 1920 (ed. E. Davison) . . . . £100/£25
Poems by Four Authors, Bowes & Bowes, 1923 . .
. . . . £200/£75
Micheldever and Other Poems, McKelvie, 1972 (350 numbered copies, wraps with d/w) . . . £75/£35

Other Titles

The Prisoners of War: A Play in Three Acts, Chatto & Windus, 1925. . . . . £75/£35
Hindoo Holiday: An Indian Journey, Chatto & Windus, 1932. . . . . £175/£75
ditto, Viking (U.S.), 1932 . . . . £75/£25
ditto, Chatto & Windus, 1952 (revised edition). . .
. . . . £30/£10
My Dog Tulip: Life with an Alsatian, Secker & Warburg, 1956 . . . . £50/£15
ditto, Fleet Publishing Corp (U.S.), 1965 (expanded edition) . . . . £15/£5

My Father and Myself, Bodley Head, 1968. . £20/£5
ditto, Coward-McCann (U.S.), 1969 (first state binding
with 'Ackerly' on spine). . . . . . . £15/£5
ditto, Coward-McCann (U.S.), 1969 (second state with
name correct). . . . . £10/£5
E.M. Forster: A Portrait, McKelvie, 1972 (wraps) .
. . . . £25
The Letters of J.R. Ackerley, Duckworth, 1975 . .
. . . . £25/£10
ditto, as *The Ackerley Letters*, Harcourt Brace (U.S.),
1975 . . . . £15/£5
My Sister and Myself, Hutchinson, 1982 . . £20/£5

Edited by Ackerley
Escapers All, Bodley Head, 1932 . . . . £25/£5

PETER ACKROYD
(b.1949)

A wide-ranging and versatile writer, Ackroyd is best
known as a novelist and biographer. His life of T.S.
Eliot won the Whitbread and Heinemann Awards for
1984, and his monumental biography of Dickens is
much acclaimed.

Novels
The Great Fire of London, Hamish Hamilton, 1982 .
. . . . £250/£30
ditto, Univ. of Chicago Press (U.S.), 1982 (wraps) £10
The Last Testament of Oscar Wilde, Hamish
Hamilton, 1983 . . . . £75/£15
ditto, Harper & Row (U.S.), 1983 . . . . £20/£5
Hawksmoor, Hamish Hamilton, 1985 . . £45/£10
ditto, Harper & Row (U.S.), 1985 . . . £25/£10
Chatterton, Hamish Hamilton, 1987. . . . £25/£5
ditto, Hamish Hamilton, 1987 (150 signed copies,
glassine d/w) . . . . £65/£45
ditto, Grove Press (U.S.), 1988 . . . . £20/£5
First Light, Hamish Hamilton, 1989. . . . £20/£5
ditto, Grove Weidenfeld (U.S.), 1989 . . . £20/£5
English Music, Hamish Hamilton, 1992 . . £15/£5
ditto, London Limited Editions, 1992 (150 signed,
numbered copies, glassine d/w). . . . £50/£35
ditto, Knopf (U.S.), 1992 . . . . . . £15/£5
ditto, The Franklin Library, 1992 (full leather, signed,
limited edition) £30
The House of Doctor Dee, Hamish Hamilton, 1993 .
. . . . £15/£5
Dan Leno and the Limehouse Golem, Sinclair-
Stevenson, 1994 . . . . £15/£5
ditto, as *The Trial of Elizabeth Cree*, Doubleday
(U.S.), 1995 . . . . £10/£5
Milton in America, Sinclair-Stevenson, 1996 . £10/£5
ditto, Doubleday (U.S.), 1997 . . . . . £10/£5
The Plato Papers, Chatto & Windus, 1999 . . £10/£5
ditto, Doubleday (U.S.), 1999 . . . . . £10/£5

Poetry
Ouch, The Curiously Strong Vol IV No.2 1971
(xeroxed copies, sheets, usually in stapled wraps) .
. . . . £200
London Lickpenny, Ferry Press, 1973 (26 signed
copies of edition of 500, illustrated card wraps) £200
ditto, Ferry Press, 1973 (474 unsigned copies of edition
of 500, illustrated card wraps) £65
Country Life, Ferry Press, 1978 (324 signed copies of
edition of 350, card wraps) £50
ditto, Ferry Press, 1978 (26 signed copies of edition of
350, with additional holograph poem, card wraps) .
. . . . £225
The Diversions of Purley, Hamish Hamilton, 1987 .
. . . . £25/£10

Biography
Ezra Pound and His World, Thames & Hudson, 1980
. . . . £25/£5
ditto, Scribner's, 1980. . . . . . . £20/£5
T.S. Eliot, Hamish Hamilton, 1984 . . . £20/£5
ditto, Simon & Schuster, 1984 . . . . £15/£5
Dickens, Sinclair-Stevenson, 1990 . . . £20/£5
ditto, London Limited Editions, 1990 (150 signed
copies, glassine d/w). . . . . . £65/£50
ditto, HarperCollins (U.S.), 1990. . . . £15/£5
Blake, Sinclair-Stevenson, 1995 . . . . £15/£5
ditto, Knopf (U.S.), 1996 . . . . . . £10/£5
The Life of Thomas Moore, Chatto & Windus, 1998 .
. . . . £10/£5
ditto, Doubleday (U.S.), 1998 . . . . . £10/£5

Miscellaneous
Notes for a New Culture: An Essay on Modernism,
Vision Press, 1976 . . . . . . £75/£20
ditto, Barnes & Noble (U.S.), 1976 . . . £50/£15
*Dressing Up, Transvestism and Drag: The History of
an Obsession*, Thames & Hudson, 1979 . £35/£15
ditto, Simon & Schuster, 1979 . . . . £25/£10
Dickens' London: An Imaginative Vision, Headline,
1987 (introduced by Peter Ackroyd) . . . £15/£5
Introduction to Dickens, Sinclair-Stevenson, 1991 .
. . . . £20/£5
ditto, Ballantine (U.S.), 1992 (wraps) £5
London: The Biography, Chatto & Windus, 2000 . .
. . . . £15/£5
ditto, Doubleday (U.S.), 2001 . . . . £10/£5
The Collection, Chatto & Windus, 2001 . . £10/£5
Albion: The Origins of the English Imagination,
Chatto & Windus, 2002 . . . . . . £10/£5

DOUGLAS ADAMS
(b.1952 d.2001)

The Hitch-Hiker's Guide To The Galaxy was heard on the radio before becoming a successful book, and finally a television series.

Novels
The Hitch-Hiker's Guide To The Galaxy, Pan, 1979 (pbk) £20
ditto, Barker, n.d. [1980] (first hardback edition) . . . . £200/£30
ditto, Harmony (U.S.), 1980 . . . . . £40/£10
The Restaurant At The End Of The Universe, Pan, 1980 (pbk) £5
ditto, Barker, 1980 (first hardback edition) . £100/£15
ditto, Harmony (U.S.), 1980 . . . . . . £30/£5
Life, The Universe and Everything, Pan, 1982 . . £5
ditto, Barker, 1982 (first hardback edition) . £75/£15
ditto, Harmony (U.S.), 1982 . . . . . . £20/£5
So Long, And Thanks For All The Fish, Pan, 1984 . . . . £20/£5
ditto, Harmony (U.S.), 1985 . . . . . . £10/£5
Dirk Gently's Holistic Detective Agency, Heinemann, 1987 . . . . £15/£5
ditto, Simon & Schuster (U.S.), 1987 . . . £10/£5
The Long Dark Tea-Time Of The Soul, Heinemann, 1988 . . . . £15/£5
ditto, Simon & Schuster (U.S.), 1988 . . . £10/£5
Mostly Harmless, Heinemann, 1992 . . . . £15/£5
ditto, Harmony (U.S.), 1992 . . . . . . £10/£5
Starship Titanic, Harmony (U.S.), 1997 (with Terry Jones) . . . . £10/£5

Collected Editions
The Hitch-Hiker's Trilogy, Harmony (U.S.), 1983 . . . . £25/£10
The Hitch-Hiker's Guide To The Galaxy: A Trilogy in Four Parts, Heinemann, 1986 . . . . £40/£10
ditto, as *The Hitch-Hiker's Quartet*, Harmony (U.S.), 1986 . . . . £25/£10
The Hitch-Hiker's Guide To The Galaxy: A Trilogy in Five Parts, Heinemann, 1995 . . . . . £10/£5
The More Than Complete Hitch-Hiker's Guide, Bonanza (U.S.), 1989 . . . . £10/£5
The Dirk Gently Omnibus, Heinemann, 2001 . £10/£5

Others
The Meaning of Liff, Pan, 1983 (with John Lloyd, pbk) £15
ditto, Harmony (U.S.), 1984 . . . . . . £10/£5
The Hitch-Hiker's Guide To The Galaxy: The Original Radio Scripts, Pan, 1985 (pbk) . . £15
ditto, Harmony (U.S.), [c.1985] (pbk) . . . £10
Last Chance To See ..., Heinemann, 1990 (with Mark Carwardine) . . . . £20/£5
ditto, Harmony (U.S.), 1992 . . . . . . £15/£5
The Deeper Meaning of Liff, Pan, 1990 (with John Lloyd) . . . . £10/£5

ditto, Harmony (U.S.), 1990 . . . . . . £10/£5
Doctor Who - Pirate Planet, Titan Books, 1994 (pbk) £5
The Salmon of Doubt: Hitchhiking the Galaxy One Last Time, Heinemann, 2002 . . . . . £10/£5
ditto, Harmony (U.S.), 2002 . . . . . . £10/£5

RICHARD ADAMS
(b.1920)

The classic *Watership Down* won the Guardian Award and Carnegie Medal. Much of Adams' best work is concerned with man's cruelty to animals. The first issue of *The Girl in a Swing* was withdrawn through fear of libel, and among the changes made was the name of the heroine.

Watership Down, Rex Collings, 1972 . £1,000/£75
ditto, Macmillan (U.S.), 1972 . . . £200/£15
ditto, Penguin, 1976 (first illustrated edition, in slipcase with d/w) . . . . £65/£15
ditto, Penguin, 1976 (deluxe illustrated edition limited to 250 signed, numbered copies, slipcase) . £750/£600
ditto, Penguin, 1976 (approx 30 copies of the above edition with an original illustration) . . . £2,000
Shardik, Allen Lane, 1974 . . . . . . £15/£5
ditto, Simon & Schuster (U.S.), [1974] . . . £10/£5
Plague Dogs, Allen Lane, 1977 . . . . . £15/£5
ditto, Knopf (U.S.), 1978 . . . . £10/£5
The Girl in a Swing, Allen Lane, 1980 (withdrawn first issue with 'Kathe Geutner') . . . . . £50/£15
ditto, Knopf (U.S.), 1980 (withdrawn issue) £40/£15
ditto, Allen Lane, 1980 (second issue, revised edition, with 'Karin Förster') . . . . £10/£5
ditto, Knopf (U.S.), 1980 (revised edition) . . £10/£5
The Iron Wolf and Other Stories, Allen Lane, 1980 . . . . £10/£5
ditto, as *The Unbroken Web: Stories & Fables*, Crown (U.S.), 1980 . . . . £10/£5
The Legend of Te Tuna, Sylvester & Orphanos, 1982 (300 of 330 signed copies) . . . . . £75/£50
ditto, Sylvester & Orphanos, 1982 (26 lettered and signed copies and 4 copies with recipient's name printed, of 330, slipcase) . . . . . £150/£100
ditto, Sidgwick & Jackson, 1986 . . . . . £10/£5
Maia, Viking, 1984 . . . . £10/£5
ditto, Knopf (U.S.), 1985 . . . . £10/£5
The Bureaucats, Viking Kestrel, 1985 . . . £20/£5
Traveller, Knopf (U.S.), 1988 . . . . . £10/£5
ditto, Hutchinson, 1988 . . . . £10/£5
Tales from Watership Down, Hutchinson, 1996 £10/£5
ditto, Knopf (U.S.), 1996 . . . . £10/£5

Poetry
The Tyger Voyage, Cape, 1976 . . . . . £20/£10
ditto, Knopf (U.S.), 1976 . . . . £20/£10
The Ship's Cat, Cape, 1977 . . . . . . £20/£10
ditto, Knopf (U.S.), 1977 . . . . £20/£10

Non Fiction

Nature Through the Seasons, Kestrel, 1975 (with Max
Hooper) . . . . £10/£5
ditto, Simon & Schuster (U.S.), 1975 . . . £10/£5
Nature Day and Night, Kestrel, 1978 (with Max
Hooper) . . . . £10/£5
ditto, Viking (U.S.), 1978. . . . . . . £10/£5
Voyage Through the Antarctic, Allen Lane, 1982
(with Ronald Lockley). . . . . . . £10/£5
ditto, Knopf (U.S.), 1983 . . . . £10/£5
The Nature Diary, Viking, 1985. . . . . £10/£5
ditto, Viking (U.S.), 1985. . . . . . . £10/£5
Day Gone By, Hutchinson, 1990. . . . . £10/£5
ditto, Knopf (U.S.), 1991 . . . . £10/£5

CHAS ADDAMS
(b.1912 d.1988)

An American cartoonist with a dark sense of humour,
who is best known for the 'Addams Family'

Cartoons

Drawn and Quartered, Random House (U.S.), 1942 .
. . . . £75/£35
ditto, Hamish Hamilton, 1943 . . . . £65/£25
Addams and Evil, Random House (U.S.), 1947 . .
. . . . £60/£25
ditto, Hamish Hamilton, 1947 . . . . £60/£25
Monster Rally, Simon & Schuster (U.S.), 1950. . .
. . . . £60/£25
ditto, Hamish Hamilton, 1951 . . . . £50/£20
Homebodies, Simon & Schuster (U.S.), 1954 £60/£25
ditto, Hamish Hamilton, 1954 . . . £50/£20
Nightcrawlers, Simon & Schuster (U.S.), 1957. . .
. . . . £60/£25
ditto, Hamish Hamilton, 1957 . . . . £50/£20
Black Maria, Simon & Schuster (U.S.), 1960 £60/£25
ditto, Hamish Hamilton, 1960 . . . . £50/£20
The Penguin Charles Addams, Penguin, 1962 (pbk) .
. . . . £10
The Groaning Board, Simon & Schuster (U.S.), 1964.
. . . . £40/£15
ditto, Hamish Hamilton, 1964 . . . . £40/£15
The Chas Addams Mother Goose, Windmill Books/
Harper (U.S.), 1967 . . . . . . £40/£15
ditto, Collins, 1967 . . . . . . £40/£15
My Crowd, Simon & Schuster (U.S.), 1970. £40/£15
ditto, Tom Stacey, 1971 . . . . . £40/£15
Favourite Haunts, Simon & Schuster (U.S.), 1976 .
. . . . £30/£10
ditto, W.H. Allen, 1977 . . . . . £30/£10
Creature Comforts, Simon & Schuster (U.S.), 1981 .
. . . . £25/£10
ditto, Heinemann, 1981 . . . . . . £25/£10
The Addams Family Album, Hamish Hamilton, 1991
(pbk) £5

The World of Chas Addams, Knopf (U.S.), 1991 . . .
. . . . £25/£10
ditto, Hamish Hamilton, 1992 . . . . £25/£10

Others

Afternoon in the Attic by John Kobler, Dodd, Mead
(U.S.), 1950 . . . . £50/£20
Dear Dead Days: A Family Album, Putnam (U.S.),
1959 . . . . £50/£20
ditto, Hamlyn, [1960] . . . . £50/£20

JAMES AGEE
(b.1909 d.1955)

U.S. poet, novelist, journalist, film critic, and social
activist, Agee led an unorthodox, hard-driving life
that resulted in an early death.

Reportage

Let Us Now Praise Famous Men, Houghton Mifflin
(U.S.), 1941 (with Walker Evans) . . £2,000/£250
ditto, Peter Owen, 1965 . . . . . . £30/£10
A Way of Seeing, Viking, 1965 (with Helen Levitt) .
. . . . £200/£50

Poetry

Permit Me Voyage, Yale Univ. Press (U.S.), 1934 . .
. . . . £500/£75
The Collected Poems of James Agee, Houghton
Mifflin (U.S.), 1968 . . . . . . £45/£15
ditto, Calder & Boyars, 1972 . . . . £30/£10

Novels

The Morning Watch, Houghton Mifflin (U.S.), 1951 .
. . . . £125/£15
ditto, Secker and Warburg, 1952. . . . £25/£5
A Death in the Family, McDowell Obolensky (U.S.),
1957 (first issue 'walking' for 'waking' on p.80) . .
. . . . £150/£20
ditto, McDowell Obolensky (U.S.), 1957 (second
issue) . . . . £45/£10
ditto, Gollancz, 1958 . . . . . . £65/£20

Others

Knoxville: Summer of 1915 for Voice and Orchestra,
by Samuel Barber (musical score) and Agee (words),
Schirmer (U.S.), 1949 . . . . . . £100
ditto, as *Knoxville: Summer 1915*, Aliquando
(Canada), 1970 (100 numbered copies, no music) .
. . . . £125
Agee on Film: Reviews and Comments, McDowell
Obolensky (U.S.), 1958 . . . . . £100/£25
ditto, Peter Owen, 1963 . . . . . £40/£15
Agee on Film, Volume Two: Five Film Scripts,
McDowell Obolensky (U.S.), 1960. . . £60/£15
ditto, Peter Owen, 1965 . . . . . £40/£15

Letters of James Agee to Father Flye, Braziller (U.S.),
1962 . . . . £25/£10
ditto, Peter Owen, 1964 . . . . £20/£5
Four Early Stories, Cummington Press (U.S.), 1964
(285 copies) . . . . £250/£175
The Collected Short Prose of James Agee, Houghton
Mifflin, 1968 . . . . £25/£5
ditto, Calder & Boyars, 1972 . . . . . £20/£5
The Last Letter of James Agee to Father Flye, Godine
(U.S.), 1969 (500 copies, wraps) £25

ROBERT AICKMAN
(b.1914 d.1981)

British short story writer, critic, lecturer and novelist.
He edited *The Fontana Book of Great Ghost Stories*
between 1964 and 1972.

Short Stories
We Are For the Dark - Six Ghost Stories, Cape, 1951
(with Elizabeth Jane Howard) . . . . £350/£125
Dark Entries, Collins, 1964 . . . . . £300/£125
Powers of Darkness, Collins, 1966 . . . £250/£100
Sub Rosa, Gollancz, 1968 . . . . . £200/£100
ditto, Gollancz, 1968 (40 signed copies). . £350/£250
Cold Hand in Mine, Gollancz, 1975 [1976] £90/£50
ditto, Scribner's (U.S.), 1975 [1977]. . £25/£10
Tales of Love and Death, Gollancz, 1977 . £125/£45
Painted Devils: Strange Stories, Scribner's (U.S.),
1979 . . . . £25/£10
Intrusions: Strange Tales, Gollancz, 1980 . £80/£50
Night Voices: Strange Stories, Gollancz, 1985 . .
. . . . £35/£10
The Wine-dark Sea, Arbor House (U.S.), 1988. . .
. . . . £20/£10
ditto, Mandarin, 1990 (pbk) £5
The Unsettled Dust, Mandarin, 1990 (pbk). . £10
The Collected Strange Stories, Tartarus/Durtro, 1999
(2 vols) . . . . £150/£75

Novels
The Late Breakfasters, Gollancz, 1964 . . £250/£75
ditto, Portway, 1978 . . . . £20/£10
The Model, Arbor House (U.S.), 1987 . . . £15/£5
ditto, Robinson, 1988 . . . . £15/£5

Canals
Know Your Waterways, Coram, [1955] (wraps) £10
ditto, Coram, [1956] . . . . £35/£10
The Story of Our Inland Waterways, Pitman, 1955 .
. . . . £25/£10

Autobiography
The Attempted Rescue, Gollancz, 1966 . . £150/£75
The River Runs Uphill, Pearson, 1986 . . £20/£10

CONRAD AIKEN
(b.1889 d.1973)

A poet and novelist, born in Savannah, Georgia,
Aiken made his name with his first collection of
verse, *Earth Triumphant*. *Selected Poems* was
awarded the 1930 Pulitzer Prize. He also wrote short
stories and novels, including the autobiographical
Ushant (1952).

Poetry
Earth Triumphant and Other Tales in Verse,
Macmillan (U.S.), 1914 . . . . £75
Turns and Movies and Other Tales in Verse,
Houghton Mifflin (U.S.), 1916 (d/w attached to
boards at spine) . . . . £125/£10
ditto, Constable, 1916 . . . . £125/£10
The Jig of Forslin: A Symphony, Four Seas (U.S.),
1916 (assumed first issue with 'r' missing in 'warm'
on p.117, line 1) £50
Nocturne of Remembered Spring and Other Poems,
Four Seas (U.S.), 1917 . . . . . . £125/£35
*The Charnel Rose; Senlin: A Biography; and Other
Poems*, Four Seas (U.S.), 1918 . . . £125/£35
ditto, as *Senlin: A Biography*, Hogarth Press, 1925 £75
The House of Dust: A Symphony, Four Seas (U.S.),
1920 . . . . £75/£25
*Punch: The Immortal Liar, Documents in His
History*, Knopf (U.S.), 1921 . . . . £125/£25
ditto, Secker, 1921 . . . . £125/£25
Priapus and the Pool, Dunster House (U.S.), 1922 (50
numbered copies) . . . . £300/£175
ditto, as *Priapus and the Pool and Other Poems*, Boni
& Liveright (U.S.), 1925 . . . . £125/£25
The Pilgrimage of Festus, Knopf (U.S.), 1923 . . .
. . . . £50/£20
Prelude, Random House (U.S.), 1929 (475 copies,
wraps). £65
Selected Poems, Scribner's (U.S.), 1929 . £125/£35
ditto, Scribner's (U.S.), 1929 (210 numbered, signed
copies in slipcase) . . . . . . £200/£125
John Deth, a Metaphysical Legend and Other Poems,
Scribner's (U.S.), 1930 . . . . . £125/£25
Gehenna, Random House (U.S.), 1930 (875 copies,
wraps). £65
The Coming Forth by Day of Osiris Jones, Scribner's
(U.S.), 1931 (with 'THE MUSIC' in caps on p.37) .
. . . . £125/£25
ditto, Scribner's (U.S.), 1931 (with 'The Music') . .
. . . . £100/£20
Preludes for Memnon, Scribner's (U.S.), 1931. . .
. . . . £75/£30
Landscape West of Eden, Dent, 1934 . . £65/£20
ditto, Scribner's (U.S.), 1935 . . . . . £65/£20
Time in the Rock: Preludes to Definition, Scribner's
(U.S.), 1936 . . . . £35/£15
And in the Human Heart, Duell, Sloan & Pearce
(U.S.), 1942 . . . . £30/£10

Brownstone Eclogues and Other Poems, Duell, Sloan
& Pearce (U.S.), 1942 . . . . . . £30/£10
The Soldier: A Poem, New Directions (U.S.), 1944 .
. . . . £45/£20
ditto, New Directions (U.S.), 1944 (wraps) . . £25
ditto, Editions PL, [1946] . . . . . £30/£10
The Kid, Duell, Sloan & Pearce (U.S.), 1947 £25/£10
ditto, John Lehmann, 1947 . . . . £25/£10
The Divine Pilgrim, Univ. of Georgia Press (U.S.),
1949 . . . . £30/£10
Skylight One: Fifteen Poems, O.U.P. (U.S.), 1949 .
. . . . £40/£10
ditto, John Lehmann, 1951 . . . . £40/£10
Collected Poems, O.U.P. (U.S.), 1953 . . £50/£20
A Letter From Li Po and Other Poems, O.U.P. (U.S.),
1955 . . . . £30/£10
Sheepfold Hill: Fifteen Poems, Sagamore Press (U.S.),
1958 . . . . £30/£10
The Morning Song of Lord Zero, O.U.P. (U.S.), 1963
. . . . £25/£10
A Seizure of Limericks, Holt, Rinehart & Winston
(U.S.), 1964 . . . . £20/£5
ditto, Allen, 1965 . . . . £20/£5
The Clerk's Journal, Eakins Press (U.S.), 1971 . .
. . . . £25/£10
ditto, Eakins Press (U.S.), 1971 (300 signed copies,
slipcase) . . . . £75/£50
Thee, Braziller (U.S.), 1967 . . . . £25/£10
ditto, Braziller (U.S.), 1967 (100 numbered copies
signed by Aiken and Baskin of 500, slipcase) . .
. . . . £125/£100
ditto, Braziller (U.S.), 1967 (400 numbered copies
signed by Aiken and Baskin of 500) . . £75/£50
ditto, Inca Books, 1973 (100 numbered copies signed
by Aiken of 500, slipcase) . . . . £125/£100
ditto, Braziller (U.S.), 1973 (400 numbered copies
signed by Aiken of 500) . . . . . £75/£50

Novels
Blue Voyage, Gerald Howe, 1927 . . . £100/£25
ditto, Scribner's (U.S.), 1927 . . . . £100/£25
ditto, Scribner's (U.S.), 1927 (125 signed copies) . .
. . . . £200/£150
Great Circle, Scribner's (U.S.), 1933 . . £100/£25
ditto, Wishart, 1933 . . . . . . £100/£25
King Coffin, Scribner's (U.S.), 1935 . . £75/£25
ditto, Dent, 1935 . . . . £100/£25
A Heart for the Gods of Mexico, Secker, 1939 . . .
. . . . £225/£50
Conversation: or a Pilgrim's Progress, Duell, Sloan &
Pearce (U.S.), 1940 . . . . . . £35/£10
ditto, Rodney, Phillips & Green, 1940 . . £35/£10
Ushant: An Essay, Duell, Sloan & Pearce (U.S.), 1952
. . . . £25/£10
ditto, Allen, 1963 . . . . £25/£10
The Collected Novels of Conrad Aiken, Holt, Rinehart
& Winston (U.S.), 1964 . . . . . . £20/£5
Three Novels, Allen, 1965 . . . . £25/£10

Short Stories
Bring! Bring! And Other Stories, Secker, 1925 . .
. . . . £175/£35
ditto, Boni & Liveright (U.S.), 1925 . . . £175/£35
Costumes By Eros, Scribner's (U.S.), 1928 . £100/£25
Among the Lost People, Scribner's (U.S.), 1934 . .
. . . . £75/£20
The Short Stories of Conrad Aiken, Duell, Sloan &
Pearce (U.S.), 1950 . . . . . . £25/£10
The Collected Short Stories of Conrad Aiken, World
Publishing Co., 1960. . . . . . . £20/£5

Children's Books
Cats and Bats and Things with Wings, Atheneum
(U.S.), 1965 . . . . £35/£10
A Little Who's Zoo of Mild Animals, Atheneum
(U.S.), 1977 . . . . £35/£10
ditto, Cape, 1977 . . . . £25

Literary Criticism
Scepticisms: Notes on Contemporary Poetry, Knopf
(U.S.), 1919 . . . . £45
A Reviewer's ABC, Meridian Books (U.S.), 1958 . .
. . . . £25/£10
*Collected Criticism of Conrad Aiken from 1916 to the
Present*, W.H. Allen, 1961 . . . . . £25/£10

Others
Mr Arcularis, Harvard Univ. Press, 1953 . £30/£10
Selected Letters of Conrad Aiken, Yale Univ. Press
(U.S.), 1978 . . . . £25/£10

JOAN AIKEN
(b.1924)

Daughter of the American poet, Conrad Aiken, Joan
is best known for her books for children, although she
also writes novels and short stories for adults.

Novels for Children
The Kingdom and the Cave, Abelard-Schuman, 1960 .
. . . . £50/£15
ditto, Doubleday (U.S.), 1974 . . . . £35/£10
The Wolves of Willoughby Chase, Cape, 1962 . . .
. . . . £100/£20
ditto, Doubleday (U.S.), 1963 . . . . £65/£10
Black Hearts in Battersea, Cape, 1965 . . £50/£15
ditto, Doubleday (U.S.), 1964 . . . . £30/£10
Nightbirds on Nantucket, Cape, 1966 . . £45/£10
ditto, Doubleday (U.S.), 1966 . . . . £20/£10
The Whispering Mountain, Cape, 1968. . £30/£10
ditto, Doubleday (U.S.), 1969 . . . . £15/£5
The Cuckoo Tree, Cape, 1971 . . . . £25/£10
ditto, Doubleday (U.S.), 1971 . . . . £15/£5
Go Saddle the Sea, Doubleday (U.S.), 1977 . £20/£5
ditto, Cape, 1978 . . . . £20/£5
The Shadow Guests, Cape, 1980. . . . £15/£5

ditto, Delacorte (U.S.), 1980 . . . . . . £10/£5
The Stolen Lake, Cape, 1981. . . . . £25/£10
ditto, Delacorte (U.S.), 1981 . . . . . . £20/£5
Bridle the Wind, Cape, 1983 . . . . . . £20/£5
ditto, Delacorte (U.S.), 1983 . . . . . . £15/£5
Dido and Pa, Cape, 1986 . . . . £20/£5
ditto, Delacorte (U.S.), 1987 . . . . . . £15/£5
The Moon's Revenge, Cape, 1987 . . . . £10
ditto, Knopf (U.S.), 1988 . . . . £10/£5
The Teeth of the Gale, Cape, 1988 . . . . £15/£5
ditto, Harper (U.S.), 1988. . . . . . . £10/£5
Is, Cape, 1992 . . . . £10/£5
ditto, Delacorte (U.S.), 1992 . . . . . . £10/£5
The Winter Sleepwalker, Cape, 1994 . . £10/£5
Cold Shoulder Road, Cape, 1995 . . . . £10/£5
ditto, Delacorte (U.S.), 1995 . . . . . . £10/£5
A Handful of Gold, Cape, 1995 . . . . . £10/£5
Moon Cake, Hodder, 1998 . . . . . . £10/£5
The Scream, Macmillan, 2002 . . . . . £10/£5

Short Stories for Children
All You've Ever Wanted and Other Stories, Cape,
1953 . . . . £50/£15
More Than You Bargained For and Other Stories,
Cape, 1955 . . . . £45/£10
ditto, Abelard-Schuman (U.S.), 1957 . . . £25/£5
A Necklace of Raindrops and Other Stories, Cape,
1968 . . . . £150/£25
ditto, Doubleday (U.S.), 1968 . . . . £100/£15
A Small Pinch of Weather and Other Stories, Cape,
1969 . . . . £25/£10
All and More, Cape, 1971 (contains *All You've Ever
Wanted* and *More Than You Bargained For*) . £20/£5
The Kingdom Under the Sea and Other Stories, Cape,
1971 . . . . £25/£10
A Harp of Fishbones and Other Stories, Cape, 1972 .
. . . . £25/£10
Arabel's Raven, BBC/Cape, 1972 . . . £75/£25
ditto, Doubleday (U.S.), 1974 . . . . £50/£15
The Escaped Black Mamba, BBC, 1973 (wraps) .
. . . . £15
All But A Few, Puffin, 1974 (wraps) £5
*Not What You Expected: A Collection of Short
Stories*, Doubleday (U.S.), 1974 . . . £30/£10
The Bread Bin, BBC, 1974 (wraps) £5
Mortimer's Tie, BBC, 1976 (wraps) £5
*A Bundle of Nerves: Stories of Horror, Suspense and
Fantasy*, Gollancz, 1976 . . . . . £45/£10
The Faithless Lollybird and Other Stories, Cape, 1977
. . . . £30/£10
ditto, Doubleday (U.S.), 1978 . . . . £25/£10
Tales of A One-Way Street and Other Stories, Cape,
1978 . . . . £25/£10
ditto, Doubleday (U.S.), 1979 . . . . . £20/£5
Mice and Mendelson, Cape, 1978 . . . . £20/£5
Mortimer and the Sword Excalibur, BBC, 1979
(wraps) £5
The Spiral Stair, BBC, 1979 (wraps) £5

*A Touch of Chill: Stories of Horror, Suspense and
Fantasy*, Gollancz, 1979 . . . . . . £20/£5
ditto, Delacorte (U.S.), 1980 . . . . . . £15/£5
Arabel and Mortimer, Cape, 1980 . . . . £20/£5
ditto, Doubleday (U.S.), 1981 . . . . . . £15/£5
Mortimer's Portrait on Glass, BBC, 1980 (wraps). £5
Mr Jones's Disappearing Taxi, BBC, 1980 (wraps) £5
*A Whisper in the Night: Stories of Horror, Suspense
and Fantasy*, Gollancz, 1982 . . . . £20/£5
ditto, Delacorte (U.S.), 1984 . . . . . . £15/£5
Mortimer's Cross, BBC/Cape, 1983 . . . . £25/£5
ditto, Harper (U.S.), 1983 . . . . . . £20/£5
The Kitchen Warriors, BBC, 1983 . . . . £15/£5
Up The Chimney Down and Other Stories, Cape, 1984
. . . . £25/£5
ditto, Harper (U.S.), 1984. . . . . . . £20/£5
Mortimer Says Nothing, Cape, 1985 . . . £25/£5
ditto, Harper (U.S.), 1985. . . . . . . £20/£5
The Last Slice of Rainbow and Other Stories, Cape,
1985 . . . . £25/£5
ditto, Harper (U.S.), 1988. . . . . . . £20/£5
Past Eight O'Clock, Cape, 1986 . . . . . £15/£5
ditto, Viking Kestrel (U.S.), 1987 . . . . £15/£5
A Foot in the Grave, Cape, 1989. . . . . £20/£5
ditto, Viking (U.S.), 1991. . . . . . . £20/£5
A Fit of Shivers, Gollancz, 1990. . . . . £25/£5
ditto, Delacorte (U.S.), 1992 . . . . . . £20/£5
Creepy Company, Gollancz, 1993 . . . . £25/£5

Adult Novels
The Silence of Herondale, Gollancz, 1965 . £30/£10
ditto, Doubleday (U.S.), 1964 . . . . . £20/£5
The Fortune Hunters, Doubleday (U.S.), 1965 . .
. . . . £30/£10
Trouble With Project X, Gollancz, 1966 . £30/£10
ditto, as *Beware of the Banquet*, Doubleday (U.S.),
1966 . . . . £20/£5
Hate Begins at Home, Gollancz, 1967 . . £30/£10
ditto, as *Dark Interval*, Doubleday (U.S.), 1967 . .
. . . . £20/£5
The Ribs of Death, Gollancz, 1967 . . . £30/£10
ditto, as *The Crystal Cow*, Doubleday (U.S.), 1968 .
. . . . £20/£5
Night Fall, Holt Rinehart (U.S.), 1969 . . £30/£10
The Embroidered Sunset, Gollancz, 1970 . £30/£10
ditto, Doubleday (U.S.), 1970 . . . . . £20/£5
Died on a Rainy Day, Gollancz, 1972 . . £30/£10
ditto, Holt Rinehart (U.S.), 1972 . . . . £20/£5
The Butterfly Picnic, Gollancz, 1972 . . £30/£10
ditto, as *A Cluster of Separate Sparks*, Doubleday
(U.S.), 1972 . . . . £20/£5
Midnight is a Place, Cape, 1974 . . . . £30/£10
ditto, Viking (U.S.), 1974. . . . . . . £20/£5
Voices in an Empty House, Gollancz, 1975 £30/£10
ditto, Doubleday (U.S.), 1975 . . . . . £20/£5
Castle Barebane, Gollancz, 1976 . . . . £30/£10
ditto, Viking (U.S.), 1976. . . . . . . £20/£5
Last Movement, Gollancz, 1977 . . . . £30/£10
ditto, Doubleday (U.S.), 1977 . . . . . £20/£5

The Five-Minute Marriage, Gollancz, 1977 . £25/£5
ditto, Doubleday (U.S.), 1978 . . . . . £20/£5
The Smile of the Stranger, Gollancz, 1978 . . £25/£5
ditto, Doubleday (U.S.), 1978 . . . . £20/£5
The Lightning Tree, Gollancz, 1980 . . £20/£5
ditto, as *The Weeping Ash*, Doubleday (U.S.), 1980 .
. . . . £15/£5
The Young Lady From Paris, Gollancz, 1978 . £20/£5
ditto, as *The Girl From Paris*, Doubleday (U.S.), 1980
. . . . £15/£5
Foul Matter, Gollancz, 1983 . . . . . £20/£5
ditto, Doubleday (U.S.), 1983 . . . . £15/£5
Mansfield Revisited, Gollancz, 1984 . . . £15/£5
ditto, Doubleday (U.S.), 1985 . . . . . £10/£5
Deception, Gollancz, 1987 . . . . . . £15/£5
ditto, as *If I Were You*, Doubleday (U.S.), 1987 £10/£5
Blackground, Gollancz, 1989 . . . . . £15/£5
ditto, Doubleday (U.S.), 1989 . . . . £10/£5
Jane Fairfax, Gollancz, 1990 . . . . £15/£5
ditto, St Martin's Press (U.S.), 1990 . . . . £15/£5
The Haunting of Lamb House, Cape, 1991 . £15/£5
ditto, St Martin's Press (U.S.), 1993 . . . . £15/£5
Eliza's Daughter, Gollancz, 1994 . . . . £10/£5
ditto, St Martin's Press (U.S.), 1994 . . . . £10/£5
Emma Watson: The Watsons Completed, Gollancz,
1996 (with Jane Austen) . . . . . . £10/£5
ditto, St Martin's Press (U.S.), 1996 . . . £10/£5
The Cockatrice Boys, Gollancz, 1996 . . £10/£5
ditto, Tor (U.S.), 1996 . . . . . . £10/£5
*The Youngest Miss Ward: A Jane Austen Entertain-
ment*, Gollancz, 1998 . . . . . . £10/£5
ditto, St Martin's Press (U.S.), 1998 . . . . £10/£5

Adult Short Stories
Armitage, Armitage, Fly Away Home, Doubleday
(U.S.), 1968 . . . . £45/£10
The Windscreen Weepers, Gollancz, 1969 . £75/£10
Smoke From Cromwell's Time and Other Stories,
Doubleday (U.S.), 1970 . . . . . . £40/£10
*The Green Flash and Other Tales of Horror,
Suspense and Fantasy*, Holt Rinehart (U.S.), 1971 .
. . . . £30/£10
*The Far Forests: Tales of Romance, Fantasy and
Suspense*, Viking (U.S.), 1977 . . . . . £20/£5
A Goose On Your Grave, Gollancz, 1987 . . £25/£5
The Erl King's Daughter, Heinemann, 1988 . £10
Voices, Hippo, 1988 (wraps) £5
*Give Yourself A Fright: Thirteen Tales of the
Supernatural*, Delacorte (U.S.), 1989 . . . £10/£5

Poetry
The Skin Spinners, Viking (U.S.), 1976 . £10/£5

Plays
Winterthing, Holt Rinehart (U.S.), 1972 . £15/£5
Winterthing and The Mooncusser's Daughter, Cape,
1973 . . . . £15/£5
The Mooncusser's Daughter, Viking (U.S.), 1974. .
. . . . £15/£5

Others
Angel Inn, Cape, 1976 (translated by Aiken from a
story by the Comtesse de Segur) . . . . £15/£5
ditto, Stemmer House, 1978 . . . . . . £15/£5
The Way To Write For Children, Elm Tree, 1982
(wraps) £5

ALAIN-FOURNIER
(b.1886 d.1914)

Alain-Fournier was the pen name of Henri Fournier,
author of one novel, *Le Grand Meaulnes*, published in
France in 1913. Often translated into English as *The
Wanderer* or *The Lost Domain*, it is a classic novel of
a lost childhood love.

The Wanderer, Houghton Mifflin (U.S.), 1928
(translated by Françoise Delisle) . . . £200/£40
ditto, Constable, 1929 . . . . . . £200/£40
*Towards the Lost Domain: Letters from London,
1905*, Carcanet, 1986 (edited and translated by W.J.
Strachan) . . . . £15/£5
Le Grand Meaulnes and Miracles, Tartarus Press,
1999 . . . . £30/£10

ALASTAIR
(b.1887 d.1969)

Pseudonym for Hans Henning Voight, an illustrator
who owes a great debt to Aubrey Beardsley, but
succeeds in offering a decadent style all of his own.

Books Illustrated by Alastair
*Forty-Three Drawings by Alastair (with a note of
Exclamation by Robert Ross)*, John Lane, 1914 (500
copies) £750
Poèmes pour Pâques, by Loïs Cendré, privately
printed, 1915 (printed anonymously by 'Celui qui
aime l'amour', 7 illustrations) £200
The Sphinx, by Oscar Wilde, John Lane, 1920 (1,000
copies, 10 illustrations) £400
Carmen, by Prosper Mérimée, Verlag Rascher
(Zurich), 1920 (50 copies on Japon paper, 12
illustrations) £750
ditto, Verlag Rascher (Zurich), 1920 (ordinary edition
of 450 copies, 12 illustrations) £200
Die Buchse der Pandora, by Frank Wedekind, George
Muller Verlag (Munich), [1921] (12 illustrations) .
. . . . £100
Erdgeist, by Frank Wedekind, George Muller Verlag
(Munich), [1921] (12 illustrations) £100
Die Rache einer Frau, by Barbey d'Aurevilly,
(Vienna), 1924 (9 illustrations) £100
Sebastian van Storck, by Walter Pater, Im Avalun
Verlag (Vienna), 1924 (480 copies, 8 illustrations) .
. . . . £200

ditto, John Lane, 1927 (1050 copies, 8 illustrations, of which one is signed in pencil by the artist) . £200

ditto, Propyläen Verlag (Frankfurt), 1974 (facsimile reprint of 1924 edition, limited to 400 copies, 8 illustrations) £50

Salome, by Oscar Wilde, G. Crès (Paris), 1922 (9 illustrations) £75

ditto, G. Crès (Paris), 1922 (100 copies on Imperial Japon paper, 9 illustrations) £500

Fifty Drawings, by Alastair, Alfred A. Knopf (U.S.), 1925 (1025 copies in box) . . . . . £300/£200

Red Skeletons, by Harry Crosby, Editions Narcisse (Paris), 1927 (ordinary edition of 337 copies, 9 illustrations) £500

ditto, Editions Narcisse (Paris), 1927 (33 copies on Imperial Japon paper, 9 illustrations) . . . £1,000

The Fall of the House of Usher, by Edgar Allan Poe, Editions Narcisse (Paris), 1928 (1 copy only on old Japon paper containing the original drawings, 5 illustrations) £20,000

ditto, Editions Narcisse (Paris), 1928 (307 copies, 5 illustrations) £750

L'Anniversaire de L'Enfant, by Oscar Wilde, Black Sun Press (Paris), 1928 (9 illustrations) . . £250

The Birthday of the Infanta, by Oscar Wilde, Black Sun Press (Paris), 1928 (100 copies, as above but text in English, 9 illustrations, slipcase). £1,250/£1,000

Manon Lescaut, by Abbé Prévost, John Lane, 1928 (1850 copies, 11 illustrations) £75

ditto, privately printed for Rarity Press, 1933 (a very poor reprint of the above, 11 illustrations). . £30

Les Liaisons Dangereuses, by Choderlos de Laclos, Black Sun Press (Paris), 1929 (2 vols, edition of 15 sets on Japon paper, 7 illustrations). . . £2,500

ditto, Black Sun Press (Paris), 1929 (ordinary edition of 1005 sets, 7 illustrations) . . . . . £250/£150

ditto, privately printed for William Godwin (U.S.), 1933 (as *Dangerous Acquaintances*, a very poor reprint of Vol. 1 of above edition) £30

Alastair: Illustrator of Decadence, Thames & Hudson (U.S.), 1979 . . . . £45/£20

Poetry

Das Flammende Tal, Hyperion Verlag (Munich), 1920 (680 copies) £450

CECIL ALDIN

(b.1870 d.1925)

A British comic illustrator in the 1890s, Aldin later became a successful sporting artist.

Spot, An Autobiography, Houlston, 1894 (14 b/w illustrations) £125

Wonderland Wonders, by Rev. John Isabell, Home Words, 1895 (frontispiece and 19 plates) . . £95

Every-Day Characters, by Winthrop Mackworth Praed, Kegan, Paul, Trench, Trubner & Co., 1896 . . . . £450

Prehistoric Man and Beast, by Henry Neville Hutchinson, Smith, Elder & Co, 1896 . . . £65

Two Little Runaways, by James Buckland, Longman, 1898 . . . . £75

Two Well-Worn Shoe Stories, Sands, 1899 (illustrations by Aldin and John Hassall) £225

A Cockney in Arcadia, by Harry Spurr, George Allen, 1899 (28 illustrations by Aldin and John Hassall) £75

Ten Little Puppy Dogs, Sands, [1902] . . . £200

A Sporting Garland, Sands, 1902 (23 colour plates) £650

Faithful Friends, Blackie, 1902 . . . . . £100

Bubble and Squeak, by P. Robinson, Isbister, 1902 . . . . £350

A Dog Day, or The Angel in the House, by Walter Emanuel, Heinemann, 1902 (28 full page black, white & red on brown plates) £125

The House Annual, Gale & Palden, 1902 . . £75

The Young Folks Birthday Book, Hills, 1902 . £50

The Snob: Some Episodes In a Mis-spent Youth, by Walter Emanuel, Lawrence & Bullen, 1904 (19 colour plates). £100

A Gay Dog: The Story of a Foolish Year, by Walter Emanuel, Heinemann, 1905 (24 colour plates) £150

The Dogs of War, by Walter Emanuel, Bradbury Agnew, [1906] (frontispiece and 11 colour plates) £200

The Happy Annual, Heinemann, 1907 (with John Hassall) £75

Old Christmas, by Washington Irving, Hodder & Stoughton, 1908 (27 colour plates, 6 b/w illustrations) £150

Farm Friends for Little Folk, Blackie, 1908 . £100

The Playtime Picture Books, Lawrence & Jellicoe, 1909 (series) . . . . £175 each

Pussy and Her Ways, Henry Frowde/Hodder & Stoughton, [1909] £200

Doggie and His Ways, Henry Frowde/Hodder & Stoughton, [1909] £200

The Black Puppy Book, Henry Frowde/Hodder & Stoughton, [1909] £225

The White Puppy Book, Henry Frowde/Hodder & Stoughton, [1909] (12 colour plates) . . . £225

The White Kitten Book, Henry Frowde/Hodder & Stoughton, [1909] (11 colour plates) . . . £225

Pickles, A Puppy Dog's Tale, Henry Frowde/Hodder & Stoughton, [1909] (24 colour plates) . . £350

The Perverse Widow, and *The Widow* by R. Steele, and Washington Irving, Heinemann, 1909 (3 colour plates). £25

Wives, and *The Henpecked Man* by Washington Irving, and R. Steele, Heinemann, 1909 (3 colour plates). £25

Bachelors, and *Bachelor's Confessions* by Washington Irving, Heinemann, 1909 (3 colour plates). £25

Rough and Tumble, Henry Frowde/Hodder & Stoughton, [1910] £350

Field Babies, Henry Frowde/Hodder & Stoughton, [1910] (24 colour plates) £200

The Twins, Henry Frowde/Hodder & Stoughton, [1910] (24 colour plates) £325

The Red Puppy Book, Henry Frowde/Hodder & Stoughton, [1910] (12 colour plates) . . . £200

My Pets, Henry Frowde/Hodder & Stoughton, [1910] £100

An Old-Fashioned Christmas Eve, by Washington Irving, Hodder & Stoughton, 1910 . . . . £50

An Old-Fashioned Christmas Day, by Washington Irving, Hodder & Stoughton, 1910 (6 colour plates) £50

The Posthumous Papers of the Pickwick Club, by Charles Dickens, Chapman & Hall/Lawrence & Jellicoe, 1910 (2 vols, vol. I with 13 colour plates, vol. II with 11 colour plates) £150

ditto, Chapman & Hall/Lawrence & Jellicoe, 1910 (as above but 250 signed copies) £250

My Book of Doggies: Stories and Pictures for Little Folk, Blackie, [1910] £100

Farm Babies, by May Byron, Henry Frowde/Hodder & Stoughton, [1911] (24 colour plates) . . . £300

Handley Cross, Or Mr. Jorrock's Hunt, by Robert Smith Surtees, Edward Arnold [1911] (12 colour plates in each of 2 vols) £100

Farmyard Puppies, Henry Frowde/Hodder & Stoughton, [1911] (12 colour plates) . . . £250

Merry and Bright, Henry Frowde/Hodder & Stoughton, [1911] (24 colour plates) . . . £350

Mac: A Story of a Dog, Henry Frowde/Hodder & Stoughton, [1912] (24 colour plates) . . . £350

The Mongrel Puppy Book, Henry Frowde/Hodder & Stoughton, [1912] (12 colour plates) . . £200

Puppy Tails, by Richard Waylett, Lawrence & Jellicoe, [1912]. £125

Black Beauty, by Anna Sewell, Jarrold, [1912] (18 colour plates). £100

ditto, Jarrold, [1912] (250 copies) £300

White-Ear and Peter: The Story of a Fox and a Fox-Terrier, by Neils Heiberg, Macmillan, 1912 (16 colour plates). £150

Cecil Aldin's Happy Family, by May Byron, Henry Frowde/Hodder & Stoughton, [1912] (6 parts, illustrated in colour). . . . . . . £75 each

ditto, Henry Frowde/Hodder & Stoughton, [1912] (single volume edition) £100

Cecil Aldin's Merry Party, by May Byron, Henry Frowde/Hodder & Stoughton, [1913] (6 parts, illustrated in colour). . . . . . . £75 each

ditto, Henry Frowde/Hodder & Stoughton, [1913] (single volume edition) £100

My Dog, by Maurice Maeterlinck, Allen, 1913 (6 colour plates). £100

Zoo Babies, by G.E. Farrow, Henry Frowde/Hodder & Stoughton, 1913 . . . . £125

The Merry Puppy Book, Milford, 1913 (36 colour plates). £275

The Underdog, by Sidney Trist, Animals' Guardian, 1913 (4 plates) £75

Cecil Aldin's Rag Book, The Animals' School Treat, by Clifton Bingham, Dean: 'Rag Book' series No. 70, [1913] (24 colour plates) £175

The Bobtail Puppy Book, Henry Frowde/Hodder & Stoughton, [1914] (12 colour plates) . . . £225

Jack and Jill, by May Byron, Henry Frowde/Hodder & Stoughton, [1914] (24 colour plates) . . . £400

The Dog Who Wasn't What He Thought He Was, by Walter Emanuel, Raphael Tuck, [1914] (24 colour plates). £250

Animal Revels, by May Byron, Henry Frowde/Hodder & Stoughton, [1915]. £100

Moufflou, by Ouida, T.C. & E.C. Jack, 1915 . £100

The Cecil Aldin Painting Books, Lawrence & Jellicoe, [1915]. £125

Jock and Some Others, by Richard Waylett, Gale & Polden, [1916] (16 colour plates) £250

Animal Frolics, by May Byron, Henry Frowde/Hodder & Stoughton, [1916]. £100

The Merry Party, Humphrey Milford, [1918] . £150

Bunnyborough, Humphrey Milford, [1919] . £275

ditto, Eyre & Spottiswoode, 1946 (15 colour plates) . . . . £75/£25

Gyp's Hour of Bliss, by Gladys Davidson, Collins, 1919 . . . . £200

The Great Adventure, Humphrey Milford, [1921] (17 colour plates). £250

Cecil Aldin Letter Books, Humphrey Milford, [1921] (6 parts) £125

Old Inns, Heinemann, 1921 (16 plates) . . £150/£75

ditto, Heinemann, 1921 (380 signed copies) . £200

Us, Humphrey Milford, [1922] . . . . £150/£75

Right Royal by John Masefield, Heinemann, 1922 (4 plates). . . . . £100/£25

Old Manor Houses, Heinemann, 1923 (12 plates) . . . . £100/£65

Jack Frost Days, Collins, 1923 (with John Hassall) . . . . £150/£75

Cathedrals and Abbey Churches of England, Eyre & Spottiswoode, 1924 (16 plates) . . . . £35/£10

ditto, Eyre & Spottiswoode, 1929 (375 signed copies) £250

Ratcatcher to Scarlet, Eyre & Spottiswoode, 1926. . . . . £125/£45

Dogs of Character, Eyre & Spottiswoode, 1927 . . . . £125/£45

ditto, Eyre & Spottiswoode, 1927 (250 signed copies with an original signed sketch) £500

A Dozen Dogs Or So, by P.R. Chalmers, Eyre & Spottiswoode, 1927 (13 colour plates) . . £150/£65

ditto, Eyre & Spottiswoode, 1927 (13 colour plates, 250 copies, signed by Aldin and Chalmers) . £300

Berkshire Vale, by Wilfred Howe-Nurse, Basil Blackwell, 1927 (22 plates). . . . . . £150/£100

The Romance of the Road, Eyre & Spottiswoode, 1928 (12 colour plates and colour map of London in front pocket) . . . . £225/£150
Sleeping Partners: A Series of Episodes, Eyre & Spottiswoode, [1929] (20 colour plates) . £300/£200
Jerry: The Story of an Exmoor Pony, by Eleanor E. Helme and Nance Paul, Eyre & Spottiswoode, [1930] (11 b/w illustrations). . . . . . . £50/£10
Roads and Vagabonds, by Kenneth Hare, Eyre & Spottiswoode, [1930] . . . . . . £175/£75
ditto, Eyre & Spottiswoode, [1930] (50 copies signed by Hare and Aldin) £225
An Artist's Model, H. F & G Witherby, 1930 (20 colour plates). . . . . £250/£175
ditto, H. F & G Witherby, 1930 (250 signed copies) £350
Riding, by Lady Hunloke, Eyre and Spottiswoode, 1931 . . . . £45/£20
Mrs Tickler's Caravan, Eyre & Spottiswoode, 1931 . . . . £75/£30
Lost, Stolen or Strayed, by Marion Ashmore, Eyre & Spottiswoode, 1931 (30 b/w illustrations and colour frontispiece) . . . . £65/£25
Flax, Police Dog, by Svend Fleuron, Eyre & Spottiswoode, [1931] (10 b/w illustrations) £65/£35
Forty Fine Ladies, Eyre & Spottiswoode, 1929 . . . . £200/£125
ditto, Eyre & Spottiswoode, 1929 (250 signed copies). £300
The Bunch Book, by James Douglas, Eyre & Spottiswoode, 1932 (51 b/w illustrations and coloured frontispiece) . . . . £50/£20
The Joker, and Jerry Again, by Eleanor E. Helme and Nance Paul, Eyre & Spottiswoode, 1932 . £45/£15
The Cecil Aldin Book, Eyre & Spottiswoode, 1932 (8 colour plates and 95 b/w illustrations) . . £75/£45
Scarlet, Blue and Green, by Duncan Fife, Macmillan, 1932 (5 colour plates, 7 half-tone and 25 b/w illustrations) . . . . £100/£50
His Apologies, by Rudyard Kipling, Doubleday Doran (U.S.), 1932 . . . . £65/£35
Dogs of Every Day, by Patrick Chalmers, Eyre & Spottiswoode, 1933 (12 full-page mono plates) . . . . £100/£65
Who's Who in the Zoo, Eyre & Spottiswoode, 1933 (4 colour plates and 35 full-page b/w illustrations) . . . . £65/£30
Scarlet to M.F.H., Eyre & Spottiswoode, 1933 (21 plates) . . . . £175/£50
Hotspur the Beagle, by John Vickerman, Constable, 1934 . . . . £65/£45
Time I Was Dead: Pages from my Autobiography, Eyre & Spottiswoode, 1934 . . . . . £65/£45
Just Among Friends, Eyre & Spottiswoode, 1934 . . . . £175/£215
How to Draw Dogs, John Lane/Bodley Head, 1935 . . . . £150/£100
Exmoor, The Riding Playground of England, Witherby, 1935 (4 plates) . . . . . £50/£20

Smuggler's Gallows, by William E.S. Hope, Eyre & Spottiswoode, 1936 . . . . . . £35/£20
Hunting Scenes, Eyre & Spottiswoode, 1936 . . . . £175/£100
Last Muster, Eyre & Spottiswoode, 1939 . £75/£45

RICHARD ALDINGTON
(b.1892 d.1962)

Richard Aldington, poet, novelist and literary scholar, is probably best known for being one of the first three Imagist poets, along with Ezra Pound and H.D.

Novels
Death of a Hero, Chatto & Windus, 1929 . £100/£40
ditto, Covici Friede (U.S.), 1929 . . . . £45/£20
ditto, Babou & Kahane (Paris), 1930 (first unexpurgated edition, 300 copies, 2 vols, tissue d/w). . . . . £400/£300
The Colonel's Daughter. A Novel, Chatto & Windus, 1931 . . . . £20/£5
ditto, Chatto & Windus, 1931 (210 signed, numbered copies) £125
ditto, Doubleday (U.S.), 1931 . . . . . £20/£5
Stepping Heavenward - A Record, Orioli (Florence), 1931 (808 signed, numbered copies) . £65/£45
ditto, Chatto & Windus, 1931 . . . . . £25/£5
All Men are Enemies: A Romance, Chatto & Windus, 1932 . . . . £20/£5
ditto, Chatto & Windus, 1933 (110 signed copies) £100
ditto, Doubleday (U.S.), 1933 . . . . . £20/£5
Women Must Work, Chatto & Windus, 1934 . £20/£5
ditto, Doubleday (U.S.), 1934 . . . . . £20/£5
Very Heaven, Heinemann, 1937 . . . . . £15/£5
ditto, Doubleday (U.S.), 1937 . . . . . £15/£5
Seven Against Reeves: A Comedy-Farce, Heinemann, 1938 . . . . £15/£5
ditto, Doubleday (U.S.), 1938 . . . . . £15/£5
Rejected Guest, Viking (U.S.), 1939. . . . £20/£5
ditto, Heinemann, 1939 . . . . £15/£5
The Romance of Casanova: a Novel, Duell, Sloan & Pearce (U.S.), 1946 . . . . £15/£5
ditto, Heinemann, 1946 . . . . £15/£5

Short Stories
Roads to Glory, Chatto & Windus, 1930 . £75/£15
ditto, Chatto & Windus, 1930 (360 numbered copies) £90
ditto, Doubleday (U.S.), 1931 . . . . £30/£10
Two Stories, Elkin Mathews & Marrot, 1930 (530 signed, numbered copies) . . . . . £65/£35
At All Costs, Heinemann, 1930 . . . . . £15/£5
ditto, Heinemann, 1930 (275 signed, numbered copies) £65
Last Straws, Hours Press (Paris), 1930 (500 numbered copies out of 700) £100

ditto, Hours Press (Paris), 1930 (200 signed, numbered copies out of 700) £150
Soft Answers, Chatto & Windus, 1932 . . . £20/£5
ditto, Chatto & Windus, 1932 (110 signed copies) £90
ditto, Doubleday (U.S.), 1932 . . . . . £20/£5

Poetry
Images (1910-1915), The Poetry Bookshop, 1915 (wraps) £200
ditto, as *Images Old and New*, Four Seas Company (U.S.), 1916 (wraps). £75
The Love of Myrrhine and Konallis And Other Prose Poems, The Clerk's Press (U.S.), 1917 (40 copies, wraps). £250
ditto, Pascal Covici (U.S.), 1926 (150 signed copies) . . . . £75/£45
ditto, Pascal Covici (U.S.), 1926 (unsigned copies) . . . . £25/£5
Reverie, A Little Book of Poems for H.D., The Clerk's Press (U.S.), 1917 (50 copies, wraps) . . . £150
Images of War, Beaumont Press, 1919 (30 numbered, signed copies, in box) £400
ditto, Beaumont Press, 1919 (50 copies on cartridge paper numbered 31 to 80) £200
ditto, Beaumont Press, 1919 (120 unsigned copies on hand-made paper, numbered 81 to 200) . . £75
ditto, Allen & Unwin, 1919 . . . . . . £20
ditto, Four Seas Company (U.S.), 1921 (wraps) £65
Images of Desire, Elkin Mathews/Riverside Press, 1919 (signed, numbered, wraps) £95
Images, The Egoist Ltd, 1919 (wraps) . . . £45
War and Love (1915-1918), Four Seas Company (U.S.), 1919 . . . . £45
The Berkshire Kennet, Curwen Press, 1923 (50 copies, wraps). £150
Collected Poems 1915-1923, Allen & Unwin, 1923 . . . . £35/£15
Exile and Other Poems, Allen & Unwin, 1923 (700 unsigned copies of 750) . . . . . £65/£25
ditto, Allen & Unwin, 1923 (50 signed copies of 750) . . . . £250/£175
A Fool i' the Forest: a Phantasmagoria, Allen & Unwin, 1924 . . . . £35/£10
Hark the Herald, Hours Press (Paris), 1928 (100 numbered, signed copies) £300
The Eaten Heart, Hours Press (Paris), 1929 (200 numbered, signed copies) £300
ditto, Chatto & Windus, 1933 . . . . £30/£10
Movietones: Invented and Set Down by Richard Aldington, 1928-1929, privately printed, 1932 (10 copies) £7,500
Love and the Luxembourg, Covici Friede (U.S.), 1930 (475 signed copies, slipcase) . . . . £45/£25
ditto, as *A Dream in the Luxembourg*, Chatto & Windus, 1930 (308 signed copies) . . . £45/£25
The Poems of Richard Aldington, Doubleday (U.S.), 1934 . . . . £15/£5
Life Quest, Chatto & Windus, 1935 . . . . £15/£5
ditto, Doubleday (U.S.), 1935 . . . . £10/£5

The Crystal World, Heinemann, 1937 . . . £10/£5
ditto, Doubleday (U.S.), 1937 . . . . . £10/£5

Others
Literary Studies and Reviews, Allen & Unwin 1924 . . . . £30/£10
ditto, Lincoln MacVeagh/Dial Press (U.S.), 1924 . . . . £30/£10
Voltaire, Routledge, 1925 . . . . . £30/£10
French Studies and Reviews, Allen & Unwin, 1926 . . . . £45/£20
ditto, Dial Press (U.S.), 1926 . . . . . £45/£20
D.H. Lawrence: An Indiscretion, Univ. of Washington Book Store (U.S.), 1927 (wraps) £25
ditto, as *D.H. Lawrence*, Chatto & Windus, 1930 (250 signed copies) £75
ditto, as *D.H. Lawrence*, Chatto & Windus, 1930 (wraps) £20
Remy de Gourment. A Modern Man of Letters, Univ. of Washington Book Store (U.S.), 1928 (wraps) £25
Balls and Another Book for Suppression, Lahr, 1930 (100 copies, wraps) £45
ditto, Lahr, 1930 (unlimited edition, wraps). . £25
Balls, privately printed, 1932 (99 + copies, single folded sheet) £200
The Squire Heinemann, 1934 . . . . . £2,750
D.H. Lawrence: A Complete List of His Works, Together with a Critical Appreciation, Heinemann, [1935?] . . . . £35/£10
Artifex: Sketches and Ideas, Chatto & Windus, 1935 . . . . £20/£5
ditto, Doubleday, 1936 . . . . . . £15/£5
W. Somerset Maugham, An Appreciation, Doubleday (U.S.), 1939 (wraps). £35
Life for Life's Sake, A Book of Reminiscences, Viking (U.S.), 1941 . . . . £40/£20
ditto, Cassell, 1968 . . . . . . £25/£10
The Duke, Being an Account of the Life and Achievements of the 1st Duke of Wellington, Viking (U.S.), 1943 . . . . £15/£5
ditto, as *Wellington*, Heinemann, 1946 . . . £15/£5
Jane Austen, Ampersand Press (U.S.), 1948 . £50
Four English Portraits 1801-1851, Evans, 1948 . . . . £20/£5
The Strange Life of Charles Waterton, Evans, 1949 . . . . £20/£5
ditto, Duell, Sloan & Pearce (U.S.), 1949 . £20/£5
D.H. Lawrence: An Appreciation, Penguin, 1950 (wraps) £5
ditto, as *D.H. Lawrence, Portrait of a Genius, But ...*, Heinemann, 1950 . . . . £25/£10
ditto, as *D.H. Lawrence, Portrait of a Genius, But ...*, Duell, Sloan & Pearce (U.S.), 1950 . . £25/£10
Pinorman: Personal Recollections of Norman Douglas, Pino Orioli, and Charles Prentice, Heinemann, 1954 . . . . £25/£10
Ezra Pound & T.S. Eliot - A Lecture, The Peacocks Press, 1954 (350 signed, numbered copies, glassine d/w, slipcase). . . . . £75/£65

ditto, The Peacocks Press, 1954 (10 trial copies, azure paper, signed) £250
A.E. Housman & W.B. Yeats: Two Lectures, The Peacocks Press, 1955 (350 copies of 360, glassine d/w) . . . . £75/£45
Lawrence L'Imposteur: T.E. Lawrence, the Legend and the Man, Amiot-Dumont (Paris), 1954 . £35
ditto, as **Lawrence of Arabia: A Biographical Enquiry**, Collins, 1955 (first issue with errata slip at p. 332) . . . . £35/£15
ditto, as **Lawrence of Arabia: A Biographical Enquiry**, Regenery (U.S.), 1955 . . . £35/£15
Introduction to Mistral, Heinemann, 1956 . . £20/£5
ditto, Southern Illinois Univ. Press (U.S.), 1960 £10/£5
Frauds, Heinemann, 1957 . . . . . . £10/£5
A Tourist's Rome, Melissa Press (France), [1960 or 1961] (wraps) £75
Portrait of a Rebel, The Life and Works of Robert Louis Stevenson, Evans, 1957 . . . . £15/£5
A Letter from Richard Aldington and a Summary Bibliography of Count Potocki's Published Works, Melissa Press (France), 1962 . . . . . £100
D.H. Lawrence in Selbstzeugnissen und Bilddokumenten, Rowohlt Taschenbuch (Hamburg), 1961 . . . . £10/£5
Selected Critical Writings 1928-60, Southern Illinois Univ. Press (U.S.), 1970 . . . . £10/£5
A Passionate Prodigality: Letters to Alan Bird from Richard Aldington 1949-1962, New York Public Library & Readers Books (U.S.), 1975 . . . £10/£5
Literary Lifelines: The Richard Aldington - Lawrence Durrell Correspondence, Faber, 1981 . . . £15/£5
ditto, Viking (U.S.), 1981 . . . . . . £15/£5

BRIAN ALDISS
(b.1925)

First published during the 1950s, Aldiss is best known for science fiction novels. He is able to push the genre to the limits of convention, however. *Barefoot in the Head* owes much to Joyce, and *A Report on Probability* is in essence an 'anti-novel'. His mainstream novel *Life in the West* was selected by Anthony Burgess as one of the 99 best novels published in England since 1945.

Novels
The Brightfount Diaries, Faber, 1955 . . £90/£40
Non-Stop, Faber, 1958 (first printing red boards) . . . . £220/£30
ditto, as **Starship**, Criterion (U.S.), 1959 . £70/£20
Vanguard from Alpha, Ace (U.S.), 1959 (paperback double with Kenneth Bulmer's *The Changeling Worlds*) £10
ditto, as **Equator**, Digit, 1961 (wraps) . . . £10

Bow Down to Nul, Ace (U.S.), 1960 (paperback double with Manly Wade Wellman's *The Dark Destroyers*) £10
ditto, as **The Interpreter**, Digit, 1961 (wraps) . £10
The Male Response, Galaxy Publishing Corp/Beacon Press (U.S.), 1961 (wraps) £40
ditto, Dobson, 1963 . . . . £40/£5
The Primal Urge, Ballantine (U.S.), 1961 (wraps) . £5
ditto, Sphere, 1967 (wraps) £5
The Long Afternoon of Earth, Signet (U.S.), 1962 (abridged, wraps) £5
ditto, as **Hothouse**, Faber, 1962 (full text) . £400/£35
The Dark Light Years, Faber, 1964 . . . £45/£10
ditto, Signet (U.S.), 1964 (wraps) £5
Greybeard, Harcourt Brace (U.S.), 1964 . £60/£10
ditto, Faber, 1964 . . . . £50/£10
Earthworks, Faber, 1965 . . . . . £40/£10
ditto, Doubleday (U.S.), 1966 . . . . . £20/£5
An Age, Faber, 1967 . . . . . . £40/£10
ditto, as **Cryptozoic**, Doubleday, 1968 . . £20/£5
Report on Probability A, Faber, 1968 . . £35/£5
ditto, Doubleday (U.S.), 1969 . . . . . £25/£5
Barefoot in the Head, Faber, 1969 . . . £55/£5
ditto, Doubleday (U.S.), 1970 . . . . . £25/£5
The Hand-Reared Boy, Weidenfeld & Nicolson, 1970 . . . . £25/£5
ditto, McCall (U.S.), 1970 . . . . . . £20/£5
A Soldier Erect, Weidenfeld & Nicolson, 1971 . £25/£5
ditto, McCann (U.S.), 1971 . . . . . £15/£5
Frankenstein Unbound, Cape, 1973 . . £40/£10
ditto, Random House (U.S.), [1974] . . . £20/£5
The Eighty-Minute Hour, Doubleday (U.S.), 1974 . . . . £15/£5
ditto, Cape, 1974 . . . . £25/£5
The Malacia Tapestry, Cape, 1976 . . . £30/£5
ditto, Harper & Row (U.S.), [1977] . . . £55/£5
Brothers of the Head, Pierrot, 1977 . . . £35/£5
ditto, Pierrot, 1977 (wraps) £15
ditto, Pierrot/Two Continents (U.S.), 1977 . £35/£5
ditto, Pierrot/Two Continents (U.S.), 1977 (wraps). £15
ditto, as **Brothers of the Head**, and **Where the Lines Converge**, Panther, 1979 (wraps) £5
Enemies of the System, Cape, 1978 . . . £15/£5
ditto, Harper & Row (U.S.), 1978 . . . £10/£5
A Rude Awakening, Weidenfeld & Nicolson, 1978 . . . . £10/£5
ditto, Random House (U.S.), 1979 . . . £10/£5
Life in the West, Weidenfeld & Nicolson, 1980 £45/£5
ditto, Carroll & Graf (U.S.), 1990 . . . £15/£5
Moreau's Other Island, Cape, 1980 . . . £20/£5
ditto, as **An Island Called Moreau**, Simon & Schuster (U.S.), 1981 . . . . £15/£5
Helliconia Spring, Cape, 1982 . . . . £25/£5
ditto, Atheneum (U.S.), 1982 . . . . . £15/£5
Helliconia Summer, Cape, 1983 . . . . £25/£5
ditto, Atheneum (U.S.), 1983 . . . . . £15/£5
Helliconia Winter, Atheneum (U.S.), 1985 . . £20/£5
ditto, Cape, 1985 . . . . £20/£5

Ruins, Century Hutchinson, 1987 . . . . . £10/£5
The Year Before Yesterday, Watts (U.S.), 1987. . .
. . . .£15/£5
ditto, as Cracken at Critical, Kerosina, 1987 . £15/£5
ditto, Kerosina, 1987 (250 signed, numbered copies,
with d/w and in slipcase with *The Magic of the Past*)
. . . . £40 the set
ditto, Kerosina, 1987 (26 lettered, ¼ leather copies) .
. . . .£125
Forgotten Life, Gollancz, 1988 . . . . . £10/£5
ditto, Atheneum (U.S.), 1989. . . . . .£10/£5
Dracula Unbound, HarperCollins (U.S.), 1991. £10/£5
ditto, Easton Press (U.S.), 1991 (priority between this
and HarperCollins edition not determined). . £60
ditto, Grafton, 1991 . . . .£10/£5
Remembrance Day, HarperCollins (U.S.), 1992 . .
. . . .£10/£5
ditto, St Martin's Press (U.S.), 1993 . . . .£10/£5
*White Mars, or, The Mind Set Free: A 21ˢᵗ Century
Utopia*, Little, Brown, 1999. . . . . £10/£5
ditto, St Martin's Press (U.S.), 1999 . . . .£10/£5
A Chinese Perspective, James Goddard, 2000 (300
copies, wraps) £10
Super-State, Orbit, 2002 . . . . £10/£5
The Cretan Teat, House of Stratus, 2002 . . £10/£5

Short Stories
Space, Time and Nathaniel, Faber, 1957 . £200/£45
ditto, as No Time Like Tomorrow, Signet (U.S.), 1959
(wraps) £10
The Canopy of Time, Faber, 1959 . . . £80/£15
ditto, as Galaxies Like Grains of Sand, Signet (U.S.),
1960 (wraps) £5
The Airs of Earth, Faber, 1963 . . . . £50/£20
ditto, as Starswarm, Signet (U.S.), 1964 (wraps) . £5
Best Science Fiction Stories of Brian W. Aldiss, Faber,
1965 . . . .£30/£5
ditto, as Who Can Replace a Man?, Harcourt Brace
(U.S.), 1966 . . . .£15/£5
*ditto. as Best Science Fiction Stories of Brian W.
Aldiss* Faber, 1971 (revised edition) . . .£15/£5
The Saliva Tree and Other Strange Growths, Faber,
1966 . . . . £65/£20
ditto, Gregg Press (U.S.), 1987 (no d/w). . . £40
Intangibles Inc. and Other Stories, Faber, 1969 . .
. . . .£30/£5
ditto, as Neanderthal Planet, Avon (U.S.), 1970.
(wraps) £5
ditto, as Neanderthal Planet, Avon, Science Fiction
Book Club (U.S.), 1970 . . . . . .£10/£5
The Moment of Eclipse, Faber, 1970 . . .£35/£5
ditto, as Moment of Eclipse, Doubleday (U.S.), 1972 .
. . . .£10/£5
The Book of Brian Aldiss, Daw Books (U.S.), 1972
(wraps) £10
ditto, as The Comic Inferno, N.E.L., 1973 (wraps) .
. . . . £5
Excommunication, Postcard Partnership (U.S.), 1975
(very short story printed on a postcard). . . £10
Last Orders, Cape, 1977 . . . .£20/£5

ditto, Carroll & Graf (U.S.), 1989 . . . .£10/£5
New Arrivals, Old Encounters, Cape, 1979 . .£20/£5
ditto, Harper & Row (U.S.), 1979 . . . .£10/£5
A Romance of the Equator, Birmingham Science
Fiction Group, 1980 (wraps) £15
Foreign Bodies, Chopmen (Singapore), 1981 .£45/£5
ditto, Chopmen (Singapore), 1981 (wraps) . . £20
Best of Aldiss, Viaduct Publications, 1983 (wraps,
magazine format) £15
Seasons in Flight, Cape, 1984 . . . . .£10/£5
ditto, Atheneum (U.S.), 1986. . . . . .£10/£5
My Country 'Tis Not Only of Thee, Aldiss
Appreciation Society, 1986 (100 signed copies) £25
The Magic of the Past, Kerosina, 1987 (350 copies,
wraps). £5
ditto, Kerosina, 1987 (250 cloth copies without jacket,
in slipcase with *Cracken at Critical*) . £40 the set
Science Fiction Blues, Avernus, 1987 (wraps,
programme booklet) £10
Science Fiction Blues, Avernus, 1988 (wraps, short
stories with poetry and stage sketches). . . £10
Best SF Stories of Brian W. Aldiss, Gollancz, 1988
(new collection) . . . .£15/£5
ditto, as Man in His Time, Atheneum (U.S.), 1989 .
. . . .£10/£5
A Romance of the Equator: Best Fantasy Stories,
Gollancz, 1989 . . . .£15/£5
ditto, Atheneum (U.S.), 1990. . . . . .£10/£5
Bodily Functions, Avernus, 1991 (100 signed copies).
. . . .£40/£20
Journey to the Goat Star, Pulphouse Publishing (U.S.),
1991 (wraps) £5
A Tupolev Too Far, HarperCollins, 1993. . £10/£5
ditto, St Martin's Press (U.S.), 1994 . . . .£10/£5
The Secret of This Book, HarperCollins, 1995 .£10/£5
ditto, as Common Clay: 20 Odd Stories, St Martin's
Press (U.S.), 1996 . . . .£10/£5
The Rain Will Stop, The Pretentious Press (U.S.), 2000
(85 signed, numbered copies, wraps) . . . £25
*Supertoys Last All Summer Long and Other Stories of
Future Time*, Orbit, 2001 (wraps) £10

Poetry
Summer 1773, The Bellvue Press (U.S.), 1976 (single
poem on a postcard).. . . . . . . £5
Pile: Petals from St Klaed's Computer, Cape, 1979
(illustrated by Mike Wilks, laminated boards, no d/w)
. . . . £10
ditto, Cape, 1979 (unspecified number signed by author
and artist on tipped-in bookplate) £15
ditto, Holt Rinehart (U.S.), 1980 . . . . . £10
Farewell to a Child, Priapus, 1982 (315 of 350
unsigned copies) £15
ditto, Priapus, 1982 (35 signed, numbered copies of
350) £25
Home Life With Cats, Grafton, 1992 (laminated
boards, no d/w) £10
At the Caligula Hotel, Sinclair Stevenson, 1995
(wraps) £15

Songs from the Steppes of central Asia: the Collected Poems of Makhtumkuli – Eighteenth century Poet Hero of Turkmenistan The society of Friends of Makhtumkuli, 1995 (translated by Dr Youssef Azemoun and versified by Aldiss) . . . . £30/£5
A Plutonian Monologue, The Frogmore Press, 2000 (200 signed, numbered copies, wraps) £5
At a Bigger House, Avernus, 2002 (20 copies with eight coloured plates from author's own paintings, wraps). £60

Non Fiction
Cities and Stones: A Traveller's Yugoslavia, Faber, 1966 . . . . £30/£5
The Shape of Further Things, Faber, 1970. . £30/£5
ditto, Doubleday (U.S.), 1971 . . . . . £15/£5
Billion Year Spree: The History of Science Fiction, Weidenfeld & Nicolson, 1973 . . . . . £15/£5
ditto, Doubleday (U.S.), 1973 . . . . . £10/£5
Science Fiction Art, N.E.L., 1975 (oversized soft cover). £35
ditto, Bounty Books (U.S.), 1975 . . . . £20
Science Fiction as Science Fiction, Bran's Head Books, 1978 (wraps). £20
This World and Nearer Ones: Essays Exploring the Familiar, Weidenfeld & Nicolson, 1979 . . £10/£5
ditto, Kent State (U.S.), 1981 (wraps) . . . £10
The Pale Shadow of Science, Serconia Press (U.S.), 1985 . . . . £30/£5
Trillion Year Spree: The History of Science Fiction, Gollancz, 1986 (with David Wingrove) . £25/£10
ditto, Gollancz, 1986 (100 signed copies of 126, slipcase) £125
ditto, Gollancz, 1986 (26 signed, lettered copies of 126) £200
ditto, Atheneum (U.S.), 1986. . . . . . £25/£5
...And the Lurid Glare of the Comet, Serconia Press (U.S.), 1986 . . . . £15/£5
Bury my Heart at W.H. Smith's, Hodder & Stoughton, 1990 . . . . £15/£5
ditto, Avernus, 1990 (250 signed, numbered copies, with six extra chapters) . . . . . £30/£10
The Detached Retina, Liverpool Science Fiction Texts and Studies, No.4, 1994 . . . . . £30/£5
ditto, Liverpool Science Fiction Texts and Studies, No.4, 1994 (wraps) £10
ditto, Syracuse Univ. Press (U.S.), 1995 (wraps) £10
The Twinkling of an Eye, Little, Brown, 1998 . £10/£5
ditto, St Martin's (U.S.), 1999 . . . . £10/£5
When the Feast is Finished, Little, Brown, 1999 . . . . £10/£5

Omnibus Editions
A Brian Aldiss Omnibus, Sidgwick & Jackson, 1969 . . . . £50/£10
Brian Aldiss Omnibus 2, Sidgwick & Jackson, 1971 . . . . £60/£10

Miscellaneous
The Life of Samuel Johnson, as edited [written] by Aldiss, Oxford Polytechnic Press, 1980 (60 signed, numbered copies) £35
Science Fiction Quiz, Weidenfeld & Nicolson, 1983 (laminated boards) £10
Sex and the Black Machine, Avernus: Titan Books, 1988 (wraps) £20
Kindred Blood at Kensington Gore, Avernus, 1992 (wraps) £15
Art After Apogee, Avernus, 2000 (50 copies signed by author and artist, hardback, no d/w) . . . £60
ditto, Avernus, 2000 (50 copies signed by author and artist, wraps) £30

MARGERY ALLINGHAM
(b.1904 d.1966)

An author of detective fiction from its 'Golden Age', whose hero is an aristocratic adventurer known as Albert Campion.

'Albert Campion' Titles
The Crime at Black Dudley, Jarrolds, 1929. . . . . £1,000/£175
ditto, as *The Black Dudley Murder*, Doubleday (U.S.), 1930 . . . . £175/£75
Mystery Mile, Jarrolds, 1930 . . . . . £750/£100
ditto, Doubleday (U.S.), 1930 . . . . £100/£25
Look to the Lady, Jarrolds, 1931. . . . £750/£100
ditto, as *The Gyrth Chalice Mystery*, Doubleday (U.S.), 1931 . . . . £75/£20
Police at the Funeral, Heinemann, 1931 . £500/£75
ditto, Doubleday (U.S.), 1932 . . . . £75/£20
Sweet Danger, Heinemann, 1933 . . . £500/£75
ditto, as *Kingdom of Death*, Doubleday (U.S.), 1933 . . . . £75/£20
Death of a Ghost, Heinemann, 1934. . . £500/£75
ditto, Doubleday (U.S.), 1934 . . . . £75/£15
Flowers for the Judge, Heinemann, 1936 . £350/£50
ditto, Doubleday (U.S.), 1936 . . . . £75/£15
Dancers in Mourning, Heinemann, 1937 . £350/£50
ditto, Doubleday (U.S.), 1937 . . . . £75/£15
The Case of the Late Pig, Hodder & Stoughton, 1937 (wraps) £175
Mr. Campion Criminologist, Doubleday (U.S.), 1937 . . . . £125/£25
The Fashion in Shrouds, Heinemann, 1938 £350/£50
ditto, Doubleday (U.S.), 1938 . . . . £65/£15
Mr Campion and Others, Heinemann, 1939 . . . . £1,000/£175
Traitor's Purse, Heinemann, 1941 . . . £275/£65
ditto, Doubleday (U.S.), 1941 . . . . £65/£15
Coroner's Pidgin, Heinemann, 1945 . . £275/£65
ditto, as *Pearls Before Swine*, Doubleday (U.S.), 1945 . . . . £75/£10

The Case Book of Mr Campion, Spivak (U.S.), 1947 .
. . . . £75
More Work for the Undertaker, Heinemann, 1948. .
. . . . £100/£20
ditto, Doubleday (U.S.), 1949 . . . . £40/£10
The Tiger in the Smoke, Chatto & Windus, 1952 . .
. . . . £45/£10
ditto, Doubleday (U.S.), 1952 . . . . . £25/£5
The Beckoning Lady, Chatto & Windus, 1955 . . .
. . . . £40/£10
ditto, as *The Estate of the Beckoning Lady*, Doubleday
(U.S.), 1955 . . . . £25/£5
Hide My Eyes, Chatto & Windus, 1958 . . £40/£10
ditto, as *Tether's End*, Doubleday (U.S.), 1958. . .
. . . . £25/£5
The China Governess, Doubleday (U.S.), 1962 . .
. . . . £35/£10
ditto, Chatto & Windus, 1963 . . . . . £25/£5
*The Mysterious Mr Campion, An Allingham
Omnibus*, Chatto & Windus, 1963 . . . . £30/£5
The Mind Readers, Morrow (U.S.), 1965 . £30/£5
ditto, Chatto & Windus, 1965 . . . . . £25/£5
Mr Campion's Lady, An Allingham Omnibus, Chatto
& Windus, 1965 . . . . £25/£5
Mr Campion's Clowns, An Allingham Omnibus,
Chatto & Windus, 1967 . . . . . . £15/£5
Cargo of Eagles, Chatto & Windus, 1968 . . £25/£5
ditto, Morrow (U.S.), 1968 . . . . . £20/£5
The Allingham Casebook, Chatto & Windus, 1969 .
. . . . £15/£5
ditto, Morrow (U.S.), 1969 . . . . . £15/£5
The Allingham Minibus, Chatto & Windus, 1973 . .
. . . . £20/£5
ditto, Morrow (U.S.), 1973 . . . . . £15/£5
ditto, as *Mr. Campion's Lucky Day and other Stories*,
Penguin, 1992 . . . . £5
ditto, Carroll & Graf (U.S.), 1992 (pbk). . . . £5
The Return of Mr Campion, Hodder & Stoughton,
1989 . . . . £10/£5
ditto, St Martin's Press (U.S.), 1990 . . . £10/£5

Books Written as 'Maxwell March'
Other Man's Danger, Collins, 1933. . . £250/£45
ditto, as *The Man of Dangerous Secrets*, Doubleday
(U.S.), 1933 . . . . £200/£35
The Rogues' Holiday, Collins, 1935. . . £250/£45
ditto, Doubleday (U.S.), 1935 . . . . £200/£35
The Shadow in the House, Collins Crime Club, 1936 .
. . . . £200/£35
ditto, Doubleday (U.S.), 1936 . . . . £200/£35

Other Crime Titles
The White Cottage Mystery, Jarrolds, 1928. £250/£45
ditto, Carroll & Graf (U.S.), 1990 (pbk). . . . £5
Black Plumes, Doubleday (U.S.), 1940 . £250/£45
ditto, Heinemann, 1940 . . . . . £250/£45
Wanted: Someone Innocent, Stamford House (U.S.),
1946 (wraps) £50
Deadly Duo, Doubleday (U.S.), 1949. . . £30/£10

ditto, as *Take Two at Bedtime*, World's Work, 1950 .
. . . . £30/£10
No Love Lost, World's Work, 1954 . . . £40/£10
ditto, Doubleday (U.S.), 1954 . . . . £25/£10
The Darings of the Red Rose, Crippen & Landru
(U.S.), 1995 (wraps) £45

Other Titles
Blackkerchief Dick, Hodder & Stoughton, 1923 . .
. . . . £750/£125
ditto, as *Black'erchief Dick*, Doubleday (U.S.), 1923 .
. . . . £500/£100
Dance of the Years, Joseph, 1943 . . . £45/£10

Plays
Water in a Sieve, French, 1925 (wraps) . . . £35
Room to Let, Crippen & Landru, 1999 (247 copies,
wraps). £35

Non Fiction
The Oaken Heart, Joseph, 1941 . . . . £75/£35
ditto, Doubleday (U.S.), 1941 . . . . £65/£25

ERIC AMBLER
(b.1909 d.1998)

A popular and influential thriller writer who deftly
directs his heroes through fast-moving plots.

The Dark Frontier, Hodder & Stoughton, 1936 . .
. . . . £5,000/£250
ditto, Mysterious Press (U.S.), 1990 . . . . £20/£5
Uncommon Danger, Hodder & Stoughton, 1937 . .
. . . . £4,500/£250
ditto, as *Background to Danger*, Knopf (U.S.), 1937 .
. . . . £750/£75
Epitaph for a Spy, Hodder & Stoughton, 1938 . . .
. . . . £3,500/£200
ditto, Knopf (U.S.), 1952 . . . . . £100/£25
Cause for Alarm, Hodder & Stoughton, 1938 . . .
. . . . £2,500/£150
ditto, Knopf (U.S.), 1939 . . . . . £500/£40
The Mask of Dimitrios, Hodder & Stoughton, 1939
. . . . £6,500/£350
ditto, as *A Coffin for Dimitrios*, Knopf (U.S.), 1939 .
. . . . £750/£75
Journey into Fear, Hodder & Stoughton, 1940. . .
. . . . £1,500/£150
ditto, Knopf (U.S.), 1940 . . . . . £450/£40
Skytip, Doubleday (U.S.), 1950 (pseud. 'Eliot Reed',
written with Charles Rhoda) . . . . £75/£15
ditto, Hodder & Stoughton, 1951. . . . £75/£15
Judgement on Deltchev, Hodder & Stoughton, 1951 .
. . . . £50/£25
ditto, Knopf (U.S.), 1951 . . . . . £25/£10
Tender to Danger, Doubleday (U.S.), 1951 (pseud.
'Eliot Reed', written with Charles Rhoda) . £75/£15

ditto, as *Tender to Moonlight*, Hodder & Stoughton,
1951 . . . . £75/£15
The Malas Affair, Collins, 1953 (pseud. 'Eliot Reed',
written with Charles Rhoda) . . . . £75/£15
The Schirmer Inheritance, Heinemann, 1953 £75/£20
ditto, Knopf (U.S.), 1953 . . . . . £45/£15
Charter to Danger, Collins, 1954 (pseud. 'Eliot Reed',
written with Charles Rhoda) . . . . £75/£15
The Night Comers, Heinemann, 1956 . . £25/£10
ditto, as *State of Siege*, Knopf (U.S.), 1956 . £25/£10
Passage of Arms, Heinemann, 1959 . . . £25/£10
ditto, Knopf (U.S.), 1959 . . . . . . £15/£5
The Light of Day, Heinemann, 1962 . . £25/£10
ditto, Knopf (U.S.), 1963 . . . . . . £15/£5
A Kind of Anger, Bodley Head, 1964 . . £25/£10
ditto, Atheneum (U.S.), 1964 . . . . . £15/£5
The Jealous God Stellar Press, 1964 (200 copies,
wraps) £50
Dirty Story, Bodley Head, 1967 . . . . £25/£10
ditto, Atheneum (U.S.), 1967 . . . . . £15/£5
The Intercom Conspiracy, Atheneum (U.S.), 1969 .
. . . . £25/£10
ditto, Weidenfeld & Nicolson, 1970 . . . £25/£10
The Levanter, Weidenfeld & Nicolson, 1972 £25/£10
ditto, Atheneum (U.S.), 1972 . . . . . £15/£5
Doctor Frigo, Weidenfeld & Nicolson, 1974 £25/£10
ditto, Atheneum (U.S.), 1974 . . . . . £15/£5
Send No More Roses, Weidenfeld & Nicolson, 1977 .
. . . . £15/£5
ditto, as *The Siege of the Villa Lipp*, Random House
(U.S.), 1977 . . . . £20/£5
The Care of Time, Farrar Straus Giroux (U.S.), 1981 .
. . . . £15/£5
ditto, Farrar Straus Giroux (U.S.), 1981 (300 signed
copies, slipcase) . . . . £50/£35
ditto, Weidenfeld & Nicolson, 1981 . . . £15/£5

Short Stories
The Army of the Shadows and Other Stories,
Eurographica (Helsinki), 1986 (350 signed copies) .
. . . . £75/£45
Waiting for Orders, Mysterious Press (U.S.), 1991 .
. . . . £15/£5
ditto, Mysterious Press (U.S.), 1991 (26 signed copies,
slipcase) . . . . £125/£100
The Story So Far, Weidenfeld & Nicolson, 1993 . .
. . . . £15/£5

Essays
The Ability to Kill and Other Pieces, Bodley Head,
1962 (first issue with essay). . . . . £125/£75
ditto, Bodley Head, 1963 (second issue). . £35/£10
ditto, The Mysterious Press (U.S.), [1987] (250 signed
copies in slipcase) . . . . £45/£35
ditto, The Mysterious Press (U.S.), [1987] (unlimited
edition in d/w) . . . . £10/£5

Autobiography
Here Lies Eric Ambler, Weidenfeld & Nicolson, 1985
. . . . £20/£5

ditto, Farrar Straus Giroux (U.S.), 1986 . . . £20/£5
ditto, Farrar Straus Giroux (U.S.), 1986 (100 signed
copies, slipcase) . . . . £50/£35

Edited by Ambler
To Catch a Spy, Bodley Head, 1964 . . . . £25/£5
ditto, Atheneum (U.S.), 1965 . . . . . £25/£5

KINGSLEY AMIS
(b.1922 d.1995)

A poet and novelist who has the ability to be satirical
and inventive whilst being thoroughly readable.

Novels
Lucky Jim, Gollancz, 1953 [1954] . . £2,000/£200
ditto, Doubleday (U.S.), 1954 . . . . £250/£35
That Uncertain Feeling, Gollancz, 1955 . £150/£20
ditto, Harcourt Brace (U.S.), 1956 . . . £50/£15
I Like it Here, Gollancz, 1958 . . . . £65/£20
ditto, Harcourt Brace (U.S.), 1958 . . . £45/£15
Take a Girl Like You, Gollancz, 1960 . . £65/£20
ditto, Harcourt Brace (U.S.), 1961 . . . £25/£10
One Fat Englishman, Gollancz, 1963 . . £25/£10
ditto, Harcourt Brace (U.S.), 1964 . . . £15/£5
The Egyptologists (with Robert Conquest), Cape, 1965
. . . . £45/£15
ditto, Random House (U.S.), 1966 . . £25/£10
The Anti-Death League, Gollancz, 1966 . £25/£10
ditto, Harcourt Brace (U.S.), 1966 . . . £15/£5
Colonel Sun, Cape, 1968 (pseud. 'Robert Markham') .
. . . . £60/£15
ditto, Harper (U.S.), 1968 . . . . . £45/£15
I Want it Now, Cape, 1968 . . . . . £20/£5
ditto, Harcourt Brace (U.S.), 1969 . . . £15/£5
The Green Man, Cape, 1969 . . . . £50/£15
ditto, Harcourt Brace (U.S.), 1970 . . . £35/£10
Girl, 20, Cape, 1971 . . . . £20/£5
ditto, Harcourt Brace (U.S.), 1972 . . . £20/£5
The Riverside Villas Murder, Cape, 1973 . . £20/£5
ditto, Harcourt Brace (U.S.), 1973 . . . £15/£5
Ending Up, Cape, 1974 . . . . . . £15/£5
ditto, Harcourt Brace (U.S.), 1974 . . . £15/£5
The Alteration, Cape, 1976 . . . . . £20/£5
ditto, Viking (U.S.), 1977 . . . . . £15/£5
Jake's Thing, Hutchinson, 1978 . . . . £15/£5
ditto, Viking (U.S.), 1979 . . . . . £15/£5
Russian Hide-and-Seek, Hutchinson, 1980 . £15/£5
Stanley and the Women, Hutchinson, 1984 . £15/£5
ditto, Summit (U.S.), 1985 . . . . . £15/£5
The Old Devils, Hutchinson, 1986 . . . £15/£5
ditto, Hutchinson/London Limited Editions, 1986 (250
signed copies, tissue jacket). . . . £50/£45
ditto, Summit (U.S.), 1986 . . . . . £10/£5
Difficulties With Girls, Hutchinson, 1988 . £10/£5
ditto, Hutchinson, 1988 (500 numbered proof copies,
wraps) £15
ditto, Summit (U.S.), 1989 . . . . . £10/£5

The Folks That Live on the Hill, Hutchinson, 1990
. . . . £10/£5
ditto, Hutchinson, 1990 (500 numbered proof copies)
. . . . £40
ditto, Summit (U.S.), 1990 . . . . . £10/£5
The Russian Girl, Hutchinson, 1992 . . £10/£5
ditto, Viking (U.S.), 1992. . . . . . £10/£5
We Are All Guilty, Reinhardt Books/Viking, 1991 . .
. . . . £10/£5
You Can't Do Both, London Limited Editions, 1994
(150 copies in glassine d/w). . . . £45/£35
ditto, Hutchinson, 1994 . . . . £10/£5
The Biographer's Moustache, Flamingo/Harper
Collins, 1995 . . . . £10/£5

Omnibus Editions
The Kingsley Amis Omnibus, Hutchinson, 1992 . .
. . . . £10/£5

Short Stories
My Enemy's Enemy, Gollancz, 1962 . . £75/£15
ditto, Harcourt Brace (U.S.), 1963 . . . £45/£10
Dear Illusion, Covent Garden Press, 1972 (500 copies,
wraps). £20
ditto, Covent Garden Press, 1972 (100 signed copies,
wraps). £75
The Darkwater Hall Mystery, Tragara Press, 1978
(150 of 165 copies, wraps) £100
ditto, Tragara Press, 1978 (15 signed copies of 165,
wraps). £250
Collected Short Stories, Hutchinson, 1980 . £15/£5
The Crime of the Century, Hutchinson, 1989 . £10/£5
ditto, Mysterious Press (U.S.), 1989 . . . . £10/£5
ditto, Mysterious Press (U.S.), 1989 (100 signed copies
in slipcase) . . . . £60/£40
Mrs Barrett's Secret and Other Stories, Hutchinson,
1993 . . . . £10/£5

Poetry
Bright November, Fortune Press, [1947] £1,000/£250
A Frame of Mind, Reading School of Art, 1953 (150
numbered copies, wraps) £450
Fantasy Poets No.22, Fantasy Press, 1954 (wraps).
. . . . £150
A Case of Samples: Poems, 1946-1956, Gollancz,
1956. . . . . £75/£30
ditto, Harcourt Brace (U.S.), 1957 . . £60/£20
Penguin Modern Poets No.2, Penguin, 1962 (with
Dom Moraes and Peter Porter, wraps) £5
The Evans Country, Fantasy Press, 1962 (wraps) £70
A Look Round the Estate: Poems, 1957-1967, Cape,
1967 . . . . £45/£15
ditto, Harcourt Brace (U.S.), 1968 . . . £20/£5
Wasted and *Kipling at Batemans*, Poem of the Month
Club, 1973 (broadsheet). £15
Collected Poems 1944-1979, Hutchinson, 1979 . .
. . . . £15/£5
ditto, Viking (U.S.), 1980. . . . . . £15/£5

Non Fiction
Socialism and the Intellectuals, Fabian Press, 1957
(wraps) £50
New Maps of Hell: A Survey of Science Fiction,
Harcourt Brace (U.S.), 1960 . . . . £45/£15
ditto, Gollancz, 1961 . . . . . . £45/£15
The James Bond Dossier, Cape, 1965 . . £50/£15
ditto, NAL (U.S.), 1965 . . . . . . £35/£10
*The Book of Bond, or Every Man His Own 007
Dossier*, Cape, 1965 (pseud. 'Lt.-Colonel William
('Bill') Tanner') . . . . £35/£10
ditto, Viking (U.S.), 1965. . . . . . £30/£10
Lucky Jim's Politics, Conservative Policy Centre,
1968 (wraps). £25
What Became of Jane Austen? and Other Questions,
Cape, 1970 . . . . £35/£10
ditto, Harcourt Brace (U.S.), 1971 . . £25/£10
On Drink, Cape, 1972. . . . . . . £35/£10
ditto, Harcourt Brace (U.S.), 1973 . . . £25/£10
Rudyard Kipling and his World, Thames & Hudson,
1975 . . . . £15/£5
ditto, Scribner's (U.S.), 1975 . . . . . £15/£5
An Arts Policy?, Centre for Policy Studies, 1979
(wraps) £10
Every Day Drinking, Hutchinson, 1983 . . £15/£5
*How's Your Glass? A Quizzical Look at Drinks and
Drinking*, Weidenfeld & Nicolson, 1984 . . £15/£5
*The Amis Collection: Selected Non-Fiction, 1954-
1990*, Hutchinson, 1990 . . . . . . £15/£5
Memoirs, Hutchinson, 1991 . . . . . £10/£5
ditto, Summit (U.S.), 1991 . . . . . £10/£5
The King's English: A Guide to Modern Usage,
HarperCollins, 1997 . . . . £10/£5
ditto, St Martin's Press (U.S.), 1998 . . . £10/£5
The Letters of Kingsley Amis, HarperCollins, 2000 .
. . . . £10/£5

MARTIN AMIS
(b.1949)

The son of Kingsley Amis, Martin had his first novel
published at the age of 24.

Novels
The Rachel Papers, Cape, 1973 . . . . £450/£100
ditto, Knopf (U.S.), 1974 . . . . . £75/£15
Dead Babies, Cape, 1975. . . . . . £300/£30
ditto, Knopf (U.S.), 1976 . . . . . £75/£15
ditto, as *Dark Secrets*, Triad, 1977 (wraps) . . £10
Success, Cape, 1978 . . . . £200/£25
ditto, Harmony (U.S.), 1987 . . . . . £20/£5
Other People: A Mystery Story, Cape, 1981 £100/£15
ditto, Viking (U.S.), 1981. . . . . . £30/£5
Money: A Suicide Note, Cape, 1984. . . £75/£15
ditto, Viking (U.S.), 1985. . . . . . £25/£5
London Fields, Cape, 1989 . . . . . £20/£5
ditto, London Limited Editions, 1989 (150 signed
copies, glassine d/w). . . . . . . £125/£100

ditto, Harmony (U.S.), 1990 . . . . . . £15/£5
Time's Arrow, or the Nature of the Offence, Cape, 1991 . . . . £20/£5
ditto, London Limited Editions, 1991 (200 signed copies, glassine d/w). . . . . . . £75/£50
ditto, Harmony (U.S.), 1991 . . . . . £15/£5
The Information, Flamingo, 1995 . . . . £15/£5
ditto, Flamingo, 1995 (350 signed, numbered copies of 376, slipcase). . . . . £75/£55
ditto, Harmony (U.S.), 1995 . . . . . . £15/£5
ditto, Harmony (U.S.), 195 (100 signed, numbered copies of 176, slipcase) . . . . . . £175/£150
ditto, Harmony (U.S.), 195 (26 signed, lettered copies of 176, slipcase) . . . . £225/£200
Night Train, Cape, 1997 . . . . £15/£5
ditto, Cape, 1997 (26 signed deluxe copies). . £175
ditto, Cape, 1997 (74 signed copies). . . . £100
ditto, Harmony (U.S.), 1998 . . . . . . £15/£5

Short Stories
Einstein's Monsters, Cape, 1987. . . . £25/£10
ditto, Harmony (U.S.), 1987 . . . . . . £20/£5
Two Stories, Moorhouse & Sorensen, 1994 (26 signed copies, bound in aluminium, of 326) . . . £450
ditto, Moorhouse & Sorensen, 1994 (100 signed copies bound in cloth of 326) £125
ditto, Moorhouse & Sorensen, 1994 (200 signed copies in card covers of 326) £50
God's Dice, Penguin, 1995 (wraps). £5
Heavy Water and Other Stories, Cape, 1998 . £15/£5
ditto, Cape, 1998 (50 copies). £100
ditto, Harmony (U.S.), 1999 . . . . . . £15/£5
The Coincidence of the Arts, Coromandel Express (Paris), 1999 (individual pages in a metal container, illustrated by 7 prints by photographer Mario Testino. 55 copies signed by Amis and Testino) . £2,000

Non Fiction
Invasion of the Space Invaders, Hutchinson, 1982 (wraps) £125
ditto, Celestial Arts (U.S.), 1982 (wraps) . £125
The Moronic Inferno and Other Visits to America, Cape, 1986 . . . . £35/£10
ditto, Viking (U.S.), 1987. . . . . . £25/£10
Visiting Mrs Nabokov and Other Excursions, Cape, 1993 . . . . £15/£5
ditto, Harmony (U.S.), 1994 . . . . . £15/£5
Experience, Cape, 2000 . . . . . £10/£5
ditto, Cape, 2000 (150 signed copies, slipcase) . . .
. . . . £125/£100
ditto, Hyperion (U.S.), 2000 . . . . . £10/£5
The War Against Cliché: Essays and Reviews 1971-2000, Cape, 2001 . . . . . . £10/£5
ditto, Hyperion /Talk Miramax (U.S.), 2001 . £10/£5
Koba the Dread, Hyperion/Talk Miramax (U.S.), 2002
. . . . £10/£5
ditto, Cape, 2002 . . . . £10/£5

SHERWOOD ANDERSON
(b.1876 d.1941)

An American novelist and short story writer, Anderson's prose style is said to have had a significant impact on the direction of twentieth-century American literature.

Novels
Windy McPherson's Son, John Lane/Bodley Head, 1916 . . . . £175
Marching Men, John Lane (U.S.), 1917. . . £100
Poor White, Huebsch (U.S.), 1920 . . . £150/£25
ditto, Cape, 1921 . . . . £250/£35
Many Marriages, Huebsch (U.S.), 1923 . £100/£20
Dark Laughter, Boni & Liveright (U.S.), 1925. . .
. . . . £100/£20
ditto, Boni & Liveright (U.S.), 1925 (370 signed, numbered copies, slipcase) . . . . . £150/£125
ditto, Jarrolds, 1926 . . . . £250/£35
Beyond Desire, Liveright (U.S.), 1932 . . £75/£15
ditto, Liveright (U.S.), 1932 (165 signed, numbered copies, slipcase) . . . . £200/£150
Kit Brandon: A Portrait, Scribner's (U.S.), 1936 . .
. . . . £50/£10
ditto, Hutchinson, 1937 . . . . . . £45/£10

Short Stories
Winesburg, Ohio: A Group of Tales of Ohio Small Town Life, Huebsch (U.S.), 1919 (yellow cloth, paper label on spine, first issue, with line 5 of p.86 reading 'lay' with broken type in 'the' in line 3 of p.251, map endpapers, top edge stained yellow) £5,000/£400
ditto, Huebsch (U.S.), 1919 (yellow cloth, paper label on spine, presumed second issue with unstained top edge) . . . . £3,000/£150
ditto, Cape, 1922 . . . . £250/£75
The Triumph of the Egg and Other Stories, Huebsch (U.S.), 1921 (first issue with top edge stained yellow)
. . . . £200/£25
ditto, Cape, 1922 . . . . £200/£45
Horses and Men: Tales, Long & Short from Our American Life, Huebsch (U.S.), 1923 (first issue with top edge stained orange). . . . . £250/£30
ditto, Cape, 1924 . . . . £150/£35
Alice and the Lost Novel, Elkin Mathews & Marrot, 1929 (350 signed copies) . . . . £75/£45
Death in the Woods and Other Stories, Liveright (U.S.), 1933 . . . . £150/£30

Poetry
Mid-American Chants, John Lane (U.S.), 1918 . . .
. . . . £350/£45
A New Testament, Boni & Liveright (U.S.), 1927 (265 signed, numbered copies, slipcase). . . £200/£150
ditto, Boni & Liveright (U.S.), 1927 (265 signed, numbered copies) . . . . . . £100/£20

Play
Winesburg and Others, Scribner's (U.S.), 1937 . .
. . . . £100/£20

Others
A Story Teller's Story, Huebsch (U.S.), 1924 £90/£15
ditto, Cape, 1925 . . . . £75/£15
The Modern Writer, The Lantern Press (U.S.), 1925
(950 copies in slipcase) . . . . . £100/£75
ditto, The Lantern Press (U.S.), 1925 (50 signed copies
on vellum, in slipcase) . . . . . . £300/£200
Sherwood Anderson's Notebook, Boni & Liveright
(U.S.), 1926 . . . . £75/£25
ditto, Boni & Liveright (U.S.), 1926 (225 signed
copies, slipcase) . . . . £175/£125
Tar: A Midwest Childhood, Boni & Liveright (U.S.),
1926 . . . . £75/£20
ditto, Boni & Liveright (U.S.), 1926 (350 signed
copies, glassine d/w, slipcase) . . . . £150/£100
Hello Towns!, Horace Liveright (U.S.), 1929 . . .
. . . . £100/£25
Nearer the Grass Roots, Westgate Press (U.S.), 1929
(500 signed copies, printed by Grabhorn Press) .
. . . . £150/£100
The American County Fair, Random House, 1930 (six
prose quartos in wraps, slipcase, 875 copies) . . .
. . . . £100/£65
Perhaps Women, Horace Liveright (U.S.), 1931 . .
. . . . £65/£15
No Swank, Centaur Press (U.S.), 1934 (1,000 copies,
glassine d/w) . . . . £75/£50
ditto, Centaur Press (U.S.), 1934 (50 signed, numbered
copies, glassine d/w) . . . . £250/£200
Puzzled America, Scribner's (U.S.), 1935 . £100/£20
A Writer's Conception of Realism, Olivet College
(U.S.), 1939 (wraps) £250
Home Town, Alliance Book Corporation (U.S.), 1940.
. . . . £125/£40
Sherwood Anderson's Memoirs, Harcourt Brace
(U.S.), 1942 . . . . £65/£15
ditto, as *The Memoirs of Sherwood Anderson*, 1969 .
. . . . £50/£15
The Sherwood Anderson Reader, Houghton Mifflin
Co. (U.S.), 1947 . . . . £45/£15
The Portable Sherwood Anderson, Viking Press
(U.S.), 1949 . . . . £30/£10
Letters of Sherwood Anderson, Little, Brown (U.S.),
1953 . . . . £30/£10
Return to Winesburg, Univ. of North Carolina (U.S.),
1967 . . . . £25/£10
*Sherwood Anderson/Gertrude Stein: Correspondence
and Personal Essays*, Univ. of North Carolina (U.S.),
1972 . . . . £25/£10
France and Anderson: Paris Notebook, 1921,
Louisiana State Univ. (U.S.), 1977 . . £25/£10
Letters to Bab, Univ. of Illinois Press (U.S.), 1985 . .
. . . . £20/£5
The Sherwood Anderson Diaries 1936-1941, Univ. of
Georgia Press (U.S.), 1987 . . . . £25/£10

Sherwood Anderson: Early Writings, Kent State Univ.
Press (U.S.), 1989 . . . . . . £25/£10
*Sherwood Anderson's Love Letters to Eleanor
Copenhaver Anderson*, Univ. of Georgia Press
(U.S.), 1989 . . . . £25/£10
*Sherwood Anderson's Secret Love Letters: For
Eleanor, a Letter a Day*, Louisiana State Univ.
(U.S.), 1991 . . . . £25/£10
Certain Last Things: Selected Short Stories, 4 walls 8
Windows (U.S.), 1992 . . . . . . £25/£10

MAYA ANGELOU
(b. 1928)

Maya Angelou is a poet, historian, author, playwright,
actress, civil-rights activist, producer and director. Her
books of autobiography have become international
bestsellers.

Autobiography
I Know Why the Caged Bird Sings, Random House
(U.S.), 1969 . . . . £200/£45
ditto, Virago, 1984 (wraps) £5
Gather Together in My Name, Random House (U.S.),
1974 . . . . £50/£15
ditto, Virago, 1985 (wraps) £5
*Singin' and Swingin' and Gettin' Merry Like
Christmas*, Random House (U.S.), 1976 . £25/£10
ditto, Virago, 1985 (wraps) £5
The Heart of a Woman, Random House (U.S.), 1981 .
. . . . £25/£10
ditto, Virago, 1986 (wraps) £5
All God's Children Need Travelling Shoes, Random
House (U.S.), 1986 . . . . £30/£10
ditto, Franklin Library (U.S.), 1986 (signed, limited
edition) £50
ditto, Virago, 1987 (wraps) £5

Essays
Wouldn't Take Nothing for my Journey Now,
Random House (U.S.), 1993 . . . . £25/£5
ditto, Virago, 1994 . . . . £10/£5
Even the Stars Look Lonesome, Random House
(U.S.), 1997 . . . . £15/£5
ditto, Virago, 1998 (300 numbered copies) . £25/£10
ditto, Virago, 1998 . . . . £10/£5

Poetry
Just Give Me a Cool Drink of Water 'fore I Diiie,
Random House (U.S.), 1971 . . . . £50/£20
ditto, Virago, 1988 (wraps) £5
Oh Pray My Wings are Gonna Fit Me Well, Random
House (U.S.), 1975 . . . . £30/£10
And Still I Rise, Random House (U.S.), 1978 £40/£15
ditto, Virago, 1986 (wraps) £5
Shaker, Why Don't You Sing?, Random House (U.S.),
1983 . . . . £30/£10

Now Sheba Sings the Song, Dutton/Dial (U.S.), 1987 .
. . . . £25/£10
ditto, Virago, 1987 . . . . £15/£5
I Shall Not Be Moved, Random House (U.S.), 1990 .
. . . . £20/£5
ditto, Virago, 1990 (wraps) £5
On the Pulse of the Morning, Random House (U.S.),
1993 (wraps) £15
Life Doesn't Frighten Me, Stewart, Tabori and Chang
(U.S.), 1993 . . . . £35/£10
The Complete Collected Poems of Maya Angelou,
Random House (U.S.), 1994 . . . . . £10/£5
ditto, Virago, 1994 . . . . £10/£5
A Brave and Startling Truth, Random House (U.S.),
1995 . . . . £15/£5
Phenomenal Woman: Four Poems Celebrating
Women, Random House (U.S.), 1994 . . . £10/£5

Children's Titles
My Painted House, My Friendly Chicken, And Me,
Clarkson Potter Inc (U.S.), 1994 . . . £25/£10
Kofi and His Magic, Clarkson Potter Inc (U.S.), 1996 .
. . . . £25/£10

EDWARD ARDIZZONE
(b.1900 d.1979)

Ardizzone studied at the Westminster School of Art
and in 1927 became a full-time artist. He is best
known for his illustrations of children's books, some
of which he wrote himself.

Children's Books Written and Illustrated by
Ardizzone
Little Tim and the Brave Sea Captain, O.U.P., [1936]
. . . . £600/£300
ditto, O.U.P. (U.S.), [1936] . . . . . £500/£250
ditto, O.U.P., 1955 (revised edition) . . . £45/£20
Lucy Brown and Mr Grimes, O.U.P., [1937] . . .
. . . . £500/£250
ditto, O.U.P., 1970 (revised edition) . . . £60/£20
ditto, Walck (U.S.), [1971] . . . . . £35/£10
Tim and Lucy go to Sea, O.U.P., [1938] . £500/£250
ditto, O.U.P., 1958 (revised edition) . . . £50/£20
ditto, Walck (U.S.), [1958] . . . . . £45/£10
Nicholas the Fast-Moving Diesel, Eyre & Spottiswoode, [1947] . . . . £450/£200
ditto, Walck (U.S.), 1959 . . . . . £45/£10
Paul, The Hero of the Fire, Penguin, 1948 (wraps) .
. . . . £45
ditto, Constable, 1962 (revised edition) . . £40/£15
ditto, Walck (U.S.), [1963] . . . . . £65/£25
Tim to the Rescue, O.U.P., 1949 . . . . £150/£45
ditto, Walck (U.S.), [196-?] . . . . . £65/£25
Tim and Charlotte, O.U.P., 1951 . . . £150/£45
ditto, Lothrop, Lee & Shepard Books (U.S.), 2000 . .
. . . . £25/£10

Tim in Danger, O.U.P., 1953 . . . . £150/£45
ditto, Walck (U.S.), [196-?] . . . . . £65/£25
Tim all Alone, O.U.P., 1956 . . . . . £100/£25
Johnny the Clockmaker, O.U.P., 1960 . . £100/£25
ditto, Walck (U.S.), 1960 . . . . . . £65/£25
Tim's Friend Towser, O.U.P., 1962 . . . £100/£25
ditto, Walck (U.S.), 1962 . . . . . . £65/£25
Peter the Wanderer, O.U.P., 1963 . . . £75/£25
ditto, Walck (U.S.), 1963 . . . . . . £65/£25
Diana and her Rhinoceros, Bodley Head, 1964 . .
. . . . £75/£25
ditto, Walck (U.S.), 1964 . . . . . . £65/£25
Sarah and Simon and No Red Paint, Constable,
[1965] . . . . £75/£25
ditto, Delacorte Press (U.S.), [1966] . . £65/£25
Tim and Ginger, O.U.P., 1965 . . . . £75/£25
ditto, Walck (U.S.), 1965 . . . . . . £65/£25
The Little Girl and the Tiny Doll, Constable, 1966
(with Aingelda Ardizzone) . . . . . £75/£25
ditto, Delacorte (U.S.), 1966 . . . . . £60/£25
Tim to the Lighthouse, O.U.P., 1968 . . £75/£25
ditto, Walck (U.S.), [1968] . . . . . £50/£20
Johnny's Bad Day, Bodley Head, 1970 . . £65/£25
Tim's Last Voyage, Bodley Head, 1972 . . £50/£20
ditto, Walck (U.S.), 1972 . . . . . . £50/£20
Ship's Cook Ginger: Another Time Story, Bodley
Head, 1977 . . . . £35/£15
ditto, Macmillan (U.S.), 1978 . . . . £35/£15
The Adventures of Tim, Bodley Head, 1977 £35/£15

Children's Books Illustrated by Ardizzone
Tom, Dick and Harriet, by Albert N. Lyons, Cresset
Press, 1937 . . . . £300/£100
Great Expectations, by Charles Dickens, Heritage
Press (U.S.), 1939 . . . . . . £100/£45
ditto, Limited Editions Club (U.S.), [1939] . £600/£350
MIMFF: the Story of a Boy Who Was Not Afraid, by
H.J. Kaeser, O.U.P., 1939 . . . . £100/£45
Peacock Pie, by Walter de la Mare, Faber, 1946 . .
. . . . £75/£40
The Pilgrim's Progress, by John Bunyan, Faber, 1947
. . . . £100/£45
Three Brothers and a Lady, by Margaret Black, Acorn
Press, 1947 . . . . £80/£35
A True and Pathetic History of Desbarollda, The
Waltzing Mouse, by Noel Langley, Lindsay
Drummond, 1947 . . . . £80/£35
Hey Nonny Yes: Passions and Conceits from
Shakespeare, edited by Hallam Fordham, Saturn
Press, 1947 . . . . £65/£25
The Life and Adventures of Nicholas Nickleby, Ealing
Studios, 1947 (promotional booklet) . . . £100
Charles Dickens' Birthday Book, edited by Enid
Dickens Hawksley, Faber, 1948 . . . £75/£25
The Otterbury Incident, by Cecil Day Lewis, Putnam,
1948 . . . . £75/£25
ditto, Viking (U.S.), 1949 . . . . . . £35/£15

The Rose and the Ring, by William Makepeace Thackeray, Guilford Press/Wilfrid David, 1948 . . . . £65/£20
MIMFF in Charge, by H.J. Kaeser, O.U.P., 1949 (translated by David Ascoli) . . . . £60/£25
The Tale of Ali Baba, Limited Editions Club (U.S.), 1949 (translated by J.C. Mardrus and E. Powys Mathers, 2,500 signed copies) £150
Somebody's Rocking My Dreamboat, by Noel Langley and Hazel Pynegar, Barker, 1949 . . . £50/£20
The Humour of Dickens, News Chronicle, 1952 £40
The Blackbird in the Lilac, by James Reeves, O.U.P., 1952 . . . . £60/£25
MIMFF Takes Over, by H.J. Kaeser, O.U.P., 1954 . . . . £50/£20
The Fantastic Tale of the Plucky Sailor and the Postage Stamp, by Stephen Corrin, Faber, 1954 . . . . £45/£20
The Little Bookroom, by Eleanor Farjeon, O.U.P., 1955 . . . . £50/£20
ditto, Walck (U.S.), 1955 . . . . . £30/£10
The Suburban Child, by James Kenward, C.U.P., 1955 . . . . £75/£25
Minnow on the Say, by Phillippa Pearce, O.U.P., 1955 . . . . £75/£25
ditto, as *The Minnow Leads to Treasure*, Gregg Press (U.S.), 1980 . . . . £25/£10
David Copperfield, by Charles DickensO.U.P., 1955 (abridged by S. Wood) . . . . . £45/£20
Bleak House, Charles Dickens, O.U.P., 1955 (abridged by S. Wood) . . . . £45/£20
Sun Slower, Sun Faster, by Meriol Trevor, Collins, 1955 . . . . £45/£20
Pigeons and Princesses, by James Reeves, Heinemann, 1956 . . . . £40/£20
Marshmallow, by Claire Newberry, Studio, 1956 £30
St Luke's Life of Christ (translated by J.B. Phillips), Collins, 1956 . . . . £45/£20
ditto, Collins, 1956 (150 signed copies, slipcase) . . . . £150/£125
Wandering Moon, by James Reeves, Heinemann, 1957 . . . . £60/£25
ditto, Dutton (U.S.), 1960. . . . . £30/£10
A Stickful of Nonpareil, by George Scurfield, C.U.P., 1956 (500 copies) £100
Hunting with Mr Jorrocks, by Robert Surtees (edited by Lionel Gough) O.U.P., 1956. . . . £75/£35
Prefabulous Animiles, by James Reeves, Heinemann, 1957 . . . . £50/£20
The School in Our Village, by Joan M. Goldman, Batsford, 1957 . . . . £50/£20
The Boy Down Kitchiner Street, by Leslie Paul, Faber, 1957 . . . . £45/£20
Lottie, by John Symonds, Bodley Head, 1957 £50/£20
Ding Dong Bell, Dobson, 1957 . . . . £65/£25
ditto, Dover (U.S.), 1969 . . . . . £30/£10
MIMFF-Robinson, by H.J. Kaeser, O.U.P., 1958 (translated by Ruth Michaelis and Jena & Arthur Ratcliff) . . . . £50/£20

The Story of Joseph, by Walter de la Mare, Faber, 1958 . . . . £40/£15
Jim at the Corner, by Eleanor Farjeon, O.U.P., 1958 . . . . £75/£30
ditto, Walck (U.S.), 1958 . . . . . £75/£30
Pinky Pye, by Eleanor Estes, Constable, 1959 £50/£20
ditto, Harcourt, Brace & World (U.S.), 1959 £45/£15
The Nine Lives of Island Mackenzie, by Ursula Moray Williams, Chatto & Windus, 1959 . . £45/£15
Titus in Trouble, by James Reeves, Bodley Head, 1959 . . . . £50/£20
ditto, Walck (U.S.), 1960 . . . . . £30/£10
Exploits of Don Quixote, by Cervantes, Blackie, [1959] (abridged by James Reeves) . . £50/£20
ditto, Bedrick Books (U.S.), 1985 . . . £20/£10
Story of Moses, by Walter de la Mare, Faber, 1959 . . . . £40/£15
Elfrida and the Pig, by John Symonds, Harrap, 1959 . . . . £60/£25
ditto, Franklin Watts (U.S.), 1959 . . . £60/£25
Holiday Trench, by Joan Ballantyne, Nelson, 1959 . . . . £35/£15
The Godstone and the Blackymor, by T.H. White, Cape, 1959 . . . . £40/£15
ditto, Putnam (U.S.), 1959 . . . . . £35/£10
The Story of Samuel and Saul, by Walter de la Mare, Faber, 1960 . . . . £50/£20
Kidnappers at Coombe, by Joan Ballantyne, Nelson, 1960 . . . . £45/£15
The Rib of the Green Umbrella, by Naomi Mitchison, Collins, 1960 . . . . £50/£20
Eleanor Farjeon's Book, edited by Eleanor Graham, Puffin, 1960 (wraps). £20
ditto, Walck (U.S.), 1966 . . . . . £35/£15
Merry England, by Cyril Ray, Vista Books, 1960 . . . . £35/£15
Italian Peepshow, by Eleanor Farjeon, O.U.P., 1960 . . . . £40/£25
ditto, Walck (U.S.), 1960 . . . . . £30/£10
The Penny Fiddle: Poems for Children, by Robert Graves, Cassell, 1960 . . . . . £125/£50
ditto, Doubleday (U.S.), 1960 . . . . £75/£20
Boyhoods of the Great Composers, O.U.P., 1960 &, 1963 (2 vols) . . . . £75/£30
Hurdy Gurdy, by James Reeves, Heinemann, 1961 . . . . £75/£30
No Mystery for the Maitlands, by Joan Ballantyne, Nelson, 1961 . . . . £60/£25
Down in the Cellar, by Nicholas Gray, Dobson, 1961 . . . . £50/£25
The Adventures of Huckleberry Finn, by Mark Twain, Heinemann, 1961 . . . . £60/£25
The Adventures of Tom Sawyer, by Mark Twain, Heinemann, 1961 . . . . £60/£25
Stories from the Bible, by Walter de la Mare, Faber, 1929 . . . . £50/£20
ditto, Knopf (U.S.), 1961 . . . . . £50/£20
The Witch Family, by Eleanor Estes, Constable, 1962 . . . . £60/£25

ditto, Harcourt Brace Jovanovich (U.S.), [1990] . .
. . . . £20/£5
Naughty Children, by Christianna Brand, Gollancz,
1962 . . . . £75/£30
ditto, Dutton (U.S.), 1963 . . . . . £50/£20
Sailor Rumbelow and Britannia, by James Reeves,
Heinemann, 1962 . . . . £75/£25
Peter Pan, by J.M. Barrie, Brockhampton Press, 1962.
. . . . £75/£30
ditto, Scribner's (U.S.), [1962] . . . . £75/£30
A Ring of Bells, by John Betjeman, Murray, 1962 . .
. . . . £60/£25
ditto, Houghton Mifflin (U.S.), 1963 . . £45/£20
The Story of Let's Make an Opera, by Eric Crosier,
O.U.P., 1962 . . . . £50/£25
The Singing Cupboard, by Dana Farralla, Blackie,
1962 . . . . £45/£20
Mrs Malone, by Eleanor Farjeon, O.U.P., 1962 . .
. . . . £60/£25
ditto, Walck (U.S.), 1962 . . . . . £45/£15
Island of Fish in the Trees, by Eva-Lis Wuorio, World
(U.S.), 1962 . . . . £60/£20
ditto, Dobson, 1964 . . . . . . £60/£20
Stig of the Dump, by Clive King, Puffin Original, 1963
(wraps) £25
Kaleidoscope, by Eleanor Farjeon, O.U.P., 1963 . .
. . . . £75/£30
ditto, Walck (U.S.), 1963 . . . . . £45/£15
Swanhilda-of-the-Swans, by Dana Farralla, Blackie,
[1964] . . . . £50/£20
Ann at Highwood Hall, by Robert Graves, Cassell,
1964 . . . . £50/£20
ditto, Doubleday (U.S.), 1964 . . . . £30/£10
Three Tall Tales, by James Reeves, Abelard-
Schumann, 1964 . . . . £50/£20
The Alley, by Eleanor Estes, Harcourt Brace (U.S.),
1964 . . . . £35/£15
Hello, Elephant, by Jan Wahl, Holt, Rinehart and
Winston (U.S.), [1964] . . . . . £50/£15
Nurse Matilda, by Christianna Brand, Brockhampton
Press, 1965 . . . . £60/£20
ditto, Dutton (U.S.), 1964 . . . . . £50/£15
The Land of Right Up and Down, by Eva-Lis Wuorio,
World (U.S.), [1964] . . . . . . £60/£15
ditto, Dobson, 1968 . . . . . . £60/£25
Open the Door, edited by Margery Fisher,
Brockhampton Press, 1965 . . . . £50/£20
The Story of Jackie Thimble, by James Reeves, Dutton
(U.S.), 1964 . . . . £50/£20
ditto, Chatto & Windus, 1965 . . . . £50/£20
Old Perisher, by Diana Ross, Faber, 1965 . £50/£20
The Old Nurse's Stocking Basket, by Eleanor Farjeon,
O.U.P., 1965 . . . . £50/£20
ditto, Walck (U.S.), 1965 . . . . . £45/£15
The Truants and Other Poems for Children, by John
Walsh, Heinemann, 1965 . . . . £50/£20
ditto, Rand McNally (U.S.), [1968] . . £45/£15
The Growing Summer, by Noel Streatfield, Collins,
1966 . . . . £70/£25

ditto, as *The Magic Summer*, Random House (U.S.),
1967 . . . . £40/£15
Long Ago When I Was Young, by E. Nesbit, Whiting
& Wheaton, 1966 . . . . £50/£20
ditto, Watts (U.S.), [1966] . . . . . £45/£15
Daddy Longlegs, by Jean Webster, Brockhampton
Press, 1966 . . . . £50/£20
The Land of Green Ginger, by Noel Langley, Puffin,
1966 (wraps) £20
ditto, Penguin Books (U.S.), [1966] £20
The Dragon, by Archibald Marshall, Warne, 1966. .
. . . . £40/£15
ditto, Dutton (U.S.), [1967] . . . . . £40/£10
The Secret Shoemaker and Other Stories, by James
Reeves, Abelard-Schumann, 1966 . . . £75/£20
Timothy's Song, by W.J. Lederer, Lutterworth Press,
1966 . . . . £40/£15
ditto, Norton (U.S.), [1965] . . . . . £40/£15
The Year Round, by Leonard Clark, Hart-Davis, 1966
. . . . £40/£15
The Muffletumps; the story of four dolls, by Jan Wahl,
Holt Rinehart and Winston (U.S.), [1966] . £40/£15
Rhyming Will, by James Reeves, Hamish Hamilton,
1967 . . . . £70/£25
ditto, McGraw-Hill (U.S.), [1968] . . . £65/£20
Travels with a Donkey, by Robert Louis Stevenson,
Folio Society, 1967 . . . . . . £35/£15
Miranda The Great, by Eleanor Estes, Harcourt Brace
(U.S.), 1967 . . . . £35/£15
ditto, Harcourt, Brace & World (U.S.), [1967] £35/£15
A Likely Place, by Paula Fox, Macmillan [1967] . .
. . . . £35/£15
ditto, Macmillan (U.S.), [1967] . . . . £35/£15
Kali and the Golden Mirror, by Eva-Lis Wuorio,
World Publishing (U.S.), 1967 . . . . £45/£20
The Stuffed Dog, by John Symonds, Barker, 1967 . .
. . . . £40/£15
Nurse Matilda Goes to Town, by Christianna Brand,
Brockhampton Press, 1967 . . . . . £40/£15
ditto, Dutton (U.S.), [1968] . . . . . £40/£10
Robinson Crusoe, by Daniel Defoe, Nonesuch Press,
1968 . . . . £40/£15
Upside-Down Willie, by Dorothy Clewes, Hamish
Hamilton, 1968 . . . . £35/£15
Special Branch Willie, by Dorothy Clewes, Hamish
Hamilton, 1969 . . . . £35/£15
The Angel and the Donkey, by James Reeves, Hamish
Hamilton, 1969 . . . . £50/£15
ditto, McGraw-Hill (U.S.), [1970] . . . £35/£15
A Riot of Quiet, by Virginia Sicotte, Holt, Rinehart and
Winston (U.S.), [1969] . . . . . £35/£10
Dick Wittington, retold by Kathleen Lines, Bodley
Head, 1970 . . . . £25/£10
ditto, Walck (U.S.), [1970] . . . . . £25/£10
Fire Brigade Willie, by Dorothy Clewes, Hamish
Hamilton, 1970 . . . . £45/£15
Home From the Sea, by Robert Louis Stevenson,
Bodley Head, 1970 (verse, selected and introduced by
Ivor Brown) . . . . £25/£10

How the Moon Began, by James Reeves, Abelard-
Schumann, 1971 . . . . £40/£15
The Old Ballad of the Babes in the Wood, Bodley
Head, 1972 . . . . £35/£10
ditto, Walck (U.S.), [1972] . . . . . £35/£10
The Second Best Children in the World, by Mary
Lavin, Longmans, 1972 . . . . . . £25/£10
ditto, Houghton Mifflin (U.S.), 1972 . . £25/£10
The Tunnel of Hugsy Goode, by Eleanor Estes,
Harcourt Brace (U.S.), 1972 . . . £25/£10
ditto, Harcourt Brace Jovanovich (U.S.), [1972] . .
. . . . £25/£10
Rain, Rain, Don't Go Away, by Shirley Morgan,
Dutton, [1972] . . . . £25/£10
The Little Fire Engine, by Graham Greene, Bodley
Head, 1973 . . . . £45/£20
ditto, Doubleday (U.S.), 1973 . . . . £45/£20
The Little Train, by Graham Greene, Bodley Head,
1973 . . . . £45/£20
ditto, Doubleday (U.S.), 1973 . . . . £45/£20
Complete Poems for Children, by James Reeves,
Heinemann, 1973 . . . . £30/£10
The Night Ride, by Aingelda Ardizzone, Bodley Head,
1973 . . . . £25/£10
ditto, Windmill Books (U.S.), 1975 . . . £25/£10
The Little Horse Bus, by Graham Greene, Bodley
Head, 1974 . . . . £50/£20
ditto, Doubleday (U.S.), 1974 . . . . £45/£20
The Little Steam Roller, by Graham Greene, Bodley
Head, 1974 . . . . £50/£20
ditto, Doubleday (U.S.), 1974 . . . . £45/£20
The Lion That Flew, by James Reeves, Chatto &
Windus, 1974 (issued without d/w). . . . £20
Nurse Matilda Goes to Hospital, by Christianna Brand,
Brockhampton Press, 1974 . . . . £45/£15
More Prefabulous Animiles, by James Reeves,
Heinemann, 1975 . . . . . . £30/£15
Ardizzone's Kilvert, Cape, 1976 . . . £25/£10
Arcadian Ballads, by James Reeves, Heinemann, 1978
. . . . £25/£10
Ardizzone's Hans Andersen, Deutsch, 1978 £35/£15
ditto, Atheneum (U.S.), 1979 . . . . £35/£15
A Child's Christmas in Wales, by Dylan Thomas,
Dent, 1978 . . . . £65/£20
ditto, Godine (U.S.), 1980 . . . . £35/£10
The James Reeves Story Book, Heinemann, 1978 . .
. . . . £25/£10
Ardizzone's English Fairy Tales, Deutsch, 1980 . .
. . . . £25/£10
The Wrong Side of the Bed, Doubleday (U.S.), 1970 .
. . . . £25/£10

Adult Books Written and Illustrated by Ardizzone
Baggage to the Enemy, Murray, 1941 . . £50/£20
*The Young Ardizzone: An Autobiographical Frag-
ment*, Studio Vista, 1970 . . . . . £30/£10
ditto, Macmillan (U.S.), 1970 . . . . £30/£10
Diary of a War Artist, Bodley Head, 1974 . £30/£10

From Edward Ardizzone's Indian Diary, Stellar Press/
Bodley Head, 1983 (225 copies, wraps) . . £75
Indian Diary, Bodley Head, 1984 . . . £25/£10

Adult Books Illustrated by Ardizzone
In a Glass Darkly, by Sheridan Le Fanu, Peter Davis,
1929 . . . . £250/£125
ditto, Peter Davis, 1929 (second impression) £100/£45
The Library, by George Crabbe, De la More Press,
1930 . . . . £75/£30
The Mediterranean, edited by Paul Bloomfield,
Cassell, 1935 . . . . £100/£35
The Local, by Maurice Gorham, Cassell, 1939 £75/£25
My Uncle Silas, by H.E. Bates, Cape, 1939. £175/£75
ditto, Graywolf Press (U.S.), 1984 . . . £25/£10
The Road to Bordeaux, by C.D. Freeman and D.
Cooper, Cresset Press, 1940. . . . . £45/£20
The Battle of France, by A. Maurois, Bodley Head,
1940 . . . . £45/£20
Women, O.U.P., 1943 (wraps) £25
The Poems of Francois Villon, Cresset Press, 1946 .
. . . . £70/£20
Back to the Local, by Maurice Gorham, Percival
Marshall, 1949 . . . . £75/£25
The Londoners, by Maurice Gorham, Percival
Marshall, 1951 . . . . £45/£20
Showmen and Suckers, by Maurice Gorham, Percival
Marshall, 1951 . . . . £45/£20
The Modern Prometheus, by Zara Nuber, Forge Press,
1952 . . . . £25/£10
The Warden, by Anthony Trollope, O.U.P., 1952 . .
. . . . £60/£25
Barchester Towers, by Anthony Trollope, O.U.P.,
1953 . . . . £60/£25
ditto, Franklin Library (U.S.), 1982 (full leather
edition) £35
Christmas Eve, by Cecil Day Lewis, Faber, 1954
(wraps) £15
The Newcomes, by William Makepeace Thackeray,
Limited Edition Club, 1954 (1,500 signed copies,
slipcase, 2 vols) . . . . £65/£45
The Tale of an Old Tweed Jacket, by Eric Keown,
Moss Bros, [1955] . . . . £75/£25
The History of Henry Esmond, by William Makepeace
Thackeray, The Limited Editions Club (U.S.), 1956
(1,500 signed, numbered copies, slipcase). £125/£75
Sugar for the Horse, by H.E. Bates, Joseph, 1957 . .
. . . . £35/£15
Brief to Counsel, by Henry Cecil, Joseph, 1957 . .
. . . . £35/£15
Not Such An Ass, by Henry Cecil, Hutchinson, 1961 .
. . . . £30/£10
Folk Songs of England, Ireland, Scotland and Wales,
by W. Cole, Doubleday (U.S.), 1961 . . £40/£15
London Since 1912, by John T. Hayes, Museum of
London, 1962 . . . . £35/£10
The Thirty-Nine Steps, by John Buchan, Dent, 1964 .
. . . . £35/£10

The Milldale Riot, by Freda P. Nichols, Ginn, 1965 .
. . . . £35/£10
Know About English Law, by Henry Cecil, Blackie,
1965 . . . . £35/£10
The Short Stories, by Charles Dickens, Limited
Edition Club (U.S.), 1971 (1,500 signed copies,
slipcase) . . . . £125/£75
Learn About English Law, by Henry Cecil, William
Luscombe, 1974 . . . . £20/£10

MICHAEL ARLEN
(b.1895 d.1956)

Born Dikran Kouyoumdjian in Bulgaria of Armenian
ancestry, Arlen became a naturalised British subject in
1922 and was a popular writer during the 20s and 30s.

Short Stories
The Romantic Lady and Other Stories, Collins, [1921]
. . . . £50/£20
ditto, Doran (U.S.), 1921 . . . . . £45/£15
These Charming People, Collins, [1923] . £40/£10
ditto, Doran (U.S.), 1924 . . . . . £35/£10
*May Fair, In Which Are Told the Last Adventures of
These Charming People*, Collins, [1925] . £40/£10
ditto, Doran (U.S.), [1925] . . . . . £25/£5
ditto, Doran (U.S.), [1925] (550 signed copies in
slipcase) . . . . £60/£40
Ghost Stories, Collins, [1927] . . . . £75/£30
Babes in the Wood, Hutchinson, [1929]. . £25/£10
ditto, Doran (U.S.), 1929 . . . . . . £20/£5
The Ancient Sin and Other Stories, Collins, 1930 . .
. . . . £20/£5
The Short Stories of Michael Arlen, Collins, 1933 .
. . . . £15/£5
*The Crooked Coronet and Other Misrepresentations
of the Real Facts of Life*, Heinemann, 1937 . £20/£5
ditto, Doran (U.S.), 1937 . . . . . . £15/£5

Novels
The London Venture, Heinemann, 1920 . £100/£20
ditto, Doran (U.S.), 1920 . . . . . £75/£20
'Piracy': A Romantic Chronicle of These Days,
Collins, [1922] . . . . £50/£10
ditto, Doran (U.S.), 1923 . . . . . £40/£10
The Green Hat: A Romance for a Few People,
Collins, 1924 . . . . £75/£20
ditto, Doran (U.S.), 1924 . . . . . £60/£15
Young Men in Love, Hutchinson, [1927] . £45/£10
ditto, Doran (U.S.), 1927 . . . . . £40/£10
Lily Christine, Hutchinson, [1928] . . £30/£15
ditto, Doran (U.S.), 1928 . . . . . £25/£10
Men Dislike Women, Heinemann, 1931. . £45/£15
ditto, Doran (U.S.), 1931 . . . . . £35/£15
A Young man Comes to London, Keliher & Co., 1931
(brochure to promote Dorchester Hotel) . . £40

Man's Mortality, Heinemann, 1933 . . . . £45/£5
ditto, Doran (U.S.), 1933 . . . . . . £25/£5
Hell! Said the Duchess: A Bed-Time Story,
Heinemann, [1934] . . . . . . £30/£10
ditto, Doran (U.S.), 1934 . . . . . . £25/£5
The Flying Dutchman, Heinemann, 1939 . . £25/£5
ditto, Doran (U.S.), 1939 . . . . . . £25/£5

Plays
The Zoo, French, 1927 (wraps, with Winchell Smith) .
. . . . £15
Good Losers, French, 1933 (wraps, with Walter
Hackett) £15
The Green Hat: A Romance, Doran (U.S.), 1925 (175
signed copies, glassine d/w and slipcase) . £75/£50

DAISY ASHFORD
(b.1881 d.1972)

Written when the author was a child, Ashford's books
are classics of unconscious humour.

The Young Visiters or, Mr Salteenas Plan, Chatto &
Windus, 1919 (Preface by J. M. Barrie) . £250/£35
ditto, Doran (U.S.), 1919 . . . . . £125/£25
Daisy Ashford: Her Book, Chatto & Windus, 1920 .
. . . . £65/£15
ditto, Doran (U.S.), 1920 . . . . . £65/£15
Love and Marriage, Hart Davis, 1965 (illustrated by
Ralph Steadman). . . . . £20/£5
Where Love Lies Deepest, Hart Davis, 1966 (illustrated
by Ralph Steadman) . . . . £20/£5
The Hangman's Daughter, O.U.P., 1983 . £10/£5

ISAAC ASIMOV
(b.1920 d.1992)

Born in Russia, Asimov was taken to the U.S. in
infancy. A hugely successful science fiction writer,
his many non-fiction writings have also served to
make scientific ideas popular and easily under-
standable.

Novels
Pebble in the Sky, Doubleday (U.S.), 1950 . £750/£85
ditto, Sidgwick & Jackson, 1968 . . . . £125/£30
The Stars, Like Dust, Doubleday (U.S.), 1951 . . .
. . . . £400/£35
ditto, Panther, 1958 (pbk). £5
ditto, Grafton, 1986 . . . . £20/£5
Foundation, Gnome Press (U.S.), 1951 . . £650/£100
ditto, Weidenfeld, 1953 . . . . . . £300/£50
Foundation and Empire, Gnome Press (U.S.), 1952 .
. . . . £450/£75

ditto, Panther, 1962 (pbk). £5
ditto, Granada, 1983 . . . . £20/£5
The Currents of Space, Doubleday (U.S.), 1952 . .
. . . . £250/£45
ditto, Boardman, 1955. . . . . . . £125/£20
Second Foundation, Gnome Press (U.S.), 1953 . .
. . . . £450/£75
ditto, Digit, 1958 (wraps) £5
ditto, Granada, 1983 . . . . £20/£5
The Caves of Steel, Doubleday (U.S.), 1954 . . .
. . . . £250/£40
ditto, Boardman, 1954. . . . . . . £135/£20
The End of Eternity, Doubleday (U.S.), 1955 . . .
. . . . £200/£15
ditto, Panther, 1959 (pbk). £5
The Naked Sun, Doubleday (U.S.), 1957 . £250/£35
ditto, Joseph, 1958. . . . . £100/£20
The Death Dealers, Avon (U.S.), 1958 (pbk) . £30
ditto, as **A Whiff of Death**, Walker (U.S.), 1968 . .
. . . . £100/£20
ditto, Gollancz, 1968 . . . . £100/£20
Fantastic Voyage, Houghton Miffin (U.S.), 1966 . .
. . . . £125/£20
ditto, Dobson, 1966 . . . . . . £125/£20
The Gods Themselves, Doubleday (U.S.), 1972 . .
. . . . £150/£25
ditto, Gollancz, 1972 . . . . . . £100/£15
Murder at the ABA, Doubleday (U.S.), 1976 £45/£10
ditto, as **Authorised Murder**, Gollancz, 1976 £45/£10
Foundation's Edge, Doubleday (U.S.), 1982 £45/£10
ditto, Whispers Press (U.S.), 1982 (1,000 signed,
numbered copies, no d/w) £125
ditto, Whispers Press (U.S.), 1982 (26 signed, lettered
copies, all edges gilt, slipcase, no d/w). . . £400
ditto, Granada, 1983 . . . . £15/£5
Robots of Dawn, Doubleday (U.S.), 1983 . £75/£25
ditto, Phantasia Press (U.S.), 1983 (750 signed,
numbered copies, slipcase and d/w) . £150/£100
ditto, Granada, 1984 . . . . £25/£5
Robots and Empire, Doubleday (U.S.), 1985 £50/£15
ditto, Phantasia Press (U.S.), 1985 (650 signed,
numbered copies, slipcase) . . . . £125/£75
ditto, Phantasia Press (U.S.), 1985 (35 signed,
numbered copies, slipcase) . . . . . £450/£400
ditto, Granada, 1985 . . . . £30/£5
Foundation and Earth, Doubleday (U.S.), 1986 . .
. . . . £25/£5
ditto, Doubleday (U.S.), 1986 (300 signed, numbered
copies, slipcase) . . . . £125/£75
ditto, Grafton, 1986 . . . . £20/£5
Fantastic Voyage II: Destination Britain, Doubleday
(U.S.), 1987 . . . . £45/£10
ditto, Doubleday (U.S.), 1987 (450 signed copies) . .
. . . . £100/£65
ditto, Grafton, 1987 . . . . . . £35/£10
Prelude to Foundation, Doubleday (U.S.), 1988 . .
. . . . £25/£5
ditto, Doubleday (U.S.), 1988 (500 signed copies,
slipcase) . . . . £100/£65

ditto, Easton Press (U.S.), 1988 (signed copies, full
leather) £100
ditto, Grafton, 1988 . . . . £15/£5
Nemesis, Doubleday (U.S.), 1989 . . . . £20/£5
ditto, Doubleday (U.S.), 1989 (500 signed copies,
slipcase) . . . . £75/£50
ditto, Doubleday (U.K.), 1989 . . . . £15/£5
Nightfall and Other Stories, Doubleday (U.S.), 1990
(with Robert Silverberg). . . . . . £20/£5
ditto, Doubleday (U.S.), 1990 (750 signed copies,
slipcase) . . . . £100/£75
ditto, as **Nightfall: Twenty SF Stories**, Gollancz, 1990
. . . . £15/£5
Child of Time, Gollancz, 1991 . . . . £15/£5
ditto, as **The Ugly Little Boy**, Doubleday (U.S.), 1992 .
. . . . £15/£5

The Positronic Man, Doubleday (U.S.), 1992 (with
Robert Silverberg) . . . . £15/£5
ditto, Gollancz, 1992 . . . . £15/£5
Forward the Foundation, Doubleday (U.S.), 1993 .
. . . . £10/£5
ditto, Doubleday (U.K.), 1993 . . . . £10/£5

Short Stories
I, Robot, Gnome Press (U.S.), 1950 . . . £600/£150
ditto, Grayson, 1952 . . . . £350/£50
The Martian Way and Other Stories, Doubleday
(U.S.), 1955 . . . . £350/£50
ditto, Dobson, 1964 . . . . . - . . £200/£35
Earth Is Room Enough, Doubleday (U.S.), 1957 . .
. . . . £175/£35
ditto, Panther, 1960 (pbk). £5
Nine Tomorrows: Tales of the Near Future,
Doubleday (U.S.), 1959 . . . . . £75/£15
ditto, Dobson, 1963 . . . . . . £50/£10
The Rest of the Robots, Doubleday (U.S.), 1964 . .
. . . . £50/£10
ditto, Dobson, 1967 . . . . . . £50/£10
Through a Glass, Clearly, New English Library, 1967
(pbk) £5
Asimov's Mysteries, Doubleday (U.S.), 1968 £45/£10
ditto, Rapp & Whiting, 1968 . . . . . £45/£10
Nightfall and Other Stories, Doubleday (U.S.), 1969 .
. . . . £100/£25
ditto, Rapp & Whiting, 1969 . . . . . £100/£25
The Early Asimov, Doubleday (U.S.), 1972 £50/£10
ditto, Gollancz, 1973 . . . . . . £35/£10
The Best of Isaac Asimov, Sidgwick & Jackson, 1973 .
. . . . £45/£10
ditto, Doubleday (U.S.), 1974 . . . . £45/£10
Tales of the Black Widowers, Doubleday (U.S.), 1974
. . . . £75/£10
ditto, Gollancz, 1975 . . . . . . £50/£10
Have You Seen These?, NESFA Press (U.S.), 1974
(500 signed, numbered copies) . . . . £125/£45
Buy Jupiter and Other Stories, Doubleday (U.S.),
1975 . . . . £75/£10
ditto, Gollancz, 1976 . . . . . . £50/£10

The Bicentennial Man and Other Stories, Doubleday
(U.S.), 1976 . . . . £75/£10
ditto, Gollancz, 1977 . . . . £50/£10
More Tales of the Black Widowers, Doubleday (U.S.),
1976 . . . . £75/£10
ditto, Gollancz, 1977 . . . . £50/£10
*The Dream; Benjamin's Dream; & Benjamin's
Bicentennial Blast*, Benjamin Franklin Keepsakes
(U.S.), 1976 (approx 200 copies) £100
Good Taste, Apocalypse Press (U.S.), 1976 (500
signed, numbered copies) £100
ditto, Apocalypse Press (U.S.), 1976 (500 facsimile
signed, numbered copies) £45
The Key Word and Other Mysteries, Walker (U.S.),
1977 . . . . £50/£10
ditto, Piccolo/Pan, 1982 (pbk) £5
The Casebook of the Black Widowers, Doubleday
(U.S.), 1980 . . . . £50/£10
ditto, Gollancz, 1980 . . . . £40/£5
Three Science Fiction Tales, Targ Editions (U.S.),
1981 (250 signed copies in plain d/w) . . £175/£125
The Complete Robot, Doubleday (U.S.), 1982 . . .
. . . . £100/£25
ditto, Granada, 1982 . . . . . . £65/£15
The Winds of Change and Other Stories, Doubleday
(U.S.), 1983 . . . . £35/£10
ditto, as *The Winds of Change*, Granada, 1983. . .
. . . . £25/£10
The Union Club Mysteries, Doubleday (U.S.), 1983 .
. . . . £25/£10
ditto, Granada, 1984 . . . . £15/£5
The Edge of Tomorrow, Tor (U.S.), 1985 . . £15/£5
ditto, Harrap, 1985 . . . . £15/£5
It's Such a Beautiful Day, Creative Education (U.S.),
1985 (no d/w) £10
Banquets of the Black Widowers, Doubleday (U.S.),
1985 . . . . £35/£10
ditto, Granada, 1985 . . . . . . £25/£10
Alternate Asimovs, Doubleday (U.S.), 1986 . £15/£5
ditto, Panther/Grafton, 1987 (pbk) £5
Science Fiction by Asimov, Davis (U.S.), 1986 (pbk) .
. . . . £5
The Best Science Fiction of Isaac Asimov, Doubleday
(U.S.), 1986 . . . . £15/£5
ditto, Grafton, 1987 . . . . £10/£5
Robot Dreams, Berkley (U.S.), 1986 . . £75/£15
ditto, Gollancz, 1987 . . . . . . £50/£15
The Best Mysteries of Isaac Asimov, Doubleday
(U.S.), 1986 . . . . £15/£5
ditto, Grafton, 1987 . . . . £15/£5
Other Worlds of Isaac Asimov, Avenel (U.S.), 1987 .
. . . . £20/£5
Sally, Creative Education (U.S.), 1988 (no d/w) £10
Azazel, Doubleday (U.S.), 1988 . . . . £20/£5
ditto, Doubleday (U.K.), 1989 . . . . £20/£5
The Asimov Chronicles: Fifty Years of Isaac Asimov,
Dark Harvest (U.S.), 1989 . . . . . £25/£10
ditto, Dark Harvest (U.S.), 1989 (52 signed, lettered
copies, slipcase) . . . . £300/£250

ditto, Dark Harvest (U.S.), 1989 (500 signed copies) .
. . . . £100/£75
ditto, Century, 1991 . . . . £15/£5
All The Troubles of the World, Creative Education
(U.S.), 1989 (no d/w) £10
Franchise, Creative Education (U.S.), 1989 (no d/w) .
. . . . £10
Robbie, Creative Education (U.S.), 1989 (no d/w) £10
Robot Visions, NAL, 1990 . . . . . £35/£10
ditto, Gollancz, 1990 . . . . £25/£5
Puzzles of the Black Widowers, Doubleday (U.S.),
1990 . . . . £25/£5
ditto, Doubleday (U.K.), 1990 . . . . £15/£5
The Complete Stories I, Doubleday (U.S.), 1990 . .
. . . . £15/£5
The Complete Stories, Harper/Collins, 1992 . £15/£5
Gold: The Final Science Fiction Collection, Harper
Collins, 1995 . . . . £10/£5
Magic: The Final Fantasy Collection, Harper (U.S.),
1996 . . . . £10/£5
ditto, Voyager, 1996 . . . . £10/£5

Children's Titles Written as 'Paul French'
David Starr: Space Ranger, Doubleday (U.S.), 1953 .
. . . . £125/£45
ditto, World's Work, 1953 . . . . . £100/£30
Lucky Starr and the Pirates of the Asteroids,
Doubleday (U.S.), 1954 . . . . . £125/£45
ditto, World's Work, 1954 . . . . . £100/£30
Lucky Starr and the Oceans of Venus, Doubleday
(U.S.), 1954 . . . . £75/£15
ditto, as *Oceans of Venus*, New English Library, 1974
(pbk) £5
Lucky Starr and the Big Sun of Mercury, Doubleday
(U.S.), 1956 . . . . £75/£15
ditto, as *The Big Sun of Mercury*, New English
Library, 1974 (pbk) £5
Lucky Starr and the Moons of Jupiter, Doubleday
(U.S.), 1957 . . . . £75/£15
ditto, as *The Moons of Jupiter*, New English Library,
1974 (pbk) £5
Lucky Starr and the Rings of Saturn, Doubleday
(U.S.), 1958 . . . . £75/£15
ditto, as *The Rings of Saturn*, New English Library,
1974 (pbk) £5

MABEL LUCIE ATTWELL
(b.1879 d.1964)

Attwell illustrated not only classic children's books
such as *Alice in Wonderland*, but drew comic strips
and produced her own books, postcards and annuals.

'Bunty and the Boo Boos' Titles
Bunty and the Boo Boos, Valentine, [1921] . £175
The Boo Boos and Bunty's Baby, Valentine, [1921] . .
. . . . £175

The Boo Boos at School, Valentine, [1921]. . £175
The Boo Boos at the Seaside, Valentine, [1921] £175
The Boo Boos at Honeysweet Farm, Valentine, [1921]
. . . . £175
The Boo Boos and Santa Claus, Valentine, [1921] .
. . . . £175

Annuals
The Lucie Attwell Annual No. 1, Partridge, 1922 £225
The Lucie Attwell Annual No. 2, Partridge, 1923 £200
The Lucie Attwell Annual No. 3, Partridge, 1924 £200
Lucie Attwell's Children's Book, Partridge, 1925-32 .
. . . . £200 each
Lucie Attwell's Annual, Dean, 1934-35, 1937-41 . .
. . . . £125 each
Lucie Attwell's Annual, Dean, 1942. . . . £100
Lucie Attwell's Annual, Dean, 1945-68. . . £75
Lucie Attwell's Annual, Dean, 1969-74. . . £50

Others Written and Illustrated by Attwell
Peggy: The Lucie Attwell Cut-Out Dressing Doll,
Valentine, [1921] £125
Stitch Stitch, Valentine, [1922] £125
Comforting Thoughts, Valentine, [1922] . . £60
Baby's Book, Raphael Tuck, [1922]. . . . £100
All About Bad Babies, John Swain, [c1925] . £75
All About the Seaside, John Swain, [c1925] . £60
All About Fairies, John Swain, [c1925] . . £65
All About the Country, John Swain, [c1925] . . £65
All About School, John Swain, [c1925] . . . £65
All About Fido, John Swain, [c1925] . . . £65
Lucie Attwell's Rainy-Day Tales, Partridge [1931]
(with other authors) £125
Lucie Attwell's Rock-Away Tales, London, 1931 (with
other authors) £100
Lucie Attwell's Fairy Book, Partridge, 1932 . £200
Lucie Attwell's Happy-Day Tales, Partridge, [1932] .
. . . . £100
Lucie Attwell's Quiet Time Tales, Partridge, [1932] .
. . . . £100
Lucie Attwell's Painting Book, Dean, [1934] . £65
Lucie Attwell's Great Big Midget Book, Dean, [1934].
. . . . £100
Lucie Attwell's Great Big Midget Book, Dean, [1935]
(different from above) £100
Lucie Attwell's Playtime Pictures, Carlton Publishing
Co, 1935 . . . . £75
Lucie Attwell's Story Book, Dean, [1943] . . £65
Lucie Attwell's Story Book, Dean, [1945] (different
from above) £65
Lucie Attwell's Jolly Book, Dean, [1953] . . £50
Lucie Attwell's Nursery Rhymes Pop-Up Book, Dean,
1958 . . . . £45
Lucie Attwell's Storytime Tales, Dean, [1959] . £30
Lucie Attwell's Book of Verse, Dean, 1960 . . £30
Lucie Attwell's Book of Rhymes, Dean, 1962 . £30
Stories for Everyday, Dean, 1964 . . . . £20
A Little Bird Told Me, Dean, 1964 . . . . £20
A Little Bird Told Me Another Story, Dean, 1966 £20

Tinie's Book of Prayers, Dean, 1967 . . . £20
Lucie Attwell's Tiny Rhymes Pop-Up Book, Dean,
1967 . . . . £35
Lucie Attwell's Tell Me A Story Pop-Up Book, Dean,
1968 . . . . £35
Lucie Attwell's Book of Rhymes, Dean, 1969 . £20

Books Illustrated by Attwell
That Little Limb, by May Baldwin, Chambers, 1905 .
. . . . £75
The Amateur Cook, by K. Burrill, Chambers, 1905 £50
Troublesome Ursula, by Mabel Quiller-Couch, Cham-
bers, 1905. . . . . £65
Dora: A High School Girl, by May Baldwin, Cham-
bers, 1906. . . . . £65
A Boy and a Secret, by Raymond Jacberns, Chambers,
1908 . . . . £40
The Little Tin Soldier, by Graham Mar, Chambers,
1909 . . . . £50
The February Boys, by Mrs Molesworth, Chambers,
1909 . . . . £60
Old Rhymes, Raphael Tuck, 1909 . . . . £45
The Old Pincushion, by Mrs Molesworth, Chambers,
1910 . . . . £60
Mother Goose, Raphael Tuck, 1910 . . . . £150
Alice in Wonderland, by Lewis Carroll, Raphael Tuck,
[1910] (12 colour plates by Attwell) . . . £200
My Dolly's House ABC, Raphael Tuck, [c.1910] . .
. . . . £150
Grimm's Fairy Tales, Cassell, [1910] (4 full-page
illustrations by Attwell) £125
Tabitha Smallways, by Raymond Jacberns, Chambers,
1911 . . . . £65
Grimm's Fairy Stories, Raphael Tuck, 1912 (12 colour
plates by Attwell) £150
Troublesome Topsy and Her Friends, by May
Baldwin, Chambers, 1913 . . . . . £50
Hans Andersen's Fairy Tales, Raphael Tuck, [1914]
(12 colour plates by Attwell) £150
A Band of Mirth, by L.T. Meade, Chambers, 1914 £50
The Water Babies, by Charles Kingsley, Raphael
Tuck, [1915] (12 colour plates by Attwell) . £200
Children's Stories from French Fairy Tales, by Doris
Ashley, Raphael Tuck, 1917 . . . . . £165
Peeping Pansy, by Marie, Queen of Roumania, Hodder
& Stoughton, [1919] (issued with d/w). . . £375
Wooden, by Archibald Marshall, Collins, [1920] £75
Peter Pan and Wendy, by J.M. Barrie, Hodder &
Stoughton, [1921] £250
The Lost Princess: A Fairy Tale, by Marie, Queen of
Roumania, Partridge, 1924 . . . . . £125
Children's Stories, Whitman Publishing Co., [c.1930].
. . . . £250

MARGARET ATWOOD
(b.1939)

Atwood is a Canadian writer, most popularly known for her prose following the success of *Cat's Eye*. A versatile writer, she works successfully in various genres.

Poetry

Double Persephone, Hawkshead Press (Canada), 1961 (wraps) £1,500
The Circle Game, Cranbrook Academy, 1964 (15 copies) £3,000
ditto, Contact Press (Canada), 1966 (50 copies) £1,000
ditto, Contact Press (Canada), 1966 (200 copies, wraps) £450
ditto, House of Anansi (Canada), 1967 (100 signed copies) £200
ditto, House of Anansi (Canada), 1967 (wraps). £25
Talismans for Children, Cranbrook Academy, 1965 . (10 copies). £2,500
Kaleidoscopes: Baroque, Cranbrook Academy, 1965 (20 copies) £2,000
Speeches for Doctor Frankenstein, Cranbrook Academy, 1966 (10 copies). £2,500
Expeditions, Cranbrook Academy, 1966 (15 copies) £2,000
The Animals in that Country, O.U.P. (Canada), 1968 . . . . £200/£45
ditto, O.U.P. (Canada), 1968 (wraps). . . . £35
ditto, Little, Brown (U.S.), [1969] . . . £45/£10
What Was in the Garden?, Unicorn (U.S.), 1969 £35
The Journals of Susanna Moodie, O.U.P. (Canada), 1970 . . . . £45
ditto, Manuel and Abel Bello-Sanchez (Canada), 1980 (20 deluxe signed copies, numbered I-XX) . £750
ditto, Manuel and Abel Bello-Sanchez (Canada), 1980 (100 signed copies) £200
ditto, Bloomsbury, 1997 (slipcase) . . . £75/£50
Oratorio for Sasquatch, Man and Two Androids: Poems for Voices, C.B.C. (Canada), 1970 . . £20
Procedures for Underground, O.U.P. (Canada), 1970 (wraps) £15
ditto, Little, Brown (U.S.), 1970 . . . . £50/£15
Power Politics, Anansi (Canada), 1971 . . £100/£25
ditto, Anansi (Canada), 1971 (wraps) . . . £25
ditto, Harper (U.S.), 1973 . . . . . . £20/£5
You Are Happy, O.U.P. (Canada), 1974. . . £25
ditto, Harper (U.S.), 1974. . . . . . £15/£5
Selected Poems, O.U.P. (Canada), 1976. . . £25
ditto, Simon & Schuster (U.S.), 1978 . . . £15/£5
Marsh, Hawk, Dreadnought, 1977 . . . . £25
Two-headed Poems, O.U.P. (Canada), 1978 . £25
ditto, Simon & Schuster (U.S.), 1980 . . . £15/£5
A Poem for Grandmothers, Square Zero Editions (U.S.), 1978 (26 copies of 126, single sheet) . £100
ditto, Square Zero Editions (U.S.), 1978 (100 copies of 126, single sheet). £40
True Stories, O.U.P. (Canada), 1981 . . . £20

ditto, Simon & Schuster (U.S.), 1982 . . £20/£10
ditto, Cape, 1982 . . . . £20/£10
Notes Towards a Poem that can Never be Written, Salamander Press (Canada), 1981 (200 numbered, signed copies, wraps) £100
Snake Poems, Salamander Press (Canada), 1983 (100 numbered, signed copies, accordion fold) . . £175
Interlunar, O.U.P. (Canada), 1984 . . . . £15
ditto, Cape, 1988 . . . . £15/£5
Selected Poems 2, O.U.P. (Canada), 1986 . . £15
ditto, Houghton Mifflin (U.S.), 1987 . . . £10/£5
ditto, as *Poems, 1976-1986*, Virago, 1992 . . £10
Selected Poems, 1966-1984, O.U.P. (Canada), 1990 . . . . £15
Poems, 1965-1975, Virago, 1991 . . . . £10
ditto, Houghton Mifflin (U.S.), 1987 . . . £10/£5
Good Bones, Harbour Front Reading Series (Canada), 1992 (150 signed copies) £15
Murder in the Dark, Virago, 1995 (wraps) . . . £5
Morning in the Burned House, McClelland & Stewart (Canada), [1995] . . . . £10/£5
ditto, Virago, 1995 (wraps) £5
ditto, Houghton Mifflin (U.S.), 1995 . . . £10/£5
Bones and Murder, Virago, 1995 (wraps) . . . £5
Eating Fire; Selected Poems, 1965-1995, Virago, 1998 . . . . £5

Novels

The Edible Woman, McClelland & Stewart (Canada), 1969 . . . . £300/£35
ditto, Deutsch, 1969 . . . . £150/£30
ditto, Little, Brown (U.S.), 1970 . . . . £75/£15
Surfacing, McClelland & Stewart (Canada), 1972 . . . . £50/£15
ditto, Deutsch, 1973 . . . . £50/£15
ditto, Simon & Schuster (U.S.), 1973 . . . £35/£5
Lady Oracle, McClelland & Stewart (Canada), 1976 . . . . £45/£10
ditto, Simon & Schuster (U.S.), 1976 . . £40/£10
ditto, Deutsch, 1977 . . . . £35/£5
Life Before Man, McClelland & Stewart (Canada), 1979 . . . . £30/£5
ditto, Simon & Schuster (U.S.), 1979 . . £15/£5
ditto, Cape, 1980 . . . . £15/£5
Bodily Harm, McClelland & Stewart (Canada), 1981 . . . . £25/£5
ditto, Simon & Schuster (U.S.), 1982 . . £10/£5
ditto, Cape, 1982 . . . . £10/£5
The Handmaid's Tale, McClelland & Stewart (Canada), 1985 . . . . £35/£10
ditto, Houghton Mifflin (U.S.), 1986 . . £25/£5
ditto, Cape, 1986 . . . . £25/£5
Cat's Eye, McClelland & Stewart (Canada), 1988 . . . . £30/£10
ditto, Doubleday (U.S.), 1989 . . . . £20/£5
ditto, Bloomsbury, 1989 . . . . . . £20/£5
Robber Bride, McClelland & Stewart (Canada), 1993 . . . . £30/£10
ditto, Doubleday (U.S.), 1993 . . . . £15/£5

ditto, Bloomsbury, 1993 . . . . £10/£5
Alias Grace, McClelland & Stewart (Canada), 1996 .
. . . . £30/£10
ditto, Doubleday (U.S.), 1996 . . . . £15/£5
ditto, Bloomsbury, 1996 . . . . £10/£5
The Margaret Atwood Omnibus, Deutsch, 1987 . .
. . . . £10/£5
The Blind Assassin, McClelland & Stewart (Canada),
2000 . . . . £30/£10
ditto, Doubleday (U.S.), 2000 . . . . . £10/£5
ditto, Bloomsbury, 2000 . . . . £10/£5

Short Stories
Dancing Girls and Other Stories, McClelland &
Stewart (Canada), 1977 . . . . . . £75/£20
ditto, Simon & Schuster (U.S.), 1982 . . . £25/£5
ditto, Cape, 1982 . . . . £25/£5
Encounters with the Element Man, Ewert (U.S.), 1982
(60 copies, boards, no d/w) £150
ditto, Ewert (U.S.), 1982 (100 copies, wraps) . £65
Murder in the Dark: Short Fictions and Prose Poems,
Coach House Press (Canada), 1983 (wraps) . £20
ditto, Cape, 1984 . . . . £15/£5
Bluebeard's Egg and Other Stories, McClelland &
Stewart (Canada), 1983 . . . . . . £50/£15
ditto, Houghton Mifflin (U.S.), 1986 . . £20/£5
ditto, Cape, 1987 . . . . £15/£5
Unearthing Suite, Grand Union Press, 1983 (175
signed, numbered copies, no d/w) £200
Hurricane Hazel and Other Stories, Eurographica
(Helsinki), 1987 (350 signed copies, wraps) . £75
Wilderness Tips, McClelland & Stewart (Canada),
1991 . . . . £15/£5
ditto, Doubleday (U.S.), 1991 . . . . . £10/£5
ditto, Bloomsbury, 1991 . . . . £10/£5
Good Bones, Coach House (Canada), 1992 . £20/£5
ditto, Bloomsbury, 1992 . . . . £10/£5
Good Bones and Simple Murders, Doubleday (U.S.),
1994 . . . . £10/£5
ditto, Doubleday (U.S.), 1994 (50 copies) £100/£75

Children's Titles
Up in the Tree, McClelland & Stewart (Canada), 1978
(no d/w) £75
Anna's Pet, Lorimer (Canada), 1980 (with Joyce
Barkhouse, no d/w) £60
For the Birds, Douglas & McIntyre (Canada), 1990
(wraps) £10
Princess Prunella and the Purple Peanut, Key Porter
Kids, 1995 . . . . £15/£5

Criticism
Survival: A Thematic Guide to Canadian Literature,
Anansi (Canada), 1972 ('first' issue binding printed
by Web. Offset Ltd., with 'first' issue dj without
blurbs on the rear panel) . . . . £175/£135
ditto, Anansi (Canada), 1972 (second issue binding
printed by T.H. Best, with 'second' issue dj with
blurbs) . . . . £35/£10

Second Words: Selected Critical Prose, Anansi
(Canada), 1982 . . . . £30/£10
ditto, Beacon Press (U.S.), 1984 . . . . . £20/£5
New Critical Essays, Macmillan, 1994 . . . £10/£5
*Strange Things: The Malevolent North in Canadian
Literature*, O.U.P., 1995 . . . . . . £10/£5

Others
Margaret Atwood: Conversations, Ontario Review
Press (Canada), 1990 . . . . £15/£5
ditto, Virago, 1991 (wraps) £10
*Winner of the Welsh Arts Council International
Writer's Prize*, Welsh Arts Council, 1982 (wraps) £5

W.H. AUDEN
(b.1907 d.1973)

Auden's early poetry was markedly left-wing, but
Christianity was the dominant influence in his later
life and art. He is considered to be one of the most
influential poets of the twentieth century.

Poetry
Poems, privately printed by Stephen Spender, 1928 (30
copies, orange wraps) £30,000
Poems, Faber, 1930 (wraps) £750
ditto, Random House (U.S.), 1934 . . . £150/£50
The Orators: an English Study, Faber, [1932] . .
. . . . £250/£75
ditto, Random House (U.S.), 1967 . . . £25/£5
The Dance of Death, Faber, 1933 . . . £150/£35
The Witnesses, privately printed, 1933 (broadside, 20
copies, illustrated by Gwen Raverat) . . . £3,000
Poem, privately printed, 1933 (22 copies, wraps) . .
. . . . £5,000
Two Poems, privately printed, 1934 (22 copies, wraps)
. . . . £5,000
Our Hunting Fathers, privately printed, 1935 (22
copies, wraps) £5,000
Sonnet, privately printed, 1935 (22 copies, wraps) . .
. . . . £5,000
Look Stranger!, Faber, 1936 . . . . . £200/£45
ditto, as *On This Island*, Random House (U.S.),
[1937] . . . . £175/£40
Spain, Faber, [1937] (wraps) £125
Deux Poemes, Hours Press (Paris), 1937 (100 copies) .
. . . . £1,000
Night Mail, G.P.O., 1938 (broadside) . . . £75
Selected Poems, Faber, 1938 . . . . . £150/£35
Journey to a War, Faber, 1939 (with Christopher
Isherwood) . . . . £200/£65
ditto, Random House (U.S.), 1939 . . . £150/£50
Another Time, Faber, 1940 . . . . . £150/£50
ditto, Random House (U.S.), 1940 . . . £125/£40
Some Poems, Faber, 1940 . . . . . £75/£20
The Double Man, Random House (U.S.), 1941 . .
. . . . £100/£25

ditto, as *New Year Letter*, Faber, 1941 . . £100/£25
Three Songs for St Cecilia's Day, privately printed,
1941 (250 copies, wraps) £300
For the Time Being, Random House (U.S.), 1944 . .
. . . . £125/£35
ditto, Faber, 1945 . . . . £125/£35
The Collected Poetry, Random House, 1945 £75/£15
Litany and Anthem for St Matthew's Day, privately
printed, 1946 (single sheet) £65
The Age of Anxiety, Random House (U.S.), [1947] .
. . . . £100/£25
ditto, Faber, 1948 . . . . £95/£25
Collected Shorter Poems 1930-1944, Faber, 1950 . .
. . . . £65/£20
Nones, Random House (U.S.), 1951 . . . £75/£20
ditto, Faber, 1952 . . . . £75/£20
Mountains, Faber Ariel Poem, 1954 (wraps) . £25
The Shield of Achilles, Random House (U.S.), 1955 .
. . . . £50/£15
ditto, Faber, 1955 . . . . £50/£15
The Old Man's Road, Voyages Press (U.S.), 1956 (50
signed copies of 750, wraps) £300
ditto, Voyages Press (U.S.), 1956 (700 unsigned copies
of 750, wraps) £75
W.H. Auden: A Selection by the Author, Penguin,
1958 (wraps) £5
ditto, as *Selected Poetry of W.H. Auden*, Modern
Library (U.S.), 1959 . . . . £15/£5
Goodbye to the Mezzogiorno, All'Insegna del Pesce
d'Oro (Spain), 1958 (1,000 numbered copies, wraps)
. . . . £50
Homage to Clio, Random House (U.S.), 1960 £45/£15
ditto, Faber, 1960 . . . . £45/£15
The Platonic Blow, Fuck You Press (U.S.), 1965 (310
copies, wraps) £125
About the House, Random House (U.S.), 1965 . . .
. . . . £45/£15
ditto, Faber, 1966 . . . . £40/£15
Collected Shorter Poems, 1927-1957, Faber, 1966. .
. . . . £75/£20
ditto, Random House (U.S.), 1967 . . . £65/£20
Marginalia, Ibex Press (U.S.), 1966 (150 signed
copies, wraps) £350
Selected Poems, Faber, 1968 (wraps) £5
Collected Longer Poems, Faber, 1968 . . £35/£10
ditto, Random House (U.S.), 1969 . . . £35/£10
City Without Walls, Faber, 1969 . . . . £30/£10
ditto, Random House (U.S.), 1970 . . . £30/£10
Natural Linguistics, Poem-of-the-month-Club, 1970
(1,000 signed copies, broadsheet) £75
Academic Graffiti, Faber, 1971 . . . . . £25/£5
ditto, Random House (U.S.), 1972 . . . . £25/£5
Epistle to a Godson, Faber, 1972 . . . £35/£10
ditto, Random House (U.S.), 1972 . . . £35/£10
The Ballad of Barnaby, no place, 1973 (broadside) .
. . . . £35
Thank You Fog: Last Poems, Faber, 1974 . £35/£10
ditto, Random House (U.S.), 1974 . . . £30/£10
Collected Poems, Faber, 1976 . . . . £35/£10

ditto, Random House (U.S.), 1976 . . . £35/£10
ditto, Franklin Library (U.S.), 1976 (full leather) £50
The English Auden, Faber, 1977 . . . . £25/£5
ditto, Random House (U.S.), 1978 . . . . £25/£5
Norse Poems, Athlone Press, 1981 . . . . £25/£5

Plays
The Dog Beneath the Skin (with Christopher
Isherwood), Faber, 1935. . . . . £175/£45
ditto, Random House (U.S.), 1935 . . . £175/£45
The Ascent of F6, Faber, 1936 (with Christopher
Isherwood) . . . . £150/£35
ditto, Random House (U.S.), 1937 . . . £125/£25
On the Frontier, Faber, [1938] (with Christopher
Isherwood) . . . . £100/£25
ditto, Random House (U.S.), 1939 . . . £75/£20

Prose
Letters from Iceland, Faber, 1937 (with Louis
MacNeice) . . . . £100/£25
ditto, Harcourt Brace (U.S.), 1937 . . . £75/£15
Education Today and Tomorrow, Hogarth Press, 1939
(with T. S. Worsley, wraps) £100
*The Enchafèd Flood or The Romantic Iconography
of the Sea*, Random House (U.S.), 1950 . £65/£15
ditto, Faber, 1951 . . . . £50/£10
Making, Knowing and Judging, O.U.P., 1956 (wraps)
. . . . £45
The Dyer's Hand, Random House (U.S.), 1962 . .
. . . . £100/£25
ditto, Faber, 1963 . . . . £65/£20
Louis MacNeice - A Memorial Address, privately
printed Faber, 1963 (1,500 copies, wraps). . £75
Selected Essays, Faber, 1964 (wraps) . . . £15
Secondary Worlds, Random House (U.S.), 1968 . .
. . . . £25/£5
ditto, Faber, 1969 . . . . £25/£5
Forewords and Afterwords, Faber, 1973 . £20/£5
ditto, Viking (U.S.), 1973. . . . . . £20/£5

Others
The Rake's Progress, Boosey & Hawkes Ltd, 1951
(libretto, with Chester Kallman, wraps) . . £75
The Magic Flute, Random House, 1956 (libretto, with
Chester Kallman) . . . . £35/£15
ditto, Faber, 1957 . . . . £35/£15
Elegy for Young Lovers, Schott, 1961 (libretto, with
Chester Kallman, wraps) £50
The Bassarids, Schott, 1966 (libretto with Chester
Kallman, wraps) £50
A Certain World, Viking (U.S.), [1970]. . £30/£10
ditto, Faber, 1971 . . . . £30/£5
Lectures on Shakespeare, Princetown Univ. Press
(U.S.), 2000 . . . . £15/£5
ditto, Faber, 2001 . . . . £15/£5

JANE AUSTEN
(b.1775 d.1817)

Generally regarded as the greatest of English women novelists, Austen's novels are particularly noted for their sparkling social comedy and accurate portrayal of human relationships.

Novels

Sense and Sensibility, T. Egerton, 1811 (3 vols in contemporary bindings) £40,000
ditto, Carey & Lea (U.S.), 1833 (2 vols). . . £2,000
Pride and Prejudice, T. Egerton, 1813 (3 vols in contemporary bindings) £25,000
ditto, as *Elizabeth Bennet, or Pride and Prejudice*, Carey & Lea (U.S.), 1832 (2 vols) £2,500
Mansfield Park, T. Egerton, 1814 (3 vols in contemporary bindings) £15,000
Emma, J. Murray, 1816 (3 vols in contemporary binding) £10,000
Northanger Abbey and Persuasion, J. Murray, 1818 (4 vols in contemporary bindings) £8,500
ditto, as Carey & Lea (U.S.), 1833 . . . . £2,000
Persuasion, Carey & Lea (U.S.), 1832 . . . £5,000

Miscellaneous

Letters, R. Bentley, 1884 (2 vols) £700
Charades, Spottiswoode & Co., 1895 (wraps) . £400
Love and Freindship (sic) *and Other Early Works (Volume the second)*, Chatto & Windus, 1922. . .
. . . . £150/£50
ditto, Chatto & Windus, 1922 (260 copies, special edition) £400
ditto, Stokes (U.S.), 1922 . . . . . £140/£40
ditto, (*Volume the First*), Clarendon Press, 1933 . .
. . . . £75/£25
ditto, (*Volume the Second*), Clarendon Press, 1951 .
. . . . £50/£20
The Watsons, Parsons, 1923 . . . . . £200/£45
ditto, Appleton (U.S.), 1923 . . . . . £200/£45
Five Letters from Jane Austen to her Niece, Fanny Knight, Clarendon Press, 1924 (250 copies) . £125
Fragment of a Novel, O.U.P., 1925 ('Sanditon') £45
ditto, O.U.P., 1925 (250 copies on handmade paper) .
. . . . £200
Lady Susan, O.U.P., 1925 . . . . . . £45
ditto, O.U.P., 1925 (250 copies on handmade paper) .
. . . . £200
Two Chapters from Persuasion, O.U.P., 1926 . £65
Plan of a Novel, Clarendon Press, 1926 (350 copies) .
. . . . £100
Letters, O.U.P., 1932 (2 vols) £100
Three Evening Prayers, Colt Press (U.S.), 1940 (300 copies) £200
Sanditon: A Facsimile of the Manuscript, O.U.P., 1975 . . . . £40/£25
ditto, Houghton Mifflin (U.S.), 1975 . . £40/£25
Jane Austen's Sir Charles Grandison, O.U.P., 1980 .
. . . . £30/£10

REV. W. AWDRY
CHRISTOPHER AWDRY
(b. 1911 d.1998, b.1940)

Thomas the Tank Engine is the most famous of all of the Rev. Awdry's railway characters, in a series which has been continued by his son, Christopher.

'Railway Series' Titles by Rev. W. Awdry

The Three Railway Engines, Edmund Ward, 1945 (illustrated by Middleton) . . . . . £125/£20
Thomas the Tank Engine, Edmund Ward, 1946 (illustrated by Payne) . . . . . . £175/£25
James the Red Engine, Edmund Ward, 1948 (illustrated by Dalby) . . . . . . £125/£20
Tank Engine Thomas Again, Edmund Ward, 1949 (illustrated by Dalby) . . . . . . £150/£25
Troublesome Engines, Edmund Ward, 1950 (illustrated by Dalby) . . . . . . £125/£20
Henry the Green Engine, Edmund Ward, 1951 (illustrated by Dalby) . . . . . . £125/£20
Toby the Tram Engine, Edmund Ward, 1952 (illustrated by Dalby) . . . . . . £125/£20
Gordon the Big Engine, Edmund Ward, 1953 (illustrated by Dalby) . . . . . . £125/£20
Edward the Blue Engine, Edmund Ward, 1954 (illustrated by Dalby) . . . . . . £125/£20
Four Little Engines, Edmund Ward, 1955 (illustrated by Dalby). . . . . £125/£20
Percy the Small Engine, Edmund Ward, 1956 (illustrated by Dalby) . . . . . . £100/£20
The Eight Famous Engines, Edmund Ward, 1957 (illustrated by Kenney) . . . . . £100/£20
Duck and the Diesel Engine, Edmund Ward, 1958 (illustrated by Kenney) . . . . . . £75/£15
The Little Old Engine, Edmund Ward, 1959 (illustrated by Kenney) . . . . . . £75/£15
The Twin Engines, Edmund Ward, 1960 (illustrated by Kenney) . . . . £75/£15
Branch Line Engines, Edmund Ward, 1961 (illustrated by Kenney) . . . . £75/£15
Gallant Old Engine, Edmund Ward, 1962 (illustrated by Kenney) . . . . £75/£15
Stepney the 'Bluebell' Engine, Edmund Ward, 1963 (illustrated by G. & P. Edwards) . . . £75/£15
Mountain Engines, Edmund Ward, 1964 (illustrated by G. & P. Edwards). . . . . . . £75/£15
Very Old Engines, Edmund Ward, 1965 (illustrated by G. & P. Edwards) . . . . £75/£15
Main Line Engines, Edmund Ward, 1966 (illustrated by G. & P. Edwards). . . . . . . £75/£15
Small Railway Engines, Kaye & Ward, 1967 (illustrated by G. & P. Edwards) . . . £75/£15
Enterprising Engines, Kaye & Ward, 1968 (illustrated by G. & P. Edwards). . . . . . £75/£15
Oliver the Western Engine, Kaye & Ward, 1969 (illustrated by G. & P. Edwards) . . . £75/£15

Duke the Lost Engine, Kaye & Ward, 1970 (illustrated by G. & P. Edwards). . . . . . . £75/£15
Tramway Engines, Kaye & Ward, 1972 (illustrated by G. & P. Edwards) . . . . £50/£10

'Railway Series' Titles by Christopher Awdry
Really Useful Engines, Kaye & Ward, 1983 (illustrated by Spong) . . . . £15/£5
James and the Diesel Engines, Kaye & Ward, 1984 (illustrated by Spong) . . . . . . £15/£5
Great Little Engines, Kaye & Ward, 1985 (illustrated by Spong). . . . . £15/£5
More about Thomas the Tank Engine, Kaye & Ward, 1986 (illustrated by Spong) . . . . . £15/£5
Gordon the High-Speed Engine, Kaye & Ward, 1987 (illustrated by Spong) . . . . . . £15/£5
Toby, Trucks and Trouble, Kaye & Ward, 1988 (illustrated by Spong) . . . . £10/£5
Thomas and the Twins, Kaye & Ward, 1989 (illustrated by Spong) . . . . £10/£5
Jock the New Engine, Kaye & Ward, 1990 (illustrated by Spong). . . . . £10/£5
Thomas and the Great Railway Show, Kaye & Ward, 1991 (illustrated by Spong) . . . . . £10/£5
Thomas Comes Home, Kaye & Ward, 1992 (illustrated by Spong). . . . . £10/£5
Henry and the Express, Kaye & Ward, 1993 (illustrated by Spong) . . . . £10/£5
Wilbert the Forest Engine, Kaye & Ward, 1994 (illustrated by Spong) . . . . £10/£5
Thomas and the Fat Controller's Engines, Kaye & Ward, 1995 (illustrated by Spong) . . . . £10/£5

ALAN AYCKBOURN
(b.1939)

A popular playwright, Ayckbourn excels at highlighting the neuroses and anxieties of the English middle-class.

Relatively Speaking, Evans, 1968 (wraps) . . £45
ditto, French (U.S.), 1968 (wraps) £15
Playbill One, edited by Alan Durband, Hutchinson Educational, 1969 (contains 'Ernie's Incredible Illucinations' wraps). £10
We Who Are About To ..., Methuen, 1970 (contains 'Countdown') (wraps) £10
How the Other Half Loves, French (U.S.), 1972 (wraps) £15
ditto, Evans, 1972 (wraps) £15
Time and Time Again, French, 1973 (wraps) . £15
ditto, French (U.S.), 1973 (wraps) £15
Absurd Person Singular, French, 1974 (wraps) £15
ditto, French (U.S.), 1974 (wraps) £15
The Norman Conquests, French, 1975 (wraps). £15
ditto, French (U.S.), 1975 (wraps) £15
ditto, Chatto & Windus, 1975 . . . . £30/£10

Absent Friends, French, 1975 (wraps) . . . £15
ditto, French (U.S.), 1975 (wraps) £15
Bedroom Farce, French, 1977 (wraps) . . . £15
ditto, French (U.S.), 1977 (wraps) £15
Three Plays, Chatto & Windus, 1977 . . £25/£10
ditto, Grove Press, 1979 . . . . . . £25/£10
Just Between Ourselves, French, 1978 (wraps). £10
ditto, French (U.S.), 1978 (wraps) £10
Ten Times Table, French, 1978 (wraps). . . £10
ditto, French (U.S.), 1978 (wraps) £10
Joking Apart, French, 1979 (wraps). . . . £15
ditto, French (U.S.), 1979 (wraps) £15
ditto, Chatto & Windus, 1979 . . . . . £15/£5
Confusions, French, 1979 (wraps) £10
ditto, French (U.S.), 1979 (wraps) £10
Sisterly Feelings, French, 1981 (wraps). . . £10
ditto, French (U.S.), 1981 (wraps) £10
ditto, Chatto & Windus, 1981 . . . . . £15/£5
Taking Steps, French, 1981 (wraps) £10
ditto, French (U.S.), 1981 (wraps) £10
Suburban Strains, French, 1982 (wraps) . . . £5
ditto, French (U.S.), 1982 (wraps) £5
Season's Greetings, French, 1982 (wraps) . . . £5
ditto, French (U.S.), 1982 (wraps) £5
Way Upstream, French, 1983 (wraps) £5
ditto, French (U.S.), 1983 (wraps) £5
Intimate Exchanges, French, 1985 (2 vols, wraps) £15
ditto, French (U.S.), 1985 (2 vols, wraps) . . £15
Chorus of Disapproval, French, 1985 (wraps) . . £5
ditto, French (U.S.), 1985 (wraps) £5
Woman in Mind, Faber, 1986 . . . . . £10/£5
ditto, Fireside (U.S.), 1986 . . . . . . £10/£5
A Small Family Business, Faber, 1987 . . . £10/£5
ditto, Faber (U.S.), 1987 . . . . . . £10/£5
Henceforward, Faber, 1988 (wraps). £5
Mr A's Amazing Maze Plays, Faber, 1989 (wraps) £5
A Man of the Moment, Faber, 1990 (wraps) . . £5
Invisible Friends, Faber, 1991 (wraps) £5
Callisto 5, Faber, 1992 (wraps) £5
My Very Own Story, Faber, 1992 (wraps) . . . £5
Wildest Dreams, Faber, 1993 (wraps) £5
Comic Potential, Faber, 1999 (wraps) £5
The Boy Who Fell into a Book, Faber, 2000 (wraps) .
. . . . £5

H.C. BAILEY
(b.1878 d.1961)

Bailey's reputation is based on his dandy detective, Reggie Fortune.

'Reggie Fortune' Short Story Collections
Call Mr Fortune, Methuen, 1921 . . . £600/£100
ditto, Dutton (U.S.), 1923. . . . . . £300/£50
Mr Fortune's Practice, Methuen, 1923 . . £450/£75
ditto, Dutton (U.S.), 1924. . . . . . £300/£50
Mr Fortune's Trials, Methuen, 1925 . . £400/£75
ditto, Dutton (U.S.), 1926. . . . . . £200/£35

Mr Fortune, Please, Methuen, 1927. . . . £400/£75
ditto, Dutton (U.S.), 1928. . . . . . £300/£35
Mr Fortune Speaking, Ward Lock, 1929 . £400/£75
ditto, Dutton (U.S.), 1931. . . . . . £300/£35
Mr Fortune Explains, Ward Lock, 1930 . £350/£50
ditto, Dutton (U.S.), 1931. . . . . . £275/£35
Case for Mr Fortune, Ward Lock, 1932 . £350/£50
ditto, Dutton (U.S.), 1932. . . . . . £275/£35
Mr Fortune Wonders, Ward Lock, 1933 . £350/£50
ditto, Dutton (U.S.), 1933. . . . . . £275/£35
Mr Fortune Objects, Gollancz, 1935 . . £400/£75
ditto, Doubleday (U.S.), 1935 . . . . £250/£35
Clue for Mr Fortune, Gollancz, 1936 . . £400/£75
ditto, as *A Clue for Mr Fortune*, Doubleday (U.S.),
1936 . . . . £250/£35
This is Mr Fortune, Gollancz, 1938 . . . £300/£45
ditto, Doubleday (U.S.), 1938 . . . . £150/£25
Mr Fortune Here, Gollancz, 1940 . . . £300/£45
ditto, Doubleday (U.S.), 1940 . . . . £150/£20

'Reggie Fortune' Novels
Shadow on the Wall, Gollancz, 1934 . . £400/£100
ditto, Doubleday (U.S.), 1934 . . . . £175/£35
Black Land, White Land, Gollancz, 1937 . £350/£75
ditto, Doubleday (U.S.), 1937 . . . . £150/£30
The Great Game, Gollancz, 1939 . . . £400/£100
ditto, Doubleday (U.S.), 1939 . . . . £150/£30
The Bishop's Crime, Gollancz, 1940 . . £225/£50
ditto, Doubleday (U.S.), 1940 . . . . £125/£30
No Murder, Gollancz, 1942 . . . . . £150/£35
ditto, as *The Apprehensive Dog*, Doubleday (U.S.),
1942 . . . . £125/£25
Mr Fortune Finds a Pig, Gollancz, 1943 . £125/£30
ditto, Doubleday (U.S.), 1943 . . . . £100/£20
The Cat's Whisker, Doubleday (U.S.), 1944 £75/£20
ditto, as *Dead Man's Effects*, Macdonald, n.d. [1945].
. . . . £67/£15
The Life Sentence, Macdonald, 1946 . . £50/£15
ditto, Doubleday (U.S.), 1946 . . . . £45/£10
Saving a Rope, Macdonald, 1948 . . . £40/£15
ditto, as *Save a Rope*, Doubleday (U.S.), 1948 £45/£10

'Joshua Clunk' Novels
Garstons, Methuen, 1930 . . . . . . £350/£60
ditto, as *The Garston Muder Case*, Doubleday (U.S.),
1930 . . . . £125/£25
The Red Castle, Ward Lock, 1932 . . . £350/£60
ditto, as *The Red Castle Mystery*, Doubleday (U.S.),
1932 . . . . £100/£20
The Sullen Sky Mystery, Gollancz, 1935 . £350/£60
ditto, Doubleday (U.S.), 1935 . . . . £75/£20
Clunk's Claimant, Gollancz, 1937 . . . £350/£60
ditto, as *The Twittering Bird Mystery*, Doubleday
(U.S.), 1937 . . . . £75/£20
The Veron Mystery, Gollancz, 1939 . . . £350/£60
ditto, as *Mr Clunk's Text*, Doubleday (U.S.), 1939 .
. . . . £65/£15
The Little Captain, Gollancz, 1941 . . . £300/£50
ditto, as *Orphan Ann*, Doubleday (U.S.), 1941 £65/£15

Dead Man's Shoes, Gollancz, 1942 . . . £250/£45
ditto, as *Nobody's Vineyard*, Doubleday (U.S.), 1942 .
. . . . £65/£15
Slippery Ann, Gollancz, 1944 . . . . £75/£20
ditto, as *The Queen of Spades*, Doubleday (U.S.), 1944
. . . . £45/£10
The Wrong Man, Doubleday (U.S.), 1945 . £45/£10
ditto, Macdonald, n.d. [1946]. . . . . £45/£10
Honour Among Thieves, Macdonald, 1947. £35/£10
ditto, Doubleday (U.S.), 1947 . . . . £35/£10
Shrouded Death, Macdonald, 1950 . . . £35/£10

Other Novel
The Man in the Cape, Benn, 1933 . . . £200/£45

BERYL BAINBRIDGE
(b.1934)

Bainbridge's books, usually controversial, often involve several deaths.

Novels
A Weekend with Claud, New Authors Limited,
Hutchinson, 1967 . . . . £125/£25
ditto, as *A Weekend with Claude*, Duckworth, 1981 .
. . . . £25/£5
ditto, Braziller (U.S.), 1981 . . . . . £30/£15
Another Part of the Wood, Hutchinson, 1968 £65/£20
ditto, Duckworth, 1979 . . . . . . £25/£5
ditto, Braziller (U.S.), 1980 . . . . . £25/£5
Harriet Said ..., Duckworth, 1972 . . . £25/£5
ditto, Braziller (U.S.), 1972 . . . . . £25/£5
The Dressmaker, Duckworth, 1973 . . . £25/£5
ditto, as *The Secret Glass*, Braziller (U.S.), 1973 . .
. . . . £25/£5
The Bottle Factory Outing, Duckworth, 1974 . £25/£5
ditto, Braziller (U.S.), 1974 . . . . . £25/£5
Sweet William, Duckworth, 1975 . . . £20/£5
ditto, Braziller (U.S.), 1975 . . . . . £20/£5
A Quiet Life, Duckworth, 1976 . . . . £20/£5
ditto, Braziller (U.S.), 1977 . . . . . £20/£5
Injury Time, Duckworth, 1977 . . . . £20/£5
ditto, Braziller (U.S.), 1977 . . . . . £20/£5
Young Adolf, Duckworth, 1978 . . . . £25/£5
ditto, Braziller (U.S.), 1979 . . . . . £20/£5
Winter Garden, Duckworth, 1980 . . . £20/£5
ditto, Braziller (U.S.), 1981 . . . . . £20/£5
Watson's Apology, Duckworth, 1984 . . £20/£5
ditto, McGraw-Hill (U.S.), 1985 . . . . £20/£5
Filthy Lucre, Duckworth, 1986 . . . . £20/£5
An Awfully Big Adventure, Duckworth, 1989 . £20/£5
ditto, HarperCollins (U.S.), 1991. . . . £20/£5
The Birthday Boys, Duckworth, 1991 . . £20/£5
ditto, Carroll & Graf (U.S.), 1991 . . . £20/£5
Every Man for Himself, Duckworth, 1996 . £20/£5
ditto, Carroll & Graf (U.S.), 1996 . . . £20/£5
Master Georgie, Duckworth, 1998 . . . £20/£5

ditto, Carroll & Graf (U.S.), 1998 . . . . £20/£5
According to Queeney, Carroll & Graf (U.S.), 2000 .
. . . . £20/£5
ditto, Little, Brown, 2001 . . . . . . £10/£5

Omnibus Editions
A Bainbridge Omnibus, Duckworth, 1989 . . £15/£5

Short Stories
Mum and Mr Armitage: Selected Stories, Duckworth,
1985 . . . . £15/£5
ditto, McGraw-Hill (U.S.), 1987 . . . . . £15/£5
Collected Stories, Penguin, 1994 (wraps) . . . £5

Travel
English Journey: or, The Road to Milton Keynes,
Duckworth, 1984 . . . . £15/£5
ditto, Braziller (U.S.), 1984 . . . . . £15/£5
Forever England: North and South, Duckworth, 1987
. . . . £15/£5
ditto, Carroll & Graf (U.S.), 1999 . . . £15/£5

Essays
Something Happened Yesterday, Duckworth, 1993
(wraps) £5
ditto, Carroll & Graf (U.S.), 1998 . . . . £10/£5

R.M. BALLANTYNE
(b.1825 d.1894)

A Scottish author, Ballantyne's first published work
was about his time as a fur trader in Canada, followed
by a series of popular adventure stories. By the time
of his death he had written over 80 books in 40 years.

*Snowflakes and Sunbeams, or The Young Fur-
Traders*, Nelson, 1856 . . . . . . £1,500
Three Little Kittens, Nelson, [1856] (pseud. 'Comus').
. . . . £125
My Mother, Nelson, 1857 (pseud. 'Comus') . £125
The Butterfly's Ball, Nelson, 1857 (pseud. 'Comus') .
. . . . £150
Mister Fox, Nelson, 1857 (pseud. 'Comus') . £125
Ungava, A Tale of Esquimaux Land, Nelson, 1858
[1857]. £125
The Coral Island, A Tale of the Pacific Ocean,
Nelson, 1858 [1857]. £6,000
The Robber Kitten, Nelson, 1858 (pseud. 'Comus') .
. . . . £125
*Martin Rattler, or A Boy's Adventures in the Forests
of Brazil*, Nelson, 1858 . . . . . . £125
Mee-a-ow! or Good Advice to Cats and Kittens,
Nelson, 1859 . . . . £125
The World of Ice, or Adventures in the Polar Regions,
Nelson, 1860 [1859]. £125
The Dog Crusoe, A Tale of the Western Prairies,
Nelson, 1861 [1860]. £200

The Golden Dream, or Adventures in the Far West,
Shaw, 1861 [1860] £200
The Gorilla Hunters, A Tale of the Wilds Of Africa,
Nelson, 1861 . . . . £1,500
The Red Eric, or The Whaler's Last Cruise: A Tale,
Routledge, 1861 . . . . £150
Man on the Ocean, A Book for Boys, Nelson, 1863
[1862]. £150
*The Wild Man of the West, A Tale of the Rocky
Mountains*, Routledge, 1863 [1862] . . . £200
Ballantyne's Miscellany, Nisbet, 1863-1886 (15 vols).
. . . . £650
*Gascoyne, The Sandal-Wood Trader, A Tale of the
Pacific*, Nisbet, 1864 [1863] £150
The Lifeboat, A Tale of Our Coast Heroes, Nisbet,
1864 . . . . £125
*Freaks on the Fells, or Three Months' Rustication:
And Why I did not Become a Sailor*, Routledge, 1865
[1864]. £100
*The Lighthouse, Being the Story of a Great Fight
Between Man and the Sea*, Nisbet, 1865 . . £75
Shifting Winds, A Tough Yarn, Nisbet, 1866 . £75
Silver Lake, or Lost in the Snow, Jackson, 1867 £75
*Fighting the Flames, A Tale of the London Fire
Brigade*, Nisbet, 1868 . . . . . . £100
*Away in the Wilderness, or Life Among the Red-
Indians and Fur-Traders of North America*, Porter
S. Coates (U.S.), 1869 . . . . . . £125
Deep Down, A Tale of the Cornish Mines, Nisbet,
1869 . . . . £125
Erling the Bold, A Tale of the Norse Sea-Kings,
Nisbet, 1869 . . . . £75
The Floating Lights of the Godwin Sands, A Tale,
Nisbet, 1870 . . . . £75
*The Iron Horse, or Life on the Line: A Tale of the
Grand National Trunk Railway*, Nisbet, 1871 £125
*The Norsemen in the West, or America Before
Columbus*, Nisbet, 1872. . . . . . £100
The Pioneers, A Tale of the Western Wilderness,
Nisbet, 1872 . . . . £100
*Black Ivory, A Tale of Adventure among the Slavers
of East Africa*, Nisbet, 1873 . . . . . £100
Life in the Red Brigade, A Story for Boys, Routledge,
[1873]. £75
The Ocean and Its Wonders, Nelson, 1874. . £45
The Pirate City, An Algerine Tale, Nisbet, 1875 £100
*Rivers of Ice, A Tale Illustrative of Alpine Adventure
and Glacier Action*, Nisbet, 1875 . . . . £75
Under the Waves, or Diving In Deep Waters, A Tale,
Nisbet, 1876 . . . . £75
*The Settler and the Savage, A Tale of Peace and War
in South Africa*, Nisbet, 1877 . . . . . £100
In the Track of the Troops, A Tale of Modern War,
Nisbet, 1878 . . . . £75
Jarwin and Cuffy, A Tale, Warne, [1878] . . £100
*Six Months at the Cape, or Letters to Periwinkle from
South Africa*, Nisbet, 1879 [1878] £100
Post Haste, A Tale of Her Majesty's Mails, Nisbet,
1880 [1879] £100

Philosopher Jack, A Tale of the Southern Seas,
Nisbet, 1880 . . . . £75
The Lonely Island, or the Refuge of the Mutineers,
Nisbet, 1880 . . . . £75
The Redman's Revenge, A Tale of the Red River
Flood, Nisbet, 1880 . . . . £100
The Collected Works of Ensign Sopht, Late of the
Volunteers, Nisbet, 1881 . . . . . £175
My Doggy and I, Nisbet, [1881] £75
The Giant of the North, or Pokings Round the Pole,
Nisbet, 1882 [1881] £100
The Kitten Pilgrims, or Great Battles and Grand
Victories, Nisbet, [1882] £100
The Battery and the Boiler, or Adventures in the Lay-
ing of Submarine Cable, Nisbet, 1883 [1882] £100
The Madman and the Pirate, Nisbet, 1883 . . £75
Battles with the Sea, or Heroes of the Lifeboat and
Rocket, Nisbet, 1883 . . . . £100
The Young Trawlers, A Story of Life and Death and
Rescue on the North Sea, Nisbet, 1884 . . £75
Dusty Diamonds Cut and Polished, A Tale of City-
Arab Life and Adventure, Nisbet, 1884 [1883] £75
Twice Bought, A Tale of the Oregon Gold Fields,
Nisbet, 1885 [1884] £75
The Rover of the Andes, A Tale of Adventure in South
America, Nisbet, 1885 . . . . . . £75
The Island Queen, A Tale of the Southern
Hemisphere, Nisbet, 1885 . . . . . £75
Red Rooney, or Last of the Crew, Nisbet, 1886 £75
The Big Otter, A Tale of the Great Nor'West,
Routledge, 1887 [1886] £75
Blue Lights, or Hot Work in the Soudan: A Tale of
Soldier Life, Nisbet, 1888 . . . . . £75
The Middy and the Moors, An Algerine Story, Nisbet,
1888 . . . . £75
The Crew of the Water Wagtail, A Story of
Newfoundland, Nisbet, [1889] £75
The Garrett and the Garden, or Low Life High Up,
and *Jeff Benson, or The Young Coastguardsman,*
Nisbet, [1890] £75
Charlie to the Rescue, A Tale of the Sea and the
Rockies, Nisbet, 1890 . . . . . . £75
The Coxswain's Bride, or The Rising Tide and Other
Tales, Nisbet, 1891 . . . . £75
The Hot Swamp, A Romance of Old Albion, Nisbet,
1892 . . . . £75
Hunted and Harried, A Tale of the Scottish
Covenanters, Nisbet, [1892] £75
The Walrus Hunters, A Romance of the Realms of
Ice, Nisbet, 1893 . . . . £75
Fighting the Whales, Blackie, [1915] . . . £25
The Jolly Kitten Book, Blackie, [1925] . £50/£20
Ballantyne Omnibus for Boys, Collins, [1932] £30/£10

J. G. BALLARD
(b.1930)

Despite shifting from avant-garde science fiction to surreal contemporary writing, Ballard is best known as the author of the controversial novel *Crash*, and *Empire of the Sun*, based on his own experiences of internment by the Japanese in World War Two.

Novels
The Wind from Nowhere, Berkley (U.S.), 1962
(wraps) £25
ditto, Doubleday (U.S.), 1965 (with *The Drowned*
World) . . . . £150/£35
ditto, Penguin, 1967 (wraps) £15
The Drowned World, Berkley (U.S.), 1962 (wraps) £25
ditto, Gollancz, 1963 . . . . £450/£75
The Burning World, Berkley (U.S.), 1964 (wraps) £25
ditto, as *The Drought,* Cape, 1965 . . . £500/£50
The Crystal World, Cape, 1966 . . . £350/£45
ditto, Farrar Straus (U.S.), 1966 . . . . £80/£10
Crash!, Cape, 1973 . . . . £900/£45
ditto, Farrar Straus (U.S.), 1973 . . . . £100/£25
Concrete Island, Cape, 1974 . . . . . £125/£30
ditto, Farrar Straus (U.S.), 1974 . . . . £50/£15
High Rise, Cape, 1975 . . . . . . £85/£15
ditto, Holt Rinehart (U.S.), 1977 . . . . £35/£5
The Unlimited Dream Company, Cape, 1979 . £65/£5
ditto, Holt Rinehart (U.S.), 1979 . . . . £25/£5
Hello America, Cape, 1981 . . . . . £40/£10
ditto, Carroll & Graf (U.S.), 1988 . . . £15/£5
Empire of the Sun, Gollancz, 1984 (first issue d/w
with two reviews on back) . . . . £45/£10
ditto, Gollancz, 1984 (second issue d/w with six
reviews) . . . . £45/£10
ditto, Gollancz, 1984 (100 signed copies, slipcase). .
. . . . £400/£300
ditto, Simon & Schuster (U.S.), 1985 . . £20/£5
The Day of Creation, Gollancz, 1987 . . £20/£5
ditto, Gollancz, 1987 (100 signed copies, slipcase). .
. . . . £125/£100
ditto, Farrar Straus (U.S.), 1988 . . . . £15/£5
Running Wild, Hutchinson, 1988 (novella) . £15/£5
ditto, Farrar Straus (U.S.), 1989 . . . . £10/£5
The Kindness of Women, Harper Collins, 1991 £10/£5
ditto, Farrar Straus (U.S.), 1991 . . . . £10/£5
Rushing to Paradise, Harper Collins/Flamingo, 1994 .
. . . . £15/£5
ditto, Picador (U.S.), 1995 . . . . . £10/£5
Cocaine Nights, Harper Collins/Flamingo, 1996 . .
. . . . £20/£5
ditto, Counterpoint (U.S.), 1998 . . . . £10/£5
Super-Cannes, Harper Collins/Flamingo, 2000. . .
. . . . £25/£5
ditto, Picador (U.S.), 2001 . . . . . £10/£5

Short Stories
Billenium and Other Stories, Berkley (U.S.), 1962
(wraps). £30

The Voices of Time and Other Stories, Berkley (U.S.), 1962 (wraps) £25
The Four-Dimensional Nightmare, Gollancz, 1963 .
. . . . £650/£125
ditto, Gollancz, 1974 (drops two stories and adds two others). . . . . £70/£15
ditto, as *The Voices of Time*, Gollancz, 1985 . £20/£5
Passport to Eternity and Other Stories, Berkley (U.S.), 1963 (wraps). £20
Terminal Beach, Berkley (U.S.), 1964 (wraps). £35
The Terminal Beach, Gollancz, 1964 (not the same as above). . . . . £450/£45
The Impossible Man and Other Stories, Berkley (U.S.), 1966 (wraps). £20
The Day of Forever, Panther, 1967 (wraps). . £20
ditto, Gollancz, 1986 (hardback). . . . . £30/£5
The Disaster Area, Cape, 1967 . . . . £275/£45
The Overloaded Man, Panther, 1967 (wraps) . £15
The Atrocity Exhibition, Cape, 1970 . . £175/£45
ditto, as Doubleday (U.S.), 1970 (edition pulped and withdrawn) . . . . . . £2,500/£2,250
ditto, as *Love and Napalm: Export USA*, Grove Press (U.S.), 1972 . . . . £45/£15
ditto, as *The Atrocity Exhibition*, Re/Search (U.S.), 1990 (wraps) £15
ditto, as *The Atrocity Exhibition*, Re/Search (U.S.), 1990 (400 signed copies) . . . . £75/£45
Chronopolis, Putnam (U.S.), 1971 . . . £75/£20
Vermilion Sands, Berkley (U.S.), 1971 (wraps) £20
ditto, Cape, 1973 . . . . £300/£35
Low Flying Aircraft, Cape, 1976 . . £125/£20
The Best Science Fiction of J.G. Ballard, Orbit/Futura, 1977 (wraps) £15
The Best Short Stories of J.G. Ballard, Holt, Rinehart and Winston, 1978 . . . . . £25/£10
The Venus Hunters, Granada, 1980 (wraps) . £30
ditto, Gollancz, 1986 . . . . . . £30/£10
Myths of the Near Future, Cape, 1982 . . £30/£10
ditto, Farrar Straus (U.S.), 1991 . . . . £15/£5
Memories of the Space Age, Arkham House (U.S.), 1988 . . . . £20/£10
War Fever, Collins, 1990. . . . . . . £10/£5
The Complete Short Stories, Flamingo, 2001 . £25/£5

Others
Why I Want to Fuck Ronald Reagan, Unicorn Bookshop, 1968 (50 signed copies of 250) . £800
ditto, Unicorn Bookshop, 1968 (200 unsigned copies of 250) £500
News from the Sun, Interzone, 1982 (100 signed copies of 750, wraps). £40
ditto, Interzone, 1982 (650 unsigned copies of 750, wraps). £15
A Users Guide to the Millennium, HarperCollins, 1996 . . . . £20/£5
ditto, Picador (U.S.), 1996 . . . . . £10/£5

IAIN BANKS
(b.1954)

The Wasp Factory was a controversial success, and Banks has become more than a cult writer. His subsequent works of fiction and science fiction often stray into the realm of the bizarre and the sinister.

Novels
The Wasp Factory, Macmillan, 1984 . . £150/£35
ditto, Houghton Mifflin (U.S.), 1984 . . . £30/£5
Walking on Glass, Macmillan, 1985. . . £50/£10
ditto, Houghton Mifflin (U.S.), 1986 . . . £20/£5
The Bridge, Macmillan, 1986 . . . . £95/£20
ditto, St Martin's Press (U.S.), 1989 . . . £15/£5
Consider Phlebas, Macmillan, 1987 . . . £50/£10
ditto, Macmillan, 1987 (176 signed copies, slipcase) .
. . . . £100/£70
ditto, St Martin's Press (U.S.), 1988 . . . £15/£5
Espedair Street, Macmillan, 1987 . . . £30/£10
The Player of Games, Macmillan, 1988. . £45/£10
ditto, Macmillan, 1988 (201 signed copies, slipcase) .
. . . . £80/£60
ditto, St Martin's Press (U.S.), 1989 . . . £10/£5
Canal Dreams, Macmillan, 1989 . . . £20/£5
ditto, Doubleday (U.S.), 1991 . . . . £10/£5
Use of Weapons, Orbit, 1990. . . . . £75/£10
ditto, Bantam (U.S.), 1992 . . . . . £10/£5
The Crow Road, Scribner's, 1992 . . . £30/£5
Complicity, Little, Brown, 1993 . . . . £20/£5
ditto, Doubleday (U.S.), 1992 . . . . £10/£5
Against a Dark Background, Orbit, 1993 . £30/£5
Feersum Endjinn, Orbit, 1994 . . . . £20/£5
ditto, Bantam (U.S.), 1995 (wraps) £5
Whit, Little, Brown, 1995. . . . . . £10/£5
Excession, Orbit, 1996 . . . . . . £10/£5
ditto, Bantam (U.S.), 1997 (wraps) £5
A Song of Stone, Abacus, 1997 . . . . £10/£5
ditto, Simon & Schuster (U.S.), 1998 . . £10/£5
Inversions, Orbit, 1998 . . . . . . £10/£5
ditto, Pocket Books (U.S.), 2000 . . . £10/£5
The Business, Little, Brown, 1999 . . . £10/£5
ditto, Simon & Schuster (U.S.), 2000 . . £10/£5
Look To Windward, Orbit, 2000. . . . £10/£5
ditto, Pocket Books (U.S.), 2001 . . . . £10/£5
Dead Air, Little, Brown, 2000 . . . . £10/£5

Others
Cleaning Up, Birmingham Science Fiction Group, 1987 (500 signed, numbered copies, wraps) . £50
The State of the Art, Ziesing (U.S.), 1989 . £15/£5
ditto, Ziesing (U.S.), 1989 (400 signed copies) £50/£20
ditto, Orbit, 1991 (further uncollected stories) . £20/£5

HELEN BANNERMAN
(b.1863 d.1946)

Born in Scotland, Bannerman married an army doctor and settled in India where she wrote *Little Black Sambo* for her own children.

The Story of Little Black Sambo, Grant Richards' 'Dumpy Books for Children', No. 4, 1899 (anonymous) £7,500
ditto, Stokes (U.S.), 1901 . . . . £2,000
The Story of Little Black Mingo, Nisbet, 1901 (anonymous) £500
ditto, Stokes (U.S.), 1901 . . . . £200
The Story of Little Black Quibba, Nisbet, 1902 (anonymous) £500
ditto, Stokes (U.S.), 1903 . . . . £200
Little Degchie-Head: An Awful Warning to Bad Babas, Nisbet, 1903 (anonymous) £250
Pat and the Spider: The Biter Bit, Nisbet, 1904 (anonymous) £200
ditto, Stokes (U.S.), 1905 . . . . £200
The Story of the Teasing Monkey, Nisbet, 1906 (anonymous) £200
ditto, Stokes (U.S.), 1907 . . . . £200
The Story of Little Black Quasha, Nisbet, 1908 (anonymous) £150
ditto, Stokes (U.S.), 1908 . . . . £150
The Story of Little Black Bobtail, Nisbet, 1909 (anonymous) £75
ditto, Stokes (U.S.), 1909 . . . . £50
The Story of Sambo and the Twins, Stokes (U.S.), 1936 . . . . £50
ditto, Nisbet, 1937 . . . . £150/£50
The Story of Little White Squibba, Chatto & Windus, 1966 . . . . £100/£25

JOHN BANVILLE
(b.1945)

A well respected Irish author, whose novel *The Book of Evidence* was shortlisted for the Booker prize.

Novels
Nightspawn, Secker & Warburg, 1970 . . £400/£50
ditto, Norton (U.S.), 1971 . . . . . £100/£35
Birchwood, Secker & Warburg, 1971 . £100/£20
ditto, Norton (U.S.), 1973 . . . . . £50/£10
Doctor Copernicus, Secker & Warburg, 1976 . . .
. . . . £150/£15
ditto, Norton (U.S.), 1976 . . . . . £35/£10
Kepler, Secker & Warburg, 1981 . . . £150/£15
ditto, Godine (U.S.), 1983 . . . . . . £25/£5
The Newton Letter: an Interlude, Secker & Warburg, 1982 . . . . £150/£15
ditto, Godine (U.S.), 1987 . . . . . . £20/£5

Mefisto, Secker & Warburg, 1986 . . . £35/£10
ditto, Godine (U.S.), 1989 . . . . . . £20/£5
The Book of Evidence, Secker & Warburg, 1989 . . .
. . . . £30/£10
ditto, Scribner's (U.S.), 1990 . . . . . £25/£5
Ghosts, Secker & Warburg, 1993 . . . £20/£5
ditto, Knopf (U.S.), 1993 . . . . . . £15/£5
Athena, Secker & Warburg, 1995 . . . £20/£5
ditto, Knopf (U.S.), 1995 . . . . . . £15/£5
The Untouchable, Picador, 1997 . . . . £20/£5
ditto, Knopf (U.S.), 1997 . . . . . . £15/£5
Eclipse, Bridgewater Press, 2000 (26 signed, lettered copies) £225
ditto, Bridgewater Press, 2000 (100 signed, numbered copies) £75
ditto, Picador, 2000 . . . . £15/£5
ditto, Knopf (U.S.), 2001 . . . . . . £15/£5
Shroud, Picador, 2002 . . . . £10/£5
ditto, Joe McCann.com., 2002 (80 signed copies, no d/w) £75

Collected Editions
The Revolutions Trilogy, Picador, 2000 . . £20/£5
Frames Trilogy, Picador, 2001 . . . . £20/£5

Short Stories
Long Lankin, Secker & Warburg, 1970 . £500/£75
ditto, Gallery Press (Dublin), 1984 (revised edition) .
. . . . £25/£5

Plays
The Broken Jug, Gallery Press (Dublin), 1987 (240 copies) . . . . £45/£15
God's Gift, Gallery Press (Dublin), 2000 . £25/£5
ditto, Gallery Press (Dublin), 2000 (wraps) . . £10

CLIVE BARKER
(b.1952)

A novelist and short story writer in the horror genre, Barker was born in Liverpool but now lives in Los Angeles. He also illustrates his own work, and writes, directs and produces for the stage and screen.

Novels
The Damnation Game, Weidenfeld & Nicolson, 1985
. . . . £75/£15
ditto, Weidenfeld & Nicolson, 1985 (250 signed, numbered copies, slipcase) . . . . £125/£75
ditto, Ace/Putnam (U.S.), 1987 . . . £25/£10
Weaveworld, Poseidon (U.S.), 1987 . . . £20/£5
ditto, Poseidon (U.S.), 1987 (500 signed, numbered copies, slipcase) . . . . £125/£75
ditto, Poseidon (U.S.), 1987 (52 signed copies lettered a-zz, slipcase) . . . . £200/£165
ditto, Collins, 1987 . . . . £20/£5

ditto, Collins, 1987 (500 signed, numbered copies, quarter leather-bound, slipcase). . . . £125/75
ditto, Collins, 1987 (26 signed, numbered copies, quarter leather-bound, all edges gilt, slipcase). . . . . £250/£200
The Great and Secret Show: The First Book of the Art, Collins, 1989 . . . .£10/£5
ditto, Collins, 1989 (500 signed, numbered copies, full leather binding, all edges gilt, velvet-lined box) . . . . £125/£75
ditto, Collins, 1989 (26 signed, lettered copies, full leather binding, all edges gilt, velvet-lined box) . . . .£200/£165
ditto, Harper & Row (U.S.), 1990 . . . .£10/£5
Imajica, HarperCollins, 1991. . . . .£10/£5
ditto, HarperCollins (U.S.), 1991. . . . .£10/£5
ditto, HarperCollins (U.S.), 1991 (500 signed copies, slipcase) . . . . £125/£75
ditto, HarperCollins (U.S.), 1991 (26 signed copies, slipcase) . . . .£200/£165
The Thief of Always: A Fable, HarperCollins, 1992 . . . .£15/£5
ditto, HarperCollins (U.S.), 1992. . . . .£15/£5
ditto, HarperCollins (U.S.), 1992 (500 signed copies, slipcase) . . . . £75/£45
ditto, HarperCollins (U.S.), 1992 (26 signed copies, slipcase) . . . .£150/£125
Everville: The Second Book of the Art, HarperCollins, 1994 . . . .£10/£5
ditto, HarperCollins, 1994 (limited edition of 2,000 numbered copies with facsimilie signature) £30/£20
ditto, HarperCollins (U.S.), 1994. . . . .£10/£5
ditto, HarperCollins (U.S.), 1994 (500 signed copies, slipcase) . . . . £100/£75
ditto, HarperCollins (U.S.), 1994 (26 signed copies, slipcase) . . . .£200/£165
Sacrament, HarperCollins, 1994 . . . . .£10/£5
ditto, HarperCollins (U.S.), 1996. . . . .£10/£5
Gallilee: A Romance, HarperCollins (U.S.), 1998 . . . .£10/£5
ditto, HarperCollins/Trice (U.S.), 1998 (26 signed copies, slipcase) . . . .£200/£165
ditto, HarperCollins/Trice (U.S.), 1998 (125 signed copies, slipcase) . . . . £100/£75
ditto, HarperCollins, 1998 . . . .£10/£5
Coldheart Canyon: A Hollywood Ghost Story, HarperCollins, 2001 . . . .£10/£5
ditto, HarperCollins (U.S.), 2001. . . . .£10/£5
ditto, HarperCollins (U.S.), 2001 (2,500 signed copies). . . . .£20/£5
ditto, HarperCollins/Trice (U.S.), 2001 (26 signed copies, slipcase) . . . .£175/£125
ditto, HarperCollins/Trice (U.S.), 2001 (150 signed copies, slipcase) . . . . £100/£75
Abarat, HarperCollins, 2002 . . . . .£10/£5
ditto, HarperCollins (U.S.), 2002. . . . .£10/£5
ditto, HarperCollins/Trice (U.S.), 2002 (175 signed copies) . . . . £100/£75

ditto, HarperCollins/Trice (U.S.), 2002 (50 signed copies with additional artwork). . . . .£175/£125

Short Stories and Novellas
Books of Blood, Vol 1, Sphere, 1984 (first issue with original covers, wraps) £15
ditto, Sphere, 1984 (second issue with Barker designed covers, wraps) £5
ditto, Weidenfeld & Nicolson, 1985 . . . £65/£15
ditto, Weidenfeld & Nicolson, 1985 (200 signed, numbered sets with vols 2 and 3, slipcase). £250/£100
ditto, Berkley Books (U.S.), 1986 (wraps) . . £10
Books of Blood, Vol 2, Sphere, 1984 (first issue with original covers, wraps) £15
ditto, Sphere, 1984 (second issue with Barker designed covers, wraps) £5
ditto, Weidenfeld & Nicolson, 1985. . . £65/£15
ditto, Berkley Books (U.S.), 1986 (wraps) . . £10
Books of Blood, Vol 3, Sphere, 1984 (first issue with original covers, wraps) £15
ditto, Sphere, 1984 (second issue with Barker designed covers, wraps) £5
ditto, Weidenfeld & Nicolson, 1985 . . . £65/£15
ditto, Berkley Books (U.S.), 1986 (wraps) . . £10
Books of Blood, Vol 4, Sphere, 1985 (first issue with original covers, wraps) £15
ditto, Sphere, 1985 (second issue with Barker designed covers, wraps) £5
ditto, Weidenfeld & Nicolson, 1985 . . . £65/£15
ditto, Weidenfeld & Nicolson, 1985 (200 signed, numbered sets with vols 5 and 6, slipcase). £250/£100
ditto, Poseidon Press (U.S.), 1986 . . . £45/£15
ditto, Scream Press (U.S.), 1987 (333 signed copies, slipcase) . . . . £65/£45
Books of Blood, Vol 5, Sphere, 1985 (first issue with original covers, wraps) £15
ditto, Sphere, 1985 (second issue with Barker designed covers, wraps) £5
ditto, Weidenfeld & Nicolson, 1985 . . . £65/£15
ditto, Poseidon Press (U.S.), 1986 . . . £45/£15
ditto, Scream Press (U.S.), 1988 (333 signed copies, slipcase) . . . . £65/£45
Books of Blood, Vol 6, Sphere, 1985 (first issue with original covers, wraps) £15
ditto, Sphere, 1985 (second issue with Barker designed covers, wraps) £5
ditto, Weidenfeld & Nicolson, 1985 . . . £65/£15
ditto, Scream Press (U.S.), 1991 (333 signed copies, slipcase) . . . . £65/£45
Books of Blood, Vol 1 and 2, Sphere, 1984 . £50/£20
Books of Blood, Vol 1, 2 and 3, Scream Press (U.S.), 1985 (250 signed numbered copies, slipcase) . £150
ditto, Scream Press (U.S.), 1985 (17 signed lettered copies, slipcase) £250
ditto, Scream Press (U.S.), 1985 (10 signed copies, slipcase) £150
ditto, Weidenfeld & Nicolson, 1987 . . . . £25/£5
ditto, Ace/Putnam (U.S.), 1988 . . . . . £25/£5

Books of Blood, Vol 1-6, Stealth Press (U.S.), 2001 .
. . . . £30/£10
ditto, Stealth Press (U.S.), 2001 (500 signed numbered
copies, slipcase) . . . . £100/£75
ditto, Stealth Press (U.S.), 2001 (52 signed lettered
copies, in wooden box with brass plate) . £350/£275
Books of Blood, Vol 4, 5 and 6, Weidenfeld &
Nicolson, 1988 . . . . £25/£5
Books of Blood, Vol 4 and 5, Weidenfeld &
Nicolson/Leisure Circle, 1985 . . . . £65/£15
Cabal: The Nightbreed, Poseidon (U.S.), 1988. £10/£5
ditto, Poseidon (U.S.), 1988 (750 signed, numbered
copies) . . . . £75/£50
ditto, Fontana, 1988 (wraps) £5
ditto, Collins, 1989 . . . . £10/£5
The Essential Clive Barker, HarperCollins, 1999 . .
. . . . £15/£5
ditto, HarperCollins (U.S.), 1999. . . . . £15/£5

Collected Plays
Incarnations, HarperPrism (U.S.), 1995 . . £10/£5
ditto, HarperCollins, 1996 . . . . . . £10/£5
Forms Of Heaven, HarperPrism (U.S.), 1997 . £10/£5
ditto, HarperCollins, 1998 . . . . . . £10/£5

PAT BARKER
(b.1943)

Pat Barker is a novelist and short story writer whose
The Ghost Road, the last of her 'Regeneration
trilogy', won the Booker Prize in 1995.

Union Street, Virago, 1982 (wraps) £20
ditto, Virago, 1982 . . . . £300/£35
ditto, Putnam (U.S.), 1983 . . . . . £50/£15
Blow Your House Down, Virago, 1984 (wraps) . .
. . . . £15
ditto, Virago, 1984 . . . . £200/£25
ditto, Putnam (U.S.), 1984 . . . . . . £45/£5
The Century's Daughter, Virago, 1986 (wraps) . £5
ditto, Virago, 1986 . . . . £50/£10
ditto, Putnam (U.S.), 1986 . . . . . . £20/£5
The Man Who Wasn't There, Virago, 1989 . £30/£5
ditto, Ballantine (U.S.), 1990 (wraps) £5
Regeneration, Viking, 1991. . . . . . £175/£35
ditto, Dutton (U.S.), 1992. . . . . . £50/£15
The Eye in the Door, Viking, 1993 . . . £100/£15
ditto, Dutton (U.S.), 1994. . . . . . . £20/£5
The Ghost Road, Viking, 1995 . . . £100/£15
ditto, Dutton (U.S.), 1995. . . . . . . £20/£5
The Regeneration Trilogy, Viking, 1996 . £10/£5
Another World, Viking, 1998 . . . . £15/£5
ditto, Farrar, Straus & Giroux (U.S.), 1999 . £10/£5
Border Crossing, Viking, 2001 . . . . £15/£5
ditto, Farrar, Straus & Giroux (U.S.), 2001 . £10/£5

ROBERT BARNARD
(b.1936)

Barnard is the author of many light and entertaining
detective novels.

'Trethowan' Novels
Sheer Torture, Collins Crime Club, 1981 . £75/£15
ditto, as ***Death by Sheer Torture***, Scribner's (U.S.),
1982 . . . . £25/£5
Death and the Princess, Collins Crime Club, 1982 .
. . . . £50/£10
ditto, Scribner's (U.S.), 1982 . . . . . £20/£5
The Missing Bronte, Collins Crime Club, 1983 . .
. . . . £50/£10
ditto, as ***The Case of the Missing Bronte***, Scribner's
(U.S.), 1983 . . . . £20/£5
Bodies, Collins Crime Club, 1986, . . . £25/£10
ditto, Scribner's (U.S.), 1986. . . . . . £10/£5
Death in Purple Prose, Collins Crime Club, 1987 . .
. . . . £25/£10
ditto, as ***The Cherry Blossom Corpse***, Scribner's
(U.S.), 1987 . . . . £10/£5

'Meredith' Novels
Unruly Son, Collins Crime Club, 1978 . . £100/£10
ditto, as ***Death of a Mystery Writer***, Scribner's (U.S.),
1979 . . . . £25/£5
At Death's Door, Collins Crime Club, 1988 £30/£10
ditto, Scribner's (U.S.), 1988. . . . . . £15/£5

'Oddie' Novels
A City of Strangers, Bantam, 1990 . . . . £20/£5
ditto, Scribner's (U.S.), 1990 . . . . £15/£5
A Fatal Attachment, Bantam, 1992 . . . £15/£5
ditto, Scribner's (U.S.), 1992. . . . . . £10/£5
A Hovering of Vultures, Bantam, 1993 . . £15/£5
ditto, Scribner's (U.S.), 1993 . . . . . £10/£5
Bad Samaritan, Collins, 1995 . . . . £15/£5
ditto, Scribner's (U.S.), 1995. . . . . . £10/£5

Other Novels
Death of an Old Goat, Collins Crime Club, 1974 . .
. . . . £250/£25
ditto, Walker (U.S.), 1977 . . . . £100/£15
A Little Local Murder, Collins Crime Club, 1976 . .
. . . . £145/£15
ditto, Scribner's (U.S.), 1983 . . . . . £25/£5
Death on the High C's, Collins Crime Club, 1977 . .
. . . . £145/£15
ditto, Walker (U.S.), 1978 . . . . £100/£10
Blood Brotherhood, Collins Crime Club, 1977 . . .
. . . . £200/£45
ditto, Walker (U.S.), 1978 . . . . £100/£10
Posthumous Papers, Collins Crime Club, 1979 . .
. . . . £75/£15
ditto, as ***Death of a Literary Widow***, Scribner's (U.S.),
1980 . . . . £25/£5

Death in a Cold Climate, Collins Crime Club, 1980 .
. . . . £75/£15
ditto, Scribner's (U.S.), 1981 . . . . . . £15/£5
Mother's Boys, Collins Crime Club, 1981 . £45/£10
ditto, as *Death of a Perfect Mother*, Scribner's (U.S.),
1981 . . . . £15/£5
Little Victims, Collins Crime Club, 1983 . £40/£10
ditto, as *School for Murder*, Scribner's (U.S.), 1984 .
. . . . £15/£5
A Corpse in a Gilded Cage, Collins Crime Club, 1984
. . . . £30/£10
ditto, Scribner's (U.S.), 1984 . . . . . £15/£5
Out of the Blackout, Collins Crime Club, 1985 £25/£5
ditto, Scribner's (U.S.), 1985 . . . . . £15/£5
The Disposal of the Living, Collins Crime Club, 1985
. . . . £20/£5
ditto, as *Fete Fatale*, Scribner's (U.S.), 1985 . £15/£5
Political Suicide, Collins Crime Club, 1986 . £20/£5
ditto, Scribner's (U.S.), 1986 . . . . . £10/£5
The Skeleton in the Grass, Collins Crime Club, 1987 .
. . . . £15/£5
ditto, Scribner's (U.S.), 1988 . . . . . £10/£5
Death and the Chaste Apprentice, Collins Crime Club,
1989 . . . . £15/£5
ditto, Scribner's (U.S.), 1989 . . . . . £10/£5
A Scandal in Belgravia, Bantam, 1991 . . . £15/£5
ditto, Scribner's (U.S.), 1991 . . . . . £10/£5
Masters of the House, Collins, 1994 . . . £15/£5
ditto, Scribner's (U.S.), 1994 . . . . . £10/£5
No Place of Safety, Collins, 1997 . . . £15/£5
ditto, Scribner's (U.S.), 1997 . . . . . £10/£5
The Corpse at the Haworth Tandoori, Collins, 1998 .
. . . . £25/£5
ditto, Scribner's (U.S.), 1999 . . . . . £10/£5
Touched by the Dead, Collins, 1999 . . . £15/£5
ditto, as *Murder in Mayfair*, Scribner's (U.S.), 2000 .
. . . . £10/£5

Short Stories
Death of a Salesperson, Collins Crime Club, 1989 .
. . . . £20/£5
ditto, Scribner's (U.S.), 1990 . . . . . £15/£5
The Habit of Widowhood, Collins, 1996 . £20/£5
ditto, Scribner's (U.S.), 1996 . . . . . £15/£5

Novels as 'Bernard Bastable'
To Die like a Gentleman, Macmillan, 1993 . £20/£5
ditto, St Martin's Press (U.S.), 1993 . . . £15/£5
Too Many Notes, Mr. Mozart, Little, Brown, 1995 .
. . . . £15/£5
ditto, Carroll & Graf (U.S.), 1995 . . . £10/£5
A Mansion and It's Murder, Carroll & Graf (U.S.),
1998 . . . . £10/£5

DJUNA BARNES
(b.1892 d.1982)

An important writer in the 1930s, her books became collector's items rather than popular successes.

Fiction
*The Book of Repulsive Women; 8 Rhythms and 5
Drawings*, Guido Bruno (U.S.), 1915 (wraps). £450
ditto, Alicat Bookshop (U.S.), 1948 (1,000 copies,
wraps). £50
A Book, Boni & Liveright (U.S.), [1923] . £300/£75
ditto, as *A Night Among the Horses*, Liveright (U.S.),
1929 . . . . £250/£50
ditto, as *Spillway*, Faber, 1962 . . . £25/£10
ditto, as *Spillway*, Harper & Row (U.S.), 1972 (wraps)
. . . . £5
Ryder, Liveright (U.S.), 1928 (3,000 copies) £150/£25
Nightwood, Faber, 1936 . . . . £200/£75
ditto, Harcourt, Brace (U.S.), 1937 . . . £125/£30
Vagaries Malicieux: Two Stories, Hallman (U.S.),
1974 (500 copies, no d/w) £40
Smoke and Other Early Stories, Sun & Moon Press
(U.S.), 1982 . . . . £35/£10
Collected Stories, Sun & Moon Press (U.S.), 1996 . .
. . . . £25/£10

Plays
The Antiphon, Faber, 1958 . . . . £85/£15
ditto, Farrar, Straus (U.S.), 1958 . . . . £65/£15
To The Dogs, The Press of the Good Mountain (U.S.),
1982 (110 copies) £200

Others
Ladies Almanack, Titus (Paris), 1928 (pseud. 'A Lady
of Fashion', 1,000 copies, wraps) . . . £275
ditto, Titus (Paris), 1928 (pseud. 'A Lady of Fashion',
40 copies on Rives paper, wraps) . . . £500
ditto, Titus (Paris), 1928 (pseud. 'A Lady of Fashion',
10 signed copies on Vergé de Vidalon, wraps) £650
ditto, Harper & Row (U.S.), 1972 . . . £25/£10
Selected Works, Farrar, Straus (U.S.), 1958 . £35/£10
ditto, Faber, 1980 . . . . £20/£10
Creatures in an Alphabet, Dial Press (U.S.), 1982 . .
. . . . £40/£10
New York, Sun and Moon Press (U.S.), 1989 £25/£10
Interviews, Sun and Moon Press (U.S.), 1986 £25/£10
Poe's Mother, Sun and Moon Press (U.S.), 1995 . .
. . . . £25/£10

JULIAN BARNES
(b.1946)

An inventive post-modernist writer, Barnes moves between genres, probing the boundaries of convention.

Novels

Metroland, Cape, 1980	£300/£45
ditto, St Martin's Press (U.S.), 1980 . . .	£75/£25
Before She Met Me, Cape, 1982	£75/£20
ditto, McGraw-Hill (U.S.), 1986 (wraps) . .	£10
Flaubert's Parrot, Cape, 1984	£225/£35
ditto, Knopf (U.S.), 1985	£35/£5
Staring at the Sun, Cape, 1986	£45/£10
ditto, London Limited Editions, 1986 (150 signed copies, glassine d/w)	£75/£60
ditto, Knopf (U.S.), 1987	£20/£5
A History of the World in 10½ Chapters, Cape, 1989	£35/£10
ditto, Knopf (U.S.), 1989	£15/£5
Talking it Over, Cape, 1991	£20/£5
ditto, London Limited Editions, 1991 (200 signed copies, glassine d/w)	£100/£80
ditto, Knopf (U.S.), 1991	£15/£5
Bodlivo Svinche, Obsidian (Bulgaria), 1992 (wraps)	£10
ditto, as *The Porcupine*, Cape, 1992 (novella) .	£15/£5
ditto, Knopf (U.S.), 1992	£10/£5
England, England, Cape, 1998	£10/£5
ditto, Knopf (U.S.), 1999	£10/£5
Love, etc, Cape, 2000	£10/£5
ditto, Knopf (U.S.), 2001	£10/£5

Novels as 'Dan Kavanagh'

Duffy, Cape, 1980	£50/£10
ditto, Pantheon (U.S.), 1986 (wraps). . . .	£5
Fiddle City, Cape, 1981	£65/£10
ditto, Pantheon (U.S.), 1986 (wraps). . . .	£5
Putting the Boot In, Cape, 1985	£25/£10
Going to the Dogs, Viking UK, 1987 . .	£25/£10
ditto, Viking (U.S.), 1987.	£10/£5
The Duffy Omnibus, Penguin, 1991	£5

Short Stories

Cross Channel, Cape, 1996	£25/£15
ditto, Cape, 1996 (50 special copies, signed and numbered)	£125
ditto, Knopf (U.S.), 1996	£15/£5

Other

Letters from London, 1990-1995, Picador, 1995 (wraps)	£5
ditto, Vintage (U.S.), 1995	£5
Something to Declare, Cape, 2002 (wraps) . . .	£5

J.M. BARRIE
(b.1860 d.1937)

Scottish author best known for his creation of Peter Pan, the boy who would never grow up.

Children's Novels

The Little White Bird, Hodder & Stoughton, 1902 (first appearance of the Peter Pan character) .	£100
ditto, Scribner's (U.S.), 1902.	£100
Peter Pan in Kensington Gardens, Hodder & Stoughton, 1906 (illustrated by Arthur Rackham, deluxe edition, 500 signed copies)	£3,000
ditto, Hodder & Stoughton, 1906 (trade edition)	£1,500
ditto, Scribner's (U.S.), 1906.	£500
ditto, Hodder & Stoughton, 1910 (24 colour plates)	£1,500
ditto, Hodder & Stoughton, 1912 (50 colour plates, 12 drawings).	£400
ditto, Hodder & Stoughton, 1912 (deluxe edition, 50 colour plates, 12 drawings)	£1,500
Peter and Wendy, Hodder & Stoughton, 1911 (illustrated by Bedford)	£150
ditto, Hodder & Stoughton, [1912] (illustrated by Arthur Rackham).	£1,250
ditto, Hodder & Stoughton, [1912] (illustrated by Arthur Rackham, 500 copies numbered 101-600).	£1,750
The Peter Pan Portfolio, Hodder & Stoughton, [1912] (500 boxed portfolios numbered 101-600, signed by the publishers)	£2,000
ditto, Hodder & Stoughton, 1912 (approx 20 boxed portfolios signed by the artist)	£6,500
ditto, Brentano's (U.S.), 1912 (300 unsigned boxed portfolios)	£2,000

Adult Novels

Better Dead, Sonnenschein & Co, 1888 [1887] (wraps)	£400
ditto, Rand/McNally (U.S.), 1891 . . .	£200
The Little Minister, Cassell, 1891 (3 vols) . .	£100
ditto, Lovell, Coryell & Co. (U.S.), [1891] .	£35
Sentimental Tommy, Cassell, 1896 . . .	£30
ditto, Scribner's (U.S.), 1896	£30
Margaret Ogilvy, Scribner's (U.S.), 1896 .	£25
ditto, Hodder & Stoughton, 1896. . . .	£25
Tommy and Grizel, Cassell, 1900	£25
ditto, Scribner's (U.S.), 1900	£25
Farewell Miss Julie Logan: A Wintry Tale, Hodder & Stoughton, 1932	£40/£10
ditto, Scribner's (U.S.), 1932.	£40/£10

Sketches and Short Stories

Auld Licht Idylls, Hodder & Stoughton, 1888 .	£45
ditto, Macmillan (U.S.), 1891	£45
ditto, Hodder & Stoughton, 1895 (50 signed copies of 550 numbered)	£200
ditto, Hodder & Stoughton, 1895 (500 unsigned copies of 550 numbered)	£50

A Window in Thrums, Hodder & Stoughton, 1889 £75
ditto, Cassell (U.S.), 1892. . . . . . . £65
ditto, as *The Sabbath Day*, Hodder & Stoughton, 1895
(issued without wrappers, a reprint of the first chapter
of *A Window in Thrums*) £35
ditto, as *Jess*, Dana Estes (U.S.), 1898 (reprint of the
first 16 stories from *A Window in Thrums*) . £35
A Holiday in Bed and Other Sketches, New York
Publishing Co. (U.S.), [1892] (wraps) . . . £350
ditto, New York Publishing Co. (U.S.), [1892] . £35
An Auld Licht Manse, John Knox (U.S.), [1893]
(wraps) £45
Two of Them, Lovell, Coryell & Co. (U.S.), 1893
(wraps) £75
A Tillyloss Scandal, Lovell, Coryell & Co. (U.S.),
1893 (first issue with address at East 10th street) £125
ditto, Lovell, Coryell & Co. (U.S.), 1893 (second issue
with address at East 16th street) £100
A Powerful Drug and Other Stories, Ogilvie (U.S.),
[1893] (wraps) £100
A Lady's Shoe, Brentano's (U.S.), 1898. . . £35
Life in A Country Manse, Ogilvie (U.S.), 1899 (bound
with The Mystery of No.13 by Helen Mathers, wraps)
. . . . £35
ditto, Neely (U.S.), 1899 (wraps). . . . £35

Plays
Richard Savage, privately printed, 1891 (wraps, title-
page serves as front cover) £1,500
The Wedding Guest, Scribners (U.S.), 1900 (copyright
copies) £1,000
ditto, Fortnightly Review, 1900 (supplement to
Fortnightly Review) £45
Walker London, French, 1907 (wraps) . . . £75
Quality Street, Hodder & Stoughton, 1913 . £40
ditto, Hodder & Stoughton, 1913 (1,000 signed copies)
. . . . £75
Half Hours, Scribner's (U.S.), 1914. . . . £25
ditto, Hodder & Stoughton, [1914] £25
The Admirable Crichton, Hodder & Stoughton, 1914
(illustrated by Hugh Thompson) £50
ditto, Hodder & Stoughton, 1914 (500 copies signed by
Thompson) £400
Der Tag, Hodder & Stoughton, [1914] . . £30
Echoes of the War, Hodder & Stoughton, [1918] £50
ditto, Scribner's (U.S.), 1918. . . . . . £45
What Every Woman Knows, Hodder & Stoughton,
[1918] (from the *Uniform Edition*) £20
Alice Sit-By-The-Fire, Hodder & Stoughton, [1919]
(from the *Uniform Edition*) £20
A Kiss for Cinderella, Hodder & Stoughton, [1920]
(from the *Uniform Edition*) . . . . £45/£20
ditto, Scribner's (U.S.), 1920 . . . . £45/£15
The Twelve Pound Look and Other Plays, [1921]
(from the *Uniform Edition*) . . . . £45/£20
The Old Lady Shows Her Medals, Hodder &
Stoughton, [1921-2] (from the *Uniform Edition*) .
. . . . £35/£10
Dear Brutus, Hodder & Stoughton, [1922] (from the
Uniform Edition). . . . . . . £45/£15

ditto, Scribner's (U.S.), 1922 . . . . . £45/£15
Mary Rose, Hodder & Stoughton, [1924] (from the
Uniform Edition). . . . . . . £45/£15
ditto, Scribner's (U.S.), 1924 . . . . . £35/£10
Representative Plays, Scribner's (U.S.), 1926 £25/£10
Plays of J.M. Barrie, Hodder & Stoughton, 1928 . .
. . . . £35/£10
Peter Pan or The Boy Who Would Not Grow Up,
Hodder & Stoughton, 1928 . . . . . £150/£45
ditto, Scribner's (U.S.), 1928 . . . . . £125/£40
Shall We Join The Ladies?, Hodder & Stoughton,
1929 . . . . £45/£15
When Wendy Grew Up, An Afterthought, Nelson,
1957 . . . . £25/£10

Others
When a Man's Single, A Tale of Literary Life, Hodder
& Stoughton, 1888 . . . . £30
ditto, Harpers (U.S.), 1889 . . . . . . £30
An Edinburgh Eleven, The 'British Weekly', 1889
(wraps) £30
My Lady Nicotine, Hodder & Stoughton, 1890. £75
ditto, Rand/McNally (U.S.), 1891 . . . . £65
Jane Annie, Chappell, 1893 (with Sir Arthur Conan
Doyle, wraps) £750
Allahakbarrie C. C., privately printed, 1893 (wraps,
title-page serves as front cover). £50
*Scotland's Lament: A Poem on the Death of Robert
Louis Stevenson, December 3rd, 1894*, privately
printed for T.J. Wise (without wrappers, 12 copies) .
. . . . £100
ditto, privately printed for Clement Shorter, 1918 (25
copies, wraps) £45
Allahakbarrie Book of Broadway Cricket for 1899,
(520 copies, Japanese vellum wraps) . . . £250
George Meredith, Constable, 1909 . . . . £40
ditto, Mosher (U.S.), 1909 . . . . . . £40
ditto, as *Neither Dorking nor the Abbey* Browne's
Bookstore (U.S.), 1910 . . . . . . £25
Charles Frohman: A Tribute, privately printed for
Clement Shorter (20 copies) £45
Shakespeare's Legacy, privately printed for Clement
Shorter, [1916] (25 copies) £45
Who Was Sarah Findlay?, privately printed for
Clement Shorter, 1917 (25 copies). . . . £45
Courage, Hodder & Stoughton, [1922] . . £75/£35
ditto, Scribner's (U.S.), 1922 . . . . . £60/£25
The Ladies' Shakespeare, privately printed for
Clement Shorter, [1925] (25 copies) . . . £45
Neil and Tintinnabulum, privately printed, 1925 (52
copies, wraps) £40
The Author, privately printed for Lawson McClung
Melish (U.S.), 1925 (20 copies). £100
Cricket, privately printed for Clement Shorter, 1926
(25 copies). £300
*The Greenwood Hat: Being a Memoir of James Anon
1885-1887*, Davies, 1937 . . . . . £60/£35
ditto, Scribner's (U.S.), 1938 . . . . . £60/£35
M'Connachie and JMB: Speeches, Davies, 1938 . .
. . . . £40/£10

Collected Editions

Thistle Edition, Scribner's (U.S.), 1896-1911 (12 vols)
. . . . £75

ditto, Scribner's (U.S.), 1896-1911 (12 vols, 150 copies
on Imperial hand-made Japan paper, vol 1 signed) .
. . . . £250

Kirriemur Edition, Hodder & Stoughton, 1913 (10
vols, limited to 1,000 sets, the first vol signed) £200

Uniform Edition of Plays, Hodder & Stoughton, 1918
(11 vols) £200

The Works of J.M. Barrie, Scribner's (U.S.), 1918 (10
vols) £100

Peter Pan Edition, Scribner's (U.S.), 1929 (14 vols,
130 signed sets of 1,000) . . . . £1,000/£500

ditto, Scribner's (U.S.), 1929 (14 vols, 870 unsigned
sets of 1,000) . . . . £750/£350

H.E. BATES
(b.1906 d.1974)

A British author of popular novels, novellas and short
stories, many of which have been adapted for
television. He is perhaps best known for the Larkin
family novels, including *The Darling Buds of May*.

Novels

The Two Sisters, Cape, 1926 . . . . . £400/£100
Catherine Foster, Cape, 1929 . . . . £300/£50
ditto, Viking (U.S.), 1929 . . . . . £250/£45
Charlotte's Row, Cape, 1931 . . . . £150/£35
ditto, Cape, 1931 (107 signed, numbered copies) £250
The Fallow Land, Cape, 1932 . . . . £125/£35
The Poacher, Cape, 1935 . . . . . £100/£25
ditto, Macmillan (U.S.), 1935 . . . . £75/£15
A House of Women, Cape, 1936 . . . . £100/£25
'Spella Ho', Cape, 1938 . . . . . £125/£20
ditto, Little, Brown (U.S.), 1938 . . . . £100/£15
Fair Stood the Wind for France, Joseph, 1944 . . .
. . . . £45/£15
ditto, Little, Brown (U.S.), 1944 . . . . £35/£10
The Cruise of the 'Breadwinner', Joseph, 1946 . .
. . . . £45/£15
The Purple Plain, Joseph, 1947 . . . . £45/£10
ditto, Little, Brown (U.S.), 1947 . . . . £45/£10
The Jacaranda Tree, Joseph, [1949] . . £40/£10
ditto, Little, Brown (U.S.), 1949 . . . . £40/£10
The Scarlet Sword, Joseph, 1950 . . . . £25/£5
ditto, Little, Brown (U.S.), 1951 . . . . £25/£5
Love for Lydia, Joseph, 1952 . . . . . £20/£5
ditto, Little, Brown (U.S.), 1952 . . . . £20/£5
The Feast of July, Joseph, 1954 . . . . £20/£5
ditto, Little, Brown (U.S.), 1954 . . . . £15/£5
The Sleepless Moon, Joseph, 1956 . . £20/£5
ditto, Little, Brown (U.S.), 1956 . . . . £15/£5
The Darling Buds of May, Joseph, 1958 . £45/£15
ditto, Little, Brown (U.S.), 1958 . . . . £40/£10
A Breath of French Air, Joseph, 1959 . . £40/£10

ditto, Little, Brown (U.S.), 1959 . . . . £35/£10
When the Green Woods Laugh, Joseph, 1960 . £25/£5
The Day of the Tortoise, Joseph, 1961 . . . £30/£5
The Crown of Wild Myrtle, Joseph, 1962 . . £15/£5
ditto, Farrar, Straus (U.S.), 1963 . . . . £15/£5
Oh! to be in England, Joseph, 1963 . . . £25/£10
ditto, Farrar, Straus (U.S.), 1964 . . . . £20/£5
A Moment in Time, Joseph, 1964 . . . £15/£5
ditto, Farrar, Straus (U.S.), 1964 . . . . £15/£5
The Distant Horns of Summer, Joseph, 1967 . £15/£5
A Little of What You Fancy, Joseph, 1970 . £25/£10
The Triple Echo, Joseph, 1970 . . . . £15/£5

Novellas and Short Stories

*The Spring Song, and In View of the Fact That ...
Two Stories*, Archer, 1927 (100 numbered, signed
copies, wraps) £350
ditto, Lantern Press (U.S.), 1927 (50 signed copies) .
. . . . £350
Day's End, Cape, 1928 . . . . . £150/£45
ditto, Viking, 1928 . . . . £65/£15
Seven Tales and Alexander, Scholartis Press, 1929 (50
signed copies of an edition of 1,000) . . £200
ditto, Scholartis Press, 1929 (950 unsigned copies of an
edition of 1,000) . . . . £125/£35
ditto, Viking (U.S.), 1930 . . . . . £125/£35
The Hessian Prisoner, Furnival Books, 1930 (550
signed copies) £100
The Tree, A Story, Blue Moon Booklets, 1930 (wraps)
. . . . £45
ditto, Blue Moon Booklets, 1930 (100 large paper
copies, wraps) £200
Mrs. Esmond's Life, privately printed, 1931 (300
signed copies) £100
ditto, privately printed, 1931 (50 signed copies, leaf of
manuscript bound in) £400
A German Idyll, Golden Cockerel Press, 1932 (307
signed copies) £275
The Black Boxer, Pharos Editions (Cape), 1932 (100
signed copies) £200
ditto, Pharos Editions (Cape), 1932 . . £75/£25
Sally Go Round the Moon, White Owl Press, 1932 .
. . . . £75/£25
ditto, White Owl Press, 1932 (129 signed copies) . .
. . . . £200
ditto, White Owl Press, 1932 (21 signed copies, with
leaf of manuscript bound in) £400
The Story Without an End and The Country Doctor,
White Owl Press, 1932 . . . . . £75/£25
ditto, White Owl Press, 1932 (105 signed copies) . .
. . . . £200
ditto, White Owl Press, 1932 (25 signed copies, leaf of
manuscript bound in) £400
The House with the Apricot and Two Other Tales,
Golden Cockerel Press, 1933 (300 signed copies). .
. . . . £250
The Woman Who Had Imagination, Cape, 1934 . . .
. . . . £100/£25
ditto, Macmillan (U.S.), 1934 . . . . £65/£20

Thirty Tales, Cape, Traveller's Library, 1934 . £20/£5
The Duet, A Story, Grayson Books, 1935 (285 signed
copies) . . . . £125/£65
Cut and Come Again: Fourteen Stories, Cape, 1935 .
. . . . £150/£35
Something Short and Sweet, Cape, 1937 . £100/£25
My Uncle Silas, Cape, 1939 . . . . . £175/£75
ditto, Graywolf Press (U.S.), 1984 . . . £25/£10
The Flying Goat, Cape, 1939 . . . . £125/£25
Country Tales, Readers Union, 1938 (tissue jacket) .
. . . . £45/£35
ditto, Cape, 1940 . . . . £45/£15
The Beauty of the Dead and Other Stories, Cape,
1940, ... £75/£25
The Greatest People in the World, Cape, 1942 (pseud.
Flying Officer 'X') . . . . £45/£15
ditto, as *There's Something in the Air*, Knopf, 1943 .
. . . . £45/£15
How Sleep the Brave and other Stories, Cape, 1943
(pseud. 'Flying Officer 'X'') . . . . £40/£15
The Daffodil Sky, Cape, 1943 . . . £40/£10
Death of a Huntsman, Joseph, 1957 . £35/£10
ditto, as *Summer in Salandar*, Little, Brown (U.S.),
1957 . . . . £25/£5
The Bride Comes to Evensford, Cape, 1943 £75/£15
Thirty-One Selected Tales, Cape, 1947 . . . £20/£5
Dear Life, Little, Brown (U.S.), 1949 . . £35/£10
ditto, Joseph, 1950. . . . . . . £35/£10
Colonel Julian and Other Stories, Joseph, 1951 . .
. . . . £45/£15
ditto, Little, Brown (U.S.), 1952 . . . . £30/£10
Twenty Tales, Cape, 1951 . . . . . £15/£5
The Nature of Love, Joseph, 1953 . . . £30/£10
Sugar for the Horse, Joseph, 1957 . . . £35/£15
The Watercress Girl and other Stories, Joseph, 1959 .
. . . . £35/£10
ditto, Little, Brown, 1959 . . . . . . £30/£5
An Aspidistra in Babylon: Four Novellas, Joseph,
1960 . . . . £25/£10
Now Sleeps the Crimson Petal and Other Stories,
Joseph, 1961 . . . . £25/£5
The Golden Oriole: Five Novellas, Joseph, 1962 . .
. . . . £25/£5
ditto, Little, Brown (U.S.), 1962 . . . . £20/£5
Seven by Five: Stories 1926-1961, Joseph, 1963 . .
. . . . £20/£10
ditto, as *The Best of H. E. Bates*, Little, Brown (U.S.),
1963 . . . . £15/£5
The Fabulous Mrs V., Joseph, 1964. . . . £20/£5
The Wedding Party, Joseph, 1965 . . . £20/£5
The Wild Cherry Tree, Joseph, 1968 . . . £20/£5
The Four Beauties, Joseph, 1968 . . . £20/£5
The Song of the Wren, Joseph, 1972 . . £15/£5
The Yellow Meads of Asphodel, Joseph, 1976 . £15/£5
A Month by the Lake & Other Stories, New Directions
(U.S.), 1987 . . . . £35/£5
Elephants Nest in a Rhubarb Tree & Other Stories,
New Directions (U.S.), 1989 . . . . £35/£5

Plays
The Last Bread, Labour Publishing Co., 1926 (wraps)
. . . . £125
The Day of Glory, Joseph, 1945 . . . . £40/£10

Children's Titles
The Seekers, Bumpus, 1926 (tissue jacket) . £100/£35
The Seasons and the Gardener, C.U.P., 1940 £75/£25
Achilles the Donkey, Dobson Books, 1962 . £100/£30
ditto, Franklin-Watts (U.S.), 1963 . . . £75/£25
Achilles and Diana, Dobson Books, 1963 . £100/£30
ditto, Franklin-Watts (U.S.), 1963 . . . £75/£25
Achilles and the Twins, Dobson Books, 1964 £75/£25
The White Admiral, Dobson Books, 1968 . £65/£20

Poetry
Song for December, privately printed, 1928 (wraps) .
. . . . £250
Christmas 1930, privately printed, 1930 (wraps) £250
Holly and Sallow, Blue Moon, 1931 (100 signed
copies, broadside) £75

Autobiography
The Vanished World, Joseph, 1969 . . . . £30/£5
ditto, Univ. of Missouri Press (U.S.), 1969 . . £30/£5
The Blossoming World, Joseph, 1971 . . . £20/£5
ditto, Univ. of Missouri Press (U.S.), 1971 . . £20/£5
The World in Ripeness, Joseph,1972 . . . £20/£5
ditto, Univ. of Missouri Press (U.S.), [1972] . £15/£5

Others
A Threshing Day, Foyle, 1931 (300 signed copies) .
. . . . £100
Flowers and Faces, Golden Cockerel Press, 1935 (325
signed copies) £300
*Through the Woods: The English Woodland - April to
April*, Gollancz, 1936 . . . . . . £100/£45
ditto, Macmillan (U.S.), 1936 . . . . £65/£25
Down the River, Gollancz, 1937 . . . . £65/£25
ditto, Henry Holt & Co. (U.S.), 1937 . . £35/£10
The Modern Short Story, Nelson, 1940 . . £40/£10
You Have Seen Their Faces, H.M.S.O., 1941
(anonymous, wraps) £35
In the Heart of the Country, Country Life, 1942
(illustrated by Tunnicliffe) . . . . . £75/£25
O More Than Happy Countryman, Country Life, 1943
(illustrated by Tunnicliffe) . . . . £45/£15
Country Life, Penguin Books, 1943 (wraps) . . £5
*There's Freedom in the Air: The Official Story of the
Allied Air Forces from the Occupied Countries*,
H.M.S.O., 1944 (anonymous, wraps) . . £35
Night Battle of Britain, H.M.S.O., 1944 (anonymous,
wraps). £35
*The Tinkers of Elstow: The Story of the Royal
Ordnance Factory*, Bemrose & Sons, 1946 . £40
ditto, Bemrose & Sons, 1946 (300 signed, numbered
copies) £300
The Country Heart, Joseph, 1949 . . . £45/£10
Edward Garnett, Parrish, 1950 . . . . £35/£10
Flower Gardening, C.U.P., 1950 (wraps) . . £10

The Country of White Clover, Joseph, 1952 . £35/£5
ditto, Joseph, 1952 (100 signed copies) . . . £250
The Face of England, Batsford Ltd, 1952 . . £25/£5
Pastoral on Paper, Medway Corrugated Paper Co.,
[1956]. . . . . £75/£15
A Love of Flowers, Joseph, 1971 . . . £15/£5
Fountain of Flowers, Joseph, 1974 . . . £15/£5

L. FRANK BAUM
(b.1856 d.1919)

An American author who had a varied career until he
started to write for children with *Mother Goose in
Prose*. Three years later he brought out the classic *The
Wonderful Wizard of Oz*. In this and its 13 sequels,
Baum was attempting to write fantasies with distinctly
American origins.

Mother Goose in Prose, Way & Williams (U.S.),
[1897]. £4,000
ditto, Duckworth, 1899 . . . . . . £1,500
Father Goose, His Book, George M Hill (U.S.), 1899 .
. . . . £3,500
ditto, Werner, 1899 . . . . £1,500
A New Wonderland, Russell (U.S.), 1900 . . £2,000
ditto, as *The Surprising Adventures of the Magical
Monarch of Mo and His People*, Bobbs-Merrill
(U.S.), [1903] £1,250
The Wonderful Wizard of Oz, Hill (U.S.), 1900 . . .
. . . . £15,000
ditto, as *The New Wizard of Oz*, Bobbs-Merrill (U.S.),
[1903]. £750
ditto, Hodder & Stoughton, 1906. . . . £1,500
The Army Alphabet, Hill (U.S.), 1900 . . £1,000
The Navy Alphabet, Hill (U.S.), 1900 . . £1,000
American Fairy Tales, Hill (U.S.), 1901 . £1,000
Dot and Tot of Merryland, Hill (U.S.), 1901 . £1,000
The Master Key: An Electrical Fairy Tale, Bobbs-
Merrill (U.S.), 1901 . . . . £600
ditto, Stevens & Brown, [1902] £500
The Life and Adventures of Santa Claus, Bobbs-
Merrill (U.S.), 1902 . . . . . . £2,500
ditto, Stevens & Brown, 1902 . . . . £2,000
*The Surprising Adventures of the Magical Monarch
of Mo and His People*, Bobbs-Merrill (U.S.), [1903].
. . . . £750
The Enchanted Island of Yew, Bobbs-Merrill (U.S.),
[1903]. £600
The Marvellous Land of Oz, Reilly & Britton (U.S.),
1904 . . . . £4,000
ditto, Revell, 1906 (copyright edition) . . £1,000
ditto, Hodder & Stoughton, 1906. . . . £400
Queen Zixi of Ix, Century (U.S.), 1905 . . £1,000
ditto, Hodder & Stoughton, 1905. . . . £750
The Woggle-Bug Book, Reilly & Britton (U.S.), 1905.
. . . . £1,000
John Dough and The Cherub, Reilly & Britton (U.S.),
1906 . . . . £600

ditto, Constable, 1906. . . . . . . £500
Ozma of Oz, Reilly & Britton (U.S.), 1907 . . £650
ditto, Hutchinson, 1942 . . . . . £100/£25
The Last Egyptian: A Romance of the Nile, Reilly &
Britton (U.S.), 1908 . . . . . . £300
Dorothy and the Wizard in Oz, Reilly & Britton (U.S.),
1908 . . . . £1,000
The Road to Oz, Reilly & Britton (U.S.), 1909 . £2,000
The Emerald City of Oz, Reilly & Britton (U.S.), 1910
. . . . £2,000
The Sea Fairies, Reilly & Britton (U.S.), 1911. £500
Sky Island, Reilly & Britton (U.S.), 1912 . . £400
The Patchwork Girls of Oz, Reilly & Britton (U.S.),
1913 . . . . £1,000
Tik-Tok of Oz, Reilly & Britton (U.S.), 1914 . £1,000
The Scarecrow of Oz, Reilly & Britton (U.S.), 1915 .
. . . . £600
Rinkitink in Oz, Reilly & Britton (U.S.), 1916 . £600
The Lost Princess of Oz, Reilly & Britton (U.S.), 1917
. . . . £750
The Tin Woodman of Oz, Reilly & Britton (U.S.),
1918 . . . . £750
The Magic of Oz, Reilly & Lee (U.S.), 1919 . £500
Glinda of Oz, Reilly & Lee (U.S.), 1920 . . £450

'BB'
(b.1905 d.1990)

'BB' was the pseudonym used by Denys James
Watkins-Pitchford, an author and illustrator of
countryside books for both adults and children.

Adult Books Written and Illustrated by 'BB'
The Sportsman's Bedside Book, Eyre & Spottiswoode,
1937 . . . . £125/£30
The Countryman's Bedside Book, Eyre &
Spottiswoode, 1941 . . . . . . £125/£25
The Idle Countryman, Eyre & Spottiswoode, 1943 .
. . . . £50/£10
The Fisherman's Bedside Book, Eyre & Spottiswoode,
1945 . . . . £75/£25
ditto, Scribner's (U.S.), 1946 . . . . £75/£25
The Wayfaring Tree, Hollis & Carter, 1945 £50/£15
The Shooting Man's Bedside Book, Eyre &
Spottiswoode, 1948 . . . . . . £65/£20
ditto, Scribner's (U.S.), 1948 . . . . £65/£20
A Stream in Your Garden, Eyre & Spottiswoode, 1948
. . . . £35/£15
Be Quiet and Go A-Angling, Lutterworth, 1949
(pseud. Michael Traherne) . . . . £275/£125
Confessions of a Carp Fisher, Eyre & Spottiswoode,
1950 . . . . £200/£75
Letters from Compton Deverell, Eyre & Spottiswoode,
1950 . . . . £45/£15
Tides Ending, Hollis & Carter, 1950 . . £175/£50
ditto, Scribner's (U.S.), 1950. . . . £150/£45
Dark Estuary, Hollis & Carter, 1953 . . £175/£50
A Carp Water (Wood Pool), Putnam, 1958 . £250/£75

Autumn Road to the Isles, Kaye, 1959 . . £60/£15
The White Road Westward, Kaye, 1961 . £60/£15
The September Road to Caithness, Kaye, 1962 . .
. . . . £60/£15
Pegasus Book of the Countryside, Hamish Hamilton,
1964 . . . . £250/£100
The Summer Road to Wales, Kaye, 1964 . £60/£15
A Summer of the Nene, Kaye, 1967 . . . £100/£35
Recollections of a Longshore Gunner, Boydell, 1976 .
. . . . £75/£20
A Child Alone: The Memoirs of 'BB', Joseph, 1978 .
. . . . £100/£35
Ramblings of a Sportsman-Naturalist, Joseph, 1979 .
. . . . £50/£15
The Naturalist's Bedside Book, Joseph, 1980 £45/£15
The Quiet Fields, Joseph, 1981 . . . . £50/£15
Indian Summer, Joseph, 1984 . . . . £50/£15
The Best of 'BB', Joseph, 1985 . . . . £50/£10
Fisherman's Folly, Boydell, 1987 (wraps) . . £15

Children's Books Written and Illustrated by 'BB'
Wild Lone: The Story of a Pytchley Fox, Eyre &
Spottiswoode, 1938 . . . . £200/£75
ditto, Scribner's (U.S.), 1938 . . . . £175/£65
Manka, The Sky Gipsy, Eyre & Spottiswoode, 1939 .
. . . . £125/£35
The Little Grey Men: A Story for the Young in Heart,
Eyre & Spottiswoode, 1942 . . . . . £100/£40
ditto, Eyre & Spottiswoode, 1946 (8 colour plates). .
. . . . £200/£75
ditto, Scribner's (U.S.), 1949 . . . . . £175/£65
Brendon Chase, Hollis & Carter, 1944 . . £100/£25
ditto, Scribner's (U.S.), 1945 . . . . . £75/£25
Down the Bright Stream, Eyre & Spottiswoode, [1948]
. . . . £125/£50
ditto, as *The Little Grey Men Go Down the Bright
Stream*, Methuen, 1977 . . . . . . £35/£10
BB's Fairy Book: Meeting Hill, Hollis & Carter, 1948
. . . . £250/£75
The Wind in the Wood, Hollis & Carter, 1952 £200/£75
The Forest of Boland Light Railway, Eyre &
Spottiswoode, 1955 . . . . £150/£45
Monty Woodpig's Caravan, Ward, 1957 . £165/£65
Ben the Bullfinch, Hamish Hamilton, 1957 . £125/£45
Wandering Wind, Hamish Hamilton, 1957 . £125/£50
Alexander, Blackwell, 1957 [1958] . . . £100/£25
Monty Woodpig and his Bubblebuzz Car, Ward, 1958
. . . . £165/£65
Mr Bumstead, Eyre & Spottiswoode, 1958 . £100/£25
The Wizard of Boland, Ward, 1959 . . . £100/£25
Bill Badger's Winter Cruise, Hamish Hamilton, 1959 .
. . . . £100/£25
Bill Badger and the Pirates, Hamish Hamilton, 1960 .
. . . . £100/£25
Bill Badger's Finest Hour, Hamish Hamilton, 1961 .
. . . . £100/£25
ditto, as *Bill Badger and the Secret Weapon*, Methuen,
1983 . . . . £35/£10
The Badgers of Bearshanks, Benn, 1961 . £100/£25

Bill Badger's Whispering Reeds Adventure, Hamish
Hamilton, 1962 . . . . £100/£25
Lepus the Brown Hare, Benn, 1962 . . . £100/£25
Bill Badger's Big Mistake, Hamish Hamilton, 1963 .
. . . . £100/£25
Bill Badger and the Big Store Robbery, Hamish
Hamilton, 1967 . . . . £100/£25
The Whopper, Benn, 1967 . . . . . £300/£150
At the Back O'Ben Dee, Benn, 1968 . . £125/£35
Bill Badger's Voyage to the World's End, Kaye &
Ward, 1969 . . . . £250/£65
The Tyger Tray, Methuen, 1971 . . . . £100/£25
The Pool of the Black Witch, Methuen, 1974 . . . .
. . . . £100/£25
Lord of the Forest, Methuen, 1975 . . . £100/£25

Other Books Illustrated by 'BB'
Sport in Wildest Britain, by H.V. Prichard, Philip
Allan, 1936 . . . . £125/£35
Winged Company, by R.G. Walmsley, Eyre &
Spottiswoode, 1940 . . . . £125/£35
England is a Village, by C.H. Warren, Eyre &
Spottiswoode, 1940 . . . . £75/£25
ditto, Dutton & Co (U.S.), 1941 . . . . £65/£20
Southern English, by E. Benfield, Eyre &
Spottiswoode, 1942 . . . . £100/£25
Narrow Boat, by L.T.C. Rolt, Eyre & Spottiswoode,
1944 . . . . £100/£25
It's My Delight, by B. Vesey-Fitzgerald, Eyre &
Spottiswoode, 1947 . . . . £50/£20
Philandering Angler, by A. Applin, Hurst & Blackett,
[1948] . . . . £75/£25
A Sportsman Looks at Eire, by J.B. Drought,
Hutchinson, 1949 . . . . £75/£20
Landmarks, by A.G. Street, Eyre & Spottiswoode,
1949 . . . . £75/£20
Red Vagabond, by G.D. Adams, Batchworth Press,
1951 . . . . £100/£30
Fairy Tales of Long Ago, by M.C. Carey, Dent, 1952 .
. . . . £75/£25
The White Foxes of Gorfenletch, by H. Tegner, Hollis
& Carter, 1954 . . . . £75/£25
The Secret of Orra, by E. Vipont, Blackwell, 1957 .
. . . . £100/£25
The Long Night, by William Mayne, Blackwell, 1957
[1958] . . . . £125/£35
The Long-Bow, by Ronald Welch, Blackwell, 1958 .
. . . . £65/£20
Sailors All by Peter Dawlish, Blackwell, 1958 £65/£20
A Snowdon Stream, by W.H. Canaway, Putnam:
Fisherman's Choice Series, 1958 . . . £100/£25
Trout Fisherman's Saga, by I.D. Owen, Putnam:
Fisherman's Choice Series, 1959 . . . £100/£25
Thirteen O'Clock by William Mayne, Blackwell, 1960.
. . . . £75/£25
Vix: The Story of a Fox Cub, by A. Windsor-Richards,
E. Benn, 1960 . . . . £100/£25
Beasts of the North Country, by H. Tegner, Galley
Press, 1961 . . . . £75/£25

Birds of the Lonely Lake, by A. Windsor-Richards,
Benn, 1961 . . . . £75/£25
Prince Prigio and Prince Ricardo, by Andrew Lang,
Dent, 1961 . . . . £75/£25
The Rogue Elephant, by Arthur Catherall, Dobson,
1962 . . . . £125/£35
ditto, Macrae Smith Company (U.S.), 1962 . £75/£25
Guns This Way, by H.W. Pearson-Rogers, Witherby,
1962 . . . . £100/£25
Granny's Wonderful Chair, by Frances Browne, Dent,
1963 . . . . £100/£25
King Todd, by N. Burke, Putnam, 1963 . . £75/£25
A Cabin in the Woods, by A. Windsor-Richards,
Friday Press, 1963 . . . . . . £100/£25
Red Ivory, by A.R. Channel, Dobson, 1964 (pseud.
Arthur Catherall). . . . . . . £75/£25
ditto, Macrae Smith Company (U.S.), 1964 . £75/£25
The Lost Princess, by George Macdonald, Dent, 1965
. . . . £35/£10
To Do With Birds, by H. Tegner, H. Jenkins, 1965 .
. . . . £25/£15
The Wild White Swan, by A. Windsor-Richards,
Friday Press, 1965 . . . . . . £100/£25
Jungle Rescue, by A.R. Channel, Dobson, 1967 . .
. . . . £75/£25
ditto, (U.S.), [1968] . . . . . . £65/£20
Great Nature Stories, by A. Windsor-Richards, E.
Benn, 1967 . . . . £45/£15
The Shadow on the Moor, by I. Alan, 8th Duke of
Northumberland, privately printed, 1967 (200 copies).
. . . . £600
Where Vultures Fly, by G. Summers, Collins, 1974 .
. . . . £35/£10
Stories of the Wild, by A.L.E. Fenton and A.W.
Richards, Benn, 1975 . . . . . £45/£15
More Stories of the Wild, by A. Windsor-Richards,
Benn, 1977 . . . . £45/£15

THE BEANO

The Beano is arguably the most famous of all British
children's comics, first appearing on 30th July 1938.
The first Beano Annual was issued in 1940

Comics
No.1, D.C. Thomson, 30th July 1938 (with Whoopee
Mask). £6,000
ditto, D.C. Thomson, 30th July 1938 (without
Whoopee Mask) £3,000
No.2, D.C. Thomson, 1938 . . . . . £500
No.3, D.C. Thomson, 1938 . . . . . £400
No.4, D.C. Thomson, 1938 . . . . . £400
No.5, D.C. Thomson, 1938 . . . . . £500
1938-39. . . . . £500 each
1940s . . . . £75 each
1941-45. . . . . £45 each

Annuals
The Beano Book 1940, D.C. Thomson . . . £3,000
The Beano Book 1941, D.C. Thomson . . . £1,000
The Beano Book 1942, D.C. Thomson . . . £1,000
The Magic Beano Book 1943, D.C. Thomson . £900
The Magic Beano Book 1944, D.C. Thomson . £500
The Magic Beano Book 1945, D.C. Thomson . £450
The Magic Beano Book 1946, D.C. Thomson . £350
The Magic Beano Book 1947, D.C. Thomson . £250
The Magic Beano Book 1948, D.C. Thomson . £250
The Magic Beano Book 1949, D.C. Thomson . £250
The Magic Beano Book 1950, D.C. Thomson . £250
The Beano Book 1951, D.C. Thomson . . . £150
The Beano Book 1952, D.C. Thomson . . . £95
The Beano Book 1953, D.C. Thomson . . . £95
The Beano Book 1954, D.C. Thomson . . . £80
The Beano Book 1955, D.C. Thomson . . . £80
The Beano Book 1956, D.C. Thomson . . . £80
The Beano Book 1957, D.C. Thomson . . . £80
The Beano Book 1958, D.C. Thomson . . . £80
The Beano Book 1959, D.C. Thomson . . . £75
The Beano Book 1960, D.C. Thomson . . . £75
The Beano Book 1961, D.C. Thomson . . . £75
The Beano Book 1962, D.C. Thomson . . . £75
The Beano Book 1963, D.C. Thomson . . . £75
The Beano Book 1964, D.C. Thomson . . . £65
The Beano Book 1965, D.C. Thomson . . . £65
The Beano Book 1966, D.C. Thomson . . . £50
The Beano Book 1967, D.C. Thomson . . . £50
The Beano Book 1968, D.C. Thomson . . . £50
The Beano Book 1969, D.C. Thomson . . . £20
The Beano Book 1970-75, D.C. Thomson . £15 each
The Beano Book 1976-80, D.C. Thomson . £10 each

AUBREY BEARDSLEY
(b.1872 d.1898)

British illustrator and writer who came to prominence
in the 1890s. His sinuous black and white illustrations
became as synonymous with the 'decadence' of the
period as did the name of Oscar Wilde. See also under
'Keynotes', 'Yellow Book' and 'The Savoy' for
further publications containing his illustrations.

Major Works
Le Morte d'Arthur, by Thomas Malory, Dent, 1893-4
(12 parts, green wraps) . . . . the set £4,500
ditto, Dent, 1893-4 (12 parts, handmade paper, grey
wraps). . . . . the set £7,500
ditto, Dent, 1893 (2 vols) £3,000
ditto, Dent, 1893 (3 vols, 300 copies, handmade paper)
. . . . £5,000
ditto, Dent, 1909 (second edition, 1 vol., 1,500 copies)
. . . . £250
ditto, Dent, 1927 (third edition, 1,600 copies) . . .
. . . . £750/£250

ditto, Dent, 1927 (portfolio of eleven unpublished designs, 300 copies) £750
Bon-Mots of Sydney Smith and R. Brinsley Sheridan, Dent, 1893 . . . . £75
ditto, Dent, 1893 (100 numbered copies, large paper issue) £400
Bon-Mots of Charles Lamb and Douglas Jerrold, Dent, 1893 . . . . £75
ditto, Dent, 1893 (100 numbered copies, large paper issue) £400
Bon-Mots of Samuel Foot and Theodore Hook, Dent, 1894 . . . . £75
ditto, Dent, 1894 (100 numbered copies, large paper issue) £400
Salomé, by Oscar Wilde, Lane & Mathews, 1894 (755 copies) £2,000
ditto, Lane & Mathews, 1894 (125 copies, on Japan vellum, large paper issue) £10,000
ditto, Melmoth & Co., 1904 (250 numbered copies) £350
ditto, Melmoth & Co., 1904 (50 numbered copies). £500
The Rape of the Lock, by Alexander Pope, [Smithers], privately printed, 1896 (1,000 copies) . . . £350
ditto, [Smithers], privately printed, 1896 (25 copies on Japanese vellum). £5,000
Lysistrata of Aristophanes, [Smithers], privately printed, 1896 (100 copies) £7,500
A Book of Fifty Drawings, Smithers, 1897 (500 copies) £300
ditto, Smithers, 1897 (50 copies on Japanese vellum) £3,000
ditto, Grolier Club (U.S.), 1923 (300 copies printed on Dutch antique paper). £200
The Pierrot of the Minute, by Ernest Dowson, Smithers, 1897 (300 copies) £400
ditto, Smithers, 1897 (30 copies on Japanese vellum) £3,000
A Second Book of Fifty Drawings, Smithers, 1898 (1,000 copies) £200
ditto, John Lane (U.S.), 1899 (1,000 copies) . £200
Mademoiselle de Maupin, by Theophile Gautier, Smithers, 1898 (portfolio, 50 numbered copies) £3,000
Volpone, by Ben Jonson, Smithers, 1898 (1,000 numbered copies) £250
ditto, Smithers, 1898 (100 numbered copies on Japanese vellum). £2,000
ditto, John Lane (U.S.), 1898 (1,000 numbered copies) £200
The Early Work of Aubrey Beardsley, Bodley Head, 1899 . . . . £350
ditto, Bodley Head, 1899 (100 copies) . . . £650
ditto, Bodley Head, 1912 . . . . £75
The Later Work of Aubrey Beardsley, Bodley Head, 1901 . . . . £350
ditto, Bodley Head, 1901 (100 copies) . . . £650
ditto, Bodley Head, 1912 . . . . £75

Under the Hill, Lane, 1904 . . . . . . £300
ditto, Lane, 1904 (50 copies on Japanese vellum) £2,500
ditto, Olympia Press (Paris), 1959 . . . £50/315
ditto, Grove Press (U.S.), 1959 . . . . £20/£10
The Uncollected Works of Aubrey Beardsley, Bodley Head, 1925 . . . . £250/£150
ditto, Bodley Head, 1925 (100 copies) . . . £600

Other Titles with Designs by Beardsley
Evelina, by Frances Burney, Dent, 1893 . . £100
Pastor Sang, by Bjornstjerne Bjornson, Longmans, 1893 . . . . £100
The Wonderful History of Virgilus the Sorceror of Rome, Nutt, 1893 . . . . £100
The Pagan Papers, by Kenneth Grahame, Mathews & Lane, 1894 (450 [615] copies) £150
Plays, by John Davidson, Mathews & Lane, 1894 £200
The Land of Heart's Desire, by W.B. Yeats, Unwin, 1894 (500 copies, wraps, presumed first state without two fleurons after 'Desire' on front cover). . £1,000
ditto, T. Fisher Unwin, 1894 (presumed second state with two fleurons) £500
ditto, Stone and Kimball (U.S.), [1894] (450 copies in glazed boards, date incorrect on title-page as 1814, frontispiece by Beardsley) £500
Baron Verdigris, by Jocelyn Quilp, Henry, 1894 £150
Lucian's True History, by Lucian, [Lawrence & Bullen], 1894 (251 numbered copies) . . . £150
ditto, by Lucian, [Lawrence & Bullen], 1894 (54 numbered copies with extra plate) £400
A London Garland, Macmillan, 1895 . . . £150
Tales of Mystery and Wonder, by Edgar Allan Poe, Stone & Kimball (U.S.), 1895 . . . . . £250
Earl Lavender, by John Davidson, Ward & Downey, 1895 . . . . £150
Young Ofeg's Ditties, by Ola Hansson, Lane, 1895 . . . . £75
Sappho, by H.T. Wharton, Lane, 1895 . . . £125
An Evil Motherhood, by Walt Ruding, Mathews, 1896 ('Black Coffee' frontispiece) £750
ditto, Mathews, 1896 ('Portrait of the Author' frontispiece) £200
ditto, Mathews, 1896 (remainder issue with 'Portrait of the Author' frontispiece glued in and 'Black Coffee' inserted or tipped in). £200
The Barbarous Britishers, by H.D.Traill, Lane, 1896 . . . . £100
The Life and Times of Madame du Barry, by Douglas, Smithers, 1897 . . . . £150
Verses, by Ernest Dowson, Smithers, 1896 (300 copies) £750
ditto, Smithers, 1896 (30 copies on Japanese vellum) £3,000
A Book of Bargains, by V. O'Sullivan, Smithers, 1896 . . . . £175
Pierrot!, by Henry de Vere Stacpoole, Lane, 1896 . . £125

My Little Lady Anne, by Mrs Egerton Castle, Lane,
1896 . . . . £100
Simplicity, by A.T.G. Price, Lane, 1896. . . £100
My Brother, by Vincent Brown, Lane, 1896 . £100
Le Comédie Humaine, Scenes of Parisian Life, by
Honoré de Balzac, Smithers, 1897 (11 vols, 250 sets)
. . . . £350
ditto, Smithers, 1897 (50 sets on Japanese vellum). .
. . . . £750
Le Comédie Humaine, Scenes of Private Life, by
Honoré de Balzac, Smithers, 1897-98 (11 vols) £300
The Souvenirs of Leonard, by Jean Leonard, Smithers,
1897 (2 vols, 250 numbered sets) £100
A History of Dancing, Gaston Vuillier, Heinemann,
1898 (2 vols, Beardsley plate in 35 numbered copies
on Japanese vellum only) £500
The House of Sin, by V. O'Sullivan, Smithers, 1897 .
. . . . £350
Decorations, in Verse & Prose, Smithers, 1899 £400
The Poems of Ernest Dowson, Lane, 1905 (edited and
with a memoir by Arthur Symons) £125

Other Titles containing Illustrations by Beardsley
Aubrey Beardsley, by Arthur Symons, Unicorn Press,
1898 . . . . £75
ditto, Dent, 1905 . . . . £25
The Last Letters of Aubrey Beardsley, ed. by John
Gray, Longmans, 1904 . . . . . . £125
Aubrey Beardsley, by Robert Ross, Lane, 1909 £75
The Beardsley Period, by O. Burdett, Bodley Head,
1925 . . . . £75/£25
ditto, Boni & Liveright (U.S.), 1925 . . . £75/£25
The Best of Beardsley, by R.A. Walker, Bodley Head,
1948 . . . . £50/£20
A Beardsley Miscellany, ed. by R.A. Walker, London,
1949 . . . . £50/£20
Beardsley: A Catalogue of an Exhibition, V&A
Museum, 1966 . . . . £15

Others
*The Story of Venus and Tanhauser, A Romantic
Novel*, Smithers, 1907 ('Under the Hill', 250
numbered copies on handmade paper, no illustrations)
. . . . £300
ditto, Smithers, 1907 ('Under the Hill', 50 numbered
copies on Japanese vellum, no illustrations) . £750
Letters to Leonard Smithers, First Editions Club, 1937
. . . . £75

SAMUEL BECKETT
(b.1906 d.1989)

An individual and experimental Irish playwright,
novelist and poet who received the Nobel Prize for
Literature in 1969. Note: reprints under different titles
do not necessarily mean the same text is reproduced
(one work is often a progression of another.)

*Our Exagmination Round His Factification for
Incamination of 'Work in Progress'*, Shakespeare &
Co (Paris), 1929 (contains essay by Beckett 'Dante...
Bruno... Vico... Joyce', 300 copies, wraps) . £300
ditto, Shakespeare & Co (Paris), 1929 (96 large paper
copies) £750
ditto, Faber, 1936 . . . . £200/£75
ditto, New Directions (U.S.), 1939 . . . £125/£50
Whoroscope, Hours Press, 1930 (200 numbered copies
of 300, wraps) £2,000
ditto, Hours Press, 1930 (100 signed, numbered copies
of 300, wraps) £4,000
ditto, Grove Press (U.S.), 1957 . . . . £45/£15
Proust, Chatto & Windus, 1931 . . . . £300/£125
ditto, Grove Press (U.S.), 1957 (250 signed copies) .
. . . . £450
ditto, Grove Press (U.S.), 1957 (wraps) . . £40
More Pricks than Kicks, Chatto & Windus, 1934 . .
. . . . £3,500/£1,500
ditto, Caldar & Boyars, 1966 (wraps) . . . £50
ditto, Caldar & Boyars, 1970 (100 signed copies,
slipcase) . . . . £150/£100
ditto, Grove Press (U.S.), 1970 . . . . £30/£10
Echo's Bones, Europa Press (Paris), 1935 (25 signed
copies) £2,500
ditto, Europa Press (Paris), 1935 (250 numbered
copies, wraps) £300
ditto, Europa Press (Paris), 1935 (50 *hors commerce*
copies) £1,000
Murphy, Routledge, 1938 . . . £4,500/£2,500
ditto, Bordas (Paris), 1947 (wraps [95 copies]) . £1,250
ditto, Éditions de Minuit/Bordas (Paris), 1947 [1951] .
. . . . £250
ditto, Grove Press (U.S.), [1957] . . . . £150/£35
ditto, Grove Press (U.S.), [1957] (100 signed copies,
acetate d/w) . . . . £1,500/£1,000
Molloy, Éditions de Minuit (Paris), 1951 (500
numbered copies, wraps) £150
ditto, Éditions de Minuit (Paris), 1951 (50 large paper
numbered copies, wraps) £2,500
ditto, Olympia Press (Paris), 1955 (wraps) . . £100
ditto, Grove Press (U.S.), 1955 . . . . £100/£35
ditto, Calder, 1959. . . . . £100/£45
Malone Meurt, Éditions de Minuit (Paris), [1951]
(wraps) £200
ditto, Éditions de Minuit (Paris), [1951] (47 numbered
copies, wraps) £2,000
ditto, as *Malone Dies*, Grove Press (U.S.), 1956 . .
. . . . £65/£35

ditto, Grove Press (U.S.), 1956 (500 numbered copies, acetate d/w) . . . . £100/£65
ditto, Calder, 1958. . . . . £100/£45
En Attendant Godot, Éditions de Minuit (Paris), 1952 (wraps) £2,000
ditto, Éditions de Minuit (Paris), 1952 (35 numbered large paper copies, wraps) £6,000
ditto, Éditions de Minuit (Paris), 1952 [1956] (30 numbered copies, six photographs, wraps). . £6,000
ditto, as *Waiting for Godot*, Grove Press (U.S.), 1954 . . . . £1,000/£250
ditto, Faber, 1956 . . . . £500/£100
L'Innommable, Éditions de Minuit (Paris), 1953 (wraps) £150
ditto, Éditions de Minuit (Paris), 1953 (50 signed copies, wraps) £2,000
ditto, as *The Unnamable*, Grove Press (U.S.), 1958 (100 numbered copies, acetate d/w) . . £225/£175
ditto, Grove Press (U.S.), 1958 (26 signed, lettered copies, acetate d/w) . . . . £2,500/£2,000
ditto, Grove Press (U.S.), 1958 (acetate d/w) . . . . £125/£100
ditto, Grove Press (U.S.), 1958 (wraps) . . . £25
ditto, Calder, 1975. . . . . £25/£10
Watt, Olympia Press (Paris), 1953 (1,100 numbered copies, wraps) £250
ditto, Olympia Press (Paris), 1953 (25 signed, lettered copies) £2,500
ditto, Grove Press (U.S.), 1953 . . . . £200/£40
ditto, Grove Press (U.S.), 1953 (100 numbered copies) £300
ditto, Grove Press (U.S.), 1953 (26 signed, lettered copies) £2,500
ditto, Olympia Press (Paris), 1958 . . . £75/£25
ditto, Calder, 1963 (wraps) £75
Nouvelles et Textes pour Rien, Éditions de Minuit (Paris), 1955 (1,100 numbered copies of 1,185, wraps). £100
ditto, Éditions de Minuit (Paris), 1955 (50 numbered *hors commerce* copies of 1,185, wraps) . . £1,500
ditto, Éditions de Minuit (Paris), 1955 (35 signed copies of 1,185, wraps) £2,500
ditto, Éditions de Minuit (Paris), 1958 (2,000 numbered copies, illustrated, wraps) . . . £65
ditto, as *Stories & Texts for Nothing*, Grove Press (U.S.), 1967 . . . . £35/£10
Tous Ceux Qui Tombent, Éditions de Minuit (Paris), 1957 (wraps) £65
ditto, as *All That Fall*, Grove Press (U.S.), 1957 . . . . £65/£30
ditto, Grove Press (U.S.), 1957 (100 numbered copies, acetate jacket) . . . . £250/£225
ditto, Grove Press (U.S.), 1957 (25 signed, numbered copies) £1,000
ditto, Faber, 1958 (wraps). £65
Fin de Partie, Éditions de Minuit (Paris), 1957 (wraps) £200
ditto, Éditions de Minuit (Paris), 1957 (large paper copies) £5,000

ditto, as *Endgame*, Faber, 1958 . . . . £150/£45
ditto, Grove Press (U.S.), 1958 . . . . £125/£45
ditto, Grove Press (U.S.), 1958 (100 signed copies) £350
From an Abandoned Work, Faber, 1958 (wraps) £65
La dernière bande, Éditions de Minuit (Paris), 1959 [1960] (wraps) £35
ditto, Éditions de Minuit (Paris), 1959 [1960] (40 numbered copies, wraps) £450
ditto, as *Krapp's Last Tape and Embers*, Faber, 1959 (wraps) £40
ditto, Evergreen (U.S.), 1960. . . . . £35/£10
Molloy, Malone Dies, The Unnamable: A Trilogy, Olympia Press (Paris), 1959 (wraps) . . . £65
ditto, Calder, 1959. . . . . £60/£20
ditto, as *Three Novels*, Grove Press (U.S.), 1959 . . . . £45/£15
Poems in English, Calder, 1961 . . . . £75/£35
ditto, Calder, 1961 (100 signed copies, slipcase) . . . . £750/£500
ditto, Grove Press (U.S.), 1963 . . . . £60/£30
ditto, as *Poèms*, Éditions de Minuit (Paris), 1968 (550 copies of 762, wraps) £125
ditto, Éditions de Minuit (Paris), 1968 (100 numbered copies of 762, wraps) £200
Comment c'est, Éditions de Minuit (Paris), 1961 (wraps) £100
ditto, Éditions de Minuit (Paris), 1961 (80 numbered copies of 88, wraps) £350
ditto, Éditions de Minuit (Paris), 1961 (8 *hors commerce* of 88 copies, wraps) £350
ditto, Éditions de Minuit (Paris), 1961 (100 of 110 copies for the 'Club l'édition originale', wraps) £350
ditto, Éditions de Minuit (Paris), 1961 (10 'H.C.' of 110 copies for the 'Club l'édition originale', wraps) £350
ditto, as *How It Is*, Calder, 1964 . . . . £60/£20
ditto, as *How It Is*, Calder, 1964 (100 signed copies, slipcase) . . . . £600/£500
ditto, Grove Press (U.S.), 1964 . . . . £60/£30
Happy Days, Grove Press (U.S.), 1961 (wraps). £40
ditto, Faber, 1962 . . . . £50/£15
ditto, as *Oh Les Beaux Jours*, Éditions de Minuit (Paris), 1963 (87 numbered large paper copies of 412, wraps). £250
ditto, as *Oh Les Beaux Jours*, Éditions de Minuit (Paris), 1963 (325 copies of 412, wraps) . . £200
ditto, as *Oh Les Beaux Jours*, Éditions de Minuit (Paris), 1963 (wraps) £65
Play and Two Short Pieces for Radio, Faber, 1964 . . . . £45/£15
ditto, as Comedie et actes diversz, Éditions de Minuit (Paris), 1966 (112 copies, wraps) . . . £400
ditto, Éditions de Minuit (Paris), 1966 (wraps) . £45
ditto, as Cascando and Other Short Dramatic Pieces, Grove Press (U.S.), 1968 (wraps) £25
Proust and Three Dialogues with Georges Duthuit, Calder, 1965 . . . . £65/£15

Imagination Morte Immaginez, Éditions de Minuit (Paris), 1965 (612 signed copies) £125
ditto, as Imagination Dead Imagine, Calder, 1965 (wraps) £35
ditto, Calder, 1965 (100 signed, numbered copies) . .
. . . . £500/£450
ditto, as All Strange Away, Gotham Book Mart (U.S.), 1976 . . . . £50/£15
ditto, Gotham Book Mart (U.S.), 1976 (200 signed, numbered copies, slipcase) . . . . £1,000/£900
ditto, Calder, 1979. . . . . £20/£5
Bing, Éditions de Minuit (Paris), 1966 (100 numbered copies of 762, wraps) £150
ditto, Éditions de Minuit (Paris), 1966 (112 numbered copies reserved for La Librairie des Éditions de Minuit, wraps) £150
ditto, Éditions de Minuit (Paris), 1966 (550 numbered copies of 762, wraps) £100
ditto, as Le Depeupleur, Éditions de Minuit (Paris), 1970 (99 copies on pure thread 'lafuma' of 399 copies) £150
ditto, Éditions de Minuit (Paris), 1970 (201 of 399 copies, numbered 100-300) £75
ditto, Éditions de Minuit (Paris), 1970 (92 numbered copies reserved for publisher) £75
ditto, Éditions de Minuit (Paris), 1970 (7 *hors commerce* copies) £200
ditto, as Séjour, Georges Richar (Paris), 1970 . £300
ditto, as The Lost Ones, Calder, 1972 . . £40/£15
ditto, Calder, 1972 (100 signed copies, slipcase) . .
. . . . £300/£250
ditto, Grove Press (U.S.), 1972 . . . . £40/£15
ditto, as The North, Enitharmon Press, 1973 (137 signed, numbered copies, wraps) £500
ditto, Enitharmon Press, 1973 (15 signed copies with three extra etchings, heavyweight paper, wraps) . .
. . . . £2,000
Eh Joe and Other Writings, Faber, 1967 . £35/£10
Come and Go, Calder, 1967 . . . . . £65/£20
ditto, Calder, 1967 (100 signed copies, slipcase) . .
. . . . £600/£550
No's Knife, Calder, 1967 . . . . . . £40/£10
ditto, Calder, 1967 (100 signed copies, 'printed A (*hors commerce*)', slipcase) . . . . . £300/£200
ditto, Calder, 1967 ('a second series of 100 numbered copies printed B and signed by the author (*hors commerce*)', slipcase) . . . . . . £300/£200
Assez, Éditions de Minuit (Paris), 1968 (112 numbered copies of 662) £125
ditto, Éditions de Minuit (Paris), 1968 (100 *hors commerce* copies of 662) £150
ditto, Éditions de Minuit (Paris), 1968 (450 numbered copies of 662, wraps) £125
Poèms, Éditions de Minuit (Paris), 1968 (550 copies, wraps). £125
ditto, Éditions de Minuit (Paris), 1978 . . . £45
Sans, Éditions de Minuit (Paris), 1969 (742 copies, wraps). £125
ditto, as Lessness, Calder, 1970 . . . . £65/£20

ditto, Calder, 1970 (100 signed copies, slipcase) . .
. . . . £600/£550
Film, Grove Press (U.S.), 1969 (wraps). . . £20
ditto, Grove Press (U.S.), 1969 (200 numbered copies)
. . . . £125
ditto, Faber, 1972 (wraps). £35
ditto, Éditions de Minuit (Paris), 1972 (342 copies) .
. . . . £150
Premier Amour, Éditions de Minuit (Paris), 1970 (92 of 399 copies) £150
ditto, Éditions de Minuit (Paris), 1970 (106 numbered large paper copies of 399) £75
ditto, Éditions de Minuit (Paris), 1970 (201 of 399 copies) £75
ditto, as First Love, Calder, 1973 . . . £40/£15
ditto, Grove Press (U.S.), 1974 . . . . £40/£15
Mercier et Camier, Éditions de Minuit (Paris), 1970 (99 numbered large paper copies of 399) . . £150
ditto, Éditions de Minuit (Paris), 1970 (92 of 399 copies, wraps) £65
ditto, Éditions de Minuit (Paris), 1970 (7 *hors commerce* copies, wraps) £300
ditto, Éditions de Minuit (Paris), 1970 (201 of 399 copies, wraps) £45
ditto, as Mercier and Camier, Calder, 1974. £45/£10
ditto, Grove Press (U.S.), 1974 . . . . £45/£15
Six Residua, Calder, 1972 (wraps) £15
Breath and Other Short Plays, Faber, 1972 £60/£25
ditto, Faber, 1972 (wraps). £15
ditto, Faber, 1972 (signed, limited edition) . . £200
Not I, Faber, 1973 (wraps) £15
ditto, as Pas Moi, Éditions de Minuit (Paris), 1975 (150 numbered copies of 242, wraps) . . . £45
ditto, Éditions de Minuit (Paris), 1975 (92 numbered copies of 242, wraps) £75
Still, M'Arte Edizioni (Milan), 1974 (30 signed copies with extra portfolio of plates, slipcase) . . . £2,000
ditto, M'Arte Edizioni (Milan), 1974 (signed copies, slipcase) £1,000
ditto, as Immobile, Éditions de Minuit (Paris), 1976 (100 numbered copies of 125, wraps) . . . £45
ditto, Éditions de Minuit (Paris), 1976 (25 *hors commerce* copies, wraps) £45
That Time, Faber, 1976 (wraps) £10
ditto, as Cette Fois, Éditions de Minuit (Paris), 1978 (100 numbered copies, wraps) £250
Footfalls, Faber, 1976 (wraps) £10
ditto, Grove Press (U.S.), 1976 . . . . £25/£10
ditto, as Pas, Éditions de Minuit (Paris), 1977 (135 numbered copies of 227, wraps) £75
Pour finir encore et autres foirades, Éditions de Minuit (Paris), 1976 (125 numbered copies, wraps) .
. . . . £75
ditto, as Foirades / Fizzles, Petersburg Press, 1976 (33 lithographs by Jasper Johns, 300 signed, numbered copies, wraps) £10,000
ditto, as For to End Yet Again and Other Fizzles, Calder, 1976 . . . . £30/£10
ditto, as Fizzles, Grove Press (U.S.), 1977 . £30/£10

Drunken Boat, Whiteknights Pres, 1976 (100 copies, translation of Rimbaud by Beckett). . . . £500
Pas Suivi de Quatre Esquisses, Éditions de Minuit (Paris), 1976 (86 copies, wraps) £75
Ends and Odds, Faber, 1977 . . . . . £25/£10
ditto, Grove Press (U.S.), 1977 . . . . . £20/£5
Collected Poems in French and English, Calder, 1977
. . . . £25/£10
Four Novellas, Calder, 1978 . . . . . £25/£10
Mirlitonnades, Éditions de Minuit (Paris), 1979 (wraps) £10
Compagnie, Éditions de Minuit (Paris), 1980 (106 numbered copies, wraps) £75
ditto, as *Company*, Calder, 1980 . . . . £25/£10
ditto, Calder, 1980 (100 signed copies, slipcase) . .
. . . . £450/£400
ditto, Grove Press (U.S.), 1980 . . . £25/£10
Rockaby and Other Short Pieces, Grove Press (U.S.), 1981 . . . . £25/£10
ditto, as *Three Occasional Pieces*, Faber, 1982. £10
ditto, as *Berceuse suivi de Impromptu d'Ohio*, Éditions de Minuit (Paris), 1982 (99 numbered large paper copies, wraps) £150
Mal vu mal dit, Éditions de Minuit (Paris), 1981 (114 numbered copies, wraps) £75
ditto, Éditions de Minuit (Paris), 1981 (99 numbered copies, wraps) £150
ditto, as *Ill Seen Ill Said*, Grove Press (U.S.), 1981 .
. . . . £25/£10
ditto, Calder, 1982. . . . . . . £25/£10
ditto, Lord John Press (U.S.), 1982 (299 signed copies of 325) £300
ditto, Lord John Press (U.S.), 1982 (26 signed, lettered copies of 325) £750
Solo suivi de Catastrophe, Éditions de Minuit (Paris), 1982 (99 numbered copies, wraps) £200
Three Occasional Pieces, Faber, 1982 (wraps) . £10
Worstward Ho, Calder, 1983 . . . . £25/£10
ditto, Grove Press (U.S.), 1983 . . . £25/£10
ditto, as *Cap au pire*, Éditions de Minuit (Paris), 1991 (wraps) £15
Disjecta, Calder, 1983. . . . . . £30/£10
ditto, Grove Press (U.S.), 1983 . . . . £15/£5
Quoi Ou, Éditions de Minuit (Paris), 1983 (99 copies, wraps) £75
ditto, as *What Where*, Faber, 1984 . . . £10
Catastrophe, Lord John Press (U.S.), 1983 (100 numbered signed copies, broadside) . . £300
ditto, Lord John Press (U.S.), 1983 (26 lettered signed copies, broadside) £1,000
Collected Shorter Plays, Faber, 1984 . . £20/£5
ditto, Grove Press (U.S.), 1984 . . . . £20/£5
Collected Poems, 1930-1978, Calder, 1984 . . £20/£5
Collected Shorter Prose, 1945-1980, Calder, 1984. .
. . . . £20/£5
The Collected Works, Grove Press (U.S.), (16 vols 200 signed, numbered sets) £1,000
As the Story Was Told, Rampant Lions Press, 1987 (325 numbered copies) £100

ditto, Calder, 1990. . . . . . . £25/£10
L'Image, Éditions de Minuit (Paris), 1988 (wraps) £40
ditto, as *The Image*, Calder, 1990 . . . £25/£10
ditto, Riverrun Press (U.S.), 1990 . . . . £20/£5
Stirrings Still, Calder/Blue Moon Books, [1988] (200 of 226 signed, numbered copies, slipcase). . £1,500
ditto, Calder/Blue Moon Books, [1988] (26 lettered, signed copies of 226, slipcase) £2,000
ditto, Calder/Blue Moon Books, [1988] (15 roman-numeraled 'hors de commerce' copies, slipcase) . .
. . . . £2,000
Le Monde et le Pantalon, Éditions de Minuit (Paris), 1989 (99 copies, wraps) £45
Nohow On, Calder, 1989 . . . . . £25/£10
ditto, Limited Editions Club (U.S.), [1989] (550 signed copies in box) £2,000
Comment dire, Éditions de Minuit (Paris), 1989 (single sheet folded) £15
Dream of Fair to Middling Women, Black Cat Press (Dublin), 1992 . . . . £25/£10
Eleutheria, Éditions de Minuit (Paris), 1995 (wraps) .
. . . . £10
ditto, Foxrock (U.S.), 1995 (250 signed, numbered copies) £125

FRANCIS BEEDING

'Francis Beeding' is the best-known pseudonym of Hilary St George Saunders (b.1898 d.1951), under which name he co-wrote crime novels with John Palmer (b.1885 d.1944).

'Francis Beeding' Novels
The Seven Sleepers, Little, Brown (U.S.), 1925 . . .
. . . . £100/£20
ditto, Hutchinson, [1925] . . . . . £100/£20
The Little White Hag, Hutchinson, [1926] . £100/£20
ditto, Little, Brown (U.S.), 1926. . . . £100/£20
The Hidden Kingdom, Hodder & Stoughton, [1927] .
. . . . £100/£20
ditto, Little, Brown (U.S.), 1927. . . . £100/£20
The House of Doctor Edwardes, Hodder & Stoughton, [1927]. . . . . £750/£50
ditto, Little, Brown (U.S.), 1928. . . . £600/£50
ditto, as *Spellbound*, World Books, 1945 . £50/£15
The Six Proud Walkers, Little, Brown (U.S.), 1928 .
. . . . £100/£20
ditto, Hodder & Stoughton, [1928] . . . £100/£20
The Five Flamboys, Hodder & Stoughton, [1929] . .
. . . . £100/£20
ditto, Little, Brown (U.S.), 1929. . . . £100/£20
Pretty Sinister, Hodder & Stoughton, [1929] £100/£20
ditto, Little, Brown (U.S.), 1929. . . . £100/£20
The Four Armourers, Little, Brown (U.S.), 1930 . .
. . . . £100/£20
ditto, Hodder & Stoughton, 1930. . . . £100/£20

The League of Discontent, Little, Brown (U.S.), 1930
. . . . £100/£20
ditto, Hodder & Stoughton, 1930. . . . £100/£20
Death Walks in Eastrepps, Hodder & Stoughton, 1931
. . . . £100/£15
ditto, Mystery League (U.S.), 1931 . . . £100/£15
The Three Fishers, Little, Brown (U.S.), 1931 £75/£10
ditto, Hodder & Stoughton, [1931] . . . £75/£10
Take It Crooked, Little, Brown (U.S.), 1932 £75/£10
ditto, Hodder & Stoughton, 1932. . . . £75/£10
Murder Intended, Little, Brown (U.S.), 1932 £75/£10
ditto, Hodder & Stoughton, 1932. . . . £75/£10
The Two Undertakers, Hodder & Stoughton, 1933 .
. . . . £65/£10
ditto, Little, Brown (U.S.), 1933 . . . . £65/£10
The Emerald Clasp, Little, Brown (U.S.), 1933 . .
. . . . £60/£10
ditto, Hodder & Stoughton, 1933. . . . £60/£10
The One Sane Man, Hodder & Stoughton, 1934 . .
. . . . £60/£10
ditto, Little, Brown (U.S.), 1934 . . . . £60/£10
Mr Bobadil, Hodder & Stoughton, 1934 . £60/£10
ditto, as *The Street of the Serpents*, Harper (U.S.),
1934 . . . . £60/£10
Death in Four Letters, Hodder & Stoughton, 1935 .
. . . . £60/£10
ditto, Harper (U.S.), 1935. . . . . . £60/£10
The Norwich Victims, Hodder & Stoughton, 1935 . .
. . . . £60/£10
ditto, Harper (U.S.), 1935. . . . . . £60/£10
The Eight Crooked Trenches, Hodder & Stoughton,
1936 . . . . £50/£10
ditto, Harper (U.S.), 1936. . . . . . £50/£10
ditto, as *Coffin for One*, Avon (U.S.), 1943(wraps)
. . . . £10
The Nine Waxed Faces, Hodder & Stoughton, 1936 .
. . . . £50/£10
ditto, Harper (U.S.), 1936. . . . . . £50/£10
Hell Let Loose, Hodder & Stoughton, 1937. £50/£10
ditto, Harper (U.S.), 1937. . . . . . £50/£10
The Erring Secretary, Hodder & Stoughton, 1937
(wraps) £15
No Fury, Hodder & Stoughton, 1937 . . £50/£10
ditto, as *Murdered: One by One*, Harper (U.S.), 1937 .
. . . . £50/£10
The Black Arrows, Hodder & Stoughton, 1938. . .
. . . . £50/£10
ditto, Harper (U.S.), 1938. . . . . . £50/£10
The Big Fish, Hodder & Stoughton, 1938 . £45/£10
ditto, as *Heads off at Midnight*, Harper (U.S.), 1938 .
. . . . £45/£10
The Ten Holy Horrors, Hodder & Stoughton, 1939 .
. . . . £45/£10
ditto, Harper (U.S.), 1939. . . . . . £45/£10
He Could Not Have Slipped, Hodder & Stoughton,
1939 . . . . £35/£10
ditto, Harper (U.S.), 1939. . . . . . £35/£10
Eleven Were Brave, Hodder & Stoughton, 1940 . .
. . . . £25/£10

ditto, Harper (U.S.), 1941. . . . . . £25/£10
Not a Bad Show, Hodder & Stoughton, 1940 £35/£10
ditto, as *The Secret Weapon*, Harper (U.S.), 1940 . .
. . . . £25/£10
The Twelve Disguises, Hodder & Stoughton, 1942. .
. . . . £35/£10
ditto, Harper (U.S.), 1942. . . . . . £35/£10
There are Thirteen, Hodder & Stoughton, 1946 . .
. . . . £25/£10
ditto, Harper (U.S.), 1946. . . . . . £25/£10

'David Pilgrim' Novels, Written with John Palmer
So Great A Man, Macmillan, 1937 . . . £35/£10
ditto, Harper (U.S.), 1937. . . . . . £35/£10
No Common Glory, Macmillan, 1941 . . .£20/£5
ditto, Harper (U.S.), 1941. . . . . . .£20/£5
The Grand Design, Macmillan, 1944 . . .£15/£5
ditto, Harper (U.S.), 1944. . . . . . .£15/£5
The Emperor's Servant, Macmillan, 1946 . .£15/£5

'Barum Browne' Novel, Written with Geoffrey Dennis
The Devil and X.Y.Z., Gollancz, 1931 . . £35/£10
ditto, Doubleday (U.S.), 1931 . . . . £35/£10

'Cornelius Coffyn' Novel, Written with John de Vere Loder
The Death Riders, Gollancz, 1935 . . . £35/£10
ditto, Knopf (U.S.), 1935 . . . . . . £35/£10

As Hilary St George Saunders
Return at Dawn, New Zealand Tourist and Publicity
Department, 1943 (wraps) £10
Per Ardua, O.U.P., 1944 . . . .£20/£5
Pioneers! Pioneers!, Macmillan, 1944 . . .£15/£5
Ford at War, Harrison & Sons, 1946 (wraps) . £10
The Left Handshake, Collins, 1948 . . . £25/£10
Valiant Voyaging, Faber, 1948 . . . . £25/£10
The Middlesex Hospital, 1745-1948, Max Parrish,
1949 (wraps) £5
The Green Beret, Joseph, 1949 . . . . .£20/£5
The Red Beret, Joseph, 1950 . . . . . .£20/£5
The Red Cross and the White, Hollis & Carter, 1949 .
. . . .£20/£5
The Sleeping Bacchus, Joseph, 1951 . . .£20/£5
Westminster Hall, Joseph, 1951 . . . . .£20/£5
Royal Air Force 1939-1945, H.M.S.O., 1953-4 (3 vols,
with Denis G. Richards, wraps . . . £40 the set

Anonymous Publications
The Battle of Britain, H.M.S.O./Ministry of
Information, 1941 (wraps) £10
ditto, Doubleday (U.S.), 1941 (wraps) . . . £10
Bomber Command, H.M.S.O./Ministry of Information,
1941 (wraps) £10
ditto, Doubleday (U.S.), 1941 (wraps) . . . £10
Air-Sea Rescue, H.M.S.O./Ministry of Information,
1942 (wraps) £10
Bomber Command Continues, H.M.S.O./Ministry of
Information, 1942 (wraps) £10

Coastal Command, H.M.S.O./Ministry of Information, 1943 (wraps) £10
ditto, Macmillan (U.S.), 1943 (wraps) . . . £10
Combined Operations, H.M.S.O./Ministry of Information, 1943 (wraps) £10
ditto, Macmillan (U.S.), 1943 (wraps) . . . £10
By Air to Battle, H.M.S.O./Ministry of Information, 1945 (wraps) £10

MAX BEERBOHM
(b.1872 d.1956)

Humorist, caricaturist, essayist and novelist, and survivor of the 1890s decadent scene.

Fiction
The Happy Hypocrite, Wayside Press (U.S.), 1896 (green wraps). £150
ditto, John Lane, 1897. . . . . £100
Zuleika Dobson, Heinemann, 1911 (first issue smooth cloth) £100
ditto, Heinemann, 1911 (second issue rough cloth). .
. . . . £75
ditto, John Lane (U.S.), 1912. . . . . £75
A Christmas Garland, Heinemann, 1912 . . £65
ditto, Dutton & Co. (U.S.), 1912 . . . . £50
Seven Men, Heinemann, 1919 . . . . £35
ditto, Knopf (U.S.), 1920 (2,000 numbered copies)
. . . . £75/£25
ditto, as *Seven Men and Two Others*, Heinemann, 1946 . . . . £15/£5
The Dreadful Dragon of Hay Hill, Heinemann, 1928 .
. . . . £75/£15

Non Fiction
The Works of Max Beerbohm, Scribner's (U.S.), 1896 (1,000 copies, of which 401 were pulped) . . £200
ditto, John Lane, 1896. . . . . . . £100
More, John Lane, 1899 . . . . . £50
Yet Again, Chapman and Hall, 1909. . . . £50
ditto, Knopf (U.S.), 1923 . . . . . £55/£20
And Even Now, Heinemann, 1920 . . £50/£10
ditto, Dutton (U.S.), 1921. . . . . £45/£10
A Peep into the Past, privately printed [Max Harzof] (U.S.), 1923 (300 copies on Japanese vellum, slipcase) . . . . £125/£100
Around Theatres, Heinemann, 1924 (2 vols) . . .
. . . . £200/£50
ditto, Knopf (U.S.), 1930 (2 vols) . . . £150/£45
A Variety of Things, Heinemann, 1928 . . £40/£10
ditto, Knopf (U.S.), 1928 (2,000 numbered copies) .
. . . . £40/£10
Lytton Strachey, C.U.P., 1943 (wraps). . . £10
ditto, Knopf (U.S.), 1943 . . . . . £25/£10
Mainly on the Air, Heinemann, 1946 . . £20/£5
ditto, Knopf (U.S.), 1947 . . . . . £15/£5
Sherlockiana: A Reminiscence of Sherlock Holmes, Hill (U.S.), 1948 (36 copies) £300

Letters Of Max Beerbohm, 1892-1956, Murray, 1988.
. . . . £10/£5
ditto, Norton (U.S.), 1989. . . . . . £10/£5
More Theatres, Hart-Davis, 1969 . . . £10/£5
ditto, Taplinger (U.S.), 1969 . . . . £10/£5
Last Theatres, Hart-Davis, 1970. . . . £10/£5
ditto, Knopf (U.S.), 1970 . . . . . £10/£5

Drawings and Caricatures
Caricatures of Twenty-Five Gentleman, Leonard Smithers, 1896 (500 copies) £500
Poet's Corner, Heinemann, 1904 . . . £250
ditto, Heinemann, 1904 (wraps) . . . £250
A Book of Caricatures, Methuen, 1907 . . £150
Cartoons: The Second Childhood of John Bull, Stephen Swift, [1911] £175
Fifty Caricatures, Heinemann, 1913. . . £100
ditto, Dutton (U.S.), 1913. . . . . . £75
A Survey, Heinemann, 1921 . . . . £125/£50
ditto, Heinemann, 1921 (275 signed, numbered copies)
. . . . £250/£175
ditto, Doubleday, 1921 . . . . £100/£50
Rossetti and His Circle, Heinemann, 1922 . £200/£65
ditto, Heinemann, 1922 (380 signed, numbered copies)
. . . . £500/£400
Things New and Old, Heinemann, 1923 . £150/£50
ditto, Heinemann, 1923 (350 signed, numbered copies, with additional signed coloured plate) . . £300/£200
Observations, Heinemann, 1925 . . . £150/£50
ditto, Heinemann, 1925 (250 copies with extra signed plate) . . . . £300/£200
The Heroes and Heroines of Bitter Sweet, [Leadley, 1931] (900 numbered copies, portfolio) . . £200

Edited by Beerbohm
Herbert Beerbohm Tree, Hutchinson, 1920. £300/£125
ditto, Dutton (U.S.), [1920] . . . . £300/£125

Collected Edition
Works, Heinemann, 1922-28 (10 vols, 780 signed, numbered sets) . . . . . . £1,500/£450

BRENDAN BEHAN
(b.1923 d.1964)

An Irish playwright, Behan spent many years in prison as a result of his IRA activities. Although released in 1947, it was in prison that he started to write, and his first success came with the publication of *The Quare Fellow* in 1956.

Plays
The Quare Fellow, Methuen, 1956 . . . £175/£45
ditto, Grove Press (U.S.), 1956 . . . £40/£20
ditto, Grove Press (U.S.), 1956 (wraps) . . £10
ditto, Grove Press (U.S.), 1956 (100 numbered copies)
. . . . £40/£20

The Hostage, Methuen, 1958. . . . . £50/£15
ditto, Grove Press (U.S.), 1958 . . . . £40/£20
ditto, Grove Press (U.S.), 1958 (wraps) . . . £10
ditto, Grove Press (U.S.), 1958 (26 signed, lettered
copies) £1,000
Borstal Boy, Random House (U.S.), 1971 . £35/£10
Richard's Cork Leg, Methuen, 1973 . . . £20/£5
ditto, Grove Press (U.S.), 1974 . . . . . £20/£5
An Giall and The Hostage, C. Smythe, 1988 . . £5

Novel
The Scarperer, Hutchinson, 1964 . . . . £20/£5
ditto, Doubleday (U.S.), 1964 . . . . . £20/£5

Others
Borstal Boy, Knopf (U.S.), 1957. . . . . £75/£20
ditto, Hutchinson, 1958 . . . . . . £75/£20
Brendan Behan's Island, Hutchinson, 1962 . £20/£5
ditto, Geis (U.S.), 1962 . . . . £15/£5
Hold Your Hour and Have Another, Hutchinson, 1963
. . . . £40/£10
ditto, Little, Brown (U.S.), 1964 . . . . £25/£10
Brendan Behan's New York, Hutchinson, 1964 £15/£5
ditto, Geis (U.S.), 1964 . . . . . . £15/£5
Confessions of an Irish Rebel, Hutchinson, 1965 . .
. . . . £20/£5
ditto, Geis (U.S.), 1966 . . . . . . £15/£5
Poems and A Play in Irish, Gallery Press (Dublin),
1981 . . . . £25/£10
After the Wake: Uncollected Prose, O'Brien Press
(Ireland), 1983 . . . . £10

HILLAIRE BELLOC
(b.1870 d.1953)

Belloc was a poet, novelist, essayist, and travel writer,
but is best known and most often collected for his
humorous verse for children.

Poetry
Verses and Sonnets, Ward & Downey, 1896 . £300
The Bad Child's Book of Beasts, Alden Press, 1896
(pseud. 'H.B.') £200
More Beasts (For Worse Children), Arnold, 1897 .
. . . . £100
The Modern Traveller, Arnold, 1898 . . . £75
A Moral Alphabet, Arnold, 1899 . . . . £75
Cautionary Tales for Children, Eveleigh Nash, 1907 .
. . . . £75
Verses, Duckworth, 1910 . . . . . . £50
More Peers, Stephen Swift, 1911 . . . £45
Sonnets and Verse, Duckworth, 1923 . . £50/£10
ditto, Duckworth, 1923 (525 signed copies). . £75
The Chanty of the Nowa, Faber, Arial Poem, 1928 £15
ditto, Faber, Arial Poem, 1928 (500 signed, large paper
copies) £50
New Cautionary Tales, Duckworth, 1930 . £125/£45

ditto, Duckworth, 1930 (110 signed copies). . £150
In Praise of Wine: A Heroic Poem, Peter Davies, 1931
. . . . £35/£10
Ladies and Gentlemen, Duckworth, 1932 . £30/£10
The Verse of Hilaire Belloc, The Nonesuch Press,
1954 (1,250 numbered copies) £35

Novels
Emmanuel Burden, Methuen, 1904 . . . . £45
Mr Clutterbuck's Election, Eveleigh Nash, 1908 £25
A Change in the Cabinet, Methuen, 1909 . . £25
Pongo and the Bull, Constable, 1910 . . . £50
The Girondin, Nelson, 1911 . . . . . £20
The Green Overcoat, Arrowsmith, 1912 . . £35
The Mercy of Allah, Chatto & Windus, 1922 £75/£20
Mr Petre, Arrowsmith, 1925 . . . . . £50/£15
ditto, McBride (U.S.), 1925 . . . . . £50/£15
The Emerald of Catherine the Great, Arrowsmith,
1926 (Illustrated by G.K. Chesterton) . . £50/£15
ditto, Harpers (U.S.), 1926 . . . . . £50/£15
The Haunted House, Arrowsmith, 1927 . £200/£65
ditto, Harper (U.S.), 1928. . . . . . £150/£50
But Soft, We Are Observed, Arrowsmith, 1928. . .
. . . . £50/£15
Belinda, Constable, 1928 . . . . . . £65/£15
The Missing Masterpiece, Arrowsmith, 1929
(Illustrated by G.K. Chesterton) . . . £100/£50
The Man Who Made Gold, Arrowsmith, 1930 £75/£15
ditto, Harper (U.S.), 1931. . . . . . £65/£15
The Post-Master General, Arrowsmith, 1932 £100/£25
ditto, Lippincott (U.S.), 1932. . . . . £75/£10
The Hedge and the Horse, Cassell, 1936 . £35/£10

History
Danton, John Nisbet & Co., 1899 . . . . £50
ditto, Putnams (U.S.), 1928 . . . . . £30/£10
Robespierre, John Nisbet & Co., 1901 . . . £40
The Eye Witness, Eveleigh Nash, 1908 . . . £40
Marie Antoinette, Methuen, 1909 . . . . £40
The French Revolution, Williams and Norgate, 1911 .
. . . . £30
The Battle of Blenheim, Stephen Swift, 1911 . £20
Malplaquet, Stephen Swift, 1911 . . . . £20
Crecy, Stephen Swift, 1911 . . . . . £20
Poitiers, Stephen Swift, 1911. . . . . £20
Waterloo, Stephen Swift, 1912 . . . . . £20
Turcoing, Stephen Swift, 1912 . . . . . £20
Warfare in England, Williams & Norgate, 1912 £20
The Book of the Bayeaux Tapestry, Chatto & Windus,
1914 . . . . £30
History of England, (Vol. 11), Catholic Publications
Society of America, 1915 . . . . . . £15
Land and Water Map of the War, Land and Water,
1915 . . . . £25
*A General Sketch of the European War: The First
Phase*, Nelson, 1915. . . . . £40
The Two Maps of Europe, Arthur Pearson, 1915 £30

The Last Days of the French Monarchy, Chapman
and Hall, 1916 . . . . £10
*A General Sketch of the European War: The Second
Phase*, Nelson, 1916. . . . . £40
The Second Year of the War, Land & Water, 1916 .
. . . . £30
The Principles of War, by Foch, Chapman & Hall,
1919 (translation) £25
Precepts and Judgements, by Foch, Chapman & Hall,
1919 (translation) £25
The Jews, Constable, 1922 . . . . £25/£10
The Campaign of 1812, Nelson, 1924 . . £35/£15
History of England Vol. 1, Methuen, 1925 . £25/£10
Miniatures of French History, Nelson, 1925 £35/£15
Mrs Markham's New History of England, Cayme
Press, 1926 . . . . £25/£10
History of England Vol. 2, Methuen, 1927 . £25/£10
Oliver Cromwell, Benn, 1927 . . . . £30/£10
History of England Vol. 3, Methuen, 1928 . £25/£10
James II, Faber & Gwyer, 1928 . . . £35/£15
ditto, as *James the Second*, Lippincott (U.S.), 1928 .
. . . . £35/£15
How the Reformation Happened, Cape, 1928 £25/£10
ditto, McBride & Co (U.S.), 1928 . . . £25/£10
Joan of Arc, Cassell, 1929 . . . . £35/£15
Richelieu, Lippincott (U.S.), 1929 . . . £30/£10
ditto, Benn, 1930 . . . . £30/£10
Wolsey, Cassell, 1930 . . . . . . £30/£10
ditto, Lippincott (U.S.), 1930 . . . . £30/£10
History of England Vol. 4, Methuen, 1931 . . £25/£5
Cranmer, Cassell, 1931 . . . . . £35/£10
ditto, Lippincott (U.S.), 1931 . . . . £35/£10
*The Tactics and Strategy of the Great Duke of
Marlborough*, Arrowsmith, 1931 . . . £45/£10
Six British Battles, Arrowsmith, 1931 . . £30/£10
Napoleon, Cassell, 1932 . . . . . £25/£10
ditto, Lippincott (U.S.), 1932 . . . . £25/£10
William the Conqueror, Peter Davies, 1933 £20/£10
Beckett, Catholic Truth Society, 1933 . . . £20/£5
Charles I, Cassell, 1933 . . . . . £25/£10
ditto, Lippincott (U.S.), 1933 . . . . £15/£10
Cromwell, Cassell, 1934 . . . . . £15/£10
A Shorter History of England, Harrap, 1934 £25/£10
Milton, Cassell, 1935 . . . . . . £35/£15
The Battleground, Cassell, 1936 . . . . £20/£5
ditto, Lippincott (U.S.), 1936 . . . . £20/£5
Characters of the Reformation, Sheed & Ward (U.S.),
1936 . . . . £15/£5
The Crusade, Cassell, 1937 . . . . £35/£10
The Crisis of Our Civilization, Cassell, 1937 (wraps) .
. . . . £10
ditto, Fordham Univ. Press (U.S.), 1937. . . £10
The Great Heresies, Sheed & Ward (U.S.), 1938 . .
. . . . £20/£5
Monarchy: A Study of Louis XIV, Cassell, 1938 . .
. . . . £25/£10
ditto, as *Louis XIV*, Harper (U.S.), 1938 . £25/£10
The Last Rally, Cassell, 1940 . . . . . £20/£5
Elizabethan Commentary, Cassell, 1942 . . £15/£5

Travel
Paris, Arnold, 1900 . . . . £25
The Path to Rome, Allen, 1902 . . . . . £25
The Old Road, Constable, 1904 . . . . . £75
Esto Perpetua, Duckworth, 1906 . . . . £45
Sussex, A.C. Black, 1906. . . . . . . £30
The Historic Thames, Dent, 1907 . . . . £65
The Pyrenees, Methuen, 1909 . . . . . £25
The River of London, Foulis, 1912 . . . . £25
The Four Men, Foulis, 1912 . . . . . . £20
The Stane Street, Constable, 1913 . . . £30/£10
The Road, Charles Hobson, 1923 . . . £25/£10
The Contrast, Arrowsmith, 1923. . . . . £15/£5
ditto, McBride (U.S.), 1924 . . . . . . £15/£5
The Cruise of the Nona, Constable, 1925 . £45/£15
ditto, Houghton Mifflin, 1925 . . . . £40/£15
The Highway and its Vehicles, The Studio, 1926 (1250
numbered copies) . . . . £50/£20
Many Cities, Constable, 1928 . . . . £25/£10
Return to the Baltic, Constable, 1938 . . £25/£10
On Sailing the Sea, Methuen, 1939 . . . . £15/£5
Places, Sheed and Ward (U.S.), 1941 . . . £15/£5
ditto, Cassell, 1942 . . . . £15/£5

Politics
Socialism and the Servile State, I.L.P., 1910 . £10
The Party System and Cecil Chesterton, Stephen
Swift, 1911 . . . . £15
The Servile State, Foulis, 1912 . . . . . £20
ditto, Henry Holt (U.S.), 1946 . . . . . £10/£5
The Free Press, Allen & Unwin, 1918 . . £25/£10
The House of Commons and the Monarchy, Allen &
Unwin, 1920 . . . . £25/£5
Economics for Helen, Arrowsmith, 1924 . £20/£10
The Political Effort, True Temperance Association,
1924 . . . . £15

Literature
Caliban's Guide to Letters, Duckworth, 1903 . £35
The Romance of Tristan and Iseult, Allen, 1903
(translation) £20
*Avril, Being Essays on the Poetry of the French
Renaissance*, Duckworth, 1904. . . . . £20
On the Place of Gilbert Chesterton in English Letters,
Sheed & Ward, 1940. . . . . £20/£5

Religion
An Open Letter on the Decay of Faith, Burns & Oates,
1906 . . . . £20
The Catholic Church and Historical Truth, W.
Watson, 1908. . . . . £10
An Examination of Socialism, Catholic Truth Society,
1908 . . . . £10
The Church and Socialism, Catholic Truth Society,
1908 . . . . £10
The Ferrer Case, Catholic Truth Society, 1909. £10
Anti-Catholic History, Catholic Truth Society, 1914 .
. . . . £10

Religion and Liberty, Catholic Truth Society, 1918 .
. . . . £10
The Catholic Church and the Purchase of Private Property, Catholic Truth Society, 1920 . . £10
A Companion to Mr Wells' Outline of History, Sheed & Ward, 1926 . . . . £25/£10
Mr Belloc Still Objects, Sheed and Ward, 1927 £15/£5
The Catholic Church and History, Burns, Oates & Washbourne, 1927 . . . . £10/£5
Survivals and New Arrivals, Sheed & Ward, 1929 .
. . . . £10/£5
ditto, Macmillan (U.S.), 1929 . . . . . £10/£5
The Case of Dr Coulton, Sheed & Ward, 1931 £10/£5
The Catholic and the War, Burns & Oates, 1940 . .
. . . . £10/£5

Essays
At the Sign of the Lion, Mosher (U.S.), 1896 (950 copies) £20
ditto, Mosher (U.S.), 1916 . . . . . £15
Hills and Seas, Methuen, 1906 . . . . . £25
On Nothing, Methuen, 1908 . . . . . . £15
On Everything, Methuen, 1909 . . . . . £15
On Anything, Methuen, 1910 . . . . . £15
On Something, Methuen, 1910 . . . . . £15
First and Last, Methuen, 1911 . . . . £10
This and That, Methuen, 1912 . . . . £10
On, Methuen, 1923 . . . . £15/£5
Hilaire Belloc: Essays, Harrap, 1926 . . . £15/£5
Short Talks with the Dead, Cayme Press, 1926 . .
. . . . £25/£10
A Conversation with an Angel, Cape, 1928. £25/£10
Conversations with a Cat, Cassell, 1930 . £25/£10
ditto, Harper & Brothers (U.S.), 1931 . . . £20/£5
Essays of a Catholic, Sheed & Ward, 1931 . . £15/£5
Nine Nines, Blackwell, 1931 . . . . . . £15/£5
An Essay on the Restoration of Property, Distributist League, 1936 . . . . £10
An Essay on the Nature of Contemporary England, Constable, 1937 . . . . £15/£5
The Silence of the Sea, Sheed & Ward (U.S.), 1940 .
. . . . £15/£5
ditto, Cassell, 1941 . . . . £15/£5

Others
Lambkin's Remains, by 'H.B.', J.C.R., 1900 . £75
The Great Inquiry, Duckworth, 1903 . . . £30
A Pamphlet, 1930, privately printed (for Belloc's 60th birthday) £65
On Translation, Clarendon Press, 1931 . . £30/£15
The Issue, Sheed & Ward, 1937 . . . . £15/£5
The Question and the Answer, Longman's Green, 1938 . . . . £15/£5
The Test in Poland, Weekly Review, 1939 . . £10

SAUL BELLOW
(b.1915)

An American novelist whose writing often addresses the problems of those living in urban areas and their place in the modern world, Bellow won the Nobel Prize for Literature in 1976.

Novels
Dangling Man, Vanguard Press (U.S.), 1944 . . .
. . . . £1,000/£200
ditto, Lehmann, 1946 . . . . £225/£35
The Victim, Vanguard Press (U.S.), 1945 . £750/£65
ditto, Lehmann, 1948 . . . . £125/£25
The Adventures of Augie March, Viking (U.S.), 1953
. . . . £350/£40
ditto, Weidenfeld & Nicolson, 1954 . . . £65/£15
Seize the Day, with Three Short Stories and a One Act Play, Viking (U.S.), 1956 . . . . . £100/£15
ditto, Weidenfeld & Nicolson, 1957 . . . £100/£15
Henderson the Rain King, Viking (U.S.), 1959 . .
. . . . £75/£15
ditto, Weidenfeld & Nicolson, 1959 . . . £75/£15
Herzog, Viking (U.S.), 1964 . . . . . £50/£10
ditto, Weidenfeld & Nicolson, 1965 . . . £50/£10
Mr Sammler's Planet, Viking (U.S.), 1970 . . £40/£5
ditto, Weidenfeld & Nicolson, 1970 . . . . £30/£5
Humboldt's Gift, Viking (U.S.), 1975 . . . £40/£5
ditto, Alison Press/Secker & Warburg, 1975 . £40/£5
The Dean's December, Harper (U.S.), 1982 . £20/£5
ditto, Harper, 1982 (500 signed copies, glassine wrapper, slipcase) . . . . . . £65/£50
ditto, Secker & Warburg, 1982 . . . . £20/£5
More Die of Heartbreak, Morrow (U.S.), 1987 £10/£5
ditto, Alison Press, 1987 . . . . . . £20/£5
Ravelstein, Viking (U.S.), 2000 . . . . £10/£5
ditto, Viking, 2000 . . . . £10/£5

Short Stories
Mosby's Memoirs and Other Stories, Viking (U.S.), 1968 . . . . £50/£15
ditto, Weidenfeld & Nicolson, 1969 . . . £20/£5
Him with His Foot in His Mouth and Other Stories, Harper (U.S.), 1984 . . . . £20/£5
ditto, Secker & Warburg, 1984 . . . . £20/£5
A Theft, Penguin, 1989 (wraps) £5
ditto, Penguin (U.S.), 1989 (wraps) £5
The Bellarosa Connection, Penguin, 1989 (wraps) £5
ditto, Penguin (U.S.), 1989 (wraps) £5
Something to Remember Me By, Secker & Warburg, 1992 . . . . £20/£5
ditto, Penguin (U.S.), 1991 (wraps) £5
The Actual, Viking, 1997. . . . . . £10/£5
ditto, Penguin (U.S.), 1997 (wraps) £5

Plays
The Last Analysis, Viking (U.S.), 1965 . . £50/£10
ditto, Weidenfeld & Nicolson, 1966 . . . £50/£10

Others

To Jerusalem and Back, Viking (U.S.), 1976 . £30/£5
ditto, Secker & Warburg, 1976 . . . . . £25/£5
The Nobel Lecture, U.S. Information Service
(Stockholm), 1977 . . . . £35
ditto, Targ editions (U.S.), 1979 (350 signed copies,
tissue wraps) . . . . £100/£65
It All Adds Up, Penguin (U.S.), 1994 . . £15/£5
ditto, Secker & Warburg, 1994 . . . . . £15/£5

LUDWIG BEMELMANS
(b.1898 d.1962)

An artist and writer in various genres, Bemelmans is
best known for his schoolgirl character, Madeline.

'Madeline' Books

Madeline, Simon & Schuster (U.S.), 1939 . £500/£150
ditto, Derek Verschoyle, 1952 . . . . £150/£35
Madeline's Rescue, Viking (U.S.), 1953 . £225/£75
ditto, Derek Verschoyle, 1953 . . . £125/£35
Madeline and the Bad Hat, Viking (U.S.), 1956 (985
signed copies) . . . . £350/£200
ditto, Viking (U.S.), 1956 . . . . . £200/£65
ditto, Deutsch, 1958 . . . . . . £150/£45
Madeline and the Gypsies, Viking (U.S.), 1959 .
. . . . £200/£65
ditto, Deutsch, 1961 . . . . . . £125/£35
Madeline in London, Viking (U.S.), 1961 . £175/£50
ditto, Deutsch, 1962 . . . . . . £100/£25
Madeline's Christmas, Viking/Kestrel (U.S.), 1985
(completed by Madeline and Barbara Bemelmans) .
. . . . £150/£35
ditto, Deutsch, 1985 . . . . . . £65/£25

Other Children's Books

Hansi, Viking (U.S.), 1934 . . . . . £200/£65
ditto, Lovat Dickson, 1935 . . . . . £125/£40
The Golden Basket, Viking (U.S.), 1936 . £200/£50
The Castle Number 9, Viking (U.S.), 1937 . £200/£50
Quito Express, Viking (U.S.), 1938 . . . £125/£30
Rosebud, Viking (U.S.), 1942 . . . . £100/£25
A Tale of Two Glimps, Columbia Broadcasting
Systems (U.S.), 1947 (wraps) £100
The Happy Place, Little, Brown (U.S.), 1952 £75/£20
The High World, Harper (U.S.), 1954 . . £75/£20
ditto, Hamish Hamilton, 1958 . . . . £50/£15
Parsley, Harper (U.S.), 1955 . . . . . £50/£15

Poetry

Fifi, Simon & Schuster (U.S.), 1940 . . . £125/£30
Sunshine, Simon & Schuster (U.S.), 1950 . £75/£30
Welcome Home, Harper (U.S.), 1960 . . £45/£15
ditto, Hamish Hamilton, 1961 . . . . £35/£10
Marina, Harper (U.S.), 1962 . . . . . £45/£15

Novels for Adults

Now I Lay Me Down to Sleep, Viking (U.S.), 1943 .
. . . . £50/£15
ditto, Viking, 1943 (500 signed copies, illustrated). .
. . . . £150/£100
ditto, Hamish Hamilton, 1944 . . . . £35/£10
The Blue Danube, Viking (U.S.), 1945 . . £25/£10
ditto, Hamish Hamilton, 1946 . . . . £25/£10
Dirty Eddie, Viking (U.S.), 1947. . . . £25/£10
ditto, Hamish Hamilton, 1948 . . . . £25/£10
The Eye of God, Viking (U.S.), 1949 . . £25/£10
ditto, as *The Snow Mountain*, Hamish Hamilton, 1950
. . . . £25/£10
The Woman of My Life, Viking (U.S.), 1957 £25/£10
ditto, Hamish Hamilton, 1957 . . . . £25/£10
Are You Hungry, Are You Cold, World (U.S.), 1960 .
. . . . £20/£5
ditto, Deutsch, 1961 . . . . £20/£5
The Street Where the Heart Lies, World (U.S.), 1963 .
. . . . £20/£5

Short Stories

Small Beer, Viking (U.S.), 1939 . . . £65/£20
ditto, Viking (U.S.), 1939 (175 signed copies) . £500
ditto, John Lane, 1940 . . . . . . £45/£10
I Love You, I Love You, I Love You, Viking (U.S.),
1942 . . . . £50/£10
ditto, Hamish Hamilton, 1943 . . . . £45/£10

Travel

The Donkey Inside, Viking (U.S.), 1941 . £25/£10
ditto, Viking (U.S.), 1941 (175 deluxe copies with
original watercolour, slipcase) . . . £250/£225
ditto, Hamish Hamilton, 1947 . . . . . £20/£5
The Best of Times, Simon & Schuster (U.S.), 1948 .
. . . . £35/£10
ditto, Cresset Press, 1949 . . . . . £30/£10
How To Travel Incognito, Little, Brown (U.S.), 1952 .
. . . . £25/£10
ditto, Hamish Hamilton, 1952 . . . . . £20/£5
Father Dear Father, Viking (U.S.), 1953 . £25/£10
ditto, Viking (U.S.), 1953 (151 signed, deluxe copies
with original watercolour) £200
ditto, Hamish Hamilton, 1953 . . . . . £20/£5
Holiday in France, Houghton Mifflin (U.S.), 1957 .
. . . . £30/£10
ditto, Deutsch, 1958 . . . . £20/£5
How To Have Europe All To Yourself, European
Travel Commission (U.S.), 1960 (wraps) . . £10
Italian Holiday, Houghton Mifflin (U.S.), 1961 .
. . . . £45/£15
On Board Noah's Ark, Viking (U.S.), 1962 . £20/£5
ditto, Collins, 1962 . . . . £20/£5

Others

My War with the United States, Viking (U.S.), 1937 .
. . . . £65/£20
ditto, Gollancz, 1938 . . . . . . £40/£15
Life Class, Viking (U.S.), 1938 . . . . £40/£10

ditto, John Lane, 1939. . . . . . . £15/£5
At Your Service, Peterson (U.S.), 1941 (wraps)   £15
Hotel Splendide, Viking (U.S.), 1941 . . £100/£25
ditto, Viking (U.S.), 1941 (305 signed, deluxe copies).
. . . . £300
ditto, Hamish Hamilton, 1942 . . . £50/£15
Hotel Bemelmans, Viking (U.S.), 1946. . £30/£10
ditto, Hamish Hamilton, 1956 . . . . £20/£5
To The One I Love the Best, Viking (U.S.), 1955 . .
. . . . £50/£15
ditto, Hamish Hamilton, 1955 . . . £30/£10
The World of Bemelmans, Viking (U.S.), 1955 . .
. . . . £25/£10
My Life in Art, Harper (U.S.), 1958 . . . £30/£10
ditto, Deutsch, 1958 . . . . £25/£5
La Bonne Table, Simon & Schuster (U.S.), 1964 . .
. . . . £20/£5
ditto, Hamish Hamilton, 1964 . . . . £20/£5

ALAN BENNETT
(b.1934)

An actor and playwright, Alan Bennett's quiet, self-effacing style has been as popular with television audiences as it has with the readers of his books.

Plays
Beyond the Fringe, Souvenir Press, 1963 . £75/£20
ditto, Random House (U.S.), 1963 . . . £50/£15
Forty Years On, Faber, 1969 . . . . . £75/£20
ditto, Faber, 1969 (wraps). £5
Getting On, Faber, 1972 . . . . . . £20/£5
ditto, Faber, 1972 (wraps). £5
Habeas Corpus, Faber, 1973 . . . . . £20/£5
ditto, Faber, 1973 (wraps). £5
The Old Country, Faber, 1978 (wraps) . . . £10
Enjoy, Faber, 1980 (wraps) £10
Office Suite: Two One-Act Plays, Faber, 1981 (wraps)
. . . . £15
Objects of Affection, BBC, 1983 (wraps) . . £10
The Writer in Disguise, Faber, 1985 (wraps) . £10
Two Kafka Plays, Faber, 1987 (wraps) . . . £5
Talking Heads, BBC, 1987 (wraps) £5
ditto, as *Single Spies and Talking Heads*, Summit
(U.S.), 1989 . . . . £15/£5

Screenplays
A Private Function, Faber, 1985 (wraps) . . £10
Prick Up Your Ears, Faber, 1987 (wraps) . . £10
The Madness of King George, Faber, 1992 (wraps) £5
ditto, Random House (U.S.), 1995 . . . . £5

Novellas and Short Stories
The Clothes They Stood Up In, Profile Books/London
Review of Books, 1998 . . . . . . £10/£5
ditto, Random House (U.S.), 1998 . . . £10/£5

Father! Father! Burning Bright, Profile Books/
London Review of Books, 2000 . . . . £10/£5
Laying On Of Hands, Profile Books/London Review
of Books, 2001 . . . . £10/£5
ditto, Picador (U.S.), 2002 . . . . . . £10/£5

Others
Writing Home, Faber, 1994 . . . . . £10/£5
ditto, Random House (U.S.), 1995 . . . £10/£5
ditto, Faber, 1998 (wraps). £5

ARNOLD BENNETT
(b.1867 d.1931)

Born in the Staffordshire Potteries, this novelist, short story writer, playwright and journalist's reputation today rests principally on his novels about the lives of ordinary people.

Novels
A Man from the North, John Lane, 1898 . . £500
Anna of the Five Towns, Chatto & Windus, 1902 £150
The Grand Babylon Hotel, Chatto & Windus, 1902 .
. . . . £250
ditto, Doran (U.S.), 1902 . . . . . . £50
ditto, as *T. Racksole and Daughter*, New Amsterdam
(U.S.), 1902 . . . . £50
The Gates of Wrath, Chatto & Windus, 1903 . £45
Leonora, Chatto & Windus, 1903 . . . . £40
ditto, Mershon (U.S.), [1903]. £20
A Great Man, Chatto & Windus, 1904 . . . £30
Teresa of Watling Street, Chatto & Windus, 1904 £25
Sacred and Profane Love, Chatto & Windus, 1905 £30
Hugo, Chatto & Windus, 1906 . . . . . £30
The Sinews of War (with Eden Philpotts), T. Werner
Laurie, 1906 . . . . £35
ditto, as *Doubloons*, McClure, Phillips & Co. (U.S.),
1906 . . . . £15
Whom God Hath Joined, David Nutt, 1906 . £15
The City of Pleasure, Chatto & Windus, 1907 . £15
The Ghost: A Fantasia on Modern Times, Chatto &
Windus, 1907. . . . . £30
ditto, Turner (U.S.), 1907. . . . . . . £30
Buried Alive, Chapman & Hall, 1908 . . . £25
The Old Wives' Tale, Chapman & Hall, 1908 . £750
ditto, Ernest Benn, 1927 (500 signed copies, 2 vols,
slipcase) £145
ditto, Hodder & Stoughton (U.S.), 1909. . . £35
The Statue (with Eden Philpotts), Cassell, 1908 £30
ditto, Moffat, Yard (U.S.), 1908 . . . . £30
The Glimpse: An Adventure of the Soul, Chapman &
Hall, 1909 . . . . £30
ditto, Appleton (U.S.), 1909 . . . . . £30
Clayhanger, Methuen, 1910 . . . . . £50
Helen with the High Hand, Chapman & Hall, 1910 .
. . . . £20
The Card, Methuen, 1911 . . . . . . £45

ditto, as *Dendry the Audacious*, Dutton (U.S.), 1911 .
. . . . £45
Hilda Lessways, Methuen, 1911 . . . . . £40
ditto, Dutton (U.S.), 1911 . . . . £25
The Regent, Methuen, 1913 . . . . . . £25
ditto, as *The Old Adam*, Doran (U.S.), 1913 . £25
The Price of Love, Methuen, 1914 . . . . £25
ditto, Harper (U.S.), 1914 . . . . £25
These Twain, Methuen, 1916 . . . . . £25
ditto, Doran (U.S.), 1915 . . . . £25
The Lion's Share, Cassell, 1916 . . . . . £20
ditto, Doran (U.S.), 1916 . . . . £20
The Pretty Lady, Cassell, 1918 . . . . . £20
ditto, Cassell, [1918] £20
The Roll Call, Hutchinson, 1918 . . . . . £15
Lilian, Cassell, 1922 . . . . £75/£15
Mr Prohack, Methuen, 1922 . . . . . £65/£15
ditto, Doran (U.S.), 1922 . . . . . . £65/£10
Riceyman Steps, Cassell, 1923 . . . . £75/£20
ditto, Doran (U.S.), 1923 . . . . . . £65/£10
The Clayhanger Family, Methuen, 1925 . £45/£15
ditto, Methuen, 1925 (200 signed copies) . . £75
Lord Raingo, Cassell, 1926 . . . . . £60/£15
ditto, Doran (U.S.), 1926 . . . . . . £60/£15
The Vanguard, Doran, 1927 . . . . . £50/£15
ditto, as *The Strange Vanguard*, Cassell, 1929 £50/£15
Accident, Doubleday (U.S.), 1928 . . . £50/£15
ditto, Cassell, 1929 . . . . £50/£15
Piccadilly, Readers Library Publishing Co., 1929 . .
. . . . £50/£15
Imperial Palace, Cassell, 1930 . . . . £50/£15
ditto, Cassell, 1930 (100 signed copies, 2 vols) . £175
Venus Rising from the Sea, Cassell, 1931 (350 numbered copies, in slipcase, signed by the artist McKnight Kauffer) £200
Dream of Destiny and *Venus Rising from the Sea*, Cassell, 1932 . . . . . . £45/£15
ditto, as *Stroke of Luck* and *Venus Rising from the Sea*, Doubleday, 1932 . . . . . £45/£15

Short Stories
The Loot of Cities, Rivers, 1904 . . . . . £400
ditto, Train (U.S.), 1972 . . . . £10/£5
The Grim Smile of the Five Towns, Chatto & Windus, 1908 . . . . £30
The Matador of the Five Towns, Methuen, 1912 £30
ditto, Doran (U.S.), [1912] £30
Elsie and the Child: A Tale of Riceyman Steps And Other Stories, Cassell, 1924 . . . £50/£15
ditto, Doran (U.S.), 1924 . . . . . . £50/£15
ditto, Cassell, 1929 (750 numbered copies, title story only, illustrated by McKnight Kauffer) . . £75
The Woman Who Stole Everything and Other Stories, Cassell, 1924 . . . . £50/£25
ditto, Doran (U.S.), [1927] . . . . . £50/£25
The Night Visitor and Other Stories, Cassell, 1931 .
. . . . £25/£10
ditto, Doubleday (U.S.), 1931 . . . . £25/£10

Plays
Polite Farces for the Drawing Room, Lamley, 1900 .
. . . . £100
ditto, Doran (U.S.), 1899 . . . . . . £30
Cupid and Commonsense, New Age Press, 1909 £20
ditto, Doran (U.S.), 1920 . . . . . . £20
What the Public Wants, Duckworth, 1909 . . £20
ditto, McClure (U.S.), 1910 . . . . . £20
The Honeymoon, Methuen, 1911 . . . . £20
Milestones (with Edward Knoblauch), Methuen, 1912 .
. . . . £20
The Great Adventure, Methuen, 1913 . . . £15
The Title, Chatto & Windus, 1918 . . . . £15
Judith, Chatto & Windus, 1919 . . . . £15
ditto, Doran U.S.), 1919 . . . . . . £15
Sacred and Profane Love, Chatto & Windus, 1919 £15
ditto, Doran (U.S.), [1920] £15
The Love Match, Chatto & Windus, 1922 . £45/£15
ditto, Doran U.S.), 1922 . . . . . £45/£15
Body and Soul, Chatto & Windus, 1922 . £45/£15
Don Juan de Marana, T. Werner Laurie, 1923 (1,000 signed copies) . . . . £75/£35
ditto, Doran (U.S.), 1923 . . . . . . £45/£15
The Bright Island, Golden Cockerel Press, 1924 (200 signed, numbered copies) £200
London Life (with Edward Knoblauch), Chatto & Windus, 1924 . . . . £65/£20
ditto, Doran U.S.), 1924 . . . . . . £65/£20
Flora, Rich & Cowan, 1933 . . . . . £40/£15
The Snake Charmer, Rich & Cowan, 1933 . £40/£15

Others
Journalism for Women: A Practical Guide, John Lane, 1896 . . . . £65
Fame and Fiction, Grant Richards, 1901 . . £50
How to Become an Author: A Practical Guide, C. Arthur Pearson, 1903 . . . . . . £30
The Truth About An Author, Constable, 1903 (anonymous) £20
ditto, Doran (U.S.), [1911] £20
The Reasonable Life, A. C. Fifield, 1907 . . £15
How to Live on 24 Hours a Day, New Age Press, 1908
. . . . £10
ditto, Doran (U.S.), 1910 . . . . . . £10
The Human Machine, New Age Press, 1908 . £10
Literary Taste: How To Form It, New Age Press, 1909
. . . . £40
The Feast of St. Friend, Hodder & Stoughton, 1911 .
. . . . £25
ditto, Doran (U.S.), 1911 . . . . . . £25
Your United States: Impressions of a First Visit, Harper (U.S.), 1912 . . . . £30
ditto, as *Those United States*, Secker, 1912 . . £30
Mental Efficiency, Doran (U.S.), 1911 . . . £10
ditto, Hodder & Stoughton, 1912 . . . . . £5
Paris Nights, Hodder & Stoughton, 1913 . . £25
ditto, Doran (U.S.), 1913 . . . . . . £20
The Plain Man and His Wife, Hodder & Stoughton, [1913] £10

ditto, Doran (U.S.), 1913 . . . . . . £10
From the Log of the Velsa, Century (U.S.), 1914 £20
ditto, Chatto & Windus, 1920 . . . . £30/£10
Friendship and Happiness, Hodder & Stoughton, 1914
. . . . £5
The Author's Craft, Hodder & Stoughton, 1914 £20
ditto, Doran (U.S.), 1914 . . . . . . £20
Over There, Methuen, 1915 . . . . . £60
ditto, Doran (U.S.), 1915 . . . . . . £45
Marriage: The Plain Man and His Wife, Hodder &
Stoughton, 1916 . . . . £5
Books and Persons, Chatto & Windus, 1917 . £15
Self and Self Management, Hodder & Stoughton,
1918 . . . . £5
ditto, Doran (U.S.), [1918] £5
Married Life: The Plain Man and His Wife, Hodder
& Stoughton, 1921 . . . . £10/£5
How to Make the Best of Life, Hodder & Stoughton,
1923 . . . . £10/£5
Mediterranean Scenes, Cassell, 1928 (1,000 numbered
copies) £25

E.F. BENSON
(b.1867 d.1940)

Benson's first book, *Dodo* was a huge success.
Known for his light society novels, especially the
'Mapp and Lucia' series. Of his supernatural fiction
The Room in the Tower is the most highly regarded.

Novels

Dodo: A Detail of Today, Methuen, 1893 (2 vols) £600
ditto, Appleton (U.S.), 1893 . . . . . £400
The Rubicon, Methuen, 1894 (2 vols) . . . £250
The Judgement Books, Osgood McIlvaine, 1895 £150
Limitations, Innes, 1896 . . . . . . £60
ditto, Harpers (U.S.), 1896 . . . . . £35
The Babe, B.A., Putnams (U.S.), 1896 . . . £60
ditto, Putnams (U.S.), 1897 . . . . . £60
The Vintage, Methuen, 1898 . . . . . £65
The Money Market, Arrowsmith, 1898 . . . £65
The Capsina, Methuen, 1899. . . . . £100
ditto, Harpers (U.S.), 1899 . . . . . £75
Mammon and Co., Heinemann, 1899 . . . £60
The Princess Sophia, Heinemann, 1900 . . £65
ditto, Harpers (U.S.), 1900 . . . . . £35
The Luck of the Vails, Heinemann, 1901 . £75
Scarlet and Hyssop, Heinemann, 1902 . . £60
ditto, Appleton (U.S.), 1902 . . . . . £30
The Book of Months, Heinemann, 1903 . . £60
ditto, Harper & Bros (U.S.), 1903 . . . . £30
An Act in a Backwater, Heinemann, 1903 . . £100
ditto, Appleton (U.S.), 1903 . . . . . £75
The Valkyries, Dean, 1903 . . . . . £100
The Relentless City, Heinemann, 1903 . . £60
ditto, Harper & Bros (U.S.), 1903 . . . . £30
The Challoners, Heinemann, 1904 . . . . £45

ditto, Lippincott (U.S.), 1904. . . . . . £25
The Image in the Sand, Heinemann, 1905 . . £60
ditto, Lippincott (U.S.), 1905. . . . . . £30
The Angel of Pain, Lippincott (U.S.), 1905. . £60
ditto, Heinemann, 1906 . . . . . . £30
Paul, Heinemann, 1906 . . . . . . £60
ditto, Lippincott (U.S.), 1906. . . . . . £30
The House of Defense, Macleod & Allen, 1906 £50
ditto, Authors and Newspapers Association (U.S.),
1906 . . . . £40
Sheaves, Stanley Paul, 1907 . . . . . £50
ditto, Doubleday (U.S.), 1907 . . . . . £30
The Blotting Book, Heinemann, 1908 . . . £50
ditto, Doubleday (U.S.), 1908 . . . . . £30
The Climber, Heinemann, 1908 . . . . £45
ditto, Doubleday (U.S.), 1909 . . . . . £30
A Reaping, Heinemann, 1909 . . . . . £50
Daisy's Aunt, Nelson, 1910 . . . . . £50
The Osbornes, Smith Elder, 1910 . . . . £45
Margery, Doubleday (U.S.), 1910 . . . . £45
ditto, as *Juggernaut*, Heinemann, 1911 . . . £35
Account Rendered, Heinemann, 1911 . . . £40
ditto, Doubleday (U.S.), 1911 . . . . . £30
Mrs Ames, Hodder & Stoughton, 1912 . . £40
The Weaker Vessel, Heinemann, 1913 . . . £40
Thorley Weir, Heinemann, 1913. . . . . £40
Dodo's Daughter: A Sequel to Dodo, Century Co.
(U.S.), 1913 . . . . £75
ditto, as *Dodo the Second*, Hodder & Stoughton, 1914
. . . . £75
Arundel, Unwin, 1914 . . . . . . £40
ditto, Doran (U.S.), [1915] £35
The Oakleyites, Hodder & Stoughton, 1915 . £40
David Blaize, Hodder & Stoughton, 1916 . . £40
ditto, Doran (U.S.), 1916 . . . . . . £35
Mike, Cassell, 1916 . . . . £45
The Freaks of Mayfair, Foulis, 1916 . . . £65
ditto, Doran (U.S.), [1918] £40
Mr Teddy, Unwin, 1917 . . . . . . £40
An Autumn Sowing, Collins, 1917 . . . . £40
ditto, Doran (U.S.), 1918 . . . . . . £30
David Blaize and the Blue Door, Hodder & Stoughton,
1918 . . . . £50
ditto, Putnam (U.S.), 1918 . . . . . £40
Up and Down, Hutchinson, 1918 . . . . £40
ditto, Doran (U.S.), 1918 . . . . . . £30
Across the Stream, Murray, 1919 . . . . £40
ditto, Doran (U.S.), 1919 . . . . . . £35
Robin Linnet, Hutchinson, 1919. . . . . £40
Queen Lucia, Hutchinson, 1920 . . . . £300/£100
ditto, Doran (U.S.), 1920 . . . . . £250/£45
Dodo Wonders, Hutchinson, 1921 . . . £200/£45
ditto, Doran (U.S.), [1921] . . . . . £200/£45
Lovers and Friends, Unwin, 1921 . . . £100/£35
Miss Mapp, Hutchinson, 1922 . . . . £275/£100
Peter, Cassell, 1922 . . . . . . £50/£15
ditto, Doran (U.S.), 1922 . . . . . . £45/£15
Colin: A Novel, Hutchinson, [1923] . . . £50/£15
ditto, Doran (U.S.), 1923 . . . . . . £45/£15

David of King's, Hodder & Stoughton, 1924   £50/£15
Alan, Unwin, 1924 . . . . £50/£15
ditto, Doran (U.S.), 1925 . . . . . £45/£15
Colin II, Hutchinson, [1925] . . . . . £50/£15
ditto, Doran (U.S.), 1925 . . . . . £45/£15
Rex, Hodder & Stoughton, 1925 . . . . £50/£15
ditto, Doran (U.S.), 1925 . . . . . . £45/£15
Mezzanine, Cassell, 1926 . . . . . . £50/£15
Pharisees and Publicans, Hutchinson, 1926 £30/£10
Lucia in London, Hutchinson, 1927 . . .£275/£100
ditto, Doubleday (U.S.), 1928 . . . . £250/£65
Paying Guests, Hutchinson, 1929 . . . £50/£15
ditto, Doubleday (U.S.), 1929 . . . . £50/£15
The Inheritor, Hutchinson, [1930] . . . £65/£25
ditto, Doubleday (U.S.), 1930 . . . . £65/£25
Mapp & Lucia, Hodder & Stoughton, 1931. £250/£75
ditto, Doran (U.S.), 1931 . . . . . . £250/£45
Secret Lives, Hodder & Stoughton, 1932 . £45/£15
ditto, Doubleday (U.S.), 1932 . . . . £45/£15
Travail of Gold, Hodder & Stoughton, 1933 £35/£15
ditto, Doubleday (U.S.), 1933 . . . . £35/£15
Raven's Brood, Barker, 1934 . . . . £45/£15
ditto, Doran (U.S.), 1934 . . . . . £35/£15
Lucia's Progress, Hodder & Stoughton, 1935 . . .
. . . . £250/£75
All About Lucia, Doubleday (U.S.), 1936 (the first four
Lucia novels in one vol.) . . . . . £65/£25
Old London, Appleton-Century (U.S.), 1937 (4 vols in
d/ws, slipcase) . . . . £100/£65
Trouble for Lucia, Hodder & Stoughton, 1939 . . .
. . . . £200/£45
ditto, Doran (U.S.), 1939 . . . . . £100/£35

Short Stories
Six Common Things, Osgood McIlvaine, 1893   £100
A Double Overture, C.H. Sergel (U.S.), 1894   £100
The Countess of Lowndes Square and Other Stories,
Cassell, 1920 . . . .£350/£125
The Male Impersonator, Elkin Mathews & Marrot,
1929 (530 signed copies) . . . . £65/£50
Desirable Residences, O.U.P., 1991 . . . .£15/£5
Fine Feathers, O.U.P., 1994 . . . . . .£15/£5

Ghost Stories
The Room in the Tower, Mills & Boon, [1912]   £300
ditto, Knopf (U.S.), 1929 . . . . . . £200/£75
Visible and Invisible, Hutchinson, 1923. .£500/£125
ditto, Doran (U.S.), 1924 . . . . . .£500/£125
'And the Dead Spake' & The Horror Horn, Doran
(U.S.), 1923 . . . . £300/£75
Expiation & Naboth's Vineyard, Doran (U.S.), 1924 .
. . . . £300/£75
The Face, Doran (U.S.), 1924 . . . .£350/£100
The Temple, Doran (U.S.), 1925 . . . .£350/£100
A Tale of an Empty House & Bagnell Terrace, Doran
(U.S.), 1925 . . . .£350/£100
ditto, as *The Tale of an Empty House*, Black Swan/
Corgi, 1985 (wraps) £5

ditto, Black Swan/Corgi, 1986 (limited edition
hardback) £25
Spook Stories, Hutchinson, [1928] . . .£600/£200
The Step, H.V. Marrot, 1930 . . . . . £200/£75
More Spook Stories, Hutchinson, [1934] .£500/£125
The Horror Horn, Panther, 1974 (wraps) . . . £5
The Flint Knife, Equation, 1988 (wraps) . . £15
The Terror by Night, Ash-Tree Press, 1998 (600
copies) . . . . £30/£10
The Passenger, Ash-Tree Press, 1999 (600 copies) .
. . . . £30/£10
Mrs Amworth, Ash-Tree Press, 2001 (600 copies) . .
. . . . £30/£10

Collaborations with Eustace Miles
Daily Training, Hurst & Blackett, 1902 . . . £45
Cricket of Abel, Hirst and Shrewsbury, Hurst &
Blackett, 1903 . . . . £75
ditto, Dutton (U.S.), 1903 . . . . . . £65
The Mad Annual, Grant Richards, 1903 . . £45
A Book of Golf, Hurst Blackett, 1903 . . . £75
Diversions Day by Day, Hurst & Blackett, 1905   £45

Non Fiction
Sketches from Marlborough, 1888 (anonymous) £125
English Figure-Skating, Bell, 1908 . . . . £200
Winter Sports in Switzerland, George Allen, 1913. .
. . . . £200
Skating Calls, Bell, 1909 . . . . . . £65
Deutschland Uber Allah, Hodder & Stoughton, 1917 .
. . . . £20
Crescent and Iron Cross, Hodder & Stoughton, 1918 .
. . . . £35
ditto, Doran (U.S.), [1918] £35
The White Eagle of Poland, Hodder & Stoughton,
1918 . . . . £30
ditto, Doran (U.S.), 1919 . . . . . . £25
Poland and Mittel-Europa, Hodder & Stoughton, 1918
. . . . £15
The Social Value of Temperance, True Temperance
Association, 1919 . . . . £15
Our Family Affairs, 1867-1896, Cassell, 1920 £35/£15
ditto, Doran (U.S.), 1921 . . . . . . £35/£15
Mother, Hodder & Stoughton, 1925 . . . £35/£15
ditto, Doran (U.S.), 1925 . . . . . . £35/£15
Sir Frances Drake, John Lane/Bodley Head, 1927. .
. . . . £35/£15
ditto, Harper (U.S.), 1927. . . . . . £30/£10
The Life of Alcibiades, Ernest Benn, 1928 . £45/£15
ditto, Appleton (U.S.), 1929 . . . . . £35/£15
Ferdinand Magellan, John Lane/Bodley Head, 1929 .
. . . . £35/£15
ditto, Harper (U.S.), 1930. . . . . . £35/£15
*Henry James: Letters to A.C. Benson/Auguste
Monod*, Elkin Mathews & Marrot, 1930 (1,050
numbered copies) £30
As We Were: A Victorian Peepshow, Longmans, 1930
. . . . £35/£15

As We Are: A Modern Revue, Longmans, 1932 . . .
. . . . £30/£15
Charlotte Brontë, Longmans, 1932 . . . £30/£15
ditto, Longmans (U.S.), 1932. . . . . £35/£15
King Edward VII, Longmans, 1933 . . . £35/£15
ditto, Longmans (U.S.), 1933. . . . . £35/£15
The Outbreak of War, Peter Davies, 1933 . £65/£20
ditto, Putnams (U.S.), 1934 . . . . . £50/£15
Queen Victoria, Longmans (U.S.), 1935 . £30/£10
ditto, Longmans, 1935 . . . . . . £30/£10
The Kaiser and English Relations, Longmans, 1934 .
. . . . £25/£10
Queen Victoria's Daughters, Appleton-Century (U.S.),
1938 . . . . £25/£10
ditto, as *Daughters of Queen Victoria*, Cassell, 1939 .
. . . . £25/£10
Final Edition: An Informal Autobiography, Longmans, 1940 . . . . £30/£15
ditto, Appleton-Century (U.S.), 1940 . . £30/£15

Others
Bensoniana: Maxims by E.F. Benson, Siegle Hill
Watteau, 1912 . . . . £65
ditto, A.L. Humphreys, 1912 . . . . . £65
Thoughts from E.F. Benson, Harrap, 1913 . . £35
Thoughts from E.F. Benson, Holden & Hardingham,
1916 (leather-bound) £75
ditto, Holden & Hardingham, 1916 (cloth bound) £30

E.C. BENTLEY
(b.1875 d.1956)

Bentley's oeuvre is very small but his first book,
Trent's Last Case, is an acknowledged classic of
detective fiction.

Novels
Trent's Last Case, Nelson, [1913] £150
ditto, as *The Woman in Black*, Century (U.S.), 1913 .
. . . . £150
Trent's Own Case, Constable, 1936 (with H. Warner
Allen) . . . . £450/£25
ditto, Knopf (U.S.), 1936 . . . . . . £150/£25
Elephant's Work, Hodder & Stoughton, 1950 £40/£10
ditto, Knopf (U.S.), 1950 . . . . £20/£5
ditto, as *The Chill*, Dell (U.S.), 1953 (wraps) . £10

Short Stories
Trent Intervenes, Nelson, 1938 . . . . £250/£35
ditto, Knopf (U.S.), 1938 . . . . . . £150/£25

LORD BERNERS
(b.1883 d.1950)

Millionaire, composer, author and eccentric.

Fiction
The Camel, Constable, 1936 . . . . . £100/£35
ditto, in *Collected Tales and Fantasies*, Turtle Point
Press (U.S.), 1999 (wraps) £10
The Girls of Radcliff Hall, privately published, 1937
(wraps) £80
Far from the Madding War, Constable, 1941 £75/£25
Count Omega, Constable, 1941 . . . . £75/£35
Percy Wallingford and Mr Pidger, Blackwell, 1941
(wraps) £150
The Romance of a Nose, Constable, 1941 . £65/£25

Autobiography
First Childhood, Constable, 1934 . . . £75/£45
ditto, Farrar & Reinhart (U.S.), 1934 . . £45/£15
A Distant Prospect, Constable, 1945 . . £45/£10

Music
Intermezzo from "The Triumph of Neptune", J. &
W. Chester, Ltd, 1927 (quarto, wraps) . . . £75
Three Songs in the German Manner, J. & W. Chester,
Ltd, [n.d.] (quarto, wraps) £95
Luna Park-Fantastic Ballet in One Act, J. & W.
Chester, Ltd, [n.d., c.1930] (quarto, wraps) . £150
Trois Chansons, J. & W. Chester, Ltd, 1920 (quarto,
wraps). £85
Suite from The Triumph of Neptune, J. & W. Chester,
Ltd, [n.d.] (quarto, wraps) £50

JOHN BETJEMAN
(b.1906 d.1984)

As a broadcasting personality, commenting on the
superficial and the middle class, Betjeman somehow
missed serious recognition for his verse during his
lifetime, despite becoming Poet Laureate in 1972.

Poetry
Mount Zion or In Touch with the Infinite, James
Press, [1931] (blue and gold patterned boards, no
d/w) £750
ditto, James Press, [1931] (striped boards, no d/w) . .
. . . . £400
Continual Dew, Murray, 1937 . . . . £200/£65
Sir John Piers by 'Epsilon', Mullingar (Ireland), 1938
(50 copies, wraps) £1,250
Old Lights for New Chancels, Murray, 1940 £125/£25
ditto, Murray, 1940 (signed, printed on blue laid paper)
. . . . £500
New Bats in Old Belfries, Murray, 1945 . £100/£25
ditto, Murray, 1945 (50 signed copies) . . . £450

Slick But Not Streamlined, Doubleday (U.S.), 1947
(ed. W.H. Auden) . . . . £100/£40
Selected Poems, Murray, 1948 . . . . £45/£15
ditto, Murray, 1948 (18 signed copies) . . . £500
Verses Turned in Aid of Public Subscription Toward the Restoration of the Church of St Katherine, Chislehampton, Oxon, St Katherine's Church, 1952
(wraps) £125
A Few Late Chrysanthemums, Murray, 1954 £75/£20
ditto, Murray, 1954 (50 signed copies) . . . £350
Poems in the Porch, S.P.C.K., 1954 (wraps) . £35
John Betjeman: A Selection, Edward Hulton Pocket Poets, 1958 (wraps) £10
Collected Poems, Murray, 1958 . . . . £40/£15
ditto, Murray, 1958 (100 signed copies, slipcase) £300
ditto, Houghton Mifflin (U.S.), 1959 . . £35/£15
Lament for Moira McCavendish, Browne Lismore [n.d.] (20 copies, wraps). £300
Summoned by Bells, Murray, 1960 . . . £30/£10
ditto, Murray, 1960 (125 signed, numbered copies) .
. . . . £450
ditto, Houghton Mifflin (U.S.), 1960 . . £25/£10
A Ring of Bells, Murray, 1962 . . . . £60/£25
ditto, Houghton Mifflin (U.S.), 1963 . . £45/£20
High and Low, Murray, 1966 . . . . £30/£10
ditto, Murray, 1966 (100 signed copies). . . £350
ditto, Houghton Mifflin (U.S.), 1967 . . £25/£10
Six Betjeman Songs, Duckworth, 1967 (wraps) £35
A Wembley Lad and The Crem, Poem of the Month Club, 1971 (signed broadsheet). £125
A Nip in the Air, Murray, 1974 . . . £25/£10
ditto, Murray, 1974 (175 signed copies). . . £225
ditto, Norton (U.S.), [1974] . . . . . £20/£10
Betjeman in Miniature, Selected Poems, Gleniffer Press, 1976 (250 copies). £65
The Best of Betjeman, Murray, 1978 . . . £20/£5
Ode on the Marriage of H.R.H. Prince Charles to Lady Diana Spencer, Warren Editions, 1981 (125 signed copies, broadsheet) £200
Five Betjeman Songs, Weinberger, 1980 (wraps) £20
Church Poems, Murray, 1981 (first issue, withdrawn, with text of 'Bristol and Clifton' poem incomplete) .
. . . . £125/£100
ditto, Murray, 1981 (second issue, poem complete) .
. . . . £25/£10
ditto, Murray, 1981 (100 copies, signed by the author and John Piper) . . . . £350/£275
Uncollected Poems, Murray, 1982 . . . £10/£5
ditto, Murray, 1982 (100 signed copies). . . £300
St Mary-le-Strand, St Mary-le-Strand, 1981 (signed broadsheet) £75
Betjeman's Cornwall, Murray, 1984 . . £35/£10
Ah Middlesex, Warren, 1984 (250 copies) . . £75

Prose
Ghastly Good Taste, Chapman & Hall, 1933 . .
. . . . £400/£175
ditto, Chapman & Hall, 1933 (200 signed copies in a slipcase) £400

ditto, Anthony Blond, 1970 . . . . . . £15/£5
ditto, Anthony Blond, 1970 (200 signed copies, slipcase) . . . . £100/£65
ditto, St. Martin's Press (U.S.), 1971. . . . £10
Cornwall Illustrated in a series of views, Architectural Press, 1934 (spiral-bound) £75
Devon, Architectural Press, 1936 (spiral-bound) £65
An Oxford University Chest, John Miles, 1938. . .
. . . . £175/£65
A Handbook on Paint, with Hugh Casson, Silicate Paint Co., 1939 . . . . £450
Antiquarian Prejudice, Hogarth Sixpenny Pamphlets No. 3, 1939 (card wraps) £45
Vintage London, Collins, 1942 . . . . £50/£20
English Cities and Small Towns, Britain in Pictures/ Collins, 1943 . . . . £20/£5
John Piper, Penguin Modern Painters, 1944 (wraps) .
. . . . £15
Murray's Buckinghamshire Architectural Guide, Murray, 1949 (edited with John Piper). . £30/£10
Murray's Berkshire Architectural Guide, Murray, 1949 (edited with John Piper) . . . £30/£10
Shropshire, Faber Shell Guide, 1951 . . £25/£10
The English Scene, C.U.P./N.B.L., 1951 (wraps) £15
First and Last Loves, Murray, 1952 . . . £100/£40
The English Town in the Last Hundred Years, C.U.P., 1956 (Rede Lecture, wraps). £25
Collins Guide to English Parish Churches, Collins, 1958 . . . . £35/£10
Ground Plan to Skyline (pseud. 'Richard M. Farran'), Newman Neame, 1960 (wraps). £25
English Churches, with Basil Clarke, Studio Vista, 1964 . . . . £25/£10
The City of London Churches, Pitkin Pictorial, 1965 (wraps) £5
Victorian and Edwardian London from Old Photographs, Batsford, 1969 . . . . . £15/£5
ditto, Viking (U.S.), 1969. . . . . . . £10
Ten Wren Churches, Editions Elector, 1970 (100 copies, folder) £150
Victorian and Edwardian Oxford from Old Photographs, with David Vaisey, Batsford, 1971. .
. . . . £15/£5
Victorian and Edwardian Brighton from Old Photographs, with J. S. Gray, Batsford, 1972 . £15/£5
London's Historic Railway Stations, Murray, 1972 .
. . . . £25/£5
A Pictorial History of English Architecture, Murray, 1972 . . . . £20/£5
ditto, Murray, 1972 (100 signed copies, slipcase) . .
. . . . £225/£200
ditto, Macmillan (U.S.), 1972 . . . . £10/£5
West Country Churches, Society of Saints Peter & Paul, 1973 (wraps) £20
Victorian and Edwardian Cornwall from Old Photographs, with A. L. Rowse, Batsford, 1974 . .
. . . . £15/£5
Plea for Holy Trinity Church, Sloane Street, Church Literature Association, 1974 . . . . . £10

Souvenir of Metroland, Warren Editions, 1977 (220 copies) £200
Archie and the Strict Baptists, Murray, 1977 £35/£15
ditto, Lippincott (U.S.), 1978 . . . . . £20/£10

ALGERNON BLACKWOOD
(b.1869 d.1951)

An important British writer of supernatural fiction, Blackwood mined all aspects of the genre, and towards the end of his life became something of a radio and television personality.

Novels

Jimbo: A Fantasy, Macmillan, 1909 . . . £75
ditto, Macmillan (U.S.), 1909 . . . . . £65
The Education of Uncle Paul, Macmillan, 1909 £65
ditto, Paget (U.S.), 1909 (abridged, wraps) . . £75
ditto, Holt (U.S.), 1914 . . . . £30
The Human Chord, Macmillan, 1910 . . . £50
The Centaur, Macmillan, 1911 . . . . . £65
A Prisoner in Fairyland, Macmillan, 1913 . . £35
ditto, Macmillan (U.S.), 1913 . . . . . £35
The Extra Day, Macmillan, 1915 . . . . £35
ditto, Macmillan (U.S.), 1915 . . . . . £35
Julius Levallon, Cassell, 1916 . . . . . £45
ditto, Dutton (U.S.), 1916 . . . . . . £40
The Wave: An Egyptian Aftermath, Macmillan, 1916.
. . . . £45
ditto, Dutton (U.S.), 1916. . . . . . . £40
The Promise of Air, Macmillan, 1918 . . . £30
ditto, Dutton (U.S.), 1918. . . . . . . £25
The Garden of Survival, Macmillan, 1918 . . £30
ditto, Dutton (U.S.), 1918. . . . . . . £25
The Bright Messenger, Cassell, 1921 . . £150/£45
ditto, Dutton (U.S.), 1922. . . . . . £150/£45

Short Story Collections

The Empty House and Other Ghost Stories, Nash, 1906 . . . . £250
ditto, Vaughan (U.S.), 1915 (limited to 500 copies) .
. . . . £100
The Listener and Other Stories, Nash, 1907 . £125
ditto, Vaughan & Gomme (U.S.), 1914 (limited to 500 copies) £100
John Silence, Physician Extraordinary, Nash, 1908 .
. . . . £250
ditto, John W. Luce (U.S.), 1909 . . . . £200
The Lost Valley and Other Stories, Nash, 1910 £300
ditto, Vaughan & Gomme (U.S.), 1914 (limited to 500 copies) . . . . £100/£50
Pan's Garden, A Volume of Nature Stories, Macmillan, 1912 . . . . £75
Ten Minute Stories, Murray, 1914 . . . £75
ditto, Dutton (U.S.), 1914. . . . . . . £75
Incredible Adventures, Macmillan, 1914 . . £75
ditto, Macmillan (U.S.), 1914 . . . . . £65

Day and Night Stories, Cassell, 1917 . . . £125
ditto, Dutton (U.S.), 1917. . . . . . . £65
The Wolves of God, Cassell, 1921 (with Wilfrid Wilson) . . . . £400/£175
ditto, Dutton (U.S.), 1921. . . . . . £350/£100
Tongues of Fire and Other Sketches, Jenkins, 1924 .
. . . . £400/£100
ditto, Dutton (U.S.), 1925. . . . . . £350/£75
Ancient Sorceries and Other Tales, Collins, [1927] .
. . . . £200/£50
The Dance of Death and Other Tales, Jenkins, 1927 .
. . . . £150/£65
ditto, Dial Press (U.S.), 1928 . . . . £75/£25
Strange Stories, Heinemann, 1929 . . . £45/£20
ditto, as *The Best Supernatural Tales of Algernon Blackwood*, Causeway Books (U.S.), 1973 (abridged facsimile of above edition) . . . . . £25/£10
Full Circle, Mathews & Marrot, 1929 (530 signed, numbered copies) . . . . £100/£50
Short Stories of Today and Yesterday, Harrap & Co, 1930 . . . . £35/£20
The Willows and Other Queer Tales, Collins, [1932] .
. . . . £150/£45
Shocks, Grayson, 1935 . . . . . . £125/£25
ditto, Dutton (U.S.), 1936. . . . . . £125/£25
The Tales of Algernon Blackwood, Secker, 1938 . .
. . . . £45/£15
ditto, Dutton (U.S.), 1939. . . . . . £45/£15
Selected Tales of Algernon Blackwood, Penguin, 1942 (wraps) £15
Selected Short Stories of Algernon Blackwood, Armed Services Editions (U.S.), [1942] (wraps) . . £20
The Doll and One Other, Arkham House (U.S.), 1946 .
. . . . £45/£20
Tales of the Uncanny and Supernatural, Nevill, 1949 .
. . . . £15/£5
ditto, Castle (U.S.), 1974 . . . . . . £15/£5
In the Realm of Terror, Pantheon Books (U.S.), 1957.
. . . . £15/£5
Selected Tales of Algernon Blackwood, John Baker, 1964 . . . . £15/£5
ditto, Dutton (U.S.), 1965. . . . . . . £15/£5
Tales of the Mysterious and Macabre, Spring Books, 1967 . . . . £10/£5
ditto, Castle (U.S.), 1974 . . . . . . £10/£5
Ancient Sorceries and Other Stories, Penguin, 1968 (wraps) £10
Best Ghost Stories of Algernon Blackwood, Dover (U.S.), 1973 (wraps). £10

Children's Books

Sambo and Snitch, Blackwell, 1927. . . £100/£75
ditto, Appleton (U.S.), 1927 . . . . £85/£65
Mr Cupboard, Blackwell, 1928 . . . £100/£75
Dudley and Gilderoy: A Nonsense, Benn, 1929 . .
. . . . £75/£25
ditto, Dutton (U.S.), 1929. . . . . . £45/£20
By Underground, Blackwell, 1930 . . . £100/£65
The Parrot and the Cat, Blackwell, 1931 . £100/£65

The Italian Conjuror, Blackwell, 1932 . . £100/£65
Maria (Of England) In the Rain, Blackwell, 1933 . .
. . . . £100/£65
Sergeant Poppett and Policeman James, Blackwell,
1934 . . . . £100/£65
The Fruit Stoners, Grayson, [1934] . . . £75/£25
ditto, Dutton (U.S.), 1935 . . . . . £65/£20
ditto, Blackwell, 1935 (extract) . . . . £65/£40
How the Circus Came to Tea, Blackwell, 1936 . .
. . . . £100/£65
The Adventures of Dudley and Gilderoy, Dutton
(U.S.), 1941 (adapted by Marion B. Cottren) £45/£15
ditto, Faber, 1941 . . . . £45/£15

Plays
Karma: A Reincarnation Play, Macmillan, 1918 (with
Violet Pearn) £50
ditto, Dutton (U.S.), 1918 . . . . . . £45
Through the Crack, French, 1925 (with Violet Pearn,
wraps) £25

Other Works
Episodes Before Thirty, Cassell, 1923 . . £200/£35
ditto, Dutton (U.S.), 1924 . . . . . £200/£35
ditto, as *Adventures Before Thirty*, Cape, 1934 . .
. . . . £40/£15

NICHOLAS BLAKE
see C. Day Lewis

ROBERT BLOCH
(b.1917 d.1994)

Author of horror and crime stories, often underlain by
a black humour. *Psycho* became the best-known of
his novels following Hitchcock's classic film.

Novels
The Scarf, Dial Press (U.S.), 1947 . . . £175/£45
ditto, New English Library, 1972 (wraps) . . £10
The Kidnapper, Lion (U.S.), 1954 (wraps) . £125
Spiderweb, Ace (U.S.), 1954 (Ace Double with David
Alexander's *The Corpse in My Bed* wraps) . £25
The Will to Kill, Ace (U.S.), 1954 (wraps) . £25
Shooting Star, Ace (U.S.), 1958 (Ace Double bound
with Bloch's *Terror In The Night And Other Stories*,
wraps) £25
Psycho, Simon & Schuster (U.S.), 1959 . £1,000/£250
ditto, Robert Hale, 1960 . . . . . £450/£100
The Dead Beat, Simon & Schuster (U.S.), 1960 . .
. . . . £75/£15
ditto, Robert Hale, 1971 . . . . . £75/£15
Firebug, Regency (U.S.), 1961 (wraps) . . £20
ditto, Corgi, 1977 (wraps). £10
The Couch, Fawcett (U.S.), 1962 (wraps) . £25
Terror, Belmont (U.S.), 1962 (wraps) . . £15

ditto, Corgi, 1964 (wraps). £10
The Star Stalker, Pyramid (U.S.), 1968 (wraps) £35
The Todd Dossier, Delacorte (U.S.), 1969 (pseud.
'Collier Young') . . . . £50/£10
ditto, Macmillan, 1969 (pseud. 'Collier Young') . .
. . . . £25/£10
It's All In Your Mind, Curtis (U.S.), 1971 (wraps) £10
Sneak Preview, Paperback Library (U.S.), 1971
(wraps) £10
Night World, Simon & Schuster (U.S.), 1972 £35/£15
ditto, Robert Hale, 1974 . . . . . . £30/£10
American Gothic, Simon & Schuster (U.S.), 1974 . .
. . . . £30/£10
ditto, W. H. Allen, 1975 . . . . . . £20/£5
Strange Eons, Whispers Press (U.S.), 1978 [1979]. .
. . . . £20/£5
ditto, Whispers Press (U.S.), 1978 [1979] (300 signed
copies, slipcase) . . . . £50/£35
There is a Serpent in Eden, Zebra Books, 1979
(wraps) £10
Psycho II, Warner Books (U.S.), 1982 (wraps) . £5
ditto, Whispers Press (U.S.), 1982 . . £20/£10
ditto, Whispers Press (U.S.), 1982 (750 signed,
numbered copies, slipcase) . . . . £75/£65
ditto, Whispers Press (U.S.), 1982 (26 signed, lettered
copies, d/w and slipcase) . . . . . £250/£200
ditto, Corgi, 1983 (wraps). £5
Twilight Zone - The Movie, Warner Books (U.S.),
1983 (wraps) £5
ditto, Transworld, 1983 (wraps) £5
Night of the Ripper, Robert Hale, 1984 . . £50/£10
ditto, Doubleday (U.S.), 1984 . . . . £50/£10
Unholy Trinity, Scream Press, 1986 . . £25/£10
ditto, Scream Press (U.S.), 1986 (250 signed,
numbered copies, slipcase) . . . . £75/£50
Lori, Tor (U.S.), 1989. . . . . . . £20/£5
Screams, Underwood/Miller, 1989 . . £25/£10
ditto, Underwood/Miller, 1989 (300 signed copies,
slipcase) . . . . £75/£45
Psycho III: The Psycho House, Tor (U.S.), 1990 . .
. . . . £20/£5
ditto, Robert Hale, 1995 . . . . . . £20/£5
The Jekyll Legacy, Tor (U.S.), 1990. . . £10/£5

Short Stories
Sea Kissed, Utopian Publications, [1945] (first issue
printed in Great Britain, wraps). . . . £750
ditto, Utopian Publications, [1945] (second issue
printed in Eire, wraps) £350
The Opener of the Way, Arkham House (U.S.), 1945 .
. . . . £350/£100
ditto, Neville Spearman, 1974 . . . . £45/£10
Terror in the Night, Ace (U.S.), 1958 (wraps) . £25
Pleasant Dreams, Arkham House (U.S.), 1960 . . .
. . . . £75/£20
ditto, Whiting & Wheaton, 1967 . . . . £45/£15
Blood Runs Cold, Simon & Schuster (U.S.), 1961 . .
. . . . £75/£10
ditto, Robert Hale, 1963 . . . . . . £50/£10
Nightmares, Belmont (U.S.), 1961 (wraps) . . £10

Yours Truly, Jack the Ripper, Belmont (U.S.), [1962] (wraps) £10
ditto, as *The House of the Hatchet*, Tandem, 1965 (wraps) £5
Atoms and Evil, Fawcett (U.S.), 1962 (wraps) . £10
ditto, Frederick Muller, 1963 (wraps) £5
ditto, Hale, 1976 (hardback) . . . . £35/£10
More Nightmares, Belmont (U.S.), [1962] (wraps) £10
Horror-7, Belmont (U.S.), 1963 (wraps) . . £10
ditto, Four Square, 1965 (wraps) £5
Bogey Men: Ten Tales, Pyramid Books (U.S.), 1963 (wraps) £10
Tales in a Jugular Vein, Pyramid Books (U.S.), 1965 (wraps) £10
ditto, Sphere, 1970 (wraps) £5
The Skull of the Marquis de Sade, Pyramid Books (U.S.), 1965 (wraps) £25
ditto, Robert Hale, 1975 . . . . £75/£20
Chamber of Horrors, Award (U.S.), 1966 (wraps) . £5
ditto, Corgi, 1977 (wraps) £5
The Living Demons, Belmont (U.S.), 1967 (wraps) £5
ditto, Sphere, 1970 (wraps) £5
Dragons and Nightmares, Mirage Press (U.S.), 1968 (1,000 numbered copies) . . . . £40/£15
Ladies' Day/This Crowded Earth, Belmont (U.S.), 1968 (wraps) £15
Bloch and Bradbury, Tower (U.S.), 1969 (wraps) . £5
ditto, Sphere, 1970 (wraps) £5
Fear Today, Gone Tomorrow, Award (U.S.), 1971 (wraps) £5
Bloch & Bradbury: Whispers From Beyond, Peacock Press (U.S.), 1972 (wraps) £10
The King of Terrors, Mysterious Press (U.S.), 1977 (250 signed copies, slipcase and d/w) . £65/£40
ditto, Mysterious Press (U.S.), 1977 . . . £25/£10
ditto, Robert Hale, 1978 . . . . . £25/£5
Cold Chills, Doubleday (U.S.), 1977 . . £20/£10
ditto, Robert Hale, 1978 . . . . . . £20/£5
The Best of Robert Bloch, Ballantine (U.S.), 1977 (wraps) £5
Out of the Mouths of Graves, Mysterious Press (U.S.), 1978 . . . . £20/£5
ditto, Mysterious Press (U.S.), 1978 (26 signed, lettered copies, slipcase) . . . . £125/£90
ditto, Mysterious Press (U.S.), 1978 (250 signed, numbered copies, slipcase) . . . . £75/£40
Such Stuff As Screams Are Made Of, Ballantine (U.S.), 1978 (wraps) £5
Mysteries Of The Worm, Zebra Books (U.S.), 1981 (wraps) £5
Lost in Time and Space With Lefty Feep, Creatures at Large Press (U.S.), 1987 (wraps) . . . £10
ditto, Creatures at Large Press (U.S.), 1987 (250 signed copies in d/w and slipcase) . . . . £50/£25
The Selected Stories of Robert Bloch, Underwood/ Muller (U.S.), 1987 (3 vols, 500 copies, slipcase, no d/ws) . . . . £20 each, £75 the set

ditto, Underwood/Muller (U.S.), 1987 (11 signed, numbered, leather-bound sets, 3 vols, slipcase, no d/ws) £600
Midnight Pleasures, Doubleday (U.S.), 1987 . £20/£5
Fear and Trembling, Tor (U.S.), 1989 (wraps). . £5
The Early Fears, Fedogan and Bremer, 1994 . £15/£5
ditto, Fedogan and Bremer, 1994 (100 signed, numbered copies, slipcase and d/w) . . £200/£150

Non Fiction
The Eighth Stage of Fandom, Advent (U.S.), 1962 (125 numbered, signed copies, no d/w) . . £125
ditto, Advent (U.S.), 1962 (200 copies) . . £100/£25
ditto, Advent (U.S.), 1962 (400 copies, wraps) . £25
The First World Fantasy Convention: Three Authors Remember, Necronomicon Press (U.S.), 1980 (wraps) £30
Out Of My Head, NESFA Press (U.S.), 1986 £25/£10
ditto, NESFA Press (U.S.), 1986 (200 signed, numbered copies, slipcase and d/w) . . £45/£30
Once Around The Bloch: An Unauthorized Autobiography, Tor (U.S.), 1993 . . . . £10/£5

EDMUND BLUNDEN
(b.1896 d.1974)

Remembered primarily as a war poet, Blunden was later inspired by his adopted county of Kent.

Poetry
Poems, privately printed, 1914 (100 copies, wraps) .
. . . . £1,250
Poems Translated from the French, privately printed, 1914 (100 copies, wraps) £650
The Barn, privately printed, 1916 (50 copies, wraps) .
. . . . £750
Three Poems, privately printed, 1916 (50 copies, wraps) £750
The Harbingers, privately printed, 1916 (200 copies, 'The Barn' and 'Three Poems' bound together, wraps)
. . . . £450
Pastorals, Erskine Macdonald, 1916 (wraps) . £100
ditto, Erskine Macdonald, 1916 (50 cloth copies) £350
The Waggoner and Other Poems, Sidgwick & Jackson, 1920 . . . . £125/£35
The Shepherd and Other Poems of Peace and War, Cobden-Sanderson, 1922 . . . . . £75/£25
ditto, Knopf (U.S.), 1922 . . . . . . £75/£25
Dead Letters, Pelican Press, 1923 (50 numbered copies, wraps) £200
To Nature, The Beaumont Press, 1923 (310 numbered copies) £50
ditto, The Beaumont Press, 1923 (80 signed, numbered copies) £150
Masks of Time: A New Collection of Poems, The Beaumont Press, 1925 (310 numbered copies) £50

ditto, The Beaumont Press, 1925 (80 signed, numbered copies) £150
The Augustan Books of Modern Poetry, Benn, 1925 (wraps) £5
English Poems, Cobden-Sanderson, 1926 . £35/£15
ditto, Knopf (U.S.), 1926 . . . . . £35/£15
Retreat, Cobden-Sanderson, 1928 . . . £45/£10
ditto, Cobden-Sanderson, 1928 (112 signed, numbered copies) £175
ditto, Doubleday (U.S.), 1928 . . . . £45/£10
Japanese Garland, The Beaumont Press, 1928 (310 numbered copies) £60
ditto, The Beaumont Press, 1928 (80 signed, numbered copies) £175
Winter Nights: A Reminiscence, Faber, 1928 (wraps) .
. . . . £10
ditto, Faber, 1928 (500 signed, numbered, large paper copies) £50
Near and Far, Cobden-Sanderson, 1929 . £25/£10
ditto, Cobden-Sanderson, 1929 (160 signed, numbered copies) £100
ditto, Harper (U.S.), 1930. . . . . . £25/£10
Poems 1914-1930, Cobden-Sanderson, 1930 £45/£10
ditto, Cobden-Sanderson, 1930 (200 signed, numbered copies) £250
ditto, Harper (U.S.), 1930. . . . . . £40/£10
Halfway House: A Miscellany of New Poems, Cobden-Sanderson, 1932 . . . . . £45/£15
ditto, Cobden-Sanderson, 1932 (70 signed, numbered copies) £175
Choice or Chance: New Poems, Cobden-Sanderson, 1934 . . . . £35/£10
ditto, Cobden-Sanderson, 1934 (45 signed, numbered copies) £175
An Elegy and Other Poems, Cobden-Sanderson, 1937
. . . . £35/£10
Poems 1930-1940, Macmillan, 1940. . . £25/£10
ditto, Macmillan (U.S.), 1940 . . . . £25/£10
Shells by a Stream: New Poems, Macmillan, 1944 .
. . . . £20/£10
After the Bombing and Other Short Poems, Macmillan, 1949 . . . . £15/£5
Eastward: A Selection of Verses, privately printed, 1950 (250 copies) £65
Poems of Many Years, Collins, 1957 . . . £20/£5
A Hong Kong House: Poems 1951-1981, Collins, 1962 . . . . £10/£5
Eleven Poems, The Golden Head Press, 1965 [1966] (wraps) £25
ditto, The Golden Head Press, 1965 [1966] (21 signed copies) £125
A Selection of the Shorter Poems, privately printed, 1966 (wraps) £10
The Midnight Skaters: Poems for Young Readers, Bodley Head, 1968 . . . . £15/£5
A Selection from the Poems, privately printed, 1969 (wraps) £10
Selected Poems, Carcanet, 1982 . . . . . £5

Overtones of War: Poems of the First World War, Duckworth, 1996. . . . . £10/£5

Prose
The Bonadventure: A Random Journal of an Atlantic Holiday, Cobden-Sanderson, 1922 . . . £50/£15
ditto, Putnam (U.S.), 1923 . . . . . £40/£10
Christ's Hospital: A Retrospect, Christophers, 1923 .
. . . . £75/£25
On the Poems of Henry Vaughan, Cobden-Sanderson, 1927 . . . . £20/£10
Undertones of War, Cobden-Sanderson, 1928 . . .
. . . . £250/£60
ditto, Doubleday (U.S.), 1929 . . . . £75/£20
ditto, The Folio Society, 1989 (slipcase). . £10/£40
Nature in English Literature, The Hogarth Press, 1929
. . . . £50/£15
ditto, Harcourt (U.S.), 1929 . . . . £40/£15
Leigh Hunt, Cobden-Sanderson, 1930 . . £30/£10
ditto, Harper (U.S.), 1930. . . . . . £30/£10
De Bello Germanico: A Fragment of Trench History, G.A. Blunden, 1930 (250 copies) £125
ditto, G.A. Blunden, 1930 (25 signed copies) . £250
Votive Tablets: Studies Chiefly Appreciative of English Authors and Books, Cobden-Sanderson, 1931 . . . . £75/£30
ditto, Cobden-Sanderson, 1931 (50 signed, numbered copies) £175
ditto, Harper (U.S.), 1931. . . . . . £75/£30
The Face of England, Longmans Green, 1932 . . .
. . . . £35/£10
We'll Shift our Ground, or Two On a Tour, Cobden-Sanderson, 1933 (with Sylvia Norman) . £30/£15
Charles Lamb and His Contemporaries, C.U.P., 1933
. . . . £15/£5
ditto, Macmillan (U.S.), 1933 . . . . £15/£5
The Mind's Eye, Cape, 1934 . . . . . £20/£5
Keat's Publisher: A Memoir of John Taylor (1781-1864), Cape, 1938 . . . . £35/£10
English Villages, Collins, 1941 . . . . £15/£5
ditto, Hastings House (U.S.), [n.d.] . . . £10/£5
Thomas Hardy, Macmillan, 1941 [1942] . £35/£15
Cricket Country, Collins, 1944 . . . . £20/£10
Shelley: A Life Story, Collins, 1946 . . . £35/£10
ditto, Viking Press (U.S.), 1947 . . . . £25/£10
John Keats, British Council, Longmans, 1950 (wraps)
. . . . £10
Charles Lamb, British Council, Longmans, 1954 (wraps) £10
War Poets 1914-1918, British Council, Longmans, 1958 (wraps) £10
Guest of Thomas Hardy, Toucan Press, 1964 (wraps) .
. . . . £15

ENID BLYTON
(b.1897 d.1968)

A prolific children's author, best known for the 'Famous Five', 'Secret Seven' and 'Noddy' books.

'Famous Five' Titles

Five on a Treasure Island: An Adventure Story, Hodder & Stoughton, 1942 . . . . £1,000/£100

Five Go Adventuring Again, Hodder & Stoughton, 1943 . . . . £850/£75

Five Run Away Together, Hodder & Stoughton, 1944.
. . . . £750/£75

Five Go To Smuggler's Top, Hodder & Stoughton, 1945 . . . . £600/£65

Five Go off in a Caravan, Hodder & Stoughton, 1946
. . . . £450/£45

Five on Kirrin Island Again, Hodder & Stoughton, 1947 . . . . £450/£35

Five Go Off to Camp, Hodder & Stoughton, 1948 . .
. . . . £450/£35

Five Get Into Trouble, Hodder & Stoughton, 1949 .
. . . . £225/£30

Five Fall into an Adventure, Hodder & Stoughton, 1950 . . . . £125/£25

Five on a Hike Together, Hodder & Stoughton, 1951 .
. . . . £125/£25

Five Have a Wonderful Time, Hodder & Stoughton, [1952]. . . . . £125/£25

Five Go Down to the Sea, Hodder & Stoughton, 1953.
. . . . £125/£20

Five Go to Mystery Moor, Hodder & Stoughton, 1954
. . . . £100/£15

Five Have Plenty of Fun, Hodder & Stoughton, 1955.
. . . . £100/£15

Five on a Secret Trail, Hodder & Stoughton, 1956 .
. . . . £100/£15

Five Go To Billycock Hill, Hodder & Stoughton, 1957
. . . . £75/£15

Five get into a Fix, Hodder & Stoughton, [1958] . .
. . . . £75/£15

The Famous Five Special, Hodder & Stoughton, 1959 (contains *Five Go Off to Camp*, *Five Go Off in a Caravan* and *Five Have a Wonderful Time*) £75/£15

Five on Finniston Farm, Hodder & Stoughton, [1960]
. . . . £75/£15

Five Go To Demon's Rocks, Hodder & Stoughton, 1961 . . . . £75/£15

Five Have a Mystery to Solve, Hodder & Stoughton, 1962 . . . . £75/£15

Five are Together Again, Hodder & Stoughton, 1963 .
. . . . £75/£15

The Famous Five Big Book, Hodder & Stoughton, 1964 (contains *Five on a Treasure Island*, *Five Go Adventuring Again* and *Five Run Away Together*) .
. . . . £75/£10

'Secret Seven' Titles

The Secret Seven, Brockhampton Press, 1949 . . . .
. . . . £125/£20

Secret Seven Adventure, Brockhampton Press, 1950 .
. . . . £65/£15

Well Done, Secret Seven, Brockhampton Press, 1951 .
. . . . £65/£15

Secret Seven on the Trail, Brockhampton Press, 1952.
. . . . £65/£15

Go Ahead Secret Seven, Brockhampton Press, 1953 .
. . . . £50/£15

Good Work, Secret Seven, Brockhampton Press, 1954
. . . . £50/£15

Secret Seven Win Through, Brockhampton Press, 1955 . . . . £50/£15

Three Cheers Secret Seven, Brockhampton Press, 1956
. . . . £50/£15

Secret Seven Mystery, Brockhampton Press, 1957 . .
. . . . £45/£15

Puzzle for the Secret Seven, Brockhampton Press, 1958 . . . . £45/£15

Secret Seven Fireworks, Brockhampton Press, 1959 .
. . . . £45/£15

Good Old Secret Seven, Brockhampton Press, 1960 .
. . . . £45/£15

Shock for the Secret Seven, Brockhampton Press, 1961
. . . . £40/£15

Look out Secret Seven, Brockhampton Press, 1962 .
. . . . £40/£15

Fun for the Secret Seven, Brockhampton Press, 1963 .
. . . . £35/£15

'Adventure' Titles

The Island of Adventure, Macmillan, 1944 . £600/£75
The Castle of Adventure, Macmillan, 1946 . £400/£35
The Valley of Adventure, Macmillan, 1947 . £250/£35
The Sea of Adventure, Macmillan, 1948 . £250/£35
The Mountain of Adventure, Macmillan, 1949. . .
. . . . £200/£25

The Ship of Adventure, Macmillan, 1950 . £125/£20
The Circus of Adventure, Macmillan, 1952. £125/£20
The River of Adventure, Macmillan, 1955 . £125/£20

'Mystery' Titles

The Mystery of the Burnt Cottage, Methuen, 1943 .
. . . . £250/£45

The Mystery of the Disappearing Cat, Methuen, 1944
. . . . £175/£45

The Mystery of the Secret Room, Methuen, 1945 . .
. . . . £125/£45

The Mystery of the Spiteful Letters, Methuen, 1946 .
. . . . £75/£20

The Mystery of the Missing Necklace, Methuen, 1947
. . . . £75/£20

The Mystery of the Hidden House, Methuen, 1948 .
. . . . £75/£15

The Mystery of the Pantomime Cat, Methuen, 1949 .
. . . . £75/£15

The Mystery of the Invisible Thief, Methuen, 1950 .
. . . . £65/£10
The Mystery of the Vanished Prince: Being the Ninth
Adventure of the Five Find-Outers and Dog,
Methuen, 1951 . . . . £65/£15
The Mystery of the Strange Bundle, Methuen, 1952 .
. . . . £50/£15
The Mystery of Holly Lane, Methuen, 1953 £50/£15
The Mystery of Tally-Ho Cottage, Methuen, 1954 . .
. . . . £50/£15
The Mystery of the Missing Man, Methuen, 1956 . .
. . . . £50/£15
The Mystery of the Strange Messages, Methuen, 1957
. . . . £50/£15
The Mystery of Banshee Towers, Methuen, 1961 . .
. . . . £50/£15

'St Clare's School' Titles
The Twins at St Clare's, Methuen, 1941 . £65/£15
The O'Sullivan Twins, Methuen, 1942 . . £65/£15
Summer Term at St Clare's, Methuen, 1943 £50/£15
Claudine at St Clare's, Methuen, 1944 . . £50/£15
The Second Form at St Clare's, Methuen, 1944 .
. . . . £50/£15
Fifth Formers at St Clare's, Methuen, 1945 £50/£15

'Malory Towers' Titles
First Term at Malory Towers, Methuen, 1946 . . .
. . . . £200/£15
The Second Form at Malory Towers, Methuen, 1947 .
. . . . £125/£15
Third Year at Malory Towers, Methuen, 1948 . . .
. . . . £75/£15
The Upper Fourth at Malory Towers, Methuen, 1949.
. . . . £75/£15
In the Fifth at Malory Towers, Methuen, 1950. . .
. . . . £75/£15
Last Term at Malory Towers, Methuen, 1951 . . .
. . . . £50/£15

'Barney Junior Mystery' Titles
The Rockingdown Mystery, Collins, [1949] £50/£15
The Rilloby Fair Mystery, Collins, [1950] . £45/£15
The Ring O'Bells Mystery, Collins, 1951 . £40/£10
The Rubadub Mystery, Collins, 1952 . . £40/£10
The Rat-A-Tat Mystery, Collins, 1956 . . £40/£10
The Ragamuffin Mystery, Collins, 1959 . £40/£10

Numbered 'Noddy' Titles
No.1, *Noddy Goes to Toyland*, Sampson Low, 1949 .
. . . . £100/£20
No.2, *Hurrah for Little Noddy*, Sampson Low, 1950 .
. . . . £75/£20
No.3, *Noddy and His Car*, Sampson Low, 1951 . .
. . . . £75/£20
No.4, *Here Comes Noddy Again!*, Sampson Low,
1951 . . . . £50/£15
No.5, *Well Done, Noddy!*, Sampson Low, 1952 . .
. . . . £50/£15

No.6, *Noddy Goes to School*, Sampson Low, 1952. .
. . . . £50/£15
No.7, *Noddy at the Seaside*, Sampson Low, 1953 . .
. . . . £50/£15
No.8, *Noddy Gets Into Trouble*, Sampson Low, 1954 .
. . . . £50/£15
No.9, *Noddy and the Magic Rubber*, Sampson Low,
1954 . . . . £50/£15
No. 10, *You Funny Little Noddy*, Sampson Low, 1955
. . . . £50/£15
No.11, *Noddy Meets Father Christmas*, Sampson Low,
1955 . . . . £50/£15
No.12, *Noddy and Tessie Bear*, Sampson Low, 1956 .
. . . . £50/£15
No.13, *Be Brave, Little Noddy*, Sampson Low, 1956 .
. . . . £50/£15
No.14, *Noddy and the Bumpy-Dog*, Sampson Low,
1957 . . . . £50/£15
No.15, *Do Look Out Noddy*, Sampson Low, 1957 . .
. . . . £50/£15
No. 16, *You're a Good Friend Noddy!*, Sampson Low,
1958 . . . . £25/£15
No.17, *Noddy Has An Adventure*, Sampson Low, 1956
. . . . £25/£15
No.18, *Noddy Goes to Sea*, Sampson Low, 1959 . .
. . . . £50/£15
No.19, *Noddy and the Bunkey*, Sampson Low, 1959 .
. . . . £50/£15
No.20, *Cheer Up Little Noddy!*, Sampson Low, 1960 .
. . . . £50/£15
No.21, *Noddy Goes to the Fair*, Sampson Low, 1960 .
. . . . £50/£15
No.22, *Mr Plod and Little Noddy*, Sampson Low, 1961
. . . . £50/£15
No.23, *Noddy and the Tootles*, Sampson Low, 1962 .
. . . . £50/£15
No.24, *Noddy and the Little Aeroplane*, Sampson
Low, 1964 . . . . £50/£15

'Noddy' Titles
Noddy's House of Books, Sampson Low, [1951] ('The
Tiny Noddy Book Nos. 1-6, in card case, no d/w)
. . . . £175 the set
The Big Noddy Book, Sampson Low, 1952 (no d/w) .
. . . . £75
Enid Blyton's Noddy's Ark of Books, Sampson Low,
[1952] (5 books, cardboard case, no d/w) £165 the set
Noddy Cut-Out Model Book, Sampson Low, 1953 .
. . . . £150
Noddy's Garage of Books, Sampson Low, [1953] (5
books, in cardboard case, no d/w) . . £165 the set
Noddy's Castle of Books, Sampson Low, [1954] (5
books, in cardboard case, no d/w) . . £165 the set
The Noddy Toy Station Book Nos. 1-5, Sampson Low,
[1956]. . . . . £150 the set
Noddy's Shop of Books Nos. 1-5, Sampson Low,
[1958]. . . . . £150 the set
Noddy's Tall Blue (Green-Orange-Pink-Red-Yellow)
Book, Sampson Low, [1960] . . . £150 the set

Strip Books (wraps, no d/ws)

Mary Mouse and the Dolls House, Brockhampton Press, [1942] £20

More Adventures of Mary Mouse, Brockhampton Press, [1943] £20

Little Mary Mouse Again, Brockhampton Press, [1944]. £15

Hallo, Little Mary Mouse, Brockhampton Press, [1945]. £15

Mary Mouse and Her Family, Brockhampton Press, [1946] £15

Here Comes Mary Mouse Again, Brockhampton Press, 1947 . . . . £15

How Do You Do, Mary Mouse, Brockhampton Press, 1946 . . . . £15

Welcome Mary Mouse, Brockhampton Press, [1950] £15

We Do Love Mary Mouse, Brockhampton Press, 1950 . . . . £15

A Prize for Mary Mouse, Brockhampton Press, [1951] £15

Hurrah for Mary Mouse, Brockhampton Press, 1951 . . . . £15

Mary Mouse and Her Bicycle, Brockhampton Press, [1952] £15

Mandy, Mops and Cubby Again, Sampson Low, 1952 . . . . £15

Mandy, Mops and Cubby Find a House, Sampson Low, 1952 . . . . £15

Mr Tumpy Plays A Trick on Saucepan, Sampson Low, 1952 . . . . £15

Mary Mouse and the Noah's Ark, Brockhampton Press, [1953] £15

Clicky the Clockwork Clown, Brockhampton Press, 1953 . . . . £15

Mandy Makes Cubby a Hat, Sampson Low, 1953 £15

Mr Tumpy in the Land of Wishes, Sampson Low, 1953 . . . . £15

Mary Mouse to the Rescue, Brockhampton Press, [1954] £15

Mandy, Mops and Cubby and the Whitewash, Sampson Low, [1955] £15

Gobo in the Land of Dreams, Sampson Low, [1955] £15

Mary Mouse in Nursery Rhyme Land, Brockhampton Press, [1955] £15

Mr Tumpy in the Land of Boys and Girls, Sampson Low, [1955] £15

Bom Book, Brockhampton Press, 1956 . . . £15

A Day With Mary Mouse, Brockhampton Press, [1956] £15

Bom The Little Toy Drummer, Brockhampton Press, 1956 . . . . £15

Mary Mouse and the Garden Party, Brockhampton Press, [1957] £15

Bom and His Magic Drumstick, Brockhampton Press, 1957 . . . . £15

Bom Goes Adventuring, Brockhampton Press, 1958 . . . . £15

Clicky Gets Into Trouble, Brockhampton Press, [1956] £15

Mary Mouse Goes to the Fair, Brockhampton Press, [1958] £15

Bom and the Rainbow, Brockhampton Press, 1959 . . . . £15

Hello Bom and Wuffy Dog, Brockhampton Press, [1959] £15

Mary Mouse Has a Wonderful Idea, Brockhampton Press, [1959] £15

Bom and the Clown, Brockhampton Press, 1959 £15

Clicky and Tiptoe, Brockhampton Press, 1960 . £15

Here Comes Bom, Brockhampton Press, [1960] £15

Mary Mouse Goes to Sea, Brockhampton Press, [1960] £15

Bom Goes to Magic Town, Brockhampton Press, 1960 . . . . £15

Bom at the Seaside, Brockhampton Press, 1961 £15

Bom Goes to the Circus, Brockhampton Press, [1961] £15

Happy Birthday Clicky, Brockhampton Press, [1961] £15

Mary Mouse Goes Out for the Day, Brockhampton Press, [1961] £15

Happy Holiday, Clicky, Brockhampton Press, 1961 . . . . £15

Fun With Mary Mouse, Brockhampton Press, 1962 . . . . £15

Mary Mouse and the Little Donkey, Brockhampton Press, [1964] £15

Written as 'Mary Pollock'

Children of Kidillin, Newnes, 1940 . . . £45/£10

Three Boys and a Circus, Newnes, 1940 . £45/£10

The Adventures of Scamp, Newnes, 1943 . £45/£10

Smuggler Ben, Laurie, 1943 . . . . £45/£10

Mischief at St Rollo's, Newnes Tower House series, 1947 . . . . £45/£10

The Secret of Cliff Castle, Newnes Tower House series, 1947 . . . . . . £45/£10

Poetry

Child Whispers, J. Saville, [1922] (wraps) . . £200

ditto, J. Saville, 1923 . . . . £225/£100

Real Fairies, J. Saville, 1923 . . . . . £225/£100

ditto, J. Saville, 1923 (wraps). £200

Silver and Gold, Nelson, [1925] . . . £225/£75

Ten Songs From Child Whispers, J. Saville, 1924 (wraps) £100

Plays

A Book of Little Plays, Nelson, 1927 . . £65/£20

The Play's the Thing: Musical Plays for Children, Home Library Book Co., [1927] . . . £250/£75

Six Enid Blyton Plays, Methuen, 1936 . £60/£15

The Wishing Bean and Other Plays, Blackwell, 1939. . . . . £50/£20

The Blyton-Sharman Musical Plays for Juniors, Wheaton, 1939 . . . . £15 each

Cameo Plays Book, No 4, Edited by Holroyd, Arnold, 1939 . . . . £25/£10
How the Flowers Grow and Other Musical Plays, Wheaton, 1939 . . . . £15
School Plays: Six Plays for School, Blackwell, 1939 .
. . . . £45/£10
Plays for Older Children, Newnes, [1940] . £45/£10
Plays for Younger Children, Newnes, [1940] £45/£10
Finding the Tickets, Evans, 1955 (wraps) . . £35
The Mother's Meeting, Evans, 1955 (wraps) . £35
Mr Sly-One and the Cats, Evans, 1955 (wraps) £35
Who Will Hold the Giant, Evans, 1955 (wraps) £35

Others
Responsive Singing Games, J. Saville, 1923 (wraps) .
. . . . £125
The Zoo Book, Newnes, [1924] . . . . £65/£30
The Enid Blyton Book of Fairies, Newnes, [1924] .
. . . . £125/£45
Sports and Games, Birn, 1924 (picture boards). £150
ditto, as *Playtime*, Birn, 1932 (picture boards) . £150
Songs of Gladness, J. Saville, 1924 (wraps) . £125
The Enid Blyton Book of Bunnies, Newnes, [1925] .
. . . . £125/£45
Reading Practice, Nos 1-5,8,9 & 11, Nelson, [1925-1926] (no d/ws) . . . . £15 each
The Enid Blyton Book of Brownies, Newnes, [1926] .
. . . . £125/£45
Tales Half Told, Nelson, 1926 . . . . £125/£45
The Bird Book, Newnes, [1926] . . . . £35/£15
The Animal Book, Newnes, [1927] . . . £35/£15
The Wonderful Adventure, Birn, 1927 (picture boards)
. . . . £300
Let's Pretend, Nelson, [1928] . . . . £75/£15
Aesop's Fables Retold, Nelson, 1928 . £50/£15
Old English Tales Retold, Nelson, 1928 . £50/£15
Pinkity's Pranks and Other Nature Fairy Stories: Retold, Nelson, 1928 . . . . . £50/£15
Tales of Brer Rabbit Retold, Nelson, 1928 . £50/£15
Enid Blyton's Nature Lessons, Evans, 1929 £50/£15
Tarrydiddle Town, Nelson, 1929. . . . £35/£15
The Book Around Europe, Birn, 1929 (picture boards)
. . . . £150
The Knights of the Round Table, Newnes, [1930] . .
. . . . £45/£15
Tales from the Arabian Nights, Retold, Newnes, [1930]. . . . . £45/£15
Tales of Ancient Greece, Newnes, [1930] . £45/£15
Tales of Robin Hood, Newnes, [1930] . . £45/£15
My First Reading Book, Birn, [1933] . . £20
Cheerio! A Book for Boys and Girls, Birn, [1933] £60
Five Minute Tales: Sixty Short Stories for Children, Methuen, 1933 . . . . £50/£15
Let's Read, Birn, [1933] £25
Read to Us, Birn, 1933 . . . . . . £25
Letters from Bobs, privately printed for Blyton, 1937 (wraps) £75
More Letters from Bobs, privately printed for Blyton, 1937 (wraps) £75

The Adventures of Odysseus: Stories from World History Retold, Evans, 1934 . . . £45/£10
The Story of the Siege of Troy: Stories from World History Retold, Evans, 1934 . . . . £45/£10
Tales of the Ancient Greeks and Persians: Stories from World History Retold, Evans, 1934 . £45/£10
Tales of the Romans: Stories from World History Retold, Evans, 1934 . . . . . . £45/£10
The Enid Blyton Poetry Book, Methuen, 1934 £50/£15
The Red Pixie Book, Newnes, [1934] . . £125/£45
Round the Year With Enid Blyton: A Year's Nature Study for Children, Evans, [1934] (94 vols, no d/ws)
. . . . £20 the set
Ten-Minute Tales: Twenty-Nine Varied Stories for Children, Methuen, 1934 . . . . £45/£10
The Old Thatch Series, Johnston, 1934-1935 (8 vols, no d/ws) . . . . £10 each
The Strange Tale of Mr Wumble, Coker, [1935] (wraps) £20
Hop, Skip and Jump, Coker, [1935] (wraps) . £20
The Talking Teapot and Other Tales, Coker, [1935] .
. . . . £35/£10
The Children's Garden, Newnes, [1935] . £45/£15
The Green Goblin Book, Newnes, [1935] . £75/£15
Hedgerow Tales, Methuen, 1935. . . . £40/£10
Nature Observation Pictures, Warne, 1935 (32 pictures in four folders) £45
Fifteen-Minute Tales: Nineteen Stories for Children, Methuen, 1936 . . . . £35/£10
The Famous Jimmy, Muller, 1936 . . . £35/£10
The Yellow Fairy Book, Newnes, [1936] . £75/£15
Adventures of the Wishing-Chair, Newnes, [1937] .
. . . . £200/£45
Enid Blyton's Sunny Stories, Newnes, 1937-1953 (wraps, new series) . . . . . . £5 each
The Adventures of Binkle and Flip, Newnes, [1936] .
. . . . £45/£15
Billy-Bob Tales, Methuen, 1936 . . . . £45/£10
Heyo, Brer Rabbit! Tales of Brer Rabbit and His Friends, Newnes, 1936 . . . . . . £75/£20
Mr Galliano's Circus, Newnes, [1938] . £125/£35
The Secret Island, Blackwell, 1938 . . £125/£20
The Old Thatch, Johnston, 1938-1939 (8 vols, second series). . . . . £10 each
Hurrah for the Circus! Being the Further Adventures of Mr Galliano and his Famous Circus, Newnes, 1939 . . . . £125/£35
Naughty Amelia Jane!, Newnes, 1939 . . £100/£25
The Enchanted Wood, Newnes, 1939 . . £125/£20
News Chronicle Boys' and Girls' Circus Book, News Chronicle, [1940] . . . . £75/£25
Boys' and Girls' Circus Book, Newnes, [1940] . .
. . . . £75/£20
Boys' and Girls' Story Book, Newnes, 1940 £75/£20
News Chronicle Boys' and Girls' Book, News Chronicle, 1940 . . . . £75/£20
The Secret of Spiggy Holes, Blackwood [1940] . .
. . . . £125/£20
Birds of Our Gardens, Newnes, 1940 . . £45/£15

The Children of Cherry-Tree Farm, Country Life, 1940 . . . . £65/£20
The Little Tree-House: Being the Adventures of Josie, Bun and Click, Newnes, [1940] . . . £100/£25
Mister Meddle's Mischief, Newnes, 1940 . £75/£20
The Naughtiest Girl in the School, Newnes, 1940 . . . . £125/£35
Twenty-Minute Tales, Methuen, 1940 . . £40/£10
Tales of Betsy-May, Methuen, 1940 . . . £45/£15
The Treasure Hunters, Newnes, 1940 . . £150/£35
Bobs Again, privately printed for Blyton, 1940 (wraps) £75
The Adventures of Mr Pink-Whistle, Newnes, 1941 . . . . £150/£35
Five O'Clock Tales: Sixty Five-Minute Stories for Children, Methuen, 1941 . . . . . £30/£10
The Further Adventures of Josie, Bun and Click, Newnes, [1941] . . . . £65/£15
The Secret Mountain: Being the Third Story of the Strange Adventures of the Secret Island Children, Blackwell, 1941 . . . . £150/£35
The Adventurous Four, Newnes, 1941 . £125/£35
The Babar Story Book, Methuen, 1941 . . £75/£15
A Calendar for Children, Newnes, 1941 . . £100
Enid Blyton's Book of the Year, Evans, 1941 £35/£10
The Children of Willow Farm: A Tale of Life on a Farm, Country Life, 1942 . . . £65/£20
The Naughtiest Girl Again, Newnes, 1942 . £125/£35
More Adventures on Willow Farm, Country Life, 1942 . . . . £65/£20
Six O'Clock Tales: Thirty-Three Short Stories for Children, Methuen, 1942 . . . . . £30/£10
Shadow, the Sheep-Dog, Newnes, 1942 . . £75/£25
The Land of Far-Beyond, Methuen, 1942 . £45/£15
I'll Tell You a Story, Macmillan, 1942 . £25/£10
I'll Tell You Another Story, Macmillan, 1942 £25/£10
Enid Blyton's Happy Story, Hodder & Stoughton, 1942 . . . . £35/£10
Hello, Mr Twiddle!, Newnes, 1942 . . . £45/£15
The Further Adventures of Brer Rabbit, Newnes, 1942 . . . . £45/£15
Enid Blyton's Little Books, Evans, [1942] (wraps). . . . . £15 each, £80 the set
Circus Days Again, Newnes, 1942 . . . £45/£15
Enid Blyton's Readers, Macmillan, 1942-50 (Books 1-12). . . . . £10 each
John Jolly At Christmas Time, Evans, 1942 (wraps) £50
The Children's Life of Christ, Methuen, 1943 £30/£10
The Secret of Killimoon, Blackwell, 1943 . £125/£35
Seven O'Clock Tales: Thirty Short Stories for Children, Methuen, 1943 . . . . . £30/£10
Dame Slap and Her School, Newnes, [1943] £45/£15
The Magic Faraway Tree, Newnes, 1943 . £250/£45
Enid Blyton's Merry Story Book, Hodder & Stoughton, 1943 . . . . £35/£10
Bimbo and Topsy, Newnes, 1943 . . . £45/£15
The Jolly Family Picture Story Books, Evans, [1943] (wraps) £25

John Jolly By the Sea, Evans, 1943 (wraps) . £50
John Jolly on the Farm, Evans, 1943 (wraps) . £50
The Toys Come to Life, Brockhampton Press, [1944] . . . . £45/£10
Billy and Betty at the Seaside, Valentine, [1944] (wraps) £60
The Boy Next Door, Newnes, 1944 . . . £125/£25
Enid Blyton's Nature Lover's Book, Evans, 1944 . . . . £45/£10
The Christmas Book, Macmillan, 1944 . . £25/£10
Come to the Circus, Brockhampton Press, [1944] . . . . £45/£10
Eight O'Clock Tales, Methuen, 1944 . . £30/£10
Enid Blyton's Jolly Story Book, Hodder & Stoughton, 1944 . . . . £35/£10
Polly Piglet, Brockhampton Press, [1944] . £45/£10
Rainy Day Stories, Evans, [1944] . . . £45/£10
Tales From the Bible, Methuen, 1944 . . £30/£10
Tales of Toyland, Newnes, 1944. . . . £45/£15
At Appletree Farm, Brockhampton Press, 1944 . . . . £45/£10
A Book of Naughty Children, Methuen, 1944 £45/£15
The Dog That Went To Fairyland, Brockhampton Press, 1944 . . . . £35/£10
Jolly Little Jumbo, Brockhampton Press, 1944. . . . . £45/£10
The Three Golliwogs, Newnes, 1944 . . £75/£25
The Blue Story Book, Methuen, 1945 . . £35/£10
Round the Clock Stories, National Magazine Co., 1945 . . . . £65/£20
The Caravan Family, Lutterworth Press, 1945 £45/£15
The Brown Family, News Chronicle, [1945] £100/£45
The Conjuring Wizard and Other Stories, Macmillan, 1945 . . . . £45/£15
The Family at Red Roofs, Lutterworth Press, 1945 . . . . £45/£15
The First Christmas, Methuen, 1945 . . £25/£10
Hollow Tree House, Lutterworth Press, 1945 £35/£15
The Naughtiest Girl is a Monitor, Newnes, 1945 . . . . £65/£20
The Runaway Kitten, Brockhampton Press, [1945] . . . . £45/£10
The Twins Go To Nursery-Rhyme Land, Brockhampton Press, [1945] . . . . £45/£15
Enid Blyton's Sunny Story Book, Hodder & Stoughton, 1945 . . . . £35/£10
The Teddy Bear's Party, Brockhampton Press, [1945] . . . . £45/£10
John Jolly at the Circus, Evans, 1945 (wraps) . £50
Amelia Jane Again, Newnes, 1946 . . . £65/£20
The Bad Little Monkey, Brockhampton Press, [1946] . . . . £45/£10
The Children at Happy House, Blackwell, 1946 . . . . £35/£15
Chimney Corner Stories, National Magazine Co., 1946 . . . . £65/£20
The Enid Blyton Holiday Book, Sampson Low, [1946] . . . . £25 each

Enid Blyton's Gay Story Book, Hodder & Stoughton, 1946 . . . . £35/£10
Josie, Click and Bun Again, Newnes, [1946] £65/£20
The Little White Duck and Other Stories, Macmillan, 1946 . . . . £35/£10
The Put-Em-Rights, Lutterworth Press, 1946 £25/£10
The Red Story Book, Methuen, 1946 . . £35/£10
Tales of Green Hedges, National Magazine Co., 1946. . . . . £65/£20
The Surprising Caravan, Brockhampton Press, 1946 . . . . £45/£10
The Train That Lost Its Way, Brockhampton Press, [1946]. . . . . £45/£10
The Folk of the Faraway Tree, Newnes, 1946 . . . . £150/£35
The Adventurous Four Again, Newnes, 1947 . . . . £100/£25
At Seaside Cottage, Brockhampton Press, [1947] . . . . £45/£10
The Green Story Book, Methuen, 1947 . . £35/£10
The Happy House Children Again, Blackwell, 1947 . . . . £35/£15
House-At-The-Corner, Lutterworth Press, 1947 . . . . £45/£15
Jinky Nature Books, Arnold, [1947] (4 vols) . . . . £15/£5 each
More About Josie, Click and Bun, Newnes, 1947 . . . . £45/£15
Enid Blyton's Lucky Story Book, Hodder & Stoughton, 1947 . . . . £35/£10
Rambles With Uncle Nat, National Magazine Co., [1947]. . . . . £65/£20
The Saucy Jane Family, Lutterworth Press, 1947 . . . . £35/£10
A Second Book of Naughty Children: Twenty-Four Short Stories, Methuen, 1947 . . £40/£15
The Smith Family, Arnold, [1947] (Books 1-3 by Blyton) . . . . £15/£5 each
Enid Blyton's Treasury, Evans, 1947 (published for Boots). . . . . £35/£10
Before I Go To Sleep: A Book of Bible Stories and Prayers for Children at Night, Latimer House, 1947. . . . . £35/£10
The Very Clever Rabbit, Brockhampton Press, 1947 . . . . £45/£10
The Little Green Duck and Other Stories, Brockhampton Press, 1947. . . . . £35/£10
Mister Icey-Cold, Blackwell, 1948 . . . £35/£10
The Adventures of Pip, Sampson Low, [1948] £35/£10
The Boy With the Loaves and Fishes, Lutterworth Press, 1948 . . . . £15/£5
Enid Blyton's Brer Rabbit Book, Latimer House, 1948 (1-8) . . . . . . £25/£10 each
Just Time For A Story, Macmillan, 1948 . £25/£10
Let's Garden, Latimer House, 1948 . . . £35/£10
Let's Have A Story, Pitkin, [1948] . . . £60/£20
The Little Button-Elves, Coker, [1948] . . £35/£10
The Little Girl at Capernaum, Lutterworth Press, 1948 . . . . £15/£5

Brer Rabbit and His Friends, Coker, 1948 . £35/£10
Enid Blyton's Bedtime Series, Brockhampton Press, 1946 (2 vols). . . . . . . £15/£5 each
Children of Other Lands, Coker, [1946] . £35/£10
Come to the Circus, Newnes, 1948 . . . £35/£10
More Adventures of Pip, Marston, [1948] . £35/£10
Now For A Story, Harold Hill, 1948. . . £25/£10
The Red-Spotted Handkerchief and Other Stories, Brockhampton Press, [1948] . . . . £35/£10
Secret of the Old Mill, Brockhampton Press, [1948] . . . . £35/£10
Six Cousins at Mistletoe Farm, Evans, 1948 £50/£15
Tales of Old Thatch, Coker, 1948 . . . £35/£10
Tales of the Twins, Brockhampton Press, [1948] . . . . £25/£5
They Ran Away Together, Brockhampton Press, [1948]. . . . . £25/£5
We Want a Story, Pitkin, [1948] . . . . £60/£20
Nature Tales, Johnston, 1948 . . . . . £20/£5
Tales After Tea, Werner Laurie, 1948 . . £35/£10
Enid Blyton's Merry Christmas Cards, Pitkin, 1948 (card covers) £50
Enid Blyton's Birthday Cards, Pitkin, 1948 (card covers) £50
Enid Blyton's Bluebell Story Book, Gifford, [1949] . . . . £45/£15
Humpty Dumpty and Belinda, Collins, [1949] £40/£10
A Book of Magic, Macmillan, 1949 . . . £25/£10
Bumpy and His Bus, Newnes, 1949 . . . £35/£15
Enid Blyton's Daffodil Story Book, Gifford, [1949] . . . . £45/£15
The Dear Old Snowman, Brockhampton Press, [1949] . . . . £35/£10
The Enid Blyton Bible Stories: Old Testament, Macmillan, 1949 . . . . £25/£10
The Enid Blyton Pictures: Old Testament, by John Turner, Macmillan, 1949 . . . . £25/£10
Jinky's Joke and Other Stories, Brockhampton Press, [1949]) . . . . £35/£10
Mr Tumpy and His Caravan, Sidgwick & Jackson, 1949 . . . . £45/£10
My Enid Blyton Bedside Book, 1-12, Barker, 1949 . . . . £45/£20 each
A Story Party at Green Hedges, Hodder & Stoughton, 1949 . . . . £35/£10
Tales After Supper, Werner Laurie, 1949 . £25/£10
A Cat In Fairyland, Pitkin, 1949 . . . £50/£15
Chuff the Chimney Sweep, Pitkin, 1949 . £50/£15
The Circus Book, Latimer House, 1949 . . £35/£10
Don't Be Silly, Mr Twiddle, Newnes, 1949 . £35/£15
Those Dreadful Children, Lutterworth Press, 1949 . . . . £45/£15
Enid Blyton's Good Morning Book, National Magazine Co., 1949 . . . . £40/£10
Oh, What A Lovely Time, Brockhampton Press, 1949 . . . . £35/£10
Robin Hood Book, Latimer House, 1949 . £35/£10
Tiny Tales, Littlebury, 1949 . . . . . £30/£10

The Strange Umbrella and Other Stories, Pitkin, [1949]. . . . . £50/£15
The Enchanted Sea and Other Stories, Pitkin, [1949]. . . . . £50/£15
A Rubbalong Tale Showbook, Werner Laurie, 1950 (complete with cut-outs). £300
Mary Mouse Showbook, Werner Laurie, 1950 (complete with cut-outs). £300
The Astonishing Ladder and Other Stories, Macmillan, 1950 . . . . £35/£10
The Magic Knitting Needles and Other Stories, Macmillan, 1950 . . . . £35/£10
The Magic Snow-Bird and Other Stories, [1950]. . . . . £50/£15
The Three Naughty Children and Other Stories, Macmillan, 1950 . . . . £35/£20
The Wishing-Chair Again, Newnes, 1950 . £65/£20
Six Cousins Again, Evans, 1950 . . . . £50/£15
Smuggler Ben, Werner Laurie, 1950 . . £25/£10
Tricky the Goblin and Other Stories, Macmillan, 1950 . . . . £35/£10
Rubbalong Tales, Macmillan, 1950 . . . £45/£15
The Pole Star Family, Lutterworth Press, 1950 . . . . £45/£15
Enid Blyton's Poppy Story Books, Gifford, [1950] . . . . £40/£15
The Seaside Family, Lutterworth Press, 1950 £45/£15
Mr Pink-Whistle Interferes, Newnes, 1950 . £35/£15
Enid Blyton's Book of the Year, Evans, 1950 £45/£15
Mister Meddle's Muddles, Newnes, 1950 . £35/£15
Enid Blyton Little Book Nos 1-6, Brockhampton Press, [1950]. . . . . £10 each
The Enid Blyton Pennant Series, Macmillan, 1950 (30 vols) . . . . £10 each
Round the Year With Enid Blyton, Evans, 1950 . . . . £45/£10
Round the Year Stories, Coker, 1950 . . £25/£10
Tales About Toys, Brockhampton Press, 1950 £35/£10
What An Adventure, Brockhampton Press, 1950 . . . . £35/£10
The Yellow Story Book, Newnes, 1950 . £35/£15
Pippy and the Gnome and Other Stories, Pitkin, 1951 . . . . £50/£15
The Proud Golliwog, Brockhampton Press, 1951 . . . . £25/£5
The Queen Elizabeth Family, Lutterworth Press, 1951 . . . . £25/£10
Benjy and the Princess and Other Stories, Pitkin, [1951]. . . . . £50/£15
The Book of Brownies, Newnes, [1951] . £35/£15
The Buttercup Farm Family, Lutterworth Press, 1951 . . . . £35/£15
Enid Blyton's Buttercup Story Book, Gifford, [1951] . . . . £35/£15
The Flying Goat and Other Stories, Pitkin, [1951] . . . . £50/£15
Enid Blyton's Gay Street Book, Latimer House, [1951] . . . . £35/£10

Josie, Click and Bun, and The Little Tree House, Newnes, [1951] . . . . £35/£15
A Picnic Party With Enid Blyton, Hodder & Stoughton, 1951 . . . . £35/£10
The Runaway Teddy Bear and Other Stories, Pitkin, [1951]. . . . . £50/£15
The Six Bad Boys, Lutterworth Press, 1951. £35/£15
'Too-Wise' the Wonderful Wizard and Other Stories, Pitkin, [1951]. . . . . £50/£15
Up The Faraway Tree, Newnes, 1951 . . £75/£25
Down at the Farm, Sampson Low, 1951 . £35/£10
Father Christmas and Belinda, Collins, 1951 £30/£10
Feefo, Tuppeny and Jinks, Staples Press, 1951 . . . . £45/£15
The Little Spinning Mouse and Other Stories, Pitkin, 1951 . . . . £50/£15
Enid Blyton's Animal Lover's Book, Evans, 1952 . . . . £45/£10
Enid Blyton's Bright Story Book, Brockhampton Press, 1952 . . . . £50/£20
The Enid Blyton Bible Pictures: New Testament, Macmillan, [1952] . . . . £25/£10
The Queer Adventure, Staples Press, 1952 . £45/£15
The Story of My Life, Pitkin, [1952]. . . £75/£25
Welcome, Josie, Click and Bun!, Newnes, 1952 . . . . £35/£15
The Very Big Secret, Lutterworth Press, 1952 £35/£15
Enid Blyton's Snowdrop Story Book, Gifford, [1952]. . . . . £35/£10
Enid Blyton's Omnibus!, Newnes, 1952 . £35/£15
Enid Blyton Tiny Strip Books, Sampson Low, [1952] . . . . £15 each
My First Enid Blyton Book, Latimer House, 1952 . . . . £30/£10
My First Nature Book, Macmillan, 1952 . £15/£5
The Children's Jolly Book, Odhams, 1952 . £30/£10
Come Along Twins, Brockhampton Press, 1952 . . . . £25/£5
The Mad Teapot, Brockhampton Press, 1952 £25/£5
The Two Sillies and Other Stories, Coker, 1952 . . . . £35/£10
The Secret of Moon Castle, Blackwell, 1953 £100/£25
Snowball the Pony, Lutterworth Press, 1953 £35/£15
The Story of Our Queen, Muller, 1953 . . £35/£10
Well Really, Mr Twiddle!, Newnes, 1953 . £35/£15
The Children's Book of Prayers, Muller, [1953] . . . . £25/£10
Enid Blyton's Christmas Story, Hamilton, [1953] (advent calendar). £30
The Enid Blyton Bible Stories: New Testament, Macmillan, 1953 [1954] (14 vols) . . . £5 each
Enid Blyton's Magazine, Evans, 1953+. . £15 each
Gobo and Mr Fierce, Sampson Low, 1953 . . £20/£5
Here Come the Twins, Brockhampton Press, 1953 . . . . £25/£5
Little Gift Books, Hackett, 1953 (translated by Blyton) . . . . £25/£10 each
Playways Annual, Lutterworth Press, 1953 (by Blyton and others) . . . . £25/£10

Visitors in the Night, Brockhampton Press, 1953 (wraps) £15

The Adventure of the Secret Necklace, Lutterworth Press, 1954 . . . . £35/£15

The Castle Without a Door and Other Stories, Pitkin, [1954] . . . . £50/£15

The Children at Green Meadows, Lutterworth Press, 1954 . . . . £35/£15

Enid Blyton's Friendly Story Book, Brockhampton Press, 1954 . . . . £25/£5

Enid Blyton's Good Morning Book, Juvenile Productions, [1954] . . . . . . £25/£10

The Greatest Book in the World, British & Foreign Bible Society, [1954] . . . . . £25/£10

The Little Toy Farm and Other Stories, Pitkin, 1954 . . . . £50/£15

Enid Blyton's Marigold Story Book, Gifford, [1954] . . . . £35/£10

Merry Mistle Meddle!, Newnes, 1954 . £35/£15

More About Amelia Jane!, Newnes, 1954 . £45/£15

Enid Blyton's Magazine Annual, Evans, [1954] £15

Little Strip Picture Books, Sampson Low, 1954 (wraps) . . . . £10 each

A Surprise for Mary, Brent Press, 1954 (wraps) £25

A Happy Birthday, Brent Press, 1954 (wraps) . £25

The Two Birthdays, Brent Press, 1954 (wraps). £25

The Wonderful Birthday, Brent Press, 1954 (wraps) £25

All About Babies, Brent Press, 1954 (wraps) £25

Tales About Toys, Brent Press, 1954 (wraps) . £25

Enid Blyton's Away Goes Sooty, Collins, [1955] . . . . £30/£10

Benjy and the Others, Latimer House, 1955 £35/£10

Bible Stories from the Old Testament, Muller, [1955]. . . . . £15/£5

Enid Blyton's Bobs, Collins, [1955]. . £30/£10

Enid Blyton's Foxglove Story Book, Gifford, [1955] . . . . £35/£10

Holiday House, Evans, [1955] . . . . £45/£10

Enid Blyton's Little Bedtime Books, Sampson Low, [1955] (8 vols) . . . . £10 each

Mischief Again!, Collins, 1955 . . . £50/£15

More Chimney Corner Stories, Macdonald, 1955 . . . . £30/£10

Mr Pink-Whistle's Party, Newnes, 1955 . £35/£15

Enid Blyton's Neddy the Little Donkey, Collins, [1955]. . . . . £30/£10

Playing At Home: A Novelty Book, Methuen, 1955 (spiral bound) £150

Run-About's Holiday, Lutterworth Press, 1955 . . . . £35/£10

Enid Blyton's Christmas With Scamp and Bimbo, Collins, [1955] . . . . . . £30/£10

Enid Blyton's Sooty, Collins, [1955] . . £30/£10

The Troublesome Three, Sampson Low, [1955] . . . . £25/£10

Enid Blyton's 'What Shall I Be?', Collins, [1955]. . . . . £20/£5

Bimbo and Blackie Go Camping, Collins, 1955 £20/£5

Enid Blyton's Favourite Book of Fables, from the Tales of La Fontaine, Collins, 1955 . . £35/£10

Golliwog Grumbled, Brockhampton Press, 1955 . . . . £30/£10

Laughing Kitten, Harvill, 1955 . . . . £25/£10

The Child Who Was Chosen, Waterlow, 1955 (wraps) £30

Let's Have a Club of Our Own, Waterlow, 1955 (wraps) £30

Enid Blyton's Animal Tales, Collins, [1956] £30/£10

The Clever Little Donkey, Collins, [1956] . £30/£10

Colin the Cow-Boy, Collins, [1956] . . . £30/£10

Four in a Family, Lutterworth Press, 1956 . £25/£10

Let's Have a Party, Harvill Press, 1958 . . £25/£10

Scamp at School, Collins, [1956] . . . £30/£10

A Story of Jesus, Macmillan, 1956 . . . . £15/£5

Enid Blyton's Bom Painting Book, Dean, [1957] . . £25/£10

Children's Own Painting Book, Odhams, 1957 £15

New Testament Picture Books, Nos 1-2, Macmillan, 1957 . . . . £10/£5 each

The Birthday Kitten, Lutterworth Press, 1958 £45/£10

Enid Blyton's Little Bedtime Books, Sampson Low, [1958] (4 vols) . . . . . . £10 each

Mr Pink-Whistle's Big Book, Evans, 1958 . £45/£15

Rumble and Chuff, Juvenile Productions, [1958] . . £45/£15

Tales After Tea, Collins, 1958 . . . . . £15/£5

Enid Blyton's Mystery Stories, Collins, 1959 . £15/£5

Enid Blyton's Dog Stories, Collins, 1959 . £15/£5

Adventure Stories, Collins, 1960. . . . . £15/£5

Adventure of the Strange Ruby, Brockhampton Press, 1960 . . . . £25/£10

Happy Day Stories, Evans, 1960. . . . £35/£10

Will the Fiddler, Instructive Arts, [1960] . £30/£10

Old Testament Picture Books, Macmillan, 1960 . . £10/£5 each

Tales At Bedtime, Collins, 1960 . . . . £15/£5

The Big Enid Blyton Book, Hamlyn, 1961 . £25/£10

The Mystery That Never Was, Collins, 1961 £25/£10

Circus Days Again, May Fair Books, 1962 . £15/£5

The Four Cousins, Lutterworth Press, 1962 £25/£10

Stories for Monday, Oliphants, 1962 (no d/w) . £35

Stories for Tuesday, Oliphants, 1962 (no d/w) . £35

The Boy Who Wanted A Dog, Lutterworth Press, 1963 . . . . £25/£10

Tales of Brave Adventure, Dean, [1963] . . £15/£5

Brer Rabbit Again, Dean, 1963 . . . . . £15/£5

The Enid Blyton Storybook for Fives to Sevens, Parrish, [1964] . . . . £35/£10

Happy Hours Story Book, Dean, [1964] . £25/£5

Enid Blyton's Sunshine Picture Story Book, World Distributors, [1964] . . . . . . £20/£5

Storytime Book, Dean, 1964 . . . . . £15/£5

Tell-A-Story Books, World Distributors, 1964 . . £15/£5 each

Trouble for the Twins, Brockhampton Press, 1964. . . . . £25/£5

Enid Blyton's Sunshine Book, Dean, [1965] . £15/£5

The Boy Who Came Back, Lutterworth Press, 1965 .
. . . . £25/£10
The Man Who Stopped to Help, Lutterworth Press,
1965 . . . . £25/£10
Easy Reader, Collins, 1965 (no d/w) £5
Enid Blyton's Brer Rabbit's A Rascal, Dean, 1965 .
. . . .£15/£5
Tales of Long Ago, Dean, 1965 . . . . .£15/£5
Enid Blyton's Pixie Tales, Collins, 1966 . .£15/£5
Enid Blyton's Pixieland Story Book, Collins, 1966 .
. . . .£15/£5
Enid Blyton's Playbook, Collins, [1966] . .£15/£5
Enid Blyton's Fireside Tales, Collins, 1966 .£15/£5
The Happy House Children, Collins, 1966 . .£15/£5
Enid Blyton's Bedtime Annual, Manchester, 1966. .
. . . .£15/£5
The Fairy Folk Story Book, Collins, 1966 . .£20/£5
Enid Blyton's Gift Book, Purnell, 1966 . . .£20/£5
Stories for Bedtime, Dean, 1966 . . . . .£15/£5
Stories for You, Dean, 1966 . . . . . .£15/£5
John and Mary, Brockhampton Press, 1966-68 (9
vols) . . . . £10/£5 each
Holiday Annual Stories, Low Marston, 1967 .£20/£5
Holiday Magic Stories, Low Maraton, 1967 .£20/£5
Holiday Pixie Stories, Low Marston, 1967 . .£20/£5
Holiday Toy Stories, Low Marston, 1967 . .£20/£5
The Playtime Story Book, Nos 1-14, World
Distributors, 1967 . . . . . £10/£5 each
Adventures on Willow Farm, Collins, 1968 .£15/£5
Brownie Tales, Collins, 1968. . . . . .£15/£5
Once Upon A Time, Collins, 1968 . . . .£15/£5
The Bear With Boot-Button Eyes and Other Stories,
Purnell, 1975 . . . .£10/£5
Dame Roundy's Stockings and Other Stories, Purnell,
1975 . . . .£10/£5
The Dog With the Long Tail and Other Stories,
Purnell, 1975 . . . .£10/£5
The Goblin and the Dragon and Other Stories,
Purnell, 1975 . . . .£10/£5
The Good Old Rocking Horse and Other Stories,
Purnell, 1975 . . . .£10/£5
The Little Sugar Mouse and Other Stories, Purnell,
1975 . . . .£10/£5
Brer Rabbit and the Tar Baby, Hodder & Stoughton,
1975 . . . .£15/£5

Edited by Enid Blyton
The Teacher's Treasury, Newnes, [1926] (3 vols) .
. . . . £30/£15 each
Sunny Stories for Little Folks, Newnes, [1926-1936]
(240 issues) . . . . £10 each
Pictorial Knowledge, Newnes, 1930 (10 vols) . . .
. . . . £100/£40 the set
Treasure Trove Readers, Wheaton, 1934-35 (the
'Junior' series compiled by Blyton, no d/ws) £10 each
Birds of the Wayside and Woodland, by Thomas A.
Coward, Warne, 1936 . . . . . . £30/£10

LUCY M. BOSTON
(b.1892 d.1990)

A British author who was inspired to write *The Children of Green Knowe* after buying the 800 year-old Grey Manor in Cambridgeshire in 1935.

'Green Knowe' Novels
The Children of Green Knowe, Faber, 1954 £225/£35
ditto, Harcourt Brace (U.S.), 1955 . . . £175/£25
The Chimneys of Green Knowe, Faber, 1958 £175/£25
ditto, as *Treasure of Green Knowe*, Harcourt Brace
(U.S.), 1958 . . . . £100/£20
The River at Green Knowe, Faber, 1959 . £175/£25
ditto, Harcourt Brace (U.S.), 1959 . . . £100/£20
A Stranger at Green Knowe, Faber, 1961 . £175/£25
ditto, Harcourt Brace (U.S.), 1961 . . . £100/£20
An Enemy at Green Knowe, Faber, 1964 . £175/£25
ditto, Harcourt Brace (U.S.), 1964 . . . £100/£20
The Stones of Green Knowe, Faber, 1976 . £65/£10
ditto, Harcourt Brace (U.S.), 1976 . . . £45/£10

Other Novels
Yew Hall, Faber, 1954 . . . . . . £75/£15
The Castle of Yew, Bodley Head, 1965 . . .£35/£5
ditto, Harcourt Brace (U.S.), 1964 . . . .£25/£5
The Sea Egg, Faber, 1967 . . . . . .£25/£5
ditto, Harcourt Brace (U.S.), 1967 . . . .£25/£5
The House that Grew, Faber, 1969 . . . .£45/£5
Persephone, Collins, 1969 . . . . . .£45/£5
Nothing Said, Faber, 1971 . . . . . .£25/£5
ditto, Harcourt Brace (U.S.), 1971 . . . .£25/£5
The Guardians of the House, Bodley Head, 1974 . .
. . . .£25/£5
ditto, Atheneum (U.S.), 1975 . . . . . .£25/£5
The Fossil Snake, Bodley Head, 1975 . . .£25/£5
ditto, Atheneum (U.S.), 1976 . . . . . .£25/£5

Poetry
Time is Undone, privately printed, 1954 (750 copies,
wraps). £25

Play
The Horned Man, Faber, 1970 . . . . .£25/£5

Autobiography
Memory in a House, Bodley Head, 1973 . £30/£10
ditto, Macmillan (U.S.), 1974 . . . . .£25/£5
Perverse and Foolish, Bodley Head, 1979 . .£25/£5
ditto, Atheneum (U.S.), 1979 . . . . . .£25/£5
Memories, Colt Books, 1992 . . . . . .£15/£5

ELIZABETH BOWEN
(b.1899 d.1973)

Anglo-Irish novelist and short story writer noted for her attention to detail and subtlety of style.

Short Stories

Encounters: Stories, Sidgwick & Jackson, 1923 . . . . £750/£175
ditto, Boni & Liveright, 1926 . . . . £125/£40
Ann Lee's and Other Stories, Sidgwick & Jackson, 1926 . . . . £500/£95
ditto, Boni & Liveright, 1926 . . . . £100/£25
Joining Charles and Other Stories, Constable, 1929 . . . . £175/£30
ditto, Dial Press, 1929 . . . . . . £100/£25
The Cat Jumps and Other Stories, Gollancz, 1934 . . . . £175/£30
Look at All Those Roses, Gollancz, 1941 . £75/£15
ditto, Knopf (U.S.), 1941 . . . . . £25/£10
The Demon Lover and Other Stories, Cape, [1945] . . . . £100/£25
ditto, as *Ivy Gripped the Steps and Other Stories*, Knopf (U.S.), 1946 . . . . . . £40/£15
Selected Stories, Fridberg (Dublin), 1946 (wraps with d/w) . . . . £20/£5
Early Stories, Knopf (U.S.), 1951 . . . £20/£5
Stories, Knopf (U.S.), 1959 . . . . . £15/£5
A Day in the Dark and Other Stories, Cape, 1965 . . . . £15/£5
ditto, Random House (U.S.), 1982 . . . £20/£5
The Collected Stories, Cape, 1981 . . . £20/£5
ditto, Random House (U.S.), 1982 . . . £20/£5

Novels

The Hotel, Constable, 1927 . . . . £250/£25
ditto, Dial Press, 1928 . . . . . £65/£15
The Last September, Constable, 1929 . £225/£25
ditto, Dial Press, 1929 . . . . . £175/£20
Friends and Relations, Constable, 1931 . £200/£25
ditto, Dial Press, 1931 . . . . . £175/£20
To the North, Gollancz, 1931 . . . £175/£20
ditto, Knopf (U.S.), 1933 . . . . . £75/£15
The House in Paris, Gollancz, 1935 . . £150/£20
ditto, Knopf (U.S.), 1936 . . . . . £75/£15
The Death of the Heart, Gollancz, 1938 . £125/£20
ditto, Knopf (U.S.), 1939 . . . . . £75/£15
The Heat of the Day, Cape, 1949 . . . £15/£5
ditto, Knopf (U.S.), 1949 . . . . . £15/£5
A World of Love, Cape, 1955 . . . . £15/£5
ditto, Knopf (U.S.), 1955 . . . . . £15/£5
The Little Girls, Cape, 1964 . . . . £15/£5
ditto, Knopf (U.S.), 1964 . . . . . £15/£5
Eva Trout, Knopf (U.S.), 1968 . . . £20/£5
ditto, Cape, 1969 . . . . . . £15/£5

Non Fiction

Bowen's Court, Longman, 1942 . . . £125/£25
ditto, Knopf (U.S.), 1942 . . . . . £45/£15
English Novelists, Collins, 1942 . . . . £20/£5

ditto, Hastings House (U.S.), 1942 . . . . £20/£5
Seven Winters, Cuala Press (Dublin), 1942 (450 numbered copies, plain glassine d/w) . £125/£100
ditto, Longman, 1943 . . . . . . £15/£5
ditto, Knopf (U.S.), 1943 . . . . . £15/£5
Anthony Trollope: A New Judgement, O.U.P., 1946 (wraps) £20
ditto, O.U.P. (U.S.), 1946 (wraps) . . . £20
ditto, O.U.P. (U.S.), 1946 (unprinted tissue d/w) . . . . £40/£30
Why Do I Write?: An Exchange of Views Between Elizabeth Bowen, Graham Greene, and V.S. Pritchett, Marshall, 1948 . . . . £125/£35
Collected Impressions, Longman, 1950 . . £25/£5
ditto, Knopf (U.S.), 1950 . . . . . £25/£5
The Shelbourne, Harrap, 1951 . . . £35/£10
ditto, as *The Shelbourne Hotel*, Knopf (U.S.), 1951 . . . . £30/£5
A Time in Rome, Longman, 1960 . . . £20/£5
ditto, Knopf (U.S.), 1960 . . . . . £20/£5
Afterthought: Pieces About Writing, Longman, 1962 . . . . £20/£5
ditto, Knopf (U.S.), 1962 . . . . . £20/£5
Pictures and Conversations, Knopf (U.S.), 1975 . . . . £20/£5
ditto, Knopf (U.S.), 1975 . . . . . £20/£5
The Mulberry Tree, Virago, 1986 . . . £15/£5
ditto, Harcourt Brace Jovanovich (U.S.), [1987] £15/£5

Children's Titles

The Good Tiger, Knopf (U.S.), 1965 . . . £35/£5
ditto, Cape, 1970 . . . . £30/£5

PAUL BOWLES
(b.1910 d.1999)

An American novelist and musician, Bowles lived in self-imposed exile in Tangier.

Novels

The Sheltering Sky, John Lehmann, 1949 £1,000/£75
ditto, New Directions (U.S.), 1949 . . . £650/£50
Let It Come Down, Random House (U.S.), 1952 . . . . £75/£15
ditto, John Lehmann, 1952 . . . . £75/£15
ditto, Black Sparrow Press (U.S.), 1980 (350 signed copies) . . . . £75/£50
The Spider's House, Random House (U.S.), 1955 . . . . £50/£10
ditto, Macdonald & Co., 1957 . . . £50/£10
Up Above the World, Simon & Schuster (U.S.), 1966 . . . . £45/£10
ditto, Peter Owen, 1967 . . . . . £45/£10

Short Stories

A Little Stone, John Lehmann, 1950 . . £200/£25
ditto, as *Call at Corazón and Other Stories*, Peter Owen, 1988 . . . . £10/£5

The Delicate Prey, Random House (U.S.), 1950 . .
. . . . £100/£20
The Hours After Noon, Heinemann, 1959 . . £35/£5
A Hundred Camels in the Courtyard, City Lights
(U.S.), 1962 (wraps) £10
The Time of Friendship, Holt, Rinehart & Winston
(U.S.), 1967 . . . . £25/£5
Pages From Coldpoint and Other Stories, Peter Owen,
1968 . . . . £35/£5
Things Gone and Things Still Here, Black Sparrow
Press (U.S.), 1977 (500 copies). . . . £35/£20
ditto, Black Sparrow Press (U.S.), 1977 (26 lettered,
signed copies) £250
ditto, Black Sparrow Press (U.S.), 1977 (250
numbered, signed copies) £150
Collected Stories 1939-1976, Black Sparrow Press
(U.S.), 1979 (750 unsigned copies, wraps) . £35
ditto, Black Sparrow Press (U.S.), 1979 (300 copies
signed by Bowles, acetate d/w) . . . . £200/£175
ditto, Black Sparrow Press (U.S.), 1979 (60 copies
signed by Bowles and Vidal, acetate d/w) . £400/£275
Midnight Mass and Other Stories, Black Sparrow
Press (U.S.), 1981 (350 signed copies). . . £75
ditto, Peter Owen, 1985 . . . . £15/£5
Unwelcome Words, Tombouctou Books (U.S.), 1988 .
. . . . £10/£5
A Thousand Days for Mokhtar, Peter Owen, 1989 .
. . . . £10/£5

Poetry

Two Poems, Modern Editions Press (U.S.), 1934
(wraps) £2,500
Next To Nothing, Starstreams (Kathmandu), 1976 (500
numbered copies, wraps) £100
Next To Nothing: Collected Poems 1926-1977, Black
Sparrow Press (U.S.), 1981 (300 signed, numbered
copies £75

Others

Yallah, Macdowell, Obolenaky (U.S.), 1956
(photographs by Haeberlin, commentary by Bowles).
. . . . £100/£30
Their Heads Are Green and Their Hands Are Blue,
Random House (U.S.), 1963 . . . . £30/£10
ditto, as *Their Heads Are Green*, Peter Owen, 1963 .
. . . . £35/£10
Without Stopping, Putnam's (U.S.), 1972 . . £15/£5
ditto, Peter Owen, 1972 . . . . . . £20/£5
Points in Time, Peter Owen, 1982 . . . . £10/£5
ditto, The Ecco Press (U.S.), 1984 . . . . £10/£5
*Two Years Beside the Strait: Tangier Journal 1987-
1989*, Peter Owen, 1990 . . . . . . £10/£5
Too Far From Home, Peter Owen, 1994 (100 signed,
numbered copies) £100

WILLIAM BOYD
(b.1952)

Born in Ghana, Boyd's first two books remain highly
collectable, although he is currently slightly out of
vogue.

A Good Man in Africa, Hamish Hamilton, 1981 . .
. . . . £450/£45
ditto, Morrow (U.S.), 1982 . . . . . £65/£20
On the Yankee Station and Other Stories, Hamish
Hamilton, 1982 . . . . £300/£35
ditto, Morrow (U.S.), 1984 . . . . £40/£10
An Ice Cream War, Hamish Hamilton, 1982 £75/£15
ditto, Morrow (U.S.), 1983 . . . . £35/£10
Stars and Bars, Hamish Hamilton, 1984 . £45/£10
ditto, Morrow (U.S.), 1985 . . . . . £30/£5
School Ties, Hamish Hamilton, 1985 . . £35/£10
ditto, Penguin, 1985 (wraps) £5
ditto, Morrow (U.S.), 1986 . . . . . £30/£5
The New Confessions, Hamish Hamilton, 1987 £25/£5
ditto, Morrow (U.S.), 1988 . . . . . £15/£5
Brazzaville Beach, Sinclair Stevenson, 1990 . £20/£5
ditto, London Limited Editions, 1990 (150 signed
copies, cellophane d/w) . . . . . £65/£60
ditto, Morrow (U.S.), 1991 . . . . . £10/£5
The Blue Afternoon, Sinclair Stevenson, 1993 . £10/£5
ditto, London Limited Editions, 1993 (150 signed
copies, cellophane d/w) . . . . . £50/£45
ditto, Knopf (U.S.), 1995 . . . . . £10/£5
Cork, Ulysses, 1994 (26 copies) £150
ditto, Ulysses, 1994 (60 copies) £100
ditto, Ulysses, 1994 (150 copies). . . . £50
Killing Lizards, Penguin, 1995 (wraps) . . . £5
The Destiny of Nathalie 'X' and Other Short Stories,
Sinclair Stevenson, 1995 . . . . . £10/£5
ditto, Knopf (U.S.), 1997 . . . . . . £10/£5
Transfigured Night, One Horse press, 1995 (wraps)
(2,000 signed, numbered copies) £30
Armadillo, Hamish Hamilton, 1998 . . . £10/£5
ditto, Knopf (U.S.), 1998 . . . . . . £10/£5
Protobiography, Bridgewater Press, 1998 (26 signed,
lettered copies of 138 copies) £100
ditto, Bridgewater Press, 1998 (100 signed, lettered
copies of 138 copies) £75
Nat Tate: An American Artist: 1928-1960, 21
Publishing, 1998 . . . . £25/£10
A Haunting, Bridgewater Press, 2000 (100 signed,
lettered copies of 138 copies) £45
ditto, Bridgewater Press, 2000 (26 signed, lettered
copies of 138 copies) £100
ditto, Bridgewater Press, 2000 (12 signed copies,
numbered I-XII, with an original signed drawing by
Boyd) £400
Any Human Heart, Hamish Hamilton, 2002 . £10/£5

KAY BOYLE
(b.1903 d.1992)

An American novelist and short story writer, Boyle lived for many years in Europe and between 1946 and 1954 was a foreign correspondent for the *New Yorker*.

Novels

Plagued by the Nightingale, Cape & Smith (U.S.), 1931 . . . . £200/£30
ditto, Lehmann, 1951 . . . . £65/£20
Year Before Last, Smith (U.S.), 1932 . £100/£25
ditto, Faber, 1932 . . . . . . £100/£25
Gentlemen, I Address You Privately, Smith & Haas (U.S.), 1933 . . . . £200/£25
ditto, Faber, 1934 . . . . £75/£25
My Next Bride, Harcourt, Brace (U.S.), 1934 £50/£20
ditto, Faber, 1935 . . . . £50/£20
Death of a Man, Harcourt, Brace (U.S.), [1936] . . . . £45/£15
ditto, Faber, 1936 . . . . £50/£20
Monday Night, Harcourt, Brace (U.S.), 1938 £125/£25
ditto, Faber, 1938 . . . . £50/£20
The Crazy Hunter: Three Short Novels, Harcourt, Brace (U.S.), 1940 . . . . . £125/£10
ditto, Faber, 1940 . . . . £25/£10
Primer for Combat, Simon & Schuster (U.S.), 1942 . . . . £25/£10
ditto, Faber, 1943 . . . . £25/£10
Avalanche, Simon & Schuster (U.S.), 1944. £25/£10
ditto, Faber, 1945 . . . . £25/£10
A Frenchman Must Die, Simon & Schuster (U.S.), 1946 . . . . £25/£10
ditto, Faber, 1946 . . . . £25/£10
1939, Simon & Schuster (U.S.), 1948 . £25/£10
ditto, Faber, 1948 . . . . £25/£10
His Human Majesty, Whittlesey House (U.S.), 1949 . . . . £25/£10
ditto, Faber, 1950 . . . . £25/£10
The Seagull on the Step, Knopf (U.S.), 1955 £25/£10
ditto, Faber, 1955 . . . . £25/£10
Generation Without Farewell, Knopf (U.S.), 1960 . . . . £25/£10
ditto, Faber, 1960 . . . . £25/£10
The Underground Woman, Doubleday (U.S.), 1975 . . . . £25/£10

Short Stories

Short Stories, Black Sun Press (France), 1929 (15 signed copies on Japan paper, wraps in tied protected boards) £1,000
ditto, Black Sun Press, 1929 (20 copies on Arches paper, wraps in tied protected boards) . . £750
ditto, Black Sun Press, 1929 (150 copies on Van Gelder paper, wraps in tied protected boards) . £600
Wedding Day and Other Stories, Cape & Smith (U.S.), 1930 . . . . £250/£25
ditto, Pharos Edition, 1932 . . . . £200/£20
The First Lover and Other Stories, Smith & Haas

(U.S.), 1933 . . . . £150/£25
ditto, Faber, 1937 . . . . £75/£25
The White Horses of Vienna and Other Stories, Harcourt, Brace (U.S.), [1936] . . . . £150/£25
ditto, Faber, 1937 . . . . £45/£10
Thirty Stories, Simon & Schuster (U.S.), 1946 . . . . £100/£200
ditto, Faber, 1948 . . . . £40/£10
The Smoking Mountain: Stories of Post-War Germany, McGraw-Hill (U.S.), 1951 . £35/£10
ditto, Faber, 1952 . . . . £35/£10
Three Short Novels, Beacon Press (U.S.), 1958 (wraps) £20
Nothing Ever Breaks Except the Heart, Doubleday (U.S.), 1966 . . . . £25/£10

Poetry

A Statement, Modern Edition Press (U.S.), 1932 (175 signed, numbered copies) £300
A Glad Day, New Directions (U.S.), 1938 . £35/£15
American Citizen: Naturalized in Leadville, Colorado, Simon & Schuster (U.S.), 1944 (wraps) . . £30
Collected Poems, Knopf (U.S.), 1962 . £25/£10
Testament for My Students, Doubleday (U.S.), 1970 . . . . £25/£10

Others

The Youngest Camel, Little, Brown (U.S.), 1939 . . . . £60/£15
ditto, Faber, 1939 . . . . £40/£15
Breaking the Silence: Why a Mother Tells Her Son about the Nazi Era, Institute of Human Relations Press (U.S.), 1962 (wraps) £20
Pinky: The Cat Who Liked to Sleep, Crowell-Collier (U.S.), 1966 . . . . £45/£15
Pinky in Persia, Crowell-Collier (U.S.), 1968 £40/£15
Being Geniuses Together, Doubleday (U.S.), 1968 (with Robert McAlmon). . . . . . £20/£5
ditto, Joseph, 1970. . . . . . . £20/£5
The Long Walk at San Francisco State and Other Essays, Grove (U.S.), 1970. . . . . £20/£5
Four Visions of America, Capra Press (U.S.), 1977 . . . . £20/£5
ditto, Capra Press (U.S.), 1977 (wraps) . . £5

MALCOLM BRADBURY
(b.1932 d.2000)

A novelist and critic, *The History Man* is his best regarded novel, satirising the university culture of the 1960s and 70s.

Novels

Eating People is Wrong, Secker & Warburg, 1959 . . . . £125/£45
ditto, Knopf (U.S.), 1960 . . . . . £45/£15
Stepping Westward, Secker & Warburg, 1965 £75/£25

ditto, Houghton & Mifflin (U.S.), 1966 . . .£15/£5
The History Man, Secker & Warburg, 1975 £50/£15
ditto, Houghton & Mifflin (U.S.), 1976 . . .£15/£5
Rates of Exchange, Secker & Warburg, 1983 .£15/£5
ditto, Knopf (U.S.), 1983 . . . .£10/£5
Doctor Criminale, Secker & Warburg, 1992 .£10/£5
ditto, Viking (U.S.), 1992. . . . . . .£10/£5
To the Hermitage, Picador, 2000 . . .£10/£5
ditto, Overlook Press (U.S.), 2000 . . . .£10/£5

Novella
Cuts, Hutchinson, 1987 . . . .£15/£5
ditto, Harper (U.S.), 1987. . . . . . .£15/£5

Short Stories
Who Do You Think You Are?, Secker & Warburg,
1976 . . . .£15/£5

Criticism etc.
Phogey! How to Have Class in a Classless Society,
Parrish, 1960 . . . .£25/£10
All Dressed Up and Nowhere to Go, Parrish, 1962. .
. . . .£25/£10
Evelyn Waugh, Oliver & Boyd, 1964 (wraps) .£25
What is a Novel?, Arnold, 1969 . . . . .£15
The Social Context of Modern English Literature,
Blackwell, 1971 . . . .£20/£5
Possibilities: Essays on the State of the Novel, O.U.P.,
1973 . . . .£10
Saul Bellow, Methuen, 1982 (wraps) . . .£10
The Modern American Novel, O.U.P., 1983 .£10/£5
ditto, Viking (U.S.), 1993. . . . . .£10/£5
Why Come to Slaka?, Secker & Warburg, 1986 £10
ditto, Penguin (U.S.), 1988 . . . . .£10
*My Strange Quest for Mensonge: Structuralism's
Hidden Hero*, Deutsch, 1987 . . . .£10/£5
ditto, Penguin (U.S.), 1988 . . . . .£10
No, Not Bloomsbury, Deutsch, 1987 . .£10/£5
ditto, Columbia Univ. Press (U.S.), 1988 .£10/£5
The Modern World: Ten Great Writers, Secker &
Warburg, 1988 . . . .£10/£5
ditto, Viking (U.S.), 1989. . . . . .£10/£5
Unsent Letters, Deutsch, 1988 . . . .£10/£5
ditto, Viking (U.S.), 1988. . . . . .£10/£5
*From Puritanism to Post-modernism: The Story of
American Literature*, Routledge, 1991 (with Richard
Ruland) . . . .£10/£5
ditto, Viking (U.S.), 1991. . . . . .£10/£5
The Modern British Novel, Secker & Warburg, 1993 .
. . . .£10/£5
Dangerous Pilgrimages, Secker & Warburg, 1995. .
. . . .£10/£5
ditto, Viking (U.S.), 1996. . . . . .£10/£5

RAY BRADBURY
(b.1920)

American author in many genres, Bradbury originally
emerged from the science fiction pulp magazines and
is considered a leading writer in the field.

Novels
Fahrenheit 451, Ballantine (U.S.), 1953 (wraps) £50
ditto, Ballantine (U.S.), 1953 . . . .£3,500/£500
ditto, Ballantine (U.S.), 1953 (author's copies in cloth)
. . . .£4,500
ditto, Ballantine (U.S.), 1953 (200 signed, numbered
copies, asbestos boards) £6,000
ditto, Hart-Davis, 1954 . . . . .£750/£65
ditto, Limited Editions Club (U.S.), 1982 (2,000
signed, numbered copies, slipcase) . . .£150/£100
ditto, Simon & Schuster (U.S.), 1994 (500 signed,
numbered copies, slipcase) . . . . .£150/£100
Dandelion Wine, Doubleday (U.S.), 1957 .£600/£35
ditto, Hart-Davis, 1957 . . . . .£200/£25
Something Wicked This Way Comes, Simon &
Schuster (U.S.), 1962 . . . . . .£300/£50
ditto, Hart-Davis, 1963 . . . . .£200/£20
ditto, Gauntlet Press (U.S.), 1999 (500 signed,
numbered copies) . . . .£65/£35
ditto, Gauntlet Press (U.S.), 1999 (52 signed, numbered
deluxe copies) . . . .£250/£200
The Novels of Ray Bradbury, Granada, 1984 .£15/£5
Death is a Lonely Business, Knopf (U.S.), 1985 . .
. . . .£20/£5
ditto, Knopf (U.S.), 1985 (70-75 signed presentation
copies) £250
ditto, Franklin Library (U.S.), 1985 (signed, limited
edition, full leather) £50
ditto, Grafton, 1986 . . . .£15/£5
*A Graveyard for Lunatics: Another Tale of Two
Cities*, Knopf (U.S.), 1990 . . . . .£15/£5
ditto, Grafton, 1990 . . . . . .£10/£5
Green Shadows, White Whale, Knopf (U.S.), 1992 .
. . . .£10/£5
ditto, Ultramarine Press (U.S.), 1992 (38 signed copies,
no d/w) £400
ditto, Harper-Collins, 1992 . . . . .£10/£5

Short Stories
Dark Carnival, Arkham House (U.S.), 1947 . . .
. . . .£1,400/£350
ditto, Hamish Hamilton, 1948 . .£400/£35
The Martian Chronicles, Doubleday (U.S.), 1950
(green binding) . . . .£750/£125
ditto, as *The Silver Locusts*, Hart-Davis, 1951 . . .
. . . .£200/£45
The Illustrated Man, Doubleday (U.S.), 1951 . .
. . . .£250/£30
ditto, Hart-Davis, 1952 . . . . .£125/£20
The Golden Apples of the Sun, Doubleday (U.S.),
1953 . . . .£250/£35
ditto, Hart-Davis, 1953 . . . . .£175/£25

The October Country, Ballantine (U.S.), 1955 . . .
. . . . £100/£30
ditto, Hart-Davis, 1956 . . . . . . £60/£25
Sun and Shadow, Quenian Press (U.S.), 1957 (90
copies, wraps) £1,000
A Medicine for Melancholy, Doubleday (U.S.), 1959 .
. . . . £40/£15
ditto, as **The Day it Rained Forever**, Hart-Davis, 1959
. . . . £125/£25
The Small Assassin, Ace/New English Library, 1962
(wraps) £10
The Machineries of Joy, Simon & Schuster (U.S.),
1964 . . . . £75/£20
ditto, Hart-Davis, 1964 . . . . . . £75/£20
The Pedestrian, Roy Squires (U.S.), [1964] (280
copies, card wraps) £100
The Vintage Bradbury, Random House (U.S.), 1965
(wraps) £10
The Autumn People, Ballantine (U.S.), 1965 (cartoons,
wraps). £10
Tomorrow Midnight, Ballantine (U.S.), 1966
(cartoons, wraps). £15
Twice Twenty-Two, Doubleday (U.S.), 1966 £125/£20
I Sing the Body Electric!, Knopf (U.S.), 1969 £50/£10
ditto, Hart-Davis, 1970 . . . . . £25/£10
Bloch and Bradbury (with Robert Bloch), Tower
(U.S.), 1969 (wraps) £5
Fever Dreams and Other Stories (with Robert Bloch),
Sphere, 1970 (wraps) £5
Selected Stories, Harrap, 1975 (ed Anthony Adams) .
. . . . £15/£5
Long After Midnight, Knopf (U.S.), 1976 . £10/£5
ditto, Hart-Davis MacGibbon, 1977 . . . £15/£5
The Best of Bradbury, Bantam (U.S.), 1976 (wraps) .
. . . . £10
To Sing Strange Songs, Wheaton, 1979. . . £10/£5
The Stories of Ray Bradbury, Knopf (U.S.), 1980 . .
. . . . £20/£10
ditto, Knopf (U.S.), 1980 (60 presentation copies) .
. . . . £450/£125
ditto, Granada, 1980 (two vols, wraps) £5
The Last Circus, and The Electrocution, Lord John
Press (U.S.), 1980 (100 deluxe of 400 signed copies,
slipcase) . . . . £200/£150
ditto, Lord John Press (U.S.), 1980 (300 of 400 signed
copies, slipcase) . . . . £75/£40
Dinosaur Tales, Bantam (U.S.), 1983 (wraps) . . £5
A Memory of Murder, Dell (U.S.), 1984 (wraps) . £5
The Toynbee Convector, Knopf (U.S.), 1988 £20/£10
ditto, Knopf (U.S.), 1988 (350 signed copies) £100/£85
ditto, Grafton, 1989 . . . . £5
The Dragon, Footsteps Press (U.S.), 1988 (26 signed,
lettered copies of 300, wraps) £100
ditto, Footsteps Press (U.S.), 1988 (numbered copies,
wraps). £45
Quicker Than The Eye, Avon (U.S.), 1996 . £10/£5
ditto, Franklin Library (U.S.), 1996 (signed, limited
edition) . . . . £100/£85
Driving Blind, Avon (U.S.), 1997 . . . . £10/£5

Poetry
*Old Ahab's Friend, and friend to Noah, Speaks His
Piece*, Squires (U.S.), 1971 (445 unsigned copies of
485, wraps) £75
ditto, Squires (U.S.), 1971 (40 signed copies of 485) .
. . . . £150
That Son of Richard III, Squires (U.S.), 1974 (400
unsigned copies of 485, wraps). £45
ditto, Squires (U.S.), 1974 (85 signed copies of 485) .
. . . . £125
Twin Hieroglyphs that Swim the River Dust, Lord
John Press (U.S.), 1978 (300 signed copies of edition
of 326) £75
ditto, Lord John Press (U.S.), 1980 (26 signed, lettered
deluxe copies) £150
The Bike Repairman, Lord John Press (U.S.), 1978
(limited edition) £45
The Poet Considers His Resources, Lord John Press
(U.S.), 1979 (200 signed copies, broadside) . £45
The Aquaduct, Squires (U.S.), 1979 (230 copies,
wraps). £45
The Attic Where The Meadow Greens, Lord John
Press (U.S.), 1980 (300 copies, signed) . . £50
ditto, Lord John Press (U.S.), 1980 (75 deluxe copies,
signed) £125
The Love Affair, Lord John Press (U.S.), 1983 (300
signed copies) . . . . £45/£30
ditto, Lord John Press (U.S.), 1983 (100 signed deluxe
copies) £100
Forever and the Earth, Croissant (U.S.), 1984 (300
signed copies, tissue d/w) £125
The Complete Poems of Ray Bradbury, Ballantine
(U.S.), 1982 . . . . £5
Beyond 1984: Remembrance of Things Future, Targ
(U.S.), 1979 (350 signed copies) . . . £75/£45
Then Is All Love? It Is, It Is!, Orange County Book
Society (U.S.), 1981 (230 signed copies, broadside) .
. . . . £40
Death Has Lost Its Charm For Me, Lord John Press
(U.S.), 1987 (150 signed copies, no d/w) . £100
With Cat for Comforter, Gibbs-Smith (U.S.), 1997 .
. . . . £20/£5

Plays
The Meadow, (in **Best One-Act Plays of, 1947-48**)
Dodd, Mead (U.S.), 1948 . . . . . £100/£25
The Anthem Sprinters and Other Antics, Dial Press
(U.S.), 1963 (wraps) £25
ditto, Dial Press (U.S.), 1963 . . . . . £75/£15
The Day it Rained Forever, French (U.S.), 1966 £20
The Pedestrian, French (U.S.), 1966 . . . £20
The Wonderful Ice Cream Suit and Other Plays,
Bantam (U.S.), 1972 (wraps) £15
ditto, Hart-Davis MacGibbon, 1973 . . . £25/£10
*Pillar of Fire and Other Plays of Today, Tomorrow
and Beyond Tomorrow*, Bantam (U.S.), 1975 (wraps)
. . . . £15

That Ghost, that Bride of Time: Excerpts from a Play-
in-Progress, Squires (U.S.), 1976 (150 signed copies
of 400, wraps) £75
ditto, Squires (U.S.), 1976 (250 unsigned copies of
400, wraps) £25

Children's Books
Switch on the Night, Pantheon (U.S.), 1955 £250/£50
ditto, Hart-Davis, 1955 . . . . . £200/£35
R is for Rocket, Doubleday (U.S.), 1962 . £100/£20
ditto, Hart-Davis, 1968 . . . . . £100/£20
S is for Space, Doubleday (U.S.), 1966 . £100/£20
ditto, Hart-Davis, 1968 . . . . . £100/£20
The Hallowe'en Tree, Knopf (U.S.), 1972 . £45/£15
ditto, Hart-Davis MacGibbon, 1973 . . . £45/£15
*When Elephants Last in the Dooryard Bloomed:
Celebrations for Almost Any Day in the Year*, Knopf
(U.S.), 1973 . . . . £25/£5
ditto, Hart-Davis MacGibbon, 1975 . . . . £20/£5
*Where Robot Mice and Robot Men Run Round in
Robot Towns: New Poems both Light and Dark*,
Knopf (U.S.), 1977 . . . . £25/£5
ditto, Granada, 1979 . . . . . . £15/£5
The Haunted Computer and the Android Pope, Knopf
(U.S.), 1981 . . . . £15/£5
ditto, Granada, 1981 . . . . . . £15/£5
Dogs Think That Every Day Is Christmas, Gibbs-
Smith (U.S.), 1997 . . . . . . £15/£5

Miscellaneous
No Man is an Island, Brandeis Univ. (U.S.), 1952
(wraps) £50
The Circus of Dr Lao and Other Improbable Stories,
Bantam, 1956 (edited by Ray Bradbury, wraps) . £5
The Essence of Creative Writing, San Antonio Public
Library (U.S.), 1962 (wraps) £5
Teacher's Guide: Science Fiction with Lewy Olfson,
Bantam (U.S.), 1969 (wraps) £10
*Madrigals for the Space Age for Mixed Chorus and
Narrator with Piano*, Associated Music Publishers
(U.S.), 1972 (music by Lalo Schifrin, wraps) . £25
Mars and the Mind of Man, Harper (U.S.), 1973 .
. . . . £15/£5
Zen and the Art of Writing, and The Joy of Writing,
Capra Press (U.S.), 1973 (250 signed copies, no d/w)
. . . . £125
The Mummies of Guanajuato, Abrams (U.S.), 1978
(photographs by Archie Lieberman) . . £50/£20
Flatland: A Romance of Many Dimensions, by Edwin
Abbott, Arion Press, 1980 (with an introduction by
Bradbury, limited edition) £100
Fantasmas Para Siempre, Ediciones Libreria (Buenos
Aires), 1980 . . . . £75/£45
ditto, as *The Ghosts of Forever*, Rizzoli (U.S.), 1981 .
. . . . £50/£30
Los Angeles, Skyline Press (U.S.), 1984 (photographs
by West Light) £5
Orange County, Skyline Press (U.S.), 1985
(photographs by Bill Ross and others) . . . £5

The Art of 'Playboy', Playboy Press, 1985 . £25/£15
*Yestermorrow: Obvious Answers to Impossible
Futures*, Capra Press (U.S.), 1991 . . . . £15/£5

JOHN BRAINE
(b.1922 d.1986)

A novelist best known for *Room at the Top*, a classic
novel of the 'Angry Young Men' School.

Room at the Top, Eyre & Spottiswoode, 1957 . . .
. . . . £250/£25
ditto, Houghton Mifflin (U.S.), 1957 . . £25/£10
The Vodi, Eyre & Spottiswoode, 1959 . . . £20/£5
Life at the Top, Eyre & Spottiswoode, 1962 £45/£10
ditto, Houghton Mifflin (U.S.), 1962 . . . £25/£5
The Jealous God, Eyre & Spottiswoode, 1964 . £10/£5
ditto, Houghton Mifflin (U.S.), 1965 . . . £10/£5
The Crying Game, Eyre & Spottiswoode, 1968 £15/£5
ditto, Houghton Mifflin (U.S.), 1968 . . . £10/£5
Stay with Me till Morning, Eyre & Spottiswoode, 1970
. . . . £10/£5
The Queen of a Distant Country, Methuen, 1972 . .
. . . . £10/£5
ditto, Coward, McCann & Geoghegan (U.S.), 1973 .
. . . . £10/£5
Writing a Novel, Eyre Methuen, 1974 . . £10/£5
ditto, Coward, McCann & Geoghegan (U.S.), 1974 .
. . . . £10/£5
The Pious Agent, Eyre Methuen, 1975 . . . £10/£5
ditto, Atheneum (U.S.), 1976 . . . . . £10/£5
Waiting for Sheila, Eyre Methuen, 1976 . . £10/£5
ditto, Routledge (U.S.), 1977 . . . . . £10/£5
Finger of Fire, Eyre Methuen, 1977 . . . . £10/£5
J.B. Priestley, Weidenfeld & Nicolson, 1979 . £10/£5
ditto, Barnes and Noble (U.S.), 1976 . . . £10/£5
One and Last Love, Eyre Methuen, 1981 . . £10/£5
The Two of Us, Methuen, 1984 . . . . . £10/£5
These Golden Days, Methuen, 1985 . . . . £10/£5

ERNEST BRAMAH
(b.1868 d.1942)

Ernest Bramah Smith is read for his Kai Lung and
Max Carrados stories, the former featuring a Chinese
philosopher, the latter a blind detective.

'Kai Lung' Titles
The Wallet of Kai Lung, Grant Richards, 1900 . £300
ditto, L.C. Page and Company (U.S.), 1900 . . £150
ditto, Grant Richards's Colonial Library, 1900 . £200
ditto, Grant Richards, 1923 (200 signed copies) . .
. . . . £175/£125
ditto, Doran (U.S.), [1923] . . . . . £150/£60

The Transmutation of Ling, Grant Richards (U.K.)/
Brentano's (U.S.), 1911 (500 copies) . . . £125
Kai Lung's Golden Hours, Grant Richards, 1922 . .
. . . . £150/£50
ditto, Doran (U.S.), 1923 . . . . . . £95/£60
ditto, Grant Richards, 1924 (200 signed copies) . .
. . . . £350/£200
The Story of Wan and the Remarkable Shrub ...,
Doubleday Doran (U.S.), 1927 (wraps) . £150
ditto, as *Kai Lung Unrolls His Mat*, Richards Press,
1928 (the above title comprises two chapters from this
book) . . . . £75/£45
ditto, Doran (U.S.), 1928 . . . . . . £75/£50
The Moon of Much Gladness, Cassell, 1932 £100/£50
ditto, as *The Return of Kai Lung*, Sheridan House
(U.S.), 1937 . . . . £75/£45
The Kai Lung Omnibus, Philip Allan, 1936 £75/£25
Kai Lung Beneath the Mulberry-Tree, Richards Press,
1940 . . . . £150/£45
ditto, Arno Press (U.S.), 1978 . . . . £15
Kin Weng and the Miraculous Tusk, City of Birmingham School of Printing, 1941 . . . . . £50
The Celestial Omnibus, Richards Press, 1963 £35/£10
Kai Lung: Six, Non-Profit Press (U.S.), 1974 (250
copies) . . . . £75/£45

'Max Carrados' Titles
Max Carrados, Methuen, 1914 . . . .£400/£150
ditto, Hyperion Press (U.S.), 1975 . . . . £20
The Eyes of Max Carrados, Grant Richards, 1923 . .
. . . .£250/£125
ditto, Doran (U.S.), 1924 . . . . . £75/£40
Max Carrados Mysteries, Hodder & Stoughton, 1927 .
. . . .£175/£100
ditto, Penguin (U.S.), 1964 . . . . . £10
The Bravo of London, Cassell, 1934 . £600/£175

'Kai Lung' & 'Max Carrados' Titles
The Specimen Case, Hodder & Stoughton, 1924 . .
. . . .£200/£50
ditto, Doran (U.S.), 1925 . . . . . £100/£45
Short Stories of Today and Yesterday, Harrap, 1929 .
. . . .£65/£20

Other Fiction
The Mirror of Kong Ho, Chapman & Hall, 1905 . .
. . . .£100/£45

ANGELA BRAZIL

(b.1868 d.1947)

A British born author of school stories for girls.

A Terrible Tomboy, Gay & Bird, 1904 . . . £125
The Fortunes of Philippa, Blackie, 1907 [1906] £100
The Third Class at Miss Kaye's, Blackie, 1909 [1908]
. . . . £100
The Nicest Girl in the School, Blackie, 1910 . £75

Bosom Friends: A Seaside Story, Nelson, [1910] £65
The Manor House School, Blackie, 1911 . . £50
A Fourth Form Friendship, Blackie, 1912 . . £50
The New Girl at St. Chad's, Blackie, 1912 . . £50
A Pair of Schoolgirls, Blackie, [1912] . . . £45
The Leader of the Lower School, Blackie, [1914] £45
The Youngest Girl in the Fifth, Blackie, [1914] £45
The Girls of St. Cyprian's, Blackie, [1914] . . £45
The School by the Sea, Blackie, [1914] . . £45
The Jolliest Term on Record, Blackie, [1915] . £40
For the Sake of the School, Blackie, [1915] . £40
The Luckiest Girl in the School, Blackie, [1916] £35
The Slap-Bang Boys, T. C. & E. G. Jack, [1917] £35
The Madcap of the School, Blackie, [1918] . £35
A Patriotic Schoolgirl, Blackie, [1918] . . . £30
For the School Colours, Blackie, [1918] . . £25
A Harum-Scarum Schoolgirl, Blackie, [1919] . £25
The Head Girl at The Gables, Blackie, [1919] . £25
Two Little Scamps and a Puppy, Nelson, [1919] £25
A Gift from the Sea, Nelson, [1920] . . . £150/£20
A Popular Schoolgirl, Blackie, [1920] . . £150/£20
The Princess of the School, Blackie, [1920] £150/£25
A Fortunate Term, Blackie, [1921] . . £150/£25
Loyal to the School, Blackie, [1921] . . £100/£20
Moniteress Merle, Blackie, [1922] . . . £150/£20
The School in the South, Blackie, [1922] . £150/£25
The Khaki Boys and Other Stories, Nelson, [1923] .
. . . . £150/£20
Schoolgirl Kitty, Blackie, [1923]. . . . £150/£20
Captain Peggie, Blackie, [1924] . . . . £125/£20
Joan's Best Chum, Blackie, [1926] . . . £125/£20
Queen of the Dormitory and Other Stories, Cassell,
[1926]. . . . . £100/£20
Ruth of St. Ronans, Blackie, [1927]. . . £100/£20
At School with Rachel, Blackie, [1928] . . £100/£20
St. Catherine's College, Blackie, [1929] . £75/£15
The Little Green School, Blackie, [1931] . £75/£15
Nesta's New School, Blackie, [1932] . . £75/£15
Jean's Golden Term, Blackie, [1934] . . £75/£15
The School at the Turrets, Blackie, [1935] . £75/£15
An Exciting Term, Blackie, [1936] . . . £65/£10
Jill's Jolliest School, Blackie, 1937 . . . £65/£10
The School on the Cliff, Blackie, [1938] . £65/£10
The School on the Moor, Blackie, [1939] . £65/£10
The New School at Scawdale, Blackie, [1940] £65/£10
Five Jolly Schoolgirls, Blackie, [1941] . . £65/£10
The Mystery of the Moated Grange, Blackie, [1942] .
. . . . £45/£10
The Secret of the Border Castle, Blackie, [1943] . .
. . . . £45/£10
The School in the Forest, Blackie, [1944] . £45/£10
Three Terms at Uplands, Blackie, [1945] . £45/£10
The School on the Loch, Blackie, [1946] . £45/£10

Plays
The Mischievous Brownie, Paterson, 'Children's
Plays' series No. 1, [1913] £40
The Fairy Gifts, Paterson, 'Children's Plays' series No.
2, [1913] £40

The Enchanted Fiddle, Paterson, 'Children's Plays' series No. 3, [1913] £40
The Wishing Princess, Paterson, 'Children's Plays' series No. 4, [1913] £40

Autobiography
My Own Schooldays, Blackie, [1925] . . £65/£15

ELINOR BRENT-DYER
(b.1894 d.1969)

Born Gladys Elinor May Dyer, this British author of stories for girls worked for many years as a teacher.

'Chalet School' Titles
The School at the Chalet, Chambers, 1925 . £500/£150
Jo of the Chalet School, Chambers, 1926 . £350/£100
The Princess of the Chalet School, Chambers, 1927 . . . . £350/£100
The Head Girl of the Chalet School, Chambers, 1928. . . . . £350/£100
The Rivals of the Chalet School, Chambers, 1929 . . . . £350/£100
Eustacia Goes to the Chalet School, Chambers, 1930 . . . . £350/£100
The Chalet School and Jo, Chambers, 1931 £250/£50
The Chalet School in Camp, Chambers, 1932 . . . . £350/£100
The Exploits of the Chalet School Girls, Chambers, 1933 . . . . £350/£100
The Chalet School and the Lintons, Chambers, 1934 . . . . £350/£100
The New House at the Chalet School, Chambers, 1935 . . . . £350/£100
Jo Returns to the Chalet School, Chambers, 1936. . . . . £350/£100
The New Chalet School, Chambers, 1938 . £250/£80
The Chalet School in Exile, Chambers, 1940 (Nazi d/w) . . . . £500/£60
The Chalet School Goes To It, Chambers, 1941 . . . . £125/£60
The Highland Twins at the Chalet School, Chambers, 1942 . . . . £125/£60
Lavender Laughs in the Chalet School, Chambers, 1943 . . . . £125/£60
Gay from China at the Chalet School, Chambers, 1944 . . . . £125/£60
Jo to the Rescue, Chambers, 1945 . . . £125/£60
The Chalet School Book for Girls, Chambers, [1947] £75
The Second Chalet School Book for Girls, Chambers, 1948 (no d/w) £75
The Third Chalet School Book for Girls, Chambers, 1949 . . . . £150/£75
Three Go to the Chalet School, Chambers, 1949 . . . . £100/£50
The Chalet School and the Island, Chambers, 1950 . . . . £100/£50

Peggy of the Chalet School, Chambers, 1950 . . . . £100/£50
Carola Storms the Chalet School, Chambers, 1951 . . . . £100/£50
The Chalet School and Rosalie, Chambers, 1951 (wraps) £75
The Wrong Chalet School, Chambers, 1952 £100/£50
Shocks for the Chalet School, Chambers, 1952 . . . . £100/£50
The Chalet School in the Oberland, Chambers, 1952 . . . . £125/£60
Bride Leads the Chalet School, Chambers, 1953 . . . . £150/£65
Changes for the Chalet School, Chambers, 1953 . . . . £125/£60
The Chalet Girls' Cook Book, Chambers, 1953 . . . . £200/£100
Joey Goes to the Oberland, Chambers, 1952 £125/£65
The Chalet School and Barbara, Chambers, 1954 . . . . £125/£50
Tom Tackles the Chalet School, Chambers, 1955 . . . . £125/£65
The Chalet School Does it Again, Chambers, 1955 . . . . £150/£75
A Chalet Girl from Kenya, Chambers, 1955 £50/£30
Mary-Lou of the Chalet School, Chambers, 1956 . . . . £100/£50
A Genius at the Chalet School, Chambers, 1956 . . . . £100/£50
A Problem for the Chalet School, Chambers, 1956 . . . . £100/£50
The New Mistress at the Chalet School, Chambers, 1957 . . . . £100/£50
Excitements at the Chalet School, Chambers, 1957 . . . . £100/£50
The Coming of Age at the Chalet School, Chambers, 1958 . . . . £100/£50
The Chalet School and Richenda, Chambers, 1958 . . . . £100/£50
Trials for the Chalet School, Chambers, 1959 . . . . £100/£50
Theodora and the Chalet School, Chambers, 1959 . . . . £100/£50
Joey and Co. in Tirol, Chambers, 1960 . . £100/£50
Ruey Richardson, Chaletian, Chambers, 1960 £125/£60
A Leader in the Chalet School, Chambers, 1961 . . . . £100/£50
The Chalet School Wins the Trick, Chambers, 1961 . . . . £100/£50
A Future Chalet School Girl, Chambers, 1962. . . . . £100/£50
The Feud in the Chalet School, Chambers, 1962 . . . . £100/£50
The Chalet School Triplets, Chambers, 1963 £100/£50
The Chalet School Reunion, Chambers, 1963 (with d/w, chart and yellow band). . . . . £200/£65
Jane and the Chalet School, Chambers, 1964 . . . . £100/£50

Redheads at the Chalet School, Chambers, 1964 . .
. . . . £100/£50
Adrienne and the Chalet School, Chambers, 1965. .
. . . . £100/£50
Summer Term at the Chalet School, Chambers, 1965.
. . . . £100/£50
Challenge for the Chalet School, Chambers, 1966. .
. . . . £100/£50
Two Sams at the Chalet School, Chambers, 1967 . .
. . . . £100/£45
Althea Joins the Chalet School, Chambers, 1969 . .
. . . . £100/£45
Prefects of the Chalet School, Chambers, 1970 . .
. . . . £125/£45

'La Rochelle' Titles
Gerry Goes to School, Chambers, 1922 . . £350/£100
ditto, Lippincott (Philadelphia), 1923 . . £350/£100
A Head Girl's Difficulties, Chambers, 1923 £350/£100
The Maids of La Rochelle, Chambers, 1924 £350/£100
Seven Scamps, Chambers, 1927 . . . . £350/£100
Heather Leaves School, Chambers, 1929 . £350/£100
Janie of La Rochelle, Chambers, 1932 . . £350/£100
Janie Steps in, Chambers, 1953 . . . . £100/£25

'Chudleigh Hold' Titles
Fardingales, Latimer House, 1950 . . . £200/£50
The 'Susannah' Adventure, Chambers, 1953 £100/£40
Chudleigh Hold, Chambers, 1954 . . . £100/£40
The Condor Crags Adventure, Chambers, 1954 . .
. . . . £100/£40
Top Secret, Chambers, 1955 . . . . . £100/£40

Other Titles
A Thrilling Term at Janeways, Nelson, 1927 . . .
. . . . £250/£100
The New Housemistress, Nelson, 1928 . . £60/£25
Judy the Guide, Nelson, 1928 . . . . £200/£75
The School by the River, Burns, Oates & Washbourne,
1930 . . . . £600/£150
The Feud in the Fifth Remove, Girl's Own Paper,
1931 . . . . £150/£50
The Little Marie-Jose, Burns, Oates & Washbourne,
1932 . . . . £600/£150
Carnation of the Upper Fourth, Girl's Own Paper,
1934 . . . . £150/£45
Elizabeth the Gallant, Butterworth, 1935 . £450/£175
Monica Turns Up Trumps, Girl's Own Paper, 1936 .
. . . . £125/£50
Caroline the Second, Girl's Own Paper, 1937 . . .
. . . . £400/£50
They Both Liked Dogs, Girl's Own Paper, 1938 . .
. . . . £400/£150
The Little Missus, Chambers, 1942 . . . £150/£50
The Lost Staircase, Chambers, 1946 . . £150/£45
Lorna at Wynyards, Lutterworth, 1947 . . £150/£45
Stepsisters for Lorna, Temple, 1948. . . £150/£45
Verena Visits New Zealand, Chambers, 1951 £250/£75
Bess on Her Own in Canada, Chambers, 1951. . .
. . . . £250/£75

Quintette in Queensland, Chambers, 1951 . £250/£75
Sharlie's Kenya Diary, Chambers, 1951 . £250/£75
Nesta Steps Out, Oliphants, 1954 . . . £100/£25
Kennelmaid Nan, Lutterworth, 1954 . . £100/£25
Beechy of the Harbour School, Oliphants, 1955 . .
. . . . £100/£25
Leader in Spite of Herself, Oliphants, 1956 £100/£25
The School at Skelton Hall, Max Parrish, 1962 . .
. . . . £125/£40
Trouble at Skelton Hall, Max Parrish, 1963 £125/£40

Short Stories
Sunday and Everyday Reading for the Young
(contains 'Jack's Revenge'), Wells, Gardner, Darton,
1914 . . . . £20
The Big Book for Girls (contains 'The Lady in the
Yellow Gown'), Humphrey Milford/O.U.P., 1925 £25
The Golden Story Book for Girls (contains 'The Lady
in the Yellow Gown'), Humphrey Milford/O.U.P.,
1931 . . . . £20
Stories of the Circus, Book 4 (contains 'Carlotta to the
Rescue', magazine), c.1931 . . . . . . £15
The Children's Circus Book (contains 'Carlotta to the
Rescue'), Associated Newspapers, (c.1934) . £30
Come to the Circus (contains 'Carlotta to the Rescue'),
P.R. Gawthorn, (c.1938). £20
The Second Coronet Book for Girls (contains
'Cavalier Maid'), Sampson Low, [n.d.] . . £15
My Favourite Story (contains 'Rescue in the Snows'),
Thames [n.d.]. £15
Sceptre Girls' Story Annual (contains 'House of
Secrets'), Purnell [n.d.] £15
Girl's Own Annual, Vol 57 (contains 'The Robins
Make Good'), Girl's Own [n.d.] £50
My Treasure Hour Bumper Annual (contains 'The
Chalet School Mystery'), Murrays Sales and Service
Co., 1970 . . . . £15

ANNE BRONTË
(b.1820 d.1849)

Not held in as much esteem as her sisters. *Agnes Grey*
was originally published alongside *Wuthering
Heights*.

Poems by Currer, Ellis and Acton Bell, Aylott &
Jones, 1846, first issue (with Charlotte and Emily
Brontë) £25,000
ditto, second issue £3,000
ditto, Smith, Elder & Co, 1846 [1848], second edition .
. . . . £1,750
ditto, Lea and Blanchard (U.S.), 1848 . . £2,000
Wuthering Heights with *Agnes Grey*, Newby, 1847
(pseud. Ellis and Acton Bell, 3 vols) . . £60,000
ditto, Harper and Brothers (U.S.), 1848 . . . £6,000
The Tenant of Wildfell Hall, Newby, 1848 (pseud.
Acton Bell, 3 vols) £40,000
ditto, Harper (U.S.), 1848 . . . . . £15,000

CHARLOTTE BRONTË
(b.1816 d.1855)

Sister to Emily and Anne, Charlotte was the only Brontë to achieve literary fame in her own lifetime. Charlotte was a champion of the female spirit, her *Jane Eyre* an enduring classic.

Poems by Currer, Ellis and Acton Bell, Aylott & Jones, 1846, first issue (with Anne and Emily Brontë)
. . . . £25,000
ditto, second issue £3,000
ditto, Smith, Elder & Co, 1846 [1848], second edition.
. . . . £1,750
ditto, Lea and Blanchard (U.S.), 1848 . . . £2,000
Jane Eyre, Smith, Elder & Co., 1847 (3 vols, first issue, with advertisements dated June, 1847) £20,000
ditto, Smith, Elder & Co., 1847 (3 vols second issue, ads dated October, 1847) £5,000
ditto, Harper (U.S.), 1848 (wraps) . . . £1,250
Shirley, Smith, Elder & Co., 1849 (3 vols) . £2,500
ditto, Harper (U.S.), 1850 (1 vol.) £400
Villette, Smith, Elder & Co., 1853 (3 vols) . £2,500
ditto, Harper (U.S.), 1853 (1 vol.) £400
The Professor, Smith, Elder & Co., 1857 (2 vols) . .
. . . . £1,000
ditto, Smith, Elder & Co., 1857 (second state, 2 vols rebound together) £250
ditto, Harper (U.S.), 1857 (1 vol.) £150

Minor Works
The Last Sketch - Emma: A Fragment, The Cornhill Magazine Vol I, 1860 . . . . . . £100
The Twelve Adventurers and Other Stories, Hodder & Stoughton, 1925 (limited to 1,000 copies). £125/£45
ditto, Hodder & Stoughton (U.S.), 1925 . . £75/£25
The Spell, O.U.P., 1931 . . . . . . £75/£35
Legends of Angria, edited by Fannie E. Ratchford, Yale Univ. Press (U.S.), 1933 . . . £65/£25
The Poems of Charlotte Brontë and Patrick Branwell Brontë, edited by T.J. Wise and J.A. Symington, O.U.P., 1934 . . . . £75/£25
The Miscellaneous and Unpublished Writings of Charlotte and Patrick Branwell Brontë, edited by T.J. Wise and J.A. Symington, O.U.P., 1934 (2 vols, 1,000 copies). . . . . £75/£25
Tales from Angria, edited by Phyllis Bentley, Collins, 1954 . . . . £45/£15
The Search After Happiness, Harvill Press, 1969 . .
. . . . £20/£5
ditto, Simon & Schuster (U.S.), 1969 . . . £20/£5
Five Novelettes, edited by Winifred Gerin, The Folio Society, 1971 (slipcase) . . . . . £20/£10
A Leaf from an Unopened Volume, The Brontë Society, 1986 (wraps) £15

EMILY BRONTË
(b.1818 d.1848)

Wuthering Heights, now regarded as a classic novel, was published shortly after Charlotte's *Jane Eyre*, and the pseudonyms used by the sisters were originally thought to conceal the identity of a single male author. Emily's poems are often seen as some of the finest lyric verse in the English language.

Poems by Currer, Ellis and Acton Bell, Aylott & Jones, 1846, first issue (with Anne and Charlotte Brontë) £25,000
ditto, second issue £3,000
ditto, Smith, Elder & Co, 1846 [1848], second edition .
. . . . £1,750
ditto, Lea and Blanchard (U.S.), 1848 . . . £2,000
Wuthering Heights with *Agnes Grey*, Newby, 1847 (pseud. Ellis and Acton Bell, 3 vols) . . £60,000
ditto, Harper and Brothers (U.S.), 1848 . . . £6,000

JOCELYN BROOKE
(b.1908 d.1966)

A novelist and poet, Brooke is considered a fine stylist.

The 'Orchid' Series
The Military Orchid, Bodley Head, 1948 . £75/£15
A Mine of Serpents, Bodley Head, 1949 . £75/£15
The Goose Cathedral, Bodley Head, 1950. £75/£15

Other Fiction
The Scapegoat, Bodley Head, 1948 . . . £75/£15
ditto, Harper (U.S.), 1949 . . . . . £25/£10
The Image of a Drawn Sword, Bodley Head, 1950 .
. . . . £60/£20
ditto, Knopf (U.S.), 1951 . . . . . . £15/£5
The Passing of a Hero, Bodley Head, 1953 £60/£15
Private View: Four Portraits, Barrie, 1954 . £40/£15
The Dog at Clambercrown, Bodley Head, 1955 . .
. . . . £75/£15
ditto, Vanguard Press (U.S.), 1955 . . . £20/£10
The Crisis in Bulgaria, or Ibsen to the Rescue!, Chatto & Windus, 1956 . . . . . £45/£10
Conventional Weapons, Faber, 1961 . . £25/£10
ditto, as *The Name of Greene*, Vanguard Press (U.S.), 1961 . . . . £20/£10

Poetry
Six Poems, privately printed, 1928 (50 signed, numbered copies, wraps) £200
December Spring, Bodley Head, 1946 . £65/£20
The Elements of Death and other poems, Hand & Flower Press, 1952 (wraps) £20

Children's Titles
The Wonderful Summer, Lehmann, 1949 . £50/£20

Non Fiction
The Wild Orchids of Britain, Bodley Head, 1950 (40 specially bound, signed copies of 1,140) £1,000/£750
ditto, Bodley Head, 1950 (1,100 copies of 1,140) .
. . . . £175/£145
The Flower in Season, Bodley Head, 1952 . £35/£15
Ronald Firbank: A Critical Study, Barker, 1951 .
. . . . £25/£10
ditto, Roy (U.S.), 1951 . . . . . . £20/£5
Elizabeth Bowen, British Council/Longmans Green, 1952 (wraps) £5
Aldous Huxley, British Council/Longmans Green, 1953 (wraps) £5
ditto, revised edition, British Council/Longmans Green, 1958 (wraps) £5
Ronald Firbank and John Betjeman, British Council/Longmans Green, 1962 (wraps) . . . £5
The Birth of a Legend, Bertram Rota, 1964 (65 signed, numbered copies, wraps) £90

RUPERT BROOKE
(b.1887 d.1915)

Born and educated at Rugby, the future war poet subsequently went up to Cambridge University. Although already a published poet, Brooke achieved his greatest fame posthumously. He died of blood-poisoning aboard ship on his way to the great engagement of the Dardanelles at the age of 28.

Poetry
The Pyramids, privately printed, 1904 (wraps) £10,000
The Bastille, privately printed by A.J. Lawrence, 1905 (wraps) £6,000
ditto, privately printed by George E. Over, [1920] (wraps) £200
Prize Compositions, privately printed, 1905 (wraps) .
. . . . £2,500
Poems, Sidgwick & Jackson, 1911 (no d/w) . £450
1914 and Other Poems, Sidgwick & Jackson, 1915 .
. . . . £300
ditto, Doubleday, Page (U.S.), 1915 (87 copyright copies, wraps) £1,500
1914, Five Sonnets, Sidgwick & Jackson, 1915 (wraps) £45
War Poems, privately printed, 1915 . . . . £45
The Collected Poems of Rupert Brooke, Lane (U.S.), 1915 (with a Memoir by Edward Marsh) . . £50
ditto, Lane (U.S.), 1915 (100 copies bound for members of the Woodberry Society) . . . £600
ditto, Sidgwick & Jackson, 1918 . . . . . £50
ditto, Riccardi Press, 1919 (1,000 numbered copies) .
. . . . £150

ditto, Riccardi Press, 1919 (13 copies bound in full vellum) £1,250
The Old Vicarage, Grantchester, Sidgwick & Jackson, 1916 (wraps) £100
Selected Poems, Sidgwick & Jackson, 1917 . £20
Fragments Now First Collected, Hartford (U.S.), 1925 (94 copies) £250
ditto, Hartford (U.S.), 1925 (5 numbered copies on vellum) £400
Twenty Poems, Sidgwick & Jackson, 1935 . £50/£20
The Poetical Works of Rupert Brooke, Faber & Faber, 1946 . . . . £35/£10
Poems, Folio Society, 1948 (slipcase) . . £25/£15
Four Poems, Scolar Press, 1974 (100 copies signed by editor of 500, slipcase) £200
ditto, Scolar Press, 1974 (400 unsigned copies of 500).
. . . . £75

Prose
The Authorship of the Later 'Appius and Virginia', privately printed, [1913] (20 copies) . . . £1,000
Lithuania, A Drama in One Act, Chicago Little Theatre (U.S.), 1915 (wraps, 200 copies) . . £350
ditto, Sidgwick & Jackson, 1935 . . . £75/£25
ditto, Sidgwick & Jackson, 1935 (wraps) . . £25
Letters from America, Scribner's (U.S.), 1916 . £25
ditto, Sidgwick & Jackson, 1916 . . . . . £25
John Webster and the Elizabethan Drama, John Lane (U.S.), 1916 . . . . £50
ditto, Sidgwick & Jackson, 1916 . . . . . £40
A Letter to the Editor of the Poetry Review, Watch Hill Press, 1929 (50 copies) £175
Democracy and the Arts, Hart-Davis, 1946 (preface by Geoffrey Keynes) . . . . . . £25/£10
ditto, Hart-Davis, 1946 (240 numbered copies) £100
The Prose of Rupert Brooke, Sidgwick & Jackson, 1956 (edited and with an introduction by Christopher Hassall) . . . . £25/£10
The Letters of Rupert Brooke, Faber & Faber, 1968 .
. . . . £30/£10
ditto, Harcourt Brace (U.S.), 1968 . . . £30/£10
Song of Love: The Letters of Rupert Brooke and Noel Olivier, Bloomsbury, 1991 . . . . £25/£10
ditto, Crown (U.S.), 1992 . . . . . . £25/£10

ANITA BROOKNER
(b.1928)

Brookner's literary novels are haunted by solitary, sad women and the failures of their relationships.

Novels
A Start in Life, Cape, 1981 . . . . . £65/£15
ditto, as *The Debut*, Linden Press (U.S.), 1981 . £15/£5
Providence, Cape, 1982 . . . . . . £75/£15
ditto, Pantheon (U.S.), 1984 . . . . . . £20/£5
Look at Me, Cape, 1983 . . . . £30/£5

ditto, Pantheon (U.S.), 1983 . . . . . . £20/£5
Hotel Du Lac, Cape, 1984 . . . . . £65/£10
ditto, Pantheon (U.S.), 1985 . . . . . . £20/£5
Family and Friends, Cape, 1985. . . . . £20/£5
ditto, London Limited Editions, 1985 (250 signed copies) . . . . £50/£45
ditto, Pantheon (U.S.), 1985 . . . . . . £20/£5
A Misalliance, Cape, 1986 . . . . . . £20/£5
ditto, as **The Misalliance**, Pantheon (U.S.), 1987 . . . . £20/£5
A Friend From England, Cape, 1987 . . . £20/£5
ditto, Pantheon (U.S.), 1988 . . . . . . £20/£5
Latecomers, Cape, 1988 . . . . £15/£5
ditto, Pantheon (U.S.), 1989 . . . . . . £15/£5
Lewis Percy, Cape, 1989 . . . . £15/£5
ditto, Pantheon (U.S.), 1990 . . . . . . £15/£5
Brief Lives, Cape, 1990 . . . . £15/£5
ditto, Random House (U.S.), 1991 . . . . £15/£5
A Closed Eye, Cape, 1991 . . . . . . £15/£5
ditto, Random House (U.S.), 1992 . . . . £15/£5
Fraud, Cape, 1992 . . . . £15/£5
ditto, Random House (U.S.), 1992 . . . . £15/£5
A Family Romance, Cape, 1993 . . . . . £15/£5
A Private View, Cape, 1994 . . . . . . £10/£5
ditto, Random House (U.S.), 1994 . . . . £10/£5
Incidents in the Rue Laugier, Cape, 1995 . £10/£5
ditto, Random House (U.S.), 1994 . . . . £10/£5
Altered States, Cape, 1996 . . . . . . £10/£5
ditto, Random House (U.S.), 1996 . . . . £10/£5
Visitors, Cape, 1997 . . . . £10/£5
ditto, Random House (U.S.), 1998 . . . . £10/£5
Falling Slowly, Viking, 1998. . . . . . £10/£5
ditto, Random House (U.S.), 1999 . . . . £10/£5
Undue Influence, Viking, 1999 . . . . . £10/£5
ditto, Random House (U.S.), 1999 . . . . £10/£5
The Bay of Angels, Viking, 2001 . . . . £10/£5
ditto, Random House (U.S.), 2001 . . . . £10/£5

Essays

Watteau, Hamlyn, 1967 . . . . . . £50/£15
The Genius of the Future: Studies in French Art Criticism, Phaidon, 1971 . . . . . £30/£10
ditto, as **The Genius of the Future: Essays in French Art Criticism**, Cornell Univ. Press (U.S.), 1988 . . . . £25/£10
Greuze: The Rise and Fall of an Eighteenth-Century Phenomenon, New York Graphic Society (U.S.), 1972 . . . . £30/£10
Jacques-Louis David, Chatto & Windus, 1980 £25/£10
ditto, Harper (U.S.), 1980 . . . . . . £25/£10
Romanticism and Its Discontent, Viking, 2000 £10/£5
ditto, Farrar Straus (U.S.), 2000 . . . . . £10/£5

FREDRIC BROWN
(b.1906 d.1972)

One of the most collectable authors of the pulp era, Brown's work is usually very original, well-plotted and fast-moving.

Novels

The Fabulous Clipjoint, Dutton (U.S.), 1947 £400/£50
ditto, Boardman, 1949 (wraps) £35
The Dead Ringer, Dutton (U.S.), 1948 . . £250/£35
ditto, Boardman, 1949 (wraps) £30
Murder Can be Fun, Dutton (U.S.), 1948 . £200/£35
ditto, Boardman, 1951. . . . . . . £75/£20
The Bloody Moonlight, Dutton (U.S.), 1949 £200/£35
ditto, as **Murder in Moonlight**, Boardman, 1949 . . . . £50/£15
The Screaming Mimi, Dutton (U.S.), 1949 . £275/£50
ditto, Boardman, 1950. . . . . . . £75/£20
What Mad Universe, Dutton (U.S.), 1949 . £200/£35
ditto, Boardman, 1951. . . . . . . £75/£20
Compliments of a Fiend, Dutton (U.S.), 1950 . . . . £200/£35
ditto, Boardman, 1951. . . . . . . £75/£20
Here Comes a Candle, Dutton (U.S.), 1950. £200/£35
ditto, Boardman, 1951. . . . . . . £75/£20
Night of the Jabberwock, Dutton (U.S.), 1950 . . . . £200/£35
ditto, Boardman, 1951. . . . . . . £75/£20
The Case of the Dancing Sandwiches, Dell (U.S.), 1951 (wraps) £200
Death Has Many Doors, Dutton (U.S.), 1951 £175/£25
ditto, Boardman, 1952. . . . . . . £75/£20
The Far Cry, Dutton (U.S.), 1951 . . . £175/£25
ditto, Boardman, 1952. . . . . . . £75/£20
We All Killed Grandma, Dutton (U.S.), 1951 £150/£25
ditto, Boardman, 1952. . . . . . . £50/£15
The Deep End, Dutton (U.S.), 1952 . . . £150/£25
ditto, Boardman, 1953. . . . . . . £50/£15
Madball, Dell (U.S.), 1953 (wraps) £50
ditto, Muller Gold Medal, 1962 (wraps) . . . £10
The Lights in the Sky are Stars, Dutton (U.S.), 1953 . . . . £125/£25
ditto, as **Project Jupiter**, Boardman, 1954 . £50/£15
His Name Was Death, Dutton (U.S.), 1954 . £125/£25
ditto, Boardman, 1955. . . . . . . £50/£15
The Wench is Dead, Dutton (U.S.), 1955 . £125/£25
Martians Go Home, Dutton (U.S.), 1955 . £150/£35
ditto, Grafton, 1987 (wraps) £10
The Lenient Beast, Dutton (U.S.), 1956. . £125/£25
ditto, Boardman, 1957. . . . . . . £50/£15
Rogue in Space, Dutton (U.S.), 1957 . . £125/£25
One For the Road, Dutton (U.S.), 1958. . £125/£25
ditto, Boardman, 1959. . . . . . . £50/£15
The Office, Dutton (U.S.), 1958 . . . . £200/£35
ditto, Dennis McMillan (U.S.), 1987 (425 copies) . . . . £40/£10
The Late Lamented, Dutton (U.S.), 1959 . £100/£20
ditto, Boardman, 1959. . . . . . . £50/£15

Knock Three-One-Two, Dutton (U.S.), 1959 £150/£35
ditto, Boardman, 1960. . . . . . . £50/£15
The Murderers, Dutton (U.S.), 1961 . . £100/£20
ditto, Boardman, 1962. . . . . . . £45/£15
The Mind Thing, Bantam (U.S.), 1961 (wraps) £15
ditto, Hamlyn, 1979 (wraps) £10
The Five-Day Nightmare, Dutton (U.S.), 1963. . .
. . . . £100/£20
ditto, as **Five Day Nightmare**, Boardman, 1963 .
. . . . £45/£15
Mrs Murphy's Underpants, Dutton (U.S.), 1963 . .
. . . . £100/£20
ditto, Boardman, 1965. . . . . . . £45/£15
4 Novels by Fredric Brown, Zomba, 1983 (*Night of the
Jabberwock, The Screaming Mimi, Knock Three-One-
Two* and *The Fabulous Clipjoint*) . . . £30/£10

Short Stories
Space on My Hands, Shasta (U.S.), 1951 . £250/£35
ditto, Corgi, 1953 (wraps). £15
Mostly Murder: Eighteen Short Stories, Dutton (U.S.),
1953 . . . . £150/£35
ditto, Boardman, 1954. . . . . . . £100/£25
Angels and Spaceships, Dutton (U.S.), 1954 £125/£25
ditto, Gollancz, 1955 . . . . £50/£15
Honeymoon in Hell, Bantam (U.S.), 1958 (wraps) £15
The Shaggy Dog and Other Murders, Dutton (U.S.),
1963 . . . . £125/£25
ditto, Boardman, 1954. . . . . . . £45/£15
Carnival of Crime, Southern Illinois Univ. Press
(U.S.), 1985 . . . . £35/£10
Nightmares and Geezenstacks, Bantam (U.S.), 1961
(wraps) £20
ditto, Corgi, 1962 (wraps). £10
Daymares, Lancer (U.S.), 1968 (wraps). . . £10
Paradox Lost, Random House (U.S.), 1973. . £25/£5
ditto, Hale, 1975 . . . . £20/£5
The Best of Fredric Brown, Doubleday (U.S.), 1976 .
. . . . £35/£10
The Best Short Stories of Fredric Brown, NEL, 1982
(wraps) £5
And the Gods Laughed, Phantasia Press (U.S.), 1987
(1,525 copies) . . . . £25/£10
ditto, Phantasia Press (U.S.), 1987 (475 numbered
copies) . . . . £50/£15

Fredric Brown in the 'Pulp Detectives'
Homicide Sanatarium, Dennis McMillan (U.S.), 1984
(300 numbered copies) . . . . . . £100/£25
Before She Kills, Dennis McMillan (U.S.), 1984 (350
numbered copies) . . . . £75/£20
Madman's Holiday, Dennis McMillan (U.S.), 1985
(350 numbered copies) . . . . . . £75/£20
The Case of the Dancing Sandwiches, Dennis
McMillan (U.S.), 1985 (400 numbered copies) . .
. . . . £75/£20
The Freak Show Murders, Dennis McMillan (U.S.),
1985 (350 numbered copies) . . . . £50/£15

30 Corpses Every Thursday, Dennis McMillan (U.S.),
1985 (375 numbered copies) . . . . £50/£15
Pardon My Ghoulish Laughter, Dennis McMillan
(U.S.), 1986 (400 numbered copies) . . £50/£15
Red is the Hue of Hell, Dennis McMillan (U.S.), 1986
(400 numbered copies) . . . . . . £50/£15
Sex Life on the Planet Mars, Dennis McMillan (U.S.),
1986 (400 numbered copies) . . . . £100/£25
Brother Monster, Dennis McMillan (U.S.), 1987 (400
numbered copies) . . . . £50/£15
Nightmare in the Darkness, Dennis McMillan (U.S.),
1987 (425 numbered copies) . . . . £50/£15
Who Was That Blonde I Saw You Kill Last Night?,
Dennis McMillan (U.S.), 1988 (450 numbered copies)
. . . . £40/£10
Three Corpse Parlay, Dennis McMillan (U.S.), 1988
(450 numbered copies) . . . . . . £40/£10
Selling Death Short, Dennis McMillan (U.S.), 1988
(450 numbered copies) . . . . . . £30/£10
Whispering Death, Dennis McMillan (U.S.), 1989
(450 numbered copies) . . . . . . £30/£10
Happy Ending, Dennis McMillan (U.S.), 1990 (450
numbered copies) . . . . £30/£10
The Water Walker, Dennis McMillan (U.S.), 1990
(425 numbered copies) . . . . . . £30/£10
The Gibbering Night, Dennis McMillan (U.S.), 1991
(425 numbered copies) . . . . . . £25/£10
The Pickled Punks, Dennis McMillan (U.S.), 1991
(450 numbered copies) . . . . . . £25/£10

Poetry
Fermented Ink, privately published (U.S.), 1932
(wraps) £750
Shadow Suite, privately published (U.S.), 1932 (wraps)
. . . . £750

Children's Title
Mitkey Astromouse, Quist (U.S. & U.K.), 1971 . .
. . . . £75/£25

JEAN de BRUNHOFF
(b.1899 d.1937)

The creator of Babar the Elephant, after his death de
Brunhoff's series of books were continued by his son,
Laurent.

Histoire de Babar le Petit Éléphant, Editions Du
Jardin Des Modes (France), 1931 . . . . £300
ditto, as **The Story of Babar, the Little Elephant**,
Smith and Haas (U.S.), 1933 . . . . . £300
ditto, Methuen, 1934 . . . . £200
Le Voyage De Babar, Editions Du Jardin Des Modes
(France), 1932 . . . . £300
ditto, as **Travels of Babar**, Smith and Haas (U.S.),
1934 . . . . £300
ditto, as **Babar's Travels**, Methuen, 1935 . . £175

Le Roi Babar, Editions Du Jardin Des Modes (France), 1933 . . . . £175
ditto, as *Babar the King*, Smith and Haas (U.S.), 1935 . . . . £175
ditto, Methuen, 1936 . . . . £175
ABC de Babar, Editions Du Jardin Des Modes (France), 1937 . . . . £175
ditto, *A B C of Babar*, Smith and Haas (U.S.), 1937 . . . . £175
ditto, as *Babar's ABC*, Methuen, 1937 . . . £175
Vacances de Zéphir, Hachette (France), 1936 . £100
ditto, as *Zephir's Holidays*, Random House, 1937 £100
ditto, as *Babar's Friend Zephir*, Methuen, 1937 £100
Babar en Famille, Hachette (France), 1938 . . £150
ditto, as *Babar and His Children*, Random House (U.S.), 1938 . . . . £150
ditto, as *Babar at Home*, Methuen, 1938 . . £150
Babar et Le Père Noël, Hachette (France), 1940 £125
ditto, as *Babar and Father Christmas*, Random House, 1940 . . . . £125
ditto, Methuen, 1940 . . . . £125

'Babar' Books by Laurent de Brunhoff
Babar and that Rascal Arthur, Methuen, 1948. £75
Picnic at Babar's, Methuen, 1950 . . . . £75
Babar's Visit to Bird Island, Methuen, 1952 . £50
Babar's Castle, Methuen, 1962 . . . . £40
Babar's French Lessons, Cape, 1965 . . £35
Babar Goes Visiting, Methuen, 1969 . . . £30
Babar Goes to America, Collins, 1969 . . . £30
Babar's Fair, Methuen, 1969 . . . £30
Babar Learns to Drive, Methuen, 1969 . . . £30
Babar Keeps Fit!, Methuen, 1970 . . . £30
Babar at the Seaside, Methuen, 1971 . . £20
Babar in the Snow, Methuen, 1971 . . . £15
Babar the Gardener, Methuen, 1971 . . £15
Babar's Birthday Surprise, Methuen, 1971. . £25
Babar's Day Out, Methuen, 1971 . . . £15
Babar and the Christmas Tree, Methuen, 1972 £15
Babar and the Doctor, Methuen, 1972 . . £15
Babar and the Professor, Methuen, 1972 . . £15
Babar Goes Camping, Methuen, 1972 . . £15
Babar and the Artist, Methuen, 1972 . . £15
Babar on the Secret Planet, Methuen, 1973 . £25
Babar the Cook, Methuen, 1973 . . . . £15
Babar the Musician, Methuen, 1973 . . £15
Babar the Pilot, Methuen, 1973 . . . . £15
Babar the Sportsman, Methuen, 1973 . . . £15
Babar and the Wully-Wully, Methuen, 1977 . £15
Babar's Mystery, Methuen, 1979 . . . £15
Babar and the Ghost, Methuen, 1981 . . £15
Babar's ABC, Methuen, 1984 . . . . £15
Babar's Book of Colour, Methuen, 1985 . . £15
Babar's Counting Book, Methuen, 1986 . . £10
Babar's Little Girl, Methuen, 1988 . . . £10
Babar's Busy Week, Methuen, 1990. . . . £10
Babar's Battle, Methuen, 1992 . . . . £10
The Rescue of Babar, Methuen, 1993 . . £10

'Serafina' books by Laurent de Brunhoff
Serafina the Giraffe, Methuen, 1964 [1965] . £25
Serafina's Lucky Find, Methuen, 1967. . . £25
Captain Serafina, Methuen, 1969 . . . . £25

JOHN BUCHAN
(b.1875 d.1940)

Prolific Scottish writer whose talents ranged across novels, biographies, essays and poetry. Buchan's Richard Hannay mystery novels are still popular, and his historical romances have attracted much praise.

Historical Romances
Sir Quixote of the Moors, Fisher Unwin, 1895 . £450
ditto, Holt (U.S.), 1895 . . . . . . £100
John Burnet of Barns, John Lane, 1898 . . £300
Grey Weather, Moorland Tales, John Lane, 1899 £250
A Lost Lady of Old Years, John Lane, 1899 . £250
Salute to Adventurers, Nelson, [1915] . . £100
ditto, Doran (U.S.), 1915 . . . . . . £65
The Path of the King, Hodder & Stoughton, [1921] .
. . . . £400/£50
ditto, Doran (U.S.), 1921 . . . . . £400/£50
Midwinter, Hodder & Stoughton, [1923] . £250/£45
ditto, Doran (U.S.), 1923 . . . . . . £200/£35
Witch Wood, Hodder & Stoughton, 1927 . £300/£50
ditto, Houghton Mifflin (U.S.), 1927 . . £100/£20
The Blanket of the Dark, Hodder & Stoughton, 1931 .
. . . . £125/£25
ditto, Houghton Mifflin (U.S.), 1931 . £50/£15
The Free Fishers, Hodder & Stoughton, 1934 . . .
. . . . £125/£25
ditto, Houghton Mifflin (U.S.), 1934 . . £50/£15

The 'Richard Hannay' Books
The Thirty-Nine Steps, Blackwood, 1915 . . £500
ditto, Doran (U.S.), 1915 . . . . . . £200
Greenmantle, Hodder & Stoughton, 1916 . . £125
ditto, Doran (U.S.), 1916 . . . . . . £65
Mr Standfast, Hodder & Stoughton, 1918 . . £150
ditto, Doran (U.S.), 1919 . . . . . . £75
The Three Hostages, Hodder & Stoughton, [1924] .
. . . . £125/£25
ditto, Houghton Mifflin (U.S.), 1924 . . £75/£20
The Courts of the Morning, Hodder & Stoughton, 1929 . . . . £300/£50
ditto, Houghton Mifflin (U.S.), 1929 . . £65/£15
The Island of Sheep, Hodder & Stoughton, 1936 . .
. . . . £75/£10

The 'Edward Leithen' Books
The Power House, Blackwood, 1916 . . . £100
ditto, Doran (U.S.), 1916 . . . . . . £75
John MacNab, Hodder & Stoughton, [1925] £300/£65
ditto, Houghton Mifflin (U.S.), 1925 . . £200/£45

The Dancing Floor, Hodder & Stoughton, [1926] . .
. . . . £200/£45
ditto, Houghton Mifflin (U.S.), 1926 . . £125/£35
The Runagates Club and Other Stories, Hodder &
Stoughton, 1928 . . . . £250/£50
ditto, Houghton Mifflin (U.S.), 1928 . . £125/£30
The Gap in the Curtain, Hodder & Stoughton, 1932 .
. . . . £250/£45
ditto, Houghton Mifflin (U.S.), 1932 . . £75/£20
Sick Heart River, Hodder & Stoughton, 1941 £75/£15
ditto, as **Mountain Meadow**, Houghton Mifflin
(U.S.),1941 . . . . £50/£10

The 'Dickson McCunn' Books
Huntingtower, Hodder & Stoughton, 1922 . £300/£50
ditto, Doran (U.S.), 1916 . . . . . . £250/£35
Castle Gay, Hodder & Stoughton, 1930 . . £200/£40
ditto, Houghton Mifflin (U.S.), 1930 . . £100/£30
The House of the Four Winds, Hodder & Stoughton,
1935 . . . . £200/£30
ditto, Houghton Mifflin (U.S.), 1935 . . £100/£30

Contemporary Adventures
The Half-Hearted, Isbister, 1900 . . . . £250
ditto, Houghton Mifflin (U.S.), 1928 . . £50/£15
The Watcher by the Threshold and Other Tales,
Blackwood, 1902 . . . . £250
ditto, Doran (U.S.), 1918 . . . . . . £250
Prester John, Nelson, 1910 . . . . . £150
ditto, Doran (U.S.), 1910 . . . . . . £125
A Prince of the Captivity, Hodder & Stoughton, 1933 .
. . . . £125/£15
ditto, Houghton Mifflin (U.S.), 1933 . . £50/£15

Miscellaneous
A Lodge in the Wilderness, Blackwood, 1906 . £450
The Moon Endureth, Tales and Fancies, Blackwood,
1912 . . . . £250
ditto, Sturgis & Walton (U.S.), 1912. . . . £125
The Island of Sheep (by 'Cadmus & Harmonia'),
Hodder & Stoughton, 1919 . . . . . £50
ditto, Houghton Mifflin (U.S.), 1920 . . £150/£45

Omnibus Editions
The Four Adventures of Richard Hannay, Hodder &
Stoughton, 1930 . . . . £50/£15
The Adventures of Sir Edward Leithen, Hodder &
Stoughton, 1933 . . . . £50/£10
Four Tales, Hodder & Stoughton, 1936. . £50/£10
The Adventures of Dickson McCunn, Hodder &
Stoughton, 1937 . . . . £50/£10
A Five-Fold Salute to Adventure, Hodder &
Stoughton, 1939 . . . . £50/£10
Adventures of Richard Hannay, Houghton Mifflin
(U.S.), 1939 . . . .£30/£5
Adventurers All, Houghton Mifflin (U.S.), 1942 . .
. . . . £100/£20

Poetry
Sir Walter Raleigh, Blackwell, 1897 (wraps) . £200
The Pilgrim Fathers, Blackwell, 1898 (wraps). £200
Poems, Scots and English, Jack, 1917 . . . £75
ditto, Jack, 1917 (50 signed, numbered large paper
copies) £750

Children's Titles
Sir Walter Raleigh, T. Nelson & Sons, [1911] . £125
The Magic Walking Stick, Hodder & Stoughton, 1932
. . . . £100/£20
ditto, Houghton Mifflin (U.S.), 1932 . . £75/£20
The Long Traverse, Hodder & Stoughton, 1941 . .
. . . . £100/£20

Non Fiction
Scholar Gipsies, John Lane, 1896 . . . . £300
Brasenose College, F.E. Robinson, 1898 . . £175
The African Colony, Blackwood, 1903 . . . £150
The Law Relating to Taxation of Foreign Income ...,
Stevens and Sons, 1905 . . . . . . £300
Some Eighteenth Century Byways and other essays,
Blackwood, 1908 . . . . £125
Nine Brasenose Worthies, Clarendon, 1909 . £175
What the Home Rule Bill Means, Smythe, 1912 £250
The Marquis of Montrose, T. Nelson & Sons, 1913 .
. . . . £45
ditto, Scribner's (U.S.), 1913 . . . . . . £35
Andrew Jameson, Lord Ardwall, Blackwood, 1913 .
. . . . £60
Britain's War By Land, OUP, 1915 . . . . £350
Nelson's History of the War, T. Nelson & Sons,
[1915-1919] (24 vols) £100
ditto, as **A History of the Great War**, Nelson, 1921-22
(4 vols, condensed version of the above) . . £60
ditto, Nelson, 1921-22 (500 numbered, signed copies, 4
vols) £150
ditto, Houghton Mifflin (U.S.), 1923 (4 vols) . £60
The Achievement of France, Methuen, 1915 . £250
Ordeal by Marriage, Clay, 1915 . . . . . £500
The Future of the War, Boyles, Sons & Watchurst,
1916 . . . . £200
The Purpose of War, Dent, 1916 . . . . £200
The Battle of Jutland, Nelson, 1916 (wraps) . £100
The Battle of The Somme, First Phase, Nelson, 1916 .
. . . . £75
The Battle of The Somme, Second Phase, Nelson,
1917 . . . . £75
The Battle of The Somme, Doran (U.S.), 1917 . £75
The Battle-Honours of Scotland, Outram, 1919 £125
**These for Remembrance, Reminiscences of Men
Killed in the War**, Medici, 1919 . . . . £500
The History of the South African Forces in France, T.
Nelson & Sons, [1920] . . . . . £150/£100
Francis and Riversdale Grenfell: A Memoir, T.
Nelson & Sons, [1920] . . . . . £100/£45
A Book of Escapes and Hurried Journeys, T. Nelson
& Sons, [1922] . . . . £150/£45

The Last Secrets: the final mysteries of exploration, T.
Nelson & Sons, [1923]. . . . . . . £150/£35
ditto, Houghton Mifflin (U.S.), 1924 . . £45/£10
***Days to Remember: the British Empire in the Great
War***, T. Nelson & Sons, 1923 (with Henry Newbolt).
. . . . £150/£35
Some Notes on Walter Scott, English Association/
OUP, 1924 (wraps) £30
Lord Minto: A Memoir, T. Nelson & Sons, [1924] .
. . . . £100/£25
Two Ordeals of Democracy, Houghton Mifflin (U.S.),
1925 . . . . £150/£50
The Man and the Book: Sir Walter Scott, Nelson,
1925 . . . . £125/£45
The History of the Royal Scots Fusiliers, 1678-1918,
T. Nelson & Sons, [1925] . . . . £150/£65
The Fifteenth (Scottish) Division, Blackwood, 1926
(with J. Stewart) . . . . £150/£50
Homilies and Recreations, T. Nelson & Sons, [1926] .
. . . . £150/£50
ditto, T. Nelson & Sons, [1926] (large paper edition,
200 signed and numbered copies) £250
Montrose, T. Nelson & Sons, [1928] . £100/£20
ditto, Houghton Mifflin (U.S.), 1928 . . £45/£15
The Causal and the Casual in History, C.U.P., 1929 .
. . . . £150/£45
Montrose and Leadership, OUP, 1930 . £150/£45
The Kirk in Scotland, 1560-1929, Hodder and
Stoughton, [1930] (with George Adam Smith) . .
. . . . £100/£25
Lord Roseberry, British Academy/Milford, 1930 .
. . . . £125/£35
The Novel and the Fairy Tale, English Association,
1931 (wraps) £35
Sir Walter Scott, Cassell, [1932] . . . £45/£10
ditto, Coward-McCann (U.S.), [1932] . £35/£10
Julius Caesar, P. Davies, 1932 . . . £45/£10
Andrew Lang and the Border, OUP, 1933 . £125/£30
The Massacre of Glencoe, P. Davies, 1933 . £125/£25
ditto, Putnam (U.S.), 1933 . . . . £100/£20
The Margins of Life, Birkbeck College, 1933) . .
. . . . £150/£60
Gordon at Khartoum, P. Davies, 1934 . . £125/£25
Oliver Cromwell, Hodder and Stoughton, [1934] .
. . . . £125/£25
ditto, Houghton Mifflin (U.S.), 1934 . £100/£20
The King's Grace: 1910-35, Hodder and Stoughton,
[1935]. . . . . £50/£15
ditto, Hodder and Stoughton, 1935 (large paper edition,
500 numbered, signed copies) £75
Men and Deeds, Peter Davies, 1935 . . . £100/£20
Augustus, Hodder and Stoughton, 1937 . . £75/£20
ditto, Houghton Mifflin (U.S.), 1937 . . £45/£10
Naval Episodes of the Great War, Nelson, 1938 .
. . . . £75/£20
The Interpreter's House, Hodder & Stoughton, 1938 .
. . . . £65/£15
Unchanging Germany, Nelson, 1939 . . £125/£35

Memory Hold-the-Door, Hodder and Stoughton, 1940
. . . . £15/£5
Comments and Characters, T. Nelson & Sons, [1940]
. . . . £100/£25
Canadian Occasions, Hodder and Stoughton, [1940] .
. . . . £65/£15
ditto, Hodder & Stoughton, 1940 (1,000 copies) £100
The Clearing House: a John Buchan Anthology,
Hodder and Stoughton, 1946 . . . . . £30/£5
Life's Adventure: a John Buchan Anthology, Hodder
and Stoughton, 1947. . . . . £30/£5

ANTHONY BUCKERIDGE
(b.1912)

Buckeridge was a teacher whose first successes were
radio plays for adults. The immortal Jennings
appeared later on, first on the radio and then in a
series of children's novels.

'Jennings' Books
Jennings Goes to School, Collins, 1950. . £75/£10
Jennings Follows a Clue, Collins, 1951 . £60/£10
Jennings' Little Hut, Collins, 1951 . . . £60/£10
Jennings and Darbishire, Collins, 1952 . £50/£10
Jennings' Diary, Collins, 1953 . . . . £50/£10
According to Jennings, Collins, 1954 . . £45/£10
Our Friend Jennings, Collins, 1955. . . £45/£10
Thanks to Jennings, Collins, 1957 . . . £40/£10
Take Jennings, for Instance, Collins, 1958. £40/£10
Jennings, as Usual, Collins, 1959 . . . £40/£10
The Trouble with Jennings, Collins, 1960 . £40/£10
Just Like Jennings, Collins, 1961 . . . £40/£10
Leave It to Jennings, Collins, 1963 . . . £40/£10
Jennings, of Course!, Collins, 1964. . . £40/£10
Especially Jennings!, Collins, 1965 . . £40/£10
A Bookful of Jennings!, Collins, 1966 (anthology) .
. . . . £40/£10
ditto, as ***The Best of Jennings***, Collins, 1972 £35/£10
Jennings Abounding, Collins, 1967 . . . . £40/£5
Jennings in Particular, Collins, 1968 . . . £40/£5
Trust Jennings!, Collins, 1969 . . . . £40/£5
The Jennings Report, Collins, 1970. . . £75/£15
Typically Jennings!, Collins, 1971 . . . £45/£10
Speaking of Jennings, Collins, 1973 . . £40/£10
Jennings at Large, Armada, 1977 (wraps) . . £15
ditto, Severn House, 1980. . . . . . £35/£10
Jennings Abounding, A Comedy with Music, French,
1980 (wraps) £5
Jennings Again!, Macmillan, 1991 . . . . £20/£5
That's Jennings, Macmillan, 1994 . . . . £20/£5
Jennings Sounds The Alarm: Seven Plays for Radio,
David Schutte, 1999 (wraps) £5
ditto, David Schutte, 1999 (100 signed copies, wraps) .
. . . . £30

Jennings Breaks the Record: Seven More Plays for Radio, David Schutte, 2000 (wraps) £5
ditto, David Schutte, 2000 (100 signed copies, wraps) .
. . . . £30
Jennings Joins the Search Party: Plays for Radio Volume 3, David Schutte, 2001 (wraps) . . . £5
ditto, David Schutte, 2001 (100 signed copies, wraps) .
. . . . £30
Jennings To the Rescue: Plays for Radio Volume 4, David Schutte, 2002 (wraps) £5
ditto, David Schutte, 2002 (100 signed copies, wraps) .
. . . . £25
Jennings And the Roman Remains: Plays for Radio Volume 5, David Schutte, 2002 (wraps) . . . £5
ditto, David Schutte, 2002 (100 signed copies, wraps) .
. . . . £25

'Rex Milligan' Books
Rex Milligan's Busy Term, Lutterworth Press, 1953 .
. . . . £40/£10
Rex Milligan Raises the Roof, Lutterworth Press, 1955
. . . . £40/£10
Rex Milligan Holds Forth, Lutterworth Press, 1955 .
. . . . £40/£10
Rex Milligan Reporting, Lutterworth Press, 1961 . .
. . . . £40/£10
Introducing Rex Milligan, David Schutte, 2002 (wraps) £5
ditto, David Schutte, 2002 (100 signed copies, wraps) .
. . . . £20

Others
A Funny Thing Happened!, Lutterworth Press, [1953]
. . . . £40/£10
While I Remember, Romansmead, 1999 (wraps) £10
ditto, David Schutte, 2002 (100 signed copies, wraps) .
. . . . £20

ANTHONY BURGESS
(b.1917 d.1993)

Born John Burgess Wilson, this inventive, satirical author often presents a bleak outlook on life. He has written very distinctive, well received novels, his best-known work being the classic *The Clockwork Orange*.

Novels
Time for a Tiger, Heinemann, 1956 . . . £700/£75
The Enemy in the Blanket, Heinemann, 1958 . . .
. . . . £300/£45
Beds in the East, Heinemann, 1959 . . . £200/£20
The Right to an Answer, Heinemann, 1960 . £150/£20
ditto, Norton (U.S.), 1961 . . . . . . £35/£10
The Doctor is Sick, Heinemann, 1960 . £150/£25
ditto, Norton (U.S.), 1966 . . . . . £35/£10
The Worm and the Ring, Heinemann, 1961 £450/£125
Devil of a State, Heinemann, 1961 . . . £100/£10

ditto, Norton (U.S.), 1962 . . . . . . £25/£5
One Hand Clapping, Peter Davies, 1961 (pseud. 'Joseph Kell') . . . . £300/£65
ditto, Knopf (U.S.), 1961 . . . . £25/£5
A Clockwork Orange, Heinemann, 1962 (black boards)
. . . . £3,000/£100
ditto, Norton (U.S.), 1963 . . . . . £400/£75
The Wanting Seed, Heinemann, 1962 . . £75/£35
ditto, Norton (U.S.), 1963 . . . . £20/£5
Honey for the Bears, Heinemann, 1963 . . £75/£10
ditto, Norton (U.S.), 1964 . . . . £20/£5
Inside Mr Enderby, Heinemann, 1963 (pseud. 'Joseph Kell') . . . . £250/£60
Nothing Like the Sun, Heinemann, 1964 . £50/£10
ditto, Norton (U.S.), 1964 . . . . . . £25/£5
The Eve of Saint Venus, Sidgwick & Jackson, 1964 .
. . . . £45/£10
ditto, Norton (U.S.), 1970 . . . . £15/£5
A Vision of Battlements, Sidgwick & Jackson, 1964 .
. . . . £45/£10
ditto, Norton (U.S.), 1966 . . . . £15/£5
Tremor of Intent, Heinemann, 1966 . . . £40/£10
ditto, Norton (U.S.), 1966 . . . . £15/£5
Enderby Outside, Heinemann, 1968 . . . £40/£10
ditto, as **Enderby**, Norton (U.S.), 1968 . . . £15/£5
MF, Cape, 1971 . . . . £30/£5
ditto, Knopf (U.S.), 1971 . . . . £15/£5
Napoleon Symphony, Cape, 1974 . . . . £30/£5
ditto, Knopf (U.S.), 1974 . . . . £15/£5
The Clockwork Testament; or Enderby's End, Hart-Davis MacGibbon, 1974 . . . . . £30/£5
ditto, Knopf (U.S.), 1974 . . . . £15/£5
Beard's Roman Women, McGraw-Hill (U.S.), 1976 .
. . . . £15/£5
ditto, Hutchinson, 1977 . . . . . . £15/£5
Abba Abba, Faber, 1977 . . . . . . £35/£5
ditto, Little, Brown (U.S.), 1977 . . . . £35/£5
1985, Hutchinson, 1978 . . . . . . £20/£5
ditto, Little, Brown (U.S.), 1978 . . . . £15/£5
Man of Nazareth, McGraw-Hill (U.S.), 1979 . £20/£5
ditto, Magnum, 1980 . . . . £15/£5
Earthly Powers, Hutchinson, 1980 . . . £30/£5
ditto, Simon & Schuster (U.S.), 1980 . . . £15/£5
The End of the World News, Hutchinson, 1982 £20/£5
ditto, McGraw-Hill (U.S.), 1983 . . . . £15/£5
Enderby's Dark Lady, Hutchinson, 1984 . . £20/£5
ditto, McGraw-Hill (U.S.), 1984 . . . . £15/£5
The Kingdom of the Wicked, Hutchinson, 1985 £20/£5
ditto, Franklin Library (U.S.), 1985 (signed, limited edition) £30
ditto, Arbor House (U.S.), 1985 . . . . £10/£5
The Pianoplayers, Hutchinson, 1986 . . £15/£5
ditto, Arbor House (U.S.), 1986 . . . . £10/£5
The Old Iron, Hutchinson, 1989 . . . . £15/£5
ditto, Random House (U.S.), 1989 . . . . £10/£5
Mozart and the Wolf Gang, Hutchinson, 1991 . £10/£5
ditto, as **On Mozart: a Paean for Wolfgang**, Ticknor and Fields (U.S.), 1991 . . . . . . £10/£5
A Dead Man in Deptford, Hutchinson, 1993 . £10/£5

Byrne, Hutchinson, 1995 . . . . . . £10/£5
ditto, Carroll & Graf (U.S.), 1997 . . . £10/£5

Short Stories
The Devil's Mode, Hutchinson, 1989 . . . £15/£5
ditto, Random House (U.S.), 1989 . . . £15/£5

Autobiography
Little Wilson and Big God, Weidenfeld & Nicolson
(U.S.), 1986 . . . . £20/£5
ditto, Heinemann, 1987 . . . . £15/£5
ditto, Franklin Library (U.S.), 1987 (signed, limited
edition) £35
You've Had Your Time, Heinemann, 1990 . . £20/£5
ditto, Grove Weidenfeld (U.S.), 1991 . . . £15/£5

Literary Criticism & Biography
English Literature: A Survey for Students, Longmans,
Green, 1958 (pseud. 'John Burgess Wilson') . . .
. . . . £100/£15
The Novel Today, Longmans, Green, 1963 (wraps) £15
Language Made Plain, English Univ. Press, 1964 . .
. . . . £35/£10
ditto, Crowell (U.S.), 1965 . . . . . £10/£5
Here Comes Everybody, Faber, 1965 . . £50/£10
The Novel Now, Faber, 1967 . . . . £25/£10
ditto, Norton (U.S.), 1967. . . . . . £15/£5
Urgent Copy, Literary Studies, Cape, 1968 . £30/£10
ditto, Norton (U.S.), 1969. . . . . . £15/£5
Shakespeare, Cape, 1970 . . . . . £25/£10
ditto, Knopf (U.S.), 1970 . . . . . . £15/£5
Joysprick, Deutsch, 1973 . . . . . £30/£10
Ernest Hemingway and His World, Thames &
Hudson, 1978. . . . . £15/£5
ditto, Scribner's (U.S.), 1978 . . . . . £10/£5
Ninety-Nine Novels, Allison & Busby, 1984 . £10/£5
ditto, Simon & Schuster (U.S.), 1984 . . . £10/£5
Flame into Being: The Life and Works of D.H.
Lawrence, Heinemann, 1985 . . . . £10/£5
ditto, Arbor House (U.S.), 1985 . . . . £10/£5
Mouthful of Air, Hutchinson, 1992 . . . £10/£5
ditto, Morrow (U.S.), 1992 . . . . . £10/£5

Miscellaneous Works
A Long Trip to Teatime, Dempsey & Squires, 1976 .
. . . . £15/£5
ditto, Stonehill (U.S.), 1976 . . . . . £10/£5
Moses: A Narrative, Dempsey & Squires, 1976 . .
. . . . £20/£5
ditto, Stonehill (U.S.), 1976 . . . . . £15/£5
New York, Time-Life Books, 1977 . . . £10/£5
The Land Where Ice-Cream Grows, Benn, 1979 . .
. . . . £10/£5
ditto, Doubleday (U.S.), 1979 . . . . £10/£5
On Going to Bed, Deutsch, 1982. . . . £10/£5
ditto, Abbeville Press (U.S.), 1982 . . . £10/£5
This Man and Music, Hutchinson, 1982 . £10/£5
ditto, McGraw-Hill (U.S.), 1983 . . . . £10/£5
Homage to Qwert Yuiop, Hutchinson, 1985 £10/£5

ditto, McGraw-Hill (U.S.), 1986 . . . . . £10/£5
Oberon Old and New, Hutchinson, 1985 . . £10/£5
Carmen, Hutchinson, 1986 . . . . . . £10/£5
Blooms of Dublin, Hutchinson, 1986 . . . £10/£5

JAMES LEE BURKE
(b.1936)

One of the biggest selling crime writers in America,
Burke is best known for his novels about Vietnam
veteran Dave Robicheaux.

'Dave Robicheaux' Books
The Neon Rain, Henry Holt & Co. (U.S.), 1987 . .
. . . . £175/£45
ditto, Mysterious/Century, 1989 . . . . £150/£25
ditto, Mysterious/Century, 1989 (wraps) . . £25
Heaven's Prisoners, Henry Holt (U.S.), 1988 . .
. . . . £100/£25
ditto, Century, 1990 . . . . £100/£25
Black Cherry Blues, Little, Brown (U.S.), 1989 . .
. . . . £75/£15
ditto, Century, 1990 . . . . £45/£10
A Morning for Flamingos, Little, Brown (U.S.), 1990
. . . . £65/£15
ditto, Century, 1992 . . . . £45/£10
A Stained White Radiance, Hyperion (U.S.), 1992. .
. . . . £45/£15
ditto, Century, 1993 . . . . £25/£10
In the Electric Mist with the Confederate Dead,
Hyperion (U.S.), 1993 . . . . £40/£10
ditto, Hyperion (U.S.), 1993 (150 signed, numbered
copies, slipcase) . . . . £100/£65
ditto, Orion, 1993 . . . . £25/£10
Dixie City Jam, Hyperion (U.S.), 1994 . . . £35/£5
ditto, Hyperion, (U.S.), 1994 (1,525 signed, numbered
copies, slipcase) . . . . £45/£30
ditto, Orion, 1994 . . . . £25/£10
Burning Angel, Hyperion (U.S.), 1995 . . £25/£10
ditto, Trice (U.S.), 1995 (150 signed, numbered copies,
slipcase), 1995 . . . . £100/£75
ditto, Orion, 1995 . . . . £15/£5
Cadillac Jukebox, Hyperion (U.S.), 1996 . £25/£10
ditto, Hyperion (U.S.), 1996 (ABA collectors edition) .
. . . . £60/£35
ditto, Trice (U.S.), 1996 (175 signed, numbered copies,
slipcase), 1996 . . . . £100/£65
ditto, Orion, 1996 . . . . £15/£5
Sunset Limited, Doubleday (U.S.), 1998 . . £20/£5
ditto, Orion, 1998 . . . . £20/£5
ditto, Scorpion Press, 1998 (110 signed, numbered
copies) £150
Purple Cane Road, Doubleday (U.S.), 2000 . £15/£5
ditto, Trice (U.S), 2000 (150 signed, numbered copies,
slipcase) . . . . £100/£75
ditto, Orion, 2000 . . . . £15/£5

Jolie Blon's Bounce, Simon & Schuster (U.S.), 2002 .
. . . . £10/£5
ditto, Trice (U.S), 2002 (150 signed, numbered copies,
slipcase) . . . . £100/£75
ditto, Orion, 2002 . . . . £10/£5

'Billy Bob Holland' Books
Cimarron Rose, Orion, 1997 . . . . . £25/£10
ditto, Hyperion (U.S.), 1997 . . . . . . £15/£5
ditto, Trice (U.S.), 1997 (150 signed, numbered copies,
slipcase) . . . . £100/£75
Heartwood, Doubleday (U.S.), 1999. . . . £20/£5
ditto, Trice (U.S), 1999 (26 signed, lettered copies,
slipcase) . . . . £150/£125
ditto, Trice (U.S), 1999 (150 signed, numbered copies,
slipcase) . . . . £100/£75
ditto, Orion, 1999 . . . . £20/£5
Bitterroot, Simon & Schuster (U.S.), 2001 . . £10/£5
ditto, Trice (U.S), 2001 (150 signed, numbered copies,
slipcase) . . . . £100/£75
ditto, Orion, 2001 . . . . £10/£5

Other Books
Half of Paradise, Houghton Mifflin (U.S.), 1965 . .
. . . . £1,250/£200
To the Bright and Shining Sun, Scribner's (U.S.),
1970 . . . . £800/£150
ditto, James Cahill (U.S.), 1992 (400 signed copies) .
. . . . £75/£45
Lay Down My Sword and Shield, Crowell (U.S.), 1971
. . . . £750/£100
Two for Texas, Pocket Books (U.S.), 1982 (wraps) £10
ditto, James Cahill (U.S.), 1992 (400 numbered, signed
copies, slipcase) . . . . £100/£75
The Lost Get-Back Boogie, Louisiana State Univ.
Press (U.S.), 1986 . . . . . . £225/£65
White Doves at Morning, Simon & Schuster (U.S.),
2003 . . . . £10/£5
ditto, Orion, 2003 . . . . £10/£5

Short Stories
The Convict, Louisiana State Univ. Press (U.S.), 1985
. . . . £1,500/£750
ditto, Louisiana State Univ. Press (U.S.), 1985 (wraps)
. . . . £100
ditto, Orion, 1995 . . . . £40/£10
Winter Light, James Cahill (U.S.), 1992 (26 signed,
lettered copies) £150
ditto, James Cahill (U.S.), 1992 (300 signed, numbered
copies) £100
Texas City 1947, Lord John Press (U.S.), 1992 (26
signed, lettered copies) £200
ditto, Lord John Press (U.S.), 1992 (275 signed,
numbered copies, slipcase) . . . . . £75/£65

W.J. BURLEY
(b.1914)

Burley worked as an engineer until he won a mature
state scholarship to Oxford where he read Zoology.
Later working as a teacher, he is famous for his
'Wycliffe' detective novels set in Cornwall.

'Wycliffe' Novels
Three Toed Pussy, Gollancz, 1968 . . . £350/£25
To Kill A Cat, Gollancz, 1970 . . . . £175/£25
ditto, Walker (U.S.), 1972 . . . . . £45/£15
Guilt Edged, Gollancz, 1971 . . . . . £150/£20
ditto, Walker (U.S.), c.1972 . . . . . £45/£15
ditto, as *Wycliffe and the Guilt Edged Alibi*, Corgi,
1994 (wraps) £10
Death in a Salubrious Place, Gollancz, 1973 £125/£15
ditto, Walker (U.S.), 1973 . . . . . . £30/£5
ditto, as *Wycliffe and Death in a Salubrious Place*,
Corgi, 1995 (wraps) £5
Death in Stanley Street, Gollancz, 1974 . £125/£15
ditto, Walker (U.S.), 1974 . . . . . . £30/£5
ditto, as *Wycliffe and Death in Stanley Street*, Corgi,
1990 (wraps) £5
Wycliffe and the Pea-Green Boat, Gollancz, 1975. .
. . . . £100/£15
ditto, Walker (U.S.), 1975 . . . . . . £30/£5
Wycliffe and the Schoolgirls, Gollancz, 1976 £85/£15
ditto, Walker (U.S.), 1976 . . . . . . £25/£5
Wycliffe and the Scapegoat, Gollancz, 1978 £75/£10
ditto, Doubleday (U.S.), 1979 . . . . . £25/£5
Wycliffe in Paul's Court, Gollancz, 1980 . £50/£10
ditto, Doubleday (U.S.), 1980 . . . . . £25/£5
Wycliffe's Wild Goose Chase, Gollancz, 1982 £45/£10
ditto, Doubleday (U.S.), 1982 . . . . . £25/£5
Wycliffe and the Beales, Gollancz, 1983 . £45/£10
ditto, Doubleday (U.S.), 1984 . . . . . £20/£5
Wycliffe and the Four Jacks, Gollancz, 1985 £35/£10
ditto, Doubleday (U.S.), 1986 . . . . . £20/£5
Wycliffe and the Quiet Virgin, Gollancz, 1986 £35/£10
ditto, Doubleday (U.S.), 1986 . . . . . £15/£5
Wycliffe and the Winsor Blue, Gollancz, 1987 £25/£10
ditto, Doubleday (U.S.), 1987 . . . . . £15/£5
Wycliffe and the Tangled Web, Gollancz, 1988 £15/£5
ditto, Doubleday (U.S.), 1989 . . . . . £15/£5
Wycliffe and the Cycle of Death, Gollancz, 1990 .
. . . . £15/£5
ditto, Doubleday (U.S.), 1991 . . . . . £15/£5
Wycliffe and the Dead Flautist, Gollancz, 1991 £15/£5
ditto, St Martin's Press (U.S.), 1992 . . . £15/£5
Wycliffe and the Last Rites, Gollancz, 1992 . £15/£5
ditto, St Martin's Press (U.S.), 1993 . . . £15/£5
Wycliffe and the Dunes Mystery, Gollancz, 1994 . .
. . . . £15/£5
ditto, St Martin's Press (U.S.), 1994 . . . £15/£5
Wycliffe and the House of Fear, Gollancz, 1995 .
. . . . £15/£5
ditto, St Martin's Press (U.S.), 1996 . . . £15/£5
Wycliffe Omnibus, Gollancz, 1996 . . . . £10/£5

Wycliffe and the The Redhead, Gollancz, 1997 £15/£5
ditto, St Martin's Press (U.S.), 1998 . . . . £15/£5
Wycliffe and the Guild of Nine, Gollancz, 2000 £15/£5

Other Novels
A Taste of Power: A Novel, Gollancz, 1966 £200/£30
Death in Willow Pattern, Gollancz, 1969 . £150/£25
ditto, Walker (U.S.), 1970 . . . . . £45/£10
The Schoolmaster, Gollancz, 1977 . . . £45/£10
ditto, Walker (U.S.), 1977 . . . . . . £20/£5
The Sixth Day: A Novel, Gollancz, 1978 . £45/£10
Charles and Elizabeth: A Gothic Novel, Gollancz,
1979 . . . . £40/£10
ditto, Walker (U.S.), 1981 . . . . . . £10/£5
The House of Care: A Novel, Gollancz, 1981 £45/£10
ditto, Walker (U.S.), 1981 . . . . . . £10/£5

Non Fiction
City of Truro, 1877-1977, O. Blackford, Truro, 1977
(wraps) £10

FRANCES HODGSON BURNETT
(b.1849 d.1924)

Novelist and children's writer, Burnett was born in
Manchester but spent many years in America, where
she died. Her sentimental children's stories have often
been filmed, with varying degrees of success.

Children's Books
Little Lord Fauntleroy, Scribner's (U.S.), 1886 (first
issue with 'De Vinne' imprint at end) . . . £750
ditto, Warne, 1886 . . . . £600
Sara Crewe; or What Happened at Miss Minchin's,
Unwin, 1887 . . . . £45
ditto, Scribner's (U.S.), 1888 . . . . . £35
ditto, as *Sara Crewe, and Editha's Burglar*, Warne,
1888 . . . . £30
Editha's Burglar, Jordan, Marsh (U.S.), 1888 . £50
Little Saint Elizabeth and Other Child Stories,
Scribner's (U.S.), 1890 . . . . . . £30
ditto, Warne, 1890 . . . . £30
Children I Have Known, Osgood McIlvaine, 1892
[1891] £30
ditto, as *Giovanni and the Other*, Scribner's (U.S.),
1892 . . . . £30
The One I Knew the Best of All, Scribner's (U.S.),
1893 . . . . £25
ditto, Warne, 1893 . . . . £25
The Captain's Youngest and Other Stories, Warne,
1894 . . . . £15
ditto, as *Piccino and Other Child Stories*, Scribner's
(U.S.), 1894 . . . . £15
Two Little Pilgrims' Progress, Scribner's (U.S.), 1895
. . . . £25
ditto, Warne, 1895 . . . . £25
A Little Princess, Scribner's (U.S.), 1905 . . £100
ditto, Warne, 1905 . . . . £125

Racketty Packetty House, Century (U.S.), 1906 £30
ditto, Warne, 1907 . . . . £30
The Troubles of Queen Silver-Bell, Century (U.S.),
1907 . . . . £30
ditto, Warne, 1907 . . . . £30
The Cozy Lion, Century (U.S.), 1907 . . . £25
ditto, Tom Stacey, 1972 . . . . £10/£5
The Spring Cleaning, Century (U.S.), 1909 . £30
ditto, Tom Stacey, 1973 . . . . £10/£5
The Land of the Blue Flower, Moffat, Yard (U.S.),
1909 . . . . £30
ditto, Putnam, 1912 . . . . £30
The Secret Garden, Stokes (U.S.), 1911 . . £500
ditto, Heinemann, 1911 . . . . £500
My Robin, Stokes (U.S.), 1912 . . . . . £500
ditto, Putnam, 1913 . . . . £25
The Lost Prince, Century (U.S.), 1915 . . . £30
ditto, Hodder & Stoughton, 1915 . . . . £30
The Little Hunchback Zia, Stokes (U.S.), 1916 £50
ditto, Heinemann, 1916 . . . . £50

Novels and Novellas for Adults
That Lass O'Lowrie's: A Lancashire Story, Warne,
[1877] £30
ditto, Scribner's (U.S.), 1887 . . . . . £75
Dolly: A Love Story, Porter & Coates (U.S.), 1877 £20
ditto, Routledge, [1877] £20
ditto, Warne, 1893 (new edition) £10
Theo: A Love Story, Peterson (U.S.), 1877 . . £20
ditto, Ward Lock, [1877] £20
ditto, Warne, 1877 (new edition) £20
ditto, as *Vagabondia*, Scribner's (U.S.), 1883 (*Theo
and Dolly*) £20
Pretty Polly Pemberton: A Love Story, Peterson (U.S.),
1877 . . . . £20
ditto, Routledge, 1878 . . . . £20
Kathleen: A Love Story, Peterson (U.S.), 1878 . £20
ditto, Routledge, 1878 . . . . £20
ditto, as *Kathleen Mavourneen*, Chatto & Windus,
1879 . . . . £20
Miss Crespigny: A Love Story, Peterson (U.S.), 1878 .
. . . . £20
ditto, Routledge, [1878] £20
Haworth's, Scribner's (U.S.), 1879 (1 vol) . . £35
ditto, Macmillan, 1879 (2 vols) £50
Louisiana, Scribner's (U.S.), 1880 . . . . £30
Louisiana, and That Lass O'Lowrie's, Macmillan,
1880 . . . . £30
A Fair Barbarian, Osgood (U.S.), 1881 . . . £25
ditto, Warne, [1881] £25
Through One Administration, Osgood & Co. (U.S.),
1883 . . . . £75
ditto, Warne, 1883 (3 vols) £75
A Woman's Will; or, Miss Defarge, Warne, 1887 £20
The Fortunes of Philippa Fairfax, Warne, 1888 £30
The Pretty Sister of Jose, Scribner's (U.S.), 1889 £25
ditto, Spencer Blackett, 1889 (wraps) . . . £25
A Lady of Quality, Scribner's (U.S.), 1896 . . £25
ditto, Warne, 1896 . . . . £25

His Grace of Ormonde, Scribner's (U.S.), 1897   £20
ditto, Warne, 1897.   .   .   .   .   .   .   £20
In Connection with the De Willoughby Claim,
Scribner's (U.S.), 1899   .   .   .   .   .   £15
ditto, Warne, 1899.   .   .   .   .   .   .   £15
The Making of a Marchioness, Stokes (U.S.), 1901   .
.   .   .   .   £20
ditto, Smith Elder, 1901   .   .   .   .   .   £15
The Methods of Lady Walderhurst, Stokes (U.S.),
1901   .   .   .   .   £20
ditto, Smith Elder, 1902   .   .   .   .   .   £20
In the Closed Room, McClure, Phillips (U.S.), 1904 £50
ditto, Hodder & Stoughton, 1904.   .   .   .   £50
The Dawn of Tomorrow, Scribner's (U.S.), 1906   £15
ditto, Warne, 1907.   .   .   .   .   .   .   £15
The Shuttle, Stokes (U.S.), 1907.   .   .   .   £15
ditto, Heinemann, 1907   .   .   .   .   .   £15
T. Tembarom, Century (U.S.), 1913.   .   .   .   £15
ditto, Hodder & Stoughton, [1913]   .   .   .   £15
The White People, Harper & Bros (U.S.), 1917   £15
ditto, Heinemann, 1920   .   .   .   .   .   . £25/£5
The Head of the House of Coombe, Stokes (U.S.),
1922   .   .   .   . £25/£5
ditto, Heinemann, 1922   .   .   .   .   . £25/£5
Robin, Stokes (U.S.), 1922   .   .   .   .   . £25/£5
ditto, Heinemann, 1922   .   .   .   . £25/£5

Short Stories for Adults
Surly Tim and Other Stories, Scribner's (U.S.), 1877 .
.   .   .   .   £20
ditto, Ward Lock, [1877] £20
Earlier Stories, Scribner's (U.S.), 1878 (2 vols)   £35
Our Neighbour Opposite, Routledge, [1878]   .   £20
Natalie and Other Stories, Warne, [1879]   .   .   £20
Lindsay's Luck, Scribner's (U.S.), 1878   .   .   £20
ditto, Routledge, 1879.   .   .   .   .   .   £20
A Quiet Life and *The Tide on the Moaning Bar*,
Peterson (U.S.), 1878   .   .   .   .   .   £20
ditto, Routledge, [1879] £20

ROBERT BURNS
(b.1759 d.1796)

A self-taught poet, Burns was as adept composing in both English and Scottish vernacular.

Poems Chiefly in the Scottish Dialect, John Wilson,
1786 .   .   .   . £1,500
ditto, John Wilson, 1786 (wraps).   .   .   £10,000
The Poetical Miscellany, Stewart & Melkie, [1800]   .
.   .   .   .   £400
The Works of Robert Burns, McCreery, 1800 (4 vols)
.   .   .   .   £300 the set
Letters Addressed to Clarinda, Stewart/Macgoun, 1802
.   .   .   .   £150
The Prose Works of Robert Burns, Mackenzie & Dent,
1819 .   .   .   .   £350

EDGAR RICE BURROUGHS
(b.1875 d.1950)

The 'Tarzan' titles are Burroughs' best-known, but his many 'Martian' and other science fiction stories are of seminal importance in the development of the genre.

'Tarzan' Titles
Tarzan of the Apes, McClurg (U.S.), 1914 .   .   .
.   .   .   .   £25,000/£1,000
ditto, Methuen, 1917 .   .   .   .   . £1,250/£350
The Return of Tarzan, McClurg (U.S.), 1915 .   .   .
.   .   .   .   £6,000/£500
ditto, Methuen, 1918 .   .   .   .   . £1,000/£250
The Beasts of Tarzan, McClurg (U.S.), 1916   .   .   .
.   .   .   .   £6,000/£500
ditto, Methuen, 1918 .   .   .   .   . £1,000/£50
The Son of Tarzan, McClurg (U.S.), 1917 .   .   .
.   .   .   .   £4,000/£250
ditto, Methuen, 1919 .   .   .   .   . £1,000/£50
Tarzan and the Jewels of Opar, McClurg (U.S.), 1918
.   .   .   .   £2,000/£250
ditto, Methuen, 1919 .   .   .   .   .   £750/£60
Jungle Tales of Tarzan, McClurg (U.S.), 1919. .   .
.   .   .   .   £1,250/£150
ditto, Methuen, 1919 .   .   .   .   .   £750/£60
Tarzan the Untamed, McClurg (U.S.), 1920   .   .   .
.   .   .   .   £2,000/£100
ditto, Methuen, 1920 .   .   .   .   .   £750/£60
Tarzan the Terrible, McClurg (U.S.), 1921.   .   .   .
.   .   .   .   £2,000/£100
ditto, Methuen, 1921 .   .   .   .   .   £750/£60
Tarzan and the Golden Lion, McClurg (U.S.), 1923 .
.   .   .   .   £2,000/£100
ditto, Methuen, 1924 .   .   .   .   .   £750/£60
Tarzan and the Ant Men, McClurg (U.S.), 1924   .   .
.   .   .   .   £2,000/£100
ditto, Methuen, 1925 .   .   .   .   .   £225/£60
The Tarzan Twins, Volland (U.S.), 1924   .   £450/£75
ditto, Collins, 1930   .   .   .   .   . £500/£100
The Eternal Lover, McClurg (U.S.), 1925 .   .   .
.   .   .   .   £2,000/£100
ditto, Methuen, 1927 .   .   .   .   . £500/£60
Tarzan, Lord of the Jungle, McClurg (U.S.), 1928   .
.   .   .   .   £2,000/£100
ditto, Cassell, 1928   .   .   .   .   .   £750/£60
Tarzan and the Lost Empire, Metropolitan (U.S.),
1929 .   .   .   .   £1,000/£50
ditto, Cassell, 1931   .   .   .   .   .   £750/£60
Tarzan at the Earth's Core, Metropolitan (U.S.), 1930
.   .   .   .   £1,000/£50
ditto, Methuen, 1938 .   .   .   .   .   £750/£60
Tarzan the Invincible, ERB Inc. (U.S.), 1931 .   .   .
.   .   .   .   £500/£45
ditto, John Lane, 1933.   .   .   .   .   £750/£60
Tarzan Triumphant, ERB Inc. (U.S.), 1932 £400/£45
ditto, John Lane, 1933.   .   .   .   .   £400/£60
Tarzan and the City of Gold, ERB Inc. (U.S.), 1933   .
.   .   .   .   £400/£45

ditto, John Lane, 1936. . . . . . . £400/£60
Tarzan and the Leopard Men, ERB Inc. (U.S.), 1935 .
. . . . £400/£45
ditto, John Lane, 1936. . . . . . . £300/£60
Tarzan and the Lion Man, ERB Inc. (U.S.), 1934 . .
. . . . £400/£45
ditto, Goulden, 1950 (wraps) £10
Tarzan's Quest, ERB Inc. (U.S.), 1936 . . £350/£40
ditto, Methuen, 1938 . . . . £300/£60
Tarzan and the Forbidden City, ERB Inc. (U.S.), 1938
. . . . £300/£30
ditto, Goulden, 1950 (wraps) £10
**Tarzan and the Tarzan Twins with Jad-Bal-Ja the
Golden Lion**, Whitman (U.S.), 1936 . . . £200
Tarzan the Magnificent, ERB Inc. (U.S.), 1939 . .
. . . . £200/£30
ditto, Methuen, 1940 . . . . £150/£50
Tarzan and the Foreign Legion, ERB Inc. (U.S.),
1947 . . . . £100/£25
ditto, W.H.Allen, 1949 . . . . . . £45/£10
Tarzan the Madman, Canaveral (U.S.), 1964 £75/£25
ditto, Four Square, 1966 (wraps) £5
Tarzan and the Castaways, Canaveral (U.S.), 1965 .
. . . . £75/£25
ditto, Four Square, 1966 (wraps) £5
Tarzan: The Lost Adventure, Dark Horse (U.S.), 1995
. . . . £10
ditto, Dark Horse (U.S.), 1995 (signed, deluxe copies).
. . . . £75/£45

'Mars' Titles
A Princess of Mars, McClurg (U.S.), 1917 . . . .
. . . . £6,000/£500
ditto, Methuen, 1920 . . . . . £1,000/£65
The Gods of Mars, McClurg (U.S.), 1918 £3,000/£200
ditto, Methuen, 1920 . . . . . . £750/£65
The Warlord of Mars, McClurg (U.S.), 1919 . . .
. . . . £3,000/£200
ditto, Methuen, 1920 . . . . . . £750/£65
Thuvia, Maid of Mars, McClurg (U.S.), 1920 . . .
. . . . £2,000/£100
ditto, Methuen, 1921 . . . . . . £650/£50
Chessmen of Mars, McClurg (U.S.), 1922 £2,000/£100
ditto, Methuen, 1923 . . . . . . £600/£50
Master Mind of Mars, McClurg (U.S.), 1928 . . .
. . . . £2,000/£100
ditto, Methuen, 1939 . . . . . . £200/£50
Fighting Man of Mars, Metropolitan (U.S.), 1931. .
. . . . £750/£50
ditto, Bodley Head, 1932 . . . . . £250/£50
Swords of Mars, ERB Inc. (U.S.), 1936 . £1,250/£75
ditto, Four Square, 1966 (wraps) £5
Synthetic Men of Mars, ERB Inc. (U.S.), 1940 . .
. . . . £400/£45
ditto, Methuen, 1941 . . . . . . £150/£40
Llana of Gathol, ERB Inc. (U.S.), 1948. . £200/£45
ditto, Four Square, 1967 (wraps) £5
John Carter of Mars, Canaveral (U.S.), 1964 £100/£20
ditto, Four Square, 1967 (wraps) £5

'Venus' Titles
Pirates of Venus, ERB Inc. (U.S.), 1934 . £400/£35
ditto, John Lane, 1935. . . . . . £200/£35
Lost on Venus, ERB Inc. (U.S.), 1935 . . £400/£25
ditto, Methuen, 1937 . . . . . . £200/£35
Carson of Venus, ERB Inc. (U.S.), 1939 . £400/£25
ditto, Goulden, 1950 (wraps) £10
Escape on Venus, ERB Inc. (U.S.), 1946 . £250/£25
ditto, Four Square, 1966 (wraps) £5
Wizard of Venus, New English Library, 1973 (wraps) .
. . . . £5

'Pellucidar' Titles
At the Earth's Core, McClurg (U.S.), 1922 . . . .
. . . . £2,000/£100
ditto, Methuen, 1923 . . . . . . £600/£50
Pellucidar, McClurg (U.S.), 1923 . £2,000/£100
ditto, Methuen, 1924 . . . . . . £600/£50
Tanar of Pellucidar, Metropolitan (U.S.), 1930 . .
. . . . £1,000/£50
ditto, Methuen, 1939 . . . . . . £400/£50
Back to the Stone Age, ERB Inc. (U.S.), 1937 . . .
. . . . £500/£35
ditto, Tandem, 1974 (wraps) £5
Land of Terror, ERB Inc. (U.S.), 1944 . £500/£35
ditto, Tandem, 1974 (wraps) £5
Savage Pellucidar, Canaveral (U.S.), 1963 . £250/£25
ditto, Tandem, 1974 (wraps) £5

'Old West' Titles
The Bandit of Hell's Bend, McClurg (U.S.), 1925 .
. . . . £2,000/£100
ditto, Methuen, 1926 . . . . . . £750/£50
The War Chief, McClurg (U.S.), 1927 . £1,500/£75
ditto, Methuen, 1926 . . . . . . £500/£45
Apache Devil, ERB Inc. (U.S.), 1933 . . £600/£50
The Oakdale Affair/The Rider, ERB Inc. (U.S.), 1937
. . . . £750/£50
The Deputy Sheriff of Comanche Country, ERB Inc.
(U.S.), 1940 . . . . £400/£35

Others
The Mucker, McClurg (U.S.), 1921 . . £3,000/£150
ditto, as **The Mucker** and **The Man Without a Soul**,
Methuen, 1921 and 1922 . . . £500/£50
The Girl from Hollywood, McCauley (U.S.), 1923. .
. . . . £2,000/£50
ditto, Methuen, 1924 . . . . . . £350/£60
The Land That Time Forgot, McClurg (U.S.), 1924 .
. . . . £4,500/£50
ditto, Methuen, 1927 . . . . . . £350/£60
The Cave Girl, McClurg (U.S.), 1925 . £1,000/£50
ditto, Methuen, 1927 . . . . . . £600/£50
The Moon Maid, McClurg (U.S.), 1926. £1,000/£50
ditto, Tom Stacey, 1972 . . . . . £50/£10
The Mad King, McClurg (U.S.), 1926 . £1,000/£50
The Outlaw of Torn, McClurg (U.S.), 1929 £600/£35
ditto, Methuen, 1929 . . . . . . £200/£20
The Monster Men, McClurg (U.S.), 1929 £2,000/£50

ditto, Tandem, 1976 (wraps) £5
Jungle Girl, ERB Inc. (U.S.), 1932 . . . £175/£50
ditto, Odhams, [1934] . . . . . . £175/£45
The Resurrection of Jimber Jaw, Argosy (U.S.), 1937
(wraps) £120
The Lad and the Lion, ERB Inc. (U.S.), 1938 . . .
. . . . £175/£50
The Scientists Revolt, Fantastic Adventures (U.S.),
July 1939 (wraps) £100
Beyond Thirty and The Man Eater, Science Fiction
and Fantasy Publications (U.S.), 1957 . . £250/£75
ditto, as **The Lost Continent**, Tandem, 1977 (wraps) £5
The Girl from Farris's, Wilma Co. (U.S.), 1959 (150
numbered copies, no d/w) £250
ditto, Wilma Co. (U.S.), 1959 (wraps) . . . £150
Tales of Three Planets, Canaveral (U.S.), 1963 . .
. . . . £150/£25
The Efficiency Expert, House of Greystoke, 1966 . .
. . . . £200
I Am A Barbarian, ERB Inc. (U.S.), 1967 . £100/£20
Pirate Blood, Ace (U.S.), 1970 (wraps) £5

WILLIAM S. BURROUGHS
(b.1914 d.1997)

A controversial American 'beat' novelist who wrote
of his experience as a heroin addict in *Junkie* and *The
Naked Lunch*. The latter became a cult classic, banned
on the grounds of obscenity.

Novels
Junkie: Confessions of an Unredeemed Drug Addict,
Ace (U.S.), 1953 (pseud. 'William Lee', bound back-
to-back with *Narcotic Agent*, wraps) . . . £400
ditto, Digit, 1957 . . . . £75
ditto, Ace (U.S.), 1964 (first separate publication) £10
ditto, David Bruce & Watson, 1973 . . . £200/£30
ditto, as **Junky**, Penguin, 1977 . . . . £5
The Naked Lunch, Olympia Press (Paris), 1959 (first
issue with green border on title page and 'Francs
1500' on back cover, wraps, with d/w) £1,250/£250
ditto, Olympia Press (Paris), 1959 (later issue with
price change stamped on the back cover, wraps, with
d/w) . . . . £600/£250
ditto, as **Naked Lunch**, Grove Press (U.S.), 1959
[1962] . . . . £225/£35
ditto, Calder, 1964 . . . . £100/£20
ditto, Grove Press (U.S.), 1984 (500 signed copies in
box) . . . . £300/£200
The Soft Machine, Olympia Press (Paris), 1961
(wraps, with d/w) . . . . . . £300/£75
ditto, Grove Press (U.S.), 1966 . . . . £100/£25
ditto, Calder & Boyars, 1968 . . . . . £75/£15
The Ticket That Exploded, Olympia Press (Paris),
1962 (wraps, with d/w) . . . . . £150/£100
ditto, Grove Press (U.S.), 1967 . . . £100/£25
ditto, Calder & Boyars, 1968 . . . . . £45/£15

Dead Fingers Talk, Calder/Olympia Press, 1963 . .
. . . . £50/£25
Nova Express, Grove Press (U.S.), 1964 . £50/£15
ditto, Cape, 1966 . . . . £45/£15
The Wild Boys: A Book of the Dead, Grove Press
(U.S.), 1971 . . . . £65/£20
ditto, Calder & Boyars, 1972 . . . . . £65/£20
Port of Saints, Covent Garden Press, 1973 [1975] (100
signed copies of 200, d/w and slipcase) . £400/£300
ditto, Covent Garden Press, 1973 [1975] (100 unsigned
copies of 200) . . . . £225/£125
ditto, Blue Wind Press (U.S.), 1980 . . . . £25/£5
ditto, Blue Wind Press (U.S.), 1980 (200 signed copies,
slipcase) . . . . £150/£125
ditto, Calder, 1983 . . . . £25/£5
Short Novels, Calder, 1978 . . . . . £35/£10
Blade Runner: A Movie, Blue Wind Press (U.S.), 1979
. . . . £125/£30
ditto, Blue Wind Press (U.S.), 1979 (100 signed,
numbered copies) . . . . . . £225/£150
ditto, Blue Wind Press (U.S.), 1979 (wraps) . £10
Cities of the Red Night, Calder, 1981 . £25/£10
ditto, Holt Rinehart (U.S.), 1981 . . . . £20/£5
ditto, Holt Rinehart (U.S.), 1981 (500 signed,
numbered copies, slipcase, no d/w) . . £150/£100
The Place of Dead Roads, Holt Rinehart (U.S.), 1983 .
. . . . £25/£5
ditto, Holt Rinehart (U.S.), 1983 (300 signed,
numbered copies, slipcase, no d/w) . . £125/£100
ditto, Calder, 1984 . . . . £25/£5
Queer, Viking (U.S.), 1985 . . . . . £20/£5
ditto, Picador, 1985 . . . . £20/£5
The Western Lands, Viking (U.S.), 1987 . £15/£5
ditto, Picador, 1988 . . . . £15/£5

Short Stories
Exterminator!, Viking (U.S.), 1973 . . . £30/£10
ditto, Calder & Boyars, 1974 . . . . . £30/£10
Early Routines, Cadmus (U.S.), 1981 (26 signed
copies of 500) £500
ditto, Cadmus (U.S.), 1981 (125 signed copies of 151,
glassine d/w) . . . . £175/£15
ditto, Cadmus (U.S.), 1981 (349 copies in wraps) £20

Poetry
The Exterminator, Auerhahn Press (U.S.), 1960 (with
Brion Gysin, wraps) £60
Minutes to Go, Two Cities Editions (Paris), 1960 (with
Brion Gysin, Gregory Corso and Sinclair Beiles,
wraps) £50

Others
Letter from a Master Addict to Dangerous Drugs,
privately published, 1957 (stapled sheets) . . £225
The Yage Letters, City Lights Books (U.S.), 1963
(with Allen Ginsburg, wraps) £65
Takis, Galleria Schwarz (Milan), 1962 (exhibition
catalogue, wraps) £25

Roosevelt After Inauguration, Fuck You Press (U.S.), 1964 (pseud. 'Willy Lee', wraps) £200
ditto, as *Roosevelt After Inauguration and Other Atrocities*, City Lights Books (U.S.), 1979 (wraps) .
. . . . £20
Time, 'C' Press (U.S.), 1965 (with Brion Gysin, 886 copies of 986, wraps) £100
ditto, 'C' Press (U.S.), 1965 (100 signed copies of 986, wraps). £500
ditto, 'C' Press (U.S.), 1965 (14 copies with page of manuscript and an original drawing by Gysin) £1,500
ditto, Urgency Press Rip-Off, 1972 (495 copies) £100
Valentine's Day Reading, American Theatre for Poets (U.S.), 1965 (wraps). £30
Health Bulletin: Apo-33, Fuck You Press (U.S.), 1965
. . . . £65
White Subway, Aloes Books [1965] (975 copies of 1,000, wraps). £60
ditto, Aloes Books, [1965] (25 signed copies of 1,000)
. . . . £500
Apo-33 Bulletin: A Metabolic Regulator, Beach Books (U.S.), 1966 (wraps). £75
So Who Owns Death TV?, Beach Books (U.S.), 1967 (first issue, 50 cent price, with Claude Pélieu and Carl Weissner, wraps). £100
The Dead Star, Nova Broadcast Press (U.S.), 1969 (wraps) £50
Fernseh-Tuberkulose, Nova Press (Frankfurt), 1969 (with Claude Pélieu and Carl Weissner, wraps) £100
Entretiens avec William Burroughs, Pierre Belfond (Paris), 1969 (by Daniel Odier, wraps). . . £25
ditto, as *The Job, Interviews with William S. Burroughs*, Grove Press (U.S.), 1970 (by Daniel Odier) .
. . . . £60/£25
ditto, Cape, 1970 (by Daniel Odier) . . . £45/£15
The Last Words of Dutch Schultz, Cape Goliard, 1970 (wraps) £35
ditto, Cape Goliard, 1970 (100 signed, numbered copies, glassine d/w). . . . . . £275/£200
ditto, as *The Last Words of Dutch Schultz: A Fiction in the Form of a Film Script*, Viking (U.S.), 1975 .
. . . . £30/£10
Ali's Smile, Unicorn Books, 1971 (99 signed copies, with record) £1,250
ditto, as *Ali's Smile/Naked Scientology*, Expanded Media Editions (Göttingen), 1978 (wraps). . £35
Electronic Revolution, 1970-71, Blackmoor Head Press, 1971 (100 signed copies of 500, wraps) £1,000
ditto, Blackmoor Head Press, 1971 (400 copies of 500, wraps). £200
Mayfair Academy Series More or Less, Urgency Press Rip Off, [1973] (650 copies, wraps) . . . £50
The Book of Breathing, Chopin, 1974 (350 numbered copies, wraps) £500
ditto, Chopin, 1974 (50 signed copies) . . . £1,250
ditto, Blue Wind Press (U.S.), 1975 (wraps) . £10
ditto, Blue Wind Press (U.S.), 1975 (175 signed copies)
. . . . £250

Cobble Stone Gardens, Cherry Valley Editions (U.S.), 1976 (50 handbound, numbered and signed copies) .
. . . . £400
ditto, Cherry Valley Editions (U.S.), 1976 (wraps) £20
The Third Mind, Viking (U.S.), 1978 . . £30/£10
ditto, Calder, 1979. . . . . £25/£10
Ah Pook is Here and Other Texts, Calder, 1979 . .
. . . . £50/£20
A William Burroughs Reader, Picador, 1982 (wraps) .
. . . . £10
The Burroughs File, City Lights Books (U.S.), 1984 .
. . . . £25/£10
ditto, City Lights Books (U.S.), 1984 (wraps) . £10
The Adding Machine, Selected Essays, Calder, 1985 .
. . . . £25/£5
ditto, Seaver Books (U.S.), 1986. . . . . £25/£5
Interzone, Picador, 1989 . . . . . £25/£10
ditto, Viking, 1989 . . . . . . £25/£10
The Letters of William S. Burroughs, 1945-59, Picador, 1993. . . . . £25/£5
ditto, Viking, 1993 . . . . £15/£5
My Education, A Book of Dreams, Picador, 1995 . .
. . . . £20/£5
ditto, Viking, 1995 . . . . £20/£5
Word Virus: The William Burroughs Reader, Grove (U.S.), 1998 . . . . £15/£5
Last Words: The Final Journals of William S. Burroughs, Grove (U.S.), 2000. . . . £15/£5
ditto, Flamingo, 2000 . . . . £15/£5

ROBERT BURTON
(b.1577 d.1640)

Although he only wrote one book, The Anatomy of Melancholy was constantly revised and expanded by Burton and subsequent editions increase in size.

The Anatomy of Melancholy, Lichfield & Short for Henry Cripps, 1621 . . . . . . £20,000

A.S. BYATT
(b.1936)

A novelist and critic, and sister of Margaret Drabble, Byatt won the Booker Prize for *Possession*, her best-known work.

Novels
The Shadow of the Sun, Chatto & Windus, 1964 . .
. . . . £300/£30
ditto, as *Shadow of a Sun*, Harcourt Brace (U.S.), 1964
. . . . £150/£20
The Game, Chatto & Windus, 1967 . . . £100/£25
ditto, Scribner's (U.S.), 1968. . . . . £75/£15
The Virgin in the Garden, Chatto & Windus, 1978 .
. . . . £75/£10
ditto, Knopf (U.S.), 1979 . . . . . . £30/£5

Still Life, Chatto & Windus and The Hogarth Press,
1985 . . . . £30/£5
ditto, Scribner's (U.S.), 1985 . . . . . £15/£5
Possession, Chatto & Windus, 1990 . . . £75/£10
ditto, Random House (U.S.), 1990 . . £65/£10
Babel Tower, Chatto & Windus, 1996 . . . £15/£5
ditto, Random House (U.S.), 1996 . . . . £15/£5
ditto, Franklin Library (U.S.), 1996 (signed, limited
edition) £45
The Biographer's Tale, Chatto & Windus, 2000 . .
. . . . £15/£5
ditto, Knopf (U.S.), 2001 . . . . £15/£5
A Whistling Woman, Chatto & Windus, 2002 . £15/£5

Short Stories and Novellas
Sugar and Other Stories, Chatto & Windus, 1987 . .
. . . . £50/£10
ditto, Scribner's (U.S.), 1987 . . . . . £45/£10
Angels and Insects, Chatto & Windus, 1992 . £15/£5
ditto, London Limited Editions, 1992 (150 signed
copies, acetate d/w) . . . . . . £75/£50
ditto, Random House (U.S.), 1992 . . . £10/£5
ditto, Franklin Library (U.S.), 1993 (signed, limited
edition) £45
Matisse Stories, Chatto & Windus, 1993 . £15/£5
ditto, Random House (U.S.), 1993 . . . £10/£5
Djinn in the Nightingale's Eye, Five Fairy Stories,
Chatto & Windus, 1994 . . . . . £10/£5
ditto, Random House (U.S.), 1994 . . . £10/£5
Elementals: Stories of Fire and Ice, Chatto & Windus,
1998 . . . . £10/£5
ditto, Random House (U.S.), 1999 . . . £10/£5

Non Fiction
Degrees of Freedom: The Novels of Iris Murdoch,
Chatto & Windus, 1965 . . . . . £75/£25
ditto, Barnes & Noble (U.S.), 1965 . . . £65/£20
Wordsworth and Coleridge in their Time, Nelson,
1970 . . . . £75/£20
ditto, Crane, Russak (U.S.), 1973 . . . £35/£10
ditto, as ***Unruly Times: Wordsworth and Coleridge in
Their Times***, Hogarth Press, 1989 . . . £10/£5
Iris Murdoch, Longman, 1970 (wraps) . . £10
ditto, Crane, Russak (U.S.), 1973 (wraps) . . £10
Ford Madox Ford and the Prose Tradition, Chatto &
Windus, 1982 . . . . £25/£10
ditto, Knopf (U.S.), 1982 . . . . . . £20/£10
Passions of the Mind, Chatto & Windus, 1991 . £15/£5
ditto, Turtle Bay (U.S.), 1992 . . . . . £10/£5
***Imagining Characters, Six Conversations with
Women Writers***, Chatto & Windus, 1995 (with Ignes
Sodre) . . . . £25/£10
ditto, as ***Imagining Characters: Conversations about
Women Writers***, Vintage Books (U.S.), 1997 . £10/£5
On Histories and Stories, Chatto & Windus, 2000 . .
. . . . £15/£5
ditto, Harvard Univ. Press (U.S.), 2000 . . £15/£5
Portraits in Fiction, Chatto & Windus, 2001 . £15/£5

ALBERT CAMUS
(b.1913 d.1960)

One of the very few international goalkeepers to have
gone on to establish an international literary
reputation, for which he was awarded the Nobel Prize
for Literature in 1957.

Novels
The Outsider, Hamish Hamilton, 1946 (translated by
Stuart Gilbert) . . . . £300/£30
ditto, as ***The Stranger***, Knopf (U.S.), 1946 . £300/£30
The Plague, Hamish Hamilton, 1948 (translated by
Stuart Gilbert) . . . . £250/£25
ditto, Knopf (U.S.), 1948 . . . . . . £200/£20
The Rebel, Hamish Hamilton, 1953 (translated by
Anthony Bower) . . . . £125/£20
ditto, Knopf (U.S.), 1954 . . . . . £100/£15
The Fall, Hamish Hamilton, 1957 (translated by Justin
O'Brien) . . . . £125/£15
ditto, Knopf (U.S.), 1957 . . . . . . £125/£15
A Happy Death, Hamish Hamilton, 1972 (translated by
Richard Howard) . . . . £20/£5
ditto, Knopf (U.S.), 1972 . . . . . . £20/£5

Short Stories
Exile and the Kingdom, Hamish Hamilton, 1958
(translated by Justin O'Brien) . . . £65/£15
ditto, Knopf (U.S.), 1958 . . . . . £65/£10

Plays
Caligula and ***Cross Purpose***, Hamish Hamilton, 1947
(translated by Justin Kaplan) . . . . £100/£15
ditto, New Directions (U.S.), 1947 . . . £60/£15
ditto, Knopf (U.S.), 1948 . . . . . £35/£10
The Possessed, Hamish Hamilton, 1960 (translated by
Justin O'Brien) . . . . £65/£15
ditto, Knopf (U.S.), 1960 . . . . . . £50/£10

Others
The Myth of Sisyphus, Hamish Hamilton, 1955
(translated by Justin O'Brien) . . . . £50/£15
ditto, Knopf (U.S.), 1955 . . . . . £45/£10
Nobel Prize Acceptance Speech, Knopf (U.S.), 1958
(translated by Justin O'Brien, wraps) . . . £40
Reflections on the Guillotine, Fridtjof-Karla (U.S.),
1959 . . . . £75/£20
Resistance, Rebellion and Death, Hamish Hamilton,
1961 (translated by Justin O'Brien) . . . £25/£5
ditto, Knopf (U.S.), 1961 . . . . . . £25/£5
Lyrical and Critical, Hamish Hamilton, 1967
(translated by Ellen Conroy Kennedy) . . . £25/£5
ditto, Knopf (U.S.), 1968 . . . . . . £25/£5
Youthful Writings, Knopf (U.S.), 1976 (translated by
Ellen Conroy Kennedy) . . . . . . £25/£5
ditto, Hamilton, 1977 . . . . £25/£5
Carnets 1935-1942, Hamish Hamilton, 1963 (translated by Justin O'Brien) . . . . . £40/£15
ditto, as ***Notebooks 1935-1942***, Knopf (U.S.), 1963 .
. . . . £40/£15

Carnets 1942-1951, Hamish Hamilton, 1965
(translated by Justin O'Brien) . . . . £40/£15
ditto, as *Notebooks 1942-1951*, Knopf (U.S.), 1965 .
. . . . £40/£15

RANDOLPH CALDECOTT
(b.1846 d.1886)

A British illustrator, Caldecott produced a series of popular picture books which are said to have had an influence on Beatrix Potter.

'Picture Books'
The Diverting History of John Gilpin, Routledge,
[1878]. £30
The House that Jack Built, Routledge, [1878] . £30
The Mad Dog, Routledge, [1879] £75
The Babes in the Wood, Routledge, [1879] . . £30
The Three Jovial Huntsmen, Routledge, [1880] £25
Sing a Song for Sixpence, Routledge, [1880] . £25
The Queen of Hearts, Routledge, [1881] . . £25
The Farmer's Boy, Routledge, [1881] . . . £25
The Milkmaid, Routledge, [1882] £30
Hey Diddle Diddle and Baby Bunting, Routledge,
[1882]. £25
The Fox Jumps Over the Parson's Gate, Routledge,
[1883]. £25
A Frog He Would A-Wooing Go, Routledge, [1883] .
. . . . £25
Come Lasses and Lads, Routledge, [1884] . £25
*Ride a Cock Horse to Banbury Cross and A Farmer
Went Trotting upon his Grey Mare*, Routledge,
[1884]. £25
An Elegy on the Glory of Her Sex, Mrs Mary Blaize,
by Dr Oliver Goldsmith, Routledge, [1885] . £25
The Great Panjandrum Himself, Routledge, [1885] .
. . . . £25
R. Caldecott's Picture Book, Vol. 1, Routledge, [1879]
(containing the first 4 'Picture Books'). . £50
R. Caldecott's Picture Book, Vol. 2, Routledge, [1881]
(containing the second 4 'Picture Books') . . £50
R. Caldecott's Collection of Pictures and Songs,
Routledge, [1881] (reissue of Caldecott's 'Picture
Book' Vols 1 and 2) £50
The Hey Diddle Diddle Picture Book, Routledge,
[1883] (contains 4 'Picture Books') . . . £50
The Panjandrum Picture Book, Routledge, [1885]
(contains 4 'Picture Books'). £50
*The Complete Collection of Randolph Caldecott's
Pictures and Songs*, Routledge, [1887] (contains all
16 'Picture Books', 800 copies). £300
R. Caldicott's Picture Books, Routledge, [1889-1892]
(contains the first 4 'Picture Books') . . . £50
*Randolph Caldecott's Second Collection of Pictures
and Songs*, Warne, [1895] (reissue of *The Hey Diddle
Diddle Picture Book* and *The Panjandrum Picture
Book*) £50

Other Titles Illustrated by Randolph Caldecott
Frank Mildmay, or The Naval Officer, by Captain
Marryat, Routledge, [1873] £50
*Baron Bruno, or The Unbelieving Philosopher and
Other Fairy Stories*, by Louisa Morgan, Macmillan,
1875 . . . . £50
*Old Christmas, From the Sketchbook of Washington
Irving*, Macmillan, 1876 . . . . . . £35
Bracebridge Hall, or The Humorists, by Washington
Irving, Macmillan, 1877 [1876] £40
What the Blackbird Said, A Story in Four Chirps, by
Mrs Frederick Locker, Routledge, 1881 . . £50
Jackanapes, by Juliana Horatia Ewing, S.P.C.K., 1884
[1883]. £25
Some of Aesop's Fables with Modern Instances,
Macmillan, 1883 . . . . £35
Daddy Darwin's Dovecote, A Country Tale, by Juliana
Horatia Ewing, S.P.C.K., [1884] £25
Lob Lie-By-The-Fire, by Juliana Horatia Ewing,
S.P.C.K., [1885] £25
Fables de la Fontaine, Macmillan, 1885 . . £35
Jack and the Beanstalk, by Hallam Tennyson,
Macmillan, 1886. . . . . £35
The Owls of Olynn Belfry, by A.Y.D., Field & Tuer,
[1886]. £35
Jackanapes, by Juliana Horatia Ewing, S.P.C.K.,
[1892] (contains *Daddy Darwin's Dovecote* and *Lob
Lie-By-The-Fire*). £25
Randolph Caldecott's Painting Book, S.P.C.K., [1895]
. . . . £50

TRUMAN CAPOTE
(b.1924 d.1984)

American short story writer and novelist whose career developed after he won the O. Henry Prize in 1946.

Novels
Other Voices, Other Rooms, Random House (U.S.),
1948 . . . . £350/£45
ditto, Heinemann, 1948 . . . . . £125/£20
ditto, Franklin Library (U.S.), 1979 (signed, limited
edition) £100
The Grass Harp, Random House (U.S.), [1951] . .
. . . . £175/£25
ditto, Heinemann, 1952 . . . . . £100/£20
Answered Prayers: The Unfinished Novel, Hamish
Hamilton, 1986 . . . . £20/£55
ditto, Random House (U.S.), 1987 . . . . £15/£5

Short Stories
A Tree of Night and Other Stories, Random House
(U.S.), 1949 . . . . £100/£25
ditto, Heinemann, 1950 . . . . . £65/£10
Breakfast at Tiffany's, Random House (U.S.), 1958 .
. . . . £300/£35
ditto, Heinemann, 1958 . . . . . £125/£20

A Christmas Memory, Random House (U.S.), 1966 (slipcase, no d/w) . . . . £100/£75
ditto, Random House (U.S.), 1966 (600 signed copies, slipcase, no d/w) . . . . £350/£300
One Christmas, Random House (U.S.), 1983 (no d/w, slipcase) . . . . £50/£30
ditto, Random House (U.S.), 1983 (500 numbered copies signed by the author) . . . . £300/£250
ditto, Hamish Hamilton, 1983 . . . . . £20/£5
Three by Truman Capote, Random House (U.S.), 1985
. . . . £20/£5

Plays
The Grass Harp, Random House (U.S.), [1952] . .
. . . . £400/£150
ditto, Dramatist Play Service, 1954 (wraps). . £10
The Thanksgiving Visitor, Random House (U.S.), 1967 (300 signed, numbered copies, slipcase). . .
. . . . £400/£300
ditto, Random House (U.S.), 1968 (slipcase) £65/£45
ditto, Hamish Hamilton, 1969 . . . . £50/£10
House of Flowers, Random House (U.S.), 1968 (with Harold Arlen) . . . . £300/£100
Trilogy: An Experiment in Multimedia, Macmillan (U.S.), 1969 (with Elinor and Frank Perry) £30/£10

Non Fiction
Local Color, Random House (U.S.), 1950 . £150/£60
ditto, Heinemann, 1950 . . . . . £35/£10
ditto, Heinemann, 1950 (200 numbered copies) £200
The Muses are Heard: An Account, Random House (U.S.), 1956 . . . . £50/£25
ditto, as *The Muses are Heard: An Account of the Porgy and Bess Visit to Leningrad*, Heinemann, 1957
. . . . £25/£10
Observations, Simon & Schuster (U.S.), 1959 (photographs by Richard Avedon, glassine d/w, slipcase) . . . . £175/£150
ditto, Weidenfeld and Nicolson, 1959 (glassine d/w, slipcase) . . . . £175/£150
In Cold Blood: A True Account of a Multiple Murder and its Consequences, Random House (U.S.), 1965 .
. . . . £25/£10
ditto, Random House (U.S.), 1965 (extra signed leaf inserted) . . . . £400/£175
ditto, Random House (U.S.), 1965 (500 signed, numbered copies, slipcase) . . . . £750/£300
ditto, Hamish Hamilton, 1966 . . . . £50/£10
The Dogs Bark: Public People and Private Places, Random House (U.S.), 1973 . . . . £20/£5
ditto, Weidenfeld and Nicolson, 1974 . . £15/£5
Then it All Came Down: Criminal Justice Today Discussed by Police, Criminals and Correcting Officers with Comments by Truman Capote, Random House (U.S.), 1976 . . . . £35/£10
Music for Chameleons, Random House (U.S.), 1980 .
. . . . £25/£10
ditto, Random House (U.S.), 1980 (350 signed copies, slipcase) . . . . £200/£150
ditto, Hamish Hamilton, 1980 . . . . £25/£10

Collections
Selected Writings of Truman Capote, Random House (U.S.), 1963 . . . . £25/£5
ditto, Hamish Hamilton, 1963 . . . . . £20/£5
A Capote Reader, Random House (U.S.), 1987. £10/£5
ditto, Hamish Hamilton, 1987 . . . . . £10/£5

PETER CAREY
(b.1943)

An Australian author of novels and stories which have been described as post-modern fables.

Novels
Bliss, Univ. of Queensland Press (Australia), 1981. . .
. . . . £100/£25
ditto, Faber, 1981 . . . . £35/£10
ditto, Harper (U.S.), 1981. . . . . . £35/£10
Illywhacker, Univ. of Queensland Press (Australia), 1985 . . . . £35/£10
ditto, Faber, 1985 . . . . £25/£5
ditto, Harper (U.S.), 1985. . . . . . £20/£5
Oscar and Lucinda, Univ. of Queensland Press (Australia), 1988 . . . . £25/£10
ditto, Faber, 1988 . . . . £20/£5
ditto, Harper (U.S.), 1988. . . . . . £20/£5
The Tax Inspector, Univ. of Queensland Press (Australia), 1991. . . . . £20/£5
ditto, Faber, 1991 . . . . £15/£5
ditto, Knopf (U.S.), 1991 . . . . . . £15/£5
ditto, Franklin Library (U.S.), 1991 (signed, limited edition) £40
The Unusual Life of Tristan Smith, Univ. of Queensland Press (Australia), 1994. . . . . £15/£5
ditto, Faber, 1994 . . . . £15/£5
ditto, Knopf (U.S.), 1995 . . . . . . £15/£5
Jack Maggs, Univ. of Queensland Press (Australia), 1997 . . . . £10/£5
ditto, Faber, 1997 . . . . £10/£5
ditto, Knopf (U.S.), 1998 . . . . . . £10/£5
True History of the Kelly Gang, Univ. of Queensland Press (Australia), 2000 . . . . . £15/£5
ditto, Faber, 2001 . . . . £10/£5
ditto, Knopf (U.S.), 2001 . . . . . . £10/£5

Short Stories
The Fat Man in History, Univ. of Queensland Press (Australia), 1974 . . . . £250/£40
ditto, Faber, 1980 . . . . £45/£10
ditto, Random House (U.S.), 1980 . . . £25/£10
War Crimes, Univ. of Queensland Press (Australia), 1979 . . . . £125/£30
Collected Stories, Faber, 1995 . . . . . £20/£5

Others
Bliss: The Screenplay, Univ. of Queensland Press (Australia), 1986. . . . . £10/£5
ditto, as *Bliss: The Film*, Faber, 1986 . . . £10/£5

A Letter to Our Son, Univ. of Queensland Press
(Australia), 1994 . . . . £35/£10
Big Bazoohley, Faber, 1995 . . . . . . £35/£5
ditto, Holt (U.S.), 1995 . . . . . . £35/£5

JOHN DICKSON CARR
(b.1906 d.1977)

Carr was one of the classic authors of 'locked room'
mysteries.

'Dr Gideon Fell' Titles
Hag's Nook, Harper (U.S.), 1933 . . £1,250/£150
ditto, Hamilton, 1933 . . . . . . £1,250/£150
The Mad Hatter Mystery, Harper (U.S.), 1933 . . .
. . . . £1,250/£150
ditto, Hamilton, 1933 . . . . . . £1,250/£150
The Eight of Swords, Harper (U.S.), 1934 £1,250/£150
ditto, Hamilton, 1934 . . . . . . £1,250/£150
The Blind Barber, Harper (U.S.), 1934 . . £850/£150
ditto, Hamilton, 1934 . . . . . . £850/£150
Death Watch, Hamilton, 1935 . . . £850/£150
ditto, Harper (U.S.), 1935 . . . . . £850/£150
The Three Coffins, Harper (U.S.), 1935 . . £850/£150
ditto, as The Hollow Man, Hamilton, 1935 . £850/£150
The Arabian Night's Murder, Hamilton, 1936 . . .
. . . . £850/£150
ditto, Harper (U.S.), 1936 . . . . . £850/£150
The Third Bullet, Hodder, 1937 (wraps) . . £100
To Wake the Dead, Hamilton, 1937 . . . £600/£75
ditto, Hamilton, 1938 . . . . . . £600/£75
The Crooked Hinge, Harper (U.S.), 1938 . £600/£75
ditto, Hamilton, 1938 . . . . . . £600/£75
The Problem of the Green Capsule, Harper (U.S.),
1939 . . . . £500/£75
ditto, as The Black Spectacles, Hamilton, 1939 . .
. . . . £500/£75
The Problem of the Wire Cage, Harper (U.S.), 1939 .
. . . . £300/£50
ditto, Hamilton, 1940 . . . . . . £300/£50
The Man Who Could Not Shudder, Harper (U.S.),
1940 . . . . £250/£40
ditto, Hamilton, 1940 . . . . . . £250/£40
The Case of the Constant Suicides, Harper (U.S.),
1941 . . . . £250/£40
ditto, Hamilton, 1941 . . . . . . £250/£40
Death Turns the Tables, Harper (U.S.), 1941 £250/£40
ditto, as The Seat of the Scornful, Hamilton, 1941. .
. . . . £250/£40
Till Death Do Us Part, Harper (U.S.), 1944 £175/£30
ditto, Hamilton, 1944 . . . . . . £175/£30
He Who Whispers, Hamilton, 1946 . . . £150/£25
ditto, Harper (U.S.), 1947 . . . . . £150/£25
The Sleeping Sphinx, Harper (U.S.), 1947 . £150/£25
ditto, Hamilton, 1947 . . . . . . £150/£25
Dr Fell, Detective and Other Stories, Harper (U.S.),
1947 (wraps) £50

Below Suspicion, Harper (U.S.), 1949 . . £65/£10
ditto, Hamilton, 1950 . . . . . . £65/£10
The Dead Man's Knock, Harper (U.S.), 1958 £35/£10
ditto, Hamilton, 1958 . . . . . . £35/£10
In Spite of Thunder, Harper (U.S.), 1960 . £35/£10
ditto, Hamilton, 1960 . . . . . . £35/£10
The House at Satan's Elbow, Harper (U.S.), 1965. .
. . . . £35/£10
ditto, Hamilton, 1965 . . . . . . £35/£10
Panic in Box C, Harper (U.S.), 1966 . . £35/£10
ditto, Hamilton, 1966 . . . . . . £35/£10
Dark of the Moon, Harper (U.S.), 1967 . . £35/£10
ditto, Hamilton, 1968 . . . . . . £35/£10

'Henri Bencolin' Titles
It Walks by Night, Harper (U.S.), 1930 . £1,750/£200
ditto, Harper (U.S.),1930 (unbroken seal on last
section) . . . . £3,000/£2,000
ditto, Harper (U.K.), 1930 . . . £1,500/£200
ditto, Harper (U.K.), 1930 (unbroken seal on last
section) . . . . £3,000/£1,250
The Lost Gallows, Harper (U.S.), 1931 . £1,500/£150
ditto, Hamilton, 1931 . . . . . £1,500/£150
Castle Skull, Harper (U.S.), 1931 . . £1,400/£200
ditto, Tom Stacey, 1973 . . . . . £100/£90
ditto, Severn House, 1976 . . . . . £10/£5
The Waxworks Murder, Hamilton, 1932 £1,500/£150
ditto, as The Corpse in the Waxworks, Harper (U.S.),
1932 . . . . £1,500/£150
The Four False Weapons, Harper (U.S.), 1937 . .
. . . . £750/£100
ditto, Hamilton, 1938 . . . . . . £750/£100
The Door to Doom and Other Detections, Harper,
1980 . . . . £10/£5
ditto, Hamilton, 1981 . . . . . . £10/£5

'Sir Henry Merrivale' Titles by 'Carter Dixon'
The Plague Court Murders, Morrow (U.S.), 1934 . .
. . . . £1,000/£150
ditto, Heinemann, 1935 . . . . £1,000/£150
The White Priory Murders, Morrow (U.S.), 1934 . .
. . . . £1,000/£150
ditto, Heinemann, 1935 . . . . £1,000/£150
The Red Widow Murders, Morrow (U.S.), 1935 . .
. . . . £1,000/£150
ditto, Heinemann, 1935 . . . . £1,000/£150
The Unicorn Murders, Morrow (U.S.), 1935 . . .
. . . . £1,000/£150
ditto, Heinemann, 1936 . . . . £1,000/£150
The Magic Lantern Murders, Heinemann, 1936 . .
. . . . £1,000/£150
ditto, as The Punch and Judy Murders, Morrow
(U.S.), 1937 . . . . £1,000/£150
The Peacock Feather Murders, Morrow (U.S.), 1937.
. . . . £750/£125
ditto, as The Ten Teacups, Morrow (U.S.), 1937 . .
. . . . £750/£125
The Judas Window, Morrow (U.S.), 1938 . £500/£100
ditto, Heinemann, 1938 . . . . . £500/£100

Death in Five Boxes, Heinemann, 1938. . £400/£75
ditto, Morrow (U.S.), 1938 . . . . . £400/£75
The Reader is Warned, Heinemann, 1939 . £750/£125
ditto, Morrow (U.S.), 1939 . . . . . £750/£125
And So To Murder, Morrow (U.S.), 1940 . £750/£125
ditto, Heinemann, 1941 . . . . . £750/£125
Murder in the Submarine Zone, Heinemann, 1940 .
 . . . . £750/£125
ditto, as *Nine–And Death Makes Ten*, Morrow (U.S.),
1940 . . . . £750/£125
The Department of Queer Complaints, Heinemann,
1940 . . . . £750/£125
ditto, Morrow (U.S.), 1940 . . . . £750/£125
Seeing is Believing, Morrow (U.S.), 1941 . £750/£125
ditto, Heinemann, 1942 . . . . . £750/£125
The Gilded Man, Morrow (U.S.), 1942 . £250/£40
ditto, Heinemann, 1942 . . . . . £250/£40
She Died a Lady, Morrow (U.S.), 1943 . £250/£40
ditto, Heinemann, 1943 . . . . . £250/£40
He Wouldn't Kill Patience, Morrow (U.S.), 1944 . .
 . . . . £150/£25
ditto, Heinemann, 1944. . . . . . £150/£25
The Curse of the Bronze Lamp, Morrow (U.S.), 1946.
 . . . . £100/£20
ditto, as *Lord of the Sorcerers*, Heinemann, 1946 . .
 . . . . £100/£20
My Late Wives, Morrow (U.S.), 1946 . £75/£15
ditto, Heinemann, 1947 . . . . . £75/£15
The Skeleton in the Clock, Morrow (U.S.), 1948 . .
 . . . . £75/£15
ditto, Heinemann, 1949 . . . . . £75/£15
A Graveyard to Let, Morrow (U.S.), 1949 . £75/£15
ditto, Heinemann, 1950 . . . . . £65/£10
Night at the Mocking Widow, Morrow (U.S.), 1950 .
 . . . . £65/£10
ditto, Heinemann, 1951 . . . . . £65/£10
Behind the Crimson Blind, Morrow (U.S.), 1952 . .
 . . . . £65/£10
ditto, Heinemann, 1952 . . . . . £65/£10
The Cavalier's Cup, Morrow (U.S.), 1953 . £65/£10
ditto, Heinemann, 1953 . . . . . £65/£10
Fear is the Same, Morrow (U.S.), 1956. . £65/£10
ditto, Heinemann, 1956 . . . . . £65/£10

Other Titles
Poison in Jest, Harper (U.S.), 1932 . . £1,000/£100
ditto, Hamilton, 1932 . . . . . £1,000/£100
The Bowstring Murders, Morrow (U.S.), 1933 (pseud.
'Carter Dixon') . . . . . £1,000/£150
ditto, Heinemann, 1934 . . . . . £1,000/£150
Devil Kinsmere, Hamilton, 1934 (pseud. 'Roger
Fairbairn') . . . . £1,000/£150
ditto, Harper (U.S.), 1934. . . . £1,000/£150
The Murder of Sir Edmund Godfrey, Hamilton, 1936.
 . . . . £250/£45
ditto, Harper (U.S.), 1936. . . . . £250/£45
The Third Bullet, Hodder, 1937 (wraps) . . £250
The Burning Court, Harper (U.S.), 1937 . £250/£45
ditto, Hamilton, 1937 . . . . . . £250/£45

Drop to His Death, Heinemann, 1939 (pseud. 'Carter
Dixon', with John Rhode) . . . . £250/£45
ditto, as *Fatal Descent*, Dodds Mead (U.S.), 1939
(pseud. 'Carter Dixon', with John Rhode) . £250/£45
The Emperor's Snuffbox, Harper (U.S.), 1942. .
 . . . . £250/£45
ditto, Hamilton, 1943 . . . . . . £250/£45
The Life of Sir Arthur Conan Doyle, Harper (U.S.),
1948 . . . . £75/£10
ditto, Hamilton, 1949 . . . . . . £65/£10
The Bride of Newgate, Harper (U.S.), 1950. £60/£20
ditto, Hamilton, 1950 . . . . . . £60/£20
The Devil in Velvet, Harper (U.S.), 1951 . £60/£20
ditto, Hamilton, 1951 . . . . . . £60/£20
The Nine Wrong Answers, Harper (U.S.), 1952 . .
 . . . . £60/£20
ditto, Hamilton, 1952 . . . . . . £60/£20
The Third Bullet and Other Stories, Harper (U.S.),
1954 . . . . £60/£20
ditto, Hamilton, 1954 . . . . . . £60/£20
The Exploits of Sherlock Holmes, Random House
(U.S.), 1954 (with Adrian Conan Doyle) . £60/£20
ditto, Murray, 1954 . . . . . . £60/£20
Captain Cut Throat, Harper (U.S.), 1955 . £60/£15
ditto, Hamilton, 1955 . . . . . . £60/£15
Patrick Butler for the Defence, Harper (U.S.), 1956 .
 . . . . £60/£15
ditto, Hamilton, 1956 . . . . . . £60/£15
Fire, Burn!, Harper (U.S.), 1957 . . . £60/£15
ditto, Hamilton, 1957 . . . . . . £60/£15
Scandal at High Chimneys, Harper (U.S.), 1959 . .
 . . . . £60/£15
ditto, Hamilton, 1959 . . . . . . £60/£15
The Witch of the Low-Tide, Harper (U.S.), 1961 . .
 . . . . £50/£10
ditto, Hamilton, 1961 . . . . . . £50/£10
The Demoniacs, Harper (U.S.), 1962 . £50/£10
ditto, Hamilton, 1962 . . . . . . £50/£10
The Men Who Explained Miracles, Harper (U.S.),
1963 . . . . £50/£10
ditto, Hamilton, 1964 . . . . . . £50/£10
Most Secret, Harper (U.S.), 1964 . . £50/£10
ditto, Hamilton, 1964 . . . . . . £50/£10
Papa La-Bas, Harper (U.S.), 1968 . £50/£10
ditto, Hamilton, 1969 . . . . . . £50/£10
The Ghost's High Noon, Harper (U.S.), 1969 £50/£10
ditto, Hamilton, 1970 . . . . . . £50/£10
Deadly Hall, Harper (U.S.), 1971 . . £45/£10
ditto, Hamilton, 1971 . . . . . . £45/£10
The Hungry Goblin, Hamilton, 1972 . £45/£10
ditto, Harper (U.S.), 1972. . . . . £45/£10
The Dead Sleep Lightly, Doubleday (U.S.), 1983 . .
 . . . . £30/£10

LEWIS CARROLL
(b.1832 d.1898)

Born Charles Lutwidge Dodgson, Carroll was a humorist and children's writer. *Alice's Adventures in Wonderland* was an immediate success.

Alice's Adventures in Wonderland, Macmillan, 1865 (withdrawn, illustrated by Sir John Tenniel) £200,000
ditto, Appleton (U.S.), 1866 (illustrated by Sir John Tenniel) £5,000
ditto, Macmillan, 1866 (illustrated by Sir John Tenniel) £3,000
ditto, as *Alice's Adventures Under Ground*, Macmillan, 1886 (red cloth) £175
ditto, as *Alice's Adventures Under Ground*, Macmillan, 1886 (variant binding) £1,750
ditto, as *Alice's Adventures in Wonderland* Macmillan, 1889 (illustrated by Gertrude Thomson, withdrawn) £300
ditto, Macmillan, 1889 (illustrated by Gertrude Thomson). £150
ditto, Harper (U.S.), 1901 (illustrated by Peter Newell) £150
ditto, Mansfield (U.S.), 1896 (illustrated by Blanche McManus) £75
ditto, Ward Lock, 1907 (illustrated by Blanche McManus) £75
ditto, Cassell, 1907 (illustrated by Charles Robinson) £150
ditto, Heinemann, [1907] (illustrated by Arthur Rackham). £300
ditto, Heinemann, [1907] (illustrated by Arthur Rackham, deluxe edition of 1,130 copies) . . £1,750
ditto, Doubleday (U.S.), [1907] (illustrated by Arthur Rackham, 550 signed copies) £1,750
ditto, Doubleday (U.S.), [1907] (illustrated by Arthur Rackham, trade edition) £300
ditto, Routledge, 1907 (illustrated by Thomas Maybank) £100
ditto, Chatto & Windus, 1907 (illustrated by Millicent Sowerby) £125
ditto, Nelson, 1908 (illustrated by Harry Rountree) £100
ditto, Raphael Tuck, [1910] (12 colour plates by Mabel Lucie Attwell) £200
ditto, Dutton (U.S.), 1929 (illustrated by Willy Pogány) . . . . £50/£15
ditto, Dutton (U.S.), 1929 (200 signed, numbered copies, illustrated by Willy Pogány) . £750/£500
ditto, Black Sun Press, Paris, 1930 (illustrated by Marie Lurencin) £2,000
ditto, Black Sun Press, Paris, 1930 (illustrated by Marie Lurencin, with extra plates) . . . £5,000
ditto, Random House (U.S.), 1969 (illustrated by Salvador Dali) £3,000
Phantasmagoria and Other Poems, Macmillan, 1869 . . . . £250

ditto, Macmillan, 1911 (miniature edition) . . £25
Through the Looking Glass, Macmillan, 1872 (illustrated by Sir John Tenniel) £300
ditto, Mansfield (U.S.), 1899 (illustrated by Blanche McManus) £50
ditto, Harper (U.S.), 1902 (illustrated by Peter Newell) £100
The Hunting of the Snark, An Agony in Eight Fits, Macmillan, 1876 . . . . £450
ditto, Chatto & Windus, 1941 (illustrated by Mervyn Peake yellow boards) . . . . . . £75/£20
ditto, Chatto & Windus, 1941 (illustrated by Mervyn Peake, large format, pink boards) . . £125/£35
Rhyme? and Reason?, Macmillan, 1883 . . £150
A Tangled Tale, Macmillan, 1885 . . . . £100
The Game of Logic, Macmillan, 1886 (with envelope, card and 9 counters. Approx 50 copies) . . £750
ditto, Macmillan, 1887 (with envelope, card and 9 counters) £500
Symbolic Logic, Macmillan, 1896 . . . . £750
Sylvie and Bruno, Macmillan, 1889 . . . . £65
Sylvie and Bruno Concluded, Macmillan, 1893 £65
Three Sunsets and Other Poems, Macmillan, 1898 £45
The Lewis Carroll Picture Book, T. Fisher Unwin, 1899 . . . . £125
Feeding the Mind, Chatto & Windus, 1907 (boards) £40
ditto, Chatto & Windus, 1907 (wraps) . . . £30
ditto, Chatto & Windus, 1907 (leather binding). £50
Bruno's Revenge, Collins, [1924] . . . £25/£10
Further Nonsense, Verse and Prose, T. Fisher Unwin, 1926 . . . . £35/£15
The Collected Verse of Lewis Carroll, Macmillan, 1932 . . . . £50/£20
For the Train, Denis Archer, 1932 . . . £75/£25
ditto, Denis Archer, 1932 (100 signed, numbered copies) . . . . £300/£15
The Rectory Umbrella and Mischmasch, Cassell & Co., 1932 . . . . £65/£20
Useful and Instructive Poetry, Butler and Tanner, 1954 . . . . £40/£10
ditto, Macmillan (U.S.), 1954 . . . . £40/£10
The Diaries of Lewis Carroll, Cassell, 1953 [1954] (2 vols) . . . . £125/£45
The Rectory Magazine, Univ. of Texas (U.S.), 1975 . . . . £20/£10
The Letters of Lewis Carroll, Macmillan, 1979 (2 vols) . . . . £45/£20
ditto, as *The Selected Letters of Lewis Carroll*, Macmillan, 1982 (1 vol.) . . . . . £15/£5
Alice in Wonderland and Through the Looking Glass, Zephyr Books (Sweden), 1946 (illustrated by Mervyn Peake, wraps with d/w) . . . . . . £200/£75
ditto, Allan Wingate, 1954 . . . . £450/£150
ditto, Schocken (U.S.), 1979 . . . . £25/£10

ANGELA CARTER
(b.1940 d.1992)

Carter was a novelist and short story writer whose work explores the territory of magic realism.

Novels

Shadow Dance, Heinemann, 1966 . . . £200/£35
ditto, as *Honeybuzzard*, Simon & Schuster (U.S.), 1966 . . . . £80/£25
The Magic Toyshop, Heinemann, 1967 . £250/£45
ditto, Simon & Schuster (U.S.), 1968 . £100/£15
Several Perceptions, Heinemann, 1968 . £200/£20
ditto, Simon & Schuster (U.S.), 1968 . £45/£10
Heroes and Villains, Heinemann, 1969 . £150/£15
ditto, Simon & Schuster (U.S.), 1969 . £35/£15
Love, Hart-Davis, 1971 . . . . . £75/£15
ditto, Chatto & Windus, 1987 (revised edition) . £20/£5
The Infernal Desire Machines of Doctor Hoffman, Hart-Davis, 1972. . . . . . . £60/£15
ditto, as *The War of Dreams*, Harcourt Brace (U.S.), 1974 . . . . £25/£10
The Passion of New Eve, Gollancz, 1977 . £35/£10
ditto, Harcourt Brace (U.S.), 1977 . . £25/£5
Nights at the Circus, Chatto & Windus, 1984 . £20/£5
ditto, Viking (U.S.), 1986. . . . . . £20/£5
Wise Children, Chatto & Windus, 1991 . . £20/£5
ditto, Farrar Straus (U.S.), 1992 . . . £10/£5

Short Stories

Fireworks: Nine Profane Pieces, Quartet, 1974 . . . . £45/£15
ditto, as *Fireworks: Nine Stories in Various Disguises*, Harper & Row (U.S.), 1981 . . . . . £15/£5
The Bloody Chamber and Other Stories, Gollancz, 1979 . . . . £50/£15
ditto, Harper (U.S.), 1979. . . . . . £20/£5
Black Venus's Tale, Next Editions, 1980 (spiral bound, wraps) £10
Black Venus, Chatto & Windus, 1985 . . £20/£5
ditto, as *Saints and Strangers*, Viking (U.S.), 1986 . . . . £20/£5
Wayward Girls and Wicked Women, Virago, 1986 (wraps) £5
American Ghosts and Old World Wonders, Chatto & Windus, 1993. . . . . . . £20/£5
Burning Your Boats, The Complete Short Stories, Chatto & Windus, 1995 . . . . . £20/£10
ditto, Holt (U.S.), 1996 . . . . . . £15/£5

Children's Fiction

Miss Z, The Dark Young Lady, Heinemann, 1970 . . . . £65/£15
ditto, Simon & Schuster (U.S.), 1970 . £65/£10
The Donkey Prince, Simon & Schuster (U.S.), 1970 . . . . £25/£10
The Fairy Tales of Charles Perrault, Gollancz, 1977 . . . . £40/£20

Martin Leman's Comic and Curious Cats, Gollancz, 1979 . . . . £20/£5
ditto, Harmony/Crown (U.S.), 1979 . . . £25/£5
The Music People, Hamish Hamilton, 1980 (with Leslie Carter). . . . . . . £15/£5
Moonshadow, Gollancz, 1982 (with Justin Todd, no d/w) £100
Sleeping Beauty and Other Favourite Fairy Tales, Gollancz, 1983 . . . . £15/£5
ditto, Schocken, 1984 . . . . £15/£5

Poetry

The Unicorn, Tlaloc, 1966 (150 copies, mimeographed sheets, stapled) £400

Others

The Sadeian Woman, Virago, 1979 . . . £75/£20
ditto, Pantheon (U.S.), 1979 . . . . . £25/£5
Nothing Sacred, Selected Writings, Virago, 1982 (wraps) £10
Come Unto These Yellow Sands, Bloodaxe Books, 1984 . . . . £65/£20
Expletives Deleted, Chatto & Windus, 1992 . £15/£5
The Curious Room, Collected Dramatic Works, Chatto & Windus, 1996 . . . . . . £15/£5
ditto, Secker & Warburg (U.S.), 1997 . . . £15/£5

RAYMOND CARVER
(b.1938 d.1988)

American short story writer and poet, Carver's work has been translated into more than twenty languages.

Fiction

Put Yourself in My Shoes, Capra (U.S.), 1974 (500 copies, wraps) £100
ditto, Capra (U.S.), 1974 (75 numbered copies in hard covers) £600
Will you Please Be Quiet, Please?, McGraw-Hill (U.S.), 1976 . . . . £250/£75
Furious Seasons and Other Stories, Capra (U.S.), 1977 (100 signed copies) . . . . £1,000/£350
ditto, Capra (U.S.), 1977 (wraps). £100
What We Talk About When We Talk About Love, Knopf (U.S.), 1981 . . . . . . £150/£20
ditto, Collins, 1982 . . . . £125/£15
The Pheasant, Metacom (U.S.), 1982 (150 signed copies, wraps) £125
ditto, Metacom (U.S.), 1982 (26 lettered signed copies, no d/w) £500
Cathedral, Knopf (U.S.), 1983 . . . . £35/£10
ditto, Collins, 1984 . . . . £35/£10
The Stories of Raymond Carver, Picador, 1985 (wraps) £10
My Father's Life, Babcock & Koontz (U.S.), 1986 (200 signed copies of 240, wraps) £75

ditto, Babcock & Koontz (U.S.), 1986 (40 signed copies of 240, wraps) £125

Those Days: Early Writings by Raymond Carver, Raven (U.S.), 1987 (100 signed, numbered copies, wraps). £125

ditto, Raven (U.S.), 1987 (26 signed, lettered copies) .
. . . . £350

ditto, Raven (U.S.), 1987 (14 signed, presentation copies, quarter leather) £500

Where I'm Calling From: New and Selected Stories, Atlantic Monthly (U.S.), 1988 . . . . £15/£5

ditto, Atlantic Monthly (U.S.), 1988 (250 signed copies, slipcase) . . . . £250/£225

ditto, Franklin Library (U.S.), 1988 (signed, limited edition) £75

ditto, Harvill, 1993 . . . . £15/£5

Elephant, Jungle Garden Press, 1988 (200 signed copies, wraps) £175

Elephant and Other Stories, Collins Harvill, 1988. .
. . . . £35/£10

Three Stories, Engdahl Typography, 1990 (400 numbered copies) . . . . . . £75/£25

Poetry

Near Klamath, English Club of Sacramento State College (U.S.), 1968 (wraps) £1,250

Winter Insomnia, Kayak (U.S.), 1970 (wraps) . £125

At Night the Salmon Move, Capra (U.S.), 1976 (100 signed hardback copies). £450

ditto, Capra (U.S.), 1976 (1000 copies, wraps) . £75

Distress Sale, Lord John Press, 1981 (150 signed copies, single printed sheet). £100

Two Poems, Scarab (U.S.), 1982 (100 signed copies, wraps). £175

This Water, Ewart (U.S.), 1985 (100 signed copies, wraps). £125

ditto, Ewart (U.S.), 1985 (36 signed, hard back copies)
. . . . £200

Where Water Comes Together with Other Water, Random House, 1985 . . . . . £25/£10

Ultramarine, Random House (U.S.), 1986 . £25/£10

Two Poems, Ewart (U.S.), 1986 (100 copies, wraps) .
. . . . £25

ditto, Ewart (U.S.), 1986 (25 signed copies, wraps)
. . . . £65

In a Marine Light: Selected Poems, Collins Harvill, 1987 . . . . £40/£15

The Painter and the Fish, Ewart (U.S.), 1988 (26 signed copies, hardcover) £250

ditto, Ewart (U.S.), 1988 (74 signed, numbered copies, wraps). £100

ditto, Ewart (U.S.), 1988 (15 signed publisher's copies, hardcover) £250

A New Path to the Waterfall, Atlantic Monthly (U.S.), 1989 . . . . £25/£10

ditto, Atlantic Monthly (U.S.), 1989 (200 copies signed by editor, slipcase). . . . . . £75/£65

ditto, Collins Harvill, 1989 . . . . £25/£10

All of Us, Collins Harvill, 1996 . . . . £30/£10

ditto, Knopf (U.S.), 1998 . . . . . £20/£10

Essays, Poems and Stories

Fires, Capra (U.S.), 1983 (250 signed, hardback copies, acetate d/w) . . . . . . £150/£135

ditto, Capra (U.S.), 1983 (wraps). . . . £15

ditto, Collins Harvill, 1985 . . . . . £25/£10

Music, Ewart (U.S.), 1985 (26 signed, lettered copies, wraps). £150

ditto, Ewart (U.S.), 1985 (100 signed, numbered copies, wraps) £75

No Heroics, Please: Uncollected Writings, Collins Harvill, 1991 . . . . £25/£10

ditto, Vintage Contemporaries (U.S.), 1992 (wraps) £10

Screenplay

Dostoevsky: A Screenplay, Capra (U.S.), 1985 (with Tess Gallagher, bound in with ***King Dog*** by Le Guin, wraps). £25

ditto, Capra (U.S.), 1985 (200 copies signed by all authors, wraps) £150

JOYCE CARY
(b.1888 d.1957)

A novelist, perhaps best known for his *The Horse's Mouth*, made into a film with Alec Guinness.

Novels

Aissa Saved, Benn, 1932 . . . . . . £400/£40

ditto, Harper & Row (U.S.), 1962 . . . £30/£10

An American Visitor, Benn, 1933 . . . £200/£20

ditto, Harper & Row (U.S.), 1961 . . . £25/£10

The African Witch, Gollancz, 1936 . . . £75/£25

ditto, Morrow (U.S.), 1936 . . . . . £25/£5

Castle Corner, Gollancz, 1938, ... £75/£20

ditto, Harper & Row (U.S.), 1963 . . . £25/£10

Mister Johnson, Gollancz, 1939 . . . . £75/£20

ditto, Harper & Row (U.S.), 1948 . . . . £20/£5

Charley Is My Darling, Joseph, 1940 . . £50/£10

ditto, Harper & Row (U.S.), 1959 . . . . £20/£5

A House of Children, Joseph, 1941 . . . £35/£10

ditto, Harper & Row (U.S.), 1955 . . . . £20/£5

Herself Surprised, Joseph, 1941 . . . . £35/£10

ditto, Harper & Row (U.S.), 1941 . . . . £20/£5

To Be a Pilgrim, Joseph, 1942 . . . . £35/£10

ditto, Harper & Row (U.S.), 1942 . . . . £20/£5

The Horse's Mouth, Joseph, 1944 . . . £150/£20

ditto, Harper & Row (U.S.), 1944. . . . £60/£10

The Moonlight, Joseph, 1946 . . . . £35/£10

ditto, Harper & Row (U.S.), 1946. . . . . £20/£5

A Fearful Joy, Joseph, 1949 . . . . . £25/£10

ditto, Harper & Row (U.S.), 1949. . . . . £20/£5

Prisoner of Grace, Joseph, 1952 . . . . £25/£10

ditto, Harper & Row (U.S.), 1952. . . . . £20/£5

Except the Lord, Joseph, 1953 . . . . . £20/£5

ditto, Harper & Row (U.S.), 1953. . . . . £20/£5

Not Honour More, Joseph, 1955. . . . . £20/£5

ditto, Harper & Row (U.S.), 1955. . . . . £20/£5

The Old Strife at Plant's, New Bodlean, 1956 (100 signed, numbered copies, wraps) . . . £60
The Horse's Mouth and The Old Strife at Plant's, George Rainbird/Joseph, 1957 (1500 copies, slipcase, acetate d/w) . . . . £50/£35
The Captive and the Free, Joseph, 1959 . £20/£10
ditto, Harper & Row (U.S.), 1959. . . . £15/£5
Spring Song and Other Stories, Joseph, 1960 £15/£10
ditto, Harper & Row (U.S.), 1960. . . . £15/£5
Cock Jarvis, Joseph, 1974 . . . . . . £10/£5
ditto, St Martin's Press (U.S.), 1975 . . . £10/£5

Poetry
Marching Soldier, Joseph, 1945 . . . . £25/£10
The Drunken Sailor: A Ballad-Epic, Joseph, 1947 .
. . . . £25/£10

Others
Power in Men, Liberal Book Club/Nicholson & Watson, 1939. . . . . £20/£10
ditto, Univ. of Washington Press (U.S.), 1963 . £15/£5
The Case for African Freedom, Secker & Warburg, 1941 . . . . £25/£10
ditto, Secker & Warburg, 1941 (revised edition) . .
. . . . £20/£10
ditto, as *The Case for African Freedom and Other Writings on Africa*, Univ. of Texas (U.S.), 1962 . .
. . . . £10/£5
Process of Real Freedom, Joseph, 1943 (wraps) £25
Britain and West Africa, Longman's Green and Co., 1946 (wraps) £25
Art and Reality, Ways of the Creative Process, C.U.P., 1958 . . . . £20/£5
ditto, Harper & Row (U.S.), 1958. . . . £20/£5
Memoir of the Bobotes, Univ. of Texas (U.S.), 1960 .
. . . . £20/£5
ditto, Joseph, 1964. . . . . £20/£5
Selected Essays, Joseph, 1976 . . . . £20/£5
ditto, St Martin's Press (U.S.), 1976 . . . £20/£5

WILLA CATHER
(b.1873 d.1947)

O Pioneers was Cather's first popular success, and serious critical recognition was to come with the award of the Pulitzer Prize for *One of Ours*, and the Prix Femina Americaine in 1933.

Novels
Alexander's Bridge, Houghton Mifflin/Riverside Press (U.S.), 1912 (blue cloth). £65
ditto, Houghton Mifflin/Riverside Press (U.S.), 1912 (later issues, other cloth colours) £40
ditto, Heinemann, 1912 . . . . . . £35
O Pioneers!, Houghton Mifflin/Riverside Press (U.S.), 1913 (tan or cream cloth) £75
ditto, Houghton Mifflin/Riverside Press (U.S.), 1913 (later issue, brown cloth) £45

ditto, Heinemann, 1913 . . . . . . £35
The Song of the Lark, Houghton Mifflin/Riverside Press (U.S.), 1915 . . . . . . £45
ditto, Murray, 1916 . . . . £25
My Ántonia, Houghton Mifflin/Riverside Press (U.S.), 1918 . . . . £45
ditto, Heinemann, 1919 . . . . . . £25
One of Ours, Knopf (U.S.), 1922 (35 signed, on Japanese vellum of 345 copies, glassine d/w) . . .
. . . . £1,500/£1,250
ditto, Knopf (U.S.), 1922 (310 signed of 345 copies, slipcase) . . . . £500/£400
ditto, Knopf (U.S.), 1922 . . . . . £100/£25
ditto, Knopf (U.S.), 1922 (250 special copies) £75/£25
ditto, Heinemann, 1923 . . . . . £75/£25
A Lost Lady, Knopf (U.S.), 1923 . . . £150/£45
ditto, Knopf (U.S.), 1923 (220 signed copies, slipcase)
. . . . £650/£550
ditto, Heinemann, 1924 . . . . . £75/£25
The Professor's House, Knopf (U.S.), 1925 (40 signed, on Japanese vellum of 225 copies, glassine d/w) . . . . £600/£500
ditto, Knopf (U.S.), 1925 (185 signed of 225 copies, slipcase) . . . . £350/£300
ditto, Knopf (U.S.), 1925 . . . . . £65/£20
ditto, Heinemann, 1925 . . . . . £35/£10
My Mortal Enemy, Knopf (U.S.), 1926 (220 signed copies, slipcase) . . . . . . £450/£350
ditto, Knopf (U.S.), 1926 . . . . . £65/£20
ditto, Heinemann, 1928 . . . . . £35/£10
Death Comes for the Archbishop, Knopf (U.S.), 1927 (50 signed copies on Japanese vellum). . . £2,000
ditto, Knopf (U.S.), 1927 (175 signed copies) . £750
ditto, Knopf (U.S.), 1927 . . . . . £75/£20
ditto, Heinemann, 1927 . . . . . £35/£10
ditto, Knopf (U.S.), 1929 (170 signed copies) . . .
. . . . £350/£250
Shadows on the Rock, Knopf (U.S.), 1931 . £75/£15
ditto, Knopf (U.S.), 1931 (199 signed, numbered copies on Japanese vellum) £600
ditto, Knopf (U.S.), 1931 (619 signed, numbered copies) . . . . £250/£200
ditto, Cassell, 1932 . . . . . . £30/£10
Lucy Gayheart, Knopf (U.S.), 1935 . . . £50/£10
ditto, Knopf (U.S.), 1935 (749 signed, numbered copies, d/w and slipcase) . . . . £250/£175
ditto, Cassell, 1935 . . . . . . £25/£10
Sapphira and the Slave Girl, Knopf (U.S.), 1940 . .
. . . . £45/£10
ditto, Knopf (U.S.), 1940 (525 signed, numbered copies) . . . . £200/£150
ditto, Cassell, 1941 . . . . £15/£5

Short Stories
The Troll Garden, McClure, Phillips & Co. (U.S.), 1905 . . . . £100
Youth and the Bright Medusa, Knopf (U.S.), 1920 .
. . . . £100/£35
ditto, Knopf (U.S.), 1920 (35 signed copies) £500/£400
ditto, Heinemann, 1921 . . . . . £75/£25

The Fear that Walks by Noonday, Phoenix Bookshop, 1931 (30 numbered copies) £500
Obscure Destinies, Knopf (U.S.), 1932 (260 signed, numbered copies, d/w and slipcase) . . £200/£150
ditto, Knopf (U.S.), 1932 . . . . . . £35/£10
ditto, Cassell, 1932 . . . . £25/£10
The Old Beauty and Others, Knopf (U.S.), 1948 . .
. . . . £30/£10
ditto, Cassell, 1956 . . . . £10/£5
Five Stories, Vintage Books (U.S.), 1956 (wraps) £100
Father Junipero's Holy Family, Robbins (U.S.), 1955 (200 copies) . . . . £250/£200
Early Stories of Willa Cather, Dodd, Mead (U.S.), 1957 . . . . £20/£10
Willa Cather's Collected Short Fiction, Univ. of Nebraska Press (U.S.), 1965 . . . . . £20/£5
Uncle Valentine and Other Stories, Univ. of Nebraska Press (U.S.), 1973 . . . . £15/£5

Poetry
April Twilights, Gorham Press (U.S.), 1903. . £200
April Twilights and Other Poems, Knopf (U.S.), 1923 (450 signed, numbered copies, slipcase) . £150/£125
ditto, Knopf (U.S.), 1923 . . . . . £50/£20
ditto, Heinemann, 1924 . . . . . £45/£15

Essays
Not Under Forty, Knopf (U.S.), 1936 . . £20/£10
ditto, Knopf (U.S.), 1936 (313 signed, numbered copies on Japanese vellum, d/w and slipcase) . £250/£200
ditto, Cassell, 1936 . . . . £20/£5

Others
My Autobiography, Stokes (U.S.), 1914 (pseud. S.S. McClure) £15
ditto, Murray, 1914 . . . . £10
December Night, Knopf (U.S.), 1933 . . £75/£35
Not Under Forty, Knopf (U.S.), 1936 . . £30/£10
ditto, Knopf (U.S.), 1936 (333 signed large paper copies) . . . . £300/£200
Willa Cather on Writing, Knopf (U.S.), 1949 £30/£10
Writing from Willa Cather's Campus Years, Univ. of Nebraska Press (U.S.), 1950 . . . . £25/£10
Willa Cather in Europe, Knopf (U.S.), 1956 . £20/£5
The Kingdom of Art: Willa Cather's First Principles and Critical Statements 1893-1902, Univ. of Nebraska Press (U.S.), 1966 . . . . £25/£10
The World and the Parish: Willa Cather's Articles and Reviews 1893-1902, Univ. of Nebraska Press (U.S.), 1970 (2 vols) . . . . . £30/£10
Willa Cather In Person, Univ. of Nebraska Press (U.S.), 1987 . . . . £20/£10

RAYMOND CHANDLER
(b.1888 d.1959)

Born in America, Chandler became a British citizen in 1907, but returned to the U.S. in 1912. A novelist and short story writer, Chandler was 45 before he started writing, and in *The Big Sleep* introduced one of the most famous fictional detectives of all time, Philip Marlowe.

Novels
The Big Sleep, Knopf (U.S.), 1939 . . £10,000/£600
ditto, Hamish Hamilton, 1939 . . . £2,000/£300
ditto, World (U.S.), 1946 (motion picture edition with photographs from the film) . . . . . £45/£10
Farewell My Lovely, Knopf (U.S.), 1940 £3,000/£250
ditto, Hamish Hamilton, 1940 . . . £1,000/£100
The High Window, Knopf (U.S.), 1942 . £2,500/£250
ditto, Hamish Hamilton, 1943 . . . £1,000/£100
The Lady in the Lake, Knopf (U.S.), 1943 . . . .
. . . . £3,000/£250
ditto, Hamish Hamilton, 1944 . . £1,000/£100
The Little Sister, Hamish Hamilton, 1949 £1,000/£150
ditto, Houghton Mifflin (U.S.), 1949 . £750/£100
The Long Goodbye, Hamish Hamilton, 1953 £500/£75
ditto, Houghton Mifflin (U.S.), 1954 . £400/£75
Playback, Hamish Hamilton, 1958 . . £75/£20
ditto, Houghton Mifflin (U.S.), 1958 . . £50/£20
Poodle Springs, Putnam (U.S.), 1989 (completed by Robert Parker) . . . . £15/£5
ditto, Macdonald, 1990 . . . . . . £15/£5
ditto, Macdonald, 1990 (250 copies signed by Parker, slipcase, no d/w) . . . . £50/£30

Short Stories
Five Murderers, Avon (U.S.), 1944 (wraps) . £175
Five Sinister Characters, Avon (U.S.), 1945 (wraps) .
. . . . £150
Finger Man and Other Stories, Avon (U.S.), [1946] (wraps) £75
Red Wind, World (U.S.), 1946 . . . £45/£10
Spanish Blood, World (U.S.), 1946 . . . £40/£10
Trouble is My Business, Penguin, 1950 (wraps) £10
ditto, Pocket Books (U.S.), 1951 . . . . £15
The Simple Art of Murder, Houghton Mifflin (U.S.), 1950 . . . . £250/£30
ditto, Hamish Hamilton, 1950 . . . £200/£30
Pick-Up on Noon Street, Pocket Books (U.S.), 1952 £15
Smart Aleck Kill, Hamish Hamilton, 1953 . £100/£25
Pearls are a Nuisance, Hamish Hamilton, 1953 (wraps) £40
ditto, Hamish Hamilton, 1953 . . . . £30/£10
ditto, as *Finger Man*, Ace Books (U.S.), 1960 . £40
Killer in the Rain, Hamish Hamilton, 1964 . £60/£15
ditto, Houghton Mifflin (U.S.), 1964 . . £50/£15
The Smell of Fear, Hamish Hamilton, 1965 £60/£15
Goldfish, Penguin, 1995 (wraps). £5
Omnibus Editions

Raymond Chandler's Mystery Omnibus, World (U.S.),
1944 . . . . £25/£10
The Raymond Chandler Omnibus, Hamish Hamilton,
1953 . . . . £65/£15
ditto, Knopf (U.S.), 1964 . . . . . £40/£10
The Second Chandler Omnibus, Hamish Hamilton,
1962 . . . . £50/£15
The Midnight Raymond Chandler, Houghton Mifflin
(U.S.), 1971 . . . . £35/£10

Others

Raymond Chandler On Writing, Houghton Mifflin
(U.S.), 1962 (wraps) £200
Raymond Chandler Speaking, Hamish Hamilton, 1962
. . . . £75/£15
ditto, Houghton Mifflin (U.S.), 1962 . . £50/£15
Chandler On Proof Reading, Merrion Press, 1963
(wraps) £200
*Chandler Before Marlowe: Raymond Chandler's
Early Prose and Poetry, 1908-1912*, Univ. of South
Carolina Press (U.S.), 1973 (wraps) . . . £15
ditto, Univ. of South Carolina Press (U.S.), 1973 (499
numbered copies, slipcase, no d/w) . . . £75
The Blue Dahlia, Southern Illinois Univ. Press, 1976 .
. . . . £45/£10
ditto, Elm Tree Books, 1976 . . . . . £20/£5
*The Notebooks of Raymond Chandler and English
Summer - A Gothic Romance*, The Ecco Press (U.S.),
1976 . . . . £45/£20
ditto, Weidenfeld & Nicolson, 1977 . . . £25/£10
Letters, Raymond Chandler and James M. Fox,
Nevile & Yellin (U.S.), 1978 (350 numbered copies,
no d/w) £45
ditto, Nevile & Yellin (U.S.), 1978 (26 lettered copies
numbered copies, no d/w) £150
The Selected Letters of Raymond Chandler, Columbia
Univ. Press (U.S.), 1981. . . . . . £40/£15
ditto, Cape, 1981 . . . . £25/£10
Backfire: Story for the Screen, Santa Barbara Press
(U.S.), 1984 (200 copies, wraps) £30
ditto, Santa Barbara Press (U.S.), 1984 (26 lettered
copies, signed by Robert Parker, slipcase, no d/w) .
. . . . £200
ditto, Santa Barbara Press (U.S.), 1984 (100 signed,
numbered copies, slipcase, no d/w) . . . £75
*Raymond Chandler's Unknown Thriller: The
Screenplay of 'Playback'*, Mysterious Press (U.S.),
1985 . . . . £30/£15
ditto, Mysterious Press (U.S.), 1985 (250 copies,
signed by Robert Parker, slipcase) . . . £100/£75
ditto, Mysterious Press (U.S.), 1985 (26 signed, lettered
copies, slipcase) . . . . £200/£175
ditto, Harrap, 1985 . . . . £20/£10
*The Raymond Chandler Papers: Selected Letters and
Nonfiction, 1909-1959*, Atlantic Monthly Press
(U.S.), 2000 . . . . £25/£10

LESLIE CHARTERIS
(b.1907 d.1993)

Leslie Charteris was born in Singapore to a Chinese
father and English mother. Educated and living in
England for several years he wrote a number of crime
novels before hitting upon the character of Simon
Templar, a gentleman burglar nicknamed 'The Saint'.
He later moved to America, and in 1941 became an
American citizen.

'Saint' Novels

Meet the Tiger!, Ward Lock, 1928 . . £2,000/£750
ditto, Doubleday (U.S.), 1929 . . . £1,500/£650
ditto, as *The Saint Meets The Tiger*, Hodder &
Stoughton, 1963 . . . . £25/£10
The Last Hero, Hodder & Stoughton, [1930] . . .
. . . . £1,000/£100
ditto, Doubleday (U.S.), 1931 . . . £750/£75
ditto, as *The Saint Closes The Case*, Hodder &
Stoughton, 1951 . . . . £45/£10
Knight Templar, Hodder & Stoughton, [1930] . . .
. . . . £1,000/£100
ditto, as *The Avenging Saint*, Hodder & Stoughton,
1949 . . . . £45/£10
ditto, as *The Avenging Saint*, Doubleday (U.S.), 1931.
. . . . £750/£75
She was a Lady, Hodder & Stoughton, 1931 . . .
. . . . £1,000/£100
ditto, as *Angels of Doom*, Doubleday (U.S.), 1932. .
. . . . £750/£75
ditto, as *The Saint Meets His Match*, Hodder &
Stoughton, 1950 . . . . £45/£10
Getaway, Hodder & Stoughton, 1932 . £1,000/£100
ditto, as *Getaway: The New Saint Mystery*, Doubleday
(U.S.), 1933 . . . . £750/£75
ditto, as *The Saint's Getaway*, Hodder & Stoughton,
1950 . . . . £40/£10
The Saint in New York, Hodder & Stoughton, 1935 .
. . . . £1,000/£100
ditto, Doubleday (U.S.), 1935 . . . . £750/£75
The Saint Overboard, Hodder & Stoughton, 1936 . .
. . . . £1,000/£100
ditto, Doubleday (U.S.), 1936 . . . . £750/£75
Thieves' Picnic, Hodder & Stoughton, 1937 £750/£75
ditto, Doubleday (U.S.), 1937 . . . . £600/£60
ditto, as *The Saint Bids Diamonds*, Hodder &
Stoughton, 1950 . . . . £45/£10
Prelude for War, Hodder & Stoughton, 1938 £450/£40
ditto, Doubleday (U.S.), 1938 . . . . £350/£30
ditto, as *The Saint Plays With Fire*, Hodder &
Stoughton, 1951 . . . . £35/£10
The Saint in Miami, Doubleday (U.S.), 1940 £350/£30
ditto, Hodder & Stoughton, 1941. . . . £175/£15
The Saint Steps In, Doubleday (U.S.), 1943 £175/£20
ditto, Hodder & Stoughton, 1944. . . . £150/£15
The Saint Sees it Through, Doubleday (U.S.), 1946 .
. . . . £100/£15
ditto, Hodder & Stoughton, 1947. . . . £100/£15

Guide to First Edition Prices, 2004/5

The Saint and the Fiction Makers, Doubleday (U.S.),
1968 . . . . £75/£10
ditto, Hodder & Stoughton, 1969. . . . £75/£10
The Saint in Pursuit, Doubleday (U.S.), 1970 . . .
. . . . £125/£25
ditto, Hodder & Stoughton, 1971. . . . £125/£25
The Saint and the People Importers, Hodder &
Stoughton, 1971 (wraps) £10
ditto, Doubleday (U.S.), 1972 . . . £100/£15
ditto, Hodder & Stoughton, 1973. . . . £125/£25
The Saint and the Hapsburg Necklace, Doubleday
(U.S.), 1976 . . . . £60/£10
ditto, Hodder & Stoughton, 1976. . . . £60/£10
Send for The Saint, Hodder & Stoughton, 1977 . .
. . . . £35/£10
ditto, Doubleday (U.S.), 1978 . . . . £35/£10
The Saint and the Templar Treasure, Doubleday
(U.S.), 1979 . . . . £35/£10
ditto, Hodder & Stoughton, 1979. . . . £35/£10
Count on The Saint, Doubleday (U.S.), 1980 . £25/£5
ditto, Hodder & Stoughton, 1980. . . . . £25/£5
Salvage for The Saint, Doubleday (U.S.), 1983 £20/£5
ditto, Hodder & Stoughton, 1983. . . . . £20/£5

'Saint' Novellas and Short Stories
Enter The Saint, Hodder & Stoughton, [1930] . . .
. . . . £1,000/£100
ditto, Doubleday (U.S.), 1931 . . . . £750/£75
Featuring The Saint, Hodder & Stoughton, 1931 . .
. . . . £1,000/£100
Alias The Saint, Hodder & Stoughton, 1931 . . .
. . . . £1,000/£100
Wanted for Murder, Doubleday (U.S.), 1931 (contains
Featuring the Saint and Alias the Saint) . £750/£75
ditto, as Paging the Saint, Jacobs (U.S.), 1945 (wraps)
. . . . £45
The Holy Terror, Hodder & Stoughton, 1932 . . .
. . . . £1,000/£100
ditto, as The Saint Versus Scotland Yard, Doubleday
(U.S.), 1932 . . . . £750/£75
ditto, as The Saint Versus Scotland Yard, Hodder &
Stoughton, 1949 . . . . £25/£10
Once More The Saint, Hodder & Stoughton, 1933. .
. . . . £1,000/£100
ditto, as The Saint and Mr Teal, Doubleday (U.S.),
1933 . . . . £750/£75
The Brighter Buccaneer, Hodder & Stoughton, 1933 .
. . . . £1,000/£100
ditto, Doubleday (U.S.), 1933 . . . . £750/£75
The Misfortunes of Mr Teal, Hodder & Stoughton,
1934 . . . . £1,000/£100
ditto, Doubleday (U.S.), 1934 . . . . £750/£75
ditto, as The Saint In London, Hodder & Stoughton,
1952 . . . . £25/£10
Boodle, Hodder & Stoughton, 1934 . £1,000/£100
ditto, The Saint Intervenes, Doubleday (U.S.), 1934 .
. . . . £750/£75
The Saint Goes On, Hodder & Stoughton, 1934 . .
. . . . £1,000/£100

ditto, Doubleday (U.S.), 1935 . . . . £750/£75
The Ace of Knaves, Hodder & Stoughton, 1937 . .
. . . . £400/£35
ditto, Doubleday (U.S.), 1937 . . . . £300/£30
Follow The Saint, Doubleday (U.S.), 1938 . £400/£35
ditto, Hodder & Stoughton, 1939. . . . £300/£30
The Happy Highwayman, Doubleday (U.S.), 1939 .
. . . . £350/£25
ditto, Hodder & Stoughton, 1939. . . . £275/£25
The Saint Goes West, Doubleday (U.S.), 1942 . . .
. . . . £125/£15
ditto, Hodder & Stoughton, 1942. . . . £75/£15
The Saint on Guard, Doubleday (U.S.), 1944 £100/£15
ditto, Hodder & Stoughton, 1945. . . . £65/£15
Call For The Saint, Doubleday (U.S.), 1948 £75/£15
ditto, Hodder & Stoughton, 1948. . . . £30/£10
Saint Errant, Doubleday (U.S.), 1948 . . £35/£10
ditto, Hodder & Stoughton, 1949. . . . £25/£10
The Saint in Europe, Doubleday (U.S.), 1953 £35/£10
ditto, Hodder & Stoughton, 1954. . . . £25/£10
The Saint on the Spanish Main, Doubleday (U.S.),
1955 . . . . £30/£10
ditto, Hodder & Stoughton, 1956. . . . £25/£10
The Saint Around the World, Doubleday (U.S.), 1956
. . . . £25/£10
ditto, Hodder & Stoughton, 1957. . . . £25/£10
Thanks to The Saint, Doubleday (U.S.), 1957 £25/£10
ditto, Hodder & Stoughton, 1958. . . . £25/£10
Señor Saint, Doubleday (U.S.), 1958 . . £25/£10
ditto, Hodder & Stoughton, 1959. . . . £25/£10
The Saint to the Rescue, Doubleday (U.S.), 1959 . .
. . . . £25/£10
ditto, Hodder & Stoughton, 1961. . . . £25/£10
Trust The Saint, Doubleday (U.S.), 1962 . £25/£10
ditto, Hodder & Stoughton, 1962. . . . £25/£10
The Saint in the Sun, Doubleday (U.S.), 1963 £25/£10
ditto, Hodder & Stoughton, 1964. . . . £25/£10
Vendetta for The Saint, Doubleday (U.S.), 1964 . .
. . . . £25/£10
ditto, Hodder & Stoughton, 1965. . . . £25/£10
The Saint on TV, Doubleday (U.S.), 1968 . £25/£10
ditto, Hodder & Stoughton, 1968. . . . £25/£10
The Saint Returns, Doubleday (U.S.), 1968 £25/£10
ditto, Hodder & Stoughton, 1969. . . . £25/£10
The Saint Abroad, Doubleday (U.S.), 1969. . £20/£5
ditto, Hodder & Stoughton, 1970. . . . . £15/£5
Catch The Saint, Hodder & Stoughton, 1975 . £15/£5
ditto, Doubleday (U.S.), 1975 . . . . . £15/£5
The Saint in Trouble, Doubleday (U.S.), 1978 . £15/£5
ditto, Hodder & Stoughton, 1979. . . . . £15/£5

Collected Editions
The First Saint Omnibus, Hodder & Stoughton, 1939.
. . . . £75/£15
ditto, Doubleday (U.S.), 1939 . . . . £75/£15
ditto, as Arrest the Saint, PermaBooks (U.S.), 1951 .
. . . . £30/£10
The Saint Two in One, Sun Dial Press (U.S.), 1942 .
. . . . £30/£5

The Saint at Large, Sun Dial Press (U.S.), 1943 . .
. . . . £30/£5
The Second Saint Omnibus, Doubleday (U.S.), 1951 .
. . . . £30/£10
ditto, Hodder & Stoughton, 1952. . . . £30/£10
Concerning The Saint, Avon (U.S.), 1958 (wraps) £25
The Saint Cleans Up, Avon (U.S.), 1959 (wraps) £25
The Saint Magazine Reader, Doubleday (U.S.), 1966 .
. . . . £15/£5
ditto, as *The Saint's Choice*, Hodder & Stoughton,
1976 . . . . £15/£5
Saints Alive, Hodder & Stoughton, 1974 . . £15/£5
The Saint: Good as Gold, The Ellery Queen Mystery
Club (U.S.), 1979 . . . . £10
The Fantastic Saint, Doubleday (U.S.), 1982 . £10/£5
ditto, Hodder & Stoughton, 1982. . . . . £10/£5
The Saint: Five Complete Novels, Avenel Books
(U.S.), 1983 . . . . £10/£5

Other Titles
X Esquire, Ward Lock, 1927 . . . . £1,250/£125
The White Rider, Ward Lock, 1928 . . . £500/£75
ditto, Doubleday (U.S.), 1930 . . . . £350/£35
Daredevil, Ward Lock, 1929 . . . . £300/£75
ditto, Doubleday (U.S.), 1929 . . . . £200/£25
The Bandit, Ward Lock, 1929 . . . . £300/£75
ditto, Doubleday (U.S.), 1930 . . . . £200/£25
Killer of Bulls, Heinemann, 1937 (with Juan Belmonte)
. . . . £75/£25
ditto, Doubleday (U.S.), 1937 . . . . £50/£15
Lady on a Train, Shaw Press (U.S.), 1945 (wraps) £65
Spanish for Fun, Hodder & Stoughton, 1964 (wraps)
. . . . £15
Paleneo: A Universal Sign Language, Hodder &
Stoughton, 1972 (wraps) £15

BRUCE CHATWIN
(b.1940 d.1989)

A travel writer and novelist, Chatwin's first book, *In Patagonia*, won both the Hawthornden Prize and the E.M. Forster Award of the American Academy of Arts and Letters.

Novels
The Viceroy of Ouidah, Cape, 1980 . . . £60/£10
ditto, Summit (U.S.), 1980 . . . . . £30/£10
On the Black Hill, Cape, 1982 . . . . £30/£10
ditto, Viking, 1982 . . . . . . £25/£10
The Songlines, Cape, 1987 . . . . . £45/£10
ditto, London Limited Editions, 1987 (150 signed
copies, glassine wrapper) . . . . . £300/£250
ditto, Viking (U.S.), 1987. . . . . . £35/£5
ditto, Franklin Library (U.S.), 1987 (signed limited
edition) £75
Utz, Cape, 1988 . . . . £15/£5
ditto, Viking (U.S.), 1989. . . . . . £10/£5

Travel
In Patagonia, Cape, 1977 (map endpapers). £500/£250
ditto, Cape, 1977 (white endpapers) . . . £350/£100
ditto, Summit (U.S.) . . . . £75/£25
Patagonia Revisited, Russell, 1985 (with Paul
Theroux) . . . . £25/£10
ditto, Russell, 1985 (250 copies, cellophane d/w) . .
. . . . £250/£200
ditto, Houghton Mifflin (U.S.), 1986 . . £20/£10
ditto, as *Nowhere Is a Place*, Sierra Club (U.S.), 1991.
. . . . £20/£10

Short Stories
The Attractions of France, Colophon Press, 1993 (26
lettered copies of 211 bound in cloth) . . . £400
ditto, Colophon Press, 1993 (175 numbered copies of
211, wraps) £75

Biography
What am I Doing Here?, Cape, 1989 . . . £25/£5
ditto, Viking (U.S.), 1989. . . . . . £20/£5
Photographs and Notebooks, Cape, 1993 . £35/£10
ditto, as *Far Journeys: Photographs and Notebooks*,
Viking (U.S.), 1993 . . . . £25/£10

Others
Animal Style: Art From East to West, Asia Society
(U.S.), 1970 (with Emma Bunker and Ann Farkas,
wraps). £30
Lady Lisa Lyon, Viking (U.S.), 1983 (Robert
Mapplethorpe, text by Chatwin, wraps) . . £20
ditto, St Martin's Press (U.S.), 1983 . . . £40/£15
ditto, Blond & Briggs, 1983 . . . . £75/£25
The Morality of Things, Typographeum (U.S.), 1993
(175 copies, no d/w) £75
*The Anatomy of Restlessness, Selected Writings,
1969-89*, Cape, 1996. . . . . . . £30/£10
ditto, Viking (U.S.), 1996. . . . . . £25/£5

GEOFFREY CHAUCER
(b.1340? d.1400)

Chaucer gave English literature its form and inspiration, and well over 500 years later his work is still outrageous and entertaining. The values suggested below are purely hypothetical!

Canterbury Tales, William Caxton, [c.1478] . . . .
. . . . £5,000,000
ditto, William Caxton, 1483 (with woodcut illustrations)
. . . . £2,500,000

JOHN CHEEVER
(b.1912 d.1982)

An American short story writer and novelist, his *Stories* won a Pulitzer Prize in 1978.

Fiction
The Way Some People Live: A Book of Stories, Random House (U.S.), 1943 . . . . £750/£125
The Enormous Radio and Other Stories, Funk & Wagnalls (U.S.), 1953 . . . . . . £150/£25
ditto, Gollancz, 1953 . . . . £75/£15
The Wapshot Chronicle, Harper (U.S.), 1957 . . .
. . . . £125/£25
ditto, Gollancz, 1957 . . . . £75/£15
ditto, Franklin Library (U.S.), 1978 (signed, limited edition) £65
The Housebreaker of Shady Hill and Other Stories, Harper (U.S.), [1958] . . . . . £125/£25
ditto, Gollancz, 1958 . . . . £75/£15
Some People, Places, and Things That Will Not Appear in My Next Novel, Harper (U.S.), 1961 . .
. . . . £100/£20
ditto, Gollancz, 1961 . . . . £75/£15
The Wapshot Scandal, Harper (U.S.), 1964 £40/£10
ditto, Gollancz, 1964 . . . . £40/£10
The Brigadier and the Golf Widow, Harper (U.S.), 1964 . . . . £40/£10
ditto, Gollancz, 1965 . . . . £40/£10
Bullet Park, Knopf (U.S.), 1969 . . . . £100/£25
ditto, Cape, 1969 . . . . £40/£10
The World of Apples, Knopf (U.S.), 1973 . £30/£10
ditto, Cape, 1974 . . . . £25/£10
Falconer, Knopf (U.S.), 1977 . . . . £25/£10
ditto, Cape, 1977 . . . . £25/£10
The Stories of John Cheever, Knopf (U.S.), 1978 . .
. . . . £25/£10
ditto, Cape, 1979 . . . . £20/£5
The Wapshot Chronicle/The Wapshot Scandal, Harper (U.S.), 1979 . . . . £30/£10
Oh, What a Paradise it Seems, Knopf (U.S.), 1982 .
. . . . £20/£5
ditto, Cape, 1982 . . . . £20/£5
The Letters of John Cheever, Simon & Schuster (U.S.), 1988 (ed. by Benjamin Cheever) . £25/£10
ditto, Cape, 1989 . . . . £20/£5
The Journals of John Cheever, Knopf (U.S.), 1991 .
. . . . £20/£5
ditto, Cape, 1991 . . . . £15/£5
Atlantic Crossings: Excerpts From The Journals of John Cheever, Ex Ophidia (U.S.), 1986 (90 copies) .
. . . . £225

Others
Homage to Shakespeare, Country Squires Books (U.S.), 1968 (150 signed, numbered copies) . . .
. . . . £125/£150
The Day the Pig Fell into the Well, Lord John Press (U.S.), 1978 (275 signed, numbered copies) . £65

ditto, Lord John Press (U.S.), 1978 (26 signed, lettered copies, slipcase) . . . . £200/£150
The Leaves, The Lion-Fish and the Bear, Sylvester & Orphanos (U.S.), 1980 (300 signed, numbered copies)
. . . . £65
ditto, Sylvester & Orphanos (U.S.), 1980 (26 signed, lettered copies, slipcase) . . . . £200/£150
ditto, Sylvester & Orphanos (U.S.), 1980 (4 signed copies bearing printed name of recipient, slipcase) .
. . . . £350/£300
The National Pastime, Sylvester & Orphanos (U.S.), 1982 (300 signed, numbered copies) . . . £65
ditto, Sylvester & Orphanos (U.S.), 1982 (26 signed, lettered copies, slipcase) . . . . £200/£150
ditto, Sylvester & Orphanos (U.S.), 1982 (4 signed copies bearing printed name of recipient, slipcase) .
. . . . £350/£300
Expelled, Sylvester & Orphanos (U.S.), 1988 (a miniature book with a Preface by Malcom Cowley, an Afterword by John Updike, designed and illustrated by Warren Chappell, 150 copies signed by Cheever, Cowley, Updike and Chappell, slipcase) . £175/£125
ditto, Sylvester & Orphanos (U.S.), 1988 (26 lettered copies, signed by contributors, slipcase) . £250/£200
ditto, Sylvester & Orphanos (U.S.), 1988 (4 copies bearing printed name of recipient, signed by contributors, slipcase) . . . . . . £350/£300

G.K. CHESTERTON
(b.1874 d.1936)

Poet, novelist, journalist and essayist, Chesterton is best remembered for his detective stories featuring Father Brown, an unassuming Catholic priest.

'Father Brown' Stories
The Innocence of Father Brown, Cassell, 1911 £275
ditto, John Lane (U.S.), 1911 . . . . . £65
The Wisdom of Father Brown, Cassell, 1914 . £100
ditto, John Lane (U.S.), 1915 . . . . . £45
The Incredulity of Father Brown, Cassell, 1926 . .
. . . . £1,500/£50
ditto, Dodd, Mead (U.S.), 1927 . . . . £500/£35
The Secret of Father Brown, Cassell, 1927 £1,500/£35
ditto, Harper & Bros (U.S.), 1928 . . . £500/£30
The Scandal of Father Brown, Cassell, 1935 . . .
. . . . £600/£25
ditto, Dodd, Mead (U.S.), 1935 . . . . £200/£25

Omnibus Editions of 'Father Brown' Stories
The Father Brown Stories, Cassell, 1929 . £250/£25
ditto, as *The Father Brown Omnibus*, Dodd, Mead (U.S.), 1933 . . . . £175/£20

Novels
The Napoleon of Notting Hill, John Lane, 1904 £100
ditto, John Lane (U.S.), 1906 . . . . . £100

The Man Who Was Thursday, Arrowsmith, [1908] .
. . . . £150
ditto, Dodd, Mead (U.S.), 1908 . . . . . £150
The Ball and the Cross, John Lane (U.S.),1909 £45
ditto, Wells Gardner, 1910 . . . . . . £40
Manalive, Nelson, 1912 . . . . . . £35
ditto, John Lane (U.S.), 1912 . . . . . £30
The Flying Inn, Methuen, 1914 . . . . . £45
ditto, John Lane (U.S.), 1914 . . . . . . £35
The Return of Don Quixote, Chatto & Windus, 1927 .
. . . . £100/£20
ditto, Dodd, Mead (U.S.), 1927 . . . . £75/£15

Short Stories
The Club of Queer Trades, Harper & Bros, 1905 £250
ditto, Harper & Bros (U.S.), 1905 . . . . £200
The Man Who Knew Too Much, Cassell, 1922 .
. . . . £450/£25
ditto, Harper & Bros (U.S.), 1922 . . . £250/£25
Tales of the Long Bow, Cassell, 1925 . . £500/£75
ditto, Dodd, Mead (U.S.), 1925 . . . . £350/£40
The Sword of Wood, Elkin Mathews & Marrott, 1928
(530 signed copies) . . . . £125/£75
The Poet and the Lunatics, Cassell, 1929 . £500/£65
ditto, Dodd, Mead (U.S.), 1929 . . . . £400/£45
Four Faultless Felons, Cassell, 1930 . £400/£45
ditto, Dodd, Mead (U.S.), 1930 . . . £300/£40
The Paradoxes of Mr Pond, Cassell, 1937 . £200/£40
ditto, Dodd, Mead (U.S.), 1937 . . . . £125/£25

Plays
Magic, A Fantastic Comedy, Secker, 1913 (wraps) £65
ditto, Martin Secker, 1913 (150 signed copies, tissue
d/w) . . . . £350/£275
ditto, Putnam's (U.S.), 1913 . . . . . £65
The Judgement of Dr. Johnson, Sheed & Ward, 1927
. . . . £75/£20
ditto, Putnam's (U.S.), 1928 . . . . . £50/£10
The Surprise, Sheed & Ward, 1952 . . £45/£15
ditto, Sheed & Ward (U.S.), 1953 . . . £45/£15

Poetry
Greybeards at Play, Brimley Johnson, 1900 . £500
The Wild Knight and Other Poems, Grant Richards,
1900 . . . . £200
The Ballad of the White Horse, Methuen, 1911 £45
ditto, Methuen, 1911 (100 signed copies, handmade
paper) £250
The Nativity, Albany (U.S.), 1911 (wraps) . . £65
Poems, Burns & Oates Ltd, 1915 . . . . £40
Wine, Water and Song, Methuen, 1915 . . . £45
The Ballad of St. Barbara and Other Verses, Cecil
Palmer, 1922 . . . . £200/£35
ditto, Putnam's (U.S.), 1923 . . . £75/£20
The Queen of Seven Swords, Sheed & Ward, 1926 .
. . . . £50/£20
Collected Poems, Cecil Palmer, 1927 . . £65/£25
ditto, Cecil Palmer, 1927 (350 signed copies, slipcase)
. . . . £150/£125

Others
The Defendant, Brimley Johnson, 1901 . . . £65
Twelve Types, Humphreys, 1902 . . . . . £65
ditto, as *Varied Types*, Dodd, Mead (U.S.), 1908 £30
Robert Browning, Macmillan, 1903 . . . . £25
G.F. Watts, Duckworth, 1904 . . . . £25
ditto, Dutton (U.S.), 1904 . . . . . . £25
Charles Dickens, Methuen, 1906 . . . . £45
ditto, as *Charles Dickens, a critical study*, Dodd, Mead
(U.S.), 1906 . . . . £35
All Things Considered, Methuen, 1908 . . . £45
Orthodoxy, John Lane, 1909 . . . . . . £30
George Bernard Shaw, John Lane/Bodley Head, 1909
. . . . £40
ditto, John Lane (U.S.), 1909 . . . . . £40
Tremendous Trifles, Methuen, 1909 . . . £45
What's Wrong with the World, Cassell, 1910 . £35
Five Types, Humphries, 1910 (wraps) . . . £35
ditto, Hole (U.S.), 1911 . . . . . . £35
Alarms and Discursions, Methuen, 1910 . . £45
ditto, Dodd, Mead (U.S.), 1911 . . . . . £40
William Blake, Duckworth, 1910 . . . £40
Appreciations and Criticisms of the Works of Dickens,
Dent & Sons, 1911 . . . . £40
ditto, Dutton (U.S.), 1911 . . . . . . £40
*The Future of Religion. Mr. G.K. Chesterton's Reply
to Mr. Bernard Shaw*, The Heritics Club (U.S.), 1911
(wraps) £50
A Miscellany of Men, Methuen, 1912 . . £40
ditto, Dodd, Mead (U.S.), 1912 . . . . . £35
Victorian Age in Literature, Williams & Norgate,
1913 . . . . £35
The Barbarism of Berlin, Cassell, 1914 (wraps) £40
ditto, as *The Appetite of Tyranny*, Dodd, Mead (U.S.),
1915 . . . . £25
London, Privately Printed for Edmund D. Brooks and
Alvin Langdon Coburn etc (U.S.), 1914 . . £500
The Crimes of England, Cecil, Palmer & Hayward,
1915 . . . . £65
ditto, Cecil, Palmer & Hayward, 1915 (wraps) . £25
Lord Kitchener, privately published, 1917 (wraps) £75
A Short History Of England, John Lane, 1917 . £35
ditto, John Lane (U.S.), 1917 . . . . . . £35
Utopia of Usurers and Other Essays, Boni & Liveright
(U.S.), 1917 . . . . £35
Irish Impressions, John Lane (U.S.), 1920 . £75/£35
The Superstition of Divorce, Chatto & Windus, 1920 .
. . . . £75/£15
The New Jerusalem, Hodder & Stoughton, 1920 . .
. . . . £125/£15
ditto, Doran (U.S.), 1921 . . . . . £125/£15
Eugenics and Other Evils, Cassell, 1922 . £125/£15
ditto, Dodd, Mead (U.S.), 1922 . . . . £125/£15
What I Saw In America, Hodder & Stoughton, 1922 .
. . . . £100/£25
Fancies Versus Fads, Methuen, 1923 . . £100/£25
ditto, Dodd, Mead (U.S.), 1923 . . . . £100/£25
St Francis of Assisi, Hodder & Stoughton, 1923 . .
. . . . £100/£25

The Superstitions of the Sceptic, Heffers, 1925 (wraps)
. . . . £45
The Everlasting Man, Dodd, Mead (U.S.), 1925 . .
. . . . £100/£25
William Cobbett, Hodder & Stoughton, 1925 £75/£15
The Outline of Sanity, Methuen, 1926 . . £75/£25
ditto, Dodd, Mead (U.S.), 1927 . . . . £75/£25
The Catholic Church and Conversion, Burns, Oates &
Washbourne, 1926 . . . . . . £75/£15
The Gleaming Cohort, Methuen, 1926 . . £75/£25
Robert Louis Stevenson, Hodder & Stoughton, [1927]
. . . . £75/£30
ditto, Dodd, Mead (U.S.), 1928 . . . . £75/£30
Generally Speaking, Methuen, 1928 . . £65/£25
*Do We Agree? A Debate Between G. K. Chesterton
and George Bernard Shaw. With Hilaire Belloc in
the Chair*, Mitchell (U.S.), 1928 . . . £75/£25
The Thing, Sheed & Ward, 1929 . . . £85/£30
ditto, Dodd, Mead (U.S.), 1930 . . . . £50/£20
The Resurrection of Rome, Hodder & Stoughton,
[1930]. . . . . £75/£30
ditto, Dodd, Mead (U.S.), 1927 . . . . £75/£30
Come to Think of It, Methuen, 1930 . £75/£25
All Is Grist, Methuen, 1931 . . . . £75/£25
ditto, Dodd, Mead (U.S.), 1932 . . . £65/£20
Chaucer, Faber & Faber, 1932 . . . £75/£25
ditto, Farrar & Rinehart (U.S.), 1932 . . £45/£15
*Sidelights on New London and Newer York and Other
Essays*, Sheed & Ward, 1933 . . . £75/£30
ditto, Dodd, Mead (U.S.), 1932 . . . £75/£30
Christendom in Dublin, Sheed & Ward, 1933 £75/£20
ditto, Sheed & Ward (U.S.), 1933 . . . £75/£20
All I Survey, Methuen, 1933 . . . . £50/£15
ditto, Dodd, Mead (U.S.), 1933 . . . . £50/£15
St. Thomas Aquinas, Hodder & Stoughton, 1933 . .
. . . . £45/£15
ditto, Sheed & Ward (U.S.), 1933 . . . £45/£15
Avowals and Denials, Methuen, 1934 . £45/£15
The Well and the Shallows, Sheed & Ward, 1933 . .
. . . . £45/£15
ditto, Sheed & Ward (U.S.), 1935 . . . £45/£15
Autobiography, Hutchinson, 1936 . . £45/£15
ditto, Hutchinson, 1936 (250 deluxe copies in slipcase)
. . . . £95/£75
ditto, Sheed & Ward (U.S.), 1936 . . . £40/£15
The Coloured Lands, Sheed & Ward, 1938. £40/£15
ditto, Sheed & Ward (U.S.), 1938 . . . £40/£15
The Common Man, Sheed & Ward, 1950 . £30/£10
ditto, Sheed & Ward (U.S.), 1950 . . £30/£10
A Handful Of Authors, Sheed & Ward, 1953 . . .
. . . . £35/£10
ditto, Sheed & Ward (U.S.), 1953 . . . £35/£10
*The Glass Walking-Stick and Other Essays from the
Illustrated London News*, Methuen, 1955. £35/£10
Lunacy and Letters, Sheed & Ward, 1958 . £35/£10
ditto, Sheed & Ward (U.S.), 1958 . . . £35/£10

PETER CHEYNEY
(b.1896 d.1951)

British author Cheyney's books may seem a little
dated now, but his brutal heroes still attract collectors
of thrillers.

Novels
This Man is Dangerous, Collins, 1936 . . £75/£15
ditto, Coward-McCann (U.S.), 1938 . . . £50/£10
Poison Ivy, Collins, 1937 . . . . . £75/£15
Dames Don't Care, Collins, 1937 . . . £75/£10
ditto, Coward-McCann (U.S.), 1938 . . . £75/£10
Can Ladies Kill?, Collins, 1938 . . . . £75/£10
The Urgent Hangman, Collins, 1938 . . £75/£10
ditto, Coward-McCann (U.S.), 1939 . . . £75/£10
Don't Get Me Wrong, Collins, 1939. . . £65/£10
Dangerous Curves, Collins, 1939 . . . £65/£10
ditto, as *Callaghan*, Belmont (U.S.), 1973 . £50/£10
You'd Be Surprised, Collins, 1940 . . . £50/£10
You Can't Keep the Change, Collins, 1940. £50/£10
ditto, Dodd Mead (U.S.), 1944 . . . £45/£10
Another Little Drink, Collins, 1940 . . £50/£10
ditto, as *A Trap For Bellamy*, Dodd Mead (U.S.), 1941
. . . . £45/£10
ditto, as **Premeditated Murder**, Avon (U.S.), 1943
(wraps) £10
Your Deal, My Lovely, Collins, 1941 . . £50/£10
It Couldn't Matter Less, Collins, 1941 . . £50/£10
ditto, Arcadia (U.S.), 1943 . . . . £40/£10
Never a Dull Moment, Collins, 1942 . . £50/£10
Sorry You've Been Troubled, Collins, 1942 £50/£10
ditto, as *Farewell to the Admiral*, Dodd Mead (U.S.),
1943 . . . . £45/£10
Dark Duet, Collins, 1942. . . . . . £45/£10
ditto, Dodd Mead (U.S.), 1943 . . . . £45/£10
ditto, as *The Counterspy Murder*, Avon (U.S.), 1944
(wraps) £10
You Can Always Duck, Collins, 1943 . . £40/£10
The Stars Are Dark, Collins, 1943 . . . £40/£10
ditto, Dodd Mead (U.S.), 1943 . . . . £40/£10
ditto, as *The London Spy Murders*, Avon (U.S.), 1944
(wraps) £10
They Never Say When, Collins, 1944 . . £30/£5
ditto, Dodd Mead (U.S.), 1945 . . . . £30/£5
The Dark Street, Collins, 1944 . . . . £25/£5
ditto, Dodd Mead (U.S.), 1944 . . . . £25/£5
ditto, as *The Dark Street Murders*, Avon (U.S.), 1946
(wraps) £10
I'll Say She Does, Collins, 1945 . . . . £20/£5
ditto, Dodd Mead (U.S.), 1946 . . . . £20/£5
Sinister Errand, Collins, 1945 . . . . £20/£5
ditto, Dodd Mead (U.S.), 1945 . . . . £20/£5
ditto, as *Sinister Murders*, Avon (U.S.), 1957 (wraps).
. . . . £10
Uneasy Terms, Collins, 1946. . . . . £20/£5
ditto, Dodd Mead (U.S.), 1947 . . . . £20/£5
Dark Hero, Collins, 1946. . . . . . £20/£5
ditto, Collins, 1946 (250 signed copies) . . £100/£65

ditto, Dodd Mead (U.S.), 1946 . . . . . £20/£5
ditto, as *The Case of the Dark Hero*, Avon (U.S.),
1947 (wraps) £20
Dark Interlude, Collins, 1947 . . . . £20/£5
ditto, Dodd Mead (U.S.), 1947 . . . . . £20/£5
ditto, as *The Terrible Night*, Avon (U.S.), 1959
(wraps) £10
The Curiosity of Etienne Macgregor, Locke, 1947 .
. . . . £20/£5
ditto, as *The Sweetheart of the Razors*, Four Square
(U.S.), 1942 (wraps). £5
Dance Without Music, Collins, 1947 . . . £20/£5
ditto, Dodd Mead (U.S.), 1948 . . . . . £20/£5
Dark Wanton, Collins, 1948 . . . . . . £20/£5
ditto, Dodd Mead (U.S.), 1949 . . . . . £20/£5
ditto, as *The Case of the Dark Wanton*, Avon (U.S.),
1948 (wraps) £10
Try Anything Twice, Collins, 1948 . . . . £20/£5
ditto, Dodd Mead (U.S.), 1948 . . . . . £20/£5
ditto, as *Undressed To Kill*, Avon (U.S.), 1959 (wraps)
. . . . £10
You Can Call It A Day, Collins, 1949 . . . £20/£5
ditto, as *The Man Nobody Saw*, Dodd Mead (U.S.),
1949 . . . . £20/£5
One Of Those Things, Collins, 1949 . . . £20/£5
ditto, Dodd Mead (U.S.), 1950 . . . . . £20/£5
ditto, as *Mistress Murder*, Avon (U.S.), 1951 (wraps) .
. . . . £10
Lady, Behave!, Collins, 1950 . . . . . £20/£5
ditto, as *Lady Beware*, Dodd Mead (U.S.), 1950 . .
. . . . £20/£5
Dark Bahama, Collins, 1950. . . . . . £20/£5
ditto, Dodd Mead (U.S.), 1951 . . . . . £20/£5
ditto, as *I'll Bring Her Back*, Eton (U.S.), 1952 £20/£5
Set Up For Murder, Pyramid (U.S.), 1950 (wraps) £5
Ladies Won't Wait, Collins, 1951 . . . . £20/£5
ditto, Dodd Mead (U.S.), 1951 . . . . . £20/£5
ditto, as *Cocktails and the Killer*, Avon (U.S.), 1957
(wraps) £10

Short Story Collections
You Can't Hit A Woman and Other Stories, Collins,
1937 . . . . £75/£10
Knave Takes Queen, Collins, 1939 . . . £65/£10
Mr Caution – Mr Callaghan, Collins, 1941 £45/£10
Dressed to Kill, Todd, 1952 . . . . . £20/£5
G Man At the Yard, Todd, 1953 . . . . . £20/£5
The Adventures of Julia and Two Other Spy Stories,
Todd, 1954 . . . . £15/£5
ditto, as *The Killing Game*, Belmont (U.S.), 1975
(wraps) £5
Velvet Johnnie and Other Stories, Collins, 1952 . .
. . . . £20/£5
Calling Mr Callaghan, Todd, 1953 . . . . £20/£5
The Mystery Blues and Other Stories, Todd, 1954. .
. . . . £20/£5
ditto, as *Fast Work*, Four Square (U.S.), 1965 (wraps).
. . . . £5

He Walked In Her Sleep and Other Stories, Todd,
1954 . . . . £20
ditto, as *MacTavish*, Belmont (U.S.), 1973 (wraps) £5
The Best Stories of Peter Cheyney, Faber, 1954 £20/£5

Short Stories Published as Pamphlets
Adventures of Alonzo Mactavish, Todd, 1943 . £20
Alonzo Mactavish Again, Todd, 1943 . . . £20
Love With A Gun and Other Stories, Todd, 1943 . .
. . . . £20
The Murder of Alonzo, Todd, 1943 . . . . £20
The Man With The Red Beard, Todd, 1943 . £20
Account Rendered, Vallencey, 1944. . . . £30
The Adventures of Julia, Poynings, 1945 . . £30
Dance Without Music, Vallencey, 1945. . . £30
Escape For Sandra, Poynings, 1945 . . . £30
Night Club, Poynings, 1945 . . . . . . £30
A Tough Spot For Cupid and Other Stories,
Vallencey, 1945 . . . . £30
Date After Dark and Other Stories, Todd, 1946 £20
G Man At the Yard, Poynings, 1946. . . . £30
Time For Caution, Foster, 1946 . . . . . £25
He Walked In Her Sleep and Other Stories, Todd,
1946 . . . . £20
The Man With Two Wives and Other Stories, Todd,
1946 . . . . £20
A Spot of Murder and Other Stories, Todd, 1946 £20
Vengeance With A Twist and Other Stories,
Vallencey, 1946 . . . . £5
You Can't Trust A Duchess and Other Stories,
Vallencey, 1946 . . . . £5
Lady In Green and Other Stories, Bantam, 1947 . £5
A Matter of Luck and Other Stories, Bantam, 1947 £5
Cocktail For Cupid and Other Stories, Bantam, 1948 .
. . . . £5
Cocktail Party and Other Stories, Bantam, 1948 . £5
Fast Work and Other Stories, Bantam, 1948 . £5
Information Received and Other Stories, Bantam,
1948 . . . . £5
The Unhappy Lady and Other Stories, Bantam, 1948 .
. . . . £5
The Lady in Tears and Other Stories, Bantam, 1949 .
. . . . £5

Miscellaneous
Three Character Sketches, Reynolds, 1927. . £25/£5
*'I Guarded Kings': The Memoirs of a Political Police
Officer*, Stanley Paul, 1935 (pseud. 'Harold Brust') .
. . . . £25/£5
*In Plain Clothes: Further Memoirs of a Political
Police Officer*, Stanley Paul, 1937 (pseud. 'Harold
Brust') . . . . £25/£5
Making Crime Pay, Faber, 1944. . . . £20/£10
No Ordinary Cheyney, Faber, 1948 . . . £20/£10

AGATHA CHRISTIE
(b.1890 d.1976)

The Queen of detective fiction, and creator of the immortal Hercule Poirot and Miss Marple.

Novels

The Mysterious Affair at Styles, John Lane (U.S.), 1920 . . . . £20,000/£4,500
ditto, John Lane, 1921. . . . . £20,000/£4,500
The Secret Adversary, John Lane, 1922. . . . .
. . . . £15,000/£2,000
ditto, Dodd, Mead (U.S.), 1922 . . £4,500/£500
Murder on the Links, John Lane, 1923 £15,000/£2,000
ditto, Dodd, Mead (U.S.), 1923 . . £4,500/£500
The Man in the Brown Suit, John Lane, 1924 . . .
. . . . £10,000/£1,000
ditto, Dodd, Mead (U.S.), 1924 . . . £2,000/£150
The Secret of Chimneys, John Lane, 1925 . . . . .
. . . . £10,000/£1,000
ditto, Dodd, Mead (U.S.), 1925 . . . £2,000/£150
The Murder of Roger Ackroyd, Collins, 1926 . . .
. . . .£12,000/£750
ditto, Dodd, Mead (U.S.), 1926 . . £3,000/£300
The Big Four, Collins, 1927 . . . . £6,500/£450
ditto, Dodd, Mead (U.S.), 1927 . . £1,500/£125
The Mystery of the Blue Train, Collins, 1928 . . .
. . . . £6,000/£450
ditto, Dodd, Mead (U.S.), 1928 . . £1,250/£100
The Seven Dials Mystery, Collins, 1929 £6,000/£450
ditto, Dodd, Mead (U.S.), 1929 . . £1,250/£100
The Murder at the Vicarage, Collins Crime Club, 1930
. . . . £5,000/£350
ditto, Dodd, Mead (U.S.), 1930 . . . £1,250/£75
Giant's Bread, Collins, 1930 (pseud. 'Mary Westmacott'). . . . . . . £1,000/£100
ditto, Doubleday (U.S.), 1930 . . . . £500/£75
The Sittaford Mystery, Collins, 1931 . £6,000/£750
ditto, as *The Murder at Hazelmoor*, Dodd, Mead (U.S.), 1931 . . . . £1,500/£100
Peril at End House, Collins Crime Club, 1931 . . .
. . . . £4,000/£350
ditto, Dodd, Mead (U.S.), 1932 . . £1,250/£100
Lord Edgware Dies, Collins Crime Club, 1933 . . .
. . . . £3,500/£250
ditto, as *Thirteen at Dinner*, Dodd, Mead (U.S.), 1933
. . . . £1,000/£100
Murder on the Orient Express, Collins Crime Club, 1934 . . . . £6,000/£1,000
ditto, as *Murder in the Calais Coach*, Dodd, Mead (U.S.), 1942 . . . . . . £1,500/£100
Why Didn't They Ask Evans?, Collins Crime Club, 1934 . . . . £4,000/£250
ditto, as *Boomerang Clue*, Dodd, Mead (U.S.), 1935 .
. . . . £1,000/£75
Murder in Three Acts, Dodd, Mead (U.S.), 1934 . .
. . . . £1,000/£75
ditto, as *Three Act Tragedy*, Collins Crime Club, 1935
. . . . £2,000/£75

Unfinished Portrait, Collins, 1934 (pseud. 'Mary Westmacott') . . . . £1,500/£65
ditto, Doubleday (U.S.), 1934 . . . . £750/£65
Death in the Clouds, Collins Crime Club, 1935 . .
. . . . £2,000/£100
ditto, as *Death in the Air*, Dodd, Mead (U.S.), 1935 .
. . . . £750/£65
The A.B.C. Murders: A New Poirot Mystery, Collins Crime Club, 1936 . . . . . £3,000/£100
ditto, Dodd, Mead (U.S.), 1936 . . . . £750/£65
Murder in Mesopotamia, Collins Crime Club, 1936 .
. . . . £3,000/£200
ditto, Dodd, Mead (U.S.), 1936 . . . . £750/£65
Cards on the Table, Collins Crime Club, 1936 . . .
. . . . £3,000/£100
ditto, Dodd, Mead (U.S.), 1936 . . . . £750/£65
Dumb Witness, Collins Crime Club, 1937 . . . .
. . . . £5,000/£125
ditto, as *Poirot Loses a Client*, Dodd, Mead (U.S.), 1937 . . . .£650/£100
Death on the Nile, Collins Crime Club, 1937 . . .
. . . . £3,000/£125
ditto, Dodd, Mead (U.S.), 1938 . . . . £650/£100
Appointment With Death: A Poirot Mystery, Collins Crime Club, 1938 . . . . . £2,000/£150
ditto, Dodd, Mead (U.S.), 1938 . . . . £650/£60
Hercule Poirot's Christmas, Collins Crime Club, 1939
. . . . £2,000/£200
ditto, as *Murder for Christmas, A Poirot Story*, Dodd, Mead (U.S.), 1939 . . . . . £1,000/£60
Murder Is Easy, Collins Crime Club, 1939 . . . .
. . . . £2,000/£100
ditto, as *Easy to Kill*, Dodd, Mead (U.S.), 1939 . .
. . . . £750/£35
Ten Little Niggers, Collins Crime Club, 1939 . . .
. . . . £5,000/£500
ditto, as *And Then There Were None*, Dodd, Mead (U.S.), 1940 . . . .£750/£100
Sad Cypress, Collins Crime Club, [1940] £1,250/£100
ditto, Dodd, Mead (U.S.), 1940 . . . . £400/£40
One, Two, Buckle My Shoe, Collins Crime Club, 1940
. . . . £1,500/£200
ditto, as *The Patriotic Murders*, Dodd, Mead (U.S.), 1941 . . . . £400/£40
Evil Under the Sun, Collins Crime Club, 1941 . . .
. . . . £1,000/£100
ditto, Dodd, Mead (U.S.), 1941 . . . . £800/£65
N or M?, Collins Crime Club, 1941 . . £1,000/£100
ditto, Dodd, Mead (U.S.), 1941 . . . . £400/£40
The Body in the Library, Collins Crime Club, 1942 .
. . . . £1,000/£100
ditto, Dodd, Mead (U.S.), 1942 . . . . £400/£40
Five Little Pigs, Collins Crime Club, 1942 . £500/£75
ditto, as *Murder in Retrospect*, Dodd, Mead (U.S.), 1942 . . . . £200/£25
The Moving Finger, Dodd, Mead (U.S.), 1942 . . .
. . . . £400/£40
ditto, Collins Crime Club, 1943 . . . . £500/£50

Death Comes as the End, Dodd, Mead (U.S.), 1942 .
. . . . £200/£25
ditto, Collins Crime Club, 1945 . . . . £150/£25
Towards Zero, Collins Crime Club, 1944 . £250/£40
ditto, Dodd, Mead (U.S.), 1944 . . . . £200/£25
Absent in the Spring, Collins, 1944 (pseud. 'Mary Westmacott') . . . . £125/£40
ditto, Farrar & Rinehart (U.S.), 1944 . . £125/£25
Sparkling Cyanide, Collins Crime Club, 1945 . . .
. . . . £125/£40
ditto, as *Remembered Death*, Dodd, Mead (U.S.), 1945
. . . . £125/£35
The Hollow, Collins Crime Club, 1946 . . £125/£40
ditto, Dodd, Mead (U.S.), 1946 . . . . £125/£25
Taken at the Flood, Collins Crime Club, 1948 . . .
. . . . £125/£40
ditto, as *There is a Tide*, Dodd, Mead (U.S.), 1948. .
. . . . £125/£25
The Rose and the Yew Tree, Heinemann, 1948 (pseud. 'Mary Westmacott') . . . . £125/£40
ditto, Rinehart (U.S.), 1948 . . . . . £125/£25
Crooked House, Collins Crime Club, 1949 . £125/£40
ditto, Dodd, Mead (U.S.), 1949 . . . . £100/£25
A Murder is Announced, Collins Crime Club, 1950 .
. . . . £125/£15
ditto, Dodd, Mead (U.S.), 1950 . . . . £100/£15
They Came to Baghdad, Collins Crime Club, 1951 .
. . . . £75/£15
ditto, Dodd, Mead (U.S.), 1951 . . . . £65/£15
Mrs McGinty's Dead, Collins Crime Club, 1952 . .
. . . . £75/£15
ditto, Dodd, Mead (U.S.), 1952 . . . . £65/£15
After the Funeral, Collins Crime Club, 1953 £65/£10
ditto, as *Funerals are Fatal*, Dodd, Mead (U.S.), 1953
. . . . £45/£10
They Do It with Mirrors, Collins Crime Club, 1951 .
. . . . £75/£15
ditto, as *Murder with Mirrors*, Dodd, Mead (U.S.), 1951 . . . . £65/£15
A Daughter's a Daughter, Heinemann, 1952 (pseud. 'Mary Westmacott') . . . . £75/£15
A Pocket Full of Rye, Collins Crime Club, 1953 . .
. . . . £60/£10
ditto, Dodd, Mead (U.S.), 1954 . . . . £45/£10
Destination Unknown, Collins Crime Club, 1954 . .
. . . . £60/£10
ditto, as *So Many Steps to Death*, Dodd, Mead (U.S.), 1955 . . . . £45/£10
Hickory, Dickory, Dock, Collins Crime Club, 1955 .
. . . . £45/£10
ditto, as *Hickory, Dickory, Death*, Dodd, Mead (U.S.), 1955 . . . . £40/£10
Dead Man's Folly, Collins Crime Club, 1956 £45/£10
ditto, Dodd, Mead (U.S.), 1956 . . . . £45/£10
The Burden, Heinemann, 1956 (pseud. 'Mary Westmacott'). . . . . £65/£10
ditto, Arbor House (U.S.), 1956 . . . . £40/£10
4.50 from Paddington, Collins Crime Club, 1957 . .
. . . . £45/£10

ditto, as *What Mrs McGillicuddy Saw!*, Dodd, Mead (U.S.), 1957 . . . . £40/£10
Ordeal by Innocence, Collins Crime Club, 1958 . .
. . . . £40/£10
ditto, Dodd, Mead (U.S.), 1958 . . . . £40/£10
Cat Among the Pigeons, Collins Crime Club, 1959 .
. . . . £40/£10
ditto, Dodd, Mead (U.S.), 1959 . . . . £30/£10
The Pale Horse, Collins Crime Club, 1961 . £25/£10
ditto, Dodd, Mead (U.S.), 1962 . . . . £25/£10
The Mirror Crack'd from Side to Side, Collins Crime Club, 1962 . . . . £25/£10
ditto, as *The Mirror Crack'd*, Dodd, Mead (U.S.), 1963 . . . . £25/£10
The Clocks, Collins Crime Club, 1963 . . . £20/£5
ditto, Dodd, Mead (U.S.), 1964 . . . . . £20/£5
A Caribbean Mystery, Collins Crime Club, 1964 . .
. . . . £20/£5
ditto, Dodd, Mead (U.S.), 1965 . . . . . £20/£5
At Bertram's Hotel, Collins Crime Club, 1965 . £20/£5
ditto, Dodd, Mead (U.S.), 1965 . . . . . £20/£5
Third Girl, Collins Crime Club, 1966 . . . £20/£5
ditto, Dodd, Mead (U.S.), 1967 . . . . . £20/£5
Endless Night, Collins Crime Club, 1967 . . £20/£5
ditto, Dodd, Mead (U.S.), 1968 . . . . . £20/£5
By the Pricking of My Thumbs, Collins Crime Club, 1968 . . . . £20/£5
ditto, Dodd, Mead (U.S.), 1968 . . . . . £20/£5
Halloween Party, Collins Crime Club, 1969 . £20/£5
ditto, Dodd, Mead (U.S.), 1969 . . . . . £20/£5
Passenger to Frankfurt, Collins Crime Club, 1970 .
. . . . £15/£5
ditto, Dodd, Mead (U.S.), 1970 . . . . . £15/£5
Nemesis, Collins Crime Club, 1971 . . . . £15/£5
ditto, Dodd, Mead (U.S.), 1971 . . . . . £15/£5
Elephants Can Remember, Collins Crime Club, 1972
. . . . £15/£5
ditto, Dodd, Mead (U.S.), 1972 . . . . . £15/£5
Postern of Fate, Collins Crime Club, 1973 . . £15/£5
ditto, Dodd, Mead (U.S.), 1973 . . . . . £15/£5
Murder on Board; Three Complete Mystery Novels, Dodd, Mead (U.S.), 1974 . . . . . £15/£5
Curtain: Hercule Poirot's Last Case, Collins Crime Club, 1975 . . . . £15/£5
ditto, Dodd, Mead (U.S.), 1975 . . . . . £15/£5
Sleeping Murder, Collins Crime Club, 1976 . £15/£5
ditto, Dodd, Mead (U.S.), 1976 . . . . . £10/£5

Short Stories
Poirot Investigates, John Lane, 1924 . £7,500/£750
ditto, Dodd, Mead (U.S.), 1924 . . . £6,000/£500
Partners in Crime, Collins, 1929 . . £4,000/£250
ditto, Dodd, Mead (U.S.), 1929 . . . £3,000/£75
Two New Crime Stories, Reader's Library, 1929 (includes 'The Underdog' by Christie). . £450/£75
The Mysterious Mr Quinn, Collins, 1930 £4,000/£250
ditto, Dodd, Mead (U.S.), 1930 . . . £3,000/£75
The Thirteen Problems, Collins Crime Club, 1932 .
. . . . £5,000/£400

ditto, as *The Tuesday Club Murders*, Dodd, Mead
(U.S.), 1933 . . . . £2,000/£50
The Hound of Death and Other Stories, Odhams,
1933 . . . . £350/£75
The Listerdale Mystery and Other Stories, Collins,
1934 . . . . £2,000/£75
Parker Pyne Investigates, Collins, 1934 £2,500/£100
ditto, as *Mr Parker Pyne, Detective*, Dodd, Mead
(U.S.), 1934 . . . . £2,500/£65
Murder in the Mews and Other Stories, Collins Crime
Club, 1937 . . . . £3,000/£250
ditto, as *Dead Man's Mirror and Other Stories*, Dodd,
Mead (U.S.), 1937 . . . . . £2,500/£150
The Regatta Mystery and Other Stories, Dodd, Mead
(U.S.), 1939 . . . . £2,000/£100
The Labours of Hercules: Short Stories, Collins
Crime Club, 1947 . . . . . . £150/£25
ditto, as *Labours of Hercules*, Dodd, Mead (U.S.),
1947 . . . . £100/£25
Witness for the Prosecution, Dodd, Mead (U.S.), 1948
. . . . £175/£25
Three Blind Mice and Other Stories, Dodd, Mead
(U.S.), 1950 . . . . £175/£25
Under Dog and Other Stories, Dodd, Mead (U.S.),
1951 . . . . £200/£25
The Adventure of the Christmas Pudding, Collins
Crime Club, 1960 . . . . . . £75/£20
Double Sin and Other Stories, Dodd, Mead (U.S.),
1961 . . . . £60/£15
Thirteen for Luck, Dodd, Mead (U.S.), 1961 £25/£10
ditto, Collins, 1966 . . . . . . £25/£10
Star over Bethlehem and Other Stories, Collins, 1965
(pseud. 'A.C. Mallowan') . . . . . £20/£5
ditto, Dodd, Mead (U.S.), 1965 . . . . £15/£5
Surprise! Surprise!, Dodd, Mead (U.S.), 1965 . £15/£5
13 Clues for Miss Marple, Dodd, Mead (U.S.), 1965 .
. . . . £20/£5
The Golden Ball and Other Stories, Dodd, Mead
(U.S.), 1971 . . . . £20/£5
Hercule Poirot's Early Cases, Collins Crime Club,
1974 . . . . £25/£5
ditto, Dodd, Mead (U.S.), 1974 . . . . £20/£5
Miss Marple's Final Cases and Others, Collins Crime
Club, 1979 . . . . £20/£5
ditto, Dodd, Mead (U.S.), 1979 . . . . £15/£5
Remembrance, Souvenir Press, 1988 . . . £15/£5

Poetry
The Road of Dreams, Bles, 1925 . . . £600/£150
ditto, as *Poems*, Collins, 1973 (glassine d/w) £50/£45
ditto, Dodd, Mead (U.S.), 1973 (glassine d/w) £45/£40

Plays
Black Coffee, Ashley, 1934 (wraps) £125
ditto, French, 1952 (wraps) £35
Ten Little Niggers, French, 1944 (wraps) . . £50
ditto, as *Ten Little Indians*, French (U.S.), 1946
(wraps) £10
Appointment with Death, French, 1945 (wraps) £50

Murder on the Nile, French, 1946 (wraps) . . £75
ditto, French (U.S.), 1946 (wraps) . . . £65
The Hollow, French, 1952 (wraps) £35
ditto, French (U.S.), 1952 (wraps) £20
The Mousetrap, French, 1954 (wraps) . . . £100
ditto, French (U.S.), 1954 (wraps) £75
Witness for the Prosecution, French (U.S.), 1954
(wraps) £40
ditto, French, 1956 (wraps) £40
The Spider's Web, French, 1957 (wraps) . . £30
ditto, French (U.S.), 1957 (wraps) £10
Towards Zero, Dramatist's Play Service (U.S.), 1957
(wraps) £50
ditto, French, 1958 (wraps) £35
Verdict, French, 1958 (wraps) £35
The Unexpected Guest, French, 1958 (wraps) . £35
Go Back for Murder, French, 1960 (wraps) . £35
Rule of Three, French, 1963 (3 vols, wraps) . £50
Akhmaton, Collins, 1973 . . . . . . £15/£5
ditto, Dodd, Mead (U.S.), 1973 . . . . £15/£5

Others
Come Tell Me How You Live, Collins, 1946 £65/£10
ditto, Dodd, Mead (U.S.), 1946 . . . £50/£10
Autobiography, Collins, 1977 . . . . . £20/£5
ditto, Dodd, Mead (U.S.), 1977 . . . . £20/£5

TOM CLANCY
(b.1947)

Clancy is considered to be a master of the 'techno
thriller'. The successful filming of his books has
widened his audience.

Fiction
The Hunt for Red October, Naval Institute Press
(U.S.), 1984 (six blurbs on back of d/w) . £450/£75
ditto, Naval Institute Press (U.S.), 1984 (eight blurbs
on back of d/w) . . . . £100/£15
ditto, Collins, 1985 . . . . . . £75/£15
Red Storm Rising, G.P. Putnam (U.S.), 1986 . £25/£5
ditto, Collins, 1987 . . . . . . £25/£5
Patriot Games, G.P. Putnam (U.S.), 1987 . £65/£15
ditto, Collins, 1987 . . . . . . £50/£15
The Cardinal of the Kremlin, G.P. Putnam (U.S.),
1988 . . . . £20/£5
ditto, Collins, 1988 . . . . . . £20/£5
Clear and Present Danger, G.P. Putnam (U.S.), 1988 .
. . . . £15/£5
ditto, G.P. Putnam (U.S), 1988 (250 signed, numbered
copies in slipcase), ... £175/£125
ditto, Collins, 1989 . . . . . . £15/£5
The Sum of All Fears, G.P. Putnam (U.S), 1991 . .
. . . . £10/£5
ditto, G.P. Putnam (U.S), 1991 (600 signed, numbered
copies in slipcase), ... £100/£75
ditto, HarperCollins, 1991 . . . . . £15/£5

Without Remorse G.P. Putnam (U.S.), 1993 . £10/£5
ditto, G.P. Putnam (U.S.), 1993 (600 signed, numbered copies in slipcase) . . . . £100/£75
ditto, HarperCollins, 1993 . . . . . £15/£5
Debt of Honor, G.P. Putnam (U.S.), 1994 . £10/£5
ditto, G.P. Putnam (U.S.), 1994 (447 signed, numbered copies in slipcase) . . . . . . £125/£100
ditto, Collins, 1994 . . . . £10/£5
Executive Orders, G.P. Putnam (U.S.), 1996 . £10/£5
ditto, G.P. Putnam (U.S.), 1996 (200 signed, numbered copies in slipcase), ... £150/£125
ditto, Collins, 1996 . . . . £10/£5
Rainbow Six, G.P. Putnam (U.S.), 1998. . . £10/£5
ditto, G.P. Putnam (U.S.), 1998 (675 signed, numbered copies in slipcase) . . . . . £225/£175
ditto, Joseph, 1998. . . . . £10/£5
The Bear and the Dragon, G.P. Putnam (U.S.), 2000 .
. . . . £10/£5
ditto, G.P. Putnam (U.S.), 2000 (425 signed, numbered copies in slipcase) . . . . . £175/£125
ditto, Joseph, 2000. . . . . £10/£5
Red Rabbit, G.P. Putnam (U.S.), 2002 . . £10/£5
ditto, G.P. Putnam (U.S.), 2002(550 signed, numbered copies in slipcase) . . . . . . £100/£75
ditto, Joseph, 2002. . . . . £10/£5

Non Fiction
Submarine, A Guided Tour inside a Nuclear Warship, G.P. Putnam, 1993 (300 signed, numbered copies, slipcase) . . . . £125/£100
ditto, Berkley (U.S.), 1993 (wraps) £5
Armored Cav: A Guided Tour of an Armoured Cavalry Regiment, Putnam (U.S.), 1994 (150 signed, numbered copies, slipcase) . . . . . £200/£150
ditto, Berkley (U.S.), 1994 (wraps) £5
ditto, as *Armoured Warfare*, HarperCollins, 1996 (wraps) £5
Fighter Wing: A Guided Tour of an Airforce Combat Wing, Berkley (U.S.), 1995 (wraps) £5
ditto, HarperCollins, 1995 (wraps) £5
SSN: Strategies of Submarine Warfare, Berkley (U.S.), 1996 (wraps) £5
Marine: A Guided Tour of a Marine Expeditionary Team, Berkley (U.S.), 1996 (wraps) £5
Airborne: A Guided Tour of an Airborne Task Force, Berkley (U.S.), 1997 (wraps) £5
Into the Storm: A Study in Command, Putnam (U.S.), 1997 (with Fred Franks Jr). . . . . £25/£10
Carrier: A Guided Tour of an Aircraft Carrier, Berkley (U.S.), 1999 (wraps) £5
Every Man a Tiger, Putnam (U.S.), 1999 (with Chuck Horner) . . . . £25/£10
Special Forces: A Guided Tour of U.S. Special Forces, Berkley (U.S.), 2001 (with John Grisham) £5
Shadow Warriors, Putnam (U.S.), 2002 (with Carl Steiner) . . . . £15/£5

JOHN CLARE
(b.1793 d.1864)

A poet who excels in his descriptions of rural life, and the thoughts and feelings of humble country people.

Poetry
Poems Descriptive of Rural Life and Scenery, Taylor & Hessey, 1820 . . . . £750
The Village Minstrel and Other Poems, Taylor & Hessey (and) Stamford: E. Drury, 1821 . . £350
The Shepherd's Calendar, Taylor, 1827 . . £350
The Rural Muse, Whittaker & Co., 1835 . . £200
Poems by John Clare, G.E. Over, 1901 (selected by Norman Gale) £50
Poems by John Clare, Frowde, 1908 (selected by Arthur Symons) £20
Poems Chiefly From Manuscript, Cobden-Sanderson, 1920 . . . . £150/£45
Madrigals and Chronicles, Beaumont Press, 1924 (398 numbered copies, edited by Edmund Blunden) .
. . . . £100

Others
The Life and Remains of John Clare, by J. L. Cherry, Warne, 1873 . . . . £100
Sketches in the Life of John Clare, Cobden-Sanderson, 1931 . . . . £100/£35
The Letters of John Clare, Routledge & Kegan Paul, 1951 . . . . £35/£10

ARTHUR C. CLARKE
(b.1917)

Clarke's much admired science fiction has successfully popularised and experimented with speculative science.

Novels
Prelude to Space, World Editions (U.S.), 1951 (wraps)
. . . . £45
ditto, Sidgwick & Jackson, 1953 . . . . £125/£35
ditto, Gnome Press (U.S.), 1954 . . . . £75/£25
The Sands of Mars, Sidgwick & Jackson, 1951 . .
. . . . £125/£35
ditto, Gnome Press (U.S.), 1952 . . . . £75/£35
Islands in the Sky, Winston (U.S.), 1952 . £125/£35
ditto, Sidgwick & Jackson, 1952 . . . . £100/£35
Against the Fall of Night, Gnome Press (U.S.), 1953 .
. . . . £125/£35
Childhood's End, Ballantine (U.S.), 1953 . £250/£75
ditto, Sidgwick & Jackson, 1954 . . . . £95/£35
Earthlight, Ballantine (U.S.), 1955 . . . £200/£75
ditto, Muller, 1955. . . . . £125/£45
The City and the Stars, Harcourt Brace (U.S.), 1956 .
. . . . £100/£35
ditto, Muller, 1956. . . . . £75/£35

The Deep Range, Harcourt Brace (U.S.), 1957 £75/£25
ditto, Muller, 1957. . . . . . . £75/£25
A Fall of Moondust, Harcourt Brace (U.S.), 1961 . .
. . . . £75/£25
ditto, Gollancz, 1961 . . . . . . £75/£25
Dolphin Island, Holt Rinehart (U.S.), 1963 . £50/£20
ditto, Gollancz, 1963 . . . . . . £50/£20
Glide Path, Harcourt Brace (U.S.), 1963 . £50/£20
ditto, Sidgwick & Jackson, 1969 . . . . £50/£20
2001: A Space Odyssey, NAL (U.S.), 1968 . £175/£45
ditto, Hutchinson, 1968 . . . . £125/£45
The Lion of Comarre, Harcourt Brace (U.S.), 1968 .
. . . . £45/£15
ditto, Gollancz, 1970 . . . . . . £45/£15
Rendezvous with Rama, Harcourt Brace (U.S.), 1973 .
. . . . £45/£15
ditto, Gollancz, 1973 . . . . . . £45/£15
Imperial Earth, Gollancz, 1975 . . . £25/£10
ditto, Harcourt Brace (U.S.), 1976 . . £25/£10
The Fountains of Paradise, Gollancz, 1979 £25/£10
ditto, Harcourt Brace (U.S.), 1979 . . . £25/£10
2010: Odyssey Two, Granada, 1982 . . . . £20/£5
ditto, Granada, 1982 (author's name misspelt 'Clark'
on title page) . . . . £75/£45
ditto, Phantasia (U.S.), 1982 (650 signed copies,
slipcase) . . . . £75/£65
ditto, Phantasia (U.S.), 1982 (26 signed, lettered
copies, leather box) . . . . . . £500/£45
ditto, Ballantine (U.S.), 1982 . . . . . £15/£5
The Songs of Distant Earth, Grafton, 1986 . £15/£5
ditto, Ballantine (U.S.), 1986 . . . . . £15/£5
2061: Odyssey Three, Ballantine (U.S.), 1988 . £15/£5
ditto, Grafton, 1988 . . . . . . £15/£5
Cradle, Gollancz, 1988 (with Gentry Lee) . £15/£5
ditto, Warner (U.S.), 1988 . . . . . £15/£5
Rama II, Gollancz, 1989 (with Gentry Lee) £20/£10
ditto, Ballantine (U.S.), 1989 . . . . . £10/£5
Beyond the Fall of Night, Putnam (U.S.), 1990 (with
Gregory Benford) . . . . £10/£5
ditto, as *Against the Fall of Night*, Gollancz, 1991 .
. . . . £10/£5
The Ghost from the Grand Banks, Bantam (U.S.),
1990 . . . . £10/£5
ditto, Gollancz, 1990 . . . . . . £10/£5
The Garden of Rama, Gollancz, 1991 (with Gentry
Lee) . . . . £10/£5
ditto, Bantam (U.S.), 1991 . . . . . £10/£5
Rama Revealed, Gollancz, 1993 (with Gentry Lee) .
. . . . £10/£5
ditto, Bantam (U.S.), 1994 . . . . . £10/£5
The Hammer of God, Gollancz, 1993 . . £10/£5
ditto, Bantam (U.S.), 1993 . . . . . £10/£5
Richter 10, Gollancz, 1996 (with Mike McQuay) . .
. . . . £10/£5
ditto, Bantam (U.S.), 1996 . . . . . £10/£5
3001: The Final Odyssey, HarperCollins, 1997 £10/£5
ditto, Ballantine (U.S.), 1997 . . . . . £10/£5
The Trigger, Voyager (HarperCollins), 1999 (with
Michael P. Kube-McDowell) . . . . £10/£5

ditto, Bantam (U.S.), 1999 . . . . . £10/£5
The Light of Other Days, Voyager (HarperCollins),
2000 (with Stephen Baxter) . . . . . £10/£5
ditto, Tor (U.S.), 2000. . . . . . . £10/£5

Stories
Expedition to Earth, Ballantine (U.S.), 1953 £175/£45
ditto, Sidgwick & Jackson, 1954 . . . . £90/£25
Reach for Tomorrow, Ballantine (U.S.), 1956 . . .
. . . . £125/£35
ditto, Gollancz, 1962 . . . . . . £75/£25
Tales from the White Hart, Ballantine (U.S.), 1957 .
. . . . £100/£25
ditto, Sidgwick & Jackson, 1972 . . . . £30/£10
The Other Side of the Sky, Harcourt Brace (U.S.),
1958 . . . . £100/£35
ditto, Gollancz, 1961 . . . . . . £35/£10
Tales of Ten Worlds, Harcourt Brace (U.S.), 1962 . .
. . . . £25/£10
ditto, Gollancz, 1963 . . . . . . £25/£10
The Nine Billion Names of God, Harcourt Brace
(U.S.), 1967 . . . . £15/£5
A Meeting with Medusa, Harcourt Brace (U.S.), 1971 .
. . . . £15/£5
The Wind from the Sun, Harcourt Brace (U.S.), 1971 .
. . . . £15/£5
Of Time and Stars, Gollancz, 1972 . . . £15/£5
The Sentinel, Berkley (U.S.), 1983 . . . £10/£5
ditto, Panther, 1985 . . . . . . £10/£5
Tales from Planet Earth, Century, 1989 . £10/£5

Miscellaneous Collections
Across the Sea of Stars, Harcourt Brace (U.S.), 1959 .
. . . . £45/£10
From the Oceans, From the Stars, Harcourt Brace
(U.S.), 1962 . . . . £50/£25
Prelude to Mars, Harcourt Brace (U.S.), 1965 £35/£10
An Arthur C. Clarke Omnibus, Sidgwick & Jackson,
1965 . . . . £25/£10
An Arthur C. Clarke Second Omnibus, Sidgwick &
Jackson, 1968 . . . . £25/£10
Best of Arthur C. Clarke: 1937-1971, Sidgwick &
Jackson, 1973 . . . . £25/£10

Non Fiction
Interplanetary Flight, Temple Press, 1950 . £150/£45
ditto, Harpers (U.S.), [1951] . . . . . £100/£25
The Exploration of Space, Temple Press, 1951 . .
. . . . £100/£25
ditto, Harpers (U.S.), 1951 . . . . . £100/£25
The Exploration of the Moon, Muller, 1954 £125/£30
The Young Traveller in Space, Phoenix House, 1954 .
. . . . £100/£25
ditto, as *Into Space*, Harpers (U.S.), 1971 (with Robert
Silverberg) . . . . £25/£5
The Coast of Coral, Muller, 1956 . . . £75/£20
ditto, Harpers (U.S.), 1956 . . . . . £75/£20
The Making of a Moon, Muller, 1957 . . £40/£10
ditto, Harpers (U.S.), 1957 . . . . . £40/£10

The Reefs of Taprobane, Muller, 1957 . .	£35/£10
ditto, Harpers (U.S.), 1957	£35/£10
Boy Beneath the Sea, Harpers (U.S.), [1958]	£50/£15
Voice Across the Sea, Muller, 1958 . . .	£50/£10
ditto, Harpers (U.S.), 1958	£50/£10
The Challenge of the Sea, Muller, 1960 .	£40/£10
ditto, Holt, Reinhart (U.S.), 1960. . . .	£40/£10
The Challenge of the Spaceship, Muller, 1960	£40/£10
ditto, Holt, Reinhart (U.S.), 1960. . . .	£40/£10
The First Five Fathoms, Harpers (U.S.), 1960	£35/£10
Indian Ocean Adventure, Barker, 1962 .	£40/£10
Profiles of the Future, Gollancz, 1962 . .	£35/£10
ditto, Harpers (U.S.), 1962	£35/£10
Man and Space, Time (U.S.), 1964 . . .	£25
The Treasure of the Great Reef, Barker, 1964	£35/£10
ditto, Harpers (U.S.), 1964	£35/£10
Indian Ocean Treasure, Harpers (U.S.), 1964 (with Mike Wilson).	£15/£5
ditto, Sidgwick and Jackson, 1972 . . .	£15/£5
Voices from the Sky, Harpers (U.S.), 1965 .	£35/£10
ditto, Gollancz, 1966	£35/£10
The Promise of Space, Hodder & Stoughton, 1968	£20/£5
ditto, Harpers (U.S.), 1968	£20/£5
Report on Planet Three and Other Speculations, Gollancz, 1972	£15/£5
ditto, Harpers (U.S.), 1972	£15/£5
The Lost Worlds of 2001, NAL (U.S.), 1972	£25/£10
ditto, Sidgwick & Jackson, 1972	£25/£10
Beyond Jupiter, Little, Brown (U.S.), 1972 (with Chesley Bonestell)	£35/£10
The View from Serendip, Random House (U.S.), 1977	£20/£5
ditto, Gollancz, 1978	£20/£5
Arthur C. Clarke's Mysterious World, Collins, 1980 (with John Fairley and Simon Welfare) .	£35/£10
1984: Spring, A Choice of Futures, Granada, 1984	£15/£5
ditto, Ballantine (Del Ray) (U.S.), 1984 . .	£15/£5
Ascent to Orbit: A Scientific Autobiography, Wiley, 1984	£30/£10
The Odyssey File, Panther, 1985 (with Peter Hyams, wraps).	£5
Arthur C. Clarke's July 20, 2019, Macmillan (U.S.), 1986	£15/£5
Astounding Days: a Science Fictional Autobiography, Gollancz, 1989	£15/£5
ditto, Bantam (U.S.), 1990	£15/£5
How the World Was One, Gollancz, 1992 .	£15/£5
ditto, Bantam (U.S.), 1992	£15/£5
The Fantastic Muse, Hilltop Press, 1992 .	£20
By Space Possessed, Gollancz, 1993 . .	£20/£5
The Snows of Olympus, Gollancz, 1994 .	£15/£5
ditto, Norton (U.S.), 1995.	£15/£5
Greetings, Carbon-Based Bipeds!, HarperCollins, 1999	£15/£5
ditto, St. Martin's Press (U.S.), 1999. . .	£15/£5

HARRY CLARKE
(b.1889 d.1931)

An Irish artist in the tradition of Beardsley, but whose detail and decoration are distinctively his own.

Illustrated by Clarke

Hans Andersen's Fairy Tales, Harrap, [1916] (125 signed copies)	£1,000
ditto, Harrap, [1916] (full leather edition) . .	£600
ditto, Harrap, [1916] (cloth edition)	£250
ditto, Bretano's (U.S.), 1916	£250
Tales of Mystery and Imagination, by Edgar Allan Poe, Harrap, 1919 (170 signed copies). . .	£2,000
ditto, Harrap, [1919] (morocco leather edition) .	£600
ditto, Harrap, [1919] (cloth edition)	£250
ditto, Bretano's (U.S.), 1919	£250
ditto, Harrap, [1923] (new edition with colour plates, antique leather)	£275
ditto, Harrap, [1923] (new edition with colour plates, cloth edition)	£350/£150
ditto, Bretano's (U.S.), 1923 (new edition with colour plates, cloth edition).	£300/£150
The Year's at the Spring, Harrap, 1920 (250 signed copies)	£600
ditto, Harrap, 1920 (cloth edition) . . .	£300/£150
ditto, Bretano's (U.S.), 1920	£250/£125
The Fairy Tales of Perrault, Harrap, [1922] (Persian levant leather edition)	£700
ditto, Harrap, [1922] (Buckram edition). .	£600/£300
ditto, Harrap, [1922] (cloth edition) . . .	£600/£250
ditto, Dodge (U.S.), [1922]	£600/£250
Faust, by Goethe, Harrap, 1925 (1,000 signed copies).	£750/£450
ditto, Harrap/Dingwall-Rock (U.S.), 1925 (1,000 signed copies)	£750/£450
Elixir of Life Being a slight account of the romantic rise to fame of a great house, John Jameson & Son Limited (Dublin), 1925	£750/£450
Selected Poems of Algernon Charles Swinburne, John Lane, 1928	£400/£125
ditto, Dodd, Mead (U.S.), 1928 . . .	£250/£125

WILLIAM COBBETT
(b.1763 d.1835)

A journalist, farmer and M.P., Cobbett was also an English civil rights activist. Many of his publications were privately printed. *Rural Rides* is his best known work.

Books

Le Tuteur Anglais, Bradford (U.S.), 1795 . .	£100
A Collection of facts and Observations Relative to the Peace with Bonaparte, Cobbett, 1801 . . .	£200
Letters to Aldington on the Fatal Effects of the Peace, Cobbett, 1802	£150

Letters to Hawkesbury on the Peace with Bonaparte, Cobbett, 1802 . . . . £100
The Political Proteus: A View of the Public Character and Conduct of R.B. Sheridan, Budd, 1804 . £150
Letters of the Late War between the United States and Great Britain, J. Belden & Co.,1815 . . . £200
Paper Against Gold, printed by J. M'Creery, 1815 (2 vols) £150
An Address to the Journeymen and Labourers of England, 1816 . . . . £75
Mr Cobbett's Address to His Countrymen, 1817 £75
A Journal of a Year's Residence in the United States, Sherwood, Neely & Jones, 1818 & 1819 (3 parts) .
. . . . £300 the set
A Grammar of the English Language, Clayton & Kingsland (U.S.), 1818 . . . . . . £200
ditto, Thomas Dolby, 1819 . . . . . . £200
The American Gardener, Charles Clement, 1821 £200
Preliminary Paper Against Gold, John M. Cobbett, 1821 . . . . £75
Cobbett's Sermons, Charles Clement, 1822 . £75
Cottage Economy, Charles Clement, 1822 . . £125
ditto, Peter Davies, 1926 (preface by G.K. Chesterton, illustrated by Eric Gill) . . . . . £20/£5
Cobbett's Collective Commentaries, J.M. Cobbett, 1822 . . . . £200
A History of the Protestant Reformation, William Cobbett, 1824 & 1827 (2 parts). . £200 the set
A French Grammar, Charles Clement, 1824 . £150
The Woodlands, William Cobbett, 1825 [1828] £150
A Treatise on Cobbett's Corn, William Cobbett, 1828.
. . . . £175
The English Gardener, William Cobbett, 1829 £150
Advice to Young Men, William Cobbett, 1829 [1830] .
. . . . £125
The Emigrant's Guide, William Cobbett, 1829 £250
Rural Rides, William Cobbett, 1830. . . . £600
History of the Regency and Reign of George IV, William Cobbett, 1830 . . . . . £125
A Spelling Book and Stepping-Stones to English Grammar, William Cobbett, 1831 . . . £125
A Geographical Dictionary of England and Wales, W.H. Cobbett, 1832 . . . . £200
Three Lectures on the Political State of Ireland, R. Byrne (Dublin), 1834 . . . . . £125
Legacy to Labourers, William Cobbett, 1834 [1835] .
. . . . £75
Legacy to Parsons, William Cobbett, 1835 . £75
Legacy to Peel, Cobbett's 'Register' Office, 1836 £75

Pamphlets
Observations on Dr Joseph Priestley's Emigration, Bradford (U.S.), 1794 . . . . . £125
A Bone to Gnaw for the Democrats, Bradford (U.S.), 1795 (2 parts). . . . . £100 the set
ditto, J. Wright, 1797 (with *A Rod for the Backs*) £600
A Kick for Bite, William Cobbett (U.S.), 1795 . £100
A New Year's Gift for the Democrats, Bradford (U.S.), 1796 . . . . £100

The Political Censor, William Cobbett (U.S.), 1796-7 (numbers 1-9) . . . . . . £250 the set
The Bloody Buoy, Benjamin Davies (U.S.), 1796 £150
The Scare-Crow, William Cobbett (U.S.), 1796 £125
The Life and Adventures of Peter Porcupine, William Cobbett (U.S.), 1796. . . . . . . £150
ditto, Nonesuch Press, 1927 (1800 numbered copies) .
. . . . £40
Life of Thomas Paine, R. Gilbert (U.S.), 1796 £150
A Letter to the Infamous Tom Paine, William Cobbett (U.S.), 1796 . . . . £100
ditto, Ogilvy & Son: London, 1797 . . . £75
Observations on the Debates in the American Congress, William Cobbett (U.S.), 1797 . . £100
ditto, Ogilvy & Son: London, 1797 . . . . £75
Selections from Porcupine's Gazette, William Cobbett (U.S.), 1797 . . . . £125
The Democratic Judge, William Cobbett (U.S.), 1798
. . . . £100
ditto, Wright, 1798 . . . . £75
A Detection of a Conspiracy, Formed by the United Irishmen, Milliken (U.S.), 1799 . . . . £125
The Cannibal's Progress or The Dreadful Horrors of French Invasion, William Cobbett, 1798 . . £125
French Arrogance, Published by Peter Porcupine (U.S.), 1798 . . . . £100
Selections from Porcupine's Gazette, William Cobbett, 1798 . . . . £125
The Trial of Republicanism, William Cobbett, 1799 .
. . . . £100
ditto, Cobbett and Morgan, 1801 . . . . £75
Cobbett's Advice, William Cobbett, 1800 . . £75
Mr Cobbett's Taking Leave of His Countrymen, William Cobbett, 1817 . . . . . . £100
The Farmer's Friend, William Cobbett, 1822 . £100
The Farmer's Wife's Friend, William Cobbett, 1822 .
. . . . £100
Reduction No Robbery, C. Clement, 1822 . . £100
Gold For Ever, C. Clement, 1825 . . . . £100
Good Friday, or The Murder of Jesus Christ by The Jews, printed for the Author, 1830 . . . £150
Surplus Population: A Comedy, William Cobbett, 1831 . . . . £125
Cobbett's Address to the Tax-Payers of England, William Cobbett, 1832 . . . . . . £100
The Rights of the Poor, William Cobbett, 1833 £75
The Flash in the Pan, William Cobbett, 1833 . £75

LIZA CODY
(b.1944)

Best known for her 'Anna Lee' novels about an everyday female detective.

Anna Lee Novels
Dupe, Collins, 1980 . . . . £300/£25
ditto, Scribner's (U.S.), 1981 . . . . . £100/£15
Bad Company, Collins, 1982 . . . . . £200/£15

ditto, Scribner's (U.S.), 1981 . . . . . £50/£15
Stalker, Collins, 1984 . . . . £80/£15
ditto, Scribner's (U.S.), 1984 . . . . . £30/£15
Headcase, Collins, 1985 . . . . . . £35/£10
ditto, Scribner's (U.S.), 1985 . . . . . £25/£15
Under Contract, Collins, 1986 . . . . £25/£10
ditto, Scribner's (U.S.), 1986 . . . . . £25/£15
Backhand, Chatto & Windus, 1991 . . . £15/£5
ditto, Little, Brown (U.S.), 1991 . . . . £15/£5

Other Novels
Rift, Collins, 1988 . . . . £45/£10
ditto, Scribner's (U.S.), 1988 . . . . . £25/£10
Bucket Nut, Chatto & Windus, 1992 . . £25/£5
ditto, Doubleday (U.S.), 1993 . . . . . £20/£5
Monkey Wrench, Chatto & Windus, 1994 . £20/£5
ditto, Mysterious Press (U.S.), 1995 . . . £15/£5
Musclebound, Bloomsbury, 1997 . . . £15/£5
ditto, Mysterious Press (U.S.), 1997 . . . £15/£5
Gimme More, Bloomsbury, 2000 (wraps) . . £10

JOHN COLLIER
(b.1901 d.1980)

A British author who spent much of his life in Hollwood, Collier is perhaps best known for his clever short fantasies and twist-in-the-tail stories, although the novel *His Monkey Wife* was also very highly regarded.

Novels
His Monkey Wife; or, Married to a Chimp, Davies, 1930 . . . . £200/£75
ditto, Appleton (U.S.), 1931 . . . . . £75/£20
No Traveller Returns, White Owl Press, 1931 (25 copies on Japanese vellum of 210 signed, numbered copies) £150
ditto, White Owl Press, 1931 (185 copies on handmade paper of 210 signed, numbered copies) . . £90
Tom's A-Cold: A Tale, Macmillan, 1933 . £200/£45
ditto, as **Full Circle**, Appleton (U.S.), 1933 . £200/£45
Defy the Foul Fiend; or, The Misadventures of a Heart, Macmillan, 1934 . . . . . £75/£25
ditto, Knopf (U.S.), 1934 . . . . . . £40/£15

Short Stories
An Epistle to a Friend, Ulysses Press, 1932 (99 signed copies) £75
ditto, Ulysses Press, 1932 (7 signed copies, each containing an original page of manuscript . . £250
Green Thoughts, William Jackson, 1932 (550 signed copies) . . . . £60/£35
The Devil and All, Nonesuch Press, 1934 (1,000 signed, numbered copies) £60
Variation on a Theme, Grayson & Grayson, 1935 (285 signed copies) . . . . £60/£40

Witch's Money, Viking Press (U.S.), 1940 (350 signed copies, tissue d/w) . . . . . . £60/£40
Presenting Moonshine, Viking (U.S.), 1941 £75/£30
ditto, Macmillan, 1941 . . . . . . £75/£30
The Touch of Nutmeg, and More Unlikely Stories, The Readers Club (U.S.), 1943 . . . . £30/£10
Fancies and Goodnights, Doubleday (U.S.), 1951 . . . . £65/£15
ditto, as **Of Demons and Darkness**, Corgi, 1965 (abridged, wraps) £5
Pictures in the Fire, Hart-Davis, 1958 . £35/£10

Collected Edition
The John Collier Reader, Knopf (U.S.), 1972 £30/£10
ditto, Souvenir Press, 1975 . . . . . . £20/£5

Poetry
Gemini, Ulysses Press, 1931 (185 signed copies) £100
ditto, Ulysses Press, 1931 (15 signed copies, each containing an original page of manuscript) . £500
ditto, Harmsworth, 1931 (glassine d/w) . . £45/£30

Others
Just The Other Day: An Informal History of Great Britain Since the War, Hamish Hamilton, 1932 (with Iain Lang). . . . . £35/£10
ditto, Harpers (U.S.), 1932 . . . . . £30/£10
Milton's Paradise Lost: Screenplay for Cinema of the Mind, Knopf (U.S.), 1973 . . . . . £30/£10

WILKIE COLLINS
(b.1824 d.1889)

A friend of Charles Dickens, Collins was a popular and skilful author of sensation fiction.

Memoirs of the Life of William Collins, R.A. Longmans, 1848 (2 vols) £1,250
Antonina, or the Fall of Rome, Bentley, 1850 (3 vols) £1,000
Rambles Beyond Railways: Notes in Cornwall Taken A-Foot, Bentley, 1851 . . . . . . £450
Mr Wray's Cash-Box, Bentley, 1852 . . . £650
Basil: A Story of Modern Life, Bentley, 1852 (3 vols). £650
Hide and Seek, Bentley, 1854 (3 vols) . . £1,000
After Dark, Smith & Elder, 1855 (3 vols) . £650
The Dead Secret, Bradbury and Evans, 1857 (2 vols) £1,000
The Queen of Hearts, Hurst & Blackett, 1859 (3 vols) £2,000
The Woman in White, Sampson Low, 1860 (3 vols) £10,000
No Name, Sampson Low, 1862 (3 vols). . . £1,500
My Miscellanies, Sampson Low, 1863 (3 vols). £1,000
Armadale, Smith, Elder & Co., 1866 (2 vols) . £650

The Moonstone, William Tinsley, 1868 (3 vols) . .
. . . . £10,000
Man and Wife, F. S. Ellis, 1870 (3 vols) . . £1,000
Poor Miss Finch, Bentley, 1872 (3 vols) . . £500
The New Magdalen, Bentley, 1873 (2 vols) . £650
Miss or Mrs? and Other Stories, Bentley, 1873 £500
The Frozen Deep and Other Tales, Bentley, 1874 (2
vols) £1,250
The Law and the Lady, Chatto & Windus, 1875 (3
vols) £750
The Two Destinies, Chatto & Windus, 1876 (2 vols) .
. . . . £650
The Haunted Hotel and My Lady's Money, Chatto &
Windus, 1879 (2 vols) £700
A Rogue's Life, Bentley, 1879 . . . . . £500
The Fallen Leaves, Chatto & Windus, 1879 (3 vols) .
. . . . £500
Jezebel's Daughter, Chatto & Windus, 1880 (3 vols) .
. . . . £500
The Black Robe, Chatto & Windus, 1881 (3 vols) . .
. . . . £500
Heart and Science, Chatto & Windus, 1883 (3 vols) .
. . . . £500
I Say No, Chatto & Windus, 1884 (3 vols) . . £450
The Evil Genius, Chatto & Windus, 1886 (3 vols) . .
. . . . £450
The Guilty River, Arrowsmith, 1886 . . £750
Little Novels, Chatto & Windus, 1887 (3 vols) . £750
The Legacy of Cain, Chatto & Windus, 1889 (3 vols) .
. . . . £400
Blind Love, Chatto & Windus, 1890 (3 vols, completed
by Walter Besant) £250
The Lazy Tour of Two Idle Apprentices, Chapman &
Hall, 1890 (in collaboration with Charles Dickens) .
. . . . £250

IVY COMPTON-BURNETT
(b.1892 d.1969)

The author of incisive, if claustrophobic domestic
novels, told principally through the dialogue of her
characters.

Dolores, Blackwood, 1911 . . . . . £400
Pastors and Masters, A Study, Heath Cranton, 1925 .
. . . . £150/£65
Brothers and Sisters, Heath Cranton, 1929 . £150/£75
ditto, Zero Press (U.S.), 1956 (includes introductory
pamphlet) . . . . £65/£10
Men and Wives, Heinemann, 1931 . . . £90/£40
ditto, Harcourt Brace (U.S.), [1939] . . £30/£10
More Women than Men, Heinemann, 1933 £90/£40
ditto, Simon & Schuster (U.S.), 1965 (with *A Family
and Its Fortune*) . . . . £20/£5
A House and its Head, Heinemann, 1935 . £90/£40
Daughters and Sons, Gollancz, 1937 . £65/£25
A Family and its Fortune, Gollancz, 1939 . £60/£25

Parents and Children, Gollancz, 1941 . . £60/£25
Elders and Betters, Gollancz, 1944 . . . £50/£20
Manservant and Maidservant, Gollancz, 1947 . . .
. . . . £40/£10
ditto, as *Bullivant and the Lamb*, Knopf (U.S.), 1948 .
. . . . £40/£10
Two Worlds and their Ways, Gollancz, 1949 £40/£10
ditto, Knopf (U.S.), 1949 . . . . . . £30/£10
Darkness and Day, Gollancz, 1951 . . . £30/£10
ditto, Knopf (U.S.), 1951 . . . . . . £30/£10
The Present and the Past, Gollancz, 1953 . . £25/£5
ditto, Messner (U.S.), 1953 . . . . . . £25/£5
Mother and Son, Gollancz, 1955 . . . £25/£5
ditto, Messner (U.S.), 1955 . . . . . . £25/£5
A Father and his Fate, Gollancz, 1957 . . . £25/£5
ditto, Messner (U.S.), 1958 . . . . . . £25/£5
A Heritage and its History, Gollancz, 1959 . . £25/£5
ditto, Simon & Schuster (U.S.), 1960 . . . £20/£5
The Mighty and their Fall, Gollancz, 1961 . . £20/£5
ditto, Simon & Schuster (U.S.), 1962 . . . £20/£5
A God and His Gifts, Gollancz, 1963 . . . £20/£5
ditto, Simon & Schuster (U.S.), 1964 . . . £20/£5
The Last and the First, Gollancz, 1971 . . . £15/£5
ditto, Knopf (U.S.), 1971 . . . . . . £10/£5
Collected Works, Gollancz, 1972 (deluxe edition of
500 sets in 19 vols) £400

CYRIL CONNOLLY
(b.1903 d.1974)

Principally a critic and literary editor, Connolly
founded the influential literary magazine *Horizon*.

The Rock Pool, Obelisk Press (Paris), 1936 (wraps) .
. . . . £600
ditto, Scribner's (U.S.), 1936 . . . . . £200/£75
ditto, Hamish Hamilton, 1947 . . . . £60/£20
Enemies of Promise, Routledge, 1938 . . £250/£50
ditto, Little, Brown (U.S.), 1939 . . . . £125/£35
The Unquiet Grave, Horizon, 1944 (500 numbered
hardback copies of 1,000, pseud. 'Palinurus') . . .
. . . . £300/£75
ditto, Horizon, 1944 (500 numbered copies of 1,000,
wraps) £125
ditto, Hamish Hamilton, [1945] (new edition) . £20/£5
ditto, Harper (U.S.), 1945 (new edition) . . £30/£5
The Condemned Playground, Routledge, [1945] . .
. . . . £25/£10
ditto, Macmillan (U.S.), 1946 . . . . . £15/£5
The Missing Diplomats, Queen Anne Press, 1952
(wraps) £30
Ideas and Places, Weidenfeld & Nicolson, 1953 . .
. . . . £25/£10
ditto, Harper (U.S.), 1953 . . . . . . £25/£10
The Golden Horizon, Weidenfeld & Nicolson, 1953 .
. . . . £15/£5
ditto, University Books (U.S.), 1955 . . . . £10/£5

Les Pavillons, Macmillan (U.S.), 1962 (with Jerome
 Zerbe). . . . . £25/£10
ditto, Hamish Hamilton, 1962 . . . . £25/£10
Previous Convictions, Hamish Hamilton, 1963. . .
 . . . . £20/£10
ditto, Harper (U.S.), 1964. . . . . . . £15/£5
*The Modern Movement: 100 Key Books from
 England, France and America, 1880-1950*, Deutsch/
 Hamilton, 1965 . . . . £45/£15
ditto, Atheneum (U.S.), 1966. . . . . £45/£15
ditto, H.R.C. (U.S.), 1971 (wraps) £20
ditto, H.R.C. (U.S.), 1971 (520 copies, cloth) . £50
The Evening Colonnade, Bruce & Watson, 1973 . .
 . . . . £10/£5
ditto, Harcourt Brace (U.S.), 1975 . . . £10/£5
*A Romantic Friendship: The Letters of Cyril Connolly
 to Noel Blakiston*, Constable, 1975 . . £15/£5
Journal and Memoir, Collins, 1983. . . . £10/£5
ditto, Ticknor & Fields (U.S.), 1984 . . . £10/£5
Shade Those Laurels, Bellew, 1990. . . £10/£5
ditto, Pantheon (U.S.), 1991 . . . . . £10/£5

JOSEPH CONRAD
(b.1857 d.1924)

Conrad served for twenty years at sea, becoming a
naturalised British subject in 1886. The sea provided
the background for a number of powerful novels. His
classic 'Heart of Darkness' was first published in
Youth: A Narrative, and Other Stories in 1902.

Novels

Almayer's Folly, T. Fisher Unwin, 1895 (first issue,
 with 'e' omitted from 'generosity' at bottom of page
 110) £1,500
ditto, T. Fisher Unwin, 1895 (second issue, corrections
 made) £100
ditto, Macmillan (U.S.), 1895 . . . . . £500
An Outcast of the Islands, T. Fisher Unwin, 1896
 ('this' for 'their' on line 31, p.26) . . . £400
ditto, Appleton (U.S.), 1896 (wraps). . . . £250
ditto, Appleton (U.S.), 1896 (green cloth) . £150
ditto, Appleton (U.S.), 1896 (deluxe edition in 3/4 roan
 and marbled boards) £400
The Children of the Sea, Dodd, Mead (U.S.), 1897 .
 . . . . £650
ditto, as *The Nigger of the Narcissus*, Heinemann,
 August 1898 (copyright edition, 7 copies, wraps). .
 . . . . £4,000
ditto, as *The Nigger of the Narcissus*, Heinemann,
 1898 (first issue: 'H' in 'Heinemann' on spine
 5.5mm, 16 pages of advertisements) . . . £400
ditto, as *The Nigger of the Narcissus*, Heinemann,
 1898 (second issue: 'Heinemann' on spine 3mm, 16
 pages of advertisements) £300
ditto, as *The Nigger of the Narcissus*, Heinemann,
 1898 (second issue: 32 pages of advertisements) £200

Lord Jim, William Blackwood, 1900 . . . £1,750
ditto, Doubleday (U.S.), 1900 . . . . . £350
Nostromo, Harper, 1904 . . . . . . £500
ditto, Harper (U.S.), 1904 . . . . . . £200
The Secret Agent, Methuen, 1907 (40 pages of adverts
 dated September). £750
ditto, Harper (U.S.), 1907. . . . . . . £200
Under Western Eyes, Methuen, 1911 . . . £350
ditto, Harper (U.S.), 1911. . . . . . . £100
Chance, Methuen, 1913 ('Methven' on spine, 32 page
 catalogue). £2,000
ditto, Methuen, 1914 ('Methuen' on spine, no
 catalogue). £1,500
ditto, Methuen, 1914 (authorised issue) . . . £500
ditto, Doubleday (U.S.), 1913 (150 copyright copies) .
 . . . . £500
ditto, Doubleday (U.S.), 1914 . . . . . £100
Victory, An Island Tale, Doubleday (U.S.), 1915 £75
ditto, Methuen, 1915 . . . . £65
The Shadow Line, Dent, 1917 . . . . . £65
ditto, Doubleday (U.S.), 1917 . . . . . £50
The Arrow of Gold, Doubleday (U.S.), 1919
 ('credentials and apparently' in line 15, p.5) . £35
ditto, Doubleday (U.S.), 1919 ('credentials and who' in
 line 15, p.5)) £25
ditto, T. Fisher Unwin, 1919 . . . . . . £45
The Rescue, Doubleday (U.S.), 1920 ($1.90 d/w) .
 . . . . £200/£25
ditto, Doubleday (U.S.), 1920 ($2.00 d/w) . £150/£25
ditto, Dent, 1920 (40 copies for private distribution) .
 . . . . £1,000
ditto, Dent, 1920 (trade edition, green cloth) £300/£35
The Rover, Doubleday (U.S.), 1923 (377 signed
 copies, slipcase) . . . . £325/£275
ditto, Doubleday (U.S.), 1923 . . . . £125/£20
ditto, T. Fisher Unwin, 1923 . . . . . £125/£20
Suspense, Dent, 1925 . . . . £150/£25
ditto, Doubleday (U.S.), 1925 (limited edition of 377
 copies, glassine d/w, slipcase) . . . . £200/£250
ditto, Doubleday (U.S.), 1925 . . . . £125/£25
The Sisters, Crosby Gaige (U.S.), 1928 (926 copies) .
 . . . . £100

Titles Written with Ford Maddox Hueffer/Ford

The Inheritors, McClure, Phillips & Co. (U.S.), 1901
 (dedicated to Boys & Christina) £3,000
ditto, McClure, Phillips & Co. (U.S.), 1901 (dedicated
 to Borys & Christina) £400
ditto, Heinemann, 1901 (top edge untrimmed, 32 pages
 adverts, publisher's device on spine with initials) £600
ditto, Heinemann, 1901 (top edge trimmed, no catalogue, publisher's device on spine with initials) £350
ditto, Heinemann, 1901 (without initials in publisher's
 device) £300
ditto, Heinemann, 1901 (remainder issue, non-pictorial
 cloth) £150
Romance, Smith Elder, 1903. . . . . . £150
ditto, McClure (U.S.), 1904 . . . . . . £125
The Nature of a Crime, Duckworth, 1924 . £125/£25
ditto, Doubleday (U.S.), 1924 . . . . £125/£25

Short Stories

Tales of Unrest, Scribner's (U.S.), 1898 . . £250
ditto, T. Fisher Unwin, 1898 (top edge gilt). . £300
ditto, T. Fisher Unwin, 1898 . . . . . . £225
Youth: A Narrative, and Other Stories, William Blackwood, 1902 (adverts dated '10/02') . £200
ditto, William Blackwood, 1902 (adverts dated '11/02')
. . . . £175
ditto, McClure, Phillips & Co. (U.S.), 1903 . . £200
Typhoon, Putnam/Knickerbocker Press, 1902 (green cloth) £400
ditto, Putnam/Knickerbocker Press, 1902 (maroon cloth) £350
ditto, as **Typhoon and Other Stories**, Heinemann, 1903 (grey cloth) £150
A Set of Six, Methuen, 1908 (first issue, adverts dated Feb. 1908, list of works including 'The Secret Agent (with Ford M. Hueffer)') £750
ditto, Methuen, 1908 (second issue, adverts dated Feb. 1908, list of works including 'The Secret Agent' with 'FORD M. HUEFFER' below) £400
ditto, Methuen, 1908 (third issue, adverts dated June. 1908) £350
'Twixt Land and Sea, Dent, 1912 (first issue with 'Secret' instead of 'Seven' on front cover). . £2,000
ditto, Dent, 1912 (second issue with 'Seven' stamped over erased 'Secret'). £200
ditto, Dent, 1912 (third issue with front cover corrected). £100
ditto, Hodder & Stoughton/Doran (U.S.), 1912 . £100
Within the Tides, Dent, 1915. . . . . . £150
Tales of Hearsay, T. Fisher Unwin, 1925 . £150/£20
ditto, Doubleday (U.S.), 1925 . . . . £150/£20

Plays

One Day More: A Play in One Act, privately printed, Clement Shorter, 1917 (25 copies, wraps) . . £1,500
ditto, Beaumont Press, 1919 (250 copies) . . £200
ditto, Beaumont Press, 1919 (24 signed copies on Japanese vellum) £2,000
ditto, Doubleday (U.S.), 1920 (377 signed copies) . .
. . . . £300
The Secret Agent: A Drama, Goulden, 1921 (wraps) .
. . . . £1,500
ditto, T. Werner Laurie, 1923 (printed for subscribers only, 1,000 signed copies) . . . . £700/£300
Laughing Anne, Moorland Press, 1923 (200 signed, numbered copies) £500
Laughing Anne and One More Day, John Castle, 1924
. . . . £75/£20
Three Plays, Methuen, 1934 (contains 'One Day More', 'The Secret Agent' and 'Laughing Anne') .
. . . . £35/£10

Miscellaneous

The Nigger of the Narcissus: A Preface, privately printed, 1902 (100 copies, wraps) . . . £1,500
The Mirror of the Sea, Methuen, [1906] . . £250
ditto, Harper (U.S.), 1906. . . . . . £100

Some Reminiscences, Eveleigh Nash, 1912. . £100
ditto, as *A Personal Record*, Harper, 1912 . . £100
Notes on Life and Letters, Dent, 1921 (33 copies, privately printed). £1,500
ditto, Dent, 1921 ('S' and 'a' missing from 'Sea', line 8 of table of contents) . . . . . . £175/£45
ditto, Dent, 1921 (corrected page on cancel leaf) . .
. . . . £150/£20
ditto, Doubleday (U.S.), 1921 . . . . £150/£20
Notes On My Books, Heinemann, 1921 (250 signed copies). £400
The Dover Patrol: A Tribute, privately printed, Canterbury, 1922 (75 copies, first state without title page, wraps) £750
ditto, privately printed, Canterbury, 1922 (75 copies, second state with added title page, wraps) . . £300
Five Letters by Joseph Conrad, privately printed, 1925 (100 numbered copies, wraps) £225
Notes by Joseph Conrad, privately printed, 1925 (100 numbered copies) £250
Last Essays, Dent, 1926 . . . . . £125/£20
ditto, Doubleday (U.S.), 1926 . . . . £120/£20
Joseph Conrad's Letters to His Wife, privately printed, 1927 (220 copies, signed by his widow) . . £200
Letters ... 1895 to 1924, Nonesuch Press, 1928 (925 numbered copies) £75
A Sketch of Joseph Conrad's Life Written by Himself, privately printed, 1939 (75 copies) . . . £150
Letters to William Blackwood, Duke Univ. Press (U.S.), 1958 . . . . £25/£10
Congo Diary and other Uncollected Pieces, Doubleday (U.S.), 1979 . . . . £20/£10

A.E. COPPARD
(b.1878 d.1957)

An acknowledged master of the short story form, Coppard is at his best in his evocation of the English countryside.

Short Stories

Adam and Eve and Pinch Me, Golden Cockerel Press, 1921 (white buckram issue of 550 signed copies). .
. . . . £150
ditto, Golden Cockerel Press, 1921 (orange boards issue of 550 signed copies). £125
ditto, Cape, 1921 . . . . £250/£100
ditto, Knopf (U.S.), 1922 . . . . . £150/£65
Clorinda Walks in Heaven, Golden Cockerel Press, 1922 . . . . £75/£25
ditto, Golden Cockerel Press, 1922 (25 signed copies on special paper). £250
The Black Dog and Other Stories, Cape, 1923 . . .
. . . . £75/£25
ditto, Knopf (U.S.), 1924 . . . . . £65/£25
Fishmonger's Fiddle, Cape, 1925 . . . £75/£25
ditto, Cape, 1925 (60 signed copies). . . . £125

ditto, Knopf (U.S.), 1925 . . . . . . £65/£25
The Field of Mustard, Cape, 1926 . . . £65/£20
ditto, Cape, 1926 (85 signed, numbered copies) £100
ditto, Knopf (U.S.), 1927 . . . . . £65/£15
Silver Circus, Cape, 1928 . . . . . £65/£15
ditto, Cape, 1928 (125 signed copies) . . £125/£100
ditto, Knopf (U.S.), 1929 . . . . . £65/£15
Count Stefan, Golden Cockerel Press, 1928 (600 signed copies) . . . . £75/£50
The Gollan, privately printed, 1929 (75 copies, wraps)
. . . . £125
The Man from Kilsheelan, Furnival Books, 1930 (550 signed copies) £35
The Hundredth Story, Golden Cockerel Press, 1931 (1,000 copies) . . . . . . £65/£45
Pink Furniture: A Tale for Lovely Children with Noble Natures, Cape, 1930 . . . . . £20/£5
ditto, Cape, 1930 (260 signed copies) . . £80/£60
The Higgler, The Chochorua Press (U.S.), [c.1930] (39 copies) £300
Fares Please! An Omnibus, Cape, 1931 £45/£15
Nixey's Harlequin, Cape, 1931 . . . £25/£10
ditto, Cape, 1931 (304 signed copies) . £40/£25
ditto, Knopf (U.S.), 1932 . . . . . £20/£10
Crotty Shinkwin, The Beauty Spot, Golden Cockerel Press, 1932 (500 numbered copies). . . £65
Cheefoo, privately printed (U.S.), 1932 . . . £150
Dunky Fitlow, Cape, 1933 . . . . £25/£10
ditto, Cape, 1933 (300 signed copies) . . £65
Ring the Bells of Heaven, White Owl Press, 1933 . .
. . . . £25/£10
ditto, White Owl Press, 1933 (150 signed copies) £50
Emergency Exit, Random House, 1934 (350 signed copies) £45
Good Samaritans, privately printed by The Spiral Press (U.S.), 1934 (100 copies) £125
Polly Oliver, Cape, 1935 . . . . £30/£10
The Ninepenny Flute: Twenty-One Tales, Macmillan, 1937 . . . . £35/£10
Tapster's Tapestry, Golden Cockerel Press, 1938 . .
. . . . £45/£30
You Never Know, Do You? and Other Tales, Methuen, 1939 . . . . £25/£10
Ugly Anna and Other Tales, Methuen, 1944 £25/£10
Selected Tales, Cape, 1946 . . . . £35/£15
Fearful Pleasures, Arkham House (U.S.), 1946 . .
. . . . £65/£15
ditto, Peter Nevill, 1951 . . . . . £25/£10
Dark-Eyed Lady: Fourteen Tales, Methuen, 1947. .
. . . . £35/£10
Collected Tales, Knopf (U.S.), 1948 . . £25/£10
Lucy in Her Pink Jacket, Peter Nevill, 1954 £25/£10
Selected Stories, Cape, 1972 . . . . . £15/£5

Poetry
Hips and Haws, Golden Cockerel Press, 1922 (500 signed copies) . . . . . . £75/£45
Pelagea and Other Poems, Golden Cockerel Press, 1926 (425 numbered copies) . . . £100/£45

Yokohama Garland and Other Poems, Centaur Press (U.S.), 1926 (500 signed, numbered copies, glassine d/w) . . . . £65/£45
Collected Poems, Cape, 1928 . . . . £30/£10
ditto, Knopf (U.S.), 1928 . . . . . £30/£10
Easter Day, [no publisher stated], [1931] (145 copies, last four lines written and signed, slipcase) £125/£100
Cherry Ripe, Hawthorn House (U.S.), 1935 (300 signed, numbered copies, slipcase) . . £60/£35
ditto, Tintern Press, 1935 (150 signed, numbered copies) £100

Others
Rummy, The Noble Game, Golden Cockerel Press, 1932 (1,000 copies, with Robert Gibbings) £75/£30
ditto, Golden Cockerel Press, 1932 (250 signed copies on handmade paper, with Robert Gibbings) . £85
ditto, Houghton Mifflin (U.S.), 1933 . . £25/£10
It's Me, O Lord!, Methuen, 1957 . . . £25/£10

BERNARD CORNWELL
(b.1944)

Cornwell's most famous creation, Richard Sharpe, is a common British infantryman who is made an officer by the Duke of Wellington during the Napoleonic Wars.

'Sharpe' Novels
Sharpe's Eagle, Collins, 1981 [1980] . . £225/£25
ditto, Viking (U.S.), 1981. . . . . £75/£15
Sharpe's Gold, Collins, 1981. . . . . £225/£20
ditto, Viking (U.S.), 1982. . . . . £75/£15
Sharpe's Company, Collins, 1982 . . £250/£35
ditto, Viking (U.S.), 1982. . . . . £75/£15
Sharpe's Sword, Collins, 1983 . . . £250/£35
ditto, Viking (U.S.), 1983 . . . . . £75/£15
Sharpe's Enemy, Collins, 1984 . . . £250/£35
ditto, Viking (U.S.), 1984. . . . . £75/£15
Sharpe's Honour, Collins, 1985. . . . £250/£25
ditto, Viking (U.S.), 1985. . . . . £75/£15
Sharpe's Regiment, Collins, 1986 . . . £200/£20
ditto, Viking (U.S.), 1986. . . . . £60/£10
Sharpe's Siege, Collins, 1987 . . . £150/£15
ditto, Viking (U.S.), 1987. . . . . £60/£10
Sharpe's Rifles, Collins, 1988 . . . £75/£10
ditto, Viking (U.S.), 1988. . . . . £60/£10
Sharpe's Revenge, Collins, 1989 . . . £75/£10
ditto, Viking (U.S.), 1989. . . . . £50/£10
Sharpe's Waterloo, Collins, 1990 . . . £75/£10
ditto, as **Waterloo**, Viking (U.S.), 1990 . . £40/£10
Sharpe's Devil, Collins, 1992 . . . £65/£10
ditto, Viking (U.S.), 1992. . . . . £35/£10
Sharpe's Battle, HarperCollins, 1995 . . £65/£10
ditto, HarperCollins (U.S.), 1995. . . £35/£10
Sharpe's Tiger, HarperCollins, 1997 . . £30/£10
ditto, HarperCollins (U.S.), 1997 (wraps) . . . £5

Sharpe's Triumph, HarperCollins, 1998 . £20/£10
ditto, HarperCollins (U.S.), 1999. . . . . £15/£5
Sharpe's Fortress, HarperCollins, 1999. . . £15/£5
ditto, HarperCollins (U.S.), 2000. . . . . £15/£5
Sharpe's Trafalgar HarperCollins, 2000 . . £15/£5
ditto, HarperCollins (U.S.), 2001. . . . . £15/£5
Sharpe's Prey, HarperCollins, 2001. . . . £15/£5
ditto, HarperCollins (U.S.), 2002. . . . . £15/£5
Sharpe's Havoc, HarperCollins, 2003 . . . £15/£5
ditto, HarperCollins (U.S.), 2003. . . . . £15/£5

'Sharpe' Short Story
Sharpe's Skirmish, HarperCollins, 1999 (wraps) £150
ditto, Sharpe Appreciation Society, 2002 (wraps) £10

'Nathaniel Starbuck Chronicles'
Rebel, HarperCollins, 1993 . . . . . £35/£10
ditto, HarperCollins (U.S.), 1993. . . . . £15/£5
Copperhead, HarperCollins, 1994 . . . £30/£10
ditto, HarperCollins (U.S.), 1994. . . . . £10/£5
Battle Flag, HarperCollins, 1995 . . . £30/£10
ditto, HarperCollins (U.S.), 1995. . . . . £10/£5
The Bloody Ground, HarperCollins, 1996 . £30/£10
ditto, HarperCollins (U.S.), 1996. . . . . £15/£5

The 'Warlord' Chronicles
The Winter King, Joseph, 1995 . . . . £75/£10
ditto, St Martin's Press (U.S.), 1996 . . . . £30/£10
Enemy of God, Joseph, 1996. . . . . . £50/£10
ditto, St Martin's Press (U.S.), 1997 . . . . £20/£5
Excalibur, Joseph, 1997 . . . . . . £30/£10
ditto, St Martin's Press (U.S.), 1998 . . . . £20/£5

Other Novels
Redcoat, Joseph, 1987 . . . . . £45/£10
ditto, Viking (U.S.), 1987. . . . . . . £20/£5
Wildtrack, Joseph, 1988 . . . . . . £35/£10
ditto, Viking (U.S.), 1988. . . . . . . £15/£5
Sea Lord, Joseph, 1989 . . . . . £35/£10
ditto, as *Killer's Wake*, Viking (U.S.), 1989 . £15/£5
Crackdown, Joseph, 1990 . . . . . £35/£10
ditto, HarperCollins (U.S.), 1990. . . . . £15/£5
Stormchild, Joseph, 1990 [1991]. . . . £35/£10
ditto, HarperCollins (U.S.), 1991. . . . . £15/£5
Scoundrel, Joseph, 1992 . . . . . £35/£10
Stonehenge, A Novel of 2000 BC, HarperCollins, 1999
. . . . £10/£5
ditto, HarperCollins (U.S.), 2000. . . . . £10/£5
Harlequin, HarperCollins, 2000 . . . . £10/£5
ditto, as *The Archer's Tale*, HarperCollins (U.S.), 2001
. . . . £10/£5
Gallows Thief, HarperCollins, 2001. . . . £10/£5
ditto, HarperCollins (U.S.), 2002. . . . . £10/£5
Vagabond, HarperCollins, 2002 . . . . £10/£5
ditto, HarperCollins (U.S.), 2002. . . . . £10/£5

PATRICIA CORNWELL
(b.1956)

With her first book, Post Mortem, Cornwell won four major awards.

'Scarpetta' Books
Postmortem, Scribner's (U.S.), 1990 . . £450/£50
ditto, Macdonald, 1990 . . . . . . £275/£35
Body of Evidence, Scribner's (U.S.), 1991 . £65/£15
ditto, Macdonald, 1991 . . . . . . £65/£15
All That Remains, Little, Brown, 1992 . . £30/£10
ditto, Scribner's (U.S.), 1992 . . . . . £25/£10
Cruel and Unusual, Scribner's (U.S.), 1993 £25/£10
ditto, Little, Brown, 1993 . . . . . . £20/£10
The Body Farm, Scribner's (U.S.), 1994 . £20/£10
ditto, Little, Brown, 1994. . . . . . £20/£10
From Potter's Field, Scribner's (U.S.), 1995 £20/£10
ditto, Little, Brown, 1995. . . . . . £20/£10
Cause of Death, Putnam (U.S.), 1996 . £20/£10
ditto, Putnam (U.S.), 1996 (185 signed, numbered copies, slipcase) . . . . £100/£65
ditto, Little, Brown, 1996. . . . . . £20/£10
Unnatural Exposure, Putnam (U.S.), 1997 . £20/£10
ditto, Putnam (U.S.), 1997 (175 signed, numbered copies, slipcase) . . . . £75/£50
ditto, Little, Brown, 1997. . . . . . £20/£10
Point of Origin, Putnam (U.S.), 1998 . . £10/£5
ditto, Putnam (U.S.), 2000 (500 signed, numbered copies, slipcase) . . . . £75/£50
ditto, Little, Brown, 1998. . . . . . £10/£5
Scarpetta's Winter Table, Wyrick & Company (U.S.), 1998 . . . . £10/£5
Black Notice, Putnam (U.S.), 1999 . . . £10/£5
ditto, Putnam (U.S.), 1999 (200 signed, numbered copies, slipcase) . . . . £75/£50
ditto, Little, Brown, 1999. . . . . . £10/£5
The Last Precinct, Putnam (U.S.), 2000. . £10/£5
ditto, Putnam (U.S.), 2000 (175 signed, numbered copies, slipcase) . . . . £75/£50
ditto, Little, Brown, 2000. . . . . . £10/£5

'Hammer' novels
Hornet's Nest, Putnam (U.S.), 1996. . . £20/£10
ditto, Little, Brown, 1996. . . . . . £20/£10
Southern Cross, Putnam (U.S.), 1999 . . £10/£5
ditto, Little, Brown, 1999. . . . . . £10/£5
Isle of Dogs, Putnam (U.S.), 2001 . . . £10/£5
ditto, Little, Brown, 2001. . . . . . £10/£5

Others
A Time for Remembering: The Ruth Bell Graham Story, Harper & Row (U.S.), 1983 . . . £100/£15
ditto, as *Ruth: A Portrait*, Hodder & Stoughton, 1998 . . . . £15/£5
Life's Little Fable, Putnam (U.S.), 1999 . £10/£5
Portrait of a Killer : Jack the Ripper - Case Closed, Putnam (U.S.), 2002 . . . . £10/£5

HUBERT CRACKANTHORPE
(b.1870 d.1896)

Crackanthorpe's reputation was based on his willingness to deal with taboo subjects such as adultery, prostitution and social degradation.

Wreckage: Seven Studies, Heinemann, 1893 . £75
ditto, Cassell (U.S.), 1894. . . . . . . £60
Sentimental Studies & A Set of Village Tales, Heinemann, 1895 . . . . £100
ditto, Putnams (U.S.), 1895 . . . . . . £75
Vignettes, A Miniature Journal of Whim and Sentiment, John Lane/ Bodley Head, 1896 . £85
Last Studies, Heinemann, 1897 . . . . . £75
The Light Sovereign: A Farcical Comedy in Three Acts, privately printed, Lady Henry Harland, 1917 (with Henry Harland) £150
Collected Stories (1893-1897) of Hubert Crackanthorpe, Scholar's facsimiles and Reprints (U.S.), 1969 . . . . £25

WALTER CRANE
(b.1845 d.1915)

A successful British artist, Crane was a colleague of William Morris, sharing many of Morris's political and artistic beliefs.

Sixpenny Toy Books
The House that Jack Built, Ward, Lock & Tyler, 1865 . . . . £300
The Comical Cat, Ward, Lock & Tyler, 1865 . £250
The Affecting Story of Jenny Wren, Ward, Lock & Tyler, 1865 . . . . £250
The Railroad Alphabet, Routledge, 1865 . . £250
The Farmyard Alphabet, Routledge, 1865 . . £250
Cock Robin, Frederick Warne, 1866. . . . £250
A Gaping-Wide-Mouth Waddling Frog, Frederick Warne, [1866] £250

'Aunt Mavor' Books
Sing A Song of Sixpence, Frederick Warne, 1866 £250
The Old Courtier, Frederick Warne, 1867 . . £250
Multiplication Rule in Verse, Routledge, [1867] £250
Chattering Jack's Picture Book, Routledge, [1867] £250
How Jessie Was Lost, Routledge, [1868] . . £250
Grammar in Rhyme, Routledge, [1868]. . . £250
Annie and Jack in London, Routledge, [1869]. £250
One, Two, Buckle My Shoe, Routledge, [1869] £250
The Fairy Ship, Routledge, 1870 . . . . £250
The Adventures of Puffy, Routledge, 1870 . . £250
This Little Pig Went To Market, Routledge, [1870] £250
King Luckieboy's Party, Routledge, 1870 . . £350
King Luckieboy's Picture Book, Routledge, 1871 £350
Routledge's Book of Alphabets, Routledge, 1871 £250

Noah's Ark Alphabet, Routledge, 1872 . . . £250
My Mother, Routledge, 1873. . . . . . £250
Ali Baba and the Forty Thieves, Routledge, 1873 £75
The Three Bears, Routledge, 1873 . . . . £250
Cinderella, Routledge, 1873 . . . . . . £250
Walter Crane's New Toy Book, Routledge, 1873 £400
Walter Crane's Picture Book, Routledge, 1874 £400
Valentine and Orson, Routledge, 1874 . . . £250
Puss in Boots, Routledge, 1874 . . . . . £250
Old Mother Hubbard, Routledge, 1874 . . £250
The Marquis of Caraba's Picture Book, Routledge, [1874]. £250
The Absurd ABC, Routledge, 1874 . . . . £200
The Frog Prince, Routledge: 'Walter Crane Shilling Series', 1874 . . . . £250
Goody Two Shoes, Routledge: 'Walter Crane Shilling Series', 1874 . . . . £250
Beauty and the Beast, Routledge: 'Walter Crane Shilling Series', 1874 . . . . £250
The Alphabet of Old Friends, Routledge: 'Walter Crane Shilling Series', 1874 . . . . . £250
Little Red Riding Hood, Routledge, 1875 . . £250
Jack and the Beanstalk, Routledge, 1875 . . £250
The Bluebeard Picture Book, Routledge, 1875. £250
Baby's Own Alphabet, Routledge, 1875 . . £250
The Yellow Dwarf, Routledge: 'Walter Crane Shilling Series', 1875 . . . . £250
The Hind in the Wood, Routledge: 'Walter Crane Shilling Series', 1875 . . . . £250
Princess Belle Etoile, Routledge: 'Walter Crane Shilling Series', 1875 . . . . £250
Aladdin's Picture Book, Routledge: 'Walter Crane Shilling Series', 1875 [1876] £250
Song of Sixpence Toy Book, Warner, [1876] . £250
The Three Bears Picture Book, Routledge, [1876] £75
The Sleeping Beauty in the Wood, Routledge, 1876 . . . . £200
Walter Crane's Picture Books Vol. 1: The Little Pig: His Picture Book, John Lane, 1895 . . . £200
Walter Crane's Picture Books Vol. 2: Mother Hubbard: Her Picture Book, John Lane, 1897 £200
Walter Crane's Picture Books Vol. 3: Cinderella's Picture Book, John Lane, 1897. . . . . £200
Walter Crane's Picture Books Vol. 4: Red Riding Hood's Picture Book, John Lane, 1898 . £200
Beauty and the Beast Picture Book, John Lane: Large Series Vol. l, 1901 . . . . £200
Goody Two Shoes Picture Book, John Lane: Large Series Vol. 2, 1901 . . . . £200
The Song of Sixpence Picture Book, John Lane: Large Series Vol. 3, 1909 . . . . . . £200
The Buckle My Shoe Picture Book, John Lane: Large Series Vol. 4, 1910 . . . . . . £200
Puss in Boots and *The Forty Thieves*, John Lane, 1914 . . . . £200
The Sleeping Beauty and *Bluebeard*, John Lane, 1914 . . . . £200
The Three Bears and *Mother Hubbard*, John Lane, 1914 . . . . £200

Books Written by Mary Molesworth,
Illustrated by Crane

Tell Me A Story, Macmillan, 1875	£70
Carrots, Macmillan, 1876.	£60
The Cuckoo Clock, Macmillan, 1877 . . .	£60
Grandmother Dear, Macmillan, 1878 . . .	£45
The Tapestry Room, Macmillan, 1879 . . .	£50
A Christmas Child, Macmillan, 1880 . . .	£50
The Adventures of Herr Baby, Macmillan, 1881	£75
Rosy, Macmillan, 1882	£45
Two Little Waifs, Macmillan, 1883	£45
Christmas-Tree Land, Macmillan, 1884 . .	£45
Us, An Old Fashioned Story, Macmillan, 1885	£45
Four Winds Farm, Macmillan, 1886 . . .	£40
Little Miss Piggy, Macmillan, 1887 . . .	£40
A Christmas Posy, Macmillan, 1888. . . .	£40
The Rectory Children, Macmillan, 1889 . .	£40
The Children of the Castle, Macmillan, 1890 .	£30
Studies and Stories, A.D. Innes, 1893 . . .	£30

Other Titles Illustrated by Crane

The New Forest: Its History and Scenery, by John de Capel Wise, Smith & Elder, 1863 . . .	£125
A Merrie Heart, by Cassell, 1871	£150
Mrs Mundi at Home, by Walter Crane, Marcus Ward, 1875	£125
The Quiver of Love: A Collection of Valentines, Marcus Ward, 1876 (with Kate Greenaway) .	£500
The Baby's Opera: Old Rhymes with New Dresses, by Walter Crane, Routledge, 1877. . . .	£125
The Baby's Bouquet, by Walter Crane, Routledge, 1878	£125
The Necklace of Princess Fiorimonde, by Mary de Morgan, Macmillan, 1880	£75
The First of May: A Fairy Masque, by John R Wise, Henry Southeran, 1881 (300 copies, signed by Crane)	£600
ditto, Henry Southeran, 1881 (folio edition, 200 copies, signed by Crane)	£750
Household Stories, by the Brothers Grimm, Macmillan, 1882	£100
Art and the Formation of Taste, by Lucy Crane, Macmillan, 1882.	£75
Pan Pipes: A Book of Old Songs, by Theodore Marzials, Routledge, 1883	£165
The Golden Primer, Parts 1 & 2, by Professor J.M.D. Meiklejohn, William Blackwood, 1884-5 (2 vols) £75
Folk and Fairy Tales, by Mrs Burton Harrison, Ward & Downey, 1885.	£75
Slateandpencilvania: Being the Adventures of Dick on a Desert Island, by Walter Crane, Marcus Ward, 1885	£175
Little Queen Annie, by Walter Crane, Marcus Ward, 1886	£175
Pothooks and Perseverance, by Walter Crane, Marcus Ward, 1886	£200
A Romance of the Three Rs, by Walter Crane, Marcus Ward, 1886	£150

The Sirens Three: A Poem, by Walter Crane, Macmillan, 1886	£150
Legends for Lionel in Pen and Pencil, by Walter Crane, Cassell, 1887	£150
The Baby's Own Aesop, by Walter Crane, Routledge, 1887	£150
Echoes of Hellas, Parts 1 & 2, by Professor George C. Warr, Marcus Ward, 1887-88 (2 vols) . . .	£175
The Happy Prince and Other Tales, by Oscar Wilde, David Nutt, 1888.	£1,500
ditto, David Nutt, 1888 (75 signed copies, large hand made paper edition)	£6,000
The Book of Wedding Days, Compiled by K.E.J. Reid, Longmans, 1889	£125
Flora's Feast: A Masque of Flowers, by Walter Crane, Cassell, 1889	£125
The Story of the Glittering Plain, by William Morris, Kelmscott Press, 1894 (250 copies) . . .	£2,000
ditto, by William Morris, Kelmscott Press, 1894 (7 copies on vellum)	£6,000
Society for the Encouragement of Arts, Manufacture and Commerce: Lectures by Walter Crane, W. Trounce, 1891	£75
Queen Summer: or the Tourney of the Lily and the Rose, by Walter Crane, Cassell, 1891 . . .	£125
ditto, by Walter Crane, Cassell, 1891 (250 large paper copies)	£600
Renascence: A Book of Verse, by Walter Crane, Elkin Mathews, 1891 (350 numbered copies) . .	£75
ditto, by Walter Crane, Elkin Mathews, 1891 (25 signed, numbered copies on Japanese vellum). £1,000
The Claims of Decorative Art, by Walter Crane, Lawrence & Bullen, 1892	£125
A Wonder Book for Boys and Girls, by Nathaniel Hawthorne, Osgood, McIlvaine, 1892 . .	£175
Columbia's Courtship, by Walter Crane, Prang & Co. (U.S.), 1893	£175
The Old Garden and Other Verses, by Margaret Delane, Osgood, McIlvaine, 1893 . . .	£75
The Tempest, by William Shakespeare, Dent, 1893 £75
Eight Illustrations to Shakespeare's The Tempest, Dent, 1893 (600 signed portfolios). . . .	£400
The History of Reynard the Fox, by F.S. Ellis, David Nutt, 1894	£100
The Merry Wives of Windsor, by William Shakespeare, George Allen, 1894	£75
Two Gentlemen of Verona, by William Shakespeare, Dent, 1894	£75
The Faerie Queen, by Edmund Spenser, George Allen, 1894-97 (issued in 19 parts). . . £750 the set
ditto, George Allen, 1897 (6 vols, 1,000 sets) . . . . £1,250 the set
A Book of Christmas Verse, Methuen, 1895 . £75
Cartoons for the Cause, Twentieth Century Press, 1896	£600
Of the Decorative Illustration of Books Old and New, by Walter Crane, Bell, 1896.	£100
The Work of Walter Crane, Virtue & Co., 1898	£125

A Floral Fantasy in an Old English Garden, by Walter Crane, Harper, 1898 . . . . . . £150
The Shepherd's Calendar, by Edmund Spenser, Harper, 1898 . . . . £100
The Bases of Design, by Walter Crane, Bell, 1898 . . . . £100
Triplets, by Walter Crane, Routledge, 1899 (500 numbered copies) £300
Don Quixote, translated by Judge Parry, Blackie, 1900 . . . . £65
Line and Form, by Walter Crane, Bell, 1900 . £50
Walter Crane's Picture Book, Frederick Warne, 1900 (750 copies, bound in vellum) £400
A Masque of Days, Cassell, 1901 . . . . £150
The Art of Walter Crane, by Paul George Konody, Bell, 1902. . . . . £250
A Flower Wedding, by Walter Crane, Cassell, 1905 . . . . £100
Flowers from Shakespeare's Garden, by Walter Crane, Cassell, 1906 . . . . £150
India Impressions, by Walter Crane, Methuen, 1907 . . . . £100
An Artists Reminiscences, by Walter Crane, Methuen, 1907 . . . . £75
A Child's Socialist Reader, by A.A. Watts, Methuen, 1907 . . . . £65
The Rosebud and Other Tales, by Arthur Kelly, Fisher & Unwin, 1909 . . . . £65
King Arthur's Knights, by H. Gilbert, Jack, 1911 £65
William Morris to Whistler, by Walter Morris, Bell, 1911 (350 copies) £250
Rumbo Rhymes, by A. Calmour, Harper, 1911. £125
Robin Hood, by H. Gilbert, Jack, 1912 . . . £65
The Story of Greece, by M. MacGregor, Jack, 1913 £65
Michael Mouse Unfolds His Tale, by Walter Crane, Yale Univ. Press (U.S.), 1956 (300 copies, slipcase) . . . . £150/£125
ditto, by Walter Crane, Merrimack/Yale Univ. Press (U.S.), 1956 (wraps). £30

JOHN CREASEY
(b.1908 d.1973)

An author whose output was prodigious, Creasey is best known for his detective fiction, especially his Inspector West and Gideon novels. He used many pseudonyms.

'Inspector West' Novels
Inspector West Takes Charge, Stanley Paul, 1942 . . . . £300/£35
ditto, Scribner's (U.S.), 1972 . . . . . £20/£5
Inspector West Leaves Town, Stanley Paul, 1943 . . . . £250/£30
ditto, as *Go Away To Murder*, Lancer (U.S.), 1972 (wraps) £5
Inspector West at Home, Stanley Paul, 1944 £250/£30

ditto, Scribner's (U.S.), 1973 . . . . . . £15/£5
Inspector West Regrets, Stanley Paul, 1945. £200/£25
ditto, Lancer (U.S.), 1971 (wraps) £5
Holiday for Inspector West, Stanley Paul, 1946 . . . . £175/£20
Battle for Inspector West, Stanley Paul, 1948 £125/£20
Triumph for Inspector West, Stanley Paul, 1948 . . . . £100/£15
ditto, as *The Case Against Paul Raeburn*, Harper (U.S.), 1958 . . . . £40/£10
Inspector West Kicks Off, Stanley Paul, 1949 . . . . £100/£15
ditto, as *Sport for Inspector West*, Lancer (U.S.), 1971 (wraps) £5
Inspector West Alone, Evans, 1950 . . . £100/£15
ditto, Scribner's (U.S.), 1975 . . . . . £15/£5
Inspector West Cries Wolf, Evans, 1950 . £100/£15
ditto, as *The Creepers*, Scribner's (U.S.), 1952 £75/£10
A Case for Inspector West, Evans, 1951 . £65/£15
ditto, as *The Figure in the Dusk*, Harper (U.S.), 1952. . . . . £50/£10
Puzzle for Inspector West, Evans, 1951. . £50/£10
ditto, as *The Dissemblers*, Scribner's (U.S.), 1967 . . . . £15/£5
Inspector West at Bay, Evans, 1952. . . £45/£10
ditto, as *The Blind Spot*, Harper (U.S.), 1954 £40/£10
A Gun for Inspector West, Hodder & Stoughton, 1953 . . . . £40/£5
ditto, as *Give A Man A Gun*, Harper (U.S.), 1954 . . . . £30/£5
Send Inspector West, Hodder & Stoughton, 1953 . . . . £40/£5
ditto, as *Send Superintendent West*, Scribner's (U.S.), 1976 . . . . £20/£5
A Beauty for Inspector West, Hodder & Stoughton, 1954 . . . . £40/£5
ditto, as *The Beauty Queen Killer*, Harper (U.S.), 1956 . . . . £20/£5
ditto, as *So Young, So Cold, So Fair*, Dell (U.S.), 1958 (wraps) £10
Inspector West Makes Haste, Hodder & Stoughton, 1955 . . . . £35/£5
ditto, as *The Gelignite Gang*, Harper (U.S.), 1956 . . . . £35/£5
Two for Inspector West, Hodder & Stoughton, 1955 . . . . £35/£5
ditto, as *Murder: One, Two, Three*, Scribner's (U.S.), 1960 . . . . £20/£5
Parcels for Inspector West, Hodder & Stoughton, 1956 . . . . £30/£5
ditto, as *Death of a Postman*, Harper (U.S.), 1957 . . . . £30/£5
A Prince for Inspector West, Hodder & Stoughton, 1956 . . . . £30/£5
ditto, as *Death of an Assassin*, Scribner's (U.S.), 1960 . . . . £25/£5
Accident for Inspector West, Hodder & Stoughton, 1957 . . . . £30/£5
ditto, as *Hit and Run*, Scribner's (U.S.), 1959 . £25/£5

Find Inspector West, Hodder & Stoughton, 1957 . .
. . . . £25/£5
ditto, as *The Trouble at Saxby's*, Harper (U.S.), 1959 .
. . . . £25/£5
Murder, London-New York, Hodder & Stoughton,
1958 . . . . £25/£5
ditto, Scribner's (U.S.), 1961 . . . . . . £20/£5
Strike for Death, Hodder & Stoughton, 1958 . £25/£5
ditto, as *The Killing Strike*, Scribner's (U.S.), 1961 .
. . . . £20/£5
Death of a Racehorse, Hodder & Stoughton, 1959. .
. . . . £25/£5
ditto, Scribner's (U.S.), 1962 . . . . . . £15/£5
The Case of the Innocent Victims, Hodder &
Stoughton, 1959 . . . . £25/£5
ditto, Scribner's (U.S.), 1966 . . . . . . £15/£5
Murder on the Line, Hodder & Stoughton, 1960 . .
. . . . £25/£5
ditto, Scribner's (U.S.), 1963 . . . . . . £20/£5
Death in Cold Print, Hodder & Stoughton, 1961 . .
. . . . £25/£5
ditto, Scribner's (U.S.), 1962 . . . . . . £20/£5
The Scene of the Crime, Hodder & Stoughton, 1961 .
. . . . £25/£5
ditto, Scribner's (U.S.), 1963 . . . . . . £20/£5
Policeman's Dread, Hodder & Stoughton, 1962 . .
. . . . £25/£5
ditto, Scribner's (U.S.), 1964 . . . . . . £20/£5
Hang the Little Man, Hodder & Stoughton, 1963 . .
. . . . £20/£5
ditto, Scribner's (U.S.), 1963 . . . . . . £20/£5
Look Three Ways at Murder, Hodder & Stoughton,
1964 . . . . £20/£5
ditto, Scribner's (U.S.), 1965 . . . . . . £20/£5
Murder, London-Australia, Hodder & Stoughton,
1965 . . . . £20/£5
ditto, Scribner's (U.S.), 1965 . . . . . . £20/£5
Murder, London-South Africa, Hodder & Stoughton,
1966 . . . . £20/£5
ditto, Scribner's (U.S.), 1966 . . . . . . £20/£5
The Executioners, Hodder & Stoughton, 1967 . £20/£5
ditto, Scribner's (U.S.), 1967 . . . . . . £20/£5
So Young to Burn, Hodder & Stoughton, 1968. £20/£5
ditto, Scribner's (U.S.), 1968 . . . . . . £20/£5
Murder, London-Miami, Hodder & Stoughton, 1969 .
. . . . £20/£5
ditto, Scribner's (U.S.), 1969 . . . . . . £20/£5
A Part for a Policeman, Hodder & Stoughton, 1970 .
. . . . £20/£5
ditto, Scribner's (U.S.), 1970 . . . . . . £20/£5
Alibi, Hodder & Stoughton, 1971 . . . . £20/£5
ditto, Scribner's (U.S.), 1971 . . . . . . £20/£5
A Splinter of Glass, Hodder & Stoughton, 1972 £20/£5
ditto, Scribner's (U.S.), 1972 . . . . . . £20/£5
The Theft of Magna Carter, Hodder & Stoughton,
1973 . . . . £20/£5
ditto, Scribner's (U.S.), 1973 . . . . . . £20/£5
The Extortioners, Hodder & Stoughton, 1974 . £20/£5
ditto, Scribner's (U.S.), 1975 . . . . . . £20/£5

A Sharp Rise in Crime, Hodder & Stoughton, 1978 .
. . . . £15/£5

'The Toff' Novels
Introducing The Toff, Long, 1938 . . . £250/£35
The Toff Goes On, Long, 1939 . . . . £175/£25
The Toff Steps Out, Long, 1939 . . . . £150/£20
Here Comes The Toff, Long, 1940 . . . £150/£20
ditto, Walker (U.S.), 1967 . . . . . . £20/£5
The Toff Breaks In, Long, 1940 . . . . £150/£20
Salute the Toff, Long, 1941 . . . . . £150/£20
ditto, Walker (U.S.), 1971 . . . . . . £20/£5
The Toff Proceeds, Long, 1941 . . . . £150/£20
ditto, Walker (U.S.), 1968 . . . . . . £15/£5
The Toff Goes to Market, Long, 1942 . . £125/£20
ditto, Walker (U.S.), 1967 . . . . . . £15/£5
The Toff is Back, Long, 1942 . . . . £125/£20
ditto, Walker (U.S.), 1974 . . . . . . £15/£5
The Toff Among the Millions, Long, 1943 . £100/£15
ditto, Walker (U.S.), 1976 . . . . . . £20/£5
Accuse the Toff, Long, 1943 . . . . . £100/£15
ditto, Walker (U.S.), 1975 . . . . . . £20/£5
The Toff and the Curate, Long, 1944 . . £100/£15
ditto, Walker (U.S.), 1969 . . . . . . £15/£5
The Toff and the Great Illusion, Long, 1944 £75/£10
ditto, Walker (U.S.), 1967 . . . . . . £15/£5
Feathers for the Toff, Long, 1945 . . . £75/£10
ditto, Walker (U.S.), 1970 . . . . . . £15/£5
The Toff and the Lady, Long, 1946 . . . . £50/£5
ditto, Walker (U.S.), 1975 . . . . . . £15/£5
The Toff on Ice, Long, 1946 . . . . . . £45/£5
ditto, as *Poison for The Toff*, Pyramid (U.S.), 1965
(wraps) £5
Hammer the Toff, Long, 1947 . . . . . £45/£5
The Toff in Town, Long, 1948 . . . . . £35/£5
ditto, Walker (U.S.), 1977 . . . . . . £15/£5
The Toff Takes Shares, Long, 1948 . . . . £35/£5
ditto, Walker (U.S.), 1972 . . . . . . £15/£5
The Toff and Old Harry, Long, 1949 . . . £35/£5
ditto, Walker (U.S.), 1970 . . . . . . £15/£5
The Toff on Board, Long, 1949 . . . . . £35/£5
ditto, Walker (U.S.), 1973 . . . . . . £15/£5
Fool The Toff, Evans, 1950 . . . . . . £35/£5
ditto, Walker (U.S.), 1966 . . . . . . £20/£5
Kill The Toff, Evans, 1950 . . . . . . £35/£5
ditto, Walker (U.S.), 1966 . . . . . . £15/£5
A Knife for The Toff, Evans, 1951 . . . . £35/£5
ditto, Pyramid (U.S.), 1965 (wraps) £5
The Toff Goes Gay, Evans, 1951 . . . . £35/£5
ditto, as *A Mask for The Toff*, Walker (U.S.), 1966 .
. . . . £15/£5
Hunt The Toff, Evans, 1952 . . . . . . £30/£5
ditto, Walker (U.S.), 1969 . . . . . . £15/£5
Call The Toff, Hodder & Stoughton, 1953 . . £30/£5
ditto, Walker (U.S.), 1969 . . . . . . £15/£5
The Toff Down Under, Hodder & Stoughton, 1953 .
. . . . £30/£5
ditto, Walker (U.S.), 1969 . . . . . . £15/£5

The Toff at Butlins, Hodder & Stoughton, 1954 . .
. . . . £30/£5
ditto, Walker (U.S.), 1976 . . . . . £15/£5
The Toff at the Fair, Hodder & Stoughton, 1954 . .
. . . . £25/£5
ditto, Walker (U.S.), 1968 . . . . . £15/£5
A Six for The Toff, Hodder & Stoughton, 1955 £25/£5
ditto, Walker (U.S.), 1969 . . . . . £20/£5
The Toff and the Deep Blue Sea, Hodder &
Stoughton, 1955 . . . . £25/£5
ditto, Walker (U.S.), 1967 . . . . . £15/£5
Make-Up for The Toff, Hodder & Stoughton, 1956 .
. . . . £25/£5
ditto, Walker (U.S.), 1967 . . . . . £20/£5
The Toff in New York, Hodder & Stoughton, 1956 .
. . . . £25/£5
ditto, Pyramid (U.S.), 1964 (wraps) £5
Model for The Toff, Hodder & Stoughton, 1957 . .
. . . . £25/£5
ditto, Pyramid (U.S.), 1965 (wraps) £5
The Toff on Fire, Hodder & Stoughton, 1957 . £25/£5
ditto, Walker (U.S.), 1966 . . . . . £15/£5
The Toff and the Stolen Tresses, Hodder & Stoughton,
1958 . . . . £25/£5
ditto, Walker (U.S.), 1965 . . . . . £15/£5
The Toff on the Farm, Hodder & Stoughton, 1958 .
. . . . £25/£5
ditto, Walker (U.S.), 1964 . . . . . £20/£5
ditto, as *Terror for The Toff*, Pyramid (U.S.), 1965
(wraps) £5
Double for The Toff, Hodder & Stoughton, 1959 . .
. . . . £25/£5
ditto, Walker (U.S.), 1965 . . . . . £20/£5
The Toff and the Runaway Bride, Hodder &
Stoughton, 1959 . . . . £25/£5
ditto, Walker (U.S.), 1964 . . . . . £20/£5
A Rocket for The Toff, Hodder & Stoughton, 1960 .
. . . . £20/£5
ditto, Pyramid (U.S.), 1964 (wraps) £5
The Toff and the Kidnapped Child, Hodder &
Stoughton, 1960 . . . . £20/£5
ditto, Walker (U.S.), 1967 . . . . . £15/£5
Follow The Toff, Hodder & Stoughton, 1961 . £20/£5
ditto, Walker (U.S.), 1967 . . . . . £20/£5
The Toff and the Teds, Hodder & Stoughton, 1961 .
. . . . £20/£5
ditto, as *The Toff and the Toughs*, Walker (U.S.),
1968 . . . . £15/£5
A Doll for The Toff, Hodder & Stoughton, 1963 . .
. . . . £20/£5
ditto, Walker (U.S.), 1965 . . . . . £20/£5
Leave it to The Toff, Hodder & Stoughton, 1963 . .
. . . . £20/£5
ditto, Pyramid (U.S.), 1965 (wraps) £5
The Toff and the Spider, Hodder & Stoughton, 1965 .
. . . . £20/£5
ditto, Walker (U.S.), 1966 . . . . . £15/£5
The Toff in Wax, Hodder & Stoughton, 1966 . £20/£5
ditto, Walker (U.S.), 1966 . . . . . £15/£5

A Bundle for The Toff, Hodder & Stoughton, 1967 .
. . . . £20/£5
ditto, Walker (U.S.), 1968 . . . . . £20/£5
Stars for The Toff, Hodder & Stoughton, 1968. £20/£5
ditto, Walker (U.S.), 1968 . . . . . £20/£5
The Toff and the Golden Boy, Hodder & Stoughton,
1969 . . . . £20/£5
ditto, Walker (U.S.), 1969 . . . . . £15/£5
The Toff and the Fallen Angels, Hodder & Stoughton,
1970 . . . . £20/£5
ditto, Walker (U.S.), 1970 . . . . . £15/£5
Vote for The Toff, Hodder & Stoughton, 1971 . £20/£5
ditto, Walker (U.S.), 1971 . . . . . £15/£5
The Toff and the Trip-Trip-Triplets, Hodder &
Stoughton, 1972 . . . . £20/£5
ditto, Walker (U.S.), 1972 . . . . . £15/£5
The Toff and the Terrified Taxman, Hodder &
Stoughton, 1973 . . . . £20/£5
ditto, Walker (U.S.), 1973 . . . . . £15/£5
The Toff and the Sleepy Cowboy, Hodder &
Stoughton, 1975 . . . . £20/£5
ditto, Walker (U.S.), 1975 . . . . . £15/£5

'The Toff' Short Stories
The Toff on the Trail, Everybody's Books, n.d.
[1940s?] (wraps) £10
Murder out of the Past, Barrington Gray, 1953 (wraps)
. . . . £10

'Department Z' Novels
The Death Miser, Melrose, 1932. . . . £400/£50
Redhead, Hurst & Blackett, 1934 . . . £350/£45
First Came a Murder, Melrose, 1934 . . £300/£40
ditto, Popular Library (U.S.), 1972 (wraps) . . . £5
Death Round the Corner, Melrose, 1935 . £300/£40
ditto, Popular Library (U.S.), 1972 (wraps) . . . £5
The Mark of the Crescent, Melrose, 1935 . £300/£40
ditto, Popular Library (U.S.), 1972 (wraps).. . . £5
Thunder in Europe, Melrose, 1936 . . . £250/£35
ditto, Popular Library (U.S.), 1972 (wraps) . . . £5
The Terror Trap, Melrose, 1936 . . . . £250/£35
ditto, Popular Library (U.S.), 1972 (wraps) . . . £5
Carriers of Death, Melrose, 1937 . . . £200/£35
ditto, Popular Library (U.S.), 1972 (wraps) . . . £5
Days of Danger, Melrose, 1937 . . . . £200/£35
ditto, Popular Library (U.S.), 1972 (wraps) . . . £5
Death Stands By, Long, 1938 . . . . £150/£25
ditto, Popular Library (U.S.), 1972 (wraps) . . . £5
Menace, Long, 1938 . . . . £150/£25
ditto, Popular Library (U.S.), 1972 (wraps) . . . £5
Murder Must Wait, Melrose, 1939 . . . £125/£20
ditto, Popular Library (U.S.), 1972 (wraps) . . . £5
Panic!, Long, 1939 . . . . £125/£20
ditto, Popular Library (U.S.), 1972 (wraps) . . . £5
Death By Night, Long, 1940 . . . . . £125/£20
ditto, Popular Library (U.S.), 1972 (wraps) . . . £5
The Island of Peril, Long, 1940 . . . . £125/£20
ditto, Popular Library (U.S.), 1976 (wraps) . . . £5
Sabotage, Long, 1941 . . . . £125/£20

ditto, Popular Library (U.S.), 1976 (wraps) . . . £5
Go Away Death, 1941. . . . . . . £125/£20
ditto, Popular Library (U.S.), 1976 (wraps) . . . £5
The Day of Disaster, Long, 1942 . . . £100/£20
Prepare for Action, Stanley Paul, 1942 . . £100/£20
ditto, Popular Library (U.S.), 1975 (wraps) . . . £5
No Darker Crime, Stanley Paul, 1943 . . £75/£15
ditto, Popular Library (U.S.), 1976 (wraps) . . . £5
Dark Peril, Stanley Paul, 1944 . . . . £50/£10
ditto, Popular Library (U.S.), 1975 (wraps) . . . £5
The Peril Ahead, Stanley Paul, 1946 . . . £40/£5
ditto, Popular Library (U.S.), 1974 (wraps) . . . £5
The League of Dark Men, Stanley Paul, 1947 . £30/£5
ditto, Popular Library (U.S.), 1975 (wraps) . . . £5
Department of Death, Evans, 1949 . . . . £30/£5
The Enemy Within, Evans, 1950. . . . . £30/£5
ditto, Popular Library (U.S.), 1977 (wraps) . . . £5
Dead or Alive, Evans, 1951 . . . . . £30/£5
ditto, Popular Library (U.S.), 1974 (wraps) . . . £5
A Kind of Prisoner, Hodder & Stoughton, 1954 £20/£5
ditto, Popular Library (U.S.), 1975 (wraps) . . . £5
The Black Spiders, Hodder & Stoughton, 1957 £20/£5
ditto, Popular Library (U.S.), 1975 (wraps) . . . £5

'Dr Palfrey' Novels
Traitor's Doom, Long, 1942 . . . . . £125/£20
ditto, Walker (U.S.), 1970 . . . . . £20/£5
The Legion of the Lost, Long, 1943 . . . £100/£15
ditto, Daye (U.S.), 1944 . . . . . £100/£15
The Valley of Fear, Long, 1943 . . . . £100/£15
ditto, as **The Perilous Country**, Walker (U.S.), 1973 .
. . . . £20/£5
Dangerous Quest, Long, 1944 . . . . £65/£10
ditto, Walker (U.S.), 1974 . . . . . £15/£5
Death in the Rising Sun, Long, 1945 . . £60/£10
ditto, Walker (U.S.), 1976 . . . . . £15/£5
The Hounds of Vengeance, Long, 1945 . £50/£10
Shadow of Doom, Long, 1946 . . . . £45/£5
The House of the Bears, Long, 1946 . . £45/£5
ditto, Walker (U.S.), 1975 . . . . . £15/£5
Dark Harvest, Long, 1947 . . . . . £35/£5
ditto, Walker (U.S.), 1977 . . . . . £15/£5
Sons of Satan, Long, 1947 . . . . . £35/£5
The Wings of Peace, Long, 1948 . . . £35/£5
ditto, Walker (U.S.), 1978 . . . . . £15/£5
The Dawn of Darkness, Long, 1949. . . . £35/£5
The League of Light, Evans, 1949 . . . £35/£5
The Man Who Shook the World, Evans, 1950 . £35/£5
The Prophet of Fire, Evans, 1951 . . . £30/£5
The Children of Hate, Evans, 1952 . . . £30/£5
ditto, as **The Killers of Innocence**, Walker (U.S.), 1971
. . . . £20/£5
The Touch of Death, Hodder & Stoughton, 1954 . .
. . . . £25/£5
ditto, Walker (U.S.), 1969 . . . . . £20/£5
The Mists of Fear, Hodder & Stoughton, 1955 . £25/£5
ditto, Walker (U.S.), 1977 . . . . . £15/£5
The Flood, Hodder & Stoughton, 1956 . . . £25/£5
ditto, Walker (U.S.), 1969 . . . . . £20/£5

The Plague of Silence, Hodder & Stoughton, 1958 .
. . . . £25/£5
ditto, Walker (U.S.), 1968 . . . . . £20/£5
The Drought, Hodder & Stoughton, 1959 . . £25/£5
ditto, Walker (U.S.), 1967 . . . . . £20/£5
The Terror, Hodder & Stoughton, 1962. . . £20/£5
ditto, Walker (U.S.), 1966 . . . . . £15/£5
The Depths, Hodder & Stoughton, 1963 . . £20/£5
ditto, Walker (U.S.), 1967 . . . . . £20/£5
The Sleep, Hodder & Stoughton, 1964 . . . £20/£5
ditto, Walker (U.S.), 1968 . . . . . £20/£5
The Inferno, Hodder & Stoughton, 1965 . . £20/£5
ditto, Walker (U.S.), 1966 . . . . . £15/£5
The Famine, Hodder & Stoughton, 1967 . . £20/£5
ditto, Walker (U.S.), 1968 . . . . . £20/£5
The Blight, Hodder & Stoughton, 1968 . . £20/£5
ditto, Walker (U.S.), 1968 . . . . . £20/£5
The Oasis, Hodder & Stoughton, 1970 . . . £20/£5
ditto, Walker (U.S.), 1970 . . . . . £20/£5
The Smog, Hodder & Stoughton, 1970 . . . £20/£5
ditto, Walker (U.S.), 1971 . . . . . £20/£5
The Unbegotten, Hodder & Stoughton, 1971 . £20/£5
ditto, Walker (U.S.), 1972 . . . . . £20/£5
The Insulators, Hodder & Stoughton, 1972. . £20/£5
ditto, Walker (U.S.), 1973 . . . . . £20/£5
The Voiceless One, Hodder & Stoughton, 1973 £20/£5
ditto, Walker (U.S.), 1974 . . . . . £20/£5
The Thunder-Maker, Hodder & Stoughton, 1976 .
. . . . £15/£5
ditto, Walker (U.S.), 1976 . . . . . £15/£5
The Whirlwind, Hodder & Stoughton, 1979 . £15/£5

'Sexton Blake' titles
The Case of the Murdered Financier, Amalgamated
Press, 1937 (wraps) £30
The Great Air Swindle, Amalgamated Press, 1939
(wraps) £30
The Man from Fleet Street, Amalgamated Press, 1940
(wraps) £30
The Case of the Mad Inventor, Amalgamated Press,
1942 (wraps) £30
Private Carter's Crime, Amalgamated Press, 1943
(wraps) £30

Other Novels
Seven Times Seven, Melrose, 1932 . . . £350/£50
Men, Maids and Murder, Melrose, 1933 . £300/£45
Four of the Best, Hodder & Stoughton, 1955 . £25/£5
The Mountain of the Blind, Hodder & Stoughton,
1960 . . . . £20/£5
The Foothills of Fear, Hodder & Stoughton, 1961. .
. . . . £20/£5
The Masters of Bow Street, Hodder & Stoughton, 1972
. . . . £20/£5
ditto, Simon & Scuster (U.S.), 1974 . . . £15/£5

Children's Titles
Ned Cartwright, Middleweight Champion, Mellifont,
1935 (pseud. 'James Marsden', wraps) . . £35

The Men Who Died Laughing, D.C. Thomson, 1935
(wraps) £25
The Killer Squad, Newnes, 1936 (wraps) . . £25
Our Glorious Term, Sampson Low, [n.d.] . £175/£25
The Captain of the Fifth, Sampson Low, [n.d.] . .
. . . . £175/£25
Blazing the Air Trail, Sampson Low, 1936 . £175/£25
The Jungle Flight Mystery, Sampson Low, 1936 . .
. . . . £175/£25
The Mystery 'Plane, Sampson Low, 1936 . £175/£25
Murder by Magic, Amalgamated Press, 1937 (wraps) .
. . . . £25
The Mysterious Mr Rocco, Mellifont, 1937 (wraps) .
. . . . £25
The S.O.S. Flight, Sampson Low, 1937. . £150/£25
The Secret Aeroplane, Sampson Low, 1937 £150/£25
The Treasure Flight, Sampson Low, 1937 . £150/£25
The Air Marauders, Sampson Low, 1937 . £150/£25
The Black Biplane, Sampson Low, 1937 . £150/£25
The Mystery Flight, Sampson Low, 1937 . £150/£25
The Double Motive, Mellifont, 1938 . . £150/£25
The Double-Cross of Death, Mellifont, 1938 (wraps) .
. . . . £25
The Missing Hoard, Mellifont, 1938 (wraps) . £25
Mystery at Manby House, North News Syndicate,
1938 (wraps) £25
The Fighting Flyers, Sampson Low, 1938 . £150/£25
The Flying Stowaways, Sampson Low, 1938 £150/£25
The Miracle 'Plane, Sampson Low, 1938 . £150/£25
Dixon Hawke, Secret Agent, D.C. Thomson, 1939
(wraps) £22
Documents of Death, Mellifont, 1939 (wraps) . £20
The Hidden Hoard, Mellifont, 1939 (wraps) . £20
Mottled Death, D.C. Thomson, 1939 (wraps) . £15
The Blue Flyer, Mellifont, 1939 (wraps) . £15
The Jumper, Northern News Syndicate, 1939 (wraps).
. . . . £15
The Mystery of Blackmoor Prison, Mellifont, 1939
(wraps) £15
The Sacred Eye, D.C. Thomson, 1939 . . £150/£25
The Ship of Death, D.C. Thomson, 1939 (wraps) £15
Peril By Air, Newnes, 1939 (wraps) £15
The Flying Turk, Sampson Low, 1939 . . £150/£25
The Monarch of the Skies, Sampson Low, 1939 . .
. . . . £125/£20
The Fear of Felix Corder, Fleetway, [n.d.] (wraps)£10
John Brand, Fugitive, Fleetway, [n.d.] (wraps) £10
The Night of Dread, Fleetway, [n.d.] (wraps) . £10
Dazzle - Air Ace No. 1, Newnes, 1940 (wraps) . £10
Dazzle and the Red Bomber, Newnes, n.d. (wraps) £10
Five Missing Men, Newnes, 1940 (wraps) . . £10
The Poison Gas Robberies, Mellifont, 1940 (wraps) .
. . . . £10
The Cinema Crimes, Pemberton, 1945 (wraps). £10
The Missing Monoplane, Sampson Low, 1947£35/£10

Novels Written as 'J.J. Marric'
Gideon's Day, Hodder & Stoughton, 1955 . £75/£15
ditto, Harper (U.S.), 1955. . . . . . £75/£15

Gideon's Week, Hodder & Stoughton, 1956 . £50/£10
ditto, Harper (U.S.), 1956. . . . . . . £50/£5
Gideon's Night, Hodder & Stoughton, 1957 . £35/£5
ditto, Harper (U.S.), 1957. . . . . . . £35/£5
Gideon's Month, Hodder & Stoughton, 1958 . £35/£5
ditto, Harper (U.S.), 1958. . . . . . . £35/£5
Gideon's Staff, Hodder & Stoughton, 1959. . £25/£5
ditto, Harper (U.S.), 1959. . . . . . . £25/£5
Gideon's Risk, Hodder & Stoughton, 1960 . . £25/£5
ditto, Harper (U.S.), 1960. . . . . . . £25/£5
Gideon's Fire, Hodder & Stoughton, 1961 . . £25/£5
ditto, Harper (U.S.), 1961. . . . . . . £25/£5
Gideon's March, Hodder & Stoughton, 1962 . £20/£5
ditto, Harper (U.S.), 1962. . . . . . . £20/£5
Gideon's Ride, Hodder & Stoughton, 1963 . . £20/£5
ditto, Harper (U.S.), 1963. . . . . . . £20/£5
Gideon's Vote, Hodder & Stoughton, 1964 . . £20/£5
ditto, Harper (U.S.), 1964. . . . . . . £15/£5
Gideon's Lot, Harper (U.S.), 1964 . . . . £20/£5
ditto, Hodder & Stoughton, 1965. . . . £20/£5
Gideon's Badge, Harper (U.S.), 1965 . . . £20/£5
ditto, Hodder & Stoughton, 1966. . . . £20/£5
Gideon's Wrath, Hodder & Stoughton, 1967 . £20/£5
ditto, Harper (U.S.), 1967. . . . . . . £20/£5
Gideon's River, Hodder & Stoughton, 1968 . £20/£5
ditto, Harper (U.S.), 1968. . . . . . . £20/£5
Gideon's Power, Hodder & Stoughton, 1969 . £20/£5
ditto, Harper (U.S.), 1969. . . . . . . £15/£5
Gideon's Sport, Hodder & Stoughton, 1970 . £15/£5
ditto, Harper (U.S.), 1970. . . . . . . £15/£5
Gideon's Art, Hodder & Stoughton, 1971 . . £15/£5
ditto, Harper (U.S.), 1971. . . . . . . £15/£5
Gideon's Men, Hodder & Stoughton, 1972 . . £15/£5
ditto, Harper (U.S.), 1972. . . . . . . £15/£5
Gideon's Press, Hodder & Stoughton, 1973 . £15/£5
ditto, Harper (U.S.), 1973. . . . . . . £15/£5
Gideon's Fog, Hodder & Stoughton, 1975 . . £15/£5
ditto, Harper (U.S.), 1975. . . . . . . £15/£5
Gideon's Drive, Hodder & Stoughton, 1976 . £15/£5
ditto, Harper (U.S.), 1976. . . . . . . £15/£5

Novels Written as 'Anthony Morton'
Meet the Baron, Harrap, 1937 . . . . £300/£35
ditto, Harrap, 1937 (12 presentation copies). . £500
ditto, as *The Man In The Blue Mask*, Lippincott
(U.S.), 1937 . . . . £300/£35
The Baron Returns, Harrap, 1937 . . . £275/£35
ditto, as *The Return of The Blue Mask*, Lippincott
(U.S.), 1937 . . . . £275/£35
The Baron Again, Sampson Low, 1938. . £250/£30
ditto, as *Salute Blue Mask*, Lippincott (U.S.), 1938 .
. . . . £250/£30
The Baron At Bay, Sampson Low, 1938 . £250/£30
ditto, as *Blue Mask at Bay*, Lippincott (U.S.), 1938 .
. . . . £250/£30
Alias the Baron, Sampson Low, 1939 . . £200/£25
ditto, as *Alias Blue Mask*, Lippincott (U.S.), 1939 . .
. . . . £200/£25
The Baron at Large, Sampson Low, 1939 . £175/£25

ditto, as *Challenge Blue Mask!*, Lippincott (U.S.), 1939 . . . . £175/£25
Versus the Baron, Sampson Low, 1940 . . £150/£20
ditto, as **The Blue Mask Strikes Again**, Lippincott (U.S.), 1940 . . . . £150/£20
Call for the Baron, Sampson Low, 1940 . £150/£20
ditto, as **Blue Mask Victorious**, Lippincott (U.S.), 1940
. . . . £150/£20
The Baron Comes Back, Sampson Low, 1943 . . .
. . . . £100/£15
Mr Quentin Investigates, Sampson Low, 1943 £65/£5
Introducing Mr Brandon, Sampson Low, 1944 £65/£5
A Case for the Baron, Sampson Low, 1945 £60/£10
ditto, Duell (U.S.), 1949 . . . . £25/£5
Reward for the Baron, Sampson Low, 1945 £60/£10
Career for the Baron, Sampson Low, 1946. . £45/£5
ditto, Duell (U.S.), 1950 . . . . £25/£5
The Baron and the Beggar, Sampson Low, 1947 .
. . . . £40/£5
ditto, Duell (U.S.), 1950 . . . . . . £25/£5
Blame the Baron, Sampson Low, 1948 . . . £40/£5
ditto, Duell (U.S.), 1951 . . . . . . £25/£5
A Rope for the Baron, Sampson Low, 1948 . £40/£5
ditto, Duell (U.S.), 1949 . . . . . . £35/£5
Books for the Baron, Sampson Low, 1949 . £40/£5
ditto, Duell (U.S.), 1952 . . . . . . £25/£5
Cry for the Baron, Sampson Low, 1950 . £35/£5
ditto, Walker (U.S.), 1970 . . . . . £20/£5
Trap the Baron, Sampson Low, 1950 . . £35/£5
ditto, Walker (U.S.), 1971 . . . . . £15/£5
Attack the Baron, Sampson Low, 1951 . . £35/£5
Shadow the Baron, Sampson Low, 1951 . . £30/£5
Warn the Baron, Sampson Low, 1952 . . £30/£5
The Baron Goes East, Sampson Low, 1953 . £30/£5
The Baron in France, Hodder & Stoughton, 1953 . .
. . . . £30/£5
ditto, Walker (U.S.), 1976 . . . . . £15/£5
Danger for the Baron, Hodder & Stoughton, 1953 .
. . . . £30/£5
ditto, Walker (U.S.), 1974 . . . . . £15/£5
The Baron Goes Fast, Hodder & Stoughton, 1954 . .
. . . . £30/£5
ditto, Walker (U.S.), 1972 . . . . . £15/£5
Nest-Egg for the Baron, Hodder & Stoughton, 1954 .
. . . . £30/£5
ditto, as **Deaf, Dumb and Blonde**, Doubleday (U.S.), 1961 . . . . £20/£5
Help from the Baron, Hodder & Stoughton, 1955 . .
. . . . £30/£5
ditto, Walker (U.S.), 1977 . . . . . £15/£5
Hide the Baron, Hodder & Stoughton, 1956 . £30/£5
ditto, Walker (U.S.), 1978 . . . . . £15/£5
Frame the Baron, Hodder & Stoughton, 1957 . £30/£5
ditto, as **The Double Frame**, Doubleday (U.S.), 1961 .
. . . . £20/£5
Red Eye for the Baron, Hodder & Stoughton, 1958 .
. . . . £30/£5
ditto, as **The Double Frame**, Doubleday (U.S.), 1960 .
. . . . £20/£5

Black for the Baron, Hodder & Stoughton, 1959 . .
. . . . £30/£5
ditto, as **If Anything Happens to Hester**, Doubleday (U.S.), 1962 . . . . £20/£5
Salute for the Baron, Hodder & Stoughton, 1960 . .
. . . . £30/£5
ditto, Walker (U.S.), 1973 . . . . . £15/£5
A Branch for the Baron, Hodder & Stoughton, 1961 .
. . . . £30/£5
ditto, as **The Baron Branches Out**, Scribner's (U.S.), 1967 . . . . £20/£5
Bad for the Baron, Hodder & Stoughton, 1962 £30/£5
ditto, as **The Baron and the Stolen Legacy**, Scribner's (U.S.), 1967 . . . . £20/£5
A Sword for the Baron, Hodder & Stoughton, 1963 .
. . . . £30/£5
ditto, as **The Baron and the Mogul Swords**, Scribner's (U.S.), 1966 . . . . £20/£5
The Baron on Board, Hodder & Stoughton, 1964 . .
. . . . £30/£5
ditto, Walker (U.S.), 1968 . . . . . £15/£5
The Baron and the Chinese Puzzle, Hodder & Stoughton, 1965 . . . . £25/£5
ditto, Scribner's (U.S.), 1966 . . . . . £25/£5
Sport for the Baron, Hodder & Stoughton, 1966 . .
. . . . £25/£5
ditto, Walker (U.S.), 1969 . . . . . £20/£5
Affair for the Baron, Hodder & Stoughton, 1967 . .
. . . . £25/£5
ditto, Walker (U.S.), 1968 . . . . . £20/£5
The Baron and the Missing Old Masters, Hodder & Stoughton, 1968 . . . . £20/£5
ditto, Walker (U.S.), 1969 . . . . . £20/£5
The Baron and the Unfinished Portrait, Hodder & Stoughton, 1969 . . . . £20/£5
ditto, Walker (U.S.), 1970 . . . . . £20/£5
Last Laugh for the Baron, Hodder & Stoughton, 1970
. . . . £15/£5
ditto, Walker (U.S.), 1971 . . . . . £20/£5
The Baron Goes A-Buying, Hodder & Stoughton, 1971 . . . . £15/£5
ditto, Walker (U.S.), 1972 . . . . . £15/£5
The Baron and the Arrogant Artist, Hodder & Stoughton, 1972 . . . . £15/£5
ditto, Walker (U.S.), 1973 . . . . . £15/£5
Burgle the Baron, Hodder & Stoughton, 1973 . £15/£5
ditto, Walker (U.S.), 1974 . . . . . £15/£5
The Baron, King-Maker, Hodder & Stoughton, 1975 .
. . . . £15/£5
ditto, Walker (U.S.), 1975 . . . . . £15/£5
Love for the Baron, Hodder & Stoughton, 1976 . .
. . . . £15/£5

Novels Written as 'Gordon Ashe'
Death on Demand, Long, 1939 . . . £125/£25
The Speaker, Long, 1939 . . . . . £125/£25
ditto, as **The Croaker**, Holt (U.S.), 1973 . £15/£5
Terror by Day, Long, 1940 . . . . £125/£20
Secret Murder, Long, 1940 . . . . £125/£20

Who Was the Jester?, Newnes, 1940 . .	£125/£20
'Ware Danger, Long, 1941	£125/£20
Murder Most Foul, Long, 1942 . . .	£100/£20
There Goes Death, Long, 1942 . . .	£100/£20
Death in High Places, Long, 1942 . .	£100/£20
Death in Flames, Long, 1943 . . .	£75/£15
Two Men Missing, Long, 1943 . . .	£75/£15
Rogues Rampant, Long, 1944 . . .	£50/£10
Death on the Move, Long, 1945 . . .	£50/£10
Invitation to Adventure, Long, 1945 .	£45/£10
Here is Danger, Long, 1946	£40/£5
Give Me Murder, Long, 1947 . . .	£30/£5
Murder Too Late, Long, 1947 . . .	£30/£5
Dark Mystery, Long, 1948	£30/£5
Engagement With Death, Long, 1948 .	£30/£5
A Puzzle in Pearls, Long, 1949 . . .	£30/£5
Kill or Be Killed, Evans, 1949 . . .	£30/£5
The Dark Circle, Evans, 1950 . . .	£30/£5
Murder With Mushrooms, Evans, 1950.	£25/£5
ditto, Holt (U.S.), 1974	£15/£5
Death in Diamonds, Evans, 1951 . .	£25/£5
Missing or Dead?, Evans, 1951 . . .	£25/£5
Death in a Hurry, Evans, 1952 . . .	£25/£5
The Long Search, Evans, 1953 . . .	£25/£5
ditto, as *Drop Dead*, Ace (U.S.), 1954 (wraps) .	£10
Sleepy Death, Evans, 1953	£25/£5
Double for Death, Evans, 1954 . . .	£20/£5
ditto, Holt (U.S.), 1969	£15/£5
Death in the Trees, Evans, 1954. . .	£20/£5
The Kidnapped Child, Evans, 1955 . .	£20/£5
ditto, Holt (U.S.), 1971	£15/£5
The Man Who Stayed Alive, Long, 1955 .	£20/£5
Day of Fear, Long, 1956	£20/£5
ditto, Holt (U.S.), 1978	£15/£5
No Need to Die, Long, 1956	£20/£5
ditto, as *You've Bet Your Life*, Ace (U.S.), 1957 (wraps)	£10
Wait for Death, Long, 1957	£20/£5
ditto, Holt (U.S.), 1972	£15/£5
Come Home to Death, Long, 1958 . .	£20/£5
ditto, as *The Pack of Lies*, Doubleday (U.S.), 1959	£20/£5
Elope to Death, Long, 1959	£20/£5
ditto, Holt (U.S.), 1977	£15/£5
Don't Let Him Kill, Long, 1960 . . .	£15/£5
ditto, as *The Man Who Laughed At Murder*, Doubleday (U.S.), 1960	£15/£5
The Crime Haters, Long, 1961 . . .	£15/£5
ditto, Doubleday (U.S.), 1960 . . .	£15/£5
Rogues Ransome, Long, 1962 . . .	£15/£5
ditto, Doubleday (U.S.), 1961 . . .	£15/£5
Death from Below, Long, 1963 . . .	£15/£5
ditto, Holt (U.S.), 1968	£15/£5
The Big Call, Long, 1964.	£15/£5
ditto, Holt (U.S.), 1975	£15/£5
A Promise of Diamonds, Long, 1965 .	£15/£5
ditto, Dodd (U.S.), 1964	£15/£5
A Taste of Treasure, Long, 1966 . .	£15/£5
ditto, Holt (U.S.), 1966	£15/£5

A Clutch of Coppers, Long, 1967 . . .	£15/£5
ditto, Holt (U.S.), 1969	£15/£5
A Shadow of Death, Long, 1968. . . .	£15/£5
ditto, Holt (U.S.), 1976	£15/£5
A Scream of Murder, Long, 1970 . .	£15/£5
ditto, Holt (U.S.), 1970	£15/£5
A Nest of Traitors, Long, 1970 . . .	£15/£5
ditto, Holt (U.S.), 1971	£15/£5
A Rabble of Rebels, Long, 1971 . . .	£15/£5
ditto, Holt (U.S.), 1972	£15/£5
A Herald of Doom, Long, 1973 . . .	£15/£5
ditto, Holt (U.S.), 1975	£15/£5
A Blast of Trumpets, Long, 1975 . .	£10/£5
ditto, Holt (U.S.), 1976	£10/£5
A Plague of Demons, Long, 1976 . .	£10/£5

Novels Written as M.E. Cooke

Fire of Death, Fiction House, 1934 (wraps) .	£10
The Black Heart, Gramol, 1935 (wraps) .	£10
The Casino Mystery, Mellifont, 1935 (wraps) .	£10
The Crime Gang, Mellifont, 1935 (wraps) . .	£10
The Death Drive, Mellifont, 1935 (wraps) . .	£10
No 1's Last Crime, Fiction House, 1935 (wraps)	£10
The Stolen Formula Mystery, Mellifont, 1935 (wraps)	£10
The Big Radium Mystery, Mellifont, 1936 (wraps)	£10
The Day of Terror, Mellifont, 1936 (wraps) .	£10
The Dummy Robberies, Mellifont, 1936 (wraps)	£10
The Hypnotic Demon, Fiction House, 1936 (wraps) .	£10
The Moat Farm Mystery, Fiction House, 1936 (wraps)	£10
The Secret Formula, Fiction House, 1936 (wraps)	£10
The Successful Alibi, Mellifont, 1936 (wraps) .	£10
The Hadfield Mystery, Mellifont, 1937 (wraps)	£10
The Moving Eye, Mellifont, 1937 (wraps) . .	£10
The Raven, Fiction House, 1937 (wraps) . .	£10
The Mountain Terror, Mellifont, 1939 (wraps)	£10
For Her Sister's Sake, Fiction House, 1938 (wraps)	£10
The Verrall Street Affair, Newnes, 1940 (wraps)	£10

Paperbacks Written as 'Margaret Cooke'

For Love's Sake, Northern News Syndicate, 1934 (wraps)	£5
Troubled Journey, Fiction House, 1937 (wraps)	£5
False Love or True, Northern News Syndicate, 1937 (wraps)	£5
Fate's Playthings, Fiction House, 1938 (wraps) .	£5
Web of Destiny, Fiction House, 1938 (wraps) .	£5
Whose Lover?, Fiction House, 1938 (wraps) .	£5
A Mannequin's Romance, Fiction House, 1938 (wraps)	£5
Love Calls Twice, Fiction House, 1938 (wraps) .	£5
The Road to Happiness, Fiction House, 1938 (wraps).	£5
The Turn of Fate, Fiction House, 1939 (wraps) .	£5
Love Triumphant, Fiction House, 1939 (wraps) .	£5
Love Comes Back, Fiction House, 1939 (wraps) .	£5

Crossroads of Love, Mellifont, 1939 (wraps) . . £5
Love's Journey, Fiction House, 1940 (wraps) . . £5

Novels Written as 'Henry St John Cooper'
The Golconda Necklace, Sampson Low, 1926 £75/£15
The Splendid Love, Sampson Low, 1932 . £50/£10
Dangerous Paths, Sampson Low, 1933 . £50/£10
Call of Love, Sampson Low, 1936 . . . £45/£10
Chains of Love, Sampson Low, 1937 . . .£30/£5
Love's Pilgrim, Sampson Low, 1937 . . .£30/£5
The Tangled Legacy, Sampson Low, 1938 . .£30/£5
The Greater Desire, Sampson Low, 1938 . .£30/£5
Love's Ordeal, Sampson Low, 1939. . . .£25/£5
The Lost Lover, Sampson Low, 1940 . . .£25/£5

Novels Written as 'Norman Deane'
Secret Errand, Hurst & Blackett, 1939 . . £125/£20
ditto, McKay (U.S.), 1974 (as by John Creasey) £15/£5
Dangerous Journey, Hurst & Blackett, 1939 £125/£20
ditto, McKay (U.S.), 1974 (as by John Creasey) £15/£5
Unknown Mystery, Hurst & Blackett, 1940. £125/£20
ditto, McKay (U.S.), 1972 (as by John Creasey) £15/£5
The Withered Man, Hurst & Blackett, 1940 £125/£20
ditto, McKay (U.S.), 1974 (as by John Creasey) £15/£5
I Am the Withered Man, Hurst & Blackett, 1941 . .
. . . . £100/£15
ditto, McKay (U.S.), 1973 (as by John Creasey) £15/£5
Where is the Withered Man?, Hurst & Blackett, 1942.
. . . . £100/£15
ditto, McKay (U.S.), 1974 (as by John Creasey) £15/£5
Return to Adventure, Hurst & Blackett, 1943 £75/£10
Gateway to Escape, Hurst & Blackett, 1944 . .£50/£5
Come Home to Crime, Hurst & Blackett, 1945. £50/£5
Play for Murder, Hurst & Blackett, 1946 . .£40/£5
The Silent House, Hurst & Blackett, 1947 . .£30/£5
Why Murder?, Hurst & Blackett, 1948 . . .£30/£5
Intent to Murder, Hurst & Blackett, 1948 . .£30/£5
The Man I Didn't Kill, Hurst & Blackett, 1950. £30/£5
Double for Death, Hurst & Blackett, 1950 . .£30/£5
Golden Death, Hurst & Blackett, 1952 . . .£25/£5
Look at Murder, Hurst & Blackett, 1952 . .£25/£5
Murder Ahead, Hurst & Blackett, 1953 . . .£25/£5
Death in the Spanish Sun, Hurst & Blackett, 1954 .
. . . .£25/£5
Incense of Death, Hurst & Blackett, 1954 . .£25/£5

Paperbacks Written as 'Elise Felcamps'
Love or Hate?, Fiction House, 1936 (wraps) . £30
True Love, Fiction House, 1937 (wraps) . . £30
Love's Triumph, Fiction House, 1937 (wraps) . £30

Novels Written as 'Robert Caine Frazer'
Kilby Takes a Risk, Pocket (U.S.), 1962 (wraps) £10
R.I.S.C., Collins, 1962 . . . .£20/£5
The Secret Syndicate, Collins, 1963 . . . .£20/£5
The Hollywood Hoax, Collins, 1964 . . .£20/£5
The Miami Mob and *Mark Kilby Stands Alone*,
Collins, 1965 . . . .£15/£5

Paperbacks Written as 'Patrick Gill'
The Fighting Footballers, Mellifont, 1937 (wraps) £25
The Laughing Lightweight, Mellifont, 1937 (wraps) .
. . . . £25
The Battle for the Cup, Mellifont, 1939 (wraps) £25
The Fighting Tramp, Mellifont, 1939 (wraps) . £25
The Mystery of the Centre-Forward, Mellifont, 1939
(wraps) £25
The £10,000 Trophy Race, Mellifont, 1939 (wraps) .
. . . . £25
The Secret Super-Charger, Mellifont, 1940 (wraps) .
. . . . £25

Novels Written as 'Michael Halliday'
Three For Adventure, Cassell, 1937. . . £125/£15
Four Find Danger, Cassell, 1937 . . . £125/£15
Two Meet Trouble, Cassell, 1938 . . . £100/£15
Murder Comes Home, Stanley Paul, 1940 . £65/£10
Heir to Murder, Stanley Paul, 1940 . . . £60/£10
Murder By the Way, Stanley Paul, 1940 . £50/£10
Who Saw Him Die?, Stanley Paul, 1941 . .£50/£5
Foul Play Suspected, Stanley Paul, 1942 . .£50/£5
Who Died at the Grange, Stanley Paul, 1942 .£45/£5
Five to Kill, Stanley Paul, 1943 . . . .£45/£5
Murder at King's Kitchen, Stanley Paul, 1943 .£45/£5
No Crime More Cruel, Stanley Paul, 1944 . .£35/£5
Who Said Murder, Stanley Paul, 1944 . . .£35/£5
Crime With Many Voices, Stanley Paul, 1945 .£35/£5
Murder Makes Murder, Stanley Paul, 1946 .£30/£5
Mystery Motive, Stanley Paul, 1947 . . . .£30/£5
ditto, McKay (U.S.), 1974 (as by Jeremy York) £15/£5
Lend a Hand to Murder, Stanley Paul, 1947 .£30/£5
First a Murder, Stanley Paul, 1948 . . . .£30/£5
ditto, McKay (U.S.), 1972 (as by Jeremy York) £15/£5
No End to Danger, Stanley Paul, 1948 . . .£30/£5
Who Killed Rebecca?, Stanley Paul, 1949 . .£30/£5
The Dying Witness, Evans, 1949. . . . .£30/£5
Dine With Murder, Evans, 1950. . . . .£30/£5
Murder Weekend, Evans, 1950. . . . .£30/£5
Quarrel With Murder, Evans, 1951 . . . .£30/£5
Take a Body, Evans, 1951 . . . . . .£30/£5
ditto, World (U.S.), 1972 (as by John Creasey) . £15/£5
Lame Dog Murder, Evans, 1952. . . . .£30/£5
ditto, World (U.S.), 1972 (as by John Creasey) . £15/£5
Murder in the Stars, Hodder & Stoughton, 1953 . .
. . . .£30/£5
Man on the Run, Hodder & Stoughton, 1953 .£25/£5
ditto, World (U.S.), 1972 (as by John Creasey) . £15/£5
Death out of Darkness, Hodder & Stoughton, 1954 .
. . . .£25/£5
ditto, World (U.S.), 1979 (as by John Creasey) . £15/£5
Out of the Shadows, Hodder & Stoughton, 1954 . .
. . . .£25/£5
ditto, World (U.S.), 1971 (as by John Creasey) £15/£5
Cat and Mouse, Hodder & Stoughton, 1955 . .£25/£5
ditto, as *Hilda, Take Heed*, Scribner's (U.S.), 1957 (as
by Jeremy York) . . . .£20/£5
Murder at End House, Hodder & Stoughton, 1955 .
. . . .£25/£5

Death of a Stranger, Hodder & Stoughton, 1957 . .
. . . . £25/£5
ditto, as *Come Here and Die*, Scribner's (U.S.), 1959
(as by Jeremy York) . . . . £20/£5
Runaway, Hodder & Stoughton, 1957 . . £25/£10
ditto, World (U.S.), 1971 (as by John Creasey). £15/£5
Murder Assured, Hodder & Stoughton, 1958 £25/£10
Missing from Home, Hodder & Stoughton, 1959 . .
. . . . £25/£5
ditto, as *Missing*, Scribner's (U.S.), 1960 (as by Jeremy
York) . . . . £20/£5
Thicker Than Water, Hodder & Stoughton, 1959 . .
. . . . £25/£5
ditto, Doubleday (U.S.), 1962 (as by Jeremy York)
. . . . £20/£5
Go Ahead with Murder, Hodder & Stoughton, 1960 .
. . . . £25/£5
ditto, as *Two For The Money*, Doubleday (U.S.), 1962
(as by Jeremy York) . . . . £20/£5
How Many to Kill?, Hodder & Stoughton, 1960 £25/£5
ditto, as *The Girl With The Leopard-Skin Bag*,
Scribner's (U.S.), 1961 . . . . . . £20/£5
The Edge of Terror, Hodder & Stoughton, 1961 . .
. . . . £25/£5
ditto, Macmillan (U.S.), 1963 (as by Jeremy York). .
. . . . £15/£5
The Man I Killed, Hodder & Stoughton, 1961 . £20/£5
ditto, Macmillan (U.S.), 1963 (as by Jeremy York). .
. . . . £15/£5
Hate to Kill, Hodder & Stoughton, 1962 . £20/£5
The Quiet Fear, Hodder & Stoughton, 1963 . £20/£5
ditto, Macmillan (U.S.), 1968 (as by Jeremy York). .
. . . . £15/£5
The Guilt of Innocence, Hodder & Stoughton, 1964 .
. . . . £20/£5
Cunning as a Fox, Hodder & Stoughton, 1965 £20/£5
ditto, Macmillan (U.S.), 1965 (as by Kyle Hunt)
. . . . £20/£5
Wicked as the Devil, Hodder & Stoughton, 1966 . .
. . . . £20/£5
ditto, Macmillan (U.S.), 1966 (as by Kyle Hunt)
. . . . £20/£5
Sly as a Serpent, Hodder & Stoughton, 1967 . £20/£5
ditto, Macmillan (U.S.), 1967 (as by Kyle Hunt) . .
. . . . £15/£5
Cruel as a Cat, Hodder & Stoughton, 1968 . £20/£5
ditto, Macmillan (U.S.), 1969 (as by Kyle Hunt) . .
. . . . £15/£5
Too Good to be True, Hodder & Stoughton, 1969 . .
. . . . £20/£5
ditto, Macmillan (U.S.), 1969 (as by Kyle Hunt) . .
. . . . £15/£5
A Period of Evil, Hodder & Stoughton, 1970 . £15/£5
ditto, World (U.S.), 1971 (as by Kyle Hunt) . £15/£5
As Lonely as the Damned, Hodder & Stoughton, 1971
. . . . £15/£5
ditto, World (U.S.), 1972 (as by Kyle Hunt) . £15/£5
As Empty as Hate, Hodder & Stoughton, 1972 . £15/£5
ditto, World (U.S.), 1972 (as by Kyle Hunt) . £15/£5

As Merry as Hell, Hodder & Stoughton, 1973 . £15/£5
ditto, World (U.S.), 1974 (as by Kyle Hunt) . £15/£5
This Man Did I Kill?, Hodder & Stoughton, 1974 . .
. . . . £10/£5
ditto, Stein (U.S.), 1974 (as by Kyle Hunt) . £10/£5
The Man Who Was Not Himself, Hodder &
Stoughton, 1976 . . . . £10/£5

Novels Written as 'Kyle Hunt'
Kill Once, Kill Twice, Simon & Schuster (U.S.), 1956.
. . . . £30/£5
ditto, Barker, 1957. . . . . £30/£5
Kill a Wicked Man, Simon & Schuster (U.S.), 1957 .
. . . . £30/£5
ditto, Barker, 1958. . . . . £30/£5
Kill My Love, Simon & Schuster (U.S.), 1958 . £25/£5
ditto, Boardman, 1959. . . . . . . £25/£5
To Kill a Killer, Random House (U.S.), 1960 . £25/£5
ditto, Boardman, 1960. . . . . . . £25/£5

Novels Written as 'Peter Manton'
Murder Manor, Wright & Brown, 1937. . £125/£20
The Greyvale School Mystery, Wright & Brown, 1937
. . . . £125/£20
Stand By For Danger, Wright & Brown, 1937. . .
. . . . £125/£20
The Circle of Justice, Wright & Brown, 1938 . . .
. . . . £100/£15
Three Days' Terror, Wright & Brown, 1938 £100/£15
The Crime Syndicate, Wright & Brown, 1939 £75/£10
Death Looks On, Wright & Brown, 1939 . £65/£10
Murder in the Highlands, Wright & Brown, 1939 . .
. . . . £50/£10
The Midget Marvel, Mellifont, 1940 (wraps) . £25
Policeman's Triumph, Wright & Brown, 1948. £30/£5
Thief in the Night, Wright & Brown, 1950 . . £30/£5
No Escape from Murder, Wright & Brown, 1953 . .
. . . . £25/£5
The Crooked Killer, Wright & Brown, 1954 . £25/£5
The Charity Killers, Wright & Brown, 1954 . £25/£5

Novels Written as 'Richard Martin'
Keys to Crime, Earl, 1947. . . . . . £35/£5
Vote to Murder, Earl, 1948 . . . . . £35/£5
Adrian and Jonathan, Hodder & Stoughton, 1954. .
. . . . £25/£5

Novels Written as 'Jeremy York'
By Persons Unknown, Bles, 1941 . . . £75/£15
Murder Unseen, Bles, 1942 . . . . . £65/£10
No Alibi, Melrose, 1943 . . . . . £50/£10
Murder in the Family, Melrose, 1944 . . £50/£10
ditto, McKay (U.S.), 1976 (as by John Creasey) £15/£5
Yesterday's Murder, Melrose, 1945 . . . . £40/£5
Find the Body, Melrose, 1945 . . . . £40/£5
ditto, Macmillan (U.S.), 1967 . . . . £15/£5
Murder Came Late, Melrose, 1946 . . . £40/£5
ditto, Macmillan (U.S.), 1969 . . . . £15/£5
Run Away To Murder, Melrose, 1947 . . . £35/£5

ditto, Macmillan (U.S.), 1970 . . . . . £15/£5
Let's Kill Uncle Lionel, Melrose, 1947 . . . £35/£5
ditto, McKay (U.S.), 1976 . . . . . . £10/£5
Close the Door on Murder, Melrose, 1948 . . £35/£5
ditto, McKay (U.S.), 1973 . . . . . £10/£5
The Gallows Are Waiting, Melrose, 1949 . . £35/£5
ditto, McKay (U.S.), 1973 . . . . . £10/£5
Death to My Killer, Melrose, 1950 . . . £30/£5
ditto, Macmillan (U.S.), 1966 . . . . £15/£5
Sentence of Death, Melrose, 1950 . . . £30/£5
ditto, Macmillan (U.S.), 1964 . . . . £15/£5
Voyage With Murder, Melrose, 1952 . . £30/£5
Safari With Fear, Melrose, 1953 . . . £25/£5
So Soon to Die, Stanley Paul, 1955 . . . £25/£5
ditto, Scribner's (U.S.), 1957 . . . . . £25/£5
Seeds of Murder, Stanley Paul, 1956 . . £25/£5
ditto, Scribner's (U.S.), 1958 . . . . . £25/£5
Sight of Death, Stanley Paul, 1958 . . . £25/£5
ditto, Scribner's (U.S.), 1959 . . . . . £25/£5
My Brother's Killer, Stanley Paul, 1958 . £25/£5
ditto, Scribner's (U.S.), 1959 . . . . . £25/£5
Hide and Kill, Long, 1959 . . . . . £25/£5
ditto, Scribner's (U.S.), 1960 . . . . . £25/£5
To Kill or to Die, Long, 1960 . . . . £20/£5
ditto, as **To Kill or Die**, Macmillan (U.S.), 1965 £15/£5

Novels Written as 'Ken Ranger'
One Shot Marriott, Sampson Low, 1938 . £125/£20
Roaring Guns, Sampson Low, 1939 . . . £125/£20

Novels Written as 'William K Reilly'
Range War, Stanley Paul, 1939 . . . . £100/£15
Two-Gun Texan, Stanley Paul, 1939 . . £100/£15
Gun Feud, Stanley Paul, 1940 . . . . £100/£15
Stolen Range, Stanley Paul, 1940 . . . £100/£15
War on Lazy K, Stanley Paul, 1941 . . . £75/£10
Outlaw's Vengeance, Stanley Paul, 1941 . £75/£10
Guns Over Blue Lake, Jenkins, 1942 . . £50/£10
Riders of Dry Gulch, Jenkins, 1943 . . . £50/£10
Long John Rides the Range, Jenkins, 1944. . £40/£5
Miracle Range, Jenkins, 1945 . . . . £30/£5
Secret of the Range, Jenkins, 1946 . . . £30/£5
Outlaws Guns, Earl, 1949 . . . . . £25/£5
Range Vengeance, Ward Lock, 1953 . . £20/£5

Novels Written as 'Tex Riley'
Two-Gun Girl, Wright & Brown, 1938 . . £125/£20
Gun-Smoke Range, Wright & Brown, 1938 £125/£20
Gunshot Mesa, Wright & Brown, 1939 . £100/£15
The Shootin' Sheriff, Wright & Brown, 1940 . . .
. . . . £100/£15
Masked Riders, Wright & Brown, 1940. . £100/£15
Rustler's Range, Wright & Brown, 1940 . £100/£15
Death Canyon, Wright & Brown, 1941 . . £75/£10
Guns on the Range, Wright & Brown, 1942 £50/£10
Range Justice, Wright & Brown, 1943 . . £40/£5
Outlaw Hollow, Wright & Brown, 1944. . £40/£5
Hidden Range, Earl, 1946 . . . . . £30/£5
Forgotten Range, Earl, 1947. . . . . £25/£5

Trigger Justice, Earl, 1948 . . . . . £25/£5
Lynch Hollow, Earl, 1949 . . . . . £25/£5

Other Pseudonymous Fiction
The Dark Shadow, Fiction House, [n.d.] (pseud.
'Rodney Mattheson', wraps) £25
The House of Ferrars, Fiction House, [n.d.] (pseud.
'Rodney Mattheson', wraps) £25
Four Motives for Murder, Newnes, 1938 (pseud.
'Brian Hope', wraps) £25
Triple Murder, Newnes, 1940 (pseud. 'Colin Hughes',
wraps) £20
Murder on Largo Island, Selwyn & Blount, 1944
(pseud. 'Charles Hogarth', with Ian Bowen) £40/£10
Danger Woman, Pocket Books (U.S.), 1966 (pseud.
'Abel Mann', wraps) £10

Non Fiction
Fighting Was My Business, by Jimmy Wilde, Joseph,
1935 (ghosted by Creasey) . . . . £75/£15
Log of a Merchant Airman, Stanley Paul, 1943 (with
John H. Lock) . . . . £50/£10
**Heroes of the Air: A Tribute to the Courage, Sacrifice
end Skill of the Men of the R.A.F.**, Dorset Wings for
Victory Committee, 1943 (wraps) £15
**The Printer's Devil: An Account of the History and
Objects of the Printers' Pension, Almshouse and
Orphan Asylum Corporation**, Hutchinson, 1943
(with Walter Hutchinson) . . . . £45/£10
Man in Danger, Stanley Paul, 1950 (pseud. 'Credo',
wraps) £10
Round the World in 465 Days, Hale, 1953 (with Jean
Creasey) . . . . £25/£10
Let's Look at America, Hale, 1956 (with Jean Creasey)
. . . . £25/£10
**They Didn't Mean to Kill: The Real Story of Road
Accidents**, Hodder & Stoughton, 1960. . . £15/£5
Optimists in Africa, Timmins, 1963 (with Jean, Martin
and Richard Creasey) . . . . . . £20/£5
African Holiday, Timmins, 1963 . . . . £20/£5
**Good, God and Man: An Outline of the Philosophy of
Selfism**, Hodder & Stoughton, 1967 . . £25/£5
Evolution to Democracy, Hodder & Stoughton, 1969 .
. . . . £15/£5

MICHAEL CRICHTON
(b.1942)

An author whose interest in science and its effects on
society is at the fore in his most successful work,
Jurassic Park.

Novels
The Andromeda Strain, Knopf (U.S.), 1969 £100/£20
ditto, Cape, 1969 . . . . £75/£15
The Terminal Man, Knopf (U.S.), 1972 . £75/£20
ditto, Cape, 1972 . . . . £65/£20

The Great Train Robbery, Knopf (U.S.), 1975 £50/£10
ditto, Cape, 1975 . . . . £45/£10
Eaters of the Dead, Knopf (U.S.), 1976 . . £40/£10
ditto, Cape, 1976 . . . . £40/£10
Congo, Knopf (U.S.), 1980 . . . . . £35/£10
ditto, Allen Lane, 1981 . . . . . . £35/£10
Sphere, Knopf (U.S.), 1987 . . . . . £25/£10
ditto, Macmillan, 1987 . . . . . . £25/£10
Jurassic Park, Knopf (U.S.), 1990 . . . £60/£10
ditto, Franklin Library (U.S.), 1990 (signed, limited edition) £250
ditto, Century, 1991 . . . . £50/£10
Rising Sun, Knopf (U.S.), 1992 . . . . . £15/£5
ditto, Century, 1992 . . . . £15/£5
Disclosure, Franklin Library (U.S.), 1993 (signed, limited edition) £60
ditto, Knopf (U.S.), 1994 . . . . £15/£5
ditto, Century, 1994 . . . . £15/£5
The Lost World, Knopf (U.S.), 1995 . . £15/£5
ditto, Century, 1995 . . . . £15/£5
Airframe, Knopf (U.S.), 1996 . . . . . £15/£5
ditto, Knopf (U.S.), 1996 (50 signed deluxe copies of 250, aluminium slipcase) . . . . . £200/£150
ditto, Knopf (U.S.), 1996 (200 signed copies of 250, slipcase) . . . . £75/£50
ditto, Franklin Library (U.S.), 1996 (signed, limited edition) £60
ditto, Century, 1996 . . . . £15/£5
Timeline, Knopf (U.S.), 1999 . . . . £15/£5
ditto, Franklin Library (U.S.), 1999 (signed, limited edition) £80
ditto, Century, 1999 . . . . £15/£5
Prey, Knopf (U.S.), 2002 . . . . £15/£5
ditto, Harper Collins, 2002 . . . . . . £15/£5

Novels Written as 'John Lange'
Odds On, New American Library/Signet (U.S.), 1966 (wraps) £150
Scratch One, New American Library/Signet (U.S.), 1967 (wraps) £65
Easy Go, New American Library/Signet (U.S.), 1968 (wraps) £65
ditto, Sphere, 1972 (wraps) £5
ditto, as *The Last Tomb*, Bantam (U.S.), 1974 (by Michael Crichton, wraps) £5
The Venom Business, World (U.S.), 1969 . £90/£25
Zero Cool, New American Library/Signet (U.S.), 1969 (wraps) £50
ditto, Sphere, 1972 (wraps) £5
Grave Descend, New American Library/Signet (U.S.), 1970 (wraps) £50
Drug of Choice, New American Library/Signet (U.S.), 1970 (wraps) £40
ditto, as *Overkill*, Sphere, 1972 (wraps) . . . £5
Binary, Knopf (U.S.), 1972 . . . . . £40/£10
ditto, Heinemann, 1972 . . . . . £40/£10

Novels Written as 'Jeffery Hudson'
A Case of Need, World (U.S.), 1968. . . . £50/£10
ditto, Heinemann, 1968 . . . . . . £50/£10

Novels Written as 'Michael Douglas'
Dealing, Knopf (U.S.), 1971 . . . . . £60/£10
ditto, Talmy Franklin, 1971 . . . . . £50/£10

Screenplays
Westworld, Bantam (U.S.), 1974 (wraps) . . £10

Non Fiction
Five Patients: The Hospital Explained, Knopf (U.S.), 1970 . . . . £60/£15
ditto, Cape, 1971 . . . . £50/£10
Jasper Johns, Abrams (U.S.), 1977 . . . £50/£20
ditto, Thames & Hudson, 1977 . . . . £45/£20
Electronic Life: How to Think About Computers, Knopf (U.S.), 1983 . . . . £50/£15
ditto, Heinemann, 1983 . . . . . . £40/£10
Travels, Knopf (U.S.), 1988 . . . . . £40/£10
ditto, Franklin Library (U.S.), 1988 (signed, limited edition) £50
ditto, Macmillan, 1988 . . . . £25/£5

EDMUND CRISPIN
(b.1921 d.1978)

Successful author of detective fiction. He was also a prolific editor of detective and science fiction anthologies.

Novels
The Case of the Gilded Fly, Gollancz, 1944 £500/£75
ditto, as *Obsequies at Oxford*, Lippincott (U.S.), 1945. . . . . £150/£45
Holy Disorders, Gollancz, 1946 . . . . £250/£25
ditto, Lippincott (U.S.), 1946 . . . . £150/£20
The Moving Toyshop, Gollancz, 1946 . £125/£20
ditto, Lippincott (U.S.), 1946 . . . . £125/£20
Swan Song, Gollancz, 1947 . . . . . £100/£20
ditto, as *Dead and Dumb*, Lippincott (U.S.), 1947 . . . . £75/£20
Love Lies Bleeding, Gollancz, 1948 . . . £75/£20
ditto, Lippincott (U.S.), 1948 . . . . . £50/£15
Buried for Pleasure, Gollancz, 1948 . . £75/£20
ditto, Lippincott (U.S.), 1948 . . . . . £50/£15
Frequent Hearses, Gollancz, 1950 . . . £75/£15
ditto, as *Sudden Vengeance*, Dodd, Mead (U.S.), 1950 . . . . £50/£10
The Long Divorce, Gollancz, 1951 . . £75/£15
ditto, Dodd, Mead (U.S.), 1951 . . . . £40/£10
ditto, as *A Noose for Her*, Spivak, 1952. . £40/£10
The Glimpses of the Moon, Gollancz, 1977 £25/£10
ditto, Walker (U.S.), 1978 . . . . . . £10/£5

Short Stories
Beware of the Trains: 16 Stories, Gollancz, 1953 . .
. . . . £75/£15
ditto, Walker (U.S.), 1962 . . . . . £40/£10
Fen Country: 26 stories, Gollancz, 1979 . £30/£10
ditto, Walker (U.S.), 1979 . . . . . £25/£10

FREEMAN WILLS CROFTS
(b.1879 d.1957)

Crofts is acknowledged as one of the first authors of detective fiction to methodically use police procedure.

'Inspector French' Novels
Inspector French's Greatest Case, Collins, 1924 . .
. . . . £1,250/£200
ditto, Seltzer (U.S.), 1925. . . . . . £600/£75
Inspector French and the Cheyne Mystery, Collins, 1926 . . . . £1,000/£150
ditto, as *The Cheyne Mystery*, Boni (U.S.), 1926 . .
. . . . £600/£75
Inspector French and the Starvel Tragedy, Collins, 1927 . . . . £1,000/£150
ditto, as *The Starvel Hollow Tragedy*, Harper (U.S.), 1927 . . . . £500/£75
The Sea Mystery, Collins, 1928 . . . £1,000/£150
ditto, Harper (U.S.), 1928. . . . . . £500/£75
The Box Office Murders, Collins, 1929 . £1,000/£150
ditto, as *The Purple Sickle Murders*, Harper (U.S.), 1929 . . . . £300/£45
Sir John Magill's Last Journey, Collins Crime Club, 1930 . . . . £1,000/£150
ditto, Harper (U.S.), 1930. . . . . . £300/£45
Mystery in the Channel, Crime Club, 1931 . . . .
. . . . £1,000/£150
ditto, as **Mystery in the English Channel**, Harper (U.S.),1931 . . . . £300/£45
Sudden Death, Crime Club, 1932 . . £1,000/£150
ditto, Harper (U.S.), 1932. . . . . . £300/£45
Death on the Way, Crime Club, 1932 . £1,000/£150
ditto, as *Double Death*, Harper (U.S.), 1932 £300/£45
The Hog's Back Mystery, Hodder & Stoughton, 1933. .
. . . . £1,000/£150
ditto, as *The Strange Case of Dr Earle*, Dodd, Mead (U.S.), 1933 . . . . £300/£45
The 12.30 from Croydon, Hodder & Stoughton, 1934 .
. . . . £1,000/£150
ditto, as *Wilful and Premeditated*, Dodd (U.S.), 1934 .
. . . . £300/£45
Mystery on Southampton Water, Hodder & Stoughton, 1934 . . . . £1,000/£150
ditto, as *Crime on the Solent*, Dodd (U.S.), 1934 . .
. . . . £300/£45
Crime at Guildford, Crime Club, 1935 . £1,000/£150
ditto, as *The Crime at Nornes*, Dodd (U.S.), 1935 . .
. . . . £300/£45

The Loss of the 'Jane Vosper', Crime Club, 1936 . .
. . . . £1,000/£150
ditto, Dodd (U.S.), 1936 . . . . . . £300/£45
Man Overboard!, Crime Club, 1936. . £1,000/£150
ditto, Dodd (U.S.), 1936 . . . . . . £300/£45
ditto, as *Cold-Blooded Murder*, Avon, 1947 (abridged, wraps). £20
Found Floating, Hodder & Stoughton, 1937 £850/£85
ditto, Dodd (U.S.), 1937 . . . . . . £300/£45
The End of Andrew Harrison, Hodder & Stoughton, 1938 . . . . £850/£85
ditto, as *The Futile Alibi*, Dodd (U.S.), 1938 £300/£50
Antidote to Venom Hodder & Stoughton, 1938. . .
. . . . £850/£85
ditto, Dodd (U.S.), 1939 . . . . . . £300/£50
Fatal Venture, Hodder & Stoughton, 1939 . £850/£85
ditto, as *Tragedy in the Hollow*, Dodd (U.S.), 1939 .
. . . . £300/£50
Golden Ashes, Hodder & Stoughton, 1940 . £850/£85
ditto, Dodd (U.S.), 1940 . . . . . . £300/£50
James Tarrant, Adventurer, Hodder & Stoughton, 1941 . . . . £850/£85
ditto, as *Circumstantial Evidence*, Dodd (U.S.), 1941
. . . . £300/£50
The Losing Game, Hodder & Stoughton, 1941 . . .
. . . . £600/£60
ditto, as *A Losing Game*, Dodd (U.S.), 1941 £350/£50
Fear Comes to Chalfont, Hodder & Stoughton, 1942 .
. . . . £400/£40
ditto, Dodd (U.S.), 1942 . . . . . . £250/£25
The Affair at Little Wokeham, Hodder & Stoughton, 1943 . . . . £350/£50
ditto, as *Double Tragedy*, Dodd (U.S.), 1943 £250/£25
Enemy Unseen, Hodder & Stoughton, 1945 £200/£25
ditto, Dodd (U.S.), 1945 . . . . . . £175/£25
Death of a Train, Hodder & Stoughton, 1946 . . .
. . . . £125/£20
ditto, Dodd (U.S.), 1947 . . . . . . £100/£20
Silence for the Murderer, Dodd (U.S.), 1948 £175/£25
ditto, Hodder & Stoughton, 1949. . . . £200/£25
Dark Journey, Dodd (U.S.), 1951 . . . £175/£25
ditto, as *French Strikes Oil*, Hodder & Stoughton, 1952 . . . . £200/£25
Anything to Declare?, Hodder & Stoughton, 1957. .
. . . . £200/£25

'Inspector French' Novel for Children
Young Robin Brand, Detective, U.L.P., 1947 £75/£25
ditto, Dodd (U.S.), 1948 . . . . . £50/£15

Other Novels
The Cask, Collins, 1920 . . . . . £3,000/£600
ditto, Seltzer (U.S.), 1924. . . . . . £750/£75
The Ponson Case, Collins, 1921 . . . £1,500/£200
ditto, Boni (U.S.), 1927 . . . . . . £750/£75
The Pit-Prop Syndicate, Collins, 1922 . £1,500/£200
ditto, Seltzer (U.S.), 1925. . . . . . £750/£75
The Groote Park Murder, Collins, 1923 £1,250/£125
ditto, Seltzer (U.S.), 1925. . . . . . £750/£75

Short Stories
The Hunt Ball Murder, Todd 1943 (wraps) . £300
Mr. Sefton, Murderer, Vallancey Press, 1944 (wraps).
. . . . £300
Murderers Make Mistakes, Hodder & Stoughton, 1947
. . . . £250/£25
Many a Slip, Hodder & Stoughton, 1955 . £300/£25
The Mystery of the Sleeping Car Express, Hodder &
Stoughton, 1956 . . . . £300/£25

RICHMAL CROMPTON
(b.1890 d.1969)

Richmal Crompton Lamburn began writing short
stories for magazines whilst working as a teacher.
When these stories were first collected together the
resultant *Just William* was an immediate success.

'William' Titles
Just William, Newnes, [1922] . . . £1,750/£200
More William, Newnes, 1922 . . . . £750/£125
William Again, Newnes, 1923 . . . . £500/£75
William the Fourth, Newnes, 1924 . . . £400/£75
Still William, Newnes, 1925 . . . . . £350/£65
William the Conqueror, Newnes, 1926 . . £350/£65
William the Outlaw, Newnes, 1927 . . . £350/£65
William in Trouble, Newnes, 1927 . . . £350/£65
William the Good, Newnes, 1928 . . . £350/£65
William, Newnes, 1929 . . . . . £450/£75
William the Bad, Newnes, 1930 . . . . £450/£75
William's Happy Days, Newnes, 1930 . . £450/£75
William's Crowded Hours, Newnes, 1931 . £450/£75
William the Pirate, Newnes, 1932 . . . £450/£75
William the Rebel, Newnes, 1933 . . . £450/£75
William the Gangster, Newnes, 1934 . . £450/£75
William the Detective, Newnes, 1935 . . £450/£75
Sweet William, Newnes, 1936 . . . . £400/£65
William the Showman, Newnes, 1937 . . £400/£65
William the Dictator, Newnes, 1938. . . £400/£65
William and A.R.P., Newnes, 1939 (title later changed
to *William's Bad Resolution*) . . . £350/£50
William and the Evacuees, Newnes, 1940 (title later
changed to *William the Film Star*) . . £650/£125
William Does His Bit, Newnes, 1941 . £400/£65
William Carries On, Newnes, 1941 . . . £300/£50
William and the Brains Trust, Newnes, 1945 . . .
. . . . £165/£45
Just William's Luck, Newnes, 1948. . . £100/£20
William the Bold, Newnes, 1950. . . . £100/£20
William and the Tramp, Newnes, 1952 . . £100/£20
William and the Moon Rocket, Newnes, 1954 . . .
. . . . £100/£20
William and the Space Animal, Newnes, 1956. . .
. . . . £100/£20
William's Television Show, Newnes, 1958 . £125/£30
William the Explorer, Newnes, 1960 . . £150/£35
William's Treasure Trove, Newnes, 1962 . £125/£30

William and the Witch, Newnes, 1964 . . £150/£35
William and the Ancient Briton, Mayfair, 1965 . .
. . . . £25/£5
William and the Monster, Mayfair, 1965 . £25/£5
William the Globetrotter, Mayfair, 1965 . £25/£5
William the Cannibal, Mayfair, 1965 . . .£25/£5
William and the Pop Singers, Newnes, 1965 £150/£35
William and the Masked Ranger, Newnes, 1966 . .
. . . . £150/£35
William the Superman, Newnes, 1968 . . £275/£65
William the Lawless, Newnes, 1970 . . . £850/£250

Adult Novels
The Innermost Room, Melrose, 1923 . . £250/£50
The Hidden Light, Hodder & Stoughton, [1924] . .
. . . . £175/£35
Anne Morrison, Jarrolds, 1925 . . . . £175/£35
The Wildings, Hodder & Stoughton, [1925] £150/£30
David Wilding, Hodder & Stoughton, [1926] £150/£30
The House, Hodder & Stoughton, [1926] . £200/£35
ditto, as *Dread Dwelling*, Boni & Liveright (U.S.),
1926 . . . . £200/£35
Millicent Dorrington, Hodder & Stoughton, [1927] .
. . . . £125/£25
Leadon Hill, Hodder & Stoughton, [1927] . £125/£25
The Thorn Bush, Hodder & Stoughton, [1928] . .
. . . . £125/£25
Roofs Off!, Hodder & Stoughton, [1928] . £100/£20
The Four Graces, Hodder & Stoughton, [1929] . .
. . . . £175/£35
Abbot's End, Hodder & Stoughton, [1929] . £175/£35
Blue Flames, Hodder & Stoughton, [1930] . £100/£20
Naomi Godstone, Hodder & Stoughton, [1930] . .
. . . . £100/£20
Portrait of a Family, Macmillan, 1931 . . £100/£20
The Odyssey of Euphemia Tracy, Macmillan, 1932 .
. . . . £100/£20
Marriage of Hermione, Macmillan, 1932 . £65/£20
The Holiday, Macmillan, 1933 . . . . £65/£20
Chedsy Place, Macmillan, 1934 . . . . £65/£20
The Old Man's Birthday, Macmillan, 1934. £65/£20
Quartet, Macmillan, 1935 . . . . . £65/£20
Caroline, Macmillan, 1936 . . . . . £65/£20
There are Four Seasons, Macmillan, 1937 . £50/£15
Journeying Wave, Macmillan, 1938. . . £65/£20
Merlin Bay, Macmillan, 1939 . . . . £65/£20
Steffan Green, Macmillan, 1940. . . . £65/£20
Narcissa, Macmillan, 1941 . . . . . £65/£20
Mrs Frensham Describes a Circle, Macmillan, 1942 .
. . . . £45/£15
Weatherley Parade, Macmillan, 1943 . . .£25/£5
Westover, Hutchinson, [1946] . . . . .£25/£5
The Ridleys, Hutchinson, [1947]. . . . .£25/£5
Family Roundabout, Hutchinson, [1948] . .£25/£5
Frost at Morning, Hutchinson, 1950 . . .£25/£5
Linden Rise, Hutchinson, 1952 . . . . .£25/£5
The Gypsy's Baby, Hutchinson, 1954 . . £50/£15
Four in Exile, Hutchinson, 1955. . . . .£30/£5
Matty and the Dearingroydes, Hutchinson, 1956 . .
. . . .£25/£5

Blind Man's Buff, Hutchinson, 1957 . . . £25/£5
Wiseman's Folly, Hutchinson, 1959. . . . £25/£5
The Inheritor, Hutchinson, 1960. . . . . £15/£5

Adult Short Stories
Kathleen and I, and, Of Course, Veronica, Hodder &
Stoughton, [1926] . . . . £125/£25
Enter—Patricia, Newnes, [1927] . . . £65/£15
A Monstrous Regiment, Hutchinson, [1927] £150/£40
Mist and Other Stories, Hutchinson, [1928] £200/£45
The Middle Things, Hutchinson, [1928] . £175/£45
Felicity Stands By, Newnes, [1928] . . . £100/£25
Sugar and Spice, Ward Lock, 1929 . . . £100/£25
Ladies First, Hutchinson, [1929]. . . . £175/£45
The Silver Birch, Hutchinson, [1931] . . £175/£45
The First Morning, Hutchinson, [1936]. . £175/£45

HARRY CROSBY
(b.1898 d.1929)

A short-lived American poet whose ambition
exceeded his ability, but whose self-published
volumes are things of great beauty.

Sonnets for Caresse, Herbert Clarke (Paris), 1925 (17
copies) £3,000
ditto, Herbert Clarke (Paris), 1926 (second edition, 27
copies) £2,000
ditto, Albert Messein (Paris), 1926 (third edition, 108
copies) £750
ditto, Editions Narcisse (Paris), 1927 (fourth edition, 44
copies) £750
Red Skeletons, Editions Narcisse (Paris), 1927 (370
copies, illustrated by Alastair) £1,250
Chariot of the Sun, At the Sign of the Sundial (Paris),
1928 (48 copies) £1,500
Shadows of the Sun, The Black Sun Press (Paris),
1928 (44 copies) £1,500
ditto, Second Series, The Black Sun Press (Paris), 1929
(44 copies) £1,500
ditto, Third Series, The Black Sun Press (Paris), 1930
(44 copies) £1,500
ditto, Black Sparrow Press (U.S.), 1977 (acetate d/w) .
. . . . £50/£45
ditto, Black Sparrow Press (U.S.), 1977 (200 numbered
copies) . . . . £100/£75
ditto, Black Sparrow Press (U.S.), 1977 (wraps) £15
Transit of Venus, The Black Sun Press (Paris), 1928
(44 copies) £1,500
ditto, The Black Sun Press (Paris), 1929 (200 copies) .
. . . . £200
Mad Queen: Tirades, The Black Sun Press (Paris),
1928 (141 copies, printed wrappers and glassine in
gold foil folder with ties) . . . . £1,000/£750
Six Poems, Latterday Pamphlets (U.S.), 1928 (225
copies, wraps) £400

The Sun, The Black Sun Press (Paris), 1929 (100
copies) £1,000
Sleeping Together, The Black Sun Press (Paris), 1929
(77 copies) £1,250
Aphrodite in Flight, The Black Sun Press (Paris), 1930
(27 copies) £2,000
The Collected Poems, Black Sun Press (Paris), 1931
(500 copies, 4 vols in box: *Chariot of the Sun*,
Introduction by D.H. Lawrence, *Transit of Venus*,
With a Preface by T.S. Eliot, *Sleeping Together*, With
a Memory of the Poet by Stuart Gilbert, *Torchbearer*,
With Notes by Ezra Pound) £1,000
War Letters, The Black Sun Press (Paris), 1932 (as
Henry Grew Crosby, 125 copies, preface by Henrietta
Crosby) £600
Shadows of the Sun: The Diaries of Harry Crosby,
Black Sparrow (U.S.), 1977 (edited by Edward
Germain, 200 numbered copies) £100
ditto, Black Sparrow (U.S.), 1977 (1,300 hardback
copies, acetate jacket) . . . . . . £65/£50
ditto, Black Sparrow (U.S.), 1977 (wraps) . . £10
Devour the Fire, Twowindows Press (U.S.), 1983 (200
numbered copies) £100

As Editor
Anthology, Maurice Darantiere (Paris), 1924 (edited by
'Henry Grew Crosby') £500
*47 Unpublished Letters From Marcel Proust to Walter
Berry*, Black Sun Press (Paris), 1930 (edited and
translated by Harry and Caresse Crosby, 50 numbered
copies on Japon, wraps). £300
ditto, Black Sun Press (Paris), 1930 (200 numbered
copies on velin d'Arches, wraps) £200

ALEISTER CROWLEY
(b.1875 d.1947)

Notorious British occultist and author of interminable
magical works. The special copies on Japanese
vellum etc were usually for presentation and will vary
in value depending upon whom they were inscribed
to.

Poetry
Aceldama, A Place to Bury Strangers In, privately
printed by Leonard Smithers, 1898 (88 copies, pseud.
'a gentleman of the University of Cambridge', wraps)
. . . . £700
ditto, privately printed by Leonard Smithers, 1898 (10
large paper copies, pseud. 'a gentleman of the
University of Cambridge', wraps) . . . £2,250
The Tale of Archais: a Romance in Verse, Kegan Paul
& Co, 1898 (250 copies, pseud. 'a gentleman of the
University of Cambridge') £350
Jezebel, privately printed, 1898 (40 copies, wraps). .
. . . . £400

ditto, privately printed, 1898 (10 copies on Japanese vellum, wraps) £2,250

Songs of the Spirit, Kegan Paul & Co, 1898 (200 copies) £300

ditto, Kegan Paul & Co, 1898 (50 signed, numbered copies) £850

Jephthah, and other mysteries, lyrical and dramatic, Kegan Paul & Co, 1899 . . . . . . £300

An Appeal to the American Republic, Kegan Paul & Co, 1899 (500 copies, wraps) £150

The Mother's Tragedy, privately printed, 1901 (500 copies) £225

The Soul of Osiris, Kegan Paul & Co, 1901 (500 copies) £350

ditto, Kegan Paul & Co, 1901 (6 copies on india paper) £1,750

Carmen Saeculare, Kegan Paul & Co, 1901 (450 copies, pseud. 'St. E. A. of M. and S', wraps) . £200

Tannhäuser, Kegan Paul & Co, 1902 . . £225

The God-Eater, A Tragedy of Satire, Watts & Co, 1903 (300 copies, wraps) £200

Summa Spes, privately printed, 1903 . . . £225

Ahab and Other Poems, privately printed at the Chiswick Press, 1903 (150 copies) £500

ditto, privately printed at the Chiswick Press, 1903 (10 copies on Japanese vellum) £1,500

ditto, privately printed at the Chiswick Press, 1903 (2 copies on vellum) £2,500

Alice: an Adultery, privately printed, 1903 (100 copies, wraps). £350

The Star and the Garter, Watts & Co, 1903 (50 copies, wraps). £400

The Sword of Song, Society for the Propagation of Religious Truth, 1904 (100 copies, wraps). . £400

The Argonauts, Society for the Propagation of Religious Truth, 1904 (200 copies, wraps). £250

In Residence: The Don's Guide to Cambridge, Elijah Johnson, 1904 (wraps) £250

Why Jesus Wept, A study of society and of the grace of God, privately printed, 1904 (wraps) . £225

Oracles, The Biography of an Art, Society for the Propagation of Religious Truth, 1905 (wraps). £350

Orpheus, A Lyrical Legend, Society for the Propagation of Religious Truth, 1905 (2 vols, various coloured boards) £400

Rosa Mundi, A poem, Renouard (Paris), 1905 (pseud. 'H.D. Carr') £225

Collected Works of Aleister Crowley, Society for the Propagation of Religious Truth, 1905, 1906 & 1907 (3 vols, wraps) £600

ditto, Society for the Propagation of Religious Truth, 1907 (1 vol.) £500

Gargoyles: being strangely wrought images of life and death, Society for the Propagation of Religious Truth, 1906 (300 copies) £200

ditto, Society for the Propagation of Religious Truth, 1906 (50 copies on handmade paper) . . . £450

Rosa Coeli, Chiswick Press, 1907 (pseud. 'H.D. Carr') £275

Rosa Inferni, Chiswick Press, 1907 (pseud. 'H.D. Carr') £275

Rodin in Rhyme, Seven Lithographs by Clot from the Water-Colours of Auguste Rodin, with a chaplet of verse by Aleister Crowley, privately printed at the Chiswick Press, 1907 (488 copies). . . . £400

Amphora, privately printed, 1908 . . . £600

ditto, Burns & Oates: London, 1908 . . . . £500

Hail Mary, Wieland & Co, [1911] £225

Clouds Without Water, 'Privately printed for circulation among ministers of religion', 1909 (pseud. 'the Rev. C. Verey', wraps). £275

The World's Tragedy, privately printed (Paris), 1910 (100 copies) £350

The Winged Beetle, privately printed, 1910 (50 signed copies) £600

ditto, privately printed, 1910 (250 unsigned copies) £350

Ambergris, Elkin Mathews, 1910 . . . £125

The High History of Good Sir Palamedes..., Wieland & Co., 1912 . . . . £100

Household Gods, A Comedy, privately printed, 1912 . . . . £150

Chicago May, privately printed (New York), 1914. . . . . £850

Songs for Italy, privately printed, 1923 (single folded sheet) £75

England, Stand Fast!, privately issued by the O.T.O., 1939 (single sheet folded) £100

Temperance, A Tract for the Times, privately issued by the O.T.O., 1939 (100 copies, wraps) . . £250

Thumbs up! A Pentagram-a Pentacle to Win the War, O.T.O., 1941 (100 copies, wraps) . . . £250

La Gauloise-Song of the Fighting French, privately printed, 1942 (single sheet folded) £75

Fun of the Fair, O.T.O., 1942 (containing errata slip and mimeographed poem 'Landed gentry') . £275

The City of God, A Rhapsody, O.T.O., 1943 (wraps, 200 copies) £275

Olla, An Anthology of Sixty Years of Song, etc., O.T.O., [1946] (500 copies). . . . . £350/£200

ditto, O.T.O., [1946] (20 copies on handmade paper) £750

Novels, Plays etc

Mortadello, or the Angel of Venice, Wieland & Co, 1912 . . . . £100

The Diary of a Drug Fiend, Collins, 1922 £2,000/£200

ditto, Dutton (U.S.), 1923. . . . . £1,000/£150

Moonchild: A Prologue, Mandrake Press, 1929 . . . . £350/£125

The Stratagem and Other Stories, Mandrake Press, [1929]. £125/175

ditto, Temple Press, 1990. . . . . . £30/£15

Erotica

White Stains, privately printed (Amsterdam), 1898 (100 copies on handmade paper, pseud. 'George Archibald Bishop') £3,250

Snowdrops From A Curate's Garden, privately printed (Paris), [c.1904] £2,250

Bagh-I-Muattar, The Scented Garden of Abdullah the Satirist of Shiraz, privately printed, 1910 (100 copies, pseud. 'the late Major Lutiy and another', wraps). £1,750

Magical Titles

Berashith – An Essay in Ontology with some remarks on Ceremonial Magic by Abhavananda, privately printed for the Sangha of the West (Paris), 1903 (200 copies, pseud. 'Abhavananda', wraps). . . . £275

The Book of the Goetia of Solomon the King, Society for the Propagation of Religious Truth, 1904 ('Translated into the English tongue by a dead hand etc', 200 copies) £400

ditto, Society for the Propagation of Religious Truth, 1904 (10 copies on Japanese vellum) . . . £850

Konx om Pax, Essays in Light, Walter Scott Publishing Co. for The Society for the Propagation of Religious Truth, 1907 (500 copies on handmade paper). £600

ditto, Walter Scott Publishing Co. for The Society for the Propagation of Religious Truth, 1907 (10 copies on Japanese vellum) £1,250

777, Walter Scott Publishing Co. for The Society for the Propagation of Religious Truth, 1909 (500 copies on handmade paper) £1,500

The Rites of Eleusis, [The Equinox:], [1910] (wraps) £100

The Holy Books, privately printed, [c.1909] (3 vols) £1,250

Book Four, Part One, Wieland & Co, 1911 (pseud. 'Frater Perdurabo', with 'Soror Virakam'). . £175

Book Four, Part Two, Wieland & Co, 1912 (pseud. 'Frater Perdurabo', with 'Soror Virakam'). . £200

Liber CCCXXXIII, The Book of Lies, Wieland & Co., 1913 . . . . £400

Liber II, The Message of the Master Therion, privately printed, 1916 . . . . . . £100

The Law of Liberty, A tract of Therion, that is a Magus, O.T.O., 1917 (single folded sheet) . £75

Book Four, Part Three, Magick, in Theory and Practice, Lecram Press (Paris), 1929 (four parts, pseud. 'Master Therion', wraps) £600

ditto, Lecram Press for Subscribers (Paris), 1929 [1930]. . . . . £500/£250

The Book of the Law, O.T.O., 1938 . . . . £275

ditto, O.T.O., 1938 (wraps) £175

The Heart of the Master, O.T.O., 1938 (pseud. 'Khaled Khan') £325

Little Essays Towards Truth, etc., privately issued by the O.T.O., [1938] £325

Liber XXI, Khing Kang King, the Classic of Purity, O.T.O., 1939 . . . . £900

Eight Lectures on Yoga, O.T.O., 1939 (pseud. 'Mahatma Guru Sri Parahamsa Shivaji') . £600/£400

The Book of Thoth, A short essay on the Tarot of the Egyptians, O.T.O., 1944 (200 signed copies, pseud. 'Master Therion') £3,250

Others

The Banned Lecture—Gilles de Rais—to have been delivered before the Oxford University Poetry Society, etc., Stephensen, [1930.] £225

The Spirit of Solitude, Mandrake Press, 1929 (2 vols). . . . . £1,000 the set

The Confessions of Aleister Crowley, Mandrake Press, 1929 (800 copies, 2 vols) £350

ditto, Cape (U.S.), 1969 . . . . . . £30/£10

ditto, Hill & Wang (U.S.), 1970 . . . . £30/£10

The Scientific Solution of the Problem of Government, O.T.O., [c.1937] (pseud. 'Comte de Fénix') £90

The Last Ritual, privately printed, [1947] (wraps) £125

Translation

Little Poems in Prose by Baudelaire, Titus (Paris), 1928 (800 copies, with 12 copper plate engravings from the original drawings by Jean de Bosschere) £400

The Key of the Mysteries, by Eliphas Levi, Rider & Co., 1959 . . . . £75/£30

E.E. CUMMINGS
(b.1894 d.1962)

An innovative American poet, much influenced by slang and jazz, whose work is characterised by unconventional punctuation and typography. He usually signed his work 'e.e. cummings'.

Poetry

Eight Harvard Poets, Gomme (U.S.), 1917. . £150

Tulips and Chimneys, Seltzer (U.S.), 1923 £1,000/£250

&, privately printed (U.S.), 1925 (111 of 333 signed copies, green gold-flecked boards, slipcase) . . . . £750/£650

ditto, privately printed (U.S.), 1925 (222 of 333 signed copies, slipcase) . . . . £600/£500

XLI Poems, Dial Press (U.S.), 1925 . . £600/£75

Is 5, Boni & Liveright (U.S.), 1926 (orange gold-flecked boards) . . . . £200/£100

ditto, Boni & Liveright (U.S.), 1926 (77 signed copies, slipcase) . . . . £1,750/£1,500

[Untitled], Covici Friede (U.S.), 1930 (491 signed copies) £500

CIOPW, Covici Friede (U.S.), 1931 (391 signed, numbered copies) £750

W [ViVa], Liveright Inc. (U.S.), 1931 . £450/£200

ditto, Liveright Inc. (U.S.), 1931 (95 signed, numbered copies, glassine d/w). £800

No Thanks, Golden Eagle Press (U.S.), 1935 (90 signed copies) £900

ditto, Golden Eagle Press (U.S.), 1935 (9 signed copies with manuscript page) £2,000

ditto, Golden Eagle Press (U.S.), 1935 (900 copies) .
. . . . £200/£75

Tom, Arrow Editions (U.S.), 1935 (1500 copies, glassine d/w) . . . . £250/£100

1/20, Roger Roughton, 1936 (tissue d/w) . £125/£100

Collected Poems, Harcourt Brace (U.S.), 1938 . . .
. . . . £150/£35

50 Poems, Duell, Sloane and Pearce, 1940 . £250/£75

ditto, Duell, Sloane and Pearce, 1940 (150 signed copies, glassine d/w slipcase) . . £1,250/£1,000

1 x 1, Holt (U.S.), 1944 . . . . . . £80/£25

ditto, Horizon, 1947 . . . . . . £45/£15

XAIPE: Seventy-One Poems, O.U.P. (U.S.), 1950. .
. . . . £65/£20

Poems, 1923-1954, Harcourt Brace (U.S.), 1954 . .
. . . . £25/£5

95 Poems, Harcourt Brace (U.S.), 1958 (300 signed copies, slipcase) . . . . £400/£250

ditto, Harcourt Brace (U.S.), 1958 . . . £25/£10

100 Selected Poems, Grove Press (U.S.), 1959 (wraps)
. . . . £20

Selected Poems, 1923-1958, Faber, 1960 . £30/£10

73 Poems, Harcourt (U.S.), 1963. . . . £45/£15

ditto, Faber, 1963 . . . . £40/£10

Complete Poems, MacGibbon & Kee, 1968 (2 vols) .
. . . . £300/£125

Complete Poems 1913-1962, Harcourt Brace (U.S.), 1972 . . . . £30/£10

Poems 1905-1962, Marchim Press, 1973 (225 numbered copies) £250

Hist Whist and Other Poems for Children, Evans, 1975 . . . . £25/£10

ditto, Liveright (U.S.), 1983 . . . . £25/£10

In Just-Spring, Little, Brown, 1988 . . . £35/£10

Complete Poems 1910-1962, Granada, 1981 (2 vols in slipcase) . . . . £50/£25

Etcetera: The Unpublished Poems, Liveright (U.S.), 1983 . . . . £45/£15

Complete Poems 1904-1962, Liveright, 1991 £20/£10

Fiction

The Enormous Room, Boni & Liveright (U.S.), 1911 (word 'shit' in last line on page 219) £2,000/£1,000

ditto, Boni & Liveright (U.S.), 1911 (word 'shit' in last line on page 219 inked out) . . . . £1,000 /£75

ditto, Cape, 1928 . . . . £250/£50

Eimi, Covici Friede (U.S.), 1933 (1,381 signed, numbered copies) . . . . . . £350/£150

Plays

Him, Boni & Liveright (U.S.), 1927 . . . £125/£25

ditto, Boni & Liveright (U.S.), 1927 (160 signed, numbered copies, slipcase) . . . . £325/£250

Anthropos, Golden Eagle Press (U.S.), 1944 (222 copies, slipcase) . . . . £150/£125

Santa Claus, Holt (U.S.), 1946 (250 signed copies, glassine d/w) . . . . £250/£200

ditto, Holt (U.S.), 1946 . . . . . . £125/£35

Others

Puella Lia, Golden Eagle Press (U.S.), 1949 (17 drawings by Cummings, Paul Klee, Picasso, Modigliani, and Kurt Roesch. Contains poem originally in *Tulips and Chimneys*) . . £150/£125

i: Six Nonlectures, Harvard Univ. Press (U.S.), 1953 .
. . . . £60/£15

ditto, Harvard Univ. Press (U.S.), 1953 (350 signed copies) . . . . £400/£250

A Miscellany, Argophile Press (U.S.), 1958 £75/£25

ditto, Argophile Press (U.S.), 1958 (75 signed, numbered copies, glassine d/w). . . £200/£150

Adventures in Value, Harcourt, Brace & World (U.S.), 1962 (50 photographs by Marion Morehouse, with text by Cummings) . . . . . . £100/£35

Fairy Tales, Harcourt Brace (U.S.), 1965 . £25/£10

Selected Letters, Harcourt Brace (U.S.), 1969 £25/£10

ditto, Deutsch, 1972 . . . . £20/£5

ROALD DAHL
(b.1916 d.1990)

Principally a children's writer, although his short stories for adults are also well known. In the past Dahl's books for children often met with disapproval due to the unpleasant ends met by some of his characters—precisely what children seem to enjoy.

Children's Titles

The Gremlins, Random House (U.S.), [1943] . . .
. . . . £3,000/£750

ditto, Collins, [1944] (boards, no d/w) . . . £700

James and the Giant Peach, Knopf (U.S.), 1961 . .
. . . . £400/£100

ditto, Allen & Unwin, 1967 (boards, no d/w) . £250

Charlie and the Chocolate Factory, Knopf (U.S.), 1964 . . . . £1,000/£250

ditto, Allen & Unwin, 1967 (boards, no d/w) . £250

The Magic Finger, Harper (U.S.), 1966. . £100/£25

ditto, Allen & Unwin, 1968 (boards, no d/w) . £75

Fantastic Mr Fox, Knopf (U.S.), 1970 . . £100/£25

ditto, Allen & Unwin, 1970 (boards, no d/w) . £75

Charlie and the Great Glass Elevator, Knopf (U.S.), 1972 . . . . £150/£25

ditto, Allen & Unwin, 1973 (boards, no d/w) . £75

Danny, The Champion of the World, Cape, 1975 . .
. . . . £100/£25

ditto, Knopf (U.S.), 1975 . . . . . £53/£15

The Wonderful Story of Henry Sugar and Six More, Cape, 1977 . . . . £75/£15

ditto, Knopf (U.S.), 1977 . . . . . £35/£15

The Enormous Crocodile, Cape, 1978 (no d/w) £65

ditto, Knopf (U.S.), 1978 . . . . . £30/£10

The Twits, Cape, 1980	£50/£10
ditto, Knopf (U.S.), 1981	£35/£10
George's Marvellous Medicine, Cape, 1981	£50/£20
ditto, Knopf (U.S.), 1982	£25/£5
Roald Dahl's Revolting Rhymes, Cape, 1983 (no d/w)	
. . . .	£65
ditto, Knopf (U.S.), 1983	£35/£10
The BFG, Cape, 1982.	£45/£10
ditto, Farrar Straus (U.S.), 1982	£25/£5
Dirty Beasts, Cape, 1983 (no d/w) . . .	£45
ditto, Farrar Straus (U.S.), 1983 . . .	£25/£10
The Witches, Cape, 1983	£60/£10
ditto, Farrar Straus (U.S.), 1983	£30/£10
The Giraffe, the Pelly and Me, Cape, 1985 (no d/w)	
. . . .	£45
ditto, Farrar Straus (U.S.), 1985 (no d/w) .	£25
Matilda, Cape, 1988	£60/£10
ditto, Viking Kestrel (U.S.), 1988 . . .	£30/£5
Rhyme Stew, Cape, 1989	£35/£5
ditto, Viking (U.S.), 1990.	£25/£5
Esio Trot, Cape, 1990.	£35/£5
ditto, Viking (U.S.), 1990.	£25/£5
Roald Dahl's Guide to Railway Safety, British Rail,	
1991 (wraps)	£5
The Vicar of Nibbleswicke, Random Century, 1991 .	
. . . .	£30/£5
ditto, Viking (U.S.), 1991.	£20/£5
The Minpins, Cape, 1991.	£25/£5
ditto, Viking (U.S.), 1991.	£15/£5
My Year, Cape, 1993	£15/£5
ditto, Viking (U.S.), 1993.	£10/£5
The Mildenhall Treasure, Cape, 1999 . .	£15/£5
ditto, Knopf (U.S.), 2000	£10/£5

Adult Novels

Sometime Never, Scribner's (U.S.), 1948 .	£200/£35
ditto, Collins, 1949	£200/£35
My Uncle Oswald, Joseph, 1979. . . .	£30/£5
ditto, Knopf (U.S.), 1980	£30/£5

Short Stories

Over to You, Reynal & Hitchcock (U.S.), 1946. . .	
. . . .	£300/£45
ditto, Hamish Hamilton, 1946	£300/£45
Someone Like You, Knopf (U.S.), 1953. .	£125/£20
ditto, Secker & Warburg, 1954	£100/£20
Kiss Kiss, Knopf (U.S.), 1960 . . .	£75/£15
ditto, Joseph, 1960.	£75/£15
A Roald Dahl Selection, Longmans (U.S.), 1960	
(wraps)	£5
Selected Short Stories, Modern Library (U.S.), 1968	
(wraps)	£35/£10
Twenty Nine Kisses from Roald Dahl, Joseph, 1969 .	
. . . .	£25/£5
Switch Bitch, Knopf (U.S.), 1974 . .	£75/£15
ditto, Joseph, 1974.	£75/£15
Tales of the Unexpected, Joseph, 1979 .	£35/£10
ditto, Random/Vintage (U.S.), 1979 (wraps) .	£5
Taste and Other Tales, Penguin, 1979 (wraps) .	£5
More Tales of the Unexpected, Joseph, 1980 .	£25/£5

The Best of Roald Dahl, Joseph, 1983 . .	£15/£5
Completely Unexpected Tales, Penguin, 1986 (wraps)	
. . . .	£5
Two Fables, Viking, 1986	£25/£10
ditto, Viking, 1986 (300 signed copies) . .	£250
ditto, Farrar Straus (U.S.), 1987 . .	£25/£10
Taste a 1934 Chateau Branaire-Ducru Tainted!,	
Redpath Press (U.S.), 1986 (wraps) . . .	£5
Ah! Sweet Mystery of Life, Joseph, 1989 .	£15/£5
ditto, Knopf (U.S.), 1989	£10/£5
The Collected Short Stories of Roald Doyle, Cape,	
1991	£20/£5
ditto, Viking (U.S.), 1991.	£15/£5
The Great Automatic Grammatizator, Viking, 1996 .	
. . . .	£15/£5
ditto, as *The Umbrella Man and Other Stories*, Viking	
(U.S.), 1996	£15/£5
Skin, Viking, 2000	£10/£5

Autobiography

Boy: Tales of Childhood, Cape, 1984 . .	£45/£10
ditto, Farrar Straus, 1984 (200 signed copies) .	£100
ditto, Farrar Straus, 1984	£35/£5
Going Solo, Cape, 1986	£15/£5
ditto, Farrar Straus, 1986	£15/£5

THE DANDY

A successful rival to *The Beano*, *The Dandy* sported
Korky the Cat on its front cover for almost fifty years.

Comics

No.1, D.C. Thomson, 1937 (with free gift) .	£3,500
ditto, D.C. Thomson, 1937 (without free gift) .	£2,500
No.2, D.C. Thomson, 1937	£750
Nos 3-10, D.C. Thomson, 1937	£400 each
1938 issues.	£75 each

Dandy Monster Comic

1939, D.C. Thomson	£2,500
1940, D.C. Thomson	£1,000
1941, D.C. Thomson	£750
1942, D.C. Thomson	£650
1943, D.C. Thomson	£500
1944, D.C. Thomson	£450
1945, D.C. Thomson	£400
1946, D.C. Thomson	£350
1947, D.C. Thomson	£300
1948, D.C. Thomson	£250
1949, D.C. Thomson	£200
1950, D.C. Thomson	£150
1951, D.C. Thomson	£100
1952, D.C. Thomson	£75

Dandy Books

1953-1960, D.C. Thomson	£50
1961-65, D.C. Thomson	£65
1966-69, D.C. Thomson	£25

LINDSEY DAVIS
(b.1949)

The author of detective novels set in Roman times, Davis was the first recipient of the Crime Writers Association Ellis Peters Historical Dagger.

The 'Falco' Series
The Silver Pigs, Sidgwick & Jackson, 1989. £300/£35
ditto, Crown (U.S.), 1989 . . . . . £40/£10
Shadows in Bronze, Sidgwick & Jackson, 1990 . .
. . . . £175/£20
ditto, Crown (U.S.), 1990 . . . . . £30/£10
Venus in Copper, Hutchinson, 1991 . . £35/£10
ditto, Crown (U.S.), 1991 . . . . . £20/£5
The Iron Hand of Mars, Hutchinson, 1992. £125/£15
ditto, Crown (U.S.), 1992 . . . . . £60/£10
Poseidon's Gold, Century, 1993 . . . . £20/£5
ditto, Century, 1993 (400 signed, numbered proof copies, wraps) . . . . £20/£5
ditto, Crown (U.S.), 1993 . . . . . . £50
Last Act in Palmyra, Century, 1994 . . . £15/£5
ditto, Mysterious Press (U.S.), 1994 . . . £15/£5
Time To Depart, Century, 1995 . . . . £15/£5
ditto, Scorpion Press, 1995 (99 signed, numbered copies) £50
ditto, Scorpion Press, 1995 (15 signed, lettered copies)
. . . . £100
ditto, Mysterious Press (U.S.), 1997 . . . £10/£5
A Dying Light in Corduba, Century, 1996 . . £10/£5
ditto, Scorpion Press, 1996 (99 signed, numbered copies) £50
ditto, Scorpion Press, 1996 (15 signed, lettered copies)
. . . . £100
ditto, Mysterious Press (U.S.), 1998 . . . £10/£5
Three Hands in the Fountain, Century, 1997 . £10/£5
ditto, Mysterious Press (U.S.), 1999 . . . £10/£5
Two For the Lions, Century, 1998 . . . £10/£5
ditto, Mysterious Press (U.S.), 1999 . . . £10/£5
One Virgin Too Many, Century, 1999 . . £10/£5
ditto, Mysterious Press (U.S.), 2000 . . . £10/£5
Ode to a Banker, Century, 2000 . . . . £10/£5
ditto, Mysterious Press (U.S.), 2001 . . . £10/£5
A Body in the Bath House, Century, 2001 . . £10/£5
ditto, Mysterious Press (U.S.), 2002 . . . £10/£5
The Jupiter Myth, Century, 2002 . . . £10/£5
ditto, Mysterious Press (U.S.), 2002 . . . £10/£5

Other Novels
The Course of Honour, Century, 1997 . . £10/£5
ditto, Mysterious Press (U.S.), 1998 . . . £10/£5

C. DAY LEWIS
(b.1904 d.1972)

An Anglo-Irish poet and critic. Cecil Day Lewis was appointed Poet Laureate in 1968. He is also remembered as a detective story writer under the pseudonym 'Nicholas Blake'.

Poetry
Beechen Virgil and Other Poems, Fortune Press, 1925 (wraps) £150
Country Comets, Martin Hopkinson, 1928 (slipcase) .
. . . . £100/£65
Transitional Poems, Hogarth Press, 1929 . £100/£40
From Feathers to Iron, Hogarth Press, 1931 £100/£40
The Magnetic Mountain, Hogarth Press, 1932 £40/£15
ditto, Hogarth Press, 1932 (100 signed, numbered copies) . . . . £200/£100
Collected Poems 1929-33, Hogarth Press, 1935 £65/£20
ditto, Random House (U.S.), 1935 . . . £50/£20
A Time to Dance and Other Poems, Hogarth Press, 1935 . . . . £75/£20
Noah and the Waters, Hogarth Press, 1936. £40/£10
ditto, Hogarth Press, 1936 (100 signed, numbered copies) . . . . £125/£75
A Time to Dance, Noah and the Waters, Random House (U.S.), 1936 . . . . . . £30/£10
Overtures to Death and Other Poems, Cape, 1938. .
. . . . £35/£10
ditto, as *Short is the Time*, Poems 1936-1943, O.U.P. (U.S.), 1945 (with *Word Over All*) . . £25/£10
Child of Misfortune, Cape, 1939. . . . £35/£10
Poems in Wartime, Cape, 1940 (250 copies, wraps) .
. . . . £65
Selected Poems, Hogarth Press, 1940 . . £60/£20
Word Over All, Cape, 1943 . . . . . £40/£10
The Augustan Poets, Eyre and Spottiswoode, 1943 (wraps) £10
Poems 1943-47, Cape, 1948 . . . . . £25/£10
ditto, O.U.P. (U.S.), 1948. . . . . . £25/£10
Collected Poems 1929-1946, Hogarth Press, 1948 .
. . . . £20/£5
Selected Poems, Penguin, 1951 . . . . . £5
An Italian Visit, Cape, 1953 . . . . . £25/£10
ditto, Harper (U.S.), 1953 . . . . . £25/£10
Collected Poems, Cape/Hogarth Press, 1954 £35/£10
Christmas Eve, Faber, 1954 (wraps) . . . £15
Pegasus and Other Poems, Cape, 1957 . . £10/£5
The Buried Day, Chatto & Windus, 1960 . £25/£10
ditto, Harper (U.S.), 1960 . . . . . £20/£10
The Gate and Other Poems, Chatto & Windus, 1962 .
. . . . £10/£5
Requiem for the Living, Harper (U.S.), 1964 . £10/£5
The Room and Other Poems, Cape, 1965 . . £10/£5
Selected Poems, Harper (U.S.), 1967 . . . £10/£5
The Abbey That Refused To Die, Dolmen Press (Dublin), 1967 (wraps) £10
The Whispering Roots, Cape, 1970 . . . £10/£5
ditto, Harper (U.S.), 1970. . . . . . £10/£5

Going My Way, Poem of the Month Club, 1970
(broadside) £5
Posthumous Poems, Whittington Press, 1979 (250
copies, slipcase) . . . . £100/£75
Complete Poems of C. Day Lewis, Stanford Univ.
Press (U.S.), 1992 . . . . £20/£10

Detective Fiction Written as 'Nicholas Blake'
A Question of Proof, Collins Crime Club, 1935 . .
. . . . £1,750/£75
ditto, Harper (U.S.), 1935 . . . . . . £600/£35
Thou Shell of Death, Collins Crime Club, 1936 . .
. . . . £1,750/£75
ditto, as **Shell of Death**, Harper (U.S.), 1936 £350/£35
There's Trouble Brewing, Collins Crime Club, 1937 .
. . . . £1,750/£50
ditto, Harper (U.S.), 1937 . . . . . . £350/£35
The Beast Must Die, Collins Crime Club, 1938 . .
. . . . £1,750/£50
ditto, Harper (U.S.), 1938 . . . . . . £300/£35
The Smiler with the Knife, Collins Crime Club, 1939 .
. . . . £1,500/£45
ditto, Harper (U.S.), 1939 . . . . . . £300/£35
Malice in Wonderland, Collins Crime Club, 1940 . .
. . . . £600/£45
ditto, as **The Summer Camp Mystery**, Harper (U.S.),
1940 . . . . £250/£35
ditto, as **Malice with Murder**, Pyramid (U.S.), 1964
(wraps) £15
ditto, as **Murder with Malice**, Carroll & Graf (U.S.),
1987 . . . . £20/£5
The Case of the Abominable Snowman, Collins Crime
Club, 1941 . . . . £300/£45
ditto, as **The Corpse in the Snowman**, Harper (U.S.),
1941 . . . . £125/£25
Minute for Murder, Collins Crime Club, 1947 . . .
. . . . £125/£35
ditto, Harper (U.S.), 1948 . . . . . £45/£15
Head of a Traveller, Collins Crime Club, 1949 £85/£20
ditto, Harper (U.S.), 1949 . . . . . £35/£10
The Dreadful Hollow, Collins Crime Club, 1953 . .
. . . . £85/£20
ditto, Harper (U.S.), 1953 . . . . . £35/£10
The Whisper in the Gloom, Collins Crime Club, 1954.
. . . . £60/£20
ditto, Harper (U.S.), 1954 . . . . . £35/£10
ditto, as **Catch and Kill**, Bestseller (U.S.), 1955
(abridged). . . . . £25/£10
A Tangled Web, Collins Crime Club, 1956. £50/£15
ditto, Harper (U.S.), 1956 . . . . . £35/£10
ditto, as **Death and Daisy Bland**, Dell (U.S.), 1960
(wraps) £10
End of Chapter, Collins Crime Club, 1957 . £50/£15
ditto, Harper (U.S.), 1957 . . . . . £35/£10
A Penknife in My Heart, Collins Crime Club, 1958 .
. . . . £50/£15
ditto, Harper (U.S.), 1959 . . . . . £35/£10
The Widow's Cruise, Collins Crime Club, 1959 . .
. . . . £40/£10

ditto, Harper (U.S.), 1959 . . . . . £30/£10
The Worm of Death, Collins Crime Club, 1961 . .
. . . . £40/£10
ditto, Harper (U.S.), 1961 . . . . . £30/£10
The Deadly Joker, Collins Crime Club, 1963 £40/£10
The Sad Variety, Collins Crime Club, 1964. £40/£10
ditto, Harper (U.S.), 1964 . . . . . £30/£10
The Morning After Death, Collins Crime Club, 1966 .
. . . . £40/£10
ditto, Harper (U.S.), 1966 . . . . . £25/£10
The Nicholas Blake Omnibus, Collins Crime Club,
1966 . . . . £25/£10
The Private Wound, Collins Crime Club, 1968 £35/£10
ditto, Harper (U.S.), 1968 . . . . . £30/£10

Other Novels
The Friendly Tree, Cape, 1936 . . . . £35/£10
ditto, Harper (U.S.), 1937 . . . . . £35/£10
Starting Point, Cape, 1937 . . . . . £35/£10
ditto, Harper (U.S.), 1938 . . . . . £35/£10

Childrens Titles
Dick Willoughby, Blackwell, 1933 . . . £450/£125
ditto, Random House (U.S.), 1938 . . . £100/£30
The Otterbury Incident, Putnam, 1948 . . £75/£25
ditto, Viking (U.S.), 1949 . . . . . £35/£15

Others
A Hope for Poetry, Blackwell, 1934 . . £35/£15
ditto, Random House (U.S.), 1935 . . . £25/£10
Revolution in Writing, Hogarth Press, 1935 (wraps) .
. . . . £25
Imagination and Thinking, British Institute of Adult
Education, 1936 (wraps) £15
**We're Not Going to do Nothing: A Reply to Mr
Aldous Huxley's Pamphlet**, The Left Review, 1936
(wraps) £35
ditto, The Left Review, 1936 (50 signed, numbered
copies, wraps) £100
Poetry for You, Blackwell, 1945 . . . . £40/£10
ditto, O.U.P. (U.S.), 1947 . . . . . £40/£10
The Poetic Image, Cape, 1947 . . . . £30/£10
ditto, O.U.P. (U.S.), 1947 . . . . . £30/£10
The Colloquial Element In English Poetry, Literary
Soc. of Newcastle, 1947 (wraps) . . . £10
Enjoying Poetry, C.U.P., 1947 (wraps) . . . £10
The Poet's Task, O.U.P., 1951 (wraps) . . . £10
Notable Images of Virtue, Ryerson Press (Canada),
1954 . . . . £20/£5
The Poet's Way of Knowledge, C.U.P., 1957 . £10/£5
The Lyric Impulse, Harvard.U.P. (U.S.), 1965 . £15/£5
ditto, Chatto & Windus, 1965 . . . . . £10/£5
A Need for Poetry, Univ. of Hull., 1968 (wraps) £10

LOUIS DE BERNIÈRES
(b.1954)

The reputation of the author's best-known book, *Captain Corelli's Mandolin*, is said to have been spread almost entirely by word of mouth.

Novels
The War of Don Emmanuel's Nether Parts, Secker & Warburg, 1990 . . . . £200/£35
ditto, Morrow (U.S.), 1990 . . . . . £25/£5
Señor Vivo and the Coca Lord, Secker & Warburg, 1991 . . . . £150/£35
ditto, Morrow (U.S.), 1991 . . . . . £25/£10
The Troublesome Offspring of Cardinal Guzman, Secker & Warburg, 1992 . . . . £125/£25
ditto, Morrow (U.S.), 1994 . . . . £20/£10
Captain Corelli's Mandolin, Secker & Warburg, 1994 (white boards) . . . . £500/£150
ditto, Secker & Warburg, 1994 (black boards) . . .
. . . . £250/£50
ditto, as *Corelli's Mandolin*, Pantheon (U.S.), 1994 .
. . . . £25/£10
Red Dog, Secker & Warburg, 2001 . . . £10/£5
ditto, Secker & Warburg, 2001 (100 signed copies) .
. . . . £100/£75
ditto, Morrow (U.S.), 1991 . . . . £25/£10

Others
Labels, One Horse Press, 1993 (2,000 signed copies, wraps). £45
A Day Out for Mehmet Erbil, Belmont Press, 1999 (26 signed, lettered copies of 276) £300
ditto, Belmont Press, 1999 (100 signed, numbered copies of 276) £175
ditto, Belmont Press, 1999 (150 signed, numbered copies of 276) £100
Günter Weber's Confession, Tartarus Press, 2001 (26 signed, numbered hardback copies of 300, in slipcase with extra print signed by artist) . . . £200
ditto, Tartarus Press, 2001 (74 signed copies of 300, wraps). £125
ditto, Tartarus Press, 2001 (200 unsigned copies of 300, wraps) £35

DANIEL DEFOE
(b.1660 d.1730)

Defoe is regarded as the father of the English novel, of modern journalism and of the art of political propaganda. He also worked for the government as a policy adviser and in undercover espionage work.

'Robinson Crusoe'
The Life and Strange Surprizing Adventures of Robinson Crusoe, W. Taylor, 1719 (first edition, first issue, anonymous) £15,000

ditto, W. Taylor, 1719 (anonymous, later impressions)
. . . . £2,000
ditto, Etchells & MacDonald, 1929 (illustrated by E. McKnight Kauffer, limited edition, 525 copies) £600
ditto, Basilisk Press, 1979 (illustrated by Edward Gordon Craig, limited edition, 500 copies, slipcase) .
. . . . £500
The Farther Adventures of Robinson Crusoe, W. Taylor, 1719 (anonymous) £10,000
Serious Reflections During the Life and Surprising Adventures of Robinson Crusoe, W. Taylor, 1720 (anonymous). £6,000
ditto, W. Mears/T. Woodward, 1726 (2 vols made up of the abridged seventh edition of *The Life and Strange Adventures of Robinson Crusoe* and the fifth edition of *The Farther Adventures of Robinson Crusoe*) £1,250
The Life and Strange Surprising Adventures of Robinson Crusoe, John Stockdale, 1790 (together with 'The Life of Daniel De Foe' and a bibliography of his writings by George Chalmers. 2 vols) . £1,250
The Life and Adventures of Robinson Crusoe, sold by J. Walter, 1790 (first joint edition of Parts I, II and III, printed at the Logographic Press, includes 'The True-Born Englishman, A Satire' and 'The Original Power of the People of England examined and asserted', 3 vols) £1,250
ditto, Constable Press, 1925 (reissued with facsimiles of Stothard's plates, as *The Life and Strange Surprising Adventures of Robinson Crusoe*, with an introduction by Charles Whibley. 3 vols, limited edition, 775 copies) £600
The Life and Adventures of Robinson Crusoe, John Major, 1831 (illustrated by George Cruikshank and Thomas Stothard, with introductory verses by Bernard Barton. 2 vols) £600
ditto, Dent, 1903 (illustrated by J. Ayton Symington) .
. . . . £50

Other Fiction
The Life ... of Captain Singleton, J. Brotherton, 1720 (anonymous). £750
Moll Flanders, W. Chetwood/T. Edling, [1722] (anonymous). £15,000
A Journal of the Plague Year, E. Nutt, 1722 (anonymous). £750
The History ... of Col. Jacque, Commonly Call'd Col. Jack, J. Brotherton, 1722 (anonymous) . . £750
The Fortunate Mistress, or ... Roxana, T. Werner, 1724 (anonymous) £750
Memoirs of a Cavalier, A. Bell, 1720 . . . £750

Non Fiction
The Shortest-Way With Dissenters, published anon, MDCCII [1702] £3,000
The History of the Union of Great Britain, Heirs and Successors of Andrew Anderson, Edinburgh 1709 (in 6 parts) £500

The Family Instructor [Vol I], Emanuel Matthews /J.
Button, 1715 (anonymous) £300
The Family Instructor [Vol II], Emanuel Matthews,
1718 (2 parts) (anonymous). £300
ditto, Thos. Longman, 1741 (first combined edition, 2
vols) £300
The Compleat English Tradesman [Vol I], Charles
Rivington, 1726 [1725] (anonymous) . . . £300
The Compleat English Tradesman [Vol II], Charles
Rivington, 1732 (2 parts, anonymous) . . . £300
ditto, C. Rivington, 1732 (first combined edition, 2
vols) £300
A Tour Thro' the Whole Island of Great Britain, G.
Strahan, 1724-27 [1726] (3 vols, anonymous) £2,500
ditto, Peter Davis, 1927 (abridged version, 2 vols,
limited edition, 1,000 copies) £300
A System of Magick, Roberts, 1727 . . . £1,500

LEN DEIGHTON
(b.1929)

Len Deighton worked as an illustrator until his first
novel was published in 1962. He is best known for his
popular thrillers and spy novels.

Novels

The Ipcress File, Hodder & Stoughton, 1962 £400/£35
ditto, Simon & Schuster (U.S.), 1963 . . £150/£35
ditto, Franklin Library (U.S.), 1988 (signed, limited
edition) £65
Horse Under Water, Cape, 1963 (with loose crossword competition) . . . . . . £150/£75
ditto, Cape, 1963 (without loose crossword competition) . . . . £75/£15
ditto, Putnam (U.S.), 1968 . . . . £65/£15
Funeral in Berlin, Cape, 1964 . . . £100/£15
ditto, Putnam (U.S.), 1965 . . . . £75/£10
Billion Dollar Brain, Putnam (U.S.), 1966 . £100/£15
ditto, Cape, 1966 . . . . . . £100/£15
An Expensive Place to Die, Putnam (U.S.), 1967 (with
wallet of documents). . . . . . £75/£30
ditto, Putnam (U.S.), 1967 (without wallet of
documents) . . . . £45/£10
ditto, Cape, 1967 (with wallet of documents) £75/£30
ditto, Cape, 1967 (without wallet of documents) £45/£5
Only When I Larf, privately printed (limited edition,
150 copies in plastic binding) £1,500
ditto, Joseph, 1968 (boards) . . . . £100/£20
ditto, Joseph, 1968 (wraps) £10
ditto, as *Only When I Laugh*, The Mysterious Press
(U.S.), 1987 (250 signed copies, slipcase, no d/w)
. . . . £75/£45
ditto, as *Only When I Laugh*, The Mysterious Press
(U.S.), 1987. . . . . £25/£10
Bomber, Cape, 1970 . . . . . . £40/£10
ditto, Harper & Row, 1970 . . . . £35/£10
Close-Up, Cape, 1972 . . . . . . £40/£10

ditto, Atheneum (U.S.), 1972. . . . . £30/£5
Spy Story, Cape, 1974. . . . . . £30/£5
ditto, Harcourt Brace (U.S.), 1974 . . . £25/£5
Yesterday's Spy, Cape, 1975 . . . . . £30/£5
ditto, Harcourt Brace (U.S.), 1975 . . . £25/£5
Twinkle, Twinkle, Little Spy, Cape, 1976 . £30/£5
ditto, as *Catch a Falling Spy*, Harcourt Brace (U.S.),
1976 . . . . £25/£5
SS-GB, Cape, 1978 . . . . . . £30/£5
ditto, Knopf (U.S.), 1979 . . . . . £25/£5
XPD, Hutchinson, 1981 . . . . . £30/£5
ditto, Knopf (U.S.), 1981. . . . . . £25/£5
Goodbye, Mickey Mouse, Hutchinson, 1982 . £30/£5
ditto, Knopf (U.S.), 1982 . . . . . £25/£5
Berlin Game, Hutchinson, 1983 . . . . £30/£5
ditto, Knopf (U.S.), 1984 . . . . . £25/£5
Mexico Set, Hutchinson, 1984 . . . . £30/£5
ditto, Knopf (U.S.), 1985 . . . . . £25/£5
London Match, Hutchinson, 1985 . . . £30/£5
ditto, Knopf (U.S.), 1986 . . . . . £25/£5
Winter, Hutchinson, 1987 . . . . . £30/£5
ditto, Knopf (U.S.), 1987 . . . . . £25/£5
Spy Hook, Hutchinson, 1988 . . . . . £25/£5
ditto, Knopf (U.S.), 1988 . . . . . £25/£5
Spy Line, Hutchinson, 1989 . . . . . £20/£5
ditto, Knopf (U.S.), 1989 . . . . . £15/£5
Spy Sinker, Hutchinson, 1989 . . . . £20/£5
ditto, HarperCollins (U.S.), 1990. . . . £15/£5
MAMista, Century, 1991 . . . . . £20/£5
ditto, HarperCollins (U.S.), 1991. . . . £15/£5
City of Gold, Century, 1992 . . . . . £20/£5
ditto, HarperCollins (U.S.), 1992. . . . £15/£5
Violent Ward, Scorpion Press, 1993 (130 signed
copies) £100
ditto, Scorpion Press, 1993 (20 deluxe signed copies) .
. . . . £175
ditto, HarperCollins, 1993 . . . . . £20/£5
ditto, HarperCollins (U.S.), 1993. . . . £15/£5
Faith, HarperCollins, 1994 . . . . . £30/£5
ditto, HarperCollins (U.S.), 1994. . . . £25/£5
Hope, Scorpion Press, 1995 (15 copies of edition of
114) £175
ditto, Scorpion Press, 1995 (99 copies of edition of
114, glassine d/w) £100
ditto, HarperCollins, 1995 . . . . . £30/£5
ditto, HarperCollins (U.S.), 1995. . . . £20/£5
Charity, HarperCollins, 1996. . . . . £30/£5
ditto, HarperCollins (U.S.), 1996. . . . £25/£5

Omnibus Editions

Game, Set and Match, Hutchinson, 1986 . £40/£10
ditto, Knopf (U.S.), 1989 . . . . . £35/£10
ditto, Hutchinson, 1986 (presentation set of 3 first
editions with *The Len Deighton Companion*, in
slipcase) £100
Hook, Line and Sinker, Hutchinson, 1991 . £10/£5
ditto, Hutchinson, 1991 (presentation set of 3 first
editions, in slipcase) £100

Short Stories
Declarations of War, Cape, 1971 (short stories) . .
. . . . £40/£10
ditto, as *Eleven Declarations of War*, Harcourt Brace
(U.S.),1975 . . . . £35/£10

Cookery Titles
Action Cook Book, Len Deighton's Guide to Eating,
Cape, 1965 (printed boards, clear d/w). . £100/£50
ditto, as *Cookstrip Cookbook*, Bernard Geis (U.S.),
1966 . . . .£10/£5
*Où Est le Garlic or Len Deighton's French Cook
Book*, Penguin, 1965 (wraps) £30
ditto, as *Où Est le Garlic or French Cooking in 50
Lessons*, Harper & Row (U.S.), 1977 . . £25/£10
ditto, as *Basic French Cooking*, Cape, 1979 £50/£15
ditto, as *Basic French Cookery Course*, Century
Hutchinson, 1990 . . . .£10/£5
ABC of French Food, Century, 1989 . . .£10/£5

Others
The Assassination of President Kennedy, Cape/
Jackdaw, 1967 (Portfolio containing 12
reproductions, 1 cut-out model and 5 broadsides, with
Rand and Loxton) £350
Len Deighton's London Dossier, Cape, 1967 £50/£20
Len Deighton's Continental Dossier, Joseph, 1968 (no
d/w) £40
Fighter: The True Story of the Battle of Britain, Cape,
1977 . . . . £45/£10
ditto, Knopf (U.S.), 1978 . . . .£10/£5
Airshipwreck, Cape, 1978 (6 postcards laid in, with
record) . . . . £175/£75
ditto, Cape, 1978 (no postcards or record) . £75/£15
ditto, Holt Rinehart (U.S.), 1979 . . . . £50/£10
*Blitzkrieg: From the Rise of Hitler to the Fall of
Dunkirk*, Cape, 1979 . . . .£30/£5
ditto, Knopf (U.S.), 1980 . . . .£30/£5
Battle of Britain, Cape, 1980. . . . . .£30/£5
ditto, Coward, McCann & Geoghegan (U.S.), 1980 .
. . . .£30/£5
*Blood, Tears and Folly: An Objective Look at World
War II*, Cape, 1993 . . . .£30/£5
ditto, HarperCollins (U.S.), 1993. . . . .£30/£5
Pests, A Play in Three Acts, Martin, 1994 (50 signed,
numbered copies of 226, slipcase) . . £75/£50
ditto, Martin, 1994 (150 signed, numbered copies of
226) . . . . £50/£40
ditto, Martin, 1994 (26 signed, lettered copies of 226) .
. . . . £200/£150

WALTER DE LA MARE
(b.1873 d.1956)

British author, poet and critic, whose delicate and
lyrical poems of fantasy and childhood are still
admired today.

Poetry
Songs of Childhood, Longmans, 1902 (pseud. 'Walter
Ramal') £350
ditto, Longmans, 1923 (enlarged and revised) £75/£20
ditto, Longmans, 1923 (310 signed copies) . £175/£100
Poems, Murray, 1906 . . . . £50
The Listeners and Other Poems, Constable, 1912 £45
ditto, Holt (U.S.), 1916 . . . . £45
A Child's Day, A Book of Rhymes, Constable, 1912 .
. . . . £100
Peacock Pie, A Book of Rhymes, Constable, 1913 £30
ditto, Constable, 1916 (illustrated by W. Heath
Robinson). £75
ditto, Constable, 1924 (250 signed copies, illustrated by
C. Lovat Fraser). £125
ditto, Holt (U.S.), 1924 (500 signed copies, illustrated
by C. Lovat Fraser) £125
The Old Men, Flying Fame, 1913 (broadside) . £30
The Sunken Garden and Other Poems, Beaumont
Press, 1917 (250 signed, numbered copies) . £75
Motley and Other Poems, Constable, 1918 . . £35
ditto, Holt (U.S.), 1918 . . . . £35
Flora: A Book of Drawings, by Pamela Bianco,
Heinemann, 1919 (with 27 poems by de la Mare) £45
ditto, Lippincott (U.S.), 1919. . . . . . £45
Poems, 1901 to 1918, Constable, 1920 (2 vols). . .
. . . . £65/£35
ditto, Constable, 1920 (210 signed, numbered sets) .
. . . . £100/£50
The Veil and Other Poems, Constable, 1921 £50/£15
ditto, Constable, 1921 (250 signed, numbered copies) .
. . . . £75
ditto, Holt (U.S.), 1922 . . . . £35
Down-Adown-Derry, A Book of Fairy Poems,
Constable, 1922 . . . . £125/£50
ditto, Constable, 1922 (325 signed, numbered copies) .
. . . . £225
ditto, Holt (U.S.), 1922 . . . . . . £75/£35
Thus Her Tale, A Poem, Porpoise Press, 1923 (50
numbered copies, wraps) £40
A Ballad of Christmas, Selwyn & Blount, 1924 (100
copies) £40
Before Dawn, Selwyn & Blount, 1924 (100 copies) .
. . . . £40
The Hostage, Selwyn & Blount, 1925 (100 copies) £40
St Andrews, A & C Black, 1926 (with Rudyard
Kipling) . . . . £45/£25
Alone, Faber, 1927 (Ariel Poem No.4, wraps) . £10
Selected Poems, Holt (U.S.), 1927 . . . £30/£10
Stuff and Nonsense and So On, Constable, 1927 . .
. . . . £45/£15

ditto, as **Stuff and Nonsense**, Faber, 1946 (enlarged and revised edition of above) . . . . . £15/£5
The Captive and Other Poems, Bowling Green Press (U.S.), 1928 (600 signed copies, glassine wraps) . .
. . . . £45/£35
Self to Self, Faber, 1928 (Ariel Poem No. 11, wraps) .
. . . . £10
ditto, Faber, 1928 (500 signed large paper copies) £45
A Snowdrop, Faber, 1929 (Ariel Poem No. 20, wraps).
. . . . £15
ditto, Faber, 1929 (500 signed large paper copies) £45
News, Faber, 1930 (Ariel Poem No. 31, wraps). £15
Poems for Children, Constable, 1930 . . £35/£10
ditto, Constable, 1930 (133 signed, numbered copies) .
. . . . £225
ditto, Holt (U.S.), 1930 (300 signed copies, slipcase) .
. . . . £175/£150
To Lucy, Faber, 1931 (Ariel Poem No. 33, wraps) £15
The Sunken Garden and Other Verses, Birmingham School of Printing, 1931 (different selection to 1917 edition) £25
Two Poems, privately printed, 1931 (100 copies, wraps). £75
Old Rhymes and New, Constable, 1932 (2 vols) .
. . . . £50/£20
The Fleeting and Other Poems, Constable, 1933 . .
. . . . £25/£15
ditto, Constable, 1933 (150 signed copies) . . £65
Poems, 1919 to 1934, Constable, 1935 . . £30/£15
This Year, Next Year, Faber, 1937 . . . . £125
ditto, Faber, 1937 (100 signed, numbered copies) . .
. . . . £450/£300
ditto, Holt (U.S.), 1937 . . . . . . £125/£65
Poems, Corvinus Press, 1937 (40 copies) . . £150
Memory and Other Poems, Constable, 1938 . £25/£5
Two Poems by Walter de la Mare and - but! - Arthur Rogers, privately printed, 1938 (200 copies) . £45
Haunted: A Poem, Linden Broadsheet No. 4, 1939 £20
Bells and Grass, a book of rhymes, Faber, 1941 . .
. . . . £50/£25
ditto, Viking (U.S.), 1942. . . . . . £50/£25
Collected Poems, Faber, 1942 . . . . £35/£10
Time Passes and Other Poems, Faber, 1942 . £25/£5
Collected Rhymes and Verses, Faber, 1944 . . £25/£5
The Burning-Glass and Other Poems, Faber, 1945 .
. . . . £20/£5
ditto, Viking (U.S.), 1945. . . . . . £20/£5
The Traveller, Faber, 1946 . . . . . £40/£20
Two Poems, Dropmore Press, 1946 . . . . £20
Rhymes and Verses, Collected Poems for Children, Holt (U.S.), 1947. . . . . . . £25/£10
Inward Companion, Faber, 1950 . . . . £25/£10
Winged Chariot, Faber, 1951 . . . . £30/£10
ditto, Viking (U.S.), 1951. . . . . . £25/£10
O Lovely England and Other Poems, Faber, 1953 . .
. . . . £30/£10
The Winnowing Dream, Faber, 1954 (Ariel Poem, wraps). £10
Selected Poems, Faber, 1954 . . . . . . £20/£5

The Morrow, privately printed, 1955 (50 copies, wraps). £25
Poems, Puffin, 1962 (wraps) £5

Children's Stories
The Three Mulla-Mulgars, Duckworth, 1910 . £45
ditto, Duckworth, 1910 (250 signed copies). . £125
ditto, Knopf (U.S.), 1919 . . . . . . £25
ditto, as **The Three Royal Monkeys**, Faber, 1935 . .
. . . . £15/£5
Broomsticks and Other Tales, Constable, 1925 (278 signed copies, slipcase) . . . . . £200/£165
ditto, Constable, 1925. . . . . . . £125/£25
ditto, Knopf (U.S.), 1930 . . . . . £100/£25
Miss Jemima, Blackwell, 1925 . . . . . £30
Lucy, Blackwell, 1925 . . . . £30
Old Joe, Blackwell, 1925. . . . . . . £30
Readings: Traditional Tales, told by de la Mare, Blackwell, 1925-28 (set of 6 vols) . . . £125
Told Again: Traditional Tales, Blackwell, 1927 . .
. . . . £65/£15
ditto, Blackwell, 1927 (260 signed copies) . . £100
ditto, Knopf (U.S.), 1927 . . . . . . £35/£10
Stories from the Bible, Faber, 1929 . . £50/£20
ditto, Faber, 1929 (300 signed copies) . . . £75
Desert Islands and Robinson Crusoe, Faber, 1930 .
. . . . £50/£15
ditto, Faber/Fountain Press, 1930 (650 signed copies) .
. . . . £75
Poems for Children, Constable, [1930] . . . £30/£5
The Dutch Cheese and The Lovely Myfanwy, Knopf (U.S.), 1931 . . . . £65/£35
The Lord Fish and Other Tales, Faber, 1933 £60/£25
ditto, Faber, 1933 (60 signed copies, d/w, slipcase) £250
This Year, Next Year, Faber, 1937 . . . £150/£50
Animal Stories, Faber, 1939 . . . . . £20/£5
Bells and Grass, Faber, 1941. . . . . . £20/£5
Mr Bumps and His Monkey, J.C. Winston (U.S.), 1942 . . . . £50/£15
The Old Lion and Other Stories, Faber, 1942 . £20/£5
The Magic Jacket and Other Stories, Faber, 1943 .
. . . . £20/£5
Collected Rhymes and Verses, Faber, 1944 . £15/£5
The Scarecrow and Other Stories, Faber, 1945 £20/£5
The Dutch Cheese and Other Stories, Faber, 1946 .
. . . . £20/£5
Collected Stories for Children, Faber, 1947 . £20/£5
Rhymes and Verses, Holt (U.S.), [1947] . £15/£5
Jack and the Beanstalk, Hulton Press, 1951 . £20/£5
Dick Whittington, Hulton Press, 1951 . . . £20/£5
Snow White, Hulton Press, 1952. . . . . £20/£5
Cinderella, Hulton Press, 1952 . . . . . £20/£5
Selected Stories and Verse, Puffin, 1952 (wraps) . £5
The Story of Joseph, Faber, 1958 (illustrated by Ardizzone) . . . . £40/£15
Story of Moses, Faber, 1959 (illustrated by Ardizzone)
. . . . £40/£15
A Penny a Day and Other Stories, Knopf (U.S.), 1960
. . . . £15/£5

Novels
Henry Brocken, Murray, 1904 . . . . . £50
ditto, Collins, 1924 (250 signed copies) . . . £50
ditto, Knopf (U.S.), 1924 . . . . . . £50/£15
The Return, Arnold, 1910 . . . . . . £150
ditto, Collins, 1922 (250 signed copies) . . . £50
ditto, Knopf (U.S.), 1922 . . . . . . £75/£25
Memoirs of a Midget, Collins, 1921 . . . £65/£20
ditto, Collins, 1921 (210 signed, numbered copies) £75
The Walter de la Mare Omnibus, Collins, 1933 . .
. . . . £25/£10

Short Stories
Story and Rhyme, Dent, 1921 . . . . £40/£15
Lispet, Lispet and Vaine, Bookman's Journal, 1923
(Vine Books No.3, 200 signed copies) . . £100
The Riddle and Other Stories, Selwyn & Blount, 1923
. . . . £75/£10
ditto, Selwyn & Blount, 1923 (310 signed copies) £65
ditto, Knopf (U.S.), 1923 . . . . . £40/£10
Ding Dong Bell, Selwyn & Blount, 1924 . £40/£10
ditto, Selwyn & Blount, 1924 (300 signed copies) . .
. . . . £60/£30
ditto, Knopf (U.S.), 1924 . . . . . £40/£10
Two Tales: 'The Green Room' and 'The
Connoisseur', Bookman's Journal, 1925 (200 signed
copies) £100
The Connoisseur and Other Stories, Collins, 1926 .
. . . . £100/£25
ditto, Collins, 1926 (250 signed copies) . . . £125
ditto, Knopf (U.S.), 1926 . . . . . £100/£20
Seaton's Aunt, Faber, 1927 (wraps) £65
At First Sight, Crosby Gaige (U.S.), 1928 (650 signed
copies) £35
On the Edge, Faber, 1930 . . . . £75/£25
ditto, Faber, 1930 (211 signed copies) . . . £125
Seven Short Stories, Faber, 1931 . . £100/£25
ditto, Faber, 1931 (100 signed copies) . . . £300
A Froward Child, Faber, 1934 . . . . £20/£5
The Wind Blows Over, Faber, 1936 . . . £75/£20
ditto, Macmillan (U.S.), 1936 . . . . £65/£20
The Nap and Other Stories, Nelson Classics, 1938 .
. . . . £20/£5
Stories, Essays and Poems, Dent, Everyman's Library,
1938 . . . . £20/£5
The Picnic and Other Stories, Faber, 1941 . . £20/£5
Best Stories of Walter de la Mare, Faber, 1942 £20/£5
The Almond Tree, Todd, 1943 . . . . . £20/£5
The Orgy, Todd, 1943 . . . . . . £20/£5
The Collected Tales of Walter de la Mare, Knopf
(U.S.), 1950 . . . . £25/£5
A Beginning and Other Stories, Faber, 1955 £50/£15
Ghost Stories, Folio Society, 1956 (slipcase) . £10/£5
Walter de la Mare: A Selection from his Writings,
Faber, 1956 . . . . £15/£5
Some Stories, Faber, 1962 . . . . . £15/£5
Eight Tales, Arkham House (U.S.), 1971 . . £25/£5

Miscellaneous
M.E. Coleridge: An Appreciation, The Guardian, 1907
(limited edition) £50
Rupert Brooke and the Intellectual Imagination,
Sidgwick & Jackson, 1919 . . . . . £25
Some Thoughts on Reading, Yellowsands Press, 1923
(340 copies) £25
The Printing of Poetry, C.U.P., 1931 (limited to 90
copies) £100
Lewis Carroll, Faber, 1932 . . . . . £50/£15
Poetry in Prose, Humphrey Milford, 1936 . £25/£10
ditto, O.U.P. (U.S.), 1937 . . . . . £25/£10
Arthur Thompson: A Memoir, privately printed, 1938
. . . . £15
An Introduction to Everyman, Dent, 1938 (400 copies)
. . . . £45
Pleasures and Speculations, Faber, 1940 . £30/£10
Private View, Faber, 1953 . . . . . £20/£5

MAURICE AND EDWARD
DETMOLD
(b.1883 d.1908, b.1883 d.1957)

Brothers who collaborated in illustrating until the
suicide of the former. Edward continued illustrating
books until the late 1920s.

Books Illustrated by Maurice and Edward Detmold
Pictures from Birdland, Dent, 1899 (24 coloured
lithographs) £600
Sixteen Illustrations of Subjects from Kipling's
'Jungle Book', Macmillan, 1903 (portfolio) . £1,000
The Jungle Book, Macmillan, 1908 (16 colour
illustrations) £250
ditto, Century (U.S.), 1913 (16 colour illustrations) .
. . . . £250

Books Illustrated by Edward Detmold
The Fables of Aesop, Hodder & Stoughton, 1909 (23
colour plates) £300
ditto, Hodder & Stoughton, 1909 (750 signed copies,
25 colour plates) £1,000
Birds and Beasts, by Camille Lemonnier, Allen, 1911
(6 colour plates) £125
The Book of Baby Beasts, by Florence E. Dugdale,
Frowde/Hodder & Stoughton, [1911] (19 colour
plates) £125
The Life of the Bee, by Maurice Maeterlinck, Allen,
1911 (13 colour plates) £250
Hours of Gladness, by Maurice Maeterlinck, Allen,
1912 (20 colour plates) £250
ditto, as *News of Spring*, Dodd, Mead (U.S.), 1913 (20
colour plates) £200
The Book of Baby Birds, by Florence E. Dugdale,
Frowde/Hodder & Stoughton, [1912] (19 colour
plates) £150

The Book of Baby Pets, by Florence E. Dugdale, Frowde/Hodder & Stoughton, [1915] (19 colour plates). £125
The Book of Baby Dogs, by Charles J. Kaberry, Frowde/Hodder & Stoughton, [1915] (colour plates). £125
Twenty-Four Nature Pictures, Dent, [1919] (portfolio) £500
Birds in Town and Village, by W.H. Hudson, Dent, 1919 (8 colour plates) £50
ditto, Dutton (U.S.), 1920. . . . . . £60/£25
The Children's Life of the Bee, Dodd, Mead (U.S.), 1919 (5 colour plates) £25
ditto, Unwin, 1920 (5 colour plates) . . . £60/£25
Our Little Neighbours, by Charles J. Kaberry, Humphrey Milford/Oxford Univ. Press, 1921, [1921] (11 colour plates) . . . . £250/£100
Fabre's Book of Insects, by J.H.C. Fabre, Hodder & Stoughton, [1921] (12 colour plates) . . £450/£150
ditto, Dodd, Mead (U.S.), 1921 (12 colour plates) . . . . £250/£100
Rainbow House for Boys and Girls, by Arthur Vine Hall, Cape, 1923 (6 colour plates) . . . £150/£45
The Arabian Nights - Tales from the Thousand and One Nights, Hodder & Stoughton, [1924] (12 colour plates) £350
ditto, Hodder & Stoughton, [1924] (100 signed copies, 12 colour plates) £1,500
ditto, Dodd, Mead (U.S.), 1925 (12 colour plates, glassine d/w and slipcase) . . . . £500/£250
The Fantastic Creatures of Edward Julius Detmold, Pan, 1976 (wraps) £15
ditto, Peacock Press/Bantam Books (U.S.), 1976 (wraps) £10
ditto, Scribner's (U.S.), 1976 . . . . £25/£10

COLIN DEXTER
(b.1930)

A crime writer whose Inspector Morse is pre-eminent among the contemporary television detectives.

Novels
Last Bus to Woodstock, Macmillan, 1975 £1,250/£75
ditto, St Martin's Press (U.S.), 1975 . . . £850/£65
Last Seen Wearing, Macmillan, 1976 . £1,000/£75
ditto, St Martin's Press (U.S.), 1976 . . . £600/£45
The Silent World of Nicholas Quinn, Macmillan, 1977 . . . . £1,000/£75
ditto, St Martin's Press (U.S.), 1977 . . . £250/£35
Service of All the Dead, Macmillan, 1979 . £250/£25
ditto, St Martin's Press (U.S.), 1980 . . . £150/£15
The Dead of Jericho, Macmillan, 1980 . . £200/£20
ditto, St Martin's Press (U.S.), 1980 . . . £150/£15
Riddle of the Third Mile, Macmillan, 1983 . £150/£15
ditto, St Martin's Press (U.S.), 1983 . . . £100/£10
The Secret of Annexe 3, Macmillan, 1986 . £100/£10
ditto, St Martin's Press (U.S.), 1987 . . . £75/£10

The Wench is Dead, Macmillan, 1989 . . . £25/£5
ditto, St Martin's Press (U.S.), 1990 . . . . £15/£5
The Jewel That Was Ours, Scorpion Press, 1991 (150 signed copies, quarter leather) £150
ditto, Scorpion Press, 1991 (20 signed deluxe copies) £300
ditto, Macmillan, 1991 . . . . £25/£5
ditto, Crown (U.S.), 1992 . . . . £10/£5
The Way Through the Woods, Macmillan, 1992 . . . . £15/£5
ditto, Scorpion Press, 1992 (150 signed copies, quarter leather) £100
ditto, Scorpion Press, 1992 (20 signed deluxe copies) £300
ditto, Crown (U.S.), 1993 . . . . . . £10/£5
Daughters of Cain, Macmillan, 1992 . . £10/£5
ditto, Crown (U.S.), 1994 . . . . . . £10/£5
Death is Now My Neighbour, Macmillan, 1996 £10/£5
ditto, as *Death is Now My Neighbor*, Crown (U.S.), 1997 . . . . £10/£5
The Remorseful Day, Macmillan, 1999 . . £10/£5
ditto, Crown (U.S.), 1999 . . . . . . £10/£5

Short Stories
Morse's Greatest Mystery and Other Stories, Macmillan, 1993 . . . . £10/£5
ditto, Scorpion Press, 1993 (99 signed copies, quarter leather) £125
ditto, Scorpion Press, 1993 (20 signed deluxe copies) £250
ditto, Crown (U.S.), 1993 . . . . . . £10/£5
Inside Story, Macmillan, 1993 (for American Express, wraps). £15
Neighbourhood Watch, Moorhouse/Sorenson, 1993 (150 numbered copies, wraps) £25
ditto, Moorhouse/Sorenson, 1993 (50 signed, numbered copies, wraps). £50
ditto, Moorhouse/Sorenson, 1993 (26 signed, numbered copies). £100
As Good as Gold, Kodak/Pan, 1994 (wraps) . . £5

Omnibus Editions
An Inspector Morse Omnibus, Macmillan, 1991 . . . . £20/£5
The Second Inspector Morse Omnibus, Macmillan, 1992 . . . . £15/£5
The Third Inspector Morse Omnibus, Macmillan, 1993 . . . . £15/£5
The Fourth Inspector Morse Omnibus, Macmillan, 1996 . . . . £15/£5

Non Fiction
Liberal Studies: An Outline Course, Pergamon Press, 1964 (written as N.C. Dexter, with E.G. Rayner, 2 vols) . . . . £20/£5 (the set)
Guide to Contemporary Politics, Pergamon Press, 1966 (written as N.C. Dexter, with E.G. Rayner) . . . . £15/£5

MICHAEL DIBDIN
(b.1947)

A popular crime writer, Dibdin is considered by some to be the next P.D. James.

The Last Sherlock Holmes Story, Cape, 1978 . . .
. . . . £350/£50
ditto, Pantheon (U.S.), 1978 . . . . . . £25/£5
A Rich Full Death, Cape, 1986 . . . . £125/£20
ditto, Vintage/Black Lizard (U.S.), 1999 (wraps) . £5
Ratking, Faber, 1988 . . . . £100/£15
ditto, Bantam (U.S.), 1989 . . . . . . £25/£5
The Tryst, Faber, 1989 . . . . £40/£5
ditto, Summit (U.S.), 1990 . . . . . . £25/£5
Vendetta, Faber, 1990 . . . . £25/£5
ditto, Doubleday (U.S.), 1991 . . . . . £15/£5
Dirty Tricks, Faber, 1991 . . . . . . £20/£5
ditto, Summit (U.S.), 1991 . . . . . £15/£5
Cabal, Faber, 1992 . . . . £20/£5
ditto, Doubleday (U.S.), 1993 . . . . £15/£5
The Dying of the Light, Faber, 1993 . . . £15/£5
ditto, Pantheon (U.S.), 1993 . . . . . £10/£5
Dead Lagoon, Faber, 1994 . . . . . £15/£5
ditto, Pantheon (U.S.), 1994 . . . . . £10/£5
Dark Spectre, Faber, 1995 . . . . . £15/£5
ditto, Pantheon (U.S.), 1995 . . . . . £10/£5
Cosi Fan Tuti, Faber, 1996 . . . . . £10/£5
ditto, Pantheon (U.S.), 1996 . . . . . £10/£5
A Long Finish, Faber, 1998 . . . . . £10/£5
ditto, Pantheon (U.S.), 1998 . . . . . £10/£5
Blood Rain, Faber, 1999 . . . . . . £10/£5
ditto, Pantheon (U.S.), 1999 . . . . . £10/£5
Thanksgiving, Faber, 2000 . . . . . £10/£5
ditto, Pantheon (U.S.), 2000 . . . . . £10/£5
And Then You Die, Faber, 2002 . . . . £10/£5

PHILIP K. DICK
(b.1928 d.1982)

Dick was an American writer of science fiction, often dealing in his work with the effects of mechanisation, hallucinogenic drugs and schizophrenic delusions.

Short Stories
A Handful of Darkness, Rich & Cowan, 1955 (first issue boards blue, lettered silver, with first issue d/w not listing *World of Chance* on rear panel). . . .
. . . . £1,000/£200
ditto, Rich & Cowan, 1955 (second issue, orange boards, lettered black) . . . . . £450/£150
ditto, Gregg Press (U.S.), 1978 (no d/w) . . £50
The Variable Man, Ace Books (U.S.), 1957 (wraps) .
. . . . £35
The Preserving Machine, Ace Books (U.S.), 1969 (wraps) £30
ditto, Gollancz, 1971 . . . . £175/£25

The Book of Philip K. Dick, Daw Books (U.S.), 1973 (wraps) £10
ditto, as *The Turning Wheel*, Coronet, 1977 (wraps) .
. . . . £10
The Best of Philip K. Dick, Ballantine (U.S.), 1977 (wraps) £10
The Golden Man, Berkeley (U.S.), 1980 (wraps) £10
I Hope I Shall Arrive Soon, Doubleday (U.S.), 1985 .
. . . . £50/£10
ditto, Gollancz, 1986 . . . . £50/£10

Novels
Solar Lottery, Ace Books (U.S.), 1955 (wraps). £35
ditto, as *World of Chance*, Rich & Cowan, 1956 . .
. . . . £2,000/£400
ditto, Gregg Press (U.S.), 1979 (no d/w). . £300
The World Jones Made, Ace Books (U.S.), 1956 (wraps) £30
ditto, Sidgwick & Jackson, 1968 . . . . £650/£150
ditto, Gregg Press (U.S.), 1979 (no d/w). . £65
The Man Who Japed, Ace Books (U.S.), 1956 (wraps)
. . . . £30
ditto, Eyre Methuen, 1978 . . . . . £175/£35
Eye in the Sky, Ace Books (U.S.), 1957 (wraps) £30
ditto, Gregg Press (U.S.), 1979 . . . . £65
The Cosmic Puppets, Ace Books (U.S.), 1957 (wraps)
. . . . £35
ditto, Severn House, 1986. . . . . £35/£10
Time Out Of Joint, Lippincott (U.S.), 1959. £600/£125
ditto, Science Fiction Book Club, 1961 . . £25/£10
Dr Futurity, Ace Books (U.S.), 1960 (wraps) . £40
Vulcan's Hammer, Ace Books (U.S.), 1960 (wraps) .
. . . . £25
ditto, Gregg Press (U.S.), 1979 . . . . £45
The Man in the High Castle, Putnam (U.S.), 1962. .
. . . . £400/£65
ditto, Penguin, 1965 (wraps) £10
ditto, Gollancz, 1975 . . . . . . £35/£10
The Game Players of Titan, Ace Books (U.S.), 1963 (wraps) £20
ditto, White Lion, 1974 . . . . . . £200/£35
Martian Time-Slip, Ballantine Books (U.S.), 1964 (wraps) £20
ditto, New English Library, 1976 . . . £175/£35
The Simulacra, Ace Books (U.S.), 1964 (wraps) £40
ditto, Eyre Methuen, 1977 . . . . . £250/£35
The Penultimate Truth, Belmont (U.S.), 1964 (wraps)
. . . . £20
ditto, Cape, 1967 . . . . £600/£75
Clans of the Alphane Moon, Ace Books (U.S.), 1964 (wraps) £20
ditto, Gregg Press (U.S.), 1979 (no d/w). . £50
The Three Stigmata of Palmer Eldritch, Doubleday (U.S.), 1965 . . . . £1,250/£150
ditto, Cape, 1966 . . . . £300/£35
Dr Bloodmoney, Ace Books (U.S.), 1965 (wraps) £20
ditto, Gregg Press (U.S.), 1977 (no d/w). . £400
Now Wait for Last Year, Doubleday (U.S.), 1966 . .
. . . . £175/£45

The Crack in Space, Ace Books (U.S.), 1966 (wraps) .
. . . . £25
ditto, Severn House, 1989. . . . . . . £30/£5
The Unteleported Man, Ace Books (U.S.), 1966
(wraps) £20
ditto, Berkley (U.S.), 1983 (wraps, revised version) .
. . . . £10
ditto, as *Lies Inc.*, Gollancz, 1984 (further revisions) .
. . . . £40/£10
The Zap Gun, Pyramid (U.S.), 1967 (wraps) . £25
ditto, Gregg Press (U.S.), 1979 . . . . £65
Counter-Clock World, Berkley (U.S.), 1967 (wraps) .
. . . . £30
ditto, White Lion, 1977 . . . . . . £150/£25
The Ganymede Takeover, Ace Books (U.S.), 1967
(with Ray Nelson, wraps) £20
ditto, Severn House, 1988. . . . . . . £40/£5
Do Androids Dream of Electric Sheep?, Doubleday
(U.S.), 1969 . . . . . . £5,000/£1,000
ditto, Rapp & Whiting, 1969. . . . . £650/£100
Ubik, Doubleday (U.S.), 1969 . . . £600/£65
ditto, Rapp & Whiting, 1970 . . . . . £175/£25
Galactic Pot-Healer, Berkeley (U.S.), 1969 (wraps) .
. . . . £20
ditto, Gollancz, 1971 . . . . . . £50/£10
A Maze of Death, Doubleday (U.S.), 1970 . £750/£100
ditto, Gollancz, 1972 . . . . £250/£35
Our Friends from Frolix 8, Ace Books (U.S.), 1970
(wraps) £15
ditto, Ace Books (U.S.), 1971 . . . . £35/£10
ditto, Kinnell, 1989 . . . . . . £50/£10
A Philip K. Dick Omnibus, Sidgwick & Jackson, 1970
. . . . £50/£15
We Can Build You, Daw Books (U.S.), 1972 (wraps) .
. . . . £10
ditto, Severn House, 1988. . . . . . . £35/£5
Flow My Tears, The Policeman Said, Doubleday
(U.S.), 1974 . . . . £275/£35
ditto, Gollancz, 1974 . . . . £200/£25
Confessions of a Crap Artist, Entwhistle Books (U.S.),
1975 (90 signed copies of 1,000, no d/w) . . £500
ditto, Entwhistle Books (U.S.), 1975 (410 copies of
1,000). £200
ditto, Entwhistle Books (U.S.), 1975 (500 copies of
1,000, wraps). £30
ditto, Magnum, 1979 (wraps). £10
Deus Irae, Doubleday (U.S.), 1976 (with Roger
Zelazny) . . . . £50/£10
ditto, Gollancz, 1977 . . . . . . £45/£10
A Scanner Darkly, Doubleday (U.S.), 1977 £35/£10
ditto, Gollancz, 1977 . . . . . . £25/£10
Valis, Bantam (U.S.), 1981 (wraps) . . . £10
ditto, Kerosina, 1987 . . . . . . £25/£10
ditto, Kerosina, 1987 (limited edition of 250 copies
with d/w, in slipcase together with the 325 copy
hardcover edition of *Cosmogony and Cosmology*,
Kerosina, 1987) £75
The Divine Invasion, Simon Schuster/Timescape
(U.S.), 1981 . . . . £25/£5

The Transmigration of Timothy Archer, Simon &
Schuster, 1982 . . . . £25/£5
ditto, Gollancz, 1982 . . . . £25/£5
The Man Whose Teeth Were Exactly Alike, Ziesling
(U.S.), 1984 . . . . £125/£35
In Milton Lumky Territory, Dragon Press, 1985 .
. . . . £40/£10
ditto, Dragon Press, 1985 (50 signed, numbered copies)
. . . . £200
ditto, Gollancz, 1986 . . . . £40/£10
Ubik: The Screenplay, Corroboree Press (U.S.), 1985 .
. . . . £100/£45
ditto, Corroboree Press (U.S.), 1985 (20 signed copies
in leather). £250
Puttering About in a Small Land, Chicago Academy
(U.S.), 1985 . . . . £25/£5
Radio Free Albemuth, Arbor House (U.S.), 1985 . .
. . . . £20/£5
ditto, Severn House, 1987. . . . . . . £20/£5
Humpty Dumpty in Oakland, Gollancz, 1986 £65/£15
Mary and the Giant, Arbor House (U.S.), 1987 £25/£5
ditto, Arbor House (U.S.), 1987 (50 copies bound in
quarter leather) £200
ditto, Gollancz, 1988 . . . . £25/£5
Collected Stories, Underwood Miller, 1987 (5 vols)
. . . . £200
ditto, Underwood Miller, 1987 (deluxe limited edition)
. . . . £350
ditto, Gollancz, 1988-90 (4 vols). . . £25/£10 each
Cosmogony and Cosmology, Kerosina, 1987 (no d/w).
. . . . £65
ditto, Kerosina, 1987 (wraps). £15
Nick and the Glimmung, Gollancz, 1988 . £25/£10
ditto, Trafalgar Square (U.S.), 1988 . . . £25/£10
The Broken Bubble, Morrow/Arbor House (U.S.),
1988 . . . . £15/£5
ditto, Gollancz, 1989 . . . . £15/£5
ditto, Ultramarine Press, 1989 (150 copies, quarter
leather) £125
ditto, Ultramarine Press, 1989 (26 copies, full leather).
. . . . £200

CHARLES DICKENS
(b.1812 d.1870)

An acclaimed and prolific author, Dickens' position
as one of the 'greats' of English literature is beyond
dispute.

*Sketches by 'Boz', Illustrative of Every-Day Life, and
Every-Day People*, John Macrone MDCCCXXXVI
1836 (2 vols, dark green cloth, Preface states
'Furnival's Inn, February 1836', 16 plates by
Cruikshank, frontispiece and 7 plates per vol) £7,000
ditto, John Macrone MDCCCXXXVI 1836 (the above
vols rebound). £2,000
*Sketches by 'Boz': Illustrative of Every-Day Life, and
Every-Day People. The Second Series*, John Macrone

MDCCCXXXVII 1837 (1 vol, pink cloth, Preface states 'December 17, 1836', 10 plates by Cruikshank) £3,000
ditto, John Macrone MDCCCXXXVII 1837 (the above rebound) £1,000
Sketches by 'Boz' Illustrative of Every-Day Life, and Every-Day People, Chapman & Hall, November 1837-June 1839 (first and second series together, 20 monthly parts, 40 plates by George Cruikshank, 2 per volume, pink wrappers) £20,000
ditto, Chapman & Hall, 1839 (first 1 vol. edition dated '1837', monthly parts bound with wrapper in glossy brown or purple cloth, with 40 plates by George Cruikshank) £2,000
Sunday Under Three Heads, Chapman & Hall, 1836 (pseud. 'Timothy Sparks', 3 illustrations plus wrapper by H.K. Browne, first edition the title appears as a heading to Chapter III on p.35 and 'hair' spelt correctly on p.7, line 15, buff wraps) . . £2,250
ditto, Chapman & Hall, 1836 (the above rebound) £750
The Village Coquettes, Richard Bentley, 1836 (wraps) £3,000
ditto, Richard Bentley, 1836 (the above rebound) £1,000
The Posthumous Papers of the Pickwick Club edited by 'Boz', Chapman & Hall, April 1836-Nov 1837 (20 monthly parts in 19. Parts I & II Illustrated by Robert Seymour, part III by R. W. Buss and parts IV-XIX/XX by Phiz. Green wrappers) . . . £5,000
ditto, Chapman & Hall, 1837 (first book edition, 1 vol, monthly parts bound with or without wrappers. 43 illustrations by R. Seymour and Phiz. Slate or purple/black cloth, first issue with 'S Veller' on p.342, line 5) £5,000
ditto, Chapman & Hall, 1837 (the above rebound) £750
ditto, Carey Lea & Blanchard (U.S.), 1837 (5 vols) £2,500
Oliver Twist; or, The Parish Boy's Progress, Richard Bentley, 1838 (pseud. 'Boz', 3 vols, illustrated by George Cruikshank, red-brown cloth, first issue with 'Rose Maylie and Oliver' plate in vol 3 showing them at fireside) £10,000
ditto, Richard Bentley, 1838 (the above rebound) £2,000
ditto, Richard Bentley, 1838 (second issue showing them at church) £2,500
ditto, Richard Bentley 1838 (second edition, or third issue, with 'Dickens' on title page, not 'Boz'). £2,000
ditto, Bradbury & Evans, January-October 1846 (10 monthly parts with illustrations by George Cruikshank, green boards) £10,000
ditto, Bradbury & Evans, MDCCCXLVI 1846 (first 1 vol. edition, with slate-coloured cloth) . . £1,750
ditto, Bradbury & Evans, MDCCCXLVI 1846 (the above rebound) £450
Sketches of Young Gentlemen, Chapman & Hall, 1838 (anonymous, 6 illustrations and cover by Phiz, blue-green paper boards) £1,500
The Memoirs of Joseph Grimaldi, Richard Bentley, 1838 (edited by 'Boz', 2 vols, 12 plates and

frontispiece to vol 1 by Cruikshank, first issue pink cloth, without border around final plate 'The Last Song'). £2,000
ditto, Richard Bentley, 1838 (as above, second issue brown cloth with border around final plate 'The Last Song'). £1,000
The Life and Adventures of Nicholas Nickleby, Chapman & Hall, April 1838-October 1839 (20 monthly parts in 19, illustrated by Phiz, green wrappers, first issue with 'vister' on p.123, line 17) £3,000
ditto, Chapman & Hall, 1839 (first book edition, monthly parts in 1 vol., illustrated by Phiz, dark olive green cloth) £2,500
ditto, Chapman & Hall, 1839 (the above rebound) £300
Sketches of Young Couples, Chapman & Hall, 1840 ('By the Author of Sketches of Young Gentlemen', 6 illustrations and cover by Phiz, grey-green paper boards) £1,000
Master Humphrey's Clock, Chapman & Hall, April 1840-Nov 1841 (by 'Boz', 88 weekly parts, illustrated by G. Cattermole, Phiz & Daniel Maclise, white wrappers). £1,750
ditto, Chapman & Hall, April 1840-Nov 1841 (20 monthly parts, illustrated as above, green wrappers) £1,500
ditto, Chapman & Hall, MDCCCXL/MDCCCXLI 1841 (first book edition, 3 vols, weekly or monthly parts, illustrated as above, brown cloth with clock on front pointing to volume numbers) . . . £750
ditto, Chapman & Hall, MDCCCXL/MDCCCXLI 1841 (as above but variant cloth, no hands on clock) £300
The Old Curiosity Shop, Chapman & Hall, 1841 (original monthly parts from 'Master Humphrey's Clock', cloth binding) £1,250
Barnaby Rudge, Chapman & Hall, 1841 (original monthly parts from 'Master Humphrey's Clock', cloth binding) £1,750
American Notes for General Circulation, Chapman & Hall, 1842 (2 vols, first issue with prelims misnumbered with p.10 (x) as 'xvi', purple cloth) £1,000
ditto, Chapman & Hall, 1842 (as above but prelims corrected). £500
Martin Chuzzlewit, Chapman & Hall, Jan 1843-July 1844 (20 monthly parts in 19, illustrated by Phiz, green wrappers) £1,250
ditto, Chapman & Hall, MDCCCXXLIV 1844 (first book edition made up of unsold monthly parts, Prussian blue cloth binding). £4,000
ditto, Chapman & Hall, MDCCCXXLIV 1844 (as above, brown cloth binding) £3,500
ditto, Chapman & Hall, MDCCCXXLIV 1844 (as above rebound) £300
A Christmas Carol, Chapman & Hall, 1843 (many variants but earliest may have title page dated 1843, brown cloth, green endpapers, and 'Stave I' on first text page) £15,000

The Chimes, Chapman & Hall, 1845 (first issue with publisher's name in title vignette) £500
ditto, Chapman & Hall, 1845 (second issue with publisher's name below title vignette) . . . £300
The Cricket on the Hearth, Bradbury & Evans, 1846 (first issue with ad. page [175] without heading 'New Editions of Oliver Twist', red cloth) . . . £500
ditto, Bradbury & Evans, 1846 (second issue) . £300
The Battle of Life: A Love Story, Bradbury & Evans, 1846 (first issue, on engraved title page 'A Love Story' in heavy type and publisher's name at bottom of page) £30,000
ditto, Bradbury & Evans, 1846 (second issue with 'A Love Story' in light type supported by cupids and publisher's name at bottom of page) . . . £5,000
ditto, Bradbury & Evans, 1846 (third issue as above but publisher's name not at bottom of page) . . £1,000
Pictures from Italy, Bradbury & Evans, 1846 (illustrations by Samuel Palmer, blue cloth) . £500
Dombey and Son, Bradbury & Evans, 1848 (20 monthly parts in 19, illustrated by Phiz, with 12 line errata slip in part V) £1,250
ditto, Bradbury & Evans, 1848 (first book edition, monthly parts bound in dark green cloth.) . . £2,000
ditto, Bradbury & Evans, 1848 (as above rebound) £300
The Haunted Man and The Ghost's Bargain, Bradbury & Evans, 1848 (date on title page '1848', red cloth with blind-stamped borders) . . . £200
ditto, Bradbury & Evans, 1848 (as above but date on title page 'MDCCCXLVIII') £1,000
The Personal History of David Copperfield, Bradbury & Evans, May 1849-Nov, 1850 (20 monthly parts in 19, illustrated by Phiz, green wrappers) . £6,000
ditto, Bradbury & Evans, 1850 (first book edition, monthly parts bound in dark green cloth) . . £5,000
A Child's History of England, Bradbury & Evans, 1852, 53, 54 (3 vols, first issue of vol. I with ad. page [211] listing 4 books plus 5 Christmas books, and vol. III with ad. page [324] 'Collected and Revised', red cloth) £1,500
ditto, Bradbury & Evans, 1852, 53, 54 (3 vols, second issue of vol. I with ad. page [211] listing this book, plus 7 books plus 5 Christmas books, and vol. III with ad page [324] 'Corrected and Revised', red cloth) £750
Bleak House, Bradbury & Evans, March 1852-Sept 1853 (20 monthly parts in 19, illustrated by Phiz, blue wrappers) £1,750
ditto, Bradbury & Evans, 1853 (first book edition, monthly parts bound in cloth) £3,000
ditto, Bradbury & Evans, 1853 (the above rebound) £250
Hard Times, Bradbury & Evans, 1854 (1 vol., green cloth, with 'Price 5/' on spine) £1,000
ditto, Bradbury & Evans, 1854 (1 vol., green cloth, no price on spine) £500
Little Dorrit, Bradbury & Evans, Dec 1855-June 1857 (20 monthly parts in 19, illustrated by Phiz, blue wrappers, errata slip in part XVI) . . . £1,500

ditto, Bradbury & Evans, 1857 (first book edition, monthly parts bound in olive green cloth),. . £2,500
A Tale of Two Cities, Chapman & Hall, June-Dec MDCCCLIX 1859 (8 parts in 7, illustrated by Phiz, first issue page 213 misnumbered '113', blue wrappers) £7,500
ditto, Chapman & Hall, 1859 (first book edition, monthly parts bound in red cloth, first issue) £7,500
ditto, Chapman & Hall, 1859 (as above in green cloth, first issue) £5,000
ditto, Chapman & Hall, 1859 (as above, rebound) £750
ditto, Chapman & Hall, 1859 (second issue with pages correctly numbered, red cloth) £5,000
ditto, Chapman & Hall, 1859 (second issue with pages correctly numbered, green cloth) £3,500
Great Expectations, Chapman & Hall, MDCCCLXI 1861 (3 vols, purple, plum or yellow-green cloth, 32 pages of ads dated May 1861) £17,500
The Uncommercial Traveller, Chapman & Hall, 1861 (ads dated December 1860, red/purple cloth) £1,250
Our Mutual Friend, Chapman & Hall, May 1864-May 1865 (20 monthly parts in 19, illustrated by Marcus Stone, green wrappers) £1,250
ditto, Chapman & Hall, 1865 (first book edition, 2 vols of monthly parts bound in brown cloth) . £1,500
ditto, Chapman & Hall, 1865 (the above rebound) £250
The Mystery of Edwin Drood, Chapman & Hall, April-Sept 1870 (unfinished, six monthly parts, illustrated by Luke Fildes with cover design by Charles Alston Collins, green wrappers) £750
ditto, Chapman & Hall, 1870 first book edition (monthly parts bound in green cloth, sawtooth border around front cover) £500
ditto, Chapman & Hall, 1870 first book edition (monthly parts bound in green cloth, no border around front cover) £200

ISAK DINESEN
(b.1885 d.1962)

Isak Dinesen was the pseudonym of Danish-born writer Karen Blixen, née Dinesen. She is perhaps best known for her autobiographical novel *Out of Africa*, although her gothic short stories are also highly regarded.

Seven Gothic Tales, Putnam, 1934 . . . £300/£50
ditto, Smith & Haas (U.S.), 1934 (by Dinesen) . . . . £100/£25
ditto, Smith & Haas (U.S.), 1934 (1010 numbered copies, with slipcase, no d/w) . . . £125/£100
Out of Africa, Putnam, 1937 (by Blixen) . . . . £1,000/£150
ditto, Random House (U.S.), 1938 . . . £250/£45
Winter's Tales, Putnam, 1942 (by Blixen) . £125/£20
ditto, Random House (U.S.), 1942 . . . £100/£20
The Angelic Avengers, Putnam, 1946 (pseud. 'Pierre Andrezei') . . . . £80/£15

ditto, Random House (U.S.), 1946 . . . £80/£15
Last Tales, Putnam, 1957 (by Dinesen) . £35/£10
ditto, Random House (U.S.), 1957 . . . £30/£10
Anecdotes of Destiny, Joseph, 1958 (by Dinesen) . .
. . . . £40/£10
ditto, Random House (U.S.), 1958 . . . £40/£10
Shadows on the Grass, Joseph, 1961 (by Dinesen). .
. . . . £30/£5
ditto, Random House (U.S.), 1961 . . . . £30/£5
On Mottoes of my Life, Ministry of Foreign Affairs
(Copenhagen), 1962 (no d/w) £20
Ehrengard, Joseph, 1963 (by Dinesen) . . £40/£10
ditto, Random House (U.S.), 1963 . . . £30/£10
Isak Dinesen: Letters from Africa: 1914-1931,
Wiedenfeld/Univ. of Chicago Press, 1981 . £35/£10
Daguerreotypes and Other Essays, Heinemann, 1974 .
. . . . £20/£5
ditto, Univ. of Chicago Press Chicago (U.S.), 1979 .
. . . . £20/£5

BENJAMIN DISRAELI
(b.1804 d.1881)

Perhaps better-known as a politician, Disraeli was
also a successful and popular novelist of the
nineteenth century.

Fiction
Vivian Grey, Colburn, 1826-27 (5 vols, anonymous) .
. . . . £1,000
The Voyage of Captain Popanilla, Colburn, 1828 £300
The Young Duke, Colburn, 1831 (3 vols) . . £750
Contarini Fleming: A Pyschological Auto-biography,
Murray, 1832 (4 vols) £500
ditto, as **The Young Venetian**, Murray, 1834 . £250
The Wondrous Tale of Alroy, and **The rise of
Iskander**, Saunders & Otley, 1833 (3 vols) . £250
A Year at Hartlebury, or The Election, Saunders &
Otley, 1834 (pseud. 'Cherry' and 'Fair Star', with
Sarah Disraeli, 2 vols) £300
Henrietta Temple, Colburn, 1836 (3 vols) . . £500
Venetia, or The Poet's Daughter, Colburn, 1837 (3
vols) £500
Coningsby, or The New Generation, Colburn, 1844 (3
vols) £500
Sybil, or The Two Nations, Colburn, 1845 (3 vols) .
. . . . £500
Tancred, or The New Crusade, Colburn, 1847 (3 vols)
. . . . £400
Lothair, Longman, 1870 (3 vols) £250
Endymion, Longman, 1880 (3 vols). . . . £250
Ixion in Heaven, Cape, 1925. . . . . £25/£10
ditto, Holt (U.S.), 1925 . . . . . . £25/£10
The Infernal Marriage, William Jackson, 1929 (850
numbered copies) . . . . . . £60/£35

Poetry
The Revolutionary Epick, Moxon, 1834 (2 vols) £250

J.P. DONLEAVY
(b.1926)

An American-born novelist and playwright,
Donleavy's first book, *The Ginger Man* was
controversial and had, at first, to be published in
Paris. He became an Irish citizen in 1967.

Novels
The Ginger Man, Olympia Press (Paris), 1955 (wraps)
. . . . £500
ditto, Neville Spearman, 1956 (expurgated text) . .
. . . . £100/£20
ditto, Olympia Press, Paris, 1958. . . . £75/£20
ditto, McDowell Obolensky (U.S.), 1958 . £40/£10
A Singular Man, Little, Brown (U.S.), 1963 £40/£10
ditto, Bodley Head, 1964 [1963] . . . . £40/£10
The Beastly Beatitudes of Balthazar B, Delacorte
(U.S.), 1968 . . . . £25/£10
ditto, Eyre & Spotiswoode, 1969. . . . £25/£10
The Onion Eaters, Delacorte (U.S.), 1971 . £25/£10
ditto, Eyre & Spotiswoode, 1971. . . . £25/£10
A Fairy Tale of New York, Delacorte (U.S.), 1973. . .
. . . . £25/£10
ditto, Eyre Methuen, 1973 . . . . . £25/£10
The Destinies of Darcy Dancer, Gentleman, Delacorte
(U.S.), 1977 . . . . £25/£10
ditto, Franklin Library (U.S.), 1977 . . . . £25
ditto, Allen Lane, 1978 . . . . . . £25/£10
Schultz, Delacorte (U.S.), 1979 . . . £25/£10
ditto, Allen Lane, 1980 . . . . . . £25/£10
Leila, Delacorte (U.S.), 1983. . . . . £25/£10
ditto, Franklin Library (U.S.), 1983 . . . . £25
ditto, Allen Lane, 1983 . . . . . . £20/£5
De Alfonce Tennis, Dutton (U.S.), 1984 . £20/£5
ditto, Weidenfeld & Nicolson, 1984 . . . £20/£5
Are You Listening, Rabbi Low, Little, Brown (U.S.),
1987 . . . . £20/£5
ditto, Viking, 1987 . . . . £20/£5
That Darcy, That Dancer, That Gentleman, Little,
Brown (U.S.), 1990 . . . . . . £20/£5
ditto, Viking, 1990 . . . . £20/£5
The Lady Who Liked to Clean Rest Rooms, Little,
Brown (U.S.), 1997 . . . . . . £20/£5
Wrong Information Given Out At Princetown, Little,
Brown (U.S.), 1998 . . . . . . £20/£5

Short Stories and Novellas
Meet My Maker the Mad Molecule, Little, Brown
(U.S.), 1964 . . . . £25/£10
ditto, Bodley Head, 1965 . . . . . £25/£10
The Saddest Summer of Samuel S, Delacorte (U.S.),
1966 . . . . £25/£10
ditto, Eyre & Spottiswoode, 1967 . . . £25/£10

Plays

The Ginger Man: A Play, Random House (U.S.), 1961
. . . . £30/£10
ditto, as *What They Did in Dublin With 'The Ginger Man': A Play*, Macgibbon & Kee, 1961 . £30/£10
Fairy Tales of New York, Random House (U.S.), 1961
. . . . £30/£10
ditto, Penguin, 1961 (wraps) £10
A Singular Man, Bodley Head, 1965 . . . £20/£5
The Plays of J.P. Donleavy, Delacorte (U.S.), 1972 .
. . . . £30/£10
ditto, Penguin, 1974 (wraps) £10

Others

The Unexpurgated Code: A Complete Manual of Survival and Manners, Delacorte (U.S.), 1975 .
. . . . £30/£10
ditto, Wildwood House, 1975 . . . . . £20/£5
Ireland: In All Her Sins And In Some Of Her Graces, Viking (U.S.), 1986 . . . . £20/£5
ditto, Joseph, 1986. . . . . £20/£5
A Singular Country, Ryan Publishing, 1989 . £20/£5
ditto, Norton (U.S.), 1990. . . . . . £20/£5
A History of the Ginger Man, Viking, 1994 £25/£10
ditto, Houghton Mifflin (U.S.), 1994 . . . £20/£5
An Author and His Image, Viking, 1997 . £25/£10

LORD ALFRED DOUGLAS
(b.1870 d.1945)

Notorious for his tempestuous affair with Oscar Wilde, Douglas was also a serious poet of some merit.

Poetry

Poemes, Mercur de France (Paris), 1896 . . £275
ditto, Mercur de France (Paris), 1896 (20 copies on Holland paper) £500
ditto, Mercur de France (Paris), 1896 (50 deluxe copies) £500
ditto, Mercur de France (Paris), 1896 (25 grande deluxe copies) £1,000
Perkin Warbeck and Some Other Poems, Chiswick Press, 1897 (50 copies) £400
Tails With a Twist: Animal Nonsense Verse, Arnold, 1898 . . . . £200
ditto, Batsford, 1979 . . . . . . £10/£5
The City of the Soul, Grant Richards, 1899 . £175
The Duke of Berwick, Smithers, [1899]. . . £100
The Placid Pug, Duckworth, 1906 . . . . £75
The Pongo Papers and the Duke of Berwick, Greening, 1907 . . . . £100
Sonnets, W.H. Smith & Son/Academy Publishing Company, 1909 . . . . £75
ditto, Arden Press, 1909 (large paper edition) . £150
Collected Poems, Martin Secker, 1919 . . . £35
ditto, Martin Secker, 1919 (200 copies, signed by the author) £200

In Excelsis, Martin Secker, 1924. . . . £200/£75
ditto, Martin Secker, 1924 (100 signed copies) . £200
Nine Poems, privately printed for A.J.A. Symons, 1926 (50 copies) £500
Selected Poems, Martin Secker, 1926 . . £25/£10
Lord Alfred Douglas [*'Selected Poems'*], Ernest Benn, 'Augustan Books of Modern Poetry', [1926] (wraps).
. . . . £5
The Duke of Berwick and Other Rhymes, Secker, 1925 . . . . £65/£15
ditto, Knopf (U.S.), 1925 . . . . . £65/£15
Collected Satires, The Fortune Press, 1926 (550 copies) £100
ditto, The Fortune Press, 1926 (250 numbered copies signed by the author) £300
Complete Poems and Light Verse, Martin Secker, 1928 . . . . £125/£35
Lyrics, Rich & Cowan, 1935 . . . . . £75/£25
ditto, Rich & Cowan, 1935 (50 copies signed by the author, cloth slipcase) £250
ditto, Richards Press, 1943 . . . . £25/£10
Sonnets, Rich & Cowan, 1935 . . . . £75/£25
ditto, Rich & Cowan, 1935 (edition limited to 50 copies signed by the author, cloth slipcase) . £250
ditto, Richards Press, 1943 . . . . £25/£10
Sonnets, Richards Press, 1943 (pocket edition). £15/£5

Prose

Oscar Wilde and Myself, Long, 1914 . . . £100
ditto, Duffield (U.S.), 1914 . . . . . £75
The Autobiography of Lord Alfred Douglas, Martin Secker, 1929 . . . . £125/£25
ditto, as *My Friendship With Oscar Wilde*, Coventry House (U.S.), 1932 . . . . . £75/£25
The True History of Shakespeare's Sonnets, Secker, 1933 . . . . £75/£25
Without Apology, Secker, 1938 . . . . £50/£20
Oscar Wilde: A Summing Up, Duckworth, 1940 . .
. . . . £75/£20
Ireland and The War Against Hitler, Richards Press, 1940 . . . . £75/£20
The Principles of Poetry, Richards Press, 1943 (1,000 copies, wraps) £20

Others

New Preface to 'The Life and Confessions of Oscar Wilde', The Fortune Press, 1925 (with Frank Harris).
. . . . £75/£45
ditto, The Fortune Press, 1925 (225 signed, numbered copies) £200
Songs of Cell, by Horatio Bottomley, Southern, 1928 (Introduction by Douglas) . . . . £45/£15
The Pantomime Man, by Richard Middleton, Rich & Cowan, 1933 (Introduction by Douglas) . £75/£25
Bernard Shaw, Frank Harris and Oscar Wilde, by Robert Harborough Sherard, Werner Laurie, 1937 (Preface by Douglas) . . . . . £45/£15

Brighton Aquatints, by John Piper, Duckworth, 1939 (Introduction by Douglas, 200 copies with uncoloured plates) £600
ditto, by John Piper, Duckworth, 1939 (55 copies with hand-coloured prints) £2,000
Wartime Harvest, by Marie Carmichael Stopes, De la Mare Press, 1944 (Preface by Douglas) . £45/£10
Salome: A Tragedy in One Act, by Oscar Wilde, Heritage Press, 1945 (translated by Douglas, with Sandglass booklet) £25

NORMAN DOUGLAS
(b.1868 d.1952)

A travel writer and novelist, Douglas's *South Wind* is perhaps his best-known novel.

Novels
South Wind, Martin Secker, 1917 . . . . £150
ditto, Dodd, Mead (U.S.), 1918 . . . . . £150
ditto, Martin Secker, 1922 (150 signed copies) . £400
ditto, Limited Editions Club (U.S.), 1932 . . £50
They Went, Chapman & Hall, 1920 . . . £125/£45
ditto, Dodd, Mead (U.S.), 1921 . . . . £125/£45
In the Beginning, privately printed (Florence), 1927 (700 signed, numbered copies) . . . . £150/£75
ditto, Chatto & Windus, 1928 . . . . £40/£15
ditto, John Day (U.S.), 1928 . . . . . £50/£20
Nerinda, G. Orioli (Florence), 1929 (475 signed, numbered copies) . . . . . . £150/£75

Short Stories
Unprofessional Tales, T. Fisher Unwin, 1901 (pseud. 'Normyx') £300

Travel/Belles Lettres
Siren Land, J.M. Dent, 1911 . . . . . . £300
ditto, Durton (U.S.), 1911. . . . . . £250
Fountains in the Sand, Martin Secker, 1912 . £100
ditto, James Pott (U.S.), 1912. . . . . £25
Old Calabria, Martin Secker, 1915 . . . . £100
Alone, Chapman & Hall, 1921 . . . . £75/£25
ditto, McBride (U.S.), 1922 . . . . £65/£25
Together, Chapman & Hall, 1923 . . . £75/£25
ditto, Chapman & Hall, 1923 (275 signed copies) £125
ditto, McBride (U.S.), 1923 . . . . £65/£25
One Day, Hours Press (Paris), 1929 (300 copies) £200
ditto, Hours Press (Paris), 1929 (200 signed copies) £350
Summer Islands, Desmond Harmsworth, 1931 £35/£15
ditto, Desmond Harmsworth, 1931 (500 numbered copies) . . . . £100/£35
ditto, Colophon (U.S.), 1931 . . . . . £25
ditto, Colophon (U.S.), 1931 (550 signed copies) £100
ditto, Corvinus Press, 1942 [1944] (45 copies, various papers and bindings). £350
Footnote on Capri, Sidgwick & Jackson, 1952 . £20/£5
ditto, McBride (U.S.), 1952 . . . . . . £20/£5

Capri Monographs
The Blue Grotto and its Literature, privately printed, 1904 (100 copies) £350
The Forestal Conditions of Capri, privately printed, 1904 (100 copies) £350
Fabio Giordano's Relation of Capri, privately printed, 1906 (250 copies) £300
Three Monographs, privately printed, 1906 (250 copies) £300
The Life of the Venerable Suor Serafina Di Dio, privately printed, 1907 (100 copies) . . . £350
Some Antiquarian Notes, privately printed, 1907 (250 copies) £300
Disiecta Membra, privately printed, 1915 (100 copies) £350
Index, privately printed, 1915 (100 copies) . . £350

Pamphlets
Zur Fauna Santorins, Leipzig, 1892 (c.50 copies, no wraps). £750
Contributions to an Avifauna of Baden, London, 1894 (c.50 copies, no wraps, pseud. 'G. Norman Douglass') £750
On the Herpetology of the Grand Duchy of Baden, London, 1894 (c.50 copies, pseud. 'G. Norman Douglass') £750
The Beaver in Norway, The Zoologist, [n.d.] . £300
Report on the Pumice Stone Industry of the Lipari Islands, H.M.S.O., 1895 (c.125 copies) . £500
ditto, Hours Press, 1928 (80 copies) £400
On the Darwinian Hypothesis of Sexual Selection, London, 1895 (25 copies, pseud. 'G. Norman Douglass') £450

Others
London Street Games, St Catherine's Press, 1916 £150
ditto, Chatto & Windus, 1931 . . . . £45/£10
ditto, Chatto & Windus, 1931 (110 signed copies) £150
D.H. Lawrence and Maurice Magnus: A Plea for Better Manners, privately printed (Florence), 1924 (wraps) £65
Experiments, privately printed (Florence), 1925 (300 signed, numbered copies) . . . . . £200/£100
ditto, Chapman & Hall, 1925. . . . . £25/£10
ditto, McBride (U.S.), 1925 . . . . . £25/£10
Birds and Beasts of the Greek Anthology, privately printed (Florence), 1927 (500 signed, numbered copies . . . . £200/£100
ditto, Chapman & Hall, 1928. . . . . £40/£20
ditto, Cape & Smith (U.S.), 1929. . . . £25/£10
Some Limericks, privately printed (Florence), 1928 (110 signed numbered copies) £250
ditto, privately printed (Florence), 1928 (750 unnumbered copies) £100
ditto, privately printed by Guy d'Isere for David Moss (U.S.), 1928 (750 numbered copies) . . . £75
ditto, privately printed (Florence), 1929 (1,000 numbered copies for subscribers) £100

How About Europe?, privately printed (Florence), 1929 (550 signed, numbered copies) . . £150/£100
ditto, Chatto & Windus, 1930 . . . . £65/£20
The Angel of Manfredonia, The Windsor Press, 1929 (225 numbered copies, no d/w) £150
Three of Them, Chatto & Windus, 1930 . £25/£10
Capri: Materials for a Description of the Island, G. Orioli (Florence), 1930 (525 signed, numbered copies) £300
ditto, G. Orioli (Florence), 1930 (103 signed copies) .
. . . . £500
Paneros, G. Orioli (Florence), 1930 (250 signed copies, slipcase) £200
ditto, Chatto & Windus, 1931 (650 numbered copies) .
. . . . £75
ditto, McBride (U.S.), 1932 (750 copies, box) £65/£50
Looking Back, Chatto & Windus, 1933 (2 vols, 535 signed, numbered sets) £150
ditto, Harcourt, Brace (U.S.), 1933 (1 vol.) . £100/£25
ditto, Chatto & Windus, 1934 (1 vol.) . . £35/£15
An Almanac, privately printed (Lisbon), 1941 (25 [c.50] signed, numbered copies) . . . £400
ditto, Secker & Warburg, 1945 . . . £25/£10
Late Harvest, Lindsay Drummond, 1946 . . £20/£5
Venus in the Kitchen, Heinemann, 1952 . £25/£5
ditto, Viking (U.S.), 1953 . . . . . . £25/£5

ERNEST DOWSON
(b.1867 d.1900)

Dowson was one of the best of the decadent poets of the 1890s. He also prepared translations and wrote short stories, before dying of tuberculosis at the age of thirty-two.

Poetry
Verses, Leonard Smithers, 1896 (300 copies. Cover design by Aubrey Beardsley) £750
ditto, Leonard Smithers, 1896 (30 copies on Japanese Vellum) £3,000
The Pierrot of the Minute, Leonard Smithers, 1897 (illustrated by Aubrey Beardsley, 300 copies printed on handmade paper) £500
ditto, Leonard Smithers, 1897 (30 copies printed on Japanese vellum) £3,000
ditto, Grolier Club (U.S.), 1923 (300 copies printed on Dutch antique paper, slipcase) £250
Decorations, in Verse & Prose, Leonard Smithers, 1899 . . . . £400
The Poems of Ernest Dowson, John Lane, 1905 (edited and with a memoir by Arthur Symons. Illustrated by Aubrey Beardsley) £125
Cynara: A Little Book of Verse, Thomas Mosher (U.S.), 1907 (950 copies, slipcase) £45
Poetical Works of Ernest Dowson, Cassell/John Lane, 1934 (edited by Desmond Flower) . . . £25/£10
ditto, Cassell's Pocket Library, 1950. . . . £10/£5

The Poems of Ernest Dowson, The Unicorn Press, 1946 . . . . £15/£5
The Poems of Ernest Dowson, Univ. of Pennsylvania Press (U.S.), 1962 (edited by Mark Longaker) £20/£5

Prose
A Comedy of Masks, Heinemann, 1893 (with Arthur Moore. Novel in 3 vols) £200
Dilemmas, Elkin Matthews, 1895 (short stories) £150
Adrian Rome, Methuen, 1899 (with Arthur Moore) .
. . . . £75
The Stories of Ernest Dowson, Univ. of Pennsylvania (U.S.), 1947 . . . . £25/£10
ditto, W.H. Allen, [1949] (edited by Mark Longaker) .
. . . . £15/£5
The Letters of Ernest Dowson, Fairleigh Dickinson (U.S.), 1967 (collected and edited by Desmond Flower & Henry Maas) . . . . . £30/£20
ditto, Cassell, 1967 . . . . £30/£20
Bouquet, Whittington Press, 1991 . . . . £90
New Letters from Ernest Dowson, Whittington Press, 1984 (220 copies, signed by Desmond Flower) £50

Translations
La Terre, by Emile Zola, Lutetian Society, 1894 £100
Majesty, by Couperus, T. Fisher Unwin, 1894 (translated with A. Teixera de Mattos) £35
La Fille Aux Yeux D'Or, by Honore de Balzac, Leonard Smithers, 1896 (illustrated by Charles Conder) £75
Memoirs of Cardinal Dubois, Leonard Smithers, 1899 (2 vols) £75
La Pucelle D'Orleans, by Voltaire, Lutetian Society, 1899 (500 sets, 2 vols) £125
The Confidantes of a King, by Edmond & Jules de Goncourt, T.N. Foulis, 1907 . . . . . £25
The Story of the Beauty and the Beast, John Lane, 1908 [1907] (illustrated by Charles Conder) . £40
Dangerous Acquaintances, by Pierre Choderlos de Laclos, Nonesuch Press, 1940 (illustrated by Charles Laborde) £40

SIR ARTHUR CONAN DOYLE
(b.1859 d.1930)

Best known, of course, for his creation of the ever-popular detective, Sherlock Holmes. Conan Doyle also wrote historical fiction, the genre of which he was most fond.

'Sherlock Holmes' Titles
A Study in Scarlet, 28th Beeton's Christmas Annual, 1887 (story contained in first 95pps, wraps) £40,000
ditto, 28th Beeton's Christmas Annual, 1887 (rebound) £15,000
ditto, Ward Lock, 1888 (first book edition, first issue with 'younger' spelt correctly in preface, wraps) .
. . . . £50,000

ditto, Ward Lock, 1888 (second issue with 'youunger', wraps). £15,000

The Sign of Four, Lippincott's Magazine, February 1890 (pp.147-223, wraps) £1,500

ditto, Lippincott's/Ward Lock, 1890, in **Six Complete Novels by Famous Authors** £750

ditto, Lippincott's/Ward Lock, 1891, in **Five Complete Novels by Famous Authors** £500

ditto, Spencer Blackett, 1890 (first book edition, first issue) £5,000

ditto, Spencer Blackett, 1890 (second issue, remainder sheets issued by Griffith Farran, with 'Griffith Farran and Co' at foot of spine). £2,500

ditto, Spencer Blackett, 1892 (third issue, remainder sheets issued by Newnes, with 'Griffith Farran and Co' on cover). £1,500

The Adventures of Sherlock Holmes, George Newnes, 1892 . . . . £2,000

ditto, Harper (U.S.), 1892 (first issue with 'if had' on page 65, line 4) £1,000

ditto, Harper (U.S.), 1892 (second issue with 'if he had') £500

The Memoirs of Sherlock Holmes, George Newnes, 1894 [1893] £1,000

ditto, Harper (U.S.), 1894 . . . . £600

The Hound of the Baskervilles, George Newnes, 1902 . . . . £2,000

ditto, McClure, Phillips (U.S.), 1902 (first issue without 'Published 1902' on copyright page) . £750

ditto, McClure, Phillips (U.S.), 1902 (second issue with 'Published 1902') £200

ditto, McClure, Phillips (U.S.), 1902 (third issue with tipped in title page with 'Illustrated') . . £150

ditto, McClure, Phillips (U.S.), 1902 (fourth issue, as third but integral title page) £75

The Return of Sherlock Holmes, McClure, Phillips (U.S.), 1905 (black cloth) £500

ditto, McClure, Phillips (U.S.), 1905 ('special edition', dark-blue cloth) £150

ditto, George Newnes, 1905 . . . . . £1,500

The Valley of Fear, Doran (U.S.), 1914. . . £300

ditto, Smith Elder, 1915 . . . . £300

His Last Bow, Murray, 1917 . . . . . £300

ditto, Doran (U.S.), 1917 (orange cloth). . . £135

ditto, Doran (U.S.), 1917 (red cloth). . . . £100

The Case-Book of Sherlock Holmes, Murray, 1927 . . . . £2,500/£300

ditto, Doran (U.S.), 1927 . . . . . . £750/£100

Novels

The Mystery of Cloomber, Ward and Downey, 1889 [1888] (wraps) £500

ditto, Fenno (U.S.), 1895 . . . . . . £75

Micah Clarke, Longmans Green, 1889 . . . £300

The Firm of Girdlestone, Chatto & Windus, 1890 (ads dated January 1890) £350

ditto, Chatto & Windus, 1890 (ads dated later) . £250

The White Company, Smith Elder, 1891 (3 vols) £3,000

ditto, Smith Elder, 1892 (1 vol.) £75

ditto, John Lovell Co (U.S.), 1891 (tan wraps) . £500

ditto, Lovell, Coryell & Co. (U.S.), 1892 (white pictorial wraps) £300

The Doings of Raffles Haw, Lovell (U.S.), 1891 £200

ditto, Cassell, 1892 . . . . £350

The Great Shadow, Arrowsmith's Christmas Annual, 1892 (pictorial wraps) £400

ditto, Arrowsmith's Christmas Annual, 1892 (cloth, brown endpapers) £150

Beyond the City, Rand McNally (U.S.), [1892]. £125

The Great Shadow, and Beyond the City, Arrowsmith [1893]. £75

ditto, Harper (U.S.), 1893 . . . . £75

The Refugees, Longmans Green, 1893 (3 vols) £3,000

ditto, Longmans Green [August], 1893 (1 vol.). £100

ditto, Harper (U.S.), 1893. . . . . . . £100

The Parasite, Constable, 1894 . . . . £150

ditto, Constable, 1894 (wraps) £150

Rodney Stone, Smith Elder, 1896 . . . . £100

ditto, Appleton (U.S.), 1896 . . . . . . £75

Uncle Bernac, Horace Cox, 1896 [Jan 1897] (wraps, copyright edition: Chapters 1-10 only). . £1,500

ditto, Smith Elder, 1897 . . . . £150

ditto, Appleton (U.S.), 1897 . . . . . . £150

A Desert Drama, being the tragedy of the Korosko, Lippincott (U.S.), 1898 . . . . . . £100

ditto, as **The Tragedy of Korosko**, Smith Elder, 1898 . . . . £100

Sir Nigel, Smith Elder, 1906 . . . . . £75

ditto, McClure, Phillips (U.S.), 1906. . . . £65

The Lost World, Hodder & Stoughton, [1912] . £650

ditto, Hodder & Stoughton, [1912] (large paper edition, 190 of 1,000 copies comprise the first issue) . £1,500

ditto, Henry Frowde/Hodder & Stoughton, [1912] (large paper edition, 810 of 1,000 copies comprise the second issue) £400

ditto, Doran (U.S.), 1912 . . . . £400

The Poison Belt, Hodder & Stoughton, 1913 . £100

ditto, Hodder/Doran (U.S.),1913 . . . . . £100

The Land Of Mist, Hutchinson, [1926] . £2,000/£200

ditto, Doran (U.S.),1926 . . . . . . £500/£50

The Maracot Deep, Murray, 1929 (novel and 3 short stories) . . . . £750/£75

ditto, Doran (U.S.),1929 . . . . . . £400/£45

Short Stories

Mysteries and Adventures, Walter Scott, [1890] £1,500

ditto, Walter Scott, [1890] (wraps) £1,000

The Captain of the Polestar, Longmans, 1890 . £300

Round the Red Lamp, Methuen, 1894 . . . £150

ditto, Appleton (U.S.), 1894 . . . . . . £125

The Exploits of Brigadier Gerard, Newnes, 1896 (advertisements dated 10/2/96) £125

ditto, Newnes, 1896 (later advertisements) . . £75

ditto, Appleton (U.S.), 1896 . . . . . . £65

The Green Flag, Smith Elder, 1900 . . . . £100

ditto, McClure, Phillips (U.S.), 1900. . . . £75

Adventures of Gerard, Newnes, 1903 . . . £75

ditto, McClure, Phillips (U.S.), 1903.	£45
The Croxley Master, A Great Tale of the Prize Ring,	
McClure, Phillips (U.S.), 1907	£50
ditto, McClure, Phillips (U.S.), 1907.	£30
Round the Fire Stories, Smith Elder, 1908	£30
ditto, McClure, Phillips (U.S.), 1908.	£30
The Last Galley, Smith Elder, 1911	£50
ditto, Doubleday (U.S.), 1911	£30
Danger, Murray, 1918	£30
ditto, Doran (U.S.), 1918	£30

Plays

Waterloo, French, 1907	£150

Collected Edition

The Crowborough Edition of the Works of Sir Arthur Conan Doyle, Doubleday, Doran (U.S.), 1930 (24 volumes, 760 signed copies) £5,000

RODDY DOYLE
(b.1958)

Doyle achieved recognition when *The Commitments* was filmed in 1991, the same year that *The Van* was shortlisted for the Booker Prize. *Paddy Clarke Ha Ha Ha* won the Booker Prize for 1993, establishing Doyle as a leading comic writer and earning him comparisons to Irish humorists O'Casey and Behan.

The Commitments, King Farouk (Dublin), 1987 (wraps)	£350
ditto, Heinemann, 1988 (wraps)	£75
ditto, Vintage (U.S.), 1989 (wraps)	£15
The Snapper, Secker, 1990	£200/£35
ditto, Penguin (U.S.), 1992 (wraps)	£10
The Van, Secker, 1991	£125/£20
ditto, Viking (U.S.), 1992.	£15/£5
The Barrytown Trilogy, Secker, 1992 (contains *The Commitments, The Snapper*, and *The Van*)	£50/£10
Paddy Clarke, Ha Ha Ha, Secker, 1993	£75/£10
ditto, Viking (U.S.), 1994.	£15/£5
The Woman Who Walked Into Doors, Cape, 1996	£20/£5
ditto, Viking (U.S.), 1996	£15/£5
A Star Called Henry, Cape, 1999	£20/£5
ditto, Viking (U.S.), 1999	£15/£5

Drama

War, Passion Machine (Dublin), 1989 (wraps)	£150
ditto, Penguin (U.S.), 1992 (wraps)	£10
Brownbread and War, Secker, 1992 (wraps)	£20
ditto, Penguin (U.S.), 1994 (wraps)	£10

Children's Titles

Not Just For Christmas, New Island Books (Dublin), 1999 (wraps)	£5
The Giggler Treatment, Scholastic Press, 2000	£20/£5
ditto, Levine/Scholastic (U.S.), 2000	£20/£5
Roger Saves Christmas, Scholastic Press, 2001	£15/£5

Others

Yeats Is Dead, Cape, 2001	£15/£5
Rory and Ita, Cape, 2002.	£15/£5

MARGARET DRABBLE
(b.1939)

Drabble's novels often explore the struggle of the individual against convention or repression. She was awarded a C.B.E. in 1980 for her services to English literature.

Novels

A Summer Bird-Cage, Weidenfeld & Nicolson, 1963	£300/£40
ditto, Morrow (U.S.), 1964	£90/£15
The Garrick Year, Weidenfeld & Nicolson, 1964	£100/£20
ditto, Morrow (U.S.), 1965	£75/£15
The Millstone, Weidenfeld & Nicolson, 1965	£75/£20
ditto, Morrow (U.S.), 1966	£50/£10
Jerusalem the Golden, Weidenfeld & Nicolson, 1967	£30/£10
ditto, Morrow (U.S.), 1967	£25/£5
The Waterfall, Weidenfeld & Nicolson, 1969	£25/£5
ditto, Knopf (U.S.), 1969	£25/£5
The Needle's Eye, Weidenfeld & Nicolson, 1972	£30/£5
ditto, Knopf (U.S.), 1972.	£25/£5
The Realms of Gold, Weidenfeld & Nicolson, 1975	£20/£5
ditto, Knopf (U.S.), 1975.	£20/£5
The Ice Age, Weidenfeld & Nicolson, 1977	£20/£5
ditto, Knopf (U.S.), 1977.	£20/£5
The Middle Ground, Weidenfeld & Nicolson, 1980	£15/£5
ditto, Knopf (U.S.), 1980.	£15/£5
The Radiant Way, Weidenfeld & Nicolson, 1987	£15/£5
ditto, Knopf (U.S.), 1987.	£15/£5
A Natural Curiosity, Viking, 1989	£15/£5
ditto, London Limited Editions, 1989 (150 signed copies, glassine d/w).	£65/£45
ditto, Viking (U.S.), 1989.	£15/£5
The Gates of Ivory, Viking, 1991	£10/£5
ditto, Viking (U.S.), 1992.	£10/£5
The Witch of Exmoor, Viking, 1996	£10/£5
ditto, Harcourt Brace (U.S.), 1996	£10/£5
The Peppered Moth, Viking, 2000	£10/£5
ditto, Harcourt Brace (U.S.), 2001	£10/£5
The Seven Sisters, Viking, 2002.	£10/£5

Non Fiction

Wordsworth, Evans, 1966	£45/£10
ditto, Arco (U.S.), 1969 (no d/w).	£25
Virginia Woolf: A Personal Debt, Aloe Editions (U.S.), 1973 (110 signed copies, wraps)	£125

Arnold Bennett: A Biography, Weidenfeld & Nicolson, 1974 . . . . £25/£5
ditto, Knopf (U.S.), 1974 . . . . . . £25/£5
A Writer's Britain: Landscape in Literature, Thames & Hudson, 1979 . . . . £25/£10
ditto, Knopf (U.S.), 1979 . . . . . . £20/£10
The Tradition of Women's Fiction: Lectures in Japan, O.U.P. (Tokyo), 1985 . . . . . £25/£5
Case for Equality, Fabian Society, 1988 . . £10
Stratford Revisited: A Legacy of the Sixties, Celandine Press, 1989 (150 signed copies, wraps) . . £35
Safe As Houses: An Examination of Home Ownership and Mortgage Tax Relief, Chatto & Windus, 1990 . . . . £5
Angus Wilson: A Biography, Secker & Warburg, 1995 . . . . £15/£5
ditto, St Martin's Press (U.S.), 1996 . . . . £10/£5

Children's Title
For Queen and Country: Britain in the Victorian Age, Deutsch, 1978 . . . . £15/£5
ditto, Seabury Press (U.S.), 1979 . . . . £10/£5

THEODORE DREISER
(b.1871 d.1945)

Considered by many to be the first exponent of Naturalism in American writing, his writing dealt with social problems and characters struggling to survive. His sympathetic treatment of a 'morally loose' woman in *Sister Carrie* was branded immoral and he suffered, principally, at the hands of his own publishers.

Novels
Sister Carrie, Doubleday (U.S.), 1900 . . . £3,500
ditto, Heinemann, 1901 . . . . . . £500
ditto, Dodge (U.S.), 1907 . . . . . . £50
Jennie Gerhardt, Harpers (U.S.), 1911 (first issue, 'is' for 'it' on page 22, line 30, 'Theodore Dreiser' on spine, mottled light blue cloth) £150
ditto, Harpers (U.S.), 1911 (second issue, text corrected, 'Dreiser' on spine) £100
The Financier, Harpers (U.S.), 1912 (first issue with 'Published October, 1912' and 'K-M' on title page) .
. . . . £150
ditto, Constable, 1927 . . . . . . £65/£15
The Titan, John Lane/ Bodley Head (U.S), 1914 £125
The 'Genius', John Lane (U.S.), 1915 (first issue, 1¼ inches thick, p.497 correctly numbered) . . £200
ditto, John Lane (U.S.), 1915 (second issue, 1½ inches thick, p.497 unnumbered) £100
ditto, Constable, 1928 . . . . £65/£15
Twelve Men, Boni & Liveright (U.S.), 1919 . £75
ditto, Constable, 1931 . . . . £65/£15
An American Tragedy, Boni & Liveright (U.S.), 1925 (2 vols, first issue, black cloth, white endpapers, slipcase) . . . . £600/£100

ditto, Boni & Liveright (U.S.), 1925 (2 vols, second issue, blue cloth, slipcase) . . . . . £500/£100
ditto, Boni & Liveright (U.S.), 1925 (795 signed copies, 2 vols, slipcase) . . . . . . £600/£150
ditto, Constable, 1926 . . . . £65/£15
A Gallery of Women, Horace Liveright (U.S.), 1929 (560 signed copies, 2 vols, slipcase) . . £200/£75
ditto, Boni & Liveright (U.S.), 1929 (2 vols) £100/£25
ditto, Constable, 1930 . . . . £65/£15
The Bulwark, Doubleday, 1946 . . . . £70/£20
ditto, Constable, 1947 . . . . £50/£15
The Stoic, Doubleday, 1947 . . . . . £65/£20

Short Stories
Free and Other Stories, Boni & Liveright (U.S.), 1918 . . . . £100
Chains: Lesser Novels and Stories, Boni & Liveright (U.S.), 1927 (440 signed, numbered copies, slipcase) . . . . £150/£75
ditto, Boni & Liveright (U.S.), 1927 . . £150/£35
ditto, Constable, 1928 . . . . £65/£15
Fine Furniture, Random House (U.S.), 1930 £40/£10

Poetry
Moods: Cadenced and Declaimed, Boni & Liveright (U.S.), 1926 (550 signed, numbered copies) . . .
. . . . £250/£150
ditto, Boni & Liveright (U.S.), 1928 . . £65/£15
ditto, Constable, 1929 . . . . £65/£15
ditto, as *Moods: Philosophic and Emotional, Cadenced and Declaimed*, Simon & Schuster (U.S.), 1935 . . . . £45/£15
The Aspirant, Random House (U.S.), 1929 (475 copies, wraps) £45
Epitaph, Heron Press (U.S.), 1929 (200 signed full leather copies, slipcase) . . . . . £250/£200
ditto, Heron Press (U.S.), 1929 (200 signed copies bound in silk, slipcase, glassine d/w) . £250/£200
ditto, Heron Press (U.S.), 1929 (700 signed copies bound in cloth, slipcase, glassine d/w) . £150/£100

Others
A Traveller at Forty, Century, 1913 . . . . £75
ditto, Grant Richards, 1914 . . . . . £65
Plays of the Natural and the Supernatural, John Lane (U.S. and U.K.), 1916 (first issue without 4 page essay by Dreiser at end of text) £100
ditto, John Lane (U.S. and U.K.), 1916 (second issue with essay) £65
A Hoosier Holiday, John Lane (U.S. and U.K.), 1916 .
. . . . £125
The Hand of the Potter: A Tragedy in Four Acts, Boni & Liveright (U.S.), 1918 . . . . . . £75
ditto, Constable, 1931 . . . . £50/£15
Hey Rub-a-Dub-Dub: A Book of the Mystery and Wonder and Terror of Life, Boni & Liveright (U.S.), 1920 . . . . £250/£45
ditto, Constable, 1931 . . . . £50/£15
A Book About Myself, Boni & Liveright (U.S.), 1922 .
. . . . £125/£45

ditto, Constable, 1929 . . . . £50/£15
ditto, as *Newspaper Days*, Boni & Liveright (U.S.),
1931 . . . . £100/£35
ditto, as *A History of Myself: Dawn*, Boni & Liveright
(U.S.), 1931 (275 signed copies, slipcase) . £225/£175
ditto, as *A History of Myself: Dawn*, Horace Liveright
(U.S.), 1931 . . . . £75/£25
ditto, as *A History of Myself: Dawn*, Constable, 1931 .
. . . . £50/£15
ditto, as *Autobiography*, Boni & Liveright (U.S.), 1965
(2 vols) . . . . £100/£25
The Color of a Great City, Boni & Liveright (U.S.),
1923 . . . . £100/£35
ditto, Constable, 1930 . . . . . . £50/£15
Dreiser Looks at Russia, Boni & Liveright (U.S.),
1928 . . . . £75/£25
ditto, Constable, 1929 . . . . . . £50/£15
The Carnegie Works at Pittsburgh, (privately printed),
1929 (150 numbered copies) £200
Tragic America, Horace Liveright (U.S.), 1931 . . .
. . . . £65/£20
ditto, Constable, 1932 . . . . . . £50/£15
America is Worth Saving, Modern Age Books, 1941 .
. . . . £65/£10
Letters of Theodore Dreiser: A Selection, Univ. of
Pennsylvania Press (U.S.), 1959 (3 vols) . . . .
. . . . £100/£35 the set
*Letters to Louise: The Correspondence of Theodore
Dreiser and H.L. Menken, 1907-1945*, Univ. of
Pennsylvania Press (U.S.), 1959 . . . £50/£20
Notes on Life, Univ. of Alabama Press (U.S.), 1974 .
. . . . £30/£10
*Dreiser-Menken Letters: The Correspondence of
Theodore Dreiser and H.L. Menken, 1907-1945*,
Univ. of Pennsylvania Press (U.S.), 1986 . £25/£10

EDMUND DULAC
(b.1882 d.1953)

A French illustrator, and rival to Arthur Rackham,
Dulac illustrated many 'gift book' editions of popular
fairy tales.

Written and Illustrated by Dulac
Lyrics Pathetic and Humorous From A to Z, Warne,
1908 (24 colour plates) £600
ditto, Warne, 1908 [1909] (portfolio of 24 plates, cloth-
covered box) £2,500
*A Fairy Garland: Being Fairy Tales from the Old
French*, Cassell, 1928 (12 colour plates) . £300/£125
ditto, Cassell, 1928 (deluxe edition, 1,000 signed
copies, slipcase and glassine d/w, 12 colour plates) .
. . . . £400/£300
ditto, Scribner's (U.S.), 1929 (12 colour plates) . .
. . . . £300/£125

Illustrated by Dulac
The Novels of the Brontë Sisters, by The Brontës,
Dent, 1905 (10 vols, 6 colour plates in each) £40 each
Fairies I Have Met, by Mrs R. Stawell, John Lane,
[1907] (8 colour plates) £75
ditto, Hodder & Stoughton, [1910] (8 colour plates) .
. . . . £75
ditto, as *My Days With the Fairies*, Hodder &
Stoughton, [1913] (8 colour plates) . . . £200
Stories from The Arabian Nights, retold by Laurence
Housman, Hodder & Stoughton, 1907 (50 colour
plates) £200
ditto, Hodder & Stoughton, 1907 (deluxe edition, 350
signed copies, 50 colour plates) £1,250
ditto, Scribner's (U.S.), 1907 . . . . . £200
The Tempest, by William Shakespeare, Hodder &
Stoughton, [1908] (40 colour plates) . . . £200
ditto, Hodder & Stoughton, [1908] (deluxe edition, 500
signed copies, 40 colour plates) £1,250
The Rubaiyat of Omar Khyyam, by Edward Fitzgerald,
Hodder & Stoughton, [1909] (20 colour plates) £250
ditto, Hodder & Stoughton, [1909] (deluxe edition, 750
signed copies, 20 colour plates) £1,000
The Sleeping Beauty, retold by Sir Arthur Quiller-
Couch, Hodder & Stoughton, [1910] (30 colour
plates) £350
ditto, Hodder & Stoughton, [1910] (deluxe edition,
1,000 signed copies, 30 colour plates) . . . £1,500
Stories from Hans Andersen, Hodder & Stoughton,
1911 (28 colour plates) £350
ditto, Hodder & Stoughton, 1911 (deluxe edition, 750
signed copies, 28 colour plates) £1,250
ditto, Hodder & Stoughton, 1911 (deluxe edition, 100
signed copies, morocco binding, 28 colour plates) .
. . . . £2,500
The Bells and Other Poems, by Edgar Allan Poe,
Hodder & Stoughton, [1912] (28 colour plates) . .
. . . . £250
ditto, Hodder & Stoughton, [1912] (deluxe edition, 750
signed copies, 28 colour plates) £800
Princess Badoura: A Tale from The Arabian Nights,
retold by Laurence Housman, Hodder & Stoughton,
[1913] (10 colour plates) £500
ditto, Hodder & Stoughton, [1913] (deluxe edition, 750
signed copies, 10 colour plates) £1,500
*Sinbad the Sailor and Other Stories from the Arabian
Nights*, Hodder & Stoughton, [1914] (23 colour
plates) £600
ditto, Hodder & Stoughton, [1914] (deluxe edition, 500
signed copies, 23 colour plates) £2,500
*Edmund Dulac's Picture-Book for the French Red
Cross*, Hodder & Stoughton, [1915] (20 colour plates)
. . . . £100
The Dreamer of Dreams, by Queen Marie of
Roumania, Hodder & Stoughton, [1915] (6 colour
plates) £50
The Stealers of Light, by Queen Marie of Roumania,
Hodder & Stoughton, 1916 (2 colour plates) . £45

Edmund Dulac's Fairy-Book, Hodder & Stoughton, [1916] (15 colour plates) £150
ditto, Hodder & Stoughton, [1916] (deluxe edition, 350 signed copies, 15 colour plates). £1,000
ditto, Hodder & Stoughton, 1919 (16 colour plates) .
. . . . £100
Tanglewood Tales, by Nathaniel Hawthorne, Hodder & Stoughton, [1918] (14 colour plates) . . £125
ditto, Hodder & Stoughton, [1918] (deluxe edition, 500 signed copies, 14 colour plates). £600
The Kingdom of the Pearl, by Leonard Rosenthal, Piazza (Paris), 1920 (1,500 copies, 10 colour plates) .
. . . . £500
ditto, Nisbet, [1920] (675 copies, 10 colour plates). .
. . . . £600/£300
ditto, Nisbet, [1920] (100 signed copies, 10 colour plates). £1,500
ditto, Brentano's (U.S.), 1920 (675 numbered copies, 10 colour plates). . . . . £600/£300
Four Plays for Dancers, by W.B. Yeats, Macmillan, 1921 (7 illustrations). . . . . . £200/£125
ditto, Macmillan (U.S.), 1921 . . . . £200/£125
The Green Lacquer Pavilion, by Helen Beauclerk, Collins, 1926 (9 illustrations) . . . £40/£20
ditto, Doran (U.S.), 1926 (9 illustrations) . £40/£20
Treasure Island, by Robert Louis Stevenson, Benn, 1927 (12 colour plates) . . . . . £500/£350
ditto, Benn, 1927 (deluxe edition, 50 signed copies, 12 colour plates). £5,000
ditto, Doran (U.S.), [1927] (12 colour plates) . . .
. . . . £450/£300
Gods and Mortals in Love, by Hugh Ross Williamson, Country Life, [1936] (9 colour plates) . £300/£150
The Daughters of the Stars, by Mary C. Crary, Hatchard, 1939 (2 colour plates) . . . £60/£30
ditto, Hatchard, 1939 (deluxe edition, 500 copies signed by author and artist, 2 colour plates) . £500
The Golden Cockerel, by Alexander Pushkin, Limited Editions Club (U.S.), [1950] (1,500 signed, numbered copies, slipcase) . . . . . £250/£150
The Marriage of Cupid and Psyche, by Walter Pater, Limited Editions Club (U.S.), [1951] (1,500 signed, numbered copies, slipcase) . . . . . £250/£150
The Masque of Comus, by John Milton, Limited Editions Club (U.S.), 1954 (1,500 numbered copies, slipcase) . . . . £250/£150

DAPHNE DU MAURIER

(b.1907 d.1989)

Du Maurier is the author of tense romances set against the background of Cornwall, her home for most of her life.

Novels
The Loving Spirit, Heinemann, 1931 . £1,250/£45
ditto, Doubleday (U.S.), 1931 . . . . £650/£25

I'll Never Be Young Again, Heinemann, 1932 . . . .
. . . . £1,250/£45
ditto, Doubleday (U.S.), 1932 . . . . £650/£25
The Progress of Julius, Heinemann, 1933 £1,000/£45
Jamaica Inn, Gollancz, 1936 . . . £3,000/£200
ditto, Doubleday (U.S.), 1936 . . £2,500/£200
Rebecca, Gollancz, 1938 . . . . . £2,750/£300
ditto, Doubleday (U.S.), 1938 . . . £1,250/£150
Frenchman's Creek, Gollancz, 1941 . . £75/£20
ditto, Doubleday (U.S.), 1942 . . . £65/£15
Hungry Hill, Gollancz, 1943 . . . . . . £30/£5
ditto, Doubleday (U.S.), 1943 . . . . . £25/£5
The King's General, Gollancz, 1946 . . . £35/£5
ditto, Doubleday (U.S.), 1946 . . . . . £35/£5
The Parasites, Gollancz, 1949 . . . . . £40/£5
ditto, Doubleday (U.S.), 1950 . . . . . £25/£5
My Cousin Rachel, Gollancz, 1951 . . . £50/£10
ditto, Doubleday (U.S.), 1952 . . . . . £40/£5
Mary Anne, Gollancz, 1954 . . . . . . £25/£5
ditto, Doubleday (U.S.), 1954 . . . . . £20/£5
The Daphne du Maurier Omnibus, Gollancz, 1956 (contains *Rebecca, Jamaica Inn* and *Frenchman's Creek*). . . . . £15/£5
The Scapegoat, Gollancz, 1957 . . . . . £25/£5
ditto, Doubleday (U.S.), 1957 . . . . . £20/£5
Castle Dor, Gollancz, 1962 (begun by Sir Arthur Quiller-Couch) . . . . £15/£5
ditto, Doubleday (U.S.), 1962 . . . . . £15/£5
The Glassblowers, Gollancz, 1963 . . . £20/£5
ditto, Doubleday (U.S.), 1963 . . . . . £15/£5
The Daphne du Maurier Tandem, Gollancz, 1964 (contains *Mary Anne* and *My Cousin Rachel*) . £15/£5
The Flight of the Falcon, Gollancz, 1965 . £15/£5
ditto, Doubleday (U.S.), 1965 . . . . . £15/£5
The House on the Strand, Gollancz, 1969 . £15/£5
ditto, Doubleday (U.S.), 1969 . . . . . £15/£5
Rule Britannia, Gollancz, 1972 . . . . £15/£5
ditto, Doubleday (U.S.), 1972 . . . . . £15/£5
Three Famous Daphne du Maurier Novels, Gollancz, 1982 (contains *The Flight of the Falcon, The House on the Strand* and *The King's General*) . £10/£5
Four Great Cornish Novels, Gollancz, 1982 (contains *Jamaica Inn, Rebecca, Frenchman's Creek* and *My Cousin Rachel*) . . . . £10/£5

Short Stories
Happy Christmas, Doubleday (U.S.), 1940 . £40/£10
ditto, Todd Publishing Co., 1943. . . . £35/£10
Come Wind, Come Weather, Heinemann, 1940 (wraps) £15
ditto, Doubleday (U.S.), 1941 (wraps) . . . £15
Consider the Lilies, Polybooks/Todd Publishing Co., 1943 (wraps). £20
Escort, Polybooks/Todd Publishing Co., 1943 (wraps)
. . . . £25
Nothing Hurts for Long; and Escort, Polybooks/Todd Publishing Co., 1943 (wraps) £20
Spring Picture, Todd Publishing Co., 1944 (no d/w) .
. . . . £25

Leading Lady, Polybooks/Vallancey Press, 1945
(wraps) £20
London and Paris, Polybooks/Vallancey Press, 1945
(wraps) £20
The Apple Tree, Gollancz, 1952 (later published as
The Birds) . . . . £100/£15
Early Stories, Todd, 1955 (wraps) £40
The Breaking Point, Gollancz, 1959 (later published as
The Blue Lenses) . . . . £30/£5
ditto, Doubleday (U.S.), 1959 . . . . £25/£5
The Treasury of du Maurier Short Stories, Gollancz,
1960 (contains *The Apple Tree* and *The Breaking
Point*) . . . . £10/£5
The Lover, Ace Wraps (U.S.), 1961 . . . . . £5
Not After Midnight, Gollancz, 1971 (later published as
Don't Look Now) . . . . . . £40/£10
Echoes from the Macabre, Gollancz, 1976 . £40/£10
ditto, Doubleday (U.S.), 1976 . . . . £35/£10
The Rendezvous, Gollancz, 1980 . . . £15/£5
Classics of the Macabre, Gollancz, 1987 . £25/£5
ditto, Gollancz, 1987 (250 signed copies in slipcase) .
. . . . £175/£150
ditto, Doubleday (U.S.), 1987 . . . . . £25/£5

Plays
Rebecca, Gollancz, 1940 . . . . . . £100/£15
The Years Between, Gollancz, 1945 . . . £30/£10
ditto, Doubleday (U.S.), 1946 . . . . £30/£10
September Tide, Gollancz, 1946 . . . . £30/£10
ditto, Doubleday (U.S.), 1950 . . . . £25/£10
The Little Photographer, French, 1979 (wraps,
adapted by Derek Hoddinott) £5
My Cousin Rachel, French, 1979 (wraps, adapted by
Diana Morgan) £5

Biographies
Gerald: A Portrait, Gollancz, 1934 . . . £50/£10
The du Mauriers, Gollancz, 1937 . . . £65/£15
ditto, Doubleday (U.S.), 1937 . . . . £65/£15
The Infernal World of Branwell Brontë, Gollancz,
1960 . . . . £20/£5
ditto, Doubleday (U.S.), 1961 . . . . £15/£5
The Golden Lads, Gollancz, 1975 . . . £20/£5
ditto, Doubleday (U.S.), 1975 . . . . £15/£5
*The Winding Stair: Francis Bacon, His Rise And
Fall*, Gollancz, 1976 . . . . £20/£5
ditto, Doubleday (U.S.), 1977 . . . . £15/£5
Growing Pains: The Shaping of a Writer, Gollancz,
1977 . . . . £20/£5
The Rebecca Notebook & Other Memories,
Doubleday (U.S.), 1980 . . . . . . £15/£5
ditto, Gollancz, 1981 . . . . £15/£5

Miscellaneous
Vanishing Cornwall, Gollancz, 1967 . . £20/£5
ditto, Doubleday (U.S.), 1967 . . . . £15/£5
ditto, Gollancz, 1981 (colour edition) . . £15/£5
ditto, Doubleday (U.S.), 1981 . . . . £10/£5

GEORGE DU MAURIER
(b.1834 d.1896)

Principally a novelist and critic, du Maurier's *Trilby*
brought the author fame. He also wrote humorous
verse.

Novels
Peter Ibbetson, Harper (U.S.), 1891 . . . . £50
ditto, Osgood, McIlvaine, 1892 (2 vols) . . £50
Trilby, Osgood, McIlvaine, 1894 (3 vols) . . £250
ditto, Harper (U.S.), 1894 . . . . . . £45
ditto, Osgood, McIlvaine, 1895 (250 signed copies, 1
vol.) £100
The Martian, Harper (U.S.), 1897 . . . . £25
ditto, Harper (U.K.), 1898 . . . . . . £25
Svengali, W.H. Allen, 1982 (first unexpurgated edition
of *Trilby*) . . . . £10/£5

Others
Gauwaine Hys Penance: A Legend of Camelot,
Bradbury & Evans, 1866 (wraps) £500
English Society at Home, Bradbury, Agnew & Co.,
1880 . . . . £75
ditto, Osgood (U.S.), 1881 . . . . . . £50
Society Pictures, Bradbury, Agnew & Co., 1890-91 (2
vols) £100
English Society, Osgood, McIlvaine, 1897 . . £75
ditto, Harper (U.S.), 1897 . . . . . . £75
Social Pictorial Satire, Harper & Bros., 1898 . £45
ditto, Harper (U.S.), 1898 . . . . . . £35
A Legend of Camelot, Bradbury, Agnew & Co., 1898
. . . . £25
ditto, Harper (U.S.), 1898 . . . . . . £25
The Young du Maurier: A Selection of his Letters,
Peter Davies, 1951 . . . . £15/£5

DOUGLAS DUNN
(b.1942)

A Scottish poet whose early work shows the influence
of Philip Larkin.

Poetry
Terry Street, Faber, 1969 . . . . . . £35/£10
ditto, Chilmark (U.S.), 1969 . . . . . £20/£5
Backwaters, The Review, 1971 (wraps) . . . £20
Night, Poem of the Month Club, 1971 (signed
broadside) £25
The Happier Life, Faber, 1972 . . . £25/£10
ditto, Chilmark (U.S.), [no date] . . . . £20/£5
Love or Nothing, Faber, 1974 (wraps) . . . £20
Corporal Punishment, Sycamore Press, 1975
(broadside) £10
Barbarians, Faber, 1979 (wraps) £15
St Kilda's Parliament, Faber, 1981 (wraps) . £15

Douglas Dunn: Writers in brief, No 18, National Book
League, 1981 (broadside) £10
Europa's Lover, Bloodaxe, 1982 (wraps) . . £10
Elegies, Faber, 1985 . . . . £15/£5
ditto, Faber, 1985 (wraps). £5
Selected Poems 1964-1983, Faber, 1986 . . £15/£5
ditto, Faber, 1986 (wraps). £5
Northlight, Faber, 1988 . . . . . . £15/£5
ditto, Faber, 1988 (wraps). £5
New and Selected Poems 1966-1988, Ecco Press
(U.S.), 1989 . . . . £10/£5
Dante's Drum-Kit, Faber, 1993 . . . . £10/£5
Garden Hints, Carnivorous Arpeggio Press, 1993 (50
numbered copies, wraps) £20
The Donkey's Ears, Faber, 2000 (wraps) . . . £5
The Year's Afternoon, Faber, 2000 (wraps) . . £5
New Selected Poems 1964-1999, Faber, 2002 . £15/£5

Prose

Secret Villages, Faber, 1985 . . . . . . £15/£5
ditto, Dodd, Mead, 1985 . . . . . . £15/£5
Boyfriends and Girlfriends, Faber, 1995 . . £10/£5

Others

*Under the Influence: Douglas Dunn on Philip
Larkin*, Edinburgh Univ. Press Library, 1987 . £10
*Poll Tax, the Fiscal Fake: Why We Should Fight the
Community Charge*, Chatto & Windus, 1990 . £10
The Topical Muse on Contemporary Poetry, Kenneth
Allott Lecture No 6, [1990] (wraps) . . . £10

LORD DUNSANY

(b.1878 d.1957)

A versatile Irish writer, Dunsany is read and
appreciated today for his contributions to the genre of
heroic fantasy.

Short Stories

The Gods of Pegana, Elkin Mathews, 1905 (drummer
blind-stamped on front cover) £400
ditto, Elkin Mathews, 1905 (no drummer on front
cover) £200
ditto, Luce (U.S.), [1916] £100
Time and the Gods, W. Heinemann, 1906 . . £150
ditto, Luce (U.S.), 1913 . . . . £75
ditto, Putnam's, 1922 [1923] (250 copies signed by
Dunsany and Sime) £275
The Sword of Welleran, George Allen, 1908 (the first
issue has 'George Allen & Sons' at base of spine)
. . . . £125
ditto, George Allen, 1908 (second issue with 'George
Allen' at base of spine) £100
ditto, Luce (U.S.), [no date] £75
A Dreamer's Tales, George Allen, 1910 . . £125
ditto, Luce (U.S.), 1911 . . . . £75

The Fortress Unvanquishable, Save for Sacnoth,
School of Arts Press, 1910 (30 copies). . . £600
Selections from the Writings of Lord Dunsany, Cuala
Press, 1912 (250 copies, Introduction by W.B. Yeats)
. . . . £225
The Book of Wonder, W. Heinemann, 1912 . £75
ditto, Luce (U.S.), 1912 . . . . £45
Fifty-One Tales, Elkin Mathews, 1915 . . . £75
ditto, Kennerly (U.S.), 1915 . . . . . . £45
Tales of Wonder, Elkin Mathews, 1916 . . . £75
ditto, as *The Last Book of Wonder*, Luce (U.S.), 1916
. . . . £60
Tales of War, Talbot Press/T. Fisher Unwin, 1918 £20
ditto, Little, Brown (U.S.), 1918 . . . . . £20
Unhappy Far Off Things, Little, Brown (U.S.), 1919 .
. . . . £20
ditto, Elkin Mathews, 1919 . . . . . . £20
Tales of Three Hemispheres, Luce (U.S.), 1919 £35
ditto, T. Fisher Unwin, 1920 . . . . . £300/£40
The Travel Tales of Mr. Joseph Jorkens, Putnam's,
1931 . . . . £200/£35
ditto, Putnam's (U.S.), 1931 . . . . £175/£35
Mr Jorkens Remembers Africa, W. Heinemann, 1934
. . . . £175/£35
ditto, Longmans (U.S.), 1934. . . . £150/£30
Jorkens Has A Large Whiskey, Putnam, 1940 . . .
. . . . £175/£35
The Fourth Book of Jorkens, Jarrolds, [1947] (first
binding black cloth).. . . . . . £100/£25
ditto, Jarrolds, [1947] (second binding blue cloth) .
. . . . £65/£15
ditto, Arkham House (U.S.), 1948 . . . £45/£15
The Man Who Ate the Phoenix, Jarrolds [1949] . .
. . . . £100/£20
The Little Tales of Smethers, Jarrolds, 1952 (first
binding black cloth) . . . . . . £75/£25
ditto, Jarrolds, 1952 (second binding green cloth) .
. . . . £65/£15
Jorkens Borrows Another Whiskey, Joseph, 1954 . .
. . . . £75/£15
The Edge of the World, Ballantine Adult Fantasy,
1970 (wraps) £5
Beyond the Fields We Know, Ballantine Adult Fantasy,
1972 (wraps) £5
*Gods, Men and Ghosts: The Best Supernatural
Fiction of Lord Dunsany*, Dover, 1972 (wraps) . £5
Over the Hills and Far Away, Ballantine Adult
Fantasy, 1974 (wraps) £5

Novels

The Chronicles of Rodriguez, Putnam's, 1922 (500
copies numbered and signed by Dunsany and Sime) .
. . . . £400/£200
ditto, as *Don Rodriguez, Chronicles of Shadow Valley*,
Putnam's (U.S.), 1924 . . . . . £125/£25
The King of Elfland's Daughter, Putnam's, 1924 (250
copies numbered and signed by Dunsany and Sime) .
. . . . £500/£350
ditto, Putnam's (U.S.), 1924 . . . . . £200/£25

The Charwoman's Shadow, Putnam's, 1926 £200/£30
ditto, Putnam's (U.S.), 1926 . . . . £200/£25
The Blessing of Pan, Putnam's, 1927 . . £250/£75
ditto, Putnam's (U.S.), 1928 . . . . £250/£75
The Curse of the Wise Woman, W. Heinemann, 1933.
. . . . £150/£30
ditto, Longman's (U.S.), 1933 . . . . £100/£25
Up in the Hills, W. Heinemann, 1935 . . £75/£15
ditto, Putnam's (U.S.), 1935 . . . . £65/£15
Rory and Bran, W. Heinemann, 1936 . . £75/£15
ditto, Putnam's (U.S.), 1937 . . . . £65/£15
My Talks with Dean Spanley, W. Heinemann, 1936 .
. . . . £75/£15
ditto, Putnam's (U.S.), 1936 . . . . £65/£15
The Story of Mona Sheehy, W. Heinemann, 1939 . .
. . . . £100/£25
ditto, Harper (U.S.), 1940 . . . . . £50/£20
Guerrilla, W. Heinemann, 1944 . . . . £35/£10
ditto, Bobbs-Merrill (U.S.), 1944 . . . . £25/£5
The Strange Journeys of Colonel Polders, Jarrolds,
1950 . . . . £50/£20
ditto, Jarrolds (U.S.), 1950 . . . . £50/£20
The Last Revolution, Jarrolds, 1951 . . . £50/£20
His Fellow Men, Jarrolds, 1952 . . . . £50/£20

Plays
Five Plays, Grant Richards, 1914 . . . . £35
ditto, Little, Brown (U.S.), 1914 . . . . £30
Plays of Gods and Men, Talbot Press, 1917 . £35
ditto, Luce (U.S.), 1917 . . . . . £30
If, Putnam's, 1921 . . . . £50/£15
ditto, Putnam's, 1921 (large paper issue) . £35
ditto, Putnam's (U.S.), 1921 . . . . £45/£15
The Laughter of the Gods, Putnam's, 1922 (from
Plays of Gods and Men, wraps) £25
The Tents of the Arabs, Putnam's, [1922] (from *Plays
of Gods and Men*, wraps) £25
The Queen's Enemies, Putnam's, 1922 (from *Plays of
Gods and Men*, wraps) £25
A Night at an Inn, Putnam's, 1922 (from *Plays of
Gods and Men*, wraps) £25
Plays of Near and Far, Putnam's, 1922 (500 copies) .
. . . . £60
ditto, Putnam's, 1923 . . . . . . £40/£15
ditto, Putnam's (U.S.), 1923 . . . . £40/£15
The Gods of the Mountain, Putnam's, 1923 (from *Five
Plays*, wraps) £15
The Golden Dome, Putnam's, 1923 (from *Five Plays*,
wraps) £15
King Argimenes and the Unknown Warrior,
Putnam's, 1923 (from *Five Plays*, wraps) . . £15
The Glittering Gate, Putnam's, 1923 (from *Five Plays*,
wraps) £15
The Lost Silk Hat, Putnam's, 1923 (from *Five Plays*,
wraps) £15
The Compromise of the King of the Golden Isles,
Putnam's, [1923] (from *Plays of Near and Far*,
wraps) £15

The Flight of the Queen, Putnam's, [1923] (from
Plays of Near and Far, wraps) £15
Cheezo, Putnam's, [1923] (from *Plays of Near and
Far*, wraps) £15
A Good Bargain, Putnam's, [1923] (from *Plays of
Near and Far*, wraps) £15
If Shakespeare Lived To-day, Putnam's, [1923] (from
Plays of Near and Far, wraps) £15
Fame and the Poet, Putnam's, [1923] (from *Plays of
Near and Far*, wraps) £15
Alexander, and Three Small Plays, Putnam's, 1925 .
. . . . £35/£15
ditto, Putnam's, 1925 (250 copies) £70
ditto, Putnam's (U.S.), 1923 . . . . £35/£15
Alexander, Putnam's, 1925 (from *Alexander, and
Three Small Plays*, wraps) £15
The Old King's Tale, Putnam's, 1925 (from
Alexander, and Three Small Plays, wraps) . £15
The Evil Kettle, Putnam's, 1925 (from *Alexander, and
Three Small Plays*, wraps) £15
The Amusements of Khan Kharuda, Putnam's, 1925
(from *Alexander, and Three Small Plays*, wraps) £15
Seven Modern Comedies, Putnam's, 1928 . £25/£10
ditto, Putnam's, 1928 (250 copies) £50
ditto, Putnam's (U.S.), 1929 . . . . £25/£10
Atlanta in Wimbledon, Putnam's, 1928 (from *Seven
Modern Comedies*, wraps) £10
The Raffle, Putnam's, 1928 (from *Seven Modern
Comedies*, wraps) £10
The Journey of the Soul, Putnam's, 1928 (from *Seven
Modern Comedies*, wraps) £10
In Holy Russia, Putnam's, 1928 (from *Seven Modern
Comedies*, wraps) £10
His Sainted Grandmother, Putnam's, 1928 (from
Seven Modern Comedies, wraps) £10
The Hopeless Passion of Mr Bunyon, Putnam's, 1928
(from *Seven Modern Comedies*, wraps) . . £10
The Jest of Hahalaba, Putnam's, 1928 (from *Seven
Modern Comedies*, wraps) £10
The Old Folk of the Centuries, Elkin Mathews &
Marrot, 1930 (100 signed copies of 900) . £200/£125
ditto, Elkin Mathews & Marrot, 1930 (800 unsigned
copies of 900) . . . . £50/£25
Lord Adrian, Golden Cockerel Press, 1933 (325
copies, glassine d/w) £200
Mr Faithful, French, [1935] (wraps) . . . £15
Plays for Earth and Air, W. Heinemann, 1937 £30/£10

Poetry
Fifty Poems, Putnam's, 1929 (250 copies) . £125/£100
ditto, Putnam's, 1929 . . . . . . £50/£20
Mirage Water, Putnam's, 1938 . . . . £45/£15
War Poems, Hutchinson, [1941] . . . . £45/£15
Wandering Songs, Hutchinson, [1943] . . £45/£15
A Journey, Macdonald, [1944] (250 copies, initialled
'D', leather-bound in slipcase, no d/w) . . £125
ditto, Macdonald, [1944] (trade edition) . . £30/£10
The Year, Jarrolds, 1946 . . . . . £30/£10
To Awaken Pegasus, George Ronald, 1949 . £40/£10

Autobiography

Patches of Sunlight, W. Heinemann, 1938 .   £40/£15
ditto, Reynal Hitchcock (U.S.), 1938 .   .   £40/£15
While the Sirens Slept, Jarrolds, [1944].   .   £30/£10
The Sirens Wake, Jarrolds, 1945.   .   .   .   £25/£10

Miscellaneous

If I Were Dictator, Methuen, 1934 .   .   .   £45/£10
My Ireland, Jarrolds, 1937 .   .   .   .   .   £30/£10
ditto, Funk & Wagnalls (U.S.), 1937.   .   .   £30/£10
ditto, Jarrolds, 1950 (revised edition) .   .   .   £20/£5
The Donnellan Lectures, 1943, W. Heinemann, 1945.
.   .   .   .   £40/£15
A Glimpse from the Watch Tower, Jarrolds, 1946 .   .
.   .   .   .   £30/£10
*The Ghosts of the Heaviside Layer and other
Phantasms*, Owlswick Press (U.S.), 1980 .   £20/£10

FRANCIS DURBRIDGE
(b.1912 d.1998)

Durbridge's sleuth, Paul Temple, started his career as
a radio detective, but moved to both film and TV, and
even comic strips. The rest of his books are likewise
fast-paced thrillers with twisting plots.

'Paul Temple' Books

Send for Paul Temple, Long, 1938 (with John Thewes)
.   .   .   .   £50/£10
Paul Temple and the Front Page Men, Long, 1939
(with Charles Hatton) .   .   .   .   .   £40/£10
News of Paul Temple, Long, [1940] (with Charles
Hatton) .   .   .   .   £45/£10
Paul Temple Intervenes, Long, [1944] (with Charles
Hatton) .   .   .   .   £45/£10
Send for Paul Temple Again!, Long, [1948] (with
Charles Hatton) .   .   .   .   .   .   £45/£10
Paul Temple and the Kelby Affair, Hodder &
Stoughton, 1970 (wraps) £10
Paul Temple and the Harkdale Robbery, Hodder &
Stoughton, 1970 (wraps) £10
The Geneva Mystery, Hodder & Stoughton, 1971
(wraps) £10
The Curzon Case, Hodder & Stoughton, 1971 . £15/£5
Paul Temple and the Margo Mystery, Hodder &
Stoughton, 1986 .   .   .   .   £10/£5
Paul Temple and the Maddison Case, Hodder &
Stoughton, 1988 .   .   .   .   £10/£5

Other Books

Back Room Girl, Long, [1950] .   .   .   £40/£10
Beware of Johnny Washington, Long, 1951   £35/£10
Design For Murder, Long, 1951 .   .   .   £35/£10
The Tyler Message, Hodder & Stoughton, 1957
(pseud. 'Paul Temple', with James Douglas
Rutherford MacConnell) .   .   .   .   £30/£10
The Other Man, Hodder & Stoughton, [1958] £30/£10

East of Algiers, Hodder & Stoughton, [1959] (pseud.
'Paul Temple', with James Douglas Rutherford
MacConnell) .   .   .   .   £30/£10
A Time of Day, Hodder & Stoughton, [1959] £30/£10
The Scarf, Hodder & Stoughton, [1960] .   £30/£10
ditto, as *The Case of the Twisted Scarf*, Dodd, Mead
(U.S.), 1961 .   .   .   .   £25/£5
The World of Tim Frazer, Hodder & Stoughton, 1962
.   .   .   .   £30/£5
ditto, Dodd, Mead (U.S.), 1962 .   .   .   .   £25/£5
Portrait of Alison, Hodder & Stoughton, 1962 £30/£10
ditto, Dodd, Mead (U.S.), 1962 .   .   .   .   £25/£5
My Friend Charles, Hodder & Stoughton, 1963 .   .
.   .   .   .   £30/£10
Tim Frazer Again, Hodder & Stoughton, 1964 .   .
.   .   .   .   £30/£5
Another Woman's Shoes, Hodder & Stoughton, 1965.
.   .   .   .   £25/£10
The Desperate People, Hodder & Stoughton, [1966] .
.   .   .   .   £25/£10
Dead to the World, Hodder & Stoughton, [1967] .   .
.   .   .   .   £25/£10
My Wife Melissa, Hodder & Stoughton, 1967 £30/£10
The Pig-Tail Murder, Hodder & Stoughton, 1969 .   .
.   .   .   .   £25/£10
A Man Called Harry Brent, Hodder & Stoughton,
1970 .   .   .   .   £25/£10
Bat Out Of Hell, Hodder & Stoughton, 1972   £25/£10
A Game of Murder, Hodder & Stoughton, 1975 .   .
.   .   .   .   £25/£10
The Passenger, Hodder & Stoughton, 1977.   £25/£10
Tim Frazer Gets the Message, Hodder & Stoughton,
1978 .   .   .   .   £20/£5
Breakaway, Hodder & Stoughton, 1981.   .   £25/£10
The Doll, Hodder & Stoughton, 1982 .   .   £25/£10

Plays

Suddenly at Home, French, 1973 (wraps) .   .   . £5
The Gentle Hook, French, 1975 (wraps) .   .   . £5
Murder With Love, French, 1977 (wraps) .   .   . £5
House Guest, French, 1982 (wraps) £5
Deadly Nightcap, French, 1986 (wraps).   .   . £5
A Touch of Danger, French, 1989 (wraps) .   .   . £5
Small Hours, French, 1991 (wraps) £5
Sweet Revenge, French, 1993 (wraps) .   .   . £5

GERALD DURRELL
(b.1925 d.1995)

Brother of Lawrence, Gerald Durrell wrote popular
travel and natural history books, and was appointed
an O.B.E. in 1983.

Non Fiction

The Overloaded Ark, Faber & Faber, 1953 .   £65/£15
ditto, Viking (U.S.), 1953.   .   .   .   .   £30/£10
Three Singles to Adventure, Hart-Davis, 1954 £45/£10

The Bafut Beagles, Hart-Davis, 1954 . . £45/£10
ditto, Viking (U.S.), 1954. . . . . . £30/£5
The Drunken Forest, Hart-Davis, 1956 . . £30/£5
ditto, Viking (U.S.), 1956. . . . . . £25/£5
My Family and Other Animals, Hart-Davis, 1956 . .
. . . . £75/£15
ditto, Viking (U.S.), 1957. . . . . £45/£10
Encounters With Animals, Hart-Davis, 1958 . £15/£5
A Zoo in My Luggage, Hart-Davis, 1960 . . £35/£5
ditto, Viking (U.S.), 1956. . . . . . £20/£5
The Whispering Land, Hart-Davis, 1961 . . £15/£5
ditto, Viking (U.S.), 1962. . . . . . £10/£5
Menagerie Manor, Hart-Davis, 1964 . . . £15/£5
ditto, Viking (U.S.), 1964. . . . . . £10/£5
Two In The Bush, Collins, 1966. . . . . £15/£5
ditto, Viking (U.S.), 1966. . . . . . £10/£5
Birds, Beasts & Relatives, Collins, 1969 . £15/£5
ditto, Viking (U.S.), 1969. . . . . . £10/£5
Fillets of Plaice, Collins, 1971 . . . . £15/£5
ditto, Viking (U.S.), 1971. . . . . . £10/£5
Catch Me a Colobus, Collins, 1972 . . . £15/£5
ditto, Viking (U.S.), 1972. . . . . . £10/£5
Beasts in My Belfry, Collins, 1973 . . . £15/£5
The Stationary Ark, Collins, 1976 . . . £15/£5
ditto, Simon & Schuster (U.S.), 1976 . . £10/£5
Golden Bats and Pink Pigeons, Collins, 1977 . £15/£5
ditto, Simon & Schuster (U.S.), 1977 . . £10/£5
The Garden of the Gods, Collins, 1978 . . £15/£5
The Amateur Naturalist, Hamish Hamilton, 1982 . .
. . . . £10/£5
ditto, as *A Practical Guide for the Amateur Naturalist*,
Knopf (U.S.), 1983 . . . . £10/£5
How To Shoot An Amateur Naturalist, Collins, 1982 .
. . . . £10/£5
ditto, Little, Brown (U.S.), 1984 . . . . £10/£5
Durrell in Russia, McDonald, 1986 (with Lee Durrell)
. . . . £10/£5
ditto, Simon & Schuster (U.S.), 1986 . . £10/£5
Ark's Anniversary, Collins, 1990 . . . £10/£5
ditto, Arcade (U.S.), 1991. . . . . . £10/£5
Gerald Durrell's Army, J. Murray, 1992 . . £10/£5
Best of Durrell, HarperCollins, 1996 . . £10/£5

Novels
Rosy is My Relative, Collins, 1968 . . . £35/£5
ditto, Viking (U.S.), 1968. . . . . . £15/£5
The Mockery Bird, Collins, 1981 . . . £15/£5
ditto, Simon & Schuster (U.S.), 1981 . . £10/£5

Short Stories
The Picnic & Suchlike Pandemonium, Collins, 1979 .
. . . . £15/£5
ditto, as *The Picnic & Other Inimitable Stories*, Simon
& Schuster (U.S.), 1980 . . . . . . £15/£5

Children's Titles
The New Noah, Collins, 1955 . . . . £30/£10
ditto, Viking (U.S.), 1964. . . . . . £20/£5
Island Zoo, Collins, 1961. . . . . . £30/£10

ditto, MacRae Smith (U.S.), 1963 . . . . £15/£5
Look at Zoos, Collins, 1961 . . . . . £25/£5
My Favourite Animal Stories, Collins, 1962 . £15/£5
The Donkey Rustlers, Collins, 1968. . . . £25/£5
ditto, Viking (U.S.), 1968. . . . . . £25/£5
The Talking Parcel, Collins, 1974 . . . . £25/£5
ditto, Lippincott (U.S.), 1975. . . . . £25/£5
Fantastic Flying Journey, Conran Octopus, 1987 . .
. . . . £15/£5
ditto, Simon & Schuster (U.S.), 1987 . . . £15/£5
Animal Family Adventures with Gerald Durrell, Price
Stern Sloan, 1988 . . . . £10/£5
Fantastic Dinosaur Adventure, Conran Octopus, 1989
. . . . £10/£5
ditto, Simon & Schuster (U.S.), 1989 . . . £10/£5
Toby the Tortoise, M. O'Mara Books, 1991 . £10/£5
ditto, Little, Brown (U.S.), 1991. . . . . £10/£5

LAWRENCE DURRELL
(b.1912 d.1990)

Novelist, poet and travel writer, much of Lawrence
Durrell's work owes a debt to the Mediterranean
where he spent most of his life.

Poetry
Quaint Fragment, Cecil Press, 1931 (red boards) . .
. . . . £15,000
ditto, Cecil Press, 1931 (blue wraps). . . £15,000
Ten Poems, Caduceus Press, 1932 (wraps) . . £2,500
ditto, Caduceus Press, 1932 (12 signed copies in cloth)
. . . . £7,500
Ballade of Slow Decay, privately printed, 1932 (single
sheet, folded). £2,000
Transition, Caduceus Press, 1934 . . . . £2,500
A Private Country, Faber, 1943 . . . . £250/£75
Cities, Plains and People, Faber, 1946 . . £100/£20
On Seeming to Presume, Faber, 1948 . . £45/£10
Deus Loci, Ischia, 1950 (200 signed copies, wraps) .
. . . . £200
The Tree of Idleness, Faber, 1955 . . . £30/£10
Selected Poems, Faber, 1956. . . . . £35/£10
ditto, Faber, 1956 (wraps). £10
ditto, Grove Press (U.S.), 1956 . . . . £35/£10
Collected Poems, Faber, 1960 . . . . £40/£10
ditto, Dutton (U.S.), 1960. . . . . . £40/£10
Beccafico Le Becfigue, La Licorne (France), 1963
(150 signed copies, wraps) £200
La Descente du Styx, La Murène (France), 1964 (250
signed copies, wraps) £150
ditto, as *Down the Styx*, Capricorn Press (U.S.), 1971
(200 of 1,000 copies) £75
ditto, as *Down the Styx*, Capricorn Press (U.S.), 1971
(800 of 1,000 copies, wraps) £25
Selected Poems, 1935-1963, Faber, 1964 (wraps) £10
The Ikons, Faber, 1966 . . . . . . £35/£5
ditto, Dutton (U.S.), 1967. . . . . . £25/£5

Nothing Is Lost, Sweet Self, Turret, 1967 (100 signed copies, wraps with d/w) . . . . . . £100/£65

In Arcadia, Turret, 1968 (100 signed copies, wraps with d/w) . . . . £100/£65

The Red Limbo Lingo, Faber, 1971 (500 numbered copies of 1,200, glassine d/w, slipcase) . £75/£45

ditto, Faber, 1971 (100 signed copies, glassine d/w, slipcase) . . . . £125/£75

ditto, Dutton (U.S.), 1971 (500 numbered copies, glassine d/w, slipcase) . . . . . £75/£45

ditto, Dutton (U.S.), 1971 (100 signed, numbered copies, glassine d/w, slipcase) . . . . £125/£75

On the Suchness of the Old Boy, Turret, 1972 (226 signed copies, wraps) £75

Vega and Other Poems, Faber, 1973 . . . £25/£5

ditto, Overlook Press (U.S.), 1973 . . . . £25/£5

Lifelines - Four Poems, Tragara Press, 1974 (15 signed copies of 115, wraps) £250

ditto, Tragara Press, 1974 (100 copies of 115, wraps) £75

ditto, Tragara Press, 1974 (25 'extra' author's copies, usually inscribed) £250

Selected Poems, Faber, 1977 . . . . . £25/£10

Collected Poems: 1931-1974, Faber, 1980 . £25/£10

ditto, Faber, 1980 (26 signed copies, with signed etching by Henry Moore, slipcase) . . . £750

ditto, Viking (U.S.), 1980. . . . . . £20/£10

Parody

Bromo Bombasts, Caduceus Press, 1933 (pseud. 'Gaffer Peeslake', 100 copies) £2,500

Novels

Pied Piper of Lovers, Cassell, 1935 . £2,000/£1,250

Panic Spring, Faber, 1937 (pseud. 'Charles Norden') . . . . £2,000/£750

ditto, Covici Friede (U.S.), 1937 . . . . £750/£250

The Black Book, Obelisk Press (Paris), 1938 (wraps) £500

ditto, Obelisk Press (Paris), 1959 (wraps and d/w) . . . . £65/£25

ditto, Dutton (U.S.), 1960. . . . . . £40/£10

ditto, Faber, 1973 . . . . £20/£5

Cefalû, Editions Poetry, 1947 . . . . £75/£25

ditto, as *The Dark Labyrinth*, Ace (U.S.), 1958 (wrappers) £10

ditto, Faber, 1961 . . . . £35/£10

Justine, Faber, 1957 . . . . £250/£65

ditto, Dutton (U.S.), 1957. . . . . . £75/£25

White Eagles over Serbia, Faber, 1957 . . £50/£25

ditto, Criterion (U.S.), 1957 . . . . . £50/£25

Balthazar, Faber, 1958 . . . . . . £175/£25

ditto, Dutton (U.S.), 1958. . . . . . £45/£10

Mountolive, Faber, 1958 . . . . . . £175/£25

ditto, Dutton (U.S.), 1959. . . . . . £45/£10

Clea, Faber, 1960 . . . . £125/£20

ditto, Dutton (U.S.), 1960. . . . . . £35/£5

The Alexandria Quartet, Faber, 1962 . . £75/£25

ditto, Faber, 1962 (500 signed copies, slipcase). . . . . £400/£250

ditto, Dutton (U.S.), 1962. . . . . . £65/£20

ditto, Dutton (U.S.), 1962 (199 signed, numbered copies) . . . . £500/£250

Tunc, Faber, 1968. . . . . £25/£5

ditto, Dutton (U.S.), 1968. . . . . . £20/£5

Nunquam, Faber, 1970 . . . . . . £25/£5

ditto, Dutton (U.S.), 1970. . . . . . £15/£5

The Revolt of Aphrodite, Faber, 1973 . . £25/£10

Monsieur, or, The Prince of Darkness, Faber, 1974 . . . . £20/£5

ditto, Viking (U.S.), 1974. . . . . . £15/£5

Livia or Buried Alive, Faber, 1978 . . . £15/£5

ditto, Viking (U.S.), 1979. . . . . . £10/£5

Constance or Solitary Practices, Faber, 1982 . £10/£5

ditto, Viking (U.S.), 1982. . . . . . £15/£5

Sebastian or Ruling Passions, Faber, 1983 . £15/£5

ditto, Viking (U.S.), 1984. . . . . . £15/£5

Quinx or The Ripper's Tale, Faber, 1985 . £15/£5

ditto, Viking (U.S.), 1985. . . . . . £10/£5

The Avignon Quintet, Faber, 1992 . . . £15/£5

Plays

Sappho, Faber, 1950 . . . . £45/£15

ditto, Dutton (U.S.), 1958. . . . . . £20/£5

An Irish Faustus, Faber, 1963 . . . . £20/£5

ditto, Dutton (U.S.), 1964. . . . . . £15/£5

ditto, Delos, 1987 (75 signed, numbered copies, no d/w) £65

Acte, Faber, 1965 . . . . £15/£5

ditto, Dutton (U.S.), 1965. . . . . . £15/£5

Short Stories

Zero and Asylum in the Snow, privately printed (Rhodes), 1946 (50 copies, wraps) . . . £500

ditto, as *Two Excursions into Reality*, Circle Editions (U.S.), 1947 . . . . £65/£25

Esprit de Corps, Faber, 1957. . . . . £50/£15

ditto, Dutton (U.S.), 1958. . . . . . £30/£10

Stiff Upper Lip, Faber, 1958 . . . . . £40/£10

ditto, Dutton (U.S.), 1959. . . . . . £30/£10

Sauve Qui Peut, Faber, 1966. . . . . £25/£5

ditto, Dutton (U.S.), 1967. . . . . . £20/£5

The Best of Antrobus, Faber, 1974 . . . £15/£5

Antrobus Complete, Faber, 1985. . . . £15/£5

Non Fiction

Prospero's Cell, Faber, 1945 . . . . . £75/£15

ditto, Dutton (U.S.), 1960. . . . . . £35/£10

Key to Modern Poetry, Nevill, 1952. . . £35/£10

Reflections on a Marine Venus, Faber, 1953 £75/£15

ditto, Dutton (U.S.), 1960. . . . . . £35/£5

Bitter Lemons, Faber, 1957 . . . . . £125/£15

ditto, Dutton (U.S.), 1958. . . . . . £65/£10

Art and Outrage, Putnam, 1959 . . . £45/£10

ditto, Dutton (U.S.), 1960. . . . . . £40/£10

Lawrence Durrell and Henry Miller: A Private Correspondence, Dutton (U.S.), 1963 . . £25/£10

ditto, Faber, 1963 . . . . £25/£10
Spirit of Place, Faber, 1969 . . . . . £35/£10
ditto, Dutton (U.S.), 1969. . . . . . £35/£10
Le Grand Suppositoire, Editions Pierre Belfond
(Paris), 1972 . . . . £15/£5
ditto, as ***The Big Supposer***, Abelard-Schuman, 1973
(English translation) . . . . £15/£5
ditto, as ***The Big Supposer***, Grove Press (U.S.), 1974 .
. . . . £15/£5
Blue Thirst, Capra Press (U.S.), 1975 (250 signed
copies, glassine d/w). . . . . . . £75/£45
ditto, Capra Press (U.S.), 1975 (10 signed, lettered
copies, glassine d/w). . . . . . . £500/£450
Sicilian Carousel, Faber, 1977 . . . . . £15/£5
ditto, Viking (U.S.), 1977. . . . . . . £15/£5
The Greek Islands, Faber, 1978 . . . . . £15/£5
ditto, Viking (U.S.), 1978. . . . . . . £15/£5
A Smile in the Mind's Eye, Wildwood House, 1980 .
. . . . £15/£5
***Literary Lifelines: The Richard Aldington - Lawrence
Durrell Correspondence***, Faber, 1981 . . . £15/£5
ditto, Viking (U.S.), 1981. . . . . . . £15/£5
The Durrell-Miller Letters: 1935-80, New Directions
(U.S.), 1988 . . . . £20/£5
ditto, Faber, 1988 . . . . £20/£5
Letters to Jean Fanchette, 1958-1963, Editions Two
Cities, 1988 (1,800 of 2,000 copies, wraps) . £15
ditto, Editions Two Cities, 1988 (200 signed copies of
2,000, wraps). £150
Caesar's Vast Ghost: Aspects of Provence, Faber,
1990 . . . . £10/£5
ditto, Arcade (U.S.), 1990. . . . . . . £10/£5

UMBERTO ECO
(b.1932)

Eco is a semiotician with an interest in the philosophical and aesthetic theories of the Middle Ages. He is best known, however, for his two novels, *The Name of the Rose*, and *Foucault's Pendulum*.

Novels
The Name of the Rose, Secker & Warburg, 1984 . .
. . . . £175/£25
ditto, Harcourt Brace (U.S.), 1984 . . . £175/£25
Travels in Hyperreality, Harcourt Brace (U.S.), 1986 .
. . . . £25/£5
Foucault's Pendulum, Secker & Warburg, 1989 . .
. . . . £35/£10
ditto, Harcourt Brace (U.S.), 1989 . . . £35/£10
ditto, Franklin Centre (U.S.), 1989 (signed, limited
edition) £50
The Island of the Day Before, Harcourt Brace (U.S.),
1994 . . . . £10/£5
ditto, Harcourt Brace (U.S.), 1994 (250 signed copies,
slipcase) . . . . £125/£100
ditto, Secker & Warburg, 1983 . . . . . £10/£5

Baudolino, Harcourt Brace (U.S.), 2002 . . £10/£5
ditto, Secker & Warburg, 2002 . . . . . £10/£5

Children's Titles (with Eugenio Carmi)
The Three Astronauts, Secker & Warburg, 1989 . .
. . . . £25/£10
ditto, Harcourt Brace (U.S.), 1989 . . . £25/£10
The Bomb and the General, Secker & Warburg, 1989
. . . . £25/£10
ditto, Harcourt Brace (U.S.), 1989 . . . £25/£10

Academic Titles
A Theory of Semiotics, Indiana Univ. Press (U.S.),
1976 . . . . £45/£20
Art and Beauty in the Middle Ages, Yale Univ. Press
(U.S.), 1986 . . . . £25/£10
Limits of Interpretation, Indiana Univ. Press (U.S.),
1990 . . . . £30/£10
Apocalypse Postponed, Indiana Univ. Press (U.S.),
1994 . . . . £30/£10
Six Walks in the Fictional Woods, Harvard Univ.
Press (U.S.), 1994 . . . . £25/£10
The Search for the Perfect Language, Blackwell,
1995 . . . . £40/£10
Serendipities: Language and Lunacy, Univ. of
Columbia Press (U.S.), 1998 . . . . . £15/£5
ditto, Weidenfeld & Nicolson, 1999 . . . . £15/£5

Others
The Picture History of Inventions, Macmillan (U.S.),
1963 (with G.B. Zorzoli) . . . . . £40/£10
The Bond Affair, Macdonald (U.S.), 1966 (with Oreste
del Buono) . . . . £75/£20
ditto, Macdonald, 1966 . . . . . . £75/£20
Reflections on The Name of the Rose, Secker &
Warburg, 1983 . . . . £20/£5
ditto, as ***Postscript to The Name of the Rose***, Harcourt
Brace (U.S.), 1984 . . . . £20/£5
How to Travel With A Salmon, Harcourt Brace (U.S.),
1989 . . . . £15/£5
Misreadings, Harcourt Brace (U.S.), 1993 (wraps) £20
ditto, Cape, 1993 . . . . £25/£10

BERESFORD EGAN
(b.1905 d.1984)

As an artist Egan's wickedly satirical black and white line drawings were at their most effective in *The Sink of Solitude*, a lampoon of the reactions to Radclyffe Hall's *The Well of Loneliness*.

Written and Illustrated by Egan
Pollen, Denis Archer, 1933 (patterned boards, glassine
d/w) . . . . £45/£35
ditto, Denis Archer, 1933 (orange boards, glassine d/w)
. . . . £35/£25

No Sense in Form: A Tragedy of Manners, Denis
Archer, 1933 . . . . £40
But The Sinners Triumph, Fortune Press, 1934 . .
. . . . £125/£35
Epitaph, A Double Bedside Book for Singular People,
Fortune Press, [1943] . . . . . £75/£30
Epilogue, A Potpourri of Prose, Verse and Drawings,
Fortune Press, [1946] . . . . . £75/£25
Bun-Ho!, Floris Bakeries Ltd, 1959 (edited and
decorated by Egan) £50
Storicards, Barrigan Press, 1960 (5 cards) £50 the set

Illustrated by Egan
The Sink of Solitude: A Broadside, preface by P.R.
Stevensen, lampoons by various hands, Hermes Press,
1928 (250 numbered, signed copies) . . . £175
ditto, Hermes Press, 1928 (wraps) £50
Policeman of The Lord: A Political Satire, Sophistocles Press, 1929 (500 numbered copies) . . £125
ditto, Sophistocles Press, 1929 (wraps) . . . £50
Les Fleurs du Mal, In Pattern and Prose, by Baudelaire, translated by C. Bower Adcock, Sophistocles
Press and T. Werner Laurie, 1929 (500 signed copies)
. . . . £150
ditto, Godwin (U.S.), 1933 (pirated edition). . £20
ditto, as *Flowers of Evil*, Sylvan Press (U.S.), 1947
(1,499 numbered copies) £40
ditto, as *Flowers of Evil*, Sylvan Press (U.S.), 1947
(claims to be limited, but unnumbered reprint) £20
Aphrodite, by Pierre Loüys, The Fortune Press, 1929
(1,075 copies) £65
Cyprian Masques, by Pierre Loüys, The Fortune Press,
1929 . . . . £65
De Sade, by Beresford Egan and Brian de Shane, The
Fortune Press, 1929 (1,600 copies). . . . £100
The Adventures of King Pausole, by Pierre Loüys,
Fortune Press, 1930 (1,200 copies). . . . £75
Income and Outcome: A Study in Personal Finance,
by Nigel Balchin, Hamish Hamilton, 1936 . £40
Pobottle, by Heavy Duty Alloys Ltd, 1935-39
(advertising, 7 vols, wraps) . . . . £150 the set

Others
Beresford Egan: An Introduction to His Work, by
Paul Allen, Scorpion Press, 1966 (limited edition) .
. . . . £35/£20
ditto, Scorpion Press, 1966 (25 signed copies, with
extra plate) . . . . £125/£100

GEORGE ELIOT
(b.1819 d.1880)

George Eliot was the pseudonym of Mary Anne
Evans, novelist, critic and poet. Her great power is her
detailed depiction of character and motivation chiefly
among middle class provincial society.

Novels
Adam Bede, Blackwood, 1859 (3 vols, original
orange/brown cloth) £4,000
ditto, Blackwood, 1859 (3 vols, rebound) . . £900
ditto, Harper (U.S.), 1859. . . . . . £300
The Mill on the Floss, Blackwood, 1860 (3 vols,
original orange/brown cloth) £1,500
ditto, Blackwood, 1860 (3 vols, rebound) . . £300
ditto, Harper (U.S.), 1860. . . . . . £200
Silas Marner, The Weaver of Raveloe, Blackwood,
1861 (original orange/brown cloth) . . . £500
ditto, Blackwood, 1861 (rebound) £150
ditto, Harper (U.S.), 1860 (boards) . . . £100
ditto, Harper (U.S.), 1860 (wraps) £200
Romola, Smith, Elder & Co., 1863 (3 vols, first issue
with 2 pages of ads at end of vol. 2, original green
cloth) £1,000
ditto, Blackwood, 1863 (3 vols, rebound) . . £200
ditto, Smith, Elder & Co., 1863 (3 vols, second issue) .
. . . . £750
ditto, Harper (U.S.), 1863. . . . . . £125
Felix Holt, The Radical, Blackwood, 1866 (3 vols,
original brown cloth) £750
ditto, Harper (U.S.), 1866. . . . . . £75
Middlemarch, A Study of Provincial Life, Blackwood,
1871-1872 (8 parts, pictorial wraps) . . £3,000
ditto, Blackwood, 1871-1872 (8 parts bound together
as vols) £2,000
ditto, Harper (U.S.), 1872 (2 vols) £50
ditto, Blackwood, 1874 (4 vols in book form) . £2,000
Daniel Deronda, Blackwood, 1874-1876 (8 parts, with
erratum slip in part 3, blue/grey wraps) . . £2,500
ditto, Blackwood, 1874-1876 (8 parts, without erratum
slip in part 3, blue/grey wraps) . . . £2,000
ditto, Blackwood, 1874-1876 (8 parts bound together
as 1 vol.) £1,250
ditto, Blackwood, 1876 (4 vols in book form) . £1,250
ditto, Harper (U.S.), 1876 (2 vols) £125

Short Stories
Scenes of Clerical Life, Blackwood, 1858 (2 vols,
original dark maroon cloth) £7,500
ditto, Blackwood, 1858 (2 vols, rebound) . . £1,000
ditto, Harper (U.S.), 1858. . . . . . £150

Essays
Impressions of Theophrastus Such, Blackwood, 1879
(original grey/brown cloth) £175
ditto, Harper (U.S.), 1879. . . . . . £75
Essays and Leaves from a Note-Book, Blackwood,
1884 (original brown cloth). £150

Poetry

The Spanish Gypsy, Blackwood, 1868 (original blue cloth) £200
ditto, Ticknor & Fields (U.S.), 1868 . . . . £75
The Legend of Jubal and Other Poems, Blackwood, 1874 . . . . £125
ditto, Osgood (U.S.), 1874 . . . . . £35

Translations

The Life of Jesus, Critically Examined by D.F. Strauss, Chapman, 1846 (3 vols, lilac or green cloth) £3,500
Feuerbach's Essence of Christianity, Chapman, 1854 (3 vols, black cloth) £1,500
ditto, Chapman, 1854 (3 vols, purple cloth) . . £1,000

T.S. ELIOT
(b.1888 d.1965)

The American-born poet, critic and dramatist lived most of his adult life in England. Eliot received both the Nobel Prize for Literature and the Order of Merit in 1948.

Poetry

Prufrock and Other Observations, Egoist Ltd, 1917 (wraps) £1,500
Poems, Hogarth Press, 1919 (early copies of 250 with 'aestival' for 'estivale' on p.13, wraps) . . £5,000
ditto, Hogarth Press, 1919 (later copies of 250 with misprints corrected p.13, wraps) £3,000
Ara Vus Prec (sic), Ovid Press, 1920 (30 signed, numbered copies) £5,000
ditto, Ovid Press, 1920 (220 numbered copies) . £2,000
ditto, Ovid Press, 1920 (10 unnumbered copies, although there were probably more) . . . £1,000
ditto, as *Poems*, Knopf (U.S.), 1920 . . £2,000/£450
The Waste Land, Boni & Liveright, 1922 (approx 500 of 1,000 copies with flexible black cloth, with 'mountain' spelt correctly on p. 41, line 339) . £4,500
ditto, Boni & Liveright, 1922 (later copies, approx 500 of 1,000, with stiff black cloth and 'a' dropped from 'mountain' on p. 41, line 339) £3,500
ditto, Boni & Liveright, 1922 (1,000 copies, with 'a' dropped from 'mountain' on p. 41, line 339) . £1,000
ditto, Hogarth Press, 1923 . . . . . £2,000
ditto, Faber, [1962] (300 numbered, signed copies) £2,000
Homage to John Dryden, Hogarth Press, 1924 (wraps) £125
Poems, 1909-1925, Faber & Gwyer, 1925 £1,500/£300
ditto, Faber & Gwyer, 1925 (85 numbered and signed copies) £3,000
ditto, Harcourt Brace (U.S.), 1932 . . . £250/£45
Journey of the Magi, Faber & Gwyer, 1927 (wraps) £75

ditto, Faber & Gwyer, 1927 (350 copies, wraps with glassine d/w) . . . . £250/£175
ditto, Rudge (U.S.), 1927 (27 copies, copyright edition) £1,250
A Song for Simeon, Faber & Gwyer, 1928 (wraps) £30
ditto, Faber & Gwyer, 1928 (500 numbered, signed large paper copies) £400
Animula, Faber, [1929] (wraps) £65
ditto, Faber, [1929] (400 numbered, signed copies, slipcase) £450
Ash-Wednesday, Faber, 1930 . . . . £200/£65
ditto, Faber/Fountain Press, 1930 (600 signed copies, glassine d/w with white paper flaps, slipcase) . £750
ditto, Putnam (U.S.), 1930 . . . . . £150/£40
Marina, Faber, [1930] (wraps) £50
ditto, Faber, [1930] (400 numbered, signed copies) £300
Triumphal March, Faber, 1931 (wraps). . . £65
ditto, Faber, 1931 (300 numbered, signed copies, no d/w) £400
Collected Poems, 1909-1935, Faber, 1936 . £45/£15
ditto, Harcourt Brace (U.S.), 1936 . . . £25/£10
Old Possum's Book of Practical Cats, Faber, 1939 . . . . £600/£75
ditto, Harcourt Brace (U.S.), 1939 . . . £400/£75
The Waste Land and Other Poems, Faber, 1940 . . . . £35/£10
ditto, Harcourt Brace (U.S.), 1955 . . . £25/£10
East Coker, New English Weekly, 1940 (stapled, unbound supplement) £750
ditto, New English Weekly, 1940 (reprint, identified as such on cover, of 500 copies) £300
ditto, Faber, 1940 (yellow wraps) £150
Burnt Norton, Faber, 1941 (wraps) £65
The Dry Salvages, Faber, 1941 (wraps) . . . £125
Little Gidding, Faber, 1942 (wraps) . . . £100
Four Quartets, Harcourt Brace (U.S.), 1943 (first issue states 'First American edition') . . £1,250/£150
ditto, Harcourt Brace (U.S.), 1943 (second issue does not state 'First American edition') . . £350/£150
ditto, Faber, 1944 . . . . £200/£45
ditto, Faber, 1960 (290 signed copies) . . . £2,000
A Practical Possum, Harvard Univ. Printing Office (U.S.), 1947 (80 numbered copies, wraps) £1250/£150
Selected Poems, Penguin, 1948 (wraps) . . . £10
ditto, Harcourt Brace (U.S.), 1967 . . . £25/£10
The Undergraduate Poems, Harvard Advocate, 1949 (unauthorised publication, 1,000 copies, wraps) £100
Poems Written in Early Youth, privately printed (Stockholm), 1950 (12 copies only) . . . £2,000
ditto, Faber, 1967 . . . . £65/£20
ditto, Farrar Straus (U.S.), 1967 . . . . £50/£15
The Complete Poems and Plays, 1909-1950, Harcourt Brace (U.S.), 1952 . . . . . £175/£45
The Cultivation of Christmas Trees, Faber, 1954 (wraps & envelope) . . . . . . £100/£65
ditto, Farrar Straus (U.S.), 1956 . . . . £35/£10
Collected Poems, 1909-1962, Faber, 1963 . £35/£10
ditto, Farrar Straus (U.S.), 1963 . . . . £35/£10

The Complete Poems and Plays, Faber, 1968 £150/£25
The Waste Land: A Facsimile and Transcript, Faber,
1971 . . . . £45/£15
ditto, Faber, 1971 (500 copies, in slipcase) . £200/£100
ditto, Harcourt Brace (U.S.), 1971 (250 copies). . .
. . . . £125/£75

Prose
Ezra Pound: His Metric and Poetry, Knopf (U.S.),
1917 . . . . £250
The Sacred Wood, Methuen, 1920 (first issue with
3mm 'Methuen' at foot of spine and d/w without
subtitle on front) . . . . £1,000/£150
ditto, Methuen, 1920 (second issue with 3.5mm
'Methuen' at foot of spine and d/w with subtitle on
front and 'Books by A. Clutton-Brock' on back). .
. . . . £400/£100
ditto, Methuen, 1920 (third issue with 8pps of ads after
p.156) . . . . £300/£50
ditto, Knopf (U.S.), 1921 . . . . . £1,000/£150
Shakespeare and the Stoicism of Seneca, O.U.P., 1927
(wraps) £250
For Lancelot Andrewes, Faber & Gwyer, 1928 . .
. . . . £200/£25
ditto, Doubleday (U.S.), 1929 . . . . £150/£15
Dante, Faber, 1929 (grey d/w) . . . . £150/£35
ditto, Faber, 1929 (125 numbered, signed copies,
glassine d/w) . . . . £750/£700
Thoughts After Lambeth, Faber, 1931 (wraps). £65
ditto, Faber, 1931 (boards) . . . . . £200/£15
Charles Whibley: A Memoir, O.U.P., 1931 (wraps) .
. . . . £40
Selected Essays, 1917-1931, Faber, 1932 . £250/£20
ditto, Faber, 1932 (115 numbered, signed copies,
cellophane d/w) . . . . . . £1,500/£1,400
ditto, Harcourt Brace (U.S.), 1932 . . £125/£20
John Dryden: The Poet, the Dramatist, the Critic,
Holliday, 1931 . . . . £125/£40
ditto, Holliday, 1931 (110 signed, numbered copies) .
. . . . £750
The Use of Poetry and the Use of Criticism, Faber,
1933 . . . . £225/£20
ditto, Harvard Univ. Press (U.S.), 1933 . . £175/£15
After Strange Gods: A Primer of Modern Heresy,
Faber, 1934 . . . . £200/£25
ditto, Harcourt Brace (U.S.), 1934 . . £125/£20
Elizabethan Essays, Faber, 1934 (first issue with
misprint 'No.21' for 'No.23' on half title) . £200/£25
ditto, Faber, 1934 (second issue with error corrected,
spine blocked in gold) . . . . . £125/£25
ditto, Faber, 1934 (third issue 18cm high, error
corrected, spine blocked in silver) . . £75/£25
Essays Ancient and Modern, Faber, 1936 . £75/£25
ditto, Harcourt Brace (U.S.), 1936 . . . £65/£15
The Idea of a Christian Society, Faber, 1939 £35/£10
ditto, Harcourt Brace (U.S.), 1940 . . . . £25/£5
Points of View, Faber, 1941 . . . . . £25/£5
The Classics and the Man of Letters, O.U.P., 1942
(wraps) £25

The Music of Poetry, Jackson and Co., 1942 (wraps) .
. . . . £45
Reunion by Destruction, Vacher & Sons, 1943 £45
What is a Classic?, Faber, 1945 (Virgil Society issue,
with statement of aims, wraps) £150
ditto, Faber, 1945 (Virgil Society issue, without
statement of aims, wraps) £75
ditto, Faber, 1945 . . . . £45/£20
On Poetry, Concord, 1947 (750 copies, not for sale,
wraps) £100
Milton, Cumberlege, 1947 (500 copies, wraps) £50
A Sermon, C.U.P., 1948 (300 copies, not for sale,
wraps) £175
Notes Towards the Definition of Culture, Faber, 1948
. . . . £45/£15
ditto, Harcourt Brace (U.S.), 1949 . . . £35/£10
From Poe to Valéry, Harcourt Brace (U.S.), 1948
(1,500 copies, not for sale, boards and envelope) . .
. . . . £75/£65
The Aims of Poetic Drama, Poets' Theatre Guild, 1949
(wraps) £45
Poetry and Drama, Harvard Univ. Press (U.S.), 1951 .
. . . . £50/£15
ditto, Faber, 1951 . . . . £45/£10
The Value and Use of Cathedrals in England Today,
Chichester Cathedral, 1952 (wraps) . . . £65
An Address to the Members of the London Library,
Queen Anne Press, 1952 (500 copies, wraps) . £60
Selected Prose, Penguin, 1953 . . . . . . £5
ditto, as *Selected Prose by T.S. Eliot*, Faber, 1975 . . .
. . . . £25/£10
American Literature and the American Language,
Washington Univ., 1953 (500 copies, wraps) . £75
The Three Voices of Poetry, National Book League,
1953 (wraps) £45
ditto, C.U.P. (U.S.), 1954 . . . . £30
Religious Drama: Mediaeval and Modern, House of
Books (U.S.), 1954 (300 numbered copies, glassine
d/w) . . . . £350/£300
ditto, House of Books (U.S.), 1954 (26 lettered and
signed copies) £1,500
The Literature of Politics, Conservative Political
Centre, 1955 (wraps) £50
The Frontiers of Criticism, Univ. of Minnesota, 1956
(10,050 copies, not for sale, wraps) . . . £35
On Poetry and Poets, Faber, 1957 . . . £45/£15
ditto, Farrar Straus (U.S.), 1957 . . . . £30/£15
Geoffrey Faber, 1889-1961, Faber, 1961 (100 copies,
not for sale) . . . . £200/£125
George Herbert, Longmans, 1962 (wraps) . . £25
*Knowledge and Experience in the Philosophy of F.H.
Bradley*, Faber, 1964 . . . . . . £40/£10
ditto, Farrar Straus (U.S.), 1964 . . . . £30/£10
To Criticize the Critic and Other Writings, Faber,
1965 . . . . £35/£10
ditto, Farrar Straus (U.S.), 1965 . . . . . £25/£5
The Letters of T.S. Eliot, Vol. 1, 1898-1922, Faber,
1988 . . . . £25/£10

ditto, Faber, 1988 (250 signed by editor, slipcase) . .
. . . . £75/£50
ditto, Harcourt Brace (U.S.), 1988 . . . £25/£10
ditto, Harcourt Brace (U.S.), 1988 (250 signed by editor, slipcase) . . . . £75/£50

Drama
Sweeney Agonistes, Faber, 1932 . . . . £125/£30
The Rock, Faber, 1934 (wraps) £100
ditto, Faber, 1934 (hardback). . . . £125/£15
ditto, Harcourt Brace (U.S.), 1934 . . . £100/£15
Murder in the Cathedral, Goulden, 1935 (750 copies, grey wraps) £350
ditto, Goulden, 1935 (750 copies, white wraps) £400
ditto, Faber, 1935 (first complete edition) . £150/£15
ditto, Harcourt Brace (U.S.), 1935 . . . £125/£15
The Family Reunion, Faber, 1939 . . £125/£25
ditto, Harcourt Brace (U.S.), 1939 . . £100/£20
The Cocktail Party, Faber, 1950 (misprint 'here' for 'her' on page 29, line 1) . . . . . £75/£25
ditto, Faber, 1950 (misprint corrected) . . £50/£15
ditto, Harcourt Brace (U.S.), 1950 (copies with pp.35-36 on uncancelled leaf) . . . . . £500/£450
ditto, Harcourt Brace (U.S.), 1950 (copies with pp.35-36 on cancel leaf) . . . . . . £50/£10
The Confidential Clerk, Faber, 1954 (first issue with 'Ihad' on p.7) . . . . £60/£20
ditto, Faber, 1954 (second issue with 'I had' on p.7) .
. . . . £50/£10
ditto, Harcourt Brace (U.S.), 1954 . . . £35/£10
The Elder Statesman, Faber, 1959 . . . £45/£10
ditto, Farrar Straus (U.S.), 1959 . . . £35/£10
Collected Plays, Faber, 1962 . . . . . £25/£10

ALICE THOMAS ELLIS
(b.1932)

An author whose novels are fashionable as well as respected, Ellis has also written a number of non fiction books.

Novels
The Sin Eater, Duckworth, 1977 . . . £45/£15
ditto, Moyar, Bell (U.S.),1998 . . . . £15/£5
The Birds of the Air, Duckworth, 1980 . . . £30/£5
ditto, Viking Press (U.S.),1981 . . . . £15/£5
The 27th Kingdom, Duckworth, 1982 . . £60/£10
ditto, Moyar, Bell (U.S.),1999 . . . . £30/£5
The Other Side of the Fire, Duckworth, 1983 . £15/£5
ditto, Elisabeth Sifton (U.S.),1984 . . . £15/£5
Unexplained Laughter, Duckworth, 1985 . . £15/£5
ditto, Harper (U.S.), 1987. . . . . . £10/£5
The Clothes in the Wardrobe, Duckworth, 1987 . .
. . . . £15/£5
The Skeleton in the Cupboard, Duckworth, 1988 . .
. . . . £15/£5
The Fly in the Ointment, Duckworth, 1989. . £15/£5

The Inn at the Edge of the World, Viking, 1990 . . .
. . . . £10/£5
ditto, Viking (U.S.), 1990. . . . . . £10/£5
Pillars of Gold, Viking, 1992. . . . . £10/£5
ditto, Moyer, Bell (U.S.), 2000 . . . . £10/£5
Fairy Tale, Viking, 1996 . . . . . . £10/£5
ditto, Moyer, Bell (U.S.), 1998 . . . . £10/£5

Cookery
Natural Baby Food: A Cookery Book, Duckworth, 1977 (pseud. 'Brenda O'Casey') . . . . £15/£5
Darling, You Shouldn't Have Gone to So Much Trouble, Cape, 1980 (pseud. 'Anna Haycraft', with Caroline Blackwood) . . . . £15/£5

Others
Home Life, Duckworth, 1986 . . . . . £10/£5
ditto, Moyer, Bell (U.S.), 1997 . . . . £10/£5
Secrets of Strangers, Duckworth, 1986 (with Tom Pitt-Aikens) . . . . £10/£5
More Home Life, Duckworth, 1987 . . . . £10/£5
Home Life 3, Duckworth, 1988 . . . . £10/£5
Loss of the Good Authority: The Cause of Delinquency, Viking (U.S.), 1989 (with Tom Pitt-Aikens).
. . . . £10/£5
Home Life 4, Duckworth, 1989 . . . . . £10/£5
A Welsh Childhood, Joseph, 1990 . . . . £10/£5
ditto, Moyer, Bell (U.S.), 1990 . . . . £10/£5

BRET EASTON ELLIS
(b.1964)

Simon & Schuster gave the author a $300,000 advance for *American Psycho* then refused to publish it after women's groups and women employees within the company protested.

Less Than Zero, Simon & Schuster (U.S.), 1985 . . .
. . . . £20/£5
ditto, Picador, 1986 (wraps) £25
Rules of Attraction, Simon & Schuster (U.S.), 1987 .
. . . . £20/£5
ditto, Picador, 1988 (wraps) £25
American Psycho, Vintage (U.S.), 1991 (wraps) £20
ditto, Picador, 1991 (wraps) £20
The Informers, Knopf (U.S.), 1994 . . . . £20/£5
ditto, Picador, 1994 . . . . £20/£5
Glamorama, Knopf (U.S.), 1999. . . . £25/£10
ditto, Picador, 1999 . . . . £25/£10

JOHN MEADE FALKNER
(b.1858 d.1932)

A British industrialist and antiquarian, Falkner turned his hand to novel writing and local history. In *The Lost Stradivarius* he created an enduring classic.

Novels

The Lost Stradivarius, Blackwood, 1895 . . £300
ditto, Appleton (U.S.), 1896 . . . . . £200
Moonfleet, Arnold, 1898 . . . . . . £350
ditto, Little, Brown (U.S.), 1951 . . . £35/£10
The Nebuly Coat, Arnold, 1903 . . . . £150
ditto, O.U.P., 1954. . . . . . . £35/£10

Poetry

Poems, Westminster Press, [c.1935] (wraps) . £30

Others

Handbook for Travellers in Oxfordshire, Murray, 1894 (anonymous) £65
A History of Oxfordshire, Murray, 1899 . . £65
Handbook for Berkshire, Edward Stanford, 1902 £30
Bath in History and Social Tradition, Murray, 1918 (anonymous) £20
A History of Durham Cathedral Library, Durham Country Advertiser, 1925 . . . . . £100

G.E. FARROW
(b.1862 d.*not known*)

An author of children's stories, somewhat in the tradition of Lewis Carroll, Farrow is perhaps collected as much for the artists who illustrated his books as on his own account.

The Wallypug of Why, Hutchinson, [1895] (illustrated by Harry Furniss, vignettes by Dorothy Furniss) £100
ditto, Dodd, Mead (U.S.), 1896 . . . . . £45
The King's Gardens: An Allegory, Hutchinson, 1896 (illustrated by A.L. Bowley) £45
The Missing Prince, Hutchinson, 1896 (illustrated by Harry Furniss, vignettes by Dorothy Furniss) . £45
ditto, Dodd, Mead (U.S.), 1897 . . . . . £25
The Wallypug in London, Methuen, 1898 [1897] (illustrated by Alan Wright). £75
Adventures in Wallypug-land, Methuen, 1898 (illustrated by Alan Wright). £65
The Little Panjandrum's Dodo, Skeffington, 1899 (illustrated by Alan Wright) £45
The Mandarin's Kite, or Little Tsu-Foo and Another Boy, Skeffington, 1900 (illustrated by Alan Wright) £30
Baker Minor and the Dragon, Pearson, 1902 [1901] (illustrated by Alan Wright) £30
The New Panjandrum, Pearson, 1902 [1901] (illustrated by Alan Wright). £30

An A.B.C. of Every-day People, Dean, [1902] (illustrated by John Hassall). £65
In Search of the Wallypug, Pearson, 1903 [1902] (illustrated by Alan Wright). £65
Absurd Ditties, Routledge, 1903 (illustrated by John Hassall) £45
Professor Philanderpan, Pearson, 1904 [1903] £35
All About the Wallypug, Raphael Tuck, [1904] £45
The Cinematograph Train and Other Stories, Johnson, 1904 (illustrated by Alan Wright) . £65
Pixie Pickles: The Adventures of Pixene and Pixette in their Woodland Haunts, Skeffington, [1904] (illustrated by H.B. Neilson) £65
Wallypug Tales, Raphael Tuck, [1904] . . . £45
Round the World A.B.C., Nister, [1904] (illustrated by John Hassall) £55
The Wallypug Birthday Book, Routledge, 1904 (illustrated by Alan Wright) £45
The Wallypug in Fogland, Pearson, 1904 (illustrated by Alan Wright) £65
Ruff and Ready, The Fairy Guide by May Byron and G.E. Farrow, Cooke, [1905] (illustrated by John Hassall) £40
The Mysterious 'Mr Punch', A School Story, Christian Knowledge Society, [1905] £30
The Wallypug Book, Traherne, [1905] . . . £50
The Wallypug in the Moon, or His Badjesty, Pearson, 1905 (illustrated by Alan Wright) £50
The Adventures of Ji, Partridge, [1906] (illustrated by G.C. Tresidder) £40
Essays in Bacon, An Autograph Book, Treherne, [1906] £40
The Escape of the Mullingong, A Zoological Nightmare, Blackie, 1907 [1906] (illustrated by Gordon Browne) £35
The Adventures of a Dodo, Unwin, [1907] (illustrated by Willy Pogány) £65
ditto, as *A Mysterious Voyage, or The Adventures of a Dodo*, Partridge, [1910] (illustrated by K.M. Roberts) £35
The Dwindleberry Zoo, Blackie, 1909 [1908] (illustrated by Gordon Browne). £35
The Mysterious Shin Shira, Hodder & Stoughton, [1915]. £25
Zoo Babies, Frowde/Hodder & Stoughton, 1913 (illustrated by Cecil Aldin) £125
Don't Tell, Cooke, [no date] (illustrated by John Hassall) £40
Ten Little Jappy Chaps, Treherne, [no date] (illustrated by John Hassall). £30

Parodies

Lovely Man, Being the Views of Mistress A. Crosspatch, Skeffington, 1904 . . . . . £40

WILLIAM FAULKNER
(b.1897 d.1962)

An American novelist who often pushed the boundaries of narrative convention, Faulkner won the Nobel Prize for Literature in 1949.

Novels

Soldier's Pay, Boni & Liveright (U.S.), 1926 . . . . £15,000/£500
ditto, Chatto & Windus, 1930 . . £1,000/£250
Mosquitoes, Boni & Liveright, 1927 (no publisher on spine, d/w printed in red on green with mosquito) . . . . £4,000/£400
ditto, Boni & Liveright, 1927 (publisher's name on spine, d/w with card players on yacht) . £2,000/£400
ditto, Garden City (U.S.), 1937 . . . . £125/£50
ditto, Chatto & Windus, 1964 . . . . £45/£20
Sartoris, Harcourt Brace (U.S.), 1929 . £2,500/£250
ditto, Chatto & Windus, 1932 (top edge stained blue) . . . . £1,250/£300
ditto, Chatto & Windus, 1932 (top edge unstained). . . . . £950/£75
The Sound and the Fury, Cape & Smith (U.S.), 1929 (unpriced d/w with 'Humanity Uprooted' priced $3.00 on rear panel) . . . . . £20,000/£2,000
ditto, Cape & Smith (U.S.), 1929 ('Humanity Uprooted' priced $3.50 on rear panel) £15,000/£2,000
ditto, Chatto & Windus, 1931 (black cloth, top edge stained red) . . . . £1,250/£250
ditto, Chatto & Windus, 1931 (mustard cloth stamped in red, top edge unstained) . . . £1,000/£150
As I Lay Dying, Cape & Smith (U.S.), 1930 (first issue with capital 'I' on p.11, line 1 not correctly aligned, stamping to boards complete and unbroken) . . . . £6,000/£600
ditto, Cape & Smith (U.S.), 1930 (second issue with capital 'I' correctly aligned). . . . £3,500/£250
ditto, Chatto & Windus, 1935 . . . £1,000/£250
Sanctuary, Cape & Smith (U.S.), 1931 . £2,500/£250
ditto, Chatto & Windus, 1931 (cloth stamped in gold, four pages of ads) . . . . . . £1,500/£350
ditto, Chatto & Windus, 1931 (cloth stamped in black, no ads) . . . . £1,150/£150
Idyll in the Desert, Random House (U.S.), 1931 (400 signed, numbered copies, glassine d/w) £1,250/£1,000
Miss Zilphia Gant, Book Club of Texas (U.S.), 1932 (300 numbered copies) £1,000
Light in August, Smith & Haas (U.S.), 1932 (tan cloth stamped in blue and orange, glassine d/w over paper d/w) . . . . £1,250/£150
ditto, Smith & Haas (U.S.), 1932 (stamped in blue only, glassine d/w over paper d/w) . . . £650/£150
ditto, Chatto & Windus, 1933 . . . . £750/£75
Pylon, Smith & Haas (U.S.), 1935 . . . £750/£75
ditto, Smith & Haas, 1935 (310 signed, numbered copies, slipcase, no d/w) . . . . £1,750/£750
ditto, Chatto & Windus, 1935 (top edge stained red, bottom edge untrimmed) . . . . £1,250/£65
ditto, Chatto & Windus, 1935 (top edge unstained, bottom edge trimmed) . . . . £1,000/£65
Absalom, Absalom!, Random House (U.S.), 1936 . . . . £1,000/£200
ditto, Random House, 1936 (300 signed, numbered copies, slipcase and d/w) . . . £4,000/£3,000
ditto, Chatto & Windus, 1937 (glassine d/w with glued-on front flaps) . . . . . . £1,000/£175
The Unvanquished, Random House (U.S.), 1938 . . . . £750/£150
ditto, Random House, 1938 (250 signed, numbered copies) £2,500
ditto, Chatto & Windus, 1938 (clear d/w with paper flaps) . . . . £600/£125
The Hamlet, Random House (U.S.), 1940 (d/w with ads for other books) . . . . . . £1,500/£150
ditto, Random House (U.S.), 1940 (d/w with reviews of this book) . . . . £1,000/£150
ditto, Random House, 1940 (250 signed, numbered copies) £3,000
ditto, Chatto & Windus, 1940 . . . . £650/£75
Intruder in the Dust, Random House (U.S.), 1948 . . . . £300/£45
ditto, Chatto & Windus, 1949 . . . . £200/£30
Notes on a Horsethief, Levee Press (U.S.), 1950 [1951] (975 signed, numbered copies, tissue d/w) . . . . £1,250/£1,000
Requiem for a Nun, Random House (U.S.), 1951 . . . . £75/£30
ditto, Random House, 1951 (750 signed, numbered copies) £1,000
ditto, Chatto & Windus, 1953 . . . . £45/£20
A Fable, Random House (U.S.), 1954 . £125/£20
ditto, Random House, 1954 (1,000 signed, numbered copies, glassine d/w, slipcase) . . £1,250/£1,000
ditto, Chatto & Windus, 1955 . . . £60/£25
The Town, Random House (U.S.), 1957 (first issue red cloth, top edge stained grey, threaded grey endpapers, d/w with '5/57' on front flap) . . . . £750/£200
ditto, Random House (U.S.), 1957 (later issues with various cloths, endpapers etc) . . . . £50/£20
ditto, Random House (U.S.), 1957 (450 signed, numbered copies, acetate d/w) . . £1,250/£1,000
ditto, Chatto & Windus, 1958 . . . . £45/£15
The Mansion, Random House (U.S.), 1959 . £50/£20
ditto, Random House (U.S.), 1959 (500 signed, numbered copies, acetate d/w, no slipcase) £750/£500
ditto, Chatto & Windus, 1961 . . . . £40/£15
The Reivers, Random House (U.S.), 1962 . £100/£20
ditto, Random House (U.S.), 1962 (500 signed, numbered copies, acetate d/w) . . . £600/£500
ditto, Chatto & Windus, 1962 . . . . £75/£15

Short Stories

These 13, Cape & Smith (U.S.), 1931 . £750/£200
ditto, Cape & Smith (U.S.), 1931 (299 signed, numbered copies, plain tissue d/w) . £2,250/£2,000
ditto, Chatto & Windus, 1933 . . . £1,000/£75

Doctor Martino and Other Stories, Smith & Haas (U.S.), 1934 . . . . £600/£250
ditto, Smith & Haas (U.S.), 1934 (360 signed, numbered copies) £1,000
ditto, Chatto & Windus, 1934 . . . . £500/£50
The Wild Palms, Random House (U.S.), 1939 (stamped in gold and green on spine) . . £750/£50
ditto, Random House (U.S.), 1939 (stamped in brown and green on spine) . . . . . . £500/£50
ditto, Random House (U.S.), 1939 (250 signed, numbered copies, glassine d/w) . £2,000/£1,750
ditto, Chatto & Windus, 1939 . . . . . £750/£40
Go Down, Moses and Other Stories, Random House (U.S.), 1942 . . . . £750/£125
ditto, Random House (U.S.), 1942 (100 signed, numbered copies) £10,000
ditto, Chatto & Windus, 1942 . . . . £300/£60
Knight's Gambit, Random House (U.S.), 1949 . . . . £125/£25
ditto, Chatto & Windus, 1951 . . . . £100/£15
Collected Stories, Random House (U.S.), 1950 . . . . £200/£25
ditto, Chatto & Windus, 1951 . . . . £150/£25
Mirrors of Chartres Street, Faulkner Studies (U.S.), 1953 (1,000 numbered copies) . . . . £200/£100
Big Woods, Random House (U.S.), 1955 . £200/£35
Jealousy and Episode, Faulkner Studies (U.S.), 1955 (500 copies, no d/w) £250
Uncle Willy and Other Stories: Volume 1 of The Collected Short Stories, Chatto & Windus, 1958 . . . . £75/£20
These Thirteen: Volume 2 of The Collected Short Stories, Chatto & Windus, 1958 . £75/£20
Dr Martino and Other Stories: Volume 3 of The Collected Short Stories, Chatto & Windus, 1958 . . . . £75/£20
Selected Short Stories, Random House Modern Library (U.S.), 1962 . . . . £35/£10
Uncollected Stories, Franklin Library (U.S.), 1979 £25
ditto, Random House (U.S.), 1979 . . . . £25/£5
ditto, Chatto & Windus, 1980 . . . . . £25/£5

Poetry
Vision in Spring, privately printed (U.S.), 1921 . . . . £20,000
The Marble Faun, Four Seas (U.S.), 1924 . . . . £15,000/£7,500
This Earth: A Poem, Equinox (U.S.), 1932 (wraps) £2,500
A Green Bough, Smith & Haas, 1933 . £400/£150
ditto, Smith & Haas, 1933 (360 signed copies, no d/w) £750

Play
The Marionettes, Univ. of Virginia Press, 1975 £20/£5
ditto, Univ. of Virginia Press, 1975 (26 lettered copies, unbound in box) £300
ditto, Univ. of Virginia Press, 1975 (100 numbered copies unbound in slipcase) £125

ditto, as *The Marionettes: A Play in One Act*, Yoknapatawpha Press, 1975 (10 lettered copies in a box) £300
ditto, as *The Marionettes: A Play in One Act*, Yoknapatawpha Press, 1975 (500 numbered copies) £75

Others
Sherwood Anderson and Other Famous Creoles, Pelican Bookshop Press, 1926 (50 copies signed by caricaturist Spratling) £3,000
ditto, Pelican Bookshop Press, 1926 (200/250 numbered copies) £1,000
ditto, Pelican Bookshop Press, 1926 (label pasted over original limitation stating 'Second Issue 150 copies January 1927') £1,000
Salmagundi, Casanova Press, 1932 (first 26 numbered copies of 525 with top edge level with boards and bottom edge untrimmed, slipcase) . . £1,000/£950
ditto, Casanova Press, 1932 (499 of 525 numbered copies in slipcase) . . . . . . £250/£200
An Address by William Faulkner, Delta State Teachers College (U.S.), 1952 (wraps) £1,500
Faulkner's Country: Tales of Yoknapatawpha County, Chatto & Windus, 1955 . . . £45/£15
New Orleans Sketches, Hokuseido Press (Tokyo), 1955 . . . . £200
ditto, Hokuseido Press (Tokyo), 1955 (wraps) . £75
ditto, Rutgers Univ. Press (U.S.), 1958 . £45/£15
ditto, Sidgwick and Jackson, 1959 . . . £35/£10
Early Prose and Poetry, Little, Brown (U.S.), 1962 . . . . £35/£10
ditto, Cape, 1963 . . . . £35/£10
Essays, Speeches, and Public Letters, Random House (U.S.), 1966 . . . . £35/£10
ditto, Chatto & Windus, 1966 . . . . £35/£10
Selected Letters, Franklin Library (U.S.), 1976 . £45
ditto, Random House (U.S.), 1977 . . . . £25/£5
ditto, Scolar Press, 1977 . . . . . . £25/£5

SEBASTIAN FAULKS
(b.1953)

Author of *Birdsong* and *Charlotte Grey*, Faulks was named Author of the Year in the British Book Awards of 1995.

Novels
A Trick of the Light, Bodley Head, 1984 . £350/£25
The Girl at the Lion d'Or, Hutchinson, 1989 £100/£10
A Fool's Alphabet, Hutchinson, 1992 . . £50/£10
ditto, Little, Brown (U.S.), 1993 . . . . . £15/£5
Birdsong, Hutchinson, 1993 . . . . . £200/£40
ditto, Random House (U.S.), 1996 . . . £35/£10
Charlotte Grey, Hutchinson, 1998 . . . . £20/£5
ditto, Random House (U.S.), 1999 . . . . £10/£5

On Green Dolphin Street, Hutchinson, 2001 . £10/£5
ditto, Random House (U.S.), 2002 . . . . £10/£5

Non Fiction
The Fatal Englishman, Hutchinson, 1996 . . £10/£5

HENRY FIELDING
(b.1707 d.1754)

Fielding's reputation rests on his novels, especially his classic *Tom Jones*, although he wrote plays, poetry and other works.

The History and the Adventures of Joseph Andrews and his friend Mr Abraham Adams, Millar, 1742 (2 vols, anonymous) £4,000
Miscellanies, privately printed by subscription, 1743 (3 vols) £600
ditto, privately printed by subscription, 1743 (250 large paper or 'royal' paper copies, 3 vols) . . . £900
The History of Tom Jones, A Foundling, Miller, 1749 (6 vols, with errata leaf in vol. 1) £2,500
Amelia, A. Millar, 1752 [1751] (4 vols). . . £750
The Life of Mr Jonathan Wild the Great, A. Millar, 1754 (first separate edition, originally printed in Vol 3 of *Miscellanies*) £300
The Works of Henry Fielding, Miller, 1762 (4 vols) .
. . . . £500

RONALD FIRBANK
(b.1886 d.1926)

An eccentric, Roman Catholic author of witty and artificial novels.

Novels
Vainglory, Grant Richards, 1915. . . . . . £150
ditto, Brentano's (U.S.), 1925 . . . . £100/£20
Inclinations, Grant Richards, 1916 . . . . £75
Caprice, Grant Richards, 1917 . . . . . £75
Valmouth, Grant Richards, 1919. . . . . £60
ditto, New Directions (U.S.), 1966 . . . £25/£10
The Flower Beneath the Foot, Grant Richards, 1923 .
. . . . £150/£60
ditto, Brentano (U.S.),1924 . . . . . £100/£25
Prancing Nigger, Brentano's (U.S.), 1924 . £200/£25
ditto, as *Sorrow in Sunlight*, Brentano's, 1924 (1,000 numbered copies) . . . . . . £150/£30
Concerning the Eccentricities of Cardinal Pirelli, Grant Richards, 1926, ... £200/£30
ditto, as *Extravaganzas*, Coward-McCann (U.S.), 1935 (with *The Artificial Princess*) . . . . £45/£15
The Artificial Princess, Duckworth, 1934 . £75/£25
ditto, Centaur Press, 1934 (60 copies) . . . £200

Three Novels, Duckworth, 1950 (contains *Vainglory, Inclinations* and *Caprice*) . . . . . £35/£15
ditto, New Directions (U.S.), [1951] . . . £35/£15

Short Stories
Odette d'Antrevernes and A Study in Temperament, Elkin Mathews, 1905 (wraps) £500
ditto, Elkin Mathews, 1905 (10 copies on Japanese vellum) £2,000
ditto, as *Odette: A Fairy Tale for Weary People*, Grant Richards, 1916 (wraps) £75
Santal, Grant Richards, 1921 (wraps) . . . £75
ditto, Bonacio & Saul with Grove Press (U.S.), 1955 .
. . . . £35/£15
Two Early Stories, Albondocani Press (U.S.), 1971 (226 copies) £40

Others
The Princess Zoubaroff - A Play, Grant Richards, 1920 . . . . £200/£45
A Letter from Arthur Ronald Firbank to Madame Albani, Centaur Press, 1934 (50 facsimile copies of letter, issued in envelope) . . . . . £100/£75
The New Rythum and Other Pieces, Duckworth, 1962
. . . . £20/£10
ditto, New Directions (U.S.),1963 . . . £20/£10
The Wind and the Roses, Alan Clodd, 1966 (poem limited to 50 copies, wraps). £75
Far Away, Typographical Lab Univ. of Iowa, 1966 (100 copies) £75
An Early Flemish Painter, The Enitharmon Press/ Miriam L. Benkowitz, 1969 (300 copies, wraps) £35
When Widows Love and *A Tragedy in Green*, The Enitharmon Press, 1980 (300 copies) . . £75/£35

Collected Editions
The Works of Ronald Firbank, Duckworth, 1929 (235 numbered sets, 5 vols) £1,000
Rainbow Edition, Duckworth, 1929-1930 (8 vols). .
. . . . £350
The Complete Ronald Firbank, Duckworth, 1961 (1 vol.) . . . . £35/£10

F. SCOTT FITZGERALD
(b.1896 d.1940)

An American novelist and short story writer synonymous with the jazz age; *The Great Gatsby* is his enduring classic.

Novels
This Side of Paradise, Scribner's (U.S.), 1920 ('Published April, 1920' on copyright page) . . .
. . . . £12,000/£1,750
ditto, Collins, 1921 . . . . . £2,250/£300
The Beautiful and Damned, Scribner's (U.S.), 1922 ('Published March, 1922' on copyright page, first issue d/w title in white outlined in black) £5,000/£300

ditto, Scribner's (U.S.), 1922 (second printing, d/w with front title letters in black) . . . £4,000/£100
ditto, Collins, 1922 . . . . . . £1,500/£200
The Great Gatsby, Scribner's (U.S.), 1925 (first issue with 'chatter' not 'echolalia' on p.60, line 16, 'northern' not 'southern' on p.119, line 22 etc, and d/w with 'jay Gatsby' on back blurb, line 14) . . .
. . . . £25,000/£2,000
ditto, Scribner's (U.S.), 1925 (second issue with 'echolalia' on p.60, line 16, 'southern' on p.119, line 22 etc, and d/w with 'Jay Gatsby' on back blurb, line 14). . . . . £15,000/£500
ditto, Chatto & Windus, 1926 (original binding) . .
. . . . £3,000/£500
ditto, Chatto & Windus, 1926 [1927] (cheap edition) .
. . . . £1,000/£100
ditto, as *The Great Gatsby: A Facsimilie of the Manuscript*, Bruccoli Clark (U.S.), 1973 (2,000 numbered copies, slipcase) . . . . £200/£150
Tender is the Night, Scribner's (U.S.), 1934 (first issue jacket with review blurbs by T.S. Eliot, Mencken and Rosenfeld on front flap) . . . . £15,000/£400
ditto, Scribner's (U.S.), 1934 (second issue jacket). .
. . . . £3,000/£400
ditto, Chatto & Windus, 1934 (original binding) . .
. . . . £1,000/£250
ditto, Chatto & Windus, 1934 [1936] (cheap edition) .
. . . . £350/£75
ditto, Scribner's (U.S.), 1951 . . . . £100/£30
ditto, Grey Walls Press, 1953. . . . £125/£30
The Last Tycoon, Scribner's (U.S.), 1941 (unfinished)
. . . . £1,000/£100
ditto, Grey Walls Press, 1949. . . . £200/£25

Short Stories

Flappers and Philosophers, Scribner's (U.S.), 1920 ('Published September, 1920' on copyright page) .
. . . . £7,000/£300
ditto, Collins, 1922 . . . . . . £2,000/£150
Tales of the Jazz Age, Scribner's (U.S.), 1922 ('Published September, 1922' on copyright page) .
. . . . £4,000/£200
ditto, Collins, 1923 . . . . . £2,000/£100
All the Sad Young Men, Scribner's (U.S.), 1926 . .
. . . . £2,500/£200
John Jackson's Arcady, Baker (U.S.), 1928 (wraps) .
. . . . £1,000
Taps at Reveille, Scribner's (U.S.), 1935 (first state, no printed price on d/w, 'Oh, catch it-Oh catch it…' on p.351, lines 29-30) . . . . £2,500/£250
ditto, Scribner's (U.S.), 1935 (second state, printed price on d/w, 'Oh, things like that happen…' on p.351, lines 29-30) . . . . . £1,750/£125
The Stories of F. Scott Fitzgerald, Scribner's (U.S.), 1951 . . . . £75/£20
ditto, Franklin Library (U.S.), 1977 (full leather edition). £25
Borrowed Time, Grey Walls Press, 1951 . £150/£35

Afternoon of an Author, privately printed, Princeton Univ. Press (U.S.), 1957. . . . . £100/£25
ditto, Scribner's (U.S.), 1958 . . . . £75/£10
ditto, Bodley Head, 1958 . . . . . £75/£20
The Mystery of Raymond Mortgage, Random House (U.S.), [1960] (750 copies, wraps) . . . £150
The Pat Hobby Stories, Scribner's (U.S.), 1962 . .
. . . . £75/£20
ditto, Penguin, 1967 . . . . £5
Dearly Beloved, Windhover Press/Univ. of Iowa (U.S.), 1969 (300 numbered copies, no d/w) . £75
The Basil and Josephine Stories, Scribner's (U.S.), 1973 . . . . £40/£10
Bits of Paradise, Scribner's (U.S.), 1974 . £35/£10
ditto, Bodley Head, 1973 . . . . . £35/£10
The Price Was High, Harcourt Brace (U.S.), 1979. .
. . . . £30/£5
ditto, Quartet, 1979 . . . . . . £25/£5

Others

The Vegetable: From President to Postman, Scribner's, 1923 . . . . . . £2,000/£100
The Crack-Up, New Directions (U.S.), 1945 (first issue title page printed in red/brown and black, edited by Edmund Wilson) . . . . . . £250/£45
ditto, New Directions ('British Empire' issue), 1945 .
. . . . £125/£35
ditto, Grey Walls Press, 1947. . . . £45/£15
The Letters of F. Scott Fitzgerald, Scribner's (U.S.), 1963 . . . . £50/£15
ditto, Bodley Head, 1964 . . . . . £40/£15
The Apprentice Fiction of F. Scott Fitzgerald, Rutgers Univ. Press (U.S.), 1965. . . . . £35/£10
Thoughtbook of Francis Scott Key Fitzgerald, Princeton Univ. Library (U.S.), 1965 (glassine d/w) .
. . . . £35/£30
F. Scott Fitzgerald in His Own Time, Kent State Univ. Press (U.S.), 1971 . . . . . . £30/£10
Dear Scott / Dear Max: The Fitzgerald-Perkins Correspondence, Scribner's (U.S.), 1971 . £30/£10
ditto, Cassell, 1973 . . . . . . £25/£10
As Ever, Scott Fitz: Letter Between F. Scott Fitzgerald and His Literary Agent Harold Ober, Lippincott (U.S.), 1972 . . . . £25/£10
ditto, Woburn, 1973 . . . . . . £25/£10
F. Scott Fitzgerald's Preface to This Side of Paradise, Windhover Press (U.S.), 1975 (150 copies) . £125
The Notebooks of F. Scott Fitzgerald, Harcourt Brace, 1978 . . . . £30/£10
The Correspondence of F. Scott Fitzgerald, Random House (U.S.), 1980 . . . . . . £30/£10
The Bodley Head F. Scott Fitzgerald, Volume 1-6, Bodley Head, 1958-1963 . . . . . £65/£20

PENELOPE FITZGERALD
(b.1916 d.2000)

A Booker Prize winning novelist, Fitzgerald's novels are humorous and understated while often painfully revealing.

Novels
The Golden Child, Duckworth, 1977 . . £175/£25
ditto, Scribner's (U.S.), 1978 . . . . £100/£15
The Bookshop, Duckworth, 1978 . . . £75/£15
ditto, as *The Book Shop*, Houghton Mifflin (U.S.), 1997 (wraps) £5
Offshore, Collins, 1979 . . . . . . £35/£5
ditto, Henry Holt (U.S.), 1979 . . . . £20/£5
Human Voices, Collins, 1980 . . . . £25/£5
ditto, Houghton Mifflin (U.S.), 1999 (wraps) . . £5
At Freddie's, Collins, 1982 . . . . . £15/£5
ditto, Godine (U.S.), 1985 . . . . . £15/£5
Innocence, Collins, 1986 . . . . . . £10/£5
ditto, Holt (U.S.), 1987 . . . . . . £10/£5
The Beginning of Spring, Collins, 1988 . £10/£5
ditto, Holt (U.S.), 1989 . . . . . . £10/£5
The Gate of Angels, Collins, 1990 . . . £10/£5
ditto, Doubleday (U.S.), 1992 . . . . £10/£5
The Blue Flower, Flamingo, 1995 . . . £10/£5
ditto, Houghton Mifflin (U.S.), 1997 . . £10/£5

Short Stories
Means of Escape, Flamingo/HarperCollins, 2000 . .
. . . . £10/£5
ditto, Houghton Mifflin (U.S.), 2000 . . £10/£5

Others
Edward Burne-Jones: A Biography, Joseph, 1975. .
. . . . £75/£20
The Knox Brothers, Macmillan, 1977 . . . £30/£5
ditto, Coward-McCann (U.S.), 1977 . . . £15/£5
Charlotte Mew and Her Friends: With a Selection of Her Poems, Collins, 1984 . . . . . £15/£5
ditto, Addison Wesley (U.S.), 1988 . . . £15/£5

JAMES ELROY FLECKER
(b.1884 d.1915)

A poet and dramatist who followed a career in the Consular Service. His play *Hassan* was lavishly and successfully produced in London in 1923-24.

Poetry
The Bridge of Fire, Elkin Mathews, 1907 (wraps, first issue with no quote) £125
ditto, Elkin Mathews, 1907 (wraps, with quote from *Sunday Times*) £75
Thirty Six Poems, Adelphi Press, 1910 . . . £75
Forty-Two Poems, Dent, 1911 . . . . . £25

The Golden Journey to Samarkand, Goschen, 1913 .
. . . . £80
ditto, Goschen, 1913 (50 signed, numbered copies) .
. . . . £1,250
The Old Ships, Poetry Bookshop, [n.d.] (wraps, first issue illustration of a ship with a mermaid on front cover) £100
ditto, Poetry Bookshop, [n.d.] (wraps, second issue illustration without mermaid on front cover) . £50
God Save the King, privately printed for Clement Shorter, [1915] (wraps, 20 copies) £150
The Burial In England, privately printed for Clement Shorter, [1915] (wraps, 20 copies) £150
The Collected Poems of James Elroy Flecker, Secker, [1916] £20
ditto, Doubleday (U.S.), 1916 . . . . . £20
Fourteen Poems, Poetry Bookshop, 1921 (50 copies) .
. . . . £150
Collected Poems, London, 1923 (500 copies) . .
. . . . £100/£25
Don Juan, London, 1925 . . . . . . £20/£10
ditto, London, 1925 (380 copies) . . . £50/£15
ditto, Knopf (U.S.), 1922 . . . . . . £20/£10

Drama
Hassan: The Story of Hassan of Bagdad and how he came to make the Golden Journey to Samarkand - A Play in Five Acts, Heinemann, 1922 . . £50/£20
ditto, Knopf (U.S.), 1922 . . . . . . £50/£20

Fiction
The King of Alsander, Goschen, 1914 (first issue in scarlet buckram) £75
ditto, Goschen, 1914 (second issue in yellow cloth) £45
ditto, Putnams (U.S.), 1914 . . . . . £20
The Last Generation: A Story of the Future, The New Age Press, 1908 (wraps). £75

Others
The Best Man, Holywell Press, 1906 (wraps) . £225
The Grecians; A Dialogue on Education, Dent, 1910 .
. . . . £25
The Scholar's Italian Book, etc., Nutt, 1911 . £25
Collected Prose, Bell, 1920 . . . . . £35/£10
The Letters of James Elroy Flecker to Frank Savery, Beaumont Press, 1926 (80 signed copies of 390) .
. . . . £250
ditto, Beaumont Press, 1926 (310 unsigned copies) .
. . . . £40

IAN FLEMING
(b.1908 d.1964)

Famous for the legendary James Bond stories. The condition of the early books is of paramount importance in determining their value.

'James Bond' Titles

Casino Royale, Cape, 1953 (first issue jacket with no *Sunday Times* blurb, price of 10s. 6d. net) . . . .
. . . . £15,000/£2,000
ditto, Macmillan (U.S.), 1954 (first issue jacket with square-cut front flap corners). . . . £2,000/£100
Live and Let Die, Cape, 1954 (first issue jacket without credit for jacket design and artwork) . £6,500/£350
ditto, Macmillan (U.S.), 1955. . . . . £500/£50
Moonraker, Cape, 1955 . . . . . £4,000/£350
ditto, Macmillan (U.S.), 1955. . . . . £500/£35
Diamonds are Forever, Cape, 1956 . . . £750/£75
ditto, Macmillan (U.S.), 1956. . . . . £300/£50
From Russia, with Love, Cape, 1957 . . £600/£45
ditto, Cape, 1957 (Book Club edition, bound from rejected first printing sheets) . . . . £75/£20
ditto, Macmillan (U.S.), 1957. . . . . £200/£20
Dr No, Cape, 1958 (brown silhouette of dancing girl on front board) . . . . £600/£45
ditto, Cape, 1958 (without silhouette) . . £600/£75
ditto, Macmillan (U.S.), 1958. . . . . £200/£20
Goldfinger, Cape, 1959 . . . . . £750/£35
ditto, Macmillan (U.S.), 1959. . . . . £250/£15
For Your Eyes Only, Cape, 1960 (short stories) . .
. . . . £750/£50
ditto, Viking (U.S.), 1960. . . . . £200/£25
Thunderball, Cape, 1961. . . . . . £400/£20
ditto, Viking (U.S.), 1961. . . . . £150/£15
The Spy Who Loved Me, Cape, 1962 . . £200/£20
ditto, Viking (U.S.), 1962. . . . . £75/£15
On Her Majesty's Secret Service, Cape, 1963 . . .
. . . . £225/£25
ditto, Cape, 1963 (250 signed copies, clear glassine d/w) . . . . £4,000/£3,500
ditto, NAL (U.S.), 1963 . . . . . £100/£15
You Only Live Twice, Cape, 1964 (first state of first impression says 'First Published 1964' on copyright page) . . . . £200/£50
ditto, Cape, 1964 (second state of the first impression says 'First Published March 1964'). . . £175/£25
ditto, NAL (U.S.), 1964 . . . . . £65/£15
The Man with the Golden Gun, Cape, 1965 (with gold blocked revolver on front cover) . £2,500/£2,400
ditto, Cape, 1965 (without gold blocked revolver on front cover) . . . . £125/£15
ditto, NAL (U.S.), 1965 . . . . . £50/£10
Octopussy and *The Living Daylights*, Cape, 1966 (short stories). . . . . £75/£10
ditto, NAL (U.S.), 1966 . . . . . £60/£10
see also *The Ivory Hammer: The Year at Sotherby's*, Longman, 1963 (Contains Bond story 'The Property of a Lady') . . . . £65/£20
ditto, Holt, Rinehart & Winston (U.S.), 1964 £40/£15

Non Fiction

The Diamond Smugglers, Cape, 1957 . . £125/£35
ditto, Macmillan (U.S.), 1958 . . . . £45/£20
Thrilling Cities, Cape, 1963 . . . . . £30/£15
ditto, NAL (U.S.), 1964 . . . . . . £15/£10
Ian Fleming Introduces Jamaica, Deutsch, 1965 . .
. . . . £20/£10
ditto, Hawthorne (U.S.), 1965 . . . . £15/£10

Children's Titles

Chitty Chitty Bang Bang, Cape, 1964-65 (3 books) .
. . . . . £100/£20 each, £750/£100 the set
ditto, Random House (U.S.), 1964. . . . . £30/£5

W. RUSSELL FLINT
(b.1880 d.1969)

An artist and illustrator, generally of elegant nudes.

King Solomon's Mines, by H. Rider Haggard, Cassell, 1905 (32 b&w plates) £150
Through the Magic Door, by A. Conan Doyle, Smith Elder, 1907 (6 b&w plates) £50
Of The Imitation of Christ, by Thomas à Kempis, Chatto & Windus, 1908 (8 colour plates) . . £40
Savoy Operas, by W.S. Gilbert, Bell, 1909 (32 colour plates). £150
The Song of Songs, Riccardi Press, 1909 (500 copies, 10 colour plates, boards) £150
ditto, Riccardi Press, 1909 (limp vellum) . £200
ditto, Riccardi Press, 1909 (17 copies, vellum, extra set of plates) £1,000
ditto, Riccardi Press, 1913 . . . . . £45
Iolanthe and Other Operas, by W.S. Gilbert, Bell, 1910 (32 colour plates) £100
The Thoughts of The Emperor Marcus Aurelius Antonius, Riccardi Press, 1910 (500 copies, boards) .
. . . . £75
ditto, Riccardi Press, 1910 (limp vellum) . . £100
ditto, Riccardi Press, 1912 . . . . . £45
The Scholar Gipsy and Thyrsis, by Matthew Arnold, Riccardi Press, 1910 (10 colour plates) . . £50
Le Morte d'Arthur, by Sir Thomas Malory, Riccardi Press, 1910-11 (4 vols, 500 numbered copies, boards)
. . . . £300
ditto, Riccardi Press, 1910-11 (limp vellum) . £600
ditto, Riccardi Press, 1910-11 (12 copies, vellum, extra set of plates) £1,500
ditto, Riccardi Press, 1912 . . . . . £75
Iolanthe, or The Peer and the Peri, by W.S. Gilbert, Bell, 1911 (8 colour plates) £35
The Mikado, by W.S. Gilbert, Bell, 1911 (8 colour plates). £125
Patience, by W.S. Gilbert, Bell, 1911 (8 colour plates)
. . . . £125
The Pirates of Penznce, by W.S. Gilbert, Bell, 1911 (8 colour plates). £125

Songs and Lyrics, by Robert Burns, Riccardi Press, 1911 . . . . £125
The Heroes, or Greek Fairy Tales for My Children, by Charles Kingsley, Riccardi Press, 1912 (500 copies, boards) £200
ditto, Riccardi Press, 1912 (limp vellum) . . £400
ditto, Riccardi Press, 1914 . . . . . . £75
Princess Ida, by W.S. Gilbert, Bell, 1912 (8 colour plates). £125
Ruddigore, by W.S. Gilbert, Bell, 1912 (8 colour plates). £125
The Gondoliers, by W.S. Gilbert, Bell, 1912 (8 colour plates). £125
The Yeomen of the Guard, by W.S. Gilbert, Bell, 1912 (8 colour plates) £125
The Canterbury Tales, by Geoffrey Chaucer, Riccardi Press, 1913 (3 vols, 500 copies, boards) . . £300
ditto, Riccardi Press, 1913 (limp vellum) . . £500
Rabbi Ben Ezra, Foulis, 1913 . . . . . £30
The Watercolours of W. Russell Flint, The Studio, 1920 . . . . £45
The Idyls of Theocritus, Bion and Moschus, Riccardi Press, 1922 (2 vols, 500 copies, boards) . . £150
ditto, Riccardi Press, 1922 (limp vellum) . . £250
The Odyssey, by Homer, Riccardi Press, 1924 (500 copies, boards) £125
ditto, Riccardi Press, 1924 (limp vellum) . . £200
Judith, Haymarket Press, 1928 (875 copies) . £75
ditto, Haymarket Press, 1928 (100 signed copies, parchment, in slipcase) . . . . . £200/£150
ditto, Haymarket Press, 1928 (12 signed copies, on vellum, extra set of 4 plates, in slipcase) £1,000/£800
W. Russell Flint, Famous Water-Colour Painters No. 2, The Studio, 1928 . . . . £45
The Book of Tobit and *History of Susanna*, Haymarket Press, 1929 (875 copies) . . . £75
ditto, Haymarket Press, 1929 (100 signed copies, parchment, in slipcase) . . . . . £200/£150
ditto, Haymarket Press, 1929 (12 signed copies, on vellum, extra set of 4 plates, in slipcase) £1,000/£800
W. Russell Flint, Modern Masters of Etching No.27, The Studio, 1931. . . . . £50
Drawings, Collins, 1950 . . . . . . £125/£75
ditto, Collins, 1950 (500 signed copies, with separate signed mounted print, in slipcase). . . £450/£400
ditto, Collins, 1950 (125 signed copies, with a titled and initialled pencil drawing, in slipcase) . . . . £1,250/£1,000
Models of Propriety, Joseph, 1951 . . . £75/£50
ditto, Joseph, 1951 (500 signed copies) . . . £100
Minxes Admonished, Golden Cockerel Press, 1955 (400 copies, quarter morocco, in slipcase). . £500
ditto, Golden Cockerel Press, 1955 (150 copies, scarlet morocco, with 8 extra plates, in slipcase) . £750/£600
One Hundred and Eleven Poems, by Robert Herrick, Golden Cockerel Press, 1955 (450 copies, slipcase) .
. . . . £400/£350
ditto, Golden Cockerel Press, 1955 (100 signed copies, 8 extra plates, slipcase) . . . . . £650/£550

Memoirs of Madame du Barry, by M.F. Pidansat de Mairobert, Folio Society, 1956 . . . . £15
Etchings and Dry Points, Catalogue Raisonne, Coinaghi, 1957 (135 signed copies, buckram). £150
ditto, Coinaghi, 1957 (half morocco) . . . £200
Pictures From An Artist's Studio, Royal Academy of Arts, 1962 (wraps) £30
ditto, Royal Academy of Arts, 1962 (cloth). . £45
Shadows in Arcady, Skilton, 1965 (500 signed copies, slipcase) . . . . £250/£200
The Lisping Goddess, Stanbrook Abbey Press, 1988 (275 signed copies in slipcase) . . . £250/£200
Breakfast in Perigord, Skilton, 1968 (525 signed copies, in slipcase) . . . . . . £250/£200
An Autobiography: In Pursuit, Medici Society, 1970 (150 of 1050 numbered copies in full morocco, slipcase) . . . . £250/£200
ditto, Medici Society, 1970 (remaining copies in quarter morocco, slipcase) . . . . . £125/£100

FORD MADOX FORD
(b.1873 d.1939)

A novelist and editor, he was actually born Ford Hermann Hueffer, although, unless noted otherwise, titles listed below were published as by either Ford Madox Ford, Ford Madox Hueffer or F. Madox Hueffer.

Novels
The Shifting of the Fire, T. Fisher Unwin, 1892 (pseud. 'H. Ford Hueffer') £250
The Benefactor, Brown, Langham & Co., 1905 £125
The Fifth Queen, Alston Rivers, 1906 . . £100
ditto, Vanguard Press (U.S.), [c.1963] . . £20/£5
Privy Seal, Alston Rivers, 1907 . . . . £75
An English Girl, Methuen & Co., 1907 . . £75
The Fifth Queen Crowned, Eveleigh Nash, 1908 £75
Mr Apollo, Methuen & Co., 1908 . . . £75
The Half Moon, Eveleigh Nash, 1909 . . £75
ditto, Doubleday Page (U.S.), 1909 . . . £75
A Call, Chatto & Windus, 1910 . . . £75
The Portrait, Methuen & Co., 1910 . . . £75
The Simple Life Limited, John Lane, 1911 (pseud. 'Daniel Chaucer') £75
Ladies Whose Bright Eyes, Constable & Co., 1911 .
. . . . £75
ditto, Doubleday Page (U.S.), 1912 . . . £75
The Panel, Constable & Co., 1912 . . . £75
ditto, as *Ring For Nancy*, Bobbs-Merrill (U.S.), 1913 (revised edition) £75
The New Humpty-Dumpty, John Lane, 1912 (pseud. 'Daniel Chaucer') £75
ditto, John Lane (U.S.), 1912. . . . . £150
Mr Fleight, Howard Latimer, 1913 . . . £50
The Young Lovell, Chatto & Windus, 1913. . £50
The Good Soldier, John Lane, 1915 . . . . £1,250

ditto, John Lane (U.S.), 1915 . . . . . . £1,000
ditto, Albert & Charles Boni (U.S.), 1927 (300 signed, numbered copies) £900
Zeppelin Nights: A London Entertainment, John Lane/Bodley Head, 1915 (with Violet Hunt) . £125
The Marsden Case, Duckworth, 1923 . . £140/£40
Some Do Not, Duckworth, 1924 . . . . £150/£40
ditto, Seltzer (U.S.), 1925 . . . . . . £100/£30
No More Parades, Duckworth, 1925 . . £250/£75
ditto, Boni (U.S.), 1925 . . . . . . £100/£25
A Man Could Stand Up, Duckworth, 1926 . £100/£25
ditto, Boni (U.S.), 1926 . . . . . £75/£15
The Last Post, The Literary Guild of America (U.S.), 1928 . . . . £75/£15
ditto, as **Last Post**, Duckworth, 1928 . . £75/£15
A Little Less Than Gods, Duckworth, [1928] £75/£20
ditto, Viking (U.S.), 1928 . . . . . £75/£20
No Enemy, Macaulay (U.S.), 1929 . . . £150/£35
When the Wicked Man, Horace Liveright (U.S.), 1931 . . . . £75/£20
ditto, Cape, 1932 . . . . £50/£20
The Rash Act, Long & Smith (U.S.), 1933 . £50/£20
ditto, Cape, 1933 . . . . £50/£20
Henry for Hugh, Lippincott (U.S.), 1934 . £50/£20
Vive le Roy, Lippincott (U.S.), 1936 . . £50/£20
ditto, George Allen & Unwin, 1937 . . £50/£20

For titles written with Joseph Conrad (*The Inheritors***, ***Romance*** and ***The Nature of a Crime***) please see under Conrad.**

Poetry
New Poems, Rudge (U.S.), 1927 (325 signed copies, glassine d/w) . . . . £225/£175
Selected Poems, Pym Randall, 1971 (1,000 copies) . . . . £45/£20
ditto, Pym Randall, 1971 (50 copies) . £200/£125

Others
The Brown Owl: A Fairy Story, Unwin, 1892 [1891] (as Ford H. Hueffer) £500
ditto, Putnam (U.S.), 1892 . . . . . £400
The Cinque Ports: A Historical and Descriptive Record, Blackwood, 1900 . . . . . £400
Rossetti: A Critical Essay on His Art, Duckworth, [1902] £30
ditto, Dutton (U.S.), 1902 . . . . . . £25
The Soul of London: A Survey of a Modern City, Rivers, 1905 . . . . £75
The Heart of the Country: A Survey of a Modern Land, Duckworth, 1906 . . . . . £50
The Critical Attitude, Duckworth, 1911 (pseud. 'Ford Madox Hueffer') £75
Henry James: A Critical Study, Secker, 1913 . £65
ditto, Dodd Mead (U.S.), 1916 . . . £50
Between St. Dennis and St. George: A Sketch of Three Civilizations, Hodder & Stoughton, 1915 £45
Women and Men, Three Mountains Press (Paris), 1923 (300 numbered copies, wraps) £350

Mister Bosphorus and the Muses; or, A Short History of Poetry in Britain, Duckworth, 1923 . £250/£100
ditto, Duckworth, 1923 (70 copies signed by artist) . . . . £500/£300
New York is Not America, Duckworth, 1927 £125/£20
ditto, Boni (U.S.), 1927 . . . . . £75/£20
New York Essays, Rudge (U.S.), 1927 (750 signed copies) £200
The English Novel, Lippincott (U.S.), 1929 £50/£15
ditto, Constable, 1930 . . . . . . £45/£15
Provence, from Minstrels to the Machine, Allen & Unwin, 1935 . . . . £40/£15
ditto, Lippincott (U.S.), 1935 . . . . £40/£15
Great Trade Route, O.U.P. (U.S.), 1937 . £35/£15
The March of Literature from Confucius to Modern Times, Dial Press (U.S.), 1938 . . £65/£25
Your Mirror to My Times, Holt Rinehart & Winston (U.S.), 1971 . . . . £15/£5

C.S. FORESTER
(b.1899 d.1966)

Best remembered for the 'Hornblower' series, and for *The African Queen*.

'Hornblower' Novels
Beat to Quarters, Little, Brown (U.S.), 1937 £500/£75
ditto, as **The Happy Return**, Joseph, 1937 £1,250/£100
A Ship of the Line, Little, Brown (U.S.), 1938 . . . . £500/£50
ditto, as **Ship of the Line** Joseph, 1938 . . £500/£50
Flying Colours (including **A Ship of the Line**), The Book Society/Joseph, 1938 . . . . £500/£50
Flying Colours, Joseph, 1938 . . . £400/£45
ditto, Little, Brown (U.S.), 1939 . . . £300/£40
Commodore Hornblower, Little, Brown (U.S.), 1945 . . . . £75/£20
ditto, as **The Commodore**, Joseph, 1945 . £75/£20
Lord Hornblower, Little, Brown (U.S.), 1946 £50/£15
ditto, Joseph, 1946 . . . . £50/£15
Mr Midshipman Hornblower, Little, Brown (U.S.), 1950 . . . . £30/£10
ditto, Joseph, 1950 . . . . £30/£10
Lieutenant Hornblower, Little, Brown (U.S.), 1952 . . . . £30/£10
ditto, Joseph, 1952 . . . . £30/£10
Hornblower and the Atropos, Little, Brown (U.S.), 1953 . . . . £30/£10
ditto, Joseph, 1953 . . . . £30/£10
Admiral Hornblower in the West Indies, Little, Brown (U.S.), 1958 . . . . . . £30/£10
ditto, as **Hornblower in the West Indies**, Joseph, 1958 . . . . £30/£10
Hornblower and the Hotspur, Little, Brown (U.S.), 1962 . . . . £20/£5
ditto, Joseph, 1962 . . . . £15/£5

Hornblower and the Crisis: An Unfinished Novel, Joseph, 1967 . . . . £20/£10
ditto, as *Hornblower During the Crisis*, Little, Brown (U.S.), 1967 . . . . £20/£10

'Hornblower' Omnibus Editions
Captain Horatio Hornblower, Little, Brown (U.S.), 1939 . . . . £100/£25
Captain Hornblower R.N., Joseph, 1939 . £100/£25
Hornblower Takes Command, Little, Brown (U.S.), 1953 . . . . £30/£10
Young Hornblower, Little, Brown (U.S.), 1960 . .
. . . . £30/£10
ditto, Joseph, 1964. . . . . £20/£5
The Indominatable Hornblower, Little, Brown (U.S.), 1963 . . . . £25/£10
Admiral Hornblower, Joseph, 1968 . . . . £25/£5

Other Novels
A Pawn Among Kings, Methuen, 1924 . £2,000/£450
Payment Deferred, Bodley Head, 1926 . £2,000/£150
ditto, Little, Brown (U.S.), 1942 . . . . £50/£15
Love Lies Dreaming, Bodley Head, 1927 . £600/£75
ditto, Bobbs-Merrill (U.S.), 1927 (first issue with 'C.E. Forester' on cover) . . . . £400/£50
The Wonderful Week, Bodley Head, 1927 . £400/£75
ditto, as *One Wonderful Week*, Bobbs-Merrill (U.S.), 1927 . . . . £300/£40
The Shadow of the Hawk, Bodley Head, 1928 . . .
. . . . £400/£75
ditto, as *The daughter of the Hawk*, Bobbs-Merrill (U.S.), 1928 . . . . £300/£40
Brown on Resolution, Bodley Head, 1929 . £400/£75
ditto, as *Single-Handed*, Putnam (U.S.), 1929 . . .
. . . . £300/£40
Plain Murder, Bodley Head, 1930 . . . £400/£75
ditto, Dell (U.S.), 1954 (wraps) £15
Death to the French, Bodley Head, 1932 . £350/£100
ditto, as *Rifleman Dodd*, Little, Brown (U.S.), 1943 .
. . . . £45/£15
The Gun, John Lane, 1933 . . . . £400/£50
ditto, as *Rifleman Dodd and the Gun*, Little, Brown (U.S.), 1933 . . . . £300/£40
The Peacemaker, Heinemann, 1934 . . £300/£40
ditto, Little, Brown (U.S.), 1934 . . . £200/£35
The African Queen, Heinemann, 1935 . £2,500/£500
ditto, Little, Brown (U.S.), 1935 . . £2,000/£500
The General, Little, Brown (U.S.), 1936 . £350/£35
ditto, Joseph, 1936. . . . . . . £350/£35
The Captain from Connecticut, Joseph, 1941 . . .
. . . . £250/£15
ditto, Little, Brown (U.S.), 1941 . . . £150/£10
The Ship, Joseph, 1943 . . . . . £200/£25
ditto, Little, Brown (U.S.), 1943 . . . £125/£15
The Bedchamber Mystery, S.J. Reginald Saunders (Canada), 1944 . . . . £175/£40
The Sky and the Forest, Joseph, 1948 . £75/£15
ditto, Little, Brown (U.S.), 1948 . . . £75/£15

Randall and the River of Time, Little, Brown (U.S.), 1950 . . . . £45/£10
ditto, Joseph, 1951. . . . . . . £45/£10
The Good Shepherd, Joseph, 1955 . . . £45/£10
ditto, Little, Brown (U.S.), 1955 . . . . £45/£10

Short Stories
The Paid Piper, Methuen, 1924 (first issue with ads dated September 1923) . . . . . £2,500/£400
ditto, Methuen, 1924 (second issue with ads dated May 1925) . . . . £2,000/£300
Two-and-Twenty, Bodley Head, 1931 . £1,250/£175
ditto, Appleton-Century Co. (U.S.), 1931 . £600/£75
The Nightmare, Little, Brown (U.S.), 1954. £60/£10
ditto, Joseph, 1954. . . . . . . £60/£15
The Man in the Yellow Raft, Joseph, 1969 £35/£10
ditto, Little, Brown (U.S.), 1969 . . . £35/£10
Gold From Crete, Little, Brown, 1970 . . £25/£10
ditto, Joseph (U.S.), 1971. . . . . £25/£10

Plays
U 97, John Lane, 1931 . . . . . £400/£50
Nurse Cavell, John Lane, 1933 . . . £300/£40
Payment Deferred, French, 1934 (wraps) . . £75

Children's Titles
Marionettes At Home, Joseph, 1936 (first issue, sienna cloth) . . . . £400/£75
ditto, Joseph, 1936 (second issue orange cloth, jacket with '3/6 net' on spine) . . . . . £250/£45
Poo-Poo and the Dragons, Little, Brown (U.S.), 1942 . . . . £300/£45
ditto, Little, Brown (U.S.), 1942 . . . £250/£40
The Barbary Pirates, Random House (U.S.), 1953 . .
. . . . £125/£20
ditto, Macdonald, 1953 . . . . . £50/£10
Hornblower Goes to Sea, Joseph, 1954 . . £45/£20
Hornblower's Triumph, Joseph, 1955 . . £45/£20

Non Fiction
Napoleon and His Court, Methuen, 1924 £1,250/£250
ditto, Dodd, Mead (U.S.), 1924 . . . £450/£100
Josephine, Napoleon's Empress, Methuen, 1925 . .
. . . . £850/£200
ditto, Methuen, 1925 (but with ads dated 1928). . .
. . . . £750/£100
ditto, Dodd, Mead (U.S.), 1924 . . . £400/£60
Victor Emmanuel II and the Union of Italy, Methuen, 1927 . . . . £500/£100
ditto, Dodd, Mead (U.S.), 1927 . . . £450/£75
Louis XIV, King of France and Navarre, Dodd, Mead (U.S.), 1928 . . . . £500/£100
ditto, Methuen, 1928 . . . . . . £500/£100
Nelson, John Lane, 1929 . . . . . £450/£75
ditto, as *Lord Nelson*, Bobbs-Merrill (U.S.), 1929 . .
. . . . £450/£75
The Voyage of the Annie Marble, John Lane, 1929 . .
. . . . £500/£125

The Annie Marble in Germany, John Lane, 1930 . . . . £500/£125
The Earthly Paradise, Joseph, 1940. . . £75/£25
ditto, as *To the Indies*, Little, Brown (U.S.), 1940 . . . . £65/£20
The Naval War of 1812, Joseph, 1957 . . £50/£20
ditto, as *The Age of Fighting Sail: The Story of the Naval War of 1812*, Doubleday (U.S.), 1956 £45/£15
Hunting the Bismark, Joseph, 1959 . . . £50/£15
ditto, as *The Last Nine Days of the Bismark*, Little, Brown (U.S.), 1959 . . . . . . £45/£15
The Hornblower Companion, Joseph, 1964 £125/£25
ditto, Little, Brown (U.S.), 1964 . . . . £125/£25
Long Before Forty, Joseph, 1967 . . . £30/£10
ditto, Little, Brown (U.S.), 1967 . . . . £25/£10

Edited by Forester
The Adventures of John Wetherell, Joseph, 1954 . . . . £45/£10
ditto, Doubleday (U.S.), 1954 . . . . £35/£10

E.M. FORSTER
(b.1879 d.1970)

A novelist and essayist, Forster's writings often reflect his loathing of public schools, imperialism, and the repression of civil liberties. His books have been popularised recently by the successful film makers Merchant and Ivory.

Novels
Where Angels Fear to Tread, Blackwood, 1905 (first issue with this title not mentioned in ads at rear) £2,000
ditto, Blackwood, 1905 (second issue with this title mentioned in ads) £1,500
ditto, Knopf (U.S.), 1920 . . . . £500/£150
The Longest Journey, Blackwood, 1907 . . £500
ditto, Knopf (U.S.), 1922 . . . . . . £400/£75
A Room with a View, Arnold, 1908 . . . . £1,000
ditto, Putnam (U.S.), 1911 . . . . . . £250
Howard's End, Arnold, 1910 (first issue with 4 pages of integral ads) £1,000
ditto, Arnold, 1910 (second issue with 8 pages of inserted ads) £750
ditto, Putnam (U.S.), 1910 . . . . . £500
A Passage to India, Arnold, 1924 . . £1,500/£400
ditto, Arnold, 1924 (200 numbered signed copies, fawn paper boards, grey slipcase). £3,500
ditto, Harcourt Brace (U.S.), 1924 . . £250/£50
ditto, as *The Manuscripts of A Passage to India*, Arnold, 1978 (1,500 copies) . . . . £35/£15
Maurice, Arnold, 1971 . . . . . . £25/£10
ditto, Norton (U.S.), 1971. . . . . . . £20/£5

Short Stories
The Celestial Omnibus and Other Stories, Sidgwick & Jackson, 1911 . . . . £200
ditto, Knopf (U.S.), 1923 . . . . . . £200/£35
The Story of the Siren, Hogarth Press, 1920 (first state with 'The Story/of the Siren' on front label, wraps) £500
ditto, Hogarth Press, 1920 (other states, wraps). £300
The Eternal Moment, Sidgwick & Jackson, 1928 (first issue cloth stamped in gold). . . . . £350/£75
ditto, Sidgwick & Jackson, 1928 (second issue cloth stamped in black) . . . . . . £325/£50
ditto, Harcourt Brace (U.S.), 1928 . . £200/£45
The Collected Tales, Knopf (U.S.), 1947 . £45/£15
ditto, as *The Collected Short Stories*, Sidgwick & Jackson, 1948 . . . . £45/£15
The Life to Come, Arnold, 1972. . . . £25/£10
ditto, Norton (U.S.), 1973. . . . . . £25/£10

Essays
Pharos and Pharillon, Hogarth Press, 1923 (900 copies, no d/w) £250
ditto, Knopf (U.S.), 1923 . . . . . . £250/£50
Anonymity: An Enquiry, Hogarth Press, 1925 (boards) £175
ditto, Hogarth Press, 1925 (wraps) . . . £75
A Letter to Madam Blanchard, Hogarth Press, 1931 (wraps) £35
ditto, Harcourt Brace (U.S.), 1932 (wraps) . . £25
Sinclair Lewis Interprets America, privately printed, 1932 (100 copies, wraps) £100
Pageant of Abinger, privately printed, 1934 (wraps) £65
Abinger Harvest, Arnold, 1936 (first issue with 'A Flood in the Office', cream d/w decorated orange) . . . . £300/£75
ditto, Arnold, 1936 (second issue without 'A Flood in the Office') . . . . £150/£20
ditto, Harcourt Brace (U.S.), 1936 . . . £75/£25
What I Believe, Hogarth Press, 1939 (wraps) . £35
Nordic Twilight, Macmillan, 1940 (wraps) . £25
The Challenge of Our Time, Marshall, 1948 £35/£10
Two Cheers for Democracy, Arnold, 1951 . £45/£15
ditto, Harcourt Brace (U.S.), 1951 . . . £45/£15

Others
The Government of Egypt, Labour Research Dept., [1920] (wraps) £300
Alexandria, A History and a Guide, Whitehead Morris, 1922 (no d/w) £500
ditto, Whitehead Morris, 1922 (revised edition with maps and plans) £75
ditto, Whitehead Morris, 1922 (250 signed copies). £500
ditto, Doubleday (U.S.), 1961 . . . . £25/£10
Aspects of the Novel, Arnold, 1927 . . . £250/£40
ditto, Harcourt Brace (U.S.), 1927 . . . £75/£20
Goldsworthy Lowes Dickinson, Arnold, 1934 . . . . £200/£30

ditto, Harcourt Brace (U.S.), 1934 . . . £150/£25
Reading as Usual, Tottenham Public Libraries, 1939
(wraps) £200
England's Pleasant Land, Hogarth Press, 1940 . .
. . . . £40/£15
Virginia Woolf, C.U.P., 1942 (wraps) . . £30
ditto, Harcourt Brace (U.S.), 1942 . . . £50/£20
The Development of English Prose Between 1918 and
1930, Jackson, 1945 (wraps) £45
Desmond McCarthy, Mill House Press, 1952 (64
copies) £250
ditto, Mill House Press, 1952 (8 copies). . . £1,000
The Hill of Devi, Arnold, 1953 . . . £65/£15
ditto, Harcourt Brace (U.S.), 1953 . . £45/£15
I Assert There is an Alternative to Humanism, The
Ethical Union, 1955 . . . . £50
Battersea Rise, privately printed (Harcourt Brace,
U.S.), 1955 . . . . £45
Marianne Thornton, Arnold, 1956 . . . £30/£10
ditto, Arnold, 1956 (200 signed copies, slipcase) £250
ditto, Harcourt Brace (U.S.), 1956 . . . . £30/£5
Tourism vs Thuggism, privately printed, 1957 (wraps)
. . . . £25
E.K. Bennett, privately printed, 1958 (wraps) . £75
A View Without a Room, Albondocani Press (U.S.),
1973 (200 numbered copies, wraps) . . . £75
Letters to Donald Windham, Campbell (Verona), 1975
(300 copies) £75
Commonplace Book, Scolar Press, 1978 (facsimile,
350 numbered copies, boxed) £100
Selected Letters, Vol. 1: 1879-1920, Collins, 1983. .
. . . . £25/£10
ditto, Harvard Univ. Press (U.S.), 1983 . £25/£10
Selected Letters, Vol. 2: 1921-1970, Collins, 1985. .
. . . . £25/£10
ditto, Harvard Univ. Press (U.S.), 1984 . . £25/£10

FREDERICK FORSYTH
(b.1938)

The author of the phenomenally successful *The Day of the Jackal*, Forsyth's forte is the tense thriller.

Novels
The Day of the Jackal, Hutchinson, 1971 . £65/£10
ditto, Viking (U.S.), 1971. . . . . . £25/£10
The Odessa File, Hutchinson, 1972 . . . £25/£5
ditto, Viking (U.S.), 1972. . . . . . £25/£5
The Dogs of War, Hutchinson, 1974 . . . £25/£5
ditto, Viking (U.S.), 1974. . . . . . £20/£5
The Shepherd, Hutchinson, 1975 . . . . £10/£5
ditto, Viking (U.S.), 1976. . . . . . £10/£5
The Devil's Alternative, Hutchinson, 1979 . . £15/£5
ditto, Viking (U.S.), 1980. . . . . . £15/£5
The Fourth Protocol, Hutchinson, 1984 . . £15/£5
ditto, Viking (U.S.), 1984. . . . . . £15/£5
The Negotiator, Bantam, 1989 . . . . £10/£5

ditto, London Limited editions, 1989 (150 signed
copies, glasssine d/w) . . . . . £65/£50
ditto, Bantam (U.S.), 1989 . . . . . £10/£5
The Deceiver, Bantam, 1991. . . . . . £10/£5
ditto, Bantam (U.S.), 1991 . . . . . £10/£5
Fist of God, Bantam, 1994 . . . . . £10/£5
ditto, Bantam (U.S.), 1994 . . . . . £10/£5
Icon, Bantam, 1996 . . . . £10/£5
ditto, Bantam (U.S.), 1996 . . . . . £10/£5
The Phantom of Manhattan, Bantam, 1999 . £10/£5
ditto, Franklin Library (U.S.), 1999 (signed, limited
edition) £40
The Veteran, Bantam, 2001 . . . . . £10/£5
ditto, Thomas Dunne/St. Martin's Press (U.S.), 2001 .
. . . . £10/£5

Short Stories
No Comebacks, Hutchinson, 1982 . . . £15/£5
ditto, Viking (U.S.), 1982. . . . . . £15/£5
ditto, Eurographica (Helsinki), 1986 (350 signed
copies, wraps with d/w) . . . . . £100/£65

Non Fiction
The Biafra Story, Penguin, 1969 (wraps) . . £30
ditto, as **The Biafra Story, The Making of an African**
Legend, Severn House, 1983 . . . . . £20/£5

DION FORTUNE
(b.1890 d.1946)

British occultist and writer of occult fiction, Fortune's books were published under her own name as well as the pseudonyms 'V.M. Steele' and 'Violet M. Firth'.

Dion Fortune Novels
The Demon Lover, Noel Douglas, [1927] . £200/£45
The Winged Bull, Williams & Norgate, 1935 . . .
. . . . £200/£45
The Goat-Foot God, Williams & Norgate, 1936 . . .
. . . . £200/£45
The Sea Priestess, Inner Light, 1938 . . £200/£45
Moon Magic, Aquarian Press, 1956 . . . £45/£20

Dion Fortune Short Stories
The Secrets of Dr Taverner, Noel Douglas, 1926 . . .
. . . . £200/£45

Dion Fortune Non Fiction
The Esoteric Philosophy of Love and Marriage, Rider,
1923 . . . . £100/£25
Esoteric Orders and Their Work, Rider, 1928 . . .
. . . . £100/£25
Sane Occultism, Rider, 1929. . . . . £75/£20
The Training and Work of an Initiate, Rider, 1930 .
. . . . £75/£20
Mystical Meditations Upon the Collects, Rider, 1930 .
. . . . £75/£20

Spiritualism in the Light of Occult Science, Rider, 1931 . . . . £75/£20
Psychic Self-Defence, Rider, 1931 . . . £100/£25
Through the Gates of Death, Inner Light, 1932 . .
. . . . £75/£20
The Mystical Qabalah, Williams & Norgate, 1935. .
. . . . £100/£25
Practical Occultism in Daily Life, Williams & Norgate, 1935 . . . . £75/£20
The Cosmic Doctrine, Inner Light, 1949 . £40/£10
Applied Magic, Aquarian Press, 1962 . £30/£10
Aspects of Occultism, Aquarian Press, 1962 £30/£10
The Magical Battle of Britain, Golden Gates Press, 1994 (wraps) £10
An Introduction to Ritual Magic, Thoth Publications, 1997 . . . . £15/£5
ditto, Thoth Publications, 1997 (wraps) £5
The Circuit of Force, Thoth Publications, 1998 (wraps) £5
Principles of Hermetic Philosophy, Thoth Publications 1999 (wraps) £5
Principles of Esoteric Healing, Sun Chalice Books (U.S.), 2000 (wraps) £5

Novels Written as 'V.M. Steele'
The Scarred Wrists, Stanley Paul, [1935] . £40/£15
Hunters of Humans, Stanley Paul, [1936] . £40/£15
Beloved of Ishmael, Stanley Paul, [1937] . £40/£15

Non Fiction Written as 'Violet M. Firth'
Machinery of the Mind, Allen & Unwin, 1922. . .
. . . . £150/£45
ditto, Dodd, Mead (U.S.), 1922 . . . £150/£45
The Psychology of the Servant Problem, C.W. Daniel, 1925 . . . . £35/£10
The Soya Bean, C.W. Daniel, 1925 . . £35/£10
The Problem of Purity, Rider, [1928] . £40/£10
Avalon of the Heart, Muller, 1934 . . £35/£10

Poetry Written as 'Violet M. Firth'
Violets, Mendip Press, [1904] £65
More Violets, Jarrold, [1906]. £65

JOHN FOWLES
(b.1926)

Fowles has become both popularly and critically acclaimed as a modern literary figure due to his experimental style and the broad humanist content of his novels.

Novels
The Collector, Cape, 1963 (trial binding of charcoal-black papered boards, no top edge stain, first issue d/w without reviews quoted) . £5,000/£4,725
ditto, Cape, 1963 (rust-coloured papered boards, matching top edge stain, first issue d/w) . £300/£25

ditto, Cape, 1963 (later issue rare d/w with reviews) . . . . £2,000/£50
ditto, Little, Brown (U.S.), 1963 . . . . £75/£25
The Magus, Little, Brown (U.S.), 1965 . £150/£25
ditto, Cape, 1966 . . . . . . £125/£25
ditto, Cape, 1977 (revised edition) . . £20/£10
ditto, Little, Brown (U.S.), 1978 (revised edition) .
. . . . £20/£10
The French Lieutenant's Woman, Cape, 1969. . .
. . . . £175/£25
ditto, Little, Brown (U.S.), 1969 . . . £125/£15
The Ebony Tower, Cape, 1974 (novellas) . £50/£10
ditto, Little, Brown (U.S.), 1974 . . . . . £35/£5
ditto, Little, Brown (U.S.), 1974 (signed issue, with a special tipped-in leaf signed by John Fowles) . . £175/£150
Daniel Martin, Little, Brown (U.S.), 1977 . £25/£5
ditto, Cape, 1977 . . . . £25/£5
Mantissa, Cape, 1982 . . . . . . £20/£5
ditto, Little, Brown (U.S.), 1982 . . . £20/£5
ditto, Little, Brown (U.S.), 1982 (500 signed copies, slipcase) . . . . £75/£50
A Maggot, Cape, 1985 . . . . . . £25/£5
ditto, Cape/London Limited Editions, 1985 (500 signed copies, glassine d/w). . . . . £75/£65
ditto, Little, Brown (U.S.), 1985 . . . . £20/£5
ditto, Little, Brown (U.S.), 1985 (260 signed copies, slipcase) £100

Other Titles
The Aristos, Little, Brown (U.S.), 1964 . . £100/£15
ditto, Cape, 1965 . . . . £400/£75
My Recollections of Kafka, Univ. of Manitoba Press, 1970 (25 copies, wraps) £250
Poems, Ecco Press (U.S.), 1973 . . . . £65/£20
Cinderella, by Perrault, translated by John Fowles, Cape, 1974 . . . . £45/£10
Shipwreck, Cape, 1974 (photographs by the Gibsons of Scilly, with text by John Fowles) . . . £30/£10
ditto, Little, Brown (U.S.), 1975 . . . . . £15/£5
Ourika, Tom Taylor (U.S.), 1977 (500 signed copies) .
. . . . £100
Islands, Cape, 1978 (photographs by Fay Godwin with text by John Fowles). . . . . . . £15/£5
ditto, Little, Brown (U.S.), 1979 . . . . . £10/£5
ditto, Little, Brown (U.S.), 1979 (160 signed, numbered copies, slipcase) . . . . . £200/£175
Conditional, Lord John Press (U.S.), 1979 (broadside, 150 numbered, signed copies) £100
The Tree, Aurum Press, 1979 (photographs with text by John Fowles) . . . . £30/£10
ditto, Little, Brown (U.S.), 1980 . . . . £25/£10
A Letter from Charles I Concerning Lyme, Lyme Regis Museum, 1980 (100 signed sets of 2 printed sheets). £125
The Enigma of Stonehenge, Cape, 1980 (photographs by Barry Brukoff with text by John Fowles) . £20/£5
ditto, Summit (U.S.), 1980 . . . . . . £20/£5

A Brief History of Lyme, Friends of the Lyme Regis Museum, 1981 (wraps). £15

The Screenplay of the French Lieutenant's Woman, Cape, 1981 (by Harold Pinter, foreword by John Fowles) . . . . £20/£5

ditto, Little, Brown (U.S.), 1981 . . . . . £20/£5

ditto, Little, Brown (U.S.), 1981 (360 signed, numbered copies, slipcase) . . . . . £125/£75

Photographs of Lyme Regis, Skelton Press, 1982 (25 signed copies) £1,000

A Short History of Lyme Regis, Dovecote Press, 1982 . . . . £25/£10

ditto, Little, Brown (U.S.), 1983 . . . . . £10/£5

Of Memories and Magpies, Tom Taylor (U.S.), 1983 (200 copies, wraps) £300

Land, Heinemann, 1985 (photographs by Fay Godwin) . . . . £45/£10

ditto, Little, Brown (U.S.), 1985 . . . £45/£10

Poor Koko, Eurographica (Helsinki), 1987 (350 signed, numbered copies, wraps) £75

The Enigma, Eurographica (Helsinki), 1987 (350 signed, numbered copies, wraps) . . . £75

Behind the Magus, Colophon Press, 1994 (26 signed, lettered copies bound in goatskin) . . . £1,000

ditto, Colophon Press, 1994 (signed copies, wraps) £150

ditto, privately printed by the author, 1995 (wraps) £150

The Nature of Nature and The Tree, Yolla Bolly Press (U.S.), 1995 (140 signed copies, boards, slipcase) . . . . £500/£450

ditto, Yolla Bolly Press (U.S.), 1995 (275 signed copies, wraps) £175

Wormholes, Colophon Press, 1998 (signed copies, slipcase) £175

ditto, Cape, 1998 . . . . £15/£5

ditto, Holt (U.S.), 1998 . . . . . £15/£5

ditto, Holt (U.S.), 1998 (150 signed copies, slipcase) . . . . £175/£150

DICK FRANCIS
(b.1920)

A former steeplechase jockey, Francis has become a highly popular and collectable thriller writer, setting his novels in the world of horse racing.

Novels

Dead Cert, Joseph, 1962 . . . . . £3,000/£250

ditto, Holt Rinehart (U.S.), 1962 . . . £1,000/£100

Nerve, Joseph, 1964 . . . . . £1,000/£50

ditto, Harper (U.S.), 1964 . . . . . . £350/£65

For Kicks, Joseph, 1965 . . . . . £750/£25

ditto, Harper (U.S.), 1965 . . . . . £125/£15

Odds Against, Joseph, 1965 . . . . . £350/£15

ditto, Harper (U.S.), 1966 . . . . . £100/£10

Flying Finish, Joseph, 1966 . . . . . £250/£25

ditto, Harper (U.S.), 1967 . . . . . £75/£10

ditto, Armchair Detective Library (U.S.), 1991 (100 signed, numbered copies) £100

Blood Sport, Joseph, 1967 . . . . . £150/£15

ditto, Harper (U.S.), 1968 . . . . . . £45/£5

Forfeit, Joseph, 1968 . . . . . . £100/£15

ditto, Harper (U.S.), 1969 . . . . . . £30/£5

Enquiry, Joseph, 1969 . . . . . £75/£10

ditto, Harper (U.S.), 1969 . . . . . £25/£5

Rat Race, Joseph, 1970 . . . . . £75/£10

ditto, Harper (U.S.), 1971 . . . . . £25/£5

Three To Show, Harper (U.S.), 1970 (contains *Dead Cert*, *Nerve* and *Odds Against*) . . . . . £20/£5

Bonecrack, Joseph, 1971 . . . . . . £50/£5

ditto, Harper (U.S.), 1972 . . . . . £15/£5

Smokescreen, Joseph, 1972 . . . . . £45/£5

ditto, Harper (U.S.), 1972 . . . . . £15/£5

Slay-Ride, Joseph, 1973 . . . . . £40/£5

ditto, Harper (U.S.), 1974 . . . . . £15/£5

Knock Down, Joseph, 1974 . . . . . £35/£5

ditto, Harper (U.S.), 1975 . . . . . £15/£5

Across the Board, Harper (U.S.), 1975 (contains *Flying Finish*, *Blood Sport* and *Enquiry*) . . . £35/£5

High Stakes, Joseph, 1975 . . . . . £35/£5

ditto, Harper (U.S.), 1976 . . . . . £15/£5

In The Frame, Joseph, 1976 . . . . . £25/£5

ditto, Harper (U.S.), 1977 . . . . . £15/£5

Risk, Joseph, 1977 . . . . . . £25/£5

ditto, Harper (U.S.), 1978 . . . . . £15/£5

Three Winners, Joseph, 1977 (contains *Dead Cert*, *Nerve* and *For Kicks*) . . . . . . £15/£5

Trial Run, Joseph, 1978 . . . . . £15/£5

ditto, Harper (U.S.), 1979 . . . . . £15/£5

Three Favourites, Joseph, 1978 (contains *Odds Against*, *Flying Finish* and *Blood Sport*) . . £10/£5

Whip Hand, Joseph, 1979 . . . . . £15/£5

ditto, Harper (U.S.), 1980 . . . . . £10/£5

Three To Follow, Joseph, 1979 (contains *Forfeit*, *Enquiry* and *Rat Race*) . . . . . £10/£5

Reflex, Joseph, 1980 . . . . . £10/£5

ditto, Putnam (U.S.), 1981 . . . . . £10/£5

Twice Shy, Joseph, 1981 . . . . . £10/£5

ditto, Putnam (U.S.), 1982 . . . . . £10/£5

Banker, Joseph, 1982 . . . . . £10/£5

ditto, Putnam (U.S.), 1983 . . . . . £10/£5

The Danger, Joseph, 1983 . . . . . £10/£5

ditto, Putnam (U.S.), 1984 . . . . . £10/£5

Two by Francis, Harper (U.S.), 1983 (contains *Forfeit* and *Slay Ride*) . . . . £10/£5

Proof, Joseph, 1984 . . . . . . £10/£5

ditto, Putnam (U.S.), 1985 . . . . . £10/£5

Break In, Joseph, 1985 . . . . . £10/£5

ditto, Putnam (U.S.), 1986 . . . . . £10/£5

Bolt, Joseph, 1986 . . . . . £10/£5

ditto, Putnam (U.S.), 1987 . . . . . £10/£5

Hot Money, Joseph, 1987 . . . . . £10/£5

ditto, Putnam (U.S.), 1988 (250 signed copies, slipcase) . . . . £100/£75

ditto, Putnam (U.S.), 1988 . . . . . £10/£5

The Edge, Joseph, 1988 . . . . £10/£5
ditto, Putnam (U.S.), 1989 . . . . . . £10/£5
Straight, Joseph, 1989 . . . . £10/£5
ditto, Joseph, 1989 (500 signed copies, bound in quarter leather, in slipcase) . . . . . £75/£60
ditto, Putnam (U.S.), 1989 . . . . . . £10/£5
Longshot, Joseph, 1990 . . . . £10/£5
ditto, Putnam (U.S.), 1990 . . . . . . £10/£5
Comeback, Joseph, 1991 . . . . £10/£5
ditto, Putnam (U.S.), 1991 . . . . . . £10/£5
Driving Force, Joseph, 1992 . . . . . . £10/£5
ditto, Putnam (U.S.), 1992 . . . . . . £10/£5
Decider, Joseph, 1993 . . . . £10/£5
ditto, Putnam (U.S.), 1993 . . . . . . £10/£5
Wild Horses, Joseph, 1994 . . . . . . £10/£5
ditto, Scorpion Press, 1994 (99 signed, numbered copies, bound in quarter leather) £75
ditto, Scorpion Press, 1994 (20 signed, lettered copies, deluxe binding) £150
ditto, Putnam (U.S.), 1994 . . . . . . £10/£5
Come to Grief, Joseph, 1995 . . . . . . £10/£5
ditto, Putnam (U.S.), 1995 . . . . . . £10/£5
To the Hilt, Joseph, 1996 . . . . £10/£5
ditto, Scorpion Press, 1996 (99 signed, numbered copies, bound in quarter leather) £75
ditto, Scorpion Press, 1996 (15 signed, lettered copies, deluxe binding) £125
ditto, Putnam (U.S.), 1996 . . . . . . £10/£5
10lb Penalty, Joseph, 1997 . . . . . . £10/£5
ditto, Putnam (U.S.), 1997 . . . . . . £10/£5
Second Wind, Joseph, 1999 . . . . . . £10/£5
ditto, Putnam (U.S.), 1999 . . . . . . £10/£5
Shattered, Joseph, 2000 . . . . £10/£5
ditto, Putnam (U.S.), 2000 . . . . . . £10/£5

Short Stories
Field of 13, Joseph, 1998 . . . . £10/£5
ditto, Putnam (U.S.), 1998 . . . . . . £10/£5

Miscellaneous
The Sport of Queens, Joseph, 1957 (autobiography) .
. . . . £300/£50
ditto, second edition (revised), Joseph, 1968 . £15/£5
ditto, Harper (U.S.), 1969 . . . . . . £45/£10
Best Racing and Chasing Stories, Faber, 1966 (edited, with an introduction by Dick Francis and John Welcome) . . . . £15/£5
The Racing Man's Bedside Book, Faber, 1969 (edited by Dick Francis and John Welcome) . . . £15/£5
Best Racing and Chasing Stories Two, Faber, 1972 (edited, with an introduction by Dick Francis and John Welcome) . . . . £15/£5
Lester: The Official Biography, Joseph, 1986 . £10/£5
ditto, Joseph, 1986 (500 signed copies, in slipcase) .
. . . . £50/£45
Great Racing Stories, Bellew, 1989 (edited by Dick Francis) . . . . £10/£5

ditto, Bellew, 1989 (deluxe 75 numbered copies, signed by Dick Francis and John Welcome; bound in full leather) £225
ditto, Bellew, 1989 (standard limited 175 numbered copies, signed by Dick Francis and John Welcome; bound in quarter leather) £300

GEORGE MACDONALD FRASER
(b.1925)

A novelist and historian, Fraser's successful 'Flashman' books have made an unlikely hero out of the bully who originally appeared in *Tom Brown's Schooldays*.

Novels
Flashman, Barrie & Jenkins, 1969 . . . £175/£25
ditto, World Publishing Co./New American Library (U.S.), 1969 . . . . £75/£20
Royal Flash, Barrie & Jenkins, 1970 . . £125/£20
ditto, Knopf (U.S.), 1970 . . . . . . £50/£20
Flash for Freedom, Barrie & Jenkins, 1971 £75/£20
ditto, Knopf (U.S.), 1972 . . . . . . £45/£20
Flashman at the Charge, Barrie & Jenkins, 1973 . .
. . . . £75/£20
ditto, Knopf (U.S.), 1973 . . . . . . £45/£20
Flashman in the Great Game, Barrie & Jenkins, 1975
. . . . £45/£15
ditto, Knopf (U.S.), 1975 . . . . . . £30/£10
Flashman's Lady, Barrie & Jenkins, 1977 . £50/£15
ditto, Knopf (U.S.), 1978 . . . . . . £30/£10
Flashman and the Redskins, Collins, 1982 . £35/£10
ditto, Knopf (U.S.), 1982 . . . . . . £25/£10
Flashman and the Dragon, Collins, 1985 . . £25/£5
ditto, Knopf (U.S.), 1986 . . . . . . £20/£5
Flashman and the Mountain of Light, Collins, 1990 .
. . . . £25/£5
ditto, Knopf (U.S.), 1991 . . . . . . £20/£5
Flashman and the Angel of the Lord, Collins, 1994 .
. . . . £25/£5
ditto, Scorpion Press, 1994 (99 signed copies, glassine d/w) . . . . £150/£125
ditto, Scorpion Press, 1994 (20 signed copies, glassine d/w) . . . . £200/£175
ditto, Knopf (U.S.), 1995 . . . . . . £10/£5
Flashman and the Tiger, and Other Extracts from the Flashman Papers, Collins, 1999 . . . . £10/£5
ditto, Knopf (U.S.), 2000 . . . . . . £10/£5

Short Stories
The General Danced at Dawn, Collins, 1970 £127/£20
ditto, Knopf (U.S.), 1973 . . . . . . £75/£10
McAuslan in the Rough, Barrie & Jenkins, 1974 .
. . . . £45/£15
ditto, Knopf (U.S.), 1974 . . . . . . £35/£10
The Sheik and the Dustbin, Collins, 1988 . £25/£10

Others

The Steel Bonnets, Barrie & Jenkins, 1971 . £300/£45
ditto, Knopf (U.S.), 1972 . . . . . . £100/£20
Mr American, Collins, 1980 . . . . £45/£10
ditto, Simon & Schuster (U.S.), 1980 . . . £25/£5
The Pyrates, Collins, 1983 . . . . £40/£10
ditto, Knopf (U.S.), 1984 . . . . . . £35/£10
The Hollywood History of the World, Joseph, 1988 .
. . . . £40/£10
ditto, Beech Tree/Morrow (U.S.), 1988 . . £25/£10
Quartered Safe Out Here, Collins, 1992 . £125/£20
The Candlemass Road, Collins, 1993 . . .£15/£5
Black Ajax, HarperCollins, 1997. . . .£15/£5
ditto, Carroll & Graf (U.S.), 1998 . . .£10/£5
The Light's on at the Signpost: Memoirs of the Movies, among Other Matters, HarperCollins, 2002 .
. . . .£15/£5

R. AUSTIN FREEMAN
(b.1862 d.1943)

In his best-known character, 'Dr Thorndyke', Freeman created a forensic detective who must surely rival Doyle's 'Sherlock Holmes'.

'Dr Thorndyke' Novels

The Red Thumb Mark, Collingwood Bros (U.S.),
[1907] £800
ditto, Collingwood Bros (U.S.), [1907] (wraps). £600
ditto, Hodder & Stoughton, 1911. . . . £50
ditto, Donald Newton (U.S.), 1911 . . . . £50
The Eye of Osiris, Hodder & Stoughton, [1911] £250
ditto, Hodder & Stoughton, [1911] (Egyptian binding, 150 copies) £500
ditto, as *The Vanishing Man*, Dodd, Mead (U.S.), 1912 . . . . £175
The Mystery of 31 New Inn, Hodder & Stoughton, 1912 . . . . £250
ditto, John C. Winston (U.S.), 1913 (4 plates not in U.K. edition) £175
A Silent Witness, John C. Winston (U.S.), 1913 £300
ditto, Hodder & Stoughton, [1914] £300
Helen Vardon's Confession, Hodder & Stoughton, [1922]. . . . . £1,250/£150
The Cat's Eye, Hodder & Stoughton, [1923] . . .
. . . . £1,000/£150
ditto, Dodd, Mead (U.S.), 1927 . . . . £500/£75
The Mystery of Angelina Frood, Hodder & Stoughton, [1924]. . . . . £1,000/£150
ditto, Dodd, Mead (U.S.), 1925 . . . . £500/£75
The Shadow of the Wolf, Hodder & Stoughton, [1925]
. . . . £1,200/£150
ditto, Dodd, Mead (U.S.), 1925 . . . . £500/£75
The D'Arblay Mystery, Hodder & Stoughton, [1926] .
. . . .£750/£100
ditto, Dodd, Mead (U.S.), 1926 . . . . £400/£50
A Certain Dr Thorndyke, Hodder & Stoughton, [1927]
. . . .£750/£100

ditto, Dodd, Mead (U.S.), 1928 . . . . £300/£45
As A Thief in the Night, Hodder & Stoughton, [1928].
. . . . £750/£75
ditto, Dodd, Mead (U.S.), 1928 . . . . £300/£45
Mr Pottermack's Oversight, Hodder & Stoughton, [1930]. . . . . £500/£60
ditto, Dodd, Mead (U.S.), 1930 . . . . £250/£45
Dr Thorndyke Investigates, Univ. of London Press, 1930 . . . . £250/£40
Pontifex, Son & Thorndyke, Hodder & Stoughton, 1931 . . . . £500/£35
ditto, Dodd, Mead (U.S.), 1931 . . . . £200/£25
When Rogues Fall Out, Hodder & Stoughton, 1932 .
. . . . £350/£35
ditto, as *Dr Thorndyke's Discovery*, Dodd, Mead (U.S.), 1932 . . . . £200/£25
Dr Thorndyke Intervenes, Hodder & Stoughton, 1933
. . . . £350/£35
ditto, Dodd, Mead (U.S.), 1933 . . . . £200/£25
For the Defence: Dr Thorndyke, Hodder & Stoughton, 1934 . . . . £350/£35
ditto, Dodd, Mead (U.S.), 1934 . . . . £200/£25
The Penrose Mystery, Hodder & Stoughton, 1936 . .
. . . . £300/£30
ditto, Dodd, Mead (U.S.), 1936 . . . . £200/£25
Felo de Se?, Hodder & Stoughton, 1937 . £300/£30
ditto, as *Death at the Inn*, Dodd, Mead (U.S.), 1937 .
. . . . £200/£25
The Stoneware Monkey, Hodder & Stoughton, 1938 .
. . . . £300/£30
ditto, Dodd, Mead (U.S.), 1939 . . . . £200/£25
Mr Polton Explains, Hodder & Stoughton, 1940 . .
. . . . £300/£30
ditto, Dodd, Mead (U.S.), 1940 . . . . £200/£25
Dr Thorndyke's Crime File, Dodd, Mead (U.S.), 1941
. . . . £200/£25
The Jacob Street Mystery, Hodder & Stoughton, 1942
. . . . £200/£25
ditto, as *The Unconscious Witness*, Dodd, Mead (U.S.), 1942 . . . . £175/£20

'Thorndyke' Story Collections

John Thorndyke's Cases, Chatto & Windus, 1909. . .
. . . . £350
ditto, as *Dr Thorndyke's Cases*, Dodd, Mead (U.S.), 1931 . . . . £75
The Singing Bone, Hodder & Stoughton, 1912. £250
ditto, Dodd, Mead (U.S.), 1923 . . . . . £125
The Great Portrait Mystery, Hodder & Stoughton, [1918]. £300
Dr Thorndyke's Case-Book, Hodder & Stoughton, [1923]. . . . . £1,000/£100
ditto, as *The Blue Scarab*, Dodd, Mead (U.S.), 1923 .
. . . . £500/£45
The Puzzle Lock, Hodder & Stoughton, [1925]. . .
. . . . £1,000/£100
ditto, Dodd, Mead (U.S.), 1926 . . . . £500/£45
The Magic Casket, Hodder & Stoughton, [1927] . .
. . . . £1,000/£75
ditto, Dodd, Mead (U.S.), 1927 . . . . £400/£35

The Famous Cases of Dr Thorndyke, Hodder & Stoughton, [1929] . . . . . . £200/£25
ditto, as *The Dr Thorndyke Omnibus*, Dodd, Mead (U.S.), 1932 . . . . £125/£20
The Best Dr Thorndyke Short Stories, Dover (U.S.), 1973 (wraps). £10
Dead Hand, Highfield Press, [1994]. . . . £5

Story Collections Written as 'Clifford Ashdown' (written with J.J. Pitcairn)
The Adventures of Romney Pringle, Ward Lock, 1902
. . . . £1,500
ditto, Oswald Train (U.S.), 1975. . . . £30/£10
The Further Adventures of Romney Pringle, Oswald Train (U.S.), 1975 . . . . . . £30/£10
From a Surgeon's Diary, Ferret Fantasy, 1975 (wraps)
. . . . £10
ditto, Oswald Train (U.S.), 1977. . . . £25/£10
The Queen's Treasure, Oswald Train (U.S.), 1975 .
. . . . £25/£10

Other Titles
The Golden Pool, Cassell, 1905 . . . . . £300
The Unwilling Adventurer, Hodder & Stoughton, [1913] £200
The Uttermost Farthing, Winston (U.S.), 1914 £75
ditto, as *A Savant's Vendetta*, Pearson, [1920] . .
. . . . £750/£75
The Exploits of Danby Croker, Duckworth, 1916 £150
The Surprising Experiences of Mr Shuttlebury Cobb, Hodder & Stoughton, [1927] . . . £1,000/£75
Flighty Phyllis, Hodder & Stoughton, [1928] £750/£50

Non Fiction
Travels and Life in Ashant and Jaman, Constable, 1898 . . . . £250
ditto, Stokes (U.S.), 1898 . . . . . . £250
Social Decay and Regeneration, Constable, 1921 . .
. . . . £100/£25

ROBERT FROST
(b.1874 d.1963)

An American poet with the distinctive voice of his own country, whose poetry often addresses the problems of a solitary character attempting to make sense of the world.

[Twilight] Five Poems, (1894) £15,000
A Boy's Will, David Nutt, 1913 ('A' binding, bronze cloth) £5,000
ditto, David Nutt, 1913 ('B' binding, cream-coloured vellum-paper boards stamped in red cloth) . £2,000
ditto, David Nutt, 1913 ('C' binding, cream-coloured linen-paper wraps stamped in black, and 8-petalled flowers) £1,250
ditto, David Nutt, 1913 ('D' binding, cream-coloured linen-paper wraps stamped in black, and 4-petalled flowers) £750

ditto, David Nutt, 1913 (135 signed, numbered copies, cream wraps) £1,500
ditto, David Nutt, 1913 (second issue, cream wraps) .
. . . . £500
ditto, Holt (U.S.), 1915 ('Aind' for 'And' on last line, p.14) £600
ditto, Holt (U.S.), 1915 (with 'And'). . . . £150
North of Boston, David Nutt, 1914 (first issue, binding 'A', with coarse green cloth) £3,000
ditto, David Nutt/Holt (U.S.), 1914 (first issue, binding 'B', UK sheets with Holt title page) . . . £1,750
ditto, David Nutt, 1914 (first issue, binding 'C', with fine green cloth) £1,250
ditto, David Nutt, 1914 (first issue, binding 'D', with blue cloth) £1,000
ditto, David Nutt, 1914 (first issue, binding 'E', with coarse green cloth, measuring 200x145mm, tall edges trimmed, rubber stamp p.iv). £750
ditto, David Nutt, 1914 (first issue, binding 'F', with coarse green cloth, measuring 195x150mm, top edge trimmed and others rough cut, rubber stamp p.iv). .
. . . . £1,250
Mountain Interval, Holt (U.S.), 1916 (first state, p.88, lines 6 and 7 repeated, p.63 line 6 from bottom 'Come' for 'Gone') . . . . . £1,250/£300
ditto, Holt (U.S.), 1916 (errors corrected) . £650/£100
Selected Poems, Holt (U.S.), 1923 . . . £650/£100
ditto, Heinemann, 1923 . . . . . £400/£50
New Hampshire, Holt (U.S.), 1923 . . . £500/£125
ditto, Holt (U.S.), 1923 (350 signed, numbered copies, slipcase) . . . . £1,000/£800
ditto, Grant Richards, 1924 . . . . £500/£75
ditto, The New Dresden Press (Hanover), 1955 (750 signed, numbered copies, semi-transparent d/w) . .
. . . . £400/£300
West-Running Brook, Holt (U.S.), 1928 (without 'First Edition' statement) . . . . . £250/£100
ditto, Holt (U.S.), 1928 (with 'First Edition' statement)
. . . . £150/£50
ditto, Holt (U.S.), 1928 (1,000 signed, numbered copies, slipcase, glassine d/w) . . . £400/£350
A Way Out: A One Act Play, Harbor Press (U.S.), 1929 (485 signed, numbered copies, glassine d/w) .
. . . . £250/£225
The Lovely Shall Be Choosers, Random House (U.S.), 1929 (475 copies, wraps) £125
The Cow's in the Corn: A One-Act Irish Play in Rhyme, Slide Mountain Press (U.S.), 1929 (91 signed, numbered copies) . . . £1,000/£600
Collected Poems of Robert Frost, Random House (U.S.), 1930 . . . . £225/£30
ditto, Random House (U.S.), 1930 (1,000 signed, numbered copies) £500
ditto, Longmans Green, 1930. . . . . £175/£25
The Lone Striker, Knopf (U.S.), 1933 (wraps in envelope). . . . . £60/£45
A Further Range, Holt (U.S.), 1936. . . £125/£15
ditto, Spiral Press (U.S.), 1936 (800 signed, numbered copies in slipcase, no d/w) £300

ditto, Cape, 1937 . . . . £75/£10
Selected Poems, Cape, 1936 . . . . £100/£15
From Snow to Snow, Holt (U.S.), 1936 (no d/w) £100
A Witness Tree, Holt (U.S.), 1942 . . . £150/£20
ditto, Spiral Press (U.S.), 1942 (735 signed, numbered
copies, slipcase) . . . . £300/£250
ditto, Cape, 1943 . . . . £100/£15
Come in and Other Poems, Holt (U.S.), 1944 £50/£15
ditto, Cape, 1944 . . . . £30/£10
ditto, as **The Pocket Book of Robert Frost's Poems**,
Pocket Books (U.S.), 1946 (wraps) . . . £10
ditto, as **The Road Not Taken**, Holt (U.S.), 1951 . .
. . . . £15/£5
A Masque of Reason, Holt (U.S.), 1945. . £50/£15
ditto, Holt (U.S.), 1945 (800 signed, numbered copies,
slipcase, no d/w) . . . . £250/£200
ditto, Cape, 1948 . . . . £30/£10
Steeple Bush, Holt (U.S.), 1947 . . . . £75/£15
ditto, Holt (U.S.), 1947 (750 signed, numbered copies,
slipcase, no d/w) . . . . £250/£200
A Masque of Mercy, Holt (U.S.), 1947 . £65/£15
ditto, Holt (U.S.), 1947 (751 signed, numbered copies,
slipcase) . . . . £250/£200
Hard Not to Be King, House of Books (U.S.), 1951
(300 signed, numbered copies) £300
The Complete Poems, Holt (U.S.), 1949 (500 signed,
numbered copies, slipcase, no d/w). . £500/£400
ditto, Limited Editions Club (U.S.), 1950 (signed, 2
vols in slipcase) . . . . £450/£350
ditto, Cape, 1951 . . . . £100/£20
A Cabin in the Clearing, Blumenthal/Spiral Press
(U.S.), 1951 (wraps) £45
Aforesaid, Holt (U.S.), 1954 (650 signed, numbered
copies, slipcase, no d/w). . . . . £500/£400
My Objection to Being Stepped On, Blumenthal/Spiral
Press (U.S.), 1957 (wraps) £45
You Come Too: Favourite Poems for Young Readers,
Holt (U.S.), 1959. . . . . . . £25/£10
ditto, Bodley Head, 1964 . . . . . £25/£10
A Wishing Well, Blumenthal/Spiral Press (U.S.), 1959
(wraps) £45
In the Clearing, Holt (U.S.), 1962 . . . £45/£10
ditto, Blumenthal/Spiral Press (U.S.), 1962 (1,500
signed, numbered copies, slipcase). . . £200/£150
The Prophets Really Prophecy as Mystics, Blumen-
thal/Spiral Press (U.S.), 1962 . . . . £25
The Letters of Robert Frost to Louis Untermeyer, Holt
(U.S.), 1963 . . . . £20/£5
ditto, Cape, 1964 . . . . £15/£5
**Robert Frost and John Bartlett: The Record of a
Friendship**, Holt (U.S.), 1963 . . . £20/£5
Selected Letters of Robert Frost, Holt (U.S.), 1964 .
. . . . £20/£5
Interviews with Robert Frost, Holt (U.S.), 1966 . .
. . . . £20/£5
ditto, Cape, 1967 . . . . £15/£5
Selected Prose of Robert Frost, Holt (U.S.), 1966 . .
. . . . £20/£5
The Poetry of Robert Frost, Holt (U.S.), 1969 . £20/£5

ditto, Cape, 1971 . . . . £15/£5
Family Letters of Robert Frost and Elinor Frost, State
Univ. of New York Press (U.S.), 1972. . . £20/£5
Robert Frost: Poetry and Prose, Holt (U.S.), 1972 .
. . . . £20/£5

GABRIEL GARCÍA MÁRQUEZ
(b.1928)

Colombian novelist and short story writer who was
awarded the Nobel Prize for Literature in 1982. His
masterpiece, *One Hundred Years of Solitude* is a
family saga that mirrors the history of Colombia and
mixes realism and fantasy.

Novels
La mala hora, ESSO Columbiana (Columbia), 1962
(wraps) £3,000
ditto, as **In Evil Hour**, Harper & Row (U.S.), 1979
. . . . £50/£15
ditto, as **In Evil Hour**, Cape, 1980 . . . £20/£5
Los funerales de la mama grande, Univ. of Veracruz
(Mexico), 1962 (wraps) £1,000
Cien años de soledad, Sudamericana (Argentine), 1967
(wraps) £3,000
ditto, as **One Hundred Years of Solitude**, Harper &
Row (U.S.), 1970 (no number row on last leaf of
book, first issue d/w with an exclamation mark at the
end of the first paragraph of text on the front flap) .
. . . . £1,500/£125
ditto, as **One Hundred Years of Solitude**, Harper &
Row (U.S.), 1970 (second issue d/w without
exclamation mark) . . . . . £1,000/£125
ditto, as **One Hundred Years of Solitude**, Cape, 1970 .
. . . . £350/£50
El otoño del patriarca, Plaza y Janes (Spain), 1975 .
. . . . £200/£30
ditto, as **The Autumn of the Patriarch**, Harper & Row
(U.S.), 1976 (number row ends in '5'!) . £75/£15
ditto, as **The Autumn of the Patriarch**, Cape, 1977 .
. . . . £30/£5
Crónica de una muerte anunciada, Editorial La Oveja
Negra (Columbia), 1981. . . . . . £40/£10
ditto, as **Chronicle of a Death Foretold**, Cape, 1983 .
. . . . £40/£10
ditto, as **Chronicle of a Death Foretold**, Knopf (U.S.),
1983 (first issue jacket cites *One Hundred Days of
Solitude*) . . . . £40/£10
The Story of a Shipwrecked Sailor, Knopf (U.S.),
1986 . . . . £35/£10
El Amor en los tiempos del colera, Editorial La Oveja
Negra (Columbia), 1985 (yellow d/w) . . £25/£10
ditto, Editorial La Oveja Negra (Columbia), 1985
(deluxe edition, blue and white d/w) . . £35/£15
ditto, Editorial La Oveja Negra (Columbia), 1985
(1,000 signed, unnumbered copies) . . £75/£35

ditto, as *Love in the Time of Cholera,* Knopf (U.S.),
1988 . . . . £40/£10
ditto, as *Love in the Time of Cholera,* Knopf (U.S.),
1988 (350 signed copies) . . . . . £300/£250
ditto, as *Love in the Time of Cholera,* Cape, 1988 . .
. . . . £40/£10
El general en su laberinto, Editorial La Oveja Negra
(Columbia), 1989 . . . . £40/£10
ditto, The General in His Labyrinth, Knopf (U.S.),
1990 . . . . £30/£10
ditto, The General in His Labyrinth, Knopf (U.S.),
1990 (350 signed, numbered copies, slipcase). . .
. . . . £250/£200
ditto, The General in His Labyrinth, Cape, 1991 . .
. . . . £25/£10
Del Amor y Otros Demonios, Grupo Editorial Norma
(Columbia), 1994 . . . . £15/£5
ditto, as *Of Love and Other Demons,* Knopf (U.S.),
1995 . . . . £15/£5
ditto, as *Of Love and Other Demons,* Cape, 1995 . .
. . . . £15/£5

Short Stories
La hojarasca, Ediciones S.L.B. (Columbia), 1955
(wraps) £3,000
ditto, as *Leaf Storm and Other Stories,* Harper & Row
(U.S.), 1972 . . . . £200/£25
ditto, as *Leaf Storm and Other Stories,* Cape, 1972 .
. . . . £50/£10
El coronel no tiene quien le escribe, Aguirre Editor
(Columbia), 1961 (wraps) £1,500
ditto, as *No One Writes to the Colonel and Other
Stories,* Harper & Row (U.S.), 1968 . £350/£30
ditto, as *No One Writes to the Colonel and Other
Stories,* Cape, 1971 . . . . . . £250/£25
*La increíble y triste historia de la candid Eréndira y
su abuela Desalmada,* Sudamericana (Argentine),
1972 (wraps) £100
ditto, as *Innocent Eréndira and Other Stories,* Harper
& Row (U.S.), 1978 . . . . . . £50/£15
ditto, as *Innocent Eréndira and Other Stories,* Cape,
1979 . . . . £45/£10
Collected Stories, Harper & Row (U.S.), 1984 £35/£10
ditto, Cape, 1991 . . . . £15/£5

Others
La aventura de Miguel Littin clandestino en Chile,
Editorial La Oveja Negra (Columbia), 1986 £40/£10
ditto, as *Clandestine in Chile, The Adventures of
Miguel Littin,* Holt (U.S.), 1987 . . . £35/£10
Noticia de un Secuestro, Grupo Editorial Norma
(Columbia), 1996 . . . . £15/£5
ditto, as *News of a Kidnapping,* Knopf (U.S.), 1997 .
. . . . £15/£5
ditto, as *News of a Kidnapping,* Cape, 1997 . £15/£5
*El Olor de la Guayaba: Conversaciones con Plinio
Apuleyo Mendoza,* Editorial La Oveja Negra
(Columbia), 1982 (wraps) £20

ALAN GARNER
(b.1934)

A writer of children's literature, the majority of
Garner's books are set in his native Cheshire. His
books are an evocative mix of myth, fantasy and
reality.

Novels
The Weirdstone of Brisingamen: A Tale of Alderley,
Collins, 1960 . . . . £350/£45
ditto, Philomel (U.S.), 1960 . . . . . £145/£25
The Moon of Gomrath, Collins, 1963 . . £175/£30
ditto, Philomel (U.S.), 1963 . . . . . £35/£10
Elidor, Collins, 1965 (Illustrated by Charles Keeping).
. . . . £150/£15
ditto, Walck (U.S.), [1965] . . . . . £25/£10
The Old Man of Mow, Collins, 1967 (Photographs by
Roger Hill) . . . . £45/£15
ditto, Doubleday (U.S.), 1967 . . . . £35/£10
The Owl Service, Collins, 1967 . . . . £125/£25
ditto, Philomel (U.S.), 1967 . . . . . £100/£15
Red Shift, Collins, 1973 . . . . . . £50/£10
ditto, Macmillan (U.S.), 1973 . . . . £35/£10
The Stone Book, Collins, 1976 (illustrated by Michael
Foreman) . . . . £15/£5
ditto, Collins (U.S.), 1976. . . . . . £15/£5
Tom Fobble's Day, Collins, 1977 (illustrated by
Michael Foreman) . . . . £15/£5
ditto, Collins (U.S.), 1979. . . . . . £15/£5
Granny Reardun, Collins, 1977 (illustrated by Michael
Foreman) . . . . £15/£5
ditto, Collins (U.S.), 1978. . . . . . £15/£5
The Aimer Gate, Collins, 1978 (illustrated by Michael
Foreman) . . . . £15/£5
ditto, Collins (U.S.), 1979. . . . . . £15/£5
The Lad of the Gad, Collins, 1980 . . . £15/£5
ditto, Philomel (U.S.), 1981 . . . . . £15/£5
The Stone Book Quartet, Collins, 1983 . . £20/£5
Strandloper, Harvill Press, 1996 . . . . £10/£5

Short Stories
The Guizer: A Book of Fools, Hamish Hamilton, 1975
. . . . £25/£5
ditto, Greenwillow (U.S.), 1976 . . . . £25/£5

Fairy Tales
Fairy Tales of Gold, Collins, 1979 (4 vols). £35/£10
ditto, Philomel (U.S.), 1980 (1 vol.) . . . £20/£5
Book of British Fairy Tales, Collins, 1984 . £15/£5
ditto, Delacorte Press (U.S.), 1984 . . . £15/£5
A Bag of Moonshine, Collins, 1986 (illustrated by
Patrick Lynch) . . . . £15/£5
ditto, Delacorte Press (U.S.), 1986 . . . £15/£5
Jack and the Beanstalk, HarperCollins, 1992 . £10/£5
Once Upon a Time, Dorling Kindersley (U.K. and
U.S.), 1993 . . . . £10/£5
Little Red Hen, Dorling Kindersley (U.K. and U.S.),
1997 . . . . £10/£5

The Well of the Wind, Dorling Kindersley (U.K. and U.S.), 1998 . . . . £10/£5

Poetry
The Breadhorse, Collins, 1975 (illustrated by Albin Trowski) . . . . £35/£15

Plays
Potter Thompson, O.U.P., 1975 . . . . . £25/£5

Miscellaneous
Holly from the Bongs: A Nativity Play, Collins, 1966 . . . . £75/£15
The Voice That Thunders: Essays and Lectures, Harvil, 1998 . . . . £10/£5

DAVID GARNETT
(b.1892 d.1981)

Principally a novelist, whose early works have a light, fantastic touch, Garnett was associated with the Bloomsbury Group. His *Aspects of Love* was recently turned into a successful stage musical.

Novels
Dope-Darling: A Story of Cocaine, Werner Laurie, [1919] (pseud. 'Leda Burke', wraps) . . . £750
Lady Into Fox, Chatto & Windus, 1922 . £100/£15
ditto, Knopf (U.S.), 1923 . . . . . £30/£10
A Man in the Zoo, Chatto & Windus, 1924 . £75/£15
ditto, Chatto & Windus, 1924 (110 signed, numbered copies) £75
ditto, Knopf (U.S.), 1924 . . . . . £30/£10
The Sailor's Return, Chatto & Windus, 1925 £50/£10
ditto, Chatto & Windus, 1925 (160 signed, numbered copies) £75
ditto, Knopf (U.S.), 1925 . . . . . £25/£10
Go She Must!, Chatto & Windus, 1927 . £50/£10
ditto, Chatto & Windus, 1927 (160 signed, numbered copies) £75
ditto, Knopf (U.S.), 1927 . . . . . £25/£10
No Love, Chatto & Windus, 1929 . . . £35/£10
ditto, Chatto & Windus, 1929 (160 signed, numbered copies) £65
ditto, Knopf (U.S.), 1929 . . . . . £25/£10
The Grasshoppers Come, Chatto & Windus, 1931 . . . . £20/£5
ditto, Chatto & Windus, 1931 (210 signed, numbered copies) £50
ditto, Brewer, Warren & Putnam (U.S.), 1931 . £20/£5
A Rabbit in the Air, Chatto & Windus, 1932 . £20/£5
ditto, Chatto & Windus, 1932 (110 signed, numbered copies) £50
ditto, Brewer, Warren & Putnam (U.S.), 1932 . £15/£5
Pocahontas, or the Nonpareil of Virginia, Chatto & Windus, 1933 . . . . £20/£5
ditto, Chatto & Windus, 1933 (550 signed, numbered copies) £50

ditto, Harcourt, Brace (U.S.), 1933 . . . . £15/£5
Beany-Eye, Chatto & Windus, 1935 . . . . £20/£5
ditto, Chatto & Windus, 1935 (110 signed, numbered copies) £50
ditto, Harcourt, Brace (U.S.), 1935 . . . . £15/£5
Aspects of Love, Chatto & Windus, 1955 . £30/£10
ditto, Harcourt, Brace (U.S.), 1955 . . . £25/£5
A Shot in the Dark, Longmans, 1958 . . . £15/£5
ditto, Little, Brown (U.S.), 1958 . . . . £15/£5
A Net for Venus, Longmans, 1959 . . . £25/£10
Two By Two: A Story of Survival, Longmans, 1963 . . . . £10/£5
ditto, Atheneum (U.S.), 1964 . . . . . £10/£5
Ulterior Motives, Longmans, 1966 . . . £10/£5
ditto, Harcourt, Brace (U.S.), 1967 . . . £10/£5
A Clean Slate, Hamish Hamilton, 1971 . . £10/£5
The Sons of the Falcon, Macmillan, 1972 . £10/£5
Plough Over the Bones, Macmillan, 1973 . £10/£5
Up She Rises, Macmillan, 1977 . . . . £10/£5
ditto, St Martin's Press (U.S.), 1977 . . . £10/£5

Short Stories
The Old Dovecote and Other Stories, Elkin Mathews & Marrot: No.8 in the Woburn Books series, 1928 (530 signed copies) . . . . . . £50/£35
A Terrible Day, William Jackson: No.9 in the Furnival Books series, 1932 (550 signed copies) . . £45
First 'Hippy' Revolution, San Marcos Press (New Mexico), 1970 (wraps) £25
Purl and Plain, Macmillan, 1973 . . . . £10/£5

Autobiography
The Golden Echo, Chatto & Windus, 1953 . £10/£5
ditto, Harcourt, Brace (U.S.), 1954 . . . £10/£5
The Flowers of the Forest, Chatto & Windus, 1955 . . . . £10/£5
ditto, Harcourt, Brace (U.S.), 1956 . . . £10/£5
Familiar Faces, Chatto & Windus, 1962 . £10/£5
ditto, Harcourt, Brace (U.S.), 1962 . . . £10/£5

Miscellaneous
Never Be a Bookseller, Knopf (U.S.), 1929 (2,000 copies, none for sale) £75
ditto, The Fleece Press, 1995 (400 copies, card covers with marbled d/w) . . . . . . £20/£10
War in the Air: September 1939 to May 1941, Chatto & Windus, 1941 . . . . £30/£10
ditto, Doubleday (U.S.), 1941 . . . . £25/£10
The Battle of Britain, Puffin Picture Book No.21, 1941 (wraps) £15
The Campaign in Greece and Crete, Chatto & Windus, 1942 (wraps) £15
A Historical Pageant of Huntingdonshire in Celebration of the Coronation of Her Majesty Elizabeth II, privately printed (Huntingdon), 1953 (souvenir programme) £20
The White/Garnett Letters, Cape, 1968 . . £15/£5
ditto, Viking (U.S.), 1968 . . . . . . £15/£5

The Master Cat: The True and Unexpurgated Story of Puss in Boots, Macmillan, 1974 . . . . £10/£5
Sir Geoffrey Keynes: A Tribute, privately printed, 1978 . . . . £10
Great Friends: Portraits of Seventeen Writers, Macmillan, 1979 . . . . £25/£10
ditto, Atheneum (U.S.), 1980 . . . . £25/£10

EVE GARNETT
(b.1900 d.1991)

Author and illustrator, principally of books for children, she is best known for the adventures of the family from One End Street.

Written and Illustrated by Garnett
The Family from One End Street, and Some of Their Adventures, Muller, 1937 . . . . . £100/£25
In and Out and Roundabout: Stories of a Little Town, Muller, 1948 . . . . £50/£10
Further Adventures of The Family from One End Street, Heinemann, 1956 . . . . . £75/£15
Holiday at the Dew Drop Inn, Heinemann, 1962 . .
. . . . £50/£10
To Greenland's Icy Mountains: The Story of Hans Egede–Explorer, Coloniser, Missionary, Heinemann, 1968 . . . . £50/£10
Lost and Found: Four Stories, Muller, 1974 £25/£10
First Affections: Some Autobiographical Chapters of Early Childhood, Muller, 1982 . . . . . £20/£5

Other Titles Illustrated by Garnett
The London Child, by Evelyn Sharp, John Lane, 1927
. . . . £45/£10
The Bad Baron of Crashbania, by Norman Hunter, Blackwell, 1932 . . . . £50
Is It Well With the Child?, Muller, 1938 . £50/£10
A Child's Garden of Verses, by Robert Louis Stevenson, Penguin, 1948 (wraps) . . . £10
A Book of the Seasons: An Anthology, O.U.P, 1952 .
. . . . £30/£10
A Golden Land: Stories, Poems, Songs New and Old, Constable, 1958 (with illustrations by others) . £15/£5

JONATHAN GASH
(b.1933)

Gash is the pseudonym of John Grant. His 'Lovejoy' novels have been adapted for television with great success, although some feel that his hero has lost his edge with this transition.

'Lovejoy' Novels
The Judas Pair, Collins Crime Club, 1977 . £300/£30
ditto, Harper & Row (U.S.), 1977 . . . £75/£10

Gold from Gemini, Collins Crime Club, 1978 . . .
. . . . £225/£25
ditto, as *Gold By Gemini*, Harper & Row (U.S.), 1978.
. . . . £65/£10
The Grail Tree, Collins Crime Club, 1979 . £175/£15
ditto, Harper & Row (U.S.), 1979 . . . £50/£10
Spend Game, Collins Crime Club, 1979. . £300/£35
ditto, Ticknor & Fields (U.S.), 1979 . . . £50/£10
The Vatican Rip, Collins Crime Club, 1981 £250/£35
ditto, Ticknor & Fields (U.S.), 1981 . . £25/£10
Firefly Gadroon, Collins Crime Club, 1982 £125/£15
ditto, St Martin's Press (U.S.), 1982 . . . £25/£10
The Sleepers of Erin, Collins Crime Club, 1983 . .
. . . . £100/£15
ditto, Dutton (U.S.), 1983. . . . . . £25/£10
The Gondola Scam, Collins Crime Club, 1984 £65/£10
ditto, St Martin's Press (U.S.), 1984 . . . .£15/£5
Pearlhanger, Collins Crime Club, 1985. . .£25/£5
ditto, St Martin's Press (U.S.), 1985 . . . .£15/£5
The Tartan Ringers, Collins Crime Club, 1986 £20/£5
ditto, as *The Tartan Sell*, St Martin's Press (U.S.), 1986 . . . .£15/£5
Moonspender, Collins Crime Club, 1986 . .£20/£5
ditto, St Martin's Press (U.S.), 1987 . . . .£15/£5
Jade Woman, Collins Crime Club, 1988 . .£20/£5
ditto, St Martin's Press (U.S.), 1989 . . . .£15/£5
The Very Last Gambado, Collins Crime Club, 1989 .
. . . .£15/£5
ditto, St Martin's Press (U.S.), 1990 . . . .£15/£5
The Great California Game, Century, 1991 . .£15/£5
ditto, St Martin's Press (U.S.), 1991 . . . .£15/£5
Lies of Fair Ladies, Scorpion Press, 1991 (20 signed, lettered copies) £175
ditto, Scorpion Press, 1991 (99 signed, numbered copies) £75
ditto, Century, 1992 . . . .£15/£5
ditto, St Martin's Press (U.S.), 1992 . . . .£15/£5
Paid and Loving Eyes, Century, 1993 . . .£15/£5
ditto, St Martin's Press (U.S.), 1993 . . . .£15/£5
The Sin Within Her Smile, Century, 1993 . .£15/£5
ditto, Viking (U.S.), 1994. . . . . . .£10/£5
The Grace in Older Women, Century, 1995 . .£15/£5
ditto, Viking (U.S.), 1995. . . . . . .£10/£5
The Possessions of a Lady, Century, 1996 . .£15/£5
ditto, Viking (U.S.), 1996. . . . . . .£15/£5
The Rich and The Profane, Macmillan, 1998 .£15/£5
ditto, Viking (U.S.), 1999. . . . . . .£15/£5
A Rag, a Bone and a Hank of Hair, Macmillan, 1999
. . . .£15/£5
ditto, Viking (U.S.), 2000. . . . . . .£15/£5
Every Last Cent, Macmillan, 2001 . . . .£10/£5

Other Titles
Streetwalker, Bodley Head, 1959 (anonymous) . .
. . . . £225/£35
ditto, Viking (U.S.), 1960. . . . . . £75/£15
The Incomer, Collins, 1981 (pseud. 'Graham Gaunt') .
. . . . £250/£35
ditto, Doubleday (U.S.), 1981 . . . . £25/£10

Mehala, Lady of Sealandings, Century, 1993 (pseud.
'Jonathan Grant') . . . . . . £25/£10
Different Women Dancing, Macmillan, 1997 (pseud.
'Jonathan Grant') . . . . £15/£5
ditto, Viking (U.S.), 1997 . . . . £15/£5
Prey Dancing, Macmillan, 1998 (pseud. 'Jonathan
Grant') . . . . £15/£5
ditto, Viking (U.S.), 1998 . . . . £15/£5

ELIZABETH GASKELL
(b.1810 d.1865)

A novelist whose work earned the respect of Dickens,
Mrs Gaskell is principally remembered for her friend-
ship with Charlotte Brontë, and her famous biography
The Life of Charlotte Brontë.

Novels
Mary Barton, A Tale of Manchester Life, Chapman &
Hall, 1848 (anonymous, 2 vols). £3,000
The Moorland Cottage, Chapman & Hall, 1850 £500
Ruth, A Novel, Chapman & Hall, 1853 (3 vols) £750
Cranford, Chapman & Hall, 1853 (by the author of
'Mary Barton, 'Ruth' etc.) £1,000
North and South, Chapman & Hall, 1855 (2 vols) . .
. . . . £600
*The Sexton's Hero and Christmas Storms and
Sunshine*, Chapman & Hall, 1855 . . . . £100
A Dark Night's Work, Smith Elder, 1863 . £375
Sylvia's Lovers, Smith Elder, 1863 (3 vols) . . £700
Wives and Daughters, An Everyday Story, Smith
Elder, 1866 (illustrated by George du Maurier, 2 vols)
. . . . £450

Short Stories
Libbie Marsh's Three Eras, A Lancashire Tale,
Hamilton, Adams & Co., 1850 . . . . . £600
Lizzie Leigh and Other Tales, Smith Elder, 1855
[1854]. £275
The Sexton's Hero, Johnson, Rawson & Co.,
Manchester, 1850 . . . . £600
Round the Sofa, Sampson Low, 1859 (2 vols) . £450
ditto, as *My Lady Ludlow and Other Tales*, Sampson
Low, 1861 (1 vol.) £275
Right at Last and Other Tales, Sampson Low, 1860 .
. . . . £275
Lois the Witch and Other Tales, Tauchnitz, 1861 £35
Cousin Phyllis and Other Tales, Smith Elder, 1865
(illustrated by George du Maurier) £275
The Grey Woman and Other Tales, Smith Elder, 1865
(illustrated by George du Maurier) £275
The Half-Brothers, Gulliver Book Co., [1943]. £25
The Squire's Story, Todd Publishing Co., 1943 £10/£5
The Cage at Cranford and Other Stories, Nelson
Classics, [1937] . . . . £10/£5
Mrs Gaskell's Tales of Mystery and Horror, Gollancz,
1978 . . . . £10/£5

Miscellaneous
The Life of Charlotte Brontë, Smith Elder, 1857 (2
vols) £600
Letters of Charlotte Brontë, privately printed, 1915 (25
copies) £150
*My Diary, The Early Years of My Daughter
Marianne*, privately printed by Clement Shorter,
1923 (50 copies, wraps) £75
Letters of Mrs Gaskell and Charles Eliot Norton,
1855-1865, O.U.P., 1932 . . . . . £30/£10
The Letters of Elizabeth Gaskell, Manchester Univ.
Press, [1966] . . . . £30/£10

Collected Editions
The Novels and Tales of Elizabeth Gaskell, Smith
Elder, 1878-82 (7 vols) £175
The Works of Elizabeth Gaskell, Smith Elder, 1906 (8
vols) £125

LEWIS GRASSIC GIBBON
(b.1901 d.1935)

'Grassic Gibbon' was the pseudonym used by the
Scot James Leslie Mitchell for his best-known works,
Sunset Song, Cloud Howe and *Grey Granite* which
together make up the *Scot's Quair* Trilogy.

Novels by 'Lewis Grassic Gibbon'
Sunset Song, Jarrolds, 1932 . . . . . £200/£30
Cloud Howe, Jarrolds, 1933 . . . . . £175/£30
Grey Granite, Jarrolds, 1934 . . . . . £150/£25
A Scot's Quair: A Trilogy of Novels, Jarrolds, 1946 .
. . . . £35/£10
The Speak O' The Mearns, Ramsey Head Press, 1982
(unfinished) . . . . £10/£5

Others by Lewis Grassic Gibbon
Niger: The Life of Mungo Park, Faber, 1934 £45/£15
*Scottish Scene: Or, The Intelligent Man's Guide to
Albyn*, Jarrolds, 1934 (with Hugh McDiarmid) . .
. . . . £45/£15
*Nine Against the Unknown: A Record of Geo-
graphical Exploration*, Jarrolds, 1934 (as 'Lewis
Grassic Gibbon and J. Leslie Mitchell') . £40/£15
A Scots Hairst: Essays and Short Stories, Hutchinson,
1967 . . . . £15/£5

Novels by 'J. Leslie Mitchell'
Stained Radiance: A Fictionist's Prelude, Jarrolds,
1930 . . . . £100/£40
*The Thirteenth Disciple, Being a Portrait and Saga of
Lalcolm Maudslay in His Adventures Through the
Dark Corridor*, Jarrolds, 1931 . . . . £100/£40
Three Go Back, Jarrolds, 1932 . . . . £100/£40
The Lost Trumpet, Jarrolds, 1932 . . . £65/£25
Image and Superscription, Jarrolds, 1933 . £50/£20
Spartacus, Jarrolds, 1933. . . . . . £30/£10
Gay Hunter, Jarrolds, 1934 . . . . . £50/£20

Short Stories by J. Leslie Mitchell
The Calends of Cairo, Jarrolds, 1931 . . £75/£25
Persian Dawns, Egyptian Nights, Jarrolds, [1933]. .
. . . . £75/£25

Other Titles by J. Leslie Mitchell
Hanno: Or, The Future of Exploration, Kegan Paul,
1928 . . . . £35/£15
The Conquest of the Maya, Jarrolds, 1934 . £45/£15

STELLA GIBBONS
(b.1902 d.1989)

Author of many novels, but collected mainly for her
first, the classic *Cold Comfort Farm*.

Novels
Cold Comfort Farm, Longmans, 1932 . . £500/£75
Bassett, Longmans, 1934 . . . . . £30/£10
Enbury Heath, Longmans, 1935 . . . £30/£10
Miss Linsey and Pa, Longmans, 1936 . . £30/£10
Nightingale Wood, Longmans, 1938 . . £30/£10
My American: A Romance, Longmans, 1939 £30/£10
The Rich House, Longmans, 1941 . . . . £25/£5
Ticky, Longmans, 1943 . . . . . . £25/£5
The Bachelor, Longmans, 1944 . . . . £25/£5
Westwood, or, The Gentle Powers, Longmans, 1946 .
. . . . £25/£5
Conference at Cold Comfort Farm, Longmans, 1949 .
. . . . £65/£15
The Matchmaker, Longmans, 1949 . . . £15/£5
The Swiss Summer, Longmans, 1951 . . . £15/£5
Fort of the Bear, Longmans, 1953 . . . . £15/£5
The Shadow of a Sorcerer, Hodder & Stoughton, 1955
. . . . £15/£5
Here Be Dragons, Hodder & Stoughton, 1956 . £15/£5
White Sand and Grey Sand, Hodder & Stoughton,
[1958]. . . . . £15/£5
A Pink Front Door, Hodder & Stoughton, [1959] . .
. . . . £15/£5
The Weather at Tregulla, Hodder & Stoughton, [1962]
. . . . £15/£5
The Wolves Were in the Sledge, Hodder & Stoughton,
1964 . . . . £15/£5
The Charmers, Hodder & Stoughton, 1965 . . £10/£5
Starlight, Hodder & Stoughton, 1967 . . . £10/£5
The Snow-Woman, Hodder & Stoughton, 1969 £10/£5
The Woods in Winter, Hodder & Stoughton, 1970 . .
. . . . £10/£5

Short Stories
Roaring Tower and Other Short Stories, Longmans,
1937 . . . . £30/£10
Christmas at Cold Comfort Farm and Other Stories,
Longmans, 1940 . . . . £50/£15
Beside the Pearly Water and Other Stories, Peter
Nevill, 1954 . . . . £20/£5

Poetry
The Mountain Beast and Other Poems, Longmans,
1930 (wraps) £40
The Priestess and Other Poems, Longmans, 1934
(wraps) £25
The Lowland Venus and Other Poems, Longmans,
1938 (wraps) £25
Collected Poems, Longmans, 1950 . . . £15/£5
ditto, The Collector's Book Club, 1950 (150 signed
copies) . . . . £40/£20
ditto, The Collector's Book Club, 1950 (5 signed
presentation copies) £100

Children's Titles
The Untidy Gnome, Longmans, 1935 . . £40/£10

GILES' ANNUALS

The distinctive cartoons drawn by Carl Giles, published in the Daily Express, have been collected
together annually.

No. 1, 1946. . . . . £200
No. 2, 1947. . . . . £225
No. 3, 1949. . . . . £175
No. 4, 1950. . . . . £175
No. 5, 1951. . . . . £150
No. 6, 1952. . . . . £75
No. 7, 1953. . . . . £75
No. 8, 1954. . . . . £65
No. 9, 1955. . . . . £50
No. 10, 1956 . . . . £25
No. 11, 1957 . . . . £25
No. 12, 1958 . . . . £25
No. 13, 1959 . . . . £25
No. 14, 1960 . . . . £15
No. 15, 1961 . . . . £15
No. 16, 1962 . . . . £15
No. 17, 1963 . . . . £15
No. 18, 1964 . . . . £15
No. 19, 1965 . . . . £15
No. 20, 1966 . . . . £15
No. 21, 1967 . . . . £10
No. 22, 1968 . . . . £10
No. 23, 1969 . . . . £10
No. 24, 1970 . . . . £5
No. 25, 1971 . . . . £5
No. 26, 1972 . . . . £5

WARWICK GOBLE
(b.1862 d.1943)

A British illustrator, Goble's work owes a great debt to Chinese and Japanese art.

Children's Books
The Grim House, by Mrs Molesworth, Nisbet, 1899 .
. . . . £35
The Water Babies, by Charles Kingsley, Macmillan, 1909 (32 colour plates) £350
ditto, Macmillan, 1909 (260 copies) £1,500
ditto, Macmillan, 1910 (16 colour plates) . . £75
Green Willow and Other Japanese Fairy Tales, by Grace James, Macmillan, 1910 (40 colour plates). .
. . . . £400
ditto, Macmillan, 1910 (500 copies) £2,000
ditto, Macmillan, 1912 (16 colour plates) . . £40
Folk Tales of Bengal, by Lal Behari Day, Macmillan, 1912 . . . . £200
ditto, Macmillan, 1912 (150 copies) £2,000
Peeps at Many Lands - Turkey, by Julius Van Millingen, A. & C. Black, 1911 (12 colour plates) £25
Stories from the Pentamerone, by Giovanni Battista Basile, Macmillan, 1911. . . . . . . £200
ditto, Macmillan, 1911 (150 copies) £1,250
The Fairy Book, by D.M. Craik, Macmillan, 1913 (32 colour plates). £250
The Book of Fairy Poetry, Dora Owen, ed., Longmans, 1920 (16 colour plates) . . . . £500/£350
Treasure Island, by Robert Louis Stevenson, Macmillan (U.S.), 1923 . . . . . . £100/£45
Kidnapped, by Robert Louis Stevenson, Macmillan (U.S.), 1925 (13 b&w full page illustrations and 3 colour plates). . . . . £100/£45

Others
The Oracle of Baal, by J. Provand Webster, Lippincott (U.S.), 1896 . . . . £100
Lad's Love, by S.R. Crockett, Bliss Sands & Co., 1897 (100 copies) £200
ditto, Hodder & Stoughton, 1902. . . . £25
The War of the Worlds, by H.G. Wells, Harpers (U.S.), 1898 (15 illustrations by Goble, frontispiece by Cosmo Rowe) £400
Constantinople, A. & C. Black, 1906 (63 colour plates) £150
The Greater Abbeys of England, Chatto & Windus, 1908 (60 colour plates) £45
Letters from an Ocean Tramp, by William Morley Punshon McFee, Cassell, 1908 . . . . . £75
Irish Ways, by Jane Barlow, Allen & Sons, 1909 (16 colour plates). £100
Turkey, A. & C. Black, 1911 (12 colour plates) £150
The Complete Poetical Works of Geoffrey Chaucer, Macmillan (U.S.), 1912 (32 colour plates). . £125
Indian Myth and Legend, by Donald A. Mackenzie, Gresham, 1913 (8 colour plates) £65

Indian Tales of the Great Ones Among Men, Women and Bird-People, by Cornelia Sohrabji, Blackie & Son (Bombay), 1916. . . . . £100
The Cistercians in Yorkshire, by Joseph Smith Fletcher, S.P.C.K., 1919. . . . . . . £45
The Alhambra, by Washinton Irving, Macmillan (U.S.), 1926 (3 colour plates) . . . . £100/£20
Todd of the Fens, by Elinor Whitney, Macmillan (U.S.), 1928 . . . . £100/£20

SIR WILLIAM GOLDING
(b.1911 d.1993)

Golding's novels often place his characters in extreme situations, facing moral dilemmas. He won the Nobel Prize for Literature in 1983.

Novels
Lord of the Flies, Faber, 1954 . . . £4,000/£450
ditto, Coward-McCann (U.S.), 1955 . . £1,000/£100
The Inheritors, Faber, 1955 . . . . . £350/£100
ditto, Harcourt Brace (U.S.), 1962 . . . £35/£15
Pincher Martin, Faber, 1956 . . . . £175/£35
ditto, as *The Two Deaths of Christopher Martin*, Harcourt Brace (U.S.), 1956. . . . . . £100/£15
Free Fall, Faber, 1959 . . . . . . £75/£20
ditto, Harcourt Brace (U.S.), 1960 . . . £25/£10
The Spire, Faber, 1964 . . . . . . £40/£10
ditto, Harcourt Brace (U.S.), 1964 . . . £15/£5
The Pyramid, Faber, 1967 . . . . . £40/£10
ditto, Harcourt Brace (U.S.), 1967 . . . £15/£5
Darkness Visible, Faber, 1979 . . . . £25/£10
ditto, Farrar Straus (U.S.), 1979 . . . £15/£5
Rites of Passage, Faber, 1980 . . . . £25/£10
ditto, Farrar Straus (U.S.), 1980 . . . £15/£5
The Paper Men, Faber, 1984. . . . . £15/£5
ditto, Farrar Straus (U.S.), 1984 . . . £15/£5
Close Quarters, Faber, 1987 . . . . . £15/£5
ditto, Farrar Straus (U.S.), 1987 . . . £15/£5
Fire Down Below, Faber, 1989 . . . . £10/£5
ditto, Farrar Straus (U.S.), 1989 . . . £10/£5
Double Tongue, Faber, 1995. . . . . £10/£5
ditto, Farrar Straus (U.S.), 1995 . . . £10/£5

Short Stories
Sometime, Never: Three Tales of Imagination, Eyre & Spottiswoode, 1956 . . . . . . £125/£35
ditto, Ballantine (U.S.), 1956 (wraps) . . . £20
The Ladder and the Tree, Marlborough College Press, 1961 (wraps) £1,500
The Scorpion God, Faber, 1971 . . . £45/£15
ditto, Harcourt Brace (U.S.), 1972 . . £25/£10

Collected Editions
To the Ends of the Earth: A Sea Trilogy ('*Rites of Passage*', '*Close Quarters*' & '*Fire Down Below*'), Faber, 1991 . . . . £20/£5
ditto, Faber, 1991 (400 signed copies, glassine d/w) .
. . . . £150/£135

Others

Poems, Macmillan, 1934 (wraps) £4,000
The Brass Butterfly, A Play in Three Acts, Faber,
1958 . . . . £150/£20
The Hot Gates and Other Occasional Pieces, Faber,
1965 . . . . £45/£10
ditto, Harcourt Brace (U.S.), 1965 . . . . £35/£5
A Moving Target, Faber, 1982 . . . . . £15/£5
ditto, Farrar Straus (U.S.), 1982 . . . . . £15/£5
Nobel Lecture, Sixth Chamber Press, 1983 (500
copies, wraps) £30
ditto, Sixth Chamber Press, 1983 (50 signed deluxe
copies, slipcase) . . . . £250/£225
An Egyptian Journal, Faber, 1985 . . . . £10/£5
ditto, Farrar Straus (U.S.), 1985 . . . . . £10/£5

SUE GRAFTON
(b.1940)

Grafton's 'alphabet' novels feature the credible
female private detective 'Kinsey Millhone'.

'Alphabet' Novels

A is for Alibi, Holt (U.S.), 1982 . . . £1,000/£100
ditto, Macmillan, 1986 . . . . . £150/£20
B is for Burglar, Holt (U.S.), 1985 . . . £750/£75
ditto, Macmillan, 1986 . . . . . £125/£20
C is for Corpse, Holt (U.S.), 1986 . . . £500/£45
ditto, Macmillan, 1987 . . . . . £75/£10
D is for Deadbeat, Holt (U.S.), 1987 . . £200/£20
ditto, Macmillan, 1987 . . . . . £75/£10
E is for Evidence, Holt (U.S.), 1988 . . . £125/£15
ditto, Macmillan, 1988 . . . . . £50/£10
F is for Fugitive, Holt (U.S.), 1989 . . . £75/£10
ditto, Macmillan, 1989 . . . . . . £25/£5
G is for Gumshoe, Holt (U.S.), 1990 . . . £25/£5
ditto, Macmillan, 1990 . . . . . . £20/£5
H is for Homicide, Holt (U.S.), 1991 . . . £20/£5
ditto, Macmillan, 1991 . . . . . . £15/£5
I is for Innocent, Holt (U.S.), 1992 . . . . £15/£5
ditto, Macmillan, 1992 . . . . . . £15/£5
J is for Judgment, Holt (U.S.), 1993 . . . £15/£5
ditto, Macmillan, 1993 . . . . . . £15/£5
K is for Killer, Holt (U.S.), 1994 . . . . £15/£5
ditto, Macmillan, 1994 . . . . . . £15/£5
L is for Lawless, Holt (U.S.), 1995 . . . . £15/£5
ditto, Macmillan, 1995 . . . . . . £15/£5
M is for Malice, Holt (U.S.), 1996 . . . £15/£5
ditto, Macmillan, 1997 . . . . . . £15/£5
N is for Noose, Holt (U.S.), 1998 . . . £15/£5
ditto, Macmillan, 1998 . . . . . . £15/£5
O is for Outlaw, Holt (U.S.), 1999 . . . £15/£5
ditto, Macmillan, 1999 (wraps) £5
P is for Peril, Putnam (U.S.), 2001 . . . . £10/£5
ditto, Macmillan, 2001 (wraps) £5
Q is for Quarry, Putnam (U.S.), 2002 . . . £10/£5

Short Stories

Kinsey and Me, Bench Press (U.S.), 1991 (300
numbered copies, slipcase) £300
ditto, Bench Press (U.S.), 1991 (26 lettered copies,
slipcase) £500

Other Novels

Keziah Dane, Macmillan (U.S.), 1967 . . £600/£35
ditto, Owen, 1968 . . . . £300/£25
The Lolly Madonna War, Owen, 1969 . . £400/£25

KENNETH GRAHAME
(b.1859 d.1932)

Grahame was successful as an essayist before he
turned to short stories and then the classic children's
novel *The Wind in the Willows*.

'Wind in the Willows' Titles

Wind in the Willows, Methuen, 1908 . . . £3,000
ditto, Scribner's (U.S.), 1908 . . . . . £300
ditto, Bodley Head, 1931 (illustrated by E.H.
Shepherd) . . . . £150/£75
ditto, Bodley Head, 1931 (illustrated by E.H. Shepherd,
275 copies signed by author and artist). £4,000/£600
ditto, Limited Editions Club (U.S.), 1940 (16 colour
plates by Arthur Rackham, deluxe 2,020 copies,
signed by the designer Bruce Rogers, cloth-backed
patterned boards) £1,500
ditto, Heritage Press (U.S.), 1940 (12 colour plates and
14 line drawings by Arthur Rackham, blue-mauve
cloth) . . . . £175/£75
ditto, Methuen, 1950 (illustrated by Arthur Rackham,
green cloth) . . . . £175/£75
ditto, Methuen, 1951 (illustrated by Arthur Rackham,
deluxe 500 copies, full white calf) £1,000
The Reluctant Dragon, Garden City Pub. Co. (U.S.),
1941 . . . . £150/£75
First Whisper of 'The Wind in the Willows', Methuen,
1944 . . . . £35/£10
Sweet Home, Methuen, 1946 . . . . . £30/£10
Toad Goes Caravanning, Methuen, 1947 . £30/£10
Bertie's Escapade, Methuen, 1949 (illustrated by E.H.
Shepherd) . . . . £75/£20
ditto, Lippincott (U.S.), 1949 . . . . . £75/£20

Other Titles

The Pagan Papers, Mathews & Lane, 1894 [1893]
(450 [615] copies, frontispiece by Aubrey Beardsley)
. . . . £150
The Golden Age, John Lane, 1895 . . . . £200
ditto, Stone and Kimball (U.S.), 1895 . . . £65
ditto, Bodley Head, 1900 [1899] (illustrated by
Maxfield Parrish, first issue with 16 pages of ads at
back dated 1895). £100
ditto, Bodley Head, 1928 (illustrated by E.H.
Shepherd). . . . . £150/£75

ditto, Bodley Head, 1928 (illustrated by E.H. Shepherd, 275 copies signed by author and artist). . . £600
Dream Days, John Lane (U.S.), 1899 [1898] (first issue with 15 pages of ads at back dated 1898) . . £200
ditto, John Lane/Bodley Head, 1902 (illustrated by Maxfield Parrish) £400
ditto, Bodley Head, 1930 (illustrated by E.H. Shepherd). . . . . £150/£75
ditto, Bodley Head, 1930 (illustrated by E.H. Shepherd, 275 copies signed by author and artist). . . £600
The Headswoman, John Lane/Bodley Head, 1898 (wraps) £45
Fun o' the Fair, Dent, 1929 (wraps) . . . £15
The Kenneth Grahame Book, Methuen, 1932 £35/£10

ROBERT GRAVES
(b.1895 d.1985)

Known particularly for his poetry, fiction and his early autobiography, *Goodbye to All That*, Graves lived on Majorca for most of his life.

Poetry
Over the Brazier, The Poetry Bookshop, 1916 (wraps)
. . . . £1,000
ditto, The Poetry Bookshop, 1917 (wraps) . . £200
ditto, The Poetry Bookshop, 1920 . . . £250/£35
Goliath and David, Chiswick Press, 1916 (200 copies, wraps). £1,750
Fairies and Fusiliers, Heinemann, 1917 . £450/£75
ditto, Knopf (U.S.), 1918 . . . . . . £300/£35
Treasure Box, [Chiswick Press, 1919] (200 copies, wraps). £750
ditto, [Chiswick Press, 1919] (200 copies, boards and d/w) £1,250
Country Sentiment, Secker, 1920 . . . £250/£45
ditto, Knopf (U.S.), 1920 . . . . . . £250/£45
The Pier-Glass, Secker, 1921 . . . £300/£75
ditto, Knopf (U.S.), 1921 (green cloth) . . £300/£45
ditto, Knopf (U.S.), 1921 (orange paper-covered boards) . . . . £250/£45
Whipperginny, Heinemann, 1923 . . . £250/£45
ditto, Knopf (U.S.), 1923 . . . . . . £250/£45
The Feather Bed, Hogarth Press, 1923 (250 copies, signed by the author) £500
Mock Beggar Hall, Hogarth Press, 1923 (no d/w) £350
Welchman's Hose, The Fleuron, 1925 (525 copies, glassine d/w) . . . . £250/£225
Poems, Benn, 1925 (wraps) £100
The Marmosite's Miscellany, Hogarth Press, 1925 (pseud. 'John Doyle') £400
ditto, Pharos Press (Canada), 1975 (80 signed copies, slipcase) . . . . £225/£200
ditto, Pharos Press (Canada), 1975 (750 signed copies, slipcase) . . . . £125/£100
Poems, 1914-1926, Heinemann, 1927 . £300/£75
ditto, Doubleday, Doran (U.S.), 1929 . £300/£75

Poems, 1914-1927, Heinemann, 1927 (115 signed, numbered copies, slipcase and d/w) . £1,000/£750
Poems, 1929, Seizin Press, 1929 (225 signed, numbered copies). £300
Ten Poems More, Hours Press (Paris), 1930 (200 signed copies) £350
Poems, 1926-1930, Heinemann, 1931 (first issue with misbound title-page). . . . . . £75/£25
To Whom Else?, Seizin Press (Majorca), 1931 (200 signed copies) £250
Poems, 1930-1933, Barker, 1933 . . . . £200
Collected Poems, Cassell, 1938 . . . . £100/£20
ditto, Random House (U.S.), 1939 . . . £100/£10
No More Ghosts: Selected Poems, Faber, 1940 . .
. . . . £50/£15
Poems, Eyre & Spottiswoode, 1943 (wraps) . £30
Poems, 1938-1945, Cassell, 1946 . . . £35/£10
ditto, Creative Age Press (U.S.), 1946 . . £35/£10
Collected Poems, 1914-1947, Cassell, 1948 £50/£15
Poems and Satires, Cassell, 1951 . . . £35/£10
Poems, 1953, Cassell, 1953 . . . . . £35/£10
ditto, Cassell, 1953 (250 signed, numbered copies, tissue d/w) . . . . £200/£175
Collected Poems, 1955, Doubleday (U.S.), 1955 . .
. . . . £35/£10
Poems Selected by Himself, Penguin, 1957 (wraps) £5
The Poems of Robert Graves, Doubleday (U.S.), 1958
. . . . £25/£5
Collected Poems, 1959, Cassell, 1959 . . £75/£35
More Poems, 1961, Cassell, 1961 . . . £20/£5
Collected Poems, Doubleday (U.S.), 1961 . £35/£10
New Poems, 1962, Cassell, 1962. . . . £25/£5
The More Deserving Cases: Eighteen Old Poems for Reconsideration, Marlborough College Press, 1962 (350 signed copies) £125
ditto, Marlborough College Press, 1962 (400 signed copies, bound in morocco) £125
Man Does, Woman Is, Cassell, 1964 . . £25/£10
ditto, Cassell, 1964 (175 copies, signed by the author).
. . . . £150/£100
ditto, Doubleday (U.S.), 1964 . . . . £25/£10
Love Respelt, Cassell, 1965 (250 signed copies) . .
. . . . £200/£150
ditto, Doubleday (U.S.), 1966 . . . . £25/£10
Collected Poems, 1965, Cassell, 1965 . . £20/£5
Seventeen Poems Missing From 'Love Respelt', privately printed, 1966 (330 copies, signed by the author) . . . . £150/£100
Colophon to 'Love Respelt', privately printed, 1967 (386 copies, signed by the author) . . . £100/£75
Poems, 1965-1968, Cassell, 1968 . . . £15/£5
Poems About Love, Cassell, 1969 . . . £25/£10
Love Respelt Again, Doubleday (U.S.), 1969 (1,000 numbered copies, signed by the author) . £75/£50
Beyond Giving, privately printed, 1969 (536 copies, signed by the author, card covers, d/w) . £75/£60
Poems, 1968-1970, Cassell, 1970 . . £20/£10
Advice from a Mother, Poem of the Month Club, 1970 (broadsheet) £25

The Green-Sailed Vessel, privately printed, 1971 (536 copies) . . . . £65/£45
Poems: Abridged for Dolls and Princes, Cassell, 1971 . . . . £25/£10
Poems, 1970-1972, Cassell, 1972 . . . £25/£10
Deya: A Portfolio, Motif Editions, 1972 (75 signed copies) £225
Timeless Meeting: Poems, privately printed, 1973 (536 signed, numbered copies) . . . . . £75/£50
At the Gate, Stellar Press (U.S.), 1974 (536 copies) . . . . £75/£50
Collected Poems, 1975, Cassell, 1975 . . £25/£10
New Collected Poems, Doubleday (U.S.), 1977 . . . . £25/£10
Across the Gulf, Late Poems, The New Seizin Press, 1992 (175 copies) £75

Fiction
My Head! My Head!, Secker, 1925 (500 copies) . . . . £350/£200
ditto, Knopf (U.S.), 1925 . . . . . £125/£50
The Shout, Mathews & Marrot, 1929 (530 signed, numbered copies) . . . . . . £175/£125
No Decency Left, Cape, 1932 (pseud. 'Barbara Rich', with Laura Riding) . . . . . £250/£100
The Real David Copperfield, Barker, 1933 (spine stamped in gold) . . . . £250/£75
ditto, Barker, 1933 (spine stamped in black) £125/£25
ditto, as *David Copperfield*, Harcourt Brace (U.S.), 1934 (abridged version condensed by Robert Graves) . . . . £45/£15
I, Claudius, Barker, 1934 (black cloth) . £750/£250
ditto, Barker, 1934 (remainder copies, orange cloth) . . . . £700/£200
ditto, Smith & Haas (U.S.), 1934 . . . £300/£25
Claudius the God and his Wife Messalina, Barker, 1934 . . . . £250/£75
ditto, Smith & Haas (U.S.), 1935 (first word on back jacket flap 'suddenly', blue cloth blind stamped on front) . . . . £200/£35
ditto, Smith & Haas (U.S.), 1935 (first word on back jacket flap 'At', dark blue cloth stamped in gold) . . . . £150/£25
Antigua, Penny, Puce, Constable/Seizin Press, 1936 . . . . £250/£75
ditto, as *The Antigua Stamp*, Random House (U.S.), 1937 . . . . £60/£15
Count Belisarius, Cassell, 1938 . . . £75/£15
ditto, Random House (U.S.), 1938 . . . £50/£10
Sergeant Lamb of the Ninth, Methuen, 1940 £75/£10
ditto, Random House (U.S.), 1941 . . £25/£10
Proceed, Sergeant Lamb, Methuen, 1941 . £75/£25
ditto, Random House (U.S.), 1941 . . . £65/£20
Wife to Mr Milton: The Story of Mary Powell, Cassell, 1943 . . . . £40/£15
ditto, Creative Age Press (U.S.), 1944 . £25/£10
The Golden Fleece, Cassell, 1944 . . . £45/£15
ditto, as *Hercules, My Shipmate*, Creative Age Press (U.S.), 1945 . . . . £35/£15

King Jesus, Creative Age Press (U.S.), 1946 £25/£10
ditto, Cassell, 1946 . . . . £25/£10
Watch the North Wind Rise, Creative Age Press (U.S.), 1949 . . . . £40/£15
ditto, as *Seven Days in New Crete*, Cassell, 1949 . . . . £35/£10
The Islands of Unwisdom, Doubleday (U.S.), 1949 . . . . £25/£10
ditto, as *The Isles of Unwisdom*, Cassell, 1950 £25/£10
Homer's Daughter, Cassell, 1955 . . . £35/£10
ditto, Doubleday (U.S.), 1955 . . . . £25/£10
Catacrok! Mostly Stories, Mostly Funny, Cassell, 1956 . . . . £30/£10
They Hanged My Saintly Billy, Cassell, 1957 £25/£10
ditto, Doubleday (U.S.), 1957 . . . . £25/£10
Collected Short Stories, Doubleday (U.S.), 1964 . . . . £30/£10
ditto, Cassell, 1965 . . . . £25/£10

Plays
John Kemp's Wager: A Ballad Opera, Blackwell, 1925 (100 signed, numbered copies) . . . £650
ditto, Blackwell, 1925 (750 unsigned copies, wraps) £125
ditto, French (U.S.), 1925 (250 copies) . . . £175

Children's Books
The Penny Fiddle: Poems for Children, Cassell, 1960 (illustrated by Edward Ardizzone) . . . £125/£50
ditto, Doubleday (U.S.), 1960 . . . . £75/£20
The Big Green Book, Crowell-Collier (U.S.), 1962 (illustrated by Maurice Sendak). . . £35/£10
ditto, Puffin, 1978 (wraps) £5
Ann at Highwood Hall: Poems for Children, Cassell, 1964 (illustrated by Edward Ardizzone) . £50/£20
ditto, Doubleday (U.S.), 1964 . . . . £30/£10
Two Wise Children, Quist (U.S.), 1967 . £35/£10
The Poor Boy Who Followed His Star, Cassell, 1968 . . . . £35/£10
ditto, Doubleday (U.S.), 1969 . . . . £35/£10
An Ancient Castle, Peter Owen, 1980 . . £20/£5
ditto, Kesend (U.S.), 1981 . . . . . £15/£5

Translations
Almost Forgotten Germany, by George Schwarz, Constable/Seizin Press, 1936 (with Laura Riding). . . . . £250/£60
The Transformation of Lucius, Otherwise Known as the Golden Ass, by Lucius Apuleius, Penguin, 1950 (2,000 signed, numbered copies, slipcase). £50/£40
ditto, Penguin, 1950 (wraps) £5
ditto, Farrar, Straus, Giroux (U.S.), 1951 . £20/£5
The Cross and the Sword from 'Enriquillio', by Manuel de Jesus Galvan, Univ. Press: Bloomington (U.S.), 1954 . . . . £45/£15
ditto, Gollancz, 1956 . . . . £45/£10
The Infant with the Globe from 'El Nino do la Bola', by Pedro de Alarcon, Trianon Press, 1955 . £25/£10
ditto, Yoseleff (U.S.), 1959 . . . . . £20/£10

Winter in Majorca, by George Sand, Cassell, 1956 .
. . . . £15/£5
ditto, Valldemosa Edition (Mallorca), 1959 (wraps) .
. . . . £10
Pharsalia, by Lucan, Penguin, 1956 (wraps) . . £5
ditto, Penguin (U.S.), 1957 . . . . . . £10/£5
The Twelve Caesars, by Suetonius, Penguin, 1957
(wraps) £5
The Anger of Achilles: Homer's Iliad, Homer,
Doubleday (U.S.), 1959. . . . . . £35/£10
ditto, Cassell, 1960 . . . . . . £20/£10
The Rubaiyat of Omar Khayyam, by Omar Khayyam,
Cassell, 1967 (with Omar Ali-Shah) . . . £20/£5
ditto, Doubleday (U.S.), 1968 . . . . . £20/£5
The Song of Songs, Clarkson Potter (U.S.), 1973 . .
. . . . £15/£5
ditto, Collins, 1973 . . . . £15/£5

Others

On English Poetry, Knopf (U.S.), 1922 . . £200/£30
ditto, Heinemann, 1922 . . . . . . £150/£25
The Meaning of Dreams, Cecil Palmer, 1924 . . .
. . . . £100/£35
ditto, Greenberg (U.S.), 1925. . . . . £50/£20
Poetic Unreason and Other Studies, Cecil Palmer,
1925 . . . . £150/£60
*Contemporary Techniques of Poetry: A Political
Analogy*, Hogarth Press, 1925 (wraps). . . £45
Another Future of Poetry, Hogarth Press, 1926 £100
Impenetrability, or the Proper Habit of English,
Hogarth Press, 1927 . . . . £200
The English Ballad: A Short Critical Survey, Benn,
1927 . . . . £75/£25
ditto, as *English and Scottish Ballads*, Heinemann,
1957 (revised edition) . . . . . . £25/£10
*Lars Porsena, or 'The Future of Swearing and
Improper Language'*, Kegan Paul, Trench, Trubner,
1927 . . . . £200/£30
ditto, Dutton (U.S.), 1927 . . . . . £175/£25
ditto, as *The Future of Swearing and Improper
Language*, Kegan Paul, Trench, Trubner, 1936
(revised edition) . . . . £25/£10
ditto, as *The Future of Swearing and Improper
Language*, Martin Brian & O'Keefe, 1972 (100
signed copies) £125
A Survey of Modernist Poetry, Heinemann, 1927 (with
Laura Riding) . . . . £75/£20
ditto, Doubleday (U.S.), 1928 . . . . £50/£15
Lawrence and the Arabs, Cape, 1927 . . £250/£30
ditto, as *Lawrence and the Arabian Adventure*,
Doubleday (U.S.), 1928 . . . . . £150/£20
A Pamphlet Against Anthologies, Cape, 1928 (with
Laura Riding) £75
ditto, Doubleday (U.S.), 1928 . . . . £75/£25
Mrs Fisher, or The Future of Humour, Kegan Paul,
Trench, Trubner, 1928 . . . . . £75/£25
ditto, Dutton (U.S.), 1928. . . . . . £75/£25

Goodbye to All That: An Autobiography, Cape, 1929
(first issue with Sassoon poem on pps. 341-343) . .
. . . . £1,250/£750
ditto, Cape, 1929 (second issue, poem replaced by
asterisks) . . . . £600/£45
ditto, Cape & Smith (U.S.), 1930. . . . £300/£35
But it Still Goes On: An Accumulation, Cape, 1930
(first impression with 'the child she bare' first para.
on p.157) . . . . £250/£100
ditto, Cape, 1930 (second impression with 'child she
bare' deleted). . . . . £150/£20
ditto, Cape & Smith (U.S.), 1931. . . . £125/£20
The Long Weekend (with Alan Hodge), Faber, 1940 .
. . . . £40/£10
ditto, Macmillan (U.S.), 1941 . . . . £35/£10
The Reader Over Your Shoulder (with Alan Hodge),
Cape, 1943 . . . . £40/£10
ditto, Macmillan (U.S.), 1943 . . . . £35/£10
The White Goddess, Faber, 1948 . . . £75/£20
ditto, Creative Age Press (U.S.), 1948 . . £65/£15
*The Common Asphodel: Collected Essays on Poetry,
1922-1949*, Hamish Hamilton, 1949 . . £75/£20
Occupation: Writer, Creative Age Press (U.S.), 1950 .
. . . . £35/£10
ditto, Cassell, 1951 . . . . £25/£10
The Nazarene Gospel Restored (with Joshua Podro),
Cassell, 1953. . . . . £100/£25
ditto, Doubleday (U.S.), 1954 . . . . £65/£15
The Greek Myths, Penguin, 1955 (2 vols, wraps) £10
ditto, Cassell, 1958 . . . . £20/£10
The Crowning Privilege: The Clark Lectures, 1954-5,
Cassell, 1955 . . . . £25/£10
ditto, Doubleday (U.S.), 1956 . . . . . £20/£5
Adam's Rib, Trianon Press, 1955 (illustrated by James
Metcalf) . . . . £50/£15
ditto, Trianon Press, 1955 (26 signed, numbered
copies, slipcase) . . . . £350/£150
ditto, Trianon Press, 1955 (250 signed, numbered
copies, slipcase) . . . . £200/£150
ditto, Yoseloff (U.S.), 1955 . . . . . £45/£15
ditto, Yoseloff (U.S.), 1955 (100 signed copies) . .
. . . . £150/£125
Jesus in Rome (with Joshua Podro), Cassell, 1957. . .
. . . . £45/£20
Steps, Cassell, 1958 . . . . £25/£10
5 Pens in Hand, Doubleday (U.S.), 1958 . . £30/£10
Food for Centaurs, Doubleday (U.S.), 1960 £45/£15
Greek Gods and Heroes, Doubleday (U.S.), 1960 . .
. . . . £25/£10
ditto, as *Myths of Ancient Greece*, Cassell, 1961 . .
. . . . £25/£10
Selected Poetry and Prose, Hutchinson, 1961 (edited
by James Reeves) . . . . £10/£5
Oxford Addresses on Poetry, Cassell, 1962. . £20/£5
ditto, Doubleday (U.S.), 1962 . . . . . £20/£5
The Siege and Fall of Troy, Cassell, 1962 (illustrated
by Walter Hodges) . . . . £15/£5
ditto, Doubleday (U.S.), 1962 . . . . . £15/£5

Hebrew Myths: The Book of Genesis, Doubleday
(U.S.), 1964 (with Raphael Patai) . . . £35/£10
ditto, Cassell, 1964 . . . . £35/£10
Majorca Observed, Cassell, 1965 . . . . £15/£5
ditto, Doubleday (U.S.), 1965 . . . . . £15/£5
Mammon and the Black Goddess, Cassell, 1965 . .
. . . . £20/£5
ditto, Doubleday (U.S.), 1965 . . . . . £20/£5
Poetic Craft and Principle, Cassell, 1967 . . £15/£5
Greek Myths and Legends, Cassell, 1968 . . £10/£5
The Crane Bag, Cassell, 1969 . . . . . £10/£5
On Poetry: Collected Talks and Essays, Doubleday
(U.S.), 1969 . . . . £20/£5
Difficult Questions, Easy Answers, Cassell, 1972 . .
. . . . £15/£5
ditto, Doubleday (U.S.), 1973 . . . . . £15/£5
Collected Letters, Moyer Bell (U.K./U.S.), 1984 &
1988 (2 vols) . . . . £50/£25

As Editor
Oxford Poetry, 1921, Blackwell, 1921 (with Alan
Porter and Richard Hughes) £200
ditto, Appleton (U.S.), 1922 . . . . £200/£75
John Skelton (Laureate), Benn, 1927 . . . £35
The Less Familiar Nursery Rhymes, Benn, 1927
(wraps) £50
T.E. Lawrence To His Biographers, Faber, 1938 (2
vols, 500 signed copies, with d/ws, in slipcase) .
. . . . £450/£400
ditto, Doubleday Doran, 1938 (2 vols, 500 signed
copies, with d/ws, in slipcase) . . . . £450/£400
The Comedies of Terence, Doubleday (U.S.), 1962 .
. . . . £25
ditto, Cassell, 1963 . . . . £10

ALASDAIR GRAY
(b.1934)

An inventive Scottish writer of bizarre tales, strangely
written.

Novels
Lanark, Canongate, 1981 . . . . . . £350/£20
ditto, Harper Colophon (U.S.), 1981 (wraps) . £10
ditto, Canongate, 1985 (1000 signed copies) £100/£65
ditto, Braziller (U.S.), 1985 . . . . . £50/£20
1982 Janine, Cape, 1984 . . . . . . £25/£5
ditto, Viking (U.S.), 1984 . . . . . . £20/£5
The Fall of Kelvin Walker, Canongate, 1985 . £20/£5
ditto, Braziller (U.S.), 1986 . . . . . £15/£5
Something Leather, Cape, 1990 . . . . £20/£5
ditto, Random House (U.S.), 1990 . . . £15/£5
McGrotty and Ludmilla, Dog and Bone, 1990 (wraps)
. . . . £10
Poor Things, Bloomsbury, 1991 . . . . . £15/£5
ditto, Harcourt (U.S.), 1992 . . . . . £15/£5
History Maker, Canongate, 1994 . . . £15/£5
ditto, Harcourt (U.S.), 1996 . . . . . £10/£5

Short Stories
The Comedy of the White Dog, Print Studio Press,
1979 (600 numbered copies, wraps) . . . £75
Unlikely Stories, Mostly, Canongate, 1983 . . £40/£5
ditto, Penguin (U.S.), 1984 . . . . . . £15/£5
Lean Tales, Cape, 1985 (with James Kelman and
Agnes Owens) . . . . £20/£5
Ten Tales Tall and True, Bloomsbury, 1993 . £10/£5
ditto, Harcourt (U.S.), 1993 . . . . . . £10/£5
Mavis Belfrage, Bloomsbury, 1996 . . . . £10/£5

Poetry
Old Negatives: Four Verse Sequences, Cape, 1989
(500 signed copies) . . . . . . £75/£35
ditto, Cape, 1989 (wraps) £5
The Artist In His World: Prints 1986-1997, by Ian
McCulloch, Argyll Publishing, 1998 (eight poems by
Gray) . . . . £35/£10
Sixteen Occasional Poems: 1990-2000, McAlpine,
2000 (wraps) £10
ditto, McAlpine, 2000 (200 signed copies, boards) . .
. . . . £75

Others
Dialogue, Scottish Theatre Magazine, 1971 . . £30
Self-portrait, Saltaire Society, 1988 (wraps) . £20
The Book of Prefaces, Bloomsbury, 2000 . . £10/£5
ditto, Bloomsbury (U.S.), 2001 . . . . . £10/£5
Why Scots Should Rule Scotland, Canongate, 1992
(wraps) £10
ditto, Canongate, 1997 (wraps) £5
5 Scottish Artists Retrospective Show, Famedram
Publishers, 1986 (five colour catalogues and an
introduction by Gray) £50
Pierre Lavalle: Paintings 1947-75, Lavalle Retrospective Group, 1990 (contains an essay by Gray,
wraps) £10

HENRY GREEN
(b.1905 d.1973)

Henry Green was the pseudonym of the novelist
Henry Vincent Yorke.

Novels
Blindness, Dent, 1926 . . . . . . £1,500/£150
ditto, Dutton (U.S.), 1926 . . . . £1,000/£125
Living, Dutton (U.S.), 1929 . . . £1,500/£150
ditto, Dent, 1929 . . . . . . £1,250/£125
Party Going, Hogarth Press, 1939 . . . £600/£100
ditto, Longman (Toronto), 1939 . . . £350/£75
ditto, Viking (U.S.), 1951 . . . . . . £35/£5
Caught, Hogarth Press, 1943 . . . . £250/£50
ditto, Macmillan (Toronto), 1943 . . . £150/£45
ditto, Viking (U.S.), 1950 . . . . . . £25/£5
Loving, Hogarth Press, 1945 . . . . . £225/£50
ditto, Macmillan (Toronto), 1945 . . . £125/£45
ditto, Viking (U.S.), 1949 . . . . . . £30/£5

Back, Hogarth Press, 1946 . . . . £150/£40
ditto, Oxford (Toronto), 1946 . . . . £60/£20
ditto, Viking (U.S.), 1950. . . . . . £25/£5
Concluding, Hogarth Press, 1948 . . £50/£15
ditto, Viking (U.S.), 1950. . . . . . £20/£5
Nothing, Hogarth Press, 1950 . . . . £40/£15
ditto, Viking (U.S.), 1950. . . . . . £15/£5
Doting, Hogarth Press, 1951 . . . . £40/£15
ditto, Viking (U.S.), 1952. . . . . . £15/£5

Others

Pack My Bag, Hogarth Press, 1940 . . . £500/£75
ditto, Macmillan (Toronto), 1940 . . . £125/£40
ditto, New Directions (U.S.), 1993 . . . . £10/£5
Surviving, The Uncollected Writings of Henry Green,
    Chatto & Windus, [1992] . . . . . . £20/£5
ditto, Viking (U.S.), 1993. . . . . . . £15/£5

KATE GREENAWAY
(b.1846 d.1901)

British author and illustrator whose first success,
Under the Window, had a major influence on
children's fashion of the time.

Infant Amusements, by William Henry Giles
    Kingston, Griffith and Farran, [1867] . . . £500
Aunt Louisa's Nursery Favourite, Warne, 1870 £450
Diamonds and Toads, Warne, [1871] . . . £1,000
ditto, McLoughlin Bros (U.S.), [no date] . . £250
The Children of the Parsonage, by Henry Courtney
    Selous, Griffith and Farran, 1874 . . . . £400
Puck and Blossom, by Rosa Mulholland, Marcus
    Ward, [1874?] £300
Fairy Gifts, by K. Knox, Griffith and Farran, [1875] .
    . . . . £250
The Fairy Spinner, by Miranda Hill, Marcus Ward,
    [1875] (illustrations unattributed) £200
ditto, Nelson (U.S.), 1875. . . . . . . £150
A Cruise in the Acorn, by Alice Jerrold, Marcus Ward,
    [1875]. £250
Turnaside Cottage, by Mary Senior Clark, Marcus
    Ward, 1875 . . . . £150
ditto, Nelson (U.S.), 1875. . . . . . . £150
Children's Songs, Marcus Ward, [1875] . . £100
Melcombe Manor, by F. Scarlet Potter, [1875]. £175
Seven Birthdays, by K. Knox, Griffith and Farran,
    1876 . . . . £225
ditto, Dutton (U.S.), [1876?] £175
A Quiver of Love: A Collection of Valentines, Marcus
    Ward, 1876 (with Walter Crane) £500
Two Little Cousins, by Alice Hepburn, Marcus Ward,
    1876 . . . . £150
What Santa Claus Gave Me, Griffith and Farran,
    [c.1876] £125
Starlight Stories, by Fanny Lablache, Griffith and
    Farran, 1876 . . . . £100

ditto, Pott, Young & Co (U.S.), 1879 . . . £75
Tom Seven Years Old, by H. Rutherford Russell,
    Marcus Ward, [1877] £150
Pretty Stories for Tiny Folks, Cassell, 1877 . £125
Woodland Romances, Cassell, Petter & Galpin, [1877]
    . . . . £150
ditto, as **The 'Little Folks' Painting Book**, Cassell,
    Petter & Galpin, [1879] (wraps) £300
Poor Nelly, by Mrs Bonavia Hunt, Cassell, 1878 £125
Topo, by G.E. Brunefille, Marcus Ward, 1878 . £125
Esther, by Geraldine Butt, Marcus Ward, 1878. £125
A Little Maid and Her Moods, by Elizabeth Stewart
    Phelps, Lothrop (U.S.), [1878] £125
Under the Window, by Kate Greenaway, Routledge,
    [1878]. £250
ditto, Routledge (U.S.), [1880] £150
Heartsease, by Charlotte M. Yonge, Macmillan, 1879.
    . . . . £150
The Heir of Redclyffe, by Charlotte M. Yonge,
    Macmillan, 1879. . . . . £150
Amateur Theatricals, by Walter Herries Pollock and
    Lady Pollock, Macmillan, 1879 . . . . £150
Trot's Journey, Worthington (U.S.), 1879 . . £150
A Favourite Album of Fun and Fancy, Cassell, Petter
    & Galpin, [1879]. £150
Christmas Snowflakes, Lothrop (U.S.), [1879]. £150
Three Brown Boys, Cassell, 1879 . . . . £150
ditto, Mallory (U.S.), 1879 . . . . . . £150
Art in the Nursery, Lothrop (U.S.), [1879] . . £150
A Book for Every Jack and Gill, Dodd, Mead (U.S.),
    [1879]. £150
Once Upon a Time, by Emma E. Brown, Lothrop
    (U.S.), [1879]. £150
The Two Gray Girls, Cassell, Petter & Galpin, [1880].
    . . . . £150
Kate Greenaway's Birthday Book for Children,
    Routledge, [1880] £150
Little Folks Out and About Book, by Chatty Cheerful
    [William Martin], Cassell, [1880] £150
Illustrated Children's Birthday Book, Mack, [1880] .
    . . . . £125
Freddie's Letter, Routledge, 1880 . . . . £125
The Youngster, by Cousin Daisy, Lippincott, [1880] .
    . . . . £125
Stevie's Visit, Dodd, Mead (U.S.), 1880. . . £125
The Purse of Gold, Dodd, Mead (U.S.), [1880] £125
The Lost Knife, Dodd, Mead (U.S.), 1880 . . £125
Little Sunbeam Stories, Cassell, Petter & Galpin,
    [1880]. £150
Pleasant Hours and Golden Days, Lupton (U.S.),
    [1880]. £125
Baby Dido, Lothrop (U.S.), [1880] (wraps) . . £125
Dumpy, by Archie Fell, Lothrop (U.S.), [1880]. £125
The Easy Book for Children, Pictorial Literature
    Society, [1880] £150
ditto, Butler (U.S.), [n.d.] £100
Five Mice in a Mousetrap, by Laura E. Richards, Estes
    Lauriat (U.S.), [1880] £125

Grandmamma's Surprise Party, Dodd, Mead (U.S.), 1880 . . . . £125
The Library, by Andrew Lang, Macmillan, 1881 £125
London Lyrics, by Frederick Locker, Chiswick Press, 1881 . . . . £125
ditto, Scribner's (U.S.), 1882 . . . . . £100
A Day in a Child's Life, Routledge, [1881] . . £200
Mother Goose, or The Old Nursery Rhymes, Routledge, [1881] (wraps) £250
ditto, Routledge, [1881] (cloth) £125
Elise, Dodd, Mead (U.S.), [1881] £125
Hide & Seek Illustrated, Dodd, Mead (U.S.), [1881] .
. . . . £125
King Christmas, Dodd, Mead (U.S.), [1881] . £125
Whose Fault Was It?, Dodd, Mead (U.S.), 1881 £125
Some Little People, Dodd, Mead (U.S.), [1881] £125
Art Hours, McLoughlin Bros (U.S.), 1882 . . £150
Steps to Art, McLoughlin Bros (U.S.), 1882 . £150
Happy Little People, by Olive Patch, Cassell, Petter & Galpin, [1882] £150
Little Ann, by Jane and Ann Taylor, Routledge, [1882]
. . . . £150
Flowers and Fancies, by B. Montgomerie Ranking and Thomas K Tully, Marcus Ward, 1882 . . . £150
The Wonderful Fan, Aunt Ella, Dutton (U.S.), 1882 .
. . . . £150
Tales from the Edda, told by Helen Zimmerman, Swan Sonneschein, [1882] £150
Papa's Little Daughters, by Mary D Brine, Cassell, Petter & Galpin, 1882 . . . . £150
Little Loving-Hearts Poem-Book, by Margaret Eleanora Tupper, Dutton (U.S.), 1882 . . . £150
Little Gatherers, Cassell, Petter & Galpin, [1882] . .
. . . . £150
Greenaway Pictures to Paint, Cassell, Petter & Galpin, [1882] £250
Jingles and Joys, by Mary D. Brine, Cassell (U.S.), 1883 . . . . £150
Baby Chatterbox, Worthington (U.S.), 1883 . £150
Art of England, by John Ruskin, George Allen, 1883 .
. . . . £150
Fors Clavigera, by John Ruskin, George Allen, 1884 .
. . . . £150
A Painting Book, Routledge, [1884]. . . . £250
Brothers of Pity, by Juliana Horatia Ewing, S.P.C.K., 1884 . . . . £150
Language of Flowers, Routledge, [1884] . . £150
A Summer at Aunt Helen's, Dodd, Mead (U.S.), 1880 [1884] £150
Baby's Birthday Book, Marcus Ward, [1894] . £150
English Spelling Book, by William Mavor, Routledge, 1885 . . . . £200
Chatterbox Hall, Worthington (U.S.), [1884] . £150
Children's Birthday Book, Marcus Ward, [1894] . .
. . . . £150
Little Castles with Big Wings, Dodd, Mead (U.S.), 1880 [1884] £150
A Painting Book, Routledge, [1884] (wraps.) . £250
Songs for the Nursery, Mack, [1884] . . . £125

Poems of Frederick Locker, White, Stokes & Allen (U.S.), [1884]. £150
Dame Wiggins of Lee and Her Seven Wonderful Cats, George Allen, 1885 . . . . £65
ditto, George Allen, 1885 (400 large paper copies). .
. . . . £225
Marigold Garden, Routledge, [1885] . . . £125
Kate Greenaway's Album, Routledge, [1885?] (8 copies, wraps) £7,500
Kate Greenaway's Alphabet, Routledge, [1885] (miniature book, card covers) £100
ditto, as *New Alphabet*, Routledge (U.S.), [1885] . .
. . . . £125
Tick, Tick, Tick and Other Rhymes, Mayer, Merkel & Ottmann (U.S.), [1885] £150
Mother Truths Melodies, by Mrs E.P. Miller, Bay State Publishing (U.S.), 1885. . . . . . .
£150
Little Patience Picture Book, Routledge, [1885] £125
A Apple Pie, Routledge, 1886 . . . . . £200
ditto, Routledge (U.S.), [1886] £200
The Queen of the Pirate Isle, by Bret Harte, Chatto & Windus, [1885] £200
ditto, Houghton Mifflin (U.S.), 1887 . . . £200
Rhymes for the Young Folk, by William Allingham, Cassell, [1886] £200
Bib and Tucker, Lothrop (U.S.), [1886]. . . £125
Christmas Dreams, by Mary D. Brine, Cassell (U.S.), [1886]. £125
Queen Victoria's Jubilee Garland, Routledge, 1887 .
. . . . £350
Lucy's Troubles, by Laurie Loring, Lothrop (U.S.), 1887 . . . . £125
Baby's Birthday Book, Marcus Ward, [1887] . £150
Orient Line Guide, Sampson Low, 1888 . . £125
Around the House, Worthington (U.S.), 1888 . £150
Pied Piper of Hamelin, by Robert Browning, Routledge, [1888] £150
The Old Farm Gate, Routledge, [1888]. . . £150
Miss Rosebud, Lothrop (U.S.), [1888] . . . £125
Kate Greenaway's Painting Book, Warne (U.S.), [1888]. £250
Kate Greenaway's Book of Games, Routledge, [1889]
. . . . £200
The Royal Progress of King Pepito, by Beatrice Cresswell, S.P.C.K., [1889] £125
Our Girls, Belford, Vlarke & Co. (U.S.), 1890 . £125
Songs of the Month, by Lucie E. Willeplait, Worthington (U.S.), 1891 . . . . . . £125
Soap Bubble Stories, by Fanny Barry, Skeffington, 1892 . . . . £125
Littledom Castle and Other Tales, by Mabel H. Spielmann, Routledge, 1903 . . . . . £200
Doll's Tea Party, Lothrop (U.S.), [1895] . . £125
Every Girl's Stories, by Grace Aguilar, Geraldine Butt and Jane Butt, Routledge, 1896. . . . . £125
Stories Witty and Pictures Pretty, Conky (U.S.), 1896.
. . . . £100
To Pass the Time, McLoughlin (U.S.), [1897] . £100

Little Folks' Speaker, Lothrop (U.S.), 1898 . £100
The April Baby's Book of Tunes, by the author of
'Elizabeth and her German Garden', Macmillan, 1900
. . . . £200
ditto, by the author of 'Elizabeth and her German
Garden', Macmillan (U.S.), 1900 . . . . £200

Calendars
Calendar of the Seasons, 1876/1877/1881/1882,
Marcus Ward . . . . £125 each
A Calendar of the Months, Marcus Ward, 1884 £125
Kate Greenaway's Calendar, 1884/1897/1899,
Routledge . . . . £150 each

Almanacks
(assuming original envelope no longer present)
1883, Routledge, [1882] £225
1884, Routledge, [1883] (wraps) £225
1885, Routledge, [1884] £200
1886, Routledge, [1885] £175
1887, Routledge, [1886] £125
1888, Routledge, [1887] £125
1889, Routledge, [1888] £150
1890, Routledge, [1889] £125
1891, Routledge, [1890] £125
1892, Routledge, [1891] £125
1893, Routledge, [1892] £125
1894, Routledge, [1893] £125
1895, Routledge, [1894] £125
1897, Routledge, [1896] (imitation leather binding) .
. . . . £500
1924, Warne, [1923] £75
1925, Warne, [1924] £75
1926, Warne, [1925] £75
1927, Warne, [1926] £75
1928, Warne, [1927] £75
1929, Warne, [1928] (imitation leather binding) £125

GRAHAM GREENE
(b.1904 d.1991)

Popularly known for his novels, Greene is equally
acclaimed as a short story writer, playwright, critic
and essayist. From his first real success, *Stamboul
Train*, he appears preoccupied with the themes of
guilt, pursuit and failure, much of which is thought to
stem from his conversion to Catholicism.

Novels
The Man Within, Heinemann, 1929 . . £3,000/£275
ditto, Doubleday (U.S.), 1929 . . . £1,500/£100
The Name of Action, Heinemann, 1930 (d/w price
7s6d and reviews of *The Man Within* on back) . .
. . . . £3,500/£400
ditto, Heinemann, 1930 (d/w price 3s6d and reviews of
current book on d/w flap) . . . . £1,500/£400
ditto, Doubleday (U.S.), 1931 . . . £1,000/£175

Rumour at Nightfall, Heinemann, 1931. £15,000/£300
ditto, Doubleday (U.S.), 1932 . . . £1,000/£100
Stamboul Train, Heinemann, 1932 (reference to 'Q.C.
Savory' on pps 77, 78, 82, 98, 131) . £3,000/£250
ditto, Heinemann, 1932 (reference to 'Quin Savory') .
. . . . £2,000/£75
ditto, as *Orient Express*, Doubleday (U.S.), 1933 . .
. . . . £1,250/£100
It's a Battlefield, Heinemann, 1934 (d/w price 7s6d) .
. . . . £1,500/£100
ditto, Heinemann, 1934 (d/w price 3/6) . £1,250/£100
ditto, Doubleday (U.S.), 1934 . . . . £600/£45
England Made Me, Heinemann, 1935 . £7,500/£250
ditto, Doubleday (U.S.), 1935 . . . . £750/£50
This Gun For Hire, Doubleday (U.S.), 1936 £750/£50
ditto, as *A Gun for Sale*, Heinemann, 1936 . . . .
. . . . £7,500/£250
Brighton Rock, Viking (U.S.), 1938 . . . £750/£50
ditto, Heinemann, 1938 . . . . . £25,000/£150
The Confidential Agent, Heinemann, 1939 . . . .
. . . . £5,000/£200
ditto, Viking (U.S.), 1939 . . . . . £750/£65
The Power and the Glory, Heinemann, 1940 . . .
. . . . £7,500/£450
ditto, as *The Labyrinthine Ways*, Viking (U.S.), 1940
(first state) . . . . £750/£250
ditto, as *The Labyrinthine Ways*, Viking (U.S.), 1940
(second state with pp.165 and 256 in correct order) .
. . . . £350/£35
The Ministry of Fear, Heinemann, 1943 £3,000/£75
ditto, Viking (U.S.), 1943 . . . . . £450/£35
The Heart of the Matter, Heinemann, 1948. £200/£20
ditto, Viking (U.S.), 1948 (750 copies 'For Friends of
the Viking Press') . . . . . . £75/£25
ditto, Viking (U.S.), 1948 . . . . . £50/£15
The Third Man, Viking (U.S.), 1950 . . £175/£15
The Third Man and *The Fallen Idol*, Heinemann,
1950 . . . . £200/£15
ditto, Eurographica (Helsinki), 1988 (500 signed
copies) . . . . £200/£150
The End of the Affair, Heinemann, 1951 . £100/£15
ditto, Viking (U.S.), 1951 . . . . . £45/£10
Loser Takes All, Heinemann, 1955 . . . £100/£15
ditto, Viking (U.S.), 1957 . . . . . £45/£10
The Quiet American, Heinemann, 1955 . . £100/£15
ditto, Viking (U.S.), 1956 . . . . . £45/£10
Our Man in Havana, Heinemann, 1958 . . £75/£10
ditto, Viking (U.S.), 1958 . . . . . £35/£10
A Burnt Out Case, Heinemann, 1961 . . . £75/£5
ditto, Viking (U.S.), 1961 . . . . . £25/£5
The Comedians, Viking (U.S.), 1966 (500 advance
copies, acetate d/w) . . . . . . £75/£50
ditto, Bodley Head, 1966 . . . . . £35/£10
ditto, Viking (U.S.), 1966 . . . . . £25/£5
Travels with My Aunt, Bodley Head, 1969 . £35/£10
ditto, Viking (U.S.), 1970 . . . . . £25/£5
The Honorary Consul, Bodley Head, 1973 . £35/£10
ditto, Viking (U.S.), 1973 . . . . . £25/£5
The Human Factor, Bodley Head, 1978 . £35/£10

ditto, Simon & Schuster (U.S.), 1978 . . . £25/£5
Dr Fischer of Geneva or The Bomb Party, Bodley Head, 1980 . . . . £20/£5
ditto, Simon & Schuster (U.S.), 1980 . . . £15/£5
ditto, Simon & Schuster (U.S.), 1980 (500 signed copies, slipcase) . . . . £150/£125
How Father Quixote Became a Monsignor, Sylvester & Orphanos (U.S.), 1980 (330 numbered copies, acetate d/w) . . . . £150/£125
Monsignor Quixote, Lester & Orpen Dennys (Canada), 1982 . . . . £20/£5
ditto, Bodley Head, 1982 . . . . . . £20/£5
ditto, Simon & Schuster (U.S.), 1982 . . £15/£5
ditto, Simon & Schuster (U.S.), 1982 (250 signed copies in slipcase) . . . . . . £150/£125
The Tenth Man, Bodley Head, 1985 . . . £15/£5
ditto, Simon & Schuster (U.S.), 1985 . . . £10/£5
The Captain and the Enemy, Reinhardt, 1988 . £15/£5
ditto, Viking (U.S.), 1988. . . . . . £10/£5

Short Stories

The Bear Fell Free, Grayson, 1935 (285 signed copies) . . . . £850/£450
The Basement Room, Cresset Press, 1935 . £500/£75
Twenty Four Stories, Cresset Press, 1939 (with James Laver and Sylvia Townsend Warner) . . £125/£30
Nineteen Stories, Heinemann, 1947 . . . £250/£45
ditto, Viking (U.S.), 1949. . . . . £150/£35
ditto, as **Twenty-One Stories**, Heinemann, 1954 (extra stories added). . . . . £100/£15
A Visit to Morin, Heinemann, [1959] (250 copies). .
. . . . £250/£125
A Sense of Reality, Bodley Head, 1963 . . £50/£15
ditto, Viking (U.S.), 1963. . . . . £35/£10
May We Borrow Your Husband?, Bodley Head, 1967
. . . . £30/£10
ditto, Bodley Head, 1967 (500 signed copies, glassine d/w) . . . . £150/£125
ditto, Viking (U.S.), 1967. . . . . £25/£10
The Collected Stories, Bodley Head/Heinemann, 1972
. . . . £30/£10
ditto, Viking (U.S.), 1973. . . . . . £15/£5
Shades of Greene, Bodley Head/Heinemann, 1975 .
. . . . £15/£5
The Last Word and Other Stories, Reinhardt, 1990 .
. . . . £10/£5

Plays

The Living Room, Heinemann, 1953 . . £175/£20
ditto, Viking (U.S.), 1954. . . . . £125/£15
The Potting Shed, Viking (U.S.), 1957 . . £175/£20
ditto, Heinemann, 1958 . . . . . £175/£20
The Complaisant Lover, Heinemann, 1959 . £150/£20
ditto, Viking (U.S.), 1961. . . . . £100/£15
Carving a Statue, Bodley Head, 1964 . £75/£15
The Return of A.J. Raffles, Heinemann, 1965 £45/£10
ditto, Bodley Head, 1975 (wraps) £10
ditto, Bodley Head, 1975 (250 signed copies) . .
. . . . £250/£150

ditto, Simon & Schuster (U.S.), 1978 . . . £25/£5
The Great Jowett, Bodley Head, 1981 (525 signed copies, glassine d/w). . . . . . £200/£150
Yes & No and For Whom the Bell Chimes, Bodley Head, 1983 (775 signed copies, glassine d/w). . .
. . . . £200/£150
Yes & No-A Play in One Act, Eurographica (Helsinki), 1984 (350 signed copies, wraps) £100

Travel

Journey Without Maps, Heinemann, 1936 . . . .
. . . . £4,000/£150
ditto, Doubleday (U.S.), 1936 . . . . £300/£45
The Lawless Roads, Longman, 1939 (red cloth, lettering in gold) . . . . £1,500/£350
ditto, Longman, 1939 (red cloth, lettering in blue) . .
. . . . £750/£75
ditto, as **Another Mexico**, Viking (U.S.), 1939 . . .
. . . . £250/£50

Children's Titles

The Little Train, Eyre & Spottiswoode, 1946 (anonymous) . . . . £450/£100
ditto, Lothrop (U.S.), 1958 . . . . £250/£50
The Little Fire Engine, Parrish, 1950 . . £250/£45
ditto, as **The Little Red Fire Engine**, Lothrop (U.S.), 1952. . . . . £100/£35
The Little Horse Bus, Parrish, 1952 . . £200/£45
ditto, Lothrop (U.S.), 1954 . . . . £75/£25
The Little Steam Roller, Parrish, 1953 . £200/£45
ditto, Lothrop (U.S.), 1955 . . . . £75/£25

Others

Babbling April, Blackwell, 1925. . . £2,250/£750
To Beg I am Ashamed, Vanguard Press (U.S.), 1938 (pseud. 'Sheila Cousins', with Ronald Matthews). .
. . . . £125/£25
ditto, Routledge, 1938. . . . . . £125/£25
Men At Work, Penguin New Writing, 1941 (wraps) .
. . . . £20
British Dramatists, Collins, 1942 . . . £40/£10
Why Do I Write?: An Exchange of Views Between Elizabeth Bowen, Graham Greene, and V.S. Pritchett, Marshall, 1948 . . . . £125/£35
The Lost Childhood, Eyre & Spottiswoode, 1951 . .
. . . . £40/£15
ditto, Viking (U.S.), 1952. . . . . £20/£5
In Search of a Character: Two African Journals, Bodley Head, 1961 . . . . . £45/£10
ditto, Viking (U.S.), 1961(600 advance copies). £65
ditto, Viking (U.S.), 1961. . . . . £45/£10
Introductions to Three Novels, Norstedt (Stockholm), 1962 (wraps) £100
The Revenge, An Autobiographical Fragment, The Stellar Press, 1963 (300 copies, wraps) . . £150
Victorian Detective Fiction, A Catalogue of the Collection made by Dorothy Glover and Graham Greene, Bodley Head, 1966 (500 signed copies). .
. . . . £250/£150

Collected Essays, Bodley Head, 1969 . . . £20/£5
ditto, Viking (U.S.), 1969 . . . . . . £15/£5
Mr Visconti, Bodley Head, 1969 (300 copies, wraps) .
. . . . £200
The Collected Edition, volumes 1-22, Heinemann &
Bodley Head, 1970-1982 (with new introductions by
the author) . . . . £250/£50
A Sort of Life, Bodley Head, 1971 . . . £15/£5
ditto, Simon & Schuster (U.S.), 1971 . . £15/£5
*The Pleasure Dome: The Collected Film Criticism,
1935-1940*, Secker & Warburg, 1972 . . £15/£5
ditto, Simon & Schuster (U.S.), 1972 . . £15/£5
The Virtue of Disloyalty, Bodley Head, 1972 (300
copies, wraps) £200
Lord Rochester's Monkey, Bodley Head, 1974. £15/£5
ditto, Viking (U.S.), 1974 . . . . . . £15/£5
*An Impossible Woman, The Memories of Dottoressa
Moor of Capri*, Bodley Head, 1975 . . £20/£5
Ways of Escape, Lester & Orpen Dennys (Canada),
1980 . . . . £25/£5
ditto, Lester & Orpen Dennys (Canada), 1980 (150
signed copies, slipcase) . . . . . £250/£225
ditto, Bodley Head, 1980 . . . . . . £10/£5
ditto, Simon & Schuster (U.S.), 1980 . . £10/£5
J'Accuse: The Darker Side of Nice, Lester & Orpen
Dennys (Toronto), 1982 (wraps and d/w) . £25/£15
ditto, Bodley Head, 1982 (wraps and d/w) . £25/£15
The Other Man: Conversations with Graham Greene,
Bodley Head, 1983 . . . . £20/£5
ditto, Simon & Schuster (U.S.), 1983 . . £20/£5
A Quick Look Behind, Sylvester & Orphanos, 1983
(300 signed, numbered copies of 330, slipcase) .
. . . . £175/£125
ditto, Sylvester & Orphanos, 1983 (26 signed, lettered
copies, plus 4 presentaton copies, of 330, slipcase) .
. . . . £250/£200
Getting to Know The General, Bodley Head, 1984 .
. . . . £15/£5
ditto, Simon & Schuster (U.S.), 1984 . . £15/£5
The Monster of Capri, Eurographica (Helsinki), 1985
(500 signed copies) . . . . . £175/£125
Why the Epigraph?, Nonesuch, 1989 (950 signed
copies, glassine d/w) . . . . . £150/£125
*Dear David, Dear Graham, A Bibliophilic Corres-
pondence*, The Alembic Press, 1989 (50 of 250
copies, slipcase) . . . . . . £175/£125
ditto, The Alembic Press, 1989 (200 of 250 copies) .
. . . . £100
Yours, etc: Letters to the Press, Reinhardt, 1989 .
. . . . £10/£5
ditto, Viking (U.S.), 1990 . . . . . . £10/£5
Reflections on Travels with My Aunt, Firsts & Co.
(U.S.), 1989 (250 signed copies, wraps) . . £150
Reflections 1923-1988, Reinhardt, 1990 . £10/£5
ditto, Viking (U.S.), 1990 . . . . . . £10/£5
A World of My Own, Reinhardt, 1992 . . £10/£5
ditto, Viking (U.S.), 1994 . . . . . . £10/£5

JOHN GRISHAM
(b.1955)

Grisham's reputation was established by his second
novel, *The Firm*. In 1990, a year before the novel was
published, Paramount Pictures purchased the film
rights for $600,000.

Novels

A Time to Kill, Wynwood (U.S.), 1989 (no mention of
The Firm on d/w) . . . . . £3,000/£450
ditto, Doubleday (U.S.), 1993 (350 signed, numbered
copies, slipcas,. 'First edition' statement incorrect) .
. . . . £500/£450
ditto, Doubleday (U.S.), 1993 ('First edition' statement
incorrect) . . . . £65/£10
ditto, Arrow, 1992 (wraps) £5
ditto, Century, 1993 . . . . . . £45/£10
The Firm, Doubleday (U.S.), 1991 . . £150/£15
ditto, Doubleday (U.S.), 1991 (350 signed, numbered
copies, slipcase) . . . . . . £500/£450
ditto, Century, 1991 . . . . . . £45/£10
The Pelican Brief, Doubleday (U.S.), 1992 . £30/£10
ditto, Doubleday (U.S.), 1993 (350 signed, numbered
copies, slipcase) . . . . . . £500/£450
ditto, Century, 1992 . . . . . . £25/£5
The Client, Doubleday (U.S.), 1993 . . . £10/£5
ditto, Doubleday (U.S.), 1993 (350 signed, numbered
copies, slipcase) . . . . . . £450/£400
ditto, Century, 1993 . . . . . . £10/£5
The Chamber, Doubleday (U.S.), 1994 . . £10/£5
ditto, Doubleday (U.S.), 1994 (350 signed, numbered
copies, slipcase) . . . . . . £250/£200
ditto, Century, 1994 . . . . . . £10/£5
The Rainmaker, Doubleday (U.S.), 1995 . £10/£5
ditto, Doubleday (U.S.), 1995 (350 signed, numbered
copies, slipcase) . . . . . . £250/£200
ditto, Century, 1995 . . . . . . £10/£5
The Runaway Jury, Doubleday (U.S.), 1996 . £10/£5
ditto, Doubleday (U.S.), 1996 (350 signed, numbered
copies, slipcase) . . . . . . £250/£200
ditto, Century, 1996 . . . . . . £10/£5
The Partner, Doubleday (U.S.), 1997 . . £10/£5
ditto, Doubleday (U.S.), 1997 (275 signed, numbered
copies, slipcase) . . . . . . £250/£200
ditto, Century, 1997 . . . . . . £10/£5
The Street Lawyer, Doubleday (U.S.), 1998 . £10/£5
ditto, Doubleday (U.S.), 1998 (250 signed, numbered
copies, slipcase) . . . . . . £250/£200
ditto, Century, 1998 . . . . . . £10/£5
The Testament, Doubleday (U.S.), 1999 . £10/£5
ditto, Doubleday (U.S.), 1999 (500 signed, numbered
copies, slipcase) . . . . . . £125/£100
ditto, Century, 1999 . . . . . . £10/£5
The Brethren, Doubleday (U.S.), 2000 (500 signed,
numbered copies, slipcase) . . . . £200/£150
ditto, Doubleday (U.S.), 2000 . . . . £10/£5
ditto, Century, 2000 . . . . . . £10/£5

A Painted House, Doubleday (U.S.), 2001 (350 signed, numbered copies, slipcase) . . . . . £150/£125
ditto, Doubleday (U.S.), 2001 . . . . . £10/£5
ditto, Century, 2001 . . . . £10/£5

Others
Special Forces: A Guided Tour of U.S. Special Forces, Berkley (U.S.), 2001 (with Tom Clancy) . £5

GEORGE and WEEDON GROSSMITH
(b.1847 d.1912, and b.1854 d.1919)

Although was their only published book, it is considered a *The Diary of a Nobody* comic classic.

The Diary of a Nobody, Arrowsmith, 1892 . . £300

THOM GUNN
(b.1929)

While not commanding the respect he once did, Gunn remains a well-regarded post-war poet.

Poetry
Poetry from Cambridge, 1951-1952, Fortune Press, 1952 . . . . £300/£65
The Fantasy Poets No. 16, Fantasy Press, 1953 (approx 300 copies, wraps) £250
Fighting Terms, Fantasy Press, 1954 (first issue with final 't' in 'thought' missed on first line of p.38) £300
ditto, Fantasy Press, 1954 (second issue, error corrected). £250
ditto, Hawks Well Press (U.S.), 1958 (1,500 copies, wraps with d/w) . . . . £125/£35
ditto, Faber, 1966 . . . . £25/£5
Poetry from Cambridge, 1952-1954, Fantasy Press, 1955 (wraps) £125
The Sense of Movement, Faber, 1957 . . £75/£10
ditto, Univ. of Chicago Press (U.S.), 1959 . £45/£10
My Sad Captains, Faber, 1961 . . . £40/£10
ditto, Univ. of Chicago Press (U.S.), 1961 . £25/£10
Selected Poems, Faber, 1962 (with Ted Hughes, wraps) £35
A Geography, Stone Wall Press (U.S.), 1966 (220 copies, wraps) £200
Positives, Faber, 1966 . . . . . . £30/£10
ditto, Univ. of Chicago Press (U.S.), 1967 . £30/£10
Touch, Faber, [1967] . . . . £25/£5
ditto, Univ. of Chicago Press (U.S.), 1968 . £25/£5
The Garden of the Gods, Pym-Randall Press (U.S.), [1968] (200 of 226, signed copies, wraps). . £65
ditto, Pym-Randall Press (U.S.), [1968] (26 signed, lettered copies of 226, wraps) £150
The Explorers, Gilbertson (U.S.), 1969 (6 copies) £300

ditto, Gilbertson (U.S.), 1969 (deluxe issue of 10 copies) £200
ditto, Gilbertson (U.S.), 1969 (special issue of 20 copies) £150
ditto, Gilbertson (U.S.), 1969 (ordinary issue of 64 copies) £75
The Fair in the Woods, Sycamore Press, 1969 (broadsheet, 500 copies) £10
Poems 1950-1966: A Selection, Faber, 1969 (wraps) £10
Sunlight, Albondocani Press (U.S.), 1969 (150 signed, numbered copies) £75
Moly, Faber, 1971 . . . . £25/£10
ditto, Farrar Straus (U.S.), 1973 . . . £20/£5
Last Days at Teddington, John Roberts Press, 1971 (broadsheet, 1,000 copies) £10
Poem After Chaucer, Albondocani Press (U.S.), 1971 (300 copies, wraps) £50
The Spell, Steane, 1973 (broadsheet, 500 copies) £10
Songbook, Albondocani Press (U.S.), 1973 (200 signed copies, wraps) £65
To the Air, Godine, 1974 (no d/w) . . . £25
Mandrakes, The Rainbow Press, [1974] (150 signed copies, slipcase) . . . . . . £250/£200
Jack Straw's Castle, Hallman, 1975 (300 copies, wraps). £15
ditto, Hallman, 1976 (100 signed hardback copies). . . . . £100/£45
ditto, as *Jack Straw's Castle and Other Poems*, Faber, 1976 (750 hardback copies). . . . . £40/£10
ditto, Faber, 1976 (100 numbered, signed hardback copies) . . . . £100/£45
ditto, Faber, 1976 (4,000 copies, wraps). . . £5
ditto, Farrar Straus (U.S.), 1976 . . . . £15/£5
The Missed Beat, Janus Press (U.S.), 1976 (50 copies, slipcase) . . . . £350/£300
ditto, Gruffyground Press, 1976 (approx 70 copies, wraps). £75
A Crab, The Pirates, 1978 . . . . . £20
Games of Chance, Abattoir, 1979 (220 copies). £50
Selected Poems 1950-1975, Faber, 1979 . . £10/£5
ditto, Farrar Straus (U.S.), 1979 . . . . £10/£5
Talbot Road, Helikon Press, 1981 (150 signed, numbered copies of 400, wraps) £35
ditto, Helikon Press, 1981 (250 numbered copies of 400, wraps) £10
The Passages of Joy, Faber, 1982 . . . £15/£5
ditto, Farrar Straus Giroux (U.S.), 1982 . . . £15/£5
Sidewalks, Albondocani Press (U.S.), 1985 (200 signed copies, wraps) £45
Lament, Doe Press (U.S.), 1985 (150 signed copies, wraps). £75
ditto, Doe Press (U.S.), 1985 (26 signed copies) £150
The Hurtless Trees, privately printed, 1986 (159 signed copies, wraps and d/w) £125
Night Sweats, Barth (U.S.), 1987 (200 signed, numbered copies, wraps) £50
ditto, Barth (U.S.), 1987 (wraps) £20

ditto, as *The Man with Night Sweats*, Faber, 1992 . . . . £15/£5
ditto, Farrar Straus Giroux (U.S.), 1992 . . . £15/£5
Undesirables, Pig Press, 1988 (50 signed copies of 550) £35
ditto, Pig Press, 1988 (500 unsigned copies of 550) £15
At the Barriers, NADJA, 1989 (26 signed copies of 100) £150
ditto, NADJA (U.S.), 1989 (74 signed copies of 100, wraps). £65
Death's Door, Red Hydra Press, 1989 (20 signed, quarter morocco copies). £250
ditto, Red Hydra Press, 1989 (60 signed copies) £150
My Mother's Pride, DIA Center for the Arts (U.S.), 1990 (broadside). £10
Unsought Intimacies, Koch (U.S.), 1991 (130 copies, slipcase) . . . . £150/£125
The Life of the Otter, Tucson Desert Museum (U.S.), 1991 (50 signed copies, broadside). . . . £35
Old Stories, Sea Cliff Press, 1992 (100 copies, wraps). £100
Collected Poems, Faber, 1993 . . . . £15/£5
ditto, Faber, 1993 (150 signed copies, slipcase). . . . . £125/£100
ditto, Farrar, Straus & Giroux (U.S.), 1994 . £15/£5
Shelf Life, Univ. of Michigan Press (U.S.), 1993 (no d/w) £10
ditto, Faber, 1994 . . . . £15/£5
Arthur In the Twilight Slot, Enitharmon Press, 1995 (75 copies, slipcase) . . . . . . £250/£225
Dancing David, Nadja (U.S.), 1995 (26 signed, lettered copies) £200
June, Wood Works (U.S.), 1998 (250 signed copies, broadside) £20
A Green Place, Occasional Works (U.S.), 1999 (with Eileen Hogan, 26 signed, lettered copies, slipcase) £250
ditto, Occasional Works (U.S.), 1999 (80 signed, numbered copies) £100
ditto, Occasional Works (U.S.), 1999 (220 numbered copies) £25

Others
The Occasions of Poetry, Faber, 1982 . . . £10/£5
ditto, North Point Press (U.S.), 1983 (wraps) . £10

H. RIDER HAGGARD
(b.1856 d.1925)

A successful British writer of heroic adventure novels, Haggard's strengths are his story-telling abilities and the authentic background to his books.

Novels
Dawn, Hurst & Blackett, 1884 (3 vols) . . . £5,000
ditto, Appleton (U.S.), 1887 (2 vols, wraps). . £2,000
ditto, Harpers (U.S.), 1887 . . . . . . £200

The Witch's Head, Hurst & Blackett, 1885 [1884] (3 vols) £6,000
ditto, Appleton (U.S.), 1885 . . . . . . £200
King Solomon's Mines, Cassell, 1885 (first issue with 'Bamamgwato' for 'Bamangwato' on line 14, p.10: 'twins to live' for 'twins live' line 27, p.122 and 'wrod' for 'word' line 29, p.307. Ads dated '5G.8.85'). £5,000
ditto, Cassell, 1885 (second issue, uncorrected, with ads dated '5G.10.85') £2,500
ditto, Cassell (U.S.), 1885 (third issue of English sheets, with no ads) £2,000
She, Harper (U.S.), 1886 (wraps) £1,000
ditto, Longmans, 1887 (first issue with 'Godness me' in line 38, p.269). £600
Jess, Smith, Elder, & Co., 1887 . . . . . £300
ditto, George Munro (U.S.), 1887 (wraps) . . £200
ditto, Harper (U.S.), 1887 . . . . . . £150
Allan Quartermain, Longmans, 1887 (first issue with no footnote on frontispiece). £450
ditto, Longmans, 1887 (112 large paper copies) £1,500
ditto, Harper (U.S.), 1887. . . . . . . £175
ditto, Harper (U.S.), 1887 (wraps) £175
Maiwa's Revenge, Longmans, 1888. . . . . £125
ditto, Harper (U.S.), 1888. . . . . . . £100
Mr Meeson's Will, Spencer Blackett, 1888 (first issue with 'Johnson' for 'Johnston' in line 1, p.284, catalogue dated October 1888). £300
ditto, Harper (U.S.), 1888. . . . . . . £125
Colonel Quaritch V.C., Longmans, 1888 (3 vols) £600
ditto, Lovell (U.S.), 1888 . . . . £50
Cleopatra, Longmans, 1889 (catalogue dated January 1889 . . . . £200
ditto, Longmans, 1889 (50 large paper copies) . £2,000
ditto, Harper (U.S.), 1889 (wraps) £175
Allan's Wife, Spencer Blackett, 1889 . . . £200
ditto, Longmans, 1889 (100 large paper copies) £2,000
Beatrice, Longman's, 1890 . . . . . . £70
ditto, George Munro (U.S.), 1890 . . . . £50
The World's Desire, Longmans, 1890 (with Andrew Lang). £35
ditto, Harper (U.S.), 1890. . . . . . . £35
Eric Brighteyes, Longmans, 1891 . . . . £40
ditto, Harper (U.S.), 1891. . . . . . . £35
Nada the Lily, Longmans, 1892 . . . . . £40
ditto, Longmans(U.S.), 1892 . . . . . . £35
Montezuma's Daughter, Longmans (U.S.), 1893 £40
ditto, Longmans, 1893 . . . . £35
The People of the Mist, Longmans, 1894 . . £75
ditto, Longmans (U.S.), 1894. . . . . . £40
Joan Haste, Longmans, 1895 . . . . . £70
ditto, Longmans (U.S.), 1895. . . . . . £40
Heart of the World, Longmans (U.S.), 1895 . £70
ditto, Longmans, 1896 . . . . £70
The Wizard, Arrowsmith, 1896 (wraps). . . £60
ditto, Longmans (U.S.), 1896 . . . . . £50
Doctor Therne, Longmans, 1898 . . . . £50
ditto, Longmans (U.S.), 1898 . . . . . £80
Allan the Hunter, Lothrop (U.S.), 1898. . . £125

Swallow, Longmans, 1899	£50
ditto, Longmans (U.S.), 1899	£80
Black Heart and White Heart, Longmans, 1900	£100
ditto, as *Elissa*, Longmans (U.S.), 1900. . .	£80
Lysbeth, Longmans, 1901	£50
ditto, Longmans (U.S.), 1901	£50
Pearl-Maiden, Longmans, 1903	£40
ditto, Longmans (U.S.), 1903	£40
Stella Fregelius, Longmans (U.S.), 1903 . .	£40
ditto, Longmans, 1904	£40
The Brethren, Cassell, 1904	£40
ditto, McClure, Phillips (U.S.), 1904 . . .	£40
Ayesha, Ward Lock, 1905	£60
ditto, Doubleday (U.S.), 1905	£40
The Way of the Spirit, Hutchinson, 1906 . .	£40
Benita, Cassell, 1906	£40
ditto, as *The Spirit of Bambatse*, Longmans (U.S.), 1906	£40
Fair Margaret, Hutchinson, 1907	£40
ditto, as *Margaret*, Longmans (U.S.), 1907 .	£40
The Ghost Kings, Cassell, 1908	£40
ditto, as *The Lady of the Heavens*, Lovell (U.S.), 1908	£40
The Yellow God, Cupples & Leon (U.S.), 1908	£40
ditto, Cassell, 1909	£40
The Lady of Blossholme, Hodder & Stoughton, 1909	£50
Morning Star, Cassell, 1910	£40
ditto, Longmans (U.S.), 1910.	£30
Queen Sheba's Ring, Eveleigh Nash, 1910. .	£300
ditto, Doubleday Page & Co (U.S.), 1910 .	£30
Red Eve, Hodder & Stoughton, 1911 . . .	£200
ditto, Doubleday (U.S.), 1911	£30
The Mahatma and The Hare, Longmans, 1911	£60
ditto, Henry Holt & Co (U.S.), 1911 . . .	£30
Marie, Cassell, 1912	£30
ditto, Longmans (U.S.), 1912.	£30
Child of Storm, Cassell, 1913	£30
ditto, Longmans (U.S.), 1913.	£30
The Wanderer's Necklace, Cassell, 1914 . .	£50
ditto, Longmans (U.S.), 1914.	£30
The Holy Flower, Ward Lock, 1915. . . .	£30
ditto, as *Allan and The Holy Flower*, Longmans (U.S.), 1915	£30
The Ivory Child, Cassell, 1916	£40
ditto, Longmans (U.S.), 1916.	£30
Finished, Ward Lock, 1917	£40
ditto, Longmans (U.S.), 1917.	£30
Love Eternal, Cassell, 1918	£30
ditto, Longmans (U.S.), 1918.	£30
Moon of Israel, Murray, 1918	£50
ditto, Longmans (U.S.), 1918.	£30
When the World Shook, Cassell, 1919 . . .	£40
ditto, Longmans (U.S.), 1919.	£30
The Ancient Allan, Cassell, 1920	£250/£35
ditto, Longmans (U.S.), 1920.	£250/£35
Smith and the Pharaohs, Arrowsmith, 1920	£300/£75
ditto, Longmans (U.S.), 1920.	£250/£35

She and Allan, Longmans (U.S.), 1921 . .	£125/£45
ditto, Hutchinson, 1921	£275/£65
The Virgin of the Sun, Cassell, 1922 . .	£100/£35
ditto, Doubleday (U.S.), 1922	£100/£25
Wisdom's Daughter, Hutchinson, 1923 . .	£200/£35
ditto, Doubleday (U.S.), 1923	£200/£35
Heu-Heu, Hutchinson, 1924	£150/£45
ditto, Doubleday (U.S.), 1924	£150/£35
Queen of the Dawn, Doubleday Page (U.S.), 1925.	£150/£35
ditto, Hutchinson, 1925	£150/£35
The Treasure of the Lake, Hutchinson, 1926	£150/£45
ditto, Doubleday (U.S.), 1926	£125/£25
Allan and the Ice Gods, Doubleday Page (U.S.), 1927	£255/£25
ditto, Hutchinson, 1927	£350/£45
Mary of Marion Isle, Hutchinson, 1929. .	£150/£45
ditto, as *Marion Isle*, Doubleday (U.S.), 1929	£100/£25
Belshazzar, Stanley Paul, 1930	£400/£55
ditto, Doubleday (U.S.), 1930	£250/£25

Non Fiction

Cetywayo and His White Neighbours, Trubner, 1882	£1,250
An Heroic Effort, 1893 (wraps)	£35
Church and State, 1895 (wraps)	£30
East Norfolk Representation, 1895 (wraps) .	£30
Lord Kimberly in Norfolk, 1895 (wraps) . .	£30
Speeches of the Earl of Iddesleigh, NSPCC, 1895 (wraps)	£30
A Visit to Victoria Hospital, 1897 (wraps) . .	£30
A Farmer's Year, Longmans, 1899	£100
ditto, Longmans, 1899 (100 numbered large paper copies)	£300
The Last Boer War, Kegan Paul, 1899 . . .	£125
ditto, as *A History of The Transvaal*, Kegan Paul (U.S.), 1899	£125
A Winter Pilgrimage, Longmans, 1901 . . .	£200
Rural England, Longmans, 1902 (2 vols) . .	£175
Rural Denmark, Longmans, 1902	£200
Rural England, Royal Institution of Great Britain, 1903 (wraps)	£30
A Gardener's Year, Longmans, 1905 . . .	£100
The Poor and the Land, Longmans, 1905 . .	£125
The Real Wealth of England, Dr Barnados, 1908 (wraps)	£25
The Royal Commission on Coast Erosion, HMSO, 1907-1911 (3 vols, wraps)	£45
Regeneration, Longmans, 1910	£30
Letters to the Right Honorable Lewis Harcourt, HMSO, 1913-1914 (2 vols, wraps). . . .	£50
A Call to Arms, 1914 (wraps)	£25
The After-War Settlement and Employment of Ex-Servicemen, Saint Catherine Press, 1916 (wraps)	£30
The Salvation Army, 1920 (wraps)	£30
The Days of My Life, Longmans, 1926 (2 vols)	£350/£150

ditto, Longmans (U.S.), 1926. . . . £250/£125
A Note on Religion, Longmans, 1927 (wraps) . £25
The Private Diaries of Sir H. Rider Haggard 1914-1925, Cassell, 1980 . . . . £15/£5
ditto, Stein & Day (U.S.), 1980 . . . . . £15/£5

KATHLEEN HALE
(b.1898 d.2000)

An artist whose reputation rests with books about a ginger tom cat, Orlando.

Books Written and Illustrated by Hale
Orlando the Marmalade Cat: A Camping Holiday, Country Life, [1938] (boards with d/w) . £200/£75
ditto, Scribner's (U.S.), [1938] (boards with d/w) . .
. . . . £175/£65
Orlando the Marmalade Cat: A Trip Abroad, Country Life, 1939 (boards with d/w) . . . £150/£75
Orlando's Evening Out, Puffin, [1941] (boards, no d/w) £50
ditto, Puffin, [1941] (wraps) £20
Orlando's Home Life, Puffin, [1942] (boards, no d/w)
. . . . £50
ditto, Puffin, [1942] (wraps) £20
ditto, Coward-McCann (U.S.), [1953] . £100/£35
Orlando the Marmalade Cat Buys A Farm, Country Life, 1942 (card covers). £150
Orlando the Marmalade Cat: His Silver Wedding, Country Life, 1944 (card covers) £150
Orlando the Marmalade Cat Becomes A Doctor, Country Life, 1944 (card covers) £150
Orlando's Invisible Pyjamas, Transatlantic Arts, [1947] (wraps) £25
Henrietta the Faithful Hen, Transatlantic Arts. [1947] (boards) £75
ditto, Coward-McCann (U.S.), [1953] . . £75/£35
Orlando the Marmalade Cat Keeps A Dog, Country Life, [1949] . . . . £300/£125
Orlando The Judge, Murray, [1950] (wraps) . £25
Orlando the Marmalade Cat: A Seaside Holiday, Country Life, 1952 . . . . £300/£125
Orlando's Zoo, Murray, [1950] (wraps). . . £25
Orlando's Country Life: A Peep Show Book, Chatto & Windus, 1950. . . . . £150
Puss in Boots: A Peep Show Book, Chatto & Windus, 1951 . . . . £150
ditto, Houghton Mifflin (U.S.), [c.1951]. . . £150
Manda the Jersey Calf, Murray, 1952 (boards) £30
ditto, as *Manda*, Coward-McCann (U.S.), [1953] . .
. . . . £75/£35
Orlando the Marmalade Cat: The Frisky Housewife, Country Life, 1956 (boards) £75
Orlando's Magic Carpet, Murray, [1958] . £75/£35
Orlando the Marmalade Cat Buys A Cottage, Country Life, 1963 (boards) £50
Orlando and the Three Graces, Murray, 1965 £50/£25

Orlando the Marmalade Cat Goes to the Moon, Murray, 1968. . . . . £45/£20
Orlando the Marmalade Cat and the Water Cats, Cape, 1972 (laminated boards, no d/w) . £40
Henrietta's Magic Egg, Allen & Unwin, 1973 (laminated boards, no d/w) £25

Other Books Illustrated by Hale
I Don't Mix Much With Fairies, by Molly Harrower, Eyre & Spottiswoode, 1928 . . . . £75/£35
Plain Jane, by Molly Harrower, Eyre & Spottiswoode, 1929 . . . . £75/£35
ditto, Coward-McCann (U.S.), 1929 . . £75/£35
Basil Seal Rides Again, by Evelyn Waugh, Chapman & Hall, 1963 (750 numbered copies signed by author)
. . . . £250/£100
ditto, Little, Brown (U.S.), 1963 (1,000 numbered copies signed by author, glassine d/w) . £225/£175

RADCLYFFE HALL
(b.1880 d.1943)

Hall's notoriety stems from the publication in 1928, and subsequent suppression in Britain for obscenity, of *The Well of Loneliness*. The book, a sympathetic study of lesbian love, was not republished in Britain until 1949.

Novels
The Forge, Arrowsmith, 1924 . . . £175/£50
The Unlit Lamp, Cassell, 1924 . . . £175/£50
ditto, Cape & Smith (U.S.), [1929] . . £100/£25
A Saturday Life, Arrowsmith, 1925 . . . £100/£30
ditto, Cape & Smith (U.S.), [1930] . . £75/£20
Adam's Breed, Cassell, 1926. . . . £100/£30
ditto, Cape & Smith (U.S.), [1929] . . £45/£10
The Well of Loneliness, Cape, 1928 (first issue with 'whip', not 'whips', on p. 50, line 13) . £450/£75
ditto, Pegasus Press (Paris), 1928 . . £125/£45
ditto, Covici Friede (U.S.), 1928 (500 numbered copies, glassine d/w, slipcase) . . . . £250/£175
ditto, Covici Friede (U.S.), 1929 (225 signed copies, 2 vols, slipcase) £250
ditto, Cape, 1932 (172 signed large paper copies) £250
The Master of the House, Cape, 1932 . £50/£15
ditto, Cape, 1932 (172 signed, numbered copies, slipcase) . . . . £250/£200
ditto, Cape & Ballou (U.S.), 1932 . . £45/£15
The Sixth Beatitude, Heinemann, 1936 . £45/£10
ditto, Heinemann, 1936 (125 signed, numbered copies, slipcase) . . . . £200/£150
ditto, Harcourt Brace (U.S.), [c.1936] . . £45/£10

Short Stories
Mrs Ogilvy Finds Herself, Heinemann, 1934 £75/£20
ditto, Harcourt Brace (U.S.), 1934 . . . £45/£10

Poetry

Twixt Earth and Stars, Bumpus, 1906 (wraps) .   £200
A Sheaf of Verses, Bumpus, 1908 (wraps) .   .   £200
Poems of Past and Present, Chapman & Hall, 1910   .
.   .   .   .   £150
Songs of Three Counties, Chapman & Hall, 1913   £60
The Forgotten Island, Chapman & Hall, 1915 .   £60

Others

Your John: Letters of Radclyffe Hall, New York
Univ. (U.S.), 1997 .   .   .   . £15/£5

PATRICK HAMILTON
(b.1904 d.1962)

Born in Sussex, Hamilton was a typically English
writer, relishing the art of understatement.

Novels

Monday Morning, Constable, 1925 .   .   . £250/£45
ditto, Houghton Mifflin (U.S.), 1925 .   . £250/£40
Craven House, Constable, 1926 .   .   .   . £200/£35
ditto, Houghton Mifflin (U.S.), 1927 .   . £200/£25
ditto, Constable, 1943 (revised edition) .   . £75/£20
Twopence Coloured, Constable, 1928 .   . £200/£35
ditto, Houghton Mifflin (U.S.), 1928 .   . £200/£30
The Midnight Bell: A Love Story, Constable, 1929
.   .   .   . £200/£25
ditto, Little, Brown (U.S.), 1930 .   .   . £200/£25
The Siege of Pleasure, Constable, 1932 .   £100/£25
ditto, Little, Brown (U.S.), 1932 .   .   . £100/£20
The Plains of Cement, Constable, 1934. .   £100/£25
ditto, Little, Brown (U.S.), 1935 .   .   . £100/£20
*Twenty Thousand Streets Under The Sky: A London
Trilogy*, Constable, 1935 .   .   .   .   . £75/£20
Impromptu in Moribundia, Constable, 1939 £200/£65
*Hangover Square, or The Man with Two Minds: A
Story of Darkest Earls Court*, Constable, 1941 .   .
.   .   .   . £1,000/£75
ditto, Random House (U.S.), 1942 .   .   . £100/£15
The Slaves of Solitude, Constable, 1947 .   £50/£15
ditto, as *Riverside*, Random House (U.S.), 1947 .   .
.   .   .   . £45/£15
The West Pier, Constable, 1951 .   .   .   . £45/£15
ditto, Doubleday (U.S.), 1952 .   .   .   . £45/£15
Mr Stimpson and Mr Gorse, Constable, 1953 .   .   .
.   .   .   . £150/£15
Unknown Assailant, Constable, 1955 .   . £100/£15

Plays

Rope: A Play, with a Preface on Thrillers, Constable,
1929 .   .   .   . £150/£30
Gaslight: A Victorian Thriller, Constable, 1939
(wraps) £25
ditto, as *Angel Street*, French (U.S.), 1942 (wraps) £15

*Money With Menaces and To The Public Danger:
Two Radio Plays*, Constable, 1939 (wraps) .   £15
This Is Impossible, French, 1942 (wraps) .   . £15
The Duke in Darkness, Constable, 1943 (wraps) £45
The Man Upstairs, Constable, 1954 .   .   . £25/£10

DASHIELL HAMMETT
(b.1894 d.1961)

American creator of tough detective fiction, his best-
known character being the private eye 'Sam Spade'.

Novels

Red Harvest, Knopf (U.S.), 1929 .   £12,500/£1,000
ditto, Knopf/Cassell, 1929 .   .   .   . £3,000/£350
The Dain Curse, Knopf (U.S.), 1929 . £12,500/£750
ditto, Knopf/Cassell, 1930 .   .   . £3,000/£350
The Maltese Falcon, Knopf (U.S.), 1930 (first issue
d/w without reviews for *Maltese Falcon*) .   .   .   .
.   .   .   . £25,000/£1,500
ditto, Knopf (U.S.), 1930 (second issue d/w with
reviews) .   .   .   .   .   . £10,000/£1,500
ditto, Knopf/Cassell, 1930 .   .   .   . £5,000/£250
The Glass Key, Knopf/Cassell, 1931. .   £4,000/£250
ditto, Knopf (U.S.), 1931 .   .   .   . £4,000/£250
The Thin Man, Knopf (U.S.), 1934 .   . £2,500/£175
ditto, Barker, 1934. .   .   .   .   . £2,000/£150
$106,000 Blood Money, Spivak (U.S.), 1943 (wraps) .
.   .   .   . £150
ditto, as *Blood Money*, World (U.S.), 1943 .   £30/£10
ditto, as *The Big Knock-over*, Spivak (U.S.), 1948
(wraps) £35

Short Stories

The Adventures of Sam Spade and Other Stories,
Spivak (U.S.), 1944 (wraps) £100
ditto, as *They Can Only Hang You Once*, Spivak
(U.S.), 1949 (wraps). £75
The Continental Op, Spivak (U.S.), 1945 (wraps) £75
The Return of the Continental Op, Spivak (U.S.),
1945 (wraps) £50
Hammett Homicides, Spivak (U.S.), 1946 (wraps) £50
Dead Yellow Women, Spivak (U.S.), 1947 (wraps) £50
Nightmare Town, Spivak (U.S.), 1948 (wraps). .   £50
The Creeping Siamese, Spivak (U.S.), 1950 (wraps) .
.   .   .   . £35
Woman in the Dark, Spivak (U.S.), 1951 (wraps) £35
ditto, Knopf (U.S.), 1988 .   .   .   .   . £15/£5
ditto, Headline, 1988 .   .   .   .   .   . £15/£5
A Man Named Thin and Other Stories, Ferman (U.S.),
1962 .   .   .   . £35
The Continental Op, Random House (U.S.), 1974 .   .
.   .   .   . £15/£5
ditto, Macmillan, 1975 .   .   .   .   . £15/£5

Omnibus Editions

Dashiell Hammet Omnibus, Knopf (U.S.), 1935 . . . . £450/£50

The Complete Dashiell Hammet, Knopf (U.S.), 1942 . . . . £200/£35

Dashiell Hammet's Mystery Omnibus, World (U.S.), 1944 . . . . £45/£10

The Dashiell Hammet Omnibus, Cassell, 1950 . . . . £75/£15

The Novels of Dashiell Hammet, Knopf (U.S.), 1965 . . . . £40/£10

The Big Knockover: Selected Stories and Short Novels, Random House (U.S.), 1966 (edited by Lillian Hellman) . . . . £10/£5

ditto, as *The Hammet Story Omnibus*, Cassell, 1966 . . . . £15/£5

Others

Creeps by Night: Chills and Thrills, John Day (U.S.), 1931 (selected by Hammett) . . . . £200/£50

ditto, as *Modern Tales of Horror*, Gollancz, 1932 . . . . £200/£50

Secret Agent X-9, Book One, David McKay (U.S.), 1943 (may have been at least partly ghost-written, printed boards, illustrations by Alex Raymond, wraps) £750

Secret Agent X-9, Book Two, David McKay (U.S.), 1943 (may have been at least partly ghost-written, printed boards, illustrations by Alex Raymond, wraps) £750

The Battle of the Aleutians, Western Defense Command (U.S.), 1944 (with Robert Colodny and Harry Fletcher, wraps) £150

THOMAS HARDY
(b.1840 d.1928)

Acknowledged as one of the great novelists, Hardy was also a prolific poet. Much of his writing is set in his native Dorset, fictionalised as 'Wessex'.

Novels

Desperate Remedies, Tinsley Bros., 1871 (3 vols, red cloth, anonymous) £20,000

ditto, Tinsley Bros., 1874 (1 vol, various coloured cloths) £1,000

ditto, Holt (U.S.), 1874 (1 vol.) £500

Under the Greenwood Tree, Tinsley Bros., 1872 (2 vols, green cloth, 'By the author of Desperate Remedies') £10,000

ditto, Tinsley Bros, 1872 (2 vols, rebound) . £1,500

ditto, Tinsley Bros., 1873 (1 vol.) £1,000

ditto, Holt (U.S.), 1874 (1 vol.) £400

A Pair of Blue Eyes, Tinsley Bros., 1873 (first issue, green cloth, 'c' missing in 'clouds' last line p.5, vol.2, 3 vols). £10,000

ditto, Tinsley Bros., 1873 (second issue, blue cloth, 3 vols) £2,500

ditto, Tinsley Bros., 1873 (3 vols, rebound). . £1,500

ditto, Holt (U.S.), 1873 (1 vol.) £500

ditto, Henry S. King, 1877 (1 vol.) £300

Far from the Madding Crowd, Holt (U.S.), 1874 (1 vol, cream cloth) £1,250

ditto, Smith, Elder, 1874 (2 vols, green cloth) £15,000

ditto, Smith, Elder, 1874 (2 vols, rebound) . £3,000

ditto, Smith, Elder, 1875 (2 vols). £1,000

ditto, Smith, Elder, 1877 (1 vol.) £200

The Hand of Ethelberta, Smith, Elder, 1876 (red/brown cloth, 2 vols, 11 illustrations by George du Maurier) £5,000

ditto, Smith, Elder, 1876 (2 vols, rebound) . £1,000

ditto, Holt (U.S.), 1876 (1 vol.) £300

ditto, Smith, Elder, 1877 (1 vol., 6 illustrations by George du Maurier) £200

The Return of the Native, Smith, Elder, 1878 (brown cloth, 3 vols) £5,000

ditto, Smith, Elder, 1878 (3 vols, rebound) . £1,000

ditto, Holt (U.S.), 1878 (1 vol.) £300

ditto, Kegan Paul, 1880 [1879] (1 vol.) . . . £200

The Trumpet-Major, Smith, Elder, 1880 (decorated red cloth, 3 vols) £10,000

ditto, Smith, Elder, 1880 (3 vols, rebound) . £1,000

ditto, Holt (U.S.), 1880 (1 vol.) £300

ditto, Samson Low, 1881 (1 vol.) £200

A Laodicean, Holt (U.S.), 1881 (1 vol.). . . £450

ditto, Samson Low, 1881 (first issue without word 'or' on half-title of vol.1, 3 vols, slate cloth) . £5,000

ditto, Samson Low, 1881 (first issue rebound, 3 vols) £750

ditto, Samson Low, 1881 (second issue with word 'or' on half-title of vol.1, 3 vols, slate cloth) . £2,000

ditto, Samson Low, 1882 (1 vol) £150

Two on a Tower, Samson Low, 1882 (3 vols, green cloth) £3,000

ditto, Samson Low, 1882 (3 vols, rebound). . £750

ditto, Holt (U.S.), 1882 (1 vol.) £250

ditto, Samson Low, 1883 (3 vols) £1,000

ditto, Samson Low, 1883 (1 vol.) £150

The Mayor of Casterbridge, Smith Elder, 1886 (2 vols) £10,000

ditto, Smith Elder, 1886 (2 vols rebound) . £2,000

ditto, Holt (U.S.), 1886 (1 vol., wraps) . . £600

ditto, Samson Low, 1887 (1 vol.) £250

The Woodlanders, Macmillan, 1887 (first binding in smooth green cloth with 2 rule border on back, first issue with ad leaf at back of vol.1, 3 vols) . £3,000

ditto, Macmillan, 1887 (first issue, 3 vols, rebound) £750

ditto, Macmillan, 1887 (second binding in pebbled green cloth with 1 rule border on back, second issue without ad leaf at back of vol.1, 3 vols) . £2,000

ditto, Harper (U.S.), 1887 (1 vol.) £250

ditto, Macmillan, 1887 (1 vol.) £100

Tess of the D'Urbervilles, Osgood McIlvaine, 1891 (3 vols) £8,000

ditto, Osgood McIlvaine, 1891 (3 vols rebound) £2,500

ditto, Harper (U.S.), 1892 (1 vol.) £500
ditto, Osgood McIlvaine, 1892 (3 vols) . . . £1,000
ditto, Osgood McIlvaine, 1892 ('fifth' [third] edition, 1 vol.) £250
Jude the Obscure, Osgood McIlvaine, 1896 [1895] (Volume VIII in the 'Wessex Novels' series, 1 vol) .
. . . . £300
ditto, Harper (U.S.), 1896 (1 vol.) £100
The Well-Beloved, Osgood McIlvaine, 1897 (Volume XVII in the 'Wessex Novels' series, 1 vol) . £125
ditto, Harper (U.S.), 1897 (1 vol.) £125

Short Stories

Fellow-Townsmen, Harper (U.S.), 1880 (cloth) £1,000
ditto, Harper (U.S.), 1880 (cloth). £500
ditto, Harper (U.S.), 1880 (wraps) £500
The Romantic Adventures of a Milkmaid, Munro's (U.S.), 1883 (wraps) £1,000
Wessex Tales, Macmillan, 1888 (2 vols) . . £1,500
ditto, Macmillan, 1889 (1 vol.) £75
A Group of Noble Dames, Osgood McIlvaine, 1891 .
. . . . £350
ditto, Harper (U.S.), 1891. . . . . £100
Life's Little Ironies, Osgood McIlvaine, 1894 . £300
ditto, Macmillan (U.S.), 1894 . . . . . . £75
A Changed Man and Other Tales, Macmillan, 1913 .
. . . . £50
ditto, Harper (U.S.), 1913. . . . . £75
Old Mrs Chundle, Crosby Gaige (U.S.), 1929 (755 numbered copies, glassine d/w). . . . £150/£125
Our Exploits at West Poley, O.U.P., 1952 . . £20/£5
ditto, O.U.P., 1952 (1050 numbered copies) £100/£65

Collection Editions

Wessex Novels Edition, Osgood McIlvaine, 1895-97 (18 vols) . . . . . . £2,750 the set, £75 each
The Writings, Autograph Edition, Harper & Bros, [1911] (153 signed copies, 20 vols) . £3,000 the set
Wessex Edition, Macmillan, 1912-31 (24 vols; maroon cloth) . . . . . £1,750 the set, £30 each
Melstock Edition, Macmillan, 1919-20 (37 vols, limited to 500 sets, signed by the author) . £5,000 the set

Magazine Serialisations

A Pair of Blue Eyes, Tinsley's Magazine, Sept 1872-July 1873 . . . . £450 (for set)
Far From the Madding Crowd, Cornhill Magazine, Jan-Sept 1874 . . . . £400 (for set)
The Hand of Ethelberta, Cornhill Magazine, July 1875-May 1876 . . . . £400 (for set)
The Return of the Native, Belgravia, Jan-December 1878 . . . . £400 (for set)
The Trumpet Major, Good Words, Jan-December 1880 . . . . £400 (for set)
A Laodicean, Harper's, December 1880-December 1881 . . . . £400 (for set)
Two on a Tower, Atlantic Monthly, May-December 1882 . . . . £400 (for set)
The Mayor of Casterbridge, Graphic, June 1885-May 1886 . . . . £500 (for set)

The Woodlanders, Macmillan's Magazine, May 1886-April 1887 . . . . £400 (for set)
Tess of the D'Urbervilles, Graphic, July-December 1891 . . . . £600 (for set)
Jude the Obscure, Harper's, December 1894-November 1895 (first instalment as 'The Simpleton', thereafter 'Hearts Insurgent') . . . £300 (for set)
The Well-Beloved, as **The Pursuit of the Well-Beloved**, Illustrated London News, October-December 1892 . . . . £250 (for set)

Poetry

Wessex Poems and Other Verses, Harper (U.S. & U.K.), 1898 . . . . £500
ditto, Harper (U.S. & U.K.), 1898 (presentation binding) £1,500
Poems Of The Past And The Present, Harper (U.S. & U.K.), 1902 . . . . £500
ditto, Harper (U.S. & U.K.), 1902 (presentation binding) £1,500
The Dynasts, Macmillan, 1904, 1906 [1905], 1908 (3 vols) £600
ditto, Macmillan, 1910 (1 vol.) £150
ditto, Macmillan, 1927 (525 signed large paper copies, 3 vols, tissue d/w, slipcase) . . . . . £600/£400
Time's Laughingstocks and Other Verses, Macmillan, 1909 . . . . £150
Song of the Soldiers, privately printed by Clement Shorter, 1914 (single sheet, 12 copies). . . £750
ditto, privately printed at Hove by E. Williams, 1914 (single sheet) £100
The Oxen, privately printed at Hove by E. Williams, 1915 (wraps) £150
Selected Poems, Macmillan, 1916 . . . . £150
ditto, Warner, 1921 . . . . £100
Moments of Vision and Miscellaneous Verses, Macmillan, 1917. . . . . £100
Collected Poems, Macmillan, 1919 . . . . £125
Late Lyrics and Earlier with Many Other Verses, Macmillan, 1922 . . . . £125/£50
The Famous Tragedy of the Queen of Cornwall, Macmillan, 1923 . . . . £200/£75
ditto, Macmillan, 1923 (1,000 numberd copies, no d/w)
. . . . £75
Human Shows, Far Phantasies, Songs, and Trifles, Macmillan, 1925 . . . . £150/£65
ditto, Macmillan (U.S.), 1925 (100 numbered copies, no d/w) £150
ditto, Macmillan (U.S.), 1925 . . . . £100/£45
Yuletide in a Younger World, Faber, 1927 (wraps)
. . . . £250
ditto, Rudge (U.S.), 1927 (27 copyright copies, wraps)
. . . . £400
Winter Words In Various Moods and Metres, Macmillan, 1928 . . . . £75/£35
ditto, Macmillan (U.S.), 1928 (500 copies, slipcase) .
. . . . £150/£125

CYRIL HARE
(b.1900 d.1958)

Hare was the main pseudonym of crime novelist Alfred Gordon Clark.

Novels

Tenant For Death, Faber, 1937	£200/£25
ditto, Dodd, Mead (U.S.), 1937	£200/£25
Death Is No Sportsman, Faber, 1938 . .	£200/£25
Suicide Excepted, Faber, 1939	£225/£25
ditto, Macmillan (U.S.), 1954	£45/£10
Tragedy At Law, Faber, 1942	£75/£15
ditto, Harcourt (U.S.), 1943	£60/£15
With a Bare Bodkin, Faber, 1946 . . .	£65/£10
When the Wind Blows, Faber, 1949 . .	£65/£10
ditto, as *The Wind Blows Death*, Little, Brown (U.S.), 1950	£65/£10
An English Murder, Faber, 1951 . . .	£65/£10
ditto, Little, Brown (U.S.), 1951	£65/£10
ditto, as *The Christmas Murder*, Spivak (U.S.), 1953	£50/£10
The Yew Tree's Shade, Faber, 1954 . .	£40/£10
ditto, as *Death Walks the Woods*, Little, Brown (U.S.), 1954	£40/£10
He Should Have Died Hereafter, Faber, 1958	£40/£10
ditto, as *Untimely Death*, Macmillan (U.S.), 1958	£40/£10

Short Stories

Best Detective Stories of Cyril Hare, Faber, 1959	£40/£5
ditto, Walker (U.S.), 1961	£25/£5
ditto, as *Death Among Friends*, Perennial (U.S.), 1984 (wraps)	£5

Children's Titles

The Magic Bottle, Faber, 1946	£45/£15

ROBERT HARRIS
(b.1953)

The best-selling author of thrillers, his non fiction books include *Selling Hitler*, an account of the forging of Hitler's diaries.

Novels

Fatherland, Hutchinson, 1992	£60/£10
ditto, Random House (U.S.), 1992 . . .	£35/£5
Enigma, Hutchinson, 1995	£40/£5
ditto, Random House (U.S.), 1995 . . .	£25/£5
Archangel, Hutchinson, 1998	£15/£5
ditto, Random House (U.S.), 1999 . . .	£10/£5

Non Fiction

A Higher Form of Killing, Chatto & Windus, 1982 (with Jeremy Paxman)	£35/£5

ditto, Hill & Wang (U.S.), 1982	£20/£5
Gotcha!: The Media, the Government, and the Falklands Crisis, Faber, 1983 (wraps) . . .	£10
The Making of Neil Kinnock, Faber, 1984 .	£10/£5
Selling Hitler, Faber, 1986	£20/£5
ditto, Pantheon (U.S.), 1986	£20/£5
Good and Faithful Servant: The Unauthorized Biography of Bernard Ingham, Faber, 1990 .	£10/£5

THOMAS HARRIS
(b.1940)

Famous since the release of the film of *The Silence of the Lambs*, aficionados also recommend that *Red Dragon* should not be overlooked.

Novels

Black Sunday, Putnam (U.S.), 1975 . . .	£125/£15
ditto, Hodder & Stoughton, 1975. . . .	£75/£10
Red Dragon, Putnam (U.S.), 1981 . . .	£50/£10
ditto, Bodley Head, 1982	£30/£10
The Silence of the Lambs, St Martin's Press (U.S.), 1988	£75/£10
ditto, Heinemann, 1988	£50/£10
Hannibal, Delacorte Press (U.S.), 1999 . .	£15/£5
ditto, Heinemann, 1988	£10/£5

L.P. HARTLEY
(b.1895 d.1972)

Novelist and short story writer, Leslie Poles Hartley's work won a number of awards, but he is best known for *The Go-Between*, an evocative portrayal of a small boy's view of Edwardian England, which won the Heinemann Foundation Award.

Novels

Simonetta Perkins, Putnam, 1925 . . .	£200/£50
ditto, Putnam (U.S.), 1925	£175/£30
The Shrimp and the Anemone, Putnam, 1944	£100/£25
ditto, as *The West Window*, Putnam (U.S.), 1945	£65/£15
The Sixth Heaven, Putnam, 1946 . . .	£45/£5
ditto, Doubleday (U.S.), 1947	£35/£5
Eustace and Hilda, Putnam, 1947 . . .	£35/£5
ditto, British Book Centre (U.S.), 1958 . .	£25/£5
The Boat, Putnam, 1950	£50/£10
ditto, Doubleday (U.S.), 1950	£45/£10
My Fellow Devils, Barrie, 1951	£30/£5
ditto, British Book Centre (U.S.), 1959 . .	£25/£5
The Go-Between, Hamilton, 1953 . . .	£45/£10
ditto, Knopf (U.S.), 1954	£30/£5
A Perfect Woman, Hamilton, 1955 . . .	£25/£5
ditto, Knopf (U.S.), 1956	£25/£5

The Hireling, Hamilton, 1957 . . . . . £25/£5
ditto, Rinehart (U.S.), 1958 . . . . . . £25/£5
Facial Justice, Hamilton, 1960 . . . . £45/£10
ditto, Doubleday (U.S.), 1961 . . . . . £25/£5
The Brickfield, Hamilton, 1964 . . . . . £20/£5
The Betrayal, Hamilton, 1966 . . . . . £15/£5
Poor Clare, Hamilton, 1968 . . . . . . £15/£5
The Love-Adept, Hamilton, 1969 . . . . £15/£5
My Sister's Keeper, Hamilton, 1970. . . . £15/£5
The Harness Room, Hamilton, 1971 . . . £15/£5
The Will and the Way, Hamilton, 1973 . . . £10/£5

Short Stories
Night Fears and Other Stories, Putnam, 1924 . . .
. . . . £350/£75
The Killing Bottle, Putnam, 1931 . . . £200/£45
The Travelling Grave, Arkham House (U.S.), 1948 .
. . . . £50/£15
ditto, Barrie, 1951 . . . . £75/£15
A White Wand and Other Stories, Hamilton, 1954. .
. . . . £50/£10
Two for the River, Hamilton, 1961 . . . £35/£10
The Collected Stories, Hamilton, 1968 . . . £15/£5
ditto, Horizon Press (U.S.), 1969. . . . . £15/£5
Mrs Carteret Receives, Hamilton, 1971 . . . £15/£5
The Collected Macabre Stories, Tartarus Press, 2001 .
. . . . £35/£10

Others
The Novelist's Responsibility, Hamilton, 1967 £25/£5

JOHN HARVEY
(b.1938)

A highly respected British author of crime novels, Harvey has also written novels under various pseudonyms such as 'John B. Harvey', 'John J. McLaglen', 'William S. Brady', 'J.D. Sandon', 'L.J. Coburn', 'J.B. Dancer', 'William M. James', 'John Hart' and 'Jon Barton'.)

'Resnick' Novels
Lonely Hearts, Viking, 1989 . . . . . £150/£25
ditto, Holt (U.S.), 1989 . . . . . . £75/£15
Rough Treatment, Viking, 1990. . . . £45/£10
ditto, Holt (U.S.), 1990 . . . . . . £30/£10
Cutting Edge, Viking, 1991 . . . . . £45/£10
ditto, Holt (U.S.), 1991 . . . . . . £30/£10
Off Minor, Viking, 1992 . . . . . . £85/£25
ditto, Holt (U.S.), 1992 . . . . . . £30/£5
Wasted Years, Viking, 1993 . . . . . £45/£5
ditto, Holt (U.S.), 1993 . . . . . . £30/£5
Cold Light, Heinemann, 1994 . . . . £15/£5
ditto, Holt (U.S.), 1994 . . . . . . £15/£5
Living Proof, Heinemann, 1995 . . . . £15/£5
ditto, Holt (U.S.), 1995 . . . . . . £15/£5
Easy Meat, Heinemann, 1996 . . . . £15/£5

ditto, Holt (U.S.), 1996 . . . . . . £15/£5
Still Water, Heinemann, 1997 . . . . . £10/£5
ditto, Holt (U.S.), 1997 . . . . . . £10/£5
Last Rites, Heinemann, 1998. . . . . . £10/£5
ditto, Holt (U.S.), 1999 . . . . . . £10/£5

'Resnick' Short Stories
Now's The Time, Slow Dancer Press, 1999 (wraps) .
. . . . £10
ditto, Slow Dancer Press, 1999 (600 hardback copies).
. . . . £25/£10
ditto, Slow Dancer Press, 1999 (400 signed hardback copies) . . . . £45/£25
ditto, Heinemann, 2002 . . . . . . £10/£5

Other Crime Fiction
Amphetamines and Pearls, Sphere, 1976 (wraps) . £5
The Geranium Kiss, Sphere, 1976 (wraps) . . £5
Junkyard Angel, Sphere, 1977 (wraps) . . . £5
Neon Madman, Sphere, 1977 (wraps) . . . £5
Frame, Magnum, 1979 (wraps) £10
ditto, Severn House, [1995] . . . . . £25/£10
Blind, Magnum, 1981 (wraps) £10
Endgame, N.E.L., 1982 (pseud. 'James Mann', wraps)
. . . . £5
Dancer Draws a Wild Card, Hale, 1985. . . £10/£5
In A True Light, Heinemann, 2001 . . . . £10/£5

NATHANIEL HAWTHORNE
(b.1804 d.1864)

Hawthorne's rarest work is *Fanshawe*, which he attempted to suppress by destroying as many copies as he could obtain.

Fanshawe, Marsh & Capen (U.S.), 1828 (anonymous, boards, purple cloth spine, paper labels) . £30,000
Twice-Told Tales, American Stationers Co./John B. Russell (U.S.), 1837 (first issue with fifth story listed in Contents as at p.78, not p.77, rose cloth). . £3,500
ditto, American Stationers Co./John B. Russell (U.S.), 1837 (first issue rebound) £1,000
Peter Parley's Universal History, American Stationers Co./John B. Russell (U.S.), 1837 (anonymous, 2 vols)
. . . . £3,000
The Gentle Boy, Weeks, Jordon/Wiley & Putnam (U.S.), 1839 (wraps). £2,500
The Sister Years, Salem Gazette (U.S.), 1839 (anonymous, wraps). £1,500
Grandfather's Chair, Peabody/Wiley & Putnam (U.S.), 1841 (cloth, paper label) . . . £500
Famous Old People, Peabody (U.S.), 1841 (cloth, paper label) £600
Liberty Tree, Peabody (U.S.), 1841 (cloth, paper label, first printing with 'Meet in a Con-' on p.25, line 2) .
. . . . £1,250

ditto, Peabody (U.S.), 1841 (second printing with 'Meet in Con-' on p.25, line 2) £400
The Celestial Rail-Road, Wilder (U.S.), 1843 (wraps). £4,000
ditto, Fish (U.S.), 1843 (wraps) £4,000
Journal of an African Cruiser, Wiley & Putnam (U.S.), 1845 (wraps) £3,000
Mosses from an Old Manse, Wiley & Putnam (U.S.), 1846 (printer given as 'R. Craighead's Power Press' verso title page, 2 vols, wraps) £4,000
ditto, Wiley & Putnam (U.S.), 1846 (1 vol., cloth) £500
The Scarlet Letter, Ticknor, Reed & Fields (U.S.), 1850 (first edition with 'reduplicate' instead of 'repudiate' on p.21, line 20 and no preface) . £5,000
ditto, Ticknor, Reed & Fields (U.S.), 1850 (second edition with with preface) £500
ditto, Ticknor, Reed & Fields (U.S.), 1850 (third edition with with 'Hobart and Robbins' on copyright page instead of 'Metcalf and Co.') . . . £150
True Stories from History and Biography, Ticknor, Reed & Fields (U.S.), 1851 (first issue with 'Cambridge: Printed by Bolles & Houghton' verso title page). £500
The House of the Seven Gables, Ticknor, Reed & Fields (U.S.), 1851 (first printing with the last letters ('t' and 'h') of the last words in lines 1 and 2 on p.149 broken) £2,500
ditto, Bohn, 1851 . . . . £750
A Wonder-Book for Girls and Boys, Ticknor, Reed & Fields (U.S.), 1852 (first issue with design at top of spine only, not entire spine). £2,000
ditto, Bohn, 1852 . . . . £400
The Snow Image and Other Tales, Bohn's Cheap Series, 1851 . . . . £200
ditto, as *The Snow Image and Other Twice-Told Tales*, Ticknor, Reed & Fields (U.S.), 1852 . £400
The Blithedale Romance, Chapman & Hall 1852 (2 vols) £400
ditto, Ticknor, Reed & Fields (U.S.), 1852 . £250
Life of Franklin Pierce, Ticknor, Reed & Fields (U.S.), 1852 (wraps) £400
ditto, Ticknor, Reed & Fields (U.S.), 1852 (cloth) £125
Tanglewood Tales, Chapman and Hall, 1853 . £500
ditto, Ticknor, Reed & Fields (U.S.), 1853 (without 'George C. Rand' imprint on title page) . £1,000
A Rill from the Town Pump, Cash (U.S.), 1857 (wraps) £1,500
Transformation, Smith, Elder, 1860 (3 vols) . £750
ditto, as *The Marble Faun*, Ticknor & Fields, 1860 (first printing with 'Preface' preceeding 'Contents', 2 vols) £500
Our Old Home, Ticknor & Fields (U.S.), 1863 (first issue with publisher's list on leaf opposite p.398) £150
ditto, Smith, Elder, 1863 (2 vols). £100
Pansie, John Camden Hotten, [1864] . . . £300

Passages from the American Note-Books of Nathaniel Hawthorne, Ticknor & Fields (U.S.), 1868 (2 vols, green cloth with spine reading 'Ticknor & Co') £250
ditto, Smith, Elder, 1868 (2 vols). £125
Passages from the English Note-Books of Nathaniel Hawthorne, Fields, Osgood (U.S.), 1870 (2 vols). £150
ditto, Strahan, 1870 (2 vols) £125
Passages from the French and Italian Note-Books of Nathaniel Hawthorne, Strahan, 1871 (2 vols) £125
ditto, Osgood (U.S.), 1872 (2 vols) £125
Septimus Felton or the Elixier of Life, Osgood (U.S.), 1872 . . . . £150
ditto, Henry S King, 1872. . . . . . . £100

SEAMUS HEANEY
(b.1939)

An acclaimed Irish poet who moved from nature poetry to political and cultural issues. Heaney was awarded the Nobel Prize for Literature in 1995.

Poetry
Eleven Poems, Festival (Belfast), 1965 (first issue, laid paper, red-violet sun, wraps) £900
ditto, Festival (Belfast), 1965 (second issue, wove paper, dark-maroon sun, wraps) £600
ditto, Festival (Belfast), 1965 (third issue, grey paper, stiff green wraps) £250
Death of a Naturalist, Faber, 1966 . . . £350/£50
ditto, O.U.P. (U.S.), 1966. . . . . . £175/£35
ditto, Faber, 1969 (wraps). £35
A Lough Neagh Sequence, Phoenix Pamphlet, Poets Press, 1969 (950 copies, wraps) £200
ditto, Phoenix Pamphlet, Poets Press, 1969 (50 signed copies, wraps) £600
Door into the Dark, Faber, 1969. . . . £450/£45
ditto, O.U.P. (U.S.), 1969. . . . . . £200/£35
ditto, Faber, 1972 (wraps). £20
Night Drive: Poems, Gilbertson, 1970 (100 signed copies) £500
ditto, Gilbertson, 1970 (25 of the above containing poem in author's hand) £1,000
ditto, Crediton, 1970 (100 signed copies, wraps) £400
A Boy Driving His Father to Confession, Sceptre Press, 1970 (150 numbered copies, wraps) . £150
ditto, Sceptre Press, 1970 (50 signed copies, wraps) £400
Land, Poem of the Month Club, 1979 (signed broadside) £75
Wintering Out, Faber, 1972 (wraps). . . . £300
ditto, Faber, 1973 . . . . £100/£20
ditto, O.U.P. (U.S.), 1973. . . . . . £100/£20
Stations, Ulsterman Publications, 1975 (wraps) £100
North, Faber, 1975 . . . . £300/£75
ditto, Faber, 1975 (wraps). £35
ditto, O.U.P. (U.S.), 1976. . . . . . £175/£35

Bog Poems, Rainbow Press, 1975 (150 signed copies, slipcase) . . . . £1,500/£1,250
In Their Element, Arts Council of Northern Ireland, 1977 (wraps) £35
Ugolino, Carpenter, 1978 (125 signed copies, hardback, no d/w) £750
Hedgeschool, Seluzicki/Janus Press (U.S.), 1979 (285 numbered copies signed by poet and artist, wraps) .
. . . . £500
After Summer, Gallery Press (Dublin), 1979 (250 signed copies) . . . . £250/£200
Field Work, Faber, 1979 . . . . . . £150/£20
ditto, Faber, 1979 (wraps). £25
ditto, Farrar Straus (U.S.), 1979 . . . £150/£20
Gravities, Charlotte Press, 1979 (wraps). . £25
Selected Poems 1965-1975, Faber, 1980 . £75/£20
ditto, Faber, 1980 (wraps). £15
ditto, Farrar Straus (U.S.), 1980 . . . £50/£10
Holly, Loughcrew, 1981 (121 signed copies, wraps) .
. . . . £200
Sweeney Praises the Trees, Kelly/Winterton Press (U.S.), 1981 (110 copies, wraps) £300
Poems and a Memoir, The Limited Editions Club (U.S.), 1982 (2,000 signed copies, slipcase) . . .
. . . . £400/£350
An Open Letter, Field Day (Derry), 1983 (wraps) £40
Sweeney Astray, Field Day (Derry), 1983 . £70/£20
ditto, Field Day (Derry), 1983 (wraps) . . £25
ditto, Faber, 1984 . . . . £35/£10
ditto, Faber, 1984 (wraps). £15
ditto, Farrar Straus (U.S.), 1984 . . . £25/£10
ditto, Farrar Straus (U.S.), 1984 (350 signed copies, slipcase) . . . . £200/£175
Station Island, Faber, 1984 . . . . £35/£10
ditto, Faber, 1984 (wraps). £15
ditto, Farrar Straus (U.S.), 1984 . . . £35/£10
Verses for a Fordham Commencement, Fordham Univ. (U.S.), 1982 (broadsheet) . . . £200
ditto, NADJA (U.S.), 1984 (200 signed, numbered copies, wraps) £200
ditto, NADJA (U.S.), 1984 (26 signed, lettered copies on hand-made paper, boards) £350
Hailstones, Gallery Press (Dublin), 1984 (250 signed copies) . . . . £350/£200
ditto, Gallery Press (Dublin), 1984 (500 unsigned copies, wraps) £75
From the Republic of Conscience, Amnesty International, 1985 (2,000 copies, wraps) . . £20
Towards a Collaboration, Arts Council of Northern Ireland, 1986 (wraps) £20
The Haw Lantern, Faber, 1987 . . . . £65/£10
ditto, Faber, 1987 (wraps). £10
ditto, Farrar Straus (U.S.), 1987 . . . £65/£10
ditto, Farrar Straus (U.S.), 1987 (250 signed copies, slipcase) . . . . £125/£100
An Upstairs Outlook, Linen Hall, 1989 (wraps) £20
Railway Children, Poems on the Underground, 1989 (200 copies, broadside) £65

The Fire Gaze, Cheltenham Festival of Literature, 1989 (broadside). £25
New Selected Poems 1966-87, Faber, 1990 . . £20/£5
ditto, Faber, 1990 (25 signed copies of 125, slipcase) .
. . . . £500/£450
ditto, Faber, 1990 (100 signed copies of 125, slipcase).
. . . . £200/£165
ditto, Faber, 1990 (wraps). £10
ditto, Farrar Straus (U.S.), 1990 . . . . £15/£5
ditto, Farrar Straus (U.S.), 1990 (200 signed copies, slipcase) . . . . £175/£150
The Place of Waiting, Scholars Press (U.S.), 1990 £10
The Tree Clock, Linen Hall, 1990 (750 copies) . .
. . . . £125/£50
ditto, Linen Hall, 1990 (100 signed copies, slipcase) .
. . . . £350/£300
The Earth House, Cheltenham Festival of Literature, 1990 (broadside). £15
Seeing Things, Faber, 1991 . . . . . £25/£5
ditto, Faber, 1991 (250 signed copies, slipcase). . .
. . . . £175/£150
ditto, Faber, 1991 (wraps). £10
Squarings, Hieroglyph Editions (Dublin), 1991 (100 signed copies in slipcase) £750
The Water Pause, Cheltenham Festival of Literature, 1991 (broadside). £15
Sweeney's Flight, Faber, 1992 . . . . £45/£10
ditto, Farrar Straus (U.S.), 1992 . . . £45/£10
Iron Spike, Ewart (U.S.), 1992 (100 signed copies, broadside) £100
The Air Station, Cheltenham Festival of Literature, 1992 (broadside). £15
The Gravel Walks, Lenoir Rhyne College, 1992 (wraps) £100
The Midnight Verdict, Gallery Press (Dublin), 1993 (925 copies) . . . . £45/£15
ditto, Gallery Press (Dublin), 1993 (75 signed copies) .
. . . . £250
Poet's Chair, Ewart (U.S.), 1993 (100 signed copies, broadside) £100
Keeping Going, Ewart (U.S.), 1993 (50 signed copies, boards, no d/w) £200
ditto, Ewart (U.S.), 1993 (150 signed copies, wraps) .
. . . . £125
Laments: Jan Kochanowski (1530-1584), Faber, 1995 (translation, with Stanislaw Baranczak) . £25/£10
ditto, Farrar Straus (U.S.), 1995 . . . £25/£10
The Spirit Level, Faber, 1996 . . . . . £15/£5
ditto, Faber, 1996 (350 numbered, signed copies, slipcase) . . . . £250/£225
ditto, Farrar Straus (U.S.), 1996 (200 signed, numbered copies with audio cassette in slipcase) . . £200/£175
ditto, Farrar Straus (U.S.), 1996 (with audio cassette in slipcase) . . . . £25/£10
Opened Ground: Poems 1966-1996, Faber, 1998 . .
. . . . £15/£5
ditto, Faber, 1998 (300 signed, numbered copies in slipcase) . . . . £300/£250
ditto, Farrar Straus (U.S.), 1998 . . . . £15/£5

Electric Light, Faber, 2001 . . . . . . £25/£5
ditto, Faber, 2001 (300 signed, numbered copies, slipcase) . . . . £250/£225

Others
The Fire i' the Flint: Reflections on the Poetry of Gerard Manley Hopkins, British Academy/O.U.P., 1975 (wraps) £45
Robert Lowell: A Memorial Lecture and an Eulogy, privately printed, 1978 (wraps) £125
The Makings of Music: Reflections on the Poetry of Wordsworth and Yeats, Univ. of Liverpool, 1978 (wraps) £35
Preoccupations: Selected Prose 1968-1978, Faber, 1980 . . . . £75/£15
ditto, Farrar Straus (U.S.), 1980 . . . . £50/£10
Among the Schoolchildren, Queen's Univ. (Belfast), 1983 (green wraps) £75
ditto, Queen's Univ. (Belfast), 1983 (blue wraps) £20
Place and Displacement, Dove Cottage, 1984 (wraps) £25
The Government of the Tongue, Faber, 1988 . £15/£5
ditto, Farrar Straus (U.S.), 1988 . . . . £15/£5
The Cure at Troy, Field Day, 1989 (500 signed copies) . . . . £200/£125
ditto, Faber, 1989 (wraps). £5
ditto, Farrar Straus (U.S.), 1991 . . . . £25/£5
The Redress of Poetry, Clarendon Press, 1990 . £15
ditto, Faber, 1995 . . . . £20/£5
ditto, Farrar Straus (U.S.), 1995 . . . . £10/£5
Dylan the Durable? On Dylan Thomas, Bennington College, 1992 (1,000 numbered copies, wraps) £25
Joy or Night, Univ. College of Swansea, 1993 (wraps) £20
Crediting Poetry, Gallery Books, 1995 (wraps). £25
Commencement Address, Univ. of North Carolina (U.S.), 1998 (100 signed copies of 500, wraps) £175
ditto, Univ. of North Carolina (U.S.), 1998 (400 unsigned copies of 500, wraps) £25
Beowulf, Faber, 1999 . . . . £15/£5
ditto, Faber, 1999 (300 signed, numbered copies, slipcase) . . . . £500/£400
ditto, Farrar Straus (U.S.), 2000 . . . . £25/£5
Finders Keepers Selected Prose 1971-2001, Faber, 2002 . . . . £15/£5

ROBERT A. HEINLEIN
(b.1907 d.1988)

An influential American science fiction writer, Heinlein was first published in *Astounding SF* magazine in 1939.

Novels
The Discovery of the Future, Novacious Press (U.S.), 1941 ('Limited First Edition' (200) on front wrapper, wraps). £1,400

ditto, Novacious Press (U.S.), 1941 (adds 'Reprint' (100) under original limitation, wraps). . . £500
Beyond This Horizon, Fantasy Press (U.S.), 1948 . . . . £200/£45
ditto, Fantasy Press (U.S.), 1948 (500 signed, numbered copies). . . . . £750/£500
Sixth Column, Gnome Press (U.S.), 1949 . £300/£35
ditto, as *The Day After Tomorrow*, Signet, 1962 (wraps) £10
ditto, as *Sixth Column*, Mayflower, 1962 (wraps) £10
The Puppet Masters, Doubleday (U.S.), 1951 £300/£75
ditto, Museum Press, 1953 . . . . . £125/£30
Universe, Dell Books (U.S.), 1951 (wraps) . £35
Double Star, Doubleday (U.S.), 1956 . £500/£100
ditto, Joseph, 1958. . . . . £200/£65
The Door into Summer, Doubleday (U.S.), 1957 . . . . £450/£75
ditto, Panther, 1960 (wraps) £5
ditto, Gollancz, 1967 . . . . . . £100/£25
Methuselah's Children, Gnome Press (U.S.), 1958 . . . . £200/£35
ditto, Gollancz, 1963 (abridged version). . £75/£20
Stranger in a Strange Land, Putnam (U.S.), 1961 (first issue with 'C22' on p. 408 and d/w priced $4.50). . . . . £1,000/£100
ditto, New English Library, 1965 . . . £150/£25
Orphans of the Sky, Gollancz, 1963 . . . £350/£75
ditto, Putnam (U.S.), 1964 . . . . . £200/£45
Glory Road, Putnam (U.S.), 1963 . . . £300/£65
ditto, New English Library, 1965 . . . £150/£20
Farnham's Freehold, Putnam (U.S.), 1964. £175/£45
ditto, Dobson, 1965 . . . . £75/£25
The Moon is a Harsh Mistress, Putnam (U.S.), 1966 . . . . £350/£45
ditto, Dobson, 1967 . . . . £75/£25
I Will Fear No Evil, Putnam (U.S.), 1970 . £125/£20
ditto, New English Library, 1971 . . . £35/£15
Time Enough For Love, Putnam (U.S.), 1973 £125/£45
ditto, New English Library, 1974 . . . £100/£35
Destination Moon, Gregg Press (U.S.), 1979 (no d/w). £65
The Number of the Beast, New English Library, 1980 . . . . £50/£10
ditto, Fawcett (U.S.), 1980 . . . . £45/£15
ditto, Fawcett (U.S.), 1980 (wraps) . . . £10
Friday, Holt Rinehart (U.S.), 1982 . . £25/£5
ditto, Ballantine/Del Ray (U.S.), 1984 (500 signed, numbered copies, slipcase) . . . . . £150/£100
ditto, New English Library, 1982 . . . £20/£5
Job, Ballantine/Del Ray (U.S.), 1984 . . £15/£5
ditto, Ballantine/Del Ray (U.S.), 1984 (750 signed, numbered copies, slipcase) . . . . . £100/£75
ditto, Ballantine/Del Ray (U.S.), 1984 (26 signed deluxe copies, slipcase) £1,000
ditto, New English Library, 1984 . . . £20/£5
The Cat Who Walks Through Walls, Putnam (U.S.), 1985 (First state with line missing on p.300, erratum sheet laid in) . . . . £25/£5

ditto, Putnam (U.S.), 1984 (350 signed, numbered copies, slipcase) . . . . £200/£150
ditto, New English Library, 1986 . . . . £20/£5
To Sail Beyond the Sunset, Ace/Putnam (U.S.), 1987 .
. . . . £20/£5
ditto, Joseph, 1987. . . . . £15/£5

Omnibus Editions
The Robert Heinlein Omnibus, Science Fiction Book Club, 1958 . . . . £25/£10
Three by Heinlein, Doubleday (U.S.), 1965 £75/£25
ditto, as *A Heinlein Triad*, Gollancz, 1966 . £35/£10
A Robert Heinlein Omnibus, Sidgwick & Jackson, 1966 . . . . £25/£10

Short Stories
The Man Who Sold the Moon, Shasta (U.S.), 1950 .
. . . . £250/£45
ditto, Shasta (U.S.), 1950 (subscriber's copy signed on tipped-in page) . . . . £750/£500
ditto, Sidgwick & Jackson, 1953 . . . . £125/£25
Waldo and Magic Inc., Doubleday (U.S.), 1950 . .
. . . . £200/£35
The Green Hills of Earth, Shasta (U.S.), 1951 . . .
. . . . £250/£45
ditto, Shasta (U.S.), 1951 (subscriber's copy signed on tipped-in page) . . . . £600/£400
ditto, Sidgwick & Jackson, 1954 . . . . £150/£35
Assignment in Eternity, Fantasy Press (U.S.), 1953 (500 numbered, signed copies) . . . £400/£250
ditto, Fantasy Press (U.S.), 1953 . . . . £200/£75
ditto, Museum Press, 1955 . . . . . £175/£50
Revolt in 2100, Shasta (U.S.), 1953 . . . £150/£25
ditto, Shasta (U.S.), 1953 (subscriber's copy signed on tipped-in page) . . . . £350/£200
ditto, Gollancz, 1964 . . . . £65/£15
The Menace from Earth, Gnome Press (U.S.), 1959 .
. . . . £150/£40
ditto, Dobson, 1966 . . . . £75/£25
The Unpleasant Profession of Jonathan Hoag, Gnome Press (U.S.), 1959 . . . . . £175/£45
ditto, Dobson, 1964 . . . . £100/£25
The Worlds of Robert Heinlein, Ace Books (U.S.), 1966 (wraps) £10
ditto, New English Library, 1970 (wraps) . . £10
The Past Through Tomorrow, Putnam (U.S.), 1967 .
. . . . £200/£50
ditto, New English Library, 1977 (2 vols) . £100/£20
Best of Robert Heinlein, Sidgwick & Jackson, 1973 .
. . . . £25/£10
The Notebooks of Lazarus Long, Putnam (U.S.), 1978 (with D F Vassallo, wraps) £15
Expanded Universe, Grosset & Dunlap (U.S.), 1980 .
. . . . £50/£15
Grumbles from the Grave, Ballantine (U.S.), 1989 .
. . . . £10/£5
Requiem, Tor, 1992 . . . . £10/£5
The Fantasies of Robert Heinlein, Tor, 1992 . £10/£5

Childrens Titles
Rocket Ship Galileo, Scribner's (U.S.), 1947 (first state d/w published at $2.00) . . . . . . £650/£75
ditto, New English Library, 1971 (wraps) . . £30
Space Cadet, Scribner's (U.S.), 1948 (first state d/w published at $2.50) . . . . £450/£45
ditto, Gollancz, 1966 . . . . £150/£35
Red Planet, Scribner's (U.S.), 1949 . . . £125/£35
ditto, Gollancz, 1963 . . . . £150/£35
Farmer in the Sky, Scribner's (U.S.), 1950 . £200/£35
ditto, Gollancz, 1962 . . . . £125/£25
Between Planets, Scribner's (U.S.), 1951 . £200/£45
ditto, Gollancz, 1968 . . . . £150/£35
The Rolling Stones, Scribner's (U.S.), 1952 £250/£45
ditto, as **Space Family Stone**, Gollancz, 1969 £125/£35
Starman Jones, Scribner's (U.S.), 1953 . . £200/£45
ditto, Sidgwick & Jackson, 1954 . . . . £65/£15
The Star Beast, Scribner's (U.S.), 1954 . . £100/£20
ditto, New English Library, 1971 . . . £65/£10
Tunnel in the Sky, Scribner's (U.S.), 1955 . £150/£50
ditto, Gollancz, 1965 . . . . £65/£15
Time for the Stars, Scribner's (U.S.), 1956 . £250/£35
ditto, Gollancz, 1963 . . . . £100/£20
Citizen of the Galaxy, Scribner's (U.S.), 1957 . . .
. . . . £200/£50
ditto, Gollancz, 1969 . . . . £75/£25
Have Space Suit - Will Travel, Scribner's (U.S.), 1958
. . . . £300/£50
ditto, Gollancz, 1970 . . . . . . £65/£20
Starship Troopers, Putnam (U.S.), 1959 £1,000/£250
ditto, New English Library, 1961 (wraps) . £100/£35
Podkayne of Mars, Putnam (U.S.), 1963 . £500/£125
ditto, New English Library, 1969 . . . £35/£10

Non Fiction
Take Back Your Government: A Practical Handbook For The Private Citizen Who Wants Democracy To Work!, Baen (U.S.), 1992 (wraps) £10
Tramp Royale, Ace (U.S.), 1992. . . . . £10/£5

JOSEPH HELLER
(b.1923 d.1999)

Heller, an American author, is chiefly known for *Catch-22*, an anti-war satire which drew on his own experience of military service.

Novels
Catch-22, Simon & Schuster (U.S.), 1961 (d/w priced $5.95). . . . . £2,000/£200
ditto, Cape, 1962 (first issue d/w with blurb about book on back) . . . . £500/£25
ditto, Cape, 1962 (second issue d/w with comments of other authors on back) . . . . . £75/£25
ditto, Franklin Library (U.S.), 1978 (signed, limited edition) £250

ditto, Simon & Schuster (U.S.), 1994 (750 signed, numbered copies, slipcase) . . . . . £250/£200
Something Happened, Knopf (U.S.), 1974 . £45/£10
ditto, Knopf (U.S.), 1974 (350 signed, numbered copies, d/w and slipcase) . . . . £150/£100
ditto, Cape, 1974 . . . . £25/£10
Good as Gold, Franklin Library (U.S.), 1979 (limited edition) £25
ditto, Franklin Library (U.S.), 1979 (signed, limited edition) £75
ditto, Simon & Schuster (U.S.), 1979 . . . £20/£5
ditto, Simon & Schuster (U.S.), 1979 (500 signed copies, acetate d/w, slipcase) . . . . £100/£75
ditto, Cape, 1979 . . . . £20/£5
God Knows, Knopf (U.S.), 1984 . . . . . £20/£5
ditto, Knopf (U.S.), 1984 (350 signed copies, d/w and slipcase) . . . . £75/£50
ditto, Cape, 1984 . . . . £10/£5
ditto, Franklin Library (U.S.), 1984 (signed limited edition) £45
Picture This, Putnam (U.S.), 1988 . . . . £15/£5
ditto, Putnam (U.S.), 1988 (250 signed copies, slipcase, no d/w) . . . . £75/£50
ditto, Macmillan, 1988 . . . . . . £15/£5
ditto, Macmillan, 1988 (50 proof copies) . . £50
Closing Time, Franklin Library (U.S.), 1994 (signed limited edition) £45
ditto, Simon & Schuster (U.S.), 1994 . . £15/£5
ditto, Simon & Schuster (U.S.), 1994 (750 signed, numbered copies, slipcase, no d/w). . . £65/£50
ditto, Simon & Schuster, 1994 . . . . £15/£5
Portrait of an Artist as an Old Man, Scribner (U.S.), 2000 . . . . £15/£5
ditto, Simon & Schuster, 2000 . . . . . £15/£5

Plays
We Bombed in New Haven, Knopf (U.S.), 1968 . .
. . . . £35/£10
ditto, Cape, 1969 . . . . £25/£5
Catch-22: A Dramatization, French (U.S.), 1971 (wraps) £25
Clevinger's Trial, French (U.S.), 1973 (wraps). £20

Non Fiction
No Laughing Matter, Knopf (U.S.), 1986 (with Speed Vogel). . . . . £25/£5
ditto, Cape, 1986 . . . . £25/£5
Now and Then, From Coney Island to Here, Franklin Library (U.S.), 1994 (signed limited edition) . £75
ditto, Knopf, 1998 . . . . £15/£5
ditto, Simon & Schuster, 1998 . . . . . £15/£5

ERNEST HEMINGWAY
(b.1899 d.1961)

One of the most famous American novelists of the twentieth century, Hemingway's great successes were *A Farewell to Arms*, set during the First World War, and *For Whom the Bell Tolls* with the Spanish Civil War as its background. He won the Nobel Prize for Literature in 1954.

Novels
The Torrents of Spring, Scribner's (U.S.), 1926 . .
. . . . £3,500/£350
ditto, Black Sun Press (Paris), 1933 (large paper edition, 125 francs, wraps) £250
ditto, Black Sun Press (Paris), 1933 (small paper edition, 10 francs, wraps) £125
ditto, Cape, 1933 . . . . £500/£50
The Sun Also Rises, Scribner's (U.S.), 1926 (first issue with 'stoppped' rather than 'stopped' on p.181, line 26, d/w with error 'In Our Times' rather than 'In Our Time'). . . . . £12,500/£2,000
ditto, Scribner's (U.S.), 1926 (second issue with errors corrected). . . . . £1,750/£150
ditto, as **Fiesta**, Cape, 1927 . . . £5,000/£1,000
A Farewell to Arms, Scribner's (U.S.), 1929 (510 signed copies, glassine d/w, slipcase) £6,000/£4,000
ditto, Scribner's (U.S.), 1929 (no disclaimer on p.[x]) .
. . . . £2,000/£200
ditto, Scribner's (U.S.), 1929 (with disclaimer on p.[x])
. . . . £750/£100
ditto, Cape, 1929 (first issue with 'seriosu' on p.66, line 28). . . . . £500/£250
ditto, Cape, 1929 (second issue with error corrected) .
. . . . £300/£50
To Have and to Have Not, Scribner's (U.S.), 1937 .
. . . . £1,000/£75
ditto, Cape, 1937 . . . . £175/£25
For Whom the Bell Tolls, Scribner's (U.S.), 1940 (first issue d/w without photographer's name on back panel) . . . . £750/£45
ditto, Scribner's (U.S.), 1940 (second issue d/w with photographer's name) . . . . . £150/£45
ditto, Cape, 1941 . . . . £250/£30
Across the River and into the Trees, Cape, 1950 . .
. . . . £125/£25
ditto, Scribner's (U.S.), 1950 (24 advance copies containing errors) £12,500
ditto, Scribner's (U.S.), 1950 (first issue d/w with yellow lettering to spine) . . . . £150/£20
ditto, Scribner's (U.S.), 1950 (second issue d/w with orange lettering to spine) . . . . £125/£20
The Old Man and the Sea, Scribner's (U.S.), 1952 .
. . . . £250/£75
ditto, Scribner's (U.S.), 1952 (30 sheets bound in black buckram for presentation, signature blind-stamped on front cover, spine gilt) £10,000
ditto, Cape, 1952 . . . . £125/£15
Islands in the Stream, Scribner's (U.S.), 1970 £45/£10

ditto, Collins, 1970 . . . . £25/£5
The Garden of Eden, Scribner's (U.S.), 1986 . £20/£5
ditto, Hamish Hamilton, 1987 . . . . . £15/£5
True at First Light, Heinemann, 1999 . . . £15/£5

Short Stories
Three Stories & Ten Poems, privately printed, Contact Publishing Co. (Paris), 1923 (300 copies, wraps) . .
. . . . £25,000
In Our Time, Three Mountains Press (Paris), 1924 (170 copies) £25,000
ditto, Boni & Liveright (U.S.), 1925 . . £4,000/£600
ditto, Scribner's (U.S.), 1932 . . . £2,000/£600
ditto, Black Sun Press (Paris), 1932 . . . £250
Men Without Women, Scribner's (U.S.), 1927 (first state weighing 15.5 ounces). . . . £3,500/£500
ditto, Scribner's (U.S.), 1927 (second state weighing 13.8 ounces) . . . . £2,000/£100
ditto, Cape, 1928 . . . . . . £1,000/£75
God Rest You Merry Gentlemen, House of Books (U.S.), 1933 (300 copies, no d/w) £1,000
Winner Take Nothing, Scribner's (U.S.), 1933. . .
. . . . £500/£100
ditto, Cape, 1934 . . . . £250/£45
The Fifth Column and The First Forty-Nine Stories, Scribner's (U.S.), 1938 . . . . . £1,000/£100
ditto, Cape, 1939 . . . . £750/£75
The First Forty-Nine Stories, Cape, 1944 . £75/£10
ditto, Franklin Library (U.S.), 1977 . . . . £100
Two Christmas Tales, Hart Press (U.S.), 1959 (150 copies, wraps) £750
The Snows of Kilamanjaro and Other Stories, Scribner's (U.S.), 1961 . . . . . . £30/£10
ditto, Penguin, 1963 (wraps) £5
The Short Happy Life of Francis Macomber and Other Stories, Penguin, 1963 (wraps) . . . £5
The Fifth Column and Four Unpublished Stories of the Spanish Civil War, Scribner's (U.S.), 1969 . .
. . . . £45/£10
The Nick Adams Stories, Scribner's (U.S.), 1972 . .
. . . . £75/£20
A Divine Gesture, A Fable, Aloe Editions (U.S.), 1974 (200 copies, wraps) £75

Others
Today is Friday, Stable Publications (U.S.), 1926 (300 numbered copies, wraps, envelope) . £1,500/£750
Introduction to Kiki of Montparnasse, Titus (U.S.), 1929 (25 copies, wraps) £2,500
Death in the Afternoon, Scribner's (U.S.), 1932 . .
. . . . £2,000/£200
ditto, Cape, 1932 . . . . £750/£75
Green Hills of Africa, Scribner's (U.S.), 1935 . . .
. . . . £1,000/£100
ditto, Cape, 1936 . . . . £500/£45
The Spanish Earth, Savage (U.S.), 1938 (1,000 numbered copies, some with pictorial endpapers, glassine d/w) . . . . . . £1,500/£1,250

ditto, Savage (U.S.), 1938 (copies of the above 1,000 but with plain endpapers, glassine d/w) . £500/£400
The Fifth Column: A Play in Three Acts, Scribner's (U.S.), 1940 . . . . £200/£25
ditto, Penguin, 1966 . . . . £5
ditto, Cape, 1968 . . . . £15/£5
Voyage to Victory, Crowell-Collier (U.S.), 1944 (wraps with d/w) . . . . £45/£20
The Essential Hemingway, Cape, 1947 . . £25/£5
The Hemingway Reader, Scribner's (U.S.), 1953 . .
. . . . £25/£5
Hemingway: The Wild Years, Dell (U.S.), 1962 (wraps) . . . . £25/£5
The Collected Poems, Library of Living Poets [Paris], [c.1955] (pirated, wraps) £150
ditto, Haskell House (U.S.), 1970 . . . £25/£10
A Moveable Feast, Scribner's (U.S.), 1964 . £65/£20
ditto, Cape, 1964 . . . . £75/£20
By-Line, Scribner's (U.S.), 1967. . . . £65/£15
ditto, Collins, 1968 . . . . £45/£15
Ernest Hemingway, Cub Reporter, Univ. of Pittsburgh Press (U.S.), 1970 . . . . £20/£5
ditto, Univ. of Pittsburgh Press (U.S.), 1970 (200 copies) . . . . £40/£20
Ernest Hemingway's Apprenticeship: Oak Park, 1916-1917, Microcard (U.S.), 1971 . . . £20/£5
ditto, Microcard (U.S.), 1971 (200 copies) . £40/£20
Bastard Sheet Note for A Farewell to Arms, Cohn (U.S.), 1971 (93 copies, single sheet) . . . £250
Eighty-Eight Poems, Harcourt Brace (U.S.), 1980 . .
. . . . £25/£10
Selected Letters, 1917-1961, Scribner's (U.S.), 1981 (edited by Carlos Barker) . . . . . £25/£10
ditto, Scribner's (U.S.), 1981 (500 copies signed by editor, glassine d/w, slipcase) . . . . £75/£50
ditto, Granada, 1981 . . . . £25/£10
Ernest Hemingway on Writing, Scribner's (U.S.), 1984 . . . . £20/£5
ditto, Granada, 1985 . . . . £15/£5
The Dangerous Summer, Scribner's (U.S.), 1985 . .
. . . . £20/£5
ditto, Hamish Hamilton, 1985 . . . . . £20/£5
Marlin, Big Fish Books (U.S.), 1992 (1,000 copies, introduction by Gabriel García Márquez) . £50/£15

G.A. HENTY
(b.1832 d.1902)

Henty was a popular nineteenth-century author of patriotic stories for boys.

A Search for a Secret, Tinsley Brothers, 1867 (3 vols, blue or green cloth) £2,000
The March to Magdala, Tinsley Brothers, 1868 (blue cloth) £2,000
All But Lost, Tinsley Brothers, 1869 (3 vols, blue cloth) £2,000

Out on the Pampas, or The Young Settlers, Griffith & Farran, 1871 [1870] (blue or brown cloth) . . £1,000
The Young Franc-Tireurs, Griffith & Farran, 1872 [1871] (blue, red or green cloth) £650
The March to Coomassie, Tinsley Brothers, 1874 (blue cloth) £500
Seaside Maidens, Tinsley Brothers, 1880 (orange cloth) £625
The Young Buglars, Griffith & Farran, 1880 [1879] (adverts dated 1879, red or green cloth) . . £500
The Cornet of Horse, Sampson Low & Marston, 1881 (adverts dated January 1881, red cloth) . . £500
In Times of Peril, Griffith & Farran, 1881 (adverts dated October 1881, red or blue cloth) . . . £700
Facing Death, Blackie, [1882] (blue or brown cloth) .
. . . . £500
Winning His Spurs, Sampson Low & Marston, 1882 (red cloth). £300
Friends Though Divided, Griffith & Farran, 1883 (adverts dated September 1883, red, blue, brown or green cloth) £400
Jack Archer, Sampson Low & Marston, 1883 (red cloth) £400
ditto, Roberts Bros (U.S.), 1884 . . . . . £350
ditto, as *The Fall of Sebastopol*, Brown (U.S.), 1892 .
. . . . £150
Under Drake's Flag, Blackie, 1883 [1882] (green or brown cloth) £200
ditto, as *Cast Ashore*, Blackie, 1906 . . . . £45
By Sheer Pluck, Blackie, 1884 [1883] (adverts dated 'New Series for 1885', red cloth) £300
With Clive in India, Blackie, 1884 [1883] (red, brown or blue cloth). £200
ditto, as *The Young Captain*, Blackie, 1906 . £50
ditto, as *Charlie Marryat*, Blackie, 1906 . . £50
The Young Colonists, Routledge, 1885 [1884] (blue and gold cloth) £200
True to the Old Flag, Blackie, 1885 [1884] (blue, grey, red or green cloth) £200
In Freedom's Cause, Blackie, 1885 [1884] (blue, brown or red cloth) £100
ditto, as *A Highland Chief*, Blackie, 1906 . . £50
St. George For England, Blackie, 1885 [1884] (brown, blue or green cloth) £100
The Lion of the North, Blackie, 1886 [1885] (brown or green cloth) £150
The Dragon and the Raven, Blackie, 1886 [1885] (brown or green cloth) £200
For Name and Fame, Blackie, 1886 [1885] (brown or grey cloth) £200
Through the Fray, Blackie, 1886 [1885] (brown or red cloth) £150
Yarns on the Beach, Blackie, 1886 [1885] (brown or red cloth) £350
The Young Carthaginian, Blackie, 1887 [1886] (blue or green cloth) £200
The Bravest of the Brave, Blackie, 1887 [1886] (red or blue cloth) £150

A Final Reckoning, Blackie, 1887 [1886] (blue or green cloth) £100
ditto, as *Among the Bushrangers*, Blackie, 1906 £50
With Wolfe in Canada, Blackie, 1887 [1886] (green, blue or red cloth). £200
The Sovereign Reader: Scenes from the Life and Reign of Queen Victoria, Blackie, [1887] (red or purple cloth) £175
In the Reign of Terror, Blackie, 1888 (red, blue, grey or green cloth) £150
Sturdy and Strong, Blackie, 1888 [1887] (red, blue or orange cloth) £150
Orange and Green, Blackie, 1888 [1887] (red, blue or orange cloth) £100
ditto, as *Cornet Walter*, Blackie, 1906 . . . £50
Bonnie Prince Charlie, Blackie, 1888 [1887] (brown or red cloth) £100
For the Temple, Blackie, 1888 [1887] (brown, red or blue cloth) £200
Gabriel Allen MP, Spencer & Blackett, [1888] (red cloth) £250
Captain Bayley's Heir, Blackie, 1889 (red, brown or blue cloth) £100
The Cat of Bubastes, Blackie, 1889 [1888] (blue, brown, grey or green cloth) £200
The Lion of St Mark, Blackie, 1889 [1888] (red, blue or grey cloth) £75
The Curse of Carne's Hold, Spencer & Blackett, 1889 (2 vols, blue cloth) £500
The Plague Ship, S.P.C.K. 'Penny Library of Fiction' series, 1889 (wraps) £600
By Pike and Dyke, Blackie, 1890 [1889] (brown or green cloth) £125
One of the 28th, Blackie, 1890 [1889] (red, brown, green or blue cloth) £200
Tales of Daring and Danger, Blackie, 1889 [1890] (blue or green cloth) £300
With Lee in Virginia, Blackie, 1890 [1889] (brown or blue cloth) £150
Those Other Animals, Henry & Co., [1891] (green cloth) £250
By England's Aid, Blackie, 1891 [1890] (blue or brown cloth) £150
By Right of Conquest, Blackie, 1891 [1890] (green or brown cloth) £100
Maori and Settler, Blackie, 1891 (brown, blue, red or green cloth) £100
A Chapter of Adventures, Blackie, 1891 [1890] (blue or grey cloth). £1,000
A Hidden Foe, Sampson Low & Marston, [1891] (2 vols, grey cloth) £2,000
The Dash for Khartoum, Scribner's (U.S.), 1891 £100
ditto, Blackie, 1892 [1891] (brown, red, grey or green cloth) £100
Held Fast for England, Scribner's (U.S.), 1891 £100
ditto, Blackie, 1892 [1891] (red, grey or brown cloth) .
. . . . £100
Redskin and Cowboy, Scribner's (U.S.), 1891 . £100

ditto, Blackie, 1892 [1891] (red, green or brown cloth)
. . . . £100
ditto, as *An Indian Raid*, Blackie, 1906. . . £50
The Ranch in the Valley, S.P.C.K. 'Penny Library of
Fiction' series, 1892 (wraps) £500
Beric the Briton, Scribner's (U.S.), 1891 . . £150
ditto, Blackie, 1893 [1892] (blue or brown cloth) £150
Condemned as Nihilist, Scribner's (U.S.), 1892 £150
ditto, Blackie, 1893 [1892] (brown or blue cloth) £150
In Greek Waters, Scribner's (U.S.), 1892 . . £100
ditto, Blackie, 1893 [1892] (grey, brown or green
cloth) £100
Tales from the Works of G.A. Henty, Blackie, 1893
(red cloth). £100
Rujub the Juggler, Chatto & Windus, 1893 (3 vols,
blue cloth) £750
A Jacobite Exile, Scribner's (U.S.), 1893 . . £200
ditto, Blackie, 1894 [1893] (brown, green, grey or blue
cloth) £200
Through the Sikh War, Scribner's (U.S.), 1893 £100
ditto, Blackie, 1894 [1893] (green cloth) . . £100
St Bartholomew's Eve, Scribner's (U.S.), 1893 £100
ditto, Blackie, 1894 [1893] (green, blue or red cloth) .
. . . . £100
A Tale of Waterloo, Worthington (U.S.), 1894 (tan
cloth) £200
Dorothy's Double, Chatto & Windus, 1894 (3 vols,
blue cloth) £750
When London Burned, Scribner's (U.S.), 1894 £200
ditto, Blackie, 1895 [1894] (blue cloth) . . . £200
Cuthbert Hartington and A Woman of the Commune,
F.V. White, 1895 (red cloth) £200
Wulf the Saxon, Scribner's (U.S.), 1894 . . £75
ditto, Blackie, 1895 [1894] (green cloth) . . £75
In the Heart of the Rockies, Scribner's (U.S.), 1894 .
. . . . £100
ditto, Blackie, 1895 [1894] (grey cloth) . . . £100
A Knight of the White Cross, Scribner's (U.S.), 1895 .
. . . . £150
ditto, Blackie, 1895 [1894] (green cloth) . . £150
Bears and Dacoits, Blackie, [1896] (green-brown cloth
with five children among flowered vine design on
front) £300
Surly Joe, Blackie, [1896] (wraps) £200
White-Faced Dick, Blackie, [1896] (limp orange cloth
cover) £200
Through Russian Snows, Scribner's (U.S.), 1895 £100
ditto, Blackie, 1896 [1895] (grey cloth) . . . £100
The Tiger of Mysore, Scribner's (U.S.), 1895 . £100
ditto, Blackie, 1896 [1895] (blue cloth) . . . £100
On the Irrawaddy, Scribner's (U.S.), 1896 . . £150
ditto, Blackie, 1897 [1896] (blue cloth) . . . £150
At Agincourt, Scribner's (U.S.), 1896 . . . £150
ditto, Blackie, 1897 (grey cloth) £150
With Cochrane the Dauntless, Scribner's (U.S.), 1896
. . . . £100
ditto, Blackie, 1897 (blue cloth) £100
The Queen's Cup, Chatto & Windus, 1897 (three vols,
green or blue cloth) £600

Among Malay Pirates, Hurst & Co. (U.S.), [1897]. .
. . . . £150
With Moore at Corunna, Scribner's (U.S.), 1897 £100
ditto, Blackie, 1898 [1897] (green or blue cloth) £100
Colonel Thorndyke's Secret, Chatto & Windus, 1898
(pink cloth) £150
With Frederick the Great, Scribner's (U.S.), 1897. .
. . . . £100
ditto, Blackie, 1898 [1897] (32pps of adverts headed
'Books for Young People' or 'Illustrated Story
Books', red cloth) £100
Under Wellington's Command, Scribner's (U.S.),
1898 . . . . £100
ditto, Blackie, 1899 [1898] (blue cloth) . . . £100
At Aboukir and Acre, Scribner's (U.S.), 1898 . £100
ditto, Blackie, 1899 [1898] (red cloth) . . . £100
Both Sides the Border, Scribner's (U.S.), 1898. £75
ditto, Blackie, 1899 [1898] (blue cloth) . . . £75
The Lost Heir, James Bowden, 1899 (green cloth). .
. . . . £150
The Golden Canon, Mershon (U.S.), 1899 (light
brown cloth) £150
On the Spanish Main, Chambers, [1899] (red wraps) .
. . . . £100
At Duty's Call, Chambers, [1899] £75
A Roving Commission, Scribner's (U.S.), 1899 £100
ditto, Blackie, 1900 [1899] (red cloth) . . . £100
Won by the Sword, Scribner's (U.S.), 1899 . . £75
ditto, Blackie, 1900 [1899] (blue cloth) . . . £75
No Surrender!, Scribner's (U.S.), 1899 . . . £100
ditto, Blackie, 1900 [1899] (red cloth) . . . £100
Do Your Duty, Blackie, [1900] (blue or green cloth) .
. . . . £150
The Soul Survivors, Chambers, [1901] (red wraps) .
. . . . £100
In the Irish Brigade, Scribner's (U.S.), 1900 . £100
ditto, Blackie, 1901 [1900] (green cloth) . . £100
Out With Garibaldi, Scribner's (U.S.), 1900 . £65
ditto, Blackie, 1901 [1900] (blue cloth) . . . £65
John Hawke's Fortune, Chapman & Hall: Young
People's Library series, 1901 (paper cover) . £65
With Buller in Natal, Scribner's (U.S.), 1900 . £65
ditto, Blackie, 1901 (blue cloth) £65
In the Hands of the Cave Dwellers, Harper (U.S.),
1900 . . . . £150
ditto, Blackie, 1903 [1902] £150
Queen Victoria, Blackie, 1901 (purple cloth) . £50
To Herat and Cabul, Scribner's (U.S.), 1901 . £65
ditto, Blackie, 1902 [1901] (blue cloth) . . . £65
With Roberts in Pretoria, Scribner's (U.S.), 1901 £150
ditto, Blackie, 1902 [1901] (red cloth) . . . £150
At the Point of the Bayonet, Scribner's (U.S.), 1901 .
. . . . £65
ditto, Blackie, 1902 [1901] (green cloth) . . £65
At Duty's Call, Chambers, [1902] (red wraps or cloth) .
. . . . £75
The Treasure of the Incas, Scribner's (U.S.), 1902 £75
ditto, Blackie, 1903 [1902] (green cloth) . . £75
With the British Legion, Scribner's (U.S.), 1902 £75

ditto, Blackie, 1903 [1902] (blue or green cloth)   £75
With Kitchener in the Soudan, Scribner's (U.S.), 1902
. . . . £65
ditto, Blackie, 1903 [1902] (red cloth)   .   .   .   £65
Through Three Campaigns, Scribner's (U.S.), 1903 .
. . . . £65
ditto, Blackie, 1904 [1903] (red cloth)   .   .   .   £65
With the Allies to Pekin, Scribner's (U.S.), 1903   £65
ditto, Blackie, 1904 [1903] (green cloth)   .   .   £65
By Conduct and Courage, Scribner's (U.S.), 1904. .
. . . . £100
ditto, Blackie, 1905 [1904] (red cloth)   .   .   .   £100
Gallant Deeds, Chambers, 1905 (white or grey cloth) .
. . . . £65
In the Hands of the Malays, Blackie, 1905 (red
boards) £65
A Soldier's Daughter, Blackie, 1906 [1905] (red, blue
or green boards) £65
ditto, as *The Two Prisoners*, Blackie, 1906 [1905] £45

JAMES HERBERT
(b.1943)

Often thought of as the British version of Stephen
King, Herbert may not have King's world-wide sales,
but he is just as successful in the United Kingdom.

Novels
The Rats, New English Library, 1974   .   .   £300/£50
ditto, as *Deadly Eyes*, Signet (U.S.), 1975 (wraps) . £5
ditto, as *The Rats*, New English Library, 1985 (limited
edition, limitation unknown)   .   .   .   .   £35/£10
The Fog, New English Library, 1975   .   . £175/£45
ditto, Signet (U.S.), 1975 (wraps) £5
ditto, New English Library, 1988 (3,000 copies)   .   .
. . . . £30/£10
The Survivor, New English Library, 1976 .   £75/£25
ditto, Signet (U.S.), 1977 (wraps) £5
ditto, New English Library, 1988 (2,000 copies) . .
. . . . £30/£10
Fluke, New English Library, 1977   .   .   . £50/£15
ditto, Signet (U.S.), 1978 (wraps) £5
The Spear, New English Library, 1978 .   .   . £25/£5
ditto, Signet (U.S.), 1980 (wraps) £5
Lair, New English Library, 1979.   .   .   . £200/£50
ditto, Signet (U.S.), 1979 (wraps) £5
ditto, New English Library, 1985 (limited edition,
limitation unknown) .   .   .   . £100/£25
The Dark, New English Library, 1980   .   . £30/£10
ditto, Signet (U.S.), 1980 (wraps) £5
ditto, New English Library, 1988 (2,000 copies)   .   .
. . . . £30/£10
The Jonah, New English Library, 1981.   .   . £25/£5
ditto, Signet (U.S.), 1981 (wraps) £5
ditto, New English Library, 1985 (limited edition,
limitation unknown) .   .   .   . £25/£5
Shrine, New English Library, 1983 .   .   .   . £25/£5

ditto, Signet (U.S.), 1985 (wraps) £5
Domain, New English Library, 1984   .   .   . £25/£5
ditto, Signet (U.S.), 1985 (wraps) £5
Moon, New English Library, 1985   .   .   .   . £20/£5
ditto, Crown (U.S.), 1985 .   .   .   .   .   . £15/£5
The Magic Cottage, Hodder & Stoughton, 1986 £15/£5
ditto, New American Library (U.S.), 1987 .   . £15/£5
Sepulchre, Hodder & Stoughton, 1987 .   .   . £15/£5
ditto, Putnam's (U.S.), 1988 .   .   .   .   . £15/£5
Haunted, Hodder & Stoughton, 1988 .   .   . £15/£5
ditto, Hodder & Stoughton, 1988 (250 signed copies,
slipcase, no d/w) .   .   .   . £75/£50
ditto, Putnam's (U.S.), 1989 .   .   .   .   . £15/£5
Creed, Hodder & Stoughton, 1990 .   .   .   . £15/£5
Portent, Hodder & Stoughton, 1992. .   .   . £15/£5
ditto, Hodder & Stoughton, 1992 (pre-publication
issue, with d/w) .   .   .   . £35/£10
ditto, Harper Prism (U.S.), 1996 .   .   .   . £15/£5
The Ghosts of Sleath, Harper Collins, 1994 . £15/£5
ditto, Harper Collins, 1994 (over-sized edition, 500
signed copies)   .   .   .   . £40/£20
ditto, Harper Prism (U.S.), 1996 .   .   .   . £15/£5
'48, Harper Collins, 1996.   .   .   .   .   .   . £15/£5
ditto, Harper Prism (U.S.), 1996 .   .   .   . £15/£5
Others, Macmillan, 1999 .   .   .   .   .   . £15/£5
ditto, Forge (U.S.), 1999 .   .   .   .   .   . £10/£5
Once..., Macmillan, 2001   .   .   .   .   . £10/£5
ditto, Tor (U.S.), 2002.   .   .   .   .   .   . £10/£5

Others
James Herbert's Dark Places, Harper Collins, 1983 .
. . . . £15/£5
The City, Pan Macmillan, 1994 (wraps).   .   .   . £5
ditto, Pan Macmillan, 1994 (1,000 copies, signed by
author and artist in silver, some with flyer)   . £25

From 1990 Hodder & Stoughton have published
Uniform Editions of the above titles, each edition
limited to 3,000 copies .   .   .   . £25/£5 each

EDWARD HERON-ALLEN
(b.1861 d.1943)

A British scientist and polymath whose writings range
from hard sciences to the occult. He wrote several
entertaining works of weird fiction under the
pseudonym of 'Christopher Blayre' which are highly
sought after by collectors.

Novels
The Princess Daphne, Belford, Clarke & Co. (U.S.),
1888 (with Selina Dolaro) £150
ditto, H.J. Drane, 1889 .   .   .   .   .   . £150
ditto, Tartarus Press, 2001 (300 numbered copies) . .
. . . . £75/£20
The Romance of a Quiet Watering-Place, Belford,
Clarke & Co. (U.S.), 1888 (pseud. 'Nora Helen
Warddel'). £100

Bella Demonia, Belford, Clarke & Co. (U.S.), [c.1889]
(ghost written for Selina Dolaro) £100
The Vengeance of Maurice Denalguez, Belford,
Clarke & Co. (U.S.), [c.1889] (ghost written for
Selina Dolaro) £100

Short Stories
Kisses of Fate. A study of mere human nature,
Belford, Clarke & Co. (U.S.), 1888 . . . £125
A Fatal Fiddle: the commonplace tragedy of a snob,
Belford, Clarke & Co. (U.S.), 1889 . . . £150
The Purple Sapphire and other Posthumous Papers,
Allan, [1921] (pseud. 'Christopher Blayre', grey
paper boards). . . . .
£250
ditto, Allan, [1921] (10 numbered presentation copies,
grey paper boards) £500
ditto, Allan, [1921] (second issue, boards with purple
cloth, gilt lettering) . . . . . . £200/£75
ditto, Allan, [1921] (later issue, purple/grey cloth with
black lettering) . . . . £200/£65
ditto, as **The Strange Papers of Dr. Blayre**, Allan,
1932 . . . . £200/£65
ditto, as **The Strange Papers of Dr. Blayre**, Arno Press
(U.S.), 1976 . . . . £35
The Cheetah-Girl, privately printed, 1923 (pseud.
'Christopher Blayre', 20 signed copies) . . £1,500
ditto, Tartarus Press, 1998 (99 numbered copies) .
. . . . £150/£100
Some Women of the University, Sorelle Nessuno,
Nubiana [Stockwell], 1934 (pseud. 'Christopher
Blayre', 100 numbered copies) £350
The Collected Strange Papers of Christopher Blayre,
Tartarus Press, 1998 . . . . £100/£30

Palmistry
Chiromancy, or the science of palmistry, Routledge &
Sons, 1883 . . . . £45
A Manual of Cheirosophy, Ward, Lock & Co., 1885 .
. . . . £25
**Practical Cheirosophy. A synoptical study of the
science of the hand, etc.**, G.P. Putnam's & Sons
(U.S.), 1887 . . . . £25

Poetry
The Love-Letters of a Vagabond, H.J. Drane, 1889
[1889]. £125

Translations and Commentaries
The Ruba'iyat of Omar Khayyam, H.S. Nichols, 1898
(1022 copies). £100
**Some Side-lights upon Edward FitzGerald's poem
'The Ruba'iyat of Omar Khayyam.'**, Nichols, 1898
(wraps) £40

The Violin
Violin-Making, as it was and is, Ward, Lock & Co.,
1884 . . . . £200
ditto, Ward, Lock & Co., [1885.]. £65

ditto, Ward, Lock & Co., 1886 (deluxe edition of 25
copies for private circulation) £500

Scientific Titles
**The Foraminifera of the Clare Island District, Co.
Mayo, Ireland**, Dublin, 1913 . . . . . £100
**The Fossil Foraminifera of the Blue Marl of the Côte
des Basques, Biarritz**, Manchester, 1919 . . £125
Barnacles in Nature and in Myth, Humphrey Milford,
1928 . . . . £125/£65

Local History
Selsey Bill: Historic and Prehistoric, Duckworth, 1911
(2 vols) £250
Journal of the Great War, Phillimore, 2002 . £20/£5

HERMANN HESSE
(b.1877 d.1962)

One of the greatest literary figures of the German-
speaking world, the Nazis banned his books, but he
was awarded the Nobel Prize for Literature in 1946.

Novels
Peter Camenzind, Fischer (Berlin), 1904 . . £300
ditto, Peter Owen/Vision Press, 1961 (translated by
W.J. Strachan) . . . . £60/£15
ditto, Farrar Straus & Giroux (U.S.), 1969 (translated
by Michael Roloff) . . . . . . £45/£10
Unterm Rad, Fischer (Berlin), 1906 . . . . £250
ditto, as **The Prodigy**, Peter Owen/Vision Press, 1957
(translated by W.J. Strachan) . . . . £60/£15
ditto, as **Beneath the Wheel**, Farrar Straus & Giroux
(U.S.), 1968 (translated by Michael Roloff) £50/£10
Gertrud, Albert Langen (Munchen), 1910 . . £200
ditto, as **Gertrude**, Peter Owen, 1955 (translated by
Hilda Rosner). . . . . £50/£10
ditto, Farrar Straus & Giroux (U.S.), 1969 . £50/£10
Roßhalde, Fischer (Berlin), 1914 . . . . £150
ditto, as **Rosshalde**, Farrar Straus & Giroux (U.S.),
1970 (translated by Ralph Manheim) . . £45/£10
ditto, Cape, 1971 . . . . £45/£10
Knulp: Drei Geschichten aus dem Leben Knulps, Farr
Fischer (Berlin), 1915 . . . . . . £150
ditto, as **Knulp**, Farrar Straus & Giroux (U.S.), 1971
(translated by Ralph Manheim). . . . £40/£10
ditto, Cape, 1972 . . . . £40/£10
Demian, Fischer (Berlin), 1919 . . . . . £300
ditto, as **In Sight of Chaos**, Seldwyla (Zurich), 1923
(translated by Stephen Hudson, no d/w) . . £350
ditto, as **Demian**, Boni & Liveright (U.S.), 1923 .
. . . . £300/£100
ditto, Peter Owen/Vision Press, 1960 (translated by
W.J. Strachan) . . . . £65/£20
Klingsor's Letzter Sommer, Fischer (Berlin), 1920 .
. . . . £750/£150

ditto, as **Klingsor's Last Summer**, Farrar Straus & Giroux (U.S.), 1970 (translated by Richard and Clara Winston) . . . . £40/£10
ditto, Cape, 1971 . . . . £15/£5
Siddhartha, Eine indische Dichtung, Fischer (Berlin), 1922 . . . . £750/£150
ditto, as **Siddhartha**, New Directions (U.S.), 1951 (translated by Hilda Rosner) . . . £40/£10
ditto, Peter Owen, 1954 . . . . . £40/£10
Der Steppenwolf, Fischer (Berlin), 1927 £2,500/£250
ditto, as **Steppenwolf**, Secker, 1929 (translated by Basil Creighton) . . . . £1,500/£100
ditto, Holt (U.S.), 1929 . . . . . £750/£75
Narziß und Goldmund, Fischer (Berlin), 1930 . . .
. . . . £1,000/£150
ditto, as **Goldmund**, Peter Owen, 1959 (translated by Geoffrey Dunlop) . . . . . £65/£10
ditto, as **Narcissus and Goldmund**, Farrar Straus & Giroux (U.S.), 1968 (translated by Ursule Molinaro) .
. . . . £50/£10
Die Morgenlandfahrt, Fischer (Berlin), 1932 . .
. . . . £750/£200
ditto, as **The Journey to the East**, Peter Owen, 1954 (translated by Hilda Rosner) . . . £65/£15
ditto, Noonday Press (U.S.), 1957 . . . £45/£10
Das Glasperlenspiel, Fretz & Wasmuth (Zurich), 1943 (2 vols) . . . . £1,500/£75
ditto, as **Magister Ludi**, Holt (U.S.), 1949 (translated by Mervyn Savill) . . . . . £45/£10
ditto, as **The Glass Bead Game**, Holt (U.S.), 1969 (translated by Richard and Clara Winston) £45/£10
ditto, Cape, 1970 . . . . £40/£10

Short Stories
Strange News from Another Star, Farrar Straus & Giroux (U.S.), 1972 (translated by Denver Lindley) .
. . . . £40/£10
ditto, Cape, 1973 . . . . £40/£10
Stories of Five Decades, Farrar Straus & Giroux (U.S.), 1975 (translated by Ralph Manheim and Denver Lindley) . . . . £30/£10
ditto, Cape, 1974 . . . . £25/£10

Others
Poems, Farrar Straus & Giroux (U.S.), 1970 (translated by James Wright) . . . . . £30/£10
ditto, Cape, 1971 . . . . £25/£10
If the War Goes On..., Farrar Straus & Giroux (U.S.), 1971 (translated by Ralph Manheim) . . £40/£10
ditto, Cape, 1972 . . . . £35/£10
Wandering, Farrar Straus & Giroux (U.S.), 1972 (translated by James Wright) . . . . £50/£15
Autobiographical Writings, Farrar Straus & Giroux (U.S.), 1972 (translated by Denver Lindley) £30/£10
ditto, Cape, 1973 . . . . £30/£10
My Belief, Farrar Straus & Giroux (U.S.), 1974 (translated by Denver Lindley and Ralph Manheim) .
. . . . £30/£10
ditto, Cape, 1976 . . . . £30/£10
Reflections, Farrar Straus & Giroux (U.S.), 1974 (translated by Ralph Manheim) . . . . £30/£10

ditto, Cape, 1972 . . . . £35/£10
Crisis, Farrar Straus & Giroux (U.S.), 1975 (translated by Ralph Manheim) . . . . . . £30/£10

PATRICIA HIGHSMITH
(b.1921 d.1995)

A cult crime writer born in Fort Worth, Texas, Highsmith began writing at the age of fifteen. She started out writing speech bubbles for comic strips such as *Superman*. Her first novel, *Strangers on a Train*, was filmed by Hitchcock in 1951. She lived in Europe during her later years and died in Switzerland.

Novels
Strangers on a Train, Harper (U.S.), 1950 . . . .
. . . . £1,250/£500
ditto, Cresset Press, 1951 . . . . . £500/£75
The Price of Salt, Coward-McCann (U.S.), 1952 (pseud. 'Claire Morgan') . . . . £250/£50
ditto, as **Carol**, Bloomsbury, 1990 . . . £15/£5
The Blunderer, Coward-McCann (U.S.), 1954 . . .
. . . . £200/£50
ditto, Cresset Press, 1956 . . . . . £175/£50
The Talented Mr Ripley, Coward-McCann (U.S.), 1955 . . . . £750/£75
ditto, Cresset Press, 1957 . . . . . £450/£75
Deep Water, Harper (U.S.), 1957 . . . £350/£45
ditto, Heinemann, 1958 . . . . . £300/£40
A Game for the Living, Harper (U.S.), 1958 £50/£20
ditto, Heinemann, 1959 . . . . . £45/£15
This Sweet Sickness, Harper (U.S.), 1960 . £40/£15
ditto, Heinemann, 1961 . . . . . £35/£10
The Cry of the Owl, Harper (U.S.), 1962 . £40/£10
ditto, Heinemann, 1963 . . . . . £35/£5
The Two Faces of January, Doubleday (U.S.), 1964 .
. . . . £40/£10
ditto, Heinemann, 1964 . . . . . £35/£5
The Glass Cell, Doubleday (U.S.), 1964 . £45/£10
ditto, Heinemann, 1965 . . . . . £45/£10
The Story-Teller, Doubleday (U.S.), 1965 . £35/£10
ditto, as **A Suspension of Mercy**, Heinemann, 1965 .
. . . . £30/£5
Those Who Walk Away, Doubleday (U.S.), 1967 . .
. . . . £30/£5
ditto, Heinemann, 1967 . . . . . £25/£5
The Tremor of Forgery, Doubleday (U.S.), 1969 . .
. . . . £20/£5
ditto, Heinemann, 1969 . . . . . £25/£5
Ripley Under Ground, Doubleday (U.S.), 1970 . .
. . . . £50/£10
ditto, Heinemann, 1971 . . . . . £40/£10
A Dog's Ransom, Knopf (U.S.), 1972 . . £30/£5
ditto, Heinemann, 1972 . . . . . £25/£5
Ripley's Game, Knopf (U.S.), 1974 . . £45/£10
ditto, Heinemann, 1974 . . . . . £35/£10
Edith's Diary, Simon & Schuster (U.S.), 1977 . £20/£5

ditto, Heinemann, 1977 . . . . £20/£5
The Boy Who Followed Ripley, Heinemann, 1980. .
. . . . £20/£5
ditto, Lippincott (U.S.), 1980. . . . . £20/£5
The People Who Knock on the Door, Heinemann,
1983 . . . . £15/£5
ditto, Penzler (U.S.), [1985] (250 signed copies,
slipcase, no d/w) . . . . £40/£30
ditto, Penzler (U.S.), [1985] . . . . . . £10/£5
Found in the Street, Heinemann, 1986 . . . £15/£5
ditto, Atlantic Monthly Press (U.S.), 1986 . . £15/£5
Ripley Under Water, Bloomsbury, 1991 . . £20/£5
ditto, London Limited Editions, 1991 (150 signed
copies, glassine d/w). . . . . . . £60/£50
ditto, Knopf (U.S.), 1992 . . . . . . £20/£5
Small G: A Summer Idyll, Bloomsbury, 1995 . £15/£5

Short Stories
The Snail-Watcher, Doubleday (U.S.), 1970 . £25/£5
ditto, as **Eleven**, Heinemann, 1970 . . . . £25/£5
Kleine Geschichten Fur Weiberfeinde, Diogenes
(Germany), 1974. . . . . £25/£10
ditto, as **Little Tales of Misogyny**, Heinemann, 1977 .
. . . . £25/£5
ditto, as **Little Tales of Misogyny**, Penzler (U.S.),
[1986] (250 signed copies, slipcase, no d/w) £30/£20
ditto, as **Little Tales of Misogyny**, Penzler (U.S.),
[1986]. . . . . £10/£5
The Animal-Lover's Book of Beastly Murder,
Heinemann, 1975 . . . . £25/£5
ditto, Penzler (U.S.), [1986] (250 signed copies,
slipcase, no d/w) . . . . £25/£15
ditto, Penzler (U.S.), [1986] . . . . . £10/£5
Slowly, Slowly in the Wind, Heinemann, 1979 . £20/£5
ditto, Penzler, [1984] (250 signed copies, slipcase and
d/w) . . . . £25/£15
ditto, Penzler, [1984] . . . . £10/£5
The Black House, Heinemann, 1981 . . . £15/£5
ditto, Penzler (U.S.), [1988] (250 signed copies,
slipcase, no d/w) . . . . . . £25/£15
ditto, Penzler (U.S.), [1988] . . . . £10/£5
Mermaids on the Golf Course and Other Stories,
Heinemann, 1985 . . . . £15/£5
ditto, Mysterious Press (U.S.), 1988 . . . . £10/£5
**The Man Who Wrote Books in His Head and Other
Stories**, Eurographica (Helsinki), 1986 (350 signed
copies, wraps and d/w) £50
Tales of Natural and Unnatural Catastrophes,
Bloomsbury, 1987 . . . . £15/£5
ditto, Atlantic Monthly Press (U.S.), 1989 . £10/£5
Where the Action Is and Other Stories, Eurographica
(Helsinki), 1989 (350 signed copies, wraps and d/w) .
. . . . £50
Tales of Obsession, Severn House, 1994 . . £10/£5

Children's Titles
Miranda the Panda is on the Verandah, Coward-
McCann (U.S.), 1958 (with Doris Sanders) £50/£15

Miscellaneous
Plotting and Writing Suspense Fiction, Writer (U.S.),
1966 . . . . £25/£10
ditto, Poplar Press, 1983 . . . . . . £10/£5

REGINALD HILL
(b.1936)

Although he has written a number of books with other
characters, often under pseudonyms, Hill is best
known for his now televised 'Dalziel (pronounced
'De-al') and Pascoe' novels.

'Dalziel and Pascoe' Novels
A Clubbable Woman, Collins Crime Club, 1970 . .
. . . . £500/£75
ditto, Countryman (U.S.), 1984 . . . . . £25/£5
An Advancement of Learning, Collins Crime Club,
1971 . . . . £300/£25
ditto, Countryman (U.S.), 1985 . . . . . £20/£5
Ruling Passion, Collins Crime Club, 1973 . £200/£25
ditto, Harper (U.S.), 1977. . . . . . £45/£10
An April Shroud, Collins Crime Club, 1975 £300/£35
ditto, Countryman (U.S.), 1986 . . . . . £15/£5
A Pinch of Snuff, Collins Crime Club, 1978 £250/£25
ditto, Harper (U.S.), 1978. . . . . . £150/£20
A Killing Kindness, Collins Crime Club, 1980 . . .
. . . . £150/£20
ditto, Pantheon (U.S.), 1981 . . . . . £25/£5
Deadheads, Collins Crime Club, 1983 . . £75/£10
ditto, Macmillan, 1984 . . . . . . £35/£10
Exit Lines, Collins Crime Club, 1984 . . £75/£10
ditto, Macmillan (U.S.), 1985 . . . . . £30/£5
Child's Play, Collins Crime Club, 1987 . . £50/£10
ditto, Macmillan (U.S.), 1987 . . . . . £25/£5
Under World, Collins Crime Club, 1988 . £40/£10
ditto, Scribner's (U.S.), 1988 . . . . . £20/£5
Bones and Silence, Collins Crime Club, 1990 . £15/£5
ditto, Delacorte (U.S.), 1990 . . . . . £15/£5
Recalled to Life, Scorpion Press, 1992 (99 signed,
numbered copies) £100
ditto, Scorpion Press, 1992 (20 signed, lettered copies)
. . . . £200
ditto, Collins Crime Club, 1992 . . . . . £25/£5
ditto, Delacorte (U.S.), 1992 . . . . . £15/£5
Pictures of Perfection, Scorpion Press, 1994 (75
signed, numbered copies) £85
ditto, Scorpion Press, 1994 (20 signed, lettered copies)
. . . . £200
ditto, Collins Crime Club, 1994 . . . . . £20/£5
ditto, Delacorte (U.S.), 1994 . . . . . £10/£5
The Wood Beyond, Scorpion Press, 1996 (85 signed,
numbered copies) £45
ditto, HarperCollins, 1996 . . . . . . £10/£5
ditto, Delacorte (U.S.), 1996 . . . . . £10/£5
On Beulah Height, Scorpion Press, 1998 (85 signed,
numbered copies) £45

ditto, HarperCollins, 1998 . . . . . £10/£5
ditto, Delacorte (U.S.), 1998 . . . . . £10/£5
Arms and the Women, HarperCollins, 2000 . £10/£5
ditto, Delacorte (U.S.), 2000 . . . . . £10/£5
Dialogues of the Dead, HarperCollins, 2001 . £10/£5
ditto, Delacorte (U.S.), 2001 . . . . . £10/£5
Death's Jest Book, HarperCollins, 2002 . . £10/£5

'Joe Sixsmith' Novels
Blood Sympathy, Collins Crime Club, 1993 . £30/£5
Born Guilty, HarperCollins, 1995 . . . . £25/£5
Killing the Lawyers, HarperCollins, 1997 . . £15/£5
Singing the Sadness, HarperCollins, 1999 . . £15/£5

Other Novels
Fell of Dark, Collins Crime Club, 1971 . . £350/£45
ditto, N.A.L. (U.S.), 1986 . . . . . . £20/£5
A Fairly Dangerous Thing, Collins Crime Club, 1972
. . . . £100/£15
ditto, Countryman (U.S.), 1983 . . . . . £15/£5
A Very Good Hater, Collins Crime Club, 1974 . . .
. . . . £100/£15
ditto, Countryman (U.S.), 1982 . . . . . £20/£5
Another Death in Venice, Collins Crime Club, 1976 .
. . . . £100/£15
ditto, NAL (U.S.), 1987 . . . . £15/£5
The Spy's Wife, Collins, 1980 . . . . . £45/£10
ditto, Pantheon (U.S.), 1980 . . . . . £20/£5
Who Guards a Prince?, Collins, 1982 . . . £40/£5
ditto, as *Who Guards the Prince?*, Pantheon 1982 .
. . . . £30/£5
Traitor's Blood, Collins, 1983 . . . . £50/£10
ditto, Countryman (U.S.), 1986 . . . . . £25/£5
No Man's Land, Collins, 1985 . . . . . £35/£5
ditto, St Martin's Press (U.S.), 1985 . . . . £25/£5
The Collaborators, Collins, 1987 . . . . £15/£5
ditto, Countryman (U.S.), 1989 . . . . . £15/£5

Short Stories
Pascoe's Ghost, Collins Crime Club, 1979 . £125/£20
There Are No Ghosts in the Soviet Union, Collins
Crime Club, 1987 . . . . £50/£10
ditto, Countryman (U.S.), 1988 . . . . . £15/£5
One Small Step, Collins Crime Club, 1990 . . £40/£5
Brother's Keeper, Eurographica, 1992 (350 signed
copies, wraps) £60
Asking for the Moon, HarperCollins, 1994 . . £20/£5
ditto, Countryman (U.S.), 1996 . . . . . £15/£5

Novels Written as 'Dick Moorland'
Heart Clock, Faber, 1973 . . . . . . £150/£25
Albion! Albion!, Faber, 1974 . . . . £75/£10

Novels Written as 'Patrick Ruell'
The Castle of the Demon, John Long, 1971 . £25/£5
ditto, Hawthorn (U.S.), 1973 . . . . . . £25/£5
ditto, as *The Turning of the Tide*, Severn House, 1999
. . . . £15/£5
Red Christmas, Long, 1972 . . . . £150/£25
ditto, Hawthorn (U.S.), 1974 . . . . £50/£10

Death Takes the Low Road, Hutchinson, 1974 . . . .
. . . . £150/£25
ditto, Mysterious Press (U.S.), 1987 . . . . £20/£5
Urn Burial, Hutchinson, 1975, ... £75/£15
ditto, Countryman (U.S.), 1987 . . . . . £15/£5
ditto, as *Beyond the Bone*, Severn House, 2000 £15/£5
The Long Kill, Methuen, 1986 . . . . . £25/£5
ditto, Countryman (U.S.), 1988 . . . . . £20/£5
Death of a Dormouse, Methuen, 1987 . . . £15/£5
ditto, Mysterious Press (U.S.), 1987 . . . . £15/£5
Dream of Darkness, Methuen, 1989 . . . £15/£5
ditto, Countryman (U.S.), 1990 . . . . . £15/£5
The Only Game, Collins, 1991 . . . . . £15/£5
ditto, Countryman (U.S.), 1993 . . . . . £15/£5

Novels Written as 'Charles Underhill'
Captain Fantom, Hutchinson, 1978 . . . . £20/£5
ditto, St Martin's Press (U.S.), 1980 . . . . £20/£5
The Forging of Fantom, Hutchinson, 1979. £200/£35

WILLIAM HOPE HODGSON
(b.1877 d.1918)

Hodgson was born in Essex and spent many of his earlier years at sea with the Merchant Marine. He is known for his ghost and horror stories, many of which have a maritime theme. Hodgson was killed in an artillery bombardment near Ypres in April, 1918.

The Boats of 'Glen Carrig ', Chapman & Hall, 1907 .
. . . . £1,250
The House on the Borderland, Chapman & Hall, 1908
. . . . £2,000
The Ghost Pirates, Stanley Paul, 1909 . . . £1,250
The Night Land, Eveleigh Nash, 1912 . . . £2,000
Poems and The Dream of X, R. Harold Paget (U.S.),
1912 (wraps) £300
Carnacki the Ghost-Finder, Eveleigh Nash, 1913 . . .
. . . . £1,250
ditto, Mycroft & Moran (U.S.), 1947 . . £100/£30
Men of the Deep Waters, Eveleigh Nash, 1914 . £900
The Luck of the Strong, Eveleigh Nash, 1916 . £400
Captain Gault, Eveleigh Nash, 1917 . . . £400
ditto, Mcbride & Co. (U.S.), 1918 . . . £200
The Calling of the Sea, Selwyn & Blount, 1920 . . .
. . . . £750/£250
The Voice of the Ocean, Selwyn & Blount, 1921 . . .
. . . . £750/£250
The House on the Borderland and Other Novels,
Arkham House (U.S.), 1946 . . . . £250/£75
Deep Waters, Arkham House (U.S.), 1967 . £125/£30
Out of the Storm, Donald Grant (U.S.), 1975 £50/£15
The Dream of X, Donald Grant (U.S.), 1977 £30/£10
Poems of the Sea, Ferret Fantasy, 1977 (50 numbered
large paper copies of 500 signed by editor) £65/£20
ditto, Ferret Fantasy, 1977 (450 copies of 500) £45/£15

The Haunted 'Pampero': Uncollected Fantasies and Mysteries, Donald Grant (U.S.), 1996 (500 numbered copies signed by editor) . . . . . £30/£10
Terrors of the Sea: Unpublished and Uncollected Fantasies, Donald M. Grant (U.S.), 1996 . £50/£15

NICK HORNBY
(b.1957)

Hornby is a successful writer due to his ability to convey with humour his passions, for example football and popular music, to readers who would not otherwise be interested.

Novels
Fever Pitch, Gollancz, 1992 . . . . . £400/£20
ditto, Penguin (U.S.), 1992 (wraps) . . . £10
ditto, as *Fever Pitch: The Screenplay*, Indigo, 1997 (wraps) £5
High Fidelity, Gollancz, 1995 . . . . £45/£5
ditto, Riverhead/Putnam (U.S.), 1995 . . £20/£5
About a Boy, Gollancz, 1998 . . . . £15/£5
ditto, Riverhead/Putnam (U.S.), 1998 . . £10/£5
How to Be Good, Viking, 2001 . . . £15/£5
ditto, Riverhead/Putnam (U.S.), 2001 . . £10/£5

Others
Contemporary American Fiction, Vision Press/St Martin's Press, 1992 . . . . . £100/£20

GEOFFREY HOUSEHOLD
(b.1900 d.1988)

'Household' is a pseudonym for Edward West. He is best known for his second novel, *Rogue Male*, although he wrote twenty thrillers and adventure stories. His work is characterised by an interest in the psychology of the chase.

Novels
The Third Hour, Chatto & Windus, 1937 . £125/£25
ditto, Little, Brown (U.S.), 1938 . . . . £100/£20
Rogue Male, Chatto & Windus, 1939 . £500/£45
ditto, Little, Brown (U.S.), 1939 . . . . £350/£40
Arabesque, Chatto & Windus, 1948 . . . £45/£10
ditto, Little, Brown (U.S.), 1948 . . . . £35/£5
The High Place, Joseph, 1950 . . . . £30/£5
ditto, Little, Brown (U.S.), 1950 . . . . £20/£5
A Rough Shoot, Joseph, 1951 . . . . £40/£5
ditto, Little, Brown (U.S.), 1951 . . . . £20/£5
A Time to Kill, Little, Brown (U.S.), 1951 . £30/£5
ditto, Joseph, 1952 . . . . £20/£5
Fellow Passenger, Joseph, 1955 . . . . £20/£5
ditto, Little, Brown (U.S.), 1955 . . . . £20/£5
Watcher in the Shadows, Joseph, 1960 . . £15/£5
ditto, Little, Brown (U.S.), 1960 . . . . £15/£5

Thing to Love, Joseph, 1963 . . . . . £15/£5
ditto, Little, Brown (U.S.), 1963 . . . . £15/£5
Olura, Joseph, 1965 . . . . £10/£5
ditto, Little, Brown (U.S.), 1965 . . . . £10/£5
The Courtesy of Death, Joseph, 1967 . . £10/£5
ditto, Little, Brown (U.S.), 1967 . . . . £10/£5
Dance of the Dwarfs, Joseph, 1968 . . . £10/£5
ditto, Little, Brown (U.S.), 1968 . . . . £10/£5
Doom's Caravan, Joseph, 1971 . . . . £10/£5
ditto, Little, Brown (U.S.), 1971 . . . . £10/£5
The Three Sentinels, Joseph, 1972 . . . £10/£5
ditto, Little, Brown (U.S.), 1972 . . . . £10/£5
The Lives and Times of Bernardo Brown, Joseph, 1973 . . . . £10/£5
ditto, Little, Brown (U.S.), 1974 . . . . £10/£5
Red Anger, Joseph, 1975 . . . . . . £10/£5
ditto, Little, Brown (U.S.), 1976 . . . . £10/£5
Hostage: London, Joseph, 1977 . . . . £10/£5
ditto, Little, Brown (U.S.), 1977 . . . . £10/£5
The Last Two Weeks of George Rivac, Joseph, 1978 . . . . £10/£5
ditto, Little, Brown (U.S.), 1978 . . . . £10/£5
The Sending, Joseph, 1980 . . . . . £10/£5
ditto, Little, Brown (U.S.), 1980 . . . . £10/£5
Summon the Bright Water, Joseph, 1981 . £10/£5
ditto, Little, Brown (U.S.), 1981 . . . . £10/£5
Rogue Justice, Joseph, 1982 . . . . . £10/£5
ditto, Little, Brown (U.S.), 1983 . . . . £10/£5
Face to the Sun, Joseph, 1988 . . . . £10/£5

Short Stories
The Salvation of Pisco Gabar, Chatto & Windus, 1938 . . . . £100/£15
ditto, Little, Brown (U.S.), 1940 . . . . £65/£5
Tales of Adventurers, Joseph, 1952 . . . £20/£5
ditto, Little, Brown (U.S.), 1952 . . . . £15/£5
The Brides of Solomon, Joseph, 1958 . . £20/£5
ditto, Little, Brown (U.S.), 1958 . . . . £15/£5
Sabres on the Sand, Joseph, 1966 . . . £10/£5
ditto, Little, Brown (U.S.), 1966 . . . . £10/£5
The Europe That Was, David & Charles, 1979 . £10/£5
ditto, St Martin's (U.S.), 1979 . . . . £10/£5
Capricorn and Cancer, Joseph, 1981 . . £10/£5
Arrows of Desire, Joseph, 1985 . . . . £10/£5
ditto, Little, Brown (U.S.), 1986 . . . . £10/£5
The Days of Your Fathers, Joseph, 1987 . £10/£5
ditto, Little, Brown (U.S.), 1987 . . . . £10/£5

Children's Titles
The Terror of Villadonga, Hutchinson, 1936 £75/£25
ditto, as *The Spanish Cave*, Little, Brown (U.S.), 1936 (revised edition) . . . . £50/£20
The Exploits of Xenophon, Random House (U.S.), 1955 . . . . £15/£5
ditto, as *Xenophon's Adventure*, Bodley Head, 1961 . . . . £10/£5
Prisoner of the Indies, Bodley Head, 1967 . £10/£5
ditto, Little, Brown (U.S.), 1967 . . . . £10/£5
Escape Into Daylight, Bodley Head, 1976 . £10/£5

A. E. HOUSMAN
(b.1859 d.1936)

Housman was both a scholar and a poet. Although his output of verse was relatively small it is very highly regarded.

Poetry
A Shropshire Lad, Kegan Paul, Trench, Trubner & Co., 1896 (first state with 'Shropshire' on the label 33mm wide) £2,500
ditto, Kegan Paul, Trench, Trubner & Co., 1896 (second state with 'Shropshire' on the label 37mm wide) £1,250
ditto, John Lane (U.S.), 1897 . . . . . £1,250
Last Poems, Grant Richards, [1922] (first issue with comma missing after 'love' and semicolon missing after 'rain' on p.52) . . . . . £150/£25
ditto, Henry Holt (U.S.), 1922 . . . . £75/£15
A Fragment, privately printed, 1930 (37 copies, two folded leaves) £125
Three Poems, privately printed, Dept of English, Univ. College, London, 1935 . . . . . . £45
[For my Funeral], C.U.P., 1936 (300 copies, two folded leaves) £40
More Poems, Cape, 1936 . . . . . £25/£10
ditto, Cape, 1936 (379 deluxe copies) . £200/£75
ditto, Knopf (U.S.), 1936 . . . . . £20/£10
Collected Poems, Cape, 1939 . . . £25/£10
ditto, Henry Holt (U.S.), 1940 . . . £25/£10
Stars, Venice, 1939 (10 copies signed by the artist, F. Prokosch, wraps) £150
The Manuscript Poems of A.E. Housman, Univ. of Minnesota Press (U.S.), 1955 . . . . £30/£15

Prose
Introductory Lecture, C.U.P., 1892 (wraps) . £350
ditto, privately printed, C.U.P., 1933 (100 copies, wraps) £100
ditto, C.U.P., 1937 . . . . £35/£10
ditto, Macmillan & C.U.P. (U.S.), 1937 . . £30/£10
The Name and Nature of Poetry, C.U.P., 1933 . . . . £45/£15
ditto, Macmillan (U.S.), 1933 . . . . £45/£15
Jubilee Address to King George V, C.U.P., 1935 (2 copies of 26 on vellum) £1,250
ditto, C.U.P., 1935 (24 copies of 26) . . . £600
Letters to E.H. Blakeney, privately printed (18 copies) £200
A.E.H., W.W., privately printed, 1944 (12 copies) £175
Thirty Letters to Witter Bynner, Knopf (U.S.), 1957 (700 copies) . . . . £45/£20
To Joseph Ishill, Oriole Press (U.S.), 1959 . £25
Selected Prose, C.U.P., 1961 . . . . £25/£10
The Confines of Criticism, C.U.P., 1969 £30/£10
Letters, Hart-Davis, 1971 . . . . . £35/£10
ditto, Harvard Univ. Press, 1971 . . £35/£10
Classical Papers, C.U.P., 1962 (3 vols) . . £50
Fifteen Letters to Walter Ashburner, Tragara Press, 1976 (125 copies) £75

ELIZABETH JANE HOWARD
(b.1923)

Howard took up writing novels and short stories after spending the war years as an Air Raid Warden in London.

Novels
The Beautiful Visit, Cape, 1950 . . . . £50/£15
ditto, Random House (U.S.), 1950 . . . . £40/£5
The Long View, Cape, 1956 . . . . . £25/£5
ditto, Reynal (U.S.), 1956 . . . . . £25/£5
The Sea Change, Cape, 1959 . . . . £20/£5
ditto, Harper (U.S.), 1960 . . . . . £20/£5
After Julius, Cape, 1965 . . . . . £15/£5
ditto, Viking (U.S.), 1965 . . . . . £15/£5
Something in Disguise, Cape, 1969 . . . £15/£5
ditto, Viking (U.S.), 1970 . . . . . £10/£5
Odd Girl Out, Cape, 1972 . . . . . £10/£5
ditto, Viking (U.S.), 1972 . . . . . £10/£5
Getting it Right, Hamish Hamilton, 1982 . £10/£5
ditto, Viking (U.S.), 1982 . . . . . £10/£5
The Light Years, Macmillan, 1990 . . . £10/£5
ditto, Pocket Books (U.S.), 1990 . . . £10/£5
Marking Time, Macmillan, 1991 . . . £10/£5
ditto, Pocket Books (U.S.), 1992 . . . £10/£5
Confusion, Macmillan, 1993 . . . . . £10/£5
ditto, Pocket Books (U.S.), 1994 . . . £10/£5
Casting Off, Macmillan, 1995 . . . . £10/£5
ditto, Pocket Books (U.S.), 1996 . . . £10/£5
Falling, Macmillan, 1999 . . . . . £10/£5

Short Stories
We Are For the Dark, Cape, 1951 (with Robert Aickman) . . . . £350/£125
Mr Wrong, Cape, 1975 . . . . . . £10/£5
ditto, Viking (U.S.), 1975 . . . . . £10/£5
Three Miles Up, Tartarus Press, 2003 . . . £25/£10

Miscellaneous
Howard and Maschler on Food, Joseph, 1987 (with Fay Maschler) . . . . £10/£5
Slipstream: A Memoir, Macmillan, 2002 . £10/£5

As Editor
The Lover's Companion, David & Charles, 1978 . . . . £15/£5
Green Shades, An Anthology of Plants, Arum, 1991 . . . . £10/£5
Marriage, An Anthology, Dent, 1997 . . £10/£5

ROBERT E. HOWARD
(b.1906 d.1936)

A Texan writer of pulp fiction, his range extended beyond his 'Conan' tales through westerns and sports stories.

'Conan' Novels
Conan the Conqueror: The Hyperborean Age, Gnome Press (U.S.), 1950 . . . . . . £250/£100
ditto, Boardman, 1954. . . . . . . £200/£50
The Return of Conan, Gnome Press (U.S.), 1957 (by L. Sprague de Camp & Bjorn Nyberg). . £125/£50
People of the Black Circle, Grant (U.S.), 1974 £35/£15
Red Nails, Grant (U.S.), 1975 . . . . £25/£10
A Witch Shall Be Born, Grant (U.S.), 1975. £25/£10
The Hour of the Dragon, Grant (U.S.), 1989 £20/£10

'Conan' Stories
The Sword of Conan: The Hyperborean Age, Gnome Press (U.S.), 1952 . . . . . . £200/£75
King Conan: The Hyperborean Age, Gnome Press (U.S.), 1953 . . . . £200/£75
The Coming of Conan, Gnome Press (U.S.), 1953.
. . . . £150/£65
Conan the Barbarian, Gnome Press (U.S.), 1954 . .
. . . . £150/£65
Tales of Conan, Gnome Press (U.S.), 1955 (with L. Sprague de Camp) . . . . . . £125/£50
Conan the Adventurer, Lancer (U.S.), 1966 (wraps) .
. . . . £10
Conan the Usurper, Lancer (U.S.), 1967 (wraps) £10
The Tower of the Elephant, Grant (U.S.), 1975 . .
. . . . £25/£10
The Devil in Iron, Grant (U.S.), 1976 . . £25/£10
Rogues in the House, Grant (U.S.), 1976 . £25/£10
Queen of the Black Coast, Grant (U.S.), 1978 £25/£10
Black Colossus, Grant (U.S.), 1979 . . . £25/£10
Jewels of Gwahlur, Grant (U.S.), 1979 . . £25/£10
The Pool of the Black One, Grant (U.S.), 1986 . .
. . . . £25/£10
The Conan Chronicles, Orbit, 1990 (two vols, wraps).
. . . . £10

Other Novels
Almuric, Ace (U.S.), 1964 (wraps) £10
ditto, N.E.L., 1971 (wraps) £5

Other Short Stories
A Gent from Bear Creek, Herbert Jenkins, 1937 . .
. . . . £2,000/£1,000
ditto, Grant (U.S.), 1966 . . . . . . £25/£5
Skull-Face and Others, Arkham House (U.S.), 1946 .
. . . . £500/£200
ditto, as Skull-Face Omnibus, Spearman, 1974 . .
. . . . £35/£20
The Dark Man and Others, Arkham House (U.S.), 1963 . . . . £145/£45

ditto, as The Dark Man Omnibus, Panther 1978 (two vols, wraps) £10
The Pride of Bear Creek, Grant (U.S.), 1966 £45/£15
King Kull, Lancer (U.S.), 1967 (wraps, with Lin Carter) £5
Bran Mak Morn, Dell (U.S.), 1969 (wraps) . . £5
ditto, Sphere, 1976 (wraps) £5
ditto, as Kull, Grant (U.S.), 1985 (revised text) £20/£10
Wolfshead, Lancer (U.S.), 1968 (wraps) . . . £5
Red Shadows, Grant (U.S.), 1968 . . . £125/£30
Red Blades of Black Cathay, Grant (U.S.), 1971 (with Tevis Clyde Smith) . . . . £75/£25
Marchers of Valhalla, Grant (U.S.), 1972 . . £20/£5
ditto, Sphere, 1977 (wraps) £5
The Vultures, Fictioneer (U.S.), 1973 . . £20/£10
The Sowers of the Thunder, Grant (U.S.), 1973 . .
. . . . £35/£10
ditto, Sphere, 1977 (wraps) £5
Worms of the Earth, Grant (U.S.), 1974 . £25/£10
ditto, Orbit/Futura, 1976 (wraps). £5
The Incredible Adventures of Dennis Dorgan, Fax (U.S.), 1974 . . . . £15/£5
The Lost Valley of Iskander, Fax (U.S.), 1974 . £15/£5
ditto, Orbit/Futura, 1976 (wraps). £5
Tigers of the Sea, Grant (U.S.), 1974 . . £20/£5
ditto, Futura, 1977 (wraps) £5
Black Vulmea's Vengeance and Other Tales of Pirates, Grant (U.S.), 1976 . . . . . £15/£5
The Iron Man and Other Tales of the Ring, Grant (U.S.), 1976 . . . . £10/£5
The Swords of Shahrazar, Fax (U.S.), 1976 . £10/£5
ditto, Orbit/Futura, 1976 (wraps). £5
Son of the White Wolf, Fax (U.S.), 1977 . . £10/£5
ditto, Futura, 1977 (wraps) £5
Three-Bladed Doom, Futura, 1977 (wraps). . . £5
Mayhem on Bear Creek, Fax (U.S.), 1979 . £15/£5
The Road to Azrael, Grant (U.S.), 1979. . . £15/£5
Lord of the Dead, Grant (U.S.), 1981 . . £15/£5
Cthulhu: The Mythos and Kindred Horrors, Baen (U.S.), 1987 . . . . £20/£10
Post Oaks and Sand Roughs, Grant (U.S.), 1991 . .
. . . . £15/£5

Poetry
Always Comes Evening, Arkham House (U.S.), 1957 .
. . . . £300/£100
Etchings in Ivory: Poems in Prose, Glenn Lord (U.S.), 1968 . . . . £150/£50
Singers in the Shadows, Grant (U.S.), 1970 (500 copies) . . . . £75/£25
Echoes from an Iron Harp, Grant (U.S.), 1972 . .
. . . . £45/£15
Rhymes of Death, McHaney (U.S.), 1975 (600 numbered copies) £40
Shadows of Dreams, Grant (U.S.), 1991 . £20/£10

L. RON HUBBARD
(b.1911 d.1986)

Although he wrote a number of very collectable science fiction titles, L. Ron Hubbard is best known as the founder of Scientology.

Novels
Buckskin Brigades, Macauley (U.S.), 1937. . . .
. . . . £2,500/£250
ditto, Wright & Brown, [1938] . . . . £750/£75
Final Blackout, Hadley Publishing (U.S.), 1948 . .
. . . . £300/£65
ditto, New Era, 1989 . . . . £15/£5
Death's Deputy, Fantasy Publishing (U.S.), 1948 . .
. . . . £150/£35
ditto, Fantasy Publishing/Gnome Press, 1959 £75/£25
Slaves of Sleep, Shasta (U.S.), 1938 . . . £250/£75
ditto, Shasta (U.S.), 1938 (250 signed copies) . . .
. . . . £1,250/£1000
Triton, Fantasy Publishing (U.S.), 1949 . . £100/£25
The Kingslayer, Fantasy Publishing (U.S.), 1949 . .
. . . . £100/£25
Typewriter in the Sky and Fear, Gnome Press (U.S.),
1951 . . . . £150/£25
ditto, Fantasy Publishing/Gnome (U.S.), 1959 £45/£20
From Death to the Stars, Fantasy Publishing (U.S.),
1953) . . . . £350/£65
Return to Tomorrow, Ace (U.S.), 1954 (wraps) £10
ditto, Panther, 1957 (wraps) £5
Fear and the Ultimate Adventure, Berkley Medallion
(U.S.), 1970 (wraps) £10
Seven Steps to the Arbiter, Major Books (U.S.), 1975
(wraps) £10
Battlefield Earth, St Martin's Press (U.S.), 1982 . .
. . . . £20/£5
ditto, Quadrant, 1984 . . . . £15/£5
Mission Earth, Bridge Publications (U.S.), 1985-87
(ten vols: 'The Invader's Plan', 'Death Quest', 'Black
Genesis', 'The Enemy Within', 'An Alien Affair',
'Fortune of Fear', 'Voyage of Vengeance', 'Disaster',
'Villainy Victorious' and 'The Doomed Planet') . .
. . . . £10/£5 each
ditto, New Era, 1986-88 (10 vols) . . £10/£5 each
ditto, Bridge Publications (U.S.), 1987 (set). . £200

Short Stories
Ole Doc Methuselah, Theta Press (U.S.), 1970 £75/£25
ditto, New Era, 1993 . . . . £10/£5
Lives You Wished to Lead but Never Dared, Theta
Books (U.S.), 1978 . . . . . . £150/£45

Dianetics
Dianetics: The Modern Science of Mental Health,
Hermitage House, 1950 . . . . . . £400/£150

RICHARD HUGHES
(b.1900 d.1976)

Hughes is best known for *A High Wind in Jamaica*, a story of children kidnapped by pirates. The novel was considered unusual for its time because of its lack of sentimentality.

Plays
The Sister's Tragedy, Blackwell, 1922 (wraps). £100
The Sister's Tragedy and Other Plays, Heinemann,
1924 . . . . £75/£20
ditto, as *A Rabbit and a Leg, Collected Plays*, Knopf
(U.S.), 1924 . . . . £45/£10

Poetry
Gipsy-Night and Other Poems, Golden Cockerell,
1922 (750 copies) . . . . . . £75/£35
ditto, Will Ransom (U.S.), 1922 (63 copies) . £200
Confessio Juvenis: Collected Poems, Chatto &
Windus, 1925 (55 signed, numbered copies) . . .
. . . . £200/£100
ditto, Chatto & Windus, 1925 . . . . £65/£20

Short Stories
A Moment of Time, Chatto & Windus, 1926 £100/£20
Burial and The Dark Child, Chatto & Windus, 1930 .
. . . . £75/£15
In The Lap of Atlas, Chatto & Windus, 1979 £25/£10
ditto, Merrimack (U.S.), 1980 . . . . £20/£10

Novels
The Innocent Voyage, Harper (U.S.), 1929 . £150/£20
ditto, as *A High Wind in Jamaica*, Chatto & Windus,
1929 . . . . £50/£15
ditto, Chatto & Windus, 1929 (150 signed copies) . .
. . . . £200
In Hazard, Chatto & Windus, 1938 . . . . £30/£5
ditto, Harper (U.S.), 1938. . . . . . . £30/£5
The Fox in the Attic, Chatto & Windus, 1961 . £20/£5
ditto, Harper (U.S.), 1961. . . . . . . £20/£5
ditto, Harper (U.S.), 1961 (unknown number of copies
with signature on tipped-in leaf) . . . £30/£15
The Wooden Shepherdess, Chatto & Windus, 1973 .
. . . . £20/£5
ditto, Harper (U.S.), 1973. . . . . . . £20/£5

Children's Titles
The Spider's Palace, Chatto & Windus, 1931 £40/£10
ditto, Chatto & Windus, 1931 (110 numbered, signed
copies) £100
ditto, Harper (U.S.), 1932. . . . . . £35/£10
Don't Blame Me and Other Stories, Chatto & Windus,
1940 . . . . £25/£5
ditto, Harper (U.S.), 1940. . . . . . . £20/£5
Gertrude's Child, Harlin Quist (U.S.), 1966 £25/£10
The Wonder Dog, Chatto & Windus, 1977 . . £20/£5

Others

Richard Hughes: An Omnibus, Harper (U.S.), 1931 .
. . . . £20/£5
The Administration of War Production, H.M.S.O.,
1955 (with J.D. Scott) £35

TED HUGHES
(b.1930 d.1998)

Hughes is chiefly known for his poetry which often
depicts the cruelties of the animal world, and the
malevolence of creatures of his own invention. In
1984 he was made Poet Laureate.

Poetry

The Hawk in the Rain, Faber, 1957 . . . £200/£50
ditto, Harper (U.S.), 1957 . . . . . £100/£35
Pike, Gehenna Press, 1959 (broadsheet, 150 signed
copies) £300
Lupercal, Faber, 1960. . . . . . £150/£45
ditto, Harper (U.S.), 1960 . . . . . £100/£25
Selected Poems, Faber, 1962 (with Thom Gunn, wraps)
. . . . £35
The Burning of the Brothel, Turret Books, 1966 (75
numbered and signed copies, wraps with d/w)
. . . . £250/£150
ditto, Turret Books, 1966 (225 unsigned copies, wraps
with d/w) . . . . £75/£45
Recklings, Turret Books, 1966 (150 numbered and
signed copies) . . . . £200/£125
Scapegoats and Rabies, Poet & Printer, 1967 (approx.
400 copies, wraps) £50
ditto, Poet & Printer, 1967 (in portfolio with three other
poetry chapbooks published by the press, wraps) £200
ditto, Poet & Printer, 1967 (26 lettered copies for the
poet, wraps) £400
Wodwo, Faber, 1967 . . . . . . £45/£10
ditto, Harper (U.S.), 1967 . . . . . £35/£10
Animal Poems, Gilbertson, 1967 (6 signed copies with
poems handwritten by Hughes) £1,000
ditto, Gilbertson, 1967 (10 signed copies with three
manuscript poems) £750
ditto, Gilbertson, 1967 (20 signed copies with one
manuscript poem) £500
ditto, Gilbertson, 1967 (63 signed, numbered copies) .
. . . . £400
Gravestones, Bartholomew, 1967 (set of 6 broadsheets,
40 sets printed) £1,500
ditto, as ***Poems***, Bartholomew, 1967 (300 copies) £150
I Said Goodbye to Earth, Turret Books, 1969
(broadsheet, 75 signed copies) £150
A Crow Hymn, Sceptre Press, 1970 (21 signed copies
for sale) £250
ditto, Sceptre Press, 1970 (64 unsigned copies). £200
The Martyrdom of Bishop Farrar, Gilbertson, 1970
(signed copies, wraps) £200

ditto, Gilbertson, 1970 (rejected printing, lines 15 and
16 of the poem transposed) £125
A Few Crows, Rougemont Press, 1970 (75 signed
copies) . . . . £350/£275
ditto, Rougemont Press, 1970 (75 unsigned copies) .
. . . . £125/£75
Crow, Faber, 1970. . . . . . . £40/£10
ditto, Harper (U.S.), 1971. . . . . £25/£10
Fighting for Jerusalem, Northumberland Arts, 1970
(poster) £25
Crow Wakes, Poet & Printer, 1971 (100 copies) £100
Eat Crow, Rainbow Press, 1971 (150 signed, numbered
copies, slipcase) . . . . . . £300/£250
Poems, Rainbow Press, 1971 (with Ruth Fainlight and
Alan Sillitoe, 300 copies, numbered and signed by all
three poets, slipcase) . . . . . . £225/£175
Selected Poems, 1957-1967, Faber, 1972 (wraps) £10
ditto, Harper (U.S.), 1973 . . . . . £50/£15
Prometheus on His Crag, Rainbow Press, 1973 (160
copies signed by Hughes and Leonard Baskin,
slipcase) . . . . £400/£325
Cave Birds, Scolar Press, 1975 (10 sheets issued in
box, 125 sets printed) £500
ditto, Faber, 1978 . . . . £25/£5
ditto, Viking (U.S.), 1978. . . . . . £25/£5
The Interrogator: A Titled Vultress, Scolar Press, 1975
. . . . £25/£10
The New World, O.U.P., 1975 . . . £25/£10
Eclipse, Sceptre Press, 1976 (50 signed copies, wraps)
. . . . £150
ditto, Sceptre Press, 1976 (200 unsigned copies, wraps)
. . . . £65
Gaudete, Faber, 1977 . . . . . . £20/£5
ditto, Harper (U.S.), 1977. . . . . . £20/£5
Chiasmadon, Janus Press (U.S.), 1977 (120 signed
copies, wraps) £250
Sunstruck, Sceptre Press, 1977 (100 signed copies) .
. . . . £150
ditto, Sceptre Press, 1977 (200 numbered copies) £60
A Solstice, Sceptre Press, 1978 (100 signed copies,
wraps). £150
ditto, Sceptre Press, 1978 (250 numbered copies,
wraps). £45
Orts, Rainbow Press, 1978 (200 numbered and signed
copies, slipcase) . . . . £300/£250
Moortown Elegies, Rainbow Press, 1978 (6 author's
copies) £1,000
ditto, Rainbow Press, 1978 (26 lettered A-Z) . £500
ditto, Rainbow Press, 1978 (143 numbered copies). .
. . . . £350
Adam and the Sacred Nine, Rainbow Press, 1979 (200
numbered and signed copies, slipcase). . £300/£250
Remains of Elmet, Rainbow Press, 1979 (numbered 1-
70, signed by Hughes and the artist, leather-bound) .
. . . . £750
ditto, Rainbow Press, 1979 (numbered 71-180, signed
by Hughes, ordinary binding) £500
ditto, Faber, 1979 . . . . £25/£10

The Threshold, Steam Press, 1979 (100 copies of 12 leaves, illustrated by Ralph Steadman, and signed by Hughes and Steadman) £400

Night Arrival of Sea-Trout, The Iron Wolf, Puma, Morrigu Press, 1979 (three broadsheets, 30 sets) £125

Brooktrout, Morrigu Press, 1979 (60 signed copies, broadsheet) £150

Pan, Morrigu Press, 1979 (60 signed copies, broadsheet) £150

Woodpecker, Morrigu Press, 1979 (60 signed copies, broadsheet) £150

Moortown, Faber, 1979 . . . . . £20/£5

ditto, Harper (U.S.), 1980 . . . . . . £20/£5

Wolverine, Morrigu Press, 1979 (75 signed copies, broadsheet) £125

Four Tales Told by an Idiot, Sceptre Press, 1979 (450 numbered copies with erratum slip) . . . £45

ditto, Sceptre Press, 1979 (100 signed copies with erratum slip) £125

In the Black Chapel, Victoria and Albert Museum, 1979 (poster) £35

Eagle, Morrigu Press, 1980 (75 signed copies, broadsheet) £125

Mosquito, Morrigu Press, 1980 (60 signed copies, broadsheet) £150

Catadrome, Morrigu Press, 1980 (75 signed copies, broadsheet) £125

Caddis, Morrigu Press, 1980 (75 signed copies, broadsheet) £125

Visitation, Morrigu Press, 1980 (75 signed copies, broadsheet) £125

A Primer of Birds, Gehenna Press, 1981 (250 copies numbered and signed by Hughes and artist, Leonard Baskin) £400

Selected Poems, 1957-1981, Faber, 1982 . £15/£5

ditto, as *New Selected Poems*, Harper (U.S.), 1982. . . . . £15/£5

River, Faber, 1983 . . . . £25/£5

ditto, Harper (U.S.), 1984 . . . . . . £20/£5

Weasels at Work, Morrigu Press, 1983 (75 signed copies, broadsheet) £100

Fly Inspects, Morrigu Press, 1983 (75 signed copies, broadsheet) £100

Mice are Funny Little Creatures, Morrigu Press, 1983 (75 signed copies, broadsheet) £100

Flowers and Insects: Some Birds and a Pair of Spiders, Faber, 1986 . . . . £25/£5

ditto, Knopf (U.S.), 1986 . . . . . £25/£5

Moortown Diary, Faber, 1989 . . . . £20/£5

ditto, Faber, 1989 (wraps) £5

Wolf-Watching, Faber, 1989 . . . . . £20/£5

ditto, Farrar, Straus and Giroux (U.S.), 1991 . £20/£5

Rain-Charm for the Duchy, Faber, 1992 . £15/£5

ditto, Faber, 1992 (280 signed copies with loose insert, 'The Unicorn', slipcase) £175

ditto, Faber, 1992 (wraps) £5

Three Books: Remains of Elmet, Cave Birds, River, Faber, 1993 . . . . £10

Elmet, Faber, 1984 . . . . . £30/£10

Earth Dances, Old Stile Press, 1994 (250 signed copies, slipcase) £200

New Selected Poems, 1957-94, Faber, 1995 . £15/£5

Ted Hughes Poetry, Collins Educational, 1997 . £10/£5

Birthday Letters, Faber, 1998 . . . . £25/£5

ditto, Faber, 1998 (300 signed copies) . . . £500

ditto, Farrar Straus Giroux (U.S.), 1998 . . . £25/£5

Children's Poetry

Meet My Folks!, Faber, 1961 . . . . £125/£25

ditto, Bobbs-Merrill (U.S.), 1973 . . . . £35/£10

The Earth-Owl and Other Moon-People, Faber, 1963 . . . . £50/£15

ditto, as *Moon Whales and Other Moon People*, Viking (U.S.), 1976 . . . . £25/£5

ditto, as *Moonwhales*, Faber, 1988 . . . . £10/£5

Nessie the Mannerless Monster, Faber, 1964 £50/£15

ditto, as *Nessie the Monster*, Bobbs-Merrill (U.S.), 1974 . . . . £25/£5

Five Autumn Songs for Children's Voices, Gilbertson, 1968 (9 copies for sale with a verse in manuscript & a watercolour) £450

ditto, Gilbertson, 1968 (27 copies with a verse in manuscript, wraps) £250

ditto, Gilbertson, 1968 (150 signed copies, wraps) £150

ditto, Gilbertson, 1968 (312 signed copies, wraps) . £25

Spring Summer Autumn Winter, Rainbow Press, 1974 (140 numbered and signed copies) £300

ditto, as *Season Songs*, Doubleday (U.S.), 1975 £20/£5

ditto, Faber, 1976 . . . . £20/£5

Earth-Moon, Rainbow Press, 1976 (226 signed and numbered copies, slipcase) . . . . £200/£165

Moon-Bells and Other Poems, Chatto & Windus, 1978 . . . . £25/£5

Under the North Star, Faber, 1981 . . . £40/£10

ditto, Viking (U.S.), 1981 . . . . . £35/£5

The Cat and the Cuckoo, Sunstone Press, [1987] (250 signed copies in d/w and slipcase) . . . £125/£50

ditto, Faber, 1991 . . . . £15/£5

Under the North Star and Others, Faber, 1990. £20/£5

The Mermaids Purse, Faber, 1991 . . . £15/£5

ditto, Knopf (U.S.), 2000 . . . . . . £15/£5

Collected Animal Poems, Faber, 1995 (4 vols) . . . . £100/£20

ditto, Faber, 1996 (1 vol.) . . . . . . £15/£5

Children's Prose

How the Whale Became, Faber, 1963 . . £65/£15

ditto, Atheneum (U.S.), 1964 . . . . . £45/£10

The Iron Man, Faber, 1968 . . . . . £50/£15

ditto, as *The Iron Giant*, Harper (U.S.), 1968 . £45/£5

What is the Truth?, Faber, 1984 . . . . £25/£5

ditto, Harper (U.S.), 1984 . . . . . £20/£5

Ffangs the Vampire Bat and the Kiss of Truth, Faber, 1986 . . . . £20/£5

Tales of the Early World, Faber, 1988 . . £20/£5

The Iron Woman, Faber, 1993 . . . . £15/£5

ditto, Dial (U.S.), 1995 . . . . . . £15/£5

Dreamfighter and Other Creation Tales, Faber, 1995.
. . . . £15/£5
Shaggy and Spotty, Faber, 1997 . . . . . £15/£5

Others
Poetry in the Making, Faber, 1967 (no d/w) . £50
ditto, as *Poetry Is*, Doubleday (U.S.), 1970 . £35/£10
Seneca's Oedipus, Faber, 1969 . . . . . £25/£5
ditto, Doubleday (U.S.), 1972 . . . . . £20/£5
The Coming of the Kings and Other Plays, Faber,
1970 . . . . £25/£5
ditto, as *Tiger's Bones and Other Plays for Children*,
Viking (U.S.), 1974 . . . . £20/£5
Shakespeare's Poem, Lexham Press, 1971 (75 signed
copies, wraps) £125
Orpheus, Dramatic Publishing Company (U.S.), 1973
(1,023 copies, wraps) £30
Henry Williamson, Rainbow Press, 1979 (200 signed
copies, wraps) £100
T.S. Eliot: A Tribute, Faber, 1987 (privately printed,
250 copies, wraps) £125
Shakespeare and the Goddess of Complete Being,
Faber, 1992 . . . . £15/£5
ditto, Farrar Straus Giroux (U.S.), 1992 . . £15/£5
Winter Pollen: Occasional Prose, Faber, 1994 . £20/£5
ditto, Picador (U.S.), 1995 . . . . . £15/£5
Difficulties of a Bridegroom, Faber, 1995 . . £20/£5
ditto, Picador (U.S.), 1995 . . . . . £15/£5
Euripides' Alcestis, Faber, 1999 . . . . . £20/£5
ditto, Farrar (U.S.), 1999 . . . . . . £15/£5

ALDOUS HUXLEY
(b.1894 d.1963)

A novelist and short story writer, much of Huxley's
work is marked by a certain despair and disgust, none
more so than his great novel of the future, *Brave New
World*.

Poetry
The Burning Wheel, Blackwell, 1916 (wraps) . £500
Jonah, Holywell, 1917 (approx 50 signed copies,
wraps) £2,000
The Defeat of Youth and Other Poems, Blackwell,
1918 (500 copies, wraps, no title page) . £250
Leda, Chatto & Windus, 1920 . . . . £150/£75
ditto, Chatto & Windus, 1920 (160 numbered and
signed copies) £250
ditto, Doran (U.S.), 1920 . . . . . £100/£45
ditto, Doran (U.S.), 1920 (361 numbered and signed
copies, slipcase) . . . . £125/£100
Selected Poems, Blackwell, 1925 . . . £75
ditto, Appleton (U.S.), 1925 . . . . £65/£15
ditto, Blackwell, 1926 (100 signed copies) . £250
Arabia Infelix, Fountain Press (U.S.)/Chatto &
Windus, 1929 (692 signed, numbered copies, glassine
d/w) . . . . £100/£75

Apennine, Slide Mountain Press (U.S.), 1930 (91
signed, numbered copies, glassine d/w) . £350/£300
The Cicadas and Other Poems, Chatto & Windus,
1931 . . . . £65/£20
ditto, Chatto & Windus, 1931 (160 signed, numbered
copies) . . . . £175/£125
ditto, Doubleday Doran (U.S.), 1931 . . £50/£15
Verses and a Comedy, Chatto & Windus, 1946. . .
. . . . £45/£15

Short Stories
Limbo, Chatto & Windus, 1920 (6 stories and a play) .
. . . . £200/£30
ditto, Doran (U.S.), 1920 . . . . . . £125/£25
Mortal Coils, Chatto & Windus, 1922 . £125/£25
ditto, Doran (U.S.), 1922 . . . . . . £75/£20
Little Mexican and Other Stories, Chatto & Windus,
1924 . . . . £125/£35
ditto, as *Young Archimedes*, Doran (U.S.), 1924 .
. . . . £75/£25
Two or Three Graces and Other Stories, Chatto &
Windus, 1926. . . . . £75/£25
ditto, Doran (U.S.), 1926 . . . . . . £50/£15
Brief Candles, Fountain Press (U.S.), 1930 (800 signed
copies) £150
ditto, Doubleday Doran (U.S.), 1930 . £65/£10
ditto, Chatto & Windus, 1930 . . . . £65/£15
Collected Short Stories, Chatto & Windus, 1957 . .
. . . . £20/£5
ditto, Harper (U.S.), 1957. . . . . . £20/£5

Novels
Crome Yellow, Chatto & Windus, 1921 . . £250/£75
ditto, Doran (U.S.), 1922 . . . . . . £175/£45
Antic Hay, Chatto & Windus, 1923 . . . £175/£40
ditto, Doran (U.S.), 1923 . . . . . . £100/£25
Those Barren Leaves, Chatto & Windus, 1925 £75/£15
ditto, Doran (U.S.), 1925 . . . . . £65/£15
ditto, Doran, 1925 (250 signed, numbered copies) £200
Point Counter Point, Chatto & Windus, 1928 . . .
. . . . £125/£25
ditto, Chatto & Windus, 1928 (256 signed, numbered
copies) £200
ditto, Doubleday Doran (U.S.), 1928 . . £75/£15
Brave New World, Chatto & Windus, 1932. . . .
. . . . £2,500/£150
ditto, Chatto & Windus, 1932 (324 signed numbered
copies) £2,000
ditto, Doubleday Doran (U.S.), 1932 . £1,250/£150
ditto, Doubleday Doran (U.S.), 1932 (250 signed
numbered copies) £1,500
Eyeless in Gaza, Chatto & Windus, 1936 . £200/£35
ditto, Chatto & Windus, 1936 (200 signed, numbered
copies) £300
ditto, Harper (U.S.), 1936. . . . . . £125/£30
After Many a Summer, Chatto & Windus, 1939 . .
. . . . £175/£35
ditto, as *After Many a Summer Dies the Swan*, Harper
(U.S.), 1939 . . . . £100/£20

Time Must Have a Stop, Chatto & Windus, 1944 . .
. . . . £45/£10
ditto, Harper (U.S.), 1945. . . . . . £35/£10
Ape and Essence, Harper (U.S.), 1948 . . . £25/£5
ditto, Chatto & Windus, 1949 . . . . . £30/£5
The Genius and the Goddess, Chatto & Windus, 1955
. . . . £25/£5
ditto, Harper (U.S.), 1955. . . . . . . £20/£5
Island, Chatto & Windus, 1962 . . . . . £20/£5
ditto, Harper (U.S.), 1962. . . . . . . £20/£5

Drama

The World of Light, Chatto & Windus, 1931 £75/£10
ditto, Chatto & Windus, 1931 (160 signed, numbered
copies) £150
ditto, Doubleday Doran (U.S.), 1931 . . £65/£10
The Gioconda Smile, Chatto & Windus, 1948 . £35/£5
ditto, Harper (U.S.), 1948. . . . . . . £30/£5

Others

On the Margin, Chatto & Windus, 1923 (first issue
with page 'vi' numbered 'v') . . . . £100/£25
ditto, Doran (U.S.), 1923 . . . . . £75/£15
Along the Road, Chatto & Windus, 1925 . £75/£20
ditto, Doran (U.S.), 1925 . . . . £40/£5
ditto, Doran, 1925 (250 signed, numbered copies,
slipcase and d/w). . . . . £200/£100
Essays New and Old, Chatto & Windus, 1926 (650
signed, numbered copies) . . . . . £150/£100
ditto, Doran (U.S.), 1927 . . . . . . £45/£10
Jesting Pilate, Chatto & Windus, 1926 . . £100/£20
ditto, Doran (U.S.), 1926 . . . . . . £75/£20
Proper Studies, Chatto & Windus, 1927 . £75/£15
ditto, Chatto & Windus, 1927 (260 signed copies) £150
ditto, Doubleday Doran (U.S.), 1928 . . £65/£15
Do What You Will, Chatto & Windus, 1929 £65/£15
ditto, Chatto & Windus, 1929 (260 signed copies) £150
ditto, Doubleday Doran (U.S.), 1929 . . £45/£10
Holy Face and Other Essays, The Fleuron Press, 1929
(300 numbered copies, slipcase) . . . £200/£175
Vulgarity in Literature, Chatto & Windus, 1930, No. 1
of the 'Dolphin's Books' . . . . . £50/£15
ditto, Chatto & Windus, 1930 (260 signed, numbered
copies) £125
Music at Night and Other Essays, Chatto & Windus,
1931 . . . . £75/£15
ditto, Chatto & Windus/Fountain Press, 1931 (842
signed, numbered copies) £50
ditto, Doubleday Doran (U.S.), 1931 . . £50/£10
Rotunda, Chatto & Windus, 1932 . . £45/£15
T.H. Huxley as a Man of Letters, Macmillan, 1932
(wraps) £50
Texts and Pretexts, Chatto & Windus, 1932 (214
signed copies) £200
ditto, Chatto & Windus, 1932 . . . . . £25/£5
ditto, Harper (U.S.), 1933. . . . . . . £25/£5
Beyond the Mexique Bay, Chatto & Windus, 1934 .
. . . . £125/£25

ditto, Chatto & Windus, 1934 (210 signed, numbered
copies) £200
ditto, Harper (U.S.), 1934. . . . . . £75/£10
The Olive Tree and Other Essays, Chatto & Windus,
1936 . . . . £50/£15
ditto, Chatto & Windus, 1936 (160 signed, numbered
copies) £200
ditto, Harper (U.S.), 1937. . . . . . £35/£10
*What Are You Going to do About It? The Case for
Constructive Peace*, Chatto & Windus, 1936 (wraps)
. . . . £75
ditto, Harper (U.S.), 1937 (wraps) £45
Ends and Means, Chatto & Windus, 1937 . £50/£15
ditto, Chatto & Windus, 1937 (160 signed, numbered
copies) £200
ditto, Harper (U.S.), 1937. . . . . . £25/£10
The Most Agreeable Vice, Ward Ritchie Press (U.S.),
1938 (500 copies, wraps) £150
Beyond the Swarm, Ward Ritchie Press (U.S.), 1939
(300 copies, wraps) £250
Words and Their Meanings, Ward Ritchie (U.S.),
1940 (wraps) £35
ditto, Ward Ritchie (U.S.), 1940 (100 signed copies for
Jake Zeitlin) . . . . £250/£200
Grey Eminence, Chatto & Windus, 1941 . £25/£5
ditto, Harper (U.S.), 1941. . . . . . . £25/£5
The Art of Seeing, Harper (U.S.), 1942 . . . £25/£5
ditto, Chatto & Windus, 1943 . . . . . £25/£5
The Perennial Philosophy, Harper (U.S.), 1945 . .
. . . . £25/£5
ditto, Chatto & Windus, 1945 . . . . . £25/£5
Science, Liberty and Peace, Harper (U.S.), 1946 . .
. . . . £15/£5
ditto, Chatto & Windus, 1947 . . . . . £20/£5
Prisons, Trianon Press (U.K.)/Zeitlin & Ver Brugge
(U.S.), 1949 (212 signed, numbered copies, slipcase)
. . . . £250/£200
ditto, Trianon Press, 1949 (1,000 unsigned copies) £50
Themes and Variations, Chatto & Windus, 1950 . .
. . . . £25/£5
ditto, Harper (U.S.), 1950. . . . . . . £20/£5
The Devils of Loudun, Chatto & Windus, 1952 £25/£5
ditto, Harper (U.S.), 1952. . . . . . . £20/£5
Joyce, the Artificer, Chiswick, 1952 (90 copies) £200
The French of Paris, Harper (U.S.), 1954 (with
Sanford Roth) . . . . £50/£15
The Doors of Perception, Chatto & Windus, 1954 . .
. . . . £45/£10
ditto, Harper (U.S.), 1954. . . . . . . £40/£10
Heaven and Hell, Chatto & Windus, 1956 . £30/£10
ditto, Harper (U.S.), 1956. . . . . . . £20/£5
Adonis and the Alphabet, Chatto & Windus, 1956. .
. . . . £15/£5
ditto, as *Tomorrow and Tomorrow and Tomorrow*,
Harper (U.S.), 1956 . . . . £15/£5
Brave New World Revisited, Chatto & Windus, 1958 .
. . . . £30/£5
ditto, Harper (U.S.), 1958. . . . . . . £25/£5
Collected Essays, Harper (U.S.), 1959 . . . £20/£5

ditto, Chatto & Windus, 1960 . . . . . £20/£5
On Art and Artists, Chatto & Windus, 1960 . £20/£5
ditto, Harper (U.S.), 1960 . . . . £15/£5
Literature and Science, Chatto & Windus, 1960 . .
. . . . £15/£5
ditto, Harper (U.S.), 1963 . . . . . . £15/£5
Letters, Chatto & Windus, 1969 . . . . £30/£10
ditto, Harper (U.S.), 1969 . . . . . . £25/£10

J. K. HUYSMANS
(b.1848 d.1907)

A Rebours, or *Against the Grain* (also translated as *Against Nature*) was not only highly sensational, but very influential, following on from his early novels which had shown a marked influence of Zola. The dates of publication of the English translations of Huysmans' work give a distorted idea of the development of this writer.

En Route, Kegan Paul, 1896 . . . . . . £75
ditto, Dutton (U.S.), 1920 . . . . . £65/£25
The Cathedral, Kegan Paul, 1898 . . . . £50
Knapsack, Collier, 1907 . . . . . . £20
Against the Grain, Lieber & Lewis (U.S.), 1922 . .
. . . . £75/£25
ditto, Fortune Press, 1931 . . . . . . £75/£25
St. Lydwine of Schiedam, Kegan Paul, 1923 £75/£35
ditto, Dutton (U.S.), 19203 . . . . . £65/£25
The Oblate, Kegan Paul, 1924 . . . . £50/£25
Down There, Boni (U.S.), 1924 . . . . £150/£25
ditto, Fortune Press, 1930 . . . . . £75/£25
The Crowds of Lourdes, Burns & Oates, 1925 £65/£25
Downstream and Other Works, Covici (U.S.), 1927 .
. . . . £100/£35
ditto, Fortune Press, 1952 . . . . . . £65/£30
Marthe, Lear (U.S.), 1948 . . . . . £40/£15
ditto, Fortune Press, 1958 . . . . . £45/£20
Grunewald, Phaidon, 1958 . . . . . £45/£20
ditto, Dutton (U.S.), 1976 . . . . . £25/£10
Parisian Sketches, Fortune Press, 1962 . . £35/£15
Émile Zola and L'Assommoir, Princeton (U.S.), 1963
. . . . £25/£10
Living Together, Fortune Press, [1971] . . £45/£20
Vatard Sisters, Univ. of Kentucky Press (U.S.), 1983 .
. . . . £25/£5
The Bievre River, Langtry Press, 1986 . . £75/£40
The Road from Decadence : From Brothel to Cloister: Selected Letters, Athlone Press, 1989 . . . £20/£5
ditto, Ohio State Univ. Press, 1989 . . . £20/£5

HAMMOND INNES
(b.1913 d.1998)

Ralph Hammond Innes' thrillers have been translated into many languages, and appear in book club and wraps editions throughout the world.

Novels
The Doppelganger, Jenkins, 1936 . . . £750/£65
Air Disaster, Jenkins, 1937 . . . . . £650/£50
Sabotage Broadcast, Jenkins, 1938 . . . £650/£50
All Roads Lead to Friday, Jenkins, 1939 . £650/£50
Wreckers Must Breathe, Collins, 1940 . . £500/£45
ditto, as *Trapped*, Putnam (U.S.), 1940 . £450/£40
The Trojan Horse, Collins, 1940 . . . £500/£45
Attack Alarm, Collins, 1941 . . . . . £500/£45
ditto, Macmillan (U.S.), 1942 . . . . £250/£25
Dead and Alive, Collins, 1946 . . . . £250/£25
The Lonely Skier, Collins, 1947 . . . . £125/£15
ditto, as *Fire In The Snow*, Harper (U.S.), 1947 . .
. . . . £100/£15
The Killer Mine, Collins, 1947 . . . . £75/£10
ditto, Harper (U.S.), 1947 . . . . . £50/£10
ditto, as *Run By Night*, Bantam (U.S.), 1951 (wraps) .
. . . . £10
Maddon's Rock, Collins, 1948 . . . . £50/£10
ditto, as *Gale Warning*, Harper (U.S.), 1948 £45/£10
The Blue Ice, Collins, 1948 . . . . . £45/£10
ditto, Harper (U.S.), 1948 . . . . . £35/£10
The White South, Collins, 1949 . . . . £45/£10
ditto, as *Survivors*, Harpers (U.S.), 1949 . £35/£10
The Angry Mountain, Collins, 1950 . . . £35/£10
ditto, Harper (U.S.), 1950 . . . . . £35/£10
Air Bridge, Collins, 1951 . . . . . £45/£10
ditto, Knopf (U.S.), 1951 . . . . . £35/£10
Campbell's Kingdom, Collins, 1952 . . . £35/£10
ditto, Knopf (U.S.), 1952 . . . . . . £25/£5
The Strange Land, Collins, 1954 . . . . £25/£5
ditto, as *The Naked Land*, Knopf (U.S.), 1954 . £25/£5
The Mary Deare, Collins, 1956 . . . . £25/£5
ditto, as *The Wreck of the Mary Deare*, Knopf (U.S.), 1956 . . . . £25/£5
The Land God Gave to Cain, Collins, 1958 . £25/£5
ditto, Knopf (U.S.), 1958 . . . . . . £25/£5
The Doomed Oasis, Collins, 1960 . . . . £30/£5
ditto, Knopf (U.S.), 1960 . . . . . . £25/£5
Atlantic Fury, Collins, 1962 . . . . . £20/£5
ditto, Random House (U.S.), 1962 . . . . £20/£5
The Strode Venturer, Collins, 1965 . . . £15/£5
ditto, Knopf (U.S.), 1965 . . . . . . £15/£5
Levkas Man, Collins, 1971 . . . . . . £15/£5
ditto, Knopf (U.S.), 1971 . . . . . . £15/£5
Golden Soak, Collins, 1973 . . . . . . £15/£5
ditto, Knopf (U.S.), 1973 . . . . . . £15/£5
North Star, Collins, 1974 . . . . . . £15/£5
ditto, Knopf (U.S.), 1975 . . . . . . £15/£5
The Big Footprints, Collins, 1977 . . . . £15/£5
ditto, Knopf (U.S.), 1977 . . . . . . £15/£5
Solomon's Seal, Collins, 1980 . . . . . £15/£5

ditto, Knopf (U.S.), 1975 . . . . £15/£5
The Black Tide, Collins, 1982 . . . . . £15/£5
ditto, Doubleday (U.S.), 1983 . . . . . £15/£5
High Stand, Collins, 1985 . . . . . . £15/£5
ditto, Atheneum (U.S.), 1986 . . . . . . £15/£5
Medusa, Collins, 1988 . . . . £15/£5
ditto, Atheneum (U.S.), 1988 . . . . . £15/£5
Isvik, Chapmans, 1991 . . . . £15/£5
ditto, St Martin's Press (U.S.), 1992 . . . £10/£5
The Delta Connection, Macmillan, 1996 . £10/£5
ditto, Thorndike Press (U.S.), 1997 . . . £10/£5

Children's Titles (pseud. 'Ralph Hammond')
Cocos Island, Collins, 1950 . . . . . £75/£15
ditto, as *Cocos Gold*, Harpers (U.S.), 1950 . £75/£15
Isle of Strangers, Collins, 1951 . . . . £75/£15
Saracen's Tower, Collins, 1952 . . . . £75/£15
ditto, as *Cruise of Danger*, Westminster Press (U.S.),
1952 . . . . £75/£15
Black Gold on the Double Diamond, Collins, 1953 .
. . . . £75/£15
ditto, as *Island of Peril*, Westminster Press (U.S.),
1953 . . . . £75/£15

Non Fiction
Harvest of Journeys, Collins, 1960 . . . . £25/£5
ditto, Knopf (U.S.), 1960 . . . . £25/£5
Scandinavia, Time-Life (U.S.), 1963 . . . £15
Sea and Islands, Collins, 1967 . . . . . £20/£5
ditto, Knopf (U.S.), 1967 . . . . £20/£5
The Conquistadores, Collins, 1969 . . . . £15/£5
ditto, Collins, 1969 (deluxe leather-bound edition) . .
. . . . £200
ditto, Knopf (U.S.), 1969 . . . . £15/£5
Hammond Innes Introduces Australia, Deutsch, 1971
. . . . £10/£5
ditto, McGraw-Hill (U.S.), 1971 . . . . £10/£5
The Last Voyage: Captain Cook's Lost Diary, Collins,
1979 . . . . £15/£5
ditto, Knopf (U.S.), 1979 . . . . £10/£5
Hammond Innes' East Anglia, Hodder & Stoughton,
1986 . . . . £15/£5

MICHAEL INNES
(b.1906 d.1994)

'Innes' is the pseudonym used by J.I.M. Stewart when
writing his many detective novels. These range from
the ingenious and urbane through to straightforward
chase novels.

Novels
Death at the President's Lodging, Gollancz, 1936 . .
. . . . £1,500/£150
ditto, as *Seven Suspects*, Dodd, Mead (U.S.), 1937 .
. . . . £650/£50
Hamlet, Revenge!, Gollancz, 1937 . . . £500/£75

ditto, Dodd, Mead (U.S.), 1937 . . . . £300/£50
Lament for a Maker, Gollancz, 1938 . . £450/£75
ditto, Dodd, Mead (U.S.), 1938 . . . . . £300/£50
Stop Press, Gollancz, 1939 . . . . . £450/£75
ditto, as *The Spider Strikes*, Dodd, Mead (U.S.), 1939
. . . . £300/£50
There Came Both Mist and Snow, Gollancz, 1940. .
. . . . £450/£75
ditto, as *A Comedy of Terrors*, Dodd, Mead (U.S.),
1940 . . . . £300/£50
The Secret Vanguard, Gollancz, 1940 . . £300/£25
ditto, Dodd, Mead (U.S.), 1941 . . . . £75/£25
Appleby on Ararat, Gollancz, 1941 . . . £400/£45
ditto, Dodd, Mead (U.S.), 1941 . . . . £75/£25
The Daffodil Affair, Gollancz, 1942. . . £250/£30
ditto, Dodd, Mead (U.S.), 1942 . . . . £75/£25
The Weight of the Evidence, Dodd, Mead (U.S.), 1943
. . . . £125/£25
ditto, Gollancz, 1944 . . . . £125/£25
Appleby's End, Gollancz, 1945 . . . . £200/£25
ditto, Dodd, Mead (U.S.), 1945 . . . . £50/£15
From London Far, Gollancz, 1946 . . . £60/£15
ditto, as *The Unsuspected Chasm*, Dodd, Mead (U.S.),
1946 . . . . £45/£5
What Happened at Hazelwood, Gollancz, 1946 . .
. . . . £50/£15
ditto, Dodd, Mead (U.S.), 1946 . . . . £50/£15
A Night of Errors, Dodd, Mead (U.S.), 1947 £65/£15
ditto, Gollancz, 1948 . . . . £50/£10
The Journeying Boy, Gollancz, 1949 . . £50/£10
ditto, as *The Case of the Journeying Boy*, Dodd, Mead
(U.S.), 1949 . . . . £35/£5
Operation Pax, Gollancz, 1951 . . . . £50/£10
ditto, as *The Paper Thunderbolt*, Dodd, Mead (U.S.),
1951 . . . . £35/£5
A Private View, Gollancz, 1952 . . . . £45/£5
ditto, as *One-Man Show*, Dodd, Mead (U.S.), 1952 .
. . . . £35/£5
ditto, as *Murder is an Art*, Avon (U.S.), 1959 (wraps) .
. . . . £10
Christmas at Candleshoe, Gollancz, 1953 . £45/£5
ditto, Dodd, Mead (U.S.), 1953 . . . . £35/£5
ditto, as *Candleshoe*, Penguin (U.S.), 1978 (wraps) £5
The Man from the Sea, Gollancz, 1955 . . £45/£5
ditto, as *Death by Moonlight*, Dodd, Mead (U.S.),
1955 . . . . £35/£5
Old Hall, New Hall, Gollancz, 1956. . . £45/£5
ditto, as *A Question of Queens*, Dodd, Mead (U.S.),
1956 . . . . £35/£5
Appleby Plays Chicken, Gollancz, 1956 . £45/£5
ditto, as *Death On a Quiet Day*, Dodd, Mead (U.S.),
1957 . . . . £35/£5
The Long Farewell, Gollancz, 1958 . . . £45/£5
ditto, Dodd, Mead (U.S.), 1958 . . . . £35/£5
Hare Sitting Up, Gollancz, 1959 . . . . £30/£5
ditto, Dodd, Mead (U.S.), 1959 . . . . £25/£5
The New Sonia Wayward, Gollancz, 1960 . £30/£5
ditto, as *The Case of Sonia Wayward*, Dodd, Mead
(U.S.), 1960 . . . . £25/£5

Silence Observed, Gollancz, 1961 . . . . £30/£5
ditto, Dodd, Mead (U.S.), 1961 . . . . . £25/£5
A Connoisseur's Case, Gollancz, 1962 . . . £30/£5
ditto, as *The Crabtree Affair*, Dodd, Mead (U.S.), 1962
. . . . £25/£5
Money from Holme, Gollancz, 1964 . . . £30/£5
ditto, Dodd, Mead (U.S.), 1965 . . . . . £25/£5
Appleby Intervenes, Dodd, Mead (U.S.), 1965 . £20/£5
The Bloody Wood, Gollancz, 1966 . . . . £25/£5
ditto, Dodd, Mead (U.S.), 1966 . . . . . £20/£5
A Change of Heir, Gollancz, 1966 . . . . £25/£5
ditto, Dodd, Mead (U.S.), 1966 . . . . . £20/£5
Appleby at Allington, Gollancz, 1968 . . . £25/£5
ditto, as *Death by Water*, Dodd, Mead (U.S.), 1968 .
. . . . £20/£5
A Family Affair, Gollancz, 1969. . . . . £25/£5
ditto, as *Picture of Guilt*, Dodd, Mead (U.S.), 1969 .
. . . . £20/£5
Death at the Chase, Gollancz, 1970 . . . . £25/£5
ditto, Dodd, Mead (U.S.), 1970 . . . . . £20/£5
An Awkward Lie, Gollancz, 1971 . . . . £20/£5
ditto, Dodd, Mead (U.S.), 1971 . . . . . £15/£5
The Open House, Gollancz, 1972 . . . . £20/£5
ditto, Dodd, Mead (U.S.), 1972 . . . . . £15/£5
Appleby's Answer, Gollancz, 1973 . . . . £20/£5
ditto, Dodd, Mead (U.S.), 1973 . . . . . £15/£5
Appleby's Other Story, Gollancz, 1974 . . . £20/£5
ditto, Dodd, Mead (U.S.), 1974 . . . . . £15/£5
The Mysterious Commission, Gollancz, 1974 . £20/£5
ditto, Dodd, Mead (U.S.), 1975 . . . . . £15/£5
The Gay Phoenix, Gollancz, 1976 . . . . £20/£5
ditto, Dodd, Mead (U.S.), 1977 . . . . . £15/£5
Honeybath's Haven, Gollancz, 1977 . . £15/£5
ditto, Dodd, Mead (U.S.), 1978 . . . . £10/£5
The Ampersand Papers, Gollancz, 1978 . £15/£5
ditto, Dodd, Mead (U.S.), 1979 . . . . . £10/£5
Going It Alone, Gollancz, 1980 . . . . £15/£5
ditto, Dodd, Mead (U.S.), 1980 . . . . . £10/£5
Lord Mullion's Secret, Gollancz, 1981 . . £15/£5
ditto, Dodd, Mead (U.S.), 1981 . . . . £10/£5
Sheikhs and Adders, Gollancz, 1982 . . £15/£5
ditto, Dodd, Mead (U.S.), 1982 . . . . . £10/£5
Appleby and Honeybath, Gollancz, 1983 . £15/£5
ditto, Dodd, Mead (U.S.), 1983 . . . . . £10/£5
Carson's Conspiracy, Gollancz, 1984 . . £15/£5
ditto, Dodd, Mead (U.S.), 1984 . . . . £10/£5
Appleby and the Ospreys, Gollancz, 1986 . £15/£5
ditto, Dodd, Mead (U.S.), 1987 . . . . . £10/£5

Short Stories
Appleby Talking, Gollancz, 1954 . . . £200/£25
ditto, as *Dead Man's Shoes*, Dodd, Mead (U.S.), 1954
. . . . £150/£15
Appleby Talks Again, Gollancz, 1956 . . . £35/£5
ditto, Dodd, Mead (U.S.), 1957 . . . . . £25/£5
The Appleby File, Gollancz, 1975 . . . . £20/£5
ditto, Dodd, Mead (U.S.), 1976 . . . . . £15/£5

CHRISTOPHER ISHERWOOD
(b.1904 d.1986)

Isherwood is usually remembered for the novels *Mr Norris Changes Trains* and *Goodbye to Berlin*. The latter included the sketch 'Sally Bowles', which was dramatised and turned into the popular musical *Cabaret.*

Novels
All the Conspirators, Cape, 1928 . . £1,500/£100
ditto, New Directions (U.S.), 1958 . . . £50/£10
The Memorial, Hogarth Press, 1932 (first binding pink, lettered blue) . . . . £450/£125
ditto, Hogarth Press, 1932 (later bindings, blue or ochre) . . . . £300/£45
ditto, New Directions (U.S.), 1946 . . . £45/£10
Mr Norris Changes Trains, Hogarth Press, 1935 . .
. . . . £2,500/£250
ditto, as *The Last of Mr Norris*, Morrow (U.S.), 1935 .
. . . . £250/£40
Sally Bowles, Hogarth Press, 1937 . . £1,250/£250
Goodbye to Berlin, Hogarth Press, 1939 £2,000/£100
ditto, Random House (U.S.), 1939 . . . £500/£75
Prater Violet, Random House (U.S.), 1945 . £150/£20
ditto, Methuen, 1946 . . . . £150/£20
The World in the Evening, Random House (U.S.), 1954 . . . . £45/£10
ditto, Methuen, 1954 . . . . £25/£5
Down There on a Visit, Simon & Schuster (U.S.), 1962
. . . . £25/£5
ditto, Methuen, 1962 . . . . £15/£5
A Single Man, Simon & Schuster (U.S.), 1964 . £20/£5
ditto, Methuen, 1964 . . . . £15/£5
A Meeting by the River, Simon & Schuster (U.S.), 1967 . . . . £15/£5
ditto, Methuen, 1967 . . . . £15/£5

Omnibus Editions
The Berlin Stories, New Directions (U.S.), 1945 . .
. . . . £125/£15
ditto, as *The Berlin of Sally Bowles*, Hogarth Press, 1975 . . . . £15/£5

Plays
The Dog Beneath the Skin, Faber, 1935 (with W.H. Auden) . . . . £175/£45
ditto, Random House (U.S.), 1935 . . . £175/£45
The Ascent of F6, Faber, 1936 (with W.H. Auden) .
. . . . £150/£35
ditto, Random House (U.S.), 1937 . . . £125/£25
On The Frontier, Faber, 1938 (with W.H. Auden). .
. . . . £100/£25
ditto, Random House (U.S.), 1939 . . . £75/£20

Poetry
People One Ought to Know, Doubleday, 1982 . £15/£5
ditto, Macmillan, 1982 . . . . £15/£5

Others
Lions and Shadows, Hogarth Press, 1938 (blue cloth lettered black) . . . . £500/£100
ditto, Hogarth Press, 1938 (blue cloth lettered gilt). .
. . . . £400/£50
ditto, New Directions (U.S.), 1948 . . . £125/£25
Journey to a War, Faber, 1939 (with W.H. Auden) .
. . . . £200/£65
ditto, Random House (U.S.), 1939 . . . £150/£50
The Condor and the Cows, Random House (U.S.), 1949 . . . . £45/£15
ditto, Methuen, 1949 . . . . £40/£10
Ramakrishna and His Disciples, Simon & Schuster (U.S.), 1965 . . . . £20/£5
ditto, Methuen, 1965 . . . . £20/£5
Exhumations, Simon & Schuster (U.S.), 1966 . £15/£5
ditto, Methuen, 1966 . . . . £15/£5
Kathleen and Frank, Simon & Schuster (U.S.), 1971 .
. . . . £10/£5
ditto, Methuen, 1971 . . . . £10/£5
Frankenstein: The True Story, Avon (U.S.), 1973 (wraps) £10
Christopher and His Kind, Farrar, Strauss and Giroux (U.S.), 1976 . . . . £10/£5
ditto, Farrar, Strauss/Sylvester & Orphanos (U.S.), 1976 (100 signed copies, slipcase) . . . £250/£200
ditto, Eyre Methuen, 1977 . . . . . £10/£5
My Guru and His Disciple, Farrar Straus (U.S.), 1980
. . . . £10/£5
ditto, Eyre Methuen, 1980 . . . . . £10/£5
October, Twelvetrees Press (U.S.), 1980 (150 numbered, signed copies, slipcase) £250
ditto, Twelvetrees Press (U.S.), 1980 (26 signed, lettered copies) £400
ditto, Twelvetrees Press (U.S.), 1980 (wraps) . £20
ditto, Methuen, 1982 (1,000 copies, wraps) . £20
Diaries, Volume One: 1939-1960, Methuen, 1996 .
. . . . £15/£5
ditto, HarperCollins (U.S.), 1997. . . . £15/£5
Lost Years: A Memoir 1945-1951, Chatto & Windus, 2000 . . . . £15/£5
ditto, HarperCollins (U.S.), 2000. . . . £15/£5

KAZUO ISHIGURO
(b.1954)

A product of Malcolm Bradbury's creative writing course at the University of East Anglia, Ishiguro's slim, studied novels have become very fashionable following the successful film adaptation of *The Remains of the Day*.

Novels
A Pale View of Hills, Faber, 1982 . . £1,000/£75
ditto, Putnam (U.S.), 1982 . . . . . £100/£20
An Artist of the Floating World, Faber, 1986 (first issue, printed by Butler and Tanner) . . £100/£10

ditto, Faber, 1986 (second issue, printed by Richard Clay) . . . . £65/£10
ditto, Putnam (U.S.), 1986 . . . . . £35/£5
The Remains of the Day, Faber, 1989 . . £125/£25
ditto, Knopf (U.S.), 1989 . . . . . . £50/£20
The Unconsoled, Faber, 1995 . . . . . £15/£5
ditto, Knopf (U.S.), 1995 . . . . . . £15/£5
When We Were Orphans, Faber, 2000 . . . £15/£5
ditto, Knopf (U.S.), 2000 . . . . . . £15/£5

Short Stories
Early Japanese Stories, Belmont Press, 2000 (50 signed deluxe copies of 300) £300
ditto, Belmont Press, 2000 (150 signed special copies of 300) £200
ditto, Belmont Press, 2000 (100 signed standard copies of 300) £100

HENRY JAMES
(b.1843 d.1916)

Highly regarded American (later British) author of early modernist fiction, often producing comedies of manners featuring the American abroad.

Novels
Roderick Hudson, Osgood (U.S.), 1876 [1875] (first binding with J.R. Osgood & Co. imprint on spine) .
. . . . £500
ditto, Houghton Mifflin (U.S.), 1876 [1875] (second binding with Houghton Mifflin imprint on spine). .
. . . . £300
ditto, Macmillan, 1879 (3 vols) £3,500
The American, Osgood (U.S.), 1877 . . . . £450
ditto, Ward Lock, 1877 (pirated U.K. first edition). .
. . . . £450
ditto, Macmillan, 1879 (authorised U.K. first edition) .
. . . . £400
Watch and Ward, Houghton Osgood (U.S.), 1878 (with blank leaf after p.129) £500
ditto, Houghton Osgood (U.S.), 1878 (without blank leaf) £250
ditto, Houghton Osgood (U.K.), 1878 (stamped 'Trübner & Co' on title page) £400
The Europeans, Macmillan, 1878 (2 vols) . . £1,250
ditto, Houghton Osgood (U.S.), 1879 . . . £450
Confidence, Chatto & Windus, 1880 [1879] (2 vols) .
. . . . £2,500
ditto, Houghton Osgood (U.S.), 1880 . . . £300
Washington Square; The Pension Beaurepas; A Bundle of Letters, Macmillan, 1881 (2 vols, first printing with last page numbered 371 and 'H.James Jr.' on spine) £2,000
ditto, Macmillan, 1881 (2 vols, second printing with last page numbered 271 and 'Henry/James Jr.' on spine, only 250 copies) £1,000

ditto, Harper (U.S.), 1881 (2 vols, frontispiece and illustrations by George Du Maurier) . . . £400
The Portrait of a Lady, Macmillan, 1881 (3 vols) . .
. . . . £4,000
ditto, Houghton Mifflin (U.S.), 1882 (first issue with full stop after 'Copyright, 1881') £300
The Bostonians, Macmillan, 1886 (3 vols) . . £3,000
ditto, Macmillan (U.S.), 1886 . . . . . £200
The Princess Casamassima, Macmillan, 1886 (3 vols)
. . . . £2,500
ditto, Macmillan (U.S.), 1886 . . . . . £250
The Reverberator, Macmillan, 1888 (2 vols) . £1,250
ditto, Macmillan (U.S.), 1888 . . . . . £200
The Tragic Muse, Houghton Mifflin (U.S.), 1890 (2 vols) £500
ditto, Macmillan, 1890 (3 vols) £1,000
The Other House, Heinemann, 1896 (2 vols) . £500
ditto, Macmillan (U.S.), 1896 . . . . . £125
The Spoils of Poynton, Heinemann, 1897 . . £200
ditto, Houghton Mifflin (U.S.), 1897 . . . £125
What Maisie Knew, Stone (U.S.), 1897 . . . £100
ditto, Heinemann, 1898 (tulips on front cover) . £400
ditto, Heinemann, 1898 (irises on front cover) . £100
In the Cage, Duckworth, 1898 . . . . . £100
ditto, Herbert S. Stone & Co. (U.S.), 1898 . . £100
The Awkward Age, Harper (U.S.), 1899 . . . £125
ditto, Heinemann, 1899 . . . . £125
The Sacred Fount, Scribner's (U.S.), 1901 (2 vols) .
. . . . £225
ditto, Methuen, 1901 . . . . £200
The Wings of the Dove, Scribner's (U.S.), 1902 (2 vols) £200
ditto, Archibald Constable, 1902 . . . . . £150
The Ambassadors, Macmillan, 1903 . . . £150
ditto, Harper (U.S.), 1903 . . . . £150
The Golden Bowl, Scribner's (U.S.), 1905 (2 vols)
. . . . £150
ditto, Methuen, 1905 . . . . £125
The Outcry, Methuen, 1911 . . . . . . £75
ditto, Scribner's (U.S.), 1911 . . . . . . £75
The Ivory Tower, Collins, 1917 . . . . . £75
ditto, Scribner's (U.S.), 1917 . . . . . . £75
The Sense of the Past, Collins, 1917 (unfinished) £75
ditto, Scribner's (U.S.), 1917 . . . . . £75

Collected Editions
The Collective Edition, Macmillan, 1883 (14 vols) .
. . . . £1,000
ditto, Macmillan, 1883 (14 vols, wraps) . . . £750
The New York Edition, Scribner's (U.S.), 1907-9, 1918 (26 vols) £5,000
ditto, Scribner's (U.S.), 1907-9 (26 vols, 156 copies on handmade paper) £8,000
ditto, Macmillan, 1883 (26 vols, made up from US sheets) £3,000

Short Stories
A Passionate Pilgrim, Osgood (U.S.), 1875 (first issue with 'J.R. Osgood & Co' on spine) £1,250

ditto, Osgood (U.S.), 1875 (second issue with 'Houghton Osgood & Co' on spine) . . . £450
ditto, Osgood (U.S.), 1875 (third issue with 'Houghton, Mifflin & Co' on spine) £200
ditto, Macmillan, 1879 (3 vols) £1,000
Daisy Miller: A Study, Harper (U.S.), 1879 (wraps, first issue lists 79 titles in Half Hour Series) . £5,000
ditto, Harper (U.S.), 1879 (cloth edition, first issue) .
. . . . £1,000
Daisy Miller: A Study and An International Episode, Four Meetings, Macmillan, 1879 (2 vols) . . £1,000
An International Episode, Harper (U.S.), 1879 (first state with line on p44 repeated as first line on p45, no.91 in Half Hour Series, wraps) £400
ditto, Harper (U.S.), 1879 (first state, cloth) . . £250
The Madonna of the Future and Other Tales, Macmillan, 1879 (2 vols) £2,000
Daisy Miller: A Comedy, privately printed, 1882 (18 copies, wraps) £2,000
ditto, Osgood (U.S.), 1883 . . . . . . £600
Tales of Three Cities, Osgood (U.S.), 1884 . . £150
ditto, Macmillan, 1884 . . . . £150
Stories Revived, Macmillan, 1885 (3 vols) . £1,000
The Aspern Papers; Louis Pallant, The Modern Warning, Macmillan, 1888 (2 vols) . . . £750
ditto, Macmillan (U.S.), 1888 . . . . . £150
A London Life; The Patagonia; The Liar; Mrs Temperley, Macmillan, 1889 (2 vols) . . . £250
ditto, Macmillan (U.S.), 1889 . . . . . £100
The Lesson of the Master; The Marriages; The Pupil; Brooksmith; The Solution; Sir Edmund Orme, Macmillan (U.S.), 1892 . . . . . . £125
ditto, Macmillan, 1892 . . . . £125
Daisy Miller and An International Episode, (U.S.), 1892 . . . . £75
ditto, (U.S.), 1892 (250 copies) £150
The Real Thing and Other Tales, Macmillan (U.S.), 1893 . . . . £150
ditto, Macmillan, 1893 . . . . . . £150
The Private Life; The Wheel of Time; Lord Beaupre; The Visits; Collaboration; Owen Wingrave, Osgood McIlvane, 1893 . . . . . . £150
ditto, Harpers (U.S.), 1893 . . . . . £150
Terminations; The Death of the Lion; The Coxon Fund; The Middle Years; The Altar of the Dead, Heinemann, 1895 . . . . £150
ditto, Harpers (U.S.), 1895 . . . . . £150
Embarrassments; The Figure in the Carpet; Glasses; The Next Time; The Way it Came, Heinemann, 1896
. . . . £150
ditto, Macmillan (U.S.), 1896 . . . . . £150
The Two Magics: The Turn of the Screw; Covering End, Heinemann, 1898 . . . . . . £200
ditto, Macmillan (U.S.), 1898 . . . . . £200
The Soft Side, Methuen, 1900 . . . . . £75
ditto, Macmillan (U.S.), 1900 . . . . . £75
The Better Sort, Methuen, 1903 . . . . . £75
ditto, Scribner's (U.S.), 1900 . . . . . £75
The Finer Grain, Scribner's (U.S.), 1910 . . £75

ditto, Methuen, 1910 . . . . £75
The Ghostly Tales of Henry James, Rutgers Univ.
Press (U.S.), 1948 [1949] . . . . . £25/£5
ditto, as *Stories of the Supernatural*, Barrie & Jenkins,
1971 . . . . £15/£5

Plays
Theatricals: Two Comedies—Tenants [and] **Disen-**
gaged, Osgood McIlvaine, 1894 . . . . £100
ditto, Harpers (U.S.), 1894 . . . . . . £100
Theatricals: Second Series—The Album; The
Reprobate, Osgood McIlvaine, 1895 . . . £75
ditto, Harpers (U.S.), 1895 [1894] £75
The Complete Plays of Henry James, Lippincott
(U.S.), 1949 . . . . £45/£15
ditto, Hart-Davis, 1949 . . . . . £45/£15

Non Fiction
French Poets and Novelists, Macmillan, 1878 . £300
Hawthorne, Macmillan, 1879 . . . . . £125
ditto, Harpers (U.S.), 1880 . . . . . £45
Portraits of Places, Macmillan, 1883 . . . £100
ditto, Osgood (U.S.), 1884 . . . . . £100
Partial Portraits, Macmillan (U.K. and U.S.), 1888 .
. . . . £100
Essays in London and Elsewhere, Harper (U.S.), 1893
. . . . £75
ditto, Osgood McIlvaine, 1893 . . . . £75
A Little Tour in France, Heinemann, 1900 . . £75
ditto, Heinemann, 1900 (150 copies on Japanese
vellum) £450
ditto, Houghton, Mifflin (U.S.), 1900 . . . £75
ditto, Cambridge Riverside Press (U.S.), 1900 (250
numbered large paper copies) £150
William Wetmore Story and His Friends, Blackwood,
1903 (2 vols) £150
ditto, Houghton, Mifflin (U.S.), 1903 (2 vols) . £150
English Hours, Heinemann, 1905 . . . . £100
ditto, Houghton, Mifflin (U.S.), 1905 . . . £100
ditto, Cambridge Riverside Press (U.S.), 1905 (400
large paper copies) £200
The American Scene, Chapman & Hall, 1907 . £75
ditto, Harpers (U.S.), 1907 . . . . . £75
Italian Hours, Heinemann, 1909. . . . . £75
ditto, Houghton, Mifflin (U.S.), 1909 . . . £75
Notes on Novelists, Dent, 1914 . . . . £50
ditto, Scribner's (U.S.), 1914 . . . . . £50
Within the Rim and Other Essays, Collins, [1919] £65
The Letters of Henry James, Macmillan, 1920 (2 vols)
. . . . £200/£45
ditto, Scribner's (U.S.), 1920 (2 vols) . £200/£45
The Painter's Eye, Hart-Davis, 1956 . . £35/£10
The House of Fiction, Hart-Davis, 1957 . £30/£10
Henry James and Edith Wharton Letters 1900-1915,
Scribner's (U.S.), 1990 . . . . . . £10/£5

Autobiography
A Small Boy and Others, Macmillan, 1913 . . £75
ditto, Scribner's (U.S.), 1913 . . . . . £75

Notes of a Son and a Brother, Macmillan, 1914 £75
ditto, Scribner's (U.S.), 1914. . . . . £75
The Middle Years, Collins, [1917] £75
ditto, Scribner's (U.S.), 1917 . . . . . £75

M.R. JAMES
(b.1862 d.1936)

A distinguished scholar and academic, James was
awarded the Order of Merit in 1930. He had a
penchant for the macabre and supernatural, and is
famous for his ghost stories.

Ghost Stories
Ghost Stories of an Antiquary, Edward Arnold, [1904]
(catalogue dated 1904) £750
ditto, Longmans (U.S.), 1905. . . . . £500
More Ghost Stories, Edward Arnold, 1911 . . £400
A Thin Ghost, Edward Arnold, 1919 . . . £125
A Warning to the Curious, Edward Arnold, 1925 £300
ditto, Longmans (U.S.), 1925. . . . . £250
Wailing Well, Mill House Press, 1928 (157 numbered
copies) £750
Collected Ghost Stories, Edward Arnold, 1931. . .
. . . . £100/£25
ditto, Longmans (U.S.), 1931. . . . £100/£25
Two Ghost Stories: A Centenary, Ghost Story Press,
1993 (200 numbered copies) £100
A Pleasing Terror: The Complete Supernatural
Writings, Ash-Tree Press (Canada), 2001 . £50/£20

Other Titles
Old Testament Legends, Longmans, 1913 . . £50
The Five Jars, Edward Arnold, 1922 . £400/£200
ditto, Longmans (U.S.), 1922. . . . £300/£150
ditto, Ash-Tree Press (Canada), 1995 . £75/£25
Abbeys, Great Western Railway, 1925 . £75/£20
ditto, Doubleday (U.S.), 1926 . . . . £75/£15
Eton and Kings, William & Norgate, 1926 . £65/£25
Suffolk and Norfolk, Dent, 1930 . . . £45/£15
Letters to a Friend, Edward Arnold, 1956 . £35/£15

Edited/Translated by M.R. James
The Apocryphal New Testament, Clarendon Press,
1924 . . . . £45/£20
Judith, Haymarket Press, 1928 (illustrated by W.R.
Flint, 875 copies). £75
ditto, Haymarket Press, 1928 (100 copies signed by
Flint, parchment, in slipcase) . . . . £200/£150
ditto, Haymarket Press, 1928 (12 copies signed by
Flint, on vellum, extra set of 4 plates, in slipcase). .
. . . . £1,000/£800
The Book of Tobit and **History of Susanna**,
Haymarket Press, 1929 (illustrated by W.R. Flint, 875
copies) £75
ditto, Haymarket Press, 1929 (100 copies signed by
Flint, parchment in slipcase) . . . . £200/£150

ditto, Haymarket Press, 1929 (12 copies signed by Flint, on vellum, extra set of 4 plates, in slipcase). . . . . £1,000/£800
Hans Andersen, Forty Stories, Faber, 1930   £30/£15
The New Testament, Dent, 1934-6 (4 vols, engravings by Eric Gill) £75

P.D. JAMES
(b.1920)

Born in Oxford but educated at Cambridge Girl's High School, P.D. James worked in the Civil Service and did not begin writing until her forties. She is famous for her detective fiction, much of which has been successfully televised.

'Adam Dalgliesh' Novels
Cover Her Face, Faber, 1962   . . . £2,500/£300
ditto, Scribner's (U.S.), 1966 . . . . . £350/£35
A Mind to Murder, Faber, 1963 . . . £2,500/£300
ditto, Scribner's (U.S.), 1967 . . . . . £350/£35
Unnatural Causes, Faber, 1967 . . . £2,000/£200
ditto, Scribner's (U.S.), 1967 . . . . £125/£20
Shroud for a Nightingale, Faber, 1971 . . £400/£75
ditto, Scribner's (U.S.), 1971 . . . . . £100/£15
The Black Tower, Faber, 1975 . . . . £150/£15
ditto, Scribner's (U.S.), 1974 . . . . . £50/£10
Death of an Expert Witness, Faber, 1977 . £100/£15
ditto, Scribner's (U.S.), 1977 . . . . . . £25/£5
A Taste for Death, Faber, 1986 . . . . . £35/£5
ditto, Scribner's (U.S.), 1986 . . . . . . £15/£5
Devices and Desires, Faber, 1989 . . . . £15/£5
ditto, Franklin Library (U.S.), 1990 (signed, limited edition) £45
ditto, Knopf (U.S.), 1990 . . . . £10/£5
Original Sin, Faber, 1994 . . . . £15/£5
ditto, London Limited Editions, 1994 (150 signed copies, acetate d/w) . . . . £100/£90
ditto, Knopf (U.S.), 1995 . . . . £10/£5
A Certain Justice, Faber, 1997 . . . . . £15/£5
ditto, Knopf (U.S.), 1997 . . . . £10/£5
Death in Holy Orders, Faber, 2001 . . . £10/£5
ditto, Knopf (U.S.), 2001 . . . . £10/£5

'Cordelia Gray' Novels
An Unsuitable Job for a Woman, Faber, 1972 . . . . £200/£25
ditto, Scribner's (U.S.), 1972 . . . . . £75/£10
The Skull Beneath the Skin, Faber, 1982 . £50/£10
ditto, Scribner's (U.S.), 1982 . . . . . £25/£5

Other Novels
Innocent Blood, Faber, 1980 . . . . . £50/£10
ditto, Scribner's (U.S.), 1980 . . . . . . £20/£5
The Children of Men, Faber, 1992 . . . . £20/£5
ditto, Knopf (U.S.), 1993 . . . . £10/£5

Omnibus Editions
P.D. James Omnibus, Faber, 1982 . . . . £15/£5
The Second P.D. James Omnibus, Faber, 1990 . . . . £10/£5
Murder in Triplicate, Scribner's (U.S.), 1980 . £15/£5

Short Stories
Murder in Triplicate, Belmont Press, 2001 (50 signed copies of 250) £100
ditto, Belmont Press, 2001 (200 signed copies of 250). £100

Non Fiction
The Maul and the Pear Tree, Constable, 1971 (with T.A. Critchley) . . . . £50/£20
ditto, Mysterious Press (U.S.), 1986 . . . . £15/£5
Bad Language in Church, Prayer Book Society, 1988 (wraps) £10
Time to Be in Earnest, A Fragment in Autobiography, Faber, 1999 . . . . £15/£5
ditto, Knopf (U.S.), 2000 . . . . £10/£5

RICHARD JEFFERIES
(b.1848 d.1887)

British essayist, novelist, and chronicler of rural life.

Novels
The Scarlet Shawl, Tinsley Bros., 1874 . . . £350
Restless Human Hearts, Tinsley Bros., 1875 (3 vols) £4500
World's End, Tinsley Bros., 1877 (3 vols) . . £400
Greene Ferne Farm, Smith, Elder & Co., 1880   £250
The Dewy Morn, Bentley, 1884 (2 vols) . . £250
After London, or Wild England, Cassell & Co., 1885 . . . . £250
Amaryllis at the Fair, Sampson, Low & Co., 1887. . . . . £125
The Early Fiction of Richard Jefferies, Simpkin, Marshall & Co., 1896 . . . . £75
ditto, 1896 (large paper, 50 numbered copies) . £125

Short Story
T.T.T., Arthur Young, 1896 (100 copies) . . £200

Children's Titles
Wood Magic, A Fable, Cassell, Petter & Galpin, 1881 (2 vols) £400
Bevis, The Story of a Boy, Sampson, Low & Co., 1882 (3 vols) £1,000

Non Fiction
Reporting, Editing and Authorship: Practical Hints for Beginners in Literature, John Snow & Co., [1873]. £750
Jack Brass, Emperor of England, Pettit & Co., 1873 . . . . £500

A Memoir of the Goddards of North Wilts Compiled from Ancient Records, Registers and Family Papers, Simmons & Botten, [1873] £750

Suez-cide!! or How Miss Britannia Bought a Dirty Puddle and Lost her Sugar Plums, John Snow, 1876 . . . . £400

The Gamekeeper at Home, or Sketches of Natural History & Rural Life, Smith, Elder & Co., 1878 (anonymous) £750

Wild Life in a Southern County, Smith, Elder & Co., 1879 (anonymous) £150

The Amateur Poacher, Smith, Elder & Co., 1879 (anonymous) £200

Hodge and His Masters, Smith, Elder & Co., 1880 (2 vols) £200

Round About a Great Estate, Smith, Elder & Co., 1880 . . . . £150

Nature Near London, Chatto & Windus, 1883 . £100

The Story of My Heart, My Autobiography, Longmans, 1883 . . . . £150

Red Deer, Longmans, 1884 . . . . . . £125

The Life of the Fields, Chatto & Windus, 1884 £75

The Open Air, Chatto & Windus, 1885 . . . £75

Field and Hedgerow, Being the Last Essays of Richard Jefferies Collected by His Widow, Longmans, Green & Co., 1889 . . . . . £75

ditto, Longmans, Green & Co., 1889 (large paper, 200 numbered copies) £125

The Toilers of the Field, Longmans, Green & Co., 1892 . . . . £25

ditto, Longmans, Green & Co., 1892 (large paper, 105 numbered copies) £75

Jefferies Land, A History of Swindon and Its Environs, Simpkin, Marshall & Co., 1896. . £75

ditto, Simpkin, Marshall & Co., 1896 (large paper, 50 numbered copies) £100

The Hills and the Vale, Duckworth, 1909 . . £25

The Nature Diaries and Notebooks of Richard Jefferies, With an Essay 'A Tangle of Autumn' Now Printed for the First Time, Grey Walls Press, 1941 . . . . £35/£15

ditto, Grey Walls Press, 1941 (large paper, 105 numbered copies) £75

Chronicles of the Hedges And Other Essays, Phoenix House, 1948 . . . . £15/£5

The Old House at Coate, Lutterworth Press, 1948 . . . . £25/£10

ditto, Harvard Univ. Press, 1948 . . . . £20/£10

Beauty Is Immortal (Felise of the Dewy Morn), With Some Hitherto Uncollected Essays and Manuscripts, Worthing Cavalcade, 1948 . . . . . . £25

Field and Farm, Essays Now Collected With Some From Manuscripts, Phoenix House, 1957 . £25/£10

Landscape and Labour, Moonraker Press, 1979 . . . . £10/£5

By the Brook, Eric & Joan Stevens, 1981 (170 numbered copies) £25

ditto, Eric & Joan Stevens, 1981 (20 leather-bound copies in slipcase) £75

The Birth of a Naturalist, Tern Press, 1985 (300 numbered copies) £50

ditto, Tern Press, 1985 (20 leather-bound copies in slipcase) . . . . £125/£100

JEROME K. JEROME
(b.1859 d.1927)

First employed as a railway clerk, then as an actor, Jerome was best known as a novelist, but was also a successful dramatist and popular journalist.

Novels

Three Men in a Boat, Arrowsmith, 1889 (first issue, address: 'Quay Street') £150

ditto, Arrowsmith, 1889 (second issue, address: '11 Quay Street') £100

ditto, Holt (U.S.), 1890 . . . . . . £75

Diary of a Pilgrimage, Arrowsmith, 1891 . . £35

ditto, Holt (U.S.), 1891 . . . . . . £25

Three Men on the Bummel, Arrowsmith, 1900 £35

Paul Kelver, Hutchinson, 1902 . . . . . £35

ditto, Dodd, Mead (U.S.), 1902 . . . . . £25

Tommy & Co, Hutchinson, 1904. . . . . £25

ditto, Dodd, Mead (U.S.), 1904 . . . . . £20

They and I, Hutchinson, 1909 . . . . . £20

ditto, Dodd, Mead (U.S.), 1909 . . . . . £15

All Roads Lead to Calvary, Hutchinson, 1919 . £15

ditto, Dodd, Mead (U.S.), 1919 . . . . . £15

Anthony John, Cassell, 1923. . . . . £35/£15

ditto, Dodd, Mead (U.S.), 1923 . . . . £35/£15

Short Stories

Told After Supper, Leadenhall Press, 1891 . . £45

ditto, Holt (U.S.), 1891 . . . . . . £40

John Ingerfield and Other Stories, McClure, 1894 . . . . £30

ditto, Holt (U.S.), 1894 . . . . . . £25

The Observations of Henry, Arrowsmith, 1901 £25

ditto, Dodd, Mead (U.S.), 1901 . . . . . £15

Tea Table Talk, Hutchinson, 1903 . . . . £15

ditto, Dodd, Mead (U.S.), 1903 . . . . . £15

The Passing of the Third Floor Back, Hurst & Blackett, 1907 . . . . £25

ditto, Dodd, Mead (U.S.), 1908 . . . . . £25

Malvina of Brittany, Cassell, 1916 . . . . £15

Plays

Barbara, Lacy, 1886 . . . . £20

Sunset, Fitzgerald (U.S.), [1888]. £20

Fennel, French, [1888] £15

Woodbarrow Farm, French, [1888] £15

The Prude's Progress, French, 1895 . . . £15

Miss Hobbs, French, 1902 . . . . . . £15

Fanny and the Servant Problem, Lacy, 1909 . £15

The Passing of the Third Floor Back, Hurst & Blackett, 1910 . . . . £20

The Master of Mrs Chilvers, Fisher Unwin, 1911 £10

Robina in Search of a Husband, Lacy, 1914 . £10
The Celebrity, Hodder & Stoughton, 1926 . £25/£10
The Soul of Nicholas Snyders, Hodder & Stoughton,
1927 . . . . £25/£10

Other Works
On Stage-and Off, Field & Tuer, 1885 . . . £75
ditto, Leadenhall Press, 1891 . . . . . . £35
The Idle Thoughts of an Idle Fellow, Field & Tuer,
1886 . . . . £100
ditto, Holt (U.S.), 1890 . . . . £50
Stage-Land, Chatto & Windus, 1889 . . . £25
ditto, Holt (U.S.), 1906 . . . . £25
Novel Notes, Leadenhall Press, 1893 . . . £35
Sketches in Lavender, Blue and Green, Longman,
1897 . . . . £25
ditto, Holt (U.S.), 1907 . . . . £25
The Second Thoughts of an Idle Fellow, Hurst &
Blackett, 1898 . . . . £25
ditto, Dodd, Mead (U.S.), 1898 . . . . . £20
American Wives and Others, Stokes (U.S.), 1904 £25
Idle Ideas in 1905, Hurst & Blackett, 1905 . . £15
The Angel and the Author—and Others, Hurst &
Blackett, 1908 . . . . £15
Thoughts from Jerome K. Jerome, Sesame Booklets,
1913 . . . . £10
A Miscellany of Sense and Nonsense, Arrowsmith,
1923 . . . . £40/£15
My Life and Times, Hodder & Stoughton, 1926 . .
. . . . £35/£15
ditto, Harper (U.S.), 1926 . . . . . £35/£15

RUTH PRAWER JHABVALA
(b.1927)

Born in Cologne, Ruth Prawer Jhabvala fled with her
Polish/Jewish family to England in 1939. She married
an Indian architect in 1951 and moved to Delhi. Her
first novel was published in 1955. She is also known
for her short stories and film scripts written for the
Merchant/Ivory partnership.

Novels
To Whom She Will, George Allen & Unwin, 1955. .
. . . . £150/£20
ditto, as Amrita, Norton (U.S.), 1956 . . £50/£10
The Nature of Passion, George Allen & Unwin, 1956.
. . . . £75/£20
ditto, Norton (U.S.), 1957. . . . . . . £25/£5
Esmond in India, George Allen & Unwin, 1958 . .
. . . . £50/£20
ditto, Norton (U.S.), 1958. . . . .£25/£5
The Householder, Murray, 1960. . . . £50/£20
ditto, Norton (U.S.), 1960. . . . . . £20/£5
Get Ready for Battle, Murray, 1962 . . . £40/£15
ditto, Norton (U.S.), 1963. . . . . . .£15/£5
A Backward Place, Murray, 1965 . . . £25/£10
ditto, Norton (U.S.), 1965. . . . . . .£15/£5

A New Dominion, Murray, 1972. . . . £25/£10
ditto, as Travellers, Harper & Row (U.S.), 1973 £15/£5
Heat and Dust, Murray, 1975 . . . . £25/£10
ditto, Harper (U.S.), 1976. . . . . . .£20/£5
In Search of Love and Beauty, Murray, 1983 .£10/£5
ditto, Morrow (U.S.), 1983 . . . . . .£10/£5
Three Continents, Murray, 1987. . . . .£10/£5
ditto, Morrow (U.S.), 1987 . . . . . .£10/£5
Poet and Dancer, Murray, 1993 . . . . .£10/£5
ditto, Doubleday (U.S.), 1993 . . . . .£10/£5
Shards of Memory, Murray, 1995 . . . .£10/£5
ditto, Doubleday (U.S.), 1995 . . . . .£10/£5

Short Stories
Like Birds Like Fishes, Murray, 1963 . . £45/£10
ditto, Norton (U.S.), 1964. . . . . . .£25/£5
A Stronger Climate, Murray, 1968 . . . £25/£10
ditto, Norton (U.S.), 1969. . . . . . .£15/£5
An Experience of India, Murray, 1971 . . £25/£10
ditto, Norton (U.S.), 1972. . . . . . .£15/£5
How I Became a Holy Mother, Murray, 1976 .£10/£5
ditto, Harper (U.S.), 1976. . . . . . .£10/£5
Out of India: Selected Stories, Morrow (U.S.), 1986 .
. . . .£10/£5
ditto, Murray, 1987 . . . .£10/£5
East Into Upper East: Plain Tales From New York
and New Delhi, Murray, 1998 . . . . .£10/£5
ditto, Counterpoint (U.S.), 1998 . . . . .£10/£5

CAPTAIN W.E. JOHNS
(b.1893 d.1968)

In 1916 Johns joined the newly formed Royal Flying
Corps, and remained in the Air Force until 1930. He
founded the monthly Popular Flying magazine in
which Captain James Bigglesworth made his first
appearance.

'Biggles' Titles
The Camels Are Coming, Hamilton, [1932] (pseud.
'William Earle') . . . . £5,000/£750
The Cruise of the Condor: A Biggles Story, Hamilton,
[1933]. . . . . £3,000/£400
'Biggles' of the Camel Squadron, Hamilton, [1934] .
. . . . £3,000/£400
Biggles Flies Again, Hamilton, [1934] . £3,000/£400
ditto, Penguin, 1941 (wraps) £200
Biggles Learns to Fly, Boys' Friend Library, 1935
(wraps) £750
ditto, Brockhampton Press, 1955 (first hardback
edition) . . . . £50/£10
Biggles Flies East, O.U.P., 1935. . . £2,500/£300
Biggles Hits the Trail, O.U.P., 1935. . £2,500/£300
Biggles in France, Boys' Friend Library, 1935 (wraps)
. . . . £750
The Black Peril: A 'Biggles' Story, Hamilton, [1935].
. . . . £3,000/£400

Biggles in Africa, O.U.P., 1936 . . . £2,500/£300

Biggles & Co, O.U.P., 1936 . . . . £2,500/£300

Biggles - Air Commodore, O.U.P., 1937 £2,500/£300

Biggles Flies West, O.U.P., 1937 . . £2,500/£300

Biggles Flies South, O.U.P., 1938 . . £2,500/£300

Biggles Goes to War, O.U.P., 1938 . . £2,500/£300

Biggles Flies North, O.U.P., 1939 . . £2,000/£250

Biggles in Spain, O.U.P., 1939 . . . £2,000/£250

The Rescue Flight: A 'Biggles' Story, O.U.P., 1939 .
. . . . £2,000/£250

Biggles in the Baltic: A Tale of the Second Great War, O.U.P., 1940 . . . . £1,750/£225

Biggles in the South Seas, O.U.P., 1940. £1,500/£200

Biggles - Secret Agent, O.U.P., 1940 . £1,500/£200

Spitfire Parade: Stories of Biggles in War-Time, O.U.P., 1941 . . . . £2,000/£350

Biggles Sees it Through, O.U.P., 1941 . £1,250/£150

Biggles Defies the Swastika, O.U.P., 1941 . . . .
. . . . £1,250/£150

Biggles in the Jungle, O.U.P., 1942 . . . £750/£100

Biggles Sweeps the Desert, Hodder & Stoughton, 1942
. . . . £250/£40

Biggles - Charter Pilot, O.U.P., 1943 . £750/£100

Biggles 'Fails to Return', Hodder & Stoughton, 1943 .
. . . . £250/£40

Biggles in Borneo, O.U.P., 1943. . . . £250/£30

Biggles in the Orient, Hodder & Stoughton, 1945 .
. . . . £200/£30

Biggles Delivers the Goods, Hodder & Stoughton, 1946 . . . . £45/£10

Sergeant Bigglesworth CID, Hodder & Stoughton, 1947 . . . . £45/£10

Biggles Hunts Big Game, Hodder & Stoughton, 1948 .
. . . . £45/£10

Biggles' Second Case, Hodder & Stoughton, 1948. .
. . . . £45/£10

Biggles Breaks the Silence, Hodder & Stoughton, 1949
. . . . £40/£10

Biggles Takes a Holiday, Hodder & Stoughton, 1949 .
. . . . £40/£10

Biggles Gets His Men, Hodder & Stoughton, 1950 .
. . . . £40/£10

Another Job for Biggles, Hodder & Stoughton, 1951 .
. . . . £35/£10

Biggles Goes to School, Hodder & Stoughton, 1951 .
. . . . £35/£10

Biggles Works It Out, Hodder & Stoughton, 1951 . .
. . . . £35/£10

Biggles - Air Detective, Marks & Spencer, 1951 (no d/w) £10

Biggles Follows On, Hodder & Stoughton, 1952 . .
. . . . £30/£10

Biggles Takes the Case, Hodder & Stoughton, 1952 .
. . . . £30/£10

Biggles and the Black Raider, Hodder & Stoughton, 1953 . . . . £45/£10

Biggles in the Blue, Brockhampton Press, 1953 . .
. . . . £50/£10

Biggles of the Special Air Police, Thames, [1953] . .
. . . . £20/£5

Biggles in the Gobi, Hodder & Stoughton, 1953 . .
. . . . £35/£10

Biggles and the Pirate Treasure and Other Biggles Adventures, Brockhampton Press, 1954 . £45/£10

Biggles Cuts it Fine, Hodder & Stoughton, 1954 . .
. . . . £35/£10

Biggles, Foreign Legionnaire, Hodder & Stoughton, 1954 . . . . £35/£10

Biggles, Pioneer Airfighter, Thames, [1954] . £20/£5

Biggles' Chinese Puzzle and Other Biggles Adventures, Brockhampton Press, 1955 . . . £50/£10

Biggles in Australia, Hodder & Stoughton, 1955 . .
. . . . £50/£10

Biggles of 266, Thames, [1956] . . . . . £20/£5

Biggles Takes Charge, Brockhampton Press, 1956 .
. . . . £50/£10

No Rest For Biggles, Hodder & Stoughton, 1956 . .
. . . . £50/£10

Biggles Makes Ends Meet, Hodder & Stoughton, 1957
. . . . £50/£10

Biggles of the Interpol, Brockhampton Press, 1957 .
. . . . £50/£10

Biggles on the Home Front, Hodder & Stoughton, 1957 . . . . £50/£10

Biggles Buries a Hatchet, Brockhampton Press, 1958 .
. . . . £50/£10

Biggles on Mystery Island, Hodder & Stoughton, [1958] . . . . £50/£10

Biggles Presses On, Brockhampton Press, 1958 £30/£5

Biggles at World's End, Brockhampton Press, 1959 .
. . . . £50/£10

Biggles' Combined Operation, Hodder & Stoughton, [1959] . . . . £50/£10

Biggles in Mexico, Brockhampton Press, 1959 £50/£10

Biggles and the Leopards of Zinn, Brockhampton Press, 1960 . . . . £50/£10

Biggles Goes Home, Hodder & Stoughton, [1960]. .
. . . . £50/£10

Biggles and the Missing Millionaire, Brockhampton Press, 1961 . . . . £50/£10

Biggles and the Poor Rich Boy, Brockhampton Press, 1961 . . . . £40/£5

Biggles Forms a Syndicate, Hodder & Stoughton, 1961 . . . . £50/£10

Biggles Goes Alone, Hodder & Stoughton, [1962]. .
. . . . £50/£10

Biggles Sets a Trap, Hodder & Stoughton, 1962 . .
. . . . £50/£10

Orchids for Biggles, Hodder & Stoughton, 1962 . .
. . . . £50/£10

Biggles and the Planet That Disappeared: A Story of the Air Police, Hodder & Stoughton, 1963 £50/£10

Biggles Flies to Work, Dean, [1963] . . . .
£20/£5

Biggles' Special Case, Brockhampton Press, 1963. .
. . . . £65/£15

Biggles Takes A Hand, Hodder & Stoughton, [1963] .
. . . . £65/£15
Biggles Takes it Rough, Brockhampton Press, 1963 .
. . . . £65/£15
Biggles and the Black Mask, Hodder & Stoughton,
1964 . . . . £125/£25
Biggles and the Lost Sovereigns, Brockhampton Press,
1964 . . . . £100/£10
*Biggles Investigates and Other Stories of the Air
Police*, Brockhampton Press, 1965 . . . £100/£10
Biggles and the Blue Moon, Brockhampton Press,
1965 . . . . £125/£20
Biggles and the Plot That Failed, Brockhampton
Press, 1965 . . . . £125/£20
*Biggles Looks Back: A Story of Biggles and the Air
Police*, Hodder & Stoughton, 1965 . . . £125/£25
Biggles Scores a Bull, Hodder & Stoughton, 1965 . .
. . . . £150/£35
Biggles in the Terai, Brockhampton Press, 1966 . .
. . . . £175/£45
Biggles and the Gun Runners, Brockhampton Press,
1966 . . . . £175/£45
Biggles and the Penitent Thief, Brockhampton Press,
1967 . . . . £175/£45
Biggles Sorts It Out, Brockhampton Press, 1967 . .
. . . . £175/£45
Biggles and the Dark Intruder, Knight, 1967 (wraps) .
. . . . £20
ditto, Brockhampton Press, 1970 . . . . £200/£15
Biggles in the Underworld, Brockhampton Press, 1968
. . . . £225/£50
The Boy Biggles, Dean, 1968 . . . . . £25/£5
Biggles and the Deep Blue Sea, Brockhampton Press,
1968 . . . . £225/£50
Biggles and the Little Green God, Brockhampton
Press, 1969 . . . . £225/£50
Biggles and the Noble Lord, Brockhampton Press,
1969 . . . . £225/£50
Biggles Sees Too Much, Brockhampton Press, 1970 .
. . . . £225/£50
Biggles of the Royal Flying Corps, Purnell, 1978 . .
. . . . £20/£5
Biggles Does Some Homework, Wright/Schofield,
1997 (300 copies, wraps) £35
Biggles Air Ace: The Uncollected Stories, Wright,
1999 (300 copies, wraps) £35

'Biggles' Omnibuses
The Biggles Omnibus, O.U.P., 1938. . £2,500/£300
The Biggles Flying Omnibus, O.U.P., 1940 . . . .
. . . . £2,500/£300
The Third Biggles Omnibus, O.U.P., 1941 . . . .
. . . . £2,500/£300
The First Biggles Omnibus, Hodder and Stoughton,
1953 . . . . £50/£10
The Biggles Air Detective Omnibus, Hodder and
Stoughton, 1956 . . . . £50/£10
The Biggles Adventure Omnibus, Hodder and
Stoughton, 1965 . . . . £50/£10

The Bumper Biggles Book, Chancellor, 1983 . £15/£5
The Best of Biggles, Chancellor, 1985 . . . £15/£5

'Worrals' Books
Worrals of the W.A.A.F., Lutterworth Press, 1941 . .
. . . . £125/£20
Worrals Carries On, Lutterworth Press, 1942 £65/£10
Worrals Flies Again, Hodder & Stoughton, 1942 . .
. . . . £50/£10
Worrals On the War-Path, Hodder & Stoughton, 1943
. . . . £45/£10
Worrals Goes East, Hodder & Stoughton, 1944 £45/£5
*Worrals of the Islands: A Story of the War in the
Pacific*, Hodder & Stoughton, 1945 . . . £45/£5
Worrals in the Wilds, Hodder & Stoughton, 1947 . .
. . . . £30/£5
Worrals Down Under, Lutterworth Press, 1948 £35/£5
Worrals Goes Afoot, Lutterworth Press, 1949 . £35/£5
Worrals In the Wastelands, Lutterworth Press, 1949 .
. . . . £35/£5
Worrals Investigates, Lutterworth Press, 1950 . £35/£5

'Gimlet' Books
King of the Commandos, Univ. of London Press, 1943
. . . . £65/£10
Gimlet Goes Again, Univ. of London Press, 1944 . .
. . . . £50/£10
Gimlet Comes Home, Univ. of London Press, 1946 .
. . . . £45/£10
Gimlet Mops Up, Brockhampton Press, 1947 £40/£10
Gimlet's Oriental Quest, Brockhampton Press, 1948 .
. . . . £40/£10
Gimlet Lends a Hand, Brockhampton Press, 1949 . .
. . . . £40/£10
Gimlet Bores In, Brockhampton Press, 1950 £40/£10
Gimlet Off the Map, Brockhampton Press, 1951 . .
. . . . £40/£10
Gimlet Gets the Answer, Brockhampton Press, 1952 .
. . . . £35/£10
Gimlet Takes a Job, Brockhampton Press, 1954 . .
. . . . £35/£10

Science Fiction Titles
*Kings of Space: A Story of Interplanetary
Explorations*, Hodder & Stoughton, 1954 . . £30/£5
Return to Mars, Hodder & Stoughton, 1955 . £25/£5
Now to the Stars, Hodder & Stoughton, 1956 . £25/£5
To Outer Space, Hodder & Stoughton, 1957 . £25/£5
The Edge of Beyond, Hodder & Stoughton, [1958] .
. . . . £25/£5
The Death Rays of Ardilla, Hodder & Stoughton,
[1959] . . . . £25/£5
*To Worlds Unknown: A Story of Interplanetary
Explorations*, Hodder & Stoughton, [1960] . £20/£5
The Quest for the Perfect Planet, Hodder &
Stoughton, 1961 . . . . £25/£5
Worlds of Wonder: More Adventures in Space,
Hodder & Stoughton, 1962 . . . . . £25/£5

The Man Who Vanished into Space, Hodder &
Stoughton, [1963] . . . . £25/£5

Other Books Written by Johns
Mossyface, 'The Weekly Telegraph Novel', 1922
(pseud. 'William Earle', wraps). . . £1,000/£125
ditto, Mellifont, 1932 (wraps) £300
ditto, Trendler/Wright, 1994 (300 numbered copies, no
d/w) £60
Modern Boys Book of Aircraft, Amalgamated Press,
1931 . . . . £65/£20
Wings: A Book of Flying Adventures, Hamilton,
[1931] (edited by Johns). . . . . £300/£35
The Pictorial Flying Course, John Hamilton, [1932]
(by Johns and H.M. Schofield) . . . £300/£75
Fighting Planes and Aces, John Hamilton, [1932]. .
. . . . £300/£75
The Spy Flyers, John Hamilton, 1933 . . £500/£125
The Raid, John Hamilton, [1935] . . . £400/£75
The Air VC's, John Hamilton, [1935] . . £350/£75
Some Milestones in Aviation, John Hamilton, [1935] .
. . . . £200/£45
Blue Blood Runs Red, Newnes, [1936] (pseud. 'Jon
Early') . . . . £2,500/£300
Modern Boy's Book of Adventure Stories, Amalgam-
ated Press, 1936 . . . . £50/£15
Ace High, Ace, 1936 . . . . . . £100/£30
Air Adventures, Ace, 1936 . . . . £100/£30
Sky High: A 'Steeley' Adventure, Newnes, [1936]. .
. . . . £450/£75
Steeley Flies Again, Newnes, [1936] . . £450/£75
Flying Stories, John Hamilton, 1937 . £100/£25
Murder By Air: A 'Steeley' Adventure, Newnes,
[1937]. . . . . £450/£75
The Passing Show, My Garden/Newnes, 1937 . .
. . . . £100/£20
Desert Night: A Romance, John Hamilton, [1938]. .
. . . . £250/£45
The Murder at Castle Deeping: A 'Steeley' Adventure,
John Hamilton, [1938] . . . . £500/£100
Champion of the Main, O.U.P., 1938 . £400/£75
Wings of Romance: A 'Steeley' Adventure, Newnes,
1939 . . . . £300/£75
Modern Boy's Book of Pirates, Amalgamated Press,
[1939]. . . . . £250/£50
The Unknown Quantity, John Hamilton, [1940] . .
. . . . £250/£50
Sinister Service: A Tale, O.U.P., 1942 . £125/£25
Comrades in Arms, Hodder & Stoughton, 1947 . .
. . . . £45/£10
The Rustlers of Rattlesnake Valley, Nelson, 1948 . .
. . . . £30/£5
Dr Vane Answers the Call, Latimer House, 1950 . .
. . . . £175/£25
Short Sorties, Latimer House, 1950 . . £175/£25
Sky Fever and Other Stories, Latimer House, [1953] .
. . . . £175/£25
Adventure Bound, Nelson, 1955 . . . . £15/£5
Adventure Unlimited, Nelson, 1957 . . . £15/£5

No Motive for Murder, Hodder & Stoughton, [1958] .
. . . . £175/£25
The Man Who Lost His Way, Macdonald, 1959 . .
. . . . £175/£25
The Biggles Book of Heroes, Parrish, 1959 . £65/£15
Adventures of the Junior Detection Club, Parrish
[1960]. . . . . £65/£15
Where the Golden Eagle Soars, Hodder & Stoughton,
[1960]. . . . . £40/£5
The Biggles Book of Treasure Hunting, Parrish, 1962
. . . . £65/£15
Out of the Blue, John Hamilton, [no date] . £100/£25

Books Illustrated by Johns
Desert Wings, by Covington Clarke, John Hamilton,
[1931]. . . . . £100/£20
Aces Up, by Covington Clarke, John Hamilton, [1931]
. . . . £45/£15
For Valour, by Covington Clarke, John Hamilton,
[1931]. . . . . £45/£15

B.S. JOHNSON
(b.1933 d.1973)

A controversial and experimental novelist, Johnson's
books have been purposefully issued with pages
which are black, blank, and containing holes. *The
Unfortunates* was published in the form of loose
sections to be shuffled and read in no particular order.

Novels
Travelling People, Constable, 1963 . . . £150/£45
ditto, Transworld, 1964 (wraps) £10
Albert Angelo, Constable, 1964 . . . . £150/£45
ditto, Panther, 1967 (wraps) £10
ditto, New Directions (U.S.), 1987 . . . £15/£5
Trawl, Secker & Warburg, 1966 . . . £100/£35
ditto, Panther, 1968 (wraps) £10
The Unfortunates, Panther [with Secker & Warburg],
1969 (27 loose sections in box). £150
House Mother Normal, Trigram Press, 1971 (26
signed, lettered copies) £400
ditto, Trigram Press, 1971 (100 signed, numbered
copies) £100
ditto, Collins, 1971 . . . . . . £50/£20
ditto, Quartet, 1973 (wraps) £10
ditto, Bloodaxe, 1984 (wraps) £10
ditto, New Directions (U.S.), 1987 . . . £15/£5
Christie Malry's Own Double Entry, Collins, 1973 .
. . . . £45/£5
ditto, Viking (U.S.), 1973. . . . . . £20/£5
See The Old Lady Decently, Collins, 1973 . £25/£5
ditto, Viking (U.S.), 1975. . . . . . £15/£5

Short Stories
Statement Against Corpses, Constable, 1964 (with
Zulfikar Ghose) . . . . £100/£25

Aren't You Rather Young to be Writing Your Memoirs?, Hutchinson, 1973 . . . . £40/£15
ditto, Hutchinson, 1973 (wraps with d/w) . £25/£15
Everyone Knows Somebody Who's Dead, Covent Garden Press, 1973 (100 signed, numbered copies of 600, wraps) £125
ditto, Covent Garden Press, 1973 (500 copies of 600, wraps). £25

Poetry
Poems, Constable, 1964 . . . . . . £175/£35
Poems Two, Trigram Press, 1972 (26 signed, lettered copies) £250
ditto, Trigram Press, 1972 (100 signed, numbered copies, acetate d/w) . . . . £100/£75
ditto, Trigram Press, 1972 (hardback) . . £25/£10
ditto, Trigram Press, 1972 (wraps) £10
A Dublin Unicorn, Byron Press, 1975 (25 signed copies of 250, wraps) £250
ditto, Byron Press, 1975 (225 unsigned copies of 250, wraps). £50

Others
Street Children, Hodder & Stoughton, 1964 (with photographs by Julia Trevelyan) . . . £30/£10
You're Human Like the Rest of Them, Penguin New English Dramatists, 1970 (wraps) £10

JAMES JOYCE
(b.1882 d.1941)

Novelist, short story writer, poet and father of modernism, Joyce's *Ulysses* and *Finnegan's Wake* revolutionised narrative form and paved the way for the modern novel.

Poetry
Holy Office, privately printed [Austria-Hungary], [1904 or 5] (broadside) £15,000
Chamber Music, Elkin Mathews, 1907 (first state 16.2 x 11cm, thick laid endpapers, signature 'c' well centred) £4,500
ditto, Elkin Mathews, 1907 (second state 15.8 x 11cm, thick wove endpapers, signature 'c' poorly centred) .
. . . . £2,750
ditto, Elkin Mathews, 1907 (third state 15.9 x 10.9cm, thin wove transparent endpapers) . . . £2,000
ditto, Cornhill Co. (U.S.), 1918 (unauthorised edition).
. . . . £175
ditto, Huebsch (U.S.), 1918 (authorised edition) £125
Gas from a Burner, privately printed [Trieste], [1912] (broadside) £15,000
Pomes Penyeach, Shakespeare and Co. (Paris), 1927 (13 specially bound copies) £2,500
ditto, Shakespeare and Co. (Paris), 1927 (with tipped-in errata slip) £300

ditto, privately printed (U.S.), 1931 (100 copies) . .
. . . . £1,000
ditto, Faber, 1933 (wraps). £100
Collected Poems, Black Sun Press (U.S.), 1936 (800 copies, glassine d/w). . . . . . . £500/£400
ditto, Black Sun Press (U.S.), 1936 (50 signed copies, tissue d/w, slipcase) . . . . . £4,000/£3,500
ditto, Black Sun Press (U.S.), 1936 (3 signed, lettered copies, tissue d/w, slipcase) £7,500
ditto, Viking (U.S.), 1937. . . . . . £350/£65

Short Stories
Dubliners, Grant Richards, 1914. . . . . . £4,500
ditto, Huebsch (U.S.), 1916 . . . . . . £2,500

Novels
A Portrait of the Artist as a Young Man, Huebsch (U.S.), 1916 . . . . £2,000
ditto, Egoist Ltd, 1916 [1917] £1,750
Ulysses, Shakespeare Press (Paris), 1922 (750 numbered copies on handmade paper of 1,000, wraps)
. . . . £12,000
ditto, Shakespeare Press (Paris), 1922 (the above 750 copy issue rebound) £5,000
ditto, Shakespeare Press (Paris), 1922 (100 signed, numbered copies of 1,000 on Dutch handmade paper, wraps). £60,000
ditto, Shakespeare Press (Paris), 1922 (150 numbered copies on Velin d'Arches paper of 1,000, wraps) . .
. . . . £25,000
ditto, Egoist Press, 1922 (2,000 numbered copies with errata slip and 4-page leaflet of press notices, wraps).
. . . . £2,500
ditto, Random House (U.S.), 1934 (first copyright printing, 100 copies). £3,000
ditto, Random House (U.S.), 1934 (second printing) .
. . . . £2,000/£200
ditto, Bodley Head, 1936 (900 copy edition) . . .
. . . . £2,000/£500
ditto, Bodley Head, 1936 (100 signed copies, slipcase)
. . . . £15,000/£12,500
ditto, Bodley Head, 1937 . . . . . £250/£100
ditto, as *Ulysses; a Facsimile of the Manuscript*, Faber & Rosenbach, 1975 (3 vols, slipcase, no d/w) . . .
. . . . £225/£175
Finnegan's Wake, Faber, 1939 . . £2,000/£300
ditto, Viking (U.S.), 1939. . . . £1,000/£100
ditto, Faber/Viking, 1939 (425 signed copies, glassine d/w, slipcase). . . . . . . £6,500/£5,000
ditto, Faber/Viking, 1939 (26 signed copies, glassine d/w, slipcase). £10,000
Stephen Hero, Cape, 1944 . . . . . £250/£75
ditto, New Directions (U.S.), 1944 . . . £200/£75

Fragments
Anna Livia Plurabelle, Crosby Gaige (U.S.), 1928 (800 signed copies, acetate d/w) . £2,000/£1,800
ditto, Crosby Gaige (U.S.), 1928 (50 unsigned copies on green paper) £1,500

ditto, Faber, 1930 (tissue d/w) . . . . £150/£100
ditto, Faber, 1930 (wraps). £65
Tales Told of Shem and Shaun, Black Sun Press (Paris), 1929 (500 copies, wraps, slipcase) £750/£600
ditto, Black Sun Press (Paris), 1929 (100 signed copies)
. . . . £6,000
ditto, Black Sun Press (Paris), 1929 (50 hors de commerce copies) £1,500
ditto, as **Two Tales of Shem and Shaun**, Faber, 1932 .
. . . . £200/£50
Haveth Childers Everywhere, Fountain Press (U.S.), 1930 (500 copies of 685, wraps with glassine d/w and slipcase) . . . . £650/£500
ditto, Fountain Press (U.S.), 1930 (75 writer's copies of 685) £1,500
ditto, Fountain Press (U.S.), 1930 (100 signed copies of 685, glassine d/w, slipcase) £4,000
ditto, Fountain Press (U.S.), 1930 (10 signed copies of 685, glassine d/w, slipcase) £5,000
ditto, Faber, 1931 (tissue d/w) . . . . £140/£125
ditto, Faber, 1931 (wraps in d/w). . . . £75/£50
The Mime of Mick Nick and the Maggies, Servire Press, 1934 (1000 copies, wraps, slipcase). £500/£400
ditto, Servire Press, 1934 (29 signed copies, wraps, slipcase) £7,500
Storiella As She is Syung, Corvinus Press, 1937 (150 numbered copies, slipcase) £2,000
ditto, Corvinus Press, 1937 (25 signed copies, slipcase)
. . . . £7,500/£7,000

Letters
The Letters Vol. I, Faber, 1957 . . . . £45/£15
ditto, Viking (U.S.), 1957. . . . . £45/£15
The Letters Vol. II, Faber, 1966 . . . . £45/£15
ditto, Viking (U.S.), 1966. . . . . . £45/£15
The Letters Vol. III, Faber, 1966 . . . £45/£15
ditto, Viking (U.S.), 1966. . . . . . £45/£15

Others
Two Essays, Gerrard Bros, 1901 (with F.J.C. Skeffington, pink wraps) £7,500
Exiles, Grant Richards, 1918 . . . . . . £500
ditto, Huebsch (U.S.), 1918 . . . . . . £250
Introducing James Joyce: A Selection of Joyce's Prose, Faber, 1942 (by T.S. Eliot) . . . £20/£5
The Critical Writings, Faber, 1959 . . . £40/£15
ditto, Viking (U.S.), 1959. . . . . . £40/£15
The Cat and the Devil, Dodd, Mead (U.S.), [1964] .
. . . . £100/£20
ditto, Faber, 1965 . . . . £100/£20

FRANZ KAFKA
(b.1883 d.1924)

A German-speaking Czech author whose name has become synonomous with the nightmarish, confused struggles of individuals against an incomprehensible system.

Novels
Der Prozess, Die Schmiede (Germany), 1925 . . .
. . . . £3,500/£750
ditto, as **The Trial**, Gollancz, 1937 (translated by Willa and Edwin Muir). . . . . . . £750/£200
ditto, Knopf (U.S.), 1937 . . . . . . £300/£75
Das Schloss, Kurt Wolff Verlag (Germany), 1926 . .
. . . . £2,500/£500
ditto, as **The Castle**, Secker, 1930 (translated by Willa and Edwin Muir). . . . . . £1,000/£200
ditto, Knopf (U.S.), 1930 . . . . . . £750/£175
Amerika, Kurt Wolff Verlag (Germany), 1927 . .
. . . . £2,500/£500
ditto, Kurt Wolff Verlag (Germany), 1927 (wraps). .
. . . . £1,000
ditto, as **America**, Routledge, 1938 (translated by Willa and Edwin Muir). . . . . . . £500/£100
ditto, New Directions (U.S.), 1946 . . . £100/£25

Novellas and Short Stories
Die Verwandlung, Kurt Wolff Verlag (Germany), 1915 (wraps). £2,500
ditto, as **The Metamorphosis**, Parton Press, 1937 (translated by A.L. Lloyd) . . . £2,500/£500
ditto, Vanguard Press (U.S.), 1946 . . . £250/£45
Beim Bau der Chinesischen Mauer, Gustav Kiepenheuer (Germany), 1931 . . . £2,000/£400
ditto, as **The Great Wall of China**, Secker, 1933 (translated by Willa and Edwin Muir) . . £500/£100
ditto, Schocken Books (U.S.), 1946 . . £100/£25
In The Penal Settlement, Secker & Warburg, 1949 (translated by Willa and Edwin Muir) . . £100/£30
Wedding Preparations in the Country, Secker & Warburg, 1954 (translated by Ernst Kaiser and Eithne Wilkins) . . . . £75/£25
Description of a Struggle, Schocken Books (U.S.), 1946 . . . . £100/£25
ditto, as **Description of a Struggle** and **The Great Wall of China**, Secker & Warburg, 1960 (with additional translations by Tania and James Stern). . £75/£25

Others
Diaries, 1910-1913, Secker & Warburg, 1948 (translated by Joseph Kresh) . . . . . £50/£25
ditto, Schocken Books (U.S.), 1948 . . . £50/£25
Diaries, 1914-1923, Secker & Warburg, 1949 (translated by M. Greenberg and H. Arendt). . £50/£25
ditto, Schocken Books (U.S.), 1949 . . . £50/£25
Letters to Milena, Secker & Warburg, 1953 (translated by Tania and James Stern) . . . £65/£20
ditto, Schocken Books (U.S.), 1953 . . . £65/£25

Letters to Felice, Schocken Books (U.S.), 1973 (translated by James Stern and Elisabeth Duckworth) . . . . £65/£25
ditto, Secker & Warburg, 1974 . . . £45/£20
Letters to Friends, Family and Editors, John Calder, 1978 (translated by Richard and Clara Winton) . . . . £45/£20
ditto, Schocken Books (U.S.), 1977 . . . £65/£25

ditto, Collins, 1955 . . . . £60/£20
A Salzburg Comedy, Weidenfeld & Nicolson, 1950 . . . . £35/£10
ditto, Ungar (U.S.), 1957 . . . . . . £25/£10

Others
When I was a Little Boy, Cape, 1959 . . . £25/£5
Let's Face It, Cape, 1963 . . . . £20/£5

ERICH KÄSTNER
(b.1899 d.1974)

A German writer in a wide range of genres, he is collected principally for his children's works, notably *Emil and the Detectives*.

Children's Books
Emil and the Detectives, Doubleday (U.S.), 1930 . . . . £175/£40
ditto, Cape, 1931 (illustrated by Walter Trier) . . . . £175/£40
Annaluise and Anton, Cape, 1932 . . . £100/£25
ditto, Dodd, Mead (U.S.), 1933 . . . . £75/£25
The 35th of May or Conrad's Ride to the South Seas, Cape, 1933 . . . . £45/£15
The Flying Classroom, Cape, 1934 . . . £75/£20
Emil and the Three Twins, Cape, 1935 . . £60/£20
ditto, Franklin Watts (U.S.), 1961 . . . £25/£10
Emil, Cape, 1949 (contains *Emil and the Detectives*, *Emil and the Three Twins* and *The 35th of May*) . . . . £15/£5
Lottie and Lisa, Cape, 1950 . . . . . £65/£20
ditto, Knopf (U.S.), 1969 . . . . . . £25/£10
Don Quixote, Messner (U.S.), [c.1957] . . £25/£10
Baron Munchhausen, Messner (U.S.), [c.1957] . . . . £25/£10
The Simpletons, Messner (U.S.), [c.1957] . £25/£10
Till Eulenspiegel the Clown, Messner (U.S.), [c.1957] . . . . £75/£20
ditto, Cape, 1967 . . . . £75/£20
Puss in Boots, Messner (U.S.), [c.1957]. . £45/£10
ditto, Cape, 1967 . . . . £45/£15
The Little Man, Cape, 1966 . . . . . £25/£10
ditto, Knopf (U.S.), 1966 . . . . . . £25/£10
The Little Man and the Little Miss, Cape, 1969 . . . . £20/£5
The Little Man and the Big Thief, Knopf (U.S.), 1969 . . . . £20/£5

Other Novels
Fabian: The Story of a Moralist, Cape, 1932 £45/£10
Three Men in the Snow, Cape, 1935 . . . £25/£5
The Missing Miniature or The Adventures of a Sensitive Butcher, Cape, 1936 . . . . £40/£10
ditto, Knopf (U.S.), 1937 . . . . . . £40/£10
The Animals' Conference, D. McKay Co. (U.S.), [c.1949] . . . . £75/£10

JOHN KEATS
(b.1795 d.1821)

Along with Wordsworth, Keats is one of the best known and most widely read of the English Romantic poets.

Poetry
Poems, Ollier, 1817 (original boards with paper label to spine) £15,000
ditto, Ollier, 1817 (rebound) £6,000
Endymion, Taylor & Hessey, 1818 (first state with one line of errata and 2 advert leaves at end, paper covered boards) £7,500
ditto, Taylor & Hessey, 1818 (first state rebound) £2,000
ditto, Taylor & Hessey, 1818 (second state with 5 lines of errata and 5 advert leaves at end) . . . £4,500
ditto, Taylor & Hessey, 1818 (second state rebound) £1,500
Lamia, Isabella, The Eve of St Agnes, and Other Poems, Taylor & Hessey, 1820 (with half title and 8 pages of adverts at end) £8,000
ditto, Taylor & Hessey, 1820 (rebound) . . £1,500
Poetical Works of Coleridge, Shelly and Keats, A. & W. Galighasi (Paris), 1829 . . . . . £1,000
ditto, A. & W. Galighasi (Paris), 1829 (rebound) £200
Poetical Works, William Smith, 1841 . . . £100
Poetical Works and Other Writings, privately printed, 1883 (4 vols) . . . . £350 the set
Ode to a Nightingale, privately printed, 1884 (edited by T.J. Wise, 25 copies, wraps). £300
ditto, privately printed, 1884 (deluxe edition, 4 copies on vellum) £750
Poems, Kelmscott Press, 1894 (300 copies, limp vellum binding) £1,500
ditto, Doves Press, 1914 (200 copies, limp vellum binding) £250
Ode, Sonnets and Lyrics, Daniel Press, 1895 (250 copies, mounted photo, wraps) £250
Lamia, Isabella, The Eve of St Agnes and Other Poems, Golden Cockerel Press, 1928 (485 numbered copies, illustrated by Robert Gibbings). . . £300
The Collected Sonnets, Halcyon Press (Maastricht), 1930 (376 copies, illustrated by J. Buckland Wright). £150
ditto, Halcyon Press (Maastricht), 1930 (35 copies on Japanese vellum). £450

La Belle Dame Sans Merci, Eragny Press, 1946 (210 copies) £500
Endymion, Golden Cockerel Press, 1947 (400 numbered copies, signed by illustrator Robert Gibbings) £300
ditto, Golden Cockerel Press, 1947 (100 numbered copies, signed by illustrator Robert Gibbings). £500

Miscellaneous
Life, Letters and Literary Remains of John Keats, Moxon, 1848 (2 vols) £600
Letters ... to Fanny Brawne, privately printed, 1878 (50 copies) £500
ditto, Scribner, Armstrong & Co (U.S.), 1878 . £75
The Letters of John Keats, Reeves & Turner, 1895 . . . . £100
Anatomical and Physiological Notebook, O.U.P., 1934 (350 copies) £75

THOMAS KENEALLY
(b.1935)

An Australian novelist whose *Schindler's Ark* won the Booker Prize before being successfully filmed as *Schindler's List*.

Novels
The Place at Whitton, Cassell (Melbourne), 1964 . . . . £300/£35
ditto, Cassell, 1964 . . . . £300/£35
ditto, Walker (U.S.), 1964 . . . . . £125/£20
The Fear, Cassell (Melbourne), 1965 . . £150/£20
ditto, Cassell, 1965 . . . . . . £150/£20
ditto, as *By The Line*, Univ. of Queensland Press, 1989 . . . . £20/£5
ditto, as *By The Line*, Sceptre, 1992 (wraps) . . £5
Bring Larks and Heroes, Cassell (Melbourne), 1967 . . . . £60/£10
ditto, Cassell, 1967 . . . . £60/£10
ditto, Viking (U.S.), 1968 . . . . . . £40/£10
Three Cheers for the Paraclete, Angus & Robertson, 1968 . . . . £45/£10
ditto, Viking (U.S.), 1969 . . . . . £35/£10
The Survivor, Angus & Robertson, 1969 . £65/£15
ditto, Viking (U.S.), 1970 . . . . . £45/£10
A Dutiful Daughter, Angus & Robertson, 1971 £25/£5
ditto, Viking (U.S.), 1971 . . . . . . £20/£5
The Chant of Jimmie Blacksmith, Angus & Robertson, 1972 . . . . £25/£5
ditto, Viking (U.S.), 1972 . . . . . . £20/£5
Blood Red, Sister Rose, Collins, 1974 . . £25/£5
ditto, Viking (U.S.), 1974 . . . . . . £20/£5
Gossip from the Forest, Collins, 1975 . . £35/£10
ditto, Harcourt Brace (U.S.), 1976 . . . £25/£5
Season in Purgatory, Collins, 1976 . . . £20/£5
ditto, Harcourt Brace (U.S.), 1977 . . . £15/£5
A Victim of the Aurora, Collins, 1977 . . . £15/£5

ditto, Harcourt Brace (U.S.), 1978 . . . . £15/£5
Passenger, Collins, 1979 . . . . £15/£5
ditto, Harcourt Brace (U.S.), 1979 . . . £15/£5
Confederates, Collins, 1979 . . . . . £15/£5
ditto, Harcourt Brace (U.S.), 1980 . . . £15/£5
Schindler's Ark, Hodder & Stoughton, 1982 £75/£20
ditto, as *Schindler's List*, Simon & Schuster (U.S.), 1982 . . . . £65/£15
The Cut-Rate Kingdom, Wildcat Press (Sydney), 1980 . . . . £40
ditto, Allen Lane, 1984 . . . . £15/£5
A Family Madness, Hodder & Stoughton, 1985 £15/£5
ditto, Simon & Schuster (U.S.), 1986 . . £15/£5
The Playmaker, Hodder & Stoughton, 1987 . £15/£5
ditto, Simon & Schuster (U.S.), 1987 . . £15/£5
Act of Grace, Chatto & Windus, 1988 (pseud. 'William Coyle') . . . . £15/£5
Towards Asmara, Hodder & Stoughton, 1989 . £15/£5
ditto, as *To Asmara*, Warner (U.S.), 1989 . £15/£5
Flying Hero Class, Hodder & Stoughton, 1991 £15/£5
ditto, Warner (U.S.), 1991 . . . . . £15/£5
Chief of Staff, Chatto & Windus, 1991 (pseud. 'William Coyle') . . . . £15/£5
A Woman of the Inner Sea, Hodder & Stoughton, 1992 . . . . £15/£5
ditto, Doubleday (U.S.), 1993 . . . . £10/£5
Jacko, The Great Intruder, Hodder & Stoughton, 1993 . . . . £15/£5
A River Town, Hodder & Stoughton, 1995 . £15/£5
ditto, Franklin Library (U.S.), 1995 (signed, limited edition) £35
ditto, Doubleday (U.S.), 1995 . . . . £10/£5
Bettany's Book, Sceptre/Hodder & Stoughton, 2000 . . . . £15/£5

Plays
Halloran's Little Boat, Penguin, 1975 (wraps) . £15
Bullie's House, Currency Press (Sydney), 1981 £20/£5

Others
Moses the Lawgiver, Harper (U.S.), 1975 . £15/£5
ditto, Collins, 1976 . . . . £15/£5
Ned Kelly and the City of the Bees, Cape, 1978 £15/£5
ditto, Godine (U.S.), 1981 . . . . . £15/£5
Outback, Hodder & Stoughton, 1983 . . £15/£5
ditto, Rand McNally & Co. (U.S.), 1984 . £15/£5
Now and in a Time To Be, Ryan Publishing, 1991. . . . . £15/£5
Ireland, Fontana, 1992 (wraps) £5
The Place Where Souls are Born, Hodder & Stoughton, 1992 . . . . £15/£5
ditto, Simon & Schuster (U.S.), 1992 . . £15/£5
The Utility Player, The Des Hasler Story, Pan Macmillan (Sydney), 1993 (wraps). £5
Our Republic, Heinemann (Melbourne), 1993 £10/£5
Memoirs from a Young Republic, Heinemann, 1993 . . . . £10/£5
Homebush Boy, A Memoir, Hodder & Stoughton, 1995 . . . . £10/£5

The Great Shame, A Story of the Irish in the Old World and the New, Chatto & Windus, 1999 . £10/£5
ditto, Doubleday (U.S.), 1992 . . . . . £10/£5
American Scoundrel, Chatto & Windus, 2002 . £10/£5
ditto, Easton Press (U.S.), 2002 (1150 signed, numbered copies) £90
ditto, Doubleday (U.S.), 2002 . . . . . £10/£5

JACK KEROUAC
(b.1922 d.1969)

The semi-autobiographical novelist of the Beat Generation in 1950s San Francisco.

Fiction

The Town and the City, Harcourt Brace (U.S.), 1950 (pseud. 'John Kerouac'). . . . . . £750/£125
ditto, Eyre & Spottiswoode, 1951 . . £500/£75
On the Road, Viking (U.S.), 1957 . . £2,500/£400
ditto, Viking (U.S.), 1957 (review copy with additional white d/w printed 'This is a copy of the first edition') . . . . £4,000/£400
ditto, Deutsch, 1958 (author photo on rear flap) . . . . £750/£100
ditto, Deutsch, 1958 (author photo on front flap) . . . . £500/£100
The Subterraneans, Grove Press (U.S.), 1958 . . . . £650/£75
ditto, Grove Press (U.S.), 1958 (100 numbered copies, no d/w) £2,000
ditto, Grove Press (U.S.), 1958 (wraps) . . £35
ditto, Deutsch, 1962 . . . . £250/£50
The Dharma Bums, Viking (U.S.), 1958 . £200/£50
ditto, Deutsch, 1959 . . . . . . £75/£25
Doctor Sax: Faust Part Three, Grove Press (U.S.), 1959 . . . . £500/£75
ditto, Grove Press (U.S.), 1959 (26 signed, lettered copies) £4,000
ditto, Grove Press (U.S.), 1959 (4 signed, numbered copies) £5,000
ditto, Evergreen, 1961 (wraps) £20
ditto, Deutsch, 1977 . . . . . . £100/£15
Maggie Cassidy, Avon (U.S.), 1959 (wraps) . £35
ditto, Panther, 1960 (wraps) £15
ditto, Deutsch, 1974 . . . . . . £125/£20
Excerpts from Visions of Cody, New Directions (U.S.), 1959 (750 signed, numbered copies) . . . £1,000
ditto, as *Visions of Cody*, McGraw-Hill (U.S.), 1972 (full text) . . . . £75/£15
ditto, Deutsch, 1973 . . . . . . £75/£15
Tristessa, Avon (U.S.), 1960 (wraps) . . . £30
ditto, World Distributors, 1963 (wraps) . . . £15
Book of Dreams, City Light Books (U.S.), 1961 (wraps) £100
Big Sur, Farrar Straus (U.S.), 1962 . . . £125/£25
ditto, Deutsch, 1963 . . . . . . £100/£20
Visions of Gerard, Farrar Straus (U.S.), 1963 £125/£25
ditto, Deutsch, 1964 (with *Tristessa*) . . £75/£15

Desolation Angels, Coward-McCann (U.S.), 1965 . . . . £150/£25
ditto, Deutsch, 1966 . . . . £100/£25
Satori in Paris, Grove Press (U.S.), 1966 . £125/£20
ditto, Deutsch, 1967 . . . . £40/£10
Vanity of Duluoz: An Adventurous Education, 1935-46, Coward-McCann (U.S.), 1968 . . . £100/£20
ditto, Deutsch, 1969 . . . . £65/£20
Pic and the Subterraneans, Grove Press (U.S.), 1971 . . . . £50/£10
ditto, Deutsch, 1973 . . . . £45/£10
Old Angel Midnight, Unicorn Press, 1976 (wraps) £25
ditto, Midnight Press (U.S.), 1985 (wraps) . . £25
Take Care of My Ghost, Ghost Press (U.S.), 1977 (with Ginsberg, wraps) £25
ditto, Ghost Press (U.S.), 1977 (200 copies signed by Ginsberg, wraps) £125
Baby Driver: A Story About Myself, St Martin's Press (U.S.), 1981 . . . . £25/£5
ditto, Deutsch, 1981 . . . . £20/£5
San Francisco Blues, Beat Books (U.S.), 1983 (wraps) £25
Two Stories, Pacific Red Car (U.S.), 1984 (100 copies, wraps). £40
The Great Western Bus Ride, Pacific Red Car (U.S.), 1984 (100 copies, wraps) £50
Celine and Other Tales, Pacific Red Car (U.S.), 1985 (100 copies, wraps) £40
The Vision of the Hooded White Angels, Pacific Red Car (U.S.), 1985 (100 copies, wraps) . . . £40
Home at Christmas, Pacific Red Car (U.S.), [no date] (wraps) £30

Poetry

Mexico City Blues, Grove Press (U.S.), 1959 . . . . £1,000/£200
ditto, Grove Press (U.S.), 1959 (26 signed, lettered copies) £4,000
ditto, Grove Press (U.S.), 1959 (4 signed, numbered copies) £5,000
Hymn - God Pray For Me, Jubilee Magazine (U.S.), [1959] (broadsheet) £150
The Scripture of the Golden Eternity, Totem Press/Corinth Books (U.S.), 1960 (wraps) . . £175
Rimbaud, City Light Books (U.S.), 1960 (broadsheet). £75
'I demand that the human race ceases multiplying its kind...', Pax #17 (U.S.), 1962 (broadsheet) . £75
Poem, Jubilee Magazine (U.S.), [1962] (broadsheet) £65
A Pun for Al Gepi, privately printed (U.S.), (100 copies, broadsheet) £250
Hugo Weber, Portents (U.S.), 1967 (200 copies, broadsheet) £150
Someday You'll be Lying, privately printed (U.S.), 1968 (broadsheet) £65
A Last Haiku, privately printed (U.S.), 1969 (broadsheet) £50
Scattered Poems, City Lights (U.S.), 1971 (wraps) £50

Trip, Trap, Grey Fox Press (U.S.), 1973 (wraps) £50
Heaven and Other Poems, Grey Fox Press (U.S.), 1977 (wraps) £50

Others
Lonesome Traveller, McGraw-Hill (U.S.), 1960 . .
. . . . £125/£20
ditto, Deutsch, 1962 . . . . £75/£15
Pull My Daisy, Grove Press (U.S.), 1961 (wraps) £75
ditto, Evergreen, 1961 (wraps) £35

KEN KESEY
(b.1935 d.2001)

An American novelist, Kesey volunteered, in the 1960s, for Government drug experiments. His *One Flew Over the Cuckoo's Nest* draws on his experience of working as an aide on a psychiatric ward in a veteran's hospital.

Novels
One Flew Over the Cuckoo's Nest, Viking (U.S.), 1962 . . . . £2,000/£100
ditto, Methuen, 1963 . . . . £300/£45
Sometimes a Great Notion, Viking (U.S.), 1964 (first issue with Viking ship on half title before title page) .
. . . . £200/£25
ditto, Viking (U.S.), 1964 (more scarce second issue with Viking ship on half title after title page) . . .
. . . . £200/£25
ditto, Methuen, 1966 . . . . . . £125/£20
Demon Box, Viking (U.S.), 1986 . . . . £25/£5
ditto, Methuen, 1986 . . . . £25/£5
The Further Inquiry, Viking (U.S.), 1990 . . £25/£5
Sailor Song, Viking (U.S.), 1992 . . . £15/£5
ditto, Black Swan, 1993 (wraps) £5
Last Go Round, Viking (U.S.), 1994 (with Ken Babbs)
. . . . £10/£5

Children's Titles
Little Tricker the Squirrel Meets Big Double the Bear, Viking (U.S.), 1990 . . . . . . £25/£10
Sea Lion, Viking (U.S.), 1991 . . . £25/£10

Others
Kesey's Garage Sale, Viking (U.S.), 1973 . £30/£10
Kesey, Northwest Review Books (U.S.), 1977 (hardback, no d/w) £50
ditto, Northwest Review Books (U.S.), 1977 (wraps) .
. . . . £15
The Day After Superman Died, Lord John Press (U.S.), 1980 (50 signed deluxe copies of 350). £150
ditto, Lord John Press (U.S.), 1980 (300 signed copies of 350) £85
Caverns, by O.U. Levon, Penguin (U.S.), 1990 (collaborative novel written by Kesey and students in his writing class at the Univ. of Oregon, wraps) £65

KEYNOTES

A series of 33 books (34 were advertised) issued by John Lane between 1893 and 1897. Nos. 1-21 and 23 have cover, title page and key designs by Aubrey Beardsley, the remainder are by Patten Wilson.

1. *Keynotes*, by George Egerton, Mathews/Lane, 1893 (500 copies in pink wraps) £300
ditto, Mathews/Lane, 1893 (600 copies in green cloth)
. . . . £100
ditto, Roberts Bros. (U.S.), 1893 . . . . £40
2. *The Dancing Faun*, by Florence Farr, Mathews/Lane, 1894 (first issue, light blue cloth, key on spine in gilt). £175
ditto, Mathews/Lane, 1894 (second issue, light green cloth, key on spine in blue) £150
ditto, Roberts Bros. (U.S.), 1894 . . . . £50
3. *Poor Folk*, by Fedor [sic] Dostoievsky, Mathews/Lane, 1894 . . . . £200
ditto, Roberts Bros. (U.S.), 1894 . . . . £65
4. *A Child of the Age*, by Francis Adams, Lane, 1894 .
. . . . £100
ditto, Roberts Bros. (U.S.), 1894 . . . . £40
5. *The Great God Pan and the Inmost Light*, by Arthur Machen, Lane, 1894 . . . . . £225
ditto, Roberts Bros. (U.S.), 1894 . . . . £150
6. *Discords*, by George Egerton, Lane, 1894 . £100
ditto, Roberts Bros. (U.S.), 1894 . . . . £40
7. *Prince Zaleski*, by M.P. Shiel, Lane, 1895 . £300
ditto, Roberts Bros. (U.S.), 1895 . . . . £150
8. *The Woman Who Did*, by Grant Allen, Lane, 1895 .
. . . . £100
ditto, Roberts Bros. (U.S.), 1895 . . . . £40
9. *Women's Tragedies*, by H.D. Lowry, Lane, 1895 .
. . . . £100
ditto, Roberts Bros. (U.S.), 1895 . . . . £40
10. *Grey Roses*, by Henry Harland, Lane, 1895. £100
ditto, Roberts Bros. (U.S.), 1895 . . . . £40
11. *At the First Corner and Other Stories*, by H.B. Marriott Watson, Lane, 1895 . . . . £100
ditto, Roberts Bros. (U.S.), 1895 . . . . £40
12. *Monochromes*, by Ella D'Arcy, Lane, 1895 £100
ditto, Roberts Bros. (U.S.), 1895 . . . . £40
13. *At the Relton Arms*, by Evelyn Sharp, Lane, 1895 .
. . . . £100
ditto, Roberts Bros. (U.S.), 1895 . . . . £40
14. *The Girl from the Farm*, by Gertrude Dix, Lane, 1895 . . . . £100
ditto, Roberts Bros. (U.S.), 1895 . . . . £40
15. *The Mirror of Music*, by Stanley V. Makower, Lane, 1895 . . . . £100
ditto, Roberts Bros. (U.S.), 1895 . . . . £40
16. *Yellow and White*, by W. Carlton Dawe, Lane, 1895 . . . . £100
ditto, Roberts Bros. (U.S.), 1895 . . . . £40
17. *The Mountain Lovers*, by Fiona MacLeod, Lane, 1895 . . . . £100
ditto, Roberts Bros. (U.S.), 1895 . . . . £40

18. *The Woman Who Didn't*, by Victoria Crosse, Lane, 1895 . . . . £100
ditto, Roberts Bros. (U.S.), 1895 . . . . . £40
19. *The Three Impostors*, by Arthur Machen, Lane, 1895 . . . . £225
ditto, Roberts Bros. (U.S.), 1895 . . . . . £150
20. *Nobody's Fault*, by Netta Syrett, Lane, 1896 £100
ditto, Roberts Bros. (U.S.), 1895 . . . . . £40
21. *The British Barbarians*, by Grant Allen, Lane, 1895 . . . . £100
ditto, Lane/Putnams (U.S.), 1895. . . . . £40
22. *In Homespun*, E. Nesbit, Lane, 1896 . . £100
ditto, Roberts Bros. (U.S.), 1896 . . . . . £40
23. *Platonic Affections*, by John Smith, Lane, 1896 .
. . . . £100
ditto, Roberts Bros. (U.S.), 1896 . . . . . £40
24. *Nets for the Wind*, by Una Taylor, Lane, 1896 . .
. . . . £100
ditto, Roberts Bros. (U.S.), 1896 . . . . . £40
25. *Where the Atlantic Meets the Land*, by Caldwell Lipsett, Lane, 1896 . . . . £100
ditto, Roberts Bros. (U.S.), 1896 . . . . . £40
26. *In Scarlet and Grey*, by Florence Henniker (contains '*The Spectre of the Real*', by F.H. and Thomas Hardy), Lane, 1896 . . . . . £200
ditto, Roberts Bros. (U.S.), 1896 . . . . . £80
27. *Maris Stella*, by Marie Clothilde Balfour, Lane, 1896 . . . . £100
ditto, Roberts Bros. (U.S.), 1896 . . . . . £40
28. *Day Books*, by Mabel E. Wotton, Lane, 1896 £100
ditto, Roberts Bros. (U.S.), 1896 . . . . . £40
29. *Shapes in the Fire*, by M.P. Shiel, Lane, 1896 £300
ditto, Roberts Bros. (U.S.), 1896 . . . . . £150
30. *Ugly Idol*, by Claud Nicholson, Lane, 1896. £100
ditto, Roberts Bros. (U.S.), 1896 . . . . . £40
31. *Kakemonos*, by W. Carlton Dawe, Lane, 1897 . .
. . . . £100
32. *God's Failures*, by J.S. Fletcher, Lane, 1897 £100
33. *A Deliverance*, by Allan Monkhouse. Not published in Keynotes series although advertised.
34. *Mere Sentiment*, A.J Dawson, Lane, 1897 . £100

FRANCIS KILVERT
(b.1840 d.1879)

(Robert) Francis Kilvert was a clergyman and diarist. Although many volumes of his diaries were destroyed by his niece after his death, those covering the period 1870-79 were edited by William Plomer and published to great acclaim.

Selections from the Diary of the Rev. Francis Kilvert, Cape, 1938-40 (3 vols edited by William Plomer) .
. . . . £200/£50 the set
ditto, Macmillan (U.S.), 1947 (1 vol.) . . £25/£10

C. DALY KING
(b.1895 d.1963)

An author of detective fiction from its 'Golden Age', King's books are unconventional, enthralling and puzzling.

Novels
Obelists at Sea, Heritage, [1932] . . . £1,500/£200
ditto, Knopf (U.S.), 1933 . . . . . £1,000/£150
ditto, Collins Crime Club, [no date] . . . £350/£35
Obelists En Route, Collins Crime Club, 1934 . . .
. . . . £1,250/£150
Obelists Fly High, Collins Crime Club, 1935 . . .
. . . . £1,250/£150
ditto, Smith & Haas (U.S.), 1935. . . . £450/£100
Careless Corpse, Collins Crime Club, 1937. . . .
. . . . £1,000/£150
Arrogant Alibi, Collins Crime Club, 1938 . . . .
. . . . £1,000/£150
ditto, Appleton (U.S.), 1939 . . . . . £350/£100
Burmuda Burial, Collins Crime Club, 1940 . . .
. . . . £1,000/£150
ditto, Funk (U.S.), 1941 . . . . . . £350/£100

Short Stories
The Curious Mt Tarrant, Collins Crime Club, 1935 .
. . . . £1,500/£150
ditto, Dover (U.S.), 1977 . . . . . . £15

STEPHEN KING
(b.1947)

One of the most successful of living writers, King's breakthrough was *Carrie*, a book which has now sold over 12 million copies.

Novels
Carrie, Doubleday (U.S.), 1974 (inner margin of p.199 has date code 'P6') . . . . . £1,000/£150
ditto, New English Library, 1974 . £1,000/£150
Salem's Lot, Doubleday (U.S.), 1975 (inner margin of p.439 with date code 'Q37', first state, first issue d/w with Father 'Cody' and price $8.95) . £1,500/£125
ditto, Doubleday (U.S.), 1975 (first state, second issue d/w with Father 'Cody' but price clipped and new price of $7.95 added) . . . . . £750/£125
ditto, Doubleday (U.S.), 1975 (second state d/w with Father 'Callahan' and unclipped price of $7.95) . .
. . . . £450/£125
ditto, New English Library, 1976 . . . £500/£60
The Shining, Doubleday (U.S.), 1977 . . £500/£75
ditto, New English Library, 1977 . . . £250/£50
Rage, Signet/New American Library (U.S.), 1977 (pseud. 'Richard Bachman', wraps) . . . £200
ditto, New English Library, 1983 (wraps) . . £150

The Stand, Doubleday (U.S.), 1978 (d/w price $12.95)
. . . . £300/£50
ditto, New English Library, 1979 . . . £200/£50
The Dead Zone, Viking (U.S.), 1979 . . £75/£20
ditto, Macdonald & Jane, 1979 . . . . £75/£20
The Long Walk, Signet/New American Library (U.S.),
1979 (pseud. 'Richard Bachman', wraps) . . £65
Firestarter, Phantasia Press (U.S.), 1980 (725 copies in
d/w and slipcase). . . . . £600/£400
ditto, Phantasia Press (U.S.), 1980 (26 lettered copies,
bound in asbestos) £6,000
ditto, Viking (U.S.), 1980. . . . . . £50/£15
ditto, Macdonald & Jane, 1980 . . . . £50/£15
Roadwork, Signet/New American Library (U.S.), 1981
(pseud. 'Richard Bachman', wraps) . . £45
ditto, New English Library, 1983 (wraps) . . £25
Cujo, Viking (U.S.), 1981 . . . . . £40/£10
ditto, Mysterious Press (U.S.), 1981 (750 numbered,
signed copies) . . . . £400/£300
ditto, Mysterious Press (U.S.), 1981 (lettered, signed
copies) £1,250
ditto, Macdonald, 1982 . . . . . . £35/£10
The Running Man, Signet/New American Library
(U.S.), 1982 (pseud. 'Richard Bachman', wraps) £50
ditto, New English Library, 1983 (wraps) . . £35
Creepshow, NAL/Plume (U.S.), 1982 (wraps) . £25
Christine, Grant (U.S.), 1983 (lettered, signed edition)
. . . . £2,500
ditto, Grant (U.S.), 1983 (1,000 signed copies, slipcase)
. . . . £400/£300
ditto, Viking (U.S.), 1983. . . . . . £35/£5
ditto, Hodder & Stoughton, 1983. . . . £35/£5
Cycle of the Werewolf, Land of Enchantment (U.S.),
1983 . . . . £300/£150
ditto, Land of Enchantment (U.S.), 1983 (8 presentation copies) £3,000
ditto, Land of Enchantment (U.S.), 1983 (250 copies,
slipcase) . . . . £600/£300
ditto, Land of Enchantment (U.S.), 1983 (100 copies
with original drawing, slipcase). . £1,250/£1,000
ditto, New English Library, 1985 (wraps) . . £10
ditto, Signet (U.S.), 1985 (wraps) . . . £10
Selected Works, Heinemann/Octopus, 1983 . £15/£5
Pet Sematary, Doubleday (U.S.), 1983 . . . £30/£5
ditto, Hodder & Stoughton, 1984. . . . £25/£5
The Talisman, Viking, 1984 (with Peter Straub) . .
. . . . £30/£5
ditto, Grant (U.S.), 1984 (70 numbered copies signed
by authors and artists, slipcase, 2 vols) £1,500/£1,000
ditto, Grant (U.S.), 1984 (1,200 signed, numbered
copies, no d/w, slipcase, 2 vols) . . £400/£300
ditto, Viking (U.K.), 1984 . . . . . £25/£5
The Eyes of the Dragon, Philtrum (U.S.), 1984 (1,000
signed copies numbered in black ink, slipcase, no
d/w) . . . . £700/£600
ditto, Philtrum (U.S.), 1984 (250 signed copies
numbered in red ink, slipcase, no d/w) £1,250/£1,000
ditto, Viking (U.S.), 1987. . . . . . £25/£5
ditto, Macdonald, 1987 . . . . . . £20/£5

Thinner, New American Library (U.S.), 1984 (pseud.
'Richard Bachman'). . . . . . . £45/£10
ditto, New English Library, 1985 (pseud. 'Richard
Bachman') . . . . £35/£10
The Bachman Books, New American Library, 1985
(pseud. 'Richard Bachman'). . . . . £45/£10
ditto, New English Library, 1986 . . . £35/£10
Silver Bullet, New American Library/Signet (U.S.),
1985 (wraps) £15
It, Hodder & Stoughton, 1986 . . . . . £30/£5
ditto, Viking (U.S.), 1986. . . . . . . £25/£5
Misery, Viking (U.S.), 1987 . . . . . . £30/£5
ditto, Hodder & Stoughton, 1987. . . . . £20/£5
The Tommyknockers, Putnam (U.S.), 1987 . £25/£5
ditto, Hodder & Stoughton, 1988. . . . . £20/£5
The Dark Half, Hodder & Stoughton, 1989 . £20/£5
ditto, Viking (U.S.), 1989. . . . . . . £20/£5
The Stand, Doubleday (U.S.), 1990 (complete and
uncut edition). . . . . £25/£5
ditto, Doubleday (U.S.), 1990 (52 signed, lettered
copies) £3,000
ditto, Doubleday (U.S.), 1990 (1,250 signed copies,
bound in full leather, in wooden box) . £1,000/£600
ditto, Hodder & Stoughton, 1990. . . . . £25/£5
Needful Things, Hodder & Stoughton, [1991] . £15/£5
ditto, Viking (U.S.), 1991. . . . . . . £15/£5
Gerald's Game, Viking (U.S.), 1992 . . . £10/£5
ditto, Hodder & Stoughton, 1992. . . . . £10/£5
Dolores Claiborne, Book Club Associates, 1992 £15/£5
ditto, Viking (U.S.), 1992. . . . . . . £15/£5
ditto, Hodder & Stoughton, 1992. . . . . £15/£5
ditto, Hodder & Stoughton, 1992 ('Special Limited
Christmas Gift Edition', slipcase) . . . £100/£50
Insomnia, Ziesing (U.S.), 1994 (1,250 signed copies,
d/w and case). . . . . £350/£250
ditto, Ziesing (U.S.), 1994 ('Gift edition', d/w and
slipcase) . . . . £75/£45
ditto, Viking (U.S.), 1994. . . . . . . £15/£5
ditto, Hodder & Stoughton, 1994. . . . . £15/£5
ditto, Hodder & Stoughton, 1994 (200 signed,
numbered copies, slipcase, no d/w). . £300/£200
Rose Madder, Hodder & Stoughton, 1994 . . £20/£5
ditto, Hodder & Stoughton, 1994 (250 signed copies,
slipcase, no d/w) . . . . £200/£150
ditto, Viking (U.S.), 1995. . . . . . . £20/£5
The Green Mile, Penguin/Signet (U.S.), 1996 (six
paperbacks) . . . . £15 the set
ditto, Penguin, 1996 (six paperbacks) . £15 the set
ditto, Penguin/Plume (U.S.), 1997 (1 vol.) . . . £5
Desperation, Grant (U.S.), 1995 (4,000 copy gift
edition) . . . . £25/£10
ditto, Grant (U.S.), 1995 (2,050 signed copies in
traycase, no d/w). . . . . £250/£200
ditto, Viking (U.S.), 1996. . . . . . . £15/£5
ditto, Hodder & Stoughton, 1996. . . . . £15/£5
Desperation and *The Regulator*, Hodder Headline, 1996
(2 vols with free 'keep you up all night' light) £35/£10
ditto, Hodder Headline, 1996 (250 sets in single
slipcase, the former signed, the latter pseud. 'Richard

Bachman', with free 'keep you up all night' light,) .
. . . .£250/£200
Bag of Bones, Simon & Schuster/Scribner's (U.S.),
1998 . . . . £10/£5
ditto, Hodder & Stoughton, 1998. . . . . £10/£5
ditto, Hodder & Stoughton, 1998 (2,000 copies with
signed bookplate) . . . . £100/£30
The Girl Who Loved Tom Gordon, Hodder &
Stoughton, 1999 . . . . £10/£5
ditto, Scribner's (U.S.), 1999 . . . . . £10/£5
Dreamcatcher, Hodder & Stoughton, 2001 . . £10/£5
ditto, Scribner's (U.S.), 2001 . . . . . . £10/£5
Black House, Random House (U.S.), 2001 (with Peter
Straub) . . . . £10/£5
ditto, HarperCollins, 2001 . . . . . . £10/£5
ditto, Grant (U.S.), 2002 (1,520 signed copies in
traycase) . . . .£250/£200
From a Buick 8, CD Publications (U.S.), 2002 (750
signed copies in traycase) . . . . .£400/£300
ditto, Hodder & Stoughton, 2002. . . . . £10/£5
ditto, Scribner's (U.S.), 2002 . . . . . . £10/£5

'Dark Tower' Series
The Gunslinger, Grant (U.S.), 1982 . . £350/£100
ditto, Grant (U.S.), 1982 (lettered, signed edition, d/w
and slipcase) . . . . . . £2,000/£1,500
ditto, Grant (U.S.), 1982 (500 numbered, signed copies,
d/w and slipcase). . . . . . £1,000/£400
ditto, Sphere, 1988 (wraps) £10
The Drawing of the Three, Grant (U.S.), 1987 £50/£10
ditto, Grant (U.S.), 1987 (800 signed copies, d/w and
slipcase) . . . .£450/£300
ditto, Grant (U.S.), 1987 (50 lettered copies, d/w and
slipcase) . . . . £1,000/£750
ditto, Sphere, 1989 (wraps) £10
The Wastelands, Grant (U.S.), 1991. . £35/£10
ditto, Grant (U.S.), 1991 (1,250 signed copies, d/w and
slipcase). . . . .£350/£200
ditto, Sphere, 1991 (wraps) £10
Wizard and Glass, Grant (U.S.), 1997 . . £35/£10
ditto, Grant (U.S.), 1991 (1,200 signed copies, d/w and
slipcase). . . . .£350/£200
ditto, Hodder & Stoughton, 1988 (wraps) . . £10
ditto, Hodder & Stoughton, 1988 (500 copies, no d/w)
. . . . £350

Short Stories
Night Shift, Doubleday (U.S.), 1978. . . £500/£60
ditto, New English Library, 1978 . . . £250/£45
Different Seasons, Viking (U.S.), 1982 . . £50/£15
ditto, Macdonald, 1982 . . . . . £40/£15
The Plant, Philtrum (U.S.), 1982 (200 signed copies,
wraps). £1,000
ditto, Philtrum (U.S.), 1982 (26 signed, lettered copies,
wraps). £2,000
The Plant - Part Two, Philtrum (U.S.), 1983 (200
copies, wraps) £1,000
ditto, Philtrum (U.S.), 1983 (26 signed, lettered copies,
wraps). £2,000

Skeleton Crew, Putnam (U.S.), 1985 . . £35/£10
ditto, as **Stephen King's Skeleton Crew**, Scream Press
(U.S.), 1985 (1,000 copies numbered in silver ink and
signed by author and artist, slipcase) . . £600/£400
ditto, Scream Press (U.S.), 1985 (69 leather-bound,
zippered copies) £2,000
ditto, Scream Press (U.S.), 1985 (17 presentation
copies) £3,000
ditto, Scream Press (U.S.), 1985 (52 lettered copies) .
. . . .£1,500
ditto, Macdonald, 1985 . . . . . . £30/£5
The Plant - Part Three, Philtrum (U.S.), 1985 (200
copies, wraps) £1,000
ditto, Philtrum (U.S.), 1985 (26 signed, lettered copies,
wraps). £1,500
My Pretty Pony, Whitney Museum of American Art
(U.S.), 1989 (250 signed, numbered copies) . £1,750
ditto, Knopf (U.S.), 1989 (slipcase) . . . £75/£25
Dolan's Cadillac, Lord John Press (U.S.), 1989 (26
lettered, signed copies) £1,500
ditto, Lord John Press (U.S.), 1989 (100 presentation
copies, quarter-bound in leather) . . . £500
ditto, Lord John Press (U.S.), 1989 (250 numbered,
signed copies, quarter-bound in leather) . . £300
ditto, Lord John Press (U.S.), 1989 (1,000 numbered,
signed copies, no d/w) £100
Four Past Midnight, Viking (U.S.), 1990 . . £20/£5
ditto, Hodder & Stoughton, 1990. . . . . £20/£5
Nightmares and Dreamscapes, Viking (U.S.), 1993 .
. . . .£15/£5
ditto, Hodder & Stoughton, 1993. . . . . £15/£5
ditto, Hodder & Stoughton, 1993 (2,000 copy gift
issue, slipcase, no d/w) . . . . . £60/£40
Umney's Last Case, Penguin (U.S.), 1995 (wraps). £5
Six Stories, Philtrum (U.S.), 1997 (900 [800] signed
copies, wraps) £600
Everything's Eventual, Scribner's (U.S.), 2002 £10/£5
ditto, Hodder & Stoughton, 2002. . . . . £10/£5

Others
Danse Macabre, Everest House (U.S.), 1981 £65/£20
ditto, Everest House (U.S.), 1981 (250 signed,
numbered copies, slipcase, tissue d/w) . . £750/£500
ditto, Everest House (U.S.), 1981 (signed, lettered
copies, slipcase, tissue d/w) . . . £1,500/£1,000
ditto, Everest House (U.S.), 1981 (35 publishers copies,
no slipcase or d/w) £1,000
ditto, Macdonald Futura, 1981 . . . . £35/£10
Letters from Hell, Lord John Press (U.S.), 1988 (500
signed, numbered copies, broadside in wraps). £150
ditto, Lord John Press (U.S.), 1988 (26 signed, lettered
copies, broadside in wraps) £225
Nightmares in the Sky, Viking (U.S.), 1988 (with f-
stop Fitzgerald) . . . . £30/£10
Storm of the Century, Pocket Books (U.S.), 1999
(wraps) £5
ditto, Book of the Month Club (U.S.), 1999. . £25/£5
Hearts in Atlantis, Hodder & Stoughton, 1999 . £15/£5
ditto, Scribner's (U.S.), 1999 . . . . . £15/£5

On Writing: A Memoir of the Craft, Scribner's (U.S.),
2000 . . . . £10/£5
ditto, Hodder & Stoughton, 2000. . . . . £10/£5

RUDYARD KIPLING
(b.1865 d.1936)

Often considered a poet of British imperialism,
Kipling's work has caused much controversy, though
poems such as *If* and his 'Jungle Book' stories remain
firmly entrenched in British colonial mythology.
Kipling won the Nobel Prize for Literature in 1907.

Poetry

Schoolboy Lyrics, privately printed at the 'Civil &
Military Gazette' Press (Lahore), 1881 (approx 25
copies with blank paper wraps and later approx 25
with brown paper wraps) £6,000
Echoes, privately printed (Lahore), 1884 (published
anonymously, with Alice Kipling, wraps) . . £2,500
Quartette, privately printed at the 'Civil & Military
Gazette' Press (Lahore), 1885 (published anonymously,
with his sister, mother and father, wraps) . . £2,500
Departmental Ditties, Civil and Military Gazette
(Lahore), 1886 (wraps) £1,000
ditto, Thacker, Spink & Co. (Calcutta), 1886 . £500
ditto, Thacker & Co. (London), 1890 . . . £125
Barrack-Room Ballads and Other Verses, Methuen,
1892 . . . . £300
ditto, Methuen, 1892 (large paper edition, 225 copies).
. . . . £500
ditto, Methuen, 1892 (deluxe edition, 30 copies on half
vellum) £1,250
ditto, Thacker, Spink and Co. (Calcutta & Bombay)
1892 . . . . £200
The Seven Seas, Appleton (U.S.), 1896 . . . £35
ditto, Methuen, 1896 . . . . £35
ditto, Methuen, 1896 (large paper edition, 150 copies).
. . . . £225
ditto, Methuen, 1896 (deluxe edition, 30 copies on half
vellum) £650
An Almanac of Twelve Sports, Heinemann, 1898
[1897]. £400
Early Verse, Macmillan, 1900 . . . . £60
The Five Nations, Methuen, 1903 . . . . £45
ditto, Methuen, 1903 (large paper edition, 200 copies).
. . . . £200
ditto, Methuen, 1903 (deluxe edition, 30 copies on full
vellum. £750
Collected Verse, Doubleday Page (U.S.), 1907 (without
index) £100
ditto, Doubleday Page (U.S.), 1907 (with index) £65
ditto, Doubleday Page (U.S.), 1910 (9 colour plates by
W. Heath Robinson) £150
ditto, Doubleday Page (U.S.), 1910 (125 signed copies,
9 colour plates by W. Heath Robinson) . . £750
ditto, Hodder & Stoughton, 1912 (500 copies) . £150

ditto, Hodder & Stoughton, 1912 (deluxe edition, 100
copies on full vellum) £450
A Song of the English, Hodder & Stoughton, [c.1909]
(30 colour plates illustrated by W. Heath Robinson) .
. . . . £200
ditto, Hodder & Stoughton, [c.1909] (deluxe edition,
500 copies signed by the artist, 30 colour plates, full
vellum) £600
ditto, Hodder & Stoughton, [c.1909] (deluxe edition,
50 copies signed by the artist and author, 30 colour
plates, full vellum) £1,000
ditto, Doubleday (U.S.), [c.1909] (30 colour plates
illustrated by W. Heath Robinson) . . . £200
ditto, Doubleday (U.S.), [c.1909] (deluxe edition, 500
copies signed by the artist, 30 colour plates, full
vellum) £600
ditto, Hodder & Stoughton, [1912] (12 colour plates) .
. . . . £45
ditto, Hodder & Stoughton/Daily Telegraph, [1915] (16
colour plates). £65
ditto, Hodder & Stoughton, [1919] (16 colour plates) .
. . . . £45
The Dead King, Hodder & Stoughton, 1910 (illustrated
by W. Heath Robinson) £75
ditto, Hodder & Stoughton, 1910 (illustrated by W.
Heath Robinson, wraps). £75
A History of England, O.U.P./Hodder & Stoughton,
1911 (quarto, with C.R.L. Fletcher) . . . £25
ditto, O.U.P./Hodder & Stoughton, 1911 (octavo
edition for schools) £15
Songs from Books, Macmillan, 1913 . . . £25
Twenty Poems, Methuen, 1918 (wraps) . . . £20
The Years Between, Methuen, 1919 . . . £25
ditto, Methuen, 1919 (Large Paper edition, 100 copies)
. . . . £200
ditto, Methuen, 1919 (deluxe edition, 30 copies on
vellum) £350
Verse: Inclusive Edition 1885-1918, Hodder &
Stoughton, 1919 (3 vols) £75
ditto, Hodder & Stoughton, 1919 (deluxe edition, 100
signed sets on vellum) £750
A Kipling Anthology: Verse, Methuen, 1922 . £20/£5
Songs for Youth, Hodder & Stoughton, [1924] £35/£10
A Choice of Songs, Methuen, 1925 . . . . £20/£5
Sea and Sussex, Macmillan, 1926 (illustrated by
Donald Maxwell) . . . . . . £50/£15
ditto, Macmillan, 1926 (500 copies on half vellum)
. . . . £250
Songs of the Sea, Macmillan, 1927 (illustrated by
Donald Maxwell) . . . . . . £50/£15
ditto, Macmillan, 1927 (500 copies on half vellum)
. . . . £250
Poems 1886-1929, Macmillan, 1929 (3 vols, illustrated
by Francis Dodd). . . . . . . £50/£20
ditto, Macmillan, 1929 (deluxe edition, 525 sets in
morocco leather). £250
East of Suez, Macmillan, 1931 (illustrated by Donald
Maxwell) . . . . £25/£10
Selected Poems, Methuen, 1931 . . . . £15/£5

Sixty Poems, Hodder & Stoughton, 1939 . . £15/£5
Verse: Definitive Edition, Hodder & Stoughton, 1940.
. . . . £25/£5
So Shall Ye Reap: Poems For These Days, Hodder &
Stoughton, 1941 . . . . £15/£5
A Choice of Kipling's Verse, Faber & Faber, 1941
(edited by T.S. Eliot) . . . . £20/£5

Children's Titles
The Jungle Book, Macmillan, 1894 . . . . £1,250
ditto, Century (U.S.), 1894 . . . . . . £1,000
The Second Jungle Book, Macmillan, 1895 . £350
ditto, Century (U.S.), 1895 . . . . . . £250
'Captains Courageous', a story of the Grand Banks,
Macmillan, 1897 . . . . £150
ditto, Century (U.S.), 1897 . . . . . . £100
Stalky and Co., Macmillan, 1899 . . . . £200
Just So Stories for Little Children, Macmillan, 1902 .
. . . . £300
ditto, Doubleday Page (U.S.), 1902 . . . . £250
Puck of Pook's Hill, Macmillan, 1906 (illustrated by
H.R. Millar) £150
ditto, Doubleday Page (U.S.), 1906 (4 colour
illustrations by Arthur Rackham) £200
Rewards and Fairies, Macmillan, 1910 . . . £50

Novels
The Light That Failed, Lippincott (U.S.), 1890 (12
chapters with happy ending, wraps) . . . £150
ditto, Macmillan, 1891 (15 chapters with unhappy
ending!) £200
The Naulahka, a story of West and East, Heinemann,
1892 (with W. Balestier) £75
Kim, Doubleday Page (U.S.), 1901 . . . . £100
ditto, Macmillan, 1901 . . . . £100

Short Stories
Plain Tales from the Hills, Thacker Spink (Calcutta),
1888 (first issue with 24 pages of adverts at end dated
'Calcutta December 1887') £500
ditto, Thacker Spink (Calcutta), 1888 (second issue
with 32 pages of adverts at end dated 'Calcutta
December 1887'). £400
ditto, John W. Lovell Co. (U.S.), 1889 . . . £125
ditto, Macmillan, 1890 . . . . £125
Soldiers Three, A.H. Wheeler (Allahabad), 1888 (first
state without cross-hatching on barrack doors on
cover, wraps). £600
ditto, A.H. Wheeler (Allahabad), 1888 (second state
with cross-hatching on barrack doors on cover,
wraps). £300
ditto, Sampson Low, 1890. . . . . . . £100
The Story of the Gadsby's, A.H. Wheeler (Allahabad),
1888 (first printing with no date on front cover,
wraps). £750
ditto, A.H. Wheeler (Allahabad), 1888 (second printing
with 1888 date on front cover, wraps) . . . £250
ditto, Sampson Low, 1890. . . . . . . £100
In Black and White, A.H. Wheeler (Allahabad), 1888
(wraps) £600

ditto, Sampson Low, 1890 (wraps) £300
Under the Deodars, A.H. Wheeler (Allahabad), 1888
(first state without shading around 'No.4' and 'One
Rupee', wraps) £1,000
ditto, A.H. Wheeler (Allahabad), 1888 (second state
with shading around 'No.4' and 'One Rupee', wraps)
. . . . £300
ditto, Sampson Low, 1890 (wraps) £100
The Phantom Rickshaw and Other Tales, A.H.
Wheeler (Allahabad), [1888] (first binding with 'A H
Wheeler' and 'Mufid I am Press' below design on
front cover, wraps) £1,000
ditto, A.H. Wheeler (Allahabad), [1888] (second
binding with 'A.H. Wheeler' and 'Mayo School of
Art' below design on front cover, wraps) . . £500
ditto, Sampson Low, 1890 (wraps) £400
Wee Willie Winkie and Other Child Stories, A.H.
Wheeler (Allahabad), 1888 (first issue, wraps) .
. . . . £1,250
ditto, A.H. Wheeler (Allahabad), 1888 (second issue
with 'Mayo School of Art' on front wrapper, wraps) .
. . . . £750
ditto, A.H. Wheeler (Allahabad), 1888 (third issue with
96 instead of 104 pages, wraps). £250
ditto, Sampson Low, 1890 . . . . . . £100
The Courting of Dinah Shad and Other Stories,
Harper (U.S.), 1890 . . . . £250
The City of Dreadful Night and Other Sketches, A.H.
Wheeler (Allahabad), 1890 (suppressed edition) . .
. . . . £1,250
ditto, as *The City of Dreadful Night and Other Places*,
A.H. Wheeler (Allahabad), 1891 (unsuppressed
edition) £350
ditto, Sampson Low, 1891 . . . . . . £100
Life's Handicap, being stories of mine own people,
Macmillan, 1891 . . . . £75
Many Inventions, Macmillan, 1893 . . . . £75
Soldier Tales, Macmillan, 1896 (reprints from *The
Story of the Gadsbys* and *In Black and White*) £75
The Day's Work, Doubleday & McClure (U.S.), 1898.
. . . . £100
ditto, Macmillan, 1898 . . . . £75
The Kipling Reader, Macmillan, 1900 . . . £30
Traffics and Discoveries, Macmillan, 1904 . . £75
They, Macmillan, 1905 (from *Traffics and Dis-
coveries*) £50
The Brushwood Boy, Macmillan, 1907 (from *The
Day's Work*) £30
Actions and Reactions, Macmillan, 1909 . . £75
Abaft the Funnel, Dodge (U.S.), 1909 . . . £150
A Diversity of Creatures, Macmillan, 1917 . . £30
Land and Sea Tales for Scouts and Guides,
Macmillan, 1923 . . . . £45/£20
Debits and Credits, Macmillan, 1926 . . £40/£15
Thy Servant A Dog, Told by Boots, Macmillan, 1930 .
. . . . £40/£15
Humorous Tales, Macmillan, 1931 . . . £40/£15
Animal Stories, Macmillan, 1932 . . . £40/£15
Limits and Renewals, Macmillan, 1932 . . £40/£15

All The Mowgli Stories, Macmillan, 1933 . £75/£25
Collected Dog Stories, Macmillan, 1934 . £35/£15
Ham and the Porcupine, Doubleday Doran (U.S.),
1935 . . . . £40/£15
The Maltese Cat, Macmillan, 1936 (from *The Day's
Work*). . . . . £50/£15
More Selected Stories, Macmillan, 1940 . £40/£15
Twenty-One Tales, Reprint Society, 1946 . . £15/£5
Ten Stories, Pan, 1947 (wraps) £5
A Choice of Kipling's Prose, Macmillan, 1952 (selected
and with an introduction by W. Somerset Maugham).
. . . . £15/£5
Complete Works: The Sussex Edition, Macmillan,
1937-1939 (35 vols) . . . . . . £2,500 the set

Others
*Something of Myself: For My Friends Known and
Unknown*, Macmillan, 1937 . . . . £75/£15
*The Letters of Rudyard Kipling, Volume 1: 1872-
1889*, Macmillan, 1990 . . . . £15/£5
*The Letters of Rudyard Kipling, Volume 2: 1890-
1899*, Macmillan, 1990 . . . . £15/£5
*The Letters of Rudyard Kipling, Volume 3: 1900-
1910*, Macmillan, 1996 . . . . £10/£5
*The Letters of Rudyard Kipling, Volume 4: 1911-
1919*, Macmillan, 1999 . . . . £10/£5

C.H.B. KITCHIN
(b.1895 d.1967)

A novelist, poet and musician, it is as the author of a
handful of detective novels that Kitchin is best
known.

Detective Novels
Death of My Aunt, Hogarth Press, 1929 . £250/£45
ditto, Harcourt Brace (U.S.), 1930 . . . £50/£10
Crime at Christmas, Hogarth Press, 1934 . £250/£45
Death of His Uncle, Constable, 1939 . . £175/£30
ditto, Perennial (U.S.), 1984 (wraps). £5
The Cornish Fox, Secker & Warburg, 1949 £125/£20

Other Novels
Streamers Waving, Hogarth Press, 1925 . £150/£45
Mr Balcony, Hogarth Press, 1927 . . . £125/£30
The Sensitive One, Hogarth Press, 1921 . £100/£20
Olive E, Constable, 1937 . . . . . . £20/£10
Birthday Party, Constable, 1938 . . . . £20/£10
The Auction Sale, Secker & Warburg, 1949 £25/£10
The Secret River, Secker & Warburg, 1956. . £20/£5
Ten Pollitt Place, Secker & Werburg, 1957. . £20/£5
The Book of Life, Davies, 1960 . . . . £15/£5
ditto, Appleton-Century-Crofts (U.S.), [1961, c1960] .
. . . . £15/£10
A Short Walk in Williams Park, Chatto & Windus,
1971 . . . . £10/£5

Short Stories
Jumping Joan and Other Stories, Secker & Warburg,
1954 . . . . £25/£5

Poetry
Curtains, Blackwell, 1919 (wraps) £75
Winged Victory, Blackwell, 1921 (wraps) . . £50

ARTHUR KOESTLER
(b.1905 d.1983)

A novelist and philosopher, all of Koestler's books
are more or less an analysis of the turmoil in Europe
in the years preceding World War Two.

Autobiography
Spanish Testament, Gollancz, 1937 . . . £200/£30
ditto, Gollancz, 1937 (Left Book Club, wraps) . £35
ditto, as *Dialogue with Death*, Macmillan (U.S.), 1942
(abridged). . . . . £50/£10
Scum of the Earth, Cape, 1941 . . . . £50/£10
ditto, Macmillan (U.S.), 1941 . . . . £25/£10
Arrow in the Blue, Collins/Hamilton, 1952 . £30/£10
ditto, Macmillan (U.S.), 1952 . . . . . £25/£5
The Invisible Writing, Collins/Hamilton, 1954 £30/£10
ditto, Macmillan (U.S.), 1954 . . . . . £25/£5
Stranger on the Square, Hutchinson, 1984 (unfinished,
by Arthur and Cynthia Koestler) . . . . £15/£5
ditto, Random House (U.S.), 1984 . . . . £15/£5

Novels
The Gladiators, Cape, 1939 . . . . . £75/£10
ditto, Macmillan (U.S.), 1939 . . . . £50/£10
Darkness at Noon, Cape, 1940 . . . £3,000/£450
ditto, Macmillan (U.S.), 1941 . . . . . £75/£15
ditto, Franklin Library (U.S.), 1970 (signed, limited
edition) £95
Arrival and Departure, Cape, 1943 . . . £35/£10
ditto, Macmillan (U.S.), 1943 . . . . . £30/£5
Thieves in the Night, Macmillan, 1946 . . £25/£5
ditto, Macmillan (U.S.), 1946 . . . . . £20/£5
The Age of Longing, Collins, 1951 . . . £20/£5
ditto, Macmillan (U.S.), 1951 . . . . . £20/£5
The Call-Girls, Hutchinson, 1972 . . . . £15/£5
ditto, Random House (U.S.), 1973 . . . . £15/£5

Essays
The Yogi and the Commissar, Cape, 1945 . . £25/£5
ditto, Macmillan (U.S.), 1945 . . . . . £15/£5
Insight and Outlook, Macmillan, 1949 . . . £15/£5
ditto, Macmillan (U.S.), 1949 . . . . . £15/£5
The Trail of the Dinosaur, Collins, 1955 . . £15/£5
ditto, Macmillan (U.S.), 1955 . . . . . £15/£5
Reflections on Hanging, Gollancz, 1957 . . £15/£5
ditto, Macmillan (U.S.), 1957 . . . . . £15/£5
The Lotus and the Robot, Hutchinson, 1960 £25/£10
ditto, Macmillan (U.S.), 1961 . . . . £25/£10

Hanged by the Neck, Penguin, 1961 (wraps) . . £5
Drinkers of Infinity: Essays 1955-1967, Hutchinson, 1968 . . . . £15/£5
ditto, Macmillan (U.S.), 1969 . . . . . £15/£5
The Lion and the Ostrich, O.U.P., 1973 (wraps) £10
The Heel of Achilles: Essays, Hutchinson, 1974 . .
. . . . £15/£5
ditto, Random House (U.S.), 1975 . . . . £15/£5
Janus: A Summing Up, Hutchinson, 1978 . . £10/£5
ditto, Random House (U.S.), 1978 . . . . £10/£5
Bricks to Babel, Hutchinson, 1980 . . . . £10/£5
ditto, Random House (U.S.), 1981 . . . . £10/£5

Non Fiction
Promise and Fulfilment, Macmillan, 1949 . . £20/£5
ditto, Macmillan (U.S.), 1949 . . . . . £15/£5
The Sleepwalkers, Hutchinson, 1959 . . . £20/£5
ditto, Macmillan (U.S.), 1959 . . . . . £15/£5
The Act of Creation, Hutchinson, 1964 . . . £20/£5
ditto, Macmillan (U.S.), 1964 . . . . . £15/£5
The Ghost in the Machine, Hutchinson, 1967 . £25/£5
ditto, Macmillan (U.S.), 1968 . . . . . £15/£5
The Case of the Midwife Toad, Hutchinson, 1971 . .
. . . . £10/£5
ditto, Random House (U.S.), 1972 . . . £15/£5
The Roots of Coincidence, Hutchinson, 1972 . £15/£5
ditto, Random House (U.S.), 1972 . . . £10/£5
The Challenge of Chance, Hutchinson, 1973 (with Alister Hardy and Robert Harvie) . . . £10/£5
ditto, Random House (U.S.), 1975 . . . £10/£5
The Thirteenth Tribe, Hutchinson, 1976 . . £10/£5
ditto, Random House (U.S.), 1976 . . . £10/£5

DEAN KOONTZ
(b.1945)

Koontz's writing career began in 1956 when, at the age of twenty, he won an *Atlantic Monthly* fiction competition. His worldwide sales amount to close on 100 million.

Novels
Star Quest, Ace (U.S.), 1968 (with *Doom of the Green Planet* by Emil Petaja, wraps) £50
The Fall of the Dream Machine, Ace (U.S.), 1969 (with *The Star Venturers*, wraps) £25
Fear That Man, Ace (U.S.), 1969 (with *Toyman* by E.C. Tubb, wraps) £20
Anti-Man, Paperback Library (U.S.), 1970 (wraps) £20
Beastchild, Lancer (U.S.), 1970 (wraps) . . £50
Dark of the Woods and *Soft Come The Dragons*, Ace (U.S.), 1970 (wraps) £25
The Dark Symphony, Lancer (U.S.), 1970 (wraps) £25
Hell's Gate, Lancer (U.S.), 1970 (wraps) . . £20
The Crimson Witch, Curtis (U.S.), 1971 (wraps) £50
A Darkness in My Soul, Daw (U.S.), 1972 (wraps) £15
ditto, Dobson, 1979 . . . . £75/£20

The Flesh in the Furnace, Bantam (U.S.), 1972 (wraps) £15
Starblood, Lancer (U.S.), 1972 (wraps) . . £15
Time Thieves, Ace (U.S.), 1972 (with *Against Arcturus* by Susan K. Putney, wraps) . . . £15
ditto, Dobson, 1977 . . . . £75/£25
Warlock, Lancer (U.S.), 1972 (wraps) . . . £15
Writing Popular Fiction, Writers' Digest Fiction (U.S.), 1973 . . . . £50/£15
A Werewolf Among Us, Ballantine (U.S.), 1973 (wraps) £15
The Haunted Earth, Lancer (U.S.), 1973 (wraps) £15
Hanging On, M. Evans (U.S.), 1973 . . £100/£25
ditto, Barrie & Jenkins, 1974 (wraps) . . . £10
Demon Seed, Bantam (U.S.), 1973 (wraps) . . £15
ditto, Corgi, 1977 (wraps). £10
After the Last Race, Athenaeum (U.S.), 1974 £75/£25
Nightmare Journey, Putnam (U.S.), 1975 . £100/£25
Night Chills, Athenaeum (U.S.), 1976 . . £100/£30
ditto, W.H. Allen, 1977 . . . . . . £75/£25
The Vision, Putnam (U.S.), 1977 . . . £80/£25
ditto, Corgi, 1980 (wraps). £10
ditto, W.H. Allen, 1988 . . . . . . £45/£15
Whispers, Putnam (U.S.), 1980 . . . £200/£50
ditto, W.H. Allen, 1981 . . . . . . £75/£25
How To Write Best-Selling Fiction, Writers' Digest Books (U.S.), 1981 . . . . . . £50/£15
ditto, Popular Press (U.S.), 1981 . . . . . £20/£5
Phantoms, Putnam (U.S.), 1983 . . . . £75/£25
ditto, W.H. Allen, 1983 . . . . . . £25/£15
Darkness Comes, W.H. Allen, 1984 . . £125/£35
ditto, as *Darkfall*, Berkeley (U.S.), 1984 . £15/£5
Twilight Eyes, Land of Enchantment (U.S.), 1985 . .
. . . . £35/£15
ditto, Land of Enchantment (U.S.), 1985 (signed, illustrated collector's edition, 50 copies) . . £350
ditto, Land of Enchantment (U.S.), 1985 (signed edition, 200 copies, d/w and slipcase) . £200/£125
ditto, W.H. Allen, 1987 . . . . . . £50/£20
Strangers, Putnam (U.S.), 1986 . . . . . £25/£5
ditto, W.H. Allen, 1987 . . . . £25/£5
Watchers, Putnam (U.S.), 1987 . . . . . £20/£5
ditto, Headline, 1987 . . . . £20/£5
Lightning, Putnam (U.S.), 1987 . . . . . £20/£5
ditto, Headline, 1988 . . . . £20/£5
Oddkins, Warner (U.S.), 1988 . . . . . £25/£10
ditto, Headline, 1988 . . . . £20/£5
Midnight, Putnam (U.S.), 1989 . . . . . £15/£5
ditto, Headline, 1989 . . . . £15/£5
Bad Place, Putnam (U.S.), 1990 . . . . . £15/£5
ditto, Putnam (U.S.), 1990 (250 signed, numbered copies, d/w and slipcase) . . . . . £125/£75
ditto, Headline, 1990 . . . . £15/£5
Cold Fire, Putnam (U.S.), 1991 . . . . . £10/£5
ditto, Putnam (U.S.), 1991 (750 signed, numbered copies, d/w and slipcase) . . . . . £100/£65
ditto, Headline, 1991 (200 signed, numbered copies) .
. . . . £125/£100
ditto, Headline, 1991 . . . . £10/£5

Hideaway, Putnam (U.S.), 1992 . . . . . £10/£5
ditto, Putnam (U.S.), 1991 (800 signed, numbered copies, d/w and slipcase) . . . . . £100/£65
ditto, Headline, 1992 . . . . £10/£5
Dragon Tears, Putnam (U.S.), 1993 . . . . £10/£5
ditto, Putnam (U.S.), 1991 (700 signed, numbered copies, d/w and slipcase) . . . . . £100/£65
ditto, Headline, 1993 . . . . £10/£5
Mr Murder, Headline, 1993 . . . . . . £10/£5
ditto, Putnam (U.S.), 1993 . . . . . . £10/£5
ditto, Putnam (U.S.), 1991 (600 signed, numbered copies, d/w and slipcase) . . . . . £100/£65
Winter Moon, Headline, 1994 . . . . . £20/£5
ditto, Ballantine (U.S.), 1994 (wraps) £5
Dark Rivers of the Heart, Charnel House, 1994 (26 signed, lettered copies, slipcase) £750
ditto, Charnel House, 1994 (500 signed, numbered copies, slipcase) £250
ditto, Knopf, 1994 . . . . £10/£5
ditto, Headline, 1994 . . . . £10/£5
Icebound, Headline, 1995 . . . . £10/£5
Strange Highways, Warner (U.S.), 1995 . . £10/£5
ditto, Headline, 1995 . . . . £10/£5
Intensity, Knopf, 1995 . . . . £10/£5
ditto, Headline, 1995 . . . . £10/£5
Ticktock, Headline, 1996 . . . . £10/£5
ditto, Ballantine (U.S.), 1996 (wraps) £5
Sole Survivor, Knopf, 1997 . . . . . . £10/£5
ditto, Headline, 1997 . . . . £10/£5
Fear Nothing, Headline, 1997 . . . . . £10/£5
ditto, Cemetery Dance (U.S.), 1998 (52 signed, lettered copies) £400
ditto, Cemetery Dance (U.S.), 1998 (698 signed, numbered copies with d/w and slipcase) . £100/£40
ditto, Bantam (U.S.), 1998 . . . . . . £10/£5
Seize the Night, Headline, 1998 . . . . £10/£5
ditto, Cemetery Dance (U.S.), 1998 (52 signed, lettered copies) £400
ditto, Cemetery Dance (U.S.), 1998 (698 signed, numbered copies with d/w and slipcase) . £100/£40
ditto, Bantam (U.S.), 1999 . . . . . . £10/£5
False Memory, Headline, 1999 . . . . . £10/£5
ditto, Cemetery Dance (U.S.), 1999 (52 signed, lettered copies) £400
ditto, Cemetery Dance (U.S.), 1999 (698 signed, numbered copies with d/w and slipcase) . £100/£40
ditto, Bantam (U.S.), 2000 . . . . . . £10/£5
From the Corner of His Eye, Headline, 2001 . £10/£5
ditto, Charnel House (U.S.), 2001 (26 signed, lettered copies) £400
ditto, Bantam (U.S.), 2001 . . . . . . £10/£5

Titles Written with Gerda Koontz
Bounce Girl, Cosmo (U.S.), 1970 . . . £30/£10
The Underground Lifestyles Handbook, Aware Press (U.S.), 1970 . . . . £25/£10
The Pig Society, Aware Press (U.S.), 1970 . £25/£10

Written as 'David Axton'
Prison of Ice, Lippincott (U.S.), 1976 . . £200/£45
ditto, W.H. Allen, 1977 . . . . . . £100/£35

Written as 'Brian Coffey'
Blood Risk, Bobbs-Merrill (U.S.), 1973 . . £150/£45
ditto, Barker, 1974 . . . . £75/£25
Surrounded, Bobbs-Merrill (U.S.), 1974 . £150/£50
ditto, Barker, 1975 . . . . £75/£25
The Wall of Masks, Bobbs-Merrill (U.S.), 1975 . . . . £100/£25
The Face of Fear, Bobbs-Merrill (U.S.), 1977 . . . . £150/£50
ditto, Peter Davis, 1978 (pseud. 'K.R. Dwyer') £75/£25
The Voice of the Night, Doubleday (U.S.), 1980 . . . . £200/£65
ditto, Robert Hale, 1981 . . . . . . £45/£15

Written as 'Deanna Dwyer'
The Demon Child, Lancer (U.S.), 1971 (wraps) £15
Legacy of Terror, Lancer (U.S.), 1971 (wraps) . £15
Children of the Storm, Lancer (U.S.), 1972 (wraps) £15
The Dark of Summer, Lancer (U.S.), 1972 (wraps) £15
Dance With the Devil, Lancer (U.S.), 1972 (wraps) £15

Written as 'K.R. Dwyer'
Chase, Random House (U.S.), 1972 . . . £125/£40
ditto, Barker, 1974 . . . . £75/£25
Shattered, Random House (U.S.), 1972 . . £150/£45
ditto, Barker, 1974 . . . . £75/£25
Dragonfly, Random House (U.S.), 1975 . £100/£30
ditto, Peter Davis, 1977 . . . . . . £45/£20

Written as 'John Hill'
The Long Sleep, Popular Library (U.S.), 1975 (wraps) £15

Written as 'Leigh Nichols'
The Key to Midnight, Pocket (U.S.), 1979 (wraps) £15
ditto, Magnum, 1980 (wraps) £10
ditto, Dark Harvest (U.S.), 1989 . . . . £25/£10
The Eyes of Darkness, Pocket (U.S.), 1981 (wraps) £10
ditto, Piatkus, 1981 . . . . £25/£5
ditto, Dark Harvest (U.S.), 1981 (400 signed, numbered copies, d/w and slipcase) . . £50/£35
The House of Thunder, Pocket (U.S.), 1982 (wraps) £10
ditto, Fontana, 1983 (wraps) £10
ditto, Dark Harvest (U.S.), 1988 (550 signed, numbered copies, d/w and slipcase) . . £50/£35
Twilight, Pocket (U.S.), 1984 (wraps) . . £10
ditto, as *The Servants of Twilight*, Fontana, 1985 (wraps) £10
ditto, as *The Servants of Twilight*, Dark Harvest (U.S.), 1988 (450 signed copies, d/w and slipcase) . . . . £50/£35

The Door to December, NAL (U.S.), 1985 (wraps, pseud. 'Richard Paige') £10
ditto, Fontana, 1987 (wraps, pseud. 'Leigh Nichols') .
. . . . £10
Shadowfires, Pocket (U.S.), 1987 (wraps) . . £10
ditto, Fontana, 1987 (wraps) £10
ditto, Collins, 1987 . . . . £45/£20
ditto, Dark Harvest (U.S.), 1990 . . . . . £10/£5

Written as 'Anthony North'
Strike Deep, Dial (U.S.), 1974 . . . . £150/£50

Written as 'Owen West'
The Funhouse, Jove (U.S.), 1980 (wraps) . . £10
ditto, Doubleday (U.S.), 1980 . . . . . £15/£5
ditto, Sphere, 1981 (wraps) £10
The Mask, Jove (U.S.), 1980 (wraps) . . . £10
ditto, Coronet/Hodder, 1983 (wraps). . . £10
ditto, Headline, 1989 . . . . £30/£10

Written as 'Aaron Wolfe'
Invasion, Laser Books (U.S.), 1975 (wraps) . £15

PHILIP LARKIN
(b.1922 d.1985)

A poet and novelist, *XX Poems* was the first of Larkin's collections to realise his own distinctive voice, although *The Less Deceived* was his first popular success.

Poetry
The North Ship, The Fortune Press, 1945 (black cloth)
. . . . £900/£225
ditto, The Fortune Press, 1945 [1965] (unauthorised second edition, red or brown cloth). . £75/£25
ditto, Faber, 1966 . . . . £45/£15
XX Poems, privately printed, 1951 (100 copies, not for sale, wraps) £1,000
The Fantasy Poets No. 21, Fantasy Press, 1954 (300 copies) £500
The Less Deceived, Marvell Press, 1955 . £450/£125
ditto, Marvell Press, 1955 (wraps) . . . £40
ditto, St Martin's Press (U.S.), 1960 . . £65/£20
The Whitsun Weddings, Faber, 1964 . . £100/£25
ditto, Random House (U.S.), 1964 . . £65/£20
The Explosion, Poem of the Month Club, 1970 (broadsheet, 1,000 signed copies) £125
High Windows, Faber, 1974 . . . . £40/£15
ditto, Farrar Straus (U.S.), 1974 . . . £25/£10
Femmes Damnées, Sycamore Press, 1978 (broadsheet)
. . . . £30
Aubade, Penstemon Press (U.S.), 1980 (250 numbered, initialled copies, wraps, in envelope) . . . £150
Collected Poems, Faber, 1988 . . . . £25/£10
ditto, Farrar Straus (U.S.), 1988 . . . . . £20/£5

Novels
Jill, The Fortune Press, 1946 . . . . £1,000/£200
ditto, Faber, 1964 . . . . £75/£25
ditto, St Martin's Press (U.S.), 1964 . . . £50/£20
A Girl in Winter, Faber, 1947 . . . £1,000/£200
ditto, St Martin's Press (U.S.), 1957 . . . £75/£20

Recordings
Listen Presents Philip Larkin Reading 'The Less Deceived', Listen/The Marvell Press, 1959 . £25
ditto, Listen/The Marvell Press, 1959 (100 copies signed by the author) £100
Philip Larkin Reads and Comments on 'The Whitsun Weddings', Listen Records, [1965]. . . . £25
British Poets of Our Time, Philip Larkin 'High Windows': Poems Read by the Author, Argo, [1975]
. . . . £25

Others
All What Jazz: A Record Diary, 1961-68, Faber, 1970
. . . . £45/£15
ditto, St Martin's Press (U.S.), 1970 . . £25/£10
Philip Larkin Talks to Eboracum, [Eboracum, 1970] (wraps) £50
The Oxford Book of Twentieth Century English Verse, O.U.P., 1973 (edited by Larkin) . £25/£10
Required Writing, Miscellaneous Pieces, 1955-1982, Faber, 1983 (wraps) £20
ditto, Farrar Straus (U.S.), 1983 . . . . . £20/£5
ditto, Faber, 1984 (hardback). . . . . £50/£15
Selected Letters of Philip Larkin, 1940-1985, Faber, 1992 . . . . £25/£10
ditto, Farrar Straus (U.S.), 1993 . . . . . £15/£5
Trouble at Willow Gables and other Fictions, Faber, 2002 . . . . £15/£5

D.H. LAWRENCE
(b.1885 d.1930)

A versatile and controversial modernist writer whose achievements have often been overshadowed by the various court cases they have provoked, especially the trial of *Lady Chatterly's Lover*.

Novels
The White Peacock, Duffield (U.S.), 1911 (first issue with integral title page and copyright date 1910) . .
. . . . £5,000
ditto, Duffield (U.S.), 1911 (second issue with tipped-in title page and copyright date 1911) . . £3,000
ditto, Heinemann, 1911 (first issue with windmill device on back cover and pages 227-30 tipped-in) .
. . . . £750
ditto, Heinemann, 1911 (second issue without windmill device, and pages 227-30 integral) £300
The Trespasser, Duckworth, 1912 (first issue with dark blue cloth) £750

ditto, Duckworth, 1912 (second issue with green cloth)
. . . . £500
ditto, Kennerley (U.S.), 1912 . . . . . . £300
Sons and Lovers, Duckworth, 1913 (first state without date on title page or with dated title page tipped-in) .
. . . . £1,000
ditto, Duckworth, 1913 (second state with dated title page integral). £750
ditto, Kennerley (U.S.), 1913 . . . . . . £300
The Rainbow, Methuen, 1915 (blue-green cloth) . .
. . . . £750
ditto, Methuen, 1915 (red or brown cloth) . . £500
ditto, Methuen, 1915 (wraps). £400
ditto, Huebsch (U.S.), 1916 . . . . . £400
The Lost Girl, Secker, 1920 (first issue, p.256 line 15 reads '...she was taken to her room...' and p.268 reads 'whether she noticed anything in the bedroom, in the beds.') . . . . £1,250/£350
ditto, Secker, 1920 (second issue, p.256 line 15 reads '...she let be.' and p.268 deletes 'in the bedroom, in the beds.'). . . . . £1,000/£100
ditto, Seltzer (U.S.), 1921 (first issue with character's name 'Cicio'). . . . . £500/£100
ditto, Seltzer (U.S.), 1921 (second issue with character's name 'Ciccio') . . . . . £500/£65
Women in Love, privately printed (U.S.), 1921 (16 or 18 signed, numbered copies of 1,250). . . £5,000
ditto, privately printed (U.S.), 1921 (1,250 unsigned, numbered, copies) £750
ditto, Secker, 1921. . . . . . . £750/£75
ditto, Secker, 1922 (50 signed copies) . . . £3,000
Aaron's Rod, Seltzer (U.S.), 1922 . . . £250/£45
ditto, Secker, 1922. . . . . . . £250/£45
Kangaroo, Secker, 1923 . . . . . . £200/£25
ditto, Seltzer (U.S.), 1923 . . . . . £175/£25
The Boy in the Bush, Secker, 1924 (with M.L. Skinner) . . . . £200/£45
ditto, Seltzer (U.S.), 1924. . . . . £200/£45
The Plumed Serpent, Secker, 1926 . . . £200/£45
ditto, Knopf (U.S.), 1926 . . . . . £200/£45
Lady Chatterly's Lover, privately printed (Florence), 1928 (1,000 signed, numbered copies, plain protective jacket). . . . . £10,000/£6,000
ditto, privately printed (Florence), 1928 (second edition, wraps with glassine d/w) . . £400/£300
ditto, privately printed (Paris), 1929 (wraps) . £200
ditto, Secker, 1932 (expurgated edition). . £750/£25
ditto, Knopf (U.S.), 1932 (expurgated edition) . . .
. . . . £650/£45
ditto, Grove Press (U.S.), 1959 (unexpurgated edition)
. . . . £50/£15
ditto, Penguin, 1960 (unexpurgated edition, wraps) £10
Mr Noon, C.U.P., 1984 . . . .£15/£5
ditto, Viking (U.S.), 1985. . . . . . .£15/£5

Short Stories and Novelettes
The Prussian Officer and Other Stories, Duckworth, 1914 (first issue, blue cloth stamped in gold with 20 pages of ads) £400

ditto, Duckworth, 1914 (second issue, light blue cloth stamped in dark blue with 16 pages of ads) . £300
ditto, Huebsch (U.S.), 1916 . . . . . . £150
England, My England, Seltzer (U.S.), 1922 £250/£75
ditto, Secker, 1924. . . . . £250/£75
The Ladybird, The Fox, The Captain's Doll, Secker, 1923 . . . . £150/£35
ditto, as **The Captain's Doll**, Seltzer (U.S.), 1923 . .
. . . . £100/£35
St Mawr, Secker, 1925 (contents say text begins on p.9) . . . . £200/£75
ditto, Secker, 1925 (contents corrected to say text begins on p.7) . . . . £150/£30
ditto, Knopf (U.S.), 1925 . . . . . . £150/£35
Glad Ghosts, Ernest Benn, 1926 (500 copies, wraps) .
. . . . £100
Sun, E. Archer, 1926 (100 copies, expurgated). £400
ditto, Black Sun Press (Paris), 1928 (15 signed copies in glassine d/w and gold slipcase, wraps) . . . .
. . . . £2,500/£2,000
ditto, Black Sun Press (Paris), 1928 (150 copies in glassine d/w and gold slipcase, wraps) . £1,000/£500
Rawdon's Roof, Mathews and Marrot, 1928 (530 signed, numbered copies) . . . . . £350/£225
The Woman Who Rode Away, Secker, 1928 £150/£30
ditto, Knopf (U.S.), 1928 . . . . . . £125/£30
The Escaped Cock, Black Sun Press (Paris), 1929 (450 numbered copies, wraps, with glassine d/w and slipcase) . . . . £450/£200
ditto, Black Sun Press (Paris), 1929 (50 signed copies on Japanese vellum, wraps, with glassine d/w and slipcase) . . . . £1,250/£750
ditto, as **The Man Who Died**, Secker, 1931 (2,000 copies) . . . . £200/£75
ditto, as **The Man Who Died**, Knopf (U.S.), 1931 . .
. . . . £200/£75
The Virgin and the Gypsy, Orioli (Florence), 1930 (810 copies, d/w and slipcase) . . . £300/£175
ditto, Secker, 1930. . . . . £100/£25
ditto, Knopf (U.S.), 1930 . . . . . . £100/£25
Love Among the Haystacks, Nonesuch Press, 1930 (1,600 numbered copies) . . . . £200/£125
ditto, Secker, 1930. . . . . £65/£15
ditto, Haldeman Julius (U.S.), 1941 (wraps) . £25
The Lovely Lady, Secker, 1932 [1933] . . £75/£25
ditto, Viking (U.S.), 1933. . . . . . £45/£20
The Tales of D.H.Lawrence, Secker, 1934 . £35/£10
A Modern Lover, Secker, 1934 . . . . £50/£15
ditto, Viking (U.S.), 1934. . . . . . £45/£15

Poetry
Love Poems and Others, Duckworth, 1913 . . £300
ditto, Kennerley (U.S.), 1913 . . . . . £150
Amores, Duckworth, 1916 (first issue with 16pps of ads) £750
ditto, Duckworth, 1916 (second issue without ads). . .
. . . . £150
ditto, Huebsch (U.S.), 1916 . . . . . £100

Look! We have come through!, Chatto & Windus,
1917 . . . . £150
ditto, Huebsch (U.S.), 1918 . . . . . £150
New Poems, Secker, 1918 (wraps) . . . £100
ditto, Huebsch (U.S.), 1920 . . . . £75
Bay, A Book of Poems, Beaumont, 1919 . . £100
ditto, Beaumont, 1919 (30 signed copies) . .£1,000
Tortoises, Seltzer (U.S.), 1921 (glassine d/w) . .
. . . .£250/£200
Birds, Beasts and Flowers, Seltzer (U.S.), 1923 . .
. . . .£350/£100
ditto, Secker, 1923. . . . .£300/£100
ditto, Cresset Press, 1923 (500 copies) . . . £125
The Collected Poems of D. H. Lawrence, Secker, 1928
(2 vols) . . . . £200/£65
ditto, Secker, 1928 (100 signed copies, d/w and
slipcase) . . . . £1,750/£1,250
Pansies, Secker, 1929. . . . . . .£125/£45
ditto, Secker, 1929 (250 signed copies) . .£750/£400
ditto, Stephenson, 1929 (10 signed copies bound in
vellum, slipcase) £3,000
ditto, Stephenson, 1929 (50 signed copies bound in full
leather, glassine d/w and slipcase) £2,000
ditto, Stephenson, 1929 (500 signed copies, wraps,
glassine d/w and slipcase) . . . . .£500/£450
ditto, privately printed [for Frieda Lawrence] (U.S.),
1954 (750 numbered copies, glassine d/w) £45/£30
ditto, privately printed [for Frieda Lawrence] (U.S.),
1954 (250 numbered copies, signed by Frieda
Lawrence, glassine d/w). . . . . .£125/£100
Nettles, Faber & Faber, 1930 (tissue d/w) . £125/£75
ditto, Faber & Faber, 1930 (wraps) £35
The Triumph of the Machine, Faber, [1930] (wraps) .
. . . . £30
ditto, Faber, [1930] (400 numbered large paper copies)
. . . . £150
Last Poems, G. Orioli (Florence), 1932 (750 copies
with d/w and slipcase . . . . . .£300/£125
ditto, Secker, 1933. . . . .£100/£25
The Ship of Death, Secker, 1933 . . . £125/£60
Poems, Heinemann, 1939 (2 vols) . . . £35/£10
Fire and Other Poems, Book Club of California, 1940
(100 copies) . . . .£300/£200
The Complete Poems, Heinemann, 1957 (3 vols) . .
. . . . £50/£25
ditto, Viking (U.S.), 1964 (2 vols, slipcase). £40/£20

Plays
The Widowing of Mrs Holroyd, Kennerley (U.S.),
1914 (500 copies) £100
ditto, Duckworth, 1914 . . . . . . £35
Touch and Go, Daniel, 1920 . . . . . £200/£35
ditto, Seltzer (U.S.), 1920. . . . . £150/£35
David, Daniel, 1926 . . . . . . £100/£25
ditto, Knopf (U.S.), 1926 . . . . . £100/£25
The Plays, Secker, 1933 . . . . . . £35/£10
A Collier's Friday Night, Secker, 1934 . . £35/£10
The Complete Plays, Heinemann, 1965 . . £25/£10
ditto, Viking (U.S.), 1965. . . . . . £25/£10

Miscellaneous
Twilight in Italy, Duckworth, 1916 . . . . £300
ditto, Huebsch (U.S.), 1916 . . . . . £175
Movements in European History, O.U.P., 1921
(pseud. 'Lawrence H. Davison') £200
Sea and Sardinia, Seltzer (U.S.), 1921 . .£750/£150
ditto, Secker, 1923. . . . . . .£1,000/£200
Psychoanalysis and the Unconscious, Seltzer (U.S.),
1921 . . . . £250/£75
ditto, Secker, 1923. . . . .£200/£50
Fantasia of the Unconscious, Seltzer (U.S.), 1922. .
. . . . £250/£65
ditto, Secker, 1923. . . . .£250/£65
Studies in Classic American Literature, Seltzer (U.S.),
1923 . . . . £250/£65
ditto, Secker, 1924. . . . .£250/£65
*Reflections on the Death of a Porcupine and Further
Essays*, Centaur Press (U.S.), 1925 (925 copies,
slipcase) . . . .£200/£150
ditto, distributed by Simpkin, Marshall, Hamilton, Kent
in the UK, 1925 (475 numbered copies) .£200/£150
Mornings in Mexico, Secker, 1927 . . . £300/£75
ditto, Knopf (U.S.), 1927 . . . . . £300/£75
The Paintings of D.H. Lawrence, The Mandrake
Press, 1929 (500 copies, slipcase) . . .£650/£500
ditto, The Mandrake Press, 1929 (10 signed copies on
Japan paper) £5,000
Pornography and Obscenity, Faber & Faber, 1929
(wraps) £25
ditto, Faber & Faber, 1929 (cloth) £75
The Story of Doctor Manente, by A.F. Grazzini, Orioli
(Florence), 1929 (2 signed copies on blue paper,
translated and with an Introduction by Lawrence) .
. . . .£1,000
ditto, G. Orioli (Florence), 1929 (200 signed copies) .
. . . . £500
ditto, G. Orioli (Florence), 1929 (1,000 unsigned,
numbered copies) . . . .£125/£100
Assorted Articles, Secker, 1930 . . . . £65/£20
ditto, Knopf (U.S.), 1930 . . . . . . £65/£20
Apropos of Lady Chatterly's Lover, Mandrake Press,
1930 . . . . £35/£15
Apocalypse, Orioli (Florence), 1931 (750 copies) .
. . . . £150/£75
ditto, Secker, 1932 (750 numbered copies) . £75/£25
ditto, Secker, 1932. . . . . £30/£10
ditto, Viking (U.S.), 1932. . . . . . £25/£10
The Letters of D.H. Lawrence, Heinemann, 1932 . .
. . . . £100/£40
ditto, Heinemann, 1932 (525 numbered parchment
bound copies) £200
ditto, Viking (U.S.), 1932. . . . . . £25/£10
Etruscan Places, Secker, 1932 . . . . £200/£45
Pornography and So On, Faber, 1936 . . £75/£25
Phoenix: The Posthumous Papers of D.H. Lawrence,
Heinemann, 1936 . . . . £35/£15
The Manuscripts of D.H. Lawrence, Los Angeles
Public Library (U.S.), 1937 (750 copies, wraps) £25

D.H. Lawrence's Letters to Bertrand Russell, Gotham
Book Mart (U.S.), 1948 (950 copies) . . £50/£20
Sex, Literature and Censorship, Twayne (U.S.), 1953
. . . . £20/£5
ditto, Heinemann, 1955 . . . . £20/£5
Collected Letters, Heinemann, 1962 . . . £40/£15
ditto, Viking (U.S.), 1962 (2 vols) . . . £30/£10
Letters to Martin Secker, privately printed, 1970 (500
numbered copies) . . . . . . £45/£15
The Letters, C.U.P., 1979 (vol. I) . . . £25/£10
The Letters, C.U.P., 1981 (vol. II) . . . £25/£10
The Letters of D.H. Lawrence & Amy Lowell, Black
Sparrow Press (U.S.), 1985 (500 copies, glassine d/w)
. . . . £35/£25
ditto, Black Sparrow Press (U.S.), 1985 (100 copies
signed by the editors) £45
ditto, Black Sparrow Press (U.S.), 1985 (26
handbound, lettered copies signed by the editors) £75

T.E. LAWRENCE
(b.1888 d.1935)

A soldier and author, Lawrence is popularly known as
'Lawrence of Arabia'. His account of the Arab
Revolt, *The Seven Pillars of Wisdom*, is seen as a
masterpiece by many.

The Seven Pillars of Wisdom, Oxford Edition, 1922 (8
copies) £40,000
ditto, London, 1924 (first proof copy) . . . £5,000
ditto, London, 1925 (second proof, 100 copies) . .
. . . . £4,000
ditto, Cranwell, Subscribers' Edition, 1926 (169
copies) £40,000
ditto, Cranwell, Subscribers' Edition, 1926 (32
incomplete copies) £20,000
ditto, Doubleday Doran (U.S.), 1926 (copyright
edition, 22 copies) £15,000
ditto, Cape, 1935 (750 copies, d/w and slipcase) . .
. . . . £2,000/£1,250
ditto, Cape, 1935 . . . . £650/£125
ditto, Cape, 1935 (60 privately issued copies) . £750
ditto, Doubleday Doran (U.S.), 1935 . £650/£125
ditto, Doubleday Doran (U.S.), 1935 (750 copies, d/w
and slipcase) . . . . £1,250/£600
Revolt in the Desert, Cape, 1927 . . . . £300/£50
ditto, Cape, 1927 (315 large paper copies) . . .
. . . . £1,500/£1,000
ditto, Doubleday Doran (U.S.), 1927 . . £300/£50
ditto, Doubleday Doran (U.S.), 1927 (250 large paper
copies, slipcase) . . . . . . £1,000/£750
The Mint, Doubleday Doran (U.S.), 1936 (pseud.
'352087 A/C Ross', U.S. copyright edition, 50
copies) £20,000
ditto, Cape, 1955 (first unexpurgated U.K. edition,
2,000 copies, no d/w, in slipcase) . . . £125/£100

ditto, Cape, 1955 (first U.K. trade edition, expurgated)
. . . . £25/£10
ditto, Doubleday Doran (U.S.), 1955 (1,000 numbered
copies, slipcase) . . . . £150/£100
ditto, Doubleday Doran (U.S.), 1957 . . . £15/£5
Crusader Castles, Golden Cockerel Press, 1936 (2
vols, 1000 copies, no d/w or slipcase) . . £1,000
ditto, *The Thesis*, Golden Cockerel Press, 1936 (75
copies) £1,250
ditto, *The Letters*, Golden Cockerel Press, 1936 (35
copies) £2,000
ditto, Doubleday Doran (U.S.), 1937 (copyright
edition) £750
The Diary of T.E. Lawrence MCMXI, Corvinus Press,
1937 (30 copies on 'Canute' paper) . . . £5,000
ditto, Corvinus Press, 1937 (40 copies on 'Medway'
paper) £3,000
ditto, Corvinus Press, 1937 (130 copies on parchment-
style paper) £2,000
ditto, Doubleday Doran (U.S.), 1937 (copyright
edition, 50 copies) £3,000
An Essay on Flecker, Corvinus Press, 1937 (26 copies,
slipcase) . . . . £2,500/£2,000
ditto, Corvinus Press, 1937 (4 copies, vellum) . £3,500
ditto, Corvinus Press, 1937 (2 copies, leather) . £5,000
ditto, Doubleday Doran (U.S.), 1937 (copyright edition
of approx 56 copies, wraps). £1,500
Two Arabic Folk Tales, Corvinus Press, 1937 (31
copies) £2,000
Secret Dispatches from Arabia, Golden Cockerel
Press, 1939 (nos. 1-30, printed on Arnold hand-made
paper, bound in white pig-skin, with supplement). .
. . . . £2,500
ditto, Golden Cockerel Press, 1939 (nos. 31-1,000,
printed on Arnold hand-made paper, bound in quarter
Niger, without supplement) £500
Men in Print, Golden Cockerel Press, 1940 (nos. 1-30,
bound in full Niger, with supplement, slipcase) . .
. . . . £1,750/£1,250
ditto, Golden Cockerel Press, 1940 (nos. 31-500) £400
The Essential T.E. Lawrence, Cape, 1951 . £35/£10
ditto, Dutton (U.S.), 1951 . . . . £35/£10
*Evolution of a Revolt, Early Postwar Writings of T.E.
Lawrence*, The Pennsylvania State Univ. Press (U.S.),
1968 . . . . £35/£15

Translations by 'J.H. Ross'
The Forest Giant, by Adrien Le Corbeau, Cape, 1924 .
. . . . £75/£25
ditto, Harper & Bros. (U.S.), 1924 (first issue with
translator incorrectly given as 'L.H. Ross') £75/£25

Translations by 'T.E. Shaw'
The Odyssey of Homer, Bruce Rogers, 1932 (530
copies, slipcase) . . . . . £1,500/£1,000
ditto, O.U.P. (U.S.), 1932. . . . . £200/£75
ditto, O.U.P. (U.S.), 1932 (32 copies) . . £4,000
ditto, O.U.P., 1935. . . . . . . £125/£45

Letters

Letters from T.E. Shaw to Bruce Rogers, privately
printed by Bruce Rogers, 1933 (200 copies, no d/w) .
. . . . £750
More Letters from T.E. Shaw to Bruce Rogers,
privately printed by Bruce Rogers, 1936 (300 copies,
no d/w) £500
A Letter from T.E. Lawrence to His Mother, Corvinus
Press, 1936 (30 copies) £1,250
Letter from T.E. Shaw to Viscount Carlow, Corvinus
Press, 1936 (17 copies) £1,000
The Letters of T.E. Lawrence, Cape, 1938 . £100/£35
ditto, Doubleday Doran (U.S.), 1939 . . £45/£15
ditto, Dent, 1988 (new edition) . . . . . £20/£5
T.E. Lawrence To His Biographers, Faber, 1938 (500
copies signed by Graves and Hart, 2 vols with d/ws,
in slipcase) . . . . £450/£400
ditto, Doubleday Doran (U.S.), 1938 (500 copies
signed by Graves and Hart, 2 vols with d/ws, in
slipcase) . . . . £450/£400
Eight Letters from T.E.L., privately printed [Corvinus
Press], 1939 (50 copies). £750
Selected Letters of T.E. Lawrence, World Books, 1941
. . . . £5
*Shaw-Ede: T.E. Lawrence's letters to H.S. Ede, 1927-
35*, Golden Cockerel Press, 1942 (nos. 1-130, bound
in full morocco, with facsimile reproductions of 5 of
the letters) £1,000
ditto, Golden Cockerel Press, 1942 (nos. 31-500) £300
*The Home Letters of T.E. Lawrence and His
Brothers*, Blackwell, 1954 . . . . . £125/£35
ditto, Macmillan (U.S.), 1954 . . . £75/£25
From a Letter of T.E. Lawrence, Officina Bodoni,
1959 (75 copies) £150
T.E.L., Five Hitherto Unpublished Letters, privately
printed, 1975 (30 copies, wraps) £150
Fifty Letters, Humanities research centre (U.S.), 1962
(wraps) £30
Letters to E.T. Leeds, Whittington Press, 1988 (650
copies, slipcase) £100

Edited by Lawrence

Minorities, Cape, 1971 . . . . . . £40/£15
ditto, Cape, 1971 (125 copies signed by C. Day-Lewis)
. . . . £300
ditto, Doubleday (U.S.), 1972 . . . . £35/£15

EDWARD LEAR
(b.1812 d.1888)

Popularly known as a nonsense poet, Lear, an
accomplished artist and travel-writer, illustrated his
own verse.

Nonsense Books

A Book of Nonsense, Thomas Maclean, 1846 (pseud.
'Derry Down Derry', 2 vols, 175 copies, wraps) . .
. . . . £50,000
ditto, Thomas Maclean, 1855 (no pseud., 2 vols, wraps)
. . . . £10,000
ditto, Routledge, 1861 (enlarged edition) . . £650
ditto, Routledge, 1861 (enlarged edition) . . £650
Nonsense Songs, Stories, Botany and Alphabets,
Robert John Bush, 1871 . . . . £750
More Nonsense, Pictures, Rhymes, Botany, Robert
John Bush, 1872 [1874] £650
*Laughable Lyrics, A Fourth Book of Nonsense
Poems, Songs, Botany, Music, etc.*, Robert John
Bush, 1877 . . . . £650
Lear's Book of Nonsense, Warner, [1875] (Juvenile
Drolleries series) £125
*The Jumblies and Other Nonsense Poems, Songs,
Botany, Music*, Warne, 1877 [1876] . . . £200
Nonsense Drolleries, Warne, 1889 . . . £150
A Nonsense Birthday Book, Warne, [1894]. . £125
Nonsense Songs and Stories, Warne, 1895 . . £100
Nonsense Songs and Laughable Lyrics, Little, Brown
(U.S.), 1899 . . . . £100
ditto, Peter Pauper Press (U.S.), 1935 (650 copies) £75
The Pelican Chorus and Other Nonsense Verses,
Warne, 1900 . . . . £125
Queery Leary Nonsense, Mills & Boon, 1911 . £65
Callico Pie, Warne, [1924] . . . . . £75/£25
Facsimile of A Nonsense Alphabet, Warne, 1926
(1,000 numbered copies) £65
The Owl and the Pussy Cat, Warne, [1924]. £75/£35
The Pobble, Hugh Sharpe, 1934 (50 copies) . £250
The Quangle Wangle's Hat, Hugh Sharp, 1933 (50
copies) £250
Edward Lear's Nonsense Songs, Chatto & Windus,
1938 . . . . £35/£15
A Book of Lear, Penguin, 1939 (wraps with d/w) £10/£5
Edward Lear's Nonsense Omnibus, Odhams, 1943 .
. . . . £25/£10
The Complete Nonsense of Edward Lear, Faber, 1947
. . . . £25/£10
Edward Lear's Nonsense Alphabet, Collins, [1949] .
. . . . £25/£15
A Nonsense Alphabet, H.M.S.O., 1952 . . . £10
Teapots and Quails and Other Nonsense, Murray,
1953 . . . . £35/£15
ditto, Harvard Univ. (U.S.), 1953 . . . £25/£10
ABC, Constable, 1965. . . . . . . £15/£5
A Book of Nonsense, Peter Owen, 1972 (illustrated by
Mervyn Peake) . . . . £25/£10
Bosh and Nonsense, Allen Lane, 1982 . . . £15/£5

Natural History

Illustrations of the Family Psittacide, or Parrots, R. Ackerman & E. Lear, 1832 (42 hand-coloured plates, in original wraps) £100,000
ditto, R. Ackerman & E. Lear, 1832 (rebound) £50,000
Gleanings from The Menagerie and Aviary at Knowsley Hall, privately printed, Knowsley, 1846 . . . . £20,000
Tortoises, Terrapins and Turtles Drawn from Life, Henry Sotheran & Joseph Baer, 1872 (with James de Carle Sowerby) £4,000
The Lear Coloured Bird Book for Children, Mills and Boon, [1912] £60
Edward Lear's Parrots, Duckworth, 1949 (12 plates) . . . . £75/£30
The Birds of Edward Lear, A Selection, Ariel Press, 1975 (1000 copies, 12 plates) . . . . £300/£175

Travel

Views in Rome and Its Environs, Thomas Maclean, 1841 (25 plates) £4,000
Illustrated Excursions in Italy, Thomas Maclean, 1846 (first series, 30 plates) £2,000
ditto, Thomas Maclean, 1846 (second series, 25 plates) £2,000
Journals of a Landscape Painter in Albania, Richard Bentley, 1851 (21 plates) £1,000
Journals of a Landscape Painter in Southern Calabria, Richard Bentley, 1852 (2 maps, 20 plates) £750
Views in the Seven Southern Ionian Islands, E. Lear, 1863 (20 plates) £5,000
ditto, Oldham, 1979 (facsimile reprint of 1,000 numbered copies, 20 plates) . . . . £100/£65
Journals of a Landscape Painter in Corsica, Robert John Bush, 1870 (41 plates). £500
Lear in Sicily, Duckworth, 1938 . . . . £35/£15
Edward Lear's Journals, A Selection, Barker, 1952 (4 plates) . . . . £45/£20
Edward Lear's Indian Journal, Jarrolds, 1953 (9 plates) . . . . £45/£20
Edward Lear in Southern Italy, Kimber, 1964 (20 plates) . . . . £100/£35
Edward Lear in Greece, Kimber, 1965 (20 plates) . . . . £100/£35
Edward Lear in Corsica, Kimber, 1966 . . £100/£35
Lear's Corfu, Corfu Travel, 1965 (8 illustrations) . . . . £25/£10

Letters

The Letters of Edward Lear, T. Fisher Unwin, 1907 (20 plates) £50
Letters ... to Chichester Fortescue Lord Carlingford, and Frances Countess Waldegrave, Duffield (U.S.), [1908]. £45
The Later Letters of Edward Lear, T. Fisher Unwin, 1911 . . . . £25

A Letter from Edward Lear to George William Curtis, Harvard Printing Office (U.S.), 1947 (660 copies, wraps). £5
Selected Letters, Clarendon Press, 1988 . . £25/£10

Others

Three Poems by Tennyson Illustrated by Edward Lear, Bousson, Valadon & Co., Scribner's & Welford, 1889 (100 copies signed by Tennyson, 24 illustrations by Lear). £5,000
Edward Lear on My Shelves, privately printed by William Osgood Field, 1933 . . . . . £500

JOHN LE CARRÉ
(b.1931)

A novelist whose thrillers have examined the grey, dubious world of Cold War spying. As the years have passed his 'fiction' is seen to have been more and more perceptive.

Novels

Call for the Dead, Gollancz, 1961 . . £6,000/£350
ditto, Walker (U.S.), 1962 . . . . £2,000/£125
A Murder of Quality, Gollancz, 1962 . £4,000/£250
ditto, Walker (U.S.), 1963 . . . . £1,500/£100
The Spy Who Came in from the Cold, Gollancz, 1963 . . . . £750/£50
ditto, Coward-McGann (U.S.), 1963. . . £100/£20
The Looking-Glass War, Heinemann, 1965 £50/£10
ditto, Coward-McGann (U.S.), 1965 . . . £25/£5
A Small Town in Germany, Heinemann, 1968 £35/£10
ditto, Coward-McCann (U.S.), 1968 (500 signed copies, tissue d/w) . . . . . . £250/£200
ditto, Coward-McCann (U.S.), 1968. . . . £20/£5
The Naive and Sentimental Lover, Hodder & Stoughton, 1971 . . . . £25/£5
ditto, Knopf (U.S.), 1971 . . . . . . £15/£5
Tinker, Tailor, Soldier, Spy, Hodder & Stoughton, 1974 . . . . £25/£5
ditto, Knopf (U.S.), 1974 . . . . . . £15/£5
The Honourable Schoolboy, Franklin Library (U.S.), 1977 (signed, limited edition) £100
ditto, Knopf (U.S.), 1977 . . . . . . £15/£5
ditto, Hodder & Stoughton, 1977. . . . £25/£5
Smiley's People, Franklin Library (U.S.), 1979 (signed, limited edition) £100
ditto, Hodder & Stoughton, 1980. . . . £35/£5
ditto, Knopf (U.S.), 1980 . . . . . . £15/£5
ditto, Knopf (U.S.), 1980 (signed sheet tipped-in) . . . . £60/£30
The Little Drummer Girl, Knopf (U.S.), 1983 . £15/£5
ditto, Knopf (U.S.), 1983 (signed sheet tipped-in) . . . . £75/£40
ditto, Book of the Month Club (U.S.), 1983 (1,048 signed copies, slipcase) . . . . . £100/£75
ditto, Hodder & Stoughton, 1983. . . . £15/£5

ditto, Pan, 1987 (739 signed copies, wraps) . .   £50
A Perfect Spy, Hodder & Stoughton, 1986 . . £15/£5
ditto, London Limited Editions/Hodder & Stoughton,
1986 (250 signed copies, glassine d/w)   . £125/£100
ditto, Knopf (U.S.), 1986 . . . . £15/£5
ditto, Knopf (U.S.), 1986 (signed sheet tipped-in) . .
. . . . £60/£30
The Russia House, Knopf (U.S.), 1989 .   . . £15/£5
ditto, Knopf (U.S.), 1989 (signed sheet tipped-in) . .
. . . . £60/£30
ditto, Hodder & Stoughton, 1989.   . . . £15/£5
ditto, Hodder & Stoughton, 1989 (collectors' edition,
500 copies, quarter leather, slipcase) . . £75/£50
ditto, London Limited Editions, 1989 (250 signed
copies, glassine d/w). . . . . . . £125/£75
The Secret Pilgrim, Hodder & Stoughton, 1991 £15/£5
ditto, Knopf (U.S.), 1991 . . . . £15/£5
ditto, Knopf (U.S.), 1991 (signed sheet tipped-in) . .
. . . . £60/£30
The Night Manager, Hodder & Stoughton, 1993 . .
. . . . £15/£5
ditto, Knopf (U.S.), 1993 . . . . £15/£5
ditto, Knopf (U.S.), 1993 (signed sheet tipped-in) . .
. . . . £50/£25
Our Game, Hodder & Stoughton, 1995 . . . . .
. . . . £125/£50
ditto, Knopf (U.S.), 1995 . . . . £10/£5
The Tailor of Panama, Hodder & Stoughton, 1996 .
. . . . £10/£5
ditto, Knopf (U.S.), 1996 . . . . £10/£5
Single and Single, Hodder & Stoughton, 1999 . £10/£5
ditto, Scribner's (U.S.), 1999 . . . . . . £10/£5
The Constant Gardener, Hodder & Stoughton, 2001 .
. . . . £10/£5
ditto, Scribner's (U.S.), 2001 . . . . . £10/£5

Collections
The Le Carré Omnibus, Gollancz, 1964 . £75/£25
The Quest for Karla, Hodder & Stoughton, 1982 . .
. . . . £25/£5
ditto, Knopf (U.S.), 1982 . . . . £15/£5

Others
The Clandestine Muse, Seluzicki (U.S.), 1986 (250
signed copies, wraps) £200
Vanishing England, Salem House (U.S.), 1987 (with
Gareth H. Davies) . . . . £35/£15
*Nervous Times: An Address Given at the Savoy
Hotel...*, Anglo-Israel Association, 1998 (250 signed,
numbered copies) £125

HARPER LEE
(b.1926)

Lee's one and only novel, *To Kill a Mockingbird* is a
landmark of 20th century American literature and is
one of the best-selling novels of all time.

Novel
To Kill a Mockingbird, Lippincott (U.S.), 1960 (first
issue d/w with author photo by Truman Capote) . .
. . . . £6,000/£1,500
ditto, Heinemann, 1963 . . . . . . £450/£75

Other
Romance and High Adventure, Cather & Brown
(U.S.), 1993 (100 signed copies, wraps) . . £750

LAURIE LEE
(b.1914 d.1997)

Lee was primarily a poet, best known for his volumes
of autobiography. *Cider with Rosie* is a nostalgic
memoir of his Gloucestershire childhood.

Autobiography
Cider with Rosie, Hogarth Press, 1959 . . £125/£20
ditto, as *The Edge of Day*, Morrow (U.S.), 1960 . .
. . . . £40/£10
As I Walked Out One Midsummer Morning, Deutsch,
1969 . . . . £20/£5
ditto, Atheneum (U.S.), 1969 . . . . . . £10/£5
A Moment of War, Viking, 1991. . . . . £10/£5
ditto, New Press (U.S.), 1991. . . . . . £10/£5
Red Sky at Sunrise, Viking, 1992 (collects above
autobiographical works). . . . . . . £10/£5

Poetry
The Sun My Monument, Hogarth Press, 1944 £75/£25
ditto, Doubleday (U.S.), 1947 . . . . . £40/£15
The Bloom of Candles, Lehmann, 1947. . £40/£15
New Poems, 1954, Joseph, 1954 . . . . £25/£10
My Many-Coated Man, Deutsch, 1955 . . £25/£10
ditto, Coward-McCann (U.S.), 1957 . . . . £15/£5
Pocket Poets, Studio Vista, 1960. . . . . . £5
15 Poems for William Shakespeare, Trustees and
Guardians of Shakespeare's Birthplace, 1964 (wraps)
. . . . £20
Pergamon Poets 10, Pergamon Press, 1970 (wraps) £5
Selected Poems, Deutsch, 1983 (wraps). £5
Fish and Water, Friends of the Cheltenham Festival,
[1991] (broadsheet) £15
Boy in Ice, Turret Bookshop, [1991] (broadsheet) £40

Plays
Peasant's Priest, Friends of Canterbury Cathedral,
1947 . . . . £30/£10
The Voyage of Magellan, Lehmann, 1948 . £100/£15

Others

Land at War, H.M.S.O., 1945 (anonymous, wraps) £30
We Made a Film in Cyprus, Longman, 1947 (with
Ralph Keene). . . . . £65/£25
Vassos the Goatherd: A Story of Cyprus, Pilot Press,
1947 . . . . £45/£15
An Obstinate Exile, privately printed (U.S.), 1951
(glassine d/w). . . . . £125/£100
A Rose for Winter: Travels in Andalusia, Hogarth
Press, 1955 . . . . £50/£10
ditto, Morrow (U.S.), 1956 . . . . . £30/£10
Epstein: A Camera Study, Deutsch, 1956 . £35/£10
ditto, Deutsch, 1956 (200 signed copies, slipcase) .
. . . . £250/£200
Man Must Move, Rathbone, 1960 . . £25/£10
ditto, as *The Wonderful World of Transportation*,
Doubleday (U.S.), 1961 (with David Lambert) £20/£5
Atlantic Fairway, Cunard Line, [1962] (wraps) £15
The Firstborn, Hogarth Press, 1964 . . . £25/£10
ditto, Morrow (U.S.), 1964 . . . . . £15/£5
Paintings and Drawings of the Gypsies of Granada,
Athelnay Books (U.S.), 1969 . . . . £10
I Can't Stay Long, Deutsch, 1975 . . . £15/£5
ditto, Atheneum (U.S.), 1976. . . . . £10/£5
Innocence in the Mirror, Morrow (U.S.), 1978 £10/£5
Two Women, Deutsch, 1983 . . . . . £10/£5

J. SHERIDAN LE FANU
(b.1814 d.1873)

Anglo-Irish writer of mystery, supernatural and
historical romances.

Novels
The Cock and Anchor, Curry, Longmans, Fraser, 1845
(anonymous, 3 vols, boards) £2,000
ditto, as *Morley Court*, Chapman & Hall, 1873 (revised
edition) £50
The Fortunes of Colonel Torlogh O'Brien,
McGlashan, Orr, 1847 (anonymous, 10 monthly parts,
wraps). £1,000
ditto, McGlashan, Orr, 1847 (anonymous, 1 vol) £500
The House by the Church-Yard, Tinsley, 1863 (3 vols,
royal blue cloth) £5,000
ditto, Tinsley, 1863 (3 vols, green cloth) . . £3,500
ditto, Carleton (U.S.), 1866 (1 vol) . . . £750
Wylder's Hand, Bentley, 1864 (3 vols) . . . £4,000
ditto, Carleton (U.S.), 1865 (1 vol) . . . £750
Uncle Silas, Bentley, 1864 (3 vols) . . . £4,000
ditto, Munro (U.S.), 1878 (1 vol). . . . £500
Guy Deverell, Bentley, 1865 (3 vols) . . . £3,000
ditto, Harper (U.S.), 1866 (1 vol) . . . £750
All in the Dark, Bentley, 1866 (2 vols, claret cloth) .
. . . . £2,000
ditto, Bentley, 1866 (presentation copies, 2 vols, white
cloth) £3,000

The Tenants of Malory, Tinsley, 1867 (3 vols) . .
. . . . £3,000
ditto, Harper (U.S.), 1867 (1 vol) . . . £750
A Lost Name, Bentley, 1868 (3 vols) . . . £3,000
Haunted Lives, Tinsley, 1868 (3 vols) . . £3,000
The Wyvern Mystery, Tinsley, 1869 (3 vols) . £3,500
Checkmate, Hurst & Blackett, 1871 (3 vols) . £4,000
ditto, Evans (U.S.), 1871. . . . . . £750
The Rose and The Key, Chapman & Hall, 1871 (3
vols) £3,000
Willing to Die, Hurst & Blackett, 1873 (3 vols) £2,000

Short Stories and Collected Editions
Ghost Stories and Tales of Mystery, McGlashan, Orr,
1851 (anonymous, red pictorial boards). . . £5,000
ditto, McGlashan, Orr, 1851 (anonymous, with gold
blocking to front board) £3,000
ditto, McGlashan, Orr, 1851 (anonymous, no gold
blocking to front board) £750
Chronicles of Golden Friars, Bentley, 1871 (3 vols) .
. . . . £4,000
In A Glass Darkly, Bentley, 1872 (3 vols) . . £4,000
ditto, Peter Davis, 1929 (illustrated by Edward
Ardizzone) . . . . £250/£125
The Purcell Papers, Bentley, 1880 (3 vols). . £3,000
The Watcher, Downey, [1894] £400
The Evil Guest, Downey, [1895]. . . . £500
Madam Crowl's Ghost, Bell, 1923 . . . £400/£100
Green Tea and Other Ghost Stories, Arkham House
(U.S.), 1945 . . . . £175/£45
*A Strange Adventure in the Life of Miss Laura
Mildmay*, Home & Van Thal, 1947 . . £25/£10
Best Ghost Stories, Dover (U.S.), 1964 (wraps) . £5
Ghost Stories and Mysteries, Dover (U.S.), 1975
(wraps) £5
Borrhomeo The Astrologer, Tragara Press
(Edinburgh), 1985 (wraps) £35

Poetry
The Poems of Joseph Sheridan Le Fanu, Downey,
1896 . . . . £200

RICHARD LE GALLIENNE
(b.1866 d.1947)

Generally disregarded simply because he survived the
1890s, Le Gallienne is not overlooked by all
collectors of the period.

Fiction
The Student and the Body-Snatcher and Other Tales,
Elkin Mathews, 1890 (with R.K. Leather). . £65
The Book-Bills of Narcissus, Frank Murray, 1891 (250
small paper copies) £45
ditto, Frank Murray, 1891 (100 large paper copies,
wraps). £75
ditto, Putnam (U.S.), 1895 . . . . . £25

Limited editions: *A Prose Fancy; with, Confessio Amantis: A Sonnet*, privately printed for Richard Le Gallienne, Elkin Mathews, John Lane, and their Friends, Christmas 1893 (700 copies, wraps) . £50

Prose Fancies, Elkin Mathews & John Lane, 1894 £15
ditto, Frank Murray, 1894 (100 large paper copies, wraps). £75
ditto, Putnam (U.S.), 1894 . . . . . £25
Prose Fancies: Second Series, John Lane, 1896 £15
ditto, Stone (U.S.), 1896 . . . . . . £15
The Quest of the Golden Girl, John Lane, 1896 £75
The Romance of Zion Chapel, John Lane, 1898 £30
Young Lives, A Tale, Arrowsmith, 1899 . . £30
ditto, John Lane (U.S.), 1896. . . . . £30
The Worshipper of the Image, John Lane, 1900 £30
Sleeping Beauty and Other Prose Fancies, John Lane, 1900 . . . . £30
The Life Romantic, Including the Love-Letters of the King, Hurst & Blackett, 1901 . . . . . £35
ditto, as *The Love-Letters of the King, or The Life Romantic*, Little, Brown (U.S.), 1901 . . . £30
Romances of Old France, Baker & Taylor Co (U.S.), [1905]. £20
Little Dinners with The Sphinx and Other Prose Fancies, Moffat, Yard (U.S.), 1907 . . . £35
ditto, John Lane, 1909. . . . . . . £25
Painted Shadows, John Lane, 1908 [1907] . . £35
ditto, Little, Brown (U.S.), 1904 . . . . . £35
The Maker of Rainbows, with Other Fairy-Tales and Fables, Harper (U.S.), 1912. . . . . . £35
The Highway to Happiness, Morningside Press (U.S.), 1913 . . . . £30
ditto, T. Werner Laurie, [1914] £30
Pieces of Eight, Collins, 1918 . . . £45/£15
ditto, Doubleday (U.S.), 1918 . . . . £45/£15
Old Love Stories Retold, John Lane, 1924 . £45/£10
ditto, Dodd, Mead and Co. (U.S.), 1925 . . £45/£10
The Magic Seas, H. Toulmin, 1930 . . . £35/£10
There Was A Ship, Doubleday (U.S.), 1930 £35/£10

Poetry
My Ladies' Sonnets and Other 'Vain and Amatorious' Verses, with Some of Graver Mood, privately printed, 1887 . . . . . . £150
ditto, privately printed, 1887 (50 signed copies) £300
Volumes in Folio, Elkin Mathews, 1889 . . £125
ditto, Elkin Mathews, 1889 (250 copies) . . £300
ditto, Elkin Mathews, 1889 (50 large paper copies) £300
English Poems, Elkin Mathews & John Lane, 1892 .
. . . . £50
A Fellowship in Song, Elkin Mathews & John Lane, 1893 (with A. Hayes and N. Gale) . . . £20
Robert Louis Stevenson: An Elegy and Other Poems, John Lane, 1895 . . . . £10
ditto, John Lane, 1895 (500 copies) £100
ditto, John Lane, 1895 (75 large paper copies) . £200
ditto, Copeland and Day (U.S.), ... £10

Holly and Mistletoe, Marcus Ward, 1896 (with E. Nesbit and N. Gale) £45
Rubaiyat of Omar Khayyam: A Paraphrase, Grant Richards, 1897 . . . . £25
Odes from the Divan of Hafiz, Duckworth, 1903 £40
Omar Repentant, Grant Richards, 1908 . . . £20
ditto, Kennerley (U.S.), [c.1908] £20
New Poems, John Lane, 1910 . . . . . £10
Orestes: A Tragedy, Kennerley (U.S.), 1910 . £20
The Lonely Dancer and Other Poems, John Lane, 1914 . . . . £10
The Silk-Hat Soldier and Other Poems, John Lane, 1915 (wraps) £20
The Junk-Man and Other Poems, Doubleday, Page & Co., 1920 . . . . £10
A Jongleur Strayed: Verses on Love and Other Matters, Sacred and Profane, Doubleday, Page & Co., 1922 (1,500 numbered copies) . . £30/£10

Non Fiction
George Meredith: Some Characteristics, Elkin Mathews, 1890 . . . . £10
The Religion of a Literary Man, Elkin Mathews & John Lane, 1893 . . . . £10
ditto, Putnam (U.S.), 1893 . . . . . . £10
Retrospective Reviews: A Literary Log, John Lane, 1896 (2 vols) £15
If I Were God, privately printed by James Bowden, 1897 . . . . £30
ditto, Crowell & Co. (U.S.), [c.1897] . . . £30
Rudyard Kipling: A Criticism, John Lane, 1900 £25
Travels in England, Grant Richards, 1900 . . £25
ditto, John Lane (U.S.), 1900. . . . . . £25
The Beautiful Life of Rome, Simpkin, Marshall, Hamilton, Kent & Co, 1900. . . . . . £10
An Old Country House, Grant Richards, 1902 . £30
ditto, Harper (U.S.), 1902. . . . . . . £30
Tristan and Isolde, Stokes (U.S.), 1909 (translated into verse by Le Gallienne) £75
October Vagabonds, John Lane, 1910 . . . £10
ditto, Kennerley (U.S.), 1910. . . . . . £10
Attitudes and Avowals, John Lane (U.S.), 1910 £10
ditto, John Lane, 1910 [1911] £10
The Loves of the Poets, Baker & Taylor Co. (U.S.), [1911]. £30
Vanishing Roads and Other Essays, Putnam, 1915 £10
ditto, Putnam (U.S.), 1915 . . . . . . £10
The Romantic 90s, Doubleday (U.S.), 1925 £50/£15
ditto, Putnam, 1926 . . . . . . £50/£15
The Romance of Perfume, Hudnut (U.S.), 1928 (boards, glassine d/w, slipcase, brochure in pocket at rear) . . . . £120/£60
Exaggerated Nationalism: An Essay, Press of the Woolly Whale (U.S.), 1935 (wraps) . . . £20
From a Paris Garret, Richards Press, 1936 . £30/£10
ditto, Washburn (U.S.), 1936 . . . . £30/£10
The Cry of the Little Peoples, privately printed, 1941 .
. . . . £25

URSULA LE GUIN
(b.1929)

An American novelist, poet and critic, Le Guin is admired for her science fiction novels and for the 'Earthsea' fantasy books for children.

Children's Titles

A Wizard of Earthsea, Parnassus Press (U.S.), 1968 (faint vertical line or smudge on title page, d/w priced $3.95) . . . . £1,250/£300

ditto, Parnassus Press (U.S.), 1968 (no line or smudge, unpriced d/w). . . . . £125/£25

ditto, Penguin Books: Puffin, 1971 (wraps, illustrated by Ruth Robbins) £10

ditto, Gollancz, 1971 . . . . . . £150/£35

The Tombs of Atuan, Atheneum (U.S.), 1971 . . . . £125/£25

ditto, Gollancz, 1972 . . . . . £100/£20

The Farthest Shore, Atheneum (U.S.), 1972 £100/£20

ditto, Gollancz, 1973 . . . . . . £65/£15

Very Far Away From Anywhere Else, Atheneum (U.S.), 1976 . . . . £25/£5

ditto, as *A Very Long Way from Anywhere Else*, Gollancz, 1976 . . . . £20/£5

Leese Webster, Atheneum (U.S.), 1979 . . £20/£5

ditto, Gollancz, 1981 . . . . . . £15/£5

The Beginning Place, Harper (U.S.), 1980 . £20/£5

ditto, as *Threshold*, Gollancz, 1980 . . . £20/£5

Visit from Dr Katz, Atheneum (U.S.), 1988 (picture book; boards). £5

ditto, Collins, 1988 . . . . £5

Catwings, Orchard (U.S.), 1988 . . . . £10/£5

Catwings Return, Orchard (U.S.), 1989. . £10/£5

Fire and Stone, Atheneum (U.S.), 1989. . £10/£5

Tehanu, Atheneum (U.S.), 1990. . . . £10/£5

ditto, Gollancz, 1990 . . . . . . £10/£5

The Adventures of Cobbler's Rune, Cheap Street (U.S.), 1982 (26 signed, lettered copies) . . £200

ditto, Cheap Street (U.S.), 1982 (250 signed, lettered copies) £50

Solomon Leviathan's 931st Trip Around the World, Cheap Street (U.S.), 1983 (26 signed, lettered copies) £200

ditto, Cheap Street (U.S.), 1983 (250 signed, lettered copies) £50

ditto, Philomel (U.S.), 1984 . . . . . £15/£5

Fish Soup, Atheneum (U.S.), 1992 . . . £10/£5

A Ride on the Red Mare's Back, Orchard (U.S.), 1992 . . . . £10/£5

Jane On Her Own, Orchard (U.S.), 1999 . £10/£5

Novels

The Left Hand of Darkness, Ace (U.S.), 1969 (wraps, no mention of Hugo and Nebula awards) . . £25

ditto, Walker (U.S.), 1969 . . . . £200/£35

ditto, Macdonald, 1969 . . . . . £100/£20

City of Illusions, Ace (U.S.), 1971 (wraps) . . £10

ditto, Gollancz, 1971 . . . . . . £65/£15

ditto, Garland (U.S.), 1975 (no d/w) £35

Rocannon's World, Ace (U.S.), 1966 (wraps) . . £5

ditto, Tandem, 1972 (wraps) £5

ditto, Garland (U.S.), 1975 (no d/w) . . . £35

Planet of Exile, Ace (U.S.), 1966 (wraps) . . . £5

ditto, Tandem, 1972 (wraps) £5

ditto, Garland (U.S.), 1975 (no d/w) £35

The Lathe of Heaven, Scribner's (U.S.), 1971 . . . . £125/£25

ditto, Gollancz, 1972 . . . . . . £65/£20

The Dispossessed, Harper (U.S.), [1974] . £125/£25

ditto, Gollancz, 1974 . . . . . . £50/£20

The Word for World is Forest, Putnam (U.S.), 1976 . . . . £25/£5

ditto, Gollancz, 1977 . . . . . . £15/£5

Malafrena, Putnam (U.S.), 1979. . . . £15/£5

ditto, Gollancz, 1980 . . . . . . £10/£5

The Eye of the Heron, Harper (U.S.), 1982. £15/£5

ditto, Gollancz, 1983 . . . . . . £10/£5

The Visionary, Capra (U.S.), 1985 (with *Wonders Hidden* by Scott Saunders, wraps) £5

Always Coming Home, Harper (U.S.), 1985 . £10/£5

ditto, Harper (U.S.), 1985 (unspecified number of signed copies with cassette in slipcase) . £100/£35

ditto, Gollancz, 1986 . . . . . . £10/£5

ditto, Gollancz, 1986 (100 signed copies with cassette in slipcase) . . . . £75/£35

The Telling, Harcourt Brace (U.S.), 2000 . £10/£5

Short Stories

From Elfland to Ploughkeepsie, Pendragon Press/ Oregon Press (U.S.), 1973 (26 signed hardback copies, no d/w) £250

ditto, Pendragon Press/Oregon Press (U.S.), 1973 (100 signed copies, wraps) £50

ditto, Pendragon Press/Oregon Press (U.S.), 1973 (650 trade copies, wraps) £15

The Wind's Twelve Quarters, Harper (U.S.), 1975. . . . . £25/£5

ditto, Gollancz, 1976 . . . . . . £20/£5

Orsinian Tales, Harper (U.S.), 1976. . . £20/£5

ditto, Gollancz, 1977 . . . . . . £10/£5

The Water is Wide, Pendragon Press (U.S.), 1976 (50 signed copies, no d/w) £100

ditto, Pendragon Press (U.S.), 1976 (950 signed copies) . . . . £15/£5

The Compass Rose, Pendragon Press/Underwood-Miller (U.S.), 1982 (550 signed copies) . £45/£25

ditto, Harper (U.S.), 1982. . . . . £30/£10

ditto, Gollancz, 1983 . . . . . . £25/£5

Gwilan's Harp, Lord John Press (U.S.), 1981 (50 signed, numbered handbound, cloth copies of 350) £100

ditto, Lord John Press (U.S.), 1981 (300 signed copies of 350, wraps in d/w) . . . . . £25/£10

Buffalo Gals and Other Animal Presences, Capra Press (U.S.), 1987 . . . . £15/£5

ditto, Gollancz, 1990 . . . . . . £10/£5

Searoad, Harper (U.S.), 1991 . . . . £10/£5

ditto, Gollancz, 1992 . . . . £10/£5
A Fisherman of the Inland Sea, Harper Prism (U.S.), 1994 (526 copies, no d/w) £25
ditto, Harper Prism (U.S.), 1994 (1,500 advance copies) . . . . £25/£10
ditto, Gollancz, 1994 . . . . £10/£5
Four Ways to Forgiveness, Easton Press, 1995 (signed limited edition) £45
ditto, Harper Prism (U.S.), 1995 . . . . . £10/£5
Unlocking the Air and Other Stories, Harper (U.S.), 1996 . . . . £10/£5

Poetry
Wild Angels, Capra Press (U.S.), 1973 (200 signed, numbered copies) £45
Hard Words and Other Poems, Harper (U.S.), 1981 .
. . . . £20/£5
Wild Oats and Fireweed, Harper (U.S.), 1988 . £10/£5
Going Out With Peacocks and Other Poems, Harper (U.S.), 1994 (wraps) £10
The Twins, The Dream/Las Gemelas, El Sueño, Arte Publico Press (U.S.), 1996 (with Diana Bellessi, wraps) £10
Sixty Odd: New Poems, Shambhala (U.S.), 1999 £10
Walking in Cornwall: A Poem for the Solstice, Portland Press (U.S.), 1996 (wraps) . . . £25

Others
Dreams Must Explain Themselves, Algol Press (U.S.), 1973 (1,000 numbered copies, wraps) . . . £15
In The Red Zone, Lord John Press, 1983 (25 signed copies) £100
ditto, Lord John Press, 1983 (50 signed deluxe copies)
. . . . £100
ditto, Lord John Press, 1983 (150 signed copies) £50
King Dog, Capra Press (U.S.), 1986 (with Tess Gallagher, bound in with *Dostoevsky: A Screenplay* by Raymond Carver, wraps) £25
ditto, Capra (U.S.), 1985 (200 copies signed by all authors, wraps) £100
Language of the Night: Essays on Fantasy and Science Fiction, Putnam (U.S.), 1979 . . . £15/£5
ditto, Women's Press, 1989 (revised edition, wraps) £5
Dancing at the Edge of the World: Thoughts on Words, Women and Places, Grove Press (U.S.), 1989
. . . . £10/£5
ditto, Gollancz, 1989 . . . . £10/£5
Findings, Ox Head Press, 1992 (26 signed, lettered copies) £125
Lorenzo Bean, Dozing, Parchment Gallery Graphics, 1998 (100 signed, numbered copies, sketch, broadsheet) £40

ROSAMOND LEHMANN
(b.1903 d.1990)

A writer whose novels often deal with the emotional development of womanhood.

Novels
Dusty Answer, Chatto & Windus, 1927 . . £125/£20
ditto, Holt (U.S.), 1927 . . . . . . £40/£10
A Note in Music, Chatto & Windus, 1930 . £35/£10
ditto, Chatto & Windus, 1930 (260 signed copies) £100
. . . . £20/£5
ditto, Holt (U.S.), 1930 . . . . £20/£5
ditto, Holt (U.S.), 1930 (300 signed copies). . £75
Invitation to the Waltz, Chatto & Windus, 1932 . .
. . . . £30/£10
ditto, Holt (U.S.), 1932 . . . . £15/£5
The Weather in the Streets, Collins, 1936 . £45/£15
ditto, Reynal Hitchcock (U.S.), 1936 . . . £15/£5
The Ballad and the Source, Collins, 1944 . . £20/£5
ditto, Reynal Hitchcock (U.S.), 1945 . . . £15/£5
The Echoing Grove, Collins, 1953 . . . £25/£5
ditto, Harcourt Brace (U.S.), 1953 . . . . £20/£5
A Sea-Grape Tree, Collins, 1976 . . . . £15/£5
ditto, Harcourt Brace (U.S.), 1977 . . . . £15/£5

Short Stories
The Gipsy's Baby and Other Stories, Collins, 1946 .
. . . . £25/£10
ditto, Reynal Hitchcock (U.S.), 1947 . . £25/£10

Others
Letter to a Sister, Hogarth Press, 1931 (wraps) . £25
ditto, Harcourt Brace (U.S.), 1932 . . . . £10
No More Music, Collins, 1939 . . . . £45/£10
ditto, Reynal Hitchcock (U.S.), 1945 . . £35/£10
A Man Seen Afar, Spearman, 1965 (with W. Tudor Pole) . . . . £20/£5
The Swan in the Evening: Fragments of an Inner Life, Collins, 1967 . . . . £15/£5
ditto, Harcourt Brace (U.S.), 1967 . . . . £15/£5
Letters from Our Daughters, College of Psychic Studies, 1972 (with Cynthia Hill Sandys, 2 vols) £20

ELMORE LEONARD
(b.1925)

Leonard had his first success in 1951 with 'Trail of the Apache'. Despite early recognition as the writer of westerns, his crime novels have become more popular in recent years, in part thanks to Hollywood. Quentin Tarantino directed 'Jackie Brown,' a film based on Leonard's novel *Rum Punch*, in 1997.

'Chili Palmer' novels
Get Shorty, Delacorte (U.S.), 1990 . . . . £20/£5
ditto, Viking, 1990 . . . . £20/£5
Be Cool, Delacorte (U.S.), 1999 . . . . £10/£5
ditto, Viking, 1999 . . . . £10/£5

'Frank Ryan' novels
Swag, Delacorte (U.S.), 1976. . . . . £200/£25
ditto, Secker & Warburg, 1976 . . . . £75/£25
Unknown Man No. 89, Delacorte (U.S.), 1977. . .
. . . . £250/£45
ditto, Secker & Warburg, 1977 . . . . £75/£25

'Raylan Givens' novels
Pronto, Delacorte, Arbor House (U.S.), 1993 . £15/£5
ditto, Viking, 1993 . . . .£15/£5
Riding the Rap, Delacorte, Arbor House (U.S.), 1995 .
. . . .£15/£5
ditto, Viking, 1995 . . . .£15/£5

Other novels
The Bounty Hunters, Houghton-Mifflin (U.S.), 1953 .
. . . . £2,500/£300
ditto, Ballantine (U.S.), 1953 (wraps) . . . £75
ditto, Hale, 1956 . . . . £750/£75
The Law at Randado, Houghton-Mifflin (U.S.), 1954 .
. . . . £1,500/£250
ditto, Hale, 1957 . . . . £500/£50
Escape from Five Shadows, Houghton-Mifflin (U.S.),
1956 . . . . £1,000/£150
ditto, Hale, 1957 . . . . £450/£50
Last Stand at Saber River, Dell (U.S.), 1959 (wraps) .
. . . . £45
ditto, as *Lawless River*, Hale, 1961 . . . £750/£75
Hombre, Ballantine (U.S.), 1961 (wraps) . . £100
ditto, Hale, 1961 . . . . £750/£75
The Big Bounce, Fawcett Gold Medal (U.S.), 1969
(wraps) £45
ditto, Hale, 1969 . . . . £450/£50
The Moonshine War, Doubleday (U.S.), 1969 . . . .
. . . . £300/£65
ditto, Hale, 1970 . . . . £250/£30
Valdez is Coming, Hale, 1969 . . . . £300/£40
ditto, Fawcett Gold Medal (U.S.), 1970 (wraps) £45
Forty Lashes Less One, Bantam (U.S.), 1972 (wraps) .
. . . . £30
Mr Majestyk, Dell (U.S.), 1974 (wraps). . . £30
Fifty-Two Pickup, Delacorte (U.S.), 1974 . £200/£25
ditto, Secker & Warburg, 1974 . . . . £125/£25
The Hunted, Dell (U.S.), 1977 (wraps) . . . £25
ditto, Secker & Warburg, 1978 . . . . £75/£25
The Switch, Bantam (U.S.), 1978 (wraps) . . £25
ditto, Secker & Warburg, 1979 . . . . £75/£25
Gunsights, Bantam (U.S.), 1979 (wraps) . . £25
City Primeval: High Noon in Detroit, Arbor House
(U.S.), 1980 . . . . £35/£10
ditto, W.H. Allen, 1981 . . . . . . £45/£15
Gold Coast, Bantam (U.S.), 1980 (wraps) . . £20
ditto, W.H. Allen, 1982 . . . . . . £25/£10
Split Images, Arbor House (U.S.), 1981. . £35/£10
ditto, W.H. Allen, 1983 . . . . . . £25/£10
Cat Chaser, Arbor House (U.S.), 1982 . . £25/£10
ditto, Viking, 1986 . . . . £25/£10
Stick, Arbor House (U.S.), 1983 . . . . £25/£10
ditto, Allen Lane, 1984 . . . . . . £25/£10

LaBrava, Arbor House (U.S.), 1983 . . . £25/£10
ditto, Viking, 1984 . . . . £25/£10
Glitz, Viking, 1985 . . . . £25/£10
ditto, Arbor House (U.S.), 1986 . . . . £25/£10
ditto, Arbor House (U.S.), 1986 (26 signed lettered
copies, slipcase) £250
ditto, Arbor House (U.S.), 1986 (500 signed copies,
slipcase) £100
Bandits, Arbor House (U.S.), 1987 . . . £25/£10
ditto, Viking, 1987 . . . . £25/£10
Touch, Arbor House (U.S.), 1987 . . . £20/£10
ditto, Viking, 1988 . . . . £20/£10
Freaky Deaky, Arbor House/Morrow (U.S.), 1988. . .
. . . . £20/£10
ditto, Viking, 1988 . . . . £20/£10
Killshot, Arbor House/Morrow (U.S.), 1989 . £15/£5
ditto, Viking, 1989 . . . .£15/£5
Maximum Bob, Delacorte, Arbor House (U.S.), 1991 .
. . . .£15/£5
ditto, Viking, 1991 . . . .£15/£5
Rum Punch, Delacorte, Arbor House (U.S.), 1992. . .
. . . .£30/£5
ditto, Viking, 1992 . . . .£30/£5
ditto, as *Jackie Brown*, Dell, Arbor House (U.S.), 1997
(wraps) £5
Out of Sight Delacorte (U.S.), 1996 . . . .£15/£5
ditto, Viking, 1996 . . . .£15/£5
Cuba Libre, Delacorte (U.S.), 1998 . . . .£10/£5
ditto, Viking, 1998 . . . .£10/£5
Pagan Babies, Delacorte (U.S.), 2000 . . .£10/£5
ditto, Viking, 2000 . . . .£10/£5
Tishomingo Blues, Morrow (U.S.), 2002 . .£10/£5

Short Stories
The Tonto Woman and other Western Stories,
Delacorte (U.S.), 1998 . . . .£15/£5
ditto, Viking, 1999 . . . .£15/£5
*When the Women Come Out to Dance: And Other
Stories*, Morrow (U.S.), 2002 . . . . .£10/£5
ditto, Viking, 2003 . . . .£10/£5

Collected Editions
Dutch Treat, Arbor House (U.S.), 1985 (contains *The
Hunted*, *Swag* and *Mr Majestyk*) . . .£15/£5
ditto, Mysterious Press (U.S.), 1985 (350 signed,
numbered copies, slipcase, no d/w). . .£30/£15
Double Dutch Treat, Arbor House (U.S.), 1985
(contains *The Moonshine War*, *Gold Coast* and *City
Primeval*). . . . .£15/£5

Other
Naked Came the Manatee, Putnam's (U.S.), 1996
(novel written with 12 other writers) . . .£10/£5

GASTON LEROUX
(b.1868 d.1927)

Celebrated in his lifetime as an author of detective fiction, Leroux's posthumous reputation is based mainly on *The Phantom of the Opera*, the basis for Andrew Lloyd Webber's hugely successful staged musical.

The Mystery of the Yellow Room, Daily Mail Sixpenny
Novels, 1908 (wraps) £30
ditto, Brentano's (U.S.), 1908 . . . . . £50
ditto, Edward Arnold, 1909 . . . . . . £40
The Double Life, Kearney (U.S.), 1909 . . . £50
ditto, Laurie, 1910 (wraps) £15
ditto, as *The Man With the Black Feather*, Hurst &
Blackett, 1912 . . . . £30
ditto, as *The Man With the Black Feather*, Small
(U.S.), 1912 . . . . £30
The Perfume of the Lady in Black, Daily Mail
Sixpenny Novels, 1909 (wraps). £25
ditto, Brentano's (U.S.), 1908 . . . . . £40
ditto, Eveleigh Nash, 1911 . . . . . . £25
The Phantom of the Opera, Mills & Boon, 1911 £300
ditto, Bobbs-Merrill (U.S.), 1911 (colour plates) £600
ditto, Grosset & Dunlap, [1925] (colour plates).
. . . . £250/£35
Balaoo, Hurst & Blackett, 1913 . . . . . £35
The Secret of the Night, Eveleigh Nash, 1914 . £35
ditto, Macaulay (U.S.), 1914 . . . . . £35
The Bride of the Sun, McBride-Nast (U.S.), 1915 £45
ditto, Hodder & Stoughton, 1918. . . . . £45
The Man Who Came Back From the Dead, Eveleigh
Nash, 1916 . . . . £35
The Floating Prison, Laurie, 1922 . . . £150/£20
ditto, as *Wolves of the Sea*, Macaulay (U.S.), 1923 .
. . . . £150/£20
The Amazing Adventures of Carolous Herbert, Mills
& Boon, 1922 . . . . £150/£20
Cheri-Bibi and Cecily, Laurie, 1923 . . . £150/£20
ditto, as *Missing Men*, Macaulay (U.S.), 1923 . .
. . . . £150/£20
The Veiled Prisoner, Mills & Boon, 1923 . £125/£15
Cheri-Bibi, Mystery Man, John Long, 1924 £125/£15
ditto, as *The Dark Road*, Macaulay (U.S.), 1924 . .
. . . . £100/£15
The Dancing Girl, John Long, 1925. . . £100/£15
ditto, as *Nomads of the Night*, Macaulay (U.S.), 1925.
. . . . £100/£15
The Burgled Heart, John Long, 1925 . £150/£25
ditto, as *The New Terror*, Macaulay (U.S.), 1926 . .
. . . . £150/£25
The Slave Bangle, John Long, 1925. . . £100/£15
ditto, as *The Phantom Clue*, Macaulay (U.S.), 1926 .
. . . . £100/£15
The Sleuth Hound, John Long, 1926 . . £100/£15
ditto, as *The Octopus of Paris*, Macaulay (U.S.), 1927
. . . . £100/£15
The Adventures of a Coquette, Laurie, 1926 £100/£15

The Masked Man, John Long, 1927. . . £100/£15
ditto, Macaulay (U.S.), 1929 . . . , , . £100/£15
The Son of Three Fathers, John Long, 1927 £75/£15
ditto, Macaulay (U.S.), 1928 . . . . . £75/£15
The New Idol, John Long, 1928. . . . . £75/£15
ditto, Macaulay (U.S.), 1929 . . . . . £75/£15
The Midnight Lady, John Long, 1930 . . £65/£15
The Man of a Hundred Masks, Cassel, 1930 £65/£15
ditto, as *The Man of a Hundred Faces*, Macaulay
(U.S.), 1930 . . . . £65/£15
The Haunted Chair, Dutton (U.S.), 1931 . £50/£10
The Missing Archduke, John Long, 1931 . £50/£10
Lady Helena, Laurie, 1931 . . . . . . £50/£10
ditto, Dutton (U.S.), 1931. . . . . . £50/£10
The Kiss That Killed, Macaulay (U.S.), 1934 £45/£10
The Machine to Kill, Macaulay (U.S.), 1935 £45/£10
Gaston Leroux's Crime Omnibus Book, Laurie, 1935
. . . . £35/£10
The Gaston Leroux Bedside Companion, Gollancz,
1980 . . . . £10/£5

DORIS LESSING
(b.1919)

Lessing's first novel is a study of a white woman's obsession with her black servant, and is the first of many novels which suggest a fascination with the private world of the mind.

'Canopus in Argos' Novels
Re: Colonised Planet 5, Shikasta, Cape, 1979 . £20/£5
ditto, Knopf (U.S.), 1979 . . . . . . £20/£5
The Marriages Between Zones Three, Four and Five,
Cape, 1980 . . . . £20/£5
ditto, Knopf (U.S.), 1980 . . . . . . £15/£5
The Sirian Experiments, Cape, 1981 . . . £15/£5
ditto, Knopf (U.S.), 1981 . . . . . . £15/£5
The Making of the Representative for Planet 8, Cape,
1982 . . . . £15/£5
ditto, Knopf (U.S.), 1982 . . . . . . £15/£5
*Documents Relating to the Sentimental Agents in the
Volyen Empire*, Cape, 1983. . . . . £15/£5
ditto, Knopf (U.S.), 1983 . . . . . . £15/£5

'Children of Violence' Novels
Martha Quest, Joseph, 1952 . . . . . £100/£25
A Proper Marriage, Joseph, 1954 . . . £45/£10
A Ripple from the Storm, Joseph, 1958 . £40/£10
Children of Violence, Volumes 1 & 2, Simon &
Schuster (U.S.), 1964 (contains *Martha's Quest* and *A
Proper Marriage*) . . . . £45/£10
Landlocked, MacGibbon & Kee, 1965 . . £40/£10
Children of Violence, Volumes 3 & 4, Simon &
Schuster (U.S.), 1966 (contains *Ripple from the Storm*
and *Landlocked*) . . . . £25/£5
The Four-Gated City, MacGibbon & Kee, 1969 £50/£10
ditto, Knopf (U.S.), 1969 . . . . . . £45/£10

'Fifth Child' Novels

The Fifth Child, Cape, 1988 . . . . . . £15/£5
ditto, Knopf (U.S.), 1988 . . . . £15/£5
Ben, in the World, Flamingo, 2000 . . . £10/£5
ditto, HarperCollins (U.S.), 2000. . . . £10/£5

Other Novels

The Grass is Singing, Joseph, 1950 . . . £350/£45
ditto, Crowel (U.S.), 1950 . . . . . £200/£25
Retreat to Innocence, Joseph, 1956 . . . £45/£10
The Golden Notebook, Joseph, 1962 . . £150/£5
ditto, Simon & Schuster (U.S.), 1962 . . £30/£5
Briefing for a Descent into Hell, Cape, 1971 . £25/£5
ditto, Knopf (U.S.), 1971 . . . . £25/£5
The Summer Before the Dark, Cape, 1973 . . £30/£5
ditto, Knopf (U.S.), 1973 . . . . £25/£5
The Memoirs of a Survivor, Octagon Press, 1974 .
. . . . £25/£5
ditto, Knopf (U.S.), 1975 . . . . £25/£5
The Diary of a Good Neighbour, Cape, 1983 (pseud.
'Jane Somers') . . . . £15/£5
ditto, Knopf (U.S.), 1983 . . . . £15/£5
If the Old Could, Cape, 1984 (pseud. 'Jane Somers') .
. . . . £15/£5
ditto, Knopf (U.S.), 1984 . . . . £15/£5
The Good Terrorist, Cape, 1985 . . . . . £15/£5
ditto, Knopf (U.S.), 1985 . . . . £15/£5
Love, Again, Flamingo, 1996. . . . . . £10/£5
ditto, HarperCollins (U.S.), 1996. . . . . £10/£5
Playing the Game, HarperCollins, 1995 (graphic
novel) £10
Mara and Dann, an Adventure, HarperCollins, 1999 .
. . . . £10/£5
ditto, HarperCollins (U.S.), 1999. . . . . £10/£5
The Sweetest Dream, Flamingo, 2001 . . £10/£5
ditto, HarperCollins (U.S.), 2002. . . . . £10/£5

Short Stories

This Was the Old Chief's Country, Joseph, 1951 . .
. . . . £125/£25
ditto, Crowel (U.S.), 1952 . . . . . £100/£20
Five: Short Novels, Joseph, 1953 . . £65/£10
The Habit of Loving, MacGibbon & Kee, 1957 £40/£10
ditto, Crowel (U.S.), 1958 . . . . . . £35/£5
A Man and Two Women, Stories, MacGibbon & Kee,
1963 . . . . £40/£10
ditto, Simon & Schuster (U.S.), 1963 . . £35/£5
African Stories, Joseph, 1964 . . £40/£10
ditto, Simon & Schuster (U.S.), 1965 . . £35/£5
The Black Madonna, Panther, 1966 (wraps) . £10
Winter in July, Panther, 1966 (wraps) . . . £10
Nine African Stories, Longman, 1968 . £35/£10
The Story of a Non-Marrying Man, Cape, 1972 . .
. . . . £25/£5
ditto, as *The Temptation of Jack Orkney*, Knopf
(U.S.), 1972 . . . . £25/£5
Collected African Stories, Joseph, 1973 (2 vols, *This
Was the Old Chief's Country* and *The Sun Between
their Feet*) . . . . £25/£5
Collected Stories, Cape, 1978 (2 vols, *To Room Nine-*

teen and *The Temptation of Jack Orkney*) . £20/£5
ditto, as *Stories*, Knopf (U.S.), 1979 . . . £20/£5
The Doris Lessing Reader, Knopf (U.S.), 1988 £10/£5
ditto, Cape, 1989 . . . . £10/£5
London Observed, HarperCollins, 1992. . . £15/£5
ditto, as *The Real Thing*, HarperCollins (U.S.), 1992 .
. . . . £15/£5
ditto, as *The Real Thing*, Ultramarine Publishing
Company (U.S.), 1992 (38 signed copies) . . £100
ditto, Ultramarine Publishing Company (U.S.), 1992
(12 signed copies in full leather) £150
Spies I Have Known and Other Stories, Cascade/
Collins Educational, 1995 . . . . . . £10/£5
The Grandmothers, Flamingo, 2003 . . . £10/£5

Others

Going Home, Joseph, 1957 . . . . . £75/£15
ditto, Ballantine (U.S.), 1968 . . . . £5
A Small Personal Voice, MacGibbon & Kee, 1957 .
. . . . £30/£10
ditto, Dutton (U.S.), 1958 . . . . . . £25/£5
Fourteen Poems, Scorpion Press, 1959 (500 copies,
wraps) £50
ditto, Scorpion Press, 1959 (50 signed copies, wraps) .
. . . . £250
In Pursuit of the English, A Documentary, Mac-
Gibbon & Kee, 1960. . . . . £20/£5
ditto, as *Portrait of the English*, Simon & Schuster
(U.S.), 1961 . . . . £15/£5
Play with a Tiger, Joseph, 1962 . . . . £60/£10
Particularly Cats, Joseph, 1967 . . . . £35/£5
ditto, Simon & Schuster (U.S.), 1967 . . . £35/£5
ditto, as *Particularly Cats... and Rufus*, Simon &
Schuster (U.S.), 1967 . . . . £20/£5
ditto, as *Particularly Cats and More Cats*, Joseph,
1989 . . . . £15/£5
ditto, as *Particularly Cats and Rufus the Survivor*,
Knopf (U.S.), 1991 . . . . £15/£5
ditto, as *The Old Age of El Magnificato*, Burford
Books (U.S.), 2000 . . . . £10/£5
ditto, as *Particularly Cats*, Flamingo, 2000 . £10/£5
Prisons We Choose to Live Inside, C.B.C. (Canada),
1986 (wraps) £10
ditto, Cape, 1987 . . . . £15/£5
ditto, Harper & Row (U.S.), 1987 . . . £15/£5
The Wind Blows Away Our Words, Picador, 1987 . .
. . . . £15/£5
ditto, Vintage (U.S.), 1987 . . . . . . £15/£5
African Laughter, HarperCollins, 1992 . . . £10/£5
ditto, HarperCollins (U.S.), 1992. . . . . £10/£5
Conversations, Ontario Review Press (U.S.), 1994. .
. . . . £15/£5
ditto, as *Putting the Questions Differently*, Flamingo,
1996 . . . . £10/£5
Under My Skin, HarperCollins, 1994 . . . £10/£5
ditto, HarperCollins (U.S.), 1994. . . . . £10/£5
Walking in the Shade, HarperCollins, 1997 . £10/£5
ditto, HarperCollins (U.S.), 1997. . . . . £10/£5
Problems, Myths and Stories, Institute for Cultural
Research, 1999 (wraps) £5

C.S. LEWIS
(b.1898 d.1963)

Arguably best known for his children's books, Lewis also wrote a handful of science fiction novels, and a great number of theological works.

Children's Titles
The Lion, The Witch and The Wardrobe, Bles, 1950 .
. . . . £5,000/£500
ditto, Macmillan (U.S.), 1950 . . . . £750/£200
Prince Caspian: The Return to Narnia, Bles, 1951 .
. . . . £1,000/£150
ditto, Macmillan (U.S.), 1951 . . . . £250/£50
The Voyage of the 'Dawn Treader', Bles, 1952 . .
. . . . £1,000/£150
ditto, Macmillan (U.S.), 1952 . . . . £250/£50
The Silver Chair, Bles, 1953 . . . . £2,500/£400
ditto, Macmillan (U.S.), 1953 . . . . £250/£50
The Horse and His Boy, Bles, 1954 . . £1,000/£150
ditto, Macmillan (U.S.), 1954 . . . . £250/£50
The Magician's Nephew, Bles, 1955 . £750/£150
ditto, Macmillan (U.S.), 1955 . . . . £250/£50
The Last Battle, Bles, 1956 . . . . . £750/£150
ditto, Macmillan (U.S.), 1956 . . . . £250/£50

Novels
Out of the Silent Planet, Bodley Head, 1938 . . .
. . . . £2,000/£400
ditto, Macmillan (U.S.), 1943 . . . . £125/£35
Perelandra, Bodley Head, 1943 . . . . £300/£75
ditto, Macmillan (U.S.), 1944 . . . . £125/£20
That Hideous Strength: A Modern Fairy-Tale for Grown-Ups, Bodley Head, 1945 . . . £200/£45
ditto, Macmillan (U.S.), 1946 . . . . £100/£25
Till We Have Faces: A Myth Retold, Bles, 1956 . .
. . . . £75/£25
ditto, Harcourt Brace & Co (U.S.), 1957 . £35/£10

Short Stories
The Dark Tower and Other Stories, Collins, 1977 . .
. . . . £35/£10
ditto, Harcourt, Brace (U.S.), 1977 . . . £30/£10

Poetry
Spirits in Bondage, Heinemann, 1919 (pseud. 'Clive Hamilton') . . . . £6,000/£2,500
Dymer, Dent, 1926 (pseud. 'Clive Hamilton') . . .
. . . . £7,500/£4,000
ditto, Dutton (U.S.), 1926 . . . . . £2,000/£250
Hamlet, the Prince or the Poem, British Academy, 1942 (wraps) £45
Poems, Bles, 1964 . . . . £50/£15
ditto, Harcourt, Brace (U.S.), 1965 . . . £25/£10
Narrative Poems, Bles, 1969 . . . . . £50/£15

Christian Titles
The Pilgrim's Regress: An Allegorical Apology for Christianity, Reason and Romanticism, Dent, 1933 .
. . . . £800/£200
The Problem of Pain, Centenary Press, 1940 £50/£15
ditto, Bles, 1943 . . . . £30/£10
ditto, Macmillan (U.S.), 1943 . . . . £25/£5
The Screwtape Letters, Bles, 1942 . . £500/£150
ditto, Saunders (U.S.), 1942 . . . . £125/£15
Broadcast Talks: Right and Wrong: A Clue to the Meaning of the Universe, and What Christians Believe, Bles, 1942 . . . . . . £75/£15
Christian Behaviour: A Further Series of Broadcast Talks, Bles, 1943 . . . . . . £75/£20
ditto, Macmillan (U.S.), 1945 . . . . £20/£5
The Abolition of Man: or Reflections on Education with Special Reference to the Teaching of English in the Upper Forms of Schools, O.U.P., 1943 £25/£10
ditto, Macmillan (U.S.), 1947 . . . . £25/£10
Beyond Personality: The Christian Idea of God, Bles, 1944 . . . . £35/£10
The Great Divorce: A Dream, Bles, 1945 £35/£10
Miracles: A Preliminary Study, Bles, 1947 . £25/£10
Vivisection, The National Anti-Vivisection Society, [1947] (wraps) £50
Mere Christianity, Bles, 1952 . . . . £75/£25
Reflections on the Psalms, Bles, 1958 . £35/£15
ditto, Harcourt Brace (U.S.), 1958 . . . £25/£10
Shall We Lose God in Outer Space?, S.P.C.K., 1959 (wraps) £65
The Four Loves, Bles, 1960 . . . . . £35/£15
ditto, Harcourt Brace (U.S.), 1960 . . . £25/£15
The World's Last Night, Harcourt Brace (U.S.), 1960 .
. . . . £30/£10
Beyond the Bright Blur, Harcourt Brace (U.S.), 1963 .
. . . . £120/£100
Letters to Malcolm chiefly on Prayer, Bles, [1964] .
. . . . £35/£15
ditto, Harcourt Brace (U.S.), 1964 . . . £25/£15
Screwtape Proposes a Toast and Other Pieces, Bles, 1965 . . . . £25/£15
Christian Reflections, Bles, 1967 . . . £35/£15
Letters to an American Lady, Eerdmans (U.S.), 1967 .
. . . . £25/£15
The Joyful Christian, Macmillan (U.S.), 1977 . £10/£5

Academic Titles
The Allegory of Love: A Study in Medieval Tradition, O.U.P., 1936 . . . . £100/£35
Rehabilitations and Other Essays, O.U.P., 1939 . .
. . . . £35/£15
The Personal Heresy: A Controversy, O.U.P., 1939 (with E.M.W. Tillyard) . . . . . £35/£10
A Preface to Paradise Lost, O.U.P., 1942 . £35/£15
Arthurian Torso, O.U.P., 1948 (with Charles Williams) . . . . £75/£35
ditto, O.U.P. (U.S.), 1948 . . . . . £75/£35
English Literature in the Sixteenth Century, Excluding Drama, O.U.P., 1954 . . . £45/£10

ditto, O.U.P. (U.S.), 1954 . . . . . . £45/£15
Studies in Words, C.U.P., 1960 . . . . . £15/£5
ditto, Macmillan (U.S.), 1960 . . . . . £10/£5
An Experiment in Criticism, C.U.P., 1961 . £35/£15
ditto, Macmillan (U.S.), 1961 . . . . £30/£10
They Asked for a Paper, Bles, 1962. . . . £15/£5
The Discarded Image, C.U.P., 1964. . . . £10/£5
Of Other Worlds, Bles, 1966 . . . . . . £10/£5
Studies in Mediaeval and Renaissance Literature,
C.U.P., 1966 . . . . £10/£5
Spenser's Images of Life, C.U.P., 1961 . . . £10/£5

Autobiography
Surprised by Joy, Bles, 1955 . . . . . £35/£15
ditto, Harcourt Brace (U.S.), 1956 . . . £30/£10
A Grief Observed, Faber, 1961 (pseud. 'N.W. Clerk') .
. . . . £50/£15
ditto, Seabury (U.S.), 1963 . . . . . £25/£10

NORMAN LEWIS
(b.1908 d.2003)

A travel writer and novelist, Lewis was hailed by
Graham Greene as one of the best writers of the
twentieth century.

Travel
Spanish Adventure, Gollancz, 1935 . . . £250/£35
ditto, Holt (U.S.), 1935 . . . . £200/£20
Sand and Sea in Arabia, Routledge, 1938 . £150/£25
A Dragon Apparent, Travels In Indo-China, Cape,
1951 . . . . £65/£20
ditto, Scribner's (U.S.), 1951 . . . . . £50/£10
Golden Earth, Travels In Burma, Cape, 1952 £50/£20
ditto, Scribner's (U.S.), 1952 . . . . . £35/£10
The Changing Sky, The Travels of a Novelist, Cape,
1959 . . . . £45/£15
ditto, Pantheon (U.S.), 1959 . . . . . £40/£10
*The Honoured Society, The Mafia Conspiracy
Observed*, Collins, 1964. . . . . . £45/£15
ditto, Putnam's (U.S.), 1964 . . . . . £40/£10
Naples '44, Collins, 1978. . . . . . £45/£15
ditto, Pantheon (U.S.), 1978 . . . . . £40/£10
Voices of the Old Sea, Hamish Hamilton, 1984 £25/£5
ditto, Viking (U.S.), 1985. . . . . . . £20/£5
A Goddess in the Stones, Travels In India, Cape, 1991
. . . . £20/£5
ditto, Holt (U.S.), 1992. . . . . £20/£5
An Empire of the East, Travels In Indonesia, Cape,
1993 . . . . £15/£5
ditto, Holt (U.S.), 1993. . . . . £15/£5

Novels
Samara, Cape, 1949 . . . . £45/£10
Within the Labyrinth, Cape, 1950 . . . . £30/£5
ditto, Carroll & Graf (U.S.), 1986. . . . . £10/£5
A Single Pilgrim, Cape, 1953 . . . . . £15/£5

ditto, Rinehart & Co. (U.S.), 1953. . . . . £15/£5
The Day of the Fox, Cape, 1955 . . . . . £15/£5
ditto, Rinehart & Co. (U.S.), 1955. . . . . £15/£5
The Volcanoes Above Us, Cape, 1957 . . . £15/£5
ditto, Pantheon (U.S.), [1957]. . . . . . £15/£5
Darkness Visible, Cape, 1960 . . . . . £15/£5
ditto, Pantheon (U.S.), 1960. . . . . . . £15/£5
The Tenth Year of the Ship, Collins, 1962 . . £15/£5
ditto, Harcourt, Brace (U.S.), 1962. . . . . £15/£5
A Small War Made to Order, Collins, 1966 . £15/£5
ditto, Harcourt, Brace (U.S.), 1966. . . . . £15/£5
Every Man's Brother, Heinemann, 1967 . . £15/£5
ditto, Morrow (U.S.), 1968. . . . . . . £15/£5
Flight from a Dark Equator, Collins, 1972. . £15/£5
ditto, Putnam (U.S.), 1972. . . . . . . £15/£5
The Sicilian Specialist, Random House (U.S.), 1974 .
. . . . £10/£5
ditto, Collins, 1975 . . . . £10/£5
The German Company, Collins, 1979 . . . £10/£5
The Cuban Passage, Collins, 1982 . . . . £10/£5
ditto, Pantheon (U.S.), 1982. . . . . . . £10/£5
A Suitable Case for Corruption, Hamish Hamilton,
1984 . . . . £10/£5
ditto, as *The Man in the Middle*, Pantheon (U.S.),
1984 . . . . £10/£5
The March of the Long Shadows, Secker & Warburg,
1987 . . . . £10/£5

Miscellaneous
Jackdaw Cake, Hamish Hamilton, 1985 . . £20/£5
ditto, as *I Came, I Saw*, Picador, 1994 (enlarged
edition) . . . . £10/£5
A View of the World, Eland, 1986 . . . . £15/£5
The Missionaries, Secker & Warburg, 1988 . £15/£5
ditto, McGraw-Hill (U.S.), 1988.. . . . . £15/£5
To Run Across the Sea, Cape, 1989 . . . . £10/£5
The World, The World, Cape, 1996 . . . . £10/£5
ditto, Holt (U.S.), 1997. . . . . £10/£5
The Happy Ant-Heap and Other Pieces, Cape, 1998 .
. . . . £10/£5

WYNDHAM LEWIS
(b.1882 d.1957)

Considered one of the most versatile writers of his
time, Lewis was also a painter of some importance.

Fiction
Tarr, Knopf (U.S.), 1918 (red cloth). . . . £300
ditto, Knopf (U.S.), 1918 (blue cloth) . . . £200
ditto, Egoist Press, 1918 . . . . £175
The Wild Body, Chatto & Windus, 1927 . £250/£35
ditto, Chatto & Windus, 1927 (85 signed copies) . .
. . . . £350/£250
ditto, Harcourt, Brace (U.S.), [1928]. . . £125/£30
The Childermass: Section 1, Chatto & Windus, 1928 .
. . . . £200/£35

ditto, Chatto & Windus, 1928 (231 signed copies) . .
. . . . £350/£250
ditto, Covici Friede (U.S.), [1928] . . . £125/£30
The Apes of God, The Arthur Press, 1930 (750 signed copies) . . . . £300/£125
ditto, Nash & Grayson, 1931 . . . . . £125/£25
ditto, Robert McBride (U.S.), 1932 . . . £125/£25
Snooty Baronet, Cassell, 1932 . . . . £300/£100
ditto, Haskell House (U.S.), 1971 . . . £10
The Revenge for Love, Cassell, 1937 . . £250/£75
ditto, Regnery (U.S.), 1952 . . . . . £40/£10
The Vulgar Streak, Robert Hale, 1941 . . £300/£100
ditto, Jubilee Books (U.S.), 1973. . . . . £20/£5
Rotting Hill, Methuen, 1951 . . . . . £75/£25
ditto, Regnery (U.S.), 1952 . . . . . £40/£10
Self Condemned, Methuen, 1954 . . . £75/£25
ditto, Regnery (U.S.), 1955 . . . . . £40/£10
The Human Age, Methuen, 1955-56 (2 vols) £50/£20
The Red Priest, Methuen, 1963 . . . . £50/£15
The Roaring Queen, Secker & Warburg, 1973 £25/£10
ditto, Secker & Warburg, 1973 (130 copies signed by Mrs Wyndham Lewis) . . . . . £150/£45
ditto, Liveright (U.S.), 1973 . . . . £25/£10
Unlucky for Pringle, Vision Press, 1973 . £25/£10
ditto, D. Lewis (U.S.), [1973] . . . . . £20/£5
Mrs Dukes' Millions, The Coach House Press (Canada), 1977 (in box) . . . . £20/£5

Plays
The Ideal Giant, Privately Printed for the London Office of the *Little Review*, 1917 . . . £1,250
Enemy of the Stars, Harmsworth, 1932 . . £200/£50

Poetry
One-Way Song, Faber, 1933 . . . . . £150/£25
ditto, Faber, 1933 (40 signed copies) . . . £1,000

Collections
The Letters, Methuen, 1963 . . . . . £45/£15
ditto, New Directions (U.S.), [1927]. . . £45/£15
A Soldier of Humour and Selected Writings, New American Library (U.S.), 1966 (wraps) . . £10
Wyndham Lewis: An Anthology of His Prose, Methuen, 1969 . . . . £30/£10

Others
Timon of Athens, Benmar & Co, 1913 (portfolio of 16 loose plates) £3,000
The Caliph's Design, Egoist Press, 1919 . . £250
ditto, Black Sparrow Press (U.S.), 1986 (176 copies, acetate d/w) £35
Fifteen Drawings, Ovid Press, 1920. . . . £150
The Art of Being Ruled, Chatto & Windus, 1926 . .
. . . . £300/£75
ditto, Harpers (U.S.), 1926 . . . . £250/£50
The Lion and the Fox, Grant Richards, 1927 . .
. . . . £500/£100
ditto, Harpers (U.S.), [1927] . . . . £350/£50
Time and Western Man, Chatto & Windus, 1927 . .
. . . . £150/£45

ditto, Harcourt, Brace (U.S.), 1928 . . . £50/£15
Paleface, Chatto & Windus, 1929 . . . £200/£45
Hitler, Chatto & Windus, 1931 . . . . . £450/£125
The Diabolical Principle and the Dithyrambic Spectator, Chatto & Windus, 1931 . . £150/£30
Doom of Youth, Robert McBride (U.S.), 1932 £200/£30
ditto, Chatto & Windus, 1932 . . . . . £500/£250
Filibusters in Barbary, Grayson, 1932 . . £250/£65
ditto, National Travel Club (U.S.), [1927] . £100/£25
Thirty Personalities and a Self-Portrait, Harmsworth, 1932 (200 signed sets, portfolio with 31 loose plates)
. . . . £750
The Old Gang and the New Gang, Harmsworth, 1933
. . . . £200/£45
ditto, Haskell House (U.S.), 1972 . . . . £10
Men Without Art, Cassell, 1934 . . . . £300/£45
ditto, Russell & Russell (U.S.), 1964. . . £25/£10
Left Wings Over Europe, Cape, 1936 . . £150/£25
ditto, Gordon Press (U.S.), 1972 . . . . . £20/£5
Count Your Dead: They Are Alive!, Lovat Dickson, 1937 . . . . £250/£45
ditto, Gordon Press (U.S.), 1972 . . . . . £20/£5
Blasting and Bombadiering, Eyre & Spottiswoode, 1937 . . . . £150/£30
ditto, Univ. of California Press (U.S.), 1967 . £20/£5
The Mysterious Mr Bull, Robert Hale, 1938 £200/£30
The Jews, Are They Human, Allen & Unwin, 1939 . .
. . . . £250/£35
ditto, Gordon Press (U.S.), 1972 . . . . . £20/£5
Wyndham Lewis The Artist, From 'Blast' to Burlington House, Laidlaw & Laidlaw, 1939. . .
. . . . £175/£45
The Hitler Cult, Dent, 1939 . . . . . £400/£100
ditto, Gordon Press (U.S.), 1972 . . . . . £20/£5
America, I Presume, Howell & Soskin (U.S.), 1940 (wraps) . . . . £125/£35
Anglosaxony: A League That Works, Ryerson (Canada), 1941 . . . . £400
America and Cosmic Man, Nicholson & Watson, 1948
. . . . £100/£25
ditto, Doubleday (U.S.), 1949 . . . . £75/£20
Rude Assignment, Hutchinson, [1950] . . £100/£25
ditto, Black Sparrow Press (U.S.), 1984 . . . £35
The Writer and the Absolute, Methuen, 1952 £75/£20
ditto, Greenwood Press (U.S.), 1975. . . . £15/£5
The Demon of Progress in the Arts, Methuen, 1954 .
. . . . £50/£10
ditto, Regnery (U.S.), 1955 . . . . . £40/£10
Wyndham Lewis on Art, Thames & Hudson, 1969. .
. . . . £50/£15
ditto, Funk & Wagnalls (U.S.), 1969. . . £45/£15
Enemy Salvoes: Selected Literary Criticism, Vision Press, 1976 . . . . £25/£10
ditto, Barnes & Noble (U.S.), 1976 . . . £45/£15
Imaginary Letters, Wyndham Lewis Society, 1977 (300 copies, wraps) £35

DAVID LINDSAY
(b.1878 d.1945)

British novelist whose curious metaphysical writings are not widely known. Among devotees, however, he is considered highly original and interesting.

Novels
A Voyage to Arcturus, Methuen, 1920 (first binding, 8 page catalogue at rear) . . . . . £2,000/£750
ditto, Methuen, 1920 (second binding without catalogue at rear). . . . . . . £1,500/£500
ditto, Gollancz, 1946 . . . . . £50/£20
ditto, Macmillan (U.S.), 1963 . . . £50/£20
The Haunted Woman, Methuen, 1922 . £1,000/£250
ditto, Gollancz, 1947 . . . . . £45/£15
ditto, Newcastle (U.S.), 1975 (wraps) . . £10
Sphinx, John Long, 1923 . . . . £1,000/£250
The Adventures of M. De Mailly, Melrose, 1926 . .
. . . . £200/£75
ditto, as *A Blade for Sale*, McBride (U.S.), 1927 . .
. . . . £150/£35
Devil's Tor, Putnam, 1932 . . . . £1,000/£150
The Violet Apple and The Witch, Chicago Review Press (U.S.), 1975 . . . . . £75/£25
The Violet Apple, Sidgwick & Jackson, [1978]. . .
. . . . £35/£10

DAVID LODGE
(b.1935)

Also a professor and literary critic, Lodge's novels are the most keenly sought after titles.

Novels
The Picturegoers, MacGibbon & Kee, 1960 £400/£45
Ginger, You're Barmy, MacGibbon & Kee 1962 . .
. . . . £350/£40
ditto, Doubleday (U.S.), 1965 . . . £50/£15
The British Museum is Falling Down, MacGibbon & Kee, 1965. . . . . £500/£50
ditto, Holt Rinehart (U.S.), 1967 . . . £45/£15
Out of the Shelter, Macmillan, 1970. . £1,000/£50
Changing Places; A Tale of Two Campuses, Secker & Warburg, 1975 . . . . . . £100/£15
ditto, Viking (U.S.), 1979. . . . . £25/£10
How Far Can You Go?, Secker & Warburg, 1980 . .
. . . . £65/£15
ditto, as *Souls and Bodies*, Morrow (U.S.), 1982 . .
. . . . £15/£5
Small World, Secker & Warburg, 1984 . . £25/£10
ditto, Macmillan (U.S.), 1985 . . . . £15/£5
Nice Work, Secker & Warburg, 1988 . . £15/£5
ditto, Viking, 1989 . . . . £15/£5
Paradise News, Secker & Warburg, 1991 . . £10/£5
ditto, Viking (U.S.), 1992. . . . . . £10/£5
Therapy, Secker & Warburg, 1995 . . . £10/£5
ditto, Viking (U.S.), 1995. . . . . . £10/£5

Thinks..., Bridgewater Press, 2001 (XII signed, Roman-numbered copies of 138) £200
ditto, Bridgewater Press, 2001 (26 signed, lettered copies of 138) £125
ditto, Bridgewater Press, 2001 (100 signed, numbered copies of 138) £65
ditto, Secker & Warburg, 2001 . . . . . £10/£5
ditto, Viking (U.S.), 2001. . . . . . . £10/£5

Short Stories and Novellas
The Man Who Wouldn't Get Up and Other Stories, Bridgewater Press, 1998 (XII signed, Roman-numbered copies of 138) £250
ditto, Bridgewater Press, 1998 (26 signed, lettered copies) £125
ditto, Bridgewater Press, 1998 (100 signed, numbered copies) £65
Home Truths, Colophon Press, 1999 (XII signed, Roman-numbered copies of 112) £125
ditto, Colophon Press, 1999 (100 signed, numbered copies) £45

Plays
The Writing Game, Secker & Warburg, 1991 (wraps). .
. . . . £5
Home Truths, Secker & Warburg, 1999 (wraps) . £5

Others
About Catholic Authors, St Paul Publications, 1958 .
. . . . £15/£5
The Language of Fiction, Routledge, 1966. . £15/£5
ditto, Columbia Univ. Press (U.S.), 1966 . £15/£5
Graham Greene, Columbia Univ. Press (U.S.), 1966 (wraps) £45
The Novelist at the Crossroads and Other Essays on Fiction and Criticism, Routledge, 1971 . £10/£5
ditto, Cornell Univ. Press (U.S.), 1971 . . £10/£5
Evelyn Waugh, Columbia Univ. Press (U.S.), 1971 (wraps) £15
Twentieth Century Literary Criticism, Longman, 1972
. . . . £10/£5
The Modes of Modern Writing: Metaphor, Metonymy and the Typology of Modern Literature, Arnold, 1977 . . . . £15/£5
ditto, Cornell Univ. Press (U.S.), 1977 . . £15/£5
Modernism, Antimodernism and Postmodernism, Univ. of Birmingham, 1977 (no d/w) . . £10
Working with Structuralism: Essays and Reviews on Nineteenth and Twentieth Century Literature, Routledge, 1981 . . . . £10/£5
Write On, Secker & Warburg, 1986 . . . £15/£5
After Bakhtin: Essays on Fiction and Criticism, Routledge, 1990 . . . . £10/£5
The Art of Fiction, Viking (U.S.), 1992. . £10/£5
The Practice of Writing, Secker & Warburg, 1996. .
. . . . £15/£5
ditto, Allen Lane/Penguin Press (U.S.), 1996 . £10/£5
Consciousness and the Novel, Secker & Warburg, 2002 . . . . £10/£5
ditto, Harvard (U.S.), 2002 . . . . . . £10/£5

JACK LONDON

(b.1876 d.1916)

The highly successful writer of many adventure stories, London took part in the Klondike gold rush of 1897 and used this experience as the background for much of his work.

Novels

A Daughter of the Snows, Lippincott (U.S.), 1902. .
. . . . £450
ditto, Isbister, 1904 . . . . £150
The Kempton-Wace Letters, Macmillan (U.S.), 1903 (with Anna Strunsky, first issue without authors names on title page) £400
ditto, Macmillan (U.S.), 1903 (second issue with authors names on title page). £150
ditto, Isbister, 1903 . . . . £75
The Call of the Wild, Macmillan (U.S.), 1903 . £850
ditto, Heinemann, 1903 . . . . . . £300
The Sea-Wolf, Macmillan (U.S.), 1904 (title page not a cancel, copyright notice dated 1904 only) . . £4,000
ditto, Macmillan (U.S.), 1904 (title page is a cancel, copyright notices dated 1903 and 1904). . . £300
ditto, Heinemann, 1904 . . . . . . £100
The Game, Macmillan (U.S.), 1905 . . . . £200
ditto, Heinemann, 1905 . . . . . . £100
White Fang, Macmillan (U.S.), 1906 (first state with title leaf integral). £200
ditto, Macmillan (U.S.), 1906 (second state with title leaf tipped-in) £100
ditto, Methuen, 1907 . . . . £75
Before Adam, Macmillan (U.S.), 1907 . . . £200
ditto, Macmillan Colonial Library Edition, 1907 £100
ditto, Werner Laurie, [1908] £100
The Iron Heel, Macmillan (U.S.), 1908 . . . £250
ditto, Everett, [1908] £75
Martin Eden, Donohoe (U.S.), 1980. . . . £250
ditto, Macmillan (U.S.), 1909 . . . . . £200
ditto, Heinemann, 1910 . . . . £75
Burning Daylight, Macmillan (U.S.), 1910 (first printing, one blank leaf follows p.374). . . £200
ditto, Macmillan (U.S.), 1910 (second printing, three blank leaves follow p.374) £100
ditto, Heinemann, 1911 . . . . £50
Adventure, Nelson, [1911] ('First published in 1911' on copyright page) £500
ditto, Nelson, [1911] ('Published in March 1911' on copyright page) £200
ditto, Macmillan (U.S.), 1911 . . . . . £75
The Abysmal Brute, The Century Co. (U.S.), 1913 . .
. . . . £125
ditto, Newnes, [1914] £65
John Barleycorn, The Century Co. (U.S.), 1913 £125
ditto, as *John Barleycorn or Alcoholic Memoirs*, Mills & Boon, 1914 . . . . £50
The Valley of the Moon, Macmillan (U.S.), 1913 £125
ditto, Mills & Boon, 1914. . . . . . . £50

The Mutiny of the Elsinor, Macmillan (U.S.), 1914 .
. . . . £250
ditto, Mills & Boon, 1915. . . . . . £75
The Scarlet Plague, Macmillan (U.S.), 1915 . £300
ditto, Mills & Boon, 1915. . . . . . £75
The Jacket, Mills & Boon, 1915 . . . . . £450
ditto, as *The Star Rover*, Macmillan (U.S.), 1915 £300
The Little Lady of the Big House, Macmillan (U.S.), 1916 . . . . £125
ditto, Mills & Boon, 1916. . . . . . £50
Jerry of the Islands, Macmillan (U.S.), 1917 . £125
ditto, Mills & Boon, 1917. . . . . . £50
Michael, Brother of Jerry, Macmillan (U.S.), 1917 .
. . . . £150
ditto, Mills & Boon, 1918. . . . . . £50
Hearts of Three, Mills & Boon, 1918 . . . £450
ditto, Macmillan (U.S.), 1920 . . . . £250/£45
The Assassination Bureau Ltd, McGraw-Hill (U.S.), 1963 (completed by Robert L. Fish) . . £30/£10
ditto, Deutsch, 1964 . . . . . . £30/£10

Short Stories

The Son of the Wolf: Tales of the Far North, Houghton, Mifflin (U.S.), 1900 (trial bindings of either grass-green cloth stamped in silver, greenish-black cloth stamped in silver, or white buckram stamped in red) £2,000
ditto, Houghton, Mifflin (U.S.), 1900 (first printing, grey cloth stamped in silver, pagination (i-viii); no blank leaf following page 252; collation: (4), 2-22(6))
. . . . £750
ditto, Houghton, Mifflin (U.S.), 1900 (second printing, grey cloth stamped in silver, pagination: (i-vi) blank leaf following page 252) £300
ditto, Houghton, Mifflin (U.S.), 1900 (third printing, as second except collation differs: 1-21(6), 22(4)) £200
ditto, Watt, 1900 . . . . £1,000
ditto, Isbister, 1902 . . . . £300
The God of His Fathers, & Other Stories, McClure, Philips (U.S.), 1901 . . . . £450
ditto, Isbister, 1902 . . . . £150
Children of the Frost, Macmillan (U.S.), 1902 . £500
ditto, Macmillan, 1902 . . . . . . £150
The Faith of Men, and Other Stories, Macmillan (U.S.), 1904 . . . . £350
ditto, Heinemann, 1904 . . . . . . £125
Tales of the Fish Patrol, Macmillan (U.S.), 1905 £250
ditto, Heinemann, 1906 . . . . . . £50
Moon-Face, and Other Stories, Macmillan (U.S.), 1906 . . . . £250
ditto, Heinemann, 1906 . . . . . . £50
Love of Life, and Other Stories, Macmillan (U.S.), 1907 . . . . £250
ditto, Everett, [1908] £75
Lost Face, Macmillan (U.S.), 1910 . . . . £250
ditto, Mills & Boon, [1915] £50
When God Laughs, and Other Stories, Macmillan (U.S.), 1911 . . . . £250
ditto, Mills & Boon, 1912. . . . . . £50

South Sea Tales, Macmillan (U.S.), 1911 . . £250
ditto, Mills & Boon, 1912. . . . . . . £50
The House of Pride and Other Tales of Hawaii,
Macmillan (U.S.), 1912 . . . . £250
ditto, Mills & Boon, 1914. . . . . . . £50
A Son of the Sun, Doubleday, Page & Co. (U.S.), 1912
. . . . £300
ditto, Mills & Boon, 1913. . . . . . . £50
Smoke Bellew, The Century Co. (U.S.), 1912 . £250
ditto, Mills & Boon, 1913. . . . . . . £50
The Night-Born, The Century Co. (U.S.), 1913 £250
ditto, Mills & Boon, 1916. . . . . . . £50
The Strength of the Strong, Macmillan (U.S.), 1914 .
. . . . £250
ditto, Mills & Boon, 1917. . . . . . . £50
The Turtles of Tasman, Macmillan (U.S.), 1916 £250
ditto, Mills & Boon, 1917. . . . . . . £50
The Human Drift, Macmillan (U.S.), 1917 . . £300
ditto, Mills & Boon, 1919. . . . . . . £75
The Red One, Macmillan (U.S.), 1918 . . . £250
ditto, Mills & Boon, 1919. . . . . . . £50
On The Makaloa Mat, Macmillan (U.S.), 1919 £200
ditto, as *Island Tales*, Mills & Boon, 1920 . £500/£75
Dutch Courage, and Other Stories, Macmillan (U.S.),
1922 . . . . £2,000/£250
ditto, Mills & Boon, 1923. . . . . . £250/£50

Others
The Cruise of the Dazzler, The Century Co. (U.S.),
1902 . . . . £1,250
ditto, Hodder & Stoughton, 1906. . . . . £350
The People of the Abyss, Macmillan (U.S.), 1903
(grey-blue cloth) £500
ditto, Macmillan (U.S.), 1903 (dark blue cloth). £200
ditto, Isbister, 1903 . . . . £125
War of the Classes, Macmillan (U.S.), 1905 . £200
ditto, Heinemann, 1905 . . . . . . £65
Scorn of Women, Macmillan (U.S.), 1906 (top edge
gilt) £1,500
ditto, Macmillan (U.S.), 1906 (top edge not gilt) £1,000
ditto, Macmillan, 1906 . . . . £250
The Road, Macmillan (U.S.), 1907 (grey cloth stamped
in gold) £300
ditto, Macmillan (U.S.), 1907 (cream cloth stamped in
black) £200
ditto, Mills & Boon, 1914. . . . . . £100
Revolution, Kerr (U.S.), [1909] (ads on p.32 headed 'A
Socialist Success', wraps) £200
ditto, Kerr (U.S.), [1909] (ads on p.32 headed 'Pocket
Library of Socialism', wraps) £150
ditto, Kerr (U.S.), [1909] (ads on p.32 headed either
'Socialist periodicals' or 'Study Socialism', wraps) .
. . . . £125
ditto, Kerr (U.S.), [1909] (ads on p.32 headed 'Socialist
Literature', wraps) £100
Revolution and Other Essays, Macmillan (U.S.), 1910
(maroon cloth) £350
ditto, Macmillan (U.S.), 1910 (brown cloth) . £200
ditto, Mills & Boon, 1920. . . . . . £100/£25

Theft: A Play in Four Acts, Macmillan (U.S.), 1910 .
. . . . £500
ditto, Macmillan, 1910 . . . . £150
The Cruise of the Snark, Macmillan (U.S.), 1911 £200
ditto, Mills & Boon, 1913. . . . . . . £50
Jack London By Himself, Macmillan (U.S.), [1913] .
. . . . £250
ditto, Mills & Boon, 1913. . . . . . . £150
The Acorn-Planter; A California Forest Play,
Macmillan (U.S.), 1916 . . . . £1,000
ditto, Mills & Boon, 1916. . . . . . . £250
Letters from Jack London, The Odyssey Press (U.S.),
1965 . . . . £40/£20

Collected Editions
The Works of Jack London, Macmillan (U.S.), 1919
(21 vols) £1,000

E.C.R. LORAC
(b.1894 d.1958)

Edith Caroline Rivett is known for her 'Golden Age'
detective fiction written under the pseudonyms of
'Lorac' (Carol backwards) and 'Carnac'.

Novels as 'E.C.R. Lorac'
The Murder on the Burrows, Sampson Low, [1931] .
. . . . £2,000/£250
ditto, Macaulay (U.S.), 1932 . . . . . £650/£100
The Affair at Thor's Head, Sampson Low, [1932]. .
. . . . £1,500/£250
The Greenwell Mystery, Sampson Low, [1932] . .
. . . . £1,500/£250
ditto, Macaulay (U.S.), 1934 . . . . . £650/£100
Death on the Oxford Road, Sampson Low, [1933] .
. . . . £1,500/£250
ditto, Macaulay (U.S.), 1934 . . . . . £650/£100
The Case of Colonel Marchand, Sampson Low,
[1933]. . . . . £1,500/£250
ditto, Macaulay (U.S.), 1933 . . . . . £650/£100
Murder in St John's Wood, Sampson Low, [1934] .
. . . . £1,250/£200
ditto, Macaulay (U.S.), 1934 . . . . . £600/£100
Murder in Chelsea, Sampson Low, [1934] . . .
. . . . £1,250/£200
ditto, Macaulay (U.S.), 1935 . . . . . £600/£100
The Organ Speaks, Sampson Low, [1935] . . .
. . . . £1,250/£200
The Death of an Author, Sampson Low, [1935] . .
. . . . £1,250/£200
ditto, Macaulay (U.S.), 1937 . . . . . £650/£100
Crime Counter Crime, Collins Crime Club, 1936 . .
. . . . £1,000/£100
Post After Post-Mortem, Collins Crime Club, 1936 .
. . . . £1,000/£100
A Pall for a Painter, Collins Crime Club, 1936 . .
. . . . £1,000/£100

Bats in the Belfry, Collins Crime Club, 1937 . . .
. . . . £1,000/£100
ditto, Macaulay (U.S.), 1937 . . . . . £650/£100
These Names Make Clues, Collins Crime Club, 1937 .
. . . . £1,000/£100
The Devil and the CID, Collins Crime Club, 1938 . .
. . . . £1,000/£100
Slippery Staircase, Collins Crime Club, 1938 . . .
. . . . £1,000/£100
John Brown's Body, Collins Crime Club, 1938 . .
. . . . £1,000/£100
Black Beadle, Collins Crime Club, 1939 £1,000/£100
Death at Dyke's Corner, Collins Crime Club, 1940 .
. . . . £650/£100
Tryst for a Tragedy, Collins Crime Club, 1940 . .
. . . . £650/£100
Case in the Clinic, Collins Crime Club, 1941 £350/£75
Rope's End, Rogue's End, Collins Crime Club, 1942 .
. . . . £200/£25
The Sixteenth Stair, Collins Crime Club, 1942 . . .
. . . . £165/£25
Death Came Softly, Collins Crime Club, 1943 . . .
. . . . £165/£25
ditto, Mystery House (U.S.), 1943 . . . £100/£25
Checkmate to Murder, Collins Crime Club, 1944 . .
. . . . £150/£25
ditto, Mystery House (U.S.), 1944 . . £100/£20
Fell Murder, Collins Crime Club, 1944 . . £150/£25
Murder by Matchlight, Collins Crime Club, 1945 . .
. . . . £150/£25
ditto, Mystery House (U.S.), 1946 . . £75/£15
Fire in the Thatch, Collins Crime Club, 1946 . .
. . . . £125/£25
ditto, Mystery House (U.S.), 1946 . . £75/£15
The Theft of the Iron Dogs, Collins Crime Club, 1946
. . . . £125/£25
ditto, as *Murderer's Mistake*, Mystery House (U.S.),
1947 . . . . £75/£15
Relative to Poison, Collins Crime Club, 1947 £125/£25
ditto, Doubleday (U.S.), 1948 . . . . £75/£15
Death Before Dinner, Collins Crime Club, 1948 . .
. . . . £125/£25
ditto, as *A Screen for Murder*, Doubleday (U.S.), 1948
. . . . £75/£15
Part for a Poisoner, Collins Crime Club, 1948 . .
. . . . £125/£25
ditto, as *Place for a Poisoner*, Doubleday (U.S.), 1949
. . . . £75/£15
Still Waters, Collins Crime Club, 1949 . . £125/£25
Policemen on the Precinct, Collins Crime Club, 1949.
. . . . £125/£25
ditto, as *And Then Put Out the Light*, Doubleday
(U.S.), 1950 . . . . £75/£15
Accident by Design, Collins Crime Club, 1950 . .
. . . . £125/£25
ditto, Doubleday (U.S.), 1951 . . . . £75/£15
Murder of a Martinet, Collins Crime Club, 1951 . .
. . . . £125/£25

ditto, as *I Could Murder Her*, Doubleday (U.S.), 1951
. . . . £75/£15
The Dog It Was That Died, Collins Crime Club, 1952.
. . . . £100/£20
ditto, Doubleday (U.S.), 1952 . . . . £65/£15
Murder in the Millrace, Collins Crime Club, 1952. .
. . . . £100/£20
ditto, as *Speak Justly of the Dead*, Doubleday (U.S.),
1953 . . . . £65/£15
Crook o'Lune, Collins Crime Club, 1953 . £100/£20
ditto, as *Shepherd's Crook*, Doubleday (U.S.), 1953 .
. . . . £65/£15
Shroud of Darkness, Collins Crime Club, 1954 . .
. . . . £100/£20
ditto, Doubleday (U.S.), 1954 . . . . £65/£15
Let Well Alone, Collins Crime Club, 1954 . £100/£20
Ask a Policeman, Collins Crime Club, 1955 £100/£20
Murder in Vienna, Collins Crime Club, 1956 £100/£20
Picture of Death, Collins Crime Club, 1957 £100/£20
Dangerous Domicile, Collins Crime Club, 1957 . .
. . . . £100/£20
Death in Triplicate, Collins Crime Club, 1958 . . .
. . . . £100/£20
ditto, as *People Will Talk*, Doubleday (U.S.), 1958 .
. . . . £50/£10
Murder on a Monument, Collins Crime Club, 1958 .
. . . . £100/£20
Dishonour Among Thieves, Collins Crime Club, 1959
. . . . £75/£20
ditto, as *The Last Escape*, Doubleday (U.S.), 1959 .
. . . . £50/£10

Novels as 'Carol Carnac'
Triple Death, Butterworth, [1936] . . £1,000/£200
Murder at Mornington, Skeffington, [1937] . . .
. . . . £1,000/£200
The Missing Rope, Skeffington, [1937] . £1,000/£200
When the Devil Was Sick, Peter Davies, 1939 . . .
. . . . £750/£150
The Case of the First-Class Carriage, Peter Davies,
1939 . . . . £650/£125
Death in the Diving Pool, Peter Davies, 1940 . . .
. . . . £500/£100
A Double for Detection, Macdonald, [1945] £125/£25
The Striped Suitcase, Macdonald, 1946 . . £125/£25
ditto, Doubleday (U.S.), 1947 . . . . £50/£15
Clue Sinister, Macdonald, 1947 . . . . £125/£25
Over the Garden Wall, Macdonald, 1948 . £125/£25
ditto, Doubleday (U.S.), 1949 . . . . £50/£15
Upstairs, Downstairs, Macdonald, 1950. . £100/£25
ditto, as *Upstairs and Downstairs*, Doubleday (U.S.),
1950 . . . . £45/£15
Copy for Crime, Macdonald, 1950 . . . £100/£25
ditto, Doubleday (U.S.), 1951 . . . . £45/£15
It's Her Own Funeral, Collins Crime Club, 1951 . .
. . . . £100/£25
Crossed Skis, Collins Crime Club, 1952. . £100/£25
Murder As A Fine Art, Collins Crime Club, 1953 . .
. . . . £100/£25

A Policeman at the Door, Collins Crime Club, 1953 .
. . . . £100/£25
ditto, Doubleday (U.S.), 1954 . . . . £45/£15
Impact of Evidence, Collins Crime Club, 1954 . . .
. . . . £100/£20
ditto, Doubleday (U.S.), 1954 . . . . £45/£15
Murder Among Members, Collins Crime Club, 1955 .
. . . . £100/£20
Rigging the Evidence, Collins Crime Club, 1955 . .
. . . . £100/£20
The Double Turn, Collins Crime Club, 1956 . . .
. . . . £75/£20
ditto, as *The Late Miss Trimming*, Doubleday (U.S.),
1957 . . . . £45/£15
The Burning Question, Collins Crime Club, 1957. .
. . . . £75/£20
Long Shadows, Collins Crime Club, 1958 . £75/£20
ditto, as *Affair at Helen's Court*, Doubleday (U.S.),
1958 . . . . £45/£15
Death of a Lady Killer, Collins Crime Club, 1959 . .
. . . . £75/£20

Novels as 'Carol Rivett'
Outer Circle, Hodder & Stoughton, 1939 . £100/£25
Time Remembered, Hodder & Stoughton, 1940 . .
. . . . £100/£25

H.P. LOVECRAFT
(b.1890 d.1937)

Born in Providence, Rhode Island (U.S.), where he
lived for the rest of his life, Lovecraft is famous for
his weird fiction. Arkham House have issued revised
and corrected editions of all the major Lovecraft
stories in recent years.

Fiction
The Crime of Crimes, Harris, 1915 (mimeographed
pamphlet). £10,000
The Shunned House, The Recluse Press (U.S.), 1928
(original unbound sheets, 300 printed of which c.75
may survive) £3,000
ditto, copies bound by R.H. Barlow (U.S.), 1934/35
(c.8 may exist) £8,000
ditto, Arkham House (U.S.), 1959 (unbound sheets, 50
sets) £2,000
ditto, Arkham House (U.S.), 1961 (bound, 100 copies,
no d/w) £2,500
ditto, Arkham House (U.S.), (counterfeit edition,
1965/66) £500
The Battle That Ended the Century, Barlow (U.S.),
1934 (50 mimeographed copies, wraps) . . £1,000
A Sonnet – The Lovecrafter, Shepherd & Wollheim
(U.S.), 1936 (16 copies). £1,000
The Cats of Ulthar, Dragon-Fly Press (U.S.), 1935 (42
copies, wraps) £1,000
The Shadow Over Innsmouth, Visionary Publishing
(U.S.), 1936 (150-200 copies) . . £2,500/£2,000

H.P.L., Corwin Stickney (U.S.), 1937 (poetry, limited
to 23 copies, wraps) £1,500
A History of the Necronomicon, Rebel Press (U.S.),
1938 (wraps). £750
ditto, Necronomicon Press (U.S.), 1977 (wraps) £15
The Outsider and Others, Arkham House (U.S.), 1939
. . . . £1,500/£500
Fungi from Yuggoth, Evans (U.S.), 1943 (approx 65
copies, wraps) £1,000
Beyond the Wall of Sleep, Arkham House (U.S.), 1943
. . . . £1,250/£400
The Weird Shadow Over Innsmouth, Bart House
(U.S.), 1944 (wraps) £45
The Dunwich Horror and Other Weird Tales, Armed
Services Edition (U.S.), 1945 (wraps) . . . £35
Best Supernatural Stories, Tower Books (U.S.), 1945.
. . . . £50/£15
The Dunwich Horror, Bart House (U.S.), 1945 (wraps)
. . . . £35
The Lurker at the Threshold, Arkham House (U.S.),
1945 (novel mainly written by Derleth) . £100/£25
ditto, Museum Press, 1948 . . . . . £200/£40
ditto, Gollancz, 1968 . . . . . . £40/£15
The Lurking Fear and Other Stories, Avon (U.S.),
1947 (wraps) £25
The Haunter of the Dark, Gollancz, 1951 . £50/£15
The Case of Charles Dexter Ward, Gollancz, 1951 .
. . . . £100/£40
The Curse of Yig, Arkham House (U.S.), 1953 (by
Zealia B. Bishop) . . . . £75/£25
The Challenge from Beyond, Evans (U.S.), 1954
(with Abraham Merritt, Robert E. Howard, Frank
Belknap Long, and C.L. Moore) £50
The Dream Quest of Unknown Kadath, Shroud (U.S.),
1955 (50 copies bound in cloth) £250
ditto, Shroud (U.S.), 1955 (1,400+ copies in wrappers,
with d/w) £60
ditto, Shroud (U.S.), 1955 (12 numbered copies
clothbound by Gerry de la Ree in 1972) . . £100
The Survivor and Others, Arkham House (U.S.), 1957
(completed by Derleth) . . . . . £75/£35
The Dunwich Horror and Others, Arkham House
(U.S.), 1963 . . . . £100/£30
Collected Poems, Arkham House (U.S.), 1963 . . .
. . . . £100/£25
At the Mountains of Madness, Arkham House (U.S.),
1964 . . . . £125/£25
ditto, Gollancz, 1966 . . . . . . £65/£20
The Colour Out Of Space, Lancer, 1964 (wraps) £10
The Lurking Fear and Other Stories, Panther, 1964
(wraps) £10
Dagon and Other Macabre Tales, Arkham House
(U.S.), 1965 . . . . £100/£20
ditto, Gollancz (U.K.), 1967 . . . . £60/£20
The Dark Brotherhood, Arkham House (U.S.), 1966 .
. . . . £65/£20
Three Tales of Horror, Arkham House (U.S.), 1967 .
. . . . £75/£25
The Shadow Out of Time, Gollancz, 1968 . £45/£15

*The Prose Poems: Ex Oblivione, Memory, Nyarla-
thotep, What the Moon Brings*, Squires (U.S.), 1969-
1970 (26 lettered copies of 125, 4 booklets in
envelopes) £200
ditto, Squires (U.S.), 1969-1970 (99 numbered copies
of 125, 4 booklets, in envelopes) £125
The Dream Quest of Unknown Kadath, Ballantine
(U.S.), 1970 (wraps). £10
The Horror in the Museum and Other Revisions,
Arkham House (U.S.), 1970 . . . . £45/£15
The Doom That Came To Sarnath, Ballantine (U.S.),
1971 (wraps) £10
The Shadow Over Innsmouth, Scholastic, 1971
(wraps) £5
The Watchers Out of Time and Others, Arkham
House (U.S.), 1974 (stories completed by Derleth) .
. . . . £45/£15
Medusa: A Portrait, Oliphant Press (U.S.), 1975 (500
numbered copies in wrappers) £20
The Statement of Randolph Carter, The Strange
Company (U.S.), 1976 (150 copies, unbound
holographic sheets in folder) £25
ditto, The Strange Company (U.S.), 1976 (30 copies
signed by the editor, unbound holographic sheets in
folder). £50
Antarktos, Fantome Press (U.S.), 1977 (150 copies,
wraps). £15
Herbert West: Reanimator, Necronomicon Press
(U.S.), 1977 (1,000 copies, wraps) . . . £10
The Lurking Fear, Necronomicon Press (U.S.), 1977
(550 copies, wraps) £15
Collapsing Cosmoses, Necronomicon Press (U.S.),
1977 (500 copies, wraps) £15
A Winter Wish and Other Poems, Whispers Press
(U.S.), 1977 (26 copies signed and lettered in
slipcase) . . . . £300/£250
ditto, Whispers Press (U.S.), 1977 (200 signed,
numbered copies in slipcase and d/w) . . £60/£30
ditto, Whispers Press (U.S.), 1977 (trade edition, 2,000
copies) . . . . £30/£15
Uncollected Prose and Poetry, Vol I, Necronomicon
Press (U.S.), 1978 (wraps) £10
ditto, Vol II, Necronomicon Press (U.S.), 1980 (wraps)
. . . . £10
ditto, Vol III, Necronomicon Press (U.S.), 1982
(wraps) £10
The Colour Out Of Space, Necronomicon Press (U.S.),
1982 (400 copies, wraps) £15
The Best of H.P. Lovecraft, Del Rey/Ballantine (U.S.),
1982 (wraps) £5
The Young Folks' Ulysses, Soft Books (U.S.), 1982
(200 copies, wraps) £10
Ashes and Others, Miskatonic Univ. Press (U.S.), 1983
(wraps) £10
The Illustrated Fungi from Yuggoth, Dream House
(U.S.), 1983 (wraps). £15
Saturnalia and Other Poems, Crypt of Cthulhu (U.S.),
1984 (wraps) £5

Juvenilia:, 1895-1905, Necronomicon Press (U.S.),
1984 (wraps) £5
The Festival, Necronomicon Press (U.S.), 1984 (50
copies, wraps) £20
Medusa and Other Poems, Crypt of Cthulhu (U.S.),
1986 (wraps) £10
At the Mountains of Madness, Grant (U.S.), 1990
(1,000 copies signed by the artist, leather binding) .
. . . . £75
The Fantastic Poetry, Necronomicon Press (U.S.),
1990 (wraps) £10
*The Battle that Ended the Century/Collapsing
Cosmoses*, Necronomicon Press (U.S.), 1992 (wraps)
. . . . £10
Crawling Chaos: Selected Works 1920-1935, Creation
Press, 1993 (wraps) £10
The Dream Cycle of H.P. Lovecraft, Ballantine/Del
Ray (U.S.), 1995 (wraps) £5
The Transition of H.P. Lovecraft, Ballantine/Del Ray
(U.S.), 1995 (wraps). £5
The Annotated H.P. Lovecraft, Dell (U.S.), 1997
(wraps) £10
Tales of H.P. Lovecraft, Ecco Press (U.S.), 1997 . .
. . . . £20/£5
More Annotated of H.P. Lovecraft, Dell (U.S.), 1999
(wraps) £10
The Ancient Track, Necronomicon Press (U.S.), 2000
(250 copies) £25
ditto, Necronomicon Press (U.S.), 2000 (800 copies,
wraps). £10

Non Fiction
Exponent of Amateur Journalism, United Amateur
Press Association (U.S.), 1915 (mimeographed
pamphlet). £2,500
Looking Backward, C.W. Smith (U.S.), 1920 (c. 40
copies, mimeographed pamphlet) . . . £2,500
The Materialist Today, Driftwind Press (U.S.), 1926
(15 copies, pamphlet) £3,500
Further Criticism of Poetry, George C. Fetter (U.S.),
1932 (pamphlet) £2,500
Charleston, H.C. Koenig (U.S.), 1936 (first state, 20-
25 copies, pamphlet) £2,000
ditto, H.C. Koenig (U.S.), 1936 (second state, 30-35
copies, pamphlet) £1,500
Some Current Motives and Practices, R.H. Barlow
(U.S.), 1936 (50-100 copies, mimeographed pam-
phlet) £1,500
Notes and the Commonplace Book, Futile Press
(U.S.), 1938 (no d/w) £1,500
Marginalia, Arkham House (U.S.), 1944 . £250/£75
Supernatural Horror in Literature, Ben Abramson
(U.S.), 1945 (no d/w) £50
Something About Cats, Arkham House (U.S.), 1949 .
. . . . £125/£45
The Lovecraft Collector's Library, S.S.R. Publications
(U.S.), 1952-55 (7 vols, 75 copies) . . . £150
The Shuttered Room and Other Pieces, Arkham
House (U.S.), 1959 . . . . . . £125/£45

Dreams and Fancies, Arkham House (U.S.), 1962. .
. . . . £125/£45
Some Notes on a Nonentity, Arkham House (U.S.),
1963 (wraps) £100
Selected Letters, Volume I, Arkham House (U.S.),
1965 . . . . £30/£10
Selected Letters, Volume II, Arkham House (U.S.),
1968 . . . . £30/£10
Hail, Klarkash-Ton!, Squires, 1971 (89 copies, wraps)
. . . . £35
Selected Letters, Volume III, Arkham House (U.S.),
1971 . . . . £100/£45
Ec'h-Pi-El Speaks, de la Ree (U.S.), 1972 (25 cloth
bound copies, no d/w) £125
ditto, de la Ree (U.S.), 1972 (475 copies, wraps) £40
Lovecraft at Last, Carrollton Clark (U.S.), 1975
('Collectors edition', 1,000 copies in slipcase) . .
. . . . £100/£65
ditto, Carrollton Clark (U.S.), 1975 (2,000 copies) £50
The Occult Lovecraft, de la Ree (U.S.), 1975 (128
numbered cloth bound copies, no d/w). . . £60
ditto, de la Ree (U.S.), 1975 (990 copies, wraps) £20
First Writings: Pawtuxet Valley Gleaner 1906,
Necronomicon Press (U.S.), 1976 (500 numbered
copies, wraps) £25
Selected Letters, Volume IV, Arkham House (U.S.),
1976 . . . . £25/£10
Selected Letters, Volume V, Arkham House (U.S.),
1976 . . . . £25/£10
The Conservative Complete 1915-1923, Necronomicon Press (U.S.), 1976 (400 copies, wraps) £25
Writings in the United Amateur 1915-1922, Necro-
nomicon Press (U.S.), 1976 (500 numbered copies,
wraps). £25
To Quebec and the Stars, Grant (U.S.), 1976 £35/£10
The Californian, Necronomicon Press (U.S.), 1977
(1,000 numbered copies, wraps) . . . £10
Writings in The Tryout, Necronomicon Press (U.S.),
1977 (1,000 numbered copies, wraps) . . . £10
Memoirs of an Inconsequential Scribbler, Necro-
nomicon Press (U.S.), 1977 (500 copies, wraps) £10
Science Versus Charlatanry, Strange Company (U.S.),
1979 (200 numbered copies, wraps) . . . £25
H.P. Lovecraft in The Eyrie, Necronomicon Press
(U.S.), 1979 (wraps). £5
The H.P. Lovecraft Christmas Book, Necronomicon
Press (U.S.), 1984 (wraps) £5
In Defence of Dagon, Necronomicon Press (U.S.),
1985 (1,000 numbered copies, wraps) £5
Uncollected Letters, Necronomicon Press (U.S.), 1986
(wraps) £5
Commonplace Book, Necronomicon Press (U.S.),
1987 (2 vols, wraps) £10
Yr Obt Servt., The Strange Company (U.S.), 1988 (200
copies, wraps) £20
European Glimpses, Necronomicon Press (U.S.), 1988
(wraps) £5
The Vivesector, Necronomicon Press (U.S.), 1990
(wraps) £5

Letters to Henry Kuttner, Necronomicon Press (U.S.),
1990 (wraps) £5
The Conservative, Necronomicon Press (U.S.), 1990
(wraps) £5
Letters to Richard Searight, Necronomicon Press
(U.S.), 1992 (wraps). £5
Autobiographical Writings, Necronomicon Press
(U.S.), 1992 (wraps). £5
Letters to Robert Bloch, Necronomicon Press (U.S.),
1993 (wraps) £5
Letters to Robert Bloch Supplement, Necronomicon
Press (U.S.), 1993 (wraps) £5
H.P. Lovecraft in The Argosy, Necronomicon Press
(U.S.), 1994 (wraps). £5
The H.P. Lovecraft Dream Book, Necronomicon Press
(U.S.), 1994 (wraps). £10
Miscellaneous Writings, Arkham House (U.S.), 1995
(wraps) . . . . £20/£5

PETER LOVESEY
(b.1936)

An author of detective fiction whose early works look
as if they will become very collectable.

'Sergeant Cribb' Mystery Series
Wobble to Death, Macmillan, 1970 . . . £150/£45
ditto, Dodd, Mead (U.S.), 1970 . . . £75/£15
The Detective Wore Silk Drawers, Macmillan, 1971 .
. . . . £50/£10
ditto, Dodd, Mead (U.S.), 1971 . . . . . £30/£5
Abracadaver, Macmillan, 1972 . . . . £50/£10
ditto, Dodd, Mead (U.S.), 1972 . . . . . £25/£5
Mad Hatter's Holiday, Macmillan, 1973 . . £45/£5
ditto, Dodd, Mead (U.S.), 1973 . . . . . £20/£5
Invitation to a Dynamite Party, Macmillan, 1974 . .
. . . . £30/£5
ditto, as *The Tick of Death*, Dodd, Mead (U.S.), 1974.
. . . . £20/£5
A Case of Spirits, Macmillan, 1975 . . . . £25/£5
ditto, Dodd, Mead (U.S.), 1975 . . . . . £15/£5
Swing, Swing Together, Macmillan, 1976 . . £25/£5
ditto, Dodd, Mead (U.S.), 1976 . . . . . £15/£5
Waxwork, Macmillan, 1978 . . . . . £20/£5
ditto, Pantheon (U.S.), 1978 . . . . . £10/£5

'Peter Diamond' Mystery Series
The Last Detective, Scorpion Press, 1991 (99 signed,
numbered copies, acetate d/w) . . . . £75/£65
ditto, Scribner's, 1991. . . . . £15/£5
ditto, Doubleday (U.S.), 1991 . . . . . £15/£5
Diamond Solitaire, Little, Brown, 1992. . . £10/£5
ditto, Mysterious Press (U.S.), 1993 . . . . £10/£5
The Summons, Little, Brown, 1995 . . . . £10/£5
ditto, Mysterious Press (U.S.), 1995 . . . . £10/£5
Bloodhounds, Little, Brown, 1996 . . . . £10/£5
ditto, Mysterious Press (U.S.), 1996 . . . . £10/£5
Upon a Dark Night, Little, Brown, 1997 . . £10/£5

ditto, Mysterious Press (U.S.), 1998 . . . . £10/£5
The Vault, Little, Brown, 1999 . . . . . £10/£5
ditto, Soho Press (U.S.), 2000 . . . . . £10/£5
Diamond Dust, Little, Brown, 2002 . . . . £10/£5
ditto, Soho Press (U.S.), 2002 . . . . . £10/£5
The House Sitter, Little, Brown, 2003 . . . £10/£5

'Albert Edward, Prince of Wales' Mystery Series
Bertie and the Tinman, Bodley Head, 1987 . £15/£5
ditto, Mysterious Press (U.S.), 1988 . . . . £10/£5
Bertie and the Seven Bodies, Mysterious Press, 1990 .
. . . . £10/£5
ditto, Mysterious Press (U.S.), 1990 . . . £10/£5
Bertie and the Crime of Passion, Little, Brown, 1993 .
. . . . £10/£5
ditto, Mysterious Press (U.S.), 1993 . . . £10/£5

Other Novels
Goldengirl, Cassell 1977 (pseud. 'Peter Lear') £20/£5
ditto, Doubleday (U.S.), 1977 . . . . . £20/£5
Spider Girl, Cassell, 1980 (pseud. 'Peter Lear') £20/£5
ditto, Viking (U.S.), 1980 . . . . . . £20/£5
The False Inspector Dew, Macmillan, 1982 . £15/£5
ditto, Pantheon (U.S.), 1982 . . . . . £10/£5
Keystone, Macmillan, 1983 . . . . . £15/£5
ditto, Pantheon (U.S.), 1983 . . . . . £10/£5
The Secret of Spandau, Joseph, 1986 (pseud. 'Peter
Lear') . . . . £15/£5
Rough Cider, Bodley Head, 1986 . . . . £15/£5
ditto, Mysterious Press (U.S.), 1987 . . . £10/£5
On the Edge, Mysterious Press, 1989 . . . £15/£5
ditto, Mysterious Press, 1989 (250 signed, numbered
proof copies, wraps) £25
ditto, Mysterious Press (U.S.), 1989 . . . £10/£5
The Reaper, Little, Brown, 2000 . . . . £10/£5
ditto, Soho Press (U.S.), 2000 . . . . £10/£5

Short Stories
Butchers and Other Stories of Crime, Macmillan,
1985 . . . . £15/£5
ditto, Mysterious Press, 1987 . . . . . £15/£5
The Staring Man and Other Stories, Eurographica
(Helsinki), 1988 (350 signed, numbered copies, wraps
with d/w) £75
Do Not Exceed the Stated Dose, Mysterious Press
(U.S.) . . . . £10/£5
ditto, Crippen & Landru, 1998 (250 signed, numbered
copies with booklet) . . . . . . £35/£25
ditto, Little, Brown, 1998 . . . . . . £10/£5
The Sedgemoor Strangler and Other Stories of Crime,
Crippen & Landru, 2001 (275 signed copies with
pamphlet *The Butler Didn't Do It*) . . £30/£15

Others
The Black Cabinet, Xanadu, 1989 . . . . £10/£5
ditto, Carroll & Graf (U.S.), 1989 . . . . £10/£5

MALCOLM LOWRY
(b.1909 d.1957)

Few of Lowry's books were published in his lifetime.
Under the Volcano is regarded as his best work.

Ultramarine, Cape, 1933 . . . . . £3,000/£300
ditto, Lippincott (U.S.), 1962 (revised edition) £75/£20
ditto, Cape, 1963 (revised edition) . . . £45/£15
Under the Volcano, Reynal & Hitchcock, 1947 . . .
. . . . £1,000/£150
ditto, Cape, 1947 . . . . £600/£100
Hear Us O Lord from Heaven Thy Dwelling Place,
Lippincott (U.S.), 1961 . . . . . . £40/£10
ditto, Cape, 1962 . . . . £35/£10
Selected Poems of Malcolm Lowry, City Lights, 1962
(wraps) £30
Selected Letters of Malcolm Lowry, Lippincott (U.S.),
1965 . . . . £35/£15
ditto, Cape, 1967 . . . . £35/£15
Lunar Caustic, Cape, 1968 . . . . . £75/£20
ditto, Cape, 1968 (wraps) £20
Dark as the Grave Wherein My Friend is Laid, New
American Library (U.S.), 1968 . . . . £35/£10
ditto, Cape, 1969 . . . . £30/£10
October Ferry to Gabriola, World (U.S.), 1970 £25/£5
ditto, Cape, 1971 . . . . £20/£5
China and Kristbjotg's Story in the Black Hills, Aloe
Editions (U.S.), 1974 (150 numbered copies, wraps) .
. . . . £65
Malcolm Lowry, Psalms and Songs, New American
Library (U.S.), 1975 . . . . £45/£15
*Notes on a Screenplay for F. Scott Fitzgerald's
Tender is the Night*, Bruccoli (U.S.), 1976 £45/£10
*Sursum Corda! The Collected Letters of Malcolm
Lowry, Volume One: 1926-46*, Cape, 1995 £25/£10
ditto, Univ. Of Toronto Press (Canada), 1995 £25/£10
*Sursum Corda! The Collected Letters of Malcolm
Lowry, Volume Two: 1946-57*, Cape, 1996 £25/£10
ditto, Univ. Of Toronto Press (Canada), 1997 £25/£10

ROSE MACAULAY
(b.1881 d.1958)

Dame Rose Macaulay is well-respected as a novelist
who can combine intelligence with humour and
compassion.

Novels
Abbots Verney, Murray, 1906 . . . . . £200
The Furnace, Murray, 1907 . . . . . £100
The Secret River, Murray, 1909 . . . . £75
The Valley Captives, Murray, 1911 . . . £65
Views and Vagabonds, Murray, 1912 . . . £65
ditto, H. Holt and Co (U.S.), 1912 . . . £50
The Lee Shore, Hodder & Stoughton, 1912. . £40
ditto, Doran (U.S.), 1912 . . . . . . £40

The Making of a Bigot, Hodder & Stoughton, 1914 .
. . . . £35
Non-Combatants and Others, Hodder & Stoughton,
1916 . . . . £30
What Not: A Prophetic Comedy, Constable, 1918 £25
Potterism: A Tragi-Farcical Tract, Collins, 1920 . .
. . . . £100/£35
ditto, Boni & Liveright (U.S.), [1920] . . £75/£30
Dangerous Ages, Collins, 1921 . . . . £100/£35
ditto, Boni & Liveright (U.S.), [1921] . . £75/£30
Mystery at Geneva, Collins, 1922 . . . £100/£35
ditto, Boni & Liveright (U.S.), [1923] . . £75/£30
Told By an Idiot, Collins, 1923 . . . . £60/£20
ditto, Boni & Liveright (U.S.), 1923 . . . £60/£20
Orphan Island, Collins, 1924 . . . . £60/£20
ditto, Boni & Liveright (U.S.), [1925] . . £60/£20
Crewe Train, Collins, 1926 . . . . £40/£15
ditto, Boni & Liveright (U.S.), 1926 . . . £45/£15
Keeping Up Appearances, Collins, 1928 . £45/£15
Staying With Relations, Collins, 1930 . . £40/£15
ditto, Liveright (U.S.), [1930] . . . . £40/£15
They Were Defeated, Collins, 1932 . . . £35/£10
ditto, as *The Shadow Flies*, Harper & Bros (U.S.),
1934 . . . . £35/£10
Going Abroad, Collins, 1934 . . . . £35/£10
ditto, Harper & Bros (U.S.), 1934 . . . £35/£10
I Would Be Private, Collins, 1937 . . . £30/£10
ditto, Harper & Bros (U.S.), 1937 . . . £30/£10
And No Man's Wit, Collins, 1940 . . . . £20/£5
ditto, Little, Brown (U.S.), 1940 . . . . . £15/£5
The World My Wilderness, Collins, 1950 . £20/£5
ditto, Little, Brown (U.S.), 1950 . . . . . £15/£5
The Towers of Trebizond, Collins, 1956 . £20/£5
ditto, Farrar, Straus (U.S.), 1957 . . . . £15/£5

Poetry
The Two Blind Countries, Sidgwick & Jackson, 1914.
. . . . £25
Three Days, Constable, 1919. . . . . £25
ditto, Dutton (U.S.), 1919. . . . . . £25

Travel
They Went to Portugal, Cape, 1946 . . . £25/£10
Fabled Shore: From the Pyrenees to Portugal,
Hamish Hamilton, 1949 . . . . . £25/£10
ditto, Farrar, Straus (U.S.), 1949 . . . . £25/£10
Pleasure of Ruins, Weidenfeld & Nicolson, 1953 . .
. . . . £45/£15
ditto, Walker (U.S.), [1966] . . . . £45/£15

Others
A Casual Commentary, Methuen, 1925 . . £35/£10
ditto, Boni & Liveright (U.S.), 1926 . . £35/£10
Catchwords and Claptrap, Hogarth Press, 1926 (no
d/w) £65
Some Religious Elements in English Literature,
Hogarth Press, 1931 . . . . . . £35/£10
ditto, Harcourt Brace (U.S.), [1931] . . £30/£10
Milton, Duckworth, 1934 . . . . . £25/£10

ditto, Harper & Row (U.S.), 1935 . . . £20/£10
Personal Pleasures, Gollancz, 1935 . . . £35/£10
ditto, Macmillan (U.S.), 1936 . . . . £25/£10
The Writings of E.M. Forster, Hogarth Press, 1938 .
. . . . £65/£20
ditto, Harcourt Brace (U.S.), 1938 . . . £50/£15
Life Among the English, Collins, 1942 . . £20/£5
Letters to a Friend: 1950 - 1952, Collins, 1961 £15/£5
ditto, Atheneum (U.S.), 1962 . . . . . £15/£5
Last Letters to a Friend, 1952 - 1958, Collins, 1962 .
. . . . £15/£5
ditto, Atheneum (U.S.), 1963 . . . . . £15/£5
Letters to a Sister, Collins, 1964 . . . . £15/£5
ditto, Atheneum (U.S.), 1964 . . . . . £15/£5

GEORGE MACDONALD
(b.1824 d.1905)

A Scottish author, Macdonald is perhaps best known
for his children's book *At the Back of the North Wind*,
and his adult fantasy *Phantastes*.

Children's Titles
Dealings with the Fairies, Strahan, 1867 (blue cloth) .
. . . . £1,500
ditto, Strahan, 1867 (green cloth) . . . £1,000
ditto, George Routledge (U.S.), 1891 . . . £500
At the Back of the North Wind, Strahan, 1871 (first
issue binding bright blue pictorial cloth stamped in
gold) £3,000
ditto, Strahan, 1871 (second issue binding without gold
frame) £2,000
ditto, George Routledge (U.S.), [c.1871] . £1,000
Ranald Bannerman's Boyhood, Strahan, 1871 £750
ditto, Lippincott (U.S.), 1879 . . . . . £400
The Princess and the Goblin, Strahan, 1872 . £1,500
ditto, Lippincott (U.S.), 1871 . . . . . £200
Gutta Percha Willie, King, 1873 . . . . £500
The Wise Woman, Strahan, 1875 . . . . £200
The Princess and the Curdie, Chatto & Windus, 1883
. . . . £750
ditto, Lippincott (U.S.), 1883 . . . . . £500
Cross Purpose and the Shadows, Blackie, 1886 £50
The Light Princess and Other Fairy Tales, Blackie,
1890 . . . . £150
ditto, Putnam (U.S.), 1893 . . . . . £100
The Golden Key, Crowell (U.S.), [1906] . . £200
ditto, Bodley Head, 1972 . . . . . £40/£10

Poetry
Within and Without: a Dramatic Poem, Longman,
1855 . . . . £1,250
ditto, Scribner's, Armstrong (U.S.), 1872 . . £250
Poems, Longman, 1857 . . . . . . £400
ditto, Dutton (U.S.), 1887 . . . . . £300
The Disciple and Other Poems, Strahan, 1867 . £250
ditto, Sunrise Books (U.S.), 1989 . . . . £10/£5

A Threefold Cord: Poem, by Three Friends, edited by MacDonald, privately printed by Hughes, [1883]. .
. . . . £350
Poetical Works, Chatto & Windus, 1893 (2 vols) £100

Translations
Twelve of the Spiritual Songs of Novalis, Strahan, 1851 . . . . £500
Exotics, Strahan, 1851 . . . . . . £500

Others
Phantastes; a Faerie Romance, Smith, Elder, 1858 .
. . . . £1,500
ditto, Loring (U.S.), 1870 . . . . . . £150
David Elginbrod, Hurst & Blackett, 1863 (3 vols) . .
. . . . £1,500
ditto, Loring (U.S.), [1863] £250
Adela Cathcart, Hurst & Blackett, 1864 (3 vols) £750
ditto, Loring (U.S.), [1864] £250
The Portent, Smith, Elder, 1864 . . . . . £350
ditto, Loring (U.S.), [1864] £200
Alec Forbes of Howglen, Hurst & Blackett, 1865 (3 vols) £750
Annals of a Quiet Neighbourhood, Hurst & Blackett, 1867 (3 vols) £750
ditto, Harper (U.S.), 1867 . . . . . . £200
Unspoken Sermons, Strahan, 1867 . . . . £450
ditto, Second series, Longmans, 1885 . . £100
ditto, Third series, Longmans, 1889 . . . £100
ditto, Sunrise Books (U.S.), 1988 . . . £10/£5
Guild Court, Hurst & Blackett, 1868 (3 vols) . £750
Robert Falconer, Hurst & Blackett, 1868 (3 vols) £750
ditto, Loring (U.S.), [1876] £200
The Seaboard Parish, Tinsley, 1868 (3 vols) . £1,000
England's Antiphon, Macmillan, [1868] . . £125
ditto, Lippincott (U.S.), [1868] £100
The Miracles of Our Lord, Strahan, 1870 . . £75
Works of Fancy and Imagination, Strahan, 1871 (10 vols, slipcase) . . . . . £2,000/£1,500
Wilfred Cumbermede, Hurst & Blackett, 1872 (3 vols) £750
ditto, Scribner's (U.S.), 1872 . . . . . £150
The Vicar's Daughter, Tinsley, 1872 (3 vols) . £750
ditto, Roberts (U.S.), 1872 . . . . . £150
Malcolm, King, 1875 (3 vols) £750
ditto, Lippincott (U.S.), 1877 . . . . . £150
St George and St Michael, King, 1876 (3 vols) £750
ditto, Ford & Co (U.S.), [1876] £150
Thomas Wingfold, Hurst & Blackett, 1876 (3 vols) .
. . . . £750
ditto, Routledge (U.S.), 1876 . . . . . £150
The Marquis of Losse, Hurst & Blackett, 1877 (3 vols)
. . . . £600
ditto, Lippincott (U.S.), 1877 . . . . . £125
Paul Faber, Hurst & Blackett, 1879 (3 vols) . £600
ditto, Lippincott (U.S.), 1879 . . . . . £125
Sir Gibbie, Hurst & Blackett, 1879 (3 vols) . . £600
ditto, Lippincott (U.S.), 1879 . . . . . £125

A Book of Strife, privately printed, 1880 . . £500
ditto, privately printed, 1882 . . . . . . £400
ditto, Longman, 1889 . . . . £200
Mary Marston, Sampson, Low, 1881 (3 vols) . £500
ditto, Appleton (U.S.), 1881 . . . . . £125
Warlock O'Glen Warlock, Lothrop (U.S.), 1881 £175
ditto, Harper & Brothers (U.S.), 1881 (wraps) . £125
ditto, as *Castle Warlock*, Sampson, Low, 1882 (3 vols)
. . . . £750
Orts, Sampson Low, 1882 . . . . . £150
Weighed and Wanting, Sampson, Low, 1882 (3 vols).
. . . . £500
ditto, Lothrop (U.S.), 1882 . . . . . £100
The Gifts of the Child Christ, Sampson Low, 1882 (2 vols) £75
Donal Grant, Kegan Paul, 1883 (3 vols) . . £500
ditto, Lothrop (U.S.), 1883 . . . . . £100
What's Mine's Mine, Kegan Paul, 1886 (3 vols) £450
ditto, Lothrop (U.S.), [1886] £100
Home Again, Kegan Paul, 1887 . . . . . £200
ditto, Appleton (U.S.), 1888 . . . . . £100
The Elect Lady, Kegan Paul, 1888 . . . . £200
ditto, Appleton (U.S.), 1888 . . . . . £100
There and Back, Kegan Paul, 1891 (3 vols) . £350
ditto, Lothrop (U.S.), [1891] £100
A Rough Shaking, Routledge (U.S.), 1890 . . £150
ditto, Blackie, 1891 . . . . £150
The Flight of the Shadow, Kegan Paul, 1891 . £150
ditto, Appleton (U.S.), 1891 . . . . . £150
The Hope of the Gospel, Ward, Lock, 1892 . £50
ditto, Appleton (U.S.), 1892 . . . . . £45
Heather and Snow, Chatto & Windus, 1893 (2 vols) .
. . . . £250
ditto, Harper (U.S.), 1893 . . . . . . £75
A Dish of Orts, Sampson Low, 1893 . . . £75
Lilith, Chatto & Windus, 1895 . . . . £300
ditto, Dodd, Mead (U.S.), 1895 . . . . £150
Salted with Fire, Hurst & Blackett, 1897 . . £75
ditto, Dodd, Mead (U.S.), 1897 . . . . £65
Far Above Rubies, Dodd, Mead (U.S.), 1899 . £65
Fairy Tales, Fifield, 1904 (five parts) . . . £125
ditto, Fifield, 1904 (1 vol.) £70

PHILIP MACDONALD
(b.1900 d.1981)

An important figure in the Golden Age of crime fiction, *The Rasp* and *The Nursemaid Who Disappeared* were selected as Haycraft-Queen Cornerstones.

Crime Novels as Philip Macdonald
The Rasp, Collins, 1924 . . . . . £1,500/£200
ditto, Dial (U.S.), 1925 . . . . . . £400/£50
The White Crow, Collins, 1928 . . . . £500/£65
ditto, Dial (U.S.), 1928 . . . . . . £200/£25
The Noose, Collins Crime Club, 1930 . . £400/£45
ditto, Dial (U.S.), 1930 . . . . . . £150/£15

The Link, Collins Crime Club, 1930. . . £350/£40
ditto, Doubleday (U.S.), 1930 . . . . £150/£15
Rynox, Collins, 1930 . . . . £350/£40
ditto, as *The Rynox Murder Mystery*, Doubleday (U.S.), 1931 . . . . £150/£15
ditto, as *The Rynox Mystery*, Collins, 1933 . . £20/£5
Persons Unknown, Doubleday (U.S.), 1931 £150/£15
ditto, as *The Maze*, Collins Crime Club, 1932 . . .
. . . . £350/£40
Murder Gone Mad, Collins Crime Club, 1931 . . .
. . . . £350/£40
ditto, Doubleday (U.S.), 1931 . . . . £150/£15
The Wraith, Doubleday (U.S.), 1931 . . £150/£15
ditto, Collins Crime Club, 1931 . . . £350/£40
The Choice, Collins Crime Club, 1931 . . £350/£40
ditto, as *The Polferry Riddle*, Doubleday (U.S.), 1931.
. . . . £150/£15
ditto, as *The Polferry Mystery*, Collins, 1932 . £25/£5
Harbour, Doubleday (U.S.), 1931 (pseud. 'Anthony
Lawless') . . . . £150/£15
ditto, Collins Crime Club, 1931 (as Philip Macdonald)
. . . . £350/£40
The Crime Conductor, Doubleday (U.S.), 1931 . .
. . . . £150/£15
ditto, Collins Crime Club, 1932 . . . . £350/£40
Rope to Spare, Collins Crime Club, 1932 . £350/£40
ditto, Doubleday (U.S.), 1932 . . . . £150/£15
Death on My Left, Collins Crime Club, 1933 £350/£40
ditto, Doubleday (U.S.), 1933 . . . . £150/£15
R.I.P., Collins Crime Club, 1933. . . . £350/£40
ditto, as *Menace*, Doubleday (U.S.), 1933 £150/£15
The Nursemaid Who Disappeared, Collins Crime
Club, 1938 . . . . £750/£100
ditto, as *Warrant for X*, Doubleday (U.S.), 1938 . .
. . . . £400/£50
The Dark Wheel, Collins Crime Club, 1948 (with A.
Boyd Correll). . . . . £75/£15
ditto, Morrow (U.S.), 1948 . . . . . £25/£10
ditto, as *Sweet and Deadly*, Zenith, 1959 (wraps) £10
Guest in the House, Doubleday (U.S.), 1955 £25/£10
ditto, Herbert Jenkins, 1956 . . . . £75/£15
ditto, as *No Time For Terror*, Bestseller, 1956 (wraps)
. . . . £10
The List of Adrian Messenger, Doubleday (U.S.),
1959 . . . . £95/£20
ditto, Herbert Jenkins, 1960 . . . . £50/£15

Crime Novels as 'Martin Porlock'
Mystery at Friar's Pardon, Collins Crime Club, 1931.
. . . . £350/£40
ditto, Doubleday (U.S.), 1932 (as Philip Macdonald) .
. . . . £150/£15
Mystery in Kensington Gore, Collins Crime Club,
1931 . . . . £350/£40
ditto, as *Escape*, Doubleday (U.S.), 1932 (as Philip
Macdonald) . . . . £150/£15
X v. Rex, Collins Crime Club, 1933 . . . £350/£40
ditto, as *The Mystery of the Dead Police*, Doubleday
(U.S.), 1933 (as 'Philip Macdonald') . . £150/£15

ditto, as *The Mystery of Mr X*, Literary Press, 1934 .
. . . . £20/£5

Crime Novels as 'Oliver Fleming'
The Ambrotox and Limping Dick, Ward Lock, 1920
(with Ronald MacDonald) . . . £750/£100
The Spandau Quid, Cecil Palmer, 1923 (with Ronald
MacDonald) . . . . £500/£50

Short Stories
Something to Hide, Doubleday (U.S.), 1952 £25/£10
ditto, as *Fingers of Fear*, Collins Crime Club, 1953 .
. . . . £75/£20
The Man Out of the Rain, Doubleday (U.S.), 1955 .
. . . . £25/£10
ditto, Herbert Jenkins, 1957 . . . . . £50/£10
Death and Chicanery, Doubleday (U.S.), 1962 £20/£5
ditto, Herbert Jenkins, 1963 . . . . . £30/£10

Other Fiction
Gentleman Bill: A Boxing Story, Herbert Jenkins,
1923 . . . . £300/£35
Queens Mate, Collins, 1926 . . . . . £300/£35
Patrol, Collins, 1927 . . . . £350/£45
Likeness of Exe, Collins, 1929 . . . . £350/£45
Moonfisher, Collins, 1931 . . . . . £350/£45
Glitter, Collins, 1934 . . . . £300/£35
Forbidden Planet, Farrar Strauss (U.S.), 1956 (as 'W.J.
Stuart') . . . . £65/£15
ditto, Corgi, 1956 (wraps). £15

ROSS MACDONALD
(b.1915 d.1983)

Macdonald is the best known of the many pseudonyms for Kenneth Millar, an American writer of
detective novels, who also writes under his own
name.

'Ross Macdonald' Novels
The Barbarous Coast, Knopf (U.S.), 1956 £1,000/£75
ditto, Cassell, 1957 . . . . £100/£20
The Doomsters, Knopf (U.S.), 1958. . . £750/£50
ditto, Cassell, 1958 . . . . £100/£15
The Galton Case, Knopf (U.S.), 1959 . . £300/£40
ditto, Cassell, 1960 . . . . £100/£15
The Ferguson Affair, Knopf (U.S.), 1960 . £300/£40
ditto, Collins, 1961 . . . . £100/£15
The Wycherly Woman, Knopf (U.S.), 1961. £300/£40
ditto, Collins Crime Club, 1961 . . . . £100/£15
The Zebra-Striped Hearse, Knopf (U.S.), 1962 . .
. . . . £125/£30
ditto, Collins Crime Club, 1963 . . . . £25/£10
The Chill, Knopf (U.S.), 1964 . . . . £125/£30
ditto, Collins Crime Club, 1964 . . . . £40/£10
The Far Side of the Dollar, Knopf (U.S.), 1965 . .
. . . . £35/£10

ditto, Collins Crime Club, 1965 . . . . £20/£10
Black Money, Knopf (U.S.), 1966 . . . £35/£10
ditto, Collins Crime Club, 1966 . . . . £25/£10
The Instant Enemy, Knopf (U.S.), 1968 . £25/£10
ditto, Collins Crime Club, 1968 . . . . £25/£10
The Goodbye Look, Knopf (U.S.), 1969 . £20/£10
ditto, Collins Crime Club, 1969 . . . . . £15/£5
The Underground Man, Knopf (U.S.), 1971 . £15/£5
ditto, Collins Crime Club, 1971 . . . . . £10/£5
Sleeping Beauty, Knopf (U.S.), 1973 . . . £15/£5
ditto, Collins Crime Club, 1973 . . . . . £10/£5
The Blue Hammer, Knopf (U.S.), 1976. . . £15/£5
ditto, Collins Crime Club, 1976 . . . . . £10/£5
Lew Archer, Private Investigator, Mysterious Press
(U.S.), 1977 (250 numbered, signed copies, acetate
d/w and slipcase). . . . . £175/£65

Other Titles as 'Ross Macdonald'
On Crime Writing, Capra Press (U.S.), 1973 (250
signed, numbered copies, no d/w) £125
ditto, Capra Press (U.S.), 1973 (wraps) . . £15
Self Portrait, Ceaselessly Into The Past, Capra Press
(U.S.), 1981 (250 signed, numbered copies, no d/w) .
. . . . £125
ditto, Capra Press (U.S.), 1981 . . . . . £15/£5

'Kenneth Millar' Novels
The Dark Tunnel, Dodd, Mead (U.S.), 1944 . . .
. . . . £3,000/£250
ditto, as *I Die Slowly*, Lion, 1955, . . £45/£10
Trouble Follows Me, Dodd, Mead (U.S.), 1946 . .
. . . . £1,500/£100
ditto, as *Night Train*, Lion, 1955. . . . . £20/£5
Blue City, Knopf (U.S.), 1947 . . . . £300/£65
ditto, Cassell, 1949 . . . . £25/£10
The Three Roads, Knopf (U.S.), 1948 . . £300/£65
ditto, Cassell, 1950 . . . . £25/£10

'John Ross Macdonald' Novels
The Drowning Pool, Knopf (U.S.), 1950 £1,000/£75
ditto, Cassell, 1952 . . . . . . £125/£15
The Way Some People Die, Knopf (U.S.), 1951 . .
. . . . £750/£75
ditto, Cassell, 1953 . . . . £50/£15
The Ivory Grin, Knopf (U.S.), 1952. . . £750/£75
ditto, Cassell, 1953 . . . . £50/£15
Meet Me at the Morgue, Knopf (U.S.), 1953 £250/£45
ditto, as *Experience with Evil*, Cassell, 1954 £25/£10
Find a Victim, Knopf (U.S.), 1954 . . . £150/£35
ditto, Cassell, 1955 . . . . £25/£10

'John Ross Macdonald' Short Stories
The Name is Archer, Bantam (U.S.), 1955 (wraps) £25

'John Macdonald' Novels
The Moving Target, Knopf (U.S.), 1949 . £450/£45
ditto, Cassell, 1951 . . . . . . £125/£25

IAN McEWAN
(b.1948)

A writer of obsessive, often explicit novels and short
stories, McEwan was the first former student of
Malcolm Bradbury's creative writing course at the
University of East Anglia to receive recognition.

Short Stories
First Love, Last Rites, Cape, 1975 . . . £350/£35
ditto, Random House (U.S.), 1975 . . . £60/£10
In Between the Sheets, Cape, 1978 . . . £175/£25
ditto, Simon & Schuster (U.S.), 1979 . . . £30/£5
The Short Stories, Cape, 1995 . . . . . . £20/£5

Novels
The Cement Garden, Cape, 1978 . . . £125/£15
ditto, Simon & Schuster (U.S.), 1978 . . . £30/£5
The Comfort of Strangers, Cape, 1981 . . . £45/£5
ditto, Simon & Schuster (U.S.), 1981 . . . £20/£5
The Child in Time, Cape, 1987 . . . . . £25/£5
ditto, London Limited Editions (150 numbered, signed
copies in glassine jacket) . . . . . £75/£60
ditto, Houghton Mifflin (U.S.), 1987 . . . £15/£5
The Innocent, Cape, 1990 . . . . . . £20/£5
ditto, Doubleday (U.S.), 1990 . . . . . £15/£5
Black Dogs, Cape, 1992 . . . . £15/£5
ditto, London Limited Editions, 1992 (150 numbered,
signed copies in glassine jacket) . . . £65/£50
ditto, Doubleday (U.S.), 1992 . . . . . £10/£5
Enduring Love, Cape, 1997 . . . . . . £10/£5
ditto, Doubleday (U.S.), 1998 . . . . . £10/£5
Amsterdam, Cape, 1998 . . . . £10/£5
ditto, Doubleday (U.S.), 1999 . . . . . £10/£5
Atonement, Cape, 2001 . . . . £10/£5
ditto, Doubleday (U.S.), 2002 (500 signed copies) . .
. . . . £100/65
ditto, Talese/Doubleday (U.S.), 2002 . . . £10/£5

Children's Titles
The Daydreamer, Cape, 1994 . . . . . £15/£5
ditto, Harper Collins (U.S.), 1994 . . . . £10/£5

Miscellaneous
British Films at the London Film Festival, Filmways,
1979 [1980] (wraps). £25
The Imitation Game: Three Plays for Television,
Cape, 1981 . . . . £40/£10
ditto, Houghton Mifflin (U.S.), 1982 . . . £20/£5
Or Shall We Die?, Cape, 1983 . . . . £35/£15
The Ploughman's Lunch, Methuen, 1985 (wraps) £10
Soursweet, Faber, 1988 (wraps) £10
A Move Abroad, Picador, 1989 (wraps). . . . £5
*Other Minds – An extract from His Forthcoming
Novel "Atonement"*, Bridgewater Press, 2001 (26
lettered, signed copies) £150
ditto, Bridgewater Press, 2001 (100 numbered, signed
copies) £50

JOHN McGAHERN
(b.1934)

A novelist and short story writer whose works, wherever they are set, always refer back to the author's native Ireland.

Novels

The Barracks, Faber, 1963	£350/£75
ditto, Macmillan (U.S.), 1964	£100/£15
The Dark, Faber, 1965	£150/£25
ditto, Knopf (U.S.), 1966	£50/£10
The Leavetaking, Faber, 1974	£50/£10
ditto, Little, Brown (U.S.), 1974 . . .	£40/£10
The Pornographer, Faber, 1979	£40/£10
ditto, Harper & Row (U.S.), 1979 . . .	£20/£5
Amongst Women, Faber, 1990	£10/£5
ditto, Viking (U.S.), 1990	£10/£5
That They May Face The Rising Sun, Faber, 2001 .
. . . .	£10/£5

Short Stories

Nightlines, Faber, 1970	£75/£15
ditto, Little, Brown (U.S.), 1971 . . .	£35/£10
Getting Through, Faber, 1978	£45/£10
ditto, Harper & Row (U.S.), 1980 . . .	£15/£5
High Ground, Faber, 1985	£25/£5
ditto, Viking (U.S.), 1987	£10/£5
The Collected Stories, Faber, 1992 . . .	£25/£10
ditto, Knopf (U.S.), 1993	£20/£5

Plays

The Power of Darkness, Faber, 1991 (wraps) . £15

ARTHUR MACHEN
(b.1863 d.1947)

A novelist, short story writer and essayist, Machen is generally read for his tales of horror and the supernatural although his work is predominantly of a mystical cast. His *Bowmen* was the origin of the 'Angels of Mons' myth in the First World War.

Poetry

Eleusinia, privately printed, 1881 (wraps) . £25,000

Novels

The Chronicle of Clemendy, Carbonnek, 1888 (250 numbered copies) £200
ditto, privately printed, Carbonnek (U.S.), 1923 (1,050 numbered, signed copies) £75
ditto, Martin Secker, 1925 [1926] (100 signed, numbered copies) £125
ditto, Martin Secker, 1925 (trade edition) . £75/£25
The Great God Pan, John Lane, 1894 . . . £225
ditto, Roberts Bros (U.S.), 1894 . . . . £150
The Three Impostors, John Lane, 1895 . . . £225
ditto, Roberts Bros (U.S.), 1895 . . . . £150

ditto, Knopf (U.S.), 1923 . . . . . . £45/£20
The Hill of Dreams, Grant Richards, 1907 (first binding without adverts after text) £150
ditto, Grant Richards, 1907 (second binding with 20 pages of adverts after text) £125
ditto, Dana Estes & Co (U.S.), 1907 . . . . £75
ditto, Martin Secker, [1922] (150 signed, numbered copies) £250
The Great Return, The Faith Press, 1915 (first issue with top edge stained red) £200
ditto, The Faith Press, 1915 (second issue with top edge unstained) £75
The Terror, Duckworth & Co., 1917 . . . £45
ditto, as *The Terror, A Mystery*, McBride (U.S.), [1917] £40
The Secret Glory, Martin Secker, 1922 . . £200/£60
ditto, Knopf (U.S.), 1923 . . . . . £150/£50
ditto, as *Chapters Five and Six of 'The Secret Glory'*, Tartarus Press, 1990 (250 numbered copies) £35/£10
ditto, Tartarus Press, 1998 (first edition of all six chapters) . . . . £25/£10
The Green Round, Ernest Benn, 1933 . . £250/£50
ditto, Arkham House (U.S.), 1968 . . . £50/£20
ditto, Tartarus Press, 2000 . . . . . £20/£5

Short Stories

The House of Souls, Grant Richards, 1906 . . £250
ditto, Dana Estes & Co (U.S.), 1906 . . . . £200
The Bowmen, Simpkin Marshall, 1915 . . . £50
ditto, Simpkin Marshall, 1915 (enlarged edition with silhouette). £45
ditto, Putnams (U.S.), 1915 (first issue with blue bowman) £50
ditto, Putnams (U.S.), 1915 (second issue with brown bowman) £45
The Shining Pyramid, Covici-McGee (U.S.), 1923 (875 numbered copies) £75
Ornaments In Jade, Knopf (U.S.), 1924 (1,000 signed, numbered copies, slipcase) . . . . . £100/£75
ditto, Tartarus Press, 1997 . . . . . £25/£10
The Shining Pyramid, Martin Secker, 1925 (different from above *Shining Pyramid*) . . . . £75/£30
ditto, Martin Secker, 1925 (250 signed, numbered copies) . . . . £225/£150
ditto, Knopf (U.S.), 1925 . . . . . . £75/£30
The Cosy Room, Rich & Cowan, 1936 . £1,000/£300
The Children of the Pool, Hutchinson & Co., 1936 .
. . . . £1,000/£300
Ritual and Other Stories, Tartarus Press, 1992 . . .
. . . . £45/£10

Essays

Strange Roads & With the Gods in Spring, The Classic Press, 1923 . . . . £50
ditto, The Classic Press, 1924 (300 signed, numbered copies) £100
The Grande Trouvaille: A Legend of Pentonville, privately printed, 1923 (250 signed, numbered copies, wraps) £100

The Collector's Craft, privately printed, 1923 (250 numbered copies, wraps) £100
ditto, privately printed, 1923 (unknown number also signed, wraps) £150
Dog and Duck, Knopf (U.S.), 1924 . . . £75/£25
ditto, Cape, [1924] (900 numbered copies) . £100/£35
ditto, Cape, [1924] (150 of above numbered and signed) . . . . £150/£100
The Glorious Mystery, Covici-McGee (U.S.), 1924 (pictorial boards). . . . . £150/£50
Dreads and Drolls, Martin Secker, 1926 . £75/£25
ditto, Martin Secker, 1926 (100 signed, numbered copies) . . . . £150/£100
ditto, Knopf (U.S.), 1927 . . . . . . £75/£25
Notes and Queries, Spurr & Swift, 1926 (265 signed, numbered copies) £125
Tom O' Bedlam and His Song, The Appellicon Press (U.S.), 1930 (200 signed copies, slipcase) . £150/£100
Beneath the Barley, privately printed, 1931 (25 signed, numbered copies, wraps) £125
The Glitter of the Brook, Postprandial Press (U.S.), 1932 (10 copies) £300
Bridles and Spurs, The Rowfant Club (U.S.), 1951 (178 numbered copies, slipcase) . . . £200/£150
ditto, The Rowfant Club (U.S.), 1951 (offprint of the Preface only 25 copies) £100
A Critical Essay, privately printed (U.S.), 1953 (50 copies) £100
A Note on Poetry, Four Ducks Press (U.S.), 1959 (50 numbered copies) £100
From the London Evening News, Four Ducks Press (U.S.), 1959 (50 numbered copies). . . . £100
The Secret of the Sangraal, Tartarus Press, 1996 (250 copies) . . . . £45/£15

Autobiography
Far Off Things, Martin Secker, 1922 (100 signed, numbered copies) £175
ditto, Martin Secker, 1922 (trade edition) . £65/£30
ditto, Knopf (U.S.), 1923 . . . . . £45/£15
Things Near and Far, Martin Secker, 1923 (100 signed, numbered copies) £175
ditto, Martin Secker, 1923 . . . . . £65/£25
ditto, Knopf (U.S.), 1923 . . . . . £45/£15
The London Adventure, Martin Secker, 1924 £65/£25
ditto, Martin Secker, 1924 (200 signed, numbered copies) £175
ditto, Knopf (U.S.), 1924 . . . . . £45/£15
In the Eighties, privately printed, 1931 . . £100
ditto, Twyn Barlwm Press, 1933 (50 numbered copies)
. . . . £50

Translations
The Heptameron, by Queen Margaret of Navarre, privately printed [Dryden Press], 1886. . . £65
ditto, as *The Fortunate Lovers,* Redway, 1887 (a selection of the above) £30
ditto, Scribner's & Welford (U.S.), 1887 . . £100

Fantastic Tales, or The Way to Attain, privately printed, Carbonnek, 1889 [1890] (500 numbered copies) £65
ditto, privately printed, Carbonnek, 1889 [1890] (large paper issue, 50 signed, numbered copies) . . £200
ditto, privately printed, Carbonnek (U.S.), 1923 (1,050 numbered, signed copies) . . . . . £75/£35
The Memoirs of Casanova, privately printed, 1894 (12 vols, 1,000 copies) £400
ditto, privately printed, 1894 (large paper issue, 50 numbered sets) £650
ditto, privately printed, 1894 (3 numbered sets, Japanese vellum). £1,000
Casanova's Escape from the Leads, Casanova Society, 1925 . . . . £50/£15
ditto, Knopf (U.S.), Borzoi Pocket Books No. 28 [1925]. . . . . £35/£10

Others
The Anatomy of Tobacco, George Redway, 1884 (pseud. 'Leolinus Siluriensis') £300
ditto, Knopf (U.S.), 1926 . . . . . £50/£20
Don Quijote de la Mancha, George Redway, 1887 (wraps) £450
Hieroglyphics, Grant Richards, 1902 . . . £125
ditto, Kennerley (U.S), 1913 . . . . . £75
ditto, Knopf (U.S), 1923 . . . . . £50/£20
The House of the Hidden Light, privately printed, 1904 (with A.E. Waite, 3 copies) £5,000
ditto, Tartarus/Ferret, 2003 . . . . . £30/£10
Dr. Stiggins, Francis Griffiths, 1906. . . £45
ditto, Knopf (U.S), 1925 . . . . . £50/£10
War and the Christian Faith, Skeffington & Son, 1918 . . . . £50
Arthur Machen, a novelist of ecstasy and sin, Walter M. Hill (U.S.), 1918 (250 copies) £150
Precious Balms, Spurr & Swift, 1924 (265 signed, numbered copies) £100
ditto, Spurr & Swift, 1924 (15 signed, lettered copies).
. . . . £200
The Canning Wonder, Chatto & Windus, 1925 . .
. . . . £65/£20
ditto, Chatto & Windus, 1925 (130 signed, numbered copies) £75
ditto, Knopf (U.S.), 1926 . . . . . £30/£10
A Preface to Casanova's Escape from the Leads, The Casanova Society, 1925 (25 copies, wraps) . £150
A Souvenir of Cadby Hall, J. Lyons and Co. Ltd, 1927
. . . . £100
Parish of Amersham, Mason, 1930 (wraps) . £45
An Introduction to J. Gawsworth: Above the River, privately printed, 1931 (12 signed, numbered copies, wraps). £250
A Few Letters from Arthur Machen, The Rowfant Club (U.S.), 1932 (170 copies) £125
ditto, Aylesford Press, 1993 (83 copies of 333, signed by Janet Machen) £30
ditto, Aylesford Press, 1993 (250 copies of 333, wraps)
. . . . £15

A.L.S., Four Ducks Press (U.S.), 1956 (50 numbered copies) £125
Starrett Vs. Machen, Autolycus Press (U.S.), 1977 £30
ditto, Autolycus Press (U.S.), 1977 (50 numbered copies) £60
Dreams and Visions, by Morchard Bishop, Caermaen Books, 1987 (wraps). £15
Selected Letters, The Aquarian Press, 1988 . . £10/£5

Collected Edition
The Caerleon Edition, Martin Secker, 1923 (9 vols) .
. . . . £600/£350

COLIN MACINNES
(b.1914 d.1976)

Chiefly read today for his 'London Trilogy' novels, which jauntily catch the changing mood of 1950s and 60s society.

Novels
To The Victors The Spoils, MacGibbon & Kee, 1950 .
. . . . £45/£15
June in Her Spring, MacGibbon & Kee, 1952 £45/£15
City of Spades, MacGibbon & Kee, 1957 . £30/£10
ditto, Macmillan (U.S.), 1958 . . . . . £20/£5
Absolute Beginners, MacGibbon & Kee, 1959 . . .
. . . . £125/£20
ditto, Macmillan (U.S.), 1960 . . . . £45/£10
Mr Love and Justice, MacGibbon & Kee, 1960 . . .
. . . . £30/£10
ditto, Dutton (U.S.), 1961. . . . . . £20/£5
All Day Saturday, MacGibbon & Kee, 1966 . £20/£5
Sweet Saturday Night, MacGibbon & Kee, 1967 . .
. . . . £20/£5
Westward to Laughter, MacGibbon & Kee, 1969 . .
. . . . £20/£5
ditto, Farrar Straus (U.S.), 1970 . . . . £15/£5
Three Years to Play, MacGibbon & Kee, 1970. £15/£5
ditto, Farrar Straus (U.S.), 1970 . . . . £10/£5
Out of the Garden, Hart-Davis MacGibbon, 1974 . .
. . . . £10/£5

Collected Editions
Visions of London, MacGibbon & Kee, 1969 . £15/£5
ditto, as *The London Novels*, Farrar Straus (U.S.),
1969 . . . . £15/£5

Essays
England, Half English, MacGibbon & Kee, 1961 . .
. . . . £30/£10
ditto, Random House (U.S.), 1962 . . . £20/£5
Posthumous Essays, Brian & O'Keefe, 1977 . £15/£5
Out of the Way: Later Essays, Brian & O'Keefe, 1980
. . . . £15/£5

Others
London: City of Any Dream, Thames & Hudson, 1962
. . . . £25/£10

Australia and New Zealand, Time (U.S.), 1966 (with the editors of *Life*) . . . . £15/£5
Loving Them Both: A Study of Bisexuality and Bisexuals, Brian & O'Keefe, 1973 . . . £25/£10
'No Novel Reader', Brian & O'Keefe, 1975 . £15/£5

ALISTAIR MACLEAN
(b.1923 d.1987)

A successful popular novelist, Maclean used wartime experiences with the Royal Navy as the background to his first novel, *HMS Ulysses*. A series of naval and military thrillers followed, characterised by an attention to detail and compelling plots.

Novels
HMS Ulysses, Collins, 1955 . . . . . £50/£10
ditto, Doubleday (U.S.), 1956 . . . . . £15/£5
The Guns of Navarone, Collins, 1957 . . £40/£10
ditto, Doubleday (U.S.), 1957 . . . . . £30/£5
South By Java Head, Collins, 1958 . . . £35/£10
ditto, Doubleday (U.S.), 1958 . . . . £25/£5
The Last Frontier, Collins, 1959. . . . £35/£10
ditto, as *The Secret Ways*, Doubleday (U.S.), 1959 .
. . . . £25/£5
Night Without End, Collins, 1960 . . . £35/£10
ditto, Doubleday (U.S.), 1960 . . . . . £25/£5
Fear is the Key, Collins, 1961 . . . . £35/£10
ditto, Doubleday (U.S.), 1961 . . . . . £25/£5
The Dark Crusader, Collins, 1961 (pseud. 'Ian Stuart')
. . . . £30/£5
ditto, as *The Blake Shrike*, Scribner's (U.S.), 1961 .
. . . . £20/£5
The Golden Rendezvous, Collins, 1962 . . £35/£10
ditto, Doubleday (U.S.), 1962 . . . . . £20/£5
The Satan Bug, Collins, 1962 (pseud. 'Ian Stuart') .
. . . . £75/£15
ditto, Scribner's (U.S.), 1962 . . . . . £45/£10
Ice Station Zebra, Collins, 1963 . . . . £60/£10
ditto, Doubleday (U.S.), 1963 . . . . . £45/£10
When Eight Bells Toll, Collins, 1966 . . £25/£5
ditto, Doubleday (U.S.), 1966 . . . . . £15/£5
Where Eagles Dare, Collins, 1967 . . . £35/£10
ditto, Doubleday (U.S.), 1967 . . . . . £30/£5
Force 10 from Navarone, Collins, 1968 . £35/£10
ditto, Doubleday (U.S.), 1968 . . . . . £30/£5
Puppet on a Chain, Collins, 1969 . . . £20/£5
ditto, Doubleday (U.S.), 1969 . . . . . £15/£5
Caravan to Vaccares, Collins, 1970. . . £20/£5
ditto, Doubleday (U.S.), 1970 . . . . . £15/£5
Bear Island, Collins, 1971 . . . . . £20/£5
ditto, Doubleday (U.S.), 1971 . . . . . £10/£5
The Way to Dusty Death, Collins, 1973. . £20/£5
ditto, Doubleday (U.S.), 1973 . . . . . £15/£5
Breakheart Pass, Collins, 1974 . . . . £20/£5
ditto, Doubleday (U.S.), 1974 . . . . . £15/£5
Circus, Collins, 1975 . . . . £15/£5
ditto, Doubleday (U.S.), 1975 . . . . . £15/£5

The Golden Gate, Collins, 1976 . . . . . £15/£5
ditto, Doubleday (U.S.), 1976 . . . . . £15/£5
Death from Disclosure, Hale, 1976 (pseud. 'Ian Stuart') . . . . £15/£5
Flood Tide, Hale, 1977 (pseud. 'Ian Stuart') . £15/£5
Sand Trap, Hale, 1977 (pseud. 'Ian Stuart') . £15/£5
Seawitch, Collins, 1977 . . . . £15/£5
ditto, Doubleday (U.S.), 1977 . . . . . £15/£5
Goodbye, California, Collins, 1978 . . . . £10/£5
ditto, Doubleday (U.S.), 1978 . . . . . £10/£5
Fatal Switch, Hale, 1978 (pseud. 'Ian Stuart') . £10/£5
A Weekend to Kill, Hale, 1978 (pseud. 'Ian Stuart') .
. . . . £10/£5
Athabasca, Collins, 1980 . . . . £10/£5
ditto, Doubleday (U.S.), 1980 . . . . . £10/£5
River of Death, Collins, 1981 . . . . . £10/£5
ditto, Doubleday (U.S.), 1982 . . . . . £10/£5
Partisans, Collins, 1982 . . . . £10/£5
ditto, Doubleday (U.S.), 1983 . . . . . £10/£5
Floodgate, Collins, 1983 . . . . £10/£5
ditto, Doubleday (U.S.), 1984 . . . . . £10/£5
San Andreas, Collins, 1984 . . . . . . £10/£5
ditto, Doubleday (U.S.), 1985 . . . . . £10/£5
The Lonely Sea, Collins, 1985 . . . . . £10/£5
ditto, Doubleday (U.S.), 1985 . . . . . £10/£5
Santorini, Collins, 1986 . . . . £10/£5
ditto, Doubleday (U.S.), 1987 . . . . . £10/£5

Others
All About Lawrence of Arabia, Allen, 1962 £75/£20
ditto, as *Lawrence of Arabia*, Random House (U.S.), 1961 . . . . £45/£10
Captain Cook, Collins, 1971 . . . . . . £15/£5
ditto, Doubleday (U.S.), 1972 . . . . . £15/£5
Alistair MacLean Introduces Scotland, Deutsch, 1972
. . . . £10/£5

LOUIS MACNEICE
(b.1907 d.1963)

A poet often associated with Auden and Spender, MacNeice employs similar devices of irony and satire.

Poetry
Blind Fireworks, Gollancz, 1929 . . . £650/£250
Poems, Faber, 1935 . . . . £200/£45
Poems, Random House (U.S.), 1937. . . £125/£25
The Earth Compels, Faber, 1938 . . . £125/£35
Autumn Journal, Faber, 1939 . . . . £250/£35
ditto, Random House (U.S.), 1939 . . . £30/£10
The Last Ditch, Cuala Press (Dublin), 1940 (450 copies, tissue d/w) . . . . £165/£125
ditto, Cuala Press (Dublin), 1940 (25 signed copies)
. . . . £400
Selected Poems, Faber, 1940 . . . . . £30/£10
Poems, 1925-1940, Random House (U.S.), 1940 . .
. . . . £25/£5

Plant and Phantom, Faber, 1941 . . . £35/£10
Springboard: Poems, 1941-44, Faber, 1944 £35/£10
ditto, Random House (U.S.), 1945 . . . £25/£5
Holes in the Sky: Poems, 1944-47, Faber, 1948 .
. . . . £30/£10
ditto, Random House (U.S.), 1949 . . . . £25/£5
Collected Poems, 1925-48, Faber, 1949 . . £35/£10
Ten Burnt Offerings, Faber, 1951 . . . £35/£10
ditto, O.U.P. (U.S.), 1953 . . . . . . £25/£5
Autumn Sequel, Faber, 1954 . . . . . £35/£10
The Other Wing, Faber, 1954 (wraps) . . . £20
Visitations, Faber, 1957 . . . . £35/£5
ditto, O.U.P. (U.S.), 1958 . . . . . . £30/£5
Eighty-Five Poems, Faber, 1959 . . . . £25/£5
ditto, O.U.P. (U.S.), 1959 . . . . . . £25/£5
Solstices, Faber, 1961 . . . . £25/£5
ditto, O.U.P. (U.S.), 1961 . . . . . . £25/£5
The Burning Perch, Faber, 1963 . . . . £25/£5
ditto, O.U.P. (U.S.), 1963 . . . . . . £25/£5
Selected Poems, Faber, 1964 . . . . . £15/£5
Collected Poems, Faber, 1966 . . . . . £20/£5
ditto, O.U.P. (U.S.), 1967 . . . . . . £15/£5

Novel
Roundabout Way, Putman, 1931 (pseud. 'Louis Malone') . . . . £450/£100

Translations
The Agamemnon of Aeschylus, Faber, 1936 £45/£10
ditto, Harcourt Brace (U.S.), 1937. . . . £35/£10
Goethe's Faust Parts I & II, Faber, 1951 . £65/£25
ditto, O.U.P. (U.S.), 1952. . . . . . £35/£15

Plays
Out of the Picture, Faber, 1937 . . . . £50/£15
ditto, Harcourt Brace (U.S.), 1938. . . . £35/£15
Christopher Columbus, Faber, 1944. . . £35/£10
The Dark Tower, Faber, 1947 . . . . £60/£15
The Mad Islands and The Administrator, Faber, 1964
. . . . £35/£10
One for the Grave, Faber, 1968 . . . . £25/£5
ditto, O.U.P. (U.S.), 1968 . . . . . . £25/£5
Persons from Porlock and Other Plays, BBC, 1969 .
. . . . £30/£10

Essays
Modern Poetry: A Personal Essay, O.U.P. (U.S.), 1938 . . . . £75/£20
The Poetry of W.B. Yeats, O.U.P., 1941 . £45/£15
ditto, O.U.P. (U.S.), 1941. . . . . . £45/£15
Meet the U.S. Army, H.M.S.O., 1943 (anonymous, wraps). £125
Varieties of Parable, C.U.P., 1965 . . . £25/£5

Children's Titles
The Penny That Rolled Away, Putnam (U.S.), 1954 .
. . . . £75/£25
ditto, as *The Sixpence That Rolled Away*, Faber, 1956
. . . . £75/£25

Autobiography

The Strings are False, Faber, 1965 . . . £35/£10

ditto, O.U.P. (U.S.), 1966. . . . . . £30/£10

Others

Letters from Iceland, Faber, 1937 (with W.H. Auden).

. . . . £100/£25

ditto, Harcourt Brace (U.S.), 1937 . . . £75/£15

Zoo, Joseph, 1938 . . . . £250/£75

I Crossed the Minch, Longman, 1938 . . £175/£35

Astrology, Aldus, 1964 . . . . . . £65/£15

ditto, Doubleday (U.S.), 1964 . . . . £45/£10

NORMAN MAILER
(b.1923)

An American novelist and journalist, Mailer excels at taking real events and subjecting them to his own fictional representation.

Novels

The Naked and the Dead, Rinehart (U.S.), 1948 . .

. . . . £1,000/£100

ditto, Wingate, 1949 (240 numbered copies) . £400

ditto, Wingate, 1949 . . . . . . £100/£30

ditto, Franklin Library (U.S.), 1979 (signed, limited edition) £95

Barbary Shore, Rinehart (U.S.), 1951 (2 d/ws issued simultaneously in red and black, and green and black)

. . . . £125/£25

ditto, Cape, 1952 . . . . £65/£15

The Deer Park, Putnam (U.S.), 1955 . . £125/£20

ditto, Wingate, 1957 . . . . . . £65/£15

An American Dream, Dial Press (U.S.), 1965 £65/£15

ditto, Deutsch, 1965 . . . . . . £35/£10

Why are We in Vietnam?, Putnam (U.S.), 1967 (with no dedication page) . . . . . . £150/£95

ditto, Putnam (U.S.), 1967 (with tipped-in dedication page) . . . . £65/£10

ditto, Weidenfeld & Nicolson, 1969 . . . £40/£5

A Transit to Narcissus, Howard Fertig (U.S.), 1978 .

. . . . £100/£45

Of Women and their Elegance, Simon & Schuster (U.S.), 1980 . . . . £40/£10

ditto, Hodder & Stoughton, 1980. . . . £40/£10

Ancient Evenings, Little, Brown (U.S.), 1983 . £25/£5

ditto, Little, Brown (U.S.), 1983 (350 signed, number-ed copies, slipcase) . . . . . £100/£65

ditto, Macmillan, 1983 . . . . . . £20/£5

Tough Guys Don't Dance, Random House (U.S.), 1984 . . . . £20/£5

ditto, Random House (U.S.), 1984 (350 signed, numbered copies, slipcase, no d/w). . . £100/£65

ditto, Franklin Library (U.S.), 1984 (signed limited edition) £45

ditto, Joseph, 1984. . . . . £20/£5

Harlot's Ghost, Random House (U.S.), 1991 (red d/w)

. . . . £50/£5

ditto, Random House (U.S.), 1991 (grey d/w) . £20/£5

ditto, Random House (U.S.), 1991 (300 signed, numbered copies, slipcase, no d/w). . . £100/£65

ditto, Joseph, 1991. . . . . £15/£5

The Gospel According to the Son, Little, Brown (U.S.), 1997 . . . . £10/£5

ditto, Little, Brown, 1997. . . . . . . £10/£5

Collections

Advertisements for Myself, Putnam (U.S.), 1959 . .

. . . . £75/£15

ditto, Deutsch, 1961 . . . . £45/£10

The Short Fiction of Norman Mailer, Dell (U.S.), 1967 (wraps) £20

The Long Patrol: 25 Years of Writing from the Work of Norman Mailer, World (U.S.), 1971 (edited by Robert F. Lucid) . . . . £35/£10

The Time of Our Time, Random House (U.S.), 1998 .

. . . . £10/£5

ditto, Little, Brown, 1998. . . . . . . £10/£5

Non Fiction

The White Negro, City Lights Books (U.S.), 1957 (35 cents cover price, wraps) £500

ditto, City Lights Books (U.S.), 1957 (50 cents cover price, wraps) £45

The Presidential Papers, Putnam (U.S.), 1963 £75/£15

ditto, Deutsch, 1964 . . . . £40/£10

Cannibals and Christians, Dial Press (U.S.), 1966. .

. . . . £50/£10

ditto, Deutsch, 1967 . . . . £30/£10

The Armies of the Night: History As a Novel, the Novel as History, NAL (U.S.), 1968 (wraps) . £15

ditto, NAL (U.S.), 1968 . . . . . . £50/£15

ditto, Weidenfeld & Nicolson, 1968 . . . £45/£10

The Idol and the Octopus: Political Writings on the Kennedy and Johnson Administrations, Dell (U.S.), 1968 (wraps) £25

Miami and the Siege of Chicago: An Informal History of the Republican and Democratic Conventions of 1968, World (U.S.), 1968 . . . . . £40/£10

ditto, as *Miami and the Siege of Chicago: An Informal History of the American Political Conventions of 1968*, Weidenfeld & Nicolson, 1968 .

. . . . £35/£5

Of A Fire on the Moon, Little, Brown (U.S.), 1970 .

. . . . £25/£5

ditto, Weidenfeld & Nicolson, 1970 . . . . £25/£5

'King of the Hill': On the Fight of the Century, NAL (U.S.), 1971 (wraps). £20

The Prisoner of Sex, Little, Brown (U.S.), 1971 (first edition d/w states $5.95 on front flap) . . £20/£5

ditto, Weidenfeld & Nicolson, 1971 . . . . £20/£5

Existential Errands, Little, Brown (U.S.), 1972 £20/£5

St. George and the Godfather, NAL (U.S.), 1972 £20

ditto, Arbor House (U.S.), 1983 . . . . . £20/£5

Marilyn, Grosset & Dunlap (U.S.), 1973 . £45/£20

ditto, Grosset & Dunlap (U.S.), 1973 (signed limited edition in slipcase) . . . . . . £175/£145
ditto, Hodder & Stoughton (U.S.), 1973 . . £45/£20
The Faith of Graffiti, Praeger Publishers (U.S.), 1974.
. . . . £40/£10
ditto, Praeger Publishers (U.S.), 1974 (350 signed copies, slipcase) . . . . £100/£75
The Fight, Little, Brown (U.S.), 1975 . . £20/£5
ditto, Hart-Davis, MacGibbon, 1976. . . . £15/£5
Some Honourable Men: Political Conventions 1960-1976, Little, Brown (U.S.), 1976 . . . . £20/£5
Genius and Lust: A Journey Through the Major Writings of Henry Miller, Grove Press (U.S.), 1976 .
. . . . £30/£10
The Executioner's Song, Little, Brown (U.S.), 1979 .
. . . . £25/£5
ditto, Hutchinson, 1979 . . . . . . £20/£5
Of a Small and Modest Malignancy, Wicked and Bristling With Dots, Lord John Press (U.S.), 1980 (300 signed, numbered copies, slipcase, no d/w) . .
. . . . £50/£35
ditto, Lord John Press (U.S.), 1980 (100 deluxe signed, numbered copies, slipcase, no d/w). . . £75/£50
Pieces and Pontifications, Little, Brown (U.S.), 1982 (wraps) £10
Huckleberry Finn, Alive at 100, Caliban Press (U.S.), 1985 (50 copies in boards) £125
ditto, Caliban Press (U.S.), 1985 (200 copies in wraps)
. . . . £65
Conversations with Norman Mailer, Univ. Press of Mississippi (U.S.), 1988. . . . . . £20/£5
How the Wimp Won the War, Lord John Press (U.S.), 1992 (26 signed, lettered copies, no d/w) . . £125
ditto, Lord John Press (U.S.), 1992 (275 signed, numbered copies, no d/w) £50
Oswald's Tale, Franklin Library, 1995 (signed limited edition) £45
ditto, Random House (U.S.), 1995 . . . £15/£5
ditto, Little, Brown, 1995. . . . . . £15/£5
Portrait of Picasso As a Young Man: An Interpretive Biography, Atlantic Monthly Press (U.S.), 1995 . .
. . . . £15/£5
ditto, Little, Brown, 1996 . . . . . . £10/£5

Poetry
Deaths for the Ladies and Other Disasters, Putnam (U.S.), 1962 . . . . £125/£25
ditto, Putnam (U.S.), 1962 (wraps) . . . £45
ditto, Deutsch, 1962 . . . . £35
Gargoyl, Guignol, False Closet, Dolmen Press (Dublin), 1964 (two page broadsheet) . . . £50

Plays
Norman Mailer's The Deer Park: A Play, Dial Press (U.S.), 1967 . . . . £100/£25
ditto, Dell (U.S.), 1967 (wraps) £10
ditto, Weidenfeld & Nicolson, 1970 . . . £35/£10

A Fragment from Vietnam, Eurographica (Helsinki), 1985 (350 signed, numbered copies, wraps with d/w)
. . . . £125/£75

Screenplays
Maidstone: A Mystery, NAL (U.S.), 1971 (wraps) £20
The Last Night, Targ Editions (U.S.), 1984 (250 signed copies, tissue d/w) . . . . £75/£50

THOMAS MANN
(b.1875 d.1955)

Arguably the most outstanding German writer of the twentieth century, he received not only critical admiration during his lifetime, but also popular success. He won the Nobel Prize for Literature in 1929.

Novels
Royal Highness, Sidgwick & Jackson, 1916 (translated by A. Cecil Curtis) . . . . . . £500/£40
ditto, Knopf (U.S.), 1916 . . . . . £350/£35
Bashan and I, Collins, 1923 (translated by H.G. Scheffauer) . . . . £150/£40
ditto, Holt (U.S.), 1923 . . . . . £100/£25
Buddenbrooks, Knopf (U.S.), 1924 (translated by H.T. Lowe-Porter, 2 vols). . . . . . £300/£75
ditto, Secker, 1924 (2 vols) . . . . . £250/£50
The Magic Mountain, Knopf (U.S.), 1927 (translated by H.T. Lowe-Porter, 2 vols, d/ws and slipcase) . .
. . . . £500/£100
ditto, Knopf (U.S.), 1927 (200 signed 2 vol sets, d/ws and slipcase) . . . . . . £2,000/£1,500
ditto, Secker, 1927 (2 vols) . . . . £400/£75
The Beloved Returns, Knopf (U.S.), 1940 (translated by H.T. Lowe-Porter) . . . . . £60/£10
ditto, Knopf (U.S.), 1940 (395 signed copies, d/w and slipcase) . . . . £350/£200
ditto, as **Lotte in Weimar**, Secker & Warburg, 1940 .
. . . . £40/£10
Doctor Faustus, Knopf (U.S.), 1948 (translated by H.T. Lowe-Porter) . . . . . . £50/£15
ditto, Secker & Warburg, 1949 . . . £40/£10
The Holy Sinner, Knopf (U.S.), 1951 (translated by H.T. Lowe-Porter) . . . . . . £25/£10
ditto, Secker & Warburg, 1952 . . . £25/£10
Confessions of Felix Krull, Knopf (U.S.), 1955 (translated by Denver Lindley) . . . . £25/£10
ditto, Secker & Warburg, 1955 . . . £25/£10

'Joseph and His Brothers'/
'Joseph and His Bretheren' Novels
Book 1: The Tales of Jacob, Knopf (U.S.), 1934 (translated by H.T. Lowe-Porter) . . . £100/£25
ditto, Secker, 1934. . . . . . . £100/£25
Book 2: The Young Joseph, Knopf (U.S.), 1935 (translated by H.T. Lowe-Porter) . . . £100/£25

ditto, Secker, 1935. . . . . . . £100/£25
Book 3: Joseph in Egypt, Knopf (U.S.), 1938
(translated by H.T. Lowe-Porter, 2 vols) . £150/£45
ditto, Secker, 1938 (2 vols) . . . . £150/£45
Book 4: Joseph the Provider, Knopf (U.S.), 1944
(translated by H.T. Lowe-Porter) . . . £50/£20
ditto, Secker & Warburg, 1945 . . . £30/£10

Novellas and Short Stories
Death in Venice and Other Stories, Knopf (U.S.),
1925 (translated by Kenneth Burke) . . £250/£50
Death in Venice, Secker, 1928 (translated by H.T.
Lowe-Porter) . . . . £250/£75
ditto, Knopf (U.S.), 1930 . . . . . £200/£45
Children and Fools, Knopf (U.S.), 1928 (translated by
H.G. Scheffauer) . . . . £150/£35
Early Sorrow, Secker, 1929 (translated by H.G.
Scheffauer) . . . . £75/£20
ditto, Knopf (U.S.), 1930 . . . . . £75/£20
Mario and the Magician, Secker, 1930 (translated by
H.T. Lowe-Porter) . . . . . . £75/£25
ditto, Knopf (U.S.), 1931 . . . . . £75/£25
Nocturnes, Equinox Cooperative Press (U.S.), 1934
(1,000 signed copies, translated by H.T. Lowe-Porter,
slipcase) . . . . £300/£200
Stories of Three Decades, Knopf (U.S.), 1936 (translated by H.T. Lowe-Porter) . . . . £45/£15
ditto, Secker & Warburg, 1936 . . . . £45/£15
The Transposed Heads, Knopf (U.S.), 1941 (translated
by H.T. Lowe-Porter) . . . . . £45/£15
ditto, Secker & Warburg, 1941 . . . £45/£15
The Tables of the Law, Knopf (U.S.), 1945 (translated
by H.T. Lowe-Porter) . . . . . £45/£15
ditto, Secker & Warburg, 1947 . . . £45/£15
The Black Swan, Knopf (U.S.), 1954 (translated by
Willard R. Trask) . . . . . . £25/£10
ditto, Secker & Warburg, 1954 . . . £25/£10

Poetry
A Christmas Poem, Equinox Cooperative Press (U.S.),
1932 (translated by Henry Hart, wraps) . . £200

Non Fiction
Three Essays, Knopf (U.S.), 1929 (translated by H.T.
Lowe-Porter) . . . . £50/£20
ditto, Secker, 1932. . . . . . . £45/£15
A Sketch of My Life, Harrison (Paris), 1930 (695
numbered copies, translated by H.T. Lowe-Porter,
slipcase) . . . . £500/£350
ditto, Knopf (U.S.), 1960 . . . . . £25/£10
ditto, Knopf (U.S.), 1961 . . . . . £25/£10
Past Masters and Other Papers, Secker, 1933 (Translated by H.T. Lowe-Porter) . . . . £45/£15
ditto, Knopf (U.S.), 1933 . . . . . £45/£15
An Exchange of Letters, Friends of Europe, 1937
(translated by H.T. Lowe-Porter, wraps) . . £35
ditto, Knopf (U.S.), 1937 (wraps) £25
ditto, Overbrook Press (U.S.), 1938 (350 copies) £45

Freud, Goethe, Wagner, Knopf (U.S.), 1937 (trans-
lated by H.T. Lowe-Porter and R. Mathias-Reil) . .
. . . . £50/£20
The Coming Victory of Democracy, Knopf (U.S.),
1938 (translated by Agnes E. Meyer) . . £40/£15
ditto, Secker & Warburg, 1938 . . . . £25/£10
This Peace, Knopf (U.S.), 1938 (translated by H.T.
Lowe-Porter) . . . . £45/£15
This War, Knopf (U.S.), 1940 (translated by Eric
Sutton) . . . . £25/£10
ditto, Secker & Warburg, 1940 . . . . £25/£10
Order of the Day, Knopf (U.S.), 1942 (translated by
H.T. Lowe-Porter, Agnes E. Meyer and Eric Sutton) .
. . . . £50/£20
Listen Germany!, Knopf (U.S.), 1943 . . £35/£10
Essays of Three Decades, Knopf (U.S.), 1947
(translated by H.T. Lowe-Porter) . . . £35/£10
ditto, Secker & Warburg, 1947 . . . . £35/£10
Last Essays, Knopf (U.S.), 1959 (translated by R. & C.
Winston and T. & J. Stern) . . . . £25/£10
ditto, Secker & Warburg, 1959 . . . . £25/£10
Letters to Paul Amann, Wesleyan Univ. Press (U.S.),
1960 (translated by R. & C. Winston) . . £25/£10
ditto, Secker & Warburg, 1961 . . . . £25/£10
The Genesis of a Novel, Knopf (U.S.), 1961 (translated
by R. & C. Winston). . . . . . . £25/£10
ditto, Secker & Warburg, 1961 . . . . £25/£10
The Letters of Thomas Mann, 1889-1955, Secker &
Warburg, 1970 (translated by R. & C. Winston, 2
vols) . . . . £35/£15
ditto, Knopf (U.S.), 1971 (2 vols) . . . £35/£15
Letters of Heinrich and Thomas Mann, 1900-1949,
Univ. of California Press, 1988 (translated by Don
Reneau and R. & C. Winston) . . . . £25/£10

KATHERINE MANSFIELD
(b.1888 d.1923)

Katherine Mansfield was born in New Zealand, where
her work was first published, but she moved to
England in 1908 in pursuit of a literary career. Best
known for her elegant short stories, Mansfield died of
tuberculosis at the age of 35.

Fiction
In a German Pension, Stephen Swift, 1911 . . .
. . . . £4,000/£2,000
ditto, Constable, 1926 (new edition) . . . £45/£15
ditto, Knopf (U.S.), 1926 . . . . . . £45/£15
Prelude, Hogarth Press, 1918 (wraps with design by
Fergusson) £1,500
ditto, Hogarth Press, 1918 (wraps with no design) .
. . . . £1,250
ditto, as **The Aloe**, Constable, 1930 (750 copies,
revised version, edited by J.M. Murry, d/w £200/£50
ditto, Knopf (U.S.), 1930 (975 numbered copies, d/w
and slipcase) . . . . £200/£50

Je ne Parle pas Francais, Heron Press, 1919 (100 copies) £1,000
Bliss and Other Stories, Constable, 1920 (p.13 numbered '3') . . . . £500/£65
ditto, Knopf (U.S.), 1923 . . . . . £300/£35
The Garden Party and Other Stories, Constable, 1922 (first issue, 'sposition' for 'position' on p.103, red d/w, blue lettering, 25 copies) . . £2,000/£1,000
ditto, Constable, 1922 (second issue, as above but orange lettering) . . . . . . £1,000/£50
ditto, Verona Press, 1939 [1947] (alternative selection of stories, lithos by Marie Laurencin, slipcase) . . . . £750/£650
ditto, Verona Press, 1939 [1947] (30 copies signed by Laurencin, slipcase) £4,000
ditto, Knopf (U.S.), 1922 . . . . . £300/£35
The Doves' Nest and Other Stories, Constable, 1923 (first issue, verso of title page blank, 25 copies) . . . . £1,000/£800
ditto, Constable, 1923 (second issue with date on verso of title page) . . . . £200/£25
ditto, Knopf (U.S.), 1923 . . . . . £75/£20
Something Childish and Other Stories, Constable, 1924 (first issue, verso of title page blank, 34 copies) . . . . £1,000/£550
ditto, Constable, 1924 (second issue with date on verso of title page) . . . . £300/£35
ditto, as *The Little Girl and Other Stories*, Knopf (U.S.), 1924 . . . . £250/£30
The Collected Stories of Katherine Mansfield, Constable, 1946 . . . . £50/£20
Selected Stories of Katherine Mansfield, O.U.P. World's Classics, 1953 (edited and with an introduction by D.M. Davin) . . . . £15/£5
Thirty-Four Short Stories, Collins, 1957 . . £15/£5
The Stories of Katherine Mansfield, O.U.P., 1985 (edited by A. Alpers) . . . . . . £15/£5

Other Works
Poems, Constable, 1923 . . . . . . £150/£45
ditto, Knopf, 1924 . . . . £125/£35
ditto, Constable, 1930 (enlarged edition) . £25/£10
The Journal of Katherine Mansfield, Constable, 1927 . . . . £45/£10
ditto, Knopf (U.S.), 1927 . . . . . £45/£10
ditto, Constable, 1954 (revised and enlarged, edited by J.M. Murry) . . . . £25/£10
The Letters of Katherine Mansfield, Constable, 1928 (2 vols, edited by J.M. Murry) . . . £40/£15
Novels and Novelists, Constable, 1930 (edited by J.M. Murry) . . . . £35/£15
ditto, Knopf (U.S.), 1930 . . . . . £35/£15
Reminiscences of Leonid Andreyev, by Maxim Gorky, Heinemann, 1931 (translation with S. S. Koteliansky, 750 numbered copies) . . . . . £75/£35
Reminiscences of Tolstoy, Chekhov and Gorky, Hogarth Press, 1934 (translation with Virginia Woolf and S.S. Koteliansky) . . . . . £30/£10

To Stanislaw Wyspianski, privately printed, 1938 (poem, limited to 100 copies, wraps) . . . £125
The Scrapbook of Katherine Mansfield, Constable, 1939 (edited by J.M. Murry) . . . . £35/£10
ditto, Knopf (U.S.), 1940 . . . . . £30/£15
Katherine Mansfield's Letters to John Middleton Murry, 1913-1922, Constable, 1951 . . £30/£10
ditto, Knopf (U.S.), 1951 . . . . . £30/£10
Katherine Mansfield, Letters and Journals, Allen Lane, 1977 (edited and with an introduction by C.K. Stead) . . . . £15/£5
The Urewera Notebook, O.U.P., 1978 (edited by Ian Gordon) . . . . £15/£5
The Collected Letters of Katherine Mansfield Vol.1, 1903-1917, O.U.P., 1984 (edited by Vincent O'Sullivan and Margaret Scott) . . . . £10/£5
ditto, Vol.2, 1918-1919, O.U.P., 1987 . . £10/£5
The Critical Writings of Katherine Mansfield, Macmillan, 1986 . . . . £10/£5

CAPTAIN FREDERICK MARRYAT
(b.1792 d.1848)

Although he was known early in his writing career for adult novels, drawing on his experiences at sea, he is perhaps best remembered for his books for children, including *Masterman Ready* and *Children of the New Forest*.

Novels
The Naval Officer, or Scenes and Adventures in the Life of Frank Mildmay, Colburn, 1829 (3 vols, anonymous) £400
ditto, Carey & A. Hart (U.S.), 1833 (2 vols) . £250
The King's Own, Colburn & Bentley, 1830 (3 vols, 'by the author of *The Naval Officer*') £300
ditto, D. Estes (U.S.), 1896 . . . . . £50
Newton Forster, or The Merchant Service, James Cochrane, 1832 (3 vols, 'by the author of *The King's Own*') £300
ditto, Lane (U.S.), 1837 (2 vols) £200
Peter Simple, Saunders & Otley, 1834 (3 vols, 'by the author of *Newton Forster*, *The King's Own*, etc.') £350
ditto, Lane (U.S.), 1837 (2 vols) £200
Jacob Faithful, Saunders & Otley, 1834 (3 vols, 'by the author of *Peter Simple*, *The King's Own*, etc.') £400
ditto, Munro (U.S.), 1878 . . . . . . £50
Japhet In Search of a Father, Saunders & Otley, 1836 (3 vols, 'by the author of *Peter Simple*, *Jacob Faithful*, etc.') £300
ditto, Munro (U.S.), 1877 . . . . . . £50
Mr Midshipman Easy, Saunders & Otley, 1836 (3 vols, 'by the author of *Japhet In Search of a Father*, *Peter Simple*, *Jacob Faithful*, etc.'). . . . £200

ditto, Appleton (U.S.), 1866 . . . . . £50

Snarleyyow, or The Dog Fiend, Colburn, 1837 (3 vols, 'by the author of *Peter Simple, Frank Mildmay*, etc.')
. . . . £300

ditto, Carey & A. Hart (U.S.), 1837 (2 vols) . £200

The Phantom Ship, Colburn, 1839 (3 vols). . £1,000

ditto, Munro (U.S.), 1877. . . . . . . £100

Poor Jack, Longman etc., Jan-Dec 1840 (12 parts) .
. . . . £300

ditto, Longman etc., 1840. . . . . . . £200

ditto, Munro (U.S.), 1878. . . . . . . £50

Masterman Ready, or The Wreck of the Pacific,
Longman etc (3 vols, vol.1 1841, vols 2&3 1842) .
. . . . £200

ditto, Appleton (U.S.), 1843 (3 vols). . . . £125

Josph Rushbrook, or The Poacher, Longman etc,
1841 (3 vols, 'by the author of *Peter Simple* etc.') .
. . . . £200

ditto, D. Estes (U.S.), 1895 . . . . . £25

Percival Keene, Colburn, 1842 (3 vols) . . . £200

ditto, Wilson (U.S.), 1842. . . . . . . £150

Narrative of the Travels and Adventures of Monsieur Violet in California, Sonora and Western Texas,
Longmans etc., 1843 (3 vols) £400

ditto, as *The Travels and Romantic Adventures of Monsieur Violet, among the Snake Indians and Wild Tribes of the Great Western Prairies*, Longman etc,
1843 . . . . £300

ditto, Harper (U.S.), 1843. . . . . . . £200

The Settlers in Canada, Longman etc, 1844 (2 vols) .
. . . . £175

ditto, D. Estes (U.S.), 1898 . . . . . £25

The Mission, or Scenes in Africa, Longmans etc, 1845
(2 vols) £200

The Privateersman, or One Hundred Years Ago,
Longman etc, 1846 (2 vols). £200

ditto, Munro (U.S.), 1877. . . . . . . £50

The Children of the New Forest, Hurst, [1847] (2 vols)
. . . . £1,000

ditto, D. Estes (U.S.), 1898 . . . . . £45

The Little Savage, Hurst (2 vols, vol.1 1848, vol.2
1849) £200

ditto, Munro (U.S.), 1877. . . . . . . £50

Valerie: An Autobiography, Colburn, 1849 (2 vols) .
. . . . £175

ditto, Munro (U.S.), 1881. . . . . . . £50

Short Stories

The Pacha of Many Tales, Carey & A. Hart (U.S.),
1834 ('by the author of *Peter Simple, Jacob Faithful*,
etc.', 2 vols) £250

ditto, Saunders & Otley, 1835 (3 vols) . . . £250

The Pirate and The Three Cutters, Longman etc, 1836
. . . . £200

ditto, Lane (U.S.), 1837 . . . . £150

Others

A Code of Signals for the Use of Vessels Employed in the Merchant Service, J. M. Richardson, 1818 £250

Suggestions for the Abolition of the Present System of Impressment in the Naval Service, Richardson, 1822
(64 page booklet, withdrawn) £500

Birman Empire: Views Taken At and Near Rangoon,
Kingsbury/Clay, 1825-6 (3 parts in portfolio, and 2
booklets) £450

Diary in America: with Remarks on its Institutions,
Longman etc, 1839 (3 vols). £200

ditto, Carey & A. Hart (U.S.), 1839 . . . . £200

A Diary in America: Part Second, Longman etc, 1839
(3 vols) £250

Olla Porida, Longman etc, 1840 (3 vols 'by the author
of *Peter Simple* etc.') £250

NGAIO MARSH
(b.1899 d.1982)

A Kiwi writer of detective fiction whose novels are considered amongst the best of the genre. She was awarded the O.B.E. in 1948 and made a D.B.E. in 1966.

Novels

A Man Lay Dead, Bles, 1934 . . . £2,000/£250

ditto, Sheridan (U.S.), 1942 . . . . . £250/£45

Enter a Murderer, Bles, 1935 . . . £1,750/£200

ditto, Pocket Books (U.S.), 1942 . . . . £250/£45

The Nursing Home Murder, Bles, 1935 (with H.
Jellett). . . . . £1,500/£175

ditto, Sheridan (U.S.), 1941 . . . . . £200/£25

Death in Ecstasy, Bles, 1936. . . . £1,000/£125

ditto, Sheridan (U.S.), 1941 . . . . . £200/£25

Vintage Murder, Bles, 1937 . . . . . £750/£100

ditto, Sheridan (U.S.), 1940 . . . . . £200/£25

Artists in Crime, Bles, 1938 . . . . . £750/£100

ditto, Furman (U.S.), 1938 . . . . . £150/£20

Death in a White Tie, Bles, 1938 . . . £750/£100

ditto, Ferman (U.S.), 1938 . . . . . £150/£20

Overture to Death, Collins Crime Club, 1939 . . .
. . . . £750/£100

ditto, Furman (U.S.), 1939 . . . . . £150/£20

Death at the Bar, Collins Crime Club, 1940 £500/£50

ditto, Little, Brown (U.S.), 1940 . . . . £75/£15

Death of a Peer, Little, Brown (U.S.), 1940 £75/£25

ditto, as *Surfeit of Lampreys*, Collins Crime Club,
1941 . . . . £500/£50

Death and the Dancing Footman, Little, Brown
(U.S.), 1941 . . . . £65/£15

ditto, Collins Crime Club, 1942 . . . £500/£50

Colour Scheme, Little, Brown (U.S.), 1943 . £45/£15

ditto, Collins Crime Club, 1943 . . . . £150/£25

Died in the Wool, Collins Crime Club, 1945 £150/£25

ditto, Little, Brown (U.S.), 1945 . . . . £65/£15

Final Curtain, Collins Crime Club, 1947 . £100/£15

ditto, Little, Brown (U.S.), 1947 . . . £50/£15

Wreath for Riviera, Little, Brown (U.S.), 1949 . . .
. . . . £45/£10

ditto, as **Swing Brother Swing**, Collins Crime Club, 1949 . . . . £75/£10
Opening Night, Collins Crime Club, 1951 . £75/£10
ditto, as **Night at the Vulcan**, Little, Brown (U.S.), 1951 . . . . £45/£10
Spinsters in Jeopardy, Little, Brown (U.S.), 1953 . .
. . . . £45/£10
ditto, Collins Crime Club, 1954 . . . . £65/£10
Scales of Justice, Collins Crime Club, 1955 £50/£10
ditto, Little, Brown (U.S.), 1955 . . . . £45/£10
Death of a Fool, Little, Brown (U.S.), 1956 £40/£10
ditto, as **Off With His Head**, Collins Crime Club, 1957
. . . . £40/£10
Singing in the Shrouds, Little, Brown (U.S.), 1958 .
. . . . £35/£10
ditto, Collins Crime Club, 1959 . . . . £35/£10
False Scent, Little, Brown (U.S.), 1959 . . £35/£10
ditto, Collins Crime Club, 1960 . . . . £35/£10
Hand in Glove, Little, Brown (U.S.), 1962 . £30/£10
ditto, Collins Crime Club, 1962 . . . . £30/£10
Dead Water, Little, Brown (U.S.), 1963 . . £30/£10
ditto, Collins Crime Club, 1964 . . . . £30/£10
Killer Dolphin, Little, Brown (U.S.), 1966 . £30/£10
ditto, as **Death at the Dolphin**, Collins Crime Club, 1967 . . . . £30/£10
Clutch of Constables, Collins Crime Club, 1968 . .
. . . . £30/£10
ditto, Little, Brown (U.S.), 1969 . . . . £30/£10
When in Rome, Collins Crime Club, 1970 . £25/£10
ditto, Little, Brown (U.S.), 1971 . . . . £25/£10
Tied up in Tinsel, Collins Crime Club, 1972 £25/£10
ditto, Little, Brown (U.S.), 1972 . . . . £25/£10
Black as He's Painted, Collins Crime Club, 1974 . .
. . . . £25/£10
ditto, Little, Brown (U.S.), 1974 . . . . £25/£10
Last Ditch, Collins Crime Club, 1977 . . £25/£10
ditto, Little, Brown (U.S.), 1977 . . . . £25/£10
Grave Mistake, Collins Crime Club, 1978 . . £20/£5
ditto, Little, Brown (U.S.), 1978 . . . . . £20/£5
Photo-Finish, Collins Crime Club, 1980 . . . £15/£5
ditto, Little, Brown (U.S.), 1980 . . . . . £15/£5
Light Thickens, Little, Brown (U.S.), 1982 . . £15/£5
ditto, Collins Crime Club, 1982 . . . . . £15/£5

W. SOMERSET MAUGHAM
(b.1874 d.1965)

For many years Maugham was better known as a playwright than as a novelist. He is also an acknowledged master of the short story.

Novels
Liza of Lambeth, T. Fisher Unwin, 1897 . . £750
ditto, Doran (U.S.), 1921 . . . . . £250/£45
ditto, Heinemann, 1947 (1,000 signed, numbered copies) . . . . £300/£150
The Making of a Saint, Page (U.S.), 1898 . £250
ditto, T. Fisher Unwin, 1898 . . . . . . £250

The Hero, Hutchinson, 1901 . . . . . . £250
Mrs Craddock, Heinemann, 1902 . . . . £225
ditto, Doran (U.S.), 1920 . . . . . £250/£45
The Merry-Go-Round, Heinemann, 1904 . £450
ditto, Doubleday, Page & Co. (U.S.), 1904 . . £400
The Bishop's Apron, Chapman & Hall, 1906 . £250
The Explorer, Heinemann, 1908 . . . . . £150
ditto, Baker and Taylor (U.S.), 1909 . . . £125
The Magician, Heinemann, 1908 . . . . £200
ditto, Duffield and Co. (U.S.), 1909 . . . . £100
Of Human Bondage, Doran (U.S.), 1915 . . £500
ditto, Heinemann, 1915 . . . . £500
The Moon and Sixpence, Heinemann, 1919 . £200
ditto, Doran (U.S.), 1919 (author's name mis-spelled as 'Maughan' on cover) £200
The Painted Veil, Doran (U.S.), 1925 . . £500/£40
ditto, Doran (U.S.), 1925 (50 signed copies of 250) .
. . . . £200
ditto, Doran (U.S.), 1925 (200 unsigned copies of 250)
. . . . £300
ditto, Heinemann, 1925 . . . . . £500/£40
Cakes and Ale, Heinemann, 1930 . . . £250/£30
ditto, Doubleday (U.S.), 1930 . . . . £200/£20
ditto, Heinemann, [1954] (eightieth birthday edition, 1,000 signed copies) £250
The Narrow Corner, Heinemann, 1932 . . £150/£20
ditto, Doubleday (U.S.), 1932 . . . . £100/£15
Theatre, Doubleday (U.S.), 1937 . . . £100/£20
ditto, Heinemann, 1937 . . . . . . £75/£15
Christmas Holiday, Heinemann, 1939 . £100/£20
ditto, Doubleday (U.S.), 1939 . . . . £75/£15
Up at the Villa, Doubleday (U.S.), 1941 . £65/£20
ditto, Heinemann, 1941 . . . . . . £75/£20
The Razor's Edge, Doubleday (U.S.), 1944 (750 signed, numbered copies, slipcase) . . . £400/£120
ditto, Doubleday (U.S.), 1944 (unlimited issue) . . .
. . . . £200/£30
ditto, Heinemann, 1944 . . . . . . £150/£25
Then and Now, Heinemann, 1946 . . . £65/£15
ditto, Doubleday (U.S.), 1946 . . . . £40/£10
Catalina, Heinemann, 1948 . . . . . £75/£15
ditto, Doubleday (U.S.), 1948 . . . . £65/£10

Short Stories
Orientations, T. Fisher Unwin, 1899 . . . £200
The Trembling of a Leaf, Doran (U.S.), 1921 . . .
. . . . £250/£30
ditto, Heinemann, 1921 . . . . . £250/£30
The Casuarina Tree, Heinemann, 1926 . . £500/£45
ditto, Doran (U.S.), 1926 . . . . . £200/£30
Ashenden: or The British Agent, Heinemann, 1928 .
. . . . £2,500/£125
ditto, Doubleday (U.S.), 1928 . . . £750/£100
Six Stories Written in the First Person Singular, Doran (U.S.), 1931 . . . . £125/£20
ditto, Heinemann, 1931 . . . . . £125/£20
Ah King, Heinemann, 1933 . . . . . £75/£10
ditto, Heinemann, 1933 (175 signed, numbered copies, slipcase) . . . . £275/£225

ditto, Doubleday (U.S.), 1933 . . . . £75/£10
Cosmopolitans: Very Short Stories, Doran (U.S.),
1936 . . . . £150/£25
ditto, Heinemann, 1936 . . . . . £150/£25
ditto, Heinemann, 1936 (175 signed, numbered copies,
slipcase) . . . . £275/£225
The Mixture as Before, Heinemann, 1940 . £100/£15
ditto, Doubleday (U.S.), 1940 . . . . £65/£10
The Unconquered, House of Books (U.S.), 1944 (300
signed, numbered copies) . . . . £300/£200
Creatures of Circumstance, Heinemann, 1947 . . .
. . . . £100/£15
ditto, Doubleday (U.S.), 1947 . . . . £65/£10
Quartet, Heinemann, 1948 . . . . £65/£15
ditto, Doubleday (U.S.), 1949 . . . . £50/£10
Trio, Heinemann, 1950 . . . . £45/£10
ditto, Doubleday (U.S.), 1950 . . . . £35/£10
Encore, Heinemann, 1952 . . . . £35/£10
ditto, Doubleday (U.S.), 1952 . . . . £30/£10
Seventeen Lost Stories by W. Somerset Maugham,
Doubleday (U.S.), 1969 . . . . . £25/£10

Plays
A Man of Honour, Chapman and Hall, 1903 (150
copies, wraps) £500
ditto, Dramatic Publishing Company (U.S.), [1912]
(wraps) £75
Lady Frederick, Heinemann, 1912 . . . . £200
ditto, Heinemann, 1912 (wraps) £75
ditto, Dramatic Publishing Company (U.S.), [1912]
(wraps) £75
Jack Straw, Heinemann, 1912 . . . . £125
ditto, Heinemann, 1912 (wraps) £65
ditto, Dramatic Publishing Company (U.S.), [1912]
(wraps) £75
Mrs Dot, Heinemann, 1912 . . . . £200
ditto, Heinemann, 1912 (wraps) £75
ditto, Dramatic Publishing Company (U.S.), [1912]
(wraps) £75
Penelope, Heinemann, 1912 . . . . £150
ditto, Heinemann, 1912 (wraps) £65
ditto, Dramatic Publishing Company (U.S.), [1912]
(wraps) £75
The Explorer, Heinemann, 1912 . . . . £125
ditto, Heinemann, 1912 (wraps) £60
ditto, Dramatic Publishing Company (U.S.), [1912]
(wraps) £75
The Tenth Man, Heinemann, 1913 . . . . £125
ditto, Heinemann, 1913 (wraps) £60
ditto, Dramatic Publishing Company (U.S.), [1913]
(wraps) £75
Landed Gentry, Heinemann, 1913 . . . . £100
ditto, Heinemann, 1913 (wraps) £50
ditto, Dramatic Publishing Company (U.S.), [1913]
(wraps) £75
Smith, Heinemann, 1913 . . . . £125
ditto, Heinemann, 1913 (wraps) £60
ditto, Dramatic Publishing Company (U.S.), [1913]
(wraps) £75

The Land of Promise, Bickers & Son, 1913 (wraps) .
. . . . £750
ditto, Doran (U.S.), 1923 . . . . . £350
The Unknown, Heinemann, 1920 (wraps) . . £100
The Circle, Heinemann, 1921 (no d/w) . . . £100
ditto, Heinemann, 1921 (wraps) £50
ditto, Doran (U.S.), [1921] . . . . £125/£30
Caesar's Wife, Heinemann, 1922 (no d/w) . . £100
ditto, Heinemann, 1922 (wraps) £60
ditto, Doran (U.S.), [1923] . . . . £100/£35
East of Suez, Heinemann, 1922 (no d/w) . . £100
ditto, Heinemann, 1922 (wraps) £45
ditto, Doran (U.S.), 1922 . . . . . £75/£30
Our Betters, Heinemann, 1923 . . . . £75
ditto, Heinemann, 1923 (wraps) £45
ditto, Doran (U.S.), 1924 . . . . . £75/£30
Home and Beauty, Heinemann, 1923 . . . £100
ditto, Heinemann, 1923 (wraps) £45
The Unattainable, Heinemann, 1923 . . . £75
ditto, Heinemann, 1923 (wraps) £45
Loaves and Fishes, Heinemann, 1924 . . . £75
ditto, Heinemann, 1924 (wraps) £45
ditto, French (U.S.), 1926 (wraps) . . . £45
The Constant Wife, Doran (U.S.), 1927 . . £125/£45
ditto, Heinemann, 1927 . . . . £125/£45
The Letter, Heinemann, 1927 . . . . £150/£30
ditto, Doran (U.S.), 1927 . . . . . £125/£25
The Sacred Flame, Doubleday (U.S.), 1928 £125/£30
ditto, Heinemann, 1928 . . . . £100/£25
The Bread-Winner, Heinemann, 1930 (no d/w) . £125
ditto, Heinemann, 1930 (wraps) £45
ditto, Doubleday (U.S.), 1931 . . . . £100/£20
For Services Rendered, Heinemann, 1932 . £100/£15
ditto, Doubleday, Doran (U.S.), 1933 . . £45/£10
Sheppey, Heinemann, 1933 . . . . £75/£15
ditto, Baker (U.S.), 1949 . . . . . £75/£15
The Noble Spaniard, Evans Brothers, 1953 (wraps) .
. . . . £30

Travel
The Land of the Blessed Virgin, Heinemann, 1905 .
. . . . £300
ditto, Knopf (U.S.), 1920 . . . . £200/£35
On a Chinese Screen, Doran (U.S.), 1922 . £150/£25
ditto, Heinemann, 1922 . . . . £200/£35
**The Gentleman in the Parlour: A Record of a
Journey from Rangoon to Haiphong**, Heinemann,
1930 . . . . £250/£40
ditto, Doubleday (U.S.), 1930 . . . . £200/£30
Don Fernando, Heinemann, 1935 . . . £150/£15
ditto, Heinemann, 1935 (175 signed, numbered copies,
slipcase) . . . . £350/£300
ditto, Doubleday (U.S.), 1935 . . . . £100/£15
Princess September and the Nightingale, O.U.P., 1939
. . . . £300/£100

Essays
Books and You, Heinemann, 1940 . . . £65/£15
ditto, Doubleday (U.S.), 1940 . . . . £65/£15

The Writer's Point of View, C.U.P., 1951 (wraps) £20
The Vagrant Mood, Heinemann, 1952 . . £25/£10
ditto, Heinemann, 1952 (500 signed copies, slipcase) .
. . . . £250/£200
ditto, Doubleday (U.S.), 1953 . . . . £25/£10
Great Novelists and Their Novels, Winston (U.S.),
1948 . . . . £45/£10
ditto, as *Ten Novels and Their Authors*, Heinemann,
1954 . . . . £30/£10

Others
The Judgement Seat, Centaur Press (U.S.), 1934 (150
copies) . . . . £300/£200
My South Sea Island, Black Cat Press (U.S.), 1936
(first issue with name spelt 'Sommerset' on title page,
wraps). £175
ditto, Black Cat Press (U.S.), 1936 (second issue with
name spelt correctly, wraps) £45
The Summing Up, Heinemann, 1938 . . £125/£20
ditto, Doubleday (U.S.), 1938 . . . £100/£15
ditto, Doubleday (U.S.), 1954 (391 signed, numbered
copies) £225
France at War, Heinemann, 1940 (wraps) . . £45
ditto, Doubleday (U.S.), 1940 . . . . £50/£15
Strictly Personal, Doubleday (U.S.), 1941 (515 signed,
numbered copies, slipcase) . . . . £225/£175
ditto, Heinemann, 1942 . . . . . £45/£15
The Inside Story of the French Collapse, Redbook
(U.S.), 1940 (wraps). £15
The Hour Before the Dawn, Doubleday (U.S.), 1942 .
. . . . £75/£20
*Of Human Bondage, with a Digression on the Art of
Fiction*, Library of Congress (U.S.), 1946 (500 signed
copies of 800, hardcover without d/w) . . . £100
ditto, Library of Congress (U.S.), 1946 (300 signed
copies of 800, hardcover without d/w) . . . £60
ditto, Library of Congress (U.S.), 1946 (wraps). £30
A Writer's Notebook, Hearst (U.S.), 1949 (no d/w) £35
ditto, Heinemann, 1949 . . . . . . £25/£5
ditto, Heinemann, 1949 (1,000 signed copies, slipcase)
. . . . £250/£200
ditto, Doubleday (U.S.), 1949 . . . . £25/£5
ditto, Doubleday (U.S.), 1949 (1,000 signed copies,
slipcase) . . . . £250/£200
Points of View, Heinemann, 1958 . . £25/£10
ditto, Doubleday (U.S.), 1959 . . . £25/£10
Purely For My Pleasure, Heinemann, 1962 £25/£10
ditto, Doubleday (U.S.), 1962 (slipcase). . £25/£10
*A Traveller in Romance: Uncollected Writings, 1901-
1964*, Blond, 1984 . . . . £15/£5
ditto, Clarkson Potter (U.S.), 1984 . . . £15/£5

ABRAHAM MERRITT
(b.1884 d.1943)

The author of exotic fantasies which are often more
extreme than those of Edgar Rice Burroughs, he was a
popular contributor to the pre-World War Two
American pulp magazines.

Novels
The Moon Pool, Putnam's (U.S.), 1919 (first printing
without advert on p 434, 'Putnam' printed on spine in
upper and lower case) . . . . . £1,000/£150
The Ship of Ishtar, Putnam's (U.S.), 1926 . . .
. . . . £1,000/£150
Seven Footprints to Satan, Boni & Liveright (U.S.),
1928 . . . . £650/£100
ditto, Richards, 1928. . . . . . . £400/£75
The Face in the Abyss, Liveright (U.S.), 1931 . .
. . . . £1,000/£150
Dwellers in the Mirage, Liveright (U.S.), 1932. . .
. . . . £1,000/£150
ditto, Skeffington, [1933]. . . . . . £500/£75
Thru the Dragon Glass, ARRA (U.S.) 1932 (wraps) .
. . . . £75
ditto, as *Through the Dragon Glass*, Doreal (U.S.),
1948 (wraps) £40
Burn Witch Burn!, Liveright (U.S.), 1932 . £750/£100
ditto, Methuen, 1934. . . . . . . £350/£50
Creep, Shadow, Doubleday, Doran (U.S.), 1934 . .
. . . . £650/£75
ditto, as *Creep, Shadow, Creep!*, Methuen, 1935 . .
. . . . £100/£25
Three Lines of Old French, Bizarre (U.S.), 1937
(wraps) £100
ditto, Doreal (U.S.), 1948 (wraps) £40
The Story Behind the Story, privately printed by the
American Weekly (U.S.), 1942 (no d/w) . . £35
The Metal Monster, Avon (U.S.), 1946 (wraps) £15
ditto, Hyperion (U.S.), 1974 (no d/w) . . . £20
The Fox Woman/The Blue Pagoda, New Collectors
(U.S.), 1946 (with Hannes Bok, nude woman
illustration) £45
ditto, New Collectors (U.S.), 1946 (with Hannes Bok,
nude man illustration) £40
The Black Wheel, New Collectors (U.S.), 1947
(completed by Hannes Bok). £35
The Drone Man, Doreal (U.S.), 1948 (wraps) . £40
Rhythm of the Spheres, Doreal (U.S.), 1948 (wraps) .
. . . . £40
The People of the Pit, Doreal (U.S.), 1948 (wraps) .
. . . . £40
The Woman of the Wood, Doreal (U.S.), 1948 (wraps)
. . . . £40
Short Stories, Doreal (U.S.), 1948 (wraps) . . £300
The Fox Woman & Other Stories, Avon (U.S.), 1949
(wraps) £20
ditto, Eshbach (U.S.), 1949 (300 copies of Avon sheets
bound in black cloth with white d/w) . . £200/£100

ditto, Eshbach (U.S.), 1949 (bound in light blue cloth
with white d/w) . . . . £250/£150
Seven Footprints to Satan/Burn Witch Burn!,
Liveright (U.S.), 1952 . . . . . . £25/£10
Dwellers in the Mirage/The Face in the Abyss,
Liveright (U.S.), 1953 . . . . . . £25/£10
The Challenge from Beyond, Evans (U.S.), 1954 (with
H.P. Lovecraft, Robert E. Howard, Frank Belknap
Long and C.L. Moore) £50
Reflections in the Moon Pool, Train (U.S.), 1985 . .
. . . . £15/£5

ARTHUR MILLER
(b.1915)

An American playwright who is perhaps best known
for *The Death of a Salesman*, about the unsuccessful
businessman Willy Loman, and *The Crucible* which
relates the Salem witch trials to the era of
McCarthyism in the USA.

Plays
All My Sons: A Play in Two Acts, Reynal & Hitchcock
(U.S.), 1947 . . . . £250/£40
ditto, Penguin, 1961 (wraps) £10
**Death of a Salesman: Certain Private Conversations
in Two Acts and a Requiem**, Viking (U.S.), 1949 .
. . . . £500/£50
ditto, Cresset, 1949 . . . . £125/£25
ditto, Limited Editions Club (U.S.), 1984 (1500 copies
signed by Miller & Leonard Baskin, in slipcase) . .
. . . . £600/£500
The Crucible: A Play in Four Acts, Viking (U.S.),
1953 . . . . £300/£30
ditto, Cresset, 1956 . . . . . . £100/£20
A View from the Bridge: Two One-Act Plays, Viking
(U.S.), 1955 . . . . £50/£10
ditto, Cresset, 1957 . . . . . . £45/£10
A Memory of Two Mondays: A Play in One Act,
Dramatists Play Service, 1956 (wraps) . . £10
Collected Plays, Viking (U.S.), 1957 . . £45/£10
ditto, Cresset, 1958 . . . . . . £45/£10
After the Fall, Viking (U.S.), 1964 . . £25/£10
ditto, Viking (U.S.), 1964 (500 signed copies, glassine
d/w and slipcase). . . . . . . £125/£75
ditto, Secker & Warburg, 1964 . . . . £25/£10
Incident at Vichy, Viking (U.S.), 1965 . . £50/£10
ditto, Secker & Warburg, 1966 . . . . £30/£10
The Price, Viking (U.S.), 1968 . . . £30/£10
ditto, Secker & Warburg, 1968 . . . . £25/£10
The Portable Arthur Miller, Viking (U.S.), 1971 (ed.
Harold Clurman). . . . . £25/£10
The Creation of the World and Other Business,
Viking (U.S.), 1973 . . . . £20/£5
The Archbishop's Ceiling, Dramatists Play Service
(U.S.), 1976 (wraps). £10
ditto, Methuen, 1984 . . . . £10/£5

The American Clock, Viking (U.S.), 1980 . . £15/£5
ditto, Methuen, 1983 . . . . £10/£5
Collected Plays, Franklin Library (U.S.), 1980 (signed
limited edition) £75
Collected Plays: Volume II, Viking (U.S.), 1981 . .
. . . . £15/£5
Elegy for a Lady, Dramatists Play Service (U.S.), 1984
(wraps) £10
ditto, Methuen, 1984 . . . . £10/£5
Some Kind of Love Story, Dramatists Play Service
(U.S.), 1984 (wraps). £10
Playing for Time, Dramatic Publishing (U.S.), 1985
(wraps) £10
**Danger: Memory! Two Plays: 'I Can't Remember
Anything' and 'Clara'**, Methuen, 1986 . £20/£5
ditto, Grove (U.S.), 1987 . . . . . £20/£10
The Golden Years, Methuen, 1989 . . . £10/£5
ditto, Dramatists Play Service (U.S.), 1990 (wraps) .
. . . . £10
The Last Yankee, Dramatists Play Service (U.S.), 1991
(wraps) £10
ditto, Methuen, 1993 (wraps). £5
The Ride Down Mt. Morgan, Viking Penguin (U.S.),
1992 (wraps) £5
ditto, Stephens (U.S.), 1991 (200 signed, numbered
copies) £75
Broken Glass, Viking Penguin (U.S.), 1994 (wraps) £5
ditto, Methuen, 1994 (wraps). £5
The Last Yankee and Broken Glass, Fireside (U.S.),
1994 . . . . £10/£5

Novels
Focus, Reynal & Hitchcock (U.S.), 1945 . £100/£20
ditto, Gollancz, 1949 . . . . . . £45/£10
The Misfits, Viking (U.S.), 1961. . . . £125/£25
ditto, Secker & Warburg, 1961 . . . . £45/£15

Short Stories
I Don't Need You Anymore, Viking (U.S.), 1967 . .
. . . . £20/£5
ditto, Secker & Warburg, 1967 . . . . . £20/£5
'The Misfits' and Other Stories, Scribner's (U.S.),
1987 . . . . £25/£10
Homely Girl, A Life, Peter Blum Books (U.S.), 1992
(100 signed copies of 1,200, slipcase, 2 vols) . . .
. . . . £300/£250
ditto, Peter Blum Books (U.S.), 1992 (1,100 copies of
1,200, slipcase, 2 vols) . . . . . £100/£75
Homely Girl, A Life, and Other Stories, Viking (U.S.),
1995 . . . . £10/£5
ditto, as **Plain Girl**, Methuen, 1995 . . . £10/£5

Others
Situation Normal, Reynal & Hitchcock (U.S.), 1944 .
. . . . £125/£25
An Enemy of the People, Viking (U.S.), 1951
(adaptation of play by Henrik Ibsen) . . . £25/£5
On Social Plays, Viking (U.S.), 1955 (introduction to
View from the Bridge, wraps) £75
Jane's Blanket, Crowell-Collier (U.S.), 1963 £250/£35

ditto, Macmillan, 1963 . . . . . . £250/£35
In Russia, Viking, 1969 (with Inge Morath) . £20/£5
ditto, Secker & Warburg, 1969 . . . . . £20/£5
In the Country, Viking, 1977 (with Inge Morath) . .
. . . . £20/£5
ditto, Secker & Warburg, 1977 . . . . . £20/£5
The Theater Essays of Arthur Miller, Viking (U.S.),
1978 (ed. Robert A. Martin) . . . . . £15/£5
Chinese Encounters, Farrar, Straus (U.S.), 1979 (with
Inge Morath) . . . . £15/£5
ditto, Secker & Warburg, 1979 . . . . . £15/£5
Salesman in Beijing, Viking (U.S.), 1984 . . £15/£5
ditto, Methuen, 1984 . . . . £15/£5
Timebends: A Life, Franklin Library (U.S.), 1987
(signed limited edition) £35
ditto, Grove (U.S.), 1987 . . . . £15/£5
ditto, Methuen, 1987 . . . . £15/£5
*Echoes Down the Corridor: Collected Essays 1944-
2000*, Methuen, 2000 (Edited by Steven R. Centola) .
. . . . £15/£5
ditto, Viking (U.S.), 2000 . . . . £15/£5

HENRY MILLER
(b.1891 d.1980)

The American Miller made his name by writing *The
Tropic of Cancer* which describes the promiscuous
lifestyle he witnessed while living in Paris. It was the
first of many of his books to be suppressed in both
America and England because of their sexual
frankness.

Fiction
The Tropic of Cancer, Obelisk Press (Paris), 1934
(first printing, copies issued in printed green and
white wrappers) £7,500
ditto, Obelisk Press (Paris), 1934 (second printing,
issued in plain wrappers with an illustrated d/w) . .
. . . . £4,000/£1,000
ditto, Medvsa (U.S.), 1940 (no d/w) £200
ditto, Grove Press (U.S.), 1961 (100 signed copies, no
d/w) £1,500
ditto, Grove Press (U.S.), 1961 . . . . . £75/£20
ditto, Calder, 1963 . . . . £45/£15
Black Spring, Obelisk (Paris), 1936 (wraps) . £1,000
ditto, Grove (U.S.), 1963 . . . . £45/£10
ditto, Calder, 1965 . . . . £30/£10
The Tropic of Capricorn, Obelisk Press (Paris), 1939
(60 francs price on spine, errata slip tipped in, wraps)
. . . . £750
ditto, Grove Press (U.S.), 1961 . . . . £75/£20
ditto, Calder, 1964 . . . . £45/£15
Sexus, Obelisk (Paris), 1949 (2 vols, 3,000 numbered
copies, no d/ws) £200
ditto, Grove Press (U.S.), 1965 . . . . £30/£10
ditto, Calder, 1969 . . . . £45/£10

Plexus, Correa (Paris), 1952 (100 numbered copies, in
French, d/w) . . . . £1,250/£1,000
ditto, Correa (Paris), 1952 (wraps) £250
ditto, Olympia (Paris), 1953 (2,000 numbered copies, 2
vols, wraps) £250
ditto, Weidenfeld & Nicolson, 1963 . . . £50/£15
ditto, Grove Press (U.S.), 1965 . . . . £25/£10
Nexus, Obelisk (Paris), 1960 (wraps) £50
ditto, Weidenfeld & Nicolson, 1964 . . . £45/£10
ditto, Grove Press (U.S.), 1965 . . . . £25/£10

Plays
Scenario (A Film with Sound), Obelisk (Paris), 1937
(200 signed copies, wraps) £1,000
*Just Wild About Harry: A Melo Melo in Seven
Scenes*, New Directions (U.S.), 1963 . . £45/£15
ditto, MacGibbon & Gee, 1964 . . . . £25/£10

Others
What Are You Going to Do About Alf?, Lecram-
Servant (Paris), 1935 (wraps) £1,500
ditto, Porter (U.S.), 1944 (wraps) £45
ditto, Turret, 1971 (100 signed copies of 350) . . .
. . . . £150/£100
ditto, Turret, 1971 (250 unsigned copies of 350) . .
. . . . £65/£15
Aller Retour New York, Obelisk (Paris), 1935 (150
signed copies, wraps) £1,000
ditto, privately printed by Ben Abramson (U.S.), 1945
(500 copies, no d/w) £65
Money and How it Gets that Way, Booster (Paris),
1938 (with author's holograph limitation and copyright note, 495 copies, wraps) £450
ditto, Booster (Paris), 1938 (without author's holograph
limitation and copyright note, 495 copies, wraps) . .
. . . . £200
Max and the White Phagocytes, Obelisk (Paris), 1938
(wraps) £750
Hamlet, Carrefour (Puerto Rico), 1939 (500 copies,
wraps) £175
ditto, Carrefour (Puerto Rico), 1939 (25 signed,
numbered copies of 500, wraps) £300
The Cosmological Eye, New Directions (U.S.), 1939
(photo of eye inset on front cover, d/w spine lettered
white, priced $2.50) . . . . £350/£45
ditto, Editions Poetry London, 1945 . . . £150/£35
Hamlet, Volume II, Carrefour (Puerto Rico), 1941
(500 copies, wraps) £175
ditto, Carrefour (Puerto Rico), 1941 (25 signed,
numbered copies of 500, wraps) £300
The World of Sex, Abrahamson (U.S.), 1940 (250
copies) . . . . £250/£175
ditto, as *The World of Sex* and *Max and the White
Phagocytes*, Calder, 1970 . . . . . £35/£10
The Colossus of Maroussi, Colt (U.S.), 1941 £200/£35
ditto, Colt (U.S.), 1941 (100 signed copies, no d/w) . .
. . . . £1,000
ditto, Secker & Warburg, 1942 . . . . £125/£25

The Wisdom of the Heart, New Directions (U.S.), 1941 . . . . £200/£30
ditto, Editions Poetry London, 1947 . . . £45/£15
The Angel is My Watermark, Holve-Barrows (U.S.), 1944 (20 copies, watercolours, wraps with clear celluloid overlay) £4,500
Sunday After the War, New Directions (U.S.), 1944 . . . . £200/£25
ditto, Editions Poetry London, 1945 . . . £50/£15
Murder the Murderer, Miller (U.S.), 1944 (wraps) £100
ditto, Delphic Press, 1946 (wraps) £75
The Plight Of The Creative Artist In The United States Of America, Bern Porter (U.S.), 1944 (950 copies signed by Porter, wraps with plain d/w) £75
Semblance of a Devoted Past, Bern Porter (U.S.), 1945 (wraps) £100
Henry Miller Miscellanea, Bern Porter (U.S.), 1945 (500 numbered copies with inscription by Miller or postcard by Miller, wraps) £300
Obscenity and the Law of Reflection, Alicat Bookshop (U.S.), 1945 (750 copies, wraps) . . £50
Echolalia, Bern Porter (U.S.), 1945 (portfolio of 12 prints, 1,000 copies) £75
ditto, Editions Poetry London, 1945 (portfolio of 12 prints, 1,000 copies) £65
Why Abstract?, New Directions (U.S.), 1945 £50/£15
Varda: The Master Builder, Bern Porter (U.S.), 1945 (wraps) £65
The Amazing and Invariable Beauford Delaney, Alicat Bookshop (U.S.), 1945 (750 copies, wraps) . £65
The Air-Conditioned Nightmare, New Directions (U.S.), 1945 (tipped in illustrations) . . £200/£40
ditto, Secker & Warburg, 1947 . . . . £150/£25
Maurizius Forever, Colt Press (U.S.), 1946 (500 copies, plain brown d/w) . . . £175/£125
ditto, as *Reflections on the Maurizius Case*, Capra Press (U.S.), 1973 (275 signed, numbered copies, no d/w) £100
Patchen: Man of Anger, Padell (U.S.), 1946 (wraps with d/w) . . . . £65/£35
Into the Night Life, Miller and Schatz (U.S.), 1947 (800 numbered, signed copies, slipcase) £1,000/£750
Remember to Remember, New Directions (U.S.), 1947 (first state with title pages divided by frontispiece photograph of author) . . . . . £200/£40
ditto, Grey Walls Press, 1952 . . . . £75/£25
The Smile at the Foot of the Ladder, Duell, Sloan & Pearce (U.S.), 1948 . . . . . . £250/£30
ditto, MacGibbon & Kee, 1966 . . . . £35/£10
The Waters Reglitterized, Kidis (U.S.), 1950 (1,000 numbered copies, wraps) £30
ditto, Village Press, 1973 (wraps) £15
Rimbaud, Mermod (France), 1952 (5,000 numbered copies, wraps) £65
ditto, as *The Time of the Assassins: A Study of Rimbaud*, New Directions (U.S.), 1956 (acetate d/w) . . . . £125/£100
ditto, Spearman, 1956 . . . . £125/£30

The Smile at the Foot of the Ladder, Duell, Sloan & Pearce (U.S.), 1948 . . . . £250/£30
The Books in My Life, Owen, 1952 . . . £100/£25
ditto, New Directions (U.S.), 1952 . . £100/£25
Nights of Love and Laughter, Signet/New American Library (U.S.), 1955 (wraps) £10
A Devil in Paradise, Signet/New American Library (U.S.), 1956 (wraps) £10
ditto, Signet, 1965 (wraps) £10
Quiet Days in Clichy, Olympia (Paris), 1956 (wraps) £500
ditto, Grove (U.S.), 1965 (wraps) £25
ditto, Calder, 1966 . . . . £30/£10
Big Sur and the Oranges of Hieronymous Bosch, New Directions (U.S.), 1957 . . . . . . £125/£25
ditto, Heinemann, 1958 . . . . . . £75/£20
The Red Notebook, Williams (U.S.), 1958 (wraps) £15
Reunion in Barcelona, Scorpion Press, 1959 (50 signed copies of 500, wraps) £250
ditto, Scorpion Press, 1959 (450 unsigned copies, wraps) £25
The Intimate Henry Miller, Signet (U.S.), 1959 (wraps) £10
The Henry Miller Reader, New Directions (U.S.), 1959 (ed. Lawrence Durrell) . . . . £35/£10
ditto, as *The Best of Henry Miller*, Heinemann, 1960 . . . . £35/£10
To Paint Is to Love Again, Cambia (U.S.), 1960 . . . . £35/£10
ditto, Cambia (U.S.), 1960 (50 signed copies) . £250
ditto, Cambia (U.S.), 1960 (wraps) £10
Journey to an Antique Land, Big Ben Press (U.S.), 1962 (wraps) £25
ditto, Village Press, 1973 (wraps) £15
Hamlet I & II, Carrefour, 1962 (wraps) . . . £45
Stand Still Like Hummingbird, New Directions (U.S.), 1962 . . . . £30/£10
ditto, Village Press, 1974 (wraps) £15
Lawrence Durrell and Henry Miller: A Private Correspondence, Dutton (U.S.), 1963 . . £25/£10
ditto, Faber, 1963 . . . . £25/£10
Henry Miller on Writing, New Directions (U.S.), 1964 (wraps) £15
Greece, Viking (U.S.), 1964 . . . . . £25/£10
ditto, Thames and Hudson, 1964 . . . . £25/£10
Henry Miller: Letters to Anais Nin, Putnam (U.S.), 1965 (wraps) . . . . £20/£5
ditto, Owen, 1965 . . . . £20/£5
Order and Chaos Chez Hans Reichel, Loujon Press (U.S.), 1966 (26 lettered and signed copies) . £500
ditto, Loujon Press (U.S.), 1966 (99 numbered and signed copies) £350
ditto, Loujon Press (U.S.), 1966 (26 lettered copies of 1,399, 'Cork' edition) £200
ditto, Loujon Press (U.S.), 1966 (1,399 'Cork' edition) £75
Insomnia: Or, the Devil at Large, Loujon (U.S.), 1971 (200 of 385 signed, numbered copies in box) . £1,250
ditto, Loujon (U.S.), 1971 (unboxed copies) . £750

My Life and Times, Playboy (U.S.), 1971 . £25/£10
ditto, Playboy (U.S.), 1971 (500 signed, numbered
copies) . . . . £100/£75
ditto, Pall Mall Press, 1972 . . . . £25/£10
Reflections on the Death of Mishima, Capra (U.S.),
1972 (200 signed, numbered copies, no d/w) . £100
ditto, Capra (U.S.), 1972 (wraps). . . . £15
*On Turning Eighty: Journey to an Antique Land:
Forward to the 'Angel is My Watermark'*, Capra
(U.S.), 1972 (200 signed, numbered copies, no d/w) .
. . . . £125
ditto, Capra (U.S.), 1972 (wraps). . . . £15
ditto, Village Press, 1973 (wraps) . . . £15
First Impressions of Greece, Capra (U.S.), 1973 (250
signed, numbered copies, no d/w) . . . £100
ditto, Capra (U.S.), 1973 (wraps). . . . £15
ditto, Village Press, 1973 (wraps) . . . £15
This is Henry Miller from Brooklyn, Nash (U.S.),
1974 (100 signed copies, plexiglass holder) . £125
ditto, Nash (U.S.), 1974 (400 unsigned copies, no
holder) £30
The Nightmare Notebook, New Directions (U.S.),
1975 (700 signed, numbered copies) . . £200/£125
*Henry Miller's Book of Friends: A Tribute to Friends
of Long Ago*, Capra (U.S.), 1976 (250 signed, numbered copies, no d/w) £125
ditto, Capra (U.S.), 1976 (26 signed, numbered copies
with original artwork by author) . . . £600
ditto, Capra (U.S.), 1976 . . . . . £25/£10
ditto, W.H. Allen, 1978 . . . . . £25/£10
ditto, as *The Complete Book of Friends*, Allison &
Busby, 1988 . . . . £20/£5
Gliding Into the Everglades, Lost Pleiade Press (U.S.),
1977 (250 signed, numbered copies, no d/w) . £100
ditto, Lost Pleiade Press (U.S.), 1977 (wraps) . £20
Mother, China, and the World Beyond, Capra (U.S.),
1977 (250 signed, numbered copies, no d/w) . £100
ditto, Capra (U.S.), 1977 (wraps). . . . £15
Four Visions of America, Capra (U.S.), 1977 (with
Jong, Sanchez and Boyle, 250 signed, numbered
copies, no d/w) £100
ditto, Capra (U.S.), 1977 (wraps). . . . £15
My Bike and Other Friends, Capra (U.S.), 1978 (250
signed, numbered copies) . . . . £125/£75
ditto, Capra (U.S.), 1978 . . . . . £25/£10
Joey, Capra (U.S.), 1979 (250 signed, numbered
copies) . . . . £100/£75
ditto, Capra (U.S.), 1979 (wraps). . . . £25
Notes on Aaron's Rod, Black Sparrow (U.S.), 1980
(250 signed, numbered copies, acetate d/w) . . .
. . . . £125/£100
ditto, Black Sparrow (U.S.), 1980 (250 signed copies).
. . . . £65/£50
ditto, Black Sparrow (U.S.), 1980 . . . . £20/£5
The World of Lawrence: A Passionate Appreciation,
Capra (U.S.), 1979 (250 signed, numbered copies) .
. . . . £75/£45
ditto, Capra (U.S.), 1979 (26 signed, lettered copies
with photo of Miller) . . . . . £125/£75

ditto, Capra (U.S.), 1979 . . . . . . £25/£10
ditto, John Calder, 1980 . . . . . £25/£10
Reflections, Capra (U.S.), 1981 (wraps). . £10
*The Paintings of Henry Miller: Paint as You Like and
Die Happy*, Capra (U.S.), 1982 (250 signed,
numbered copies) . . . . . . £125/£75
ditto, Chronicle Books (U.S.), 1982 (wraps) . £30
Opus Pistorum, Grove (U.S.), 1983 . . . £25/£10
ditto, Allen, 1984 . . . . £10/£5
From Your Capricorn Friend, New Directions (U.S.),
1984 . . . . £20/£5
Dear, Dear Brenda, Morrow (U.S.), 1986 . . £20/£5
Letters from Henry Miller to Hoki Tokuda Miller,
Freundlich Books (U.S.), 1987 . . . . £25/£10
ditto, Hale, 1990 . . . . £15/£5
The Durrell-Miller Letters: 1935-80, New Directions
(U.S.), 1988 . . . . £20/£5
ditto, Faber, 1988 . . . . £20/£5
Letters to Emil, New Directions (U.S.), 1989 . £20/£5
ditto, Carcanet, 1990 . . . . . . £20/£5
Crazy Cock, Grove Weidenfeld (U.S.), 1991 . £15/£5
ditto, HarperCollins, 1992 . . . . . £15/£5
Moloch: Or This Gentile World, Grove (U.S.), 1992 .
. . . . £15/£5
ditto, HarperCollins, 1992 . . . . . £15/£5
The Mezzotints, Jackson (U.S.), 1993 (26 private
copies, no d/w) £200
ditto, Jackson (U.S.), 1993 (100 numbered copies) £65
ditto, Jackson (U.S.), 1993 (400 library copies). £10
ditto, Jackson (U.S.), 1993 (100 economy) . . £10
Writers Three: A Literary Exchange, Jackson (U.S.),
1995 . . . . £15/£5
ditto, Jackson (U.S.), 1995 (100 numbered copies) £35
Henry Miller and James Laughlin: Selected Letters,
Norton (U.S.), 1996 . . . . . . £15/£5
ditto, Constable, 1996 . . . . . . £10/£5
*The Colossus of Armenia: G.I. Gurdjieff and Henry
Miller with Five Previously Unpublished Miller
Letters to Pham Công Thiên*, Jackson (U.S.), 1998
(100 numbered copies) £75
*Henry Miller and Elmer Gertz: Selected Letters 1965-
1975*, Jackson (U.S.), 1998(100 numbered copies) .
. . . . £75

A.A. MILNE
(b.1882 d.1956)

Milne was a freelance journalist in London, then
assistant editor of *Punch*, before becoming a full-time
writer from 1918. He is famous for his plays and
children's books, although he also wrote novels, short
stories, poetry and essays.

Children's Titles
Once on a Time: A Fairy Story, Hodder & Stoughton,
1917 (illustrated by H.M. Brock) £150
ditto, Hodder & Stoughton, [1925] (illustrated by
Charles Robinson) . . . . . . £125/£25

When We Were Very Young, Methuen, 1924 (verse, illustrated by E.H. Shepard). . . £5,000/£1,000
ditto, Methuen, 1924 (verse, illustrated by E.H. Shepard, 100 numbered copies, signed by the author and artist) . . . . £6,000/£4,000
ditto, Dutton (U.S.), 1924 (100 numbered copies, signed by the author and artist) . . £3,500/£2,500
ditto, Dutton (U.S.), 1924 (400 deluxe copies) . . . . £1,000/£450
ditto, Methuen, 1974 (300 numbered copies, signed by Christopher Milne) . . . . . . £500/£150
Vespers: A Poem, Methuen, [1924] (illustrated by E.H. Shepard, music by H. Fraser-Simson) . £150/£50
Fourteen Songs, Methuen, 1924 (illustrated by E.H. Shepard, music by H. Fraser-Simson) . . £200/£75
Make-Believe: A Children's Play in a Prologue and Three Acts, Methuen, 1925 . . . . £100/£25
A Gallery of Children, Stanley Paul, 1925 (illustrated by H. Willebeek le Mair) . . . . . £500/£100
ditto, Stanley Paul, 1925 (500 numbered copies, signed by the author) . . . . . £1,000/£500
The King's Breakfast, Methuen, 1925 (illustrated by E.H. Shepard, music by H. Fraser-Simson) £200/£50
Winnie-the-Pooh, Methuen, 1926 (stories, illustrated by E.H. Shepard) . . . . . . £2,500/£500
ditto, Methuen, 1926 (deluxe edition: red, green or blue leather binding, in slipcase) . . . £3,000/£2,500
ditto, Methuen, 1926 (350 copies, signed by the author and artist, d/w and slipcase) . . . £5,000/£3,500
ditto, Methuen, 1926 (20 special copies, signed by the author and artist) £7,500
ditto, Dutton (U.S.), 1926 (200 numbered copies, signed by the author and artist) . £3,500/£2,500
ditto, Dutton (U.S.), 1926. . . . . £1,000/£500
ditto, Methuen, 1973 (illustrated in colour by E.H. Shepard) . . . . £75/£15
ditto, Methuen, 1976 (stories, illustrated by E.H. Shepard, 300 numbered copies, signed by Christopher Milne). . . . . £600/£300
Teddy Bear and Other Songs From 'When We Were Very Young', Methuen, 1926 (illustrated by E.H. Shepard, music by H. Fraser-Simson) . . £200/£75
ditto, Methuen, 1926 (100 numbered copies, signed by the author, artist and composer, d/w and slipcase) . . . . £750/£450
Now We Are Six, Methuen, 1927 (verse, illustrated by E.H. Shepard) . . . . £750/£125
ditto, Methuen, 1927 (deluxe edition: red, blue or green leather binding, in slipcase) . . . £1,500/£1,000
ditto, Methuen, 1927 (200 numbered copies, signed by the author and artist). . . . . £2,000/£1,000
ditto, Methuen, 1927 (20 special copies, signed by the author and artist) £3,500
ditto, Dutton (U.S.), 1927 (200 signed copies, acetate d/w) . . . . £1,750/£1,000
ditto, Dutton (U.S.), 1928. . . . . . £250/£75
ditto, Methuen, 1976 (300 numbered copies, signed by Christopher Milne) . . . . . . £400/£150

Songs from 'Now We Are Six', Methuen, 1927 (music by H. Fraser-Simson) . . . . . £200/£50
ditto, Methuen, 1927 (100 signed copies) . . £750
More Very Young Songs, Methuen, 1928 . £200/£75
ditto, Methuen, 1928 (100 numbered copies, signed by the author, artist and composer, d/w and slipcase) £750
The House at Pooh Corner, Methuen, 1928 (stories, illustrated by E.H. Shepard). . . . £1,000/£250
ditto, Methuen, 1928 (350 numbered copies, signed by the author and artist). . . . . £4,000/£2,500
ditto, Methuen, 1928 (20 special copies, signed by the author and artist) £6,000
ditto, Methuen, 1928 (deluxe edition: red, green or blue leather binding, in slipcase) £2,500
ditto, Dutton (U.S.), 1928 (250 numbered copies, signed by the author and artist) . . £2,000/£1,250
ditto, Dutton (U.S.), 1928. . . . . . £250/£75
ditto, Methuen, 1974 (illustrated in colour by E.H. Shepard) . . . . £60/£20
The Christopher Robin Calendar 1929, Methuen 'Ephemerides' series, [1928] (verse, illustrated by E.H. Shepard) £125
The Christopher Robin Story Book, Methuen, 1928 (selections from *When We Were Very Young*, *Now We Are Six*, *Winnie-the-Pooh* and *The House at Pooh Corner*, new preface by the author) . £400/£75
The Hums of Pooh, Methuen, 1929 (illustrated by E.H. Shepard, music by H. Fraser-Simson) . . £200/£45
ditto, Methuen, 1929 (100 numbered copies, signed by the author and artist and composer, d/w and slipcase) . . . . £750/£500
Toad of Toad Hall: A Play Taken from Kenneth Grahame's 'The Wind in the Willows', Methuen, 1929 . . . . £100/£25
ditto, Methuen, 1929 (200 numbered copies, signed by Kenneth Grahame and A. A. Milne) . £1,000/£500
Tales of Pooh, Methuen: 'Modern Classics' series, [1930] (selections from *Winnie-The-Pooh* and *The House at Pooh Corner*, illustrated by E.H. Shepard) . . . . £200/£65
The Christopher Robin Birthday Book, Methuen, 1930 (selections from *When We Were Very Young*, *Now We Are Six*, *Winnie-the-Pooh* and *The House at Pooh Corner*, illustrated by E.H. Shepard) . . £150/£50
The Christopher Robin Verses, Methuen, 1932 (contains *When We Were Very Young* and *Now We Are Six*, illustrated by E.H. Shepard) . £250/£100
Introducing Winnie-the-Pooh, Methuen, 1947 £75/£35
The World of Pooh, Methuen, 1958 . . £100/£35
The World of Christopher Robin, Methuen, 1959 . . . . £100/£35
Prince Rabbit and The Princess Who Could Not Laugh, Ward Lock, 1966 (illustrated by Mary Shepard) . . . . £35/£15
The Pooh Story Book, Methuen, 1967 . . £60/£20
The Christopher Robin Verse Book, Methuen, 1969 (illustrated by E.H. Shepard) . . . . £60/£20

Adult Novels

Mr Pim, Hodder & Stoughton, 1921.　.　. £75/£25
The Red House Mystery, Methuen, 1922　£1,500/£250
Chloe Marr, Methuen, 1946.　.　.　.　.　£45/£10
ditto, Dutton (U.S.), 1946.　.　.　.　.　£45/£10

Adult Short Stories

The Secret and Other Stories, Methuen/Fountain Press
　(U.S.), 1929 (742 signed copies, no d/w)　.　. £250
Birthday Party and Other Stories, Dutton (U.S.), 1948.
　.　.　.　.　.　.　.　.　.　.　.　£25/£10
ditto, Methuen, 1949　.　.　.　.　.　. £25/£10
A Table Near the Band, Methuen, 1950　. £35/£15

Plays

First Plays, Chatto & Windus, 1919 (contains 'Wurzel-
　Flummery', 'The Lucky One', 'The Boy Comes
　Home', 'Belinda' and 'The Red Feathers')　£25/£10
Second Plays, Chatto & Windus, 1921 (contains
　'Make-Believe', 'Mr Pim Passes By', 'The
　Camberley Triangle', 'The Romantic Age' and 'The
　Stepmother').　.　.　.　.　.　.　.　. £25/£10
Three Plays, Putnam (U.S.), 1922 (contains 'The
　Dover Road', 'The Truth about Blayds' and 'The
　Great Broxopp')　.　.　.　.　.　.　. £25/£10
ditto, Chatto & Windus, 1923　.　.　.　. £25/£10
Success, Chatto & Windus, 1923.　.　.　. £25/£10
The Man in the Bowler Hat, French (U.K./U.S.), 1923
　(wraps)　.　.　.　.　.　.　.　.　.　. £15
Four Plays, Chatto & Windus, 1926 (contains 'To
　Have the Honour, Meet the Prince', 'Ariadne',
　'Portrait of a Gentleman in Slippers' and 'Success')　.
　.　.　.　.　.　.　.　.　.　.　.　£25/£10
More Plays, Chatto & Windus, 1935 (contains 'The
　Ivory Doors', 'The Fourth Wall' and 'Other People's
　Lives')　.　.　.　.　.　.　.　.　.　. £20/£5
Four Plays, Penguin, 1939 (contains 'To Have the
　Honour', 'Belinda', 'The Dover Road' and 'Mr Pim
　Passes By', wraps)　.　.　.　.　.　.　. £5
The Ugly Duckling, French, 1941 (wraps)　.　. £10
Before the Flood, French (U.K./U.S.), 1951 (wraps)　.
　.　.　.　.　.　.　.　.　.　.　.　. £10

Poetry

For the Luncheon Interval: Cricket and Other Verses,
　Methuen, 1925 (wraps)　.　.　.　.　.　. £35
Behind the Lines, Methuen, 1940　.　.　£25/£10
The Norman Church, Methuen, 1948　.　.　£25/£10

Others

Lovers in London, Alston Rivers, 1905.　.　.　£75
The Day's Play, Methuen, 1910 (sketches)　.　.　£20
The Holiday Round, Methuen, 1912 (sketches)　£20
Once a Week, Methuen, 1914　.　.　.　.　£15
Happy Days, George H. Doran (U.S.), 1915　.　£15
Not That It Matters, Methuen, 1919.　.　.　£15
If I May, Methuen, 1920.　.　.　.　.　. £30/£15
The Sunny Side, Methuen, 1921.　.　.　.　£30/£15
The Ascent of Man, Ernest Benn, 1928.　.　£30/£15

By Way of Introduction, Methuen, 1929　.　£30/£15
ditto, Dutton (U.S.), 1929 (166 signed, large paper
　copies)　.　.　.　.　.　.　.　.　.　. £250
Those Were the Days, Methuen, 1929　.　. £30/£10
Two People, Methuen, 1931.　.　.　.　. £30/£10
Four Days Wonder, Methuen, 1933.　.　. £30/£10
Peace with Honour, Methuen, 1934.　.　. £25/£10
Miss Elizabeth Bennett, Chatto & Windus, 1936　.　.
　.　.　.　.　.　.　.　.　.　.　.　£30/£10
It's Too Late Now, Methuen, 1939　.　.　. £30/£10
War With Honour, Macmillan, 1940　.　. £30/£10
War Aims Unlimited, Methuen, 1941 (wraps)　.　£15
The Pocket Milne, Dutton (U.S.),1941　.　. £25/£10
ditto, Methuen, 1942　.　.　.　.　.　.　. £20/£5
Year In, Year Out, Methuen, 1952　.　.　. £25/£10

GLADYS MITCHELL

(b.1901 d.1983)

From the Golden Age of Detective Fiction, Mitchell's
unconventional sleuth, 'Beatrice Adela Lestrange
Bradley' was already elderly when she made her first
appearance in 1929. Her last case is recorded in 1984,
by which time she may have been 125 years old.

Novels

Speedy Death, Gollancz, 1929　.　.　.　. £750/£125
ditto, Dial Press (U.S.), 1929　.　.　.　. £650/£100
The Mystery of a Butcher's Shop, Gollancz, 1929.　.
　.　.　.　.　.　.　.　.　.　.　.　£650/£100
ditto, Dial Press (U.S.), 1930.　.　.　.　. £500/£65
The Longer Bodies, Gollancz, 1930.　.　. £450/£50
The Saltmarsh Murders, Gollancz, 1932　. £450/£50
ditto, Macrae-Smith (U.S.), 1933.　.　.　. £400/£45
Death at the Opera, Grayson, 1934　.　.　. £400/£45
ditto, as *Death in the Wet*, Macrae-Smith (U.S.), 1934
　.　.　.　.　.　.　.　.　.　.　.　£250/£30
The Devil at Saxon Wall, Grayson, 1935　. £250/£35
Dead Men's Morris, Joseph, 1936　.　.　. £250/£35
Come Away Death, Joseph, 1937　.　.　. £250/£35
St Peter's Finger, Joseph, 1938　.　.　.　. £175/£30
ditto, St Martin's Press (U.S.), 1987.　.　. £15/£5
Printer's Error, Joseph, 1939　.　.　.　. £175/£25
Brazen Tongue, Joseph, 1940　.　.　.　. £175/£25
Hangman's Curfew, Joseph, 1941　.　.　. £175/£25
When Last I Died, Joseph, 1941.　.　.　. £175/£30
ditto, Knopf (U.S.), 1942.　.　.　.　.　. £125/£10
Laurels are Poison, Joseph, 1942　.　.　. £175/£30
The Worsted Viper, Joseph, 1943　.　.　. £175/£30
Sunset Over Soho, Joseph, 1943.　.　.　. £150/£20
My Father Sleeps, Joseph, 1944.　.　.　. £150/£20
The Rising of the Moon, Joseph, 1945　.　. £150/£20
ditto, St Martin's Press (U.S.), 1985.　.　. £15/£5
Here Comes a Chopper, Joseph, 1946　.　. £150/£20
Death and the Maiden, Joseph, 1947　.　. £150/£20
The Dancing Druids, Joseph, 1948　.　.　. £125/£15
ditto, St Martin's Press (U.S.), 1986.　.　.　. £10/£5

Tom Brown's Body, Joseph, 1949 . . .	£125/£15
Groaning Spinney, Joseph, 1950 . . .	£100/£10
The Devil's Elbow, Joseph, 1951 . . .	£100/£10
The Echoing Strangers, Joseph, 1952 . .	£75/£10
Merlin's Furlong, Joseph, 1953	£75/£10
Faintly Speaking, Joseph, 1954	£75/£10
ditto, St Martin's Press (U.S.), 1986	£10/£5
Watson's Choice, Joseph, 1955	£50/£10
ditto, McKay (U.S.), 1976	£10/£5
Twelve Horses and The Hangman's Noose, Joseph, 1956	£50/£10
ditto, British Book Centre (U.S.), 1958 . .	£15/£5
ditto, as *Hangman's Noose*, Severn House, 1983	£10/£5
The Twenty-Third Man, Joseph, 1957 . .	£50/£10
Spotted Hemlock, Joseph, 1958	£50/£10
ditto, St Martin's Press (U.S.), 1985 . . .	£10/£5
The Man Who Grew Tomatoes, Joseph, 1959	£50/£10
ditto, British Book Centre (U.S.), 1959 . . .	£15/£5
Say it with Flowers, Joseph, 1960 . . .	£40/£5
ditto, London House (U.S.), 1960 . . .	£15/£5
The Nodding Canaries, Joseph, 1961 . .	£40/£5
My Bones Will Keep, Joseph, 1962 . . .	£35/£5
ditto, British Book Centre (U.S.), 1962 . .	£10/£5
Adders on the Heath, Joseph, 1963 . . .	£35/£5
ditto, British Book Centre (U.S.), 1963 . .	£10/£5
Death of a Delft Blue, Joseph, 1964. . .	£35/£5
ditto, British Book Centre (U.S.), 1965 . .	£10/£5
ditto, as *Death in Amsterdam*, Severn House, 1990	£10/£5
Pageant of a Murder, Joseph, 1965 . . .	£35/£5
ditto, British Book Centre (U.S.), 1965 . .	£10/£5
The Croaking Raven, Joseph, 1966 . . .	£35/£5
Skeleton Island, Joseph, 1967	£35/£5
Three Quick and Five Dead, Joseph, 1968 .	£15/£5
Dance to Your Daddy, Joseph, 1969. . .	£35/£5
Gory Dew, Joseph, 1970	£35/£5
Lament for Letto, Joseph, 1971	£35/£5
A Nearse on May-Day, Joseph, 1972 . .	£35/£5
The Murder of Busy Lizzie, Joseph, 1973 .	£25/£5
A Javelin for Jonah, Joseph, 1974 . . .	£25/£5
Winking at the Brim, Joseph, 1975 . . .	£25/£5
ditto, McKay (U.S.), 1977	£10/£5
Convent on Styx, Joseph, 1975	£25/£5
Late, Late in the Evening, Joseph, 1976 .	£25/£5
Noonday and Night, Joseph, 1977 . . .	£25/£5
Fault in the Structure, Joseph, 1977 . . .	£25/£5
Wraiths and Changelings, Joseph, 1978 . .	£25/£5
Mingled with Venom, Joseph, 1978 . . .	£25/£5
Nest of Vipers, Joseph, 1979	£20/£5
The Mudflats of the Dead, Joseph, 1979 .	£20/£5
Uncoffin'd Clay, Joseph, 1980	£20/£5
ditto, St Martin's Press (U.S.), 1981 . . .	£10/£5
The Whispering Knights, Joseph, 1980 . .	£20/£5
The Death-Cap Dancers, Joseph, 1981 . .	£20/£5
ditto, St Martin's Press (U.S.), 1981 . . .	£10/£5
Lovers, Make Moan, Joseph, 1982 . . .	£15/£5
Here Lies Gloria Mundy, Joseph, 1982 . .	£15/£5
ditto, St Martin's Press (U.S.), 1983	£10/£5

Death of a Burrowing Mole, Joseph, 1982 .	£15/£5
The Greenstone Griffins, Joseph, 1983 . .	£15/£5
Cold, Lone and Still, Joseph, 1983	£10/£5
No Winding Sheet, Joseph, 1984 . . .	£10/£5
The Crozier Pharoahs, Joseph, 1984 . . .	£10/£5

Novels Written as 'Stephen Hockaby'

Marsh Hay, Grayson, 1933	£175/£30
Seven Stars and Orion, Grayson, 1934 . .	£150/£25
Gabriel's Hold, Grayson, 1935	£150/£25
Shallw Brown, Joseph, 1936	£125/£15
Grand Master, Joseph, 1939	£125/£15

Novels Written as 'Malcolm Torre'

Heavy as Lead, Joseph, 1966.	£25/£5
Late and Cold, Joseph, 1967	£25/£5
Your Secret Friend, Joseph, 1968 . . .	£35/£10
Churchyard Salad, Joseph, 1969 . . .	£35/£10
Shades of Darkness, Joseph, 1970 . . .	£35/£10
Bismark's Herrings, Joseph, 1971 . . .	£35/£10

MARGARET MITCHELL
(b.1900 d.1949)

Gone With the Wind was the result of ten years' work, a distillation of all of the American Civil War stories Mitchell had heard. Her 1,000 page novel won the Pulitzer Prize, has sold over 25 million copies and is translated into 27 different languages.

Gone With the Wind, Macmillan (U.S.), 1936 (d/w with *Gone With the Wind* listed in second column of book list on back panel)	£4,000/£200
ditto, Macmillan (U.S.), 1936 (d/w with *Gone With the Wind* listed at top of list in first column on back panel).	£750/£200
ditto, Macmillan, 1936	£300/£75

NAOMI MITCHISON
(b.1897 d.1999)

A novelist with a long career, her works of the 1920s and 30s are held in highest esteem, especially those which evoke classical Greece and Rome. Mitchison also wrote a great deal of fiction for children.

Novels

The Conquered, Cape, 1923	£125/£25
ditto, Harcourt Brace (U.S.), 1923 . .	£100/£20
Cloud Cuckoo Land, Cape, 1925 . . .	£50/£15
ditto, Harcourt Brace (U.S.), 1926 . . .	£45/£15
The Corn King and the Spring Queen, Cape, 1931 (illustrated by Z. Stryjenska)	£30/£15
ditto, Harcourt Brace (U.S.), [n.d.] . .	£25/£10
We Have Been Warned, Constable, 1935 .	£30/£15
ditto, The Vanguard Press (U.S.), [1936]	£25/£10

Beyond this Limit, Cape, 1935 . . . . £65/£25
The Blood of the Martyrs, Constable, 1939 . £40/£10
ditto, McGraw-Hill (U.S.), 1939 . . . . £35/£10
The Bull Calves, Cape, 1947 (illustrated by Louise
Richard Annand). . . . . . . £40/£10
Lobsters on the Agenda, Gollancz, 1952 . £25/£10
Behold Your King, Muller, 1957. . . . £25/£10
Memoirs of a Spacewoman, Gollancz, 1962 £150/£35
When We Become Men, Collins, 1965 . . £20/£5
Cleopatra's People, Heinemann, 1972 . . £15/£5
Solution Three, Dobson, 1973 . . . . £15/£5
ditto, Warner (U.S.), 1975 (wraps) £5
Not By Bread Alone, Marion Boyars, 1983 . £15/£5
Early in Orcadia, R. Drew, 1987 . . . £10/£5
The Oath Takers, Balnain Books, 1991 . . £10/£5
Sea-Green Ribbons, Balnain Books, 1991 . £10/£5

Short Stories
When the Bough Breaks and Other Stories, Cape,
1924 . . . . £50/£15
ditto, Harcourt Brace (U.S.), 1924 . . . £40/£15
Black Sparta, Greek Stories, Cape, 1928 . £50/£15
ditto, Harcourt Brace (U.S.), [n.d.] . . . £40/£15
Barbarian Stories, Cape, 1929 . . . £30/£10
ditto, Harcourt Brace (U.S.), 1929 . . . £25/£10
The Powers of Light, Pharos, 1932 (illustrations by
Eric Kennington). . . . . . . £65/£20
Images of Africa, Canongate, 1980 . . . . £15/£5
*What Do You Think of Yourself? Scottish Short
Stories*, P. Harris, 1982 . . . . . . £10/£5
Beyond this Limit, Selected Shorter Fiction, Scottish
Academic Press, 1986 . . . . . . £10/£5

Short Stories and Poetry
The Delicate Fire, Cape, 1933 . . . . £75/£20
ditto, Harcourt Brace (U.S.), 1933 . . . £65/£15
The Fourth Pig, Constable, 1936 . . . £35/£10
Five Men and a Swan, Allen & Unwin, 1957 . £15/£5
A Girl Must Live, R. Drew, 1990 . . . . £10/£5

Poetry
The Laburnum Branch, Cape, 1926 . . £50/£15
ditto, Harcourt Brace (U.S.), 1926 . . . £45/£15
The Alban Goes Out, Raven Press, 1939 (engravings
by Gertrude Hermes, wraps) £65
The Cleansing of the Knife and Other Poems,
Canongate, 1978 . . . . £15/£5

Plays
The Price of Freedom, Cape, 1931 (with Lewis
Gielgud) . . . . £35/£10
As It Was in the Beginning, Cape, 1939 (with Lewis
Gielgud) . . . . £15/£5
Spindrift, French, 1951 (with Denis Macintosh, wraps)
. . . . £10

Children's Titles
Nix-Nought-Nothing: Four Plays for Children, Cape,
1928 . . . . £35/£10
ditto, Harcourt Brace (U.S.), 1929 . . . . £25/£5

The Hostages and Other Stories for Boys & Girls,
Cape, 1930 . . . . £25/£10
ditto, Harcourt Brace (U.S.), [1931] . . . . £20/£5
Boys and Girls and Gods, Watts, 1931 . . £20/£5
Kate Crackernuts: a Fairy Play for Children, Alden
Press, 1931 (300 numbered, signed copies, wraps) .
. . . . £45
An End and a Beginning and Other Plays, Constable,
1937 . . . . £15/£5
ditto, as *Historical Plays for Schools*, Constable, 1939
(2 vols) . . . . £15/£5
*Nix-Nought-Nothing and Elfin Hill: Two Plays for
Children*, Cape, 1948 . . . . £15/£5
The Big House, Faber, 1950 . . . . . . £25/£5
Travel Light, Faber, 1952. . . . . . . £20/£5
Graeme and the Dragon, Faber, 1954 . . . £20/£5
The Swan's Road, Naldrett Press, 1954 . . £20/£5
The Land the Ravens Found, Collins, 1955 . £20/£5
To The Chapel Perilous, Allen & Unwin, 1955 £20/£5
Little Boxes, Faber, 1956. . . . . . . £20/£5
The Far Harbour, Collins, 1957. . . . . £15/£5
Judy and Lakshmi, Collins, 1959 . . . . £15/£5
The Rib of the Green Umbrella, Collins, 1960
(illustrated by Edward Ardizzone) . . . £50/£20
The Young Alexander the Great, Max Parrish, 1960 .
. . . . £15/£5
ditto, Roy (U.S.), [1961] . . . . . . £10/£5
Karensgaard: The Story of a Danish Farm, Collins,
1961 . . . . £15/£5
The Young Alfred the Great, Max Parrish, 1962 . .
. . . . £15/£5
ditto, Roy (U.S.), [1963] . . . . . . £10/£5
The Fairy Who Couldn't Tell a Lie, Collins, 1963. .
. . . . £15/£5
Alexander the Great, Longman, 1964 . . £10/£5
Henry and Crispies, Department of Education (New
Zealand), 1964 . . . . £10/£5
A Mochudi Family, Department of Education (New
Zealand), 1965 . . . . £10/£5
Ketse and the Chief, Nelson, 1965 . . . £10/£5
ditto, Nelson (U.S.), 1967. . . . . . . £10/£5
Friends and Enemies, Collins, 1966 . . . £10/£5
ditto, John Day Co. (U.S.), [1968] . . . . £10/£5
Highland Holiday, Department of Education (New
Zealand), 1967 . . . . £10/£5
The Big Surprise, Kaye & Ward, 1967 . . £10/£5
African Heroes, Bodley Head, 1968. . . . £15/£5
ditto, Farrar Straus Giroux (U.S.), 1968 . . £15/£5
Don't Look Back, Kaye & Ward, 1969 . . £10/£5
The Family at Ditlabeng, Collins, 1969. . £10/£5
ditto, Farrar, Straus & Giroux (U.S.), [1970] . £10/£5
Sun and Moon, Bodley Head, 1970 . . . . £10/£5
ditto, Dutton (U.S.), [1973] . . . . . £10/£5
Sunrise Tomorrow: A Story of Botswana, Collins,
1973 . . . . £10/£5
ditto, Farrar, Straus & Giroux (U.S.), [1973] . £10/£5
The Danish Teapot, Kaye & Ward, 1973 . . £15/£5
Snake, Collins, 1976 . . . . £10/£5
The Little Sister, O.U.P. (South Africa), 1976 . £10/£5

The Wild Dogs, O.U.P. (South Africa), 1977 . £10/£5
The Brave Nurse, and Other Stories, OUP (South Africa), 1977 . . . . £10/£5
The Two Magicians, Dobson, 1978 (with G.R. Mitchison) . . . . £10/£5
The Vegetable War, Hamish Hamilton, 1980 . £10/£5
The Sea Horse, Hamish Hamilton, 1980 . . £10/£5

Non Fiction

Anna Comnena, Howe, 1928 . . . . £35/£10
Comments on Birth Control, Faber, 1930 (tissue d/w).
. . . . £30/£15
ditto, Faber, 1930 (wraps). £15
Naomi Mitchison's Vienna Diary, Gollancz, 1934. .
. . . . £20/£5
ditto, Smith and Haas (U.S.), 1934 . . . . £20/£5
The Home and Changing Civilisation, Bodley Head, 1934 . . . . £25/£5
Socrates, Hogarth Press, 1937 (with Richard Crossman) . . . . £35/£10
The Moral Basis of Politics, Constable, 1938 . £20/£5
ditto, Kennikat Press (U.S.), [1971] . . . £10/£5
The Kingdom of Heaven, Heinemann, 1939 . £15/£5
Man and Herring, A Documentary, Serif Books, 1949 (with Denis Macintosh) . . . . . . £20/£5
Highlands and Islands, Unity Publishing, 1954 £20/£5
Other People's Worlds, Secker & Warburg, 1958 . .
. . . . £20/£5
A Fishing Village on the Clyde, O.U.P., 1960 (with George Patterson) . . . . £15/£5
Presenting Other People's Children, Hamlyn, 1961 .
. . . . £10/£5
Return to the Fairy Hill, Heinemann, 1966. . £10/£5
ditto, John Day Co. (U.S.), [1966] . . . . £10/£5
The Africans, Blond, 1970 . . . . . £25/£10
A Life for Africa, Bram Fischer, Merlin Press, 1973 .
. . . . £10/£5
Small Talk, Memories of an Edwardian Childhood, Bodley Head, 1973 . . . . £15/£5
Oil for the Highlands?, Fabian Society, 1974 (wraps).
. . . . £10
All Change Here, Girlhood and Marriage, Bodley Head, 1975 . . . . £10/£5
Sittlichkeit, Birkbeck College, [1975] (wraps) . . £5
You May Well Ask, A Memoir 1920-1940, Gollancz, 1979 . . . . £15/£5
Mucking Around, Five Continents over Fifty Years, Gollancz, 1981 . . . . £10/£5
Margaret Cole, 1883-1980, The Fabian Society, 1982 (wraps) £5
Among You Taking Notes, The Wartime Diary of Naomi Mitchison, 1939-1945, Gollancz, 1985 £20/£5
Saltire Self-Portraits, Saltire Society, 1986 (wraps) .
. . . . £5

MARY RUSSELL MITFORD
(b.1787 d.1855)

Our Village is Mitford's classic, although it is only one book among verse, sketches, novels and short stories. She supported her father through her writing after he had ruined the family through his extravagance.

Poetry

Poems, Longman, Hurst, Rees and Orme, 1810 £800
Christina: The Maid of the South Seas - A Poem, Valpy & Rivington, 1811 . . . . . . £200
Watlington Hill, A.J. Valpy, 1812 (wraps) . . £100
Narrative Poems on the Female Character in the Various Relations of Life, Vol.1, Rivington, 1813 .
. . . . £200
Dramatic Scenes, Sonnets and Other Poems, Geo. B Whittaker, 1827 . . . . £75

Sketches

Our Village, G. & W.B. Whittaker, 1824-32 (5 vols) .
. . . . £500
ditto, E. Bliss (U.S.), 1826 (3 vols) £250
ditto, Macmillan, 1893 (illustrated by Hugh Thomson, 1 vol) £25
ditto, Macmillan, 1893 (470 large paper copies, illustrated by Hugh Thomson, 1 vol) . . . £300
Belford Regis, Bentley, 1835 (3 vols) . . . £200

Novels

Atherton and Other Tales, Hurst & Blackett, 1854 (3 vols) £200
ditto, Ticknor and Fields (U.S.), 1854 (3 vols) . £175

Plays

Julian, a tragedy in five acts, W.B. Gilley (U.S.), 1823
. . . . £50
Foscari, Whittaker, 1826, ... £50
Foscari and Julian, Whittaker, 1827. . . . £50
Charles I, John Duncombe, 1834 . . . . £35
Sadak and Kalasrade, Lyceum Opera House, 1835 .
. . . . £75
Dramatic Works, Hurst & Blackett, 1854 (2 vols) £50

Short Stories

American Stories, First Series, Whittaker, Treacher, 1831 (3 vols) £175
Country Stories, Saunders & Otley, 1837 . . £125
ditto, Macmillan (U.S.), 1896 . . . . . £50

Others

Lights and Shadows of American Life, Colborn & Bentley, Treacher, 1832 (3 vols) £200
The Works: Prose and Verse, James Crissy (U.S.), 1841 . . . . £150
Recollections of a Literary Life; or, Books, Places, and People, R. Bentley, 1852 (3 vols) . . . £200
ditto, Harpers (U.S.), 1852 . . . . . . £50

The Life of Mary Russell Mitford, related in a
selection from her letters to her friends, R. Bentley,
1870 (3 vols) £100
Memoirs and Letters of Charles Boner, with letters of
Mary Russell Mitford to him..., R. Bentley, 1871 (2
vols) £45
Letters of Mary Russell Mitford, Second Series,
Bentley, 1872 (edited by Henry Chorley, 2 vols) £100
The Friendships of Mary Russell Mitford, Hurst and
Blackett, 1882 (2 vols) £50
ditto, Harper & Brothers (U.S.), 1882 . . . £45
Correspondence with Charles Boner and John
Ruskin, Unwin, 1914 (edited by Elizabeth Lee) £20
Elizabeth Barrett to Miss Mitford; the unpublished
letters..., Murray, 1954 . . . . . . £25/£10
ditto, Yale Univ. Press (U.S.), 1954 . . . £25/£10

NANCY MITFORD
(b.1904 d.1973)

Although she was also a biographer, Mitford's
satirical novels of aristocratic life are her most
appreciated works.

Novels
Highland Fling, Hamish Hamilton, 1931 . £250/£65
Christmas Pudding, Thornton Butterworth, 1932 . .
. . . . £250/£50
Wigs on the Green, Thornton Butterworth, 1935 . .
. . . . £250/£50
Pigeon Pie: A Wartime Receipt, Hamish Hamilton,
1940 . . . . £250/£45
ditto, British Book Centre (U.S.), 1959 . . £35/£10
The Pursuit of Love, Hamish Hamilton, 1945 . . .
. . . . £225/£30
ditto, Random House (U.S.), 1946 . . . £50/£15
Love in a Cold Climate, Hamish Hamilton, 1949 . .
. . . . £65/£15
ditto, Random House (U.S.), 1949 . . . £45/£10
The Blessing, Hamish Hamilton, 1951 . . £40/£15
ditto, Random House (U.S.), 1951 . . . £30/£10
Don't Tell Alfred, Hamish Hamilton, 1960 . £35/£10
ditto, Harper (U.S.), 1960 . . . . . . £25/£10
The Nancy Mitford Omnibus, Hamish Hamilton, 1956
(contains The Pursuit Of Love, Love In A Cold
Climate and The Blessing) . . . . . . £10/£5

Biography
Madame de Pompadour, Hamish Hamilton, 1954 . .
. . . . £25/£10
ditto, Random House (U.S.), 1954 . . . £25/£10
Voltaire in Love, Hamish Hamilton, 1957 . £25/£10
ditto, Harper (U.S.), 1957 . . . . . £25/£10
The Sun King: Louis XIV at Versailles, Hamish
Hamilton, 1966 . . . . £25/£5
ditto, Harper (U.S.), 1966 . . . . . . £20/£5

ditto, Arcadia Press, 1970 (265 signed copies, slipcase)
. . . . £125/£75
Frederick the Great, Hamish Hamilton, 1970 . £20/£5
ditto, Harper (U.S.), 1970 . . . . . . £20/£5

Play
The Little Hut, Hamish Hamilton, 1951. . £35/£15
ditto, Random House (U.S.), 1953 . . . £25/£10

Essays
The Water Beetle, Hamish Hamilton, 1962 . £35/£10
ditto, Harper (U.S.), 1962 . . . . . £30/£10
A Talent to Annoy: Essays, Journalism and Reviews,
Hamish Hamilton, 1986 . . . . £10/£5
ditto, Beaufort Books (U.S.), 1987 . . . . £10/£5

Translation
The Princess de Cleeves, by Madame de Lafayette,
Hamish Hamilton, 1950 . . . . £35

Editor
The Ladies of Alderley, Chapman & Hall, 1938 . .
. . . . £45/£15
The Stanleys of Alderley, Chapman & Hall, 1939 . .
. . . . £45/£15
Noblesse Oblige, Hamish Hamilton, 1956 . £40/£15
ditto, Harper (U.S.), 1956 . . . . . £30/£10

NICHOLAS MONSARRAT
(b.1910 d.1979)

Although more than simply the author of sea stories,
Monsarrat's great achievements are the novel The
Cruel Sea, and his history of seafaring, Master
Mariner.

Novels
Think of Tomorrow, Hurst & Blackett, 1934 £65/£15
At First Sight, Hurst & Blackett, 1935 . . £65/£15
The Whipping Boy, Jarrolds, 1936 . . . £45/£10
This is the Schoolroom, Cassell, 1939 . . £25/£10
ditto, Knopf (U.S.), 1940 . . . . . . £25/£10
The Cruel Sea, Cassell, 1951. . . . . £75/£15
ditto, Knopf (U.S.), 1951 . . . . . . £50/£10
The Story of Esther Costello, Cassell, 1953. £25/£10
ditto, Knopf (U.S.), 1951 . . . . . . £25/£10
Castle Garac, Knopf (U.S.), 1955 . . . £20/£5
ditto, Pan, 1968 (wraps) £5
The Tribe That Lost It's Head, Cassell, 1956 . £20/£5
ditto, Sloane (U.S.), 1956. . . . . . £20/£5
The Nylon Pirates, Cassell, 1960 . . . . £20/£5
ditto, Sloane (U.S.), 1960. . . . . . £20/£5
The White Rajah, Cassell, 1961 . . . . £20/£5
ditto, Sloane (U.S.), 1961. . . . . . £15/£5
The Time Before This, Cassell, 1962 . . £15/£5
ditto, Sloane (U.S.), 1962. . . . . . £15/£5

Smith and Jones, Cassell, 1963 . . . . . £15/£5
ditto, Sloane (U.S.), 1963 . . . . £15/£5
A Fair Day's Work, Cassell, 1964 . . . . £15/£5
ditto, Sloane (U.S.), 1964 . . . . £15/£5
Something to Hide, Cassell, 1965 . . . . £15/£5
ditto, Sloane (U.S.), 1966 . . . . £15/£5
The Pillow Fight, Cassell, 1965 . . . . . £15/£5
ditto, Sloane (U.S.), 1965 . . . . £15/£5
Richer Than All His Tribe, Cassell, 1968 . £15/£5
ditto, Morrow (U.S.), 1969 . . . . . . £15/£5
The Kapillan of Malta, Cassell, 1973 . . £15/£5
ditto, Morrow (U.S.), 1974 . . . . . . £15/£5
The Master Mariner, Volume 1: Running Proud,
Cassell, 1978 . . . . £20/£5
ditto, Morrow (U.S.), 1979 . . . . . . £20/£5
The Master Mariner, Volume 2: Drunken Ship,
Cassell, 1980 . . . . £20/£5
ditto, Morrow (U.S.), 1981 . . . . . . £20/£5

Short Stories
Depends What You Mean By Love, Cassell, 1947 . .
. . . . £25/£10
ditto, Knopf (U.S.), 1948 . . . . . . £25/£10
ditto, as *HMS Marlborough Will Enter Harbour*,
Panther, 1956 (wraps) £5
HMS Marlborough Will Enter Harbour, Cassell, 1952
. . . . £15/£5
The Ship That Died of Shame, Cassell, 1959 . £20/£5
ditto, Sloane (U.S.), 1959 . . . . . . £20/£5
Monsarrat At Sea, Cassell, 1975 . . . . £15/£5
ditto, Morrow (U.S.), 1976 . . . . . . £10/£5

Autobiography
My Brother Denys: A Memoir, Cassell, 1948 £30/£10
ditto, Knopf (U.S.), 1949 . . . . . . £25/£10
H.M. Corvette, Cassell, 1942 (wraps) . . £10
ditto, Lippincott (U.S.), 1943 . . . . £30/£10
East Coast Corvette, Cassell, 1943 (wraps) . £10
ditto, Lippincott (U.S.), 1943 . . . . £30/£10
Corvette Command, Cassell, 1944 (wraps) . . £10
Three Corvettes, Cassell, 1945 . . . £25/£10
H.M. Frigate, Cassell, 1948 (wraps) . . . £10
Canada Coast To Coast, Cassell, 1955 . . £20/£5
Life is a Four Letter Word, Volume 1: Breaking In,
Cassell, 1966 . . . . £15/£5
Life is a Four Letter Word, Volume 2: Breaking Out,
Cassell, 1970 . . . . £15/£5
Breaking In, Breaking Out, Morrow, 1971 . £15/£5

Other
To Stratford, With Love, McLelland & Stewart
(Canada), 1963 (wraps) £10

MICHAEL MOORCOCK
(b.1939)

A wide-ranging author writing predominantly in the
fields of science fiction and fantasy.

'Elric of Melniboné' Titles
The Stealer of Souls, Neville Spearman, 1963 (orange
boards) . . . . £140/£45
ditto, Neville Spearman, 1963 (green boards) £70/£20
Stormbringer, Herbert Jenkins, 1965 . . £175/£50
ditto, DAW (U.S.), 1977 (revised edition, wraps) . £5
The Sleeping Sorceress, New English Library, 1971 .
. . . . £25/£5
ditto, as *The Vanishing Tower*, DAW (U.S.), 1977
(wraps) £5
ditto, as *The Vanishing Tower*, Archival Press (U.S.),
1981 (no d/w, in illustrated red slipcase) . £50/£30
ditto, as *The Vanishing Tower*, Archival Press (U.S.),
1981 (150 signed copies, no d/w, in brown slipcase) .
. . . . £150/£90
Elric of Melniboné, Hutchinson, 1972 . . . £35/£5
ditto, as *The Dreaming City*, Lancer (U.S.), 1972 (cut
text, wraps) £5
ditto, as *Elric of Melniboné*, Blue Star (U.S.), 1977 (no
d/w, in red slipcase) . . . . £50/£30
ditto, as *Elric of Melniboné*, Blue Star (U.S.), 1977
(150 signed copies, no d/w, in brown slipcase) . .
. . . . £150/£90
Elric: The Return to Melnibone [sic.], Unicorn, 1973
(graphic, illustrated by Philippe Druillet, outsized
wraps) £60
ditto, as *Elric: The Return to Melniboné*, Jayde
Design, 1997 (outsized wraps) £10
The Jade Man's Eyes, Unicorn, 1973 (wraps) . £15
The Sailor on the Seas of Fate, Quartet, 1976 . £20/£5
The Weird of the White Wolf, DAW (U.S.), 1977
(wraps) £5
The Bane of the Black Sword, DAW (U.S.), 1977
(wraps) £5
Elric at the End of Time, Paper Tiger, 1987 (illustrated
by Rodney Matthews) . . . . . . £15/£5
ditto, Paper Tiger, 1987 (outsized wraps) . . £10
The Fortress of the Pearl, Gollancz, 1989 . £15/£5
The Revenge of the Rose, Grafton, 1991 . £15/£5
The Dreamthief's Daughter, Earthlight, 2001 . £15/£5
ditto, American Fantasy (U.S.), 2001 (600 signed
copies, slipcase) . . . . £85/£50
ditto, American Fantasy (U.S.), 2003 [dated 2001] (26
signed copies, no d/w, in traycase) . . . £350/£200
The Skrayling Tree: The Albino in America, Warner
(U.S.), 2003 . . . . £15/£5

'The Roads Between the Worlds' Titles
The Fireclown, Compact, 1965 (wraps) . . . £15
ditto, as *The Winds of Limbo*, Paperback Library
(U.S.), 1969 (wraps) £5
The Twilight Man, Compact, 1966 (wraps) . . £15
ditto, as *The Shores of Death*, Sphere, 1970 (wraps) .
. . . . £5

The Wrecks of Time, Ace (U.S.), [1967] (cut text, with 'Tramontane' by Emil Petaja, wraps) £5
ditto, as *The Rituals of Infinity*, Arrow, 1971 (full text, wraps). £5
ditto, as *The Wrecks of Time*, Roc, 1994 (full text, wraps). £5

'Kane of Old Mars' Titles
Warriors of Mars, Compact, 1965 (wraps, pseud. 'Edward P. Bradbury') £15
ditto, as *The City of the Beast*, Lancer (U.S.), [1970] (wraps, as Michael Moorcock) £5
ditto, as *City of the Beast or Warriors of Mars*, DAW (U.S.), 1979 (wraps, as Michael Moorcock, with new introduction) £5
Blades of Mars, Compact, 1965 (wraps, pseud. 'Edward P. Bradbury') £15
ditto, as *The Lord of the Spiders*, Lancer (U.S.), [1971] (wraps, as Michael Moorcock) £5
Barbarians of Mars, Compact, 1965 (wraps, pseud. 'Edward P. Bradbury') £15
ditto, as *Masters of the Pit*, New English Library, 1971 (wraps, as Michael Moorcock) £5
N.B. All 'Bradbury' titles also published as Michael Moorcock, Ace (U.S.), 1991 (wraps) . . £5 each

'Nick Allard'/'Jerry Cornell' Titles
The LSD Dossier, by Roger Harris, Compact, 1966 (rewritten by Moorcock, wraps) £30
Somewhere in the Night, Compact, 1966 (wraps, pseud. 'Bill Barclay') £30
ditto, as *The Chinese Agent*, Macmillan (U.S.), 1970 (revised edition, as Michael Moorcock) . £30/£5
Printer's Devil, Compact, 1966 (wraps, pseud. 'Bill Barclay') £25
ditto, as *The Russian Intelligence*, Savoy, 1980 (revised edition, wraps, as Michael Moorcock, illustrated by Harry Douthwaite) £10
ditto, as *The Russian Intelligence*, New English Library, 1983 (revised text, as Michael Moorcock, no illustrations) . . . . £20/£5

'Hawkmoon' ('The History of the Runestaff') Titles
The Jewel in the Skull, Lancer (U.S.), 1967 (wraps) .
. . . . £10
ditto, White Lion, 1973 . . . . £20/£5
ditto, DAW (U.S.), 1977 (revised edition, wraps) . £5
Sorcerer's Amulet, Lancer (U.S.), 1968 (wraps) £10
ditto, as *The Mad God's Amulet*, Mayflower, 1969 (wraps) £5
ditto, as *The Mad God's Amulet*, White Lion, 1973 .
. . . . £20/£5
ditto, as *The Mad God's Amulet*, DAW (U.S.), 1977 (revised edition, wraps) £5
Sword of the Dawn, Lancer (U.S.), 1968 (wraps) £10
ditto, as *The Sword of the Dawn*, White Lion, 1973 .
. . . . £20/£5
ditto, as *The Sword of the Dawn*, DAW (U.S.), 1977 (revised edition, wraps) £5

The Secret of the Runestaff, Lancer (U.S.), 1969 (wraps) £10
ditto, as *The Runestaff*, Mayflower, 1969 (wraps) . £5
ditto, as *The Runestaff*, White Lion, 1974 . . £20/£5
ditto, as *The Runestaff*, DAW (U.S.), 1977 (revised edition, wraps) £5

'Jerry Cornelius' Titles
The Final Programme, Avon (U.S.), 1968 (cut text, wraps). £15
ditto, Allison & Busby, 1969 (full text, Mal Dean d/w) . . . . £45/£10
ditto, Gregg Press (U.S.), 1976 (full text, with Norman Spinrad introduction, no d/w) £30
ditto, Allison & Busby, 1976 (full text, Richard Glyn Jones d/w) . . . . £20/£5
ditto, Fontana, 1979 (revised edition, wraps) . . £5
A Cure for Cancer, Allison & Busby, 1971 (lettered d/w) . . . . £45/£10
ditto, Allison & Busby, 1976 [dated 1971] (pictorial d/w) . . . . £20/£10
ditto, Fontana, 1979 (revised edition, wraps) . . £5
The English Assassin, Allison & Busby, 1972 (multiple-figure d/w) . . . . . £45/£10
ditto, Allison & Busby, 1976 (single-figure d/w) . .
. . . . £20/£5
ditto, Fontana, 1979 (revised edition, wraps) . . £5
The Lives and Times of Jerry Cornelius, Allison & Busby, 1976 . . . . £25/£5
ditto, Harrap, 1987 (expanded edition) . . . £15/£5
ditto, Grafton, 1987 (expanded edition) . . £5
The Adventures of Una Persson and Catherine Cornelius in the Twentieth Century, Quartet, 1976 .
. . . . £25/£5
ditto, Quartet, 1976 (wraps) £10
The Condition of Muzak, Allison & Busby, 1977 . .
. . . . £30/£5
ditto, Allison & Busby, 1977 (wraps) . . . £10
ditto, Allison & Busby, 1977 (with blurbs on d/w) . .
. . . . £15/£5
ditto, Gregg Press (U.S.), 1978 (with Charles Platt introduction, no d/w) £30
ditto, Fontana, 1978 (revised edition [no note of revision], wraps) £5
The Great Rock 'n' Roll Swindle, Virgin, 1980 ('newspaper'). £35
ditto, Virgin, 1981 (wraps, with new introduction) £10
The Entropy Tango, New English Library, 1981 . .
. . . . £15/£5
Firing the Cathedral, PS Publishing, 2002 (400 signed copies) £25
ditto, PS Publishing, 2002 (500 signed copies, wraps) .
. . . . £10

'Sailing to Utopia' Titles
The Ice Schooner, Sphere, 1969 (wraps) . . . £5
ditto, Harper & Row (U.S.), 1977 (revised edition). .
. . . . £30/£5
ditto, Harrap, 1985 (re-revised edition) . . . £15/£5

The Black Corridor, Ace (U.S.), 1969 (cut text, wraps)
. . . . £10
ditto, Mayflower, 1969 (full text, wraps) . . . £5
ditto, Ace [book club] (U.S.), 1970 (cut text) . £15/£5
The Distant Suns, Unicorn, 1975 (with pseud. 'Philip
James' [Cawthorn], wraps) £10
ditto, New English Library, 1989 (wraps, with new
introduction) £5

'Karl Glogauer' Titles
Behold the Man, Allison & Busby, 1969 (novel) . .
. . . . £25/£5
ditto, as *Behold the Man: The Thirtieth Anniversary
Edition*, Mojo Press (U.S.), 1996 (novella) . £20/£5
Breakfast in the Ruins: A Novel of Inhumanity, New
English Library, 1972 . . . . £25/£5

'The Eternal Champion' Titles
The Eternal Champion, Dell (U.S.), 1970 (wraps) £5
ditto, Harper & Row (U.S.), 1978 (revised edition).
. . . . £35/£5
Phoenix in Obsidian, Mayflower, 1970 (wraps) . £5
ditto, as *The Silver Warriors*, Dell (U.S.), 1973 (wraps)
. . . . £5
The Swords of Heaven, The Flowers of Hell,
HM/Simon & Schuster (U.S.), 1979 (graphic novel,
illustrated by Howard V. Chaykin, outsized wraps) .
. . . . £50
Das Ewige Schwert, Bastei Lübbe (Germany), 1986
(wraps) £10
ditto, as *The Dragon in the Sword*, Ace (U.S.), 1986
(cut text) . . . . £20/£5
ditto, as *The Dragon in the Sword*, Grafton, 1987 (full
text) . . . . £20/£5

'Corum' ('The Coming of Chaos') Titles
The Knight of Swords, Mayflower, 1971 (wraps) £5
ditto, Allison & Busby, 1977 . . . . . £15/£5
The Queen of the Swords, Berkley (U.S.), 1971
(wraps) £5
The King of the Swords, Berkley (U.S.), 1971 (wraps)
. . . . £5

'A Nomad of the Time Streams' Titles
The Warlord of the Air, Ace (U.S.), 1971 (wraps) £10
ditto, New English Library, 1971 (censored text) . .
. . . . £20/£5
The Land Leviathan, Quartet, 1974 . . . . £20/£5
ditto, Quartet, 1974 (wraps) £10
The Steel Tsar, Granada, 1981 (wraps) . . . £5

'The Dancers at the End of Time' Titles
An Alien Heat, MacGibbon & Kee, 1972 . £40/£10
The Hollow Lands, Harper & Row (U.S.), 1974 £15/£5
Legends from the End of Time, Harper & Row (U.S.),
1976 . . . . £15/£5
The End of All Songs, Harper & Row (U.S.), 1976 .
. . . . £25/£5
The Transformation of Miss Mavis Ming, W.H. Allen,
1977 . . . . £50/£10

ditto, as *A Messiah at the End of Time*, DAW (U.S.),
1978 (wraps) £5
'Corum' ('The Prince with the Silver Hand') Titles
The Bull and the Spear, Allison & Busby, 1973 . .
. . . . £35/£5
The Oak and the Ram, Allison & Busby, 1973. £35/£5
The Sword and the Stallion, Berkley (U.S.), 1974
(wraps) £5
ditto, Allison & Busby, 1974 . . . . . . £25/£5

'Hawkmoon' ('Count Brass') Titles
Count Brass, Mayflower, 1973 (wraps) £5
The Champion of Garathorm, Mayflower, 1973
(wraps) £5
The Quest for Tanelorn, Mayflower, 1975 (wraps) £5

'The Hawklords' Titles
The Time of the Hawklords, Aidan Ellis, 1976 (with
Michael Butterworth) . . . . . . £50/£10
ditto, Collector's Guide Publishing (Canada), 1995
(wraps, as Michael Butterworth only) . . . £10
Queens of Deliria, Star, 1977 (by Michael
Butterworth, wraps) £10
Ledge of Darkness, Collector's Guide Publishing
(Canada), 1994 (outsized wraps, by Bob Walker
[illustrator] with Michael Butterworth, in four-CD
box set [Griffin Music], *Hawkwind: 25 Years On*) .
. . . . £70 for complete box set

'Colonel Pyat' Titles
Byzantium Endures, Secker & Warburg, 1981 . £25/£5
The Laughter of Carthage, Secker & Warburg, 1984 .
. . . . £20/£5
Jerusalem Commands, Cape, 1992 (buff endpapers) .
. . . . £15/£10
ditto, Cape, 1992 (white endpapers) . . . £15/£5

'Von Bek' Titles
The War Hound and the World's Pain, Timescape
(U.S.), 1981 . . . . £30/£5
The City in the Autumn Stars, Grafton, 1986 . £20/£5

'The Second Ether' Titles
Blood: A Southern Fantasy, Millennium, 1995 £20/£5
ditto, Millennium, 1995 (wraps) £10
Fabulous Harbours, Millennium, 1995 . . £40/£10
ditto, Millennium, 1995 (wraps) £10
The War Amongst the Angels, Orion, 1996 . £30/£5
ditto, Orion, 1996 (wraps) £10

Other Novels
Caribbean Crisis, Fleetway, 1962 (wraps, pseud.
'Desmond Reid'). £50
The Sundered Worlds, Compact, 1965 (wraps). £15
ditto, as *The Blood Red Game*, Sphere, 1970 (wraps) .
. . . . £5
ditto, as *The Sundered Worlds*, Roc, 1992 (revised
edition, wraps) £5
Gloriana, or The Unfulfill'd Queen, Allison & Busby,
1978 . . . . £45/£10

ditto, as *La Saga di Gloriana*, Mondadori (Italy), 1991 (revised edition, cut text, wraps) £10
ditto, as *Gloriana; or, The Unfulfill'd Queen*, Phoenix House, 1993 (revised edition, full text, wraps) . £5
The Real Life Mr Newman, A.J. Callow, 1979 (500 copies, wraps) £10
The Golden Barge, Savoy, 1979 (wraps, illustrated by James Cawthorn). £15
ditto, New English Library, 1983 (no full-page illustrations) . . . . £20/£5
The Brothel in Rosenstrasse, New English Library, 1982 . . . . £20/£5
Mother London, Secker & Warburg, 1988 . . £15/£5
The Birds of the Moon: A Travellers' Tale, Jayde Design, 1995 (wraps) £5
The Adventure of the Dorset Street Lodger, Number Two Dorset Street, [1996] (no d/w) . . . £150
Michael Moorcock's Multiverse, DC Comics (U.S.), 1999 (graphic, with Walter Simonson, Mark Reeve & John Ridgway [illustrators], outsized wraps) . £15
King of the City, Scribner, 2000 . . . . . £20/£5
ditto, Scribner, 2000 (wraps) £10
Silverheart, Earthlight, 2000 (with Storm Constantine) . . . . £20/£5

Short Stories
The Deep Fix, Compact, 1966 (wraps, pseud. 'James Colvin') £15
The Time Dweller, Hart Davis, 1969 . . £70/£20
The Singing Citadel, Mayflower, 1970 (wraps) . £5
Moorcock's Book of Martyrs, Quartet, 1976 (wraps) £5
ditto, as *Dying for Tomorrow*, DAW (U.S.), 1978 (wraps) £5
Sojan, Savoy, 1977 (wraps, ISBN 0-7045-0241-0). £5
ditto, Savoy, 1977 (wraps, with variant ISBN 0-352-33000-7 on inside back cover) £5
My Experiences in the Third World War, Savoy, 1980 (wraps) £10
Elric at the End of Time, New English Library, 1984 . . . . £20/£5
The Opium General and Other Stories, Harrap, 1984 . . . . £15/£5
Casablanca, Gollancz, 1989 . . . . . £15/£5
Elric: Tales of the White Wolf (by Moorcock & others), White Wolf (U.S.), 1994 (edited by Edward E. Kramer & Richard Gilliam) . . . . . £15/£5
Lunching with the Antichrist, Mark V. Ziesing (U.S.), 1995 . . . . £25/£5
ditto, Mark V. Ziesing (U.S.), 1995 (300 signed copies, in slipcase) . . . . £65/£40
Pawn of Chaos: Tales of the Eternal Champion (by Moorcock & others), White Wolf (U.S.), 1996 (edited by Edward E. Kramer, wraps) £10
Tales from the Texas Woods, Mojo Press (U.S.), 1997 . . . . £15/£5
London Bone, Scribner, 2001 (wraps) . . . £10

'The Tale of the Eternal Champion' Omnibus Editions
Von Bek, Millennium, 1992 (with errata slip) £60/£15
ditto, Millennium, 1992 (wraps, with errata slip) £15
ditto, Millennium, 1995 . . . . £20/£5
ditto, White Wolf (U.S.), 1995 (differing content) . . . . £20/£5
The Eternal Champion, Millennium, 1992 . . £30/£5
ditto, Millennium, 1992 (wraps) £15
ditto, White Wolf (U.S.), 1994 (differing content) . . . . £20/£5
Hawkmoon, Millennium, 1992 (revised texts) . £20/£5
ditto, Millennium, 1992 (revised texts, wraps) . £10
Corum, Millennium, 1992 . . . . £20/£5
ditto, Millennium, 1992 (wraps) £10
ditto, as *Corum: The Coming of Chaos*, Millennium, 1996 (wraps) £5
ditto, as *Corum: The Coming of Chaos*, White Wolf (U.S.), 1997 . . . . £15/£5
Sailing to Utopia, Millennium, 1993 . . £30/£5
ditto, Millennium, 1993 (wraps) £15
A Nomad of the Time Streams, Millennium, 1993 (revised edition) . . . . £30/£5
ditto, Millennium, 1993 (revised edition, wraps) £15
The Dancers at the End of Time, Millennium, 1993 (revised edition) . . . . £25/£5
ditto, Millennium, 1993 (revised edition, wraps) £10
Elric of Melniboné, Millennium, 1993 (revised) . . . . £30/£5
ditto, Millennium, 1993 (revised, wraps) . . £15
ditto, as *Elric: Song of the Black Sword*, White Wolf (U.S.), 1995 . . . . £20/£5
The New Nature of the Catastrophe (by Moorcock & others), Millennium, 1993 (edited with Langdon Jones) . . . . £25/£5
ditto, Millennium, 1993 (wraps) £10
ditto, Orion, 1997 (differing content, wraps) . . £5
The Prince with the Silver Hand, Millennium, 1993 . . . . £15/£5
ditto, Millennium, 1993 (wraps) £10
ditto, as *Corum: The Prince with the Silver Hand*, White Wolf (U.S.), 1999 . . . . . £15/£5
Legends from the End of Time, Millennium, 1993 (revised edition, cut text) . . . . . £15/£5
ditto, Millennium, 1993 (revised edition, cut text, wraps). £10
ditto, Orion, 1997 (full text, wraps) £5
ditto, White Wolf (U.S.), 1999 (full text) . £15/£5
Stormbringer, Millennium, 1993 (revised) . £25/£5
ditto, Millennium, 1993 (revised, wraps) . . £10
ditto, as *Elric: The Stealer of Souls*, White Wolf (U.S.), 1998 (re-revised) . . . . . £20/£5
Earl Aubec and Other Stories, Millennium, 1993 . . . . £25/£5
ditto, Millennium, 1993 (wraps) £10
ditto, White Wolf (U.S.), 1999 (differing content) . . . . £15/£5
Count Brass, Millennium, 1993 . . . . . £20/£5
ditto, Millennium, 1993 (wraps) £10

The Roads Between the Worlds, White Wolf (U.S.),
1996 (revised) . . . . £15/£5
Kane of Old Mars, White Wolf (U.S.), 1998 . £15/£5

Other Omnibus Editions
The Swords Trilogy, Berkley (U.S.), 1977 (wraps). £5
ditto, Gregg Press (U.S.), 1980 (with introduction by
Richard Gid Powers, no d/w) £30
ditto, as *The Swords of Corum*, Grafton, 1986 . £15/£5
ditto, as *Corum: The Prince in the Scarlet Robe*,
Gollancz, 2002 (wraps) £5
The Cornelius Chronicles, Avon (U.S.), 1977 (wraps)
. . . . £10
ditto, as *The Cornelius Quartet*, Phoenix House, 1993
(revised texts) . . . . £20/£5
ditto, as *The Cornelius Quartet*, Phoenix House, 1993
(revised texts, wraps) £15
The Chronicles of Corum, Berkley (U.S.), 1978
(wraps) £5
ditto, Grafton, 1986 . . . . £15/£5
The History of the Runestaff, Granada, 1979 . £30/£5
*The Black Corridor/The Adventures of Una Persson
and Catherine Cornelius*, Dial Press (U.S.), [1980]
(wraps) £10
Warrior of Mars, New English Library, 1981 . £30/£5
The Dancers at the End of Time, Granada, 1981 . .
. . . . £30/£5
The Nomad of Time, Nelson Doubleday [book club]
(U.S.), [1982]. . . . . £15/£5
The Elric Saga Part One, Nelson Doubleday [book
club] (U.S.), [1984] . . . . £15/£5
The Elric Saga Part Two, Nelson Doubleday [book
club] (U.S.), 1984 . . . . £15/£5
The Chronicles of Castle Brass, Granada, 1985 £15/£5
The Cornelius Chronicles Vol. II, Avon (U.S.), 1986
(wraps) £5
The Cornelius Chronicles Vol. III, Avon (U.S.), 1987
(wraps) £5
The Cornelius Chronicles Book One, Fontana, 1988
(revised texts, cut, wraps) £5
The Cornelius Chronicles Book Two, Fontana, 1988
(revised texts, cut, wraps) £5
Tales from the End of Time, Guild America [book
club] (U.S.), [1989] . . . . £15/£5
A Cornelius Calendar, Phoenix House, 1993 . £20/£5
ditto, Phoenix House, 1993 (wraps) £15
Behold the Man and Other Stories, Phoenix House,
1994 . . . . £20/£5
ditto, Phoenix House, 1994 (wraps) . . . £10
Elric, Gollancz, 2001 (wraps) £5
The Elric Saga Part Three, Science Fiction Book Club
(U.S.), 2002 . . . . £15/£5

Boxed Sets
The History of the Runestaff, Mayflower, [1973]
(wraps, in slipcase) £10
Mighty Moorcock, Quartet, [1974] (wraps, in slipcase)
. . . . £10
Multi-Dimensional Moorcock, Quartet, [1975] (wraps,
in slipcase) £10

The Chronicles of Count Brass, Mayflower/Granada,
[1977] (wraps, in slipcase) £10
ditto, as *The Chronicles of Castle Brass*, Granada,
[1978] (wraps, in slipcase) £10
The Dancers at the End of Time, Mayflower, [1978]
(wraps, in slipcase) £10
The Jerry Cornelius Quartet, Fontana, [1979] (wraps,
in slipcase) £25
The Books of Corum, Granada, [1980] (wraps, in
slipcase) £10

Non Fiction
Epic Pooh, British Fantasy Society, 1978 (500 copies,
wraps). £10
The Retreat from Liberty, Zomba, 1983 (wraps) £20
Letters from Hollywood, Harrap, 1986 . . . £20/£5
*Wizardry and Wild Romance: A Study of Epic
Fantasy*, Gollancz, 1987 . . . . . £20/£5
ditto, Gollancz, 1987 (wraps). £10
Fantasy: The 100 Best Books, Xanadu, 1988 (with
James Cawthorn, plain green boards, white d/w) . .
. . . . £15/£5
ditto, Xanadu, 1988 (50 signed copies, decorated green
boards, clear d/w) . . . . £70/£20
Death Is No Obstacle, Savoy, 1992 (with Colin
Greenland) . . . . £30/£5

BRIAN MOORE
(b.1921)

An Irish author of novels which deal powerfully with
the torments of guilt and sexual obsession in relation
to Catholicism.

Novels
Wreath for a Redhead, Harlequin (Canada), 1951
(pseud. 'Michael Bryan', wraps) £300
ditto, as *Sailor's Leave*, Pyramid Books (U.S.), 1953
(wraps) £75
The Executioners, Harlequin (Canada), 1951 (pseud.
'Michael Bryan', wraps). £100
French For Murder, Fawcett (U.S.), 1954 (pseud.
'Bernard Mara', wraps) £65
ditto, L. Miller & Sons, 1954 (pseud. 'Bernard Mara',
wraps). £65
A Bullet for My Lady, Fawcett (U.S.), 1955 (pseud.
'Bernard Mara', wraps) £65
ditto, Muller, 1956 (pseud. 'Bernard Mara', wraps) £65
Judith Hearne, Deutsch, 1955 . . . . £500/£75
ditto, as *The Lonely Passion of Judith Hearne*, Little,
Brown (U.S.), 1956 . . . . . . £175/£35
ditto, McClelland & Stewart (Canada), 1964 (wraps) .
. . . . £35
This Gun for Gloria, Dell (U.S.), 1956 (pseud.
'Bernard Mara', wraps) £45
ditto, Muller, 1956 (pseud. 'Bernard Mara', wraps) £35
Intent to Kill, Dell (U.S.), 1956 (pseud. 'Michael
Bryan', wraps) £45

ditto, Eyre & Spottiswoode, 1956 (pseud. 'Michael Bryan') . . . . £150/£45
The Feast of Lupercal, Little, Brown (U.S.), 1957. . . . . £150/£25
ditto, Deutsch, 1958 . . . . . . £150/£25
ditto, as *A Moment of Love*, Longacre, 1960 £25/£10
Murder in Majorca, Dell (U.S.), 1957 (pseud. 'Michael Bryan', wraps). £45
ditto, Eyre & Spottiswoode, 1958 (pseud. 'Michael Bryan') . . . . £75/£20
The Luck of Ginger Coffey, Little, Brown (U.S.), 1960 . . . . £100/£25
ditto, McClelland & Stewart (Canada), 1960 £100/£10
ditto, Deutsch, 1960 . . . . . . £100/£15
An Answer from Limbo, Little, Brown (U.S.), 1962 . . . . £65/£20
ditto, McClelland & Stewart (Canada), 1962 £65/£10
ditto, Deutsch, 1963 . . . . . . £50/£15
The Emperor of Ice-Cream, Viking Press (U.S.), 1965 . . . . £35/£10
ditto, McClelland & Stewart (Canada), 1965 £35/£10
ditto, Deutsch, 1966 . . . . . . £30/£10
I Am Mary Dunne, McClelland & Stewart (Canada), 1968 . . . . £30/£10
ditto, Viking Press (U.S.), 1968 . . . . £30/£10
ditto, Cape, 1968 . . . . £30/£10
Fergus, Holt Rinehart (U.S.), 1970 . . . . £25/£5
ditto, McClelland & Stewart (Canada), 1970 . £25/£5
ditto, Cape, 1971 . . . . £25/£5
The Revolution Script, McClelland & Stewart (Canada), 1971 . . . . £25/£5
ditto, Holt Rinehart (U.S.), 1971 . . . . £20/£5
ditto, Cape, 1971 . . . . £20/£5
Catholics, McClelland & Stewart (Canada), 1972 . . . . £20/£5
ditto, Cape, 1972 . . . . £20/£5
ditto, Holt Rinehart (U.S.), 1973 . . . . £15/£5
The Great Victorian Collection, Farrar Straus (U.S.), 1975 . . . . £20/£5
ditto, McClelland & Stewart (Canada), 1975 . £20/£5
ditto, Cape, 1975 . . . . £20/£5
The Doctor's Wife, Farrar Straus (U.S.), 1976 . £20/£5
ditto, McClelland & Stewart (Canada), 1976 . £20/£5
ditto, Cape, 1976 . . . . £20/£5
The Mangan Inheritance, Farrar Straus (U.S.), 1979 . . . . £20/£5
ditto, McClelland & Stewart (Canada), 1979 . £20/£5
ditto, Cape, 1979 . . . . £20/£5
The Temptation of Eileen Hughes, Farrar Straus (U.S.), 1981 . . . . £20/£5
ditto, McClelland & Stewart (Canada), 1981 . £20/£5
ditto, Cape, 1981 . . . . £20/£5
Cold Heaven, Holt Rinehart (U.S.), 1983. . . £20/£5
ditto, McClelland & Stewart (Canada), 1983 . £20/£5
ditto, Cape, 1983 . . . . £20/£5
Black Robe, Dutton (U.S.), 1985. . . . . £25/£5
ditto, McClelland & Stewart (Canada), 1985 . £25/£5
ditto, Cape, 1985 . . . . £25/£5

ditto, Cape, 1985 (50 numbered, signed copies, bound by Kenny's of Galway, slipcase) . . . £100/£75
The Color of Blood, Dutton (U.S.), 1987 . . £10/£5
ditto, McClelland & Stewart (Canada), 1987 . £10/£5
ditto, as **The Colour of Blood**, Cape, 1987 . . £15/£5
Lies of Silence, Bloomsbury, 1990 . . . . £15/£5
ditto, London Limited Editions, 1990 (250 numbered, signed copies, acetate d/w) . . . . . £65/£55
ditto, McClelland & Stewart (Canada), 1990 . £15/£5
ditto, Doubleday (U.S.), 1990 . . . . . £10/£5
No Other Life, Bloomsbury, 1993 . . . . £10/£5
ditto, Knopf (Canada), 1993 . . . . . . £15/£5
ditto, Doubleday (U.S.), 1993 . . . . . £10/£5
The Statement, Knopf (Canada), 1995 . . . £15/£5
ditto, Bloomsbury, 1995 . . . . £10/£5
ditto, Dutton (U.S.), 1996. . . . . . . £10/£5
The Magician's Wife, Knopf (Canada), 1997 . £10/£5
ditto, Bloomsbury, 1997 . . . . £10/£5
ditto, Dutton (U.S.), 1998. . . . . . . £10/£5

Short Stories
Two Stories, California State Univ. (U.S.), 1978 (300 signed, numbered copies) £65
ditto, California State Univ. (U.S.), 1978 (26 lettered copies) £100

Others
Canada, Time Life International (U.S.), 1965 (no d/w) £15

WILLIAM MORRIS
(b.1834 d.1896)

Poet, artist and socialist, Morris excelled in many of the fields in which he attempted to combat ugliness, no more so than in book production through his private press, the Kelmscott Press.

The Defence of Guenevere and Other Poems, Bell & Daldy, 1858 . . . . £500
ditto, Bell & Daldy, 1875. . . . . . . £100
ditto, Bell & Daldy, 1875 (25 large paper copies) £350
ditto, Kelmscott Press, 1892 (300 copies) . . £1,500
ditto, Kelmscott Press, 1892 (10 copies on vellum). £7,000
The Life and Death of Jason, Bell & Daldy, 1867. . . . . £250
ditto, Bell & Daldy, 1867 (25 large paper copies) £750
ditto, Roberts Bros (U.S.), 1867 . . . . . £100
ditto, Kelmscott Press, 1895 (200 copies) . . £5,000
The Earthly Paradise, F.S. Ellis, 1868-70 (4 parts - 1 & 2 together - 3 vols) £1,250
ditto, F.S. Ellis, 1868-70 (25 large paper copies) £2,000
ditto, Roberts Bros (U.S.), 1868 . . . . . £100
ditto, Roberts Bros (U.S.), 1871 (4 parts in 3 vols) £200
ditto, Kelmscott Press, 1896-97 (225 copies, 8 vols) £3,000

ditto, Kelmscott Press, 1896-97 (6 copies on vellum, 8 vols) £10,000

The Story of Grettir the Strong, F.S. Ellis, 1869 (translated by Morris & Magnusson) . . . £250

ditto, F.S. Ellis, 1869 (25 large paper copies) . £750

The Story of Volsangs and Niblungs, F.S. Ellis, 1870 (translated by Morris & Magnusson) . . . £250

ditto, F.S. Ellis, 1870 (25 large paper copies) . £750

Love is Enough, Ellis & White, 1873 [1872] . £100

ditto, Kelmscott Press, 1897 [1898] (300 copies) £3,000

Three Northern Love Stories and Other Tales, Ellis & White, 1873 (translated by Morris & Magnusson) £200

ditto, F.S. Ellis, 1873 (large paper copies) . £600

ditto, Roberts Bros (U.S.), 1873 . . . . £100

The Aenids of Virgil, Done into English Verse, Ellis & White, 1876 (translation, 2 vols) . . . £250

ditto, Ellis & White, 1876 (25 large paper copies, 2 vols) £650

The Story of Sigurd the Volsung, and the Fall of the Niblungs, Ellis & White, 1877 [1876] . . £250

ditto, Ellis & White, 1877 [1876] (25 large paper copies) £650

ditto, Roberts Bros (U.S.), 1877 . . . . £100

ditto, Kelmscott Press, 1898 (160 copies) . £2,500

Hopes and Fears for Art, Ellis & White, 1882 . £75

ditto, Ellis & White, 1882 (large paper copies) . £250

ditto, Roberts Bros (U.S.), 1882 . . . . £100

Chants for Socialists, Socialist League, 1885 (wraps) £100

Pilgrims of Hope, privately printed by H. Buxton Forman, 1886. . . . . £250

The Odyssey of Homer, Done into English Verse, Reeves & Turner, 1887 (translation, 2 vols) . £150

The Aims of Art, The Commonweal, 1887 (wraps) £75

The Tables Turned, The Commonweal, 1887 (wraps). £75

Signs of Change, Reeves & Turner, 1888 . . £125

True and False Society, Socialist League, 1888 (wraps) £95

A Dream of John Ball, and A King's Lesson, Reeves & Turner, 1888 . . . . £200

ditto, Reeves & Turner, 1888 (large paper copies) £650

ditto, Kelmscott Press, 1892 (300 copies) . £2,000

ditto, Kelmscott Press, 1892 (11 copies on vellum). £8,000

ditto, Roycroft Shop (U.S.), 1898 . . . £100

ditto, Roycroft Shop (U.S.), 1898 (100 copies on Whatman paper) £200

A Tale of the House of the Wolfings and All the Kindreds of the Mark, Reeves & Turner, 1889 £125

ditto, Reeves & Turner, 1888 (100 large paper copies). £400

ditto, Roberts Bros (U.S.), 1890 . . . . £125

The Roots of the Mountains, Reeves & Turner, 1889 [1890]. £125

ditto, Reeves & Turner, 1889 [1890] (250 copies on Whatman Paper) £1,500

News From Nowhere, Roberts Bros (U.S.), 1890 £100

ditto, Reeves & Turner, 1891. . . . . £100

ditto, Reeves & Turner, 1891 (wraps) . . . £125

ditto, Reeves & Turner, 1888 (250 large paper copies). £300

ditto, Kelmscott Press, 1892 (300 copies) . £1,500

ditto, Kelmscott Press, 1892 (10 copies on vellum). £7,500

The Story of Gunnlaug the Worm Tounge, Chiswick Press, 1891 (75 copies, translated by Morris & Magnusson) £750

The Story of the Glittering Plain, Reeves & Turner/ Kelmscott Press, 1891 (200 copies, slipcase) . £2,500

ditto, Kelmscott Press, 1891 (6 copies on vellum) £6,000

ditto, Kelmscott Press, 1894 (250 copies, illustrated by Walter Crane) £3,000

ditto, Kelmscott Press, 1894 (7 copies on vellum) £10,000

ditto, Reeves & Turner, 1891. . . . . £100

ditto, Roberts Bros (U.S.), 1891 . . . . £100

Poems by the Way, Reeves & Turner, 1891. . £100

ditto, Reeves & Turner, 1891 (100 large paper copies). £300

ditto, Kelmscott Press, 1891 (300 copies) . £1,500

ditto, Kelmscott Press, 1891 (13 copies on vellum). £5,000

The Order of Chivalry & L'Ordene de Chevalerie, Kelmscott Press, 1892 [1893] (225 copies, the latter translated by Morris). £2,000

Gothic Architecture, Kelmscott Press, 1893 (1,500 copies) £350

A Tale of King Florus and the Fair Jehane, Kelmscott Press, 1893 (350 copies, translated by Morris) £1,000

Socialism: It's Growth and Outcome, Swan Sonnenschein, 1893 (350 copies, translated by Morris) £450

Of the Friendship of Amis and Amilie, Kelmscott Press, 1894 (500 copies, translated by Morris) £600

The Tale of the Emperor Coustans and of Oversea, Kelmscott Press, 1894 (with E. Belfort Bax, 525 copies) £1,000

The Wood Beyond the World, Kelmscott Press, 1894 (350 copies) £2,000

ditto, Kelmscott Press, 1894 (8 copies on vellum) £7,500

ditto, Lawrence and Bullen, 1895 . . . . £75

ditto, Roberts Bros (U.S.), 1895 . . . . £75

A Tale of Beowulf, Kelmscott Press, 1895 (300 copies, translated by Morris). £2,500

Child Christopher and Goldilind the Fair, Kelmscott Press, 1895 (600 copies, 2 vols) . . . £850

ditto, Kelmscott Press, 1895 (12 copies on vellum). £2,500

Old French Romances, George Allen, 1896 (translation) £65

The Well at the World's End, Kelmscott Press, 1896 (350 copies) £3,000

ditto, Longman's Green, 1896 (2 vols) . . £200

ditto, Longman's Green (U.S.), 1896 (2 vols) . £200

The Water of the Wondrous Isles, Kelmscott Press,
1897 (250 copies) £2,500
ditto, Kelmscott Press, 1897 (6 copies on vellum) . .
. . . .£6,500
ditto, Longman's Green, 1897 . . . . £100
ditto, Longman's Green (U.S.), 1897 . . . £100
The Sundering Flood, Kelmscott Press, 1897 (300
copies) £1,500
ditto, Kelmscott Press, 1897 (10 copies on vellum). .
. . . .£5,000
*A Note By William Morris on His Aims in Founding
the Kelmscott Press*, Kelmscott Press, 1896 (525
copies) £600

TONI MORRISON
(b.1931)

In 1993 Toni Morrison became the first African-
American to win the Nobel Prize for Literature. Many
of her books have achieved bestseller status in the
U.S. after having been promoted by Oprah Winfrey
on her television Book Club.

Novels
The Bluest Eye, Holt Rinehart & Winston (U.S.), 1970
. . . . £2,750/£400
ditto, Chatto & Windus, 1979 . . . . £150/£25
Sula, Knopf (U.S.), 1974 . . . . . . £500/£75
ditto, Allen Lane, 1974 . . . . . . £145/£25
Song of Solomon, Knopf (U.S.), 1977 . . £60/£15
ditto, Chatto & Windus, 1978 . . . . £35/£10
Tar Baby, Franklin Library (U.S.), 1981 (signed,
limited edition) £45
ditto, Knopf (U.S.), 1981 . . . . . . £25/£10
ditto, Chatto & Windus, 1981 . . . . £25/£10
A Brief Vignette from Tar Baby, Toothpaste Press
(U.S.), 1982 (broadside, 90 signed copies) . £200
Beloved, Knopf (U.S.), 1987 . . . . . £25/£10
ditto, Chatto & Windus, 1987 . . . . £25/£10
Jazz, Franklin Library (U.S.), 1992 . . . . £35
ditto, Knopf (U.S.), 1992 . . . . . . £20/£5
ditto, Chatto & Windus, 1992 . . . . £15/£5
Paradise, Chatto & Windus, 1998 . . . £10/£5
ditto, Chatto & Windus, 1998 . . . . £10/£5

Children's Titles
The Big Box, Hyperion, 1999 . . . . £10/£5
The Book of Mean People, Hyperion, 2002 . £10/£5

Others
Playing in the Dark, Harvard Univ. Press (U.S.), 1992
. . . .£15/£5
ditto, Pan Books, 1993 (wraps) £5
The Nobel Lecture in Literature & Acceptance, Knopf
(U.S.), 1994 (no d/w) £10
ditto, Chatto & Windus, 1994 . . . . £10
The Dancing Mind, Knopf (U.S.), 1996 . . £10/£5

JOHN MORTIMER
(b.1923)

A playwright and barrister, Mortimer was called to
the Bar in 1948 and became a QC in 1966. Rumpole,
his fictional, incorrigible barrister, has been successfully and popularly televised.

Novels
Charade, Bodley Head, 1947. . . . . £75/£15
ditto, Viking (U.S.), 1986. . . . . . .£10/£5
Rumming Park, Lane, 1948 . . . . . £75/£15
Answer Yes or No, Lane, 1950 . . . . £65/£10
ditto, as *The Silver Hook*, Morrow (U.S.), 1950 £30/£5
Like Men Betrayed, Collins, 1953 . . . .£30/£5
ditto, Lippincott (U.S.), 1954. . . . . .£30/£5
The Narrowing Stream, Collins, 1954 . . .£25/£5
ditto, Viking (U.S.), 1989. . . . . . .£10/£5
Three Winters, Collins, 1956. . . . . .£25/£5
Will Shakespeare: The Untold Story, Hodder, 1977 .
. . . .£20/£5
ditto, Delacourt (U.S.), 1978 . . . . . £15/£5
Paradise Postponed, Viking, 1985 . . . .£15/£5
ditto, Viking (U.S.), 1985. . . . . . .£15/£5
Summer's Lease, Viking, 1988 . . . . £25/£5
ditto, Viking (U.S.), 1988. . . . . . .£20/£5
ditto, Franklin Library (U.S.), 1988 (signed limited
edition) £25
ditto, London Limited Editions, 1988 (250 signed
copies) £35
Titmuss Regained, Viking, 1990. . . . .£15/£5
ditto, Viking (U.S.), 1990. . . . . . .£10/£5
Dunster, Viking, 1992 . . . .£10/£5
ditto, Viking (U.S.), 1993. . . . . . .£10/£5
Felix in the Underworld, Viking, 1997 . . .£10/£5
ditto, Viking (U.S.), 1997. . . . . . .£10/£5
The Sound of Trumpets, Viking, 1998 . . .£10/£5
ditto, Viking (U.S.), 1999. . . . . . .£10/£5

Short Stories
Rumpole of the Bailey, Penguin, 1978 (wraps) . £20
ditto, Penguin (U.S.), 1980 (wraps) £10
ditto, Armchair Detective Library (U.S.), 1991 (100
signed copies, slipcase) £45
The Trials of Rumpole, Penguin, 1979 (wraps) £10
ditto, Penguin (U.S.), 1981 (wraps) . . . £10
Rumpole's Return, Penguin, 1981 (wraps) . . £10
ditto, Penguin (U.S.), 1982 (wraps) . . . £10
Rumpole for the Defence, Penguin, 1982 (wraps) . £5
Rumpole and the Golden Thread, Penguin (U.S.),
1983 (wraps) £10
Rumpole's Last Case, Penguin, 1987 (wraps) . £10
ditto, Penguin (U.S.), 1988 (wraps) . . . £10
Rumpole and the Age of Miracles, Penguin, 1988
(wraps) £10
ditto, Penguin (U.S.), 1989 (wraps) . . . £10
Rumpole à la Carte, Viking, 1990 . . . £20/£5
ditto, Viking (U.S.), 1990. . . . . . .£15/£5
Rumpole on Trial, Viking, 1992. . . . .£15/£5

ditto, Penguin (U.S.), 1992 . . . . . . £15/£5
Rumpole and the Angel of Death, Viking, 1995 . .
. . . . £10/£5
ditto, Penguin (U.S.), 1996 . . . . . . £10/£5
Rumpole Rests His Case, Viking, 2001 . . . £10/£5
ditto, Viking (U.S.), 2001 . . . . £10/£5

Plays
Three Plays, Elek, 1958 . . . . . . £30/£10
ditto, Grove Press (U.S.), 1962 . . . . . £20/£5
The Wrong Side of the Park, Heinemann, 1960 £20/£5
Lunch Hour, French, 1960 (wraps) £10
Lunch Hour and Other Plays, Methuen, 1960 . £20/£5
Two Stars For Comfort, Methuen, 1962 . £15/£5
A Flea in Her Ear, French, 1967 (wraps) . . . £5
ditto, French (U.S.), 1967 (wraps) £5
The Judge, Methuen, 1967 . . . . . . £10/£5
Five Plays, Methuen, 1970 . . . . . . £10/£5
Come As You Are: Four Short Plays, Methuen, 1971 .
. . . . £10/£5
A Voyage Round My Father, Methuen, 1971 . £20/£5
Knightsbridge, French, 1973 (wraps) £5
Collaborations, Methuen, 1973 . . . . . £10/£5
The Fear of Heaven, French, 1978 (wraps). . . £5
Heaven and Hell, French, 1978 (wraps) . . . £5
Edwin and Other Plays, Penguin, 1984 (wraps) . £5
Three Boulevard Farces, Penguin, 1985 (wraps) . £5

Collected Editions
Rumpole, Allen Lane, 1980 . . . . . . £10/£5
Regina v. Rumpole, Allen Lane, 1981 . . £10/£5
The First Rumpole Omnibus, Penguin, 1983 . £10/£5
The Second Rumpole Omnibus, Viking, 1987 . £10/£5
ditto, Penguin (U.S.), 1988 . . . . . £10/£5
The Rapstone Chronicles, Viking, 1991 . £10/£5
The Best of Rumpole, Viking, 1993 . . . £10/£5

Autobiography
Clinging to the Wreckage, Weidenfeld & Nicolson,
1982 . . . . £15/£5
ditto, Ticknor & Fields (U.S.), 1982 . . . £15/£5
Murderers and Other Friends, Viking, 1994 . £10/£5
ditto, Viking (U.S.), 1994 . . . . . . £10/£5

Others
With Love and Lizards, Joseph, 1957 (written with
Penelope Mortimer) . . . . £30/£10
No Moaning at the Bar, Bles, 1957 (pseud. 'Geoffrey
Lincoln') . . . . £35/£10
In Character, Allen Lane, 1983 . . . . £15/£5
Character Parts, Viking, 1986 . . . . £15/£5

IRIS MURDOCH
(b.1919 d.1999)

A novelist and philosopher, Murdoch employed a blend of realism and symbolism in her highly regarded novels.

Novels
Under the Net, Chatto & Windus, 1954 . £1,000/£150
ditto, Viking (U.S.), 1954 . . . . . . £125/£25
The Flight from the Enchanter, Chatto & Windus,
1956 . . . . £500/£75
ditto, Viking (U.S.), 1956 . . . . . . £125/£20
The Sandcastle, Chatto & Windus, 1957 . £200/£65
ditto, Viking (U.S.), 1957 . . . . . . £50/£15
The Bell, Chatto & Windus, 1958 . . . £75/£25
ditto, Viking (U.S.), 1958 . . . . . . £20/£5
A Severed Head, Chatto & Windus, 1961 . £65/£20
ditto, Viking (U.S.), 1961 . . . . . . £20/£5
An Unofficial Rose, Chatto & Windus, 1962 £35/£10
ditto, Viking (U.S.), 1962 . . . . . . £20/£5
The Unicorn, Chatto & Windus, 1963 . £25/£10
ditto, Viking (U.S.), 1963 . . . . . . £15/£5
The Italian Girl, Chatto & Windus, 1964 . £25/£10
ditto, Viking (U.S.), 1964 . . . . . . £15/£5
The Red and the Green, Chatto & Windus, 1965 . .
. . . . £20/£5
ditto, Viking (U.S.), 1965 . . . . . . £15/£5
The Time of the Angels, Chatto & Windus, 1966 . .
. . . . £20/£5
ditto, Viking (U.S.), 1966 . . . . . . £15/£5
The Nice and the Good, Chatto & Windus, 1968 . .
. . . . £20/£5
ditto, Viking (U.S.), 1968 . . . . . . £15/£5
Bruno's Dream, Chatto & Windus, 1969 . £20/£5
ditto, Viking (U.S.), 1969 . . . . . . £15/£5
A Fairly Honourable Defeat, Chatto & Windus, 1970.
. . . . £20/£5
ditto, Viking (U.S.), 1970 . . . . . . £15/£5
An Accidental Man, Chatto & Windus, 1971 . £20/£5
ditto, Viking (U.S.), 1972 . . . . . . £15/£5
The Black Prince, Chatto & Windus, 1973 . £20/£5
ditto, Viking (U.S.), 1973 . . . . . . £15/£5
The Sacred and Profane Love Machine, Chatto &
Windus, 1974 . . . . £20/£5
ditto, Viking (U.S.), 1974 . . . . . . £15/£5
A Word Child, Chatto & Windus, 1975 . . £20/£5
ditto, Viking (U.S.), 1975 . . . . . . £15/£5
Henry and Cato, Chatto & Windus, 1976 . £20/£5
ditto, Viking (U.S.), 1976 . . . . . . £15/£5
The Sea, the Sea, Chatto & Windus, 1978 . £20/£5
ditto, Viking (U.S.), 1978 . . . . . . £15/£5
Nuns and Soldiers, Chatto & Windus, 1980 . £15/£5
ditto, Viking (U.S.), 1981 . . . . . . £10/£5
The Philosopher's Pupil, Chatto & Windus, 1983 . .
. . . . £15/£5
ditto, Viking (U.S.), 1983 . . . . . . £10/£5
The Good Apprentice, Chatto & Windus, 1985. £15/£5

ditto, London Limited Editions, 1985 (250 signed copies, glassine d/w). . . . . . . £75/£65
ditto, Viking (U.S.), 1985. . . . . . . £10/£5
The Book and the Brotherhood, Chatto & Windus, 1987 . . . . £10/£5
ditto, Viking (U.S.), 1988. . . . . . . £10/£5
ditto, Franklin Library (U.S.), 1988 (signed limited edition) £50
The Message to the Planet, Chatto & Windus, 1989 . . . . £10/£5
ditto, London Limited Editions, 1989 (150 signed copies, d/w). . . . . . . £75/£65
ditto, Viking (U.S.), 1990. . . . . . . £10/£5
Green Knight, Chatto & Windus, 1993 . . £10/£5
ditto, Viking (U.S.), 1994. . . . . . . £10/£5
Jackson's Dilemma, Chatto & Windus, 1995 . £10/£5
ditto, Viking (U.S.), 1995. . . . . . . £10/£5

Plays

A Severed Head, Chatto & Windus, 1964 (with J. Priestley) . . . . £50/£20
The Italian Girl, French, 1969 (with James Saunders) £40
The Three Arrows and The Servants and the Snow: Two Plays, Chatto & Windus, 1973 . £65/£10
ditto, Viking (U.S.), 1974. . . . . . . £25/£5
Three Plays, Chatto & Windus, 1989 (*The Black Prince*, *The Three Arrows* and *The Servants & The Snow*) . . . . £35/£10
Joanna Joanna, A Play in Two Acts, Colophon Press, 1994 (12 signed copies of 143, leather, slipcase) £200
ditto, Colophon Press, 1994 (125 numbered, signed copies of 143) £100
ditto, Colophon Press, 1994 (6 lettered, signed copies of 143) £350
One Alone, Colophon Press, 1995 (26 lettered, signed copies) £200
ditto, Colophon Press, 1995 (6 roman numeraled, signed copies, wraps) £350
ditto, Colophon Press, 1995 (200 numbered, signed copies, wraps) £65

Poetry

A Year of Birds, Compton Press, 1978 (350 signed, numbered copies, no d/w) £2,000
ditto, Compton Press, 1978 (50 signed, numbered copies, no d/w, with extra set of proof engravings, box) £400
ditto, Chatto & Windus, 1984 . . . . £35/£10
Something Special, Four Poems and a Story, Eurographica (Helsinki), 1990 (350 signed, numbered copies, wraps in d/w) . . . . . £100/£75
ditto, Chatto & Windus, 1999 . . . . £15/£5

Others

Sartre: Romantic Rationalist, Bowes & Bowes, 1953 . . . . £150/£30
ditto, Yale Univ. Press (U.S.), 1953 . . . £75/£20

The Sovereignty of Good, C.U.P., 1967 (wraps) £65
ditto, Routledge, 1971 (containing extra essays) . . . . £65/£25
ditto, Schocken Books (U.S.), 1971 . . . . £15/£5
The Fire and the Sun: Why Plato Banished the Artists, O.U.P., 1977. . . . . . . £30/£10
The Servants, O.U.P., 1980 (125 copies, libretto) £750
Reynolds Stone, Warren Editions, 1981 (300 signed copies of 750, wraps) £100
ditto, Warren Editions, 1981 (unsigned copies of 750, wraps). £30
Acastos: Two Platonic Dialogues, Chatto & Windus, 1986 . . . . £15/£5
ditto, Viking (U.S.), 1987. . . . . . . £15/£5
The Existential Political Myth, Delos Press, 1989 (45 signed copies of 270, wraps, slipcase) . . . £75
ditto, Delos Press, 1989 (225 numbered copies of 270, wraps, slipcase). £45
Metaphysics as a Guide to Morals, Chatto & Windus, 1992 . . . . £20/£5
ditto, Allen Lane (U.S.), 1993 . . . . £10/£5
Existentialists and Mystics, Delos Press, 1993 (100 signed copies of 500, wraps, slipcase) . . . £50
ditto, Delos Press, 1993 (400 numbered copies of 500, wraps). £35
Existentialists and Mystics: Writings on Philosophy and Literature, Chatto & Windus, 1997. . . £10/£5
ditto, Allen Lane (U.S.), 1998 . . . . £10/£5

VLADIMIR NABOKOV
(b.1899 d.1977)

A naturalised American novelist, short story writer and poet, Nabokov's first published works were written in his native Russian and were critically acclaimed. During the second half of his career, he achieved a somewhat notorious success with *Lolita*.

Novels
Camera Obscura, Long, 1936 (pseud. 'Vladimir Nabokoff-Sirin', translated by Winifred Roy). . . . . £12,000/£2,000
ditto, as *Laughter in the Dark*, Bobbs Merrill (U.S.), 1938 (pseud. 'Vladimir Nabokoff', revised edition) . . . . £1,000/£250
ditto, as *Laughter in the Dark*, Weidenfeld & Nicolson, 1961 . . . . £100/£25
Despair, Long, 1937 (pseud. 'Vladimir Nabokoff-Sirin') . . . . £12,000/£2,000
ditto, Putnam (U.S.), 1966 (revised edition). £100/£35
ditto, Weidenfeld & Nicolson, 1966 (revised edition) . . . . £100/£35
The Real Life of Sebastian Knight, New Directions (U.S.), 1941 (woven red burlap, no d/w) . £350
ditto, New Directions (U.S.), 1941 (smooth red cloth) . . . . £200/£75
ditto, Editions Poetry, 1945 . . . . . . £200/£25
Bend Sinister, Holt (U.S.), 1947 . . . . £150/£50

ditto, Weidenfeld & Nicolson, 1960 . . . £100/£35
Lolita, Olympia Press (Paris), 1955 (2 vols, 'Francs: 900' on back cover, wraps) £3,500
ditto, Putnam (U.S.), 1958 (d/w bears only distinction between trade and book club copies) . . £500/£40
ditto, Weidenfeld & Nicolson, 1959 . . . £300/£45
ditto, as **The Annotated Lolita**, McGraw-Hill (U.S.), 1970 (edited by Alfred Appel) . . . . £20/£10
ditto, as **The Annotated Lolita**, Weidenfeld & Nicolson, 1971 . . . . £20/£10
Pnin, Doubleday (U.S.), 1957 . . . . £165/£45
ditto, Heinemann, 1957 . . . . . . £125/£35
Invitation to a Beheading, Putnam (U.S.), 1959 .
. . . . £75/£15
ditto, Weidenfeld & Nicolson, 1960 . . . £50/£15
Pale Fire, Putnam (U.S.), 1962 . . . . £125/£35
ditto, Weidenfeld & Nicolson, 1962 . . . £100/£15
The Gift, Putnam (U.S.), 1963 . . . . £35/£15
ditto, Weidenfeld & Nicolson, 1963 . . . £35/£15
The Defence, Weidenfeld & Nicolson, 1964 £35/£15
ditto, as **The Defense**, Putnam (U.S.), 1964 . £35/£15
The Eye, Phaedra (U.S.), 1965 . . . . £35/£15
King, Queen, Knave, McGraw-Hill (U.S.), 1968 . .
. . . . £35/£15
ditto, Weidenfeld & Nicolson, 1968 . . . £35/£15
Ada or Ardor: A Family Chronicle, McGraw-Hill (U.S.), 1969 . . . . £25/£10
ditto, Weidenfeld & Nicolson, 1969 . . . £25/£10
Mary, McGraw-Hill (U.S.), 1970 . . . . £20/£5
ditto, Weidenfeld & Nicolson, 1971 . . . . £20/£5
Glory, McGraw-Hill (U.S.), 1971 . . . . £20/£5
ditto, Weidenfeld & Nicolson, 1972 . . . . £20/£5
Transparent Things, McGraw-Hill (U.S.), 1972 . .
. . . . £20/£5
ditto, Weidenfeld & Nicolson, 1973 . . . . £20/£5
Look at the Harlequins!, McGraw-Hill (U.S.), 1974 .
. . . . £20/£5
ditto, Weidenfeld & Nicolson, 1975 . . . . £20/£5
The Enchanter, Harper (U.S.), 1986 . . . £20/£5
ditto, Picador, 1987 . . . . £15/£5

Short Stories
Nine Stories/Direction Two, New Directions (U.S.), 1947 (wraps) £150
Nabokov's Dozen: A Collection of Thirteen Stories, Doubleday (U.S.), 1958 . . . . . . £100/£35
ditto, Heinemann, 1959 . . . . . . £75/£25
ditto, as **Spring in Fialta**, Popular Library (U.S.), 1959 (wraps) £20
Nabokov's Quartet, Phaedra (U.S.), 1966 . £25/£10
ditto, Weidenfeld & Nicolson, 1967 . . . £25/£10
A Russian Beauty and Other Stories, McGraw-Hill (U.S.), 1973 . . . . £25/£10
ditto, Weidenfeld & Nicolson, 1973 . . . £25/£10
Tyrants Destroyed and Other Stories, McGraw-Hill (U.S.), 1975 . . . . £20/£10
ditto, Weidenfeld & Nicolson, 1975 . . . £20/£10
Details of a Sunset and Other Stories, McGraw-Hill (U.S.), 1976 . . . . £20/£10

ditto, Weidenfeld & Nicolson, 1976 . . . £20/£10
The Stories of Vladimir Nabokov, Knopf (U.S.), 1995
. . . . £15/£5
ditto, Weidenfeld & Nicolson, 1996 . . . . £15/£5

Collected Edition
Nabokov's Congeries, Viking Press (U.S.), 1968 . .
. . . . £20/£5

Poetry
Poems, Doubleday (U.S.), 1959 . . . . £175/£45
ditto, Weidenfeld & Nicolson, 1961 . . £100/£35
Poems and Problems, McGraw-Hill (U.S.), 1970 . .
. . . . £50/£20
ditto, Weidenfeld & Nicolson, 1972 . . . £45/£15

Plays
The Waltz Invention: A Play in Three Acts, Phaedra (U.S.), 1966 . . . . £30/£10
Lolita: A Screenplay, McGraw-Hill (U.S.), 1974 . .
. . . . £25/£10
The Man from the USSR and Other Plays, Harcourt Brace (U.S.), 1984 . . . . £20/£5
ditto, Weidenfeld & Nicolson, 1985 . . . . £20/£5

Others
Nikolai Gogol, New Directions (U.S.), 1944 (first issue, tan cloth with brown lettering, 5 titles listed on verso of half title, d/w with $1.50 price) . £225/£45
ditto, New Directions (U.S.), 1944 (second issue, tan cloth with blue lettering, 14 titles listed on verso of half title, d/w with $2.00 price and 14 titles on rear flap) . . . . £100/£35
ditto, Editions Poetry, 1947 . . . . . £125/£35
Three Russian Poets: Selections from Pushkin, Lermentov and Tyutchev, New Directions (U.S.), 1944 (new translations by Nabokov, grey paper boards, grey d/w with brown lettering, at '$1.00') .
. . . . £125/£45
ditto, New Directions (U.S.), 1944 (tan stapled wraps with blue-grey d/w lettered in brown, at '$.50') . .
. . . . £75/£15
ditto, as **Pushkin, Lermentov and Tyutchev: Poems**, Drummond, 1947 . . . . £65/£15
A Hero of Our Time, by Mihail Lermentov, Doubleday (U.S.), 1958 (translated by Vladimir Nabokov, wraps)
. . . . £15
The Song of Igor's Campaign, Vintage (U.S.), 1960 (translated by Vladimir Nabokov, wraps) . . £10
ditto, Weidenfeld & Nicolson, 1961 . . . £30/£10
Eugene Onegin: A Novel in Verse, by Aleksandr Pushkin, Pantheon (U.S.), 1964 (translation and commentary by Vladimir Nabokov, 4 vols, slipcase) .
. . . . £150/£75
Notes on Prosody From the Commentary to his translation of Pushkin's Eugene Onegin, Routledge, 1965 . . . . £25/£5
ditto, Princetown Univ. Press (U.S.), 1969 . £25/£5
Strong Opinions, McGraw-Hill (U.S.), 1973 £25/£10
ditto, Weidenfeld & Nicolson, 1974 . . . . £20/£5

The Nabokov/Wilson Letters:, 1940-1971, Harper & Row (U.S.), 1979 . . . . £20/£5
ditto, Weidenfeld & Nicolson, 1979 . . . . £20/£5
Lectures on Literature, Harcourt Brace (U.S.), 1980 .
. . . . £25/£5
ditto, Weidenfeld & Nicolson, 1980 . . . . £20/£5
Lectures on Russian Literature, Harcourt Brace (U.S.), 1981 . . . . £25/£5
ditto, Weidenfeld & Nicolson, 1982 . . . . £20/£5
Lectures on Don Quixote, Harcourt Brace (U.S.), 1983
. . . . £20/£5
ditto, Weidenfeld & Nicolson, 1983 . . . . £15/£5
Nabokov's Butterflies: Unpublished and Uncollected Writings, Beacon Press (U.S.), 2000 . . . £20/£5
ditto, Beacon Press (U.S.), 2000 (240 signed copies, slipcase) . . . . £150/£100
ditto, Allen Lane, 2000 . . . . £15/£5

Autobiography
Conclusive Evidence: A Memoir, Harper (U.S.), 1951
. . . . £200/£50
ditto, as *Speak, Memory: A Memoir*, Gollancz, 1951 (first issue blue-green cloth, black stamping, no *Daily Mail* device on spine or at bottom of front flap) . .
. . . . £300/£50
ditto, Gollancz, 1951 (second issue blue cloth, gilt stamping, with *Daily Mail* device on spine and at bottom of front flap) . . . . . . £150/£20
ditto, as *Speak, Memory: An Autobiography*, Putnam (U.S.), 1966 (revised edition) . . . £50/£20
ditto, as *Speak, Memory: An Autobiography*, Weidenfeld & Nicolson, 1967 (revised edition) . £25/£10
Selected Letters, 1940-1977, Harcourt Brace (U.S.), 1989 . . . . £20/£5
ditto, Weidenfeld & Nicolson, 1990 . . . . £20/£5

SHIVA NAIPAUL
(b.1945 d.1985)

A Trinidadian novelist, Shiva Naipaul's three novels effectively mix satire and compassion.

Novels
Fireflies, Deutsch, 1970 . . . . . . £100/£20
ditto, Knopf (U.S.), 1971 . . . . . £45/£15
The Chip-Chip Gatherers, Deutsch, 1973 . £50/£20
ditto, Knopf (U.S.), 1973 . . . . . . £25/£5
A Hot Country, Hamilton, 1983 . . . . £15/£5
ditto, as *Love and Death in a Hot Country*, Viking (U.S.), 1984 . . . . £10/£5

Short Stories
The Adventures of Gurudeva, Deutsch, 1976 £35/£10

Travel
North of South: An African Journey, Deutsch, 1978 .
. . . . £30/£5
ditto, Simon & Schuster (U.S.), 1979 . . £20/£5

Black and White, Hamilton, 1980 . . . . £20/£5
ditto, as *Journey to Nowhere: A New World Tragedy*, Simon & Schuster (U.S.), 1981 . . . . £15/£5
Beyond the Dragon's Mouth: Stories and Pieces, Hamilton, 1984 . . . . £15/£5
ditto, Viking (U.S.), 1985 . . . . . . £10/£5
An Unfinished Journey, Hamilton, 1986 . £15/£5
ditto, Viking (U.S.), 1987 . . . . . . £10/£5

V.S. NAIPAUL
(b.1932)

A distinguished Trinidadian novelist, V.S. Naipaul uses such twentieth century uncertainties as imperialism and colonialism as the motivation behind his work. He won the Nobel Prize for Literature in 2001.

Novels
The Mystic Masseur, Deutsch, 1957 . . . £300/£65
ditto, Vanguard Press (U.S.), 1959 . . . £125/£15
The Suffrage of Elvira, Deutsch, 1958 . . £500/£125
A House for Mr Biswas, Deutsch, 1961 . . £500/£75
ditto, McGraw-Hill (U.S.), 1962 . . . . £125/£15
Mr Stone and the Knights Companion, Deutsch, 1963
. . . . £125/£35
ditto, Macmillan (U.S.), 1964 . . . . £50/£15
The Mimic Men, Deutsch, 1967 . . . . £75/£20
ditto, Macmillan (U.S.), 1967 . . . . £40/£15
In a Free State, Deutsch, 1971 . . . . £65/£20
ditto, Knopf (U.S.), 1971 . . . . . . £25/£10
Guerrillas, Deutsch, 1975 . . . . . . £20/£5
ditto, Knopf (U.S.), 1975 . . . . . . £15/£5
A Bend in the River, Deutsch, 1979 . . . £20/£5
ditto, Knopf (U.S.), 1979 . . . . . . £15/£5
The Enigma of Arrival, Viking, 1987 . . £15/£5
ditto, Knopf (U.S.), 1987 . . . . . . £10/£5
A Way in the World: A Sequence, Heinemann, 1994 .
. . . . £15/£5
ditto, Knopf (U.S.), 1994 (advance copy, signed, in slipcase) . . . . £45/£25
ditto, Knopf (U.S.), 1994 . . . . . . £10/£5
Half a Life, Picador, 2001 . . . . . £10/£5
ditto, Picador, 2001 (50 signed, numbered, uncorrected proof copies, wraps) £100
ditto, Knopf (U.S.), 2001 . . . . . . £10/£5

Short Stories
Miguel Street, Deutsch, 1959 . . . . £300/£50
ditto, Vanguard Press (U.S.), 1960 . . £125/£25
A Flag on the Island, Deutsch, 1967 . £40/£15
ditto, Macmillan (U.S.), 1968 . . . . £35/£10

Others
The Middle Passage, Deutsch, 1962 . . £150/£20
ditto, Macmillan (U.S.), 1963 . . . . £65/£20
An Area of Darkness: An Experience of India, Deutsch, 1964 . . . . £65/£20
ditto, Macmillan (U.S.), 1965 . . . . £50/£15

The Loss of El Dorado, Deutsch, 1969 . . £35/£10
ditto, Knopf (U.S.), 1970 . . . . . . £25/£10
The Overcrowded Barracoon, Deutsch, 1972 £45/£15
ditto, Knopf (U.S.), 1972 . . . . . . £35/£10
India: A Wounded Civilisation, Deutsch, 1977. . .
. . . . £35/£10
ditto, Knopf (U.S.), 1977 . . . . . . £25/£10
The Return of Eva Peron with *The Killings in Trinidad*, Deutsch, 1980 . . . .£20/£5
ditto, Knopf (U.S.), 1980 . . . .£15/£5
Congo Diaries, Sylvester & Orphanos, 1980 (300 signed, numbered copies, no d/w) £75
Among the Believers: An Islamic Journey, Deutsch, 1981 . . . .£20/£5
ditto, Franklin Library (U.S.), 1981 (signed limited edition) £45
ditto, Knopf (U.S.), 1981 . . . .£15/£5
Finding the Centre: Two Narratives, Deutsch, 1984 .
. . . .£15/£5
ditto, Knopf (U.S.), 1984 . . . .£15/£5
A Turn in the South, Viking, 1989 . . . .£15/£5
ditto, Knopf (U.S.), 1989 . . . .£15/£5
ditto, Franklin Library (U.S.), 1989 (signed limited edition) £40
India: A Million Mutinies Now, Heinemann, 1990 .
. . . .£15/£5
ditto, London Limited Editions, 1990 (150 signed, numbered copies) £50
ditto, Viking (U.S.), 1991. . . . . . .£10/£5
Conversations with V.S. Naipaul, Univ. Press of Mississippi (U.S.), 1995 . . . . . .£20/£5
Beyond Belief: Islam Excursions Among the Converted Peoples, Little, Brown, 1998 . .£15/£5
ditto, Random House (U.S.), 1998 . . . .£10/£5
Letters Between a Father and a Son, Little, Brown, 1999 . . . .£10/£5
ditto, as *Between Father and Son: Family Letters*, Knopf (U.S.), 2000 . . . .£10/£5
Reading and Writing: An Essay, New York Review of Books (U.S.), 2000 . . . .£15/£5
The Writer and the World: Essays, Picador, 2002 . .
. . . .£10/£5
ditto, Knopf (U.S.), 2002 . . . .£10/£5

VIOLET NEEDHAM
(b.1876 d.1967)

A children's author, Violet Needham was 63 before her first book was published.

The Black Riders, Collins, 1939 . . . . £150/£50
The Emerald Crown, Collins, 1940 . . . £100/£35
The Stormy Petrel, Collins, 1942 . . . £100/£35
The Horn of Merlyns, Collins, 1943. . . £75/£25
The Woods of Windri, Collins, 1944 . . £45/£10
The House of the Paladin, Collins, 1945 . £35/£10
The Changeling of Monte Lucio, Collins, 1946 . .
. . . . £35/£10

The Bell of the Four Evangelists, Collins, 1947 . .
. . . . £50/£10
The Boy in Red, Collins, 1948 . . . . £35/£10
The Betrayer, Collins, 1950 . . . . . £35/£10
Pandora of Parrham Royal, Collins, 1951 . £100/£25
The Avenue, Collins, 1952 . . . . . £45/£10
How Many Miles to Babylon, Collins, 1953 £100/£25
Adventures at Hampton Court, Lutterworth Press, 1954 . . . . £75/£15
Richard and the Golden Horse Shoe, Collins, 1954 .
. . . . £125/£25
The Great House of Estraville, Collins, 1955 £125/£25
The Secret of the White Peacock, Collins, 1956 . .
. . . . £100/£20
Adventures at Windsor Castle, Lutterworth Press, 1957
. . . . £100/£15
The Red Rose of Ruvina, Collins, 1957. . £75/£20

KAY NIELSEN
(b.1886 d.1957)

A Danish illustrator, Nielsen moved to London in 1911, and was commissioned to illustrate Quiller-Couch's *In Powder and Crinoline* by Hodder & Stoughton, followed by a series of 'Gift Books'.

In Powder and Crinoline, Old Fairy Tales, retold by Sir Arthur Quiller-Couch, Hodder & Stoughton, [1913]. £600
ditto, Hodder & Stoughton, [1913] (large paper edition) £1,250
ditto, Hodder & Stoughton, [1913] (deluxe edition, 500 signed copies) £3,000
ditto, as *Twelve Dancing Princesses and Other Fairy Tales*, George H. Doran (U.S.), [1923]. . . £450
East of the Sun and West of the Moon, Old Tales from the North, retold by Peter C. Asbjörnsen and Jorgen Moe, Hodder & Stoughton, [1914]. . £2,000
ditto, Hodder & Stoughton, [1914] (deluxe edition, 500 signed copies) £5,000
ditto, George H. Doran (U.S.), [1914] . . .£1,000
Hans Andersen's Fairy Tales, Hodder & Stoughton, [1924]. . . . . £1,500/£750
ditto, Hodder & Stoughton, [1924] (deluxe edition, approx 250 of 500 signed copies, issued with d/w) .
. . . . £3,500/£1,500
ditto, Hodder & Stoughton, [1924] (deluxe edition, approx 250 of 500 signed copies, white vellum binding) £2,500
ditto, Doran (U.S.), 1924 . . . . . £1,000/£250
Hansel and Gretel and Other Stories, Hodder & Stoughton, [1925] £750
ditto, Hodder & Stoughton, [1925] (600 signed copies, cream buckram binding). £3,000
ditto, Doran (U.S.), [1925] £600
ditto, Doran (U.S.), [1925] (600 signed copies). £2,500

Red Magic: A Collection of the World's Best Fairy Tales from all Countries, edited by Romer Wilson, Cape, 1930 . . . . £750/£250

PATRICK O'BRIAN
(b.1914 d.2000)

Born in England as Richard Patrick Russ, the author later changed his name to O'Brian and claimed to be Irish. His 'Jack Aubrey' series of novels deals with the larger-than-life hero's naval career.

'Jack Aubrey' Novels
Master and Commander, Lippincott (U.S.), 1969 . . . . £300/£65
ditto, Collins, 1970 . . . . £750/£125
Post Captain, Collins, 1972 . . . . . £500/£45
ditto, Lippincott (U.S.), 1972 . . . . . £250/£35
H.M.S. Surprise, Collins, 1973 . . . £350/£45
ditto, Lippincott (U.S.), 1973 . . . . £150/£35
The Mauritius Command, Collins, 1977 . £300/£45
ditto, Stein & Day (U.S.), 1978 . . . £150/£35
Desolation Island, Collins, 1978 . . . £275/£40
ditto, Stein & Day (U.S.), 1979 . . . £125/£25
The Fortune of War, Collins, 1979 . . . £225/£40
ditto, Norton (U.S.), 1991 (wraps) . . . £25
The Surgeon's Mate, Collins, 1980 . . . £500/£65
ditto, Norton (U.S.), 1992 (wraps) . . . £25
The Ionian Mission, Collins, 1981 . . . £400/£50
ditto, Norton (U.S.), 1992 (wraps) . . . £20
Treason's Harbour, Collins, 1983 . . . £250/£45
ditto, Norton (U.S.), 1992 (wraps) . . . £20
The Far Side of the World, Collins, 1984 . £200/£40
ditto, Norton (U.S.), 1992 (wraps) . . . £20
The Reverse of the Medal, Collins, 1986 . £175/£35
ditto, Norton (U.S.), 1992 (wraps) . . . £20
The Letter of Marque, Collins, 1988 . . £150/£35
ditto, Norton (U.S.), 1990 . . . . . £25/£10
The Thirteen-Gun Salute, Collins, 1989 . £145/£35
ditto, Norton (U.S.), 1991 . . . . . £25/£10
The Nutmeg of Consolation, Collins, 1991 [1990]. . . . . £100/£25
ditto, Norton (U.S.), 1991 . . . . . £25/£10
Clarissa Oakes, Harper Collins, 1992 . £65/£20
ditto, as *The Truelove*, Norton (U.S.), 1992 . £25/£10
The Wine-Dark Sea, Harper Collins, 1993 . £50/£15
ditto, Norton (U.S.), 1993 . . . . . . £15/£5
The Commodore, Harper Collins, 1994 . £50/£15
ditto, Norton (U.S.), 1994 . . . . . . £15/£5
ditto, Norton (U.S.), 1994 (200 signed, numbered copies, slipcase) . . . . . . £200/£150
The Yellow Admiral, Norton (U.S.), 1996 . £20/£5
ditto, Harper Collins, 1997 . . . . . £25/£10
The Hundred Days, Harper Collins, 1998 . £20/£5
ditto, Norton (U.S.), 1998 . . . . . . £15/£5
Blue at the Mizzen, Norton (U.S.), 1999 . £15/£5
ditto, Harper Collins, 1999 . . . . . £15/£5

Other Novels
Caesar: The Life Story of a Panda Leopard, Putnam, 1930 (pseud. 'Richard Patrick Russ', illustrated by Harry Rowntree) . . . . £2,000/£600
ditto, British Library, 1999 (250 signed copies, with *Hussein*, no d/ws, 2 vols in slipcase) . . £250/£150
ditto, British Library, 1999 . . . . . £15/£5
ditto, Norton (U.S.), 1999 . . . . . . £10/£5
ditto, HarperCollins, 2000 . . . . . . £10/£5
Hussein: An Entertainment, Oxford U.P., 1938 . . . . £2,000/£600
ditto, British Library, 1999 (250 signed copies, with *Caesar*, no d/ws, 2 vols in slipcase) . . £250/£150
ditto, British Library, 1999 . . . . . £15/£5
ditto, Norton (U.S.), 1999 . . . . . . £10/£5
ditto, HarperCollins, 2000 . . . . . . £10/£5
Three Bear Witness, Secker & Warburg, 1952 . . . . £800/£100
ditto, as *Testimonies*, Harcourt, Brace & Co. (U.S.), [1952] . . . . £500/£65
ditto, as *Testimonies*, Harper Collins, 1994 . £20/£5
The Catalans, Harcourt, Brace & Co. (U.S.), [1953] . . . . £800/£75
ditto, as *The Frozen Flame*, Hart-Davis, 1953 . . . . £1,000/£100
Richard Temple, Macmillan, 1962 . . . £350/£50

Short Stories
The Last Pool and Other Stories, Secker & Warburg, 1950 . . . . £750/£100
The Walker and Other Stories, Harcourt, Brace & Co. (U.S.), [1955] . . . . £150/£45
ditto, as *Lying in the Sun and Other Stories*, Hart-Davis, 1956 (slightly different contents) . £175/£50
The Chian Wine and Other Stories, Collins, 1974 . . . . £125/£30
Collected Short Stories, Harper Collins, 1994 £50/£15
ditto, as *The Rendezvous and Other Stories*, Norton (U.S.), 1994 . . . . £40/£15

Children's Titles
The Road to Samarcand, Hart-Davis, 1954 . £250/£35
The Golden Ocean, Hart-Davis, 1956 . . £350/£45
ditto, John Day (U.S.), 1957 . . . . . £250/£35
The Unknown Shore, Hart-Davis, 1959 . £175/£40

Non Fiction
Men-Of-War, Collins, 1974 . . . . . £75/£20
ditto, Norton (U.S.), 1995 . . . . . . £15/£10
Pablo Ruiz Picasso: A Biography, Collins, 1976 . . . . £75/£25
ditto, as *Picasso: Pablo Ruiz Picasso: A Biography*, Putnam (U.S.), [1976] . . . . . . £75/£25
Joseph Banks: A Life, Collins Harvill, 1987 £65/£20
ditto, Godine (U.S.), 1992 . . . . . £35/£10

Translations

The Quicksand War, by Lucian Bodard, Faber, 1967 .
. . . . £75/£20
The Italian Campaign, by Michael Mohart, Weidenfeld, 1967 . . . . £75/£20
The Woman Destroyed, by Simone De Beauvoir, Collins, 1969 . . . . £25/£5
ditto, Putnam (U.S.), 1969 . . . . £15/£5
Papillon, by Henri Charriere, Hart-Davis, 1970 . .
. . . . £40/£10
ditto, Morrow (U.S.), 1970 . . . . . . £30/£5

Editor

A Book of Voyages, Home & Van Thal, 1947 . . . .
. . . . £350/£75

EDNA O'BRIEN
(b.1932)

An Irish novelist and short story writer, often concentrating on the position of women in society. Her novels are a blend of bleakness and quiet joy.

Novels

The Country Girls, Hutchinson, 1960 . . £80/£15
ditto, Knopf (U.S.), 1960 . . . . . . £50/£10
The Lonely Girl, Cape, 1962 . . . . . £40/£10
ditto, Random House (U.S.), 1962 . . . £30/£10
ditto, as *The Girl With Green Eyes*, Penguin, 1964 (wraps) £5
Girls in Their Married Bliss, Cape, 1964 . . £20/£5
ditto, Houghton Mifflin (U.S.), 1968 . . £15/£5
August is a Wicked Month, Cape, 1965 . . £20/£5
ditto, Simon & Schuster (U.S.), 1965 . . £15/£5
Casualties of Peace, Cape, 1966 . . . . £25/£5
ditto, Simon & Schuster (U.S.), 1967 . . £15/£5
A Pagan Place, Weidenfeld & Nicolson, 1970 . £20/£5
ditto, Knopf (U.S.), 1970 . . . . . . £15/£5
Night, Weidenfeld & Nicolson, 1972 . . £15/£5
ditto, Knopf (U.S.), 1973 . . . . . . £15/£5
Johnnie, I Hardly Knew You, Weidenfeld & Nicolson, 1977 . . . . £15/£5
ditto, as *I Hardly Knew You*, Doubleday (U.S.), 1978 .
. . . . £10/£5
The High Road, Weidenfeld & Nicolson, 1988 £15/£5
ditto, London Limited Editions, 1988 (150 signed copies, tissue d/w) . . . . . . £50/£40
ditto, Farrar Straus (U.S.), 1988 . . . . £10/£5
Time and Tide, Viking, 1992 . . . . . £10/£5
ditto, Farrar Straus (U.S.), 1992 . . . . £10/£5
House of Splendid Isolation, Weidenfeld & Nicolson, 1994 . . . . £10/£5
ditto, Farrar Straus (U.S.), 1994 . . . . £10/£5
Down by the River, Weidenfeld & Nicolson, 1995 . .
. . . . £10/£5
ditto, Farrar Straus (U.S.), 1997 . . . . £10/£5

Wild Decembers, Weidenfeld & Nicolson, 1999 £10/£5
ditto, Houghton Mifflin (U.S.), 2000 . . . £10/£5
In the Forest, Weidenfeld & Nicolson, 2002 . £10/£5
ditto, Houghton Mifflin (U.S.), 2002 . . . £10/£5

Short Stories

The Love Object, Cape, 1968 . . . . . £30/£5
ditto, Knopf (U.S.), 1969 . . . . . . £25/£5
A Scandalous Woman, Weidenfeld & Nicolson, 1974.
. . . . £15/£5
ditto, Harcourt Brace (U.S.), 1974 . . . £10/£5
Mrs Reinhardt and Other Stories, Weidenfeld & Nicolson, 1978 . . . . £15/£5
ditto, as *A Rose in the Heart*, Doubleday (U.S.), 1979.
. . . . £10/£5
Returning, Weidenfeld & Nicolson, 1982 . . £15/£5
A Fanatic Heart, Franklin Library (U.S.), 1984 (signed, limited edition) £20
ditto, Farrar Straus (U.S.), 1984 . . . . £10/£5
ditto, Weidenfeld & Nicolson, 1985 . . . £10/£5
Lantern Slides, Weidenfeld & Nicolson, 1990 . £10/£5
ditto, Farrar Straus (U.S.), 1990 . . . . £10/£5

Collected Editions

The Collected Edna O'Brien, Collins, 1978 . £15/£5
Some Irish Loving, Weidenfeld & Nicolson, 1979 . .
. . . . £15/£5
ditto, Harper (U.S.), 1979 . . . . . . £10/£5
The Country Girls Trilogy and Epilogue, Farrar Straus (U.S.), 1986 . . . . £10/£5
ditto, Cape, 1987 . . . . £10/£5

Children's Titles

The Dazzle, Hodder & Stoughton, 1981 . . £15/£5
Christmas Treat, Hodder & Stoughton, 1982 . £10/£5
Tales for Telling: Irish Folk and Fairy Stories, Pavilion, 1986 . . . . £10/£5
ditto, Atheneum (U.S.), 1986 . . . . . £10/£5

Plays

A Pagan Place, Faber, 1973 . . . . . £25/£10
Virginia, Hogarth Press, 1981 (wraps) . . . £15
ditto, Harcourt Brace (U.S.), 1981 . . . £15/£5

Others

Zee & Co, Weidenfeld & Nicolson, 1971 . £30/£10
Mother Ireland, Weidenfeld & Nicolson, 1976 . £15/£5
ditto, Harcourt Brace (U.S.), 1976 . . . £15/£5
Arabian Days, Horizon Press (U.S.), 1977 . £10/£5
ditto, Quartet, 1977 . . . . £10/£5
James and Nora, Lord John Press (US), 1981 (26 signed, lettered copies of 276, slipcase) . £75/£65
ditto, Lord John Press (U.S.), 1981 (250 signed, numbered copies of 276) . . . . £50/£40
Vanishing Ireland, Cape, 1986 (photos by Richard Fitzgerald) . . . . £25/£10
James Joyce, Weidenfeld & Nicolson, 1999 . £15/£5
ditto, Viking (U.S.), 1999 . . . . . . £15/£5

FLANN O'BRIEN
(b.1911 d.1966)

An Irish novelist and journalist, his first novel, *At Swim-Two-Birds*, was hailed by many as a masterpiece in the tradition of Joyce's *Ulysses*.

Novels

At Swim-Two-Birds, Longmans, 1939 (black cloth) .
. . . . £3,000/£1,000
ditto, Longmans, 1939 (second issue, grey-green cloth)
. . . . £2,000/£150
ditto, Pantheon (U.S.), 1939 [1951] . . . £200/£25
An Beal Bocht, An Press Naisiunta (Dublin), 1941
(pseud. 'Myles na gCopaleen', wraps) . . . £400
ditto, translated as *The Poor Mouth*, Hart-Davis MacGibbon, 1973 (illustrated by Ralph Steadman) .
. . . . £75/£15
ditto, Hart-Davis MacGibbon, 1973 (130 copies signed by Ralph Steadman) £500
ditto, Viking (U.S.), 1974 . . . . £45/£10
The Hard Life: An Exegesis of Squalor, MacGibbon & Kee, 1961 . . . . £100/£20
ditto, Pantheon (U.S.), 1962 . . . . £50/£15
The Dalkey Archive, MacGibbon & Kee, 1964. . .
. . . . £80/£15
ditto, Macmillan (U.S.), 1965 . . . £45/£10
The Third Policeman, MacGibbon & Kee, 1967 . .
. . . . £75/£15
ditto, Walker & Co (U.S.), 1967. . . . £45/£10

Others

Cruiskeen Lawn, Irish Times (Dublin), 1943 (pseud. 'Myles na gCopaleen', wraps) £400
Faustus Kelly, Cahill (Dublin), 1943 (wraps) . £500
The Best of Myles, a Selection from 'Cruiskeen Lawn', MacGibbon & Kee, 1968 . . . £75/£15
ditto, Walker & Co (U.S.), 1968 . . . . £45/£10
Stories and Plays, Hart-Davis MacGibbon, 1973 . .
. . . . £50/£10
ditto, Viking (U.S.), 1976. . . . . £45/£10
Further Cuttings from 'Cruiskeen Lawn', Hart-Davis MacGibbon, 1976 . . . . . . £40/£10
ditto, Dalkey Archive Press (U.S.), 2000 . . . £5
The Various Lives of Keats and Chapman and The Brother, Hart-Davis MacGibbon, 1976 . £40/£10
The Hair of the Dogma: A Further Selection from 'Cruiskeen Lawn', Hart-Davis MacGibbon, 1977 .
. . . . £40/£10
A Flann O'Brien Reader, Viking (U.S.), 1978 £25/£10
Myles Away from Dublin, Granada, 1985 . £20/£10

LIAM O'FLAHERTY
(b.1896 d.1984)

Irish novelist and short story writer, *The Informer* was selected as a Haycraft-Queen Cornerstone.

Novels

Thy Neighbour's Wife, Cape, 1923 . . . £250/£30
ditto, Boni & Liveright (U.S.), 1924 . . . £125/£25
The Black Soul, Cape, 1924 . . . . £150/£25
ditto, Boni & Liveright (U.S.), 1924 . . . £65/£15
The Informer, Cape, 1925 . . . . £2,000/£500
ditto, Knopf (U.S.), 1925 . . . . . . £750/£75
Mr Gilhooey, Cape, 1926 . . . . . . £65/£20
ditto, Harcourt Brace (U.S.), 1927 . . . £50/£15
The Assassin, Cape, 1928 . . . . . £100/£15
ditto, Cape, 1928 (150 signed, numbered copies) . .
. . . . £250/£175
ditto, Harcourt Brace (U.S.), 1928 . . . £65/£10
The House of Gold, Cape, 1929 . . . £75/£15
ditto, Harcourt Brace (U.S.), 1929 . . . £45/£10
Return of the Brute, Mandrake Press, 1929. £250/£35
ditto, Harcourt Brace (U.S.), 1930 . . . £100/£15
The Puritan, Cape, 1931 [1932] . . . £100/£15
ditto, Harcourt Brace (U.S.), 1932 . . . £50/£20
The Ecstasy of Angus, Joiner & Steele, 1931 (365 signed copies, glassine d/w). . . . . £125/£100
Skerrett, Gollancz, 1932 . . . . . . £75/£10
ditto, Long & Smith (U.S.), 1932 . . . £45/£10
The Martyr, Gollancz, 1933 . . . . . £75/£15
ditto, Macmillan (U.S.), 1933 (expurgated edition). .
. . . . £45/£10
Hollywood Cemetery, Gollancz, 1935 . £250/£30
Famine, Gollancz, 1937 . . . . . . £75/£20
ditto, Random House (U.S.), 1937 . . . £50/£15
Land, Gollancz, 1946 . . . . £35/£10
ditto, Random House (U.S.), 1946 . . . . £25/£5
Insurrection, Gollancz, 1950. . . . . £25/£10
ditto, Little, Brown (U.S.), 1951 . . . . . £20/£5
The Wilderness, Wolfhound Press (Dublin), 1979 (wraps) £5
ditto, Wolfhound Press (Dublin), 1979 (hardback with d/w) . . . . £25/£10
ditto, Wolfhound Press (Dublin), 1979 (50 signed, numbered copies) £75

Short Stories

Spring Sowing, Cape, 1924 . . . . . £75/£25
ditto, Knopf (U.S.), 1926 . . . . . . £50/£15
The Tent, Cape, 1926 (blue cloth) . . . £65/£25
ditto, Cape, 1926 (dark green cloth) . . . £55/£15
The Fairy Goose and Two Other Stories, Crosby Gaige (U.S.) & Faber & Gwyer (U.K.), 1927 (1,190 signed copies, tissue jacket). . . . . £65/£45
ditto, Crosby Gaige (U.S.) & Faber & Gwyer (U.K.), 1928 (12 signed copies on blue handmade paper). .
. . . . £200

ditto, Crosby Gaige (U.S.) & Faber & Gwyer (U.K.), 1928 (12 signed copies on green handmade paper) .
. . . . £200
Red Barbara and Other Stories, Crosby Gaige (U.S.) & Faber & Gwyer (U.K.), 1928 (600 signed, numbered copies). £75
ditto, Crosby Gaige (U.S.) & Faber & Gwyer (U.K.), 1928 (9 signed copies on grey handmade paper) . .
. . . . £250
The Mountain Tavern and Other Stories, Cape, 1929.
. . . . £45/£15
ditto, Harcourt Brace (U.S.), 1929 . . . £45/£15
The Wild Swan and Other Stories, Joiner & Steele: 'Furnival Books', 1932 (550 signed copies) £75/£50
The Short Stories of Liam O'Flaherty, Cape, 1937 .
. . . .£25/£5
Two Lovely Beasts, Gollancz, 1948 . . . .£20/£5
ditto, Devin-Adair (U.S.), 1950 . . . .£15/£5
Duil, Sainseal & Dill, 1953 (Gaelic). . . .£15/£5
The Stories of Liam O'Flaherty, Devin-Adair (U.S.), 1956 . . . .£15/£5
The Pedlar's Revenge, Wolfhound Press (Dublin), 1976 . . . .£20/£5

Pamphlets
Civil War, E. Archer, 1925 (100 signed copies, wraps)
. . . . £150
The Terrorist, E. Archer, 1926 (100 signed copies, wraps). £150
Darkness: A Tragedy in Three Acts, E. Archer, 1926 (100 signed copies, wraps) £150
ditto, E. Archer, 1926 (12 copies with cast-list). £350
The Child Of God, E. Archer, 1926 (100 signed copies, wraps). £150
ditto, E.Archer (25 signed large paper copies) . £300
A Tourist's Guide to Ireland, Mandrake Press, [1929]
. . . . £75/£50
Joseph Conrad, E. Lahr: 'Blue Moon Booklet', 1930 .
. . . . £45
ditto, E. Lahr: 'Blue Moon Booklet', 1930 (100 large paper copies). £95
A Cure for Unemployment, E. Lahr: 'Blue Moon Booklet', 1931 . . . . £45
ditto, E. Lahr: 'Blue Moon Booklet', 1931 (100 large paper copies). £95
ditto, E. Lahr/Julian Press (U.S.), 1931 . . . £35

Others
The Life of Tim Healy, Cape, 1927 . . . £75/£20
ditto, Harcourt Brace (U.S.), 1927 . . . £50/£15
Two Years, Cape, 1930 . . . . . . £35/£10
ditto, Harcourt Brace (U.S.), 1930 . . . £35/£10
I Went to Russia, Cape, 1931 . . . . £30/£10
ditto, Harcourt Brace (U.S.), 1931 . . . £30/£10
Shame the Devil, Grayson & Grayson, 1934 £30/£10
ditto, Grayson & Grayson, 1934 (single page from original manuscript bound in) . . . .£150/£125

JOHN O'HARA
(b.1905 d.1970)

A short story writer and novelist who recorded the minutiae of American life.

Novels
Appointment In Samarra, Harcourt Brace (U.S.), 1934
. . . . £2,000/£125
ditto, Faber & Faber, 1935 . . . . £1,250/£150
Butterfield 8, Harcourt Brace (U.S.), 1935 . £250/£45
ditto, Cresset Press, 1951 . . . . . . £45/£10
Hope of Heaven, Harcourt Brace (U.S.), 1939 . . . .
. . . . £300/£35
ditto, Faber & Faber, 1939 . . . . . £100/£25
A Rage to Live, Random House, 1949 . . £75/£20
ditto, Cresset Press, 1950 . . . . . . £25/£10
The Farmer's Hotel, Random House, 1951. £25/£10
ditto, Cresset Press, 1953 . . . . . . £15/£5
Ten North Frederick, Random House (U.S.), 1955 .
. . . . £50/£10
ditto, Cresset Press, 1956 . . . .£15/£5
A Family Party, Random House (U.S.), 1956 £25/£10
ditto, Cresset Press, 1957 . . . .£15/£5
From The Terrace, Random House (U.S.), 1958 . .
. . . . £25/£10
ditto, Cresset Press, 1959 . . . .£15/£5
Ourselves to Know, Random House (U.S.), 1960 . .
. . . .£15/£5
ditto, Cresset Press, 1960 . . . .£10/£5
Sermons and Soda Water, Random House (U.S.), 1960 (boxed set) . . . . £25/£10
ditto, Cresset Press, 1961 (boxed set) . . .£15/£5
The Big Laugh, Random House (U.S.), 1962 .£10/£5
ditto, Cresset Press, 1962 . . . .£10/£5
Elizabeth Appleton, Random House (U.S.), 1963 . .
. . . .£10/£5
ditto, Cresset Press, 1963 . . . .£10/£5
The Lockwood Concern, Random House (U.S.), 1965
. . . .£10/£5
ditto, Hodder & Stoughton, 1967. . . . .£10/£5
The Instrument, Random House (U.S.), 1967 .£10/£5
ditto, Hodder & Stoughton, 1968. . . . .£10/£5
Appointment in Samara, Hope of Heaven, Butterfield 8, Random House (U.S.), 1968 . . . .£10/£5
The Ewings, Random House (U.S.), 1972 . .£10/£5
ditto, Hodder & Stoughton, 1972. . . . .£10/£5
The Second Ewings, Bloomfield Hills MI and Columbia SC (U.S.), 1977 . . . . . .£10/£5

Short Stories
The Doctor's Son and Other Stories, Harcourt Brace (U.S.), 1935 . . . . £1,000/£150
Files on Parade, Harcourt Brace, 1939 (first state with the foreword on a tipped-in page) . . . £150/£25
Pal Joey, Duell, Sloan & Pearce (U.S.), 1940 £200/£25
ditto, Cresset Press, 1952 . . . . . . £100/£15
Pipe Night, Duell, Sloan & Pearce (U.S.), 1945 . . .
. . . . £100/£20

ditto, Faber & Faber, 1946 . . . . . £45/£10
Here's O'Hara, Duell, Sloan & Pearce (U.S.), 1946 .
. . . . £30/£10
Hellbox, Random House (U.S.), 1947 . . £30/£10
ditto, Faber & Faber, 1952 . . . . . . £15/£5
All The Girls He Wanted, Avon (U.S.), 1949 . £15/£5
The Great Short Stories of John O'Hara, Bantam
(U.S.), 1956 . . . . £5
The Selected Short Stories of John O'Hara, Modern
Library (U.S.), 1956 . . . . £10/£5
Assembly, Random House (U.S.), 1961 . . . £20/£5
ditto, Cresset Press, 1962 . . . . . . £10/£5
The Cape Cod Lighter, Random House (U.S.), 1962 .
. . . . £20/£5
The Hat on the Bed, Random House (U.S.), 1963 . .
. . . . £10/£5
ditto, Cresset Press, 1964 . . . . . . £10/£5
49 Stories, Modern Library (U.S.), 1963 . . £10/£5
The Horse Knows the Way, Random House (U.S.),
1964 . . . . £10/£5
ditto, Cresset Press, 1965 . . . . . . £10/£5
Waiting for Winter, Random House (U.S.), 1966 . .
. . . . £10/£5
ditto, Hodder & Stoughton, 1967 . . . . £10/£5
And Other Stories, Random House (U.S.), 1968 . .
. . . . £10/£5
ditto, Hodder & Stoughton, 1969 . . . . £10/£5
Lovey Childs, Random House (U.S.), 1969 . £10/£5
ditto, Hodder & Stoughton, 1970 . . . . £10/£5
The O'Hara Generation, Random House (U.S.), 1969
. . . . £10/£5
The Time Element and Other Stories, Random House
(U.S.), 1972 . . . . £10/£5
ditto, Hodder & Stoughton, 1972 . . . . £10/£5
The Good Samaritan and Other Stories, Random
House (U.S.), 1974 . . . . £10/£5
ditto, Hodder & Stoughton, 1974 . . . . £10/£5
Two By O'Hara, Harcourt, Brace, Jovanovich (U.S.),
1979 . . . . £10/£5
The Collected Stories of John O'Hara, Random
House (U.S.), 1984 . . . . £10/£5

Others

Pal Joey: Libretto and Lyrics, Random House (U.S.),
1952 . . . . £75/£25
Sweet and Sour, Random House, 1954 . . £25/£10
ditto, Cresset Press, 1955 . . . . . . £25/£10
Five Plays, Random House (U.S.), 1961 . . £25/£5
ditto, Cresset Press, 1962 . . . . . . £25/£5
My Turn, Random House (U.S.), 1966 . . £25/£10
An Artist Is His Own Fault, Southern Illinois Univ.
Press, 1977 . . . . £20/£5

EUGENE O'NEILL
(b.1888 d.1953)

An American playwright whose experimental work
has been a major influence on modern American
theatre. He won the Nobel Prize for Literature in
1936.

Plays

Thirst and Other One-Act Plays, Gorham Press (U.S.),
1914 . . . . £1,500/£400
Before Breakfast, Frank Shay (U.S), 1916 (wraps) .
. . . . £250
*The Moon of the Caribees and Six Other Plays of the
Sea*, Boni & Liveright (U.S.), 1919 . £1,000/£200
ditto, Cape, 1923 . . . . £50/£10
Gold, Boni & Liveright (U.S.), 1920 [1921] £300/£75
Beyond the Horizon, Boni & Liveright (U.S.), 1921 .
. . . . £500/£100
ditto, as *Beyond the Horizon and Gold*, Cape, 1924 .
. . . . £250/£35
The Emperor Jones, Diff'rent, The Straw, Boni &
Liveright (U.S.), 1921 . . . . . £500/£75
ditto, as *Plays First Series: The Emperor Jones,
Diff'rent, The Straw*, Cape, 1922 . . . £250/£35
The Emperor Jones, Stuart Kidd (U.S.), 1921 (wraps)
. . . . £50
ditto, Cape, 1925 . . . . £50/£10
Boni & Liveright (U.S.), 1928 (775 signed, numbered
copies, illustrated, d/w and slipcase) . . £300/£175
The Hairy Ape, Anna Christie, The First Man, Boni
& Liveright (U.S.), 1922 . . . . . £500/£75
ditto, as *The Hairy Ape and Other Plays*, Cape, 1923 .
. . . . £150/£35
Anna Christie, Cape, 1923 . . . . . £200/£25
ditto, Boni & Liveright (U.S.), 1930 (775 signed,
numbered copies, illustrated, d/w and slipcase) . .
. . . . £250/£175
ditto, Boni & Liveright (U.S.), 1930 (12 signed copies
in morocco with original lithograph) . . . £1,000
All God's Chillun' Got Wings, and Welded, Boni &
Liveright (U.S.), 1924 . . . . . £350/£50
ditto, as *All God's Chillun' Got Wings, Desire under
the Elms and Welded*, Cape, 1925 . . . £200/£25
Desire Under the Elms, Boni & Liveright (U.S.), 1925
. . . . £550/£50
ditto, Cape, 1925 . . . . £75/£15
*The Great God Brown, The Fountain, The Moon of
the Caribees and Other Plays*, Boni & Liveright
(U.S.), 1926 . . . . £400/£50
ditto, Cape, 1926 . . . . £200/£25
Marco Millions, Boni & Liveright (U.S.), 1927 . .
. . . . £200/£30
ditto, Boni & Liveright (U.S.), 1927 (450 signed
copies, slipcase) . . . . £200/£150
ditto, Cape, 1927 . . . . £75/£15
Lazarus Laughed, Boni & Liveright (U.S.), 1927 . .
. . . . £200/£20

ditto, Boni & Liveright (U.S.), 1927 (775 signed copies, slipcase) . . . . £200/£150
Strange Interlude, Boni & Liveright (U.S.), 1928 . .
. . . . £250/£25
ditto, Boni & Liveright (U.S.), 1928 (775 signed copies, slipcase) . . . . £200/£150
ditto, Cape, 1928 . . . . £100/£20
The Hairy Ape, Boni & Liveright (U.S.), 1929 (775 signed copies, slipcase and d/w) . . . £200/£125
Dynamo, Boni & Liveright (U.S.), 1929 . £75/£15
ditto, Boni & Liveright (U.S.), 1929 (775 signed copies, slipcase) . . . . £200/£150
Mourning Becomes Electra, Boni & Liveright (U.S.), 1931 . . . . £100/£45
ditto, Boni & Liveright (U.S.), 1931 (550 signed copies, slipcase) . . . . £250/£175
ditto, Boni & Liveright (U.S.), 1931 (50 signed presentation copies) £350
ditto, Cape, 1932 . . . . £100/£20
Ah, Wilderness!, Random House (U.S.), 1933 . . .
. . . . £150/£25
ditto, Random House (U.S.), 1933 (325 signed copies, slipcase). . . . . £300/£250
Days Without End, Random House (U.S.), 1934 . .
. . . . £100/£25
ditto, as *Ah, Wilderness! and Days Without End*, Cape, 1934 . . . . £40/£10
The Iceman Cometh, Random House (U.S.), 1946. .
. . . . £100/£25
ditto, Cape, 1947 . . . . £45/£15
ditto, Limited Editions Club (U.S.), 1982 (2,000 copies illustrated and signed by Leonard Baskin, with lithograph, slipcase) . . . . . . £100/£45
Lost Plays of Eugene O'Neill, New Fathoms Press (U.S.), 1950 . . . . £75/£15
A Moon for the Misbegotten, Random House (U.S.), 1952 . . . . £100/£15
ditto, Cape, 1953 . . . . £25/£10
Nine Plays by Eugene O'Neill, Modern Library (U.S.), 1954 . . . . £75/£15
Long Day's Journey Into Night, Yale Univ. Press (U.S.), 1956 . . . . £150/£25
ditto, Cape, 1956 . . . . £30/£10
A Touch of the Poet, Yale Univ. Press (U.S.), 1957 .
. . . . £75/£15
ditto, Cape, 1957 . . . . £25/£5
Hughie, Yale Univ. Press (U.S.), 1959 . . £75/£10
ditto, Cape, 1962 . . . . £25/£5
More Stately Mansions, Yale Univ. Press (U.S.), 1964
. . . . £75/£15
ditto, Cape, 1965 . . . . £25/£5
The Calms of Capricorn – A Preliminary Edition, Volume 1: The Scenario, Volume 2: The Play, Yale Univ. Press (U.S.), 1981 (wraps) £10
ditto, as *The Calms of Capricorn*, Tichnor & Fields (U.S.), 1982 . . . . £25/£10
Eugene O'Neill: The Unfinished Plays, Continuum (U.S.), 1988 . . . . £15/£5

The Unknown O'Neill: Unpublished and Unfamiliar Writings of Eugene O'Neill, Yale Univ. Press (U.S.), 1988 . . . . £15/£5
Eugene O'Neill: Complete Plays, Library of America (U.S.), 1988 . . . . £20/£5

Others
A Bibliography of the Works of Eugene O'Neill and The Collected Poems of Eugene O'Neill, Random House (U.S.), 1931 . . . . . . £75/£10
Inscriptions: Eugene O'Neill to Carlotta Monterey O'Neill, Yale Univ. Press (U.S.), 1960 (500 numbered copies, slipcase) . . . . . £200/£150
Poems: 1912-1944, Yale Univ. Press (U.S.), 1979 . .
. . . . £15/£5
ditto, Cape, 1980 . . . . £15/£5
Work Diary: 1924-1943, Yale Univ. Press (U.S.), 1981
. . . . £15/£5
Eugene O'Neill At Work: Newly Released Ideas for Plays, Ungar (U.S.), 1981 . . . . . £15/£5
The Theatre We Worked For: The Letters of Eugene O'Neill to Kenneth MacGowran, Yale Univ. Press (U.S.), 1982 . . . . £75/£10
Love, Admiration and Respect: The O'Neill-Commins Correspondence, Duke Univ. Press (U.S.), 1986 . . .
. . . . £50/£10
As Ever, Gene: The Letters of Eugene O'Neill to George Jean Nathan, Fairleigh Univ. Press (U.S.), 1987 . . . . £15/£5
Selected Letters of Eugene O'Neill, Yale Univ. Press (U.S.), 1988 . . . . £35/£10

JOE ORTON
(b.1933 d.1967)

Orton's black farces are a skilful blend of the crude and the clever. His irreverence and ear for comic dialogue are unique.

Plays
Entertaining Mr Sloane, Hamish Hamilton, 1964 . .
. . . . £150/£25
ditto, Grove Press (U.S.), 1965 (wraps) . . . £25
Loot, Methuen, 1967 . . . . . . £125/£15
ditto, Methuen, 1967 (wraps). £20
ditto, Grove Press (U.S.), 1968 . . . . £20
Crimes of Passion, Methuen, 1967 . . . £75/£15
ditto, Methuen, 1967 (wraps). £15
ditto, Grove Press (U.S.), 1968 . . . . £15
What the Butler Saw, Methuen, 1969 . . £100/£15
ditto, Methuen, 1969 (wraps). £15
ditto, Grove Press (U.S.), 1969 . . . . £15
Funeral Games and The Good and Faithful Servant, Methuen, 1970 . . . . £65/£10
ditto, Methuen, 1970 (wraps). £10
Joe Orton: The Complete Plays, Eyre Methuen, 1976.
. . . . £25/£10

ditto, Grove Press (U.S.), 1977 . . . . . £10
Fred and Madge & The Visitors, Nick Hern, 1998 .
. . . . £10/£5

Screenplay
Up Against It, Eyre Methuen, 1979 (wraps) . £15
ditto, Grove Press (U.S.), 1979 (wraps) . . . £15

Novels
Head to Toe, Blond, 1971 . . . . . . £25/£5
ditto, St Martins Press (U.S.), 1971 . . . . £20/£5
Between Us Girls, Nick Hern, 1998 . . . . £10/£5
The Boy Hairdresser, and Lord Cucumber: Two
Novels, Nick Hern, 1999 (with Kenneth Halliwell) .
. . . . £10/£5

Others
The Orton Diaries, Methuen, 1986 . . . . £15/£5
ditto, Harper & Row (U.S.), 1986 . . . . £10/£5

GEORGE ORWELL
(b.1903 d.1950)

A left-wing novelist, essayist and journalist, Orwell, a pseudonym for Eric Blair, is famous for his bleak political satires *Animal Farm* and *Nineteen Eighty Four.*

Novels
Burmese Days, Harper (U.S.), 1934 . . £2,500/£200
ditto, Gollancz, 1935 . . . . . . £3,000/£300
A Clergyman's Daughter, Gollancz, 1935 . . . .
. . . . £4,000/£400
ditto, Harper (U.S.), 1936 . . . . £2,500/£200
Keep the Aspidistra Flying, Gollancz, 1936 . . .
. . . . £2,500/£200
ditto, Harcourt Brace (U.S.), 1956 . . . £75/£15
Coming Up for Air, Gollancz, 1939 . £2,000/£150
ditto, Harcourt Brace (U.S.), 1950 . . . £75/£25
Animal Farm, Secker, 1945 . . . £1,750/£100
ditto, Harcourt Brace (U.S.), 1946 . . . £75/£25
Nineteen Eighty-Four, Secker, 1949 (red d/w). . .
. . . . £1,250/£100
ditto, Secker, 1949 (green d/w) . . . £1,000/£100
ditto, Harcourt Brace (U.S.), 1949 (red d/w) £250/£25
ditto, Harcourt Brace (U.S.), 1949 (blue d/w) £125/£25

Non Fiction
Down and Out in Paris and London, Gollancz, 1933 .
. . . . £3,000/£250
ditto, Harper (U.S.), 1933. . . . . £1,250/£200
The Road to Wigan Pier, Gollancz, 1937 (Left Book
Club Edition). £50
ditto, Gollancz, 1937 . . . . . . £1,000/£125
ditto, Gollancz, 1937 (200 copies of the Left Book
Club Edition bound separately, without the preface) .
. . . . £200

ditto, Supplementary Left Book Club Edition (part one
only, plus photographs) £200
ditto, Harcourt Brace (U.S.), 1958 . . . £50/£15
Homage to Catalonia, Secker, 1938 . . £2,000/£175
ditto, Harcourt Brace (U.S.), 1952 . . . £50/£15
The Lion and the Unicorn, Secker, 1941 (Searchlight
Books, No.1) . . . . £75/£20
James Burnham and the Managerial Revolution,
Socialist Book Centre, 1946 (wraps) . . . £400

Essays
Inside the Whale, Gollancz, 1940 . . £1,000/£75
Critical Essays, Secker, 1946. . . . . £75/£15
ditto, as **Dickens, Dali and Others**, Reynal (U.S.),
1946 . . . . £50/£15
The English People, Collins, 1947 . . . £45/£10
Shooting an Elephant, Secker, 1950 . . £45/£10
ditto, Harcourt Brace (U.S.), 1950 . . . £40/£10
Such, Such Were the Joys, Harcourt Brace (U.S.),
1953 . . . . £50/£15
ditto, as **England, Your England**, Secker, 1953 . .
. . . . £45/£15
The Decline of the English Murder and Other Essays,
Penguin, 1965 (wraps) £10
The War Broadcasts, BBC/Duckworth, 1985 . £15/£5
The War Commentaries, BBC/Duckworth, 1985 . .
. . . . £15/£5

Selected and Collected Editions
The Orwell Reader, Harcourt Brace (U.S.), 1956 . .
. . . . £35/£10
Selected Essays, Penguin, 1957 (wraps). . . £10
Selected Writings, Heinemann, 1958 . . . £15/£5
The Collected Essays, Journalism and Letters, Secker,
1968 (4 vols) . . . . £150/£45
ditto, Harcourt Brace (U.S.), 1968 (4 vols) £145/£40
**The Penguin Complete Longer Non-fiction of George
Orwell**, Penguin, 1983 (wraps) £5

JOHN OSBORNE
(b.1929 d.1994)

The author of *Look Back in Anger*, which won the 1956 Evening Standard Award for Best Play, is best known for his 'kitchen sink' dramas.

Plays
Look Back in Anger, Evans, 1957 (wraps) . . £30
ditto, Faber, 1957 . . . . £60/£15
ditto, Criterion (U.S.), 1957 . . . . £40/£10
The Entertainer, Faber, 1957 . . . . £40/£10
ditto, Criterion (U.S.), 1958 . . . . . £30/£5
Epitaph for George Dillon, Faber, 1958 (with Anthony
Creighton) . . . . £25/£10
ditto, Criterion (U.S.), 1958 . . . . . £15/£5
The World of Paul Slickey, Faber, 1959 . £25/£10
ditto, Criterion (U.S.), 1961 . . . . . £15/£5

A Subject of Scandal and Concern: A Play for
Television, Faber, 1961 . . . . £35/£15
Luther, Faber, 1961 . . . . £25/£10
ditto, Dramatic Publishing Co. (U.S.), 1961. . £15/£5
Plays for England, Faber, 1963 . . . . £25/£10
ditto, Criterion (U.S.), 1964 . . . . . . £15/£5
Inadmissible Evidence, Faber, 1965. . . £25/£10
ditto, Grove Press (U.S.), 1965 . . . . . £15/£5
A Patriot for Me, Faber, 1966 . . . . £25/£10
ditto, Random House (U.S.), 1970 . . . . £15/£5
Time Present and *Hotel in Amsterdam*, Faber, 1968 .
. . . . £20/£5
The Right Prospectus: A Play for Television, Faber,
1970 . . . . £15/£5
Very Like a Whale, Faber, 1971 . . . . . £15/£5
West of Suez, Faber, 1971 . . . . . . £15/£5
The Gift of Friendship, Faber, 1972. . . . £15/£5
A Sense of Detachment, Faber, 1973 . . . £15/£5
*The End of Me Old Cigar, a play, and Jill and Jack, a
play for television*, Faber, 1975. . . . . £15/£5
Watch It Come Down, Faber, 1975 . . . . £15/£5
You're Not Watching Me, Mummy, and *Try a Little
Tenderness*, Faber, 1978 . . . . . . £15/£5
A Better Class of Person and *God Rot Tunbridge
Wells*, Faber, 1985 . . . . £15/£5
Dejavu, Faber, 1992 . . . . £10/£5

Autobiography
*A Better Class of Person: An Autobiography 1929-
1956*, Faber, 1981. . . . . £20/£5
ditto, Dutton (U.S.), 1981. . . . . . . £15/£5
*Almost a Gentleman: An Autobiography, Vol II, 1955
-1966*, Faber, 1991 . . . . £15/£5

Translations/Adaptations
A Bond Honoured, Faber, 1966 (from Lope de Vega's
La Fianza Satisfecha) . . . . . . £20/£5
Hedda Gabler, Faber, 1972 (Ibsen) . . . £15/£5
The Picture of Dorian Gray: A Moral Entertainment,
Faber, 1973 (Oscar Wilde). . . . . £15/£5
A Place Calling Itself Rome, Faber, 1973 (based on
Shakespeare's *Coriolanus*). . . . . . £15/£5
Strindberg's 'The Father' and *Ibsen's 'Hedda
Gabler'*, Faber, 1989. . . . . . . £10/£5

Others
Look Back in Anger, Four Square Books, 1960
(novelisation by John Burke, wraps) . . . £5
The Entertainer, Four Square Books, 1960
(novelisation by John Burke, wraps) . . . £5
Tom Jones: A Film Script, Faber, 1964. . £20/£5
ditto, Grove Press (U.S.), 1964 . . . . £10/£5
Damn You, England: Collected Prose, Faber, 1994 .
. . . . £10/£5

WILFRED OWEN
(b.1893 d.1918)

Owen suffered trench fever and concussion in World
War One and was diagnosed 'shell-shocked'. While
waiting to return to the trenches he drafted and
revised his best poems, but was killed in action only a
week before the Armistice.

Poetry
Poems, Chatto & Windus, 1920 . . . £1,750/£250
ditto, Huebsch (U.S.), n.d. [1921] . . . £850/£200
The Poems of Wilfred Owen, Chatto & Windus, 1931.
. . . . £200/£50
ditto, Viking (U.S.), 1931. . . . . . £125/£45
Thirteen Poems, Gehenna Press (U.S.), 1956
(illustrated by Shahn and Baskin, 400 copies signed
by Baskin, no d/w) £250
ditto, Gehenna Press (U.S.), 1956 (35 copies with
portrait proof, signed by both artists) . . . £1,000
The Collected Poems of Wilfred Owen, Chatto &
Windus, 1963. . . . . £30/£10
ditto, New directions (U.S.), 1964 . . . £25/£10
The Complete Poems and Fragments, Chatto &
Windus, 1983 (2 vols, d/ws and slipcase) . £100/£50
ditto, Norton (U.S.), 1984 (2 vols, d/ws and slipcase) .
. . . . £100/£50

Others
Collected Letters, O.U.P., 1967 . . . . £125/£50

DOROTHY PARKER
(b.1893 d.1967)

An American poet, short story writer and critic,
Parker's work is characterised by her sophisticated
and sardonic wit.

Poetry
Enough Rope, Boni & Liveright (U.S.), 1926 . . .
. . . . £750/£75
Sunset Gun, Boni & Liveright (U.S.), 1928. £50/£20
ditto, Boni & Liveright (U.S.), 1928 (250 signed,
numbered copies) . . . . £300/£200
Death and Taxes, Viking Press (U.S.), 1931 £65/£25
ditto, Viking Press (U.S.), 1931 (250 signed, numbered
copies) . . . . £300/£200
*Not So Deep As A Well, The Collected Poems of
Dorothy Parker*, Viking Press (U.S.), 1936 £40/£15
ditto, Hamish Hamilton, 1937 . . . . £40/£15

Short Stories
Laments For The Living, Viking Press (U.S.), 1930 .
. . . . £100/£20
ditto, Longmans, 1930 . . . . . . £100/£20
After Such Pleasures, Viking Press (U.S.), 1933 . .
. . . . £100/£20

ditto, Viking Press (U.S.), 1933 (250 signed copies,
slipcase) . . . . £350/£300
ditto, Longmans, Green, 1934 . . . . £100/£20
Here Lies, Viking Press (U.S.), 1939 . . . £30/£5
ditto, Longmans, 1939 . . . . £30/£5

THOMAS LOVE PEACOCK
(b.1785 d.1866)

Although he also wrote poetry, Peacock is
remembered as the author of a number of unique, if
odd novels.

Poetry
Palmyra and Other Poems, Richardson, 1806 . £600
The Genius of the Thames, Hookham, 1810 . £300
The Philosophy of Melancholy, Hookham, 1812 £300
Sir Hornbook, or Childe Launcelot's Expedition,
Sharpe & Hailes, 1814 (anonymous) . . £1,000
The Round Table, or King Arthur's Feast, John
Arliss, 1817 (anonymous) £1,000
Rhododaphne, or The Thessalian Spell, Hookham,
1818 (anonymous) £300
ditto, Carey & Son (U.S.), 1818 . . . . £125
Paper Money Lyrics, Reynell, 1837 (100 copies,
anonymous) £500

Novels
Headlong Hall, Hookham, 1816 (anonymous) . £750
Melincourt, Hookham, 1817 (anonymous, 3 vols) . .
. . . . £750
Nightmare Abbey, Hookham, 1818 ('By the Author of
Headlong Hall') £1,000
Maid Marian, Hookham, 1822 ('By the Author of
Headlong Hall') £700
The Misfortunes of Elphin, Hookham, 1829 ('By the
Author of Headlong Hall') £500
Crotchet Castle, Hookham, 1831 ('By the Author of
Headlong Hall') £500
Gryll Grange, Parker, Son, & Bourn, 1861
(anonymous) £250

Others
Gl'Ingannati, The Deceived and Aelia Laelia Crispis,
Chapman & Hall, 1862 (translated by Peacock) £100
Memoirs of Shelley, Frowde, 1909 . . . . £45
The Works of Thomas Love Peacock, Richard
Bentley, 1875 (3 vols) £200

Collected Editions
The Works of Thomas Love Peacock, Bentley, 1875 (3
vols, edited by Henry Cole) £300
*The Halliford Edition of the Works of Thomas Love
Peacock*, Constable, 1923-24 (675 sets, 10 vols,
edited by H.F.B. Brett-Smith and C.E. Jones) . £500

MERVYN PEAKE
(b.1911 d.1968)

Peake's strength in both his writing and drawing is in
the creation of atmosphere through often grotesque
detail. Some of his verse is of the nonsense school.

Poetry
Shapes and Sounds, Chatto & Windus, 1941 £200/£50
ditto, Transatlantic (U.S.), 1941 . . . . £200/£50
Rhymes Without Reason, Eyre & Spottiswoode, 1944
. . . . £150/£30
The Glassblowers, Eyre & Spottiswoode, 1950. . .
. . . . £125/£30
The Rhyme of the Flying Bomb, Dent, 1962 £75/£15
Poems and Drawings, Keepsake Press, 1965 (150
copies, wraps) £250
A Reverie of Bone, Rota, 1967 (320 copies, wraps with
d/w) . . . . £175/£75
Selected Poems, Faber, 1972 . . . . . £35/£10
A Book of Nonsense, Owen, 1972 . . . £35/£10
ditto, Dufour (U.S.), 1975 . . . . . £30/£10
Twelve Poems, 1939-1960, Bran's Head, 1975 (350
numbered copies, wraps with glassine d/w) £175/£150
Swans Die and Towers Fall, Grasshopper Press, 1973
(100 copies, broadside) £150

Novels
Titus Groan, Eyre & Spottiswoode, 1946 (first issue
book, first issue jacket with no quotes). . £300/£50
ditto, Eyre & Spottiswoode, 1946 (second issue book
on cheaper paper, with jacket containing quotes from
reviews and stating 'Second Impression') . £175/£35
ditto, Reynal and Hitchcock (U.S.), 1946 . £75/£20
Gormenghast, Eyre & Spottiswoode, 1950 . £200/£35
ditto, Weybright & Talley (U.S.), 1967 . . £45/£10
Mr Pye, Heinemann, 1953 . . . . . £75/£20
Titus Alone, Eyre & Spottiswoode, 1959 . £150/£30
ditto, Weybright & Talley (U.S.), 1967 . . £45/£10
Boy in Darkness, Wheaton, 1976 (wraps) . . £40
ditto, Hodder, 1996 . . . . £15/£5

Children's Titles
Captain Slaughterboard Drops Anchor, Country Life,
1939 . . . . £3,000/£1,500
ditto, Eyre & Spottiswoode, 1945 . . . £300/£75
ditto, Macmillan (U.S.), 1967 . . . . £30/£10
Letters from a Lost Uncle from Polar Regions, Eyre &
Spottiswoode, 1948 (d/w in form of envelope) . .
. . . . £175/£75

Other Books
The Craft of the Lead Pencil, Wingate, 1946 (no d/w)
. . . . £60
The Drawings of Mervyn Peake, Grey Walls Press,
1949 . . . . £100/£60
Figures of Speech, Gollancz, 1954 . . . £50/£20
The Drawings of Mervyn Peake, Davis-Poynter, 1974
. . . . £30/£10

Mervyn Peake: Writings and Drawings, Academy,
1974 . . . . £25/£10
ditto, St Martin's Press (U.S.), 1974 . . . £25/£10
Peake's Progress: Selected Writings and Drawings,
John Lane, 1979 . . . . £20/£10
ditto, Overlook Press (U.S.), 1981 . . . £20/£10

Books Illustrated by Peake
Ride a Cock-Horse, and other nursery rhymes, Chatto
& Windus, 1940 . . . . £350/£75
ditto, Transatlantic (U.S.), 1944 . . . . £250/£45
The Hunting of the Snark, An agony in eight fits, by
Lewis Carroll, Chatto & Windus, 1941 (yellow
boards) . . . . £75/£20
ditto, by Lewis Carroll, Chatto & Windus, 1941 (large
format, pink boards) . . . . £125/£35
The Adventures of The Young Soldier in search of
The Better World, by C[yril] E[dwin] M[itchinson]
Joad, Faber & Faber, 1943 . . . . . £65/£20
ditto, Arco (U.S.), 1944 . . . . . . £50/£15
All This and Bevin Too, by Quentin Crisp, Nicholson
& Watson, 1943 (wraps) £150
ditto, Mervyn Peake Society, 1978 (40 copies signed
by Crisp) £200
The Rime of the Ancient Mariner, by Samuel Taylor
Coleridge, Chatto & Windus, 1943 . . . £45/£15
Prayers and Graces, A little book of extraordinary
piety, by Allan M. Laing, Gollancz, 1944 . £50/£15
Witchcraft in England, by Christina Hole, Batsford
1945 . . . . £50/£10
ditto, Scribner's (U.S.), 1947 . . . . £45/£10
Alice's Adventures in Wonderland and Through the
Looking-Glass, by Lewis Carroll, Zephyr Books
(Sweden), 1946 (wraps with d/w) . . . £200/£75
ditto, Allan Wingate, 1954 . . . . . £450/£150
ditto, Schocken (U.S.), 1979 . . . . £25/£10
Quest for Sita, by Maurice Collis, Faber, 1946 (500
copies) . . . . £250/£175
ditto, John Day (U.S.), 1947 . . . . £75/£45
Household Tales, by Brothers Grimm, Eyre &
Spottiswoode, 1946 . . . . . . £100/£35
ditto, Schocken (U.S.), 1979 . . . . £25/£10
Dr Jekyll & Mr Hyde, by Robert Louis Stevenson, The
Folio Society, 1948 . . . . £45/£10
ditto, Duchesne, 1948 . . . . . . £45/£10
Treasure Island, by Robert Louis Stevenson, Eyre &
Spottiswoode, 1949 . . . . . . £45/£10
ditto, Schocken (U.S.), 1979 . . . . £25/£10
ditto, Schocken (U.S.), 1979 (wraps) £5
Thou Shalt Not Suffer a Witch and Other Stories, by
Dorothy K. Haynes, Methuen, 1949 . . £75/£25
The Swiss Family Robinson, by Johann R. Wyss,
Heirloom Library, [1949] . . . . . £35/£10
ditto, Chanticleer Press Inc. (U.S.), [1950] . £35/£10
The Wonderful Life & Adventures of Tom Thumb, by
Paul Britten Austin, Radiotjänst (Radio Sweden),
1954 (2 vols, wraps) £125
Men: A Dialogue Between Women, by Allegra Sander,
Cresset Press, 1955 (translated by Vyvyan Holland) .
. . . . £30/£10

Under the Umbrella Tree, The Oxford English Course
for Secondary Schools, by H[enry] B[urgess] Drake,
Oxford Univ. Press, 1957 . . . . . £20
More Prayers and Graces, A second little book of
unusual piety, by Allan M. Laing, Gollancz, 1957 .
. . . . £40/£15
The Pot of Gold and Two Other Tales, by Aaron
Judah, Faber, 1959 . . . . . . £30/£10
Droll Stories, by Honoré de Balzac, The Folio Society,
1961 (translated by Alec Brown, slipcase). £20/£10
Mervyn Peake/Oscar Wilde, by Oscar Wilde, Gordon,
Spilstead, 1980 (200 numbered copies, slipcase) .
. . . . £100/£75
ditto, Sidgwick & Jackson, 1980 . . . . £15/£5
Sketches from Bleak House, Methuen, 1983 £25/£10
A Book of Nonsense, by Edward Lear, Peter Owen,
1972 . . . . £25/£10

ELLIS PETERS
(b.1913 d.1995)

Edith Pargeter has written many books under her own
name and such pseudonyms as 'Jolyon Carr' and
'Peter Benedict'. However, it is as 'Ellis Peters' that
she is best known, giving the world a literary sleuth
who is also a Benedictine monk, the now televised
'Brother Cadfael'.

'Brother Cadfael' Novels
A Morbid Taste for Bones: A Mediaeval Whodunnit,
Macmillan, 1977 . . . . . . £1,000/£75
ditto, Morrow (U.S.), 1978 . . . . £450/£35
One Corpse Too Many, Macmillan, 1979 . £500/£75
ditto, Morrow (U.S.), 1980 . . . . £250/£25
Monk's Hood, Macmillan, 1980 . . . £400/£75
ditto, Morrow (U.S.), 1981 . . . . £100/£15
Saint Peter's Fair, Macmillan, 1981 . . £300/£50
ditto, Morrow (U.S.), 1981 . . . . £100/£15
The Leper of Saint Giles, Macmillan, 1981. £250/£40
ditto, Morrow (U.S.), 1982 . . . . £100/£15
The Virgin in the Ice, Macmillan, 1982. . £200/£25
ditto, Morrow (U.S.), 1983 . . . . £75/£15
The Sanctuary Sparrow, Macmillan, 1983 . £175/£20
ditto, Morrow (U.S.), 1983 . . . . £65/£10
The Devil's Novice, Macmillan, 1983 . . £175/£20
ditto, Morrow (U.S.), 1984 . . . . £65/£10
Dead Man's Ransom, Macmillan, 1984. . £100/£15
ditto, Morrow (U.S.), 1985 . . . . £50/£10
The Pilgrim of Hate, Macmillan, 1984 . . £100/£15
ditto, Morrow (U.S.), 1984 . . . . £40/£5
An Excellent Mystery, Macmillan, 1985 . £100/£15
ditto, Morrow (U.S.), 1985 . . . . £30/£5
The Raven in the Foregate, Macmillan, 1986 £75/£10
ditto, Morrow (U.S.), 1986 . . . . £20/£5
The Rose Rent, Macmillan, 1986 . . . £50/£10
ditto, Morrow (U.S.), 1986 . . . . £20/£5
The Hermit of Eyton Forest, Headline, 1987 £40/£10

ditto, Mysterious Press (U.S.), 1988 . . . . £20/£5
The Confession of Brother Haluin, Headline, 1988 .
. . . . £40/£10
ditto, Mysterious Press (U.S.), 1989 . . . . £20/£5
The Heretic's Apprentice, Headline, 1989 . £35/£10
ditto, Mysterious Press (U.S.), 1990 . . . . £20/£5
The Potter's Field, Headline, 1989 . . . £25/£10
ditto, Mysterious Press (U.S.), 1990 . . . . £20/£5
The Summer of the Danes, Headline, 1991. £25/£10
ditto, Mysterious Press (U.S.), 1990 . . . . £20/£5
The Holy Thief, Headline, 1992 . . . . . £20/£5
ditto, Mysterious Press (U.S.), 1993 . . . . £20/£5
Brother Cadfael's Penance, Headline, 1994 . £15/£5
ditto, Headline, 1994 (97 signed, numbered uncorrected proof copies, wraps) £100

'Brother Cadfael' Short Stories
A Rare Benedict, Headline, 1988 . . . . £35/£10
ditto, Mysterious Press (U.S.), 1989 . . . . £25/£5

The 'Felse' Series
Death and the Joyful Woman, Collins Crime Club,
1961 . . . . £250/£25
ditto, Doubleday (U.S.), 1961 . . . . £100/£25
Flight of a Witch, Collins Crime Club, 1964 £200/£25
ditto, Mysterious Press (U.S.), 1991 . . . . £20/£5
A Nice Derangement of Epitaphs, Collins Crime Club,
1965 . . . . £175/£25
ditto, as **Who Lies Here?**, Morrow (U.S.), 1966 . .
. . . . £125/£25
The Piper on the Mountain, Collins Crime Club, 1966
. . . . £75/£15
ditto, Morrow (U.S.), 1966 . . . . . £45/£10
Black is the Colour of My True-Love's Heart, Collins
Crime Club, 1967 . . . . . . £50/£15
ditto, Morrow (U.S.), 1967 . . . . . £45/£10
The Grass Widow's Tale, Collins Crime Club, 1968 .
. . . . £75/£15
ditto, Morrow (U.S.), 1968 . . . . . £45/£10
The House of Green Turf, Collins Crime Club, 1969 .
. . . . £50/£10
ditto, Morrow (U.S.), 1969 . . . . . £30/£10
Mourning Raga, Macmillan, 1969 . . . £50/£10
ditto, Morrow (U.S.), 1970 . . . . . £20/£5
The Knocker on Death's Door, Macmillan, 1970 . .
. . . . £45/£10
ditto, Morrow (U.S.), 1971 . . . . . £20/£5
Death to the Landlords!, Macmillan, 1972 . £35/£10
ditto, Morrow (U.S.), 1972 . . . . . £20/£5
City of Gold and Shadows, Macmillan, 1973 £30/£10
ditto, Morrow (U.S.), 1974 . . . . . £20/£5
Rainbow's End, Macmillan, 1978 . . . £30/£10
ditto, Morrow (U.S.), 1979 . . . . . £20/£5

Novels as Edith Pargeter
Hortensius, Friend of Nero, Lovat Dickson, 1936 (125
signed copies) . . . . £500/£250
ditto, Greystone Press (U.S.), 1937 . . . £200/£35
Iron-Bound, Lovat Dickson, 1936 . . . £450/£50

The City Lies Foursquare, Heinemann, 1939 £175/£25
ditto, Reynall & Hitchcock (U.S.), 1939. . £125/£25
Ordinary People, Heinemann, 1941 . . . £100/£15
She Goes to War, Heinemann, 1942 . . . £100/£15
The Eighth Champion of Christendom, Heinemann,
1945 . . . . £75/£15
Reluctant Odyssey, Heinemann, 1946 . . £75/£15
Warfare Accomplished, Heinemann, 1947 . £75/£15
By This Strange Fire, Reynal & Hitchcock (U.S.),
1948 . . . . £50/£15
ditto, as **By Firelight**, Heinemann, 1948. . £50/£15
The Fair Young Phoenix, Heinemann, 1948 £45/£15
Lost Children, Heinemann, 1948 . . . £45/£15
Fallen into the Pit, Heinemann, 1951 . . £45/£15
Holiday with Violence, Heinemann, 1952 . £45/£15
This Rough Magic, Heinemann, 1953 . . £45/£15
Most Loving Mere Folly, Heinemann, 1953 £45/£15
The Soldier at the Door, Heinemann, 1954 . £45/£15
A Means of Race, Heinemann, 1956 . . £45/£15
The Heaven Tree, Heinemann, 1960 . . £40/£15
ditto, Doubleday (U.S.), 1960 . . . . . £25/£5
The Green Branch, Heinemann, 1962 . . £35/£10
The Scarlet Seed, Heinemann, 1963 . . . £35/£10
A Bloody Field by Shrewsbury, Macmillan, 1972 . .
. . . . £35/£10
ditto, Viking (U.S.), 1973 . . . . . £25/£5
Sunrise in the West, Macmillan, 1974 . . £35/£10
The Dragon at Noonday, Macmillan, 1975 . £35/£10
The Hounds of Sunset, Macmillan, 1976 . £35/£10
Afterglow and Nightfall, Macmillan, 1977 . £35/£10
The Marriage of Meggotta, Macmillan, 1979 £35/£10
ditto, Viking (U.S.), 1979 . . . . . £25/£5

Short Stories written as Edith Pargeter
The Assize of the Dying, Heinemann, 1958 . £75/£15
ditto, Doubleday (U.S.), 1958 . . . . £45/£10
The Lily Hand, Heinemann, 1965 . . . £100/£15

Novels written as 'Ellis Peters'
Death Mask, Collins Crime Club, 1959 . . £200/£35
ditto, Doubleday (U.S.), 1960 . . . . £125/£25
The Will and the Deed, Collins Crime Club, 1960 . .
. . . . £125/£20
ditto, as **Where There's a Will**, Doubleday (U.S.), 1960
. . . . £100/£15
Funeral of Figaro, Collins Crime Club, 1962 £75/£15
ditto, Morrow (U.S.), 1964 . . . . . £45/£10
The Horn of Roland, Macmillan, 1974 . . £65/£15
ditto, Morrow (U.S.), 1974 . . . . . £40/£10
Never Pick Up Hitchhikers!, Macmillan, 1976 . . .
. . . . £50/£10
ditto, Morrow (U.S.), 1976 . . . . . £30/£10

Novels written as 'Jolyon Carr'
Murder in the Dispensary, Herbert Jenkins, 1938 . .
. . . . £250/£45
ditto, Post Mortem Books (U.S.), 1999 (350 signed,
numbered copies, no d/w) £25
Freedom for Two, Herbert Jenkins, 1938 . £250/£45

Death Comes by Post, Herbert Jenkins, 1940   £250/£45
Masters of the Parachute Mail, Herbert Jenkins, 1940
. . . . £250/£45

Novels written as 'John Redfern'
The Victim Needs a Nurse, Jarrolds, 1940 . £250/£45

Others
The Coast of Bohemia, Heinemann, 1950 (by Edith
Pargeter) . . . . £100/£25
Shropshire, A Memoir of the English Countryside,
Macdonald, 1990. . . . . . . £30/£10
ditto, Mysterious Press (U.S.), 1993 . . . £35/£10
Strongholds and Sanctuaries, Sutton, 1993   £35/£10

HAROLD PINTER
(b.1930)

A playwright who created, in his best work, a
'comedy of menace'; claustrophobic situations in
which there is an indefinable threat hanging over the
characters.

Plays
The Birthday Party, Encore Publishing, [1959] (wraps)
. . . . £150
The Birthday Party and Other Plays, Methuen, 1960
(*The Dumb Waiter* & *The Room*) . . . £65/£15
The Caretaker, Encore Publishing, 1960 (wraps) £100
ditto, Methuen, 1960 . . . . . . £65/£15
ditto, Methuen, 1960 (wraps). £15
ditto, Grove (U.S.), 1960 . . . . . £25/£10
A Night Out, French, 1961 (wraps) £25
ditto, Grove (U.S.), 1967 . . . . . . £30/£5
A Slight Ache and Other Plays, Methuen, 1961 .
. . . . £40/£10
The Birthday Party and The Room, Grove (U.S.),
1961 . . . . £25/£10
The Collection, French, 1962 . . . . £15
Three Plays, Grove (U.S.), 1962 (*A Slight Ache, The
Collection* and *The Dwarfs*) . . . . . £25/£5
The Collection and The Lover, Methuen, 1963 . .
. . . . £35/£10
The Lover, Dramatists Play Service (U.S.), 1965 £15
The Dwarfs and Eight Review Sketches, Dramatists
Play Service (U.S.), 1965 (wraps) £20
The Homecoming, Methuen, 1965 . . . . £30/£5
ditto, Grove (U.S.), 1966 . . . . . . £25/£5
ditto, as **The Homecoming: Images**, by Harold Cohen,
Cohen, 1968 (175 numbered copies, nine lithographs,
slipcase) . . . . £100/£75
ditto, Cohen, 1968 (25 copies, additional set of plates,
slipcase) . . . . £175/£125
Tea Party, Methuen, 1965 . . . . . £25/£5
ditto, Vanista (Zagreb), 1965 (280 numbered copies,
wraps). £50
ditto, Grove (U.S.), 1966 . . . . . . £20/£5

**The Lover, Tea Party, The Basement: Two Plays & A
Filmscript**, Grove (U.S.), 1967 . . . . £35/£10
Tea Party and Other Plays, Methuen, 1967. . £20/£5
**A Night Out, Night School, Revue Sketches: Early
Plays**, Grove, 1967 . . . . £25/£10
Landscape, Pendragon Press, 1968 (2,000 numbered
copies, no d/w) £45
Landscape and Silence, Methuen, 1969. . . £30/£5
ditto, Grove (U.S.), 1970 . . . . . . £25/£5
Old Times, Methuen, 1971 . . . . . . £25/£5
ditto, Karnac, 1971 (150 signed, numbered copies) .
. . . . £125
ditto, Grove (U.S.), 1973 . . . . . . £20/£5
Monologue, Covent Garden Press, 1973 . £25/£10
ditto, Covent Garden Press, 1973 (100 signed copies in
slipcase) . . . . £125/£100
No Man's Land, Methuen, 1975. . . . . £25/£5
ditto, Karnac, 1975 (150 signed, numbered copies,
glassine d/w) £100
ditto, Grove (U.S.), 1975 . . . . £20/£5
Betrayal, Methuen, 1978 . . . . . . £20/£5
ditto, Grove (U.S.), 1979 . . . . £15/£5
The Hothouse, Methuen, 1980 . . . . £20/£5
ditto, Grove (U.S.), 1980 . . . . £15/£5
Family Voices, Next Editions/Faber, 1981 (spiral
bound in wraps) £15
ditto, Grove (U.S.), 1981 . . . . . . £15/£5
Other Places, Methuen, 1982 . . . . . £15/£5
ditto, Grove (U.S.), 1983 . . . . £10/£5
One for the Road, Methuen, 1985 . . . . £15/£5
Mountain Language, Faber, 1988 . . . £15/£5
ditto, Grove (U.S.), 1988 . . . . £10/£5
The Heat of the Day, Faber, 1989 . . . £15/£5
ditto, Grove (U.S.), 1990 . . . . . . £10/£5
Party Time, Faber, 1991 . . . . . . £15/£5
ditto, Grove (U.S.), 1993 (wraps) £5
Moonlight, Faber, 1993 . . . . . . £10/£5
ditto, Grove (U.S.), 1993 (wraps) £5
Ashes to Ashes, Faber, 1996 (wraps) . . . £5
ditto, Grove (U.S.), 1997 (wraps) £5

Omnibus Editions
Plays 1-4, Methuen, 1975-1981 (4 vols). . £50/£20
ditto, as **Complete Works, Volumes 1-4**, Grove, 1977-
1981 (4 vols) . . . . £50/£20

Poetry
Poems, Enitharmon Press, 1968 (wraps, with erratum
slip) £25
ditto, Enitharmon Press, 1968 (200 signed copies, no
d/w) £125
ditto, Enitharmon Press, 1971 (enlarged edition,
boards) £25
ditto, Enitharmon Press, 1971 (wraps) . . . £15
ditto, Enitharmon Press, 1971 (100 signed copies) .
. . . . £100
Poems and Prose, 1949-1977, Grove Press, 1978 . .
. . . . £20/£5
ditto, Methuen, 1978 . . . . £20/£5

ditto, as *Collected Poems and Prose*, Methuen, 1986 .
. . . . £15/£5
I Know The Place, Greville Press, 1979 (500 signed
copies, no d/w) £45
11 Early Poems, Greville Press, 1992 (wraps) . £15

Novel
The Dwarfs, Faber, 1990 . . . . £20/£5
ditto, London Limited Editions, 1990 (150 signed
copies) £75
ditto, Grove (U.S.), 1990 . . . . £20/£5

Others
Mac, Pendragon Press, 1968 (2,000 numbered copies,
no d/w) £30
Five Screenplays, Methuen, 1971 . . . £40/£10
ditto, Methuen, 1971 (wraps). £10
ditto, Karnac, 1971 (150 signed, numbered copies, no
d/w) £150
ditto, Grove (U.S.), 1973 . . . . . . £30/£10
The Proust Screenplay, Grove (U.S.), 1977 . £15/£5
ditto, Methuen, 1978 . . . . £15/£5
The Screenplay of the French Lieutenant's Woman,
Cape, 1981 . . . . £20/£5
ditto, Little, Brown (U.S.), 1981 . . . . £20/£5
ditto, Little, Brown (U.S.), 1981 (360 signed,
numbered copies, slipcase) . . . . £125/£75
*The French Lieutenant's Woman and Other
Screenplays*, Methuen, 1982 . . . . . £20/£5
The Comfort of Strangers and Other Screenplays,
Faber, 1990 . . . . £15/£5
Various Voices - Prose, Poetry, Politics 1948-1998,
Faber, 1998 . . . . £15/£5
ditto, Grove Press (U.S.), 1998 . . . . . £15/£5

SYLVIA PLATH
(b.1932 d.1963)

An American poet whose poems display an ironic
tone and an undercurrent of terror. Married to Ted
Hughes, she committed suicide in 1963.

Sculptor, Grecourt Review, 1959 (25 copies, wraps) .
. . . . £1,250
A Winter Ship, Tragara Press (Edinburgh), 1960
(anonymous leaflet) £1,500
The Colossus, Heinemann, 1960. . . £1,250/£150
ditto, as *The Colossus and Other Poems*, Knopf (U.S.),
1962 . . . . £200/£45
ditto, Heinemann, 1967 . . . . . . £15/£5
Ariel, Faber, 1965 . . . . £400/£30
ditto, Harper (U.S.), 1966 . . . . . £100/£15
Uncollected Poems, Turret Books, 1965 (150 copies,
wraps). £350
Wreath for a Bridal, Sceptre Press, 1970 (150 copies,
wraps). £75

Million Dollar Month, Sceptre Press, 1971 (150
copies, wraps) £75
Fiesta Melons, Rougemont Press, 1971 (75 copies of
150, signed by Ted Hughes) . . . . £300/£225
ditto, Rougemont Press, 1971 (75 unsigned copies of
150) . . . . £200/£125
Child, Rougemont Press, 1971 (325 copies, wraps with
d/w) . . . . £75/£40
Crystal Gazer and Other Poems, Rainbow Press, 1971
(300 copies, slipcase) . . . . . . £200/£125
ditto, Rainbow Press, 1971 (80 morocco bound copies)
. . . . £750
ditto, Rainbow Press, 1971 (20 vellum bound copies) .
. . . . £1,000
Lyonesse, Rainbow Press, 1971 (300 copies bound in
quarter leather, slipcase). . . . . . £200/£150
ditto, Rainbow Press, 1971 (90 copies bound in full
calf) £750
ditto, Rainbow Press, 1971 (10 bound in vellum) . .
. . . . £1,000
Crossing the Water, Faber, 1971. . . . £75/£15
ditto, as *Crossing the Water: Transitional Poems*,
Harper (U.S.), 1971 . . . . £50/£15
Winter Trees, Faber, 1971 . . . . £35/£10
ditto, Harper (U.S.), 1972. . . . . . . £25/£5
Pursuit, Rainbow Press, 1973 (100 numbered copies,
with an etching and drawings by Leonard Baskin,
slipcase) . . . . £1,000/£750
Two Poems, Sceptre Press, [1980] (225 of 300 copies,
wraps). £35
ditto, Sceptre Press, [1980] (75 'especial' of 300
copies, wraps) £75
Two Uncollected Poems, Anvil Press, 1980 (450
copies, wraps) £30
Collected Poems, Faber, 1981 . . . . . £30/£5
ditto, Harper (U.S.), 1981. . . . . . . £20/£5
Dialogue Over a Ouija Board, Rainbow Press, 1981
(140 copies, slipcase) . . . . . . £275/£200
The Green Rock, Embers Handpress, 1982 (160
numbered copies, wraps, slipcase) £150

Novel
The Bell Jar, Heinemann, 1963 (pseud. 'Victoria
Lucas') . . . . £1,750/£500
ditto, Faber, 1966 (as 'Sylvia Plath'). . . £500/£50
ditto, Harper (U.S.), 1971 (as 'Sylvia Plath') £75/£15

Plays
Three Women: A Monologue for Three Voices, Turret
Books, 1968 (180 copies, glassine d/w) . £300/£200

Children's Title
The Bed Book, Faber, 1976 (illustrations by Quentin
Blake). . . . . £125/£30
ditto, Harper (U.S.), 1976. . . . . £75/£15

Others
The Art of Sylvia Plath: A Symposium, Faber, 1970 .
. . . . £65/£20
Letters Home, Harper (U.S.), 1975 . . . . £25/£5

ditto, Faber, 1976 . . . .£25/£5
***Johnny Panic and the Bible of Dreams and Other
Writings***, Faber, 1977 . . . . . £50/£10
ditto, as ***Johnny Panic and the Bible of Dreams: Short
Stories, Prose and Diary Excerpts***, Harper (U.S.),
1979 . . . . £50/£10
A Day in June: an Uncollected Short Story, Embers
Handpress, 1981 (160 numbered copies, wraps) £175
The Journals of Sylvia Plath, Dial Press (U.S.), 1982 .
. . . . £25/£10
***The Magic Mirror: A Study of the Doublein Two of
Dostoevsky's Novels***, Embers Handpress, 1989 (50
copies, 'Oxford Hollow' binding, slipcase) £300/£200
ditto, Embers Handpress, 1989 (176 copies, in d/w) .
. . . .£175/£100
The Journals of Sylvia Plath 1950-1962, Faber, 2000.
. . . .£25/£5

EDGAR ALLAN POE
(b.1809 d.1849)

An American poet and short story writer, Poe is best
known for often anthologised horror tales such as
'The Fall of the House of Usher'. 'The Murder in the
Rue Morgue' signalled the birth of the detective
fiction genre.

Poetry
Tamerlane and Other Poems, Calvin F.S. Thomas
(U.S.), 1827 ('by a Bostonian', wraps). . £200,000
ditto, Redway, 1884 (100 copies) £2,500
Al AAraaf, Tamerlane and Minor Poems, Hatch &
Dunning (U.S.), 1829 . . . . . £75,000
Poems, Elam Bliss (U.S.), 1831 (claims wrongly to be
the second edition) £25,000
The Raven and Other Poems, Wiley & Putnam (U.S.),
1845 (first issue with 'T.B. Smith, Stereotyper' on
copyright page, wraps) £65,000
ditto, Wiley & Putnam, 1845 (cloth). . . £50,000

Fiction
The Narrative of Arthur Gordon Pym of Nantucket,
Harper Bros. (U.S.), 1838 (anonymous) . .£3,000
ditto, Wiley & Putnam, 1838 (cloth). . . .£2,000
Tales of the Grotesque and Arabesque, Lea &
Blanchard (U.S.), 1840 (page 213 wrongly numbered,
2 vols). £17,500
ditto, Lea & Blanchard (U.S.), 1840 (page 213
correctly numbered, 2 vols) £12,500
ditto, Lea & Blanchard (U.S.), 1840 (page 213
correctly numbered, 1 vol.) £7,500
***The Murders in the Rue Morgue, and the Man that
was Used Up***, William H. Graham (U.S.), 1843
(wraps) £15,000
The Tales, Wiley & Putnum (U.S.), 1845 (wraps) .
. . . . £30,000
ditto, Wiley & Putnam, 1845 . . . . £15,000
Eureka, A Prose Poem, Putnam (U.S.), 1848 . £2,500

Others
The Conchologist's First Book, Haswell, Barrington &
Baswell (U.S.), 1839 (coloured plates). . .£1,500
ditto, Haswell, Barrington & Baswell (U.S.), 1839
(uncoloured plates) £1,000
ditto, 1840 (second edition) £250
Mesmerism, 'In Articulo Mortis', Short & Co., 1846
(wraps) £1,750

WILLY POGÁNY
(b.1882 d.1955)

A Hungarian illustrator who, at his best, was an equal
to Rackham and Dulac.

The Welsh Fairy Book, by W. Jenkyn Thomas, Unwin,
[1907] (100 illustrations by Pogány) . . . £150
ditto, Stokes (U.S.), 1913. . . . . . £150
The Adventures of a Dodo, by G.E. Farrow, Unwin,
[1907] (70 illustrations by Pogány). . . . £65
Milly and Olly, by Mrs Humphry Ward, Unwin, 1907
(48 illustrations by Pogány). £40
Confessions of an English Opium Eater, by Thomas
De Quincey, Collins, [1908] £30
Faust, J.W. von Goethe, Hutchinson, 1908 (30 full
page colour plates) £150
ditto, Hutchinson, 1908 (deluxe edition limited to 250
copies, signed by the artist, 31 full page colour plates)
. . . .£1,250
A Treasury of Verse for Little Children, Harrap,
[1908]. £100
Rubaiyat of Omar Khayyam, Harrap, [1909] (24
colour illustrations by Pogány) £150
ditto, Harrap, [1909] (525 signed copies) . . £500
ditto, Harrap, [1909] (25 deluxe, signed copies) £1,500
Tanglewood Tales, by Nathaniel Hawthorne, Unwin,
[1909]. £50
Norse Wonder Tales, by Sir George Dasent, Collins,
[1909]. £20
Gisli the Outlaw, by Sir George Dasent, Harrap, [1909]
. . . . £20
The Blue Lagoon, by H. de Vere Stacpoole, Unwin,
1910 . . . . £175
Folk Tales from Many Lands, by Lilian Gask, Harrap,
1910 . . . . £100
ditto, Crowell (U.S.), 1910 . . . . . £75
The Witch's Kitchen, by Gerald Young, Harrap,
[1910]. £40
The Rime of the Ancent Mariner, by S.T. Coleridge,
Harrap, 1910 (20 mounted colour plates) . . £650
ditto, Crowell (U.S.), 1910 . . . . . £250
ditto, Harrap, 1910 (525 signed, numbered copies). .
. . . .£2,000
ditto, Harrap, 1910 (25 deluxe, signed copies) . £2,500
Tannhauser, by T.W. Rolleston (after R. Wagner),
Harrap, [1911] £150

ditto, Harrap, [1911] (525 signed, numbered copies) .
. . . . £500
Parsifal, by T.W. Rolleston (after R. Wagner), Harrap,
1912 . . . . £150
ditto, Harrap, 1912 (525 signed, numbered copies). .
. . . . £500
The Fairies and the Christmas Child, by Lilian Gask,
Harrap, [1912] £40
Atta Troll, by Heinrich Heine, Sidgwick & Jackson,
1913 . . . . £60
The Hungarian Fairy Book, by Nandor Pogány,
Unwin, 1913 . . . . £125
Forty-Four Turkish Fairy Tales, by Ignacz Kunos,
Harrap, [1913] £50
ditto, Harrap, [1913] (leather-bound edition) . £70
The Tale of Lohengrin, by T.W. Rolleston (after R.
Wagner), Harrap, [1913] £150
ditto, Harrap, [1913] (525 signed, numbered copies) .
. . . . £500
Willy Pogány Children, Harrap, [1914] (5 volumes:
*Children at the Pole, Hiawatha, Red Riding Hood,
Robinson Crusoe* and *The Three Bears*) . £75 each
The Children in Japan, by Grace Bartruse, Harrap,
[1915]. £20
Cinderella, by E.L. Elias, Harrap, [1915] . . £40
The Gingerbread Man, by Lionel Fable, Harrap,
[1915]. £50
Mother Goose, [anon.], Harrap, [1915] . . . £30
More Tales from The Arabian Nights, by Frances J.
Olcott, Holt (U.S.), 1915 . . . . . £45
Home Book of Verse for Young Children, edited by
B.E. Stevenson, Holt (U.S.), 1915 . . . . £25
Stories to Tell the Little Ones, by Sara Cone Bryant,
Houghton Mifflin (U.S.), 1918 . . . . . £25
ditto, Harrap, 1918 . . . . £25
The King of Ireland's Son, by Padraic Colum,
Macmillan (U.S.), 1916 . . . . . . £25
ditto, Harrap, 1920 . . . . £50/£25
Bible Stories to Read and Tell, by Frances J. Olcott,
Houghton Mifflin (U.S.), 1916 . . . . . £15
Tales of the Persian Genii, by Frances J. Olcott,
Houghton Mifflin (U.S.), 1917 . . . . . £30
ditto, Harrap, 1919 . . . . £25
Gulliver's Travels, by Jonathan Swift, Macmillan
(U.S.), 1917 . . . . £50
ditto, Harrap, 1919 . . . . £50
Little Tailor of the Winding Way, by Gertrude
Crownfield, Macmillan (U.S.), 1917 . . . £20
Polly's Garden, by Helen Ward Banks, Macmillan
(U.S.), 1918 . . . . £30
The Adventures of Odysseus and the Tale of Troy, by
Padraic Colum, Macmillan (U.S.), 1918 . . £50
ditto, Harrap, 1920 . . . . £100/£50
Children's Plays, by Eleanor & Ada Skinner, Appleton
(U.S.), 1919 . . . . £20
ditto, Appleton, 1919 . . . . £20
Uncle Davie's Children, by Agnes McClelland
Daulton, Macmillan (U.S.), 1920 . . . £50/£20

The Children of Odin: A Book of Northern Myths, by
Padraic Colum, Macmillan (U.S.), 1920 . £65/£25
ditto, Harrap, 1922 . . . . £65/£25
*The Golden Fleece, and the Heroes Who Lived Before
Achilles*, by Padraic Colum, Macmillan (U.S.), 1921.
. . . . £65/£25
The Adventures of Haroun el Raschid, by Frances J.
Olcott, Holt (U.S.), 1923 . . . . . £65/£25
The Song of Bilitis, by Pierre Louys, Macy-Massius
(U.S.), 1926 (2,000 copies signed by Pogány). . .
. . . . £150/£75
Fairy Flowers, by Isidora Newman, Holt (U.S.), 1926.
. . . . £300/£200
ditto, Milford, [1926] . . . . £300/£200
George Washington Goes Around the World, by
Margaret L. Thomas, Nelson (U.S.), 1927 . £50/£25
ditto, Nelson, 1927 . . . . £40/£15
Looking Out For Jimmie, by Helen H. Flanders,
Dutton (U.S.), 1927 . . . . £50/£25
ditto, Dent, [1928] . . . . £50/£25
Tisza Tales, by Rosika Schwimmer, Doubleday Doran
(U.S.), 1928 . . . . £70/£40
Alice's Adventures in Wonderland, by Lewis Carroll,
Dutton (U.S.), 1929 . . . . £50/£15
ditto, Dutton (U.S.), 1929 (200 signed, numbered
copies) . . . . £750/£500
Willy Pogány's Mother Goose, Nelson (U.S.), [1929] .
. . . . £200/£125
ditto, Nelson, [1929] . . . . £200/£125
ditto, Nelson (U.S.), [1929] (500 signed copies) £650
Casanova Jones, by Joseph Anthony, Century (U.S.),
1930 . . . . £65/£20
Magyar Fairy Tales, by Nandor Pogány, Dutton
(U.S.), 1930 . . . . £100/£65
The Kasidah of Haji Abdu El-Yezdi, McKay (U.S.),
1931 . . . . £100/£65
The Light of Asia, by Edwin Arnold, McKay (U.S.),
1932 . . . . £75/£30
The Song Celestial, by Edwin Arnold, McKay (U.S.),
1934 . . . . £75/£30
My Poetry Book, edited by G.T. Huffard and L.M.
Carlisle, Winston (U.S.), 1934 . . . . £45/£15
The Wimp and the Woodle, by Helen von Kolnitz
Hyer, Suttonhouse (U.S.), 1935. . . . £65/£30
The Goose Girl of Nurnberg, by H.S. Hawley, Sutton-
house (U.S.), 1936 . . . . £65/£30
Coppa Hamba, by Blanche Ambrose, Suttonhouse
(U.S.), 1936 . . . . £65/£30
How Santa Found the Cobbler's Shop, by Margaretta
Harmon, Suttonhouse (U.S.), 1936. . . £65/£30
Sonnets from the Portugese, by Elizabeth Barrett
Browning, Crowell (U.S.), 1936 . . . £75/£25
The Golden Cockerel, by Alexander Pushkin, Nelson
(U.S.), 1938 . . . . £75/£25
Peterkin, by Elaine and Willy Pogány, McKay (U.S.),
1940 . . . . £125/£45
Bookplates, Original Etchings, Castle (U.S.), 1940 .
. . . . £65/£30

Rubaiyat of Omar Khyyam, McKay (U.S.), 1942 . .
. . . . £45/£25
The Frenzied Prince: Being Heroic Stories of Ancient Ireland, by Padraic Colum, McKay (U.S.), 1943 . .
. . . . £45/£20
Running Away with Nebby, by Philis Garrard, McKay (U.S.), 1944 . . . . £35/£10
Willy Pogány's Drawing Lessons, McKay (U.S.), 1946 (no d/w) £45
ditto, as *The Art of Drawing*, A.S. Barnes (U.S.)/ Yoseloff (U.K.), 1968 . . . . . . £35/£15
Willy Pogány's Water-Colour Lessons, McKay (U.S.), 1950 . . . . £40/£20
Willy Pogány's Oil Painting Lessons, McKay (U.S.), 1954 . . . . £40/£20

BEATRIX POTTER
(b.1866 d.1943)

British author and illustrator. *The Tale of Peter Rabbit* was first written down in a letter to the son of one of her governesses. It was later privately printed in an edition of 250 copies, the first of a highly successful series of books for the very young.

The Tale of Peter Rabbit, privately printed, [1901] (250 copies, flat spine) £50,000
ditto, privately printed, 1902 (200 copies, round spine) £15,000
ditto, Warne, [1902] (trade edition, cloth) . . £4,000
ditto, Warne, 1902 (trade edition, boards) . . £3,000
ditto, Warne, 1902 (deluxe edition) £5,000
ditto, Warne, 1993 (boxed set containing facsimiles of the 1901 first edition, the first Warne cloth-bound edition of 1902, and the original 'Peter Rabbit' letter from Beatrix Potter, 750 numbered sets) . £200/£125
The Tailor of Gloucester, privately printed, 1902 (500 copies) £6,500
ditto, Warne, 1903 (trade edition) . . . £3,000
ditto, Warne, 1903 (deluxe edition) £6,000
ditto, Warne, 1903 (art cloth binding) . . . £5,000
ditto, Warne, 1903 (facsimile of the original manuscript and illustrations, 1,500 numbered copies in box) . . . . £75/£45
ditto, Warne, 1969 (facsimile of the original manuscript) £45
The Tale of Squirrel Nutkin, Warne, 1903 . . £1,500
ditto, Warne, 1903 (deluxe edition) . . . £7,500
ditto, Warne, 1903 (art cloth binding) . . . £3,000
The Tale of Benjamin Bunny, Warne, 1904 . £1,500
ditto, Warne, 1904 (deluxe edition) . . . £3,500
The Tale of Two Bad Mice, Warne, 1904 . £800
ditto, Warne, 1904 (deluxe edition) £3,500
The Tale of Mrs Tiggy-Winkle, Warne, 1905 . £800
ditto, Warne, 1905 (deluxe edition) £5,000
The Pie and the Patty Pan, Warne, 1905 (large format) £1,000

ditto, Warne, 1905 (deluxe edition) £4,000
The Tale of Mr Jeremy Fisher, Warne, 1906 . £750
ditto, Warne, 1906 (deluxe edition) £4,500
The Story of a Fierce Bad Rabbit, Warne, 1906 (panorama) £900
The Story of Miss Moppet, Warne, 1906 (panorama) £900
The Tale of Tom Kitten, Warne, 1907 . . . £750
ditto, Warne, 1907 (deluxe edition) £4,500
The Tale of Jemima Puddle-Duck, Warne, 1908 £750
ditto, Warne, 1908 (deluxe edition) £5,000
The Roly-Poly Pudding, Warne, 1908 (large format) £750
ditto, as *The Tale of Samuel Whiskers*, Warne, [1926] £250
The Tale of the Flopsy Bunnies, Warne, 1909 . £1,250
ditto, Warne, 1909 (deluxe edition) . . . £5,000
Ginger and Pickles, Warne, 1909 (large format) £500
The Tale of Mrs Tittlemouse, Warne, 1910. . £650
ditto, Warne, 1910 (deluxe edition) £4,500
Peter Rabbit's Painting Book, Warne, [1911] . £650
The Tale of Timmy Tiptoes, Warne, 1911 . . £650
ditto, Warne, 1911 (deluxe edition) £2,250
The Tale of Mr Tod, Warne, 1912 . . . . £650
The Tale of Pigling Bland, Warne, 1913 . . £650
Appley Dapply's Nursery Rhymes, Warne, 1917 £650
Tom Kitten's Painting Book, Warne, 1917 . . £500
The Tale of Johnny Town-Mouse, Warne, [1918] £650
Cecily Parsley's Nursery Rhymes, Warne, 1922 (small format) £750
Jemima Puddle-Duck's Painting Book, Warne, [1925] £400
Peter Rabbit's Almanac for 1929, Warne, [1928] £1,000
The Fairy Caravan, McKay (U.S.), 1929 . £150
ditto, privately printed, 1929 (100 copies) . . £4,500
ditto, Warne, 1952. . . . . . . £100/£50
The Tale of Little Pig Robinson, Warne, [1930] (large format) . . . . £750/£250
Sister Anne, McKay (U.S.), 1932 . . . . £250
Wag-By-Wall, Warne, [1944] (100 copies) . . £500
Jemima Puddle-Duck's Painting Book, From the Original Designs by B. Potter, Warne [1954]. £75
Jeremy Fisher's Painting Book, From the Original Designs by B. Potter, Warne, [1954] . . . £75
Peter Rabbit's Painting Book, From the Original Designs by B. Potter, Warne, [1954] . . . £75
Tom Kitten's Painting Book, From the Original Designs by B. Potter, Warne, [1954] . . . £75
The Tale of the Faithful Dove, Warne, [1955] (100 copies, illustrated by Marie Angel). . . . £1,000
The Sly Old Cat, Warne, 1971 (issued with d/w) . . . . £40/£10
The Tale of Tupenny, Warne, 1973 (illustrated by Marie Angel). . . . . £30/£5

EZRA POUND
(b.1885 d.1972)

An American poet, Pound is generally acknowledged as one of the prime movers of modern poetry.

Poetry

A Lume Spento, Antonini (Venice), 1908 (150 copies, wraps). £30,000
ditto, New Directions (U.S.), 1965 (acetate d/w) . .
. . . . £45/£15
ditto, Faber, 1965 . . . . £25/£5
A Quinzane for this Yule, Pollock & Co, 1908 (100 copies, wraps) £20,000
ditto, printed for Elkin Mathews, 1908 (100 copies, wraps). £10,000
Personae, Elkin Mathews, 1909 (500 copies, first issue binding with the five lines of type on spine measuring 2 cm) £600
ditto, Elkin Mathews, 1909 (500 copies, second issue binding with type on spine measuring 1.5 cm) £500
ditto, Boni & Liveright (U.S.), 1926 . . . £1,000/£150
Exultations, Elkin Mathews, 1909 (500 copies) £400
Provença, Small Maynard (U.S.), [1910] (200 copies, tan boards stamped in dark brown). . . . £500
ditto, Small Maynard (U.S.), [1917] (later issue, tan boards stamped in green) £100
Canzoni, Elkin Mathews, 1911 (grey cloth, author's name on cover) £400
ditto, Elkin Mathews, 1911 (brown boards, without author's name on cover). £200
Ripostes, Stephen Swift, 1912 . . . . £500
ditto, Small Maynard (U.S.), 1913 . . . £250
Lustra, Elkin Mathews, [1916] (200 numbered copies, unexpurgated version for private circulation) . £1,000
ditto, Elkin Mathews, 1916 (expurgated trade edition).
. . . . £600
ditto, Knopf (U.S.), 1917 . . . . . £1,250/£400
Pavannes and Divisions, Knopf (U.S.), 1918 (first binding, blue cloth stamped in gold) . . . £150
ditto, Knopf (U.S.), 1918 (later bindings stamped in green). £100
ditto, Peter Owen, 1960 . . . . . £35/£10
Quia Pauper Amavi, The Egoist, [1919] (100 signed copies, handmade paper) £2,250
ditto, The Egoist, [1919] (10 signed copies, roman numerals). £5,000
ditto, The Egoist, [1919] £400
The Fourth Canto, Ovid Press, 1919 (40 copies for private circulation) £6,000
Hugh Selwyn Mauberley, Ovid Press, 1920 (165 unsigned copies) £2,500
ditto, Ovid Press, 1920 (35 signed copies) . £5,000
Umbra, Elkin Mathews, 1920 . . . £400/£150
ditto, Elkin Mathews, 1920 (100 signed copies) £2,500
ditto, Elkin Mathews, 1920 (signed, lettered copies) .
. . . . £5,000
Poems, 1918-21, Boni & Liveright (U.S.), 1921 . .
. . . . £500/£175

Indiscretions; Or, Une Revue de Deux Mondes, Three Mountains Press, 1923 (300 numbered copies) £750
ditto, Three Mountains Press, 1923 (300 numbered copies, unbound sheets) £300
A Draft of XVI Cantos, Three Mountains Press, 1925 (90 copies) £1,500
A Draft of Cantos 12-27, Three Mountain Press, 1928
. . . . £500
Selected Poems, Faber, 1928 (100 signed copies) . .
. . . . £2,000
ditto, Faber, 1928 . . . . £350/£100
A Draft of XXX Cantos, Hours Press, 1930 (200 unsigned copies) £1,500
ditto, Hours Press, 1930 (10 signed copies) . £7,500
ditto, Farrar & Rinehart (U.S.), 1933 ('shit' on page 62). £1,000
ditto, Farrar & Rinehart (U.S.), 1933 ('sh-t' on page 62). . . . . £250/£45
ditto, Faber, 1933 . . . . £175/£35
Imaginary Letters, Black Sun Press (Paris), 1930 (50 signed copies on Japanese vellum, wraps with glassine d/w and slipcase) . . £2,500/£2,000
ditto, Black Sun Press (Paris), 1930 (300 copies, wraps with glassine d/w and slipcase) . . . . £500/£350
Eleven New Cantos: XXXI-XLI, Farrar & Rinehart (U.S.), 1934 . . . . £150/£40
ditto, as *Draft of Cantos XXXI-XLI*, Faber, 1935 . .
. . . . £125/£30
Homage to Sextus Propertius, Faber, 1934. £150/£45
The Fifth Decad of Cantos, Faber, 1937 . £150/£45
ditto, Farrar & Rinehart (U.S.), 1937 . . £100/£25
ditto, New Directions (U.S.), 1940 . £100/£25
Cantos LII-LXXI, Faber, 1940 . . . . £200/£45
ditto, New Directions (U.S.), 1940 (500 copies with envelope and pamphlet) . . . . . £200/£75
ditto, New Directions (U.S.), 1940 (500 copies without envelope and pamphlet) . . . . . £100/£35
The Pisan Cantos, New Directions (U.S.), 1948 . .
. . . . £250/£65
ditto, Faber, 1949 . . . . £250/£50
Section: Rock-Drill, Pesce d'Oro (Milan), 1955 £200
ditto, New Directions (U.S.), 1956 . . . £45/£15
ditto, Faber, 1957 . . . . £45/£15
Diptych Rome-London, New Directions (U.S.), 1957 (125 signed copies in slipcase) . . . £1,000/£650
ditto, Faber, 1957 (50 signed copies in slipcase) . .
. . . . £1,250/£1,000
ditto, Vanni Scheiwiller (Italy), 1957 (25 signed copies in slipcase) . . . . £2,000/£1,750
Thrones, Pesce d'Oro (Milan), 1959 (300 copies) £125
ditto, New Directions (U.S.), 1959 . . . £45/£15
ditto, Faber, 1960 . . . . £45/£15
The Cantos, Faber, 1964 (all 109 cantos) . £45/£10
Cavalcanti Poems, New Directions (U.S.), [1966] (200 signed copies, glassine d/w, slipcase) £1,500/£1,250
ditto, Faber, [1966] (190 signed copies in slipcase). .
. . . . £1,000/£850
Drafts and Fragments of Cantos CX-CXVII, New Directions (U.S.), 1969 . . . . . £45/£15

ditto, New Directions (U.S.), 1969 (200 signed,
numbered copies, slipcase) . . . . . £500/£400
ditto, Stone Wall Press (U.S.), 1969 (10 signed,
numbered copies, slipcase) . . . . £1,000/£850
ditto, Faber, 1970 (200 signed, numbered copies,
slipcase) . . . . £300/£250
ditto, Faber, 1970 . . . . £40/£15

Others
The Spirit of Romance, Dent, 1910 . . . . £300
ditto, Dutton (U.S.), 1910. . . . . . . £200
Cathay, Elkin Mathews, 1915 (wraps) . . . £350
Gaudier-Brzeska, Bodley Head, 1916 (with design on
front cover) £500
ditto, Bodley Head, 1916 (without design on front
cover) £250
ditto, Lane (U.S.), 1916 . . . . £350
Instigations, Boni & Liveright (U.S.), 1920 . .
. . . . £1,000/£200
Antheil and the Treatise on Harmony, Three
Mountains Press (Paris), 1924 (360 copies, wraps) .
. . . . £500
ditto, Three Mountains Press (Paris), 1924 (40 copies,
Arches paper, wraps) £1,000
ditto, Contact Editions/Three Mountains Press (Paris),
1924 (unsold copies of above, wraps) . . . £500
ditto, Pascal Covici (U.S.), 1927 . . . £200/£50
How to Read, Harmsworth, 1931 . . £225/£35
ABC of Economics, Faber, 1933. . . . £150/£35
ditto, New Directions (U.S.), 1940 . . . £75/£25
ABC of Reading, Routledge, 1934 . . £150/£35
ditto, Yale Univ. Press (U.S.), 1934 . . . £100/£25
Make it New, Faber, 1934 . . . . . £150/£35
ditto, New Directions (U.S.), 1935 . . . £100/£25
Social Credit, Nott, [1935 or 37?] (wraps) . . £150
Polite Essays, Faber, 1937 . . . . . £150/£35
ditto, New Directions (U.S.), 1940 . . . £100/£25
Guide to Kulchur, Faber, 1938 . . . . £150/£35
ditto, New Directions (U.S.), 1938 . . . £100/£25
Patria Mia, Seymour, 1950 . . . . . £100/£25
ditto, Owen (U.S.), 1962 . . . . . £45/£15
The Letters of Ezra Pound, Harcourt Brace (U.S.),
1950 . . . . £50/£10
ditto, Faber, 1951 . . . . £45/£10
The Translations of Ezra Pound, Faber, 1953 £50/£15
ditto, New Directions (U.S.), 1953 . . . £50/£15
Literary Essays of Ezra Pound, Faber, 1954 £40/£10
ditto, New Directions (U.S.), 1954 . . . £40/£10
*Impact, Essays on Ignorance and the Decline of
American Civilisation*, Regenery (U.S.), 1960 . .
. . . . £35/£10
Pound/Joyce, New directions (U.S.), 1967 . £25/£10
ditto, Faber, 1968 . . . . £25/£10
Selected Prose, 1909-65, Faber, 1973 . . £25/£10
ditto, New Directions (U.S.), 1975 . . . £25/£10
An Autobiographical Outline, NADJA, 1980 (200
copies, wraps) £45
Pound/Ford, Faber, 1982. . . . . . £25/£10

ANTHONY POWELL
(b.1905 d.2000)

As a novelist Powell is best known for the series of
novels having the general title *Dance to the Music of
Time*.

'Dance to the Music of Time' Novels
A Question of Upbringing, Heinemann, 1951 . . .
. . . . £650/£100
ditto, Scribner's (U.S.), 1951. . . . . £250/£35
A Buyer's Market, Heinemann, 1952 . . £800/£125
ditto, Scribner's (U.S.), 1953 . . . . £250/£35
The Acceptance World, Heinemann, 1955 . £500/£65
ditto, Farrar Straus (U.S.), 1956 . . . £200/£35
At Lady Molly's, Heinemann, 1957 . . . £100/£20
ditto, Little, Brown (U.S.), 1958 . . . . £50/£10
Casanova's Chinese Restaurant, Heinemann, 1960 .
. . . . £75/£15
ditto, Little, Brown (U.S.), 1960 . . . . £30/£10
The Kindly Ones, Heinemann, 1962. . . £50/£15
ditto, Little, Brown (U.S.), 1962 . . . . £20/£5
The Valley of Bones, Heinemann, 1964. . £50/£15
ditto, Little, Brown (U.S.), 1964 . . . . £20/£5
The Soldier's Art, Heinemann, 1966 . . £35/£10
ditto, Little, Brown (U.S.), 1966 . . . . £20/£5
The Military Philosophers, Heinemann, 1968 £35/£10
ditto, Little, Brown (U.S.), 1969 . . . . £20/£5
Books Do Furnish a Room, Heinemann, 1971 £30/£10
ditto, Little, Brown (U.S.), 1971 . . . . £10/£5
Temporary Kings, Heinemann, 1973 . . £25/£10
ditto, Little, Brown (U.S.), 1963 . . . . £15/£5
Hearing Secret Harmonies, Heinemann, 1975 £25/£10
ditto, Little, Brown (U.S.), 1975 . . . . £10/£5
All twelve *Dance to the Music of Time* novels £3,000

Other Novels
Afternoon Men, Duckworth, 1931 . . £2,750/£300
ditto, Holt (U.S.), 1932 . . . . . £2,250/£300
Venusberg, Duckworth, 1932 . . £2,000/£300
ditto, as *Venusberg & Agents and Patients*, Periscope/
Holliday (U.S.), 1952 . . . . . . £100/£15
From a View to a Death, Duckworth, 1933. . . .
. . . . £1,750/£250
ditto, as *Mr Zouch: Superman*, Vanguard Press (U.S.),
1934 . . . . £1,000/£100
ditto, Little, Brown (U.S.), 1964 . . . . £20/£5
Agents and Patients, Duckworth, 1936 . £1,500/£200
ditto, Holliday (U.S.), 1952 . . . . . £25/£5
What's Become of Waring, Cassell, 1939 £2,500/£200
ditto, Little, Brown (U.S.), 1963 . . . . £20/£5
O, How the Wheel Becomes It, Heinemann, 1983 . .
. . . . £25/£5
ditto, Holt Rinehart (U.S.), 1983 . . . . £15/£5
The Fisher King, Heinemann, 1985 . . . £30/£5
ditto, Norton (U.S.), 1986. . . . . . £15/£5

Autobiography
Infants of the Spring, Heinemann, 1976 . £25/£5
ditto, Holt Rinehart (U.S.), 1976 . . . . £20/£5

Messengers of the Day, Heinemann, 1978 . . £25/£5
ditto, Holt Rinehart (U.S.), 1978 . . . . . £20/£5
Faces in My Time, Heinemann, 1980 . . . £20/£5
ditto, Holt Rinehart (U.S.), 1981 . . . . . £15/£5
The Strangers all are Gone, Heinemann, 1982 . £20/£5
ditto, Holt Rinehart (U.S.), 1983 . . . . . £15/£5

Others
Caledonia: A Fragment, privately printed, 1934 (100 copies) £2,500
John Aubrey and His Friends, Heinemann, 1948 . .
. . . . £45/£10
ditto, Scribner's (U.S.), 1949 . . . . . £40/£10
The Garden of God and The Rest I'll Whistle, Heinemann, 1971 . . . . £25/£5
ditto, Little, Brown (U.S.), 1971. . . . . £20/£5
Under Review, Further Writings on Writers, 1946-1989, Heinemann, 1991 . . . . £15/£5
ditto, Univ. of Chicago (U.S.), 1991 . . . £15/£5
Journals, 1982-1986, Heinemann, 1995 . £10/£5
Journals, 1987-1989, Heinemann, 1996 . . £10/£5
A Reference for Mellors, Moorhouse and Sorensen, 1994 (26 signed copies of 326, quarter goatskin, slipcase) . . . . £500/£400
ditto, Moorhouse and Sorensen, 1994 (100 signed copies of 326) £200
ditto, Moorhouse and Sorensen, 1994 (200 copies of 326, wraps) £45

JOHN COWPER POWYS
(b.1872 d.1963)

Novelist, poet and essayist, Powys's romances are very highly rated by his readers, although his work has never received much general literary recognition.

Novels
Wood and Stone, A Romance, G.A. Shaw (U.S.), 1915
. . . . £65
ditto, Heinemann, [1917] £65
Rodmoor, A Romance, G.A. Shaw, 1916 . . £75
Ducdame, Doubleday Page (U.S.), 1925 . £200/£35
ditto, Grant Richards, 1925 . . . . . £200/£35
Wolf Solent, Simon & Schuster (U.S.), 1929 (2 vols, slipcase) . . . . £125/£30
ditto, Cape, 1929 (1 vol.) . . . . . £125/£25
A Glastonbury Romance, Simon & Schuster (U.S.), 1932 . . . . £75/£25
ditto, Simon & Schuster (U.S.), 1932 (204 signed, numbered copies, no d/w) £325
ditto, John Lane, 1933 (1 vol.) . . . . £75/£25
Weymouth Sands, Simon & Schuster (U.S.), 1934. .
. . . . £75/£25
ditto, as *Jobber Skald*, John Lane, 1935 (revised text) .
. . . . £50/£20
ditto, Cape, 1963 (unexpurgated version) . £20/£5
Maiden Castle, Simon & Schuster (U.S.), 1936 . .
. . . . £65/£15

ditto, Cassell, 1937 . . . . £65/£15
Morwyn, or The Vengeance of God, Cassell, 1937 .
. . . . £75/£25
Owen Glendower, Simon & Schuster (U.S.), 1940 (2 vols) . . . . £100/£30
ditto, John Lane, 1941 (1 vol.) . . . . £75/£25
Porius, Macdonald, 1951 . . . . . . £75/£15
ditto, Macdonald, 1951 (200 signed copies). . £300
ditto, Philosophical Library (U.S.), 1952 . £45/£15
The Inmates, Macdonald, 1952 . . . . £75/£15
ditto, Philosophical Library (U.S.), 1952 . £45/£15
Atlantis, Macdonald, 1954 . . . . . £75/£15
The Brazen Head, Macdonald, 1956 . . £65/£15
All or Nothing, Macdonald, 1960 . . . £35/£10
ditto, Colgate Univ. Press (U.S.), 1960 . . £35/£10
Real Wraiths, Village, 1974 (wraps). . . . £10
You and Me, Village, 1975 (wraps) £10
After My Fashion, Picador, 1980 (wraps) . . £10
Three Fantasies, Carcanet, 1985. . . . . £15/£5

Short Stories
The Owl, the Duck and - Miss Rowe! Miss Rowe!, Black Archer Press (U.S.), 1930 (250 signed copies, slipcase) . . . . £150/£125
ditto, Village, 1975 (wraps) £10
Up and Out, Macdonald, 1957 . . . . £45/£10
ditto, Village, 1974 (wraps) (with *The Mountains of the Moon*) £10

Poetry
Corinth, privately printed, 1891 ('English Verse' on front cover, wraps) £2,000
Odes and Other Poems, Rider & Co., 1896 . . £350
Poems, Rider & Co., 1899 . . . . . . £250
Wolf's-Bane, Rhymes, G.A. Shaw (U.S.), 1916 . £65
Mandragora, Poems, G.A. Shaw, 1917 . . . £100
Samphire, Poems, T. Selzer (U.S.), 1922 . £75/£35
Lucifer, A Poem, Macdonald, 1956 (560 signed, numbered copies, acetate d/w) . . . £135/£100
John Cowper Powys: A Selection from His Poems, Macdonald, 1964. . . . . . . £35/£10
ditto, Colgate Univ. Press (U.S.), 1964 (slipcase) . .
. . . . £35/£10

Others
The War and Culture, G.A. Shaw (U.S.), 1914 (boards) £50
ditto, G.A. Shaw (U.S.), 1914 (wraps) . . . £45
ditto, as *The Menace of German Culture*, 1915 . £50
Visions and Revisions: A Book of Literary Devotions, G.A. Shaw (U.S.), 1915 . . . . . . £20
ditto, Macdonald, 1955 . . . . . . £25/£10
Confessions of Two Brothers, Manas Press (U.S.), 1916 (with Llewelyn Powys) £25
One Hundred Best Books, G.A. Shaw (U.S.), 1916 .
. . . . £20
Suspended Judgements, Essays on Books and Sensations, G.A. Shaw (U.S.), 1916 . . . £20

The Complex Vision, Dodd, Mead (U.S.), 1920 . .
. . . . £100/£25
The Art of Happiness, Haldeman-Julius, 1923 (wraps)
. . . . £25
Psychoanalysis and Morality, Jessica Colbert (U.S.),
1923 (350 signed, numbered copies of 500) . £75
ditto, Jessica Colbert (U.S.), 1923 (unsigned copies) .
. . . . £25
ditto, Random House, 1925 (approximately 50 copies
of the above were rebound and signed by J.C. Powys)
. . . . £45
ditto, Village, 1975 (wraps) £5
The Religion of a Sceptic, Dodd, Mead (U.S.), 1925
(1,000 copies) . . . . . . £45/£15
ditto, Village, 1975 (wraps) £5
The Secret of Self-Development, Haldeman-Julius,
1926 (wraps) £25
The Art of Forgetting the Unpleasant, Haldeman-
Julius, 1928 (wraps) £25
The Meaning of Culture, Norton (U.S.), 1929 £30/£10
ditto, Cape, 1930 . . . . £30/£10
In Defence of Sensuality, Simon & Schuster (U.S.),
1930 . . . . £50/£15
ditto, Gollancz, 1930 . . . . . . £40/£10
Debate! Is Modern Marriage a Failure?, Discussion
Guild (U.S.), 1930 (with Bertrand Russell) . £1,000
Dorothy M. Richardson, Joiner & Steele, 1931 . .
. . . . £75/£15
ditto, Joiner & Steele, 1931 (60 signed, numbered
copies) . . . . £175/£125
A Philosophy of Solitude, Simon & Schuster (U.S.),
1933 . . . . £40/£10
Autobiography, Simon & Schuster (U.S.), 1934 . .
. . . . £30/£10
ditto, Bodley Head, 1934 . . . . . £30/£10
The Art of Happiness, Simon & Schuster (U.S.), 1935
(not the 1923 version) . . . . £30/£10
ditto, Bodley Head, 1935 . . . . . £30/£10
Enjoyment of Literature, Simon & Schuster (U.S.),
1938 . . . . £30/£10
ditto, as *The Pleasures of Literature*, Cassell, 1938
(contains one extra essay) . . . . £30/£10
Mortal Strife, Cape, 1941. . . . . £25/£10
The Art of Growing Old, Cape, 1944 . . £25/£10
Dostoievsky, John Lane, 1946 . . . £25/£10
Pair Dadeni, or The Cauldron of Rebirth, Druid Press,
1946 . . . . £40/£15
Obstinate Cymric, Essays 1935-47, Druid Press, 1947.
. . . . £40/£15
Rabelais, John Lane, 1948 . . . . . £25/£5
ditto, Philosophical Library (U.S.), 1951 . £20/£5
In Spite Of, A Philosophy for Everyman, Macdonald,
1952 . . . . £20/£5
ditto, Philosophical Library (U.S.), 1953 . £20/£5
*The Letters of John Cowper Powys to Louis
Wilkinson, 1935-1956*, Macdonald, 1958 . £20/£5
Homer and the Aether, Macdonald, 1959 . £15/£5
Letters to Nicholas Ross, Bertram Rota, 1971 £25/£10
Two & Two, Village Press, 1974. . . . £10

Letters to Henry Miller, Village Press, 1975 . £25
Letters to His Brother Llewellyn, 1902-1939, Village
Press, 1975 (2 vols) £20

LLEWELYN POWYS
(b.1884 d.1939)

Although he wrote three novels, the author's
reputation rests upon his collected essays, many
detailing his observations of Africa.

Novels
Apples Be Ripe, Harcourt Brace (U.S.), 1930 £50/£20
ditto, Longman, 1930 . . . . . . £50/£20

Essays
Ebony and Ivory, American Library Service (U.S.),
1923 . . . . £75/£20
ditto, Grant Richards, 1923 . . . . £65/£15
Thirteen Worthies, American Library Service (U.S.),
1923 . . . . £75/£20
ditto, Grant Richards, 1924 . . . . £65/£15
Honey and Gall, Haldeman-Julius (U.S.), 1924 (wraps)
. . . . £20
Cup Bearers of Wine and Hellebore, Haldeman-Julius
(U.S.), 1924 (wraps). £20
Black Laughter, Harcourt Brace (U.S.), 1924 £80/£25
ditto, Grant Richards, 1925 . . . . £80/£25
The Cradle of God, Harcourt Brace (U.S.), 1929 . .
. . . . £30/£10
ditto, Cape, 1924 . . . . £30/£10
The Pathetic Fallacy, Longmans Green, 1930 £30/£10
Impassioned Clay, Longmans Green (U.S.), 1931 . .
. . . . £65/£25
ditto, Longmans Green, 1930. . . . . £50/£15
Now that the Gods are Dead, Equinox Press (U.S.),
1932 (400 signed copies) £200
ditto, Bodley Head, 1949 . . . . . £35/£10
Glory of Life, Golden Cockerel Press, 1934 (277
numbered copies) £500
ditto, Golden Cockerel Press, 1934 (2 copies on
vellum) £5,000
ditto, John Lane, 1938. . . . . . £45/£10
Earth Memories, John Lane, 1934 . . £35/£15
ditto, Norton (U.S.), 1938 . . . . . £25/£10
Damnable Opinions, Watts, 1935 . . £35/£10
Dorset Essays, Bodley Head, 1935 . . £40/£15
The Twelve Months, Bodley Head, 1936 . £75/£20
ditto, Bodley Head, 1936 (100 signed copies) . £300
Somerset Essays, Bodley Head, 1937 . £40/£15
A Baker's Dozen, Trovillion Press (U.S.), 1940 (493
signed, numbered copies, in slipcase) . . £75/£45
ditto, Bodley Head, 1941 . . . . . £25/£10
Old English Yuletide, Trovillion Press (U.S.), 1940
(202 numbered copies, signed by the printers, in
slipcase) . . . . £125/£100
Swiss Essays, Bodley Head, 1947 . . . £25/£10

Somerset and Dorset Essays, Bodley Head, 1957 . .
. . . . £20/£10

Autobiography
Skin for Skin, Harcourt Brace (U.S.), 1925 . £45/£10
ditto, Cape, 1927 (900 signed, numbered copies) . .
. . . . £60/£25
The Verdict of Bridlegoose, Harcourt Brace (U.S.),
1926 . . . . £35/£10
ditto, Cape, 1927 (900 signed, numbered copies) . .
. . . . £40/£25
Love and Death, Bodley Head, 1939 . . £45/£15
ditto, Simon & Schuster (U.S.), 1941 . . £30/£10

Others
Henry Hudson, John Lane, 1927 (1000 copies) . .
. . . . £45/£15
ditto, Harper & Brothers (U.S.), 1928 . . £35/£10
Out of the Past, Grey Bow Press, 1928 (25 copies) .
. . . . £200
A Pagan's Pilgrimage, Harcourt Brace (U.S.), 1931 .
. . . . £30/£10
The Life & Times of Anthony A. Wood, Wishart &
Co., 1932 . . . . £30/£10
Rats in the Sacristy, Watts & Co., 1937 . . £25/£10
The Book of Days, Golden Cockerel Press, 1937 (300
copies) £200
ditto, Golden Cockerel Press, 1937 (nos. 1-55 bound in
red leather & signed by artist) £300
ditto, Golden Cockerel Press, 1937 (nos. 1-5 on lamb's
vellum, bound in red leather & signed by artist) . .
. . . . £1,250
The Letters of Llewelyn Powys, Bodley Head, 1943 .
. . . . £25/£10
*Advice to a Young Poet, Letters Between Llewelyn
Powys and Kenneth Hopkins*, Bodley Head, 1949
(issued as a volume in the Uniform Edition of the
Works of Llewelyn Powys) . . . . . £25/£10
So Wild a Thing, Letters to Gamel Woolsey, Ark
Press, 1973 . . . . £25/£10

T.F. POWYS
(b.1875 d.1953)

The author of a number of eccentric novels which
offer a highly personal and idiosyncratic view of both
God and human nature.

Novels
Black Bryony, Chatto & Windus, 1923 . . £75/£15
ditto, Knopf (U.S.), 1923 . . . . . £50/£10
Mark Only, Chatto & Windus, 1924 . . . £50/£10
ditto, Knopf (U.S.), 1924 . . . . . £40/£10
Mr Tasker's Gods, Chatto & Windus, 1925 . £50/£10
ditto, Knopf (U.S.), 1925 . . . . . £40/£10
Mockery Gap, Chatto & Windus, 1925 . . £45/£10
ditto, Knopf (U.S.), 1925 . . . . . £35/£10
Innocent Birds, Chatto & Windus, 1926 . £45/£10

ditto, Knopf (U.S.), 1926 . . . . . . £35/£10
Mr Weston's Good Wine, Chatto & Windus, 1927 (660
copies) . . . . £200/£65
ditto, Viking (U.S.), 1928. . . . . . £40/£10
ditto, Chatto & Windus, 1928. . . . . £40/£10
Kindness in a Corner, Chatto & Windus, 1930. . . .
. . . . £40/£10
ditto, Chatto & Windus, 1930 (206 signed, numbered
copies) £65
ditto, Viking (U.S.), 1930. . . . . . . £35/£5
Unclay, Chatto & Windus, 1931 . . . . £40/£10
ditto, Chatto & Windus, 1931 (large paper edition of
160 copies) £65
ditto, Viking (U.S.), 1932. . . . . . . £35/£5
The Market Bell, Brynmill, 1990 . . . . £20/£5

Short Stories
The Left Leg, Chatto & Windus, 1923 . . £50/£10
ditto, Knopf (U.S.), 1923 . . . . . . £40/£10
A Stubborn Tree, privately printed, 1926 (100 copies,
wraps). £175
Feed My Swine, E. Archer, 1926 (100 copies) . £75
A Strong Girl, E. Archer, 1926 (100 copies) . £100
What Lack I Yet?, E. Archer, 1926 . . . . £35
ditto, E. Archer, 1926 (100 signed, numbered copies) .
. . . . £100
ditto, E. Archer, 1926 (25 signed, numbered copies on
Japanese vellum). £200
The Rival Pastors, E. Archer, 1927 (100 signed,
numbered copies, in envelope) . . . . £100/£75
The House with the Echo, Chatto & Windus, 1928 .
. . . . £50/£10
ditto, Chatto & Windus, 1928 (206 numbered, signed
copies) £145
ditto, Viking (U.S.), 1929. . . . . . £40/£10
The Dewpond, Elkin Matthews, 1928 (530 signed,
numbered copies) . . . . £50/£30
Fables, Viking Press (U.S.), 1929 . . . £40/£10
ditto, Chatto & Windus, 1929 (750 signed copies) . .
. . . . £100/£45
Christ in a Cupboard, Blue Moon Booklets no. 5, 1930
(500 numbered, signed copies, wraps) . . . £45
ditto, Blue Moon Booklets no. 5, 1930 (100 small-
format copies 'for presentation', wraps) . . £40
The Key of the Field, Furnival Books no.1, 1930 (550
signed copies) . . . . £125/£50
The White Paternoster, Chatto & Windus, 1930 . .
. . . . £35/£10
ditto, Chatto & Windus, 1930 (310 copies) . . £100
ditto, Viking, 1931 . . . . £35/£10
Uriah on the Hill, Minority Press, 1930 (wraps, in
envelope) . . . . £45/£35
Uncle Dottery, Douglas Cleverdon, 1930 (350
numbered, signed copies, with engravings by Gill) .
. . . . £250/£10
ditto, Douglas Cleverdon, 1930 (nos. 1-50, containing
extra set of prints) £600
The Only Penitent, Chatto & Windus, 1931 £30/£10

ditto, Chatto & Windus, 1931 (large paper edition of 160 signed, numbered copies) £65
When Thou Wast Naked, Golden Cockerel Press, 1931 (edition of 500 numbered, signed copies) . . £150
The Tithe Barn, privately printed, 1932 (350 signed, numbered copies) £45
ditto, privately printed, 1932 (50 copies on Japanese vellum, bound in white buckram) £175
The Two Thieves, Chatto & Windus, 1932 . £50/£15
ditto, Chatto & Windus, 1932 (85 signed, numbered copies) £115
ditto, Viking, 1933 . . . . £25/£10
No Painted Plumage, Chatto & Windus, 1934 £35/£10
Captain Patch, Chatto & Windus, 1935 . . £35/£10
Make Thyself Many, Grayson & Grayson, 1935 (285 signed, numbered copies) . . . . . £125/£45
Goat Green, Golden Cockerel Press, 1937 (150 signed, numbered copies, slipcase) . . . . . £200/£125
ditto, Golden Cockerel Press, 1937 . . . £45/£15
Bottle's Path, Chatto & Windus, 1946 . . £25/£10
God's Eyes A-Twinkle, Chatto & Windus, 1947 . .
. . . . £25/£10
Rosie Plum, And Other Stories, Chatto & Windus, 1966 . . . . £25/£10
Two Stories, Brimmell, 1967 (525 numbered copies) .
. . . . £75
ditto, Brimmell, 1967 (25 numbered copies on hand-made paper, signed by Reynolds Stone) . £400/£300
Three Short Stories, Dud Noman Press, 1971 (150 numbered copies, acetate d/w) . . . £45/£30

Others
An Interpretation of Genesis, privately printed, 1907 (100 copies) £400
ditto, Chatto & Windus, 1929 (490 signed copies, slipcase) . . . . £125/£75
ditto, Viking (U.S.), 1929 (260 signed copies, slipcase)
. . . . £125/£75
The Soliloquy of a Hermit, G.A. Shaw (U.S.), 1916 .
. . . . £65
ditto, as **The Soliloquies of a Hermit**, Melrose, 1918 .
. . . . £35

TERRY PRATCHETT
(b.1948)

Author of the hugely successful 'Discworld' novels, which began with *The Colour of Magic*.

'Discworld' Novels
The Colour of Magic, Colin Smythe, 1983 (with or without alternative reviews pasted on to flap) . . .
. . . . £5,000/£500
ditto, St Martin's Press (U.S.), 1983 . . £300/£30
ditto, Colin Smythe, 1989 (new edition) . . £50/£15
The Light Fantastic, Colin Smythe, 1986 £2,000/£250
ditto, NAL/Signet (U.S.), 1988 (wraps) . . . £10

Equal Rites, Gollancz/Colin Smythe, 1987 . . . . .
. . . . £1,000/£150
ditto, NAL/Signet (U.S.), 1988 (wraps) . . . £10
Mort, Gollancz/Colin Smythe, 1987 . . £250/£25
ditto, NAL/Signet (U.S.), 1989 (wraps) . . . £10
Sourcery, Gollancz/Colin Smythe, 1988 . £200/£20
ditto, NAL/Signet (U.S.), 1989 (wraps) . . £10
Wyrd Sisters, Gollancz, 1988. . . . . . £125/£15
ditto, NAL/Roc (U.S.), 1990 (wraps) £5
Pyramids, Gollancz, 1989 . . . . . £75/£15
ditto, NAL/Roc (U.S.), 1989 (wraps) £5
Guards! Guards!, Gollancz, 1989 . . . £50/£10
Eric, Gollancz, 1990 (large format) . . . £45/£10
ditto, NAL/Roc (U.S.), 1995 (wraps) £5
Moving Pictures, Gollancz, 1990 . . . £45/£10
ditto, NAL/Roc (U.S.), 1992 (wraps) £5
Reaper Man, Gollancz, 1991. . . . . £35/£10
ditto, NAL/Roc (U.S.), 1992 (wraps) £5
Witches Abroad, Gollancz, 1991. . . . £35/£10
ditto, NAL/Roc (U.S.), 1993 (wraps) £5
Small Gods, Gollancz, 1992 . . . . . . £25/£5
Last Continent, Doubleday, 1998 . . . . £10/£5
ditto, HarperPrism (U.S.), 1999 . . . . £10/£5
Carpe Jugulum, Doubleday, 1998 . . . . £10/£5
ditto, HarperPrism (U.S.), 1999 . . . . £10/£5
The Fifth Elephant, Doubleday, 1999 . . £10/£5
ditto, HarperCollins (U.S.), 2000. . . . £10/£5
Truth, Doubleday, 2000 . . . . £10/£5
ditto, HarperCollins (U.S.), 2000. . . . . £10/£5
Thief of Time, Doubleday, 2001 . . . . £10/£5
ditto, HarperCollins (U.S.), 2001. . . . . £10/£5
The Last Hero, Gollancz, 2001 (illustrated by Paul Kidby) . . . . £10/£5
ditto, Gollancz, 2001 (deluxe edition signed by author and artist, no d/w) £35
ditto, HarperCollins (U.S.), 2001 . . . . £10/£5
Night Watch, Doubleday, 2002 . . . . £10/£5
ditto, HarperCollins (U.S.), 2002. . . . . £10/£5

Children's 'Discworld' Titles
The Amazing Maurice and His Educated Rodents, Doubleday, 2001. . . . . £10/£5
ditto, HarperCollins (U.S.), 2002. . . . . £10/£5
The Wee Free Men, Doubleday, 2003 . . . £10/£5
ditto, HarperCollins (U.S.), 2003. . . . . £10/£5

'Discworld' Related Titles
The Streets of Ankh-Morpork, Corgi, 1993 (wraps, with booklet, with Stephen Briggs). . . . £10
The Discworld Companion, Gollancz, 1994 (with Stephen Briggs) . . . . £15/£5
The Discworld Mapp, Corgi, 1995 (wraps, with Stephen Briggs) £10
The Pratchett Portfolio, Gollancz, 1996 (wraps, with Paul Kidby) £10
Discworld's Unseen University Diary, 1998, Gollancz, 1997 (with Stephen Briggs and Paul Kidby) . £15
A Tourist Guide to Lancre, Corgi, 1998 (with Stephen Briggs, Paul Kidby, wraps. First issue has cancel page correcting errors). £25

Terry Pratchett Collector's Edition Discworld 1999 Day-To-Day Calendar, Ink Group, 1998 (deskpad with plastic holder in box, illustrated by Paul Kidby). £15
Discworld's Ankh-Korpork City Watch Diary 1999, Gollancz, 1998 (with Stephen Briggs and Paul Kidby) £15
Death's Domain: A Discworld Mapp, Corgi, 1999 (wraps, with Paul Kidby) £10
The Science of Discworld, Ebury Press, 1999 (with Ian Stewart & Jack Cohen) . . . . . . £30/£10
Nanny Ogg's Cookbook, Doubleday, 1999 (with Stephen Briggs, Tina Hannan and Paul Kidby, no d/w) £15
Discworld Assassins' Guild Yearbook and Diary 2000, Gollancz, 1999 . . . . £10
The Science of Discworld II, Ebury Press, 2002 (with Ian Stewart & Jack Cohen) . . . . . . £10/£5

The 'Bromeliad' Trilogy
Truckers, Doubleday, 1989 . . . . . . £20/£5
ditto, Delacorte Press (U.S.), 1990 . . . £20/£5
Diggers, Doubleday, 1990 . . . . . . £15/£5
ditto, Delacorte Press (U.S.), 1991 . . . £15/£5
Wings, Doubleday, 1990 . . . . £15/£5
ditto, Delacorte Press (U.S.), 1991 . . . £15/£5

'Johnny Maxwell' Novels
Only You Can Save Mankind, Doubleday, 1992 . . . . £20/£5
Johnny and the Dead, Doubleday, 1993 . £15/£5
Johnny and the Bomb, Doubleday, 1996 . £15/£5

Collections
The Bromeliad, Delacorte (U.S.), 1991 (contains *Truckers*, *Diggers* and *Wings*) . . . . £15/£5
ditto, Doubleday, 1998 . . . . . . £15/£5
The Johnny Maxwell Trilogy, Science Fiction Book Club (U.S.), 1996 (contains *Only You Can Save Mankind*, *Johnny and the Dead*, *Johnny and the Bomb*, with poster) . . . . . £15/£5
Death Trilogy, Gollancz, 1998 (contains *Mort*, *Reaper Man* and *Soul Music*) . . . . . . £10/£5
Rincewind the Wizzard, Science Fiction Book Club (U.S.), 1999 (contains *The Colour of Magic*, *The Light Fantastic*, *Sourcery* and *Eric*) . . . £10/£5
The City Watch, Gollancz, 1999 (contains *Guards! Guards!*, *Men At Arms* and *Feet of Clay*) . . £10/£5
The Colour of Magic/The Light Fantastic, Colin Smythe, 1999. . . . . £10/£5
Gods Trilogy, Gollancz, 2000 (contains *Pyramids*, *Small Gods* and *Hogfather*) . . . . . £10/£5

Others
The Carpet People, Colin Smythe, 1971 . £600/£75
The Dark Side of the Sun, Colin Smythe, 1976 . . . . £500/£65
ditto, St Martin's Press (U.S.), 1976 . . . £60/£10
ditto, Doubleday, 1994 . . . . £10/£5
ditto, Doubleday, 1994 (500 signed copies) . £50/£25

STRATA, Colin Smythe, 1981 . . . . £450/£100
ditto, St Martin's Press (U.S.), 1981 . . . £50/£10
ditto, Doubleday, 1994 . . . . . . £10/£5
ditto, Doubleday, 1994 (500 signed copies) . £50/£25
The Unadulterated Cat, Gollancz, 1989 (wraps) £15
Good Omens, Gollancz, 1990 (with Neil Gaiman) . . . . £30/£5
ditto, Workman (U.S.), 1990 . . . . . £30/£5

ANTHONY PRICE
(b.1928)

A crime novelist and journalist, Price won the Crime Writers Association's Silver Dagger award with his first book, *The Labyrinth Makers*, and later the Gold Dagger with *Other Paths to Glory*.

Novels
The Labyrinth Makers, Gollancz, 1970 . . £300/£50
ditto, Doubleday (U.S.), 1971 . . . . £45/£10
The Alamut Ambush, Gollancz, 1971 . . £100/£25
ditto, Doubleday (U.S.), 1972 . . . . . £25/£5
Colonel Butler's Wolf, Gollancz, 1972 . . £75/£20
ditto, Doubleday (U.S.), 1973 . . . . . £25/£5
October Men, Gollancz, 1973 . . . . £75/£15
ditto, Doubleday (U.S.), 1974 . . . . . £25/£5
Other Paths to Glory, Gollancz, 1974 . . £75/£15
ditto, Doubleday (U.S.), 1975 . . . . . £25/£5
Our Man in Camelot, Gollancz, 1975 . . £75/£15
ditto, Doubleday (U.S.), 1976 . . . . . £25/£5
War Game, Gollancz, 1976 . . . . . £65/£10
ditto, Doubleday (U.S.), 1977 . . . . . £25/£5
The '44 Vintage, Gollancz, 1978 . . . £65/£10
ditto, Doubleday (U.S.), 1979 . . . . . £20/£5
Tomorrow's Ghost, Gollancz, 1979 . . . £50/£10
ditto, Doubleday (U.S.), 1979 . . . . . £12/£5
The Hour of the Donkey, Gollancz, 1980 . £45/£10
Soldier No More, Gollancz, 1981 . . . £35/£10
ditto, Doubleday (U.S.), 1982 . . . . . £15/£5
The Old Vengeful, Gollancz, 1982 . . . £20/£5
ditto, Doubleday (U.S.), 1983 . . . . . £15/£5
Gunner Kelly, Gollancz, 1983 . . . . . £20/£5
ditto, Doubleday (U.S.), 1984 . . . . . £15/£5
Sion Crossing, Gollancz, 1984 . . . . £15/£5
ditto, Mysterious Press (U.S.), 1985 . . . £10/£5
ditto, Mysterious Press (U.S.), 1985 (26 signed, lettered copies, slipcase) . . . . £45/£20
ditto, Mysterious Press (U.S.), 1985 (250 signed, numbered copies, slipcase) . . . . . £35/£15
Here Be Monsters, Gollancz, 1985 . . . £15/£5
ditto, Mysterious Press (U.S.), 1986 . . . . £10/£5
ditto, Mysterious Press (U.S.), 1986 (26 signed, lettered copies, slipcase) . . . . £50/£20
ditto, Mysterious Press (U.S.), 1986 (250 signed, numbered copies, slipcase) . . . . . £35/£15
For the Good of the State, Gollancz, 1986 . . £15/£5
ditto, Mysterious Press (U.S.), 1987 . . . . £10/£5

ditto, Mysterious Press (U.S.), 1987 (26 signed, lettered
copies, slipcase) . . . . £45/£20
ditto, Mysterious Press (U.S.), 1987 (250 signed,
numbered copies, slipcase) . . . . £35/£15
A New Kind of War, Gollancz, 1987 . . £15/£5
ditto, Mysterious Press (U.S.), 1988 . . . £10/£5
A Prospect of Vengeance, Gollancz, 1988 . . £10/£5
ditto, The Armchair Detective (U.S.), 1990 . . £10/£5
ditto, The Armchair Detective (U.S.), 1990 (100 signed
copies, slipcase) . . . . £30/£15
The Memory Trap, Gollancz, 1989 . . . . £10/£5
ditto, The Armchair Detective (U.S.), 1991 . . £10/£5
ditto, The Armchair Detective (U.S.), 1991 (100 signed
copies, slipcase) . . . . £30/£15

Non Fiction
The Eyes of the Fleet, Hutchinson, 1990 . . £10/£5
ditto, Norton (U.S.), 1996. . . . . . . £10/£5

J.B. PRIESTLEY
(b.1894 d.1984)

Priestley was born in Bradford, the son of an
elementary schoolmaster, and became a clerk after
leaving school. He served with distinction in the West
Riding and Devonshire Regiments during the First
World War, afterwards studying politics and history
at Cambridge. His output was prodigious, including
many non fiction titles.

Novels
Adam in Moonshine, Heinemann, 1927. . £125/£45
ditto, Harpers (U.S.), 1927 . . . . . £125/£45
Benighted, Heinemann, 1927. . . . . £125/£30
ditto, as *The Old Dark House*, Harpers, 1928 £125/£30
Farthing Hall (with Hugh Walpole), Macmillan, 1929
. . . . £65/£10
ditto, Doubleday, Doran (U.S.), 1929 . . £65/£10
The Good Companions, Heinemann, 1929 . £75/£15
ditto, Harpers (U.S.), 1929 . . . . . £75/£15
Angel Pavement, Heinemann, 1930 . . . £65/£15
ditto, Heinemann, 1930 (1,025 signed copies, slipcase)
. . . . £100/£65
ditto, Harpers (U.S.), 1930 . . . . . £50/£10
Faraway, Heinemann, 1932 . . . . . £45/£10
ditto, Harpers (U.S.), 1932 . . . . . £45/£10
I'll Tell You Everything: A Frolic, Macmillan (U.S.),
1932 (with Gerald Bullett) . . . . . £65/£25
ditto, Heinemann, 1933 . . . . . . £65/£25
Wonder Hero, Heinemann, 1933. . . . £45/£10
ditto, Heinemann, 1933 (175 signed, numbered copies)
. . . . £75
ditto, Harpers (U.S.), 1933 . . . . . £45/£10
*They Walk in the City: The Lovers in the Stone
Forest*, Heinemann, 1936 . . . . . £30/£10
ditto, Harpers (U.S.), 1936 . . . . . £30/£10

The Doomsday Men: An Adventure, Heinemann, 1938
. . . . £50/£10
ditto, Harpers (U.S.), 1938 . . . . . £50/£10
Let the People Sing, Heinemann, 1939 . . £25/£10
ditto, Harpers (U.S.), 1940 . . . . . . £25/£5
Black-Out in Gretley: A Story of - and for - Wartime,
Heinemann, 1942 . . . . £45/£15
ditto, Harpers (U.S.), 1942 . . . . . £40/£14
*Daylight on Saturday: A Novel about an Aircraft
Factory*, Heinemann, 1943 . . . . . £25/£10
ditto, Harpers (U.S.), 1943 . . . . . £25/£10
Three Men in New Suits, Heinemann, 1945 . £20/£5
ditto, Harpers (U.S.), 1945 . . . . . . £20/£5
Bright Day, Heinemann, 1946 . . . . . £20/£5
ditto, Harpers (U.S.), 1946 . . . . . . £20/£5
Jenny Villiers: A Story of the Theatre, Heinemann,
1947 . . . . £20/£5
ditto, Harpers (U.S.), 1947 . . . . . . £20/£5
Festival at Farbridge, Heinemann, 1951 . . £20/£5
ditto, as *Festival*, Harpers (U.S.), 1951 . . £20/£5
The Magicians, Heinemann, 1954 . . . . £15/£5
ditto, Harpers (U.S.), 1954 . . . . . . £15/£5
Low Notes on a High Level: A Frolic, Heinemann,
1954 . . . . £15/£5
ditto, Harpers (U.S.), 1954 . . . . . . £15/£5
Saturn Over the Water, Heinemann, 1961 . £20/£5
ditto, Doubleday (U.S.), 1961 . . . . . £20/£5
The Shapes of Sleep: A Topical Tale, Heinemann,
1962 . . . . £20/£5
ditto, Doubleday (U.S.), 1962 . . . . . £20/£5
Sir Michael and Sir George, Heinemann, 1964 £10/£5
ditto, Little, Brown (U.S.), 1965 . . . . £10/£5
Lost Empires, Heinemann, 1965 . . . . £20/£5
ditto, Little, Brown (U.S.), 1965 . . . . £20/£5
Salt is Leaving: A Detective Story, Pan, 1966 (wraps) .
. . . . £5
ditto, Harpers (U.S.), 1975 . . . . . . £10/£5
It's an Old Country, Heinemann, 1967 . . £10/£5
ditto, Little, Brown (U.S.), 1967 . . . . £10/£5
The Image Men, Heinemann, 1968-9 (2 vols, *Out of
Town* and *London End*). . . . . . £20/£5
ditto, Little, Brown (U.S.), 1969 (1 vol.) . . £10/£5
Found, Lost, Found or The English Way of Life,
Heinemann, 1976. . . . . £10/£5
ditto, Hall (U.S.), 1976 . . . . £10/£5

Short Stories
The Town Major of Miraucourt, Heinemann, 1930 .
. . . . £40/£10
ditto, Heinemann, 1930 (525 copies signed by the
author, in slipcase) . . . . £75/£50
Albert Goes Through, Heinemann, 1933 . £25/£10
ditto, Harpers (U.S.), 1933 . . . . . . £25/£5
Going Up (stories and sketches), Heinemann, 1933 .
. . . . £30/£5
The Other Place, Heinemann, 1953 . . . £100/£25
ditto, Harpers (U.S.), [1954] . . . . . £75/£20

The Thirty-First of June: A tale of true love, enter-
prise and progress in the Arthurian and ad-atomic
ages, Heinemann, 1961 . . . . £20/£5
ditto, Doubleday (U.S.), 1962 . . . . . £15/£5
Snoggle: A Story for Anybody Between 9 and 90,
Heinemann, 1971 . . . . £10/£5
ditto, Harcourt Brace (U.S.), [1972] . . . . £10/£5
The Carfit Crisis and Two Other Stories, Heinemann,
1975 . . . . £10/£5
ditto, Stein & Day (U.S.), 1976 . . . . . £10/£5

Plays
The Good Companions, French, 1931 (wraps) . £15
Dangerous Corner, Heinemann, 1932 . . £45/£10
ditto, French (U.S.), 1932 . . . . . £45/£10
The Roundabout, Heinemann, 1933 . . . . £20/£5
Laburnum Grove, Heinemann, 1934 . . . £20/£5
Eden End, Heinemann, 1934 . . . . . . £15/£5
Duet in Floodlight, Heinemann, 1935 . . . £15/£5
Cornelius, Heinemann, 1935 . . . . . . £15/£5
Spring Tide, Heinemann, 1936 (as by George Bilham
and 'Peter Goldsmith') . . . . £15/£5
Bees on the Boat Deck, Heinemann, 1936 . £15/£5
Time and the Conways, Heinemann, 1937 . . £15/£5
Mystery at Greenfingers, Heinemann, 1937 . £15/£5
I Have Been Here Before, Heinemann, 1937 . £15/£5
People At Sea, Heinemann, 1937 . . . . £15/£5
When We Are Married, Heinemann, 1938 . . £15/£5
Johnson Over Jordan, Heinemann, 1939 . . £15/£5
The Long Mirror, Heinemann, 1940 . . . £15/£5
Goodnight, Children, Heinemann, 1942 . . £15/£5
Desert Highway, Heinemann, 1944 . . . £15/£5
How Are They At Home?, Heinemann, 1944 . £15/£5
They Came To A City, Heinemann, 1944 . . £15/£5
Music At Night, Heinemann, 1947 . . . £10/£5
An Inspector Calls, Heinemann, 1947 . . . £10/£5
The Rose and Crown, French, 1947 (wraps) . £10
The Linden Tree, Heinemann, 1948 . . . . £10/£5
The High Toby, Penguin, 1948 . . . . £10/£5
The Golden Fleece, Heinemann, 1948 . . £10/£5
Home is Tomorrow, Heinemann, 1949 . . . £10/£5
Ever Since Paradise, Heinemann, 1950 . . . £10/£5
Summer's Day Dream, Heinemann, 1950 . . £10/£5
Bright Shadow, Heinemann, 1950 . . . £15/£5
Dragon's Mouth, Heinemann, 1952 . . . . £10/£5
Private Rooms, French, 1953 (wraps) . . . £10/£5
Treasure on Pelican, Heinemann, 1953 . . . £10/£5
A Glass of Bitter, French, 1954 (wraps) . . . £5
Mr Kettle and Mrs Moon, Heinemann, 1955 . £10/£5
The Glass Cage, Heinemann, 1957 . . . . £10/£5
A Severed Head, Chatto & Windus, 1964 (with Iris
Murdoch) . . . . £50/£20

Poetry
The Chapman of Rhymes, Alexander Moring, 1918 .
. . . . £100

V.S. PRITCHETT
(b.1900 d.1997)

A writer and critic, Pritchett's books range widely
through many genres encompassing travel, essays,
short stories, novels and memoirs.

Novels
Clare Drummer, Benn, 1929 . . . . . £200/£45
Shirley Sanz, Gollancz, 1932 . . . . £175/£35
ditto, as *Elopement into Exile*, Little, Brown (U.S.),
1932 . . . . £125/£25
Nothing Like Leather, Chatto & Windus, 1935 .
. . . . £175/£35
ditto, Macmillan (U.S.), 1935 . . . £100/£25
Dead Man Leading, Chatto & Windus, 1937 £175/£35
ditto, Macmillan (U.S.), 1937 . . . . £65/£15
Mr Beluncle, Chatto & Windus, 1951 . . £50/£15
ditto, Harcourt Brace (U.S.), 1951 . . . . £25/£5

Short Stories
The Spanish Virgin and Other Stories, Benn, 1930 .
. . . . £300/£45
You Make Your Own Life, Chatto & Windus, 1938 .
. . . . £250/£35
It May Never Happen and Other Stories, Chatto &
Windus, 1945 . . . . £75/£15
ditto, Reynal (U.S.), 1947 . . . . . £50/£10
Collected Stories, Chatto & Windus, 1956 . £40/£10
The Sailor, The Sense of Humour and Other Stories,
Knopf (U.S.), 1956 . . . . £35/£10
When My Girl Comes Home, Chatto & Windus, 1961
. . . . £25/£5
ditto, Knopf (U.S.), 1961 . . . . . . £25/£5
The Key to My Heart, Chatto & Windus, 1963 . £25/£5
ditto, Random House (U.S.), 1964 . . . . £25/£5
The Saint and Other Stories, Penguin, 1966 (wraps) .
. . . . £5
Blind Love and Other Stories, Chatto & Windus, 1969
. . . . £15/£5
ditto, Random House (U.S.), 1970 . . . £15/£5
The Camberwell Beauty and Other Stories, Chatto &
Windus, 1974 . . . . £15/£5
ditto, Random House (U.S.), 1974 . . . £15/£5
Selected Stories, Chatto & Windus, 1978 . £10/£5
ditto, Random House (U.S.), 1978 . . . £10/£5
On the Edge of the Cliff, Random House (U.S.), 1979
. . . . £15/£5
ditto, Chatto & Windus, 1980 . . . . £10/£5
Collected Stories, Random House (U.S.), 1982 . £10/£5
ditto, Chatto & Windus, 1982 . . . . £10/£5
More Collected Stories, Random House (U.S.), 1983 .
. . . . £10/£5
ditto, Chatto & Windus, 1983 . . . . £10/£5
The Other Side of the Frontier, A V.S. Pritchett
Reader, Clark, 1984 (wraps) £5
A Careless Widow and Other Stories, Chatto &
Windus, 1989 . . . . £10/£5
ditto, Random House (U.S.), 1989 . . . . £10/£5

Complete Short Stories, Chatto & Windus, 1990 . .
. . . . £10/£5
ditto, as *Complete Collected Stories*, Random House
(U.S.), 1991 . . . . £10/£5

Autobiography
A Cab at the Door, Chatto & Windus, 1968 . £20/£5
ditto, Random House (U.S.), 1968 . . . . £20/£5
Midnight Oil, Chatto & Windus, 1971 . . . £15/£5
ditto, Random House (U.S.), 1972 . . . . £15/£5
Autobiography, English Association, 1977 (wraps) £5

Biography
Balzac, Chatto & Windus, 1973 . . . . £25/£10
ditto, Knopf (U.S.), 1973 . . . . . . £25/£10
*The Gentle Barbarian, The Life and Work of
Turgenev*, Chatto & Windus, 1977. . . . £20/£5
ditto, Random House (U.S.), 1977 . . . . £20/£5
Chekhov: A Spirit Set Free, Hodder & Stoughton,
1988 . . . . £20/£5
ditto, Random House (U.S.), 1988 . . . . £20/£5

Others
Marching Spain, Benn, 1928 . . . . £400/£45
ditto, Left Book Club, 1928 (wraps) £45
In My Good Books, Chatto & Windus, 1942 £40/£15
The Living Novel, Chatto & Windus, 1946 . £30/£10
ditto, Reynal (U.S.), 1947. . . . . . £30/£10
Build the Ships, HMSO, 1947 (wraps) . . . £25
*Why Do I Write?: An Exchange of Views Between
Elizabeth Bowen, Graham Greene, and V.S.
Pritchett*, Marshall, 1948 . . . . . £125/£35
Books in General, Chatto & Windus, 1953 . . £20/£5
ditto, Harcourt Brace (U.S.), 1954 . . . £20/£10
The Spanish Temper, Chatto & Windus, 1954 £20/£5
ditto, Knopf (U.S.), 1954 . . . . . . £20/£5
London Perceived, Chatto & Windus, 1962
(photographs by Evelyn Hofer) . . . £25/£10
ditto, Harcourt Brace (U.S.), 1962 . . . £25/£10
Foreign Faces, Chatto & Windus, 1964. . . £15/£5
New York Proclaimed, Chatto & Windus, 1965
(photographs by Evelyn Hofer). . . . £20/£5
ditto, Harcourt Brace (U.S.), 1965 . . . £20/£5
The Working Novelist, Chatto & Windus, 1965 .
. . . . £15/£5
Dublin, A Portrait, Bodley Head, 1967 . . . £20/£5
ditto, Harper & Row (U.S.), 1967 (photographs by
Evelyn Hofer) . . . . £20/£5
George Meredith and English Comedy, Random
House (U.S.), 1969 . . . . £10/£5
ditto, Chatto & Windus, 1970 . . . . £10/£5
The Myth Makers, Chatto & Windus, 1979. . £10/£5
ditto, Random House (U.S.), 1979 . . . . £10/£5
The Tale Bearers, Chatto & Windus, 1980 . £10/£5
ditto, Random House (U.S.), 1980 . . . . £10/£5
The Turn of the Years, Russell, 1982 (illustrated by
Reynolds Stone, glassine wraps) . . . . £20/£5
ditto, Russell, 1982 (150 copies signed by author and
artist) . . . . £125/£100

ditto, Random House (U.S.), 1982 . . . . £20/£5
ditto, Random House (U.S.), 1982 (500 copies signed
by author and artist, slipcase) . . . . £100/£75
A Man of Letters, Chatto & Windus, 1985 . . £10/£5
ditto, Random House (U.S.), 1985 . . . . £10/£5
At Home and Abroad, Chatto & Windus, 1989. £10/£5
ditto, North Point Press (U.S.), 1989. . . . £10/£5
Lasting Impressions, Chatto & Windus, 1990 . £10/£5
ditto, Random House (U.S.), 1990 . . . . £10/£5
Complete Essays, Chatto & Windus, 1991 . . £10/£5
ditto, as *Complete Collected Essays*, Random House
(U.S.), 1991 . . . . £10/£5

MARCEL PROUST
(b.1871 d.1922)

The subject of Proust's work is his own past, which
he recreates through an evocation of its smell, taste
and sound.

'À la Recherche du Temps Perdu'
Swann's Way, Chatto & Windus, 1922 (translated by
C.K. Scott Moncrief, 2 vols) . . . . £150/£50
ditto, Thomas Seltzer (U.S.), 1922 (2 vols) . £75/£25
Within a Budding Grove, Chatto & Windus, 1924
(translated by C.K. Scott Moncrief, 2 vols) £125/£35
ditto, Thomas Seltzer (U.S.), 1924 (2 vols) . £75/£25
The Guermantes Way, Chatto & Windus, 1925
(translated by C.K. Scott Moncrief, 2 vols) £125/£35
ditto, Thomas Seltzer (U.S.), 1925 (2 vols) . £75/£25
Cities of the Plain, Alfred A. Knopf, 1925 (translated
by C.K. Scott Moncrief, 2,230 numbered copies, 2
vols) . . . . £100/£35
ditto, Boni (U.S.), 1927 (2,000 numbered copies, 2
vols) . . . . £100/£50
The Captive, Alfred A. Knopf, 1929 (translated by
C.K. Scott Moncrief, 2 vols) . . . . £100/£35
ditto, Boni (U.S.), 1929 . . . . . . £75/£25
The Sweet Cheat Gone, Alfred A. Knopf, 1930
(translated by C.K. Scott Moncrief) . . £50/£20
ditto, Boni (U.S.), 1930 . . . . . . £75/£25
ditto, as *Albertine Gone*, Chatto & Windus, 1989
(translated by Terence Kilmartin) . . . £15/£5
Time Regained, Chatto & Windus, 1931 (1,300
numbered copies, translated by Stephen Hudson) . .
. . . . £75/£35
Remembrance of Things Past, Chatto & Windus/
Alfred A. Knopf, 1922-31 (12 vols) . £1,000/£300

Others
*47 Unpublished Letters from Marcel Proust to Walter
Berry*, Black Sun Press (Paris), 1930 (edited and
translated by Harry and Caresse Crosby, 50 numbered
copies on Japon, wraps). £300
ditto, Black Sun Press (Paris), 1930 (200 numbered
copies on velin d'Arches, wraps) £200

Marcel Proust: A Selection from His Miscellaneous Writings, Allan Wingate, 1948 (translated by Gerard Hopkins) . . . . £30/£10
Letters to a Friend, The Falcon Press, 1949 £30/£10
Pleasures and Regrets, Crown (U.S.), 1948 £35/£10
ditto, Dobson, 1950 (translated by Louise Varese) . .
. . . . £35/£10
Letters of Marcel Proust, Random House (U.S.), 1949 (translated by Mina Curtis) . . . . £30/£10
ditto, Chatto & Windus, 1950 . . . . £30/£10
The Letters of Marcel Proust to Antoine Bibescu, Thames and Hudson, [1953] (translated by Gerard Hopkins) . . . . £30/£10
ditto, Thames & Hudson, [1953] (500 copies signed by translator) . . . . £50/£25
Jean Santeuil, Weidenfeld & Nicolson, 1955 (translated by Gerard Hopkins) . . . . £45/£10
ditto, Simon & Schuster (U.S.), 1956 . . £45/£10
Letters to His Mother, Rider, 1956 . . . £30/£10
ditto, Citadel (U.S.), 1957. . . . . . £30/£10
By Way of Saint-Beuve, Chatto & Windus, 1958 (translated by Sylvia Townsend Warner) . £40/£20
On Reading, Souvenir Press (U.S.), 1971 . . . £15/£5
ditto, Souvenir Press, 1972 (translated by Jean Autret and William Burford) . . . . . . £15/£5
Selected Letters: 1880-1903, Collins, 1983 (translated by Ralph Manheim) . . . . £15/£5
ditto, Doubleday (U.S.), 1983 . . . . . £15/£5
On Reading Ruskin, Yale Univ. Press (U.S.), 1987 .
. . . . £15/£5
Selected Letters, Volume II: 1904-1909, Collins, 1989 (translated by Terence Kilmartin) . . . . £15/£5
ditto, O.U.P. (U.S.), 1989. . . . . . £15/£5

PHILIP PULLMAN
(b.1946)

Pullman has won the Carnegie Medal, the Guardian Children's Fiction Award, the Smarties Prize and the Children's Book of the Year award, and *The Amber Spyglass* gained him wide recognition when it won the Whitbread Book of the Year Prize.

'His Dark Materials' Trilogy
Northern Lights, Scholastic, 1995 . . £5,000/£500
ditto, as *The Golden Compass*, Knopf (U.S.), 1996 .
. . . . £175/£25
The Subtle Knife, Scholastic, 1997 . . £1,000/£100
ditto, Knopf (U.S.), 1997. . . . . . £125/£15
The Amber Spyglass, Knopf (U.S.), 2001 . . £30/£5
ditto, Scholastic, 2001. . . . . £30/£5

'Sally Lockhart' Titles
The Ruby in the Smoke, O.U.P., 1985 . . £650/£50
ditto, Knopf (U.S.), 1987 . . . . . £200/£25
The Shadow in the Plate, O.U.P., 1986 . . £500/£50

ditto, as *Shadow in the North*, Knopf (U.S.), 1988. .
. . . . £65/£10
The Tiger in the Well, Knopf (U.S.), 1990 . £100/£10
ditto, Viking, 1991 . . . . £250/£25
The Tin Princess, Puffin/O.U.P., 1994 (wraps). £20
ditto, Knopf (U.S.), 1994 . . . . . . £250/£20

Others
The Haunted Storm, New English Library, 1971 . .
. . . . £200/£25
Galatea, Gollancz, 1978 . . . . . . £150/£30
ditto, Dutton (U.S.), 1979. . . . . . £75/£15
Count Karlstein, Chatto & Windus, 1982 . £350/£30
ditto, as *Count Karlstein or The Ride of the Demon Huntsman*, Knopf (U.S.), 1998. . . . £100/£10
How to be Cool, Heinemann, 1987 . . . . £25/£5
Spring-Heeled Jack: A Story of Bravery and Evil, Doubleday, 1989. . . . . £250/£30
ditto, Knopf (U.S.), 1990 . . . . . £100/£10
The Broken Bridge, Macmillan, 1990 . . £35/£10
ditto, Knopf (U.S.), 1992 . . . . £20/£5
The White Mercedes, Pan Macmillan, 1992 £75/£10
ditto, Knopf (U.S.), 1993 . . . . £35/£5
The Wonderful Story of Aladdin and the Enchanted Lamp, Deutsch, 1993 . . . . . £50/£10
Sherlock Holmes and the Adventure of the Limehouse Horror, Nelson, 1992 . . . . . £20/£5
The New Cut Gang: Thunderbolt's Waxwork, Viking, 1994 (no d/w) £150
The New Cut Gang: The Gas-Fitter's Ball, Viking, 1995 (no d/w) £150
The Firework-Maker's Daughter, Doubleday, 1995 (no d/w) £125
ditto, Levine/Scholastic Press (U.S.), 1999 . . £25/£5
Clockwork, or All Wound Up, Doubleday, 1996 (no d/w) £45
ditto, Levine/Scholastic Press (U.S.), 1998 . . £15/£5
Mossycoat, Scholastic Hippo, 1998 (wraps, illustrated by Peter Bailey) £5
I Was a Rat, Doubleday, 1999 (no d/w, illustrated by Peter Bailey) £15
ditto, Knopf (U.S.), 2000 . . . . . . £15/£5

BARBARA PYM
(b.1913 d.1980)

The author of delicate, sad comedies, often set against a background of middle class church-going characters.

Novels
Some Tame Gazelle, Cape, 1950. . . . £300/£75
ditto, Dutton (U.S.), 1983. . . . . . £15/£5
Excellent Women, Cape, 1952 . . . . £225/£45
ditto, Dutton (U.S.), 1978. . . . . . £20/£5
Jane and Prudence, Cape, 1953 . . . . £225/£45
ditto, Dutton (U.S.), 1981. . . . . . £10/£5

Less Than Angels, Cape, 1955 . . . . £200/£45
ditto, Vanguard (U.S.), 1957 . . . . . £35/£10
A Glass of Blessings, Cape, 1959 . . . £175/£40
ditto, Dutton (U.S.), 1980 . . . . . . £10/£5
No Fond Return of Love, Cape, 1961 . . £150/£40
ditto, Dutton (U.S.), 1982 . . . . . . £10/£5
Quartet in Autumn, Macmillan, 1977 . . £35/£10
ditto, Dutton (U.S.), 1978 . . . . . . £20/£5
The Sweet Dove Died, Macmillan, 1978 . . £30/£5
ditto, Dutton (U.S.), 1979 . . . . . . £10/£5
A Few Green Leaves, Macmillan, 1980 . . £25/£5
ditto, Dutton (U.S.), 1980 . . . . . . £10/£5
An Unsuitable Attachment, Macmillan, 1982 . £25/£5
ditto, Dutton (U.S.), 1982 . . . . . . £10/£5
Crampton Hodnet, Macmillan, 1985 . . £15/£5
ditto, Dutton (U.S.), 1985 . . . . . . £10/£5
An Academic Question, Macmillan, 1986 . . £10/£5
ditto, Dutton (U.S.), 1986 . . . . . . £10/£5
Civil to Strangers, Macmillan, 1987 . . . £10/£5
ditto, Dutton (U.S.), 1988 . . . . . . £10/£5

Journals
*A Very Private Eye, An Autobiography in Diaries and
Letters*, Macmillan, 1984 . . . . . . £20/£5
ditto, Dutton (U.S.), 1984 . . . . . . £15/£5

ELLERY QUEEN

'Ellery Queen' was the pseudonym for Frederic
Dannay (b.1905 d.1982) and Manfred B. Lee (b.1905
d.1971), as well as the name of their fictional
detective, who also wrote detective fiction. They also
penned a handful of 'Barnaby Ross' novels. A
number of 'Ellery Queen' novels were ghost written
by other writers.

'Ellery Queen' Novels by Dannay and Lee
The Roman Hat Mystery, Stokes (U.S.), 1929 . . .
. . . . £5,000/£400
ditto, Gollancz, 1929 . . . . . £1,000/£100
The French Powder Mystery, Stokes (U.S.), 1930 . .
. . . . £3,000/£200
ditto, Gollancz, 1930 . . . . £500/£65
The Dutch Shoe Mystery Stokes (U.S.), 1931 . . .
. . . . £1,750/£150
ditto, Gollancz, 1931 . . . . £350/£45
The Greek Coffin Mystery, Stokes (U.S.), 1932 . .
. . . . £1,500/£150
ditto, Gollancz, 1932 . . . . £250/£35
The Egyptian Cross Mystery, Stokes (U.S.), 1932 . .
. . . . £1,500/£150
ditto, Gollancz, 1933 . . . . £250/£35
The American Gun Mystery, Stokes (U.S.), 1933 . .
. . . . £1,000/£75
ditto, Gollancz, 1933 . . . . £200/£35
ditto, as *Death at the Rodeo*, Mercury, 1951 £45/£10

The Siamese Twin Mystery, Stokes (U.S.), 1933 . .
. . . . £1,000/£75
ditto, Gollancz, 1934 . . . . £200/£35
The Chinese Orange Mystery, Stokes (U.S.), 1934 .
. . . . £1,000/£75
ditto, Gollancz, 1934 . . . . £200/£35
The Spanish Cape Mystery, Stokes (U.S.), 1935 . .
. . . . £750/£75
ditto, Gollancz, 1935 . . . . £200/£35
Halfway House, Stokes (U.S.), 1936 . . £250/£30
ditto, Gollancz, 1936 . . . . £150/£20
The Door Between, Stokes (U.S.), 1937 . . £350/£35
ditto, Gollancz, 1937 . . . . £200/£20
The Devil To Pay, Stokes (U.S.), 1938 . . £250/£30
ditto, Gollancz, 1938 . . . . £150/£20
The Four of Hearts, Stokes (U.S.), 1938 . £350/£35
ditto, Gollancz, 1939 . . . . £175/£20
The Dragon's Teeth, Stokes (U.S.), 1939 . £250/£30
ditto, Gollancz, 1939 . . . . £175/£20
ditto, as *The Virgin Heiress*, Pocket Books, 1954 £20
Calamity Town, Gollancz, 1942 . . . . £250/£20
ditto, Little, Brown (U.S.), 1942 . . . £125/£20
There Was an Old Woman, Little, Brown (U.S.), 1943
. . . . £250/£20
ditto, Gollancz, 1944 . . . . £75/£15
ditto, as *The Quick and the Dead*, Pan, 1961 . £10
The Murderer is a Fox, Little, Brown (U.S.), 1945 .
. . . . £100/£15
ditto, Gollancz, 1945 . . . . £50/£10
Ten Days' Wonder, Little, Brown (U.S.), 1948 £75/£15
ditto, Gollancz, 1948 . . . . £50/£10
Cat of Many Tails, Little, Brown (U.S.), 1949 £75/£15
ditto, Gollancz, 1949 . . . . £50/£10
Double, Double, Little, Brown (U.S.), 1950 . £65/£10
ditto, Gollancz, 1950 . . . . £45/£10
ditto, as *The Case of the Seven Murders*, Pocket
(U.S.), 1958 (wraps) £10
The Origin of Evil, Little, Brown (U.S.), 1951 £65/£10
ditto, Gollancz, 1951 . . . . £45/£10
The Lamp of God, Dell (U.S.), 1951 (wraps) . £25
The King is Dead, Little, Brown (U.S.), 1952 £75/£10
ditto, Gollancz, 1952 . . . . £45/£10
The Scarlet Letters, Little, Brown (U.S.), 1953 . .
. . . . £50/£10
ditto, Gollancz, 1953 . . . . £40/£10
The Glass Village, Little, Brown (U.S.), 1954 £50/£10
ditto, Gollancz, 1954 . . . . £50/£10
Inspector Queen's Own Case, Simon & Schuster
(U.S.), 1956 . . . . £50/£10
ditto, Gollancz, 1956 . . . . £35/£5
The Finishing Stroke, Simon & Schuster (U.S.), 1958
. . . . £50/£10
ditto, Gollancz, 1958 . . . . £35/£5
A Study in Terror, Lancer (U.S.), 1966 (written with
Paul W. Fairman) £15
ditto, as *Sherlock Holmes Versus Jack the Ripper*,
Gollancz, 1967 . . . . £150/£35
Face to Face, NAL (U.S.), 1967 . . . £45/£10
ditto, Gollancz, 1967 . . . . £35/£5

Cop Out, World (U.S.), 1969 . . . . . £45/£10
ditto, Gollancz, 1969 . . . . £35/£5
The Last Woman in His Life, World (U.S.), 1970 . .
. . . . £40/£10
ditto, Gollancz, 1970 . . . . £30/£5
A Fine and Private Place, World (U.S.), 1971 . £35/£5
ditto, Gollancz, 1971 . . . . £25/£5

Omnibus Editions
The Ellery Queen Omnibus, Grosset & Dunlap (U.S.),
1932 (contains *The Roman Hat Mystery*, *The French
Powder Mystery*, *The Dutch Shoe Mystery*) £75/£20
The Ellery Queen Omnibus, Gollancz, 1934 (contains
The French Powder Mystery, *The Dutch Shoe Mystery*
and *The Greek Coffin Mystery*) . . . . £75/£20
The New York Murders: An Ellery Queen Omnibus,
Little, Brown and Co. (U.S.), 1958 (contains *Cat of
Many Tails*, *The Scarlet Letters* and *The American
Gun Mystery* . . . . £35/£10

'Ellery Queen' Short Stories
The Adventures of Ellery Queen, Stokes (U.S.), 1934 .
. . . . £600/£75
ditto, Gollancz, 1935 . . . . £175/£30
The New Adventures of Ellery Queen, Stokes (U.S.),
1940 . . . . £500/£65
ditto, Gollancz, 1940 . . . . £150/£25
The Case Book of Ellery Queen, Spivak (U.S.), 1945
(wraps) £50
The Case Book of Ellery Queen, Gollancz, 1949
(different from above) . . . . . . £45/£10
Calendar of Crime, Little, Brown (U.S.), 1952 £65/£15
ditto, Gollancz, 1952 . . . . . . £50/£10
QBI: Queen's Bureau of Investigation, Little, Brown
(U.S.), 1954 . . . . £40/£10
ditto, Gollancz, 1955 . . . . £30/£5
Queen's Full, Random House (U.S.), 1965 . . £25/£5
ditto, Gollancz, 1966 . . . . £25/£5
QED: Queen's Experiments in Detection, New
American Library (U.S.), 1968 . . . . . £25/£5
ditto, Gollancz, 1969 . . . . £25/£5

'Ellery Queen' Non Fiction Titles
Queen's Quorum, Little, Brown (U.S.), 1951 £100/£25
ditto, Gollancz, 1953 . . . . . . £65/£25
In the Queen's Parlour, Simon & Schuster (U.S.),
1957 . . . . £35/£10
ditto, Gollancz, 1957 . . . . . . £30/£10

'Barnaby Ross' Titles
The Tragedy of X, Viking (U.S.), 1932 . . £200/£60
ditto, Cassell & Co., 1932 . . . . . £150/£45
The Tragedy of Y, Viking (U.S.), 1932 . . £200/£60
ditto, Cassell & Co., 1932 . . . . . £150/£45
The Tragedy of Z, Viking (U.S.), 1933 . . £200/£60
ditto, Cassell & Co., 1933 . . . . . £150/£45
Drury Lane's Last Case, Viking (U.S.), 1933 . . .
. . . . £175/£40
ditto, Cassell & Co., 1933 . . . . . £150/£35

'Ellery Queen' Novels by Other Writers
The Last Man Club, Whitman (U.S.), 1940. £200/£35
ditto, Pyramid, 1968 (with *The Murdered Millionaire*,
wraps) £5
Ellery Queen, Master Detective, Grosset & Dunlap
(U.S.), 1941 . . . . £65/£10
ditto, as *The Vanishing Corpse*, Pyramid, 1968
(wraps) £5
The Penthouse Mystery, Grosset (U.S.), 1941 £65/£10
The Murdered Millionaire, Whitman (U.S.), 1942. .
. . . . £200/£35
The Perfect Crime, Grosset (U.S.), 1942 . £65/£10
Dead Man's Tale, Pocket Books (U.S.), 1961 (by
Stephen Marlowe, wraps) £10
ditto, Four Square, 1967 (wraps) £5
Death Spins the Platter, Pocket Books (U.S.), 1962
(by Richard Deming, wraps) £10
ditto, Gollancz, 1975 . . . . . . £40/£10
The Scrolls of Lysis, Simon & Schuster (U.S.), 1962 .
. . . . £35/£10
The Player on the Other Side, Random House (U.S.),
1963 (by Theodore Sturgeon) . . . . £45/£10
ditto, Gollancz, 1963 . . . . £35/£5
Murder With a Past, Pocket Books (U.S.), 1963 (by
Talmage Powell, wraps) £10
Kill as Directed, Four Square, 1963 (wraps) . . £5
Wife or Death, Four Square, 1963 (wraps) . . £5
And on the Eighth Day, Random House (U.S.), 1964
(by Avram Davidson) . . . . . . £45/£10
ditto, Gollancz, 1964 . . . . £35/£5
The Golden Goose, Pocket Books (U.S.), 1964 (wraps)
. . . . £10
ditto, Four Square, 1967 (wraps) £5
The Four Johns, Pocket Books (U.S.), 1964 (by Jack
Vance, wraps) £5
ditto, as *Four Men Called John*, Gollancz, 1976 . .
. . . . £25/£5
Blow Hot Blow Cold, Pocket Books (U.S.), 1964
(wraps) £10
The Duke of Chaos, Pocket Books (U.S.), 1964
(wraps) £10
The Last Score, Pocket Books (U.S.), 1964 (wraps) .
. . . . £10
The Copper Frame, Pocket Books (U.S.), 1965
(wraps) £10
ditto, Four Square, 1968 (wraps) £5
The Fourth Side of the Triangle, Random House
(U.S.), 1965 (by Avram Davidson) . . . £45/£10
ditto, Gollancz, 1965 . . . . £35/£5
The Killer Touch, Pocket Books (U.S.), 1965 (wraps).
. . . . £10
Beware the Young Stranger, Pocket Books (U.S.),
1965 (wraps) £10
A Room To Die In, Pocket Books (U.S.), 1965 (by
Jack Vance, wraps) £10
ditto, Kinnell, 1987 . . . . £20/£5
The Madman Theory, Pocket Books (U.S.), 1965 (by
Jack Vance, wraps) £10
ditto, Kinnell, 1988 . . . . £20/£5

Why So Dead?, Popular Library (U.S.), 1966 (wraps) .
. . . . £5
ditto, Four Square, 1966 (wraps). £5
Shoot the Scene, Dell (U.S.), 1966 (wraps). . . . £5
Where is Bianca?, Popular Library (U.S.), 1966
(wraps) £5
ditto, Four Square, 1966 (wraps). £5
Who Spies, Who Kills?, Popular Library (U.S.), 1966
(wraps) £5
ditto, Four Square, 1967 (wraps). £5
Losers, Weepers, Dell (U.S.), 1966 (wraps). . . £5
How Goes the Murder?, Popular Library (U.S.), 1967
(wraps) £5
Which Way to Die?, Popular Library (U.S.), 1967
(wraps) £5
The House of Brass, NAL (U.S.), 1968 (by Theodore
Sturgeon) . . . . £45/£10
ditto, Gollancz, 1968 . . . . £35/£5
What's In The Dark, Popular Library (U.S.), 1968 (by
Richard Deming, wraps). £5
ditto, as *When Fell the Night*, Gollancz, 1970 £40/£10
Guess Who's Coming to Kill You?, Lancer (U.S.),
1968 (wraps) £5
The Campus Murders, Lancer (U.S.), 1969 (wraps) £5
Kiss and Kill, Dell (U.S.), 1969 (wraps). . . . £5
The Black Hearts Murders, Lancer (U.S.), 1970
(wraps) £5
The Blue Movie Murders, Lancer (U.S.), 1972 (by
Edward D. Hoch, wraps) £5
ditto, Gollancz, 1973 . . . . £30/£5

JONATHAN RABAN
(b.1942)

Raban's early works are academic, but he now has a
considerable reputation as a travel writer.

Travel Titles
Soft City, Hamish Hamilton, 1974 . . . . £30/£5
ditto, Dutton (U.S.), 1974. . . . . . . £25/£5
Arabia Through the Looking Glass, Collins, 1979
. . . . £25/£5
ditto, as *Arabia: A Journey Through the Labyrinth*,
Simon & Schuster (U.S.), 1979 . . . . . £20/£5
Old Glory: An American Voyage, Collins, 1981 . .
. . . . £20/£5
ditto, Simon & Schuster (U.S.), 1981 . . . £15/£5
Coasting, Collins, 1986 . . . . £15/£5
ditto, Simon & Schuster (U.S.), 1987 . . . £15/£5
Hunting Mr Heartbreak, Collins, 1990 . . . £10/£5
ditto, Harper Collins (U.S.), 1991 . . . . £10/£5
Passage to Juneau: A Sea and Its Meanings, Picador,
1999 . . . . £10/£5
ditto, Pantheon (U.S.), 1999 . . . . . £10/£5

Novels
Foreign Land, Collins, 1985 . . . . . . £25/£5
ditto, Viking (U.S.), 1985. . . . . . . £20/£5

Bad Land: An American Romance, Picador, 1996 .
. . . . £15/£5
ditto, Pantheon (U.S.), 1996 . . . . . £15/£5

Academic Titles
The Technique of Modern Fiction, Arnold, 1968 . .
. . . . £100/£25
ditto, Univ. of Notre Dame Press (U.S.), 1968 (wraps).
. . . . £10
Huckleberry Finn, Arnold, 1968 . . . £50/£10
The Society of the Poem, Harrap, 1971 . . . £25/£5

Others
For Love and Money, Collins, 1987. . . . £25/£5
ditto, Harper & Row (U.S.), 1989 . . . . £20/£5
God, Man and Mrs Thatcher, Chatto & Windus
(wraps) £10

ARTHUR RACKHAM
(b.1867 d.1939)

A highly successful illustrator, Rackham's early gift
books are his most sought after titles, especially in
deluxe editions.

To the Other Side, by Thomas Rhodes, George Philip,
1893 (wraps, also illustrated by Alfred Bryan) £400
The Dolly Dialogues, by Anthony Hope, Westminster
Gazette Library: Volume One, [July] 1894 (4 half-
tone illustrations, wraps, first issue with 'Dolly'
running head). £200
ditto, Westminster Gazette Library: Volume One,
[July] 1894 (4 half-tone illustrations, wraps, second
issue with 'The Dolly Dialogues' running head) . .
. . . . £150
ditto, Westminster Gazette Library: Volume One,
[August] 1894 (4 half-tone illustrations, cloth edition)
. . . . £150
ditto, Holt (U.S.), 1894 (frontispiece illustration only).
. . . . £125
The Sketch-Book of Geoffrey Crayon, by Washington
Irving, Putnams (U.S.), 1894 (2 vols, 3 illustrations
by Rackham, many others by various artists, 1,000
numbered sets, red cloth) £350
ditto, Putnams, [1895] (2 vols, 1 further illustration by
Rackham). £175
The Illustrated Guide to Wells-next-the-Sea, by
Lingwood Lemmon, Jarrolds, [1894] (49 b&w
illustrations, illustrated wraps) £350
ditto, Jarrolds, [1894] (red cloth issue, date on title
page) £200
Sunrise-Land - Rambles in Eastern England, by Mrs
Alfred Berlyn, Jarrolds, 1894 (71 vignette
illustrations, mauve pictorial cloth). . . . £250
ditto, Jarrolds, 1894 (cheaper edition, white boards) .
. . . . £125

ditto, as *East Coast Health Resorts*, Jarrolds, 1894 (14 illustrations reprinted from above, red cloth) . £125

Isis Very Much Unveiled, by Edmund Garrett, Westminster Gazette, 1894 (1 b&w illustration, wraps). £100

Souvenir of Sir Henry Irving, Drane, 1895 (1 half-tone drawing by Rackham, many others by various artists, wraps). £125

The Homes and Haunts of Thomas Carlyle, Westminster Gazette, 1895 (1 sketch by Rackham, many others by various artists, blue cloth) . . £100

The New Fiction and Other Papers, by The Philistine, Westminster Gazette, 1895 (1 b&w illustration) £100

A London Garland, Macmillan, 1895 (1 illustration by Rackham, many others by various artists, cream cloth) £75

ditto, Macmillan, 1895 (bound in vellum, slipcase). . . . . £200/£150

The Wonderful Visit, by H.G. Wells, Dent, 1895 (design on upper board by Rackham, red cloth) £350

Tales of a Traveller, by Washington Irving, Putnams, 1895 (2 vols, 5 half-tone illustrations, white or light blue cloth) £125

ditto, Putnams, 1895 (150 copies, light brown full calf) £250

The Zankiwank and the Bletherwitch, Dent, 1896 (24 b&w illustrations, dark green cloth) . . . £2,250

ditto, Dutton (U.S.), 1896 . . . . . . £2,000

Bracebridge Hall, by Washington Irving, Putnams (U.S.), 1896 (2 vols, 5 illustrations by Rackham, many others by various artists, dark blue cloth) £100

ditto, Putnams (U.S.), 1896 (2 vols, 100 copies signed by publishers, light brown full calf) . . . £250

The Money Spinner and Other Character Notes, by Henry Seaton Merriman and S.G. Tallentyre, Smith Elder, 1896 (12 half tone illustrations, red calf) £200

In the Evening of His Days - A Study of Mr Gladstone in Retirement, Westminster Gazette, 1896 (10 b&w illustrations by Rackham, some by other artists, grey/blue cloth) £175

Captain Castle, by Carlton Dawe, Smith Elder, 1897 (frontispiece by Rackham, dark blue cloth) . £250

The Grey Lady, by Henry Seaton Merriman, Smith Elder, 1897 (12 half tone illustrations, lavender-grey cloth) £250

Two Old Ladies, Two Foolish Fairies and a Tom Cat, The Surprising Adventures of Tuppy and Tue, by Maggie Browne, Cassell, 1897 (4 colour, 19 b&w illustrations, various colours of cloth) . . £500

ditto, as *The Surprising Adventures of Tuppy & Tue*, Cassell, 1904 (4 colour illustrations, 10 b&w drawings and 12 drawings in text) £200

Charles O'Malley, The Irish Dragoon, by Charles Lever, Service & Paton, 1897 (16 b&w illustrations, maroon cloth) £300

ditto, Putnams (U.S.), 1897 . . . . . £200

Through A Glass Lightly, by T.T. Greg, Dent, 1897 (title page sketch by Rackham, bound in yellow silk). £125

The Castle Inn, by Stanley J. Wellman, Smith, Elder, 1898 (frontispiece by Rackham, dark blue cloth) £125

Evelina, by Frances Burney, George Newnes, 1898 (16 b&w illustrations, first issue with one page advert at rear, grey/blue cloth). £150

ditto, George Newnes, 1898 (second issue with two page advert at rear) £100

The Ingoldsby Legends, [by R.H. Barham], J.M. Dent, 1898 (12 colour, 90 b&w illustrations, gilt lettering on cover and spine, dark green cloth) . . . £200

ditto, J.M. Dent, 1907 (second edition, revised and enlarged, 24 colour plates, 12 tinted illustrations, 66 drawings in text) £200

ditto, J.M. Dent, 1907 (560 signed copies) . . £1,500

ditto, Dutton (U.S.), 1907 (trade edition) . £150

ditto, Dutton (U.S.), 1907 (50 signed copies) . £2,000

East Coast Scenery, by William J. Tate, Jarrolds, 1899 (7 b&w illustrations, pictorial eggshell green boards) £150

Feats on the Fjords, by Harriet Martineau, J.M. Dent, 1898 (colour frontispiece and 11 b&w illustrations, blue leather edition) £125

ditto, J.M. Dent, 1898 (blue cloth edition) . . £75

ditto, as *Feats on the Fjord and Merdhin*, Dent: Everyman Library, [1910] (3 additional b&w plates). £60

ditto, J.M. Dent, 1914 (plates coloured) . . £40

Tales from Shakespeare, by Charles and Mary Lamb, J.M. Dent, 1899 (colour frontispiece and 11 b&w illustrations, blue leather edition) £150

ditto, J.M. Dent, 1899 (blue cloth edition) . £100

ditto, J.M. Dent, 1909 (deluxe second edition, revised and enlarged, 13 colour illustrations, 2 b&w illustrations, 20 chapter headings and 14 tailpieces, 750 signed copies) £1,250

ditto, J.M. Dent, 1909 (trade edition of above, less one colour plate) £200

ditto, Dutton (U.S.), 1909 . . . . . . £150

A World In A Garden, by R Neish, J.M. Dent, 1899 (chapter headings and tailpieces by Rackham, and illustrations by Jessie Macgregor, pink cloth) . £75

The Bee-Blowaways, by Agnes Grozier Herbertson, Cassell, [1900] (16 illustrations, green cloth) . £650

Gardens Old And New, Newnes, 1900 (3 vols, with designs by Rackham in first two vols, green cloth) £100

Gulliver's Travels, by Jonathan Swift, J.M. Dent, 1900 (colour frontispiece and 11 b&w illustrations, blue leather edition) £125

ditto, J.M. Dent, 1900 (blue cloth edition) . . £75

ditto, J.M. Dent, 1909 (deluxe second edition, revised and enlarged, 13 colour plates, 2 b&w illustrations, 7 chapter heads and tailpieces, 750 signed copies with extra plate) £1,250

ditto, J.M. Dent, 1909 (trade edition of above, less one colour plate) £150

ditto, Dutton (U.S.), 1909 . . . . . . £125

Fairy Tales of the Brothers Grimm, Freemantle, 1900 (cover design, endpapers, colour frontispiece and 99 b&w illustrations) £300
ditto, Lippincott (U.S.), [1902] £250
ditto, Constable, 1909 (second edition, revised and enlarged, 40 colour plates, 45 b&w illustrations) £750
ditto, Constable, 1909 (deluxe edition, 750 signed copies) £3,000
ditto, as *Hansel & Gretel and Other Tales* and *Snowdrop and Other Tales*, by the Brothers Grimm, Constable, 1920 (dark blue cloth) . . . £500/£250
ditto, Dutton (U.S.), 1920 . . . . . £500/£250
Animal Antics, Partridge, 1901 (1 b&w drawing by Rackham). £75
Queen Mab's Fairy Realm, Newnes, 1901 (2 full page illustrations and three within the text by Rackham, with illustrations by other artists, dark blue cloth) .
. . . . £250
The Argonauts of the Amazon, by C.R. Kenyon, W. & R. Chambers, 1901 (6 half tone illustrations, light blue cloth) £100
ditto, Dutton (U.S.), 1901. . . . . . . £100
The Life of a Century, Newnes, 1901 (12 parts, with 3 line and 3 wash drawings by Rackham in part 4, wraps). £125
Mysteries of Police and Crime, by Major Arthur Griffiths, Cassell, 1901 (3 vols, with illustrations by Rackham in vols 1 and 2, along with other artists, green cloth) £100
More Tales of the Stumps, Horace Bleackley, Ward Lock, 1902 (11 b&w illustrations, blue cloth). £200
Faithful Friends, Blackie, 1902 (6 colour illustrations by Rackham, with other artists, pictorial boards) £125
Brains and Bravery, Being Stories told by ..., G.A. Henty, W. & R. Chambers, [1903] (8 half tone illustrations, red or blue cloth) £125
ditto, W. & R. Chambers, 1903 (later edition, green cloth) £100
The Grey House on the Hill, by Hon. Mrs Greene, Thomas Nelson, [1903] (8 colour illustrations, pink cloth) £100
Littledom Castle and Other Tales, by Mrs M.H. Speilmann, George Routledge, 1903 (9 full page and 3 text drawings, red cloth) £200
ditto, Dutton (U.S.), 1903 . . . . . . £200
Plays for Little Folks, Cassell, 1903 (2 coloured illustrations and 2 b&w drawings by Rackham, with other artists, grey-green cloth) £100
The Greek Heroes, Cassell, 1903 (4 colour, 8 b&w illustrations, limp green buckram) £100
The Venture, Baillie, 1905 [1904] (1 illustration by Rackham, with other artists) £100
Two Years Before the Mast, by Richard Henry Dana, Collins, [1904] (8 colour plates, green or pink cloth).
. . . . £75
ditto, Winston (U.S.), 1903 (tan or light blue cloth) £75
Where Flies the Flag, by Henry Harbour, Collins, [1904] (6 colour plates, red or blue cloth) . . £75

Molly Bawn, by Mrs Hungerford, George Newnes: Newnes Sixpenny Novels, [1904] (8 b&w illustrations, wraps) £125
The Peradventures of Private Pagett, by Major W.P. Drury, Chapman & Hall, 1904 (8 b&w illustrations, orange-red cloth). £125
Little Folks Picture Album, by S.H. Hamer, 1904 (1 colour illustration by Rackham, with other artists, green or brown cloth) £100
Red Pottage, by Mary Cholmondeley, George Newnes: Newnes Sixpenny Novels, [1904] (8 half tone illustrations, wraps) £125
Penrose's Pictorial Annual, 1905 (vols 11 and 23 each contain a colour plate by Rackham from *Rip Van Winkle* and *Cinderella*, with other artists, pictorial cloth) . . £100 for each of the two relevant volumes
The Infants Magazine, 1905 (3 b&w illustrations by Rackham, with other artists, pictorial card boards) .
. . . . £125
The Children's Christmas Treasury, Dent, [1905] (2 illustrations by Rackham from *Ingoldsby Legends*, with other artists, white cloth) £100
The 'Old' Water Colour Society, Offices of the Studio, 1905 (1 illustration by Rackham, with other artists, green or grey cloth) £100
Rip van Winkle, by Washington Irving, Heinemann, 1905 (frontispiece and 50 colour plates, green cloth) .
. . . . £750
ditto, Heinemann, 1905 (special binding, green leather)
. . . . £1,000
ditto, Heinemann, 1905 (deluxe edition, 250 signed copies, pictorial full vellum) £3,500
ditto, Doubleday (U.S.), 1905 (trade edition) . £500
ditto, Heinemann, 1916 (only 24 plates, but new drawings added) £250
ditto, Doubleday (U.S.), 1916 . . . . . £250
Kingdoms Curious, by Myra Hamilton, Heinemann, 1905 (4 b&w illustrations by Rackham, with other artists, tan cloth) £350
The Little Folks Fairy Book, Cassell, 1905 (1 full page and 8 text illustrations by Rackham, with other artists, red or blue boards) £350
The Children's Hour, Newnes, 1906 (1 b&w illustration by Rackham, with other artists, green cloth) £350
Peter Pan in Kensington Gardens, by J.M. Barrie, Hodder & Stoughton, 1906 (frontispiece and 49 colour plates, deluxe edition, 500 signed copies, full vellum) £3,000
ditto, Hodder & Stoughton, 1906 (trade edition, russet cloth) £1,000
ditto, Scribner (U.S.), 1906 (green cloth) . . £500
ditto, Hodder & Stoughton, 1910 (24 colour plates) .
. . . . £1,500
ditto, Hodder & Stoughton, 1912 (50 colour plates, 12 drawings) £400
ditto, Hodder & Stoughton, 1912 (deluxe edition, 50 colour plates, 12 drawings) £1,500

Puck of Pook's Hill, by Rudyard Kipling, Doubleday (U.S.), 1906 (4 colour illustrations, dark green cloth).
. . . . £200
The Children and the Pictures, by Pamela Tennant, Heinemann, 1907 (title page illustration by Rackham, pink cloth) £100
Alice's Adventures in Wonderland, by Lewis Carroll, William Heinemann, [1907] (13 colour plates, 14 b&w illustrations, deluxe edition of 1,130 copies, white buckram) £1,750
ditto, William Heinemann, [1907] (trade edition, green cloth) £300
ditto, Doubleday (U.S.), [1907] (550 signed copies, green boards). £1,750
ditto, Doubleday (U.S.), [1907] (trade edition, red cloth) £300
Tales and Talks About Animals, Blackie, 1907 (5 colour plates and 3 text illustrations by Rackham, with other artists, pictorial boards) . . . £100
ditto, as *Faithful Friends*, Blackie, 1913 . . £65
Good Night, by Eleanor Gates, Thomas Y. Cromwell (U.S.), [1907] (5 colour illustrations, grey pictorial cloth) £125
Auld Acquaintance, Dent, 1907 (2 illustrations from *The Zankiwank* and *Haddon Hall Library*, grey pictorial cloth) £100
The Land of Enchantment, by Alfred E. Bonser, Cassell, 1907 (frontispiece and 12 half tone illustrations, 24 drawings in text, first binding, green cloth) £200
ditto, Cassell, 1907 (second binding, cocoa cloth) £150
Featherweights, Hodder & Stoughton, 1908 (frontispiece and mounted cover label by Rackham, wraps) .
. . . . £150
The Cotter's Saturday Night, by Robert Burns, Hewetson, 1908 (frontispiece by Rackham, imitation vellum) £75
A Midsummer Night's Dream, by William Shakespeare, William Heinemann, 1908 (40 colour plates and 30 b&w drawings, tan cloth) . . £450
ditto, William Heinemann, 1908 (special binding in brown calf) £600
ditto, William Heinemann, 1908 (deluxe edition, 1,000 signed copies, full vellum) £1,750
ditto, Doubleday (U.S.), 1908 (trade edition, grey boards) £250
ditto, by William Shakespeare, Limited Editions Club (U.S.), 1939 (6 new colour illustrations, deluxe 1,950 copies) £500
Henry IV, Part II, by William Shakespeare, Harrap, 1908 (frontispiece by Rackham) £75
Macbeth, by William Shakespeare, Harrap, 1908 (frontispiece by Rackham) £75
The Odd Volume, by Simpkin etc, 1908 (1 illustration by Rackham from *Ingoldsby Legends*, with other artists, red wraps) £100
Undine, by De La Motte Fouque, William Heinemann, 1909 (15 colour plates, 30 b&w drawings, blue cloth)
. . . . £200

ditto, William Heinemann, 1909 (deluxe edition, 1,000 signed copies, full vellum) £1,250
ditto, Doubleday (U.S.), 1909 (trade edition, grey boards) £200
ditto, Doubleday (U.S.), 1909 (250 signed, numbered copies, brown boards) £1,250
The Rainbow Book, by Mrs M.H. Spielmann, Chatto & Windus, 1909 (15 coloured illustrations by Rackham, with other artists, coral cloth) . . £100
The Book of Betty Barber, by Maggie Browne, Duckworth, [1910] (6 colour illustrations, 14 b&w drawings, brown cloth with plate on cover) . £500
ditto, Badger (U.S.), 1914. . . . . . . £200
Stories of King Arthur, by A.L. Haydon, Cassell, 1910 (4 colour and 2 b&w illustrations, red cloth) . £75
Children's Treasury of Great Stories, Daily Express, 1910 (6 colour and 5 b&w illustrations by Rackham, with other artists, blue and black marbled cloth) £75
The Rhinegold and The Valkyrie, by Richard Wagner, William Heinemann, 1910 (34 colour and 14 b&w illustrations, brown buckram) £200
ditto, William Heinemann, 1910 (deluxe edition, 1,150 signed copies, full vellum) £1,000
ditto, Doubleday (U.S.), 1910 (trade edition, grey boards) £200
ditto, Doubleday (U.S.), 1910 (deluxe edition, 150 signed copies, brown boards) £1,500
Siegfried and The Twilight of the Gods, by Richard Wagner, William Heinemann, 1911 (30 colour and 9 b&w illustrations, brown buckram) . . . £200
ditto, William Heinemann, 1911 (deluxe binding in limp suede) £1,000
ditto, William Heinemann, 1911 (deluxe edition, 1,150 signed copies, full vellum) £1,000
ditto, Doubleday (U.S.), 1911 (trade edition, grey boards) £200
ditto, Doubleday (U.S.), 1911 (deluxe edition, 150 signed copies, brown boards) £1,500
ditto, as *The Ring of the Niblung*, Heinemann, 1939 (48 colour illustrations, blue-green cloth) . £150/£100
ditto, as *The Ring of the Niblung*, Garden City (U.S.), 1939 . . . . £150/£100
Aesop's Fables, William Heinemann, 1912 (13 colour plates, 53 drawings, green cloth) £250
ditto, William Heinemann, 1912 (deluxe edition, 1,450 signed copies, white buckram) £1,250
ditto, Doubleday (U.S.), 1912 (trade edition, green cloth) £250
ditto, Doubleday (U.S.), 1912 (deluxe edition, 250 signed copies, brown boards) £1,250
The Peter Pan Portfolio, Hodder & Stoughton, [1912] (500 boxed portfolios of 12 plates numbered 101-600, signed by publishers) £2,000
ditto, Hodder & Stoughton, 1912 (approx 20 boxed portfolios signed by the artist) £6,500
ditto, Brentano's (U.S.), 1912 (300 unsigned boxed portfolios) £2,000
The Little White Bird, by J.M. Barrie, Scribners (U.S.), 1912 (2 of 3 colour plates are by Rackham) . £450

Mother Goose: The Old Nursery Rhymes, William Heinemann, 1913 (13 colour plates, 85 drawings, grey cloth) £250
ditto, William Heinemann, 1913 (deluxe edition, 1,130 signed copies, white cloth) £1,500
ditto, Century (U.S.), 1913 (black cloth) . . £200
Arthur Rackham's Book of Pictures, William Heinemann, 1913 (44 colour plates and 10 drawings, grey-green cloth). £350
ditto, William Heinemann, 1913 (deluxe edition, 1,030 signed copies, white cloth) £1,000
ditto, William Heinemann, 1913 (30 inscribed copies with original drawing) £4,000
ditto, Century Co. (U.S.), 1913 (trade edition, tan cloth) £300
Princess Mary's Gift Book, Hodder & Stoughton, 1914 (1 mounted plate and 5 drawings by Rackham, with other artists, white or blue cloth) . . . £100
ditto, Hodder & Stoughton, 1914 (bound in full brown leather) £125
King Albert's Book, Hodder & Stoughton, 1914 (1 mounted colour plate by Rackham, with other artists, white cloth) £100
ditto, Hodder & Stoughton, 1914 (bound in quarter brown calf) £100
ditto, International News (U.S.), 1914 . . £100
Imagina, by Julia Ellsworth Ford, Duffield, 1914 (2 colour illustrations, blue cloth) £200
A Christmas Carol, by Charles Dickens, Heinemann, 1915 (12 colour plates and 20 drawings, olive green cloth) £350
ditto, Heinemann, 1915 (special binding in antique brown leather) £450
ditto, Heinemann, 1915 (deluxe edition, 525 signed copies, full vellum) £1,500
ditto, Lippincott (U.S.), 1915 (trade edition, red or lavender cloth) £250
ditto, Lippincott (U.S.), 1915 (deluxe edition, 100 signed copies, full vellum) £1,500
The Queen's Gift Book, Hodder & Stoughton, 1915 (1 colour plate and 2 drawings by Rackham, with other artists, light blue cloth) £100
The Allies' Fairy Book, Heinemann, 1916 (12 colour illustrations and 24 drawings, slate blue cloth) £125
ditto, Heinemann, 1916 (deluxe 525 signed copies, blue cloth) £1,000
ditto, Lippincott (U.S.), 1916 (green or red cloth) £125
ditto, Lippincott (U.S.), 1916 (deluxe 525 signed copies, blue cloth) £1,000
ditto, as *A Fairy Book*, Doubleday (U.S.), 1923 (11 colour illustrations and 20 drawings) . . . £75
Little Brother and Little Sister, by the Brothers Grimm, Constable, 1917 (12 colour illustrations, 43 drawings, light green cloth) £450
ditto, Constable, 1917 (deluxe 525 signed copies, including one extra colour plate laid in and signed, light grey cloth) £2,000
ditto, Dodd, Mead (U.S.), 1917 (red or blue cloth) £350

The Romance of King Arthur, And his Knights of the Round Table, by Thomas Malory and Alfred Pollard, Macmillan, 1917 (16 colour illustrations, 7 full-page drawings, 63 drawings in text, dark blue cloth) £300
ditto, Macmillan, 1917 (deluxe 500 signed copies, full vellum) £1,500
ditto, Macmillan (U.S.), 1917 (trade edition, green cloth) £250
ditto, Macmillan (U.S.), 1917 (deluxe 250 signed copies, full vellum) £1,500
English Fairy Tales, by Flora Annie Steel, Macmillan, 1918 (16 colour illustrations and 41 drawings, red cloth) £150
ditto, Macmillan, 1918 (deluxe edition limited to 500 signed copies, full vellum) £1,500
ditto, Macmillan (U.S.), 1918 (trade edition, red cloth) £150
ditto, Macmillan (U.S.), 1918 (250 unsigned deluxe copies, white calf) £250
The Springtide of Life: Poems of Childhood, by Algernon Charles Swinburne, Heinemann, 1918 (8 colour plates and 52 drawings, green cloth) . £100
ditto, Lippincott (U.S.), 1918 (green cloth) . . £100
ditto, Heinemann, 1918 (publishers special binding of dark green mottled leather) £125
ditto, Heinemann, 1918 (deluxe 765 signed copies, extra colour plate, vellum-backed cream boards) £750
ditto, Heinemann, 1918 [1925] (later issue, as trade edition but top edge not gilt) £30
Cinderella, by Charles Perrault, Heinemann, 1919 (colour frontispiece, 16 silhouette illustrations, pictorial boards) £150
ditto, Heinemann, 1919 (hand made paper copies, 525 signed copies, extra silhouette in colour, green boards with tan cloth spine) £650
ditto, Heinemann, 1919 (deluxe 'vellum' 325 signed copies, printed on Japanese vellum, vellum-backed cream boards) £1,000
ditto, Lippincott (U.S.), 1919 (trade edition) . £150
Snickerty Nick and the Giant, by Julia Ellsworth Ford, Moffat, Yard & Co (U.S.), 1919 (3 coloured plates and 10 drawings, light blue cloth) . . . £500
ditto, Suttonhouse (U.S.), 1933 (new edition, with music by C.A. Ridgeway) £150
Some British Ballads, by various, Constable, [1919] (16 colour plates and 24 drawings, light blue cloth) .
. . . . £125
ditto, Constable, [1919] (575 deluxe signed copies, vellum-backed cream boards) £800
ditto, Dodd Mead (U.S.), [1919] (trade edition, dark blue cloth) £125
ditto, Constable, [1924] (with 'Heinemann' at the foot of the spine) . . . . £100/£35
Irish Fairy Tales, by James Stephens, Macmillan, 1920 (16 colour illustrations, 21 drawings, green cloth) .
. . . . £500/£300
ditto, Macmillan, 1920 (deluxe 520 signed copies, vellum-backed white boards) £1,000
ditto, Macmillan (U.S.), 1920 . . . . £500/£300

The Sleeping Beauty, by Charles Perrault, Heinemann, 1920 (colour frontispiece, 4 silhouettes, 41 drawings, pictorial boards with red cloth backstrip) . £300/£150
ditto, Heinemann, 1920 (deluxe 625 signed copies, extra silhouette drawing, vellum-backed cream boards) £650
ditto, Lippincott (U.S.), 1920. . . . . £350/£200
Comus, by John Milton, Heinemann, [1921] (24 colour illustrations, 37 drawings, green cloth). . £500/£150
ditto, Heinemann, [1921] (deluxe 550 signed copies, vellum-backed cream boards) £500
ditto, Doubleday (U.S.), [1921] . . . £350/£200
A Dish of Apples, by Eden Phillpotts, Hodder & Stoughton, 1921 (3 colour illustrations, 23 drawings, grey cloth) . . . . £250/£100
ditto, Hodder & Stoughton, 1921 (deluxe 500 copies signed by author and artist, cream buckram) . £600
ditto, Hodder & Stoughton, 1921 (55 copies on Batchelor's Kelmscott paper) £1,500
A Wonder Book, by Nathaniel Hawthorne, Hodder & Stoughton, [1922] (24 colour illustrations and 20 drawings, red cloth) . . . . £300/£150
ditto, Hodder & Stoughton, [1922] (deluxe 600 signed copies, cream buckram). £1,000
ditto, Doran (U.S.), [1922] (orange-red cloth) . . .
. . . . £300/£150
Drawings In Pen and Pencil, by George Sheringham, The Studio, 1922 (1 illustration with work by others, grey-green cloth). . . . . £250/£100
ditto, by George Sheringham, The Studio, 1922 (250 numbered copies, full vellum) . . . £250/£100
British Book Illustration, by Malcolm C. Salaman, The Studio, 1923 (1 colour and 2 b&w illustrations with work by others, tan cloth) . . . . £250/£100
The Windmill, Heinemann, 1923 (1 colour picture by Rackham, with other artists, orange boards with brown cloth back) £75
ditto, Heinemann (U.S.), 1923 (as above but top edge gilt) £75
Annual of Advertising Art, Book Service Co. (U.S.), 1924 (1 colour picture by Rackham, with other artists, grey boards with tan cloth back) £75
The Book of the Queen's Dolls' House, Methuen, 1924 (2 vols, limited to 1,500 copies, containing 1 Rackham illustration, with other artists, blue boards with tan cloth back) £150
ditto, Methuen, 1924 (1 volume cheap edition, blue boards) £75
Where the Blue Begins, by Christopher Morley, Heinemann, [1925] (4 coloured plates, 16 drawings, blue cloth) . . . . £250/£100
ditto, Heinemann, [1925] (deluxe 175 signed copies, vellum-style boards). £1,000
ditto, Doubleday (U.S.), 1922 [1925] (blue cloth) . .
. . . . £250/£100
ditto, Doubleday (U.S.), 1922 [1925] (100 signed copies, black cloth) £1,500
Poor Cecco, by Margery Williams Bianco, George H. Doran (U.S.), 1925 (deluxe 105 copies signed by the

author, 7 colour plates, 24 drawings, slipcase, vellum-style spine and blue boards). . . £4,000/£3,500
ditto, George H. Doran (U.S.), 1925 (first trade issue with pictorial endpapers, blue cloth) . . £400/£250
ditto, George H. Doran (U.S.), 1925 (second trade issue with plain endpapers) . . . . . . £250/£100
ditto, Chatto & Windus, 1925 [May, 1926] (yellow cloth) . . . . £300/£150
A Road to Fairyland, by Erica Fay, Putnams, 1926 (colour frontispiece only, grey cloth with blue lettering) . . . . £250/£150
ditto, Putnams (U.S.), 1926 (red cloth with gilt lettering) . . . . £250/£150
The Tempest, by William Shakespeare, Heinemann/ Doubleday, 1926 (21 colour plates, 25 drawings, olive green or grey-black cloth). . . . £300/£150
ditto, Heinemann/ Doubleday, 1926 (deluxe 520 signed copies, vellum-style boards with vellum spine) £1,250
'Now Then', Pearson, 1927 (1 full page drawing, red pictorial wraps) £100
The Lonesomest Doll, by Abbie Farwell Brown, Houghton Mifflin (U.S.), 1928 (4 rose and turquoise, and 26 b&w drawings, tan pictorial cloth). £600/£350
The Legend of Sleepy Hollow, by Washington Irving, Harrap, 1928 (8 colour and 30 b&w drawings, green cloth) . . . . £225/£125
ditto, Harrap, 1928 (deluxe 375 signed copies, full vellum) £1,000
ditto, Harrap, 1928 (publisher's special binding, grey or brown leather). £250
ditto, McKay (U.S.), 1928 (trade edition, brown cloth)
. . . . £225/£125
ditto, McKay (U.S.), 1928 (125 signed, numbered copies, full vellum) £1,250
Not All the Truth, by Lewis Melville, Jarrolds, 1928 (1 b&w drawing, with other artists, light blue cloth). .
. . . . £250/£100
A New Book of Sense and Nonsense, Dent, 1928 (11 b&w drawings, green or orange cloth) . £250/£100
Peter Pan Retold For Little People, Hodder & Stoughton, 1929 (6 colour illustrations and 15 drawings within text, green or orange cloth) £125/£50
ditto, Scribners (U.S.), 1929 . . . . . £125/£50
The Vicar of Wakefield, by Oliver Goldsmith, Harrap, 1929 (12 colour and 22 b&w illustrations, dark green cloth) . . . . £250/£100
ditto, Harrap, 1929 (deluxe 775 signed copies, full vellum) £750
ditto, Harrap, 1929 (publisher's special binding, olive persian morocco) £250
ditto, McKay (U.S.), 1929 . . . . . £250/£100
The Outline of Literature, Newnes, 1930 (1 colour plate from Rip Van Winkle, with work by other artists, red or blue half leather) . . . . £100/£35
The Sun Princess, Shaw, [c.1930] (1 full page drawing and 2 in text from *Queen Mab's Fairy Realm*, 1901, with work by other artists, coloured pictorial boards).
. . . . £100/£35

The Chimes, by Charles Dickens, with an introduction by Edward Wagenknecht, Limited Editions Club (U.K./U.S.), 1931 (6 full-page and 14 smaller b&w drawings, 1,500 copies signed by the artist, tan buckram in pictorial slipcase) . . . . £450/£350

The Night Before Christmas, by Clement C. Moore, Harrap, 1931 (4 coloured plates, 17 b&w drawings, wraps with d/w) . . . . £100/£65

ditto, Harrap, 1931 (deluxe 550 signed copies, limp vellum in slipcase) . . . . . . £1,000/£800

ditto, Lippincott (U.S.), 1931 (green cloth) . £100/£65

The Compleat Angler, by Izaak Walton, Harrap, 1931 (12 colour and 25 b&w illustrations, dark blue cloth).
. . . . £400/£200

ditto, Harrap, 1931 (deluxe 775 signed copies, full vellum) £1,000

ditto, Harrap, 1931 (10 copies with signed watercolour, full vellum) £4,000

ditto, Harrap, 1931 (publisher's special binding, dark green or brown leather) £400

ditto, McKay (U.S.), 1931 (grey-blue cloth) £400/£200

The King of the Golden River, by John Ruskin, Harrap, 1932 (4 colour and 15 drawings, wraps with d/w) . . . . £100/£65

ditto, Harrap, 1932 (deluxe 570 signed copies, limp vellum) £650

ditto, Harrap, 1932 (9 copies with original drawing) .
. . . . £6,000

ditto, Lippincott (U.S.), 1932 (red cloth with pictorial panel) . . . . £100/£65

Fairy Tales, by Hans Andersen, Harrap, 1932 (8 colour and 19 b&w drawings, rose-red cloth) . . £300/£150

ditto, Harrap, 1932 (deluxe 525 signed copies, full vellum) £2,000

ditto, Harrap, 1932 (publisher's special binding, full morocco) £300

ditto, McKay (U.S.), 1932 . . . . . £300/£150

Oxted, Limpsfield and Neighbourhood, Lewis G Fry, editor, printed by Godwin, 1932 (5 b&w drawings, and head and tailpieces, slate green boards with grey-blue cloth spine) £75

Goblin Market, by Christina Rossetti, Harrap, 1933 (4 colour and 19 b&w illustrations, wraps with d/w) .
. . . . £200/£75

ditto, Harrap, 1933 (deluxe 410 signed copies, limp vellum, slipcase) . . . . £750/£600

ditto, Harrap, 1933 (10 copies with drawing) . . £6,000

ditto, Lippincott (U.S.), 1933 (red boards with pictorial panel) . . . . £150/£75

Raggle-Taggle, by Walter Starkie, John Murray, 1933 (title page drawing and frontispiece, green cloth) . .
. . . . £125/£45

ditto, Dutton (U.S.), 1933 (green cloth) . . £125/£45

The Arthur Rackham Fairy Book, by various, Harrap, 1933 (8 colour and 60 b&w illustrations, red cloth) .
. . . . £250/£125

ditto, Harrap, 1933 (deluxe 460 signed copies, full vellum) £1,750

ditto, Harrap, 1933 (10 signed copies with original watercolour, full vellum) £10,000

ditto, Lippincott (U.S.), 1933 (red cloth) . £250/£125

River & Rainbow, by Walter Carroll, Forsyth, 1934 (title page illustration, pictorial wraps) . . . £125

The Old Water-Colour Society's Club, Old Water-Colour Society, 1934 (one plate from *The Compleat Angler*, mottled tan boards) . . . . . £125/£45

The Pied Piper of Hamelin, by Robert Browning, Harrap, 1934 (4 colour and 14 b&w illustrations, wraps with d/w) . . . . £125/£60

ditto, Harrap, 1934 (deluxe 410 signed copies, limp vellum) £1,000

ditto, Lippincott (U.S.), 1934 (red or green cloth with pictorial panel) . . . . £125/£50

Spanish Raggle-Taggle, by Walter Starkie, John Murray, 1934 (title page drawing and frontispiece, red cloth) . . . . £125/£45

ditto, Dutton (U.S.), 1933 (red cloth) . . £125/£45

English Illustration, by James Thorpe, Faber, 1935 (1 b&w illustration, purple cloth) . . . . £125/£60

Tales of Mystery and Imagination, by Edgar Allan Poe, Harrap, 1935 (12 colour, 17 full page b&w and 11 small illustrations, grey-black cloth) . £400/£250

ditto, Harrap, 1935 (deluxe 460 signed copies, full vellum) £1,500

ditto, Harrap, 1935 (publisher's special binding, dark blue morocco) £400

ditto, Lippincott (U.S.), 1935 (red cloth) . £400/£250

Arthur Rackham, A Bibliography, by Sarah Briggs Latimore and Grace Clark Haskell, Suttonhouse (U.S.), 1936 (colour frontispiece and 14 b&w illustrations, turquoise cloth) . . . . £100/£60

ditto, Suttonhouse (U.S.), 1936 (550 numbered copies, pink cloth, slipcase) . . . . £175/£125

Don Gypsy, by Walter Starkie, John Murray, 1936 (title page drawing and frontispiece, tan cloth) . .
. . . . £125/£45

Peer Gynt, by Henrik Ibsen, Harrap, 1936 (12 colour and numerous b&w text illustrations, orange-brown cloth) . . . . £300/£150

ditto, Harrap, 1936 (deluxe 460 signed copies, full vellum) £850

ditto, Harrap, 1936 (publisher's special binding, green morocco) £250

ditto, Lippincott (U.S.), 1936 (orange cloth) £300/£150

The Far Familiar, by Percy MacKaye, Richards, 1938 (frontispiece by Rackham, blue cloth) . . £125/£45

The Wind in the Willows, by Kenneth Grahame, Limited Editions Club (U.S.), 1940 (16 colour plates, deluxe 2,020 copies, signed by the designer Bruce Rogers, cloth-backed patterned boards) . . £1,250

ditto, Heritage Press (U.S.), 1940 (12 colour plates and 14 line drawings, blue-mauve cloth) . . £175/£75

ditto, Methuen, 1950 (green cloth) . . £175/£75

ditto, Methuen, 1951 (deluxe 500 copies, full white calf) £1,000

'Haddon Hall Library' Titles
(illustrated by Rackham and other artists)
Wild Life in Hampshire Highlands, by George A.B.
Dewar, Dent, 1899 . . . . £50
ditto, Dent, 1899 (deluxe edition, 150 numbered
copies) £125
Fly Fishing, by Sir Edward Grey, Dent, 1899 . £75
ditto, Dent, 1899 (deluxe edition, 150 numbered
copies) £250
Our Gardens, by S. Reynolds Hole, Dent, 1899 £40
ditto, Dent, 1899 (deluxe edition, 150 numbered
copies, signed by Hole) £125
Our Forests and Woodlands, by John Nisbet, Dent,
1900 . . . . £35
ditto, Dent, 1900 (deluxe edition, 150 numbered
copies) £125
Hunting, by J. Otho Paget, Dent, 1900 . . . £50
ditto, Dent, 1900 (deluxe edition, 150 numbered
copies) £175
Outdoor Games, Cricket & Golf, by Hon R.H.
Lyttelton, Dent, 1901 . . . . £75
ditto, Dent, 1901 (deluxe edition, 150 numbered
copies) £175
Bird Watching, by Edmund Selous, Dent, 1901. £50
ditto, Dent, 1901 (deluxe edition, 150 numbered
copies) £125
Shooting, by Alexander Innes Shand, Dent, 1902 . £50
ditto, Dent, 1902 (deluxe edition, 150 numbered
copies) £175
Farming, by W.M. Todd, Dent, 1903 . . . £35
ditto, Dent, 1903 (deluxe edition, 150 numbered
copies) £125

ANN RADCLIFFE
(b.1764 d.1823)

Despite her inability to bring any of her characters to
life, Radcliffe excelled in her descriptions of scenes
of mystery and terror. The best known writer of the
Gothic school, without whom there would probably
be no Frankenstein or Dracula, she nevertheless
rationalised all of her supernatural manifestations
until the final novel, *Gaston de Blondeville*.

Novels
The Castles of Athlin and Dunbayne, Hookham, 1789
(anonymous) £2,500
A Sicilian Romance, Hookham & Carpenter, 1790
(anonymous) £3,000
The Romance of the Forest, Hookham, 1791 (3 vols,
'By the Authoress of 'A Sicilian Romance,', &c...') .
. . . . £2,500
*The Mysteries of Udolpho, a Romance; interspersed
with some pieces of poetry*, Robinson, 1794 (4 vols) .
. . . . £2,000
*The Italian, or the Confessional of the Black
Penitents*, Cadell & Davies, 1797 (3 vols). . £400

Gaston de Blondeville, and *St Alban's Abbey, A
Metrical Tale*, Colburn, 1826 (4 vols) . . . £1,000

Poetry
The Poems of Mrs A. Radcliffe, Bounden, 1815 . .
. . . . £1,000
The Poems of Mrs Ann Radcliffe, Smith, 1816 £750
The Poetical Works of Ann Radcliffe, Colburn &
Bentley, 1834. . . . . £500

Travel
A Journey Made in the Summer of 1794..., Robinson,
1795 . . . . £1,000

IAN RANKIN
(b.1960)

A Scottish crime writer who has lost his cult status as
he has become progressively more successful,
Rankin's novels are still vivid portrayals of
contemporary city life.

'Rebus' Novels
Knots & Crosses, Bodley Head, 1987 . £1,500/£150
ditto, Doubleday (U.S.), 1987 . . . . £350/£40
Hide & Seek, Barrie & Jenkins, 1991 . £300/£30
ditto, Penzler Books (U.S.), [1994] . . . £45/£10
Wolfman, Century, 1992 . . . . . £175/£25
Strip Jack, Orion, 1992 . . . . . £300/£25
ditto, St Martin's Press (U.S.), 1994 . . £65/£10
The Black Book, Orion, 1993 . . . . £100/£10
ditto, Penzler Books (U.S.), 1994 . . £45/£10
Mortal Causes, Orion, 1994 . . . . £100/£10
ditto, Simon & Schuster (U.S.), 1995 . . . £30/£5
Let It Bleed, Orion, 1995 . . . . . £400/£50
ditto, Simon & Schuster (U.S.), 1996 . . . £30/£5
Black & Blue, Orion, 1997 . . . . . £400/£50
ditto, St Martin's Press (U.S.), 1997 . . . £25/£5
The Hanging Garden, Orion, 1998 . . . £25/£5
ditto, Scorpion Press, 1998 (75 signed, numbered
copies) £75
ditto, Scorpion Press, 1998 (15 signed, lettered copies)
. . . . £200
ditto, St Martin's Press (U.S.), 1998 . . . . £25/£5
Dead Souls, Orion, 1999 . . . . . . £15/£5
ditto, St Martin's Press (U.S.), 1999 . . . £15/£5
Set in Darkness, Orion, 2000. . . . . . £15/£5
ditto, St Martin's Press (U.S.), 2000 . . . £15/£5
The Falls, Orion, 2001 . . . . . . £15/£5
ditto, St Martin's Press (U.S.), 2001 . . . . £15/£5
Resurrection Men, Orion, 2001 . . . . . £10/£5
ditto, Little, Brown (U.S.), 2003 . . . . £10/£5
Beggars Banquet, Orion, 2002 . . . . £15/£5
ditto, Scorpion Press, 2002 (99 signed, numbered
copies) £75

Novellas and Short Stories

A Good Hanging & Other Stories, Century, 1992 . .
. . . . £75/£15
ditto, St Martin's Press (U.S.), 2002 . . . . £15/£5
Death Is Not The End, Orion, 1998 . . . £25/£10
Herbert in Motion & Other Stories, Revolver, 1997
(200 numbered, signed copies, wraps) . . . £100

Other Novels

The Flood, Polygon, 1986 . . . . . £800/£75
Watchman, Bodley Head, 1988 . . . . £450/£30
Westwind, Barrie & Jenkins, 1990 . . . £125/£15

Novels written as 'Jack Harvey'

Witch Hunt, Headline, 1993 . . . . . £300/£35
Bleeding Hearts, Headline, 1994 . . . £500/£45
Blood Hunt, Headline, 1995 . . . . . £600/£50

ARTHUR RANSOME
(b.1884 d.1967)

Author of the much loved 'Swallows and Amazons'
series of books for children, Arthur Ransome also
wrote for adults.

'Swallows and Amazons' Titles

Swallows and Amazons, Cape, 1930 . £3,000/£300
ditto, Cape, 1931 (illustrated by Clifford Webb) . .
. . . . £400/£35
ditto, Lippincott (U.S.), 1931 . . . . . £500/£25
Swallowdale, Cape, 1931 . . . . . £2,250/£250
ditto, Lippincott (U.S.), 1932 . . . . . £200/£35
Peter Duck, Cape, 1932 . . . . . £1,250/£150
ditto, Lippincott (U.S.), 1933 . . . . . £200/£35
Winter Holiday, Cape, 1933 . . . . £1,250/£150
ditto, Lippincott (U.S.), [1934] . . . . . £200/£35
Coot Club, Cape, 1934 . . . . . £1,250/£150
ditto, Lippincott (U.S.), 1935 . . . . . £200/£35
Pigeon Post, Cape, 1936 . . . . . . £600/£75
ditto, Lippincott (U.S.), 1937 . . . . . £150/£35
We Didn't Mean to Go to Sea, Cape, 1937 . £450/£50
ditto, Macmillan (U.S.), 1938 . . . . £150/£35
Secret Water, Cape, 1939 . . . . . £400/£40
ditto, Macmillan (U.S.), 1940 . . . . £150/£35
The Big Six, Cape, 1940 . . . . . £400/£40
ditto, Macmillan (U.S.), 1941 . . . . £150/£30
Missee Lee, Cape, 1941 . . . . . £400/£40
ditto, Macmillan (U.S.), 1942 . . . . £150/£30
The Picts and the Martyrs, or Not Welcome At All,
Cape, 1943 . . . . £150/£30
ditto, Macmillan (U.S.), 1943 . . . . £125/£25
Great Northern, Cape, 1947 . . . . . £150/£30
ditto, Macmillan (U.S.), 1948 . . . . £125/£25

Other Children's Titles

Pond and Stream, Treherne, 1906 . . . . £150
The Child's Book of the Seasons, Treherne, 1906 £150
The Things in Our Garden, Treherne, 1906 . £150
Highways and Byways in Fairyland, Pinafore Library,
[1906] £175
The Imp and the Elf and the Ogre, Nisbet, 1910 £150
The Hoofmarks of the Faun, Martin Secker, 1911 .
. . . . £150
Old Peter's Russian Tales, T. C. & E. C. Jack, 1916 .
. . . . £150
ditto, Nelson (U.S.), [1938] . . . . . £75/£25
Aladdin and His Wonderful Lamp, Nisbet, [1919] .
. . . . £250
ditto, Nisbet, [1919] (250 signed copies) . . £1,000
ditto, Brentano's (U.S.), 1920 . . . . £300/£200

Adult Titles

The Souls of the Streets, Brown Langham, 1904 £400
The ABC of Physical Culture, Drane, 1904 . £50
The Stone Lady, Brown Langham, 1905 . . £125
Bohemia in London, Chapman & Hall, 1907 . £100
ditto, Dodd, Mead (U.S.), 1907 . . . . . £75
A History of Storytelling, Jack, 1909 . . . £125
Edgar Allan Poe, Secker, 1910 . . . . . £125
ditto, Mitchell Kennerley (U.S.), 1910 . . . £100
Oscar Wilde, Secker, 1912 . . . . . £100
ditto, Mitchell Kennerley (U.S.), 1913 . . . £100
Portraits and Speculations, Macmillan, 1913 . £65
The Elixir of Life, Methuen, 1915 . . . . £75
Six Weeks in Russia in 1919, Allen & Unwin, 1919
(wraps) £100
*The Soldier and Death: A Russian Folk Tale Told in
English*, J. C. Wilson, 1920 (wraps) . . . £45
ditto, Huebsch (U.S.), 1922 . . . . . £75/£25
The Crisis in Russia, Allen & Unwin, 1921 £125/£50
ditto, Huebsch (U.S.), 1921 . . . . £100/£30
Racundra's First Cruise, Allen & Unwin, 1923 . .
. . . . £750/£250
ditto, Huebsch (U.S.), 1923 . . . . . £450/£150
The Chinese Puzzle, Allen & Unwin, 1927 . £300/£100
ditto, Houghton Mifflin (U.S.), 1927 . . £300/£100
Rod and Line, Cape, 1929 . . . . . £500/£125
Mainly About Fishing, A. & C. Black, 1959 . . .
. . . . £300/£100
The Autobiography of Arthur Ransome, Cape, 1976 .
. . . . £25/£5

FORREST REID
(b.1875 d.1947)

An author whose evocations of his native Ulster landscape, and youth, are tinged with the supernatural.

Novels

The Kingdom of Twilight, Fisher Unwin, 1904. £250
The Garden God, David Nutt, 1905 . . . . £1,000
The Bracknels, Edward Arnold, 1911 . . . £150
ditto, as *Denis Bracknel*, Faber, 1947 (revised edition)
. . . . £25/£10
Following Darkness, Edward Arnold, 1912 . £150
The Gentle Lover, Edward Arnold, 1913 . . £150
At the Door of the Gate, Edward Arnold, 1915. £150
The Spring Song, Edward Arnold, 1916 . . £150
ditto, Houghton Miflin (U.S.), 1917 . . . £100
Pirates of the Spring, Talbot Press/Fisher Unwin, 1919
[1920]. £125
ditto, Houghton Miflin (U.S.), 1920 . . . £200/£75
Pender Among the Residents, Collins, 1922 £250/£100
ditto, Houghton Miflin (U.S.), 1923 . . . £200/£75
Demophon, Collins, 1927 . . . . . . £200/£75
Uncle Stephen, Faber, 1931 . . . . . £65/£20
Brian Westby, Faber, 1934 . . . . . £65/£20
The Retreat, Faber, 1936 . . . . . . £65/£20
Peter Waring, Faber, 1937 . . . . . £65/£20
Young Tom, Faber, 1944 . . . . . . £40/£10
Tom Barber, Pantheon (U.S.), 1955 (contains *Uncle Stephen*, *Young Tom* and *The Retreat*) . . . £25/£5

Short Stories

A Garden by the Sea, Talbot Press/Fisher Unwin, 1918
. . . . £125

Others

W.B. Yeats, A Critical Study, Secker, 1915 . . £75
ditto, Dodd, Mead (U.S.), 1915 . . . . £65
Apostate, Constable, 1926 (50 signed copies) . £400
ditto, Constable, 1926 . . . . . . £75/£20
ditto, Houghton Mifflin (U.S.), 1926 . . £75/£20
ditto, Faber, 1947 (engravings by Reynolds Stone). .
. . . . £75/£20
Illustrators of the Sixties, Faber & Gwyer, 1928 . .
. . . . £150/£100
Walter de la Mare, A Critical Study, Faber, 1929 . .
. . . . £50/£20
ditto, Holt (U.S.), 1929 . . . . . £45/£20
Private Road, Faber, 1940 . . . . . £50/£15
Retrospective Adventures, Faber, 1941 . £45/£10
Notes and Impressions, The Mourne Press, 1942 . .
. . . . £125/£50
Poems from the Greek Anthology, Faber, 1943 £25/£5
The Milk of Paradise, Faber, 1946 . . . £25/£5
The Suppressed Dedication and Envoy of The Garden God, D'Arch Smith, [1970's?] (105 numbered copies, wraps). £45

RUTH RENDELL
(b.1930)

A novelist and short story writer, Rendell is popularly known for the 'Wexford' detective stories and novels. Other fiction written under her own name Ruth Rendell explores wider issues of criminal maladjustment, while the 'Barbara Vine' books tend to investigate darker psychological motivation.

'Wexford' Novels

From Doon with Death, Long, 1964 . £2,000/£150
ditto, Doubleday (U.S.), 1965 . . . . £350/£30
A New Lease of Death, Long, 1967 . . . £750/£45
ditto, Doubleday (U.S.), 1967 . . . £150/£15
Wolf to the Slaughter, Long, 1967 . £2,250/£100
ditto, Doubleday (U.S.), 1968 . . . . £150/£15
The Best Man to Die, Long, 1969 . . . £650/£40
ditto, Doubleday (U.S.), 1970 . . . . £75/£15
A Guilty Thing Surprised, Hutchinson, 1970 £350/£25
ditto, Doubleday (U.S.), 1970 . . . . £60/£10
No More Dying, Then, Hutchinson, 1971 . £175/£25
ditto, Doubleday (U.S.), 1972 . . . . £35/£10
Murder Being Once Done, Hutchinson, 1972 . .
. . . . £175/£20
ditto, Doubleday (U.S.), 1972 . . . £35/£10
Some Lie and Some Die, Hutchinson, 1973 £150/£15
ditto, Doubleday (U.S.), 1973 . . . . £30/£10
Shake Hands for Ever, Hutchinson, 1975 . £125/£15
ditto, Doubleday (U.S.), 1975 . . . . £30/£10
A Sleeping Life, Hutchinson, 1978 . . . . £65/£5
ditto, Doubleday (U.S.), 1978 . . . . £15/£5
Put on by Cunning, Hutchinson, 1981 . . . £50/£5
ditto, as *Death Notes*, Pantheon (U.S.), 1981 . £10/£5
The Speaker of Mandarin, Hutchinson, 1983 . £30/£5
ditto, Pantheon (U.S), 1983 . . . . . £10/£5
An Unkindness of Ravens, Hutchinson, 1985 . £25/£5
ditto, Pantheon (U.S.), 1985 . . . . . £10/£5
The Veiled One, Hutchinson, 1988 . . . £20/£5
ditto, Pantheon (U.S.), 1988 . . . . . £10/£5
Kissing the Gunner's Daughter, Hutchinson, 1992 .
. . . . £15/£5
ditto, Warner (U.S.), 1992 . . . . . £10/£5
Simisola, Hutchinson, 1994 . . . . . £15/£5
ditto, Crown (U.S.), 1995 . . . . . £10/£5
Road Rage, Hutchinson, 1997 . . . . . £15/£5
ditto, Scorpion Press, 1997 (99 signed copies) . £75
ditto, Crown (U.S.), 1997 . . . . . . £10/£5
ditto, Franklin Library (U.S.), 1997 (signed, limited edition) £30
Harm Done, Hutchinson, 1999 . . . . . £15/£5
ditto, Scorpion Press, 1999 (99 signed copies) . £75
ditto, Scorpion Press, 1999 (15 signed, lettered copies)
. . . . £300
ditto, Crown (U.S.), 1999 . . . . . . £10/£5
Babes in the Wood, Hutchinson, 2002 . . . £15/£5

Omnibus Editions

Wexford: An Omnibus, Hutchinson, 1988 . . £20/£5

A Second Wexford Omnibus, Hutchinson, 1988 . .
. . . . £10/£5
The Third Wexford Omnibus, Hutchinson, 1989 . .
. . . . £10/£5
The Fourth Wexford Omnibus, Hutchinson, 1990 .
. . . . £10/£5
The Fifth Wexford Omnibus, Hutchinson, 1991 . .
. . . . £10/£5

Other Novels
To Fear a Painted Devil, Long, 1965 . £1,000/£100
ditto, Doubleday (U.S.), 1965 . . . . £150/£15
Vanity Dies Hard, Long, 1965 . . . £650/£45
ditto, as *In Sickness and in Health*, Doubleday (U.S.),
1966 . . . . £100/£15
The Secret House of Death, Long, 1968 . £750/£45
ditto, Doubleday (U.S.), 1969 . . . . £100/£15
One Across, Two Down, Hutchinson, 1971 . £350/£25
ditto, Doubleday (U.S.), 1971 . . . £50/£10
The Face of Trespass, Hutchinson, 1974 . £150/£15
ditto, Doubleday (U.S.), 1974 . . . £25/£10
A Demon in My View, Hutchinson, 1976 . £125/£15
ditto, Doubleday (U.S.), 1977 . . . £25/£10
A Judgement in Stone, Hutchinson, 1977 . £100/£10
ditto, Doubleday (U.S.), 1978 . . . . £20/£5
Make Death Love Me, Hutchinson, 1979 . £50/£10
ditto, Doubleday (U.S.), 1979 . . . . £40/£5
The Lake of Darkness, Hutchinson, 1980 . £25/£10
ditto, Doubleday (U.S.), 1980 . . . . £10/£5
Master of the Moor, Hutchinson, 1981 . . £20/£5
ditto, Pantheon (U.S.), 1982 . . . . £10/£5
The Killing Doll, Hutchinson, 1984 . . £20/£5
ditto, Pantheon (U.S.), 1984 . . . . £10/£5
The Tree of Hands, Hutchinson, 1984 . . £20/£5
ditto, Pantheon (U.S.), 1985 . . . . £10/£5
Live Flesh, Hutchinson, 1986 . . . . £20/£5
ditto, Pantheon (U.S.), 1986 . . . . £10/£5
A Dark Adapted Eye, Viking, 1986 (pseud. 'Barbara
Vine') . . . . £20/£5
ditto, Bantam (U.S.), 1986 (wraps) £5
A Fatal Inversion, Viking, 1987 (pseud. 'Barbara
Vine') . . . . £15/£5
ditto, Bantam (U.S.), 1987 (wraps) £5
Heartstones, Hutchinson, 1987 . . . . £15/£5
ditto, Harper (U.S.), 1987 . . . . . £10/£5
Talking to Strange Men, Hutchinson, 1987 . . £15/£5
ditto, Harper (U.S.), 1987 . . . . . £10/£5
The House of Stairs, Viking, 1988 (pseud. 'Barbara
Vine') . . . . £15/£5
ditto, Crown (U.S.), 1989 . . . . . £10/£5
The Bridesmaid, Hutchinson, 1989 . . . £15/£5
ditto, Mysterious Press (U.S.), 1989 . . . £10/£5
Gallowglass, Viking, 1990 (pseud. 'Barbara Vine') .
. . . . £15/£5
ditto, Crown (U.S.), 1990 . . . . . £10/£5
Going Wrong, Hutchinson, 1990 . . . . £15/£5
ditto, Mysterious Press (U.S.), 1990 . . . £10/£5
King Solomon's Carpet, Viking, 1991 (pseud. 'Barbara
Vine') . . . . £15/£5

ditto, Crown (U.S.), 1992 . . . . £10/£5
Asta's Book, Viking, 1993 (pseud. 'Barbara Vine') .
. . . . £15/£5
ditto, Scorpion Press, 1993 (99 signed copies) . £100
ditto, Scorpion Press, 1993 (20 lettered copies) . £250
ditto, as *Anna's Book*, Harmony (U.S.), 1993 . £10/£5
The Crocodile Bird, Hutchinson, 1993 . . . £10/£5
ditto, London Limited Editions, 1993 (150 signed
copies, glassine d/w) . . . . . £75/£65
ditto, Crown (U.S.), 1993 . . . . . . £10/£5
No Night is Too Long, Viking, 1994 (pseud. 'Barbara
Vine') . . . . £10/£5
ditto, Harmony (U.S.), 1994 . . . . . £10/£5
The Brimstone Wedding, Harmony (U.S.), 1995
(pseud. 'Barbara Vine') . . . . . £10/£5
ditto, Viking, 1996 . . . . £10/£5
The Keys to the Street, Hutchinson, 1996 . . £10/£5
ditto, Crown (U.S.), 1996 . . . . . . £10/£5
The Chimney Sweeper's Boy, Viking, 1998 (pseud.
'Barbara Vine') . . . . £10/£5
ditto, Harmony (U.S.), 1998 . . . . . £10/£5
A Sight for Sore Eyes, Hutchinson, 1998 . . £10/£5
ditto, Crown (U.S.), 1998 . . . . . . £10/£5
ditto, Scorpion Press, 1998 (99 signed copies) . £75
Grasshopper, Harmony (U.S.), 2000 (pseud. 'Barbara
Vine') . . . . £10/£5
ditto, Viking, 2000 . . . . £10/£5
Adam and Eve and Pinch Me, Hutchinson, 2001 . .
. . . . £10/£5
ditto, Crown (U.S.), 2001 . . . . . . £10/£5
The Blood Doctor, Viking, 2002 (pseud. 'Barbara
Vine') . . . . £10/£5
ditto, Shaye Areheart Books (U.S.), 2002 . . £10/£5

Short Stories
The Fallen Curtain and Other Stories, Hutchinson,
1976 . . . . £100/£25
ditto, Doubleday (U.S.), 1976 . . . . £50/£15
Means of Evil and Other Stories, Hutchinson, 1979 .
. . . . £30/£10
ditto, Doubleday (U.S.), 1980 . . . £20/£5
The Fever Tree and Other Stories, Hutchinson, 1982 .
. . . . £40/£10
ditto, Pantheon (U.S.), 1983 . . . . £20/£5
The New Girlfriend and Other Stories, Hutchinson,
1985 . . . . £20/£5
ditto, Pantheon (U.S.), 1986 . . . . . £10/£5
Three Cases for Inspector Wexford, Eurographica
(Helsinki), 1986 (350 signed copies, wraps) . £100
Collected Short Stories, Hutchinson, 1987 . . £10/£5
ditto, Pantheon (U.S.), 1988 . . . . . £10/£5
The Copper Peacock and Other Stories, Hutchinson,
1991 . . . . £15/£5
ditto, Mysterious Press (U.S.), 1991 . . . £10/£5
Blood Lines: Long and Short Stories, Hutchinson,
1995 . . . . £10/£5
ditto, Crown (U.S.), 1996 . . . . . . £10/£5
Piranha to Scurfy and Other Stories, Hutchinson,
2000 . . . . £10/£5
ditto, Crown (U.S.), 2002 . . . . . . £10/£5

Unguarded Hours, Pandora Press, 1990 (contains 'The Strawberry Tree' by Rendell, and 'Flesh and Grass' by Helen Simpson) . . . . £10/£5

Non Fiction
Matters of Suspense, Eurographica (Helsinki), 1986 (350 signed copies, wraps) £75
Ruth Rendell's Suffolk, Muller, 1989 . . . £25/£5
Undermining the Central Line, Chatto & Windus, 1989 (with Colin Ward, signed, wraps) . . £35
ditto, Chatto & Windus, 1989 (unsigned copies) £10

JEAN RHYS
(b.1890 d.1979)

Powerfully clear and imaginative writing peoples Rhys's novels with strong female characters, although the protagonists are often lonely and lacking in direction.

Novels
Postures, Chatto & Windus, 1928 . . £1,250/£100
ditto, as *Quartet*, Simon & Schuster, 1929 . £750/£75
After Leaving Mr Mackenzie, Cape, 1931 . £750/£125
ditto, Knopf (U.S.), 1931 . . . . . . £400/£45
Voyage in the Dark, Constable, 1934 . . £500/£65
ditto, Morrow (U.S.), 1935 . . . . £400/£45
Good Morning, Midnight, Constable, 1939. £500/£75
ditto, Harper & Row (U.S.), [1970] . . . . £20/£5
Wide Sargasso Sea, Deutsch, 1966 . . . £75/£15
ditto, Norton (U.S.), 1966. . . . . . £75/£15

Short Stories
The Left Bank and Other Stories, Cape, 1927 . . . . £750/£75
ditto, Harper (U.S.), 1927 . . . . . £500/£50
Tigers Are Better Looking, Deutsch, 1968 . £50/£15
ditto, Harper (U.S.), 1974 . . . . . £25/£10
Sleep It Off Lady, Deutsch, 1976 . . . £20/£5
ditto, Harper (U.S.), 1976 . . . . . . £20/£5

Translation
Perversity, by Francis Carco, Covici (U.S.), 1928 (translation credited to Ford Madox Ford but in fact Jean Rhys). . . . . £500/£100

Others
My Day, Three Pieces, Frank Hallman (U.S.), 1975 (wraps) £15
ditto, Frank Hallman (U.S.), 1975 (750 copies) £65/£30
ditto, Frank Hallman (U.S.), 1975 (26 signed, lettered copies) £175
Letters, 1931-1966, Deutsch, 1984 . . . £15/£5
ditto, Viking (U.S.), 1984 . . . . . . £15/£5
Smile Please, An Unfinished Biography, Deutsch, 1979 . . . . £15/£5
ditto, Harper (U.S.), 1980 . . . . . . £15/£5

ANNE RICE
(b.1941)

Interview with the Vampire started life as a cult best-seller and found itself two decades later as a Hollywood film.

The 'Vampire' Chronicles
Interview with the Vampire, Knopf (U.S.), 1976 . . . . £600/£45
ditto, Macdonald/Raven Books, 1976 . . £150/£15
The Vampire Lestat, Knopf (U.S.), 1985 . £150/£35
ditto, Futura Books, 1986 (wraps) £5
ditto, Macdonald, 1987 (first hardback) . . £45/£10
The Queen of the Damned, Knopf (U.S.), 1988 . . . . £45/£10
ditto, Ultramarine Press (U.S.), 1988 (150 signed, numbered copies) £250
ditto, Macdonald, 1988 . . . . . . £45/£10
The Tale of the Body Thief, Knopf (U.S.), 1992 . . . . £25/£5
ditto, Chatto & Windus, 1992 . . . . £20/£5
Memnoch the Devil, Knopf (U.S.), 1995 . £15/£5
ditto, Trice (U.S.), 1995 (26 signed, lettered copies) £250
ditto, Trice (U.S.), 1995 (50 signed copies in full leather). £200
ditto, Trice (U.S.), 1995 (425 signed, numbered copies). £100
ditto, Chatto & Windus, 1995 . . . . . £15/£5
Pandora, Knopf (U.S.), 1998. . . . . . £10/£5
ditto, Trice (U.S.), 1998 (26 signed, lettered copies, bound in full leather) £500
ditto, Trice (U.S.), 1998 (50 signed, deluxe copies, quarterbound in leather) £200
ditto, Trice (U.S.), 1998 (250 signed, numbered copies) £75
ditto, Chatto & Windus, 1998 . . . . . £10/£5
The Vampire Armand, Knopf (U.S.), 1998 . £10/£5
ditto, Trice (U.S.), 1998 (26 signed, lettered copies, bound in full leather) £500
ditto, Trice (U.S.), 1998 (50 signed, deluxe copies, quarterbound in leather) £200
ditto, Trice (U.S.), 1998 (250 signed, numbered copies) £75
ditto, Chatto & Windus, 1998 . . . . . £10/£5
Vittorio the Vampire, Knopf (U.S.), 1999 . £10/£5
ditto, Trice (U.S.), 1999 (250 signed, numbered copies) £75
ditto, Franklin Library (U.S.), 1999 (signed limited edition) £35
ditto, Chatto & Windus, 1999 . . . . . £10/£5
Merrick, Franklin Library (U.S.), 2000 (signed limited edition) £35
ditto, Knopf (U.S.), 2000 . . . . £10/£5
ditto, Chatto & Windus, 2000 . . . . . £10/£5
Blood and Gold, Knopf (U.S.), 2001 . . . £10/£5
ditto, Chatto & Windus, 2001 . . . . . £10/£5
Blackwood Farm, Knopf (U.S.), 2002 . . . £10/£5
ditto, Chatto & Windus, 2002 . . . . . £10/£5

The 'Witch' Chronicles
The Witching Hour, Knopf (U.S.), 1990 . . £20/£5
ditto, Chatto & Windus, 1991 . . . . . £15/£5
Lasher, Knopf (U.S.), 1993 . . . . . £20/£5
ditto, Chatto & Windus, 1993 . . . . . £15/£5
Taltos, Lives of the Mayfair Witches, Knopf (U.S.),
1994 . . . . £20/£5
ditto, Trice (U.S.), 1994 (500 signed, numbered
copies). £200
ditto, Chatto & Windus, 1994 . . . . . £15/£5

Ghost Novels
Servant of the Bones, Knopf (U.S.), 1996 . . £50/£5
ditto, Trice (U.S.), 1996 (26 signed, lettered copies) .
. . . . £250
ditto, Trice (U.S.), 1996 (50 signed copies in full
leather) £200
ditto, Trice (U.S.), 1996 (425 signed, numbered copies)
. . . . £100
ditto, Chatto & Windus, 1996 . . . . . £30/£5
Violin, Chatto & Windus, 1997 . . . . £45/£10
ditto, Trice (U.S.), 1997 (26 signed, lettered copies) .
. . . . £250
ditto, Trice (U.S.), 1997 (50 signed copies in full
leather) £200
ditto, Trice (U.S.), 1997 (325 signed, numbered copies)
. . . . £100
ditto, Knopf (U.S.), 1997 . . . . . £45/£10

Historical Novels
The Feast of All Saints, Simon & Schuster (U.S.),
1979 . . . . £100/£25
ditto, Arrow, 1991 (wraps) £5
Cry to Heaven, Knopf (U.S.), 1982 . . . £60/£10
ditto, Chatto & Windus, 1990 . . . . £40/£10
The Mummy, or Ramses the Damned, Ballantine
Books (U.S.), 1989 . . . . £150/£25
ditto, Ballantine Books (U.S.), 1989 (wraps) . £10
ditto, Chatto & Windus, 1989 . . . . £150/£25

Novels written as 'Anne Rampling'
Exit to Eden, Arbor House (U.S.), 1985. . £65/£15
ditto, Macdonald, 1986 . . . . . £45/£10
Belinda, Arbor House (U.S.), 1986 . . . £40/£10
ditto, Macdonald, 1987 . . . . . . £25/£5

Novels written as 'A.N. Roquelaure'
The Claiming of Sleeping Beauty, Dutton (U.S.), 1983
. . . . £150/£35
ditto, Future Books, 1987 (wraps) £5
ditto, Macdonald, 1988 . . . . . . £25/£5
Beauty's Punishment, Dutton (U.S.), 1984 . £200/£35
ditto, Futura Books, 1987 (wraps) . . . £10
Beauty's Release, Dutton (U.S.), 1985 . . £125/£35
ditto, Future Books, 1988 (wraps) . . . £10

FRANK RICHARDS
(b.1876 d.1961)

Under the pseudonym of 'Frank Richards', Charles
Hamilton created the everlasting, rotund schoolboy,
Billy Bunter.

'Billy Bunter' Titles
Billy Bunter of Greyfriars School, Skilton, 1947 . .
. . . . £75/£15
Billy Bunter's Banknote, Skilton, 1948 . . £60/£10
Billy Bunter's Barring-Out, Skilton, 1948 . £50/£10
Billy Bunter's Christmas Party, Skilton, 1949 £50/£10
Billy Bunter in Brazil, Skilton, 1949 . . £50/£10
Billy Bunter's Benefit, Skilton, 1950 . . £50/£10
Billy Bunter among the Cannibals, Skilton, 1950 . .
. . . . £45/£10
Billy Bunter's Postal Order, Skilton, 1951 . £45/£10
Billy Bunter Butts In, Skilton, 1951. . . £45/£10
Billy Bunter and the Blue Mauritius, Skilton, 1952 .
. . . . £50/£10
Billy Bunter's Beanfeast, Cassell, 1952. . £45/£10
Billy Bunter's Brain-Wave, Cassell, 1953 . £45/£10
Billy Bunter's First Case, Cassell, 1953 . £45/£10
Billy Bunter the Bold, Cassell, 1954. . . . £30/£5
Bunter Does His Best, Cassell, 1954 . . . £30/£5
Billy Bunter's Double, Cassell, 1955 . . . £30/£5
Backing Up Billy Bunter, Cassell, 1955. . . £30/£5
Lord Billy Bunter, Cassell, 1956. . . . . £25/£5
The Banishing of Billy Bunter, Cassell, 1956 . £25/£5
Billy Bunter's Bolt, Cassell, 1957 . . . . £25/£5
Billy Bunter Afloat, Cassell, 1957 . . . . £25/£5
Billy Bunter's Bargain, Cassell, 1958 . . . £20/£5
Billy Bunter the Hiker, Cassell, 1958 . . . £20/£5
Bunter Out of Bounds, Cassell, 1959 . . . £20/£5
Bunter Comes for Christmas, Cassell, 1959 . £20/£5
Bunter the Bad Lad, Cassell, 1960 . . . . £20/£5
Bunter Keeps It Dark, Cassell, 1960 . . . £20/£5
Billy Bunter's Treasure-Hunt, Cassell, 1961 . £20/£5
Billy Bunter at Butlins, Cassell, 1961 . . . £20/£5
ditto, Butlins Beaver Club edition, 1961 . . £15/£5
Bunter the Ventriloquist, Cassell, 1961 . . £20/£5
Bunter the Caravanner, Cassell, 1962 . . . £20/£5
Billy Bunter's Bodyguard, Cassell, 1962 . . £20/£5
Big Chief Bunter, Cassell, 1963 . . . . £20/£5
Just Like Bunter, Cassell, 1963 . . . . £20/£5
Bunter the Stowaway, Cassell, 1964. . . . £20/£5
Thanks to Bunter, Cassell, 1964. . . . . £20/£5
Bunter the Sportsman, Cassell, 1965 . . . £20/£5
Bunter's Last Fling, Cassell, 1965 . . . . £20/£5

Title Written as 'Hilda Richards'
Bessie Bunter of Cliff House School, Skilton, 1949 .
. . . . £45/£10

'Jack' Titles
Jack Of All Trades, Mandeville, 1930 . . . £25/£5
Jack's The Lad, Spring Books, 1957 . . . £10/£5
Jack of the Circus, Spring Books, 1957. . . £10/£5

Tom Merry Titles

The Secret of the Study, Mandeville, 1949 (pseud. 'Martin Clifford') . . . . £10/£5
Talbot's Secret, Mandeville, 1949 . . . . £10/£5
Tom Merry and Co of St Jim's, Mandeville, 1949 (pseud. 'Martin Clifford') . . . . . £10/£5
Rallying Round Gussy, Mandeville, 1950 (pseud. 'Martin Clifford') . . . . £10/£5
The Scapegrace of St Jim's, Mandeville, 1951 (pseud. 'Martin Clifford') . . . . £10/£5
The Rivals of Rookwood, Mandeville, 1951 (pseud. 'Owen Conquest') . . . . £10/£5
Tom Merry's Secret, Mandeville, 1952 (pseud. 'Martin Clifford') . . . . £10/£5
Tom Merry's Rival, Mandeville, 1952 (pseud. 'Martin Clifford') . . . . £10/£5
Trouble for Tom Merry, Spring Books, 1953 . £10/£5
Down and Out, Spring Books, 1953 . . . . £10/£5
Cardew's Catch, Spring Books, 1954 . . . £10/£5
The Disappearance of Tom Merry, Spring Books, 1954 . . . . £10/£5
Through Thick and Thin, Spring Books, 1955 . £10/£5
Tom Merry's Triumph, Spring Books, 1956 . £10/£5
Tom Merry and Co, Caravanners, Spring Books, 1956 . . . . £10/£5

Other Titles as 'Martin Clifford'

The Man from the Past, Hamilton, 1952 . . £10/£5
Who Ragged Railton?, Hamilton, 1952 . . . £10/£5
Skimpole's Snapshot, Hamilton, 1952 . . . £10/£5
Trouble for Trimble, Hamilton, 1952 . . . £10/£5
D'Arcy in Danger, Hamilton, 1952 . . . . £10/£5
D'Arcy on the Warpath, Hamilton, 1952 . . £10/£5
D'Arcy's Disappearance, Hamilton, 1952 . . £10/£5
Darcy the Reformer, Hamilton, 1952 . . . £10/£5
Darcy's Day Off, Hamilton, 1952 . . . . £10/£5

Other Titles

The Secret of the School, Merrett, 1946 . . £10/£5
The Black Sheep of Sparshott, Merrett, 1946 . £10/£5
First Man In, Merrett, 1946 . . . . . . £10/£5
Looking After Lamb, Merrett, 1946 . . . . £10/£5
The Hero of Sparshott, Merrett, 1946 . . . £10/£5
Pluck Will Tell, Merrett, 1946 . . . . . £10/£5
Top Study at Topham, Matthew, 1947 . . £10/£5
Bunny Binks on the Warpath, Matthew, 1947 . £10/£5
The Dandy of Topham, Matthew, 1947 . . . £10/£5
Sent to Coventry, Matthew, 1947 . . . . £10/£5
The Lone Texan, Atlantic, 1954 . . . . . £10/£5

W. HEATH ROBINSON
(b.1872 d.1944)

A British author and illustrator, Robinson did not find his own distinctive style until *The Adventures of Uncle Lubin*. He is popularly known for his illustrations of preposterous inventions.

Written and Illustrated by Heath Robinson

The Adventures of Uncle Lubin, Grant Richards, 1902 . . . . £1,000
ditto, Grant Richards, 1925 (new edition) . £100/£35
The Child's Arabian Nights, Grant Richards, 1903 . . . . £300
Bill the Minder, Constable, 1912 . . . . £450
ditto, Constable, 1912 (380 signed copies bound in vellum) £1,250
ditto, Holt (U.S.), 1912 . . . . . . £400
Peter Quip in Search of a Friend, S.W. Partridge, [1922]. £1,000
Some Frightful War Pictures, Duckworth, 1915 £150
ditto, Duckworth, 1915 (wraps) £150
Hunlikely, Duckworth, 1916 . . . . . . £150
The Saintly Hun, Duckworth, [1917] (wraps) . £150
Flypapers, Duckworth, 1919 (wraps) . . . £175
Get On With It, Duckworth, [1920] (with J. Birch, wraps). £200
A Jamboree of Laughter, Jones, [1920] (wraps) £150
The Home Made Car, Duckworth, [1921] (wraps). £150
Motor Mania, The Motor Owner, [1921] (wraps) £175
Quaint and Selected Pictures, Duckworth, [1922] (with J. Birch, wraps) £200
Humours of Golf, Methuen, [1925] (pictorial boards). £250
The Heath Robinson Calendar, Delgardo, 1933-36 . . . . £75 each
Absurdities, Hutchinson, [1934] £150
ditto, Hutchinson, [1934] (deluxe edition) . . £250
ditto, Hutchinson, [1934] (250 signed copies) . £400
Railway Ribaldry, G.W.R., 1935 (wraps) . . £100
My Line of Life, Blackie, 1938 . . . . £150/£60
Let's Laugh, A Book of Humorous Inventions, Hutchinson, [1939] . . . . £75/£25
Heath Robinson at War, Methuen, 1942 . £200/£75
The Penguin Heath Robinson, Penguin, 1966 (wraps) £10
Inventions, Duckworth, 1973 . . . . . £15/£5
The Gentle Art of Advertising, Duckworth, 1979 . . . . £15/£5
Great British Industries, Duckworth, 1985 . . £10/£5

Illustrated by Heath Robinson

Danish Fairy Tales and Legends, by H. C. Andersen, Bliss Sands & Co., 1897. . . . . . . £100
The Life and Exploits of Don Quixote, by Cervantes, Bliss Sands & Co., 1897. . . . . . . £100

The Pilgrim's Progress, by John Bunyan, Bliss Sands & Co., 1897 . . . . £60
The Giant Crab and Other Tales from Old India, by W.H.D. Rouse, Nutt, 1897 . . . . . . £350
The Queen's Story Book, edited by L. Gomme, Constable, 1898 . . . . £60
The Arabian Nights Entertainments, Newnes/ Constable, 1899 . . . . £100
Fairy Tales from Hans Christian Andersen, Dent, 1899 . . . . £150
The Talking Thrush, by W.H.D. Rouse, Dent, 1899 .
. . . . £300
The Poems of Edgar Allan Poe, Bell, 1900. . £300
ditto, Bell, 1900 (75 copies on Japanese vellum) £750
Tales for Toby, by A.R. Hope, Dent, 1900 . . £45
The Adventures of Don Quixote, by Cervantes, Dent, 1902 . . . . £75
Mediaeval Stories, by H. Schuck, Sands, 1902 . £65
The Surprising Travels and Adventures of Baron Munchausen, by R.E. Raspe, Grant Richards, 1902 .
. . . . £150
Tales from Shakespeare, by C. and M. Lamb, Sands, [1902]. £100
Rama and the Monkeys, edited by G. Hodgson, Dent, 1903 . . . . £100
The Works of Mr Francis Rabelais, Grant Richards, 1904 (2 vols) £300
Stories from Chaucer, edited by J.H. Kelman, Jack [1905]. £25
Two Memoirs of Barry Lydon and Men's Wives, by W.M. Thackeray, Caxton, [1906] . . . £65
Stories from the Iliad, edited by Jeanie Lang, Jack [1906]. £25
Stories from the Odyssey, edited by Jeanie Lang, Jack [1906]. £25
The Monarchs of Merry England, by Roland Carse, Alf Cooke, [1907] (4 vols, wraps) £200
More Monarchs of Merry England, by Roland Carse, T. Fisher Unwin, [1908]. £175
Twelfth Night, by W. Shakespeare, Hodder & Stoughton, [1908] £200
ditto, Hodder & Stoughton, [1908] (350 signed copies, bound in vellum). £650
A Song of the English, by Rudyard Kipling, Hodder & Stoughton, [c.1909] (30 colour plates). . . £200
ditto, Hodder & Stoughton, [c.1909] (deluxe edition, 500 copies signed by the artist, 30 colour plates, full vellum) £600
ditto, Hodder & Stoughton, [c.1909] (deluxe edition, 50 copies signed by the artist and author, 30 colour plates, full vellum) £1,000
ditto, Doubleday (U.S.), [c.1909] (30 colour plates) .
. . . . £200
ditto, Doubleday (U.S.), [c.1909] (deluxe edition, 500 copies signed by the artist, 30 colour plates, full vellum) £600
ditto, Hodder & Stoughton, [1912] (12 colour plates) .
. . . . £45

ditto, Hodder & Stoughton/Daily Telegraph, [1915] (16 colour plates). £65
ditto, Hodder & Stoughton, [1919] (16 colour plates) .
. . . . £45
The Collected Verse of Rudyard Kipling, Doubleday Page (U.S.), 1910 (9 colour plates). . . . £150
ditto, Doubleday Page (U.S.), 1910 (125 signed copies)
. . . . £750
The Dead King, by Rudyard Kipling, Hodder & Stoughton, 1910 . . . . £75
ditto, Hodder & Stoughton, 1910 (wraps) . . £75
Hans Andersen's Fairy Tales, Constable, 1913 £500
ditto, Constable, 1913 (100 signed copies, bound in vellum) £1,750
A Midsummer Night's Dream, by W. Shakespeare, Constable, 1914 . . . . £350
ditto, Constable, 1914 (150 of 250 signed copies bound in green boards) £1,250
ditto, Constable, 1914 (100 of 250 copies bound in vellum) £2,000
The Water Babies, by Charles Kingsley, Constable, 1915 . . . . £100
ditto, Houghton Mifflin (U.S.), 1915 . . . £75
Peacock Pie, by Walter de la Mare, Constable, 1916 .
. . . . £75
ditto, Holt (U.S.), 1924 . . . . . £100/£20
Old Time Stories, by C. Perrault, Constable, 1921 . .
. . . . £300/£200
Topsy Turvey Tales, by E.S. Munro, John Lane, 1923 .
. . . . £300/£150
The Incredible Adventures of Professor Branestawm, by Norman Hunter, John Lane, 1933 . . £250/£75
Balbus, A Latin Reading Book, by G.M. Lyne, E. Arnold, 1934 . . . . £75/£25
Heath Robinson's Book of Goblins, Hutchinson, [1934]. . . . . £400/£200
Once Upon A Time, by L.M.C. Clopet, Muller, 1934 .
. . . . £250/£125
How to Live in a Flat, by K.R.G. Browne, Hutchinson, [1936]. . . . . £125/£35
How to be a Perfect Husband, by K.R.G. Browne, Hutchinson, [1937] . . . . . . £125/£35
How to Make a Garden Grow, by K.R.G. Browne, Hutchinson, [1938] . . . . . . £125/£35
How to be a Motorist, by K.R.G. Browne, Hutchinson, [1939]. . . . . £125/£35
Mein Rant, by Richard F. Patterson, Blackie, 1940 .
. . . . £100/£30
How to make the Best of Things, by Cecil Hunt, Hutchinson, [1940] . . . . . . £75/£20
How to Build a New World, by Cecil Hunt, Hutchinson, [1941] . . . . £75/£20
How to Run a Communal Home, by Cecil Hunt, Hutchinson, [1943] . . . . . . £75/£20

SAX ROHMER
(b.1886 d.1959)

'Rohmer' was the pseudonym for Arthur Ward. Many of his exotic thrillers follow the devilish exploits of the sinister 'Dr Fu Manchu'.

'Fu Manchu' Novels

The Mystery of Fu Manchu, Methuen, 1913 . £300
ditto, as *The Insidious Dr Fu Manchu*, McBride (U.S.), 1913 . . . . £150
The Return of Dr Fu Manchu, McBride (U.S.), 1916.
. . . . £150
ditto, as *The Devil Doctor*, Methuen, 1916 . . £125
The Si-Fan Mysteries, Methuen, 1917 . . . £100
ditto, as *The Hand of Fu Manchu*, McBride (U.S.), 1917 . . . . £100
The Daughter of Fu Manchu, Crime Club (U.S.), 1931 . . . . £250/£35
ditto, Cassell, 1931 . . . . £250/£35
The Mask of Fu Manchu, Crime Club (U.S.), 1932 .
. . . .£500/£100
ditto, Cassell, 1933 . . . .£500/£100
Fu Manchu's Bride, Crime Club (U.S.), 1933 . .
. . . . £400/£75
ditto, as *The Bride of Fu Manchu* Cassell, 1933 . .
. . . . £400/£75
The Trail of Fu Manchu, Crime Club (U.S.), 1934 .
. . . . £200/£25
ditto, Cassell, 1934 . . . . . . £400/£30
President Fu Manchu, Crime Club (U.S.), 1936 . .
. . . . £200/£25
ditto, Cassell, 1936 . . . . . . £250/£25
The Drums of Fu Manchu, Crime Club (U.S.), 1939 .
. . . . £350/£75
ditto, Cassell, 1939 . . . . . . £350/£75
The Island of Fu Manchu, Crime Club (U.S.), 1941 .
. . . . £750/£35
ditto, Cassell, 1941 . . . . . . £750/£35
Shadow of Fu Manchu, Crime Club (U.S.), 1948 . .
. . . . £200/£30
ditto, Jenkins, 1949 . . . . . . £300/£30
Re-Enter Dr Fu Manchu, Fawcett (U.S.), 1957 (wraps) £20
ditto, Herbert Jenkins, 1957 . . . . . £300/£20
Emperor Fu Manchu, Herbert Jenkins, 1959 £150/£20
ditto, Fawcett (U.S.), 1959 (wraps) . . . £20
The Wrath of Fu Manchu, Tom Stacey, 1973 £65/£15
ditto, Daw (U.S.), 1975 (wraps) £10

Omnibus Editions

The Book of Fu Manchu, Hurst & Blackett, 1929 . .
. . . .£500/£100
ditto, McBride (U.S.), 1929 (different contents) . .
. . . .£500/£100
The Golden Scorpion Omnibus, Grosset & Dunlap (U.S.), 1938 . . . . £100/£25
The Sax Rohmer Omnibus, Grosset & Dunlap (U.S.), 1938 . . . . £100/£25

Other Novels

10.30 Folkestone Express, Lloyds Home Novels No. 41, [no date] £1,000
The Sins of Severac Bablon, Cassell, 1914 . . £150
ditto, Bookfinger (U.S.), 1967 (no d/w) . . . £20
The Yellow Claw, McBride (U.S.), 1915 . . £30
ditto, Methuen, 1915 . . . . £45
Brood of the Witch Queen, Pearson, 1918 . . £50
ditto, Doubleday (U.S.), 1924 . . . . . £30
The Orchard of Tears, Methuen, 1919 . . £75
ditto, Bookfinger (U.S.), 1970 (no d/w) . . . £20
The Quest of the Sacred Slipper, Pearson, 1919 £40
ditto, Doubleday (U.S.), 1919 . . . . . £40
Dope, Cassell, 1919 . . . . £35
ditto, McBride (U.S.), 1919 . . . . . £35
The Golden Scorpion, Methuen, 1919 . . . £35
ditto, McBride (U.S.), 1920 . . . . . £600/£35
The Green Eyes of Bast, Cassell, 1920 . . £500/£30
ditto, McBride (U.S.), 1920 . . . . . £400/£30
Bat-Wing, Cassell, 1921 . . . . . . £200/£30
ditto, as *Bat Wing*, Doubleday (U.S.), 1921. £200/£30
Fire-Tongue, Cassell, 1921 . . . . . £500/£30
ditto, Doubleday (U.S.), 1922 . . . . . £500/£30
Grey Face, Cassell, 1924 . . . . . . £200/£30
ditto, Doubleday (U.S.), 1924 . . . . .£200/£30
Yellow Shadows, Cassell, 1925 . . . . £250/£40
ditto, Doubleday (U.S.), 1926 . . . . . £250/£40
Moon of Madness, Doubleday (U.S.), 1927 £250/£40
ditto, Cassell, 1927 . . . . £250/£40
She Who Sleeps, Doubleday (U.S.), 1928 . £250/£40
ditto, Cassell, 1928 . . . . £250/£40
The Emperor of America, Crime Club (U.S.), 1929 .
. . . . £300/£50
ditto, Cassell, 1929 . . . . £300/£50
The Day the World Ended, Crime Club (U.S.), 1930 .
. . . . £250/£40
ditto, Cassell, 1930 . . . . £250/£40
Yu'an Hee See Laughs, Crime Club (U.S.), 1932 . .
. . . . £250/£40
ditto, Cassell, 1932 . . . . £250/£40
The Bat Flies Low, Crime Club (U.S.), 1935 £250/£50
ditto, Cassell, 1935 . . . . £300/£50
White Velvet, Doubleday (U.S.), 1936 . . £250/£40
ditto, Cassell, 1936 . . . . £250/£40
Seven Sins, McBride (U.S.), 1943 . . . £150/£35
ditto, Cassell, 1944 . . . . £150/£35
Hangover House, Random House (U.S.), 1914 . .
. . . . £125/£20
ditto, Herbert Jenkins, 1950 . . . . . £125/£20
Nude in Mink, Fawcett (U.S.), 1950 (wraps) . £25
ditto, as *Sins of Sumuru*, Herbert Jenkins, 1951 . .
. . . . £125/£20
ditto, Bookfinger (U.S.), 1977 (no d/w) . . . £20
Sinister Madonna, Fawcett (U.S.), 1950 (wraps) £20
ditto, Herbert Jenkins, 1956 . . . . . £125/£20
Wulfheim, Jarrolds, 1950 (pseud. 'Michael Furey') .
. . . . £150/£35
ditto, Bookfinger (U.S.), 1972 (no d/w) . . . £20
Samuru, Fawcett (U.S.), 1951 (wraps) . . . £20

ditto, as *Slaves of Sumuru*, Herbert Jenkins, 1952 (different ending) . . . . £125/£20
ditto, Bookfinger (U.S.), 1979 (no d/w) . . . £20
Fire Goddess, Fawcett (U.S.), 1952 (wraps) . £25
ditto, as *Virgin in Flames*, Herbert Jenkins, 1953 . .
. . . . £125/£20
ditto, Bookfinger (U.S.), 1978 (no d/w) . . . £20
The Moon is Red, Herbert Jenkins, 1954 . £125/£20
ditto, Bookfinger (U.S.), 1976 (no d/w) . . . £20
Return of Samura, Fawcett (U.S.), 1954 (wraps) £20
ditto, as *Sand and Satin*, Herbert Jenkins, 1955 . .
. . . . £125/£20
ditto, Bookfinger (U.S.), 1978 (no d/w) . . . £20

Short Stories
The Exploits of Captain O'Hagan, Jarrolds, 1916. .
. . . . £400
ditto, Bookfinger (U.S.), 1968 (no d/w) . . . £20
Tales of Secret Egypt, Methuen, 1918 . . . £350
ditto, McBride (U.S.), 1919 . . . . . . £300
The Dream Detective, Jarrolds, 1920 . . £750/£200
ditto, Doubleday (U.S.), 1925 . . . . £500/£100
The Haunting of Low Fennel, Pearson, 1920 . . .
. . . . £750/£125
Tales of Chinatown, Cassell, 1922 . . . £650/£75
ditto, Doubleday (U.S.), 1922 . . . . £650/£75
Tales of East and West, Cassell, 1932 . £350/£75
ditto, Crime Club (U.S.), 1933 . . . . £200/£25
Salute to Bazarada, Cassell, 1939 . . . £125/£25
Egyptian Nights, Hale, 1944 (text presented as novel).
. . . . £125/£25
ditto, as *Bim-Bashi Baruk of Egypt*, McBride (U.S.),
1944 (text presented as short stories) . . £125/£25
The Secret of Holm Peel, and Other Strange Stories,
Ace (U.S.), 1970 (wraps) £10

Non Fiction Titles
Pause!, Greening, 1910 (anonymous) . . . £500
Little Tich, Greening, 1911 . . . . . . £500
The Romance of Sorcery, Methuen, 1914 . . £400
ditto, Dutton (U.S.), 1915. . . . . . . £300

FREDERICK ROLFE
(BARON CORVO)
(b.1860 d.1913)

The author of a number of almost indigestible semi-autobiographical novels, Rolfe had an unbelievably self-destructive paranoia. He is read for his 'Toto' tales and for the minor classic *Hadrian the Seventh*. Sadly, he only really reached the level of genius in his vituperative letters to self-created enemies.

Tarcissus: The Boy Martyr of Rome, privately printed, 1880 [1881] (wraps). £2,000
Stories Toto Told Me, Bodley Head, 1898 (wraps). .
. . . . £350

The Attack on St. Winefride's Well, privately printed, [1898] (anonymous, wraps). £1,000
In His Own Image, Bodley Head, 1901 (first printing with 1 advert leaf at end) £150
ditto, Knopf (U.S.), 1925 . . . . . . £65/£20
Chronicles of the House of Borgia, Grant Richards, 1901 . . . . £200
ditto, Dutton (U.S.), 1901. . . . . . . £150
Hadrian the Seventh, Chatto & Windus, 1904 (first issue purple cloth with title and drawing stamped in white). £500
ditto, Chatto & Windus, 1904 (second issue with title and drawing blind stamped). £300
ditto, Knopf (U.S.), 1925 . . . . . £75/£25
Don Tarquinio, Chatto & Windus, 1905 (first binding violet cloth) £250
ditto, Chatto & Windus, 1905 (second binding red cloth) £150
Don Renato, An Ideal Content, Francis Griffiths, 1909
. . . . £400
ditto, Chatto & Windus, 1963 (200 large paper copies in slipcase) . . . . £125/£75
ditto, Chatto & Windus, 1963 . . . . £40/£15
The Weird of the Wanderer, by Prospero and Caliban, William Rider, 1912 . . . . £300
The Bull Against the Enemy of the Anglican Race, Corvine Society, 1929 (50 copies, wraps) . . £225
Hubert's Arthur, by Prospero and Caliban, Cassell, 1935 . . . . £175/£50
The Desire and Pursuit of the Whole, Cassell, [1934] (first binding, dark green cloth). . . . £175/£65
ditto, Cassell, [1934] (second binding, light green cloth, no d/w). £30
ditto, New Directions (U.S.), 1953 . . . £25/£10
Three Tales of Venice, The Corvine Press, [1950] (150 numbered copies) £400
Amico di Sandro, A Fragment of a Novel, The Peacocks Press, 1951 (150 numbered copies). £250
ditto, The Peacocks Press, 1951 (10 numbered copies on parchment paper of 150). £750
Letters to Grant Richards, The Peacocks Press, 1951 (200 numbered copies, no d/w) £150
ditto, The Peacocks Press, 1951 (10 numbered copies on azure handmade paper of 200) . . . £750
The Cardinal Prefect of Propaganda, Nicholas Vane, 1957 (262 copies) £150
ditto, Nicholas Vane, 1957 (12 lettered copies of 262) .
. . . . £750
Nicholas Crabbe, Chatto & Windus, 1958 . £35/£10
ditto, Chatto & Windus, 1958 (215 numbered, large paper copies in slipcase). . . . . . £125/£100
ditto, New Directions (U.S.), 1958 . . . £15/£5
The Centenary Edition of the Letters of Frederick William Rolfe, Nicholas Vane, 1959 . . . £225
Letters to Pirie Gordon and Leonard Moore, Nicholas Vane, 1959-60 (350 copies, 2 vols) . . . £450
A Letter to Father Beauclerk, Tragara Press (Edinburgh), 1960 (20 copies) £400

Letters to Leonard Moore, Cecil & Amelia Woolf, 1960 (260 numbered copies) £100
ditto, Cecil & Amelia Woolf, 1960 (16 lettered copies on handmade paper of 260) £600
Letters of Baron Corvo to Kenneth Grahame, The Peacocks Press, 1962 (40 copies) £300
Without Prejudice - One Hundred Letters from Frederick William Rolfe, Baron Corvo to John Lane, privately printed for Allen Lane, 1963 (600 copies, plain d/w) . . . . £150/£125
A Letter to a Small Nephew Named Claude, Iowa City, 1964 (134 copies) £300
Letters to James Walsh, Bertram Rota, 1972 (500 copies) £75
Ballade of Boys Bathing, Tragara Press (Edinburgh), 1972 (200 numbered copies) £75
Collected Poems of Fr Rolfe, Baron Corvo, Cecil & Amelia Woolf, 1974 . . . . £25/£10
ditto, Cecil & Amelia Woolf, 1974 (200 numbered copies) £75
The Reverse Side of the Coin, Tragara Press (Edinburgh), 1974 (95 copies) £75
The Venice Letters, Cecil & Amelia Woolf, 1966 (25 copies) £250
ditto, Cecil & Amelia Woolf, 1974 . . . £100/£25
ditto, Cecil & Amelia Woolf, 1974 (200 numbered copies, slipcase) . . . . £100/£65
ditto, Cecil & Amelia Woolf, 1987 (first illustrated edition) . . . . £15/£5
ditto, Cecil & Amelia Woolf, 1987 (100 numbered copies) £100
The Armed Hands, and Other Stories, Cecil & Amelia Woolf, 1974 . . . . £20/£5
ditto, Cecil & Amelia Woolf, 1974 (200 numbered copies) £75
Aberdeen Interval, Tragara Press (Edinburgh), 1975 (140 copies) £50
Different Aspects: Frederick William Rolfe and the Foreign Office, Tragara Press (Edinburgh), 1977 (125 copies) £50
Frederick Rolfe and 'The Times' 4-12 Feb, 1901, Tragara Press (Edinburgh), 1975 (175 copies) £45
Letters to Harry Bainbridge, Enitharmon Press, 1977 (350 of 395 copies) £40
ditto, Enitharmon Press, 1977 (45 numbered copies of 395) £150

Miscellaneous
The Rubaiyat of Umar Khaiyam, John Lane, 1903 (translated by Rolfe) £150
Agricultural and Pastoral Prospects of South Africa, by Col. Owen Thomas, Archibald Constable, 1904 (ghost-written by Rolfe) £500

J.K. ROWLING
(b.1965)

Rowling's series of books about a young wizard, 'Harry Potter', is not only a modern publishing phenomenon in terms of the huge sales of her books, but also because of the prices commanded by the first edition of her first title.

Harry Potter and the Philosopher's Stone, Bloomsbury, 1997 (laminated boards, no d/w, 500 copies) £15,000
ditto, Bloomsbury, 1997 (proofs, wraps, 200 copies) £4,000
ditto, Bloomsbury, 1999 (collector's edition, no d/w) £250
ditto, as *Harry Potter and the Sorcerer's Stone*, Levine/Scholastic (U.S.), 1998 . . £2,000/£1,500
ditto, Levine/Scholastic (U.S.), 2000 (collector's edition, no d/w) £75
Harry Potter and the Chamber of Secrets, Bloomsbury, 1998 . . . . . £2,000/£1,500
ditto, Bloomsbury, 1999 (collector's edition, no d/w) £100
ditto, Levine/Scholastic (US), 1999 . . . £75/£25
Harry Potter and the Prisoner of Azkaban, Bloomsbury, 1999 (first issue with 'Joanne Rowling' on verso title page) . . . . . £2,000/£1,600
ditto, Bloomsbury, 1999 (collector's edition, no d/w) £1,500
ditto, Levine/Scholastic (US), 1999 . . . £40/£10
Harry Potter and the Goblet of Fire, Bloomsbury, 2000 . . . . £20/£5
ditto, Bloomsbury, 2000 (collector's edition, no d/w) £75
ditto, Levine/Scholastic (US), 2000 . . . . £20/£5
ditto, Levine/Scholastic (US), 2000 (25 copies with original artwork and certificate) . £2,000/£1,950

RUPERT
see Mary Tourtel

SALMAN RUSHDIE
(b.1947)

Salman Rushdie, purveyor of post-modernist pyrotechnics, was born in Bombay but migrated to Britain in 1965. His writing is often described as 'magic realism', and has brought him great literary respect.

Novels
Grimus, Gollancz, 1975 . . . . . . £250/£35
ditto, Overlook Press (U.S.), 1979 . . . £150/£20
Midnight's Children, Knopf (U.S.), 1981 . £500/£35
ditto, Cape, 1981 . . . . £450/£45
Shame, Cape, 1983 . . . . £25/£10
ditto, Knopf (U.S.), 1983 . . . . £25/£5

The Satanic Verses, Viking, 1988 . . . . £75/£20
ditto, Viking, 1988 (100 arabic numbered copies) £500
ditto, Viking (U.S.), 1988. . . . . £35/£10
ditto, Penguin, 1988 (suppressed edition, wraps) £350
The Moor's Last Sigh, Cape, 1995 . . . . £15/£5
ditto, Cape, 1995 (200 signed copies, no d/w) . £100
ditto, Cape, 1995 (2,500 copies in slipcase with
facsimilie signature) . . . . £65/£45
ditto, Pantheon (U.S.), 1995 . . . . . . £10/£5
ditto, Pantheon (U.S.), 1995 (1,000 signed advance
reading copies, wraps, in slipcase) . . £75/£50
The Ground Beneath Her Feet, Cape, 1999 . £15/£5
ditto, Cape, 1999 (150 signed copies, full leather-
bound, in slipcase) . . . . £200/£150
ditto, Holt (U.S.), 1999 . . . . £10/£5
Fury, Cape, 2001 . . . . £10/£5
ditto, Random House (U.S.), 2001 . . . . £10/£5

Children's Title
Haroun and the Sea of Stories, Granta, 1990 . £15/£5
ditto, Granta, 1990 (251 signed copies) . . . £150
ditto, Viking (U.S.), 1991. . . . . . . £10/£5

Short Stories
Two Stories, privately printed, 1989 (60 signed copies
of 72) £750
ditto, privately printed, 1989 (12 specially bound,
signed copies of 72) £1,750
East, West, Cape, 1994 . . . . . . £15/£5
ditto, Pantheon (U.S.), 1994 .. . . . . £10/£5

Others
The Jaguar Smile: A Nicaraguan Journey, Picador,
1987 . . . . £10/£5
ditto, Viking (U.S.), 1987. . . . . . . £10/£5
Is Nothing Sacred?, Granta, 1990 . . . £10/£5
Imaginary Homelands: Essays and Criticism, Granta,
1991 . . . . £10/£5
ditto, Viking (U.S.), 1991. . . . . . . £10/£5
The Wizard of Oz, B.F.I., 1992 (wraps) . . . £15
Step Across This Line: Collected Non-Fiction 1992-
2002, Cape, 2002 . . . . £10/£5
ditto, Random House (U.S.), 2002 . . . £10/£5

VITA SACKVILLE-WEST
(b.1892 d.1962)

The Land brought Vita Sackville-West recognition,
winning her the Hawthornden Prize. A writer of both
poetry and prose, she was also a passionate gardener.
It is said the she was the model for Virginia Woolf's
Orlando.

Novels
Heritage, Collins, 1919 . . . . . . £650/£125
ditto, Doran (U.S.), 1919 . . . . . . £500/£100
The Dragon in Shallow Waters, Collins, 1921 . . .
. . . . £650/£125

ditto, Putnam's (U.S.), 1922 . . . . . £500/£100
Challenge, Doran (U.S.), 1923 . . . . £500/£125
Grey Wethers, Heinemann, 1923. . . . £350/£65
ditto, Doran (U.S.), 1923 . . . . . . £350/£65
Seducers in Equador, Hogarth Press, 1924 . £350/£65
ditto, Doran (U.S.), 1925 . . . . . . £350/£65
The Edwardians, Hogarth Press, 1930 . . £300/£50
ditto, Hogarth Press, 1930 (125 signed copies, no d/w)
. . . . £450
ditto, Doran (U.S.), 1930 . . . . . . £250/£45
All Passion Spent, Hogarth Press, 1931 . . £300/£50
ditto, Doran (U.S.), 1931 . . . . . . £200/£35
Family History, Hogarth Press, 1932 . . £300/£50
ditto, Doubleday Doran (U.S.), 1932 . . £250/£35
The Death of Noble Godavary and Gottfried Kunstler,
Benn, 1932 (wraps) £25
The Dark Island, Hogarth Press, 1934 . . £300/£50
ditto, Doran (U.S.), 1934 . . . . . . £250/£35
Grand Canyon, Joseph, 1942 . . . . £65/£20
ditto, Doran (U.S.), 1942 . . . . . . £50/£15
Devil at Westease, Doubleday Doran (U.S.), 1947 . .
. . . . £300/£50
The Easter Party, Joseph, 1953 . . . . £35/£15
ditto, Doubleday (U.S.), 1953 . . . . £30/£10
No Signposts in the Sea, Joseph, 1961 . . £25/£10
ditto, Doubleday (U.S.), 1961 . . . . . £20/£5

Short Stories
The Heir, privately printed, [1922] (100 signed copies)
. . . . £400
ditto, Heinemann, 1922 . . . . . . £300/£50
Thirty Clocks Strike the Hour and Other Stories,
Doubleday Doran (U.S.), 1934 . . . . £450/£65

Poetry
Chatterton, privately printed, 1909 (wraps) . . £4,000
Constantinople, Eight Poems, privately printed,
Complete Press, 1915 (wraps) £400
Poems of West and East, John Lane, 1917 . . £125
Orchard and Vineyard, John Lane, 1921 . £325/£125
The Land, Heinemann, 1926 . . . . . £300/£45
ditto, Heinemann, 1926 (125 copies, slipcase) . . .
. . . . £750/£500
ditto, Doubleday (U.S.), 1927 . . . . £200/£30
King's Daughter, Hogarth Press, 1929 . £150/£30
ditto, Doubleday (U.S.), 1930 . . . . £125/£25
Sissinghurst, Hogarth Press, 1931 (500 signed,
numbered copies, hand-printed by the Woolfs, no
d/w) £400
Invitation to Cast Out Care, Faber, 1931 . £50/£20
ditto, Faber, 1931 (200 copies) £150
V. Sackville-West, Benn, 1931 (wraps) . . £10
Collected Poems, Volume One, Hogarth Press, 1933 .
. . . . £150/£50
ditto, Hogarth Press, 1933 (150 copies) . . . £300
ditto, Doubleday (U.S.), 1934 . . . . £100/£30
Solitude, Hogarth Press, 1938 . . . . £75/£25
Selected Poems, Hogarth Press, 1941 . . £45/£15
The Garden, Joseph, 1946 . . . . . £60/£20

ditto, Joseph, 1946 (750 signed copies, plain d/w) . .
. . . . £450/£300
ditto, Doubleday (U.S.), 1946 . . . . £50/£20

Travel
Passenger to Tehran, Hogarth Press, 1926 . £500/£100
Twelve Days, Hogarth Press, 1928 . . . £500/£100
ditto, Doubleday (U.S.), 1928 . . . . £400/£75

Gardening
Some Flowers, Cobden-Sanderson, 1937 . £75/£30
ditto, Abrams (U.S.), 1993 . . . . . . £10/£5
Country Notes, Joseph, 1939 . . . . . £75/£30
ditto, Harper (U.S.), 1940 . . . . . . £40/£10
Country Notes in Wartime, Hogarth Press, 1940 . .
. . . . £65/£15
ditto, Doubleday Doran (U.S.), 1941 . . £50/£10
In Your Garden, Joseph, 1951 . . . . £45/£15
Hidcote Manor Garden, Country Life, 1952 £30/£10
In Your Garden Again, Joseph, 1953 . . £45/£15
More For Your Garden, Joseph, 1955 . . £35/£10
Even More For Your Garden, Joseph, 1958 £35/£10
A Joy of Gardening, Harper & Row (U.S.), 1958 . .
. . . . £25/£10
ditto, Harper (U.S.), 1958 . . . . . £25/£10
V. Sackville-West's Garden Book, Joseph, 1968 . .
. . . . £20/£5
ditto, Atheneum (U.S.), 1968 . . . . . £15/£5
The Illustrated Garden Book, Joseph, 1986 . £15/£5
ditto, Atheneum (U.S.), 1986 . . . . . £15/£5

Historical and Biographical
Knole and the Sackvilles, Heinemann, 1922 £500/£65
ditto, Doran (U.S.), [1924] . . . . . £350/£45
Aphra Benn, The Incomparable Astrea, Gerald Howe,
1927 . . . . £100/£35
ditto, Viking (U.S.), 1928 . . . . . £75/£30
Andrew Marvell, Faber, 1929 . . . . £65/£20
ditto, Faber, 1929 (75 signed copies) . . . £200
Saint Joan of Arc, Cobden-Sanderson, 1936 £45/£15
ditto, Cobden-Sanderson, 1936 (120 copies) . £150
ditto, Doubleday (U.S.), 1936 . . . . £35/£10
Joan of Arc, Hogarth Press, 1937 . . . £65/£10
Pepita, Hogarth Press, 1937 . . . . . £100/£15
ditto, Doubleday (U.S.), 1937 . . . . £35/£10
English Country Houses, Collins, 1941 . . £35/£10
ditto, Random House (U.S.), 1949 . . . . £15/£5
The Eagle and the Dove, Joseph, 1943 . . £30/£10
ditto, Doubleday (U.S.), 1944 . . . . £30/£10
Daughter of France, Joseph, 1959 . . . £30/£10
ditto, Doubleday (U.S.), 1959 . . . . £30/£10

Others
The Diary of the Lady Anne Clifford, Heinemann,
1923 (edited by V. Sackville-West) . . £150/£40
Rilke, Hogarth Press, 1931 (translation) . . £75/£20
The Women's Land Army, Joseph, 1944 . £75/£20
Nursery Rhymes, Dropmore Press, 1947 (550 copies) .
. . . . £200/£45

ditto, Dropmore Press, 1947 (25 signed copies of the
above) . . . . £1,250/£1,000
ditto, Joseph, 1950 . . . . £50/£15
Faces: Profiles of Dogs, Harvill Press, 1961 £25/£10
Dearest Andrew, Letters to Andrew Reiber, 1951-62,
Joseph, 1979 . . . . £20/£10
ditto, Scribner's (U.S.), 1979 . . . . . £15/£5
Letters from V. Sackville-West to Virginia Woolf,
Joseph, 1984 . . . . £20/£5
ditto, Morrow (U.S.), 1985 . . . . . £15/£5

SAKI
(b.1870 d.1916)

'Saki' was a pseudonym adopted by H.H. Munro for
his predominantly humorous novels and short stories.
Although his writing is whimsical and satirical, some
critics have noted a darker undercurrent indicative of
an alienated outsider.

Novels
Mrs Elmsley, Constable, 1911 (as Hector Munro) £200
The Unbearable Bassington, John Lane, 1912 . £75
When William Came, John Lane, 1913 . . . £65
The Collected Novels and Plays, John Lane/Bodley
Head, 1933 . . . . £35/£15

Short Stories
Reginald, Methuen, 1904 . . . . . . £175
Reginald in Russia and Other Sketches, Methuen,
1910 . . . . £125
The Chronicles of Clovis, John Lane, 1911 . . £125
Beasts and Superbeasts, John Lane, 1914 . . £100
The Toys of Peace, John Lane/Bodley Head, 1919 . .
. . . . £40
The Square Egg and Other Sketches, John Lane/
Bodley Head, 1924 . . . . £125/£40
The Collected Short Stories, John Lane/Bodley Head,
1930 . . . . £25/£10

Others
The Rise of the Russian Empire, Grant Richards, 1900
. . . . £200
The Westminster Alice, Westminster Gazette, 1902
(wraps) £200
ditto, Westminster Gazette, 1902 (boards) . . £150

J.D. SALINGER
(b.1919)

Essentially a one-novel novelist, the author of *The Catcher in the Rye* was born in New York. He now lives in Cornish, New Hampshire.

Novels
The Catcher in the Rye, Little, Brown (U.S.), 1951 .
. . . . £6,000/£600
ditto, Hamish Hamilton, 1951 . . . . £600/£65

Short Stories
Nine Stories, Little, Brown (U.S.), 1953 £1,500/£150
ditto, as *For Esme - With Love and Squalor and Other Stories*, Hamish Hamilton, 1953 . . . £250/£35
Franny and Zooey, Little, Brown (U.S.), 1961 £75/£20
ditto, Heinemann, 1962 . . . . . . £65/£15
Raise High the Roof Beam, Carpenters and Seymour: An Introduction, Little, Brown (U.S.), 1963 (first issue with no dedication page) . . . . £750/£600
ditto, Little, Brown (U.S.), 1963 (second issue with dedication page before half title) . . . £100/£15
ditto, Heinemann, 1963 . . . . . . £75/£15
The Complete and Uncollected Short Stories of J.D. Salinger, no publisher named, 1974 (2 vols, wraps, first vol. saddle-stitched and the second vol. perfect bound, pirated edition) £500

SAPPER
(b.1888 d.1937)

'Sapper' was the pseudonym of Herman Cyril McNeile, whose greatest literary creation was 'Bulldog Drummond', a character whose exploits were continued by NcNeile's friend Gerald Fairlie to the original author's plots.

'Bulldog Drummond' Titles
Bull-Dog Drummond: The Adventures of a Demobilised Officer Who Found Peace Dull, Hodder & Stoughton, [1920]. . . . . . £1,000/£75
ditto, Doran (U.S.), 1920 . . . . . £1,000/£75
The Black Gang, Hodder & Stoughton, [1922]. . .
. . . . £300/£25
ditto, Doran (U.S.), 1922 . . . . . . £200/£20
The Third Round, Hodder & Stoughton, [1924] . .
. . . . £300/£20
ditto, as *Bull-Dog Drummond's Third Round*, Doran (U.S.), 1920 . . . . £200/£20
The Final Count, Hodder & Stoughton, [1926] . .
. . . . £300/£20
ditto, Doran (U.S.), 1926 . . . . . . £300/£20
The Female of the Species, Hodder & Stoughton, [1928]. . . . . £300/£20
ditto, Doubleday (U.S.), 1928 . . . . £300/£20

ditto, as *Bulldog Drummond and the Female of the Species*, Sun Dial (U.S.), 1943 . . . . £45/£10
Temple Tower, Hodder & Stoughton, [1929] £300/£20
ditto, Doubleday (U.S.), 1929 . . . . £300/£20
The Return of Bulldog Drummond, Hodder & Stoughton, 1932 . . . . £200/£15
ditto, as *Bulldog Drummond Returns*, Doubleday (U.S.), 1932 . . . . £200/£15
Knock-Out, Hodder & Stoughton, 1933 . . £200/£15
ditto, as *Bulldog Drummond Strikes Back*, Doubleday (U.S.), 1933 . . . . £200/£15
Bulldog Drummond At Bay, Hodder & Stoughton, 1935 . . . . £200/£15
ditto, Doubleday (U.S.), 1935 . . . . £200/£15
Challenge, Hodder & Stoughton, 1937 . £200/£15
ditto, Doubleday (U.S.), 1937 . . . . £200/£15

Collected Editions
Bulldog Drummond: His Four Rounds With Carl Peterson, Hodder & Stoughton, 1937 . . £200/£15
Sapper: The Best Short Stories, Dent, 1984 . £25/£5

Other Novels
Jim Maitland, Hodder & Stoughton, 1923 . £200/£25
ditto, Doubleday (U.S.), 1924 . . . . £200/£25
Tiny Carteret, Hodder & Stoughton, 1930 . £200/£25
ditto, Doubleday (U.S.), 1930 . . . . £200/£25
The Island of Terror, Hodder & Stoughton, 1931 . .
. . . . £100/£15
ditto, as *Guardians of the Treasure*, Doubleday (U.S.), 1931 . . . . £100/£15

Other Short Stories
Sergeant Michael Cassidy, R.E., Hodder & Stoughton, 1915 . . . . £45
ditto, as *Michael Cassidy, Sergeant*, Doran (U.S.), 1916 . . . . £45
The Lieutenant and Others, Hodder & Stoughton, 1915 . . . . £45
Men, Women and Guns, Hodder & Stoughton, 1916 .
. . . . £40
ditto, Doran (U.S.), 1916 . . . . £40
The Fatal Second, Doran (U.S.), 1916 (wraps). £75
The Motor-Gun, Doran (U.S.), 1916 (wraps) . £75
No Man's Land, Hodder & Stoughton, 1917 . £30
ditto, Doran (U.S.), 1917 . . . . £30
The Human Touch, Hodder & Stoughton, 1918 £30
ditto, Doran (U.S.), 1918 . . . . £30
Mufti, Hodder & Stoughton, 1919 . . . . £45
ditto, Doran (U.S.), 1919 . . . . £45
The Truce of the Bear, Doran (U.S.), 1919 (wraps) .
. . . . £75
The Dinner Club, Hodder & Stoughton, [1923] . .
. . . . £150/£20
ditto, Doran (U.S.), [1923] . . . . . £150/£20
Mark Danver's Sin, and *The Madman of Coral Reef Lighthouse*, Doran (U.S.), 1923 (wraps) . . £75
Molly's Aunt at Angmering, Doran (U.S.), 1923 (wraps) £75

Peter Cornish's Revenge, Doran (U.S.), 1923 (wraps). £75

The Man in Ratcatcher and Other Stories, Hodder & Stoughton, [1924] . . . . £150/£20

ditto, Doran (U.S.), [1924] . . . . . £150/£20

Bulton's Revenge, Doran (U.S.), 1924 (wraps). £75

The Ducking of Herbert Folton, and *Coincidence*, Doran (U.S.), 1924 (wraps) £75

A Scrap of Paper, Doran (U.S.), 1924 (wraps) . £75

That Bullet Hole has a History!, Doran (U.S.), 1924 (wraps) £75

The Valley of the Shadow, Doran (U.S.), 1924 (wraps) £75

Out of the Blue, Hodder & Stoughton, [1925] . . . . £150/£15

ditto, Doran (U.S.), 1925 . . . . . . £150/£15

A Native Superstition, Doran (U.S.), 1925 (wraps) £75

The Other Side of the Wall, Doran (U.S.), 1925 (wraps) £75

The Professor's Christmas Party, and *A Student of the Obvious*, Doran (U.S.), 1925 (wraps) . . £75

A Question of Identity, Doran (U.S.), 1925 (wraps) £75

Who Was This Woman?, Two Photographs, and *The Ring of Hearts*, Doran (U.S.), 1925 (wraps) . £75

Word of Honour, Hodder & Stoughton, [1926] . . . . £150/£15

ditto, Doran (U.S.), 1926 . . . . . . £150/£15

The Eleventh Hour, Doran (U.S.), 1926 (wraps) £75

The Loyalty of Peter Drayton, and *Mrs Peter Skeffington's Revenge*, Doran (U.S.), 1926 (wraps) £75

The Message, Doran (U.S.), 1926 (wraps) . . £75

The Rout of the Oliver Samuelsons, Doran (U.S.), 1926 (wraps) £75

The Rubber Stamp, and *A Matter of Voice*, Doran (U.S.), 1926 (wraps). £75

The Saving Clause, Doran (U.S.), 1926 (wraps) £75

The Taming of Sydney Marsham, Doran (U.S.), 1926 (wraps) £75

Three of a Kind, and *The Haunting of Jack Burnham*, Doran (U.S.), 1926 (wraps). £75

Word of Honour, Doran (U.S.), 1926 (wraps) . £75

Jim Brent, Hodder & Stoughton, [1927] . £150/£15

The Saving Clause, Hodder & Stoughton, [1927] . . . . £150/£15

Shorty Bill, Hodder & Stoughton, [1927] . £150/£15

An Act of Providence, Doran (U.S.), 1927 (wraps) £75

Billie Finds the Answer, Doran (U.S.), 1927 (wraps) £75

The Diamond Hair Slide, Doran (U.S.), 1927 (wraps). £75

Dilemma, Doran (U.S.), 1927 (wraps) . . . £75

A Hundred Per Cent, Doran (U.S.), 1927 (wraps) £75

Once Bit, Twice Hit, Doran (U.S.), 1927 (wraps) £75

Relative Values, Doran (U.S.), 1927 (wraps) . £75

When Carruthers Laughed, Doran (U.S.), 1927 (wraps) £75

John Walters, Hodder & Stoughton, [1928] £150/£15

The Hidden Witness, Doubleday (U.S.), 1929 (wraps) £75

A Question of Mud, Doubleday (U.S.), 1929 (wraps) £75

The Undoing of Mrs Cransby, Doubleday (U.S.), 1929 (wraps) £75

Sapper's War Stories, Hodder & Stoughton, 1930 . . . . £150/£20

The Finger of Fate, Hodder & Stoughton, 1931 . . . . £150/£15

ditto, Doran (U.S.), [1931] . . . . . £150/£15

The Great Magor Diamond, and *The Creaking Door*, Doubleday (U.S.), 1931 (wraps) £75

The Haunted Rectory, Doubleday (U.S.), 1931 (wraps) £75

The Missing Chauffeur, Doubleday (U.S.), 1931 (wraps) £75

The Brides of Mertonbridge Hall, Doubleday (U.S.), 1932 (wraps) £75

A Matter of Tar, Doubleday (U.S.), 1932 (wraps) £75

Uncle James's Golf Match, Hodder & Stoughton, 1932 . . . . £175/£75

Ronald Standish, Hodder & Stoughton, 1933 £150/£20

The Man in Yellow, and *The Empty House*, Doubleday (U.S.), 1933 (wraps) £75

When Carruthers Laughed, Hodder & Stoughton, 1934 . . . . £150/£15

ditto, Doran (U.S.), [n.d.] . . . . . . £150/£15

51 Stories, Hodder & Stoughton, 1931 . . £100/£10

Ask For Ronald Standish, Hodder & Stoughton, 1936 . . . . £150/£35

'Bulldog Drummond' Titles by Gerald Fairlie

Bulldog Drummond on Dartmoor, Hodder & Stoughton, 1938 . . . . £125/£20

ditto, Hillman-Curl (U.S.), 1939 . . . . £100/£15

Bulldog Drummond Attacks, Hodder & Stoughton, 1939 . . . . £125/£20

ditto, Gateway (U.S.), 1940 . . . . . £100/£15

Captain Bulldog Drummond, Hodder & Stoughton, 1945 . . . . £45/£10

Bulldog Drummond Stands Fast, Hodder & Stoughton, 1947 . . . . £30/£10

Hands Off Bulldog Drummond, Hodder & Stoughton, 1949 . . . . £25/£10

Calling Bulldog Drummond, Hodder & Stoughton, 1951 . . . . £25/£10

The Return of the Black Gang, Hodder & Stoughton, 1954 . . . . £25/£10

SARBAN
(b.1910 d.1989)

Pseudonym used by John W. Wall, a diplomat for
many years stationed in the Middle-East.

Ringstones and other Curious Tales, Davies, 1951 .
.   .   .   .   £125/£30
ditto, Coward-McCann (U.S.), [1951] .   . £100/£30
ditto, Tartarus Press, 2000 (350 copies) . .   £30/£10
The Sound of His Horn, Davies, 1952 .   . £300/£45
ditto, Ballantine (U.S.), 1960 (wraps)   .   .   . £10
ditto, Tartarus Press, 1999 (350 numbered copies) .   .
.   .   .   . £100/£35
The Doll Maker, Davies, 1953 .   .   .   . £350/£75
ditto, Ballantine (U.S.), 1960 (wraps)   .   .   . £10
ditto, Tartarus Press, 1999 (250 numbered copies) .   .
.   .   .   . £100/£25
The Sacrifice, Tartarus Press, 2002 (350 copies) .   .
.   .   .   .   £30/£10

SIEGFRIED SASSOON
(b.1886 d.1967)

A poet and author of autobiography and semi-
autobiographical novels, his *Memoirs of a Fox-
Hunting Man* won both the Hawthenden and Tait
Black Memorial Prizes.

Novels
Memoirs of a Fox-Hunting Man, Faber, 1928
(anonymous) .   .   .   . £500/£75
ditto, Faber, 1928 (260 signed, numbered copies) .   .
.   .   .   . £650/£400
ditto, Faber, 1929 (300 signed, numbered copies,
illustrated)   .   .   .   .   .   . £1,250/£1,000
ditto, Faber, 1929 (illustrated)   .   .   . £100/£25
ditto, Coward-McCann (U.S.), 1929 .   .   . £75/£15
Memoirs of an Infantry Officer, Faber, 1930 £125/£25
ditto, Faber, 1930 (750 signed copies) .   .   . £200
ditto, Coward-McCann (U.S.), 1930 .   .   . £75/£15
ditto, Faber, 1931 (illustrated by Freedman, 320 signed
copies, d/w and slipcase)   .   .   . £1,000/£650
ditto, Faber, 1931 (illustrated by Freedman, 12 signed
copies) £1,500
Sherston's Progress, Faber, 1936 .   .   . £100/£20
ditto, Faber, 1936 (300 signed copies)   .   .   . £200
ditto, Doubleday (U.S.), 1936   .   .   .   . £65/£10
The Complete Memoirs of George Sherston, Faber,
1937 .   .   .   . £40/£10
ditto, Doubleday (U.S.), 1937   .   .   . £30/£10

Poetry
An Ode for Music, privately printed, 1912 (50 copies)
.   .   .   . £1,250
The Daffodil Murderer, Richmond, 1913 (wraps) £400

The Old Huntsman, Heinemann, 1917 (with errata
slip) £100
ditto, Dutton (U.S.), 1917.   .   .   .   .   . £100
Counter-Attack, Heinemann, 1918 (wraps) .   . £250
ditto, Heinemann, 1918   .   .   .   .   . £125
ditto, Dutton (U.S.), 1918.   .   .   .   . £100
The War Poems of Siegfried Sassoon, Heinemann,
1919 .   .   .   . £75
Recreations, privately printed, 1923 (75 copies of 81) .
.   .   .   . £500
ditto, privately printed, 1923 (6 copies of 81) . £750
Selected Poems, Heinemann, 1925 .   .   . £65/£20
Satirical Poems, Heinemann, 1926 .   . £300/£50
ditto, Viking (U.S.), 1926.   .   .   . £200/£45
Nativity, Faber, 1927 (350 numbered copies, wraps) .
.   .   .   . £35
ditto, Faber, 1927 (wraps). £15
ditto, William Edwin Rudge (U.S.), 1927 (27 copies to
secure copyright). £125
The Heart's Journey, Heinemann and Crosby Gaige
(U.S.), 1928 (590 signed copies)   .   . £200/£125
ditto, Heinemann and Crosby Gaige (U.S.), 1928 (9
copies on green paper) £600
ditto, Heinemann, 1928   .   .   .   .   . £75/£20
ditto, Harper (U.S.), 1929.   .   .   .   . £45/£15
To My Mother, Faber, 1928 .   .   .   . £40/£15
ditto, Faber, 1928 (500 signed large paper copies) £125
In Sicily, Faber, 1930 .   .   .   .   .   . £40/£15
ditto, Faber, 1928 (110 signed copies)   .   . £150
Poems by Pinchbeck Lyre, Duckworth, 1931 (glassine
d/w) .   .   .   . £55/£50
To the Red Rose, Faber, 1931(wraps)   .   .   . £25
ditto, Faber, 1931 (400 signed copies)   .   . £125
Prehistoric Burials, Knopf (U.S.), 1932 (Borzoi Chap
Book) £35
The Road to Ruin, Faber, 1933 .   .   . £60/£15
Vigils, [Douglas Cleverdon], 1934 (272 signed copies,
Niger morocco) £200
ditto, Heinemann, 1935   .   .   .   .   . £60/£15
ditto, Viking (U.S.), 1936.   .   .   . £40/£10
Rhymed Ruminations, Faber, 1940 .   . £35/£10
ditto, Viking (U.S.), 1941.   .   .   . £25/£10
Poems Newly Selected, Faber, 1940 .   . £25/£10
Collected Poems, Faber, 1947   .   .   . £40/£15
ditto, Viking (U.S.), 1949.   .   .   . £30/£10
Sequences, Faber, 1956 .   .   .   .   . £30/£10
ditto, Viking (U.S.), 1957.   .   .   . £25/£10
Collected Poems, 1908-1956, Faber, 1961 . £20/£10
An Octave, privately printed, 1966 (350 copies, wraps,
slipcase) .   .   .   . £75/£50

Others
The Old Century and Seven More Years, Faber, 1938.
.   .   .   . £65/£20
ditto, Viking (U.S.), 1939.   .   .   . £35/£10
The Weald of Youth, Faber, 1941 .   . £40/£10
ditto, Viking (U.S.), 1942.   .   .   . £25/£10
Siegfried's Journey, Faber, 1945 .   . £35/£10
ditto, Viking (U.S.), 1946.   .   .   . £15/£5
Meredith, Constable, 1948 .   .   .   . £20/£10

ditto, Viking (U.S.), 1948. . . . . . £20/£10
The Path to Peace, Stanbrook Abbey Press, 1960 (500 copies, quarter vellum) £250
Something About Myself by Siegfried Sassoon, aged 11, Stanbrook Abbey Press, 1966 (350 copies, wraps) £50
Diaries, 1920-1922, Faber, 1981. . . . £30/£15
Diaries, 1915-1918, Faber, 1983. . . . £25/£10
Diaries, 1923-1925, Faber, 1984. . . . £20/£10
Siegfried Sassoon: Letters to Max Beerbohm with a Few Answers, Faber, 1986 . . . . £20/£5

THE SAVOY

After leaving *The Yellow Book*, Aubrey Beardsley joined with Arthur Symons to produce *The Savoy*, published by Leonard Smithers. Smithers later bound and published sets of all 8 issues in pictorial cloth in 3 volumes.

No.1, January 1896 (including Christmas card). £150
No.1, January 1896 (without Christmas card) . £100
No.2, April, 1896 . . . . £75
No.3, July, 1896 . . . . £75
No.4, August, 1896 . . . . £75
No.5, September, 1896 . . . . £75
No.6, October, 1896 . . . . £75
No.7, November 1896. . . . . £75
No.8, December 1896. . . . . £75
All 8 issues, 3 vols. £1,500

DOROTHY L. SAYERS
(b.1893 d.1957)

Principally a writer of detective fiction, Sayers' novels follow the exploits of 'Lord Peter Wimsey'.

Novels
Whose Body?, Boni & Liveright (U.S.), 1923 (first issue without 'Inc.' after Boni & Liveright on title page) . . . . £3,000/£400
ditto, Unwin, 1923. . . . . . . £1,750/£350
Clouds of Witness, Unwin, 1926. . . £1,750/£250
ditto, as **Clouds of Witnesses**, Dial Press (U.S.), 1927 . . . . £1,250/£175
Unnatural Death, Benn, 1927 . . . £1,750/£250
ditto, as **The Dawson Pedigree**, Dial Press (U.S.), 1928 . . . . £1,250/£250
The Unpleasantness at the Bellona Club, Benn, 1928. . . . . £2,500/£250
ditto, Payson & Clarke (U.S.), 1928 . . £1,000/£150
The Documents in the Case, Benn, 1930 (with Robert Eustace) . . . . £1,000/£100
ditto, Brewer & Warren (U.S.), 1930 . . £600/£50
Strong Poison, Gollancz, 1930 . . . £1,000/£100

ditto, Brewer & Warren (U.S.), 1930 . . £750/£65
The Five Red Herrings, Gollancz, 1931 £1,000/£100
ditto, as **Suspicious Characters**, Brewer & Warren (U.S.), 1931 . . . . £750/£65
Have His Carcase, Gollancz, 1932 . . £1,000/£65
ditto, Brewer & Warren (U.S.), 1932 . . £600/£45
Murder Must Advertise, Gollancz, 1933 £1,000/£65
ditto, Harcourt (U.S.), 1933 . . . . . £600/£45
The Nine Tailors, Gollancz, 1934 . . £1,000/£45
ditto, Harcourt (U.S.), 1934 . . . . . £600/£40
Gaudy Night, Gollancz, 1935 . . . . £750/£40
ditto, Harcourt (U.S.), 1936 . . . . . £500/£40
Busman's Honeymoon, Harcourt (U.S.), 1937 . . . . £500/£40
ditto, Gollancz, 1937 . . . . £500/£40
Thrones, Dominations, Hodder & Stoughton, 1998 (completed by Jill Paton Walsh) . . . £30/£10
ditto, St Martin's Press (U.S.), 1998 . . . £30/£10

Short Stories
Lord Peter Views the Body, Gollancz, 1928 . . . . £1,250/£100
ditto, Payson & Clarke (U.S.), 1929 . . . £750/£65
Hangman's Holiday, Gollancz, 1933 . . £750/£45
ditto, Harcourt (U.S.), 1933 . . . . . £500/£35
In the Teeth of the Evidence, Gollancz, 1939 £600/£45
ditto, Harcourt (U.S.), 1940 . . . . . £500/£35
ditto, Gollancz, 1972 (3 additional stories) . £25/£5
Lord Peter, A Collection of All the Lord Peter Wimsey Stories, Harper & Row (U.S.), 1972 . £30/£10
ditto, Harper & Row (U.S.), 1972 (adds 'Talboys') . . . . £25/£10
Talboys, Harper & Row (U.S.), 1972 (wraps) . £50
Striding Folly, New English Library, 1973 (wraps) £10

Collaborations
The Floating Admiral, Hodder and Stoughton, [1931] . . . . £750/£125
ditto, Doubleday (U.S.), 1932 . . . . £500/£30
Ask a Policeman, Barker, [1933] . . . £600/£100
ditto, Morrow (U.S.), 1933 . . . . . £500/£65
The Scoop and **Behind the Screen**, Gollancz, 1983 . . . . £25/£10
No Flowers by Request, Gollancz, 1984 . £25/£10

Poetry
Op. 1, Blackwell, 1916 (wraps) £400
Catholic Tales and Christian Songs, Blackwell, 1918 (wraps and d/w) . . . . £175/£100

Plays
Busman's Honeymoon, Gollancz, 1937. . £400/£75
ditto, Gollancz, 1937 (wraps). £150
ditto, Harcourt Brace (U.S.), 1937 . . . £300/£65
The Zeal of Thy House, Gollancz, 1937 . £35/£10
ditto, Harcourt Brace (U.S.), 1937 . . . £30/£10
The Devil to Pay, Gollancz, 1937 . . . £35/£15
ditto, Harcourt Brace (U.S.), 1941 . . . £25/£10

He that Should Come, Gollancz, 1939 (wraps in d/w) .
. . . . £20/£10
The Man Born to be King, Gollancz, 1943 . £60/£15
ditto, Harpers (U.S.), 1943 . . . . . £25/£10
The Just Vengeance, Gollancz, 1946 . . £35/£10
ditto, Gollancz, 1946 (wraps). £15
Four Sacred Plays, Gollancz, 1948 . . . . £15/£5
The Emperor Constantine, Gollancz, 1951 . . £20/£5

Essays
Begin Here, Gollancz, 1940 . . . . . £75/£25
ditto, Harcourt (U.S.), 1941 . . . . . £35/£10
The Mind of the Maker, Methuen, 1941 . £25/£10
ditto, Harcourt (U.S.), 1941 . . . . . . £15/£5
Unpopular Opinions, Gollancz, 1946 . . £25/£10
ditto, Harcourt (U.S.), 1947 . . . . . . £15/£5
Creed or Chaos and Other Essays, Methuen, 1947 .
. . . . £15/£5
ditto, Harcourt (U.S.), 1949 . . . . . . £15/£5
Introductory Papers on Dante, Methuen, 1954. . .
. . . . £50/£15
ditto, Harpers (U.S.), 1955 . . . . £45/£10
Further Papers on Dante, Methuen, 1957 . £45/£10
ditto, Harpers (U.S.), 1957 . . . . £45/£10
The Poetry of Search and the Poetry of Statement,
Gollancz, 1963 . . . . £15/£5
Christian Letters to a Post-Christian World, William
Eerdmans (U.S.), 1969 . . . . £15/£5
A Matter of Eternity, William Eerdmans (U.S.), 1973 .
. . . . £15/£5
ditto, Mowbray, 1973 . . . . £15/£5
Wilkie Collins: A Critical and Bibliographical Study,
Univ. of Toledo (U.S.), 1977 . . . . . £20/£5

Children's Title
Even the Parrot, Methuen, 1944 . . . . £40/£10

Others
Papers Relating to the Family of Wimsey, privately
printed, Humphrey Milford, [1936] (approximately
500 copies, wraps) £350
*Account of Lord Mortimer Wimsey, Hermit of the
Wash*, 'Printed by M. Bryan, 1816' [O.U.P., 1937]
(250 copies, wraps) £500
The Wimsey Family, A Fragmentary History,
Gollancz, 1977 . . . . £35/£10

JACK SCHAEFER
(b.1907 d.1991)

Author of *Shane*, one of the most famous 'westerns'
of all time.

Novels
Shane, Houghton Mifflin (U.S.), 1949 . £2,500/£250
ditto, Deutsch, 1954 . . . . £150/£25

First Blood, Houghton Mifflin/Ballantine (U.S.), 1953
. . . . £450/£40
ditto, Deutsch, 1954 . . . . £125/£20
The Canyon, Houghton, Mifflin/Ballantine (U.S.),
1953 . . . . £200/£25
ditto, Deutsch, 1955 . . . . £100/£15
Company of Cowards, Houghton, Mifflin (U.S.), 1957
. . . . £125/£10
ditto, Deutsch, 1958 . . . . £45/£10
Monte Walsh, Houghton Mifflin (U.S.), 1963 £150/£20
ditto, Deutsch, 1965 . . . . £45/£10
The Short Novels of Jack Schaefer, Houghton, Mifflin
(U.S.), 1967 . . . . £45/£10
Mavericks, Houghton, Mifflin (U.S.), 1967 . £100/£15
ditto, Deutsch, 1968 . . . . £35/£10

Short Stories
The Big Range, Houghton, Mifflin/Ballantine (U.S.),
1953 . . . . £200/£45
ditto, Deutsch, 1955 . . . . £125/£20
The Pioneers, Houghton, Mifflin (U.S.), 1954 . . .
. . . . £150/£25
ditto, Deutsch, 1957 . . . . £100/£15
The Kean Land, Houghton, Mifflin (U.S.), 1959 . .
. . . . £75/£15
ditto, Deutsch, 1960 . . . . £65/£10
The Plainsmen, Houghton, Mifflin (U.S.), 1963 . .
. . . . £65/£10
The Collected Stories of Jack Schaefer, Houghton,
Mifflin (U.S.), 1966 . . . . £75/£10

Children's Titles
Old Ramon, Houghton, Mifflin (U.S.), 1960 £150/£20
Stubby Pringle's Christmas, Houghton, Mifflin (U.S.),
1964 . . . . £100/£15

Others
The Great Endurance Horse Race, Stagecoach Press
(U.S.), 1963 (750 numbered copies) . . £45/£20
Heroes Without Glory, Houghton, Mifflin (U.S.), 1965
. . . . £25/£10
ditto, Deutsch, 1966 . . . . £15/£5
Adolphe Francis Bandelier, The Press of the
Territorian (U.S.), 1966 (1,000 copies, wraps) £20
New Mexico, Coward-McCann (U.S.), 1967 £40/£10
An American Bestiary, Houghton, Mifflin (U.S.), 1975
. . . . £15/£5
Conversations With a Pocket Gopher, Capra Press
(U.S.), 1978 (wraps) £15
ditto, Capra Press (U.S.), 1978 (26 signed, lettered
hardback copies, no d/w) £300
Edited by Shaefer
Out West, Houghton, Mifflin (U.S.), 1955 . £35/£10
ditto, Deutsch, 1959 . . . . £30/£10

PAUL SCOTT
(b.1920 d.1978)

Scott only received proper recognition for his writing when in 1977 he won the Booker Prize with *Staying On*. Not the early 1980s did he achieve wide popular recognition when his 'Raj' books were filmed as *The Jewel in the Crown*.

'The Raj Quartet'
The Jewel in the Crown, Heinemann, 1966. £150/£35
ditto, Morrow (U.S.), 1966 . . . . . £45/£10
The Day of the Scorpion, Heinemann, 1968 £100/£25
ditto, Morrow (U.S.), 1968 . . . . £35/£10
The Towers of Silence, Heinemann, 1971 . £75/£20
ditto, Morrow (U.S.), 1972 . . . . . £25/£5
A Division of the Spoils, Heinemann, 1975 . £75/£20
ditto, Morrow (U.S.), 1975 . . . . . £25/£5

Other Novels
Johnnie Sahib, Eyre & Spottiswoode, 1952 £150/£25
The Alien Sky, Eyre & Spottiswoode, 1953. £75/£20
ditto, as *Six Days In Marapore*, Doubleday (U.S.), 1953 . . . . £35/£10
A Male Child, Eyre & Spottiswoode, 1956 . £50/£15
ditto, Dutton (U.S.), 1957. . . . . . £35/£10
The Mark of the Warrior, Eyre & Spottiswoode, 1956 . . . . £50/£15
ditto, Morrow (U.S.), 1958 . . . . . £20/£5
The Chinese Love Pavilion, Eyre & Spottiswoode, 1960 . . . . £25/£10
ditto, as *The Love Pavilion*, Morrow (U.S.), 1962 . . . . £20/£5
The Birds of Paradise, Eyre & Spottiswoode, 1962 . . . . £25/£10
ditto, Morrow (U.S.), 1962. . . . . . £20/£5
The Bender, Secker & Warburg, 1963 . . £25/£10
ditto, Morrow (U.S.), 1963. . . . . . £20/£5
The Corrida at San Feliu, Secker & Warburg, 1964 . . . . £25/£10
ditto, Morrow (U.S.), 1964. . . . . . £20/£5
Staying On, Heinemann, 1977 . . . . £75/£15
ditto, Morrow (U.S.), 1977. . . . . . £35/£5

Poetry
I, Gerontius, Favil Press, 1941 (wraps) . . . £400

Others
After the Funeral, Whittington Press/Heinemann, 1979 (200 copies signed by illustrator) £125
My Appointment with the Muse: Essays 1961-1975, Heinemann, 1986 . . . . £25/£10

ANNA SEWELL
(b.1820 d.1878)

Black Beauty was Anna Sewell's only novel, written in an attempt to encourage the better treatment of horses.

Black Beauty: His Grooms and Companions. The Autobiography of a Horse, Jarrold, 1877 . . £3,500
ditto, American Humane Education Society (U.S.), 1890 (orange printed wraps) £750
ditto, American Humane Education Society (U.S.), 1890 (buff boards) £500

TOM SHARPE
(b.1928)

Tom Sharpe became a full-time novelist in 1971 with the publication of *Riotous Assembly*. His books have been filmed, with varying degrees of success.

Novels
Riotous Assembly, Secker & Warburg, 1971 £250/£25
ditto, Viking (U.S.), 1971. . . . . . £65/£15
Indecent Exposure, Secker & Warburg, 1973 . . . . £150/£20
ditto, Atlantic Monthly Press (U.S.), 1973 (wraps) £10
Porterhouse Blue, Secker & Warburg, 1974 £150/£20
ditto, Prentice-Hall (U.S.), 1974 . . . . £65/£15
Blott on the Landscape, Secker & Warburg, 1975 . . . . £45/£10
ditto, Random House (U.S.), 1985 . . . . £10/£5
Wilt, Secker & Warburg, 1976 . . . . £35/£10
ditto, Random House (U.S.), 1984 . . . . £10/£5
The Great Pursuit, Secker & Warburg, 1977 . £20/£5
ditto, Harper (U.S.), 1978. . . . . . £15/£5
The Throwback, Secker & Warburg, 1978 . . £20/£5
ditto, Random House (U.S.), 1985 . . . . £10/£5
The Wilt Alternative, Secker & Warburg, 1979 £20/£5
ditto, Random House (U.S.), 1984 . . . . £10/£5
Ancestral Vices, Secker & Warburg, 1980 . . £20/£5
ditto, St Martin's Press (U.S.), 1980 . . . . £15/£5
Vintage Stuff, Secker & Warburg, 1982. . . £20/£5
ditto, Random House (U.S.), 1985 . . . . £10/£5
Wilt on High, Secker & Warburg, 1984. . . £15/£5
ditto, Random House (U.S.), 1985 . . . . £10/£5
Granchester Grind, A Porterhouse Chronicle, Secker & Warburg, 1995 . . . . £10/£5
The Midden, Deutsch/Secker & Warburg, 1996 £10/£5
ditto, Overlook (U.S.), 1997 . . . . . £10/£5

GEORGE BERNARD SHAW
(b.1856 d.1950)

Primarily a playwright, Shaw's dramatic works are often satirical attacks on convention and cant. His many other writings are also highly political. In 1925 he was awarded the Nobel Prize for Literature, but he later declined offers of a peerage and the Order of Merit.

Novels

Cashel Byron's Profession, The Modern Press, 1886 (larger issue measuring approx. 24.8 x 15.4 cm, wraps). £1,250
ditto, The Modern Press, 1886 (smaller issue measuring approx. 23.3 x 14.8 cm, wraps). .£1,000
ditto, Stone (U.S.), 1901 . . . .£100
An Unsocial Socialist, Swan, Sonnenschein, Lowrey & Co., 1887 (first state with Shaw's first novel given incorrectly as 'The Confessions of Bryn Cashel's...' and publisher's name spelt wrong on spine) . £1,250
ditto, Swan, Sonnenschein, Lowrey & Co., 1887 (second state with errors corrected). . . . £750
ditto, Brentano's (U.S.), 1900 . . . . . £75
Love Among the Artists, Stone (U.S.), 1905 . £250
ditto, Constable, 1914. . . . . £100
The Irrational Knot, Constable, 1905 . . . £65
ditto, Brentano's (U.S.), 1905 . . . . . £65
Immaturity, Constable, 1931 . . . . . £65/£15
Unfinished Novel, Constable, 1958 (950 copies) . . . . £30/£20

Plays

Widowers' Houses, Henry and Co, 1893 . . £750
Plays Pleasant and Unpleasant, Grant Richards, 1898 (2 vols) £100
ditto, Brentano's (U.S.), 1905 (2 vols) . . £65
Three Plays for Puritans, Grant Richards, 1901 £50
John Bull's Other Island, and *Major Barbara*, Constable and Co., 1907 (also contains *How He Lied to Her Husband*) £30
Man and Superman, Constable, 1903 . . . £30
ditto, Brentano's (U.S.), 1905 . . . . . £25
The Doctor's Dilemma, Getting Married, and *The Shewing-Up of Blanco Posnet*,Constable & Co, 1911 . . . . £25
ditto, Brentano's (U.S.), 1911 . . . . . £25
Pygmalion, privately printed, 1912 (title page reads 'Rough Proof-Unpublished', wraps) . . . £750
Androcles and the Lion, privately printed, 1913 (50 copies, title page reads 'Rough Proof-Unpublished', wraps). £500
Androcles and the Lion, Overruled, Pygmalion, Constable, 1916 . . . . £25
ditto, Brentano's (U.S.), 1916 . . . . . £25
Misalliance, The Dark Lady of the Sonnets, and *Fanny's First Plays*, Constable, 1914 . . . £25
ditto, Brentano's (U.S.), 1914 . . . . . £25
Heartbreak House, Great Catherine, and *Playlets of the War*, Constable, 1919 . . . . . £25

ditto, Brentano's (U.S.), 1919 . . . . . £20
Back to Methuselah. A Metabiological Pentateuch, Brentano's (U.S.), 1921 . . . . . £50/£15
ditto, Constable, 1922 . . . . £50/£15
Saint Joan: a chronicle play in six scenes and an epilogue, Constable, 1924 . . . . . £200/£30
ditto, Constable, 1924 (750 copies, with sketches by C. Ricketts) . . . .£500/£150
ditto, Brentano's (U.S.), 1924 . . . . £150/£45
The Apple Cart, a political extravaganza, Constable, 1930 . . . . £65/£15
ditto, Brentano's (U.S.), 1931 . . . . £50/£10
Too True To Be Good, Village Wooing, and *On the Rocks*, Constable, [1934] . . . . . £45/£15
ditto, Dodd, Mead (U.S.), 1934 . . . . £35/£10
The Simpleton of the Unexpected Isles, The Six of Calais, and *The Six Millionairess*, Constable, 1936 . . . . £40/£10
ditto, Dodd, Mead (U.S.), 1936 . . . . £35/£10
'In Good King Charles's Golden Days', Constable, 1939 . . . . £35/£10
ditto, Dodd, Mead (U.S.), 1947 . . . . £25/£10
Buoyant Billions, Constable, 1949 (1,000 numbered copies of 1,025) £35
ditto, Constable, 1949 (25 lettered copies of 1,025) £200
Buoyant Billions, Farfetched Fables, and *Shakes Versus Shav*, Constable, 1950 . . . . £25/£10

Political Writings

A Manifesto, Fabian Society Tract No. 2, 1884 (wraps) £100
To Provident Landlords and Capitalists, Fabian Society Tract No. 3, 1885 (anonymous, wraps) £75
The True Radical Programme, Fabian Society Tract No. 6, 1887 (anonymous, wraps) £75
Fabian Essays in Socialism, Fabian Society, 1889. . . . . £100
ditto, Brown (U.S.), 1904 . . . . £75
Anarchism Versus State Socialism, Henry Seymour, 1889 . . . . £75
What Socialism Is, Fabian Society Tract No. 13, 1890 (anonymous, wraps) £75
The Legal Eight Hours Question, R. Forder, 1891 (wraps) £75
Fabian Election Manifesto, Fabian Society Tract No. 40, 1892 (anonymous, wraps) £100
The Fabian Society: What it has Done, etc, Fabian Society Tract No. 41, 1892 (wraps) . . . £75
Vote! Vote! Vote!, Fabian Society Tract No. 43, 1892 (anonymous, wraps) £75
The Impossibilities of Anarchism, Fabian Society Tract No. 45, 1893 (wraps) £75
A Plan of Campaign for Labour, Fabian Society Tract No. 49, 1894 (wraps) £75
Report on Fabian Policy, Fabian Society Tract No. 70, 1896 (anonymous, wraps) £50
Women as Councillors, Fabian Society Tract No. 93, 1900 (wraps) £75

Fabianism and the Empire: A Manifesto, Grant
Richards, 1900 (wraps) £100
Socialism for Millionaires, Fabian Society Tract No.
107, 1901 (wraps) £50
Common Sense of Municipal Trading, Constable,
1904 . . . . £50
Election Address, Fabian Society, 1904 (wraps) £50
Fabianism and the Fiscal Question, Fabian Society
Tract No. 116, 1904 (wraps) £35
Is Free Trade Alive or Dead?, George Standring, 1906
. . . . £75
Rent and Value, Fabian Society Tract No. 142, 1909
(wraps) £35
Socialism and Superior Brains, Fabian Society Tract
No. 146, 1910 (wraps) £45
ditto, Lane (U.S.), 1910 . . . . . . £45
The Case for Equality, Address to the Political &
Economic Circle National Liberal Club, 1913 (wraps)
. . . . £35
Common Sense about The War, 'New Statesman'
supplement, 1914 (wraps) £75
How to Settle the Irish Question, Talbot and Constable
(Dublin), 1917 (first issue blue wraps) . . . £100
ditto, Talbot and Constable (Dublin), 1917 (second
issue green wraps) £65
Peace Conference Hints, Constable, 1919 (wraps) £35
Socialism and Ireland, 'New Commonwealth'
supplement, 1919 (wraps) £25
Ruskin's Politics, Ruskin Centenary Council, 1921 £50
A Discarded Defence of Roger Casement, privately
printed by Clement Shorter, 1922 (25 copies). £200
The Unprotected Child & The Law, The Six Point
Group, [1923] (wraps) £65
Bernard Shaw and Fascism, Favil Press, 1927. £15
The Intelligent Woman's Guide to Socialism,
Constable, 1928 ('were' for 'was' line 5, p.442) . .
. . . . £150/£25
ditto, Brentano's (U.S.), 1928 . . . . £100/£20
The League of Nations, Fabian Society Tract No. 226,
1929 (wraps) £35
Bernard Shaw and Karl Marx, Random House, 1930
(575 copies, slipcase) . . . . . £65/£50
A Little Talk on America, Friends of the Soviet Union,
1931 (50 copies) £100
The Black Girl in Search of God, Constable, 1932 .
. . . . £45/£10
ditto, Dodd, Mead (U.S.), 1933 . . . £35/£10
A Political Madhouse in America and Nearer Home,
Constable, 1933 . . . . £75
The Future of Political Science in America, Dodd,
Mead (U.S.), 1933 . . . . . . £65/£20
Are We Heading for War?, Labour Party, 1934
(wraps) £30
Everybody's Political What's What?, Constable, 1944
. . . . £45/£10
ditto, Dodd, Mead (U.S.), 1944 . . . £35/£10
Fabian Essays, C. Allen & Unwin, 1948 . £20/£5
Shaw on Censorship, Shavian Tract No. 3, 1955 £25
The Matter with Ireland, Hart-Davis, 1962 £25/£10

ditto, Hill & Wang (U.S.), 1962 . . . . £25/£10
The Road to Equality, Beacon Press (U.S.), 1971 . .
. . . . £20/£5

Other Prose
Quintessence of Ibsenism, Walter Scott, 1891 . £125
ditto, Brentano's (U.S.), 1904 . . . . . £35
ditto, Constable, 1913 (extended edition) . . £25
On Going to Church, Roycraft Printing Shop (U.S.),
1896 . . . . £100
ditto, Roycraft Printing Shop (U.S.), 1896 (26 copies
on Japanese vellum) £1,000
The Perfect Wagnerite, Grant Richards, 1898 . £125
ditto, Stone (U.S.), 1899 . . . . £50
Dramatic Opinions and Essays, Constable, 1907 (2
vols) £30
*Statement of the Evidence in Chief of G.B.S. Before
the Joint Select Committee on Stage Plays*, privately
printed, 1909 . . . . £200
Nine Answers, privately printed by Jerome Kern
(U.S.), 1923 (62 copies) £200
ditto, privately printed by Jerome Kern (U.S.), 1923
(150 copies) £100
Music in London 1890-94, Constable, 1931 (3 vols) .
. . . . £100/£45
Prefaces, Constable, 1934 . . . . £30/£10
London Music in 1888-1889, Dodd, Mead (U.S.),
1937 (pseud. 'Bassetto'). . . . . £45/£15
Sixteen Self-Sketches, Constable, 1949 . £35/£10
ditto, Dodd, Mead (U.S.), 1949 . . . £35/£10
How to Become a Musical Critic, Hart-Davis, 1960 .
. . . . £25/£10
ditto, Hill & Wang (U.S.), [1961] . . £25/£10
Shaw on Shakespeare, Dutton (U.S.), 1961 £25/£10
ditto, Cassell, 1962 . . . . . . £25/£10
Shaw on Religion, Constable, 1967 . . . £20/£5
ditto, Dodd, Mead (U.S.), [1967]. . . . £20/£5
The Diaries, 1885-1897, Pennsylvania State Univ.
Press, 1986 (2 vols) . . . . . . £30/£10

MARY SHELLEY
(1797-1851)

Famous for *Frankenstein* of course, but her few other
works are also keenly sought by collectors. There is
apparently some doubt about her authorship of the
first title.

Poetry
Mounseer Nongtonpaw, Baldwin, Juvenile Series,
1808 (wraps) £5,000
ditto, Baldwin, Juvenile Series, 1808 (rebound) . .
. . . . £1,500

Fiction
Frankenstein, or, the Modern Prometheus,
Lackington, Hughes, Harding, Mayor & Jones, 1818
(anonymous, original boards, paper labels, 3 vols) .
. . . . £75,000

ditto, Lackington, Hughes, Harding, Mayor & Jones, 1818 (rebound, 3 vols) £20,000
ditto, Whitaker, 1823 (second edition, 2 vols) . £5,000
ditto, Carey, Lea and Blanchard (U.S.), 1833 £20,000
Valperga, or the Life and Adventures of Castruccio, Prince of Lucca, Whitaker, 1823 (3 vols) . . £1,250
The Last Man, Colburn, 1826 ('By the Author of Frankenstein', 3 vols) £2,000
The Fortunes of Perkin Warbeck, Colburn and Bentley, 1830 (3 vols) £2,000
Lodore, Bentley, 1835 ('By the Author of Frankenstein', 3 vols). £1,000
ditto, Wallis & Newell (U.S.), 1835 . . . . £1,000
Falkner, Sanders and Ottley, 1837 ('The Author of 'Frankenstein;' 'The Last Man,' &c.' 3 vols) . £600
ditto, Harper (U.S.), 1837. . . . . . . £600
Mathilde, 1959 (unfinished) . . . . . £30/£10
Collected Tales and Stories, Johns Hopkins Univ. Press (U.S.), [1976] . . . . £30/£10

Others

History of a Six Weeks' Tour, Hookham, 1817 (anonymous, co-written by Percy Bysshe Shelley) .
. . . . £1,500
Lives of the Most Eminent Literary and Scientific Men of Italy, Spain, and Portugal, Longman, 1835-37 (3 vols, with others, published as part of *The Cabinet of Biography*) £125
Lives of the Most Eminent Literary and Scientific Men of France, Longman, 1838-39 (2 vols, with others, published as part of *The Cabinet of Biography*) £125
Rambles in Germany and Italy, 1840, 1842 and 1843, Moxon, 1844 (2 vols) £300

M.P. SHIEL
(b.1865 d.1947)

The author of fantasy and science fiction, Matthew Phipps Shiel's short stories are rather luxuriant. His 'Prince Zaleski' tales, for example, offer a detective far more decadent than that other drug-taking dilettante, 'Sherlock Holmes'.

Short Stories

Prince Zaleski, John Lane, 1895 . . . . . £300
ditto, Roberts Brothers (U.S.), 1895 . . . . £150
ditto, Tartarus Press, 2002 . . . . . £25/£10
Shapes in the Fire, John Lane, 1896 . . . . £300
ditto, Roberts Brothers (U.S.), 1896 . . . . £150
ditto, Tartarus Press, 2000 . . . . . £40/£15
The Pale Ape, T. Werner Laurie, [1911] . . £400
Here Comes the Lady, The Richards Press, [1928].
. . . . £350/£150
The Invisible Voices, The Richards Press, 1935 (with John Gawsworth) . . . . . . £350/£100
ditto, Vanguard Press (U.S.), 1936 . . . £300/£50
The Best Short Stories of M.P. Shiel, Gollancz, 1948 .
. . . . £45/£15

Xélucha and Others, Arkham House (U.S.), 1975 . . .
. . . . £20/£5
Prince Zaleski and Cummings King Monk, Mycroft & Moran (U.S.), 1977 . . . . £20/£5

Novels

The Rajah's Sapphire, Ward, Lock & Bowden, 1896 .
. . . . £400
ditto, Highflyer Press (U.S.), 1981 (no d/w). . £45
The Yellow Danger, Grant Richards, 1898 . . £250
ditto, R.F. Fenno & Co. (U.S.), 1899 . . . £225
Contraband of War, Grant Richards, 1899 . . £125
ditto, The Gregg Press (U.S.), 1968 (no d/w) . £20
Cold Steel, Grant Richards, 1899 . . . . £150
ditto, Brentano's (U.S.), 1900 . . . . . £150
ditto, Gollancz, 1929 (revised edition, 105 signed copies, half vellum) £300
The Man Stealers, Hutchinson & Co., 1900 . £150
ditto, Lippincott (U.S.), 1900 . . . . . £125
The Lord of the Sea, Grant Richards, 1901 . . £175
ditto, Frederick A. Stokes Co. (U.S.), 1901 . . £150
ditto, Gollancz, 1929 (revised edition, 105 signed copies, half vellum) £350
The Purple Cloud, Chatto & Windus, 1901 . . £350
ditto, Gollancz, 1929 (revised edition, 105 signed copies, half vellum) £400
ditto, Vanguard Press (U.S.), 1930 (revised) £50/£15
The Weird o' It, Grant Richards, 1902 . . . £350
Unto the Third Generation, Chatto & Windus, 1903 .
. . . . £300
The Evil That Men Do, Ward, Lock & Co. Ltd, 1904 .
. . . . £300
The Lost Viol, Edward J. Clode (U.S.), 1905 (first issue with 'Edward J. Clode' on spine). . . £250
ditto, Edward J. Clode (U.S.), 1905 (second issue with 'E.J. Clode' on spine) £200
ditto, Ward, Lock & Co. Ltd, 1905 (copyright edition)
. . . . £400
ditto, Ward, Lock & Co. Ltd, 1908 . . . . £100
The Yellow Wave, Ward, Lock & Co. Ltd, 1905 (author's name spelt 'Sheil' on title page) . . £250
ditto, Ward, Lock & Co. Ltd., 1905 (author's name spelt correctly on title page). £150
ditto, Thomas Langton (Canada), 1905 (author's name spelt 'Sheil' on title page) £125
The Last Miracle, T. Werner Laurie, 1906 [1907] £125
The White Wedding, T. Werner Laurie, [1908]. £100
The Isle of Lies, T. Werner Laurie, [1909] . . £100
This Knot of Life, Everett & Co., [1909] . . £125
The Dragon, Grant Richards, 1913 (advance copy, green cloth) £250
ditto, Grant Richards, 1913 . . . . . . £100
ditto, Edward J. Clode (U.S.), 1914 . . . . £75
ditto, as *The Yellow Peril*, Gollancz, 1929 (revised edition, 105 signed copies, half vellum) . . £300
Children of the Wind, Grant Richards, 1923 £250/£50
ditto, Knopf (U.S.), 1923 . . . . . £225/£45
How The Old Woman Got Home, The Richards Press, 1927 . . . . £150/£40

ditto, Vanguard Press (U.S.), 1928 . . . £125/£25
Dr Krasinski's Secret, The Vanguard Press (U.S.),
1929 . . . . £150/£30
ditto, Jarrolds, 1930 . . . . £150/£30
The Black Box, The Vanguard Press (U.S.), 1930 . .
. . . . £200/£30
ditto, The Richards Press, 1931 . . . . £175/£25
Say Au R'Voir But Not Goodbye, Ernest Benn Ltd,
1933 (wraps) £45
This Above All, The Vanguard Press (U.S.), 1933 . .
. . . . £75/£20
ditto, as **Above All Else**, Lloyd Cole, 1943 . £65/£15
The Young Men Are Coming, Allen & Unwin, 1937 .
. . . . £75/£20
ditto, Vanguard Press (U.S.), 1937 . . . £75/£20

Others
Richards Shilling Selection from Edwardian Poets -
M.P. Shiel, The Richards Press, 1936 (wraps)   £45
Science, Life and Literature, Williams & Norgate Ltd,
1950 . . . . £30/£15

NEVIL SHUTE
(b.1899 d.1961)

A popular novelist, and scientist, Shute's *On the Beach*, about the survivors of a nuclear holocaust, is arguably his most important work.

Novels
Marazan, Cassell, 1926 . . . . . £1,250/£125
ditto, Ballantine (U.S.), 1970 (wraps) £5
So Disdained, Cassell, 1926 . . . . £1,000/£100
ditto, as **The Mysterious Aviator**, Houghton Mifflin
(U.S.), 1928 . . . . £1,000/£100
Lonely Road, Heinemann, 1932 . . . . £650/£75
ditto, Ballantine (U.S.), 1970 (wraps) £5
Ruined City, Heinemann, 1938 . . . . £650/£75
ditto, as **Kindling**, Morrow (U.S.), 1938 . . £400/£45
What Happened to the Corbetts, Heinemann, 1939 .
. . . . £500/£50
ditto, as **Ordeal**, Morrow (U.S.), 1939 . . £350/£50
An Old Captivity, Heinemann, 1940 . . . £200/£25
ditto, Morrow (U.S.), 1940 . . . . £200/£25
Landfall, Heinemenn, 1940 . . . . £100/£25
ditto, Morrow (U.S.), 1940 . . . . £100/£25
Pied Piper, Heinemann, 1942 . . . . £60/£15
ditto, Morrow (U.S.), 1942 . . . . £50/£15
Pastoral, Heinemann, 1944 . . . . £60/£15
ditto, Morrow (U.S.), 1944 . . . . £50/£15
Most Secret, Heinemann, 1945 . . . . £60/£15
ditto, Morrow (U.S.), 1945 . . . . £50/£15
The Chequer Board, Heinemann, 1947 . . £50/£10
ditto, Morrow (U.S.), 1947 . . . . £40/£10
No Highway, Heinemenn, 1948 . . . £50/£10
ditto, Morrow (U.S.), 1948 . . . . £40/£10
A Town Like Alice, Heinemann, 1950 . . £75/£15
ditto, as **Legacy**, Morrow (U.S.), 1950 . . £40/£10

Round the Bend, Heinemann, 1951 . . . £30/£10
ditto, Morrow (U.S.), 1951 . . . . . £30/£10
The Far Country, Heinemann, 1952. . . £30/£10
ditto, Morrow (U.S.), 1952 . . . . . £30/£10
In the Wet, Heinemann, 1953 . . . . £30/£10
ditto, Morrow (U.S.), 1953 . . . . . £30/£10
Requiem for a Wren, Heinemann, 1955. . . £40/£5
ditto, as **The Breaking Wave**, Morrow (U.S.), 1955 .
. . . . £35/£5
Beyond the Black Stump, Heinemann, 1956 . £30/£5
ditto, Morrow (U.S.), 1956 . . . . . £25/£5
On the Beach, Heinemann, 1957 . . . . £35/£5
ditto, Morrow (U.S.), 1957 . . . . . £25/£5
The Rainbow and the Rose, Heinemann, 1958 . £25/£5
ditto, Morrow (U.S.), 1958 . . . . . £20/£5
Trustee from the Toolroom, Heinemann, 1960. £20/£5
ditto, Morrow (U.S.), 1960 . . . . . £20/£5
Stephen Morris, Heinemann, 1961 . . . £20/£5
ditto, Morrow (U.S.), 1961 . . . . . £20/£5

Autobiography
Slide Rule, Heinemann, 1954 . . . . £65/£10
ditto, Morrow (U.S.), 1954 . . . . . £65/£10

Drama
Viland the Good, Heinemann, 1946 . . . £300/£35
ditto, Morrow (U.S.), 1946 . . . . . £100/£20

ALAN SILLITOE
(b.1928)

A novelist and poet, Sillitoe's reputation rests principally on *Saturday Night and Sunday Morning*.

Novels
Saturday Night and Sunday Morning, Allen, 1958 .
. . . . £150/£25
ditto, Knopf (U.S.), 1958 . . . . . £75/£15
The General, Allen, 1960. . . . . . £35/£5
ditto, Knopf (U.S.), 1960. . . . . . £30/£5
Key to the Door, Macmillan, 1961 . . . £25/£5
ditto, Knopf (U.S.), 1961 . . . . . £25/£5
The Death of William Posters, Macmillan, 1965 .
. . . . £20/£5
ditto, Knopf (U.S.), 1965 . . . . . £20/£5
A Tree on Fire, Macmillan, 1967 . . . £20/£5
ditto, Knopf (U.S.), 1967 . . . . . £20/£5
A Start in Life, Allen, 1970 . . . . £20/£5
ditto, Scribner's (U.S.), 1971 . . . . £20/£5
Travels in Nihilon, Allen, 1971 . . . . £20/£5
ditto, Scribner's (U.S.), 1972 . . . . £20/£5
Raw Material, Allen, 1972 . . . . . £20/£5
ditto, Scribner's (U.S.), 1973 . . . . £20/£5
Flame of Life, Allen, 1974 . . . . . £20/£5
The Widower's Son, Allen, 1976 . . . £15/£5
ditto, Harper (U.S.), 1977. . . . . . £15/£5
The Storyteller, Allen, 1979 . . . . . £15/£5

ditto, Simon & Schuster (U.S.), 1980 . . . £15/£5
Her Victory, Granada, 1982 . . . . . £15/£5
ditto, Watts (U.S.), 1982 . . . . . . £15/£5
The Lost Flying Boat, Granada, 1983 . . £15/£5
ditto, Little, Brown (U.S.), 1983 . . . £15/£5
Down from the Hill, Granada, 1984 . . . £10/£5
Life Goes On, Granada, 1985 . . . . £10/£5
Out of the Whirlpool, Hutchinson, 1987 . £10/£5
ditto, Harper (U.S.), 1988 . . . . . . £10/£5
The Open Door, Grafton, 1989 . . . . £10/£5
Last Loves, Grafton, 1990 . . . . . £10/£5
Leonard's War – A Love Story, Harper Collins, 1991 .
. . . . £10/£5
Snowstop, Harper Collins, 1993 . . . . £10/£5
The Broken Chariot, Flamingo, 1998 . . £10/£5
Birthday, Flamingo, 2001 . . . . . £10/£5

Poetry
Without Beer or Bread, Outpost Publications, 1957
(wraps) £200
The Rats and Other Poems, Allen, 1960 . £25/£10
A Falling out of Love and Other Poems, Allen, 1964 .
. . . . £15/£5
Love in the Environs of Voronezh, Macmillan, 1968 .
. . . . £10/£5
ditto, Doubleday (U.S.), 1968 . . . . £10/£5
Poems, Rainbow Press, 1971 (with Ted Hughes and
Ruth Fainlight, 300 copies, numbered and signed by
all three poets, slipcase) . . . . . £225/£175
Shaman and Other Poems, Turret Books, 1973 (500
signed copies) . . . . £35/£20
Barbarians and Other Poems, Turret Books, 1973
(500 signed copies) . . . . . . £35/£20
From Canto Two of 'The Rats', published by the
author, 1973 (wraps). £15
Storm: New Poems, Allen, 1974. . . . £25/£10
Snow on the North Side of Lucifer, Sceptre Press,
1979 (150 copies, wraps) £25
ditto, Allen, 1979 . . . . £20/£5
More Lucifer, Booth, 1980 (125 numbered copies,
wraps). £25
Sun Before Departure: Poems, 1974-1984, Granada,
1984 . . . . £10/£5
Tides and Stone Walls, Grafton, 1986 . . £10/£5
Three Poems, Worlds Press, 1988 (75 signed copies of
200, wraps) £40
ditto, Worlds Press, 1988 (125 unsigned copies of 200,
wraps). £20
Shylock The Writer, Turret, 1991 (broadside) . £30
The Mentality of the Picaresque Hero, Turret, 1993
(500 copies, wraps) £25

Short Stories
The Loneliness of the Long Distance Runner, Allen,
1959 . . . . £150/£50
ditto, Knopf (U.S.), 1959 . . . . . £100/£25
The Ragman's Daughter, Allen, 1963 . . £25/£5
ditto, Knopf (U.S.), 1963 . . . . . £20/£5
Guzman Go Home, Macmillan, 1968 . . £20/£5

ditto, Doubleday (U.S.), 1968 . . . . £15/£5
Men, Women, and Children, Allen, 1973 . £15/£5
ditto, Scribner's (U.S.), 1974. . . . . £15/£5
The Second Chance and Other Stories, Cape, 1981 .
. . . . £10/£5
ditto, Simon & Schuster (U.S.), 1981 . . £10/£5
The Far Side of the Street, W.H. Allen, 1988 . £15/£5
Collected Stories, Flamingo, 1995 . . . £15/£5
Ron Delph and His Fight with King Arthur, Clarion
Tales, 1996 (wraps) £45
ditto, Clarion Tales, 1996 (150 signed copies, boards,
no d/w) £60
ditto, Clarion Tales, 1996 (59 signed copies with loose
print, boards, no d/w) £75
Alligator Playground, A Collection of Short Stories,
Flamingo, 1997 . . . . £15/£5

Plays
All Citizens are Soldiers, Macmillan, 1969 (adaptation
with Ruth Fainlight) . . . . . . £25/£10
ditto, Dufour (U.S.), 1969 (wraps) . . . £10
Three Plays, Allen, 1978 . . . . . . £10/£5

Children's Titles
The City Adventures of Marmalade Jim, Macmillan,
1967 (wraps) £15
Big John and the Stars, Robson, 1977 (wraps). £10
The Incredible Fencing Fleas, Robson, 1978 (wraps).
. . . . £10
Marmalade Jim at the Farm, Robson, 1982 (wraps) .
. . . . £10
Marmalade Jim and the Fox, Robson, 1984 (wraps) .
. . . . £10

Others
Chopin's Winter In Majorca, By Luis Ripoll, Mossen
Allcover (Spain), 1955 (translated by Sillitoe, wraps)
. . . . £5
The Road to Volgograd, Allen, 1964 . . £25/£5
ditto, Knopf (U.S.), 1964 . . . . . £20/£5
Mountains and Caverns, Allen, 1975 . . £15/£5
The Saxon Shore Way, Hutchinson, 1983 . £15/£5
Alan Sillitoe's Nottinghamshire, Grafton, 1987 £10/£5
Every Day of the Week: An Alan Sillitoe Reader, W.
H. Allen, 1987 . . . . £10/£5
Life Without Armour, An Autobiography, Harper-
Collins, 1995 . . . . £10/£5
*Leading the Blind: A Century of Guide Book Travel
1815-1914*, Picador, 1995 . . . . . £10/£5
ditto, Macmillan (U.S.), 1995 . . . . £10/£5

GEORGES SIMENON
(b.1903 d.1989)

Born in Belgium, Simenon's literary output was prodigious, and much of it has not been translated into English. He is known especially for his 'Inspector Maigret' novels.

Maigret Novels
The Crime of Inspector Maigret, Covici (U.S.), 1932 .
. . . . £1,000/£150
ditto, as Introducing Inspector Maigret, Hurst and Blackett, 1933 . . . . £750/£75
The Strange Case of Peter the Lett, Covici (U.S.), 1933 . . . . £400/£50
The Crossroads Murders, Covici (U.S.), 1933 . . .
. . . . £400/£50
Inspector Maigret Investigates, Hurst and Blackett, 1933 (the two above titles) . . . . . £450/£45
The Triumph of Inspector Maigret, Hurst and Blackett, 1934 . . . . £450/£45
The Patience of Maigret, George Routledge & Sons, 1939 . . . . £175/£25
ditto, Harcourt Brace (U.S.), 1940 . . . £175/£25
Maigret Travels South, George Routledge & Sons, 1940 . . . . £175/£25
ditto, Harcourt Brace (U.S.), 1940 . . £175/£25
Maigret Abroad, George Routledge & Sons, 1940 . .
. . . . £150/£20
ditto, Harcourt Brace (U.S.), 1940 . . . £150/£20
Maigret to the Rescue, George Routledge & Sons, 1940 . . . . £125/£20
ditto, Harcourt Brace (U.S.), 1941 . . . £125/£20
Maigret Keeps a Rendez-Vous, George Routledge & Sons, 1940 . . . . £100/£20
ditto, Harcourt Brace (U.S.), 1941 . . . £100/£20
Maigret Sits It Out, George Routledge & Sons, 1941 .
. . . . £100/£20
ditto, Harcourt Brace (U.S.), 1941 . . . £100/£20
Maigret and M. L'Abbé, George Routledge & Sons, 1941 . . . . £100/£20
ditto, Harcourt Brace (U.S.), 1942 . . . £75/£20
Maigret on Holiday, Routledge and Kegan Paul, 1950
. . . . £25/£5
ditto, as No Vacation for Maigret, Doubleday (U.S.), 1953 . . . . £25/£5
Maigret Right and Wrong, Hamish Hamilton, 1954 .
. . . . £25/£5
Maigret and the Strangled Stripper, Doubleday (U.S.), 1954 . . . . £20/£5
Maigret and the Killers, Doubleday (U.S.), 1954 . .
. . . . £20/£5
ditto, as Maigret and the Gangsters, Hamish Hamilton, 1974 . . . . £20/£5
Maigret and the Young Girl, Hamish Hamilton, 1955.
. . . . £25/£5
ditto, as Inspector Maigret and the Dead Girl, Doubleday (U.S.), 1955 . . . . . . £25/£5
The Fugitive, Doubleday (U.S.), 1955 . . . £25/£5

Maigret and the Burglar's Wife, Hamish Hamilton, 1955 . . . . £25/£5
ditto, Doubleday (U.S.), 1956 . . . . . £25/£5
Inspector Maigret in New York's Underworld, Doubleday (U.S.), 1956. . . . . . . £25/£5
Maigret's Revolver, Hamish Hamilton, 1956 . £25/£5
ditto, Harcourt Brace (U.S.), 1984 . . . £10/£5
My Friend Maigret, Hamish Hamilton, 1956 . £25/£5
ditto, as The Methods of Maigret, Doubleday (U.S.), 1957 . . . . £25/£5
Maigret Goes to School, Hamish Hamilton, 1957 . .
. . . . £25/£5
ditto, Harcourt Brace (U.S.), 1988 . . . . £10/£5
Maigret's Little Joke, Hamish Hamilton, 1957 . £25/£5
ditto, as None of Maigret's Business, Doubleday (U.S.), 1958 . . . . £25/£5
Maigret and the Old Lady, Hamish Hamilton, 1958 .
. . . . £25/£5
Maigret's First Case, Hamish Hamilton, 1958 . £25/£5
Maigret has Scruples, Hamish Hamilton, 1959. £25/£5
Maigret and the Reluctant Witnesses, Hamish Hamilton, 1959 . . . . £25/£5
ditto, Harcourt Brace (U.S.), 1989 . . . £10/£5
Madame Maigret's Own Case, Doubleday (U.S.), 1959 . . . . £25/£5
ditto, as Madame Maigret's Friend, Hamish Hamilton, 1960 . . . . £25/£5
Maigret Takes a Room, Hamish Hamilton, 1960 . .
. . . . £25/£5
ditto, as Maigret Rents a Room, Doubleday (U.S.), 1961 . . . . £25/£5
Maigret in Court, Hamish Hamilton, 1961 . . £25/£5
ditto, Harcourt Brace (U.S.), 1983 . . . £10/£5
Maigret Afraid, Hamish Hamilton, 1961 . . £25/£5
ditto, Harcourt Brace (U.S.), 1983 . . . £15/£5
Maigret in Society, Hamish Hamilton, 1962 . £25/£5
Maigret's Failure, Hamish Hamilton, 1962. . £25/£5
Maigret's Memoirs, Hamish Hamilton, 1963 . £25/£5
ditto, Harcourt Brace (U.S.), 1985 . . . £15/£5
Maigret and the Lazy Burglar, Hamish Hamilton, 1963 . . . . £25/£5
Maigret's Special Murder, Hamish Hamilton, 1964 .
. . . . £25/£5
ditto, as Maigret's Dead Man, Doubleday (U.S.), 1964
. . . . £25/£5
Maigret and the Saturday Caller, Hamish Hamilton, 1964 . . . . £25/£5
ditto, Harcourt Brace (U.S.), 1991 . . . £10/£5
Maigret Loses His Temper, Hamish Hamilton, 1965 .
. . . . £25/£5
ditto, Harcourt Brace (U.S.), 1974 . . . £20/£5
Maigret Sets a Trap, Hamish Hamilton, 1965 . £25/£5
ditto, Harcourt Brace (U.S.), 1972 . . . £20/£5
Maigret on the Defensive, Hamish Hamilton, 1966 .
. . . . £25/£5
ditto, Harcourt Brace (U.S.), 1981 . . . £15/£5
Maigret and the Headless Corpse, Hamish Hamilton, 1967 . . . . £25/£5
ditto, Harcourt Brace (U.S.), 1968 . . . £25/£5

Maigret and the Nahour Case, Hamish Hamilton,
1967 . . . . £25/£5
ditto, Harcourt Brace (U.S.), 1982 . . . . £10/£5
Maigret's Pickpocket, Hamish Hamilton, 1968. £25/£5
ditto, Harcourt Brace (U.S.), 1968 . . . . £25/£5
Maigret Has Doubts, Hamish Hamilton, 1968 . £25/£5
ditto, Harcourt Brace (U.S.), 1982 . . . . £10/£5
Maigret In Vichy, Harcourt Brace (U.S.), 1968 £25/£5
ditto, as *Maigret Takes the Waters*, Hamish Hamilton,
1969 . . . . £25/£5
Maigret and the Minister, Hamish Hamilton, 1969 .
. . . . £20/£5
ditto, as *Maigret and the Calame Report*, Harcourt
Brace (U.S.), 1969 . . . . £20/£5
Maigret Hesitates, Hamish Hamilton, 1970 . . £20/£5
ditto, Harcourt Brace (U.S.), 1970 . . . . £20/£5
Maigret's Boyhood Friend, Hamish Hamilton, 1970 .
. . . . £20/£5
ditto, Harcourt Brace (U.S.), 1970 . . . £20/£5
Maigret and the Wine Merchant, Hamish Hamilton,
1971 . . . . £20/£5
ditto, Harcourt Brace (U.S.), 1975 . . . . £20/£5
Maigret and the Killer, Hamish Hamilton, 1971 £20/£5
ditto, Harcourt Brace (U.S.), 1971 . . . . £20/£5
Maigret and the Madwoman, Hamish Hamilton, 1972
. . . . £20/£5
ditto, Harcourt Brace (U.S.), 1972 . . . . £20/£5
Maigret and the Flea, Hamish Hamilton, 1972. £20/£5
ditto, as *Maigret and the Informer*, Harcourt Brace
(U.S.), 1973 . . . . £20/£5
Maigret and Monsieur Charles, Hamish Hamilton,
1973 . . . . £20/£5
Maigret and the Dosser, Hamish Hamilton, 1973 . .
. . . . £20/£5
ditto, as *Maigret and the Bum*, Harcourt Brace (U.S.),
1973 . . . . £20/£5
Maigret and the Millionaires, Hamish Hamilton, 1974
. . . . £20/£5
ditto, Harcourt Brace (U.S.), 1974 . . . . £20/£5
Maigret and the Loner, Hamish Hamilton, 1975 . .
. . . . £20/£5
ditto, Harcourt Brace (U.S.), 1975 . . . . £20/£5
Maigret and the Man on the Boulevard, Hamish
Hamilton, 1975 . . . . £20/£5
ditto, as *Maigret on the Bench*, Harcourt Brace (U.S.),
1975 . . . . £20/£5
Maigret and the Black Sheep, Hamish Hamilton, 1976
. . . . £20/£5
ditto, Harcourt Brace (U.S.), 1976 . . . £20/£5
Maigret and the Ghost, Hamish Hamilton, 1976 .
. . . . £20/£5
ditto, as *Maigret and the Apparition*, Harcourt Brace
(U.S.), 1976 . . . . £20/£5
Maigret and the Spinster, Hamish Hamilton, 1977 .
. . . . £20/£5
ditto, Harcourt Brace (U.S.), 1977 . . . . £20/£5
Maigret and the Hotel Majestic, Hamish Hamilton,
1977 . . . . £20/£5
ditto, Harcourt Brace (U.S.), 1978 . . . . £20/£5

Maigret in Exile, Hamish Hamilton, 1978 . . £15/£5
ditto, Harcourt Brace (U.S.), 1979 . . . . £15/£5
Maigret and the Toy Village, Hamish Hamilton, 1978.
. . . . £15/£5
ditto, Harcourt Brace (U.S.), 1979 . . . . £15/£5
Maigret's Rival, Hamish Hamilton, 1979 . . £15/£5
ditto, Harcourt Brace (U.S.), 1980 . . . . £15/£5
Maigret in New York, Hamish Hamilton, 1979. £15/£5
Maigret and the Coroner, Hamish Hamilton, 1980 .
. . . . £15/£5
Maigret and the Mad Killers, Doubleday (U.S.), 1980
. . . . £15/£5
Maigret and the Death of a Harbor-Master, Harcourt
Brace (U.S.), 1989 . . . . £15/£5
Maigret and the Fortuneteller, Harcourt Brace (U.S.),
1989 . . . . £15/£5
Maigret and the Flemish Shop, Harcourt Brace (U.S.),
1990 . . . . £15/£5
Maigret and the Tavern by the Seine, Harcourt Brace
(U.S.), 1990 . . . . £15/£5

'Maigret' Short Stories
Maigret's Christmas, Hamish Hamilton, 1976 . £30/£5
ditto, Harcourt Brace (U.S.), 1977 . . . . £30/£5
Complete Maigret Short Stories, Hamish Hamilton,
1976 . . . . £25/£5
Maigret's Pipe, Hamish Hamilton, 1977 . . £25/£5
ditto, Harcourt Brace (U.S.), 1978 . . . . £25/£5

Other Novels
The Disintegration of J.P.G. George, Routledge &
Sons, 1937 . . . . £450/£75
In Two Latitudes, George Routledge & Sons, 1942 .
. . . . £150/£25
Affairs of Destiny, George Routledge & Sons, 1942 .
. . . . £100/£20
ditto, Harcourt Brace (U.S.), 1944 . . . £100/£20
The Man who Watched the Trains Go By, George
Routledge & Sons, 1942. . . . . . £100/£15
ditto, Reynal & Hitchcock (U.S.), 1946 . . £50/£10
Havoc by Accident, George Routledge & Sons, 1943 .
. . . . £100/£15
ditto, Harcourt Brace (U.S.), 1943 . . . £75/£15
Escape in Vain, George Routledge & Sons, 1943 . .
. . . . £75/£15
ditto, Harcourt Brace (U.S.), 1944 . . . £75/£15
On the Danger Line, George Routledge & Sons, 1944
. . . . £75/£15
ditto, Harcourt Brace (U.S.), 1944 . . . £75/£15
The Shadow Falls, George Routledge & Sons, 1945 .
. . . . £75/£15
ditto, Harcourt Brace (U.S.), 1945 . . . £75/£15
The Lost Moorings, George Routledge & Sons, 1946 .
. . . . £50/£10
ditto, as *Blind Alley*, Routledge & Kegan Paul, 1946 .
. . . . £50/£10
Black Rain, Reynal & Hitchcock (U.S.), 1947 £50/£10
ditto, Routledge & Kegan Paul, 1949 . . £50/£10
First Born, Reynal & Hitchcock (U.S.), 1947 £45/£10

Magnet of Doom, George Routledge & Sons, 1948 .
. . . . £50/£10
Chit of a Girl, Routledge & Kegan Paul, 1949 . . .
. . . . £50/£10
A Wife at Sea, Routledge & Kegan Paul, 1949 . . .
. . . . £50/£10
The Snow Was Black, Prentice-Hall (U.S.), 1950 . .
. . . . £35/£10
ditto, as *The Stain on the Snow*, Routledge & Kegan
Paul, 1953 . . . . £35/£10
Strange Inheritance, Routledge & Kegan Paul, 1950 .
. . . . £35/£10
Poisoned Relations, Routledge & Kegan Paul, 1950 .
. . . . £35/£10
The Strangers in the House, Routledge & Kegan Paul,
1951 . . . . £35/£10
ditto, Doubleday (U.S.), 1954 . . . . . £25/£5
The Window over the Way, Routledge & Kegan Paul,
1951 . . . . £35/£10
The Heart of a Man, Prentice-Hall (U.S.), 1951 . .
. . . . £35/£10
Act of Passion, Prentice-Hall (U.S.), 1952 . £35/£10
ditto, Routledge & Kegan Paul, 1953 . . £35/£10
The House by the Canal, Routledge & Kegan Paul,
1952 . . . . £35/£10
The Burgomaster of Furnes, Routledge & Kegan Paul,
1952 . . . . £35/£10
The Trial of Bébé Donge, Routledge & Kegan Paul,
1952 . . . . £35/£10
Aunt Jeanne, Routledge & Kegan Paul, 1953 . . .
. . . . £35/£10
ditto, Harcourt Brace (U.S.), 1983 . . . . £10/£5
The Girl in his Past, Prentice-Hall (U.S.), 1953 . .
. . . . £35/£10
ditto, Hamish Hamilton, 1976 . . . . . £10/£5
Four Days in a Lifetime, Prentice-Hall (U.S.), 1953 .
. . . . £35/£10
ditto, Hamish Hamilton, 1977 . . . . . £10/£5
Belle, New American Library (U.S.), 1954 . £35/£10
Across the Street, Routledge & Kegan Paul, 1954 . .
. . . . £35/£10
ditto, Harcourt Brace (U.S.), 1992 . . . . £10/£5
Ticket of Leave, Routledge & Kegan Paul, 1954 . .
. . . . £35/£10
Tidal Wave, Doubleday (U.S.), 1954 . . £35/£10
ditto, as *Violent Ends*, Hamish Hamilton, 1954 (drops
one story) . . . . £30/£10
*Destinations: The Hitchhiker and The Burial of
Monsieur Bouvet*, Doubleday (U.S.), 1955 £30/£10
Danger Ahead, Hamish Hamilton, 1955 . £30/£10
A Sense of Guilt, Hamish Hamilton, 1955 (contains
Chez Krull and *The Heart of a Man*) . . £30/£10
The Magician and The Widow, Doubleday (U.S.),
1955 . . . . £35/£10
ditto, as *The Magician* only, Hamish Hamilton, 1974 .
. . . . £10/£5
Witnesses And The Watchmaker, Doubleday (U.S.),
1956 . . . . £35/£10

The Judge and the Hatter, Hamish Hamilton, 1956
(contains *The Witnesses* and *The Hatter's Ghosts*) .
. . . . £25/£5
ditto, as *The Hatter's Phantoms*, Harcourt Brace
(U.S.), 1976 (single novel only) . . . . £15/£5
The Sacrifice, Hamish Hamilton, 1956 . . £25/£5
The Little Man from Archangel, Hamish Hamilton,
1957 . . . . £25/£5
The Stowaway, Hamish Hamilton, 1957 . . £25/£5
The Son, Hamish Hamilton, 1958 . . . . £25/£5
Inquest on Bouvet, Hamish Hamilton, 1958 . £25/£5
The Negro, Hamish Hamilton, 1959 . . . . £25/£5
Striptease, Hamish Hamilton, 1959 . . . . £25/£5
ditto, Harcourt Brace (U.S.), 1989 . . . . £10/£5
In Case of Emergency, Doubleday (U.S.), 1958 £25/£5
ditto, Hamish Hamilton, 1960 . . . . . £20/£5
Sunday, Hamish Hamilton, 1960 . . . . . £20/£5
ditto, Harcourt Brace (U.S.), 1966 (with *The Little Man
from Archangel*) . . . . £20/£5
The Premier, Hamish Hamilton, 1961 . . . £20/£5
The Widower, Hamish Hamilton, 1961 . . . £20/£5
ditto, Harcourt Brace (U.S.), 1982 . . . . £20/£5
The Fate of the Malous, Hamish Hamilton, 1962 . .
. . . . £20/£5
Pedigree, Hamish Hamilton, 1962 . . . . £20/£5
ditto, London House (U.S.), 1963 . . . . £20/£5
Account Unsettled, Hamish Hamilton, 1962 . £20/£5
A New Lease of Life, Hamish Hamilton, 1963 . £20/£5
The Iron Staircase, Hamish Hamilton, 1963 . £20/£5
ditto, Harcourt Brace (U.S.), 1977 . . . . £15/£5
The Patient, Hamish Hamilton, 1963 . . . £20/£5
ditto, as *The Bells of Bicetre*, Harcourt Brace (U.S.),
1964 . . . . £20/£5
The Accomplices, Harcourt Brace (U.S.), 1964 . £20/£5
ditto, Hamish Hamilton, 1966 . . . . . £20/£5
The Train, Hamish Hamilton, 1964 . . . . £20/£5
The Door, Hamish Hamilton, 1964 . . . . £20/£5
ditto, Harcourt Brace (U.S.), 1964 . . . . £20/£5
The Blue Room, Harcourt Brace (U.S.), 1964 . £20/£5
ditto, Hamish Hamilton, 1965 . . . . . £20/£5
Three Beds in Manhattan, Doubleday (U.S.), 1964 .
. . . . £20/£5
ditto, Hamish Hamilton, 1976 . . . . . £15/£5
The Man with the Little Dog, Hamish Hamilton, 1965
. . . . £20/£5
ditto, Harcourt Brace (U.S.), 1989 . . . . £10/£5
The Little Saint, Harcourt Brace (U.S.), 1965 . £20/£5
ditto, Hamish Hamilton, 1966 . . . . . £20/£5
The Cat, Harcourt Brace (U.S.), 1967 . . . £20/£5
ditto, Hamish Hamilton, 1972 . . . . . £15/£5
The Confessional, Hamish Hamilton, 1967 . . £20/£5
ditto, Harcourt Brace (U.S.), 1968 . . . . £20/£5
Monsieur Monde Vanishes, Hamish Hamilton, 1967 .
. . . . £20/£5
ditto, Harcourt Brace (U.S.), 1977 . . . . £15/£5
The Old Man Dies, Harcourt Brace (U.S.), 1967 . .
. . . . £20/£5
ditto, Hamish Hamilton, 1968 . . . . . £20/£5
The Neighbours, Hamish Hamilton, 1968 . . £20/£5

The Prison, Hamish Hamilton, 1969 . . . £20/£5
ditto, Harcourt Brace (U.S.), 1969 . . . . £20/£5
Big Bob, Hamish Hamilton, 1969 . . . . £20/£5
ditto, Harcourt Brace (U.S.), 1981 . . . . £15/£5
The Man on the Bench in the Barn, Hamish Hamilton,
1970 . . . . £15/£5
ditto, Harcourt Brace (U.S.), 1970 . . . £15/£5
November, Hamish Hamilton, 1970 . . . . £15/£5
ditto, Harcourt Brace (U.S.), 1970 . . . £15/£5
The Rich Man, Hamish Hamilton, 1971 . . £15/£5
ditto, Harcourt Brace (U.S.), 1971 . . . . £15/£5
Teddy Bear, Hamish Hamilton, 1971 . . . £15/£5
ditto, Harcourt Brace (U.S.), 1972 . . . . £15/£5
The Disappearance of Odile, Hamish Hamilton, 1972.
. . . . £15/£5
ditto, Harcourt Brace (U.S.), 1972 . . . £15/£5
The Glass Cage, Hamish Hamilton, 1973 . £15/£5
ditto, Harcourt Brace (U.S.), 1973 . . . £15/£5
The Innocents, Hamish Hamilton, 1973. . . £15/£5
ditto, Harcourt Brace (U.S.), 1974 . . . £15/£5
The Venice Train, Hamish Hamilton, 1974 . £15/£5
ditto, Harcourt Brace (U.S.), 1974 . . . £15/£5
Betty, Harcourt Brace (U.S.), 1974 . . . £15/£5
ditto, Hamish Hamilton, 1975 . . . . £15/£5
The Others, Hamish Hamilton, 1975 . . . £15/£5
The House on Quai Notre Dame, Harcourt Brace
(U.S.), 1975 . . . . £15/£5
The Bottom of the Bottle, Hamish Hamilton, 1977. .
. . . . £15/£5
The Girl with a Squint, Hamish Hamilton, 1978 . .
. . . . £15/£5
ditto, Harcourt Brace (U.S.), 1978 . . . £15/£5
The Family Lie, Hamish Hamilton, 1978 . £15/£5
ditto, Harcourt Brace (U.S.), 1978 . . . £15/£5
The Night Club, Hamish Hamilton, 1979 . £15/£5
ditto, Harcourt Brace (U.S.), 1979 . . . £15/£5
The Grandmother, Hamish Hamilton, 1980 . £10/£5
ditto, Harcourt Brace (U.S.), 1980 . . . £10/£5
The Delivery, Hamish Hamilton, 1981 . . £10/£5
ditto, Harcourt Brace (U.S.), 1981 . . . £10/£5
The Long Exile, Hamish Hamilton, 1983 . £10/£5
ditto, Harcourt Brace (U.S.), 1983 . . . £10/£5
The Lodger, Hamish Hamilton, 1983 . . £10/£5
ditto, Harcourt Brace (U.S.), 1983 . . . £10/£5
The Reckoning, Hamish Hamilton, 1984 . £10/£5
ditto, Harcourt Brace (U.S.), 1984 . . . £10/£5
The Couple from Poitiers, Hamish Hamilton, 1985 .
. . . . £10/£5
ditto, Harcourt Brace (U.S.), 1985 . . . £10/£5
Justice, Harcourt Brace (U.S.), 1985 . . £10/£5
The Outlaw, Hamish Hamilton, 1986 . . £10/£5
ditto, Harcourt Brace (U.S.), 1987 . . . £10/£5
Maigret and the YellowDog, Harcourt Brace (U.S.),
1987 . . . . £10/£5
Uncle Charles, Hamish Hamilton, 1988. . . £10/£5
ditto, Harcourt Brace (U.S.), 1987 . . . £10/£5
The Rules of the Game, Harcourt Brace (U.S.), 1989 .
. . . . £10/£5
ditto, Hamish Hamilton, 1989 . . . . £10/£5

Donadieu's Will, Harcourt Brace (U.S.), 1991 . £10/£5

Collected Editions
African Trio, Hamish Hamilton, 1979 . . . £15/£5
ditto, Harcourt Brace (U.S.), 1979 . . . . £15/£5
The White Horse Inn, Hamish Hamilton, 1980. £15/£5
ditto, Harcourt Brace (U.S.), 1980 . . . . £20/£5

Other Short Stories
The Little Doctor, Hamish Hamilton, 1978 . . £15/£5
ditto, Harcourt Brace (U.S.), 1981 . . . . £15/£5

Autobiography
When I was Old, Harcourt Brace (U.S.), 1971 . £30/£5
ditto, Hamish Hamilton, 1972 . . . . . £30/£5
Letters to my Mother, Hamish Hamilton, 1976 . £25/£5
ditto, Harcourt Brace (U.S.), 1976 . . . . £25/£5
Intimate Memoirs, Hamish Hamilton, 1984 . £25/£5
ditto, Harcourt Brace (U.S.), 1984 . . . . £25/£5

EDITH SITWELL
(b.1887 d.1964)

A poet and critic, Edith Sitwell co-founded the
anthology *Wheels* with her brothers Osbert and
Sacheverell in 1916, as a revolt against contemporary
poetry. A penchant for experimentation and an
eccentric and outrageous dress-sense made her a well-
known literary figure.

Poetry
The Mother and Other Poems, Blackwell, 1915 (500
copies) £750
Twentieth Century Harlequinade and Other Poems,
Blackwell, 1916 (with Osbert Sitwell, 500 copies,
wraps). £250
Clown's Houses, Blackwell, 1918 (750 copies, wraps)
. . . . £150
The Wooden Pegasus, Blackwell, 1920 (750 copies) .
. . . . £225/£65
Façade, Favil Press, 1922 (150 signed copies, wraps) .
. . . . £600
Bucolic Comedies, Duckworth, 1923 . . £50/£15
The Sleeping Beauty, Duckworth, 1924. . £65/£20
ditto, Knopf, 1924 . . . . £50/£15
Troy Park, Duckworth, 1925. . . . . £65/£20
ditto, Knopf, 1925 . . . . £45/£15
Poor Young People, The Fleuron, 1925 (with Osbert &
Sacheverell Sitwell, 375 numbered copies) £150/£65
The Augustan Books of Modern Poetry: Edith Sitwell,
Benn, 1926 . . . . £10
Elegy on Dead Fashion, Duckworth, 1926 (225 signed
copies) . . . . £200/£100
Rustic Elegies, Duckworth, 1927 . . . £65/£15
ditto, Knopf, 1927. . . . . £45/£15
Popular Song, Faber & Gwyer, 1928 (wraps) . £15

ditto, Faber & Gwyer, 1928 (500 signed, numbered copies) £65
Five Poems, Duckworth, 1928 (275 copies) £150/£45
Gold Coast Customs and Other Poems, Duckworth, 1929 . . . . £45/£10
ditto, Houghton Mifflin Co. (U.S.), 1929 . £45/£10
In Spring, privately printed, 1931 (290 signed copies).
. . . . £65
Jane Barston, 1719-1746, Faber, 1931 (wraps) £15
ditto, Faber, 1931 (250 signed copies) . . . £50
Epithalamium, Duckworth, 1931 (900 copies, wraps).
. . . . £20
ditto, Duckworth, 1931 (100 signed copies). . £50
Five Variations on a Theme, Duckworth, 1933 . .
. . . . £40/£10
Street Songs, Macmillan, 1942 . . . . £25/£10
Green Song and Other Poems, Macmillan, 1944 . .
. . . . £25/£10
ditto, Vanguard Press (U.S.), 1946 . . . . £50
The Shadow of Cain, John Lehmann, 1947. . £20/£5
Poor Men's Music, Fore Publications, 1950 (wraps) .
. . . . £10
Gardeners and Astronomers, Macmillan, 1953 £20/£5
ditto, Vanguard Press (U.S.), 1953 . . . . £20/£5
The Outcasts, Macmillan, 1962 . . . . . £20/£5
ditto, as *Music and Ceremonies*, Vanguard Press (U.S.), 1963 . . . . £20/£5

Collected Poetry
Collected Poems, Duckworth, 1930 . . . £100/£25
ditto, Duckworth, 1930 (320 signed copies). £300/£75
Selected Poems, Duckworth, 1936 . . . £45/£15
Poems Old and New, Faber, 1940 . . . £25/£10
The Song of the Cold, Macmillan, 1945 . . £15/£5
ditto, Vanguard Press (U.S.), 1948 . . . . £15/£5
The Canticle of the Rose, Macmillan, 1949. . £15/£5
ditto, Vanguard Press (U.S.), 1949 . . . . £15/£5
Façade and Other Poems, 1920-1935, Duckworth, 1950 . . . . £15/£5
Selected Poems, Penguin, 1952 (wraps). . . . £5
Collected Poems, Vanguard Press (U.S.), 1954. £20/£5
ditto, Duckworth, 1957 . . . . £20/£5
The Pocket Poets, Vista, 1960 (wraps) £5

Autobiography
Taken Care Of, Hutchinson, 1965 . . . . £15/£5
ditto, Atheneum (U.S.), 1965. . . . . . £15/£5

Others
Poetry and Criticism, Hogarth Press, 1925 (wraps) £45
ditto, Holt (U.S.), 1926 . . . . £35
Alexander Pope, Faber, 1930 . . . . £30/£10
ditto, Faber, 1930 (220 signed copies, d/w and slipcase)
. . . . £300/£125
ditto, Cosmopolitan Book Corp (U.S.), 1930 £30/£10
The Pleasures of Poetry, Duckworth, 1930, 1931,1932 (3 vols) . . . . £150/£50
Bath, Faber, 1932 . . . . £35/£10
ditto, Harrison Smith (U.S.), 1932 . . . £35/£10

The English Eccentrics, Faber, 1933 . . £150/£45
ditto, Vanguard Press (U.S.), 1957 . . . £25/£10
Aspects of Modern Poetry, Duckworth, 1934 . £20/£5
Victoria of England, Faber, 1936 . . . £75/£15
ditto, Houghton Mifflin (U.S.), 1936 . . £30/£10
I Live Under a Black Sun, Gollancz, 1937 . £75/£20
ditto, Doubleday (U.S.), 1938 . . . . £65/£15
Trio: Dissertations on Some Aspects of National Genius, Macmillan, 1938 (with Osbert and Sacheverell Sitwell) . . . . £40/£10
English Women, Collins, 1942 . . . . £25/£10
A Poet's Notebook, Macmillan, 1943 . . £15/£5
ditto, Little, Brown (U.S.), 1950 . . . . . £15/£5
Fanfare for Elizabeth, Macmillan, 1946 . £15/£5
ditto, Macmillan (U.S.), 1946 . . . . . £15/£5
The Queens and the Hive, Macmillan, 1962 . £15/£5
ditto, Little, Brown (U.S.), 1962 . . . . . £15/£5
Selected Letters, Macmillan, 1970 . . . . £10/£5
ditto, Vanguard Press (U.S.), 1970 . . . . £10/£5

OSBERT SITWELL
(b.1892 d.1969)

A poet and novelist, Osbert, brother to Edith and Sacheverell, also wrote a number of volumes of family memoirs.

Poetry
Twentieth Century Harlequinade and Other Poems, Blackwell, 1916 (with Edith Sitwell, 500 copies, wraps). £250
The Winstonburg Line, Hendersons, 1919 (wraps) .
. . . . £150
Argonaut and Juggernaut, Chatto & Windus, 1919 .
. . . . £25
ditto, Knopf (U.S.), 1920 . . . . . . £65/£20
At the House of Mrs Kinfoot, Favil Press, 1921 (101 signed copies, wraps) £250
Out of the Flame, Grant Richards, 1923 . £50/£15
Poor Young People, The Fleuron, 1925 (with Edith & Sacheverell Sitwell, 375 numbered copies) £150/£65
Winter the Huntsman, The Poetry Bookshop, 1927 .
. . . . £15
England Reclaimed, Duckworth, 1927 . . £45/£10
ditto, Duckworth, 1927 (165 signed copies). £125/£65
ditto, Little, Brown (U.S.), 1949 . . . . £45/£10
Miss Mew, Mill House Press, 1929 (101 signed copies)
. . . . £150
Collected Satires and Poems, Duckworth, 1931 . .
. . . . £30/£10
ditto, Duckworth, 1931 (110 signed copies). £100/£65
Three-Quarter Length Portrait of Michael Arlen, Heinemann, 1931 (520 signed copies) . . £150/£40
Three-Quarter Length Portrait of the Viscountess Wimborne, Cambridge, 1931 (57 signed copies) £250
Mrs Kimber, Macmillan, 1937 (500 copies) £65/£25

Selected Poems, Old and New, Duckworth, 1943 . .
. . . . £20/£5
Four Songs of the Italian Earth, Banyan Press (U.S.),
1945 (260 copies, wraps) £75
Demos the Emperor, Macmillan, 1949 (wraps). £10
ditto, Macmillan, 1949 (500 signed copies, wraps) £35
Wrack at Tidesend, Macmillan, 1952 . . . £20/£5
ditto, Caedmon Publishers (U.S.), 1953 . . . £20/£5
On the Continent, Macmillan, 1958 . . . . £20/£5
Poems About People, Duckworth, 1965. . . £20/£5

Autobiography
Left Hand, Right Hand!, Little, Brown (U.S.), 1944 .
. . . . £25/£5
ditto, Macmillan, 1945 . . . . £20/£5
The Scarlet Tree, Little, Brown (U.S.), 1946 . £15/£5
ditto, Macmillan, 1946 . . . . £15/£5
Great Morning, Little, Brown (U.S.), 1947 . . £15/£5
ditto, Macmillan, 1948 . . . . £15/£5
Laughter in the Next Room, Little, Brown (U.S.),
1948 . . . . £15/£5
ditto, Macmillan, 1949 . . . . £15/£5
Noble Essences, Little, Brown (U.S.), 1950. . £15/£5
ditto, Macmillan, 1950 . . . . £15/£5

Others
Who Killed Cock Robin?, C.W. Daniel, 1921 (wrapper
pasted to spine) £125
ditto, C. W. Daniel, 1921 (wrapper pasted to bords) .
. . . . £100
Triple Fugue, Grant Richards, 1924 . . . £65/£20
ditto, Doran (U.S.), 1925 . . . . . . £50/£10
Discursions on Travel, Art and Life, Grant Richards,
1925 . . . . £25/£10
ditto, Doran (U.S.), [1925] . . . . . . £25/£10
Before the Bombardment, Duckworth, 1926 £25/£10
ditto, Doran (U.S.), 1926 . . . . . . £25/£10
All At Sea, Duckworth, 1927 (with Sacheverell Sitwell)
. . . . £50/£15
ditto, Doran (U.S.), 1928 . . . . . . £50/£15
The People's Album of London Statues, Duckworth,
1928 (with Nina Hamnett) . . . . . £65/£15
ditto, Duckworth, 1928 (116 signed copies). . £250
The Man Who Lost Himself, Duckworth, 1929 . .
. . . . £30/£10
ditto, Coward-McCann (U.S.), 1930 . . . £30/£10
Dumb Animal and Other Stories, Duckworth, 1930 .
. . . . £25/£10
ditto, Duckworth, 1930 (110 signed copies). £75/£45
ditto, Lippincott (U.S.), 1931. . . . . £25/£10
Dickens, Chatto & Windus, 1932 . . . £25/£10
ditto, Chatto & Windus, 1932 (110 signed copies) £125
Winters of Content, Duckworth, 1932 . . £35/£10
ditto, Lippincott (U.S.), 1932. . . . . £25/£10
Miracle on Mount Sinai: A Satyrical Novel,
Duckworth, 1933. . . . . £50/£10
Brighton, Faber, 1935 (with Margaret Barton) £30/£10
Penny Foolish. A Book of Tirades and Panegyrics,
Macmillan, 1935 . . . . £35/£10

Those Were the Days: Panorama with Figures,
Macmillan, 1938 . . . . £15/£5
*Trio: Dissertations on Some Aspects of National
Genius*, Macmillan, 1938 (with Edith and Sacheverell
Sitwell) . . . . £40/£10
Escape with Me: An Oriental Sketch Book, Mac-
millan, 1939 . . . . £35/£10
ditto, Harrison-Hilton (U.S.), 1940 . . . £30/£10
Open the Door!, Macmillan, 1941 . . . £30/£10
ditto, Smith & Durrell (U.S.), 1941 . . . £25/£10
A Place of One's Own, Macmillan, 1941 . £25/£10
Gentle Caesar: A Play in Three Acts, Macmillan, 1942
(with R. J. Minney) . . . . £25/£10
Sing High! Sing Low!, Macmillan, 1944 . £20/£5
A Letter to My Son, Home & Van Thal, 1944 (wraps
with d/w) . . . . £15/£5
*The True Story of Dick Whittington: A Christmas
Story for Cat Lovers*, Home & Van Thal, 1945 . .
. . . . £30/£10
Alive - Alive-Oh! and Other Stories, Pan, 1947 (wraps)
. . . . £5
*The Novels of George Meredith and Some Notes on
the English Novel*, O.U.P., 1947 (wraps) . . . £5
Death of a God and Other Stories, Macmillan, 1949 .
. . . . £15/£5
Collected Stories, Duckworth/Macmillan, 1952 £15/£5
ditto, Harper (U.S.), 1953. . . . . . £15/£5
The Four Continents, Macmillan, 1954. . £15/£5
ditto, Harper (U.S.), 1954. . . . . . £15/£5
Fee Fi Fo Fum! A Book of Fairy Stories, Macmillan,
1959 . . . . £25/£10
A Place of One's Own and Other Stories, Icon, 1961
(wraps) £5
Tales My Father Taught Me, Hutchinson, 1962 . .
. . . . £20/£5
ditto, Little, Brown (U.S.), [1962] . . . . £15/£5
Pound Wise, Hutchinson, 1963 . . . . £15/£5
ditto, Little, Brown (U.S.), [1963] . . . . £15/£5
Queen Mary and Others, Joseph, 1974 . . £15/£5
ditto, John Day (U.S.), 1975 . . . . . £15/£5

SACHEVERELL SITWELL

(b.1897 d.1988)

A more 'traditional' poet than his brother Osbert and
sister Edith, Sacheverell's most important writings
were on art and music criticism.

Poetry
The People's Palace, Blackwell, 1918 (400 copies,
wraps). £150
Doctor Donne and Gargantua, First Canto, Favil
Press, 1921 (101 signed, numbered copies, wraps) .
. . . . £125
The Hundred and One Harlequins, Grant Richards,
1922 . . . . £50/£20
The Parrot, The Poetry Bookshop, 1923 . . £35

The Thirteenth Caesar and Other Poems, Grant
Richards, 1924 . . . . £65/£25
Exalt the Eglantine and Other Poems, The Fleuron,
1924 (370 copies) . . . . £125/£50
Poor Young People, The Fleuron, 1925 (with Osbert &
Edith Sitwell, 375 numbered copies) . . £150/£65
The Cyder Feast and Other Poems, Duckworth, 1927.
. . . . £35/£15
ditto, Duckworth, 1927 (165 signed copies). £125/£50
ditto, Doran (U.S.), 1927 . . . . . £50/£15
*The Augustan Books of Modern Poetry: Sacheverell
Sitwell*, Benn, 1928 . . . . £10
Two Poems, Ten Songs, Duckworth, 1929 (275 signed
copies) £125
Dr Donne & Gargantua: The First Six Cantos,
Duckworth, 1930. . . . . £25/£10
ditto, Duckworth, 1930 (215 signed copies). . £125
*Canons of Giant Art: Twenty Torsos in Heroic
Landscapes*, Faber, 1933 . . . . . £35/£10
Collected Poems, Duckworth, 1936 . . . . £20/£5
Selected Poems, Duckworth, 1948 . . . . £10/£5

Autobiography
Journey to the Ends of Time, Cassell, 1959 . £20/£5
ditto, Random House (U.S.), 1959 . . . . £20/£5

Others
Southern Baroque Art, Grant Richards, 1924 £45/£15
All Summer in a Day, Duckworth, 1926 . £35/£10
ditto, Doran (U.S.), 1926 . . . . . £35/£10
All At Sea, Duckworth, 1927 (with Osbert Sitwell) .
. . . . £50/£15
ditto, Doran (U.S.), 1928 . . . . . £50/£15
German Baroque Art, Duckworth, 1927 . £40/£15
ditto, Doran (U.S.), 1928 . . . . . £40/£15
*A Book of Towers and Other Buildings of Southern
Europe*, Etchells & Macdonald, 1928 (350 numbered
copies) £175
The Gothick North, Duckworth, 1929/30 (3 vols: *The
Visit of the Gypsies; These Sad Ruins; The Fair-
Haired Victory*) . . . . £125/£50
ditto, Houghton Mifflin (U.S.), 1929 (1 vol.) £30/£10
ditto, Duckworth, 1938 (1 vol.) . . . . £30/£10
Beckford and Beckfordism, An Essay, Duckworth,
1930 (265 signed copies) £65
Far from My Home: Stories Long and Short,
Duckworth, 1931. . . . . £25/£10
ditto, Duckworth, 1931 (110 signed copies). . £85
Spanish Baroque Art, Duckworth, 1931 . £30/£10
Mozart, Peter Davies, 1932 . . . . . £25/£10
ditto, Appleton (U.S.), 1932 . . . . £25/£10
Liszt, Faber, 1934 . . . . £20/£10
ditto, Houghton Mifflin (U.S.), 1934 . . £20/£10
Touching the Orient: Six Sketches, Duckworth, 1934.
. . . . £35/£10
A Background for Domenico Scarlatti, 1685-1757,
Faber, 1935 . . . . £25/£10
Dance of the Quick and the Dead, Faber, 1936 . .
. . . . £65/£20

ditto, Houghton Mifflin (U.S.), 1937 . . £25/£10
Conversation Pieces, Batsford, 1936 . . £65/£20
ditto, Scribner's (U.S.), 1937 . . . . £65/£20
Narrative Pictures, Batsford, 1937 . . . £75/£25
ditto, Scribner's (U.S.), 1938 . . . . £65/£20
La Vie Parisienne: A Tribute to Offenbach, Faber,
1937 . . . . £25/£10
ditto, Houghton Mifflin (U.S.), 1938 . . £25/£10
*Trio: Dissertations on Some Aspects of National
Genius*, Macmillan, 1938 (with Osbert and Edith
Sitwell) . . . . £40/£10
Roumanian Journey, Batsford, 1938 . . . £25/£5
Edinburgh, Faber, 1938 . . . . . . £25/£10
German Baroque Sculpture, Duckworth, 1938 . .
. . . . £50/£20
The Romantic Ballet in Lithographs of the Time,
Faber, 1938 . . . . £125/£65
Old Fashioned Flowers, Country Life, 1939 £100/£30
ditto, Scribner's (U.S.), 1939 . . . . . £20/£5
Mauretania: Warrior, Man and Woman, Duckworth,
1940 . . . . £40/£10
Poltergeists, Faber, 1940 . . . . . . £45/£15
ditto, University Books (U.S.), 1959 . . . £20/£10
Sacred and Profane Love, Faber, 1940 . . £25/£10
Valse des Fleurs, Faber, 1941 . . . . £20/£10
ditto, Fairfax Press, 1980 (60 signed, numbered with
roman numerals, deluxe copies of 400) . . £10
ditto, Fairfax Press, 1980 (340 copies of 400) . £10
Primitive Scenes and Festivals, Faber, 1942 £40/£10
*The Homing of the Winds and Other Passages in
Prose*, Faber, 1942 . . . . £25/£5
Splendours and Miseries, Faber, 1943 . . £25/£10
British Architects and Craftsmen, Batsford, 1945 . .
. . . . £25/£10
ditto, Scribner's (U.S.), 1946 . . . . £25/£10
The Hunters and the Hunted, Macmillan, 1947 . .
. . . . £30/£10
ditto, Macmillan (U.S.), 1947 . . . . £25/£10
The Netherlands, Batsford, 1948 . . . £25/£10
Morning, Noon & Night in London, Macmillan, 1948
. . . . £20/£5
Theatrical Figures in Porcelain, Curtain Press, 1949 .
. . . . £40/£20
Spain, Batsford, 1950 . . . . . . £30/£10
Cupid and the Jacaranda, Macmillan, 1952 . £25/£5
Truffle Hunt, Robert Hale, 1953. . . . £20/£5
Fine Bird Books, Collins, 1953 (with Handasyde
Buchanan and James Fisher) . . . £500/£350
ditto, Collins, 1953 (295 signed copies, slipcase) . .
. . . . £1,250/£750
ditto, Atlantic Monthly Press (U.S.), 1990 . £25/£10
Portugal and Madeira, Batsford, 1954 . . £20/£5
Selected Works, Bobbs-Merrill (U.S.), 1953 . £25/£5
Selected Works, Robert Hale, 1955 (different selection
from above title) . . . . £25/£5
Great Flower Books, Collins, 1956 . . . £400/£200
ditto, Collins, 1956 (with Wilfrid Blunt and Patrick M.
Synge, 295 signed copies, slipcase) . £1,000/£750
ditto, Witherby, 1990 . . . . . . £25/£10

ditto, Atlantic Monthly Press (U.S.), 1990 . £25/£10
Denmark, Batsford, 1956. . . . . . £30/£10
ditto, Hastings House (U.S.), 1956 . . . £30/£10
Arabesque and Honeycomb, Robert Hale, 1957 . .
. . . . £30/£10
ditto, Random House (U.S.), 1958 . . . . £20/£5
Malta, Batsford, 1958. . . . . . . £35/£10
Bridge of the Brocade Sash, Weidenfeld & Nicolson,
1959 . . . . £25/£10
ditto, World (U.S.), 1959 . . . . . . £25/£10
Golden Wall and Mirador: From England to Peru,
Weidenfeld & Nicolson, 1961 . . . . £35/£10
ditto, World (U.S.), 1961 . . . . . . £25/£10
The Red Chapels of Banteai Srei, Weidenfeld &
Nicolson, 1962 . . . . £35/£15
Monks, Nuns and Monasteries, Weidenfeld &
Nicolson, 1965 . . . . £30/£10
ditto, Holt, Rinehart and Winston (U.S.), 1965 £25/£10
Southern Baroque Revisited, Weidenfeld & Nicolson,
1967 . . . . £35/£10
ditto, as Baroque and Rococo, Putnam's (U.S.), 1967 .
. . . . £35/£10
Gothic Europe, Weidenfeld & Nicolson, 1969 . £20/£5
ditto, Holt, Rinehart & Winston (U.S.), 1969 . £20/£5
For Want of the Golden City, Thames and Hudson,
1973 . . . . £20/£5
ditto, John Day (U.S.), 1973 . . . . . . £20/£5

CLARK ASHTON SMITH
(b.1893 d.1961)

An American poet and author of fantasy fiction, Clark
Ashton Smith was a member of the circle of writers
surrounding H.P. Lovecraft. His work is recognisable
by its rich vocabulary.

The Star-Treader and Other Poems, A.M. Robertson
(U.S.), 1912 . . . . £200
Odes and Sonnets, The Book Club of California
(U.S.), 1918 (300 numbered copies) . . . £300
Ebony and Crystal, Auburn Journal Press (U.S.), 1922
(500 signed, numbered copies, no d/w) . . £300
Sandalwood, privately printed (U.S.), 1925 (250
signed, numbered copies, wraps) £500
The Immortals of Mercury, Stellar Publishing
Corporation (U.S.), 1932 (wraps) £100
The Double Shadow and Other Fantasies, Auburn
Journal Press (U.S.), 1933 (wraps) £200
The White Sybil, Fantasy Publications (U.S.), 1935
(wraps) £125
Nero and Other Poems, Futile Press (U.S.), 1937 (dark
tan boards with the title printed on the front and the
spine covered in a light tan tape) . . . £175
ditto, Futile Press (U.S.), 1937 (with two inserts: a
three-page printing of David Warren Ryder's 'The
Price of Poetry' from *Controversy*, and an offprint of
Smith's poem, 'Adventure'). £250

Out of Space and Time, Arkham House (U.S.), 1942 .
. . . . £750/£150
ditto, Spearman, 1971 . . . . £50/£15
Lost Worlds, Arkham House (U.S.), 1944 . £250/£75
ditto, Spearman, 1971 . . . . £45/£10
Genius Loci and Other Tales, Arkham House (U.S.),
1948 . . . . £95/£35
ditto, Spearman, 1972 . . . . £40/£10
The Ghoul and the Seraph, Gargoyle Press (U.S.),
1950 (85 numbered copies, wraps) . . . £300
The Dark Chateau, Arkham House (U.S.), 1958 . .
. . . . £350/£125
Spells and Philtres, Arkham House (U.S.), 1958 . .
. . . . £300/£125
Abominations of Yondo, Arkham House (U.S.), 1960 .
. . . . £100/£35
ditto, Spearman, 1972 . . . . £40/£10
Hesperian Fall, Clyde Beck (U.S.), 1961 (wraps) . .
. . . . £150
The Hill of Dionysus: A Selection, Squires, 1962 (100
hardback copies, half cloth, no d/w) . . . £175
ditto, Squires, 1962 (manuscript edition, 15 hardback
copies in full cloth with poem signed by Smith, no
d/w) £300
ditto, Squires, 1962 (wraps) £125
Cycles, Squires, 1963 (wraps) £65
?Donde Duermos, Eldorado? y Otros Poemas, Squires
(U. S.), 1963 (176 copies, poems in Spanish, wraps) .
. . . . £200
Nero: An Early Poem, Squires (U.S.), 1964 (381
copies, wraps) £50
ditto, Squires (U.S.), 1964 (50 numbered copies,
wraps). £150
Poems in Prose, Arkham House (U.S.), 1964 £125/£40
Tales of Science and Sorcery, Arkham House (U.S.),
1964 . . . . £100/£30
The Tartarus of the Suns, Squires, 1970 (165 copies,
wraps). £125
The Palace of Jewels, Squires, 1970 (167 copies,
wraps). £125
In the Ultimate Valleys, Squires, 1970 (160 copies,
wraps). £125
To George Sterling: Five Poems, Squires, 1970 (199
copies, wraps) £125
Other Dimensions, Arkham House (U.S.), 1970 . .
. . . . £65/£25
Zothique, Ballantine, 1970 (wraps) . . . £15
The Mortuary, Squires, 1971 (180 copies, wraps) £65
Selected Poems, Arkham House (U.S.), 1971 £100/£30
Hyperborea, Ballantine, 1971 (wraps) . . £15
Sadastor, Squires, 1972 (108 copies, wraps) . £125
Xiccarph, Ballantine, 1972 (wraps) . . . £15
Planets and Dimensions, Mirage (U.S.), 1973 (500
numbered copies) . . . . £65/£30
ditto, Mirage (U.S.), 1973 (wraps) . . . £30
Poseidonis, Ballantine, 1973 (wraps) . . . £15
From the Crypts of Memory, Squires, 1973 (198
copies, wraps) £100

The Fantastic Art of Clark Ashton Smith, Mirage (U.S.), 1973 (wraps) £45
Grotesques and Fantastiques, De la Ree (U.S.), 1973 (600 numbered copies, wraps) £45
ditto, De la Ree (U.S.), 1973 (50 hardback copies) . .
. . . . £100
Klarkash-Ton and Monstro Ligriv, De la Ree (U.S.), 1974 (500 numbered copies, wraps) . . . £45
ditto, De la Ree (U.S.), 1974 (50 copies in black buckram) £125
The Titans in Tartarus, Squires, 1974 (320 copies, wraps) £75
A Song From Hell, Squires, 1975 (296 copies, wraps)
. . . . £75
The Potion of Dreams, Squires, 1975 (292 copies, wraps) £75
The Fanes of Dawn, Squires, 1976 (303 copies, wraps)
. . . . £75
Seer of the Cycles, Squires, 1976 (321 copies, wraps) .
. . . . £75
The Burden of the Suns, Squires, 1977 (295 copies, wraps) £75
The Fugitive Poems of Clark Ashton Smith: Xiccarph Edition, Squires, 1974-1977: (contains: *The Titans in Tartarus*, *A Song From Hell*, *The Potion of Dreams*, *The Fanes of Dawn*, *Seer of the Cycles*, *The Burden of the Suns*, all printed on large paper, in a Gray Parrot traycase, and with a tipped in signed poetry manuscript by C.A.S. from the series, limited to 51 copies) £500
The Black Book of Clark Ashton Smith, Arkham House (U.S.), 1979 . . . . £50
The City of the Singing Flame, Timescape, 1981 (wraps) £10
The Last Incantation, Timescape, 1982 (wraps) £10
The Monster of the Prophecy, Timescape, 1983 (wraps) £10
Clark Ashton Smith: Letters to H.P. Lovecraft, Necronomicon Press, 1987 (wraps) . . . £15
Mother of Toads, Necronomicon Press, 1987 (wraps) .
. . . . £15
The Dweller in the Gulf, Necronomicon Press, 1987 (wraps) £30
The Vaults of Yoh-Vombis, Necronomicon Press, 1988 (wraps) £10
The Monster of the Prophecy, Necronomicon Press, 1988 (wraps) £10
Nostalgia of the Unknown, Necronomicon Press, 1988 (wraps) £10
The Witchcraft of Ulua, Necronomicon Press, 1988 (wraps) £10
Xeethra, Necronomicon Press, 1988 (wraps) . £10
A Rendezvous in Averoigne, Arkham House (U.S.), 1988 . . . . £35/£10
Strange Shadows, Greenwood Press, 1989 (no d/w) .
. . . . £100
The Hashish-Eater, Necronomicon Press, 1989 (wraps) £15
ditto, Donald Sidney-Fryer, 1990 (wraps) . . £45

The Devil's Notebook, Starmont House, 1990 . £100
ditto, Starmont House, 1990 (wraps). . . . £25
Tales of Zothique, Necronomicon Press, 1995 (wraps)
. . . . £10
Live from Auburn: The Elder Tapes, Necronomicon Press, 1995 (cassette with booklet) £30
The Book of Hyperborea, Necronomicon Press, 1996 (wraps) £10

STEVIE SMITH
(b.1902 d.1971)

A poet and novelist, Smith often illustrated her work with naive line drawings somewhat in the style of Edward Lear.

Novels
Novel on Yellow Paper, Cape, 1936 . . . £450/£40
ditto, Morrow (U.S.), 1937 . . . . . £175/£35
Over the Frontier, Cape, 1938 . . . . £225/£35
The Holiday, Chapman & Hall, 1949 . . £125/£30
ditto, Smithers (U.S.), 1950 . . . . . £100/£25

Poetry
A Good Time was Had by All, Cape, 1937 . £200/£40
Tender Only to One, Cape, 1938 . . . £125/£25
Mother, What is Man?, Cape, 1942 . . . £100/£25
Harold's Leap, Chapman & Hall, 1950 . . £65/£15
Not Waving but Drowning, Deutsch, 1957 . £150/£25
Selected Poems, Longman, 1962 . . . . £35/£10
ditto, New Directions (U.S.), 1964 (wraps) . . £10
The Frog Prince and Other Poems, Longman, 1966 .
. . . . £35/£10
ditto, as *The Best Beast*, Knopf, 1969 . £35/£10
Francesca in Winter, Poem of the Month Club, 1970 (signed broadsheet) £45
Two in One, Longman, 1971 . . . . . £25/£10
Scorpion and Other Poems, Longman, 1971 £25/£10
Collected Poems, Lane, 1975 . . . . . £75/£10
ditto, O.U.P. (U.S.), 1976 . . . . . . £40/£10

Others
Cats in Colour, Batsford, 1959 . . . . . £20/£5
ditto, Viking (U.S.), 1959 . . . . . . £15/£5
Me Again: Uncollected Writings, Virago, 1981 £20/£5
ditto, Farrar Straus (U.S.), 1982 . . . . £15/£5
Stevie Smith: A Selection, Faber, 1983 . . £10/£5
ditto, Faber (U.S.), 1982 . . . . . . £10/£5

C.P. SNOW
(b.1905 d.1980)

Possessing a Ph.D in Chemistry, C.P. Snow wrote a number of technical papers before becoming well known for his detective novels, the first of which was published in 1932. He was awarded a C.B.E. in 1943 and a knighthood in 1957. He accepted a Life Peerage in 1964.

'Strangers and Brothers' Titles
Strangers and Brothers, Faber, 1940 (later re-titled
George Passant) . . . . . . £1,500/£200
ditto, Scribner's (U.S.), 1960 . . . . . £35/£10
The Light and the Dark, Faber, 1947 . . £65/£15
ditto, Macmillan (U.S.), 1948 . . . . . £40/£5
Time of Hope, Faber, 1949 . . . . . £50/£10
ditto, Macmillan (U.S.), 1950 . . . . . £40/£5
The Masters, Macmillan, 1951 . . . . £45/£10
ditto, Macmillan (U.S.), 1951 . . . . . £35/£5
The New Men, Macmillan, 1954. . . . . £35/£5
ditto, Scribner's (U.S.), 1954 . . . . . . £30/£5
Homecomings, Macmillan, 1956 . . . £30/£10
ditto, as *Homecoming*, Scribner's (U.S.), 1956 . £25/£5
The Conscience of the Rich, Macmillan, 1958 . £20/£5
ditto, Scribner's (U.S.), 1958. . . . . . £15/£5
The Affair, Macmillan, 1960 . . . . . £20/£5
ditto, Scribner's (U.S.), 1960 . . . . . £15/£5
Corridors of Power, Macmillan, 1964 . . £15/£5
ditto, Scribner's (U.S.), 1964 . . . . . £10/£5
The Sleep of Reason, Macmillan, 1968 . . £15/£5
ditto, Scribner's (U.S.), 1969 . . . . . £10/£5
Last Things, Macmillan, 1970 . . . . £10/£5
ditto, Scribner's (U.S.), 1970 . . . . . £10/£5
Strangers and Brothers, Macmillan, 1972 (omnibus
edition, 3 vols) . . . . £35/£10
ditto, Scribner's (U.S.), 1972 (3 vols) . . £35/£10

Other Novels
Death Under Sail, Heinemann, 1932 . £1,000/£200
ditto, Scribner's (U.S.), 1959 . . . . . £350/£30
New Lives for Old, Gollancz, 1933 (anonymous) . .
. . . . £250/£65
The Search, Gollancz, 1934 . . . . £45/£10
ditto, Bobbs-Merrill (U.S.), 1935. . . . £35/£10
The Malcontents, Macmillan, 1972 . . . £10/£5
ditto, Scribner's (U.S.), 1972 . . . . . £10/£5
In Their Wisdom, Macmillan, 1974 . . . £10/£5
ditto, Scribner's (U.S.), 1974 . . . . . £10/£5
A Coat of Varnish, Macmillan, 1979 . . . £10/£5
ditto, Scribner's (U.S.), 1979 . . . . . £10/£5
ditto, Franklin Library (U.S.), 1979 (signed, limited
edition) £25

Others
Richard Aldington, Heinemann, [1938] (wraps) £40
Two Cultures and the Scientific Revolution, C.U.P.,
1959 (wraps) £20
ditto, C.U.P. (U.S.), 1959 . . . . . . £20/£5

Science and Government, Harvard Univ. Press (U.S.),
1961 . . . . £10/£5
Variety of Men, Macmillan, 1968 . . . . £15/£5
ditto, Scribner's (U.S.), 1968 . . . . . £15/£5
The State of Siege, Scribner's (U.S.), 1969 . £10/£5
Public Affairs, Macmillan, 1971. . . . . £10/£5
ditto, Scribner's (U.S.), 1971 . . . . . £10/£5
Trollope, Macmillan, 1975 . . . . . £15/£5
ditto, Scribner's (U.S.), 1975 . . . . . £10/£5
The Realists, Macmillan, 1978 . . . . £10/£5
ditto, Scribner's (U.S.), 1978 . . . . . £10/£5
The Physicists, Macmillan, 1981. . . . . £10/£5
ditto, Little, Brown (U.S.), 1981 . . . . £10/£5

ALEXANDER SOLZHENITSYN
(b.1918)

Since being deported from Russia Solzhenitsyn has lost some of his mystique, although none of his reputation, as a fine writer. He won the Nobel Prize for Literature in 1970.

Novels
One Day in the Life of Ivan Denisovich, Praeger
(U.S.), 1963 . . . . £125/£25
ditto, Dutton (U.S.), 1963. . . . . . £100/£20
ditto, Gollancz, 1963 . . . . . . £100/£20
We Never Make Mistakes: Two Short Novels, Univ. of
South Carolina (U.S.), 1963. . . . £100/£25
ditto, Sphere, 1972 (wraps) £5
For the Good of the Cause, Praeger (U.S.), 1964 . .
. . . . £45/£10
ditto, Pall Mall Press, 1964 . . . . . . £15/£5
The First Circle, Harper & Row (U.S.), 1968 £45/£10
ditto, Collins, 1968 . . . . £35/£10
Cancer Ward, Dial Press (U.S.), 1968 (1 vol.) £35/£10
ditto, Bodley Head, 1968-1969 (2 vols) . . £65/£20
August 1914, Bodley Head, 1972 . . . £35/£10
ditto, Farrar Straus (U.S.), 1972 . . . £35/£10
The Gulag Archipelago, Harper (U.S.), 1974 . £20/£5
ditto, Collins, 1974 . . . . £20/£5
The Gulag Archipelago, 2, Harper (U.S.), 1975 . .
. . . . £15/£5
ditto, Collins, 1975 . . . . £15/£5
The Gulag Archipelago, 3, Harper (U.S.), 1976 £15/£5
ditto, Collins, 1978 . . . . £15/£5
November 1916: The Red Wheel/Knot II, Farrar Straus
(U.S.), 1998 . . . . £10/£5
ditto, Cape, 1999 . . . . £10/£5

Plays
The Love-Girl and the Innocent, Bodley Head, 1969 .
. . . . £25/£5
ditto, Farrar Straus (U.S.), 1970 . . . . £20/£5
Candle in the Wind, Univ. of Minnesota (U.S.), 1973 .
. . . . £15/£5
ditto, Bodley Head/O.U.P., 1973 . . . . £15/£5

Victory Celebrations, Bodley Head, 1983 . . £10/£5
Prisoners, Bodley Head, 1983 . . . . . £10/£5
Three Plays, Farrar Straus (U.S.), 1986 . . . £15/£5

Others
Stories and Prose Poems, Bodley Head, 1971 . £15/£5
ditto, Farrar Straus (U.S.), 1971 . . . . . £15/£5
'One Word of Truth ...', Bodley Head, 1972 (wraps) .
. . . . £15
ditto, as *A World Split Apart*, Harper (U.S.), 1979 . .
. . . . £10/£5
Letter to Soviet Leaders, Index on Censorship, 1974
(wraps) £5
ditto, Harper (U.S.), 1974. . . . . . . £10/£5
From under the Rubble, Little, Brown (U.S.), 1975 .
. . . . £10/£5
ditto, Collins, 1975 . . . . £10/£5
Lenin in Zurich, Farrar Straus (U.S.), 1976 . . £10/£5
ditto, Bodley Head, 1976 . . . . £10/£5
Warning to the Western World, Bodley Head/BBC,
1976 (wraps) £10
ditto, as *Speeches to the Americans*, Farrar Straus
(U.S.), 1976 . . . . £10/£5
A World Split Apart, Harper (U.S.), 1978 . . £15/£5
ditto, as *Alexander Solzhenitsyn Speaks to the West*,
Bodley Head, 1979 . . . . £10/£5
The Mortal Danger, Bodley Head, 1980 . . £10/£5
ditto, Harper (U.S.), 1980. . . . . . . £10/£5
The Oak and the Calf, Harper (U.S.), 1980. . £10/£5
ditto, Bodley Head, 1980 . . . . £10/£5
*The Russian Question at the End of the Twentieth
Century*, Farrar Straus Giroux (U.S.), 1995 . £10/£5
ditto, HarperCollins, 1995 . . . . . £10/£5

Poetry
Prussian Nights, Collins/Harvill, 1977 . . . £15/£5
ditto, Farrar Straus (U.S.), 1977 . . . . . £15/£5

MURIEL SPARK
(b.1918)

A novelist, poet and short story writer, Spark's first
novel, *The Comforters*, was very well received. All of
her novels are written with elegance and detachment,
and are full of black humour and irony.

Novels
The Comforters, Macmillan, 1957 . . . £400/£40
ditto, Lippincott (U.S.), 1957. . . . . £300/£35
Robinson, Macmillan, 1958 . . . . . £150/£30
ditto, Lippincott (U.S.), 1958. . . . . £75/£20
Memento Mori, Macmillan, 1959 . . . £125/£30
ditto, Lippincott (U.S.), 1959. . . . . £75/£20
The Ballad of Peckham Rye, Macmillan, 1960. . .
. . . . £75/£20
ditto, Lippincott (U.S.), 1960. . . . . £30/£10
The Bachelors, Macmillan, 1960 . . . £45/£15

ditto, Lippincott (U.S.), 1961. . . . . . £15/£5
The Prime of Miss Jean Brodie, Macmillan, 1961. . .
. . . . £150/£25
ditto, Lippincott (U.S.), 1962. . . . . £75/£20
The Girls of Slender Means, Macmillan, 1963 £45/£10
ditto, Knopf (U.S.), 1963 . . . . £15/£5
The Mandelbaum Gate, Macmillan, 1965 . . £20/£5
ditto, Knopf (U.S.), 1965 . . . . £15/£5
The Public Image, Macmillan, 1968 . . . £20/£5
ditto, Knopf (U.S.), 1968 . . . . £15/£5
The Driver's Seat, Macmillan, 1970. . . . £20/£5
ditto, Knopf (U.S.), 1970 . . . . £15/£5
Not to Disturb, Macmillan, 1971. . . . . £20/£5
ditto, Observer Books, 1971 (500 signed copies,
glassine d/w) . . . . £125/£100
ditto, Viking (U.S.), 1972. . . . . . . £15/£5
The Hothouse by the East River, Macmillan, 1973 .
. . . . £15/£5
ditto, Viking (U.S.), 1973. . . . . . . £15/£5
The Abbess of Crewe: A Modern Morality Tale,
Macmillan, 1974 . . . . £15/£5
ditto, Viking (U.S.), 1974. . . . . . . £15/£5
The Takeover, Macmillan, 1976 . . . . £15/£5
ditto, Viking (U.S.), 1976. . . . . . . £10/£5
Territorial Rights, Macmillan, 1979. . . . £10/£5
ditto, Coward-McCann (U.S.), 1979. . . . £10/£5
Loitering With Intent, Bodley Head, 1981 . £10/£5
ditto, Coward-McCann (U.S.), 1981. . . . £10/£5
The Only Problem, Bodley Head, 1984. . . £10/£5
ditto, Franklin Library (U.S.), 1984 (signed, limited
edition) £35
ditto, Coward-McCann (U.S.), 1984. . . . £10/£5
A Far Cry from Kensington, Constable, 1988 . £10/£5
ditto, London Limited Editions, 1988 (150 signed,
numbered copies, glassine d/w). . . . £65/£50
ditto, Houghton Mifflin (U.S.), 1988 . . . £10/£5
Symposium, Constable, 1990. . . . . . £10/£5
ditto, Houghton Mifflin (U.S.), 1990 . . . £10/£5
Reality and Dreams, Constable, 1996 . . . £10/£5
ditto, Houghton Mifflin (U.S.), 1996 . . . £10/£5
Aiding and Abetting, Viking, 2000 . . . . £10/£5
ditto, Doubleday (U.S.), 2001 . . . . . £10/£5

Omnibus Editions
The Muriel Spark Omnibus, Volume 1, Constable,
1993 . . . . £10/£5
The Muriel Spark Omnibus, Volume 2, Constable,
1994 . . . . £10/£5
The Muriel Spark Omnibus, Volume 3, Constable,
1996 . . . . £10/£5
The Muriel Spark Omnibus, Volume 4, Constable,
1997 . . . . £10/£5

Poetry
Out of a Book, Millar & Burden, [1933] (broadside,
pseud. 'Muriel Camberg') £1,000
The Fanfarlo, Hand & Flower Press, 1952 (first issue,
wraps printed in red) £75
ditto, Hand & Flower Press, 1952 (second issue, wraps
printed in blue) £50

Collected Poems I, Macmillan, 1967 . . £25/£10
ditto, Knopf (U.S.), 1968 . . . . . . £25/£10
Going Up to Sotheby's and Other Poems, Granada, 1982 (wraps) £10

Short Stories
The Go-Away Bird and Other Stories, Macmillan, 1958 . . . . £175/£35
ditto, Lippincott (U.S.), 1960 . . . . £45/£15
The Seraph and the Zambesi, Lippincott (U.S.), 1960 (privately printed, wraps) £45
Collected Stories, Macmillan, 1967 . . . . £20/£5
ditto, Knopf (U.S.), 1968 . . . . £15/£5
Bang-Bang You're Dead and Other Stories, Granada, 1982 (wraps) £10
The Stories of Muriel Spark, Dutton (U.S.), 1985 . .
. . . . £10/£5
ditto, Bodley Head, 1987 . . . . £10/£5
The Portobello Road and Other Stories, Eurographica (Helsinki), 1990 (350 signed copies, wraps) . £75
Harper and Wilton, Colophon Press, 1996 (100 signed copies of 110) £75
ditto, Colophon Press, 1996 (10 roman numbered copies for the author, signed, of 110) . . . £450

Children's Titles
The Very Fine Clock, Knopf (U.S.), 1968 . £45/£20
ditto, Macmillan, 1969 . . . . . . £25/£10
The French Window & The Small Telephone, Colophon Press, 1993 (105 signed copies). . £75
ditto, Colophon Press, 1994 (12 signed copies, leather)
. . . . £200

Plays
Voices at Play, Macmillan, 1961 . . . . . £25/£5
ditto, Lippincott (U.S.), 1962 . . . . . £10/£5
Doctors of Philosophy, Macmillan, 1963 . . £25/£5
ditto, Knopf (U.S.), 1966 . . . . £10/£5

Others
Reassessment, Reassessment Pamphlet No.1, [1948] (single sheet, folded). £500
Child of Light: A Reassessment of Mary Wollstone-craft Shelley, Tower Bridge, 1951 . . . £100/£25
ditto, Folcroft Library Editions (U.S.), 1976 . £20/£5
Emily Brontë: Her Life and Work, Owen, 1953 (with Derek Stanford) . . . . £75/£20
ditto, Coward-McCann (U.S.), 1966 . . . . £25/£5
John Masefield, Nevill, 1953 . . . . £45/£10
ditto, Folcroft Library Editions (U.S.), 1977 . £20/£5
The Essence of the Brontës, Owen, 1993 . . £15/£5

Autobiography
Curriculum Vitae: A Volume of Autobiography, Constable, 1992 . . . . £10/£5
ditto, Houghton Mifflin (U.S.), 1993 . . . £10/£5

STEPHEN SPENDER
(b.1909 d.1995)

Early in his poetic career Spender displays a lyricism which he did not continue. In later years he put more of his energies into critical works.

Poetry
Nine Experiments by S.H.S.: Being Poems Written at the Age of Eighteen, hand-printed by Spender, 1928 (wraps) £50,000
Twenty Poems, Blackwell, 1930 (75 signed copies of 135, wraps) £600
ditto, Blackwell, 1930 (55 unsigned copies of 135, wraps). £400
Poems, Faber, 1933 . . . . £125/£25
ditto, Random House (U.S.), 1934 . . . £100/£20
Vienna, Faber, 1934 . . . . £125/£25
ditto, Random House (U.S.), 1935 . . . £100/£15
The Still Centre, Faber, 1939 . . . . £75/£15
Selected Poems, Faber, 1940 . . . . . £30/£10
Ruins and Visions, Faber, 1942 . . . £65/£20
ditto, Random House (U.S.), 1942 . . . £50/£10
Spiritual Exercises, Curwen Press, 1943 (125 copies, wraps). £175
Poems of Dedication, Faber, 1947 . . . £30/£10
ditto, Random House (U.S.), 1947 . . . £25/£10
The Edge of Being, Faber, 1949 . . . . £30/£10
ditto, Random House (U.S.), 1949 . . . £25/£10
Sirmione Peninsula, Faber, 1954 (wraps) . . £25
Collected Poems, 1928-1953, Faber, 1955 . £25/£10
ditto, Random House (U.S.), 1955 . . . £25/£10
Inscriptions, Poetry Book Society, 1958 (wraps) £20
Selected Poems, Random House (U.S.), 1964 . £15/£5
ditto, Faber, 1965 . . . . £15/£5
The Generous Days, Godine (U.S.), 1969 (50 signed & numbered copies, wraps) £75
ditto, Faber, 1971 . . . . £25/£5
ditto, Random House (U.S.), 1971 . . . . £25/£5
Art Student, Poem of the Month Club, 1970 (single sheet) £20
Recent Poems, Anvil Press Poetry, 1978 (400 signed copies, wraps) £40
Collected Poems, 1928-1985, Faber, 1985 . . £20/£5
Dolphins, Faber, 1994 . . . . £15/£5
ditto, Faber, 1994 (150 signed copies) . . . £75
ditto, St Martin's Press (U.S.), 1994 . . . £15/£5

Novels
The Backward Son, Hogarth Press, 1940 . £150/£40
The Temple, Faber, 1988 . . . . . . £15/£5
ditto, Grove Press (U.S.), 1988 . . . . £15/£5

Short Stories
The Burning Cactus, Faber, 1936 . . . £50/£15
ditto, Random House (U.S.), 1936 . . . £45/£15
Engaged in Writing and The Fool and The Princess, Hamish Hamilton, 1958 . . . . . . £25/£5
ditto, Farrar Straus (U.S.), 1958 . . . . £25/£5

Plays
Trial of a Judge, Faber, 1938 . . . . £35/£10
ditto, Random House (U.S.), 1938 . . . £30/£10
Danton's Death, Faber, 1939 (adaptation with
    Goronwy Rees) . . . . £35/£10
Oedipus Trilogy, Faber, 1985 . . . . . £15/£5
ditto, Random House (U.S.), 1985 . . . . £15/£5

Prose
The Destructive Element, Cape, 1935 . . £100/£25
ditto, Houghton Mifflin (U.S.), 1935 . . £100/£25
Forward from Liberalism, Gollancz, 1937 . £50/£15
ditto, Left Book Club, 1937 (wraps) £25
ditto, Random House (U.S.), 1937 . . . £25/£10
The New Realism: A Discussion, Hogarth Press, 1939
    (wraps) £30
Life and the Poet, Secker & Warburg, 1942 . £20/£5
Citizens in War - And After, Harrap, 1945 . £50/£10
European Witness: Impressions of Germany in 1945,
    Hamish Hamilton, 1946 . . . . . . £20/£5
ditto, Reynal & Hitchcock (U.S.), 1946 . . £20/£5
Poetry Since 1939, Longmans, Green, 1946 (wraps) .
    . . . . £15
Returning to Vienna 1947: Nine Sketches, Banyan
    Press (U.S.), 1947 (500 signed copies, wraps). £100
World Within World, Hamish Hamilton, 1951 . £15/£5
ditto, Harcourt Brace (U.S.), 1951 . . . . £10/£5
Learning Laughter, A Study of Children in Israel,
    Weidenfeld & Nicolson, 1952 . . . . . £15/£5
ditto, Harcourt Brace (U.S.), 1953 . . . £15/£5
The Creative Element, Hamish Hamilton, 1953 . .
    . . . . £10/£5
ditto, British Book Center (U.S.), 1954 . . £10/£5
The Making of a Poem, Hamish Hamilton, 1955 . .
    . . . . £20/£5
The Struggle of the Modern, Hamish Hamilton, 1963.
    . . . . £15/£5
ditto, Univ. of California Press (U.S.), 1954 . £15/£5
The Year of the Young Rebel, Weidenfeld & Nicolson,
    1969 . . . . £15/£5
ditto, Random House (U.S.), 1969 . . . £10/£5
*Love-Hate Relations: A Study of Anglo-American
    Sensibilities*, Hamish Hamilton, 1974 . . £10/£5
ditto, Random House (U.S.), 1974 . . . . £10/£5
T.S. Eliot, Fontana, 1975 (wraps) £5
ditto, Viking (U.S.), 1976 . . . . . . £20/£5
*The Thirties and After: Poetry, Politics and People,
    1933-75*, Fontana, 1975 (wraps) £5
ditto, Random House (U.S.), 1978 . . . £10/£5
Henry Moore Sculptures in Landscape, Studio Vista,
    1978 (illustrated by Geoffrey Shakerley) . £30/£10
Letters to Christopher, Black Sparrow Press (U.S.),
    1980 (wraps) £20
ditto, Black Sparrow Press (U.S.), 1980 (1,000 copies,
    glassine d/w) . . . . £25/£20
ditto, Black Sparrow Press (U.S.), 1980 (200
    numbered, signed copies) £35
ditto, Black Sparrow Press (U.S.), 1980 (50 hand-
    bound, numbered and signed copies, slipcase) . .
    . . . . £45/£35

China Diary, Thames & Hudson, 1982 . . £30/£10
ditto, Abrams (U.S.), 1982 . . . . . . £15/£5
Journals, 1939-83, Faber, 1985 . . . . . £10/£5
ditto, Faber, 1985 (150 signed copies, no d/w, slipcase)
    . . . . £75/£50
ditto, Random House (U.S.), 1986 . . . . £10/£5
ditto, Franklin Library (U.S.), 1985 (signed, limited
    edition) £25

Others
*W.H. Auden, A Memorial Address Delivered at Christ
    Church Cathedral, Oxford on 27 October, 1973*,
    Faber, 1975 (wraps) £75
W.H. Auden, A Tribute, Weidenfeld & Nicolson, 1975
    . . . . £15/£5
ditto, Macmillan (U.S.), 1975 . . . . . £10/£5

MICKEY SPILLANE
(b.1918)

An important and influential U.S. mystery writer,
Spillane's books introduced violence and sex to a
post-World War Two audience.

I, The Jury, Dutton (U.S.), 1947 . . . £2,000/£200
ditto, Collins (U.S.), 1948 (wraps) £100
ditto, Barker, 1952 . . . . £500/£35
My Gun Is Quick, Dutton (U.S.), 1950 . £1,000/£75
ditto, Barker, 1951 . . . . £200/£20
Vengeance Is Mine, Dutton (U.S.), 1950 . £750/£35
ditto, Barker, 1951 . . . . £200/£20
One Lonely Night, Dutton (U.S.), 1951 . . £750/£25
ditto, Barker, 1952 . . . . £175/£20
The Big Kill, Dutton (U.S.), 1951 . . . £600/£30
ditto, Barker, 1952 . . . . £150/£15
The Long Wait, Dutton (U.S.), 1951 . . £600/£30
ditto, Barker, 1953 . . . . £150/£15
Kiss Me, Deadly, Dutton (U.S.), 1952 . . £400/£35
ditto, Barker, 1953 . . . . £100/£15
The Deep, Dutton (U.S.), 1961 . . . . £45/£10
ditto, Barker, 1961 . . . . £35/£10
The Girl Hunters, Dutton (U.S.), 1962 . . £35/£10
ditto, Barker, 1962 . . . . £30/£10
Me, Hood!, Corgi, 1963 (wraps) £5
ditto, Signet (U.S.), 1969 (wraps) £5
The Snake, Dutton (U.S.), 1964 . . . . £25/£10
ditto, Barker, 1964 . . . . £25/£10
The Day of the Guns, Dutton (U.S.), 1964 . £25/£10
ditto, Barker, 1965 . . . . £25/£10
Return of the Hood, Corgi, 1964 (wraps) . . . £5
The Flier, Corgi, 1964 (wraps) £5
Bloody Sunrise, Dutton (U.S.), 1965 . . £25/£10
ditto, Barker, 1965 . . . . £25/£10
The Death Dealers, Dutton (U.S.), 1965 . . £25/£10
ditto, Barker, 1966 . . . . £25/£10
Killer Mine, Corgi, 1965 (wraps) £5
ditto, Signet (U.S.), 1968 (wraps) £5
The Twisted Thing, Dutton (U.S.), 1966 . £25/£10

ditto, Barker, 1966. . . . . . . £25/£10
The By-Pass Control, Dutton (U.S.), 1966 . £25/£10
ditto, Barker, 1967. . . . . £25/£10
The Body Lovers, Dutton (U.S.), 1967 . . £25/£10
ditto, Barker, 1967. . . . . £25/£10
The Delta Factor, Dutton (U.S.), 1969 . £25/£10
ditto, Corgi, 1969 (wraps). £5
The Tough Guys, Signet (U.S.), 1961 . . . . £5
Survival . . . Zero!, Dutton (U.S.), 1970. . £25/£10
ditto, Corgi, 1970 (wraps). £5
The Erection Set, Dutton (U.S.), 1972 . . £25/£10
ditto, Allen, 1972 . . . . £25/£10
The Last Cop Out, Dutton (U.S.), 1973 . . . £20/£5
ditto, Allen, 1973 . . . . £20/£5
Vintage Spillane, Allen, 1974 . . . . . £20/£5
Tomorrow I Die, Mysterious Press (U.S.), 1984 (250 signed, numbered copies) . . . . £35/£20
ditto, Mysterious Press (U.S.), 1984 (26 signed, numbered copies) . . . . . . £100/£65
The Killing Man, Dutton (U.S.), 1989 . . . £15/£5
ditto, Heinemann, 1990 . . . . £15/£5
Black Alley, Dutton (U.S.), 1996. . . . . £15/£5

Children's Titles
The Day the Sea Rolled Back, Dutton (U.S.), 1979 .
. . . . £15/£5
ditto, Methuen, 1980 . . . . £15/£5
The Ship That Never Was, Bantam (U.S.), 1982 (wraps) £5

GERTRUDE STEIN
(b.1874 d.1946)

Although an American woman of letters, Stein lived in France from 1903 until her death.

Fiction
Three Lives: Stories of the Good Anna, Melanctha, and the Gentle Lena, The Grafton Press (U.S.), 1909
. . . . £750
ditto, John Lane (U.S.), 1909 (300 copies with sheets from the above edition) £500
ditto, Bodley Head, 1920 . . . . . £250/£5
The Making of Americans, Being a History of a Family's Progress, Contact Editions/The Three Mountains Press (Paris), [1925] (400 of 500 copies, wraps). £750
ditto, Boni (U.S.), 1925 (100 of 500 copies) . £1,000
A Book Concluding with As a Wife Has a Cow: A Love Story, Galerie Simon (Paris), 1926 (102 signed copies, wraps) £2,000
ditto, Galerie Simon (Paris), 1926 (10 signed copies on Japanese vellum, wraps). £10,000
Lucy Church Amiably, Imprimerie Union (Paris), 1930
. . . . £250/£175
ditto, Something Else Press (U.S.), 1969 (100 of 500 copies) . . . . £30/£10

Ida: A Novel, Random House (U.S.), 1941 . £100/£25
Brewsie and Willie, Random House (U.S.), 1946 . .
. . . . £35/£10
Blood on the Dining Room Floor, Banyan Press (U.S.), 1948 (26 copies, glassine d/w and slipcase) .
. . . . £300/£250
ditto, Banyan Press (U.S.), 1948 (600 copies, glassine d/w and slipcase). . . . . . . £175/£150
Things as They Are: A Novel in Three Parts, Banyan Press (U.S.), 1950 (26 copies, glassine d/w) . . .
. . . . £300/£250
ditto, Banyan Press (U.S.), 1950 (490 copies, glassine d/w) . . . . £150/£125
Mrs. Reynolds, and Five Early Novelettes, Yale Univ. Press (U.S.), 1952 . . . . . . £25/£10
A Novel of Thank You, Yale Univ. Press (U.S.), 1958.
. . . . £25/£10

Plays
Geography and Plays, Four Seas (U.S.), 1922 (first binding with lettering on front cover) . . . £300
ditto, Four Seas (U.S.), 1922 (second binding without lettering on front cover) £200
A Village: Are You Ready Yet Not Yet, Editions de la Galerie Simon (Paris), 1928 (90 signed copies, wraps)
. . . . £1,250
Operas and Plays, Plain Edition (Paris), 1932 (wraps, slipcase) £350
Four Saints in Three Acts, Random House (U.S.), 1934 (music by Virgil Thomson) . . . £50/£20
A Wedding Bouquet: Ballet, J. & W. Chester, Ltd, 1936 (music by Lord Berners, wraps) . . . £150
In Savoy; or Yes Is for a Very Young Man, Pushkin Press, 1946 (wraps) £30
The Mother of Us All, Music Press (U.S.), 1947 (music by Virgil Thomson, wraps) £100
Last Operas and Plays, Rinehart (U.S.), 1949 £30/£10

Poetry and Prose Poems
Tender Buttons: Objects, Food, Rooms, Claire Marie (U.S.), 1914 . . . . £750
Have They Attacked Mary. He Giggled, Temple (U.S.), 1917 (200 copies, red wraps) . . . £500
Before the Flowers of Friendship Fade Friendship Faded, Plain Edition (Paris), 1931 (120 signed copies, wraps) £1,000
Two (Hitherto Unpublished) Poems, Banyan Press/ Gotham Book Mart (U.S.), 1914 (wraps) . . £125
Stanzas in Meditation and Other Poems (1929-1933), Yale Univ. Press (U.S.), 1956 . . . . £25/£10

Other Titles
Portrait of Mabel Dodge, Galileiana (Florence), 1912 (300 copies, wraps) £1,000
Composition as Explanation, Hogarth Press, 1926 .
. . . . £125
An Elucidation, Transition (Paris), 1927 (wraps) £125
Useful Knowledge, Payson & Clarke (U.S.), 1928 . .
. . . . £250/£30
ditto, John Lane/Bodley Head, 1929 . . . £200/£30

An Acquaintance with Description, Seizin Press, 1929
(225 signed copies) £750
Dix Portraits, Éditions de la Montagne (Paris), [1930]
(illustrated by Picasso and others, 10 signed copies) .
. . . . £2,000
ditto, Éditions de la Montagne (Paris), [1930] (25
signed copies) £1,250
ditto, Éditions de la Montagne (Paris), [1930] (65
signed copies) £1,000
ditto, Éditions de la Montagne (Paris), [1930] (402
signed copies) £250
How to Write, Plain Edition (Paris), 1931 . . £125
The Autobiography of Alice B. Toklas, Harcourt Brace
(U.S.), 1933 . . . . £300/£30
ditto, Bodley Head, 1933 . . . . . £200/£30
*Matisse, Picasso, and Gertrude Stein, with Two
Shorter Stories*, Plain Edition (Paris), 1933 (wraps
with glassine d/w and slipcase . . . . £275/£225
Portraits and Prayers, Random House (U.S.), 1934
(cellophane d/w) . . . . £200/£150
Lectures in America, Random House (U.S.), 1935 (top
edge stained grey, with frontispiece) . . £250/£65
ditto, Random House (U.S.), 1935 (top unstained, no
frontispiece) . . . . £200/£15
Narration: Four Lectures, Univ. of Chicago Press
(U.S.), 1935 . . . . £200/£45
ditto, Univ. of Chicago Press (U.S.), 1935 (120 signed
copies in slipcase) . . . . £650/£500
*The Geographical History of America, or, The
Relation of Human Nature to the Human Mind*,
Random House (U.S.), 1936 . . . £1,000/£250
Everybody's Autobiography, Random House (U.S.),
1937 . . . . £150/£25
ditto, Heinemann, 1938 . . . . . . £100/£15
Picasso, Librairie Floury (Paris), 1938 (wraps). £150
ditto, Batsford, 1938 . . . . £100/£25
ditto, Scribner's (U.S.), 1939 . . . . . £75/£20
The World Is Round, Young Scott (U.S.), 1939
(illustrated by Clement Hurd) . . . . £150/£35
ditto, Young Scott (U.S.), 1939 (350 signed copies,
slipcase) . . . . £500/£400
ditto, Batsford, 1939 . . . . £100/£25
Paris France, Scribner's (U.S.), 1940 . . £100/£25
ditto, Batsford, 1940 . . . . £75/£20
What Are Masterpieces, Conference Press (U.S.), 1940
. . . . £100/£25
ditto, Conference Press (U.S.), 1940 (50 signed copies)
. . . . £750/£500
Wars I Have Seen, Random House (U.S.), 1945 . .
. . . . £35/£10
ditto, Batsford, 1945 . . . . £25/£10
The Stein First Reader, and Three Plays, Fridberg,
1946 . . . . £30/£10
ditto, Houghton Mifflin, 1948 . . . . . £30/£10
Selected Writings, Random House (U.S.), 1946 . .
. . . . £25/£10
Four in America, Yale Univ. Press, 1947 . £45/£15
Literally True, Holland (U.S.), 1947 (folded leaflet) .
. . . . £30

*Two: Gertrude Stein and Her Brother and Other
Early Portraits (1908-1912)*, Yale Univ. Press, 1951.
. . . . £45/£15
Bee Time Vine and Other Pieces (1913-1927), Yale
Univ. Press, 1953 . . . . £45/£15
As Fine as Melanctha (1914-1930), Yale Univ. Press,
1954 . . . . £45/£15
Painted Lace and Other Pieces (1914-1937), Yale
Univ. Press, 1955 . . . . £45/£15
To Bobchen Haas, Warren Press (U.S.), 1956 (second
state after suppression of first state, folded card) £25
Alphabets and Birthdays, Yale Univ. Press, 1957 . .
. . . . £45/£15
On Our Way, Simon & Schuster (U.S.), 1959 (100
copies, wraps) £50
Fernhurst, Q.E.D., and Other Early Writings, Boni &
Liveright (U.S.), 1972 . . . . . . £25/£10
ditto, Peter Owen, 1972 . . . . . . £25/£10
A Primer for the Gradual Understanding of Stein,
Black Sparrow Press (U.S.), 1971 (60 copies,
slipcase) £200
ditto, Black Sparrow Press (U.S.), 1971 (500 copies) .
. . . . £75/£50
Reflections on the Atomic Bomb, Black Sparrow Press
(U.S.), 1974 (50 copies, with a copy of *Literally True*)
. . . . £75/£45
ditto, Black Sparrow Press (U.S.), 1974 (750 copies) .
. . . . £50/£20
Dear Sammy: Letters from Stein and Alice B. Toklas,
Houghton Mifflin (U.S.), 1977 . . . . £25/£10

JOHN STEINBECK
(b.1902 d.1968)

An American novelist, *The Grapes of Wrath* is
perhaps his best-known work, and was later made into
a classic film. He was awarded the Nobel Prize for
Literature in 1962.

Novels

Cup of Gold: A Life of Henry Morgan, Buccaneer,
McBride (U.S.), 1929 (first issue, top edges stained
blue and 'First published August, 1929' on copyright
page) . . . . £15,000/£1,000
ditto, Covici Friede (U.S.), 1929 (second issue, using
McBride sheets, maroon cloth) . . . £2,500/£750
ditto, Heinemann, 1937 . . . . £1,250/£150
The Pastures of Heaven, Brewer (U.S.), 1932 . . .
. . . . £2,750/£500
ditto, Allan, 1933 . . . . . . £1,000/£150
To a God Unknown, Ballou (U.S.), 1933 £4,500/£750
ditto, Heinemann, 1935 . . . . . . £750/£150
Tortilla Flat, Covici Friede (U.S.), 1935 £3,000/£150
ditto, Covici Friede (U.S.), 1935 (500 advance review
copies in wraps) £750
ditto, Heinemann, 1935 . . . . . . £750/£125
In Dubious Battle, Covici Friede (U.S.), 1936 . . .
. . . . £2,000/£150

ditto, Covici Friede (U.S.), 1936 (99 signed, numbered copies, tissue d/w and black slipcase) £6,000/£4,500
ditto, Heinemann, 1936 . . . . . . £650/£75
Of Mice and Men, Covici Friede (U.S.), 1937 (first state with line ending 'pendula' on page 9 and a dot between the numbers on page 88) . . £1,500/£500
ditto, Covici Friede (U.S.), 1937 (second state with line ending 'loosely' on page 9 and no dot between the numbers on page 88). . . . . . . £250/£150
ditto, Heinemann, 1937 . . . . . £1,000/£45.
The Grapes of Wrath, Viking (U.S.), 1939 . . . .
. . . . £3,000/£200
ditto, Heinemann, 1939 . . . . . . £500/£35
The Moon is Down, Viking (U.S.), 1941 (first state with large dot between 'talk' and 'this' on p.112, line 11). . . . . £300/£65
ditto, Viking (U.S.), 1941 (second state with large dot removed) . . . . £150/£15
ditto, Heinemann, 1942 . . . . . £150/£20
Cannery Row, Viking (U.S.), 1945 (first issue, buff cloth) . . . . £750/£75
ditto, Viking (U.S.), 1945 (second issue, yellow cloth).
. . . . £200/£25
ditto, Heinemann, 1945 . . . . . . £150/£20
The Wayward Bus, Viking (U.S.), 1947. . £150/£20
ditto, Heinemann, 1947 . . . . . . £100/£15
The Pearl, Viking (U.S.), 1947 . . . £250/£20
ditto, Heinemann, 1948 . . . . . £75/£10
Burning Bright, Viking (U.S.), 1950 . . £100/£15
ditto, Heinemann, 1951 . . . . . . £35/£10
East of Eden, Viking (U.S.), 1952 . . £650/£75
ditto, Viking (U.S.), 1952 (1,500 signed, numbered copies) . . . . £1,250/£850
ditto, Heinemann, 1952 . . . . . . £150/£25
Sweet Thursday, Viking (U.S.), 1954 . . £75/£15
ditto, Heinemann, 1954 . . . . . £50/£10
The Short Reign of Pippin IV: A Fabrication, Viking (U.S.), 1957 . . . . £75/£10
ditto, Heinemann, 1957 . . . . . . £35/£10
The Winter of Our Discontent, Viking (U.S.), 1961 .
. . . . £50/£10
ditto, Viking (U.S.), 1961 (500 copies) . . £250/£65
ditto, Heinemann, 1961 . . . . . . £30/£5

Short Stories
Saint Katy the Virgin, Covici Friede (U.S.), 1936 (199 signed, numbered copies, glassine d/w) £1,250/£1,000
The Red Pony, Covici Friede (U.S.), 1937 (699 signed copies, slipcase) . . . . . £2,000/£1,250
ditto, Covici Friede (U.S.), 1937 (signed, lettered copies, slipcase) . . . . . £3,000/£2,000
ditto, Viking (U.S.), 1945 (enlarged edition, slipcase, no d/w) . . . . £150/£125
The Long Valley, Viking (U.S.), 1938 . . £650/£40
ditto, Heinemann, 1939 . . . . . £200/£25
How Edith McGillcuddy Met R.L.S., Rowfant Club (U.S.), 1943 (152 copies) . . . £1,750/£1,250

Plays
Of Mice and Men: A Play in Three Acts, Covici Friede (U.S.), 1937 . . . . . £1,000/£150
The Moon is Down: A Play in Two Parts, Dramatists Play Service (U.S.), 1942 . . . . . £350
ditto, English Theatre Guild, 1943 . . . . £125

Screenplays
The Forgotten Village, Viking (U.S.), 1941 £125/£20
Viva Zapata!, Edizioni Filmcritica (Italy), 1952 £45
ditto, Viking (U.S.), 1975 (wraps) £25
ditto, Yolla Bolly Press (U.S.), 1991 (190 numbered copies signed by the artist, slipcase) . . . £600
ditto, Yolla Bolly Press (U.S.), 1991 (40 signed deluxe copies signed by the artist, with *Zapata The Man, The Myth, and The Mexican Revolution*, also signed) . .
. . . . £1,250
ditto, Heinemann, 1991 . . . . . . £75/£25

Others
Sea of Cortez: A Leisurely Journal of Travel and Research, Viking (U.S.), 1941 (with Edward F. Ricketts) . . . . £600/£65
ditto, Viking (U.S.), 1941 (advance proof copy, wraps)
. . . . £1,000
ditto, as *The Log from the Sea of Cortez*, Viking (U.S.), 1951 . . . . £200/£20
ditto, as *The Log from the Sea of Cortez*, Heinemann, 1958 . . . . £1255/£20
Bombs Away: The Story of a Bomber Team, Viking (U.S.), 1942 (photographs by John Swope) £150/£25
A Russian Journal, Viking (U.S.), 1948 (photographs by Robert Capa) . . . . £75/£20
ditto, Heinemann, 1949 . . . . . . £50/£15
Once There Was a War, Viking (U.S.), 1958 £75/£20
ditto, Heinemann, 1959 . . . . . . £50/£15
Travels With Charley in Search of America, Viking (U.S.), 1962 . . . . £50/£15
ditto, Heinemann, 1962 . . . . . . £40/£10
Speech Accepting the Nobel Prize for Literature, Viking (U.S.), 1962 (wraps with d/w, 3,200 copies) .
. . . . £175/£100
America and Americans, Viking (U.S.), 1966 £40/£10
ditto, Heinemann, 1966 . . . . . . £35/£10
Journal of a Novel: The 'East of Eden' Letters, Viking (U.S.), 1969 . . . . . . £25/£10
ditto, Viking (U.S.), 1969 (600 copies, glassine wraps and slipcase) . . . . £150/£125
ditto, Heinemann, 1970 . . . . . . £25/£10
Steinbeck: A Life in Letters, Viking (U.S.), 1975 . .
. . . . £20/£5
ditto, Viking (U.S.), 1975 (1,000 numbered copies, slipcase, no d/w) . . . . £50/£40
ditto, Heinemann, 1975 . . . . . . £20/£5
The Acts of King Arthur and His Noble Knights, Farrar Straus (U.S.), 1976 . . . . . £20/£5
ditto, Heinemann, 1977 . . . . . . £20/£5
Working Days: The Journal of 'The Grapes of Wrath', Viking (U.S.), 1988 . . . . £20/£5

COUNT ERIC STENBOCK
(b.1860 d.1895)

The most self-conscious of all 1890s decadents, Stenbock impressed his contemporaries by his personality and wealth rather than by his morbidly sensitive and self-financed poetry and prose.

Poetry
Love, Sleep and Dreams, Shrimpton & Son/Simpkin Marshall & Co., 1881[?]. £1,000
Myrtle, Rue and Cypress, privately printed by Hatchards, 1883 . . . . £1,000
ditto, Hermitage Books, 1992 (60 numbered copies) .
. . . . £100
The Shadow of Death, The Leadenhall Press, 1893 .
. . . . £1,000
On the Freezing of the Baltic Sea, privately printed for Timothy d'Arch Smith, 1961 . . . . . £50
The Collected Poems of Count Stenbock, Durtro Press, 2001 (with 'Ballad of Creditors' tipped in). . £50

Short Stories
Studies of Death: Romantic Tales, David Nutt, 1894 .
. . . . £1,250
ditto, Durtro Press, 1996 [1997] (300 numbered copies)
. . . . £100
The True Story of a Vampire, Tragara Press (Edinburgh), 1989 (110 numbered copies). . £75
The Child of the Soul, Durtro Press, 1999 . . £35
La Mazurka Des Revenants: A Serious Extravaganza In Six Parts, Durtro Press, 2002 (164 numbered copies, wraps) £75
A Secret Kept, Durtro Press, 2002 (200 numbered copies, wraps) £75

Other
The Myth of Punch, Durtro Press, 1999 (120 numbered copies, wraps) £75

LAURENCE STERNE
(b.1713 d.1768)

Although Sterne was a vicar, his parishioners apparently saw little of him after he became a celebrity.

The Case of Elijah, York, 1747 . . . . . £350
The Abuses of Conscience, York, 1750 . . . £350
A Political Romance (The History of a Good Warm Watchcoat), London, 1759 . . . . . £350
The Life and Opinions of Tristram Shandy, Gentleman, Ravanat & Dodsley, 1760-67 (9 vols) . . . £6,500

The Sermons of Mr Yorick, Dodsley, [1760-69] (7 vols) £400
A Sentimental Journey Through France and Italy, Becket/Hondt, 1768 (pseud. 'Mr Yorick', 2 vols). .
. . . . £1,000
ditto, Becket/Hondt, 1768 (350 large paper copies) .
. . . . £1,250
Letters from Mr Yorick to Eliza, Kearsley, 1775 £175
Letters to His Friends on Various Occasions, Johnson, 1775 . . . . £175
Letters to His Most Intimate Friends, Beckett, 1775 (3 vols) . . . . £350 the set

ROBERT LOUIS STEVENSON
(b.1850 d.1894)

A novelist, essayist and poet, many of Stevenson's romances have become classics of English literature, although such novels as *Treasure Island* and *Kidnapped* are often relegated to the category of children's fiction.

Fiction
New Arabian Nights, Chatto & Windus, 1882 (2 vols)
. . . . £1,000
ditto, Holt (U.S.), 1882 . . . . . . £250
Treasure Island, Cassell, 1883 (first issue with 'Dead Man's Chest' not capitalised on pp. 2 and 7; with 'rain' for 'vain' in the last line p.40; the 'a' not present in line 6, p.63; the '8' etc) £6,000
ditto, Roberts Bros (U.S.), 1884 . . . . £1,250
Prince Otto, Chatto & Windus, 1885 . . . £250
ditto, Scribner's (U.S.), 1902 . . . . . £125
The Dynamiter, More New Arabian Nights, Longmans Green & Co., 1885 (with Fanny van de Grift Stevenson, boards) £250
ditto, Longmans Green & Co., 1885 (with Fanny van de Grift Stevenson, wraps) £275
ditto, Holt (U.S.), 1885 . . . . . . £200
The Strange Case of Dr Jekyll and Mr Hyde, Scribner's (U.S.), 1886 (wraps). . . . £2,500
ditto, Scribner's (U.S.), 1886 (boards) . . . £1,750
ditto, Longmans Green & Co., 1886 (wraps, first issue with date on upper cover changed by hand to 1886) .
. . . . £3,000
ditto, Longmans Green & Co., 1886 (boards) . £2,000
Kidnapped, Cassell, 1886 (with folding frontispiece map, first issue with 'business' in line 11, p.40) . .
. . . . £1,000
ditto, Cassell, 1886 (with folding frontispiece map, second issue with 'pleasure' in line 11, p.40) . £450
ditto, Scribner's (U.S.), 1886 (boards, with folding frontispiece map, 8 pages of ads) . . . £500
ditto, Scribner's (U.S.), 1886 (wraps, no ads) . £300
The Merry Men and Other Tales, Chatto & Windus, 1887 . . . . £175
ditto, Scribner's (U.S.), 1887 . . . . . £175

The Black Arrow, Scribner's (U.S.), 1888 (wraps) . .
. . . . £350
ditto, Scribner's (U.S.), 1888 (boards) . . . £200
ditto, Cassell, 1888 (wraps) £250
ditto, Cassell, 1888 (boards) £150
The Master of Ballantrae, Cassell, 1889 . . £250
ditto, Scribner's (U.S.), 1889 (boards) . . . £200
ditto, Scribner's (U.S.), 1889 (wraps) . . . £200
The Wrong Box, Longmans Green & Co., 1889 (with
L. Osbourne). £125
ditto, Scribner's (U.S.), 1889 . . . . . £125
The Wrecker, Cassell, 1892 (with L. Osbourne) £100
ditto, Scribner's (U.S.), 1892 . . . . . £75
Three Plays, D. Nutt, 1892 (with W. Henley) . £75
ditto, D. Nutt, 1892 (with W. Henley, 30 copies on
Japanese vellum). £500
ditto, D. Nutt, 1892 (with W. Henley, 100 copies on
Dutch handmade paper). £250
Catriona, Cassell, 1893 . . . . £150
Island Nights' Entertainments, Scribner's (U.S.), 1893
. . . . £125
ditto, Cassell, 1893 . . . . £125
The Ebb-Tide, Stone & Kimball (U.S.), 1894 . £45
ditto, Heinemann, 1894 (with L. Osbourne). . £45
Valima Letters, Methuen, 1895 . . . . . £50
Weir of Hermiston, Chatto & Windus, 1896 . £50
ditto, Scribner's (U.S.), 1896 . . . . . £45
St. Ives, Scribner's (U.S.), 1897 (with Quiller Couch) .
. . . . £75
ditto, Heinemann, 1898 (with Quiller Couch) . £50

Poetry
A Child's Garden of Verses, Longmans Green & Co.,
1885 . . . . £3,000
ditto, Scribner's (U.S.), 1885 . . . . . £750
Underwoods, Chatto & Windus, 1887 . . . £50
ditto, Scribner's (U.S.), 1887 . . . . . £50
Ballads, Scribner's (U.S.), 1890 . . . . £50
ditto, Chatto & Windus, 1890 . . . . . £50
Songs of Travel and Other Verses, Chatto & Windus,
1896 . . . . £40
Verses by R.L.S., privately printed, The De Vinne
Press (U.S.), 1912 (100 presentation copies) . £300

Non Fiction
The Pentland Rising, Elliot, 1866 (anonymous, wraps)
. . . . £2,500
The Charity Bazaar, privately printed, 1868 (signed,
wraps). £750
ditto, privately printed, 1868 (unsigned, wraps) £500
An Inland Voyage, Kegan Paul, 1878 . . . £750
ditto, Roberts Bros (U.S.), 1883 . . . . . £250
Edinburgh: Picturesque Notes, Seeley & Co., 1879 .
. . . . £225
Travels With a Donkey in the Cevennes, Kegan Paul,
1879 . . . . £400
ditto, Roberts Bros (U.S.), 1879 . . . . . £250
Virginibus Puerisque, Kegan Paul, 1881 . . £150
ditto, Scribner's (U.S.), 1887 . . . . . £75

The Graver and the Pen, or Scenes from Nature with
Appropriate Verses by ...., Osbourne & Co, 1882
(wraps) £500
Familiar Studies of Men and Books, Chatto &
Windus, 1882. . . . . £125
ditto, Chatto & Windus, 1882 (100 large paper copies)
. . . . £200
The Silverado Squatters, Chatto & Windus, 1883 (first
issue lacking 'his' on penultimate line, p.140) £350
Memories and Portraits, Chatto & Windus, 1887 £50
ditto, Scribner's (U.S.), 1887. . . . . . £35
Memoir of Fleeming Jenkin, Scribner's (U.S.), 1887 .
. . . . £45
ditto, Longmans, 1912 . . . . £25
Father Damien, An Open Letter, privately printed
(Australia), 1890 (wraps, 25 copies) . . . £1,500
ditto, privately printed (Edinburgh), 1890 (unbound
sheets in portfolio, 30 copies) £750
ditto, Chatto & Windus, 1890 (wraps) . . . £300
In the South Seas, Cassell (copyright edition), 1890 .
. . . . £1,000
ditto, Edinburgh Edition, 1896 (with 15 of 35 letters) .
. . . . £75
ditto, Scribner's (U.S.), 1896 . . . . . . £75
ditto, Chatto & Windus, 1900 . . . . . £35
Across the Plains, Chatto & Windus, 1892 . . £100
ditto, Chatto & Windus, 1892 (100 large paper copies)
. . . . £200
ditto, Allen Press (U.S.), 1950 (200 copies). . £150
A Footnote to History, Cassell, 1892 . . . £40
ditto, Scribner's (U.S.), 1892 . . . . . . £40
The Amateur Emigrant, Stone & Kimball (U.S.), 1895
. . . . £25
Essays of Travel, Chatto & Windus, 1905 . . £20
ditto, Scribner's (U.S.), 1905 . . . . . . £20
Essays in the Art of Writing, Chatto & Windus, 1905 .
. . . . £20
ditto, Scribner's (U.S.), 1905 . . . . . . £20
Lay Morals and Other Papers, Chatto & Windus, 1911
. . . . £20
ditto, Scribner's (U.S.), 1915 . . . . . . £15
Records of a Family of Engineers, Chatto & Windus,
1912 . . . . £15

BRAM STOKER
(b.1847 d.1912)

Born and educated in Dublin, Stoker was the author
of a number of novels of mystery and romance, the
most famous of which was *Dracula*.

Novels
The Snake's Pass, Harpers (U.S.), 1890 (wraps) £750
ditto, Sampson Low, 1891 [1890] £750
The Watter's Mou', De Vinne & Co. (U.S.), 1894 . .
. . . . £350
ditto, Constable, 1895 . . . . £350

The Shoulder of Shasta, Constable, 1895 . . £500
Dracula, Constable, 1897 (first issue integral blank leaf at rear and no advertisement) £12,500
ditto, Constable, 1897 (second issue with ad. for *Shoulder of Shasta* on p.392) £6,000
ditto, Doubleday & McClure (U.S.), 1899 . . £4,000
Miss Betty, Pearson, 1898 . . . . . . £400
The Mystery of the Sea, Doubleday (U.S.), 1902 £300
ditto, Heinemann, 1902 . . . . . . £300
The Jewel of Seven Stars, Heinemann, 1903 . £400
ditto, Harpers (U.S.), 1904 . . . . . . £200
The Man, Heinemann, 1905 . . . . . . £350
ditto, Century (U.S.), 1905 . . . . . . £200
Lady Athlyne, Heinemann, 1908 . . . . . £300
The Lady of the Shroud, Heinemann, 1909. . £350
The Lair of the White Worm, Rider, 1911 . . £350

Short Stories
Under the Sunset, Sampson Low, 1882 [1881]. £300
Snowbound, Collier, 1908 (wraps) £75
Dracula's Guest and Other Weird Stories, Routledge, 1914 . . . . £300
ditto, Hillman-Curl (U.S.), 1937 . . . . . £200
The Dualists, Tragara Press (Edinburgh), 1986 (wrappers) £45

Non Fiction
The Duties of the Clerks of Petty Sessions in Ireland, John Falconer, 1879 . . . . £200
A Glimpse of America, Sampson Low, 1886 (wraps) .
. . . . £65
Personal Reminiscences of Henry Irving, Heinemann, 1906 (two vols) £75
ditto, Macmillan (U.S.), 1906 . . . . . £75
Famous Impostors, Sidgwick and Jackson, 1910 . .
. . . . £100
ditto, Sturgis & Walton (U.S.), 1910. . . . £100

TOM STOPPARD
(b.1937)

A prolific playwright, Stoppard was born in Czechoslovakia, taken to Singapore as an infant, and finished his education in England.

Plays
Rosencrantz and Guildenstern are Dead, Faber, 1967
. . . . £750/£50
ditto, Faber, 1967 (wraps). £50
ditto, Grove Press (U.S.), 1967 . . . . £250/£35
The Real Inspector Hound, Faber, 1968 . £300/£45
ditto, Faber, 1968 (wraps). £35
ditto, Grove Press (U.S.), 1969 (wraps) . . . £30
Enter a Free Man, Faber, 1968 . . . . £150/£35
ditto, Faber, 1968 (wraps). £25
ditto, Grove Press (U.S.), 1972 (wraps) . . . £20

Albert's Bridge and If You're Glad I'll be Frank: Two Plays for Radio, Faber, 1969 (wraps) . . . £35
Albert's Bridge, French, 1969 (wraps) . . . £10
After Magritte, Faber, 1971 (wraps). . . . £50
ditto, Grove Press (U.S.), 1972 (wraps) . . . £20
Jumpers, Faber, 1971 . . . . £100/£20
ditto, Faber, 1971 (wraps). £30
ditto, Grove Press (U.S.), 1972 . . . . £45/£10
Artist Descending a Staircase and Where Are They Now?: Two Plays for Radio, Faber, 1973 . £125/£20
ditto, Faber, 1973 (wraps). £25
Travesties, Faber, 1975 . . . . . . £75/£20
ditto, Faber, 1975 (wraps). £25
ditto, Grove Press (U.S.), 1975 (wraps) . . . £20
Dirty Linen and New-Found-Land, Ambiance/Almost Free Playscript, 1976 (wraps) £35
ditto, Inter Action, 1976 (1,000 signed, numbered copies, wraps) £50
ditto, Grove Press (U.S.), 1976 . . . . £45/£10
ditto, Faber, 1976 (wraps). £20
The Fifteen Minute Hamlet, French, 1976 (wraps) £25
Albert's Bridge & Other Plays, Grove Press (U.S.), 1977 . . . . £35/£5
Every Good Boy Deserves Favour and Professional Foul, Faber, 1978 . . . . £125/£15
ditto, Faber, 1978 (wraps). £20
ditto, Grove Press (U.S.), 1978 . . . . £50/£10
Night and Day, Faber, 1978 . . . . £40/£10
ditto, Grove Press (U.S.), 1979 . . . . £25/£10
Undiscovered Country, Faber, 1980 (wraps) . £45
Dogg's Hamlet, Cahoot's Macbeth, Inter-Action, 1979 (2,000 numbered copies, wraps) £35
ditto, Faber, 1980 (wraps). £20
On the Razzle, Faber, 1981 (wraps) £20
The Real Thing, Faber, 1982 (wraps) £15
ditto, Faber, 1982 (500 signed copies, broadside) £125
ditto, Faber (U.S.), 1984 (revised edition) . . £20/£5
The Dog It was That Died and Other Plays, Faber, 1983 (wraps) £15
Four Plays for Radio, Faber, 1984 (wraps). . £10
Squaring the Circle, Faber, 1984 (wraps) . . £10
ditto, Faber (U.S.), 1985 (wraps). £10
Rough Crossing, Faber, 1985 (wraps) . . . £10
Hapgood, Faber, 1988 (wraps) £10
Radio Plays 1964-1983, Faber, 1990 (wraps) . £10
In the Native State, Faber, 1991 (wraps) . . £10
Television Plays, 1965-84, Faber, 1993 . . £35/£10
Indian Ink, Faber, 1995 . . . . . . £30/£10
ditto, Faber, 1995 (wraps). £10

Novels
Lord Malquist and Mr Moon, Blond, 1966. £75/£15
ditto, Knopf (U.S.), 1968 . . . . . . £25/£10

Others
Rosencrantz and Guildenstern Are Dead: The Film, Faber, 1991 (wraps) £15

DAVID STOREY
(b.1933)

A novelist and playwright, much of Storey's writing considers the problems of working class characters as they move into middle class surroundings and/or a mid-life crisis.

Novels

This Sporting Life, Longmans, 1960 . .	£200/£30
ditto, Macmillan (U.S.), 1960	£65/£10
Flight into Camden, Longmans, 1961 .	£100/£20
ditto, Macmillan (U.S.), 1961	£45/£10
Radcliffe, Longmans, 1963	£40/£10
ditto, Coward-McCann (U.S.), 1964	. £25/£5
Pasmore, Longman, 1972	. £15/£5
ditto, Dutton (U.S.), 1974.	. £10/£5
A Temporary Life, Lane, 1973	. £15/£5
ditto, Dutton (U.S.), 1974.	. £10/£5
Saville, Cape, 1976	. £20/£5
ditto, Harper (U.S.), 1977.	. £10/£5
A Prodigal Child, Cape, 1982	. £15/£5
ditto, Dutton (U.S.), 1982.	. £10/£5
Present Times, Cape, 1984	. £15/£5
A Serious Man, Cape, 1998	. £10/£5
As It Happened, Cape, 2002	. £10/£5

Plays

The Restoration of Arnold Middleton, Cape, 1967. .	
. . . .	£30/£10
In Celebration, Cape, 1969	£30/£10
ditto, Grove Press (U.S.), 1975	. £15/£5
The Contractor, Cape, 1970	. £20/£5
ditto, Random House (U.S.), 1971 . . .	. £15/£5
Home, Cape, 1970.	. £15/£5
ditto, Random House (U.S.), 1971 . . .	. £10/£5
The Changing Room, Cape, 1972 . . .	. £10/£5
ditto, Random House (U.S.), 1972 . . .	. £10/£5
The Farm, Cape, 1973	. £10/£5
Cromwell, Cape, 1973	. £10/£5
Life Class, Cape, 1975	. £10/£5
Mother's Day, Cape, 1977	. £10/£5
Early Days, Penguin, 1980 (wraps) . . .	£10
Sisters, Penguin, 1980 (wraps)	£10
The March on Russia, French, 1989 (wraps) .	£10

Humour

Edward, Lane, 1973	. £15/£5

Poetry

Storey's Lives: Poems, 1951-1991, Cape, 1992	£15/£5

GILES LYTTON STRACHEY
(b.1880 d.1932)

Lytton Strachey was educated at Liverpool and Cambridge Universities and became a prominent member of the Bloomsbury Group. Best known for biographies, he also wrote poetry, reviews and essays.

Landmarks in French Literature, Williams and Norgate, 1912 (first issue with top edge stained green and 8 pages of ads)	£75
ditto, Williams and Norgate, 1912 (second issue with top edge stained red).	£25
ditto, Holt (U.S.), 1912	£25
Eminent Victorians, Chatto & Windus, 1918 .	£50
ditto, Putnam (U.S.), 1918	£30
Queen Victoria, Chatto & Windus, 1921 .	£100/£35
ditto, Harcourt (U.S.), 1921	£75/£25
Books and Characters, Chatto & Windus, 1922 . .	
. . . .	£50/£20
ditto, Harcourt (U.S.), 1922	£35/£15
Pope: The Leslie Stephen Lecture, C.U.P., 1925 . .	
. . . .	£35/£10
ditto, Harcourt (U.S.), 1926	£30/£10
Elizabeth and Essex, Chatto & Windus, 1928 £50/£15	
ditto, Harcourt Brace/Crosby Gaige (U.S.), 1928 . .	
. . . .	£30/£10
ditto, Harcourt Brace/Crosby Gaige (U.S.), 1928 (1,060 signed copies)	£75
Portraits in Miniature, Chatto & Windus, 1931 . .	
. . . .	£50/£15
ditto, Chatto & Windus, 1931 (260 signed copies) £150	
ditto, Harcourt (U.S.), 1931	£30/£10
Characters and Commentaries, Chatto & Windus, 1933	£45/£15
ditto, Harcourt (U.S.), 1933	£30/£10
Virginia Woolf and Lytton Strachey: Letters, Hogarth Press, 1956	£125/£25
ditto, Harcourt (U.S.), 1956	£45/£15
Spectatorial Essays, Chatto & Windus, 1964 . £15/£5	
ditto, Harcourt (U.S.), 1965	£10/£5
Ermyntrude and Esmeralda, Blond, 1969 (17 illustrations by Erté)	£35/£10
ditto, Blond, 1969 (250 copies signed by Erté, slipcase)	£125/£100
ditto, Stein & Day (U.S.), 1969	£25/£10
Lytton Strachey by Himself, Heinemann, 1971 (edited Michael Holroyd)	. £15/£5
ditto, Holt, Rinehart & Winston (U.S.), 1971 . £10/£5	
Lytton Strachey: The Really Interesting Question, Weidenfeld & Nicolson, 1972 (edited Paul Levy). .	
. . . .	. £15/£5
ditto, Coward-McCann (U.S.), 1973	. £15/£5
The Shorter Strachey, O.U.P., 1980 (edited Michael Holroyd)	. £10/£5

MONTAGUE SUMMERS
(b.1880 d.1948)

A strange but scholarly character, Summers published many books on the supernatural as well as 17th century theatre and the Gothic novel.

Major Works

The Marquis de Sade, The British Society for the Study of Sex Psychology, 1920 (wraps) . . £75

The History of Witchcraft and Demonology, Kegan Paul, 1926 . . . . £125/£50

ditto, Knopf (U.S.), 1926 . . . . . £100/£35

The Geography of Witchcraft, Kegan Paul, 1927 . . . . £100/£35

ditto, Knopf (U.S.), 1927 . . . . . £100/£35

Essays in Petto, Fortune Press, [1928] . . £150/£75

ditto, Fortune Press, [1928] (70 signed, numbered copies) £200

The Discovery of Witches, Cayme Press, 1928 (wraps) £65

The Vampire: His Kith and Kin, Kegan Paul, 1928 . . . . £100/£30

ditto, Dutton (U.S.), 1929. . . . . £100/£30

The Vampire in Europe, Kegan Paul, 1929. £125/£30

ditto, Dutton (U.S.), 1929. . . . . £100/£30

The Werewolf, Kegan Paul, 1933 . . . £200/£45

ditto, Dutton (U.S.), 1934. . . . . £175/£40

The Restoration Theatre, Kegan Paul, 1934 £45/£20

ditto, Macmillan (U.S.), 1934 . . . . £35/£20

A Bibliography of the Restoration Drama, Fortune Press, [1935] . . . . £45/£20

ditto, Fortune Press, [1935] (250 copies) . £65/£35

ditto, Fortune Press, [1943] (revised and enlarged edition) . . . . £30/£10

The Playhouse of Pepys, Kegan Paul, 1935. £45/£15

ditto, Macmillan (U.S.), 1935 . . . . £40/£15

A Popular History of Witchcraft, Kegan Paul, 1937 . . . . £75/£25

ditto, Dutton (U.S.), 1937. . . . . £75/£25

The Gothic Quest, Fortune Press, [1938] (950 copies, no d/w) £150

A Gothic Bibliography, Fortune Press, [1940] (750 copies) £175

ditto, Russell & Russell (U.S.), 1964 (no d/w) . £50

Witchcraft and Black Magic, Rider, [1946] £50/£20

ditto, Causeway (U.S.), 1974 . . . . £30/£15

The Physical Phenomena of Mysticism, Rider, [1950] . . . . £35/£15

ditto, Barnes & Noble (U.S.), 1950 . . . £25/£10

The Galanty Show: An Autobiography, Cecil Woolf, 1980 . . . . £30/£10

Letters to an Editor, Tragara Press (Edinburgh), 1986 (145 numbered copies, wraps) £25

Others

Antinous and Other Poems, Sisley's, [1907] . £250

ditto, Cecil Woolf, 1995 . . . . . . £15/£5

The Source of Southerne's The Fatal Marriage, C.U.P., 1916 (wraps) £45

The Double Dealer, [Incorporated Stage Society], [1916] (wraps) £35

Orrey's The Tragedy of Zoroastres, C.U.P., 1917 (wraps) £45

Love for Love, [Incorporated Stage Society], [1917] (wraps) £35

A Great Mistress of Romance, Royal Society of Literature, [1917] (wraps) £45

The Way of the World, [Incorporated Stage Society], [1918] (wraps) £35

Jane Austen: An Appreciation, Royal Society of Literature, [1918] (wraps) £45

The Provok'd Wife, Incorporated Stage Society, [1919] (wraps) £35

R.S. SURTEES
(b.1805 d.1864)

A British sporting novelist and journalist whose most successful character is arguably 'Mr Jorrocks', a good-humoured and vulgar Cockney grocer who loves to hunt.

Fiction

Jorrocks's Jaunts and Jollities, Spiers, 1838 (illustrated by Phiz) £300

ditto, Ackermann, 1843 (15 coloured illustrations by Henry Alken, first state) £750

ditto, Ackermann, 1843 (15 coloured illustrations by Henry Alken, second state with ads announcing a new edition of *The Life of John Mytton*). . . . £500

Handley Cross; or, Mr Jorrocks's Hunt, Colburn, 1843 (3 vols) £300

ditto, Bradbury & Evans, 1853 (17 monthly parts, illustrated by John Leech) . . . £1,250 the set

ditto, Bradbury & Evans, 1854 (1 vol.) . . . £200

Hillingdon Hall; or The Cockney Squire, Colburn, 1845 (3 vols) £200

Hawbuck Grange; or, The Sporting Adventures of Thomas Scott, Esq., Longmans, 1847 (illustrated by Phiz) £250

Mr Songe's Sporting Tour, Bradbury & Evans, 1852-3 (13 [12] monthly parts, illustrated by John Leech) . . . . £750 the set

ditto, Bradbury & Evans, 1853 (1 vol.) . . . £200

Ask Mamma; or, The Richest Commoner in England, Bradbury & Evans, 1857-8 (13 [12] monthly parts, illustrated by John Leech) £1,000

ditto, Bradbury & Evans, 1858 (1 vol.) . . . £125

Plain or Ringlets?, Bradbury & Evans, 1858-60 (13 [12] monthly parts, illustrated by John Leech) £600

ditto, Bradbury & Evans, 1860 (1 vol.) . . . £200

ditto, Bradbury & Evans, 1860 (1 vol., wraps) . £600

Mr Facey Romford's Hounds, Bradbury & Evans, 1864-5 (13 [12] monthly parts, illustrated by John Leech). £750
ditto, Bradbury & Evans, 1865 (1 vol.) . . . £200

Non Fiction
The Horseman's Manual, being a treatise on Soundness, the law of Warranty, and generally on the laws relating to Horses, Miller, 1831 . . £300
ditto, Treadway (U.S.), 1832 . . . . . . £300
The Analysis of the Hunting Field, Ackermann, 1846 (colour plates by Henry Alken, first issue in green cloth) £750
ditto, Ackermann, 1846 (colour plates by Henry Alken, second issue in red cloth) £500
Hints to Railway Travellers, wraps, 1852 . . £100

GRAHAM SWIFT
(b.1949)

A novelist whose reputation was based largely on *Waterland* until *Last Orders* won the 1996 Booker Prize.

Novels
The Sweet Shop Owner, Allen Lane, 1980 . £300/£45
ditto, Washington Square (U.S.), 1985 (wraps). £10
Shuttlecock, Allen Lane, 1981 . . . . £250/£30
ditto, Washington Square (U.S.), 1985 (wraps). £10
Waterland, Heinemann, 1983 . . . . £75/£10
ditto, Poseidon (U.S.), 1984 . . . . . . £20/£5
Out of This World, Viking, 1988 . . . £25/£5
ditto, Poseidon (U.S.), 1988 . . . . . £15/£5
Ever After, Picador, 1992 . . . . . £15/£5
ditto, Knopf (U.S.), 1992 . . . . . £10/£5
Last Orders, Picador, 1996 . . . . . £15/£5
ditto, Knopf (U.S.), 1996 . . . . . £10/£5

Short Stories
Learning to Swim and Other Stories, London Magazine Editions, 1982 . . . . . £350/£45
ditto, Poseidon (U.S.), 1982 . . . . £30/£10

A.J.A. SYMONS
(b.1900 d.1941)

A biographer, bibliographer and book collector, Symons' masterpiece is *The Quest for Corvo*.

A Bibliography of the First Editions of Books by William Butler Yeats, First Edition Club, 1924 (500 copies) . . . . £75/£30
Frederick Baron Corvo, Sette of Odd Volumes, 1927 (199 copies, wraps) £300
Emin: The Governor of Equatoria, The Fleuron, 1928 (300 copies) £65

ditto, Falcon Press, 1950 . . . . . . £25/£10
An Episode in the Life of the Queen of Sheba Rediscovered by A.J.A. Symons, privately printed, 1929 (150 copies, wraps) £100
H.M. Stanley, Duckworth, 1933 . . . . £45/£15
ditto, Falcon Press, 1950 . . . . . . £25/£10
The Quest for Corvo, Cassell, 1934 . . . £175/£25
ditto, Macmillan (U.S.), 1934 . . . . £100/£15
The Nonesuch Century; An Appraisal, Nonesuch Press, 1936 (with F. Meynell & D. Flower, 750 copies) . . . . £650/£500
Essays and Biographies, Cassell, 1969 (edited by Julian Symons) . . . . £25/£10
A.J.A. Symons to Wyndham Lewis: Twenty-Four Letters, Tragara Press, 1982 (120 copies, wraps) £35
Two Brothers: Fragments of a Correspondence, Tragara Press, 1985 (105 copies, wraps) . . £45
ditto, Tragara Press, 1985 (25 copies, signed by Julian Symons, wraps) £75

JULIAN SYMONS
(b.1912 d.1994)

A novelist and critic, Symons' speciality is detective fiction. He co-founded the Crime Writers Association in 1953.

Novels
The Immaterial Murder Case, Gollancz, 1945 . . . . £125/£25
ditto, Macmillan (U.S.), 1957 . . . . £50/£15
A Man Called Jones, Gollancz, 1947 . . £75/£15
Bland Beginning, Gollancz, 1949 . . . £75/£15
ditto, Harper (U.S.), 1949. . . . . . £40/£10
The 31st of February, Gollancz, 1950 . . £75/£15
ditto, Harper (U.S.), 1950. . . . . . £40/£10
The Broken Penny, Gollancz, 1952 . . . £65/£10
ditto, Harper (U.S.), 1953. . . . . . £35/£5
The Narrowing Circle, Gollancz, 1954 . . £65/£10
ditto, Harper (U.S.), 1954. . . . . . £35/£5
The Paper Chase, Collins Crime Club, 1956 £65/£10
ditto, as *Bogue's Fortune*, Harper (U.S.), 1957. £35/£5
The Colour of Murder, Collins Crime Club, 1957 . . . . £50/£10
ditto, Harper (U.S.), 1957. . . . . . £35/£5
The Gigantic Shadow, Collins Crime Club, 1958 . . . . £45/£5
ditto, as *Pipe Dream*, Harper, 1958 . . . £30/£5
The Progress of a Crime, Collins Crime Club, 1960 . . . . £35/£5
ditto, Harper (U.S.), 1960. . . . . . £25/£5
The Killing of Francie Lake, Collins Crime Club, 1962 . . . . £35/£5
ditto, as *The Plain Man*, Harper, 1962 . . . £25/£5
The End of Solomon Grundy, Collins Crime Club, 1964 . . . . £35/£5
ditto, Harper (U.S.), 1964. . . . . . £25/£5

The Belting Inheritance, Collins Crime Club, 1965 .
. . . . £35/£5
ditto, Harper (U.S.), 1965. . . . . . . £25/£5
The Man Who Killed Himself, Collins Crime Club, 1967 . . . . £35/£5
ditto, Harper (U.S.), 1967. . . . . . . £25/£5
The Man Whose Dreams Came True, Collins Crime Club, 1968 . . . . £35/£5
ditto, Harper (U.S.), 1969. . . . . . . £25/£5
The Man Who Lost His Wife, Collins Crime Club, 1970 . . . . £30/£5
ditto, Harper (U.S.), 1971. . . . . . . £25/£5
The Players and the Game, Collins Crime Club, 1971 . . . . £30/£5
ditto, Harper (U.S.), 1972. . . . . . . £25/£5
The Plot Against Roger Rider, Collins Crime Club, 1973 . . . . £20/£5
ditto, Harper (U.S.), 1973. . . . . . . £15/£5
A Three Pipe Problem, Collins Crime Club, 1975 . .
. . . . £20/£5
ditto, Harper (U.S.), 1975. . . . . . . £15/£5
The Blackheath Poisonings, Collins Crime Club, 1978
. . . . £20/£5
ditto, Harper (U.S.), 1979. . . . . . . £15/£5
Sweet Adelaide, Collins Crime Club, 1980 . . £20/£5
ditto, Harper (U.S.), 1980. . . . . . . £15/£5
The Detling Murders, Macmillan, 1982. . . £20/£5
ditto, as *The Detling Secret*, Viking, 1983 . . £15/£5
The Name of Annabel Lee, Macmillan, 1983 . £20/£5
ditto, Viking (U.S.), 1983. . . . . . . £15/£5
The Criminal Comedy of the Contented Couple, Macmillan, 1985 . . . . £15/£5
ditto, as *A Criminal Comedy*, Viking (U.S.), 1986 . .
. . . . £10/£5
The Kentish Manor Murders, Macmillan, 1988 £15/£5
ditto, Viking (U.S.), 1988. . . . . . . £10/£5
Death's Darkest Face, Macmillan, 1990 . . £15/£5
ditto, Viking (U.S.), 1990. . . . . . . £10/£5
Something Like a Love Affair, Macmillan, 1992 . .
. . . . £15/£5
ditto, Mysterious Press (U.S.), 1992 . . . . £10/£5
Playing Happy Families, Macmillan, 1994 . . £15/£5
ditto, Mysterious Press (U.S.), 1995 . . . . £10/£5
A Sort of Virtue, Macmillan, 1996 . . . . £10/£5

Omnibus
The Julian Symons Omnibus, Collins, 1966 . £15/£5

Short Stories
Murder, Murder, Fontana, 1961 (wraps) . . £10
Francis Quarles Investigates, Panther, 1965 (wraps) .
. . . . £10
The Tigers of Subtopia and Other Stories, Macmillan, 1981 . . . . £30/£5
ditto, Viking (U.S.), 1983. . . . . . . £20/£5
Somebody Else and Other Stories, Eurographica (Helsinki), 1990 (wraps). £35
Portraits of the Missing, Deutsch, 1991. . . £20/£5

Murder Under the Mistletoe, Severn House, 1993 . .
. . . . £15/£5
The Man Who Hated Television and Other Stories, Macmillan, 1995. . . . . £10/£5

Poems
Confusions About X, Fortune Press, [1939]. £125/£35
The Second Man, Routledge, 1943 . . . £75/£20
The Object of an Affair and Other Poems, Tragara Press, 1974 (25 signed copies, wraps) . . . £75
ditto, Tragara Press, 1974 (65 copies, wraps) . £45
The Thirties and the Nineties, Carcanet, 1990 (wraps)
. . . . £5

Others
A.J.A. Symons: His Life and Speculations, Eyre & Spottiswoode, 1950 . . . . £40/£15
Thomas Carlyle. The Life and Times of a Prophet, Gollancz Ltd., 1951 . . . . £15/£5
Horatio Bottomley: A Biography, The Cresset Press, 1955 . . . . £15/£5
The General Strike, The Cresset Press, 1957 £25/£10
The Thirties. A Dream Revolved, The Cresset Press, 1960 (wraps) £35
Reasonable Doubt: Some Criminal Cases, The Cresset Press, 1960 . . . . £25/£10
The Detective Story in Britain, Longmans, Green & Co., 1962 (wraps) £10
Buller's Campaign, The Cresset Press, 1963 £25/£10
Critical Occasions, Hamish Hamilton, 1966 £25/£10
England's Pride: The Story of the Gordon Relief Expedition, Hamish Hamilton, 1965 . £25/£10
Portrait of an Artist: Conan Doyle, Whizzard Press/ Deutsch, 1979 . . . . £25/£10
ditto, Mysterious Press (U.S.), 1979 . . . £25/£10
The Modern Crime Story, Tragara Press, 1980 (125 signed copies, wraps) £45
ditto, Eurographica (Helsinki), 1988 (350 signed copies, wraps) £35
1948 and 1984, Tragara Press, 1984 (135 copies, wraps). £35
Two Brothers: Fragments of a Correspondence, Tragara Press, 1985 (105 copies, wraps) . . £45
ditto, Tragara Press, 1985 (25 copies, signed by Julian Symons, wraps) £75
Makers of the New, Deutsch, 1987 . . . £10/£5
ditto, Random House (U.S.), 1987 . . . . £10/£5
Oscar Wilde: A Problem in Biography, Yellow Barn Press (U.S.), 1988 (200 copies). £65

JOSEPHINE TEY
(b.1897 d.1952)

'Josephine Tey' was the pseudonym under which British author Elizabeth Mackintosh wrote popular mystery novels. She had been previously successful as 'Gordon Daviot', writing historical plays.

Novels by 'Josephine Tey'

A Shilling for Candles, Methuen, 1936 . .	£500/£75
ditto, Macmillan (U.S.), 1954	£25/£10
Miss Pym Disposes, Peter Davies, 1946 . .	£150/£20
ditto, Macmillan (U.S.), 1948	£75/£10
The Franchise Affair, Peter Davies, 1948 .	£200/£20
ditto, Macmillan (U.S.), 1948	£50/£10
Brat Farrar, Peter Davies, 1949	£150/£20
ditto, Macmillan (U.S.), 1950	£20/£5
ditto, as *Come and Kill Me*, Pocket Books (U.S.), 1950 (wraps)	£10
To Love and Be Wise, Peter Davies, 1950 .	£150/£20
ditto, Macmillan (U.S.), 1951	£20/£5
The Daughter of Time, Peter Davies, 1951 .	£150/£20
ditto, Macmillan (U.S.), 1952	£20/£5
The Singing Sands, Peter Davies, 1952 . .	£150/£20
ditto, Macmillan (U.S.), 1953	£20/£5

Novels by 'Gordon Daviot'

The Man In The Queue, Methuen, 1929 .	£700/£125
ditto, Dutton (U.S.), 1929	£500/£50
ditto, Peter Davies, 1953 (as 'Josephine Tey')	£25/£10
ditto, as *Killer in the Crowd*, Mercury (U.S.), 1954 (as 'Josephine Tey')	£25/£10
Kif, An Unvarnished History, Benn, 1929 .	£50/£15
ditto, Appleton (U.S.), 1929	£50/£15
The Expensive Halo, Benn, 1931 . . .	£50/£15
ditto, Appleton (U.S.), 1931	£50/£15
The Privateer, Peter Davies, 1952 . . .	£25/£5
ditto, Macmillan (U.S.), 1952	£20/£5

Other Titles by 'Gordon Daviot'

Richard of Bordeaux, Gollancz, 1933 . .	£25/£5
The Laughing Woman, Gollancz, 1934 . .	£25/£5
Queen of Scots, Gollancz, 1934	£25/£5
The Stars Bow Down, Duckworth, 1939 .	£25/£5
Leith Sands, And Other Short Plays, Duckworth, 1946	£25/£5
Plays, In Three Volumes, Peter Davies, 1953-54	£25/£5
Claverhouse, Collins, 1937	£25/£5

W.M. THACKERAY
(b.1811 d.1863)

Charlotte Brontë's favourite author, Thackeray's most famous work is *Vanity Fair*.

Novels

Vanity Fair: A Novel Without a Hero, Bradbury & Evans, 1848 (20 parts in 19; yellow wraps) .	£4,000
ditto, Bradbury & Evans, 1848 (first book edition, made up of the original parts; with the woodcut [later suppressed] of Lord Steyne on page 336) . .	£2,500
ditto, Harper & Bros (U.S.), 1848 . . .	£1,500
The History of Pendennis, His Fortunes and Misfortunes, His Friends and His Greatest Enemy, Bradbury & Evans, 1850 (24 parts in 23; yellow wraps).	£2,000
ditto, Bradbury & Evans, 1849[-50] (2 vols) .	£1,250
ditto, Harper & Bros (U.S.), 1855	£1,500
The History of Henry Esmond, Esq. A Colonel In the Service of Her Majesty Q. Anne. Written by Himself, Smith Elder, 1852 (3 vols)	£500
ditto, Harper & Bros (U.S.), 1852 (wraps) . .	£300
The Newcomes: Memoirs of a Most Respectable Family, Bradbury & Evans, 1853-55 (24 parts in 23, yellow wraps)	£1,250
ditto, Bradbury & Evans, 1854[-55] (2 vols) .	£750
ditto, Harper & Bros (U.S.), 1855	£100
The Memoirs of Barry Lyndon, Esq., of The Kingdom of Ireland, Appleton (U.S.), 1853 (2 vols). .	£1,500
ditto, Bradbury & Evans, 1856 (wraps). . .	£500
The Virginians: A Tale of the Last Century, Bradbury & Evans, 1859 (24 parts, yellow wraps) . .	£750
ditto, Bradbury & Evans, 1858[-59] (2 vols) .	£500
ditto, Harper & Bros (U.S.), 1859 . . .	£100
Lovel the Widower, Harper & Bros (U.S.), 1860	£250
ditto, Smith Elder, 1861	£250
The Adventures of Philip on His Way Through the World; Shewing Who Robbed Him, Who Helped Him, and Who Passed Him By, Smith Elder, 1862 (3 vols)	£400
ditto, Harper & Bros (U.S.), 1862	£65
Denis Duval, Smith Elder, 1867	£250

Christmas Books

Mrs Perkins's Ball, Chapman & Hall, [1847] (pseud. 'Mr M.A. Titmarsh').	£400
'Our Street', Chapman & Hall, 1848 (pseud. 'Mr M.A. Titmarsh', wraps)	£400
Doctor Birch and His Young Friends, Chapman & Hall, 1849 (pseud. 'Mr M.A. Titmarsh', wraps)	£400
The Kicklebury's on the Rhine, Chapman & Hall, 1850 (pseud. 'Mr M.A. Titmarsh')	£400
The Rose and the Ring, or, The History of Prince Gigilo and Prince Bulbo: A Fireside Pantomime for Great and Small Children, Chapman & Hall, 1855 (pseud. 'Mr M.A. Titmarsh')	£500
Christmas Books, Chapman & Hall, 1857 . .	£250

Tales and Sketches
The Yellowplush Papers, Harper & Bros. (U.S.), 1848
(brown boards with brown cloth spine) . . £1,000
ditto, Harper & Bros (U.S.), 1848 (green cloth wraps).
. . . . £1,500
Comic Tales and Sketches, Hugh Cunningham, 1841
(pseud. 'Mr Michael Angelo Titmarsh'; no reference
to *Vanity Fair*) £750
The Book of Snobs, Punch Office, 1848 (wraps) £350
ditto, Appleton (U.S.), 1852 . . . . . £100
The Great Hoggarty Diamond, Harper & Bros (U.S.),
1848 (first issue with '82 Cliff Street' on title page,
wraps). £1,500
*The History of Samuel Titmarsh and the Great
Hoggarty Diamond*, Bradbury & Evans, 1849 £350
Rebecca and Rowena: A Romance Upon Romance,
Chapman & Hall, 1850 (pseud. 'Mr Michael Angelo
Titmarsh') £350
A Shabby Genteel Story, Appleton (U.S.), 1852 £350
ditto, Bradbury & Evans, 1857 (wraps) . . . £350
The Fatal Boots and *Cox's Diary*, Bradbury & Evans,
1855 (wraps) £350
The Little Dinner at Timmins's and *The Bedford-Row
Conspiracy*, Bradbury & Evans, 1856 (wraps) £350
The Memoirs of Mr Charles J. Yellowplush and *The
Diary of C. Jeames de la Pluche, Esq.*, Bradbury &
Evans, 1856 (wraps). £350
The Fitz-Boodle Papers and *Men's Wives*, Bradbury &
Evans, 1857 (wraps). £350

Non Fiction
The Paris Sketch Book, John Macrone, 1840 (pseud.
'Mr Titmarsh', 2 vols) £750
The Irish Sketch Book, John Macrone, 1843 (pseud.
'Mr Titmarsh', 2 vols) £750
*Notes of a Journey from Cornhill to Grand Cairo, By
Way of Lisbon, Athens, Constantinople, and
Jerusalem*, Chapman & Hall, 1846 (pseud. 'Mr M.A.
Titmarsh') £500
ditto, Wiley & Putnam. (U.S.), 1846 . . . . £300
*The English Humorists of the Eighteenth Century: A
Series of Lectures Delivered in England, Scotland
and the United States of America*, Smith Taylor,
1853 . . . . £250
ditto, Harper & Bros (U.S.), 1853 . . . . £150
*The Four Georges: Sketches of Manners, Morals,
Court and Town Life*, Harper Bros (U.S.), 1860 £250
ditto, Smith Elder, 1861 . . . . £250
The Roundabout Papers, Smith Elder, 1863 . £250
ditto, Harper & Bros (U.S.), 1863 . . . . £150

Collected Editions
The Works of William Makepeace Thackeray, Smith
Elder 'Library Edition', 1869-86 (24 vols) . £500
The Works of William Makepeace Thackeray, Smith
Elder/Ritchie Edition, 1898-99 (24 vols) . . £400
The Oxford Thackeray, O.U.P./Saintsbury Edition,
O.U.P, [1908] (17 vols) £250

The Works of William Makepeace Thackeray, Smith
Elder 'Centenary Biographical Edition', 1910-11 (26
vols) £750

PAUL THEROUX
(b.1941)

An American novelist and travel writer, Theroux first
came to the attention of the critics with the
publication of *The Great Railway Bazaar* and *The Old
Patagonian Express*.

Novels
Waldo, Houghton Mifflin (U.S.), 1967 . . £175/£30
ditto, Bodley Head, 1968 . . . . . . £150/£25
Fong and the Indians, Houghton Mifflin (U.S.), 1968
. . . . £125/£35
ditto, Hamish Hamilton, 1976 . . . . £65/£20
Girls at Play, Houghton Mifflin (U.S.), 1969 £100/£20
ditto, Bodley Head, 1969 . . . . . . £45/£15
Murder in Mount Holly, Ross, 1969 . £2,250/£300
Jungle Lovers, Houghton Mifflin (U.S.), 1971 £75/£20
ditto, Bodley Head, 1971 . . . . . . £75/£20
Saint Jack, Bodley Head, 1973 . . . . £40/£10
ditto, Houghton Mifflin (U.S.), 1973 . . . £40/£10
The Black House, Hamish Hamilton, 1974 . . £30/£5
ditto, Houghton Mifflin (U.S.), 1974 . . . £25/£5
The Family Arsenal, Hamish Hamilton, 1976 . £30/£5
ditto, Houghton Mifflin (U.S.), 1976 . . . £30/£5
Picture Palace, Hamish Hamilton, 1978 . . £25/£5
ditto, Houghton Mifflin (U.S.), 1978 . . . £25/£5
The Mosquito Coast, Hamish Hamilton, 1981 . £25/£5
ditto, Houghton Mifflin (U.S.), 1982 . . . £20/£5
ditto, Houghton Mifflin (U.S.), 1982 (350 signed
copies, slipcase) . . . . £100/£65
Doctor Slaughter, Hamish Hamilton, 1984 . . £20/£5
ditto, as *Half Moon Street*, Houghton Mifflin (U.S.),
1984 . . . . £20/£5
O-Zone, Hamish Hamilton, 1986 . . . . £20/£5
ditto, Putnam (U.S.), 1986 . . . . . £15/£5
My Secret History, Hamish Hamilton, 1989 . £15/£5
ditto, London Limited Editions, 1989 (150 signed,
numbered copies) £75
ditto, Putnam (U.S.), 1989 . . . . . £15/£5
Dr De Marr, Hutchinson, 1990 . . . . £15/£5
Chicago Loop, Hamish Hamilton, 1990 . . £15/£5
ditto, Random House (U.S.), 1991 . . . £15/£5
Millroy the Magician, Hamish Hamilton, 1993 £10/£5
ditto, Random House (U.S.), 1994 . . . £10/£5
My Other Life, Hamish Hamilton, 1996 . . £10/£5
ditto, Houghton Mifflin (U.S.), 1996 . . £10/£5
Kowloon Tong, Hamish Hamilton, 1997 . £10/£5
ditto, Houghton Mifflin (U.S.), 1997 . . £10/£5
ditto, Franklin Library (U.S.), 1998 (1,350 signed
copies) £40
The Collected Short Novels, Hamish Hamilton, 1998 .
. . . . £10/£5

Hotel Honolulu, Hamish Hamilton, 2000 . . £10/£5
ditto, Houghton Mifflin (U.S.), 2001 . . . £10/£5

Short Stories

Sinning with Annie and Other Stories, Houghton
Mifflin (U.S.), 1972 . . . . £100/£20
ditto, Hamish Hamilton, 1975 . . . . £65/£15
The Consul's File, Hamish Hamilton, 1977 . £25/£5
ditto, Houghton Mifflin (U.S.), 1977 . . . £20/£5
World's End, Hamish Hamilton, 1980 . . . £15/£5
ditto, Houghton Mifflin (U.S.), 1980 . . . £15/£5
The London Embassy, Hamish Hamilton, 1982 £10/£5
ditto, Houghton Mifflin (U.S.), 1983 . . . £10/£5
The Collected Stories, Viking (U.S.), 1997 . . £10/£5

Travel

The Great Railway Bazaar: By Train Through Asia,
Hamish Hamilton, 1975 . . . . . . £100/£25
ditto, Houghton Mifflin (U.S.), 1975 . . £65/£20
*The Old Patagonian Express: By Train Through the
Americas*, Hamish Hamilton, 1979. . . . £20/£5
ditto, Houghton Mifflin (U.S.), 1979 . . . £20/£5
The Kingdom by the Sea, Hamish Hamilton, 1983. .
. . . . £15/£5
ditto, Houghton Mifflin (U.S.), 1983 . . . £15/£5
ditto, Houghton Mifflin (U.S.), 1983 (250 signed,
numbered copies, slipcase) . . . . . £65/£40
Sailing through China, Russell, 1984 (150 [400]
signed copies, glassine d/w). . . . . £75/£65
ditto, Hamish Hamilton, 1984. . . . . . £15/£5
ditto, Houghton Mifflin (U.S.), 1984 . . . £15/£5
Patagonia Revisited, Russell, 1985 (with Bruce
Chatwin) . . . . £25/£10
ditto, Russell, 1985 (250 copies, cellophane d/w) .
. . . . £250/£200
ditto, Houghton Mifflin (U.S.), 1986 . . £20/£10
ditto, as *Nowhere Is a Place*, Sierra Club (U.S.), 1991.
. . . . £20/£10
Sunrise with Seamonsters, Hamish Hamilton, 1985 .
. . . . £10/£5
ditto, Houghton Mifflin (U.S.), 1985 . . . £10/£5
The Imperial Way, Hamish Hamilton, 1985 (photographs by Steve McCurry) . . . . . £10/£5
ditto, Houghton Mifflin (U.S.), 1985 . . . £10/£5
Riding the Iron Rooster: By Train Through China,
Hamish Hamilton, 1988. . . . . . . £10/£5
ditto, Putnam (U.S.), 1988 . . . . . . £10/£5
*Travelling the World, The Illustrated Travels of Paul
Theroux*, Sinclair-Stevenson, 1990. . . . £10/£5
ditto, Random House (U.S.), 1991 . . . . £10/£5
The Happy Isles of Oceana: Paddling the Pacific,
Hamish Hamilton, 1992 . . . . £10/£5
ditto, Putnam (U.S.), 1992 . . . . . . £10/£5
The Pillars of Hercules, Hamish Hamilton, 1995 . .
. . . . £10/£5
ditto, Putnam (U.S.), 1995 . . . . . . £10/£5
Fresh Air Fiend: Travel Writings, 1985-2000,
Houghton Mifflin (U.S.), 2000 . . . . £15/£5
ditto, Hamish Hamilton, 2000 . . . . £10/£5

Dark Star Safari: Overland from Cairo to Cape Town,
Hamish Hamilton, 2002 . . . . £10/£5
ditto, Houghton Mifflin (U.S.), 2003 . . . £10/£5

Others

V.S. Naipaul: An Introduction to his Work, Deutsch,
1972 . . . . £1,000/£150
ditto, Africana (U.S.), 1972 . . . . £1,250/£150
A Christmas Card, Hamish Hamilton, 1978 . £10/£5
ditto, Houghton Mifflin (U.S.), 1978 . . . £10/£5
London Snow, Russell, 1979 (450 signed copies,
glassine d/w) . . . . £100/£85
ditto, Hamish Hamilton, 1980 . . . . . £15/£5
ditto, Houghton Mifflin (U.S.), 1980 . . . £15/£5
The Turn of the Years, Russell, 1982 (150 signed
copies) £150
The Shortest Day of the Year: A Christmas Fantasy,
Sixth Chamber Press, 1986 (175 signed copies) £60
ditto, Sixth Chamber Press, 1986 (26 signed copies on
handmade paper). £100
The White Man's Burden, A Play in Two Acts,
Hamish Hamilton, 1987 . . . . £15/£5
Sir Vidia's Shadow, Hamish Hamilton, 1998 . £10/£5
ditto, Houghton Mifflin (U.S.), 1998 . . . £10/£5

DYLAN THOMAS
(b.1914 d.1953)

Notorious Fitzrovian poet and playwright, Thomas
died after taking morphine and drinking around a
dozen whiskies in the White Horse Tavern in
Greenwich Village, New York.

18 Poems, The Sunday Referee/The Parton Bookshop,
1934 (first issue, c.250 copies, flat spine, no
advertisment leaf between half title and title) . . .
. . . . £2,500/£1,000
ditto, The Sunday Referee/The Parton Bookshop, 1934
(second issue, c.250 copies, round-backed spine, with
advertisment leaf between half title and title) . . .
. . . . £1,000/£300
Twenty-Five Poems, Dent, 1936 . . . . £700/£150
The Map of Love: Verse and Prose, Dent, 1939 (first
issue in mauve cloth with very smooth texture, gilt
blocking, top edge stained) . . . . £325/£225
ditto, Dent, 1939 (second issue in plum-coloured cloth
with course texture, gilt blocking, top edge stained) .
. . . . £200/£100
ditto, Dent, 1939 (third issue, blue blocking, top edge
stained) . . . . £125/£75
ditto, Dent, 1939 (fourth issue, blue blocking, top edge
unstained). . . . . £75/£25
The World I Breathe, New Directions (U.S.), 1939
(first state binding with a single star to each side of
the title on the spine). . . . . . £500/£200
ditto, New Directions (U.S.), 1939 (second state
binding, with five stars on the spine) . . £350/£100

Portrait of the Artist as a Young Dog, Dent, 1940 . .
. . . . £300/£75
ditto, New Directions (U.S.), 1940 . . . £200/£45
From In Memory of Ann Jones, Caseg Press, [1942]
(500 copies, broadside) £300
New Poems, New Directions (U.S.), 1943 (paper
boards, d/w) . . . . £200/£75
ditto, New Directions (U.S.), 1943 (wraps in d/w) . .
. . . . £125/£75
Deaths and Entrances, Dent, 1946 . . . £250/£75
ditto, Gregynog Press, 1984 (250 copies, John Piper
illustrated edition, in slipcase). . . . . £250/£100
ditto, Gregynog Press, 1984 (28 roman numbered
copies, in slipcase). . . . . . . £1,000/£900
Selected Writings of Dylan Thomas, New Directions
(U.S.), 1946 . . . . £125/£25
Twenty-Six Poems, Dent/New Directions, [1950] (Nos
I-X signed, numbered copies of 150, printed on
Japanese vellum, in slipcase) £6,000
ditto, Dent/New Directions, [1950] (Nos 11-60 signed,
numbered copies of 150, slipcase) £2,000
ditto, Dent/New Directions, [1950] (Nos 61-147
signed, numbered copies of 150, slipcase). . £2,000
In Country Sleep and Other Poems, New Directions
(U.S.), 1952 . . . . £200/£65
ditto, New Directions (U.S.), 1952 (100 signed,
numbered copies, in slipcase) . . £2,000/£1,750
Collected Poems, 1934-1952, Dent, 1952 . £75/£15
ditto, Dent, 1952 (65 signed, numbered copies). £2,000
ditto, New Directions (U.S.), 1953 . . £65/£10
The Doctors and the Devils, Dent, 1953 . £30/£5
ditto, New Directions (U.S.), 1953 . . . £25/£5
Two Epigrams Of Fealty, privately printed for
members of the Court of Redonda, 1947 (30
numbered copies, folded leaflet) £250
Galsworthy and Gawsworth, privately printed for
members of the Court of Redonda, [1953] (30
numbered copies, folded leaflet) £250
Under Milk Wood: A Play for Voices, Dent, 1954 . .
. . . . £100/£15
ditto, New Directions (U.S.), 1954 . . . £45/£10
Quite Early One Morning, Dent, 1954 . . £75/£15
ditto, New Directions (U.S.), 1954 . . . £65/£15
Conversation About Christmas, New Directions
(U.S.), 1954 (wraps, in envelope) . . . £125/£95
Adventures in the Skin Trade and Other Stories, New
Directions (U.S.), 1955 . . . . . . £100/£20
ditto, Putnam, 1955 . . . . £100/£20
A Prospect of the Sea, Dent, 1955 . . . £40/£10
A Child's Christmas in Wales, New Directions (U.S.),
1954 [1955]. . . . . £75/£20
ditto, New Directions (U.S.), [1969] (100 copies,
illustrated by Fritz Eichenberg, with signed portfolio)
. . . . £350/£200
ditto, New Directions (U.S.), [1969] (trade edition
illustrated by Fritz Eichenberg). . . . £35/£10
ditto, Dent, 1978 (illustrated by Edward Ardizzone) .
. . . . £65/£20

ditto, Godine (U.S.), 1980 (illustrated by Ardizzone) .
. . . . £35/£10
Letters to Vernon Watkins, Dent/Faber, 1957 £30/£10
ditto, New Directions (U.S.), 1957 . . . £25/£10
The Beach of Falesa, Stein & Day (U.S.), 1963 (film
script) . . . . £30/£10
ditto, Cape, 1964 . . . . £25/£10
Twenty Years A-Growing, Dent, 1964 (film script) .
. . . . £25/£10
Rebecca's Daughters, Triton, 1965 (film script with a
foreword by Sidney Box) . . . . . . £25/£5
ditto, Little, Brown (U.S.), 1965 . . . . £25/£5
Me and My Bike, McGraw-Hill (U.S.), 1965 £45/£15
ditto, Triton, 1965 (film script) . . . . £35/£10
ditto, Triton, 1965 (500 copies, in slipcase) . £75/£50
The Doctor and the Devils and Other Scripts, New
Directions (U.S.), 1966 . . . . . . £20/£5
Selected Letters of Dylan Thomas, Dent, 1966. . .
. . . . £25/£10
ditto, New Directions (U.S.), 1967 . . . £25/£10
The Notebooks of Dylan Thomas, New Directions
(U.S.), 1967 . . . . £25/£10
ditto, as *Poet in the Making: The Notebooks of Dylan
Thomas*, Dent, 1968 . . . . £25/£10
Twelve More Letters, Turret Books, 1969 (175 copies,
acetate d/w) . . . . £65/£55
ditto, Turret Books, 1969 (26 lettered copies, acetate
d/w) . . . . £125/£100
Dylan Thomas: Early Prose Writings, Dent, 1971 . .
. . . . £20/£5
ditto, New Directions (U.S.), 1972 . . . . £20/£5
The Death of the King's Canary, Hutchinson, 1976
(with John Davenport) . . . . . . £15/£5
ditto, Viking (U.S.), 1976. . . . . . . £15/£5
*Drawings to Poems by Dylan Thomas by Ceri
Richards*, Enitharmon Press, 1980 (180 copies) £75
Collected Letters, Dent, 1985. . . . . £25/£10
ditto, Macmillan (U.S.), 1976 . . . . £25/£10
Dylan Thomas: The Notebook Poems, 1930-1934,
Dent, 1989 . . . . £25/£10
Dylan Thomas: The Broadcasts, Dent, 1991 . £15/£5
Dylan Thomas: The Filmscripts, Dent, 1995 . £15/£5

EDWARD THOMAS
(b.1878 d.1917)

Not a 'war poet', although he did die in the First
World War, Thomas's love of nature comes through
in his best work.

Poetry
Six Poems, Pear Tree Press, [1916] (pseud. 'Edward
Eastway', copies in boards of total edition of 100) .
. . . . £1,500
ditto, Pear Tree Press, [1916] (pseud. 'Edward
Eastway', copies in wraps of total edition of 100). .
. . . . £1,500

ditto, Pear Tree Press, 1927 . . . . . . £250
Poems, Selwyn & Blount, 1917 (525 copies, pseud. 'Edward Eastway') £400
ditto, Holt (U.S.), 1917 (525 copies). . . . £350
Last Poems, Selwyn & Blount, 1918 . . . £300
Collected Poems, Selwyn & Blount, 1920 . £250/£75
ditto, Selwyn and Blount, 1920 (deluxe edition, 100 copies) £600
ditto, Seltzer (U.S.), 1921. . . . . . £200/£65
Augustan Books of Modern Poetry - Edward Thomas, Benn, [1926] (wraps) £10
Selected Poems, Gregynog Press, 1926 (275 copies) .
. . . . £200
ditto, Gregynog Press, 1926 (25 specially bound copies) £1,000
Two Poems, Ingpen & Grant, 1927 (85 copies). £400
Collected Poems, Ingpen & Grant, 1928 . £75/£25
The Last Sheaf, Cape, [1928] . . . . £45/£20

Others
The Woodland Life, Blackwood, 1897 (first issue, red cloth) £500
ditto, Blackwood, 1897 (second issue, blue/green buckram) £400
ditto, Blackwood, 1897 (second issue, smooth green cloth) £300
Horae Solitaire, Duckworth, 1902 (300 copies) £200
ditto, Dutton (U.S.), [1902] £150
Oxford, A. & C. Black, [1903] £50
ditto, A. & C. Black, [1903] (deluxe edition, 300 copies) £200
Rose Acre Papers, Langham, 1904 . . . . £100
Beautiful Wales, A. & C. Black, 1905 . . . £75
The Heart of England, Dent, 1906 . . . . £50
ditto, Dutton (U.S.), [1906] £40
Richard Jefferies, Hutchinson, 1909 . . . £50
ditto, Little, Brown (U.S.), 1909 . . . . . £40
The South Country, Dent, 1909 . . . . . £50
Rest and Unrest, Duckworth, 1910 . . . . £45
ditto, Dutton (U.S.), 1910. . . . . . . £45
Rose Acre Papers, Duckworth, 1910 . . . £35
Feminine Influence on the Poets, Secker, 1910 £45
ditto, John Lane (U.S.), 1911. . . . . . £35
Windsor Castle, Blackie & Son, 1910 . . . £45
The Isle of Wight, Blackie & Son, 1911. . . £45
Light and Twilight, Duckworth, 1911 . . . £30
Maurice Maeterlink, Methuen, [1911] . . . £30
Celtic Stories, Clarendon Press, 1911 . . . £75
The Tenth Muse, Secker, [1911]. £35
Algernon Charles Swinburne, Secker, 1912 . £35
George Borrow, Chapman & Hall, 1912 . . £25
Lafcadio Hearn, Houghton Mifflin (U.S.), 1912 £20
ditto, Constable, 1912. . . . . £20
Norse Tales, Clarendon Press, 1912 . . . . £45
The Icknield Way, Constable, 1913 . . . . £75
The Country, Batsford, [1913] £50
The Happy-Go-Lucky Morgans, Duckworth, [1913] .
. . . . £200
Walter Pater, Secker, 1913 . . . . . . £25

In Pursuit of Spring, Nelson, [1914] . . . £75
Four and Twenty Blackbirds, Duckworth, [1915] £40
The Life of the Duke of Marlborough, Chapman & Hall, 1915 . . . . £20
Keats, Jack, 1916 . . . . £15
ditto, Dodge (U.S.), [1916] £15
A Literary Pilgrim in England, Dodd, Mead (U.S.), 1917 . . . . £25
ditto, Methuen, [1917] £20
Cloud Castle, Duckworth, [1922] . . . £100/£25
ditto, Dutton (U.S.), [1923] . . . . . £65/£15
Essays of Today and Yesterday, Harrap, [1926] (wraps) £20
Chosen Essays, Gregynog Press, 1926 (350 copies) .
. . . . £75
The Childhood of Edward Thomas, Faber, 1938 £25
The Friend of the Blackbird, Pear Tree Press, 1938 .
. . . . £50
The Prose of Edward Thomas, Falcon Press, 1948 .
. . . . £30/£10
Letters from Edward Thomas to Gordon Bottomley, O.U.P., 1968 . . . . £20/£5
Autumn Thoughts, Tragara Press, 1975 (190 numbered copies, wraps) £45
The Diary of Edward Thomas, Whittington Press, 1977 (575 copies, slipcase) . . . . £100/£75
Edward Thomas on the Countryside: A Selection, Faber, 1977 . . . . £10/£5
Edward Thomas: A Centenary Celebration, Eric and Joan Stevens, 1978 (75 copies signed by the artist) .
. . . . £75
Four Letters to Frederick Evans, Tragara Press, 1978 (150 numbered copies, wraps) £40
Reading out of Doors, Tragara Press, 1978 (110 numbered copies, wraps) £35
The Chessplayers, and other essays, Whittington Press, 1981 (375 copies). £75
A Selection of Letters to Edward Garnett, Tragara Press, 1981 (175 numbered copies, wraps) . £40
The Letters of Edward Thomas to Jesse Berridge, Enitharmon, 1981 . . . . £25
The Fear of Death, Tragara Press, 1982 (95 numbered copies, wraps) £45
A Sportsman's Tale, Tragara Press, 1983 (125 numbered copies, wraps) £40
A Handful of Letters: Edward and Helen Thomas, Tragara Press, 1985 (wraps). £20

FLORA THOMPSON
(b.1877 d.1947)

Flora Thompson's autobiographical writings are popularly collected together as *Lark Rise to Candleford*. Her descriptions of countryside life are precise and unsentimental.

Poetry
Bog Myrtle and Peat, Allan, 1921 (wraps) . . £75

Prose
Guide to Liphook, Bramshott and Neighbourhood,
Williams, 1925 (wraps) £30
Lark Rise, O.U.P., 1939 . . . . . . £75/£20
Over to Candleford, O.U.P., 1941 . . . £65/£15
Candleford Green, O.U.P., 1943. . . . £65/£15
Lark Rise to Candleford, O.U.P., 1945 . . £75/£20
ditto, Crown (U.S.), 1983. . . . . . . £15/£5
Still Glides the Stream, O.U.P., 1948 . . £40/£10
ditto, Crown (U.S.), 1984 . . . . £15/£5
A Country Calendar, O.U.P., 1979 . . . £15/£5
The Peverel Papers, Century, 1986 . . . . £15/£5

HENRY DAVID THOREAU
(b.1817 d.1862)

The two books published by Thoreau during his lifetime were not a success, but since his death *Walden* has come to be regarded in the U.S. as a classic.

A Week on the Concord and Merrimack Rivers,
Munroe & Co. (U.S.), 1849 . . . . . . £4,000
ditto, Ticknor & Fields (U.S.), 1862 (reissue of Munroe
sheets). £2,000
ditto, Ticknor & Fields (U.S.), 1868 . . . £250
Walden, Ticknor & Fields (U.S.), 1854 . . . £6,000
ditto, Ticknor & Fields (U.S.), 1862 . . . . £300
ditto, Douglas, 1884 . . . . £450
Excursions, Ticknor & Fields (U.S.), 1863 . . £300
The Maine Woods, Ticknor & Fields (U.S.), 1864 (in
the first issue the books listed in the adverts are
priced) £300
Cape Cod, Ticknor & Fields (U.S.), 1865 . . £300
Letters to Various Persons, Ticknor & Fields (U.S.),
1865 . . . . £250
A Yankee in Canada, Ticknor & Fields (U.S.), 1866 .
. . . . £1,000
Early Spring in Massachusetts, Houghton, Mifflin
(U.S.), 1881 . . . . £250
Summer from the Journal, Houghton, Mifflin (U.S.),
1884 . . . . £250
Winter from the Journal, Houghton, Mifflin (U.S.),
1888 . . . . £250
Autumn from the Journal, Houghton, Mifflin (U.S.),
1892 . . . . £250

Familiar Letters, Houghton, Mifflin (U.S.), 1894 £150
ditto, Houghton, Mifflin (U.S.), 1894 (150 deluxe
copies). £200
Poems of Nature, John Lane (U.K.)/Houghton, Mifflin
(U.S.), 1895 . . . . £300
Some Unpublished Letters, Marion Press (U.S.), 1899
(150 copies) £200
The Service, Goodspeed (U.S.), 1902 (500 copies) £125
ditto, Goodspeed (U.S.), 1902 (25 copies on Japan
vellum) £250
The First and Last Journeys of Thoreau, Bibliophile
Society (U.S.), 1904 (489 copies, slipcase) £250/£200
Sir Walter Raleigh, Bibliophile Society (U.S.), 1905
(489 copies, slipcase) . . . . £250/£200
The Writings, Houghton, Mifflin (U.S.), 1906
('Walden Edition', blue cloth, 20 vols). . . £1,000
ditto, Houghton, Mifflin (U.S.), 1906 ('Manuscript
Edition Edition', 400 of 600 numbered sets, green
cloth with leaf of manuscript bound in, 20 vols) . .
. . . . £4,000
ditto, Houghton, Mifflin (U.S.), 1906 ('Manuscript
Edition Edition', approx 200 of 600 copies, custom
bindings and extra set of frontispieces, 20 vols) . .
. . . . £6,000
Unpublished Poems by Bryant and Thoreau,
Bibliophile Society (U.S.), 1907 (470 copies,
slipcase) . . . . £100/£150
Two Thoreau Letters, [Edwin Bliss Hill (U.S.), 1916]
(c.250 copies, wraps) £125
The Moon, Houghton, Mifflin (U.S.), 1927 (500
copies, slipcase) . . . . £125/£100
The Transmigration of the Seven Brahmans, Rudge
(U.S.), 1931 (200 copies, slipcase) . . . £175/£150
ditto, Rudge (U.S.), 1932 (1,000 copies) . £100/£25
Collected Poems, Packard and Co. (U.S.), 1943 .
. . . . £100/£50
Consciousness in Concord, Houghton, Mifflin (U.S.),
1958 . . . . £50/£20
The Correspondence, New York Univ. Press (U.S.),
1958 . . . . £100/£35

COLIN THUBRON
(b.1939)

Popularly considered a travel writer, Thubron's novels are also critical and commercial successes.

Travel
Mirror to Damascus, Heinemann, 1967. . £75/£15
ditto, Little, Brown (U.S.), 1968 . . . . £50/£10
The Hills of Adonis: A Quest In Lebanon, Heinemann, 1968 . . . . £25/£5
ditto, Little, Brown (U.S.), 1969 . . . . . £20/£5
Jerusalem, Heinemann, 1969 . . . . . £25/£5
ditto, Little, Brown (U.S.), 1969 . . . . . £20/£5
Journey into Cyprus, Heinemann, 1975. . £40/£10

Istanbul, Time Life (Amsterdam), 1978 (with others) .
. . . . £25
The Venetians, Time Life (Amsterdam), 1980 (with others). £10
The Ancient Mariners, Time Life (Amsterdam), 1981 (with others) £10
Among the Russians, Heinemann, 1983. . £30/£10
ditto, as *Where the Nights are Longest: Travels by Car Through Western Russia*, Random House (U.S.), 1984 . . . .£20/£5
Behind the Wall: A Journey Through China, Heinemann, 1987 . . . . £25/£10
ditto, Atlantic Monthly Press (U.S.), 1988 . .£15/£5
The Silk Road—China: Beyond the Celestial Kingdom, Pyramid, 1989 . . . . . £45/£20
ditto, Simon & Schuster (U.S.), 1989 . . £45/£20
The Lost Heart of Asia, Heinemann, 1994 . .£15/£5
ditto, HarperCollins (U.S.), 1994. . . . . £10/£5
In Siberia, Chatto & Windus, 1999 . . . .£15/£5
ditto, HarperCollins (U.S.), 1999. . . . .£10/£5

Novels
The God in the Mountain, Heinemann, 1977 £30/£10
ditto, Norton (U.S.), 1977. . . . . . .£20/£5
Emperor, Heinemann, 1978 . . . . . .£30/£10
A Cruel Madness, Heinemann, 1984 . . .£15/£5
ditto, Atlantic Monthly Press (U.S.), 1985 . .£10/£5
Falling, Heinemann, 1989 . . . . . .£10/£5
ditto, Atlantic Monthly Press (U.S.), 1990 . .£10/£5
Turning Back the Sun, Heinemann, 1991 . .£10/£5
ditto, HarperCollins (U.S.), 1992. . . . .£10/£5
Distance, Heinemann, 1996 . . . . . .£10/£5
To the Last City, Chatto & Windus, 2002 . .£10/£5

Others
The Royal Opera House, Covent Garden, Hamish Hamilton, 1982 . . . .£10/£5

JAMES THURBER
(b.1894 d.1961)

An American short story writer and cartoonist whose best-known character, Walter Mitty, takes refuge in his daydreams from a confusing modern world.

Fiction
Is Sex Necessary? Or Why Do You Feel the Way You Do, Harper (U.S.), 1929 (with E.B. White) . . .
. . . . £1,000/£200
ditto, Heinemann, 1930 . . . . . . £500/£100
The Owl in the Attic and Other Perplexities, Harper (U.S.), 1931 . . . .£750/£100
ditto, Harper, 1931 . . . .£400/£45
The Seal in the Bedroom and Other Predicaments, Harper (U.S.), 1932 . . . .£500/£75
ditto, Harper, 1932 . . . .£250/£35

My Life and Hard Times, Harper (U.S.), 1933 . . .
. . . . £250/£35
ditto, Harper, 1933 . . . .£100/£25
The Middle-Aged Man on the Flying Trapeze, Harper (U.S.), 1935 . . . .£250/£35
ditto, Hamish Hamilton, 1935 . . . .£100/£25
Let Your Mind Alone! And Other More or Less Inspirational Pieces, Harper (U.S.), 1937 . £250/£35
ditto, Hamish Hamilton, 1937 . . . .£100/£25
The Last Flower: A Parable in Pictures, Harper (U.S.), 1939 . . . .£150/£25
ditto, Hamish Hamilton, 1939 . . . . £75/£20
Cream of Thurber, Hamish Hamilton, 1939 £45/£15
Fables for Our Time and Famous Poems Illustrated, Harper (U.S.), 1940 . . . .£150/£25
ditto, Hamish Hamilton, 1940 . . . . £75/£20
My World–And Welcome To It, Harcourt Brace (U.S.), 1942 . . . . £250/£40
ditto, Hamish Hamilton, 1942 . . . . £125/£25
Thurber's Men, Women and Dogs, Harcourt Brace (U.S.), 1943 . . . .£125/£25
ditto, Hamish Hamilton, 1943 . . . . £65/£15
The Thurber Carnival, Harper (U.S.), 1945 £100/£20
ditto, Hamish Hamilton, 1945 . . . . £50/£10
The Beast in Me and Other Animals, Harcourt Brace (U.S.), 1948 . . . . £45/£15
ditto, Hamish Hamilton, 1949 . . . . £25/£10
The Thurber Album: A New Collection of Pieces About People, Simon & Schuster (U.S.), 1952 . .
. . . . £45/£15
ditto, Hamish Hamilton, 1952 . . . . £25/£10
Thurber Country: A New Collection of Pieces About Males and Females, Simon & Schuster (U.S.), 1953 .
. . . . £35/£10
ditto, Hamish Hamilton, 1953 . . . . .£20/£5
Thurber's Dogs, Simon & Schuster (U.S.), 1955 £30/£5
ditto, Hamish Hamilton, 1955 . . . . .£20/£5
A Thurber Garland, Hamish Hamilton, 1955 £25/£10
Further Fables for Our Time, Simon & Schuster (U.S.), 1956 . . . .£25/£5
ditto, Hamish Hamilton, 1956 . . . . .£20/£5
Alarms and Diversions, Harper (U.S.), 1957 .£25/£5
ditto, Hamish Hamilton, 1957 . . . . .£20/£5
Lanterns and Lances, Harper (U.S.), 1961 . .£25/£5
ditto, Hamish Hamilton, 1961 . . . . .£20/£5
Credos and Curios, Harper (U.S.), 1962 . .£25/£5
ditto, Hamish Hamilton, 1962 . . . . .£20/£5
Vintage Thurber, Hamish Hamilton, 1963 (2 vols) .
. . . . £40/£10
Thurber and Company, Harper (U.S.), 1966 .£25/£5
ditto, Hamish Hamilton, 1967 . . . . .£20/£5

Children's Books
Many Moons, Harcourt Brace (U.S.), 1943 (illustrated by Louis Slobodkin). . . . . . . £200/£45
ditto, Hamish Hamilton, 1945 . . . .£150/£40
ditto, Joseph & Roe (U.S.), 1958 (illustrated by Philip Reed, 250 copies signed by illustrator). . . £125
The Great Quillow, Harcourt Brace (U.S.), 1944 (illustrated by Doris Lee) . . . . . £100/£25

The **White Deer**, Harcourt Brace (U.S.), 1945
(illustrated by Thurber and Don Freeman) . £50/£15
ditto, Hamish Hamilton, 1946 . . . . £40/£15
The **13 Clocks**, Simon & Schuster (U.S.), 1950
(illustrated by Mark [Marc] Simont) . . £100/£15
ditto, Hamish Hamilton, 1951 . . . . £40/£15
The **Wonderful O**, Simon & Schuster (U.S.), 1957
(illustrated by Marc Simont) . . . . £45/£15
ditto, Hamish Hamilton, 1958 . . . . £40/£15

Plays
'Oh My, Omar': A Musical Comedy, Ohio State Univ.
(U.S.), 1921 (with Hayward M. Andersen, wraps) .
. . . . £400
Many Moons, Ohio State Univ. (U.S.), 1922 (wraps) .
. . . . £350
Tell Me Not: A Two Act Musical Comedy, Ohio State
Univ. (U.S.), 1924 (wraps) £350
The Male Animal, Random House (U.S.), 1940 (with
Elliott Nugent) . . . . £125/£35
ditto, Hamish Hamilton, 1950 . . . . £35/£10

Non Fiction
Thurber on Humour, Ohioana Library Association
(U.S.), 1953 (wraps). £45
The Years with Ross, Little, Brown (U.S.), 1959 . .
. . . . £25/£10
ditto, Hamish Hamilton, 1959 . . . . £25/£10
Selected Letters of James Thurber, Little, Brown,
1981 (edited by Helen Thurber & Edward Weeks) .
. . . . £15/£5
ditto, Franklin Library (U.S.), 1981 (limited edition) .
. . . . £20
ditto, Hamish Hamilton, 1982 . . . . £15/£10
*Collecting Himself, James Thurber on Writing,
Writers, Humor & Himself*, Harper, 1989 (edited by
Michael J. Rosen) . . . . £10/£5
Thurber On Crime, Mysterious Press (U.S.), 1989
(edited by Robert Lopresti) . . . . . £10/£5

WILLIAM M. TIMLIN
(b.1892 d.1943)

Although Timlin illustrated works by other authors,
he will be best remembered for the beautiful fantasy
The Ship That Sailed to Mars, which he wrote and
illustrated himself.

Novels
The Ship That Sailed to Mars, Harrap, [1923] . . .
. . . . £3,000/£2,000
ditto, Stokes (U.S.), 1923 . . . . £3,000/£2,000
South Africa, A. & C. Black, [1927] . . £30/£10
Out of the Crucible, Cassell, 1929 . . . . £20/£5

J.R.R. TOLKIEN
(b.1892 d.1973)

John Ronald Reuel Tolkien was born in South Africa
but educated in Britain. He was appointed Professor
of Anglo-Saxon at Oxford in 1925 and published a
number of related academic works. He is best known
for his novels dealing with the mythical land of
'Middle-Earth'.

'Middle-Earth' Novels
The Hobbit, Allen & Unwin, 1937 . £17,500/£2,000
ditto, Houghton Mifflin (U.S.), 1938 £5,000/£1,000
*The Fellowship of the Ring, being the First Part of
'The Lord of the Rings'*, Allen & Unwin, 1954 . .
. . . . £4,000/£500
ditto, Houghton Mifflin (U.S.), 1954 . £1,500/£250
*The Two Towers, being the Second Part of 'The Lord
of the Rings'*, Allen & Unwin, 1954 . £3,000/£400
ditto, Houghton Mifflin (U.S.), 1955 . £1,250/£200
*The Return of the King, being the Third Part of 'The
Lord of the Rings'*, Allen & Unwin, 1955. . . .
. . . . £3,000/£400
ditto, Houghton Mifflin (U.S.), 1956 . £1,250/£200
The Lord of the Rings, Allen & Unwin, 1962 (first
combined edition, three books in grey box) £100/£65
ditto, Allen & Unwin, 1964 (deluxe combined edition,
three books bound in buckram, decorated box) . .
. . . . £125/£75
The Silmarillion, Allen & Unwin, 1977 (printed by
either Billing & Sons or William Clowes) . £45/£10
ditto, Houghton Mifflin (U.S.), 1977 . . £35/£10

History of 'Middle-Earth' Titles
The Book of Lost Tales, Part 1, Allen & Unwin, 1983
. . . . £25/£10
ditto, Houghton Mifflin (U.S.), 1984 . . £25/£10
The Book of Lost Tales, Part 2, Allen & Unwin, 1984
. . . . £25/£10
ditto, Houghton Mifflin (U.S.), 1984 . . £25/£10
*The Book of Lost Tales, Part 3: The Lays of
Beleriand*, Allen & Unwin, 1985 . . . £25/£10
ditto, Houghton Mifflin (U.S.), 1985 . . £25/£10
*The Book of Lost Tales, Part 4: The Shaping of
Middle-Earth*, Allen & Unwin, 1986 . . £25/£10
ditto, Houghton Mifflin (U.S.), 1986 . . £25/£10
The Lost Road and Other Writings, Unwin Hyman,
1987 . . . . £25/£10
ditto, Houghton Mifflin (U.S.), 1987 . . £25/£10
*The Return of the Shadow: The History of the Lord of
the Rings, Part 1*, Unwin Hyman, 1988 . £25/£10
ditto, Houghton Mifflin (U.S.), 1988 . . £25/£10
*Treason in Isengard: The History of the Lord of the
Rings, Part 2*, Unwin Hyman, 1989 . . £25/£10
ditto, Houghton Mifflin (U.S.), 1989 . . £25/£10
*The War of the Ring: The History of the Lord of the
Rings, Part 3*, Unwin Hyman, 1990 . . £25/£10
ditto, Houghton Mifflin (U.S.), 1990 . . £25/£10

Sauron Defeated: The History of the Lord of the
Rings, Part 4, Unwin Hyman, 1992 . . £25/£10
ditto, Houghton Mifflin (U.S.), 1992 . . £25/£10

Other 'Middle-Earth' Titles
The Adventures of Tom Bombadil and Other Verses
from 'The Red Book', Allen & Unwin, 1962 . . .
. . . . £100/£20
ditto, Houghton Mifflin (U.S.), 1963 . . £60/£15
The Road Goes Ever On: A Song Cycle, Houghton
Mifflin (U.S.), 1967 . . . . £35/£10
ditto, Allen & Unwin, 1968 . . . . . £35/£10
Bilbo's Last Song, Houghton Mifflin (U.S.), 1974 .
. . . . £25/£5
ditto, Allen & Unwin, 1974 (poster) £10
Unfinished Tales, Allen & Unwin, 1980 . £35/£10
ditto, Houghton Mifflin (U.S.), 1980 . . £35/£10

Other Prose
Farmer Giles of Ham, Allen & Unwin, 1949 £200/£45
ditto, Houghton Mifflin (U.S.), 1950 . . £75/£15
Tree and Leaf, Allen & Unwin, 1964 . . £100/£20
ditto, Houghton Mifflin (U.S.), 1965 . . £35/£10
The Tolkien Reader, Ballantine (U.S.), 1966 £25/£10
Smith of Wootton Major, Allen & Unwin, 1967 £35
ditto, Houghton Mifflin (U.S.), 1967 . . £30/£10
The Father Christmas Letters, Allen & Unwin, 1976 .
. . . . £15/£5
ditto, Houghton Mifflin (U.S.), 1976 . . £15/£5
Pictures by J.R.R. Tolkien, Allen & Unwin, 1979 . .
. . . . £25/£10
ditto, as The Pictures of J.R.R. Tolkien, Houghton
Mifflin (U.S.), 1979 . . . . £25/£10
Poems and Stories, Allen & Unwin, 1980 . £25/£5
ditto, Houghton Mifflin (U.S.), 1980 . . £15/£5
Letters, Allen & Unwin, 1981 . . . . £15/£5
ditto, Houghton Mifflin (U.S.), 1981 . . £15/£5
Mr Bliss, Allen & Unwin, 1982 . . . . £15/£5
ditto, Houghton Mifflin (U.S.), 1983 . . £15/£5
Finn and Hengest: The Fragment and the Episode,
Allen & Unwin, 1983 . . . . . . £15/£5
ditto, Houghton Mifflin (U.S.), 1983 . . £15/£5

Other Poetry
Songs for the Philologists, privately printed, 1936. .
. . . . £1,250
The Homecoming of Beorhtnoth, Allen & Unwin,
1975 . . . . £15/£5

Academic Titles
A Middle English Vocabulary, O.U.P., 1922 (first
issue with ads dated October 1921, 186 ornaments in
cover design, wraps) £450
ditto, O.U.P., 1922 (second issue with ads undated, 184
ornaments in cover design, wraps) £225
ditto, O.U.P. (U.S.), 1922 . . . . . . £75
Sir Gawain and the Green Knight, O.U.P., 1925 (with
errata slip) . . . . £200/£75
ditto, O.U.P. (U.S.), 1925 . . . . . . £75

Beowulf: The Monsters and the Critics, British
Academy, [1936] (wraps) £100
ditto, Folcroft Editions (U.S.), 1972 . . . . £10
Sir Gawain and the Green Knight, Pearl, and Sir
Orfeo, Allen & Unwin, 1975 . . . . £15/£5
ditto, Houghton Mifflin (U.S.), 1975 . . £15/£5

MARY TOURTEL
(b.1873 d.1948)

Rupert Bear was the best-known creation of this
British author and illustrator. Rupert first appeared in
the Daily Express in 1920. Tourtel stopped working
on the cartoon strip in 1935 due to failing eyesight.
The very collectable series of Rupert Annuals began
in the following year after the strip was taken over by
Alfred Bestall. It is now drawn by John Harrold.

'Rupert' Annuals
1936, Daily Express, 1936 (with d/w) . . . £2,000
ditto, Daily Express, 1936 (without d/w) . . £350
1937, Daily Express, 1937 . . . . . . £350
1938, Daily Express, 1938 . . . . . . £300
1939, Daily Express, 1939 . . . . . . £350
1940, Daily Express, 1940 . . . . . . £400
1941, Daily Express, 1941 . . . . . . £450
1942, Daily Express, 1942 (wraps) . . . £500
1943, Daily Express, 1943 (wraps) . . . £350
1944, Daily Express, 1944 (wraps) . . . £300
1945, Daily Express, 1945 (wraps) . . . £250
1946, Daily Express, 1946 (wraps) . . . £200
1947, Daily Express, 1947 (wraps) . . . £200
1948, Daily Express, 1948 (wraps) . . . £75
1949, Daily Express, 1949 (wraps) . . . £75
1950-59, Daily Express, 1950-59 (boards) . £75 each
1960-68, Daily Express, 1960-68 ('magic painting'
pages not coloured in) . . . . . . £100 each
1960-68, Daily Express, 1960-68 ('magic painting'
pages coloured in) . . . . £35 each
1969, Daily Express, 1969 . . . . . . £20
1970-89, Daily Express, 1970-89 . . . . £5
1990, Daily Express, 1990 (anniversary issue) . £10
1991-97, Daily Express, 1991-97 . . . £5 each

'Rupert' Annuals - Facsimiles
1936, Daily Express, 1985 . . . . . £100/£45
1937, Daily Express, 1986 . . . . . . £80
1938, Daily Express, 1989 . . . . . . £100
1939, Daily Express, 1991 . . . . . . £30
1940, Daily Express, 1992 . . . . . . £15
1941, Daily Express, 1993 (in slipcase) . . £20/£10
1942, Daily Express, 1994 (in slipcase) . . £50/£20

'Monster Rupert' Annuals
Monster Rupert, Sampson Low, [1931] (Rupert with
wolf) £900

Monster Rupert, Sampson Low, [1932] (Rupert on log) £750
Monster Rupert, Sampson Low, [1933] (Rupert with bird) £750
Monster Rupert, Sampson Low, [1934] (Rupert with small boy in storeroom) £750
Monster Rupert, Sampson Low, [1948] (Rupert on log, with d/w) £35
Monster Rupert, Sampson Low, [1949] (Rupert with fox, with d/w) £35
Monster Rupert, Sampson Low, [1950] (Rupert helping boy out of hole, with d/w, with all cut-outs intact) £50
Monster Rupert, Sampson Low, [1953] (with all cut-outs intact) £40

'Rupert' Books
The Adventures of Rupert the Little Lost Bear, Nelson, [1921] £900
The Little Bear and the Fairy Child, Nelson, [1922] £1,000
Margot the Midget and Little Bear's Christmas, Nelson, [1922] £850
The Little Bear and the Ogres, Nelson, 1922 . £850
'Rupert Little Bear's Adventures', Sampson Low, 1924-25 (3 books) . . . . £800 each
'Rupert - Little Bear Series', Sampson Low, 1925-27 (6 books) . . . . £600 each
'Little Bear Library' Titles, Sampson Low, [1928-1936] (numbered 1-46) . . . . £150/£50 each
The Rupert Story Book, Sampson Low, [1938] £450
Rupert Little Bear: More Stories, Sampson Low, [1939]. £450
Rupert Again, Sampson Low, [1940] . . . £450

'Adventure' Titles *(all in card covers)*
No. 1, Daily Express £40
Nos. 2-9, Daily Express . . . . . . £15 each
No. 10, Daily Express. . . . . . £25 each
Nos. 11-30, Daily Express . . . . . £20 each
Nos. 31-40, Daily Express . . . . £25 each
Nos. 41-45, Daily Express . . . . £50 each
Nos. 46-48, Daily Express . . . . £60 each
No. 49, Daily Express. £100
No. 50, Daily Express. £125

Daily Express Children's Annuals
Daily Express Children's Annual, 1930, Lane, 1930 . . . . £125
Daily Express Children's Annual, 1931, Lane, 1931 . . . . £125
Daily Express Children's Annual, 1932, Lane, 1932 . . . . £100
Daily Express Children's Annual, 1933, Lane, 1933 . . . . £100
Daily Express Children's Annual, 1934, Lane, 1934 . . . . £100
Daily Express Children's Annual, 1935, Lane, 1935 . . . . £125

Other Collectable Titles by Mary Tourtel
A Horse Book, Grant Richards 'Dumpy Books for Children' series No. 10, 1901, ... £150
The Humpty Dumpty Book, Nursery Rhymes Told in Pictures, Treherne, [1902] £150
The Three Little Foxes, Grant Richards 'Dumpy Books for Children' series No. 21, 1903 . . £150

WILLIAM TREVOR
(b.1928)

A novelist and short story writer, Trevor's work often deals with the corruption of innocence.

Novels
A Standard of Behaviour, Hutchinson, 1958 . . . . £600/£200
ditto, Sphere, 1967 (revised edition, wraps). . £10
The Old Boys, Bodley Head, 1964 . . . £175/£35
ditto, Viking (U.S.), 1964. . . . . . £75/£15
The Boarding House, Bodley Head, 1965 . £125/£35
ditto, Viking (U.S.), 1965. . . . . . . £75/£15
The Love Department, Bodley Head, 1966 £125/£35
ditto, Viking (U.S.), 1967. . . . . . £65/£15
Mrs Eckdorf in O'Neill's Hotel, Bodley Head, 1969 . . . . £65/£15
ditto, Viking (U.S.), 1970. . . . . . £45/£10
Miss Gomez and the Brethren, Bodley Head, 1971 . . . . £65/£15
Elizabeth Alone, Bodley Head, 1973 . . £50/£15
ditto, as *Dreaming*, Stellar Press, 1973 (extract from *Elizabeth Alone*, 225 copies, wraps with d/w) . . . . £135/£100
ditto, Viking (U.S.), 1974. . . . . . £35/£10
The Children of Dynmouth, Bodley Head, 1976 . . . . £35/£10
ditto, Viking (U.S.), 1977. . . . . . . £15/£5
Other People's Worlds, Bodley Head, 1980 . £20/£5
ditto, Viking (U.S.), 1981. . . . . . . £10/£5
Fools of Fortune, Bodley Head, 1983 . . . £20/£5
ditto, Bodley Head, 1983 (50 numbered, signed copies, bound by Kenny's of Galway, slipcase) . . £75
ditto, Viking (U.S.), 1983. . . . . . . £10/£5
The Silence in the Garden, Bodley Head, 1988 £15/£5
ditto, London Limited Editions, 1988 (150 numbered, signed copies, glassine d/w). . . . . £75/£50
ditto, Viking (U.S.), 1988. . . . . . . £10/£5
Felicia's Journey, Viking (U.K.), 1994. . . £10/£5
ditto, Viking (U.S.), 1995. . . . . . . £10/£5
Death in Summer, Viking (U.K.), 1998. . . £10/£5
ditto, Viking (U.S.), 1998. . . . . . . £10/£5
The Story of Lucy Gault, Viking, 2002 . . . £10/£5
ditto, Viking (U.S.), 2002. . . . . . . £10/£5

Short Stories
The Day We Got Drunk on Cake, Bodley Head, 1967. . . . . £500/£40

ditto, Viking (U.S.), 1968 . . . . . . £75/£15
The Ballroom of Romance, Bodley Head, 1972 . .
. . . . £125/£35
ditto, Viking (U.S.), 1972 . . . . . . £45/£10
The Last Lunch of the Season, Covent Garden Press, 1973 (100 numbered, signed copies of 600, wraps) .
. . . . £75
ditto, Covent Garden Press, 1973 (500 copies of 600, wraps) £40
Angels at the Ritz and Other Stories, Bodley Head, 1975 . . . . £45/£15
ditto, Viking (U.S.), 1976 . . . . . . £25/£10
Old School Ties, Lemon Tree Press, 1976 . £75/£20
Lovers of Their Time and Other Stories, Bodley Head, 1978 . . . . £30/£10
ditto, Bodley Head, 1978 (extract, 225 copies, wraps) .
. . . . £125
ditto, Viking (U.S.), 1978 . . . . . . £20/£5
The Distant Past, Poolbeg Press (Dublin), 1979 (wraps) £20
Beyond the Pale, Bodley Head, 1981 . . £20/£5
ditto, Viking (U.S.), 1982 . . . . . . £10/£5
The News From Ireland and Other Stories, Bodley Head, 1986 . . . . £25/£5
ditto, Bodley Head, 1986 (50 numbered, signed copies, bound by Kenny's of Galway, slipcase) . . £125
ditto, Viking (U.S.), 1986 . . . . . . £15/£5
Nights at the Alexandria, Hutchinson, 1987 . £15/£5
ditto, Harper (U.S.), 1987 . . . . . . £10/£5
Family Sins and Other Stories, Bodley Head, 1990 .
. . . . £10/£5
ditto, Viking (U.S.), 1990 . . . . . . £10/£5
The Collected Stories, Viking (U.K.), 1990 . £15/£5
ditto, Viking (U.K.), 1990 (100 signed copies) . . .
. . . . £150/£75
ditto, Viking (U.S.), 1992 . . . . . . £15/£5
Two Lives, Viking (U.K.), 1991 (contains 'Reading Turgenev' & 'My House in Umbria') . . £10/£5
ditto, Viking (U.S.), 1991 . . . . . . £10/£5
Outside Ireland: Selected Stories, Penguin, 1995 (wraps) £5
Marrying Damian, Colophon Press, 1995 (175 numbered, signed copies, wraps) £50
ditto, Colophon Press, 1994 (26 signed copies, slipcase) . . . . £125/£100
After Rain, Viking, 1996 . . . . . . £15/£5
ditto, Viking (U.S.), 1996 . . . . . . £10/£5
The Piano Tuner's Wives, Clarion Press, 1996 (99 copies signed by author and illustrator out of 499 copies, with additional signed proof of one of the illustrations laid in) £100
ditto, Clarion Press, 1996 (150 copies numbered and signed by author and illustrator, of 499 copies) £65
ditto, Clarion Press, 1996 (250 copies numbered out of 499 copies) £30
Death of a Professor, Colophon Press, 1997 (200 numbered, signed copies, wraps) £30
ditto, Colophon Press, 1997 (26 signed copies, slipcase) . . . . £125/£100

Low Sunday, 1950, Colophon Press, 2000 (200 numbered, signed copies, wraps) £40
ditto, Colophon Press, 2000 (26 signed copies, slipcase) . . . . £125/£100
The Hill Bachelors, Viking (U.K.), 2000 . . £15/£5
ditto, Viking (U.S.), 2000 . . . . £15/£5

Plays
The Girl, French, 1968 (wraps) £25
The Old Boys, Poynter, 1971 (wraps) . . . £25
Going Home, French, 1972 (wraps) £10
A Night With Mrs Da Tonka, French, 1972 (wraps) .
. . . . £10
Marriages, French, 1973 (wraps) £10
Scenes from an Album, Co-op Books (Dublin), 1981 (wraps) £15

Children's Title
Juliet's Story, O'Brien Press (Dublin), 1991 £25/£10
ditto, Bodley Head, 1992 . . . . £15/£5
ditto, Simon & Schuster (U.S.), 1992 . . £10/£5

Others
A Writer's Ireland, Viking (U.S.), 1984 . . £15/£5
ditto, Thames & Hudson, 1984 . . . . . £15/£5
Excursions in the Real World, Hutchinson, 1993 . .
. . . . £15/£5
ditto, Hutchinson/London Limited Editions, 1993 (150 signed copies) . . . . £65/£75
ditto, Knopf (U.S.), 1994 . . . . £10/£5

ANTHONY TROLLOPE
(b.1815 d.1882)

Trollope's two most important series of novels are based around the fictitious cathedral town of Barchester. Arguably his greatest contribution to society, however, was the introduction of the pillar-box.

Novels
The Macdermots of Ballycoran, Newby, 1847 (3 vols)
. . . . £6,000
The Kellys and the O'Kelleys, Colburn, 1848 (3 vols) .
. . . . £4,000
La Vendée, Colburn, 1850 (3 vols) £3,000
The Warden, Longman, 1855 (first issue with ads dated September 1854) £2,000
ditto, Longman, 1855 (later issue with ads dated March 1956 or no ads) £1,250
ditto, Longman, 1855 (later issue with ads dated October 1959) £1,000
Barchester Towers, Longman, 1857 (first issue with brick-red endpapers, some with ads dated 1857, 3 vols) £7,500
ditto, Longman, 1857 (second issue with brown endpapers, ads dated 1860, 3 vols) . . . £4,500

The Three Clerks, Bentley, 1858 (3 vols) . . £2,000
Doctor Thorne, Chapman & Hall, 1858 (first edition with 'mamma' on p.18, line 15, 3 vols) . . £7,500
ditto, Chapman & Hall, 1858 (second edition with 'mommon' on p.18, line 15, 3 vols) . . . £650
The Bertrams, Chapman & Hall, 1859 (3 vols). £2,000
Castle Richmond, Chapman & Hall, 1860 (first issue with 16 pages of ads dated February 1860, 3 vols) .
. . . . £2,500
ditto, Chapman & Hall, 1860 (second issue with 32 pages of ads dated May 1860, 3 vols) . . . £1,000
Framley Parsonage, Smith Elder, 1861 (3 vols) £3,000
Orley Farm, Chapman & Hall, 1862 (20 parts, wraps).
. . . . £6,000
ditto, Chapman & Hall, 1862 (2 vols) . . . £3,000
Rachel Ray, Chapman & Hall, 1863 (2 vols) . £1,250
The Small House at Allington, Smith Elder, 1864 (2 vols) £2,000
Can You Forgive Her, Chapman & Hall, 1864-65 (20 parts, wraps). £4,000
ditto, Chapman & Hall, 1864, 1865 (2 vols) . £2,000
Miss Mackenzie, Chapman & Hall, 1865 (2 vols) . .
. . . . £2,000
The Belton Estate, Chapman & Hall, 1866 (3 vols) .
. . . . £2,500
Nina Balakta, Blackwood, 1867 (anonymous, 2 vols).
. . . . £2,000
The Last Chronicle of Barset, Smith Elder, 1866-67 (32 parts, wraps). £5,000
ditto, Smith Elder, 1867 (2 vols) £1,500
The Claverings, Smith Elder, 1867 (2 vols). . £750
Linda Tressel, Blackwood, 1868 (2 vols) . . £750
Phineas Finn, The Irish Member, Virtue, 1869 (2 vols) £1,000
He Knew He Was Right, Strahan, 1868-69 (32 parts, wraps). £3,000
ditto, Strahan, 1869 (2 vols) £1,500
The Vicar of Bullhampton, Bradbury, Evans, 1869-70 (11 parts, wraps). £2,500
ditto, Bradbury, Evans, 1870 . . . . . . £750
The Struggles of Brown, Jones and Robinson, Smith Elder, 1870 . . . . £750
Sir Harry Hotspur of Humblethwaite, Hurst and Blackett, 1871 . . . . £1,000
Ralph the Heir, Hurst and Blackett, 1870-71 (19 parts, wraps). £2,500
ditto, Hurst and Blackett, 1871 (3 vols) . . . £2,000
The Golden Lion of Granpere, Tinsley, 1872 . £650
The Eustace Diamonds, Harpers (U.S.), 1872 (wraps)
. . . . £1,000
ditto, Chapman & Hall, 1873 (3 vols) . . . £750
Phineas Redux, Chapman & Hall, 1874 (2 vols) £750
Lady Anna, Chapman & Hall, 1874 (2 vols) . £2,000
Harry Heathcote of Gangoil, Sampson Low, 1874 .
. . . . £500
The Way We Live Now, Chapman & Hall, 1874-75 (20 parts, wraps). £3,000
ditto, Chapman & Hall, 1875 (2 vols) . . . £1,000

The Prime Minister, Chapman & Hall, 1875-76 (8 parts, wraps or cloth) £1,500
ditto, Chapman & Hall, 1876 (4 vols) . . . £1,000
The American Senator, Chapman & Hall, 1877 (3 vols) £1,500
Is He Popenjoy?, Chapman & Hall, 1878 (3 vols) . .
. . . . £1,000
An Eye for an Eye, Chapman & Hall, 1879 (2 vols) .
. . . . £750
John Caldigate, Chapman & Hall, 1879 (first binding grey cloth, 3 vols) £1,250
ditto, Chapman & Hall, 1879 (second binding dark green cloth, 3 vols) £1,000
Cousin Henry, Chapman & Hall, 1879 (2 vols) £750
The Duke's Children, Chapman & Hall, 1880 (3 vols)
. . . . £1,000
Dr Wortle's School, Chapman & Hall, 1881 (2 vols) .
. . . . £1,000
Ayala's Angel, Chapman & Hall, 1881 (3 vols) £2,000
Kept in the Dark, Chatto & Windus, 1882 (2 vols). .
. . . . £1,000
Marion Fay, Chapman & Hall, 1882 (3 vols) . £1,500
The Fixed Period, Blackwood, 1882 (2 vols) . £1,000
Mr Scarborough's Family, Chatto & Windus, 1883 (3 vols) £1,250
The Landleaguers, Chatto & Windus, 1883 (3 vols) .
. . . . £1,450
An Old Man's Love, Blackwood, 1884 (2 vols) £750
The Noble Jilt, Constable, 1923 (500 copies) . . .
. . . . £250/£100

Short Stories

Tales of All Countries, Chapman & Hall, 1861. £750
Tales of All Countries: Second Series, Chapman & Hall, 1863 . . . . £750
Lotta Schmidt and Other Stories, Strahan, 1867 £650
Why Frau Frohmann Raised Her Prices and Other Stories, Ibister, 1882 (1 vol) £1,000
ditto, Ibister, 1882 (2 vols) £750

Others

The West Indies and the Spanish Main, Chapman & Hall, 1859 . . . . £500
North America, Chapman & Hall, 1862 (2 vols) . . .
. . . . £1,000
Hunting Sketches, Chapman & Hall, 1865 . . £500
Travelling Sketches, Chapman & Hall, 1866 . £500
Clergymen of the Church of England, Chapman & Hall, 1866 . . . . £450
An Editor's Tales, Strahan, 1870 . . . . £450
The Commentaries of Caesar, Blackwood, 1870 £300
Australia and New Zealand, Chapman & Hall, 1873 (2 vols) £750
South Africa, Chapman & Hall, 1878 (2 vols) . £500
How the 'Mastiffs' Went to Iceland, Virtue, 1878 . .
. . . . £650
Thackeray, Macmillan, 1879 . . . . . . £200
The Life of Cicero, Chapman & Hall, 1880 (2 vols) .
. . . . £250
Lord Palmerston, Ibister, 1882 . . . . . £250

An Autobiography, Blackwood, 1883 (first issue with smooth red cloth, 2 vols) £600
ditto, Blackwood, 1883 (second issue with ribbed red cloth, 2 vols) £300
London Tradesmen, Mathews & Marrot, 1927 £75/£25
The New Zealander, Clarendon Press, 1972   £25/£10

MARK TWAIN
(b.1835 d.1910)

A U.S. humourist, novelist and travel writer, 'Twain' was the pen name of Samuel Langhorne Clemens.

The Celebrated Jumping Frog of Calaveras Country and Other Sketches, Webb (U.S.), 1867 (first issue with single leaf of ads on cream paper inserted before title page, last line on p.66 with 'life' unbroken, last line on p.198 with 'this' unbroken). . .   £10,000
ditto, Webb (U.S.), 1867 (second issue with no ads and type broken or worn) £2,000
ditto, Routledge, 1867 (wraps) £3,000
The Innocents Abroad or The New Pilgrim's Progress, American Publishing Company (U.S.), 1868 (first issue, pp.xvii-xviii lacking page reference numbers; p.xviii with last entry reading 'Thankless Devotion - A Newspaper Valedictory'; p.129 with no illustration; p.643 reading Chapter XLI & p.654 reading 'Personal History') £1,000
ditto, Hotten, [1870] (2 vols) £750
ditto, as **Mark Twain's Pleasure Trip on the Continent**, Hotten, [1870] (1 vol.) £400
Mark Twain's (Burlesque) Autobiography & First Romance, Sheldon & Co. (U.S.), 1871 (first issue with no advert for Ball, Black & Co on verso title, wraps). £450
ditto, Sheldon & Co. (U.S.), 1871 (first issue, cloth) .
. . . .   £300
ditto, Hotten, [1871] (cloth) £250
ditto, Hotten, [1871] (wraps) £200
Memoranda From the Galaxy, Backas (Toronto), 1871 . . . .£1,000
Eye Openers/Good Things, Hotten, [1871] (wraps and cloth) £175
Screamers/A Gathering, Hotten, [1871] (wraps and cloth) £175
Roughing It, Routledge, 1872 (2 vols) . . .   £650
ditto, American Publishing Company (U.S.), 1872 . .
. . . .   £650
The Innocents at Home, Routledge, 1872 .   £600
A Curious Dream and Other Sketches, Routledge, [1872]. £600
Mark Twain's Sketches, Routledge, 1872 .   £500
The Choice Humorous Works, Hotten, [1873] .   £400
The Gilded Age, American Publishing Company (U.S.), 1874 (3 vols). £1,000
ditto, Routledge, 1874 (3 vols) £900

Mark Twain's Sketches. Number One, American News Co. (U.S.), [1874] (wraps, first state with rear wrapper blank) £650
ditto, American News Co. (U.S.), [1874] (wraps, second state with insurance ads on rear wrapper) £500
Sketches, New and Old, American Publishing Company (U.S.), 1875 . . . .   £300
Old Times on the Mississippi, Belford (Toronto), 1876 . . . .   £400
Information Wanted and Other Sketches, Routledge (U.S.), 1876 . . . .   £350
The Adventures of Tom Sawyer, Chatto & Windus, 1876 . . . .£6,000
ditto, American Publishing Company (U.S.), 1876 . .
. . . . £10,000
A True Story, and the Recent Carnival of Crime, Osgood (U.S.), 1877. . . . .   £700
Punch, Brother, Punch, Slote, Woodman (U.S.), 1878 (wraps and cloth) £500
ditto, Livingstone, 1878 (wraps) £400
A Tramp Abroad, American Publishing Company (U.S.), 1880 (first state with frontispiece captioned 'Moses') £750
ditto, American Publishing Company (U.S.), 1880 (second state with frontispiece captioned 'Titian's Moses') £250
ditto, Chatto & Windus, 1880 (2 vols) . . .   £400
Conversation, As It Was It Was by the Social Fireside in the Time of the Tudors, [Gunn (U.S.), 1880] (4 copies) £20,000
ditto, Charles Erskine Scott Wood (U.S.), 1882 (50 copies) £10,000
The Prince and the Pauper: A Tale for Young People of All Ages, Chatto & Windus, 1881 . . .£1,000
ditto, Osgood (U.S.), 1882 . . . . . .£1,000
The Stolen White Elephant, Chatto & Windus, 1882 (first state, list of books on verso half title does not mention *The White Elephant*) £300
ditto, Chatto & Windus, 1882 (second state, list of books on verso half title mentions *The White Elephant*) £150
ditto, Osgood (U.S.), 1882 . . . . . .   £150
Life on the Mississippi, Chatto & Windus, 1883   £500
ditto, Osgood (U.S.), 1883 . . . . . .£1,000
The Adventures of Huckleberry Finn, Chatto & Windus, 1884. . . . .£1,250
ditto, Webster (U.S.), 1885 (blue cloth) . .£4,500
ditto, Webster (U.S.), 1885 (green cloth) .£3,000
Mark Twain's Library of Humour, Chatto & Windus, 1888 . . . .   £400
ditto, Webster (U.S.), 1888 . . . . . .   £500
A Connecticut Yankee in King Arthur's Court, Webster (U.S.), 1889 . . . .£1,000
ditto, as **A Yankee at the Court of King Arthur**, Chatto & Windus, 1889 . . . .   £250
The American Claimant, Webster (U.S.), 1892   £200
ditto, Chatto & Windus, 1892 . . . . .   £125
Merry Tales, Webster (U.S.), 1892 . . . .   £350

The $1,000,000 Bank Note, Webster (U.S.), 1893 . .
. . . . £200
ditto, Chatto & Windus, 1893 . . . . . £125
Tom Sawyer Abroad, Chatto & Windus, 1894 . £500
ditto, Webster (U.S.), 1894 . . . . . . £650
The Tragedy of Pudd'nhead Wilson and the Comedy of Those Extraordinary Twins, Chatto & Windus, 1894 . . . . £300
ditto, American Publishing Company (U.S.), 1894 . .
. . . . £400
Personal Recollections of Joan of Arc, Harper (U.S.), 1896 . . . . £200
Tom Sawyer Abroad/Tom Sawyer, Detective/And Other Stories, Harper (U.S.), 1896 . . . . £1,000
Tom Sawyer, Detective, Chatto & Windus, 1897 £400
How to Tell a Story and Other Essays, Harper (U.S.), 1897 . . . . £250
Following the Equator, American Publishing Company (U.S.), 1897 . . . . . . £200
ditto, American Publishing Company (U.S.), 1897 (250 numbered, signed copies) £3,000
ditto, as *More Tramps Abroad*, Chatto & Windus, 1897 . . . . £150
The Man That Corrupted Hadleyburg, Harper (U.S.), 1900 . . . . £150
ditto, Chatto & Windus, 1900 . . . . . £100
To the Person Sitting in Darkness, Anti-Imperialist League (U.S.), 1901 (wraps) £350
A Double Barrelled Detective Story, Harper (U.S.), 1902 . . . . £100
ditto, Chatto & Windus, 1902 . . . . . £75
My Debut as a Literary Person, American Publishing Company, 1903 (vol. 23 in a collected edition) £100
A Dog's Tale, National Anti-Vivesection Society, 1903 (wraps) £250
ditto, Harper (U.K. & U.S.), 1904 . . . . £100
Extracts from Adam's Diary, Harper (U.K. & U.S.), 1904 . . . . £100
King Leopold's Soliloquy, Warren (U.S.), 1905 £75
Eve's Diary, Harper (U.K. & U.S.), 1906 . . £100
What Is Man?, De Vinne Press (U.S.), 1906 (anonymous, 250 copies) £1,000
The $30,000 Bequest, Harper (U.K. & U.S.), 1906 . . . . £75
Christian Science, Harper (U.K. & U.S.), 1907. £200
A Horse's Tale, S.P.C.A./Harper (U.K. & U.S.), 1907. . . . . £50
Is Shakespeare Dead? From My Autobiography, Harper (U.K. & U.S.), 1909 . . . . . £100
Extract from Captain Stormfield's Visit to Heaven, Harper (U.S.), 1909 . . . . £100
Queen Victoria's Jubilee, [privately printed, 1910] .
. . . . £500
Mark Twain's Speeches, Harper (U.S.), 1910 . £100
The Mysterious Stranger, a Romance, Harper (U.S.), 1916 . . . . £100
Mark Twain's Letters, Harper (U.S.), [1917] (2 vols) .
. . . . £100
ditto, Harper (U.S.), [1917] (350 copies, 2 vols) £200

The Curious Republic of Gondour and Other Whimsical Sketches, Boni & Liveright (U.S.), 1919 .
. . . . £75
Europe and Elsewhere, Harper (U.S.), 1923 £200/£50
Mark Twain's Autobiography, Harper (U.S.), 1924 (2 vols, slipcase and d/ws) . . . . . . £200/£65
Mark Twain's Notebook, Harper (U.S.), 1935 . . .
. . . . £150/£50

BARRY UNSWORTH
(b.1930)

Unsworth is not as widely known as he might be, despite *Sacred Hunger* being jointly awarded the 1992 Booker Prize.

Novels
The Partnership, Hutchinson New Authors, 1966 . .
. . . . £275/£50
The Greeks Have a Word For It, Hutchinson, 1967 .
. . . . £100/£20
The Hide, Gollancz, 1970 . . . . £75/£20
ditto, Norton (U.S.), 1996. . . . . . £10/£5
Mooncranker's Gift, Lane, 1973. . . . £65/£10
ditto, Houghton Mifflin (U.S.), 1974 . . £20/£5
The Big Day, Joseph, 1976 . . . . £25/£5
ditto, Mason/Charter (U.S.), 1976 . . . £15/£5
Pascali's Island, Joseph, 1980 . . . . £25/£5
ditto, as *The Idol Hunter*, Simon & Schuster (U.S.), 1980 . . . . £15/£5
The Rage of the Vulture, Granada, 1982 . £20/£5
ditto, Houghton Mifflin (U.S.), 1982 . . £15/£5
Stone Virgin, Hamish Hamilton, 1985 . . £20/£5
ditto, Houghton Mifflin (U.S.), 1986 . . £15/£5
Sugar and Rum, Hamish Hamilton, 1988 . £20/£5
Sacred Hunger, Hamish Hamilton, 1992 . £75/£10
ditto, Hamish Hamilton, 1992 (wraps) . . . £10
ditto, Doubleday (U.S.), 1992 . . . . £15/£5
Morality Play, Hamish Hamilton, 1995 . . £15/£5
ditto, Doubleday (U.S.), 1995 . . . . £10/£5
After Hannibal, Hamish Hamilton, 1996 . £15/£5
ditto, Doubleday (U.S.), 1997 . . . . £10/£5
Losing Nelson, Hamish Hamilton, 1999 . . £10/£5
ditto, Doubleday (U.S.), 1999 . . . . £10/£5
The Songs of the Kings, Hamish Hamilton, 2002 . .
. . . . £10/£5
ditto, Random House (U.S.), 2003 . . . £10/£5

JOHN UPDIKE
(b.1932)

American novelist, short story writer and critic, Updike has the reputation of a keen observer of American life.

Poetry

The Carpentered Hen and Other Tame Creatures, Harper (U.S.), 1958 (first issue d/w with '...a wife and two small children' on the rear inside flap) . . . . £500/£45
ditto, as *Hoping for a Hoopoe*, Gollancz, 1959. . . . . £150/£25
Telephone Poles and Other Poems, Knopf (U.S.), 1963 . . . . £75/£20
ditto, Deutsch, 1964 . . . . £45/£10
Dog's Death, Scott (U.S.), 1965 (100 signed copies, broadside) £125
Bath After Sailing, Country Squires Books, 1968 (125 signed copies, wraps) £350
The Angels, King & Queen Press (U.S.), 1968 (150 copies, wraps in envelope) . . . . £600/£500
On Meeting Authors, Wickford Press (U.S.), 1968 (250 copies, wraps) £500
Midpoint and Other Poems, Knopf (U.S.), 1969 . . . . £75/£15
ditto, Knopf (U.S.), 1969 (350 signed copies in d/w) . . . . £150/£95
ditto, Deutsch, 1969 . . . . £45/£10
The Dance of the Solids, Scientific American (U.S.), [1970] (wraps) £750
Seventy Poems, Penguin, 1971 (wraps) . . . £15
Six Poems, Aloe Editions (U.S.), 1973 (26 signed, lettered copies, wraps) £450
ditto, Aloe Editions (U.S.), 1973 (100 signed, numbered copies, wraps) £200
Cunts, Hallman (U.S.), 1974 (26 signed, lettered copies) £450
ditto, Hallman (U.S.), 1974 (250 signed, numbered copies) £175
Query, Albondocani and Ampersand (U.S.), 1974 (greeting card, 400 [75] copies). . . . £150
Flirt, International Poetry Forum, 1975 (approx 500 copies, broadside) £65
Sunday in Boston, Rook Press (U.S.), 1975 (100 copies signed by author and illustrator, broadside) £125
ditto, Rook Press (U.S.), 1975 (100 copies signed by author only, broadside) £100
ditto, Rook Press (U.S.), 1975 (100 unsigned copies, broadside) £65
Scenic, Roxburghe Club (U.S.), 1976 (150 copies, broadside) £150
Tossing and Turning, Knopf (U.S.), 1977 . . £20/£5
ditto, Deutsch, 1977 . . . . £15/£5
Raining at Magens Bay, John Updike Newsletter (U.S.), 1977 (200 numbered copies, broadside) £25

From the Journal of a Leper, Lord John Press (U.S.), 1978 (26 signed, lettered copies) £200
ditto, Lord John Press (U.S.), 1978 (300 signed, numbered copies) £100
Sixteen Sonnets, Ferguson (U.S.), 1979 (250 signed, numbered copies, wraps) £125
ditto, Ferguson (U.S.), 1979 (26 signed, lettered copies) £200
An Oddly Lovely Day Alone, Waves Press (U.S.), 1979 (276 numbered copies, broadside) £25
Styles of Bloom, Palaemon (U.S.), 1982 (81 signed, numbered copies, broadside) £100
Spring Trio, Palaemon (U.S.), 1982 (150 numbered, signed copies, wraps) £100
Jester's Dozen, Lord John Press, 1984 (50 signed, numbered copies of 200) £100
ditto, Lord John Press, 1984 (150 signed, numbered copies of 200) £75
Facing Nature, Knopf (U.S.), 1985 . . . £15/£5
ditto, Deutsch, 1986 . . . . £10/£5
A Pear Like a Potato, Santa Susanna Press (U.S.), 1986 (broadside, 26 signed, lettered copies) . £75
ditto, Santa Susanna Press (U.S.), 1986 (broadside, 100 signed copies) £45
Two Sonnets, Northouse & Northouse (U.S.), 1987 (40 signed, Roman numbered copies) £250
ditto, Northouse & Northouse (U.S.), 1987 . . £40
On the Move, Bits Press (U.S.), 1988 (120 signed copies, wraps) £125
Recent Poems, 1986-1990, Eurographica (Helsinki), 1990 (350 signed, numbered copies, wraps) . £125
Collected Poems 1953-1993, Knopf (U.S.), 1993 . . . . £15/£5
ditto, Hamish Hamilton, 1993 . . . . . £15/£5
Down Time, Firefly Press (U.S.), 1997 (30 copies signed by author and illustrator, broadside) . £150
ditto, Firefly Press (U.S.), 1997 (60 copies signed by author, broadside) £125

Novels

The Poorhouse Fair, Knopf (U.S.), 1959 (first issue d/w with one paragraph of copy only on back flap) . . . . £200/£35
ditto, Gollancz, 1959 . . . . £100/£15
Rabbit, Run, Knopf (U.S.), 1960 (first issue d/w with 16-line blurb on front flap) . . . . . £500/£45
ditto, Deutsch, 1961 . . . . £100/£15
ditto, Franklin Library (U.S.), 1977 (signed, limited edition) £50
The Centaur, Knopf (U.S.), 1963 . . £100/£20
ditto, Deutsch, 1963 . . . . £45/£15
Of the Farm, Knopf (U.S.), 1965 . . . £75/£10
ditto, Deutsch, 1966 . . . . £50/£5
Couples, Knopf (U.S.), 1968 . . . . . £35/£5
ditto, Deutsch, 1968 . . . . £25/£5
Rabbit Redux, Knopf (U.S.), 1971 . . . £50/£10
ditto, Knopf (U.S.), 1971 (350 signed copies, slipcase, clear d/w) . . . . £250/£200
ditto, Deutsch, 1972 . . . . £30/£5

ditto, Franklin Library (U.S.), 1981 (signed, limited edition) £45
A Month of Sundays, Knopf (U.S.), 1975 . . £25/£5
ditto, Knopf (U.S.), 1975 (450 signed, numbered copies, slipcase, d/w) . . . . . . £125/£75
ditto, Deutsch, 1975 . . . . £20/£5
Marry Me: A Romance, Knopf (U.S.), 1976 . £20/£5
ditto, Knopf (U.S.), 1976 (300 signed, numbered copies, slipcase, d/w) . . . . . £100/£65
ditto, Franklin Library (U.S.), 1976 (signed limited edition) £50
ditto, Deutsch, 1977 . . . . £15/£5
The Coup, Knopf (U.S.), 1978 . . . . . £15/£5
ditto, Knopf (U.S.), 1978 (350 signed, numbered copies, slipcase, d/w) . . . . . £100/£65
ditto, Deutsch, 1979 . . . . £10/£5
Rabbit is Rich, Knopf (U.S.), 1981 . . . . £30/£5
ditto, Knopf (U.S.), 1981 (350 signed copies, slipcase, d/w) . . . . £200/£150
ditto, Deutsch, 1982 . . . . £25/£5
Bech is Back, Knopf (U.S.), 1982 . . . . £15/£5
ditto, Knopf (U.S.), 1982 (500 signed, numbered copies, slipcase, d/w) . . . . . £100/£65
ditto, Deutsch, 1983 . . . . £10/£5
The Witches of Eastwick, Knopf (U.S.), 1984 £35/£10
ditto, Knopf (U.S.), 1984 (350 signed copies, glassine d/w and slipcase). . . . . £125/£100
ditto, Franklin Library (U.S.), 1984 (signed limited edition) £45
ditto, Deutsch, 1984 . . . . £25/£10
Roger's Version, Knopf (U.S.), 1986 . . . £10/£5
ditto, Knopf (U.S.), 1986 (350 signed copies, glassine d/w and slipcase). . . . . . . £125/£100
ditto, Franklin Library (U.S.), 1986 (signed limited edition) £35
ditto, Deutsch, 1986 . . . . £10/£5
S, Knopf (U.S.), 1988 . . . . £10/£5
ditto, Knopf (U.S.), 1986 (350 signed copies, glassine d/w and slipcase). . . . . . . £125/£100
ditto, Deutsch, 1988 . . . . £10/£5
Rabbit at Rest, Knopf (U.S.), 1990 . . . . £20/£5
ditto, Knopf (U.S.), 1990 (350 signed copies, glassine d/w and slipcase). . . . . . . £150/£125
ditto, Franklin Library (U.S.), 1990 (signed, limited edition) £50
ditto, Deutsch, 1991 . . . . £15/£5
Brazil, Knopf (U.S.), 1994 . . . . . £15/£5
ditto, Franklin Library (U.S.), 1994 (signed, limited edition) £35
ditto, Hamish Hamilton, 1994 . . . . . £15/£5
In the Beauty of the Lilies, Knopf (U.S.), 1996 £15/£5
ditto, Franklin Library (U.S.), 1996 (signed, limited edition) £35
ditto, Hamish Hamilton, 1996 . . . . . £15/£5
Toward the End of Time, Knopf (U.S.), 1997 . £10/£5
ditto, Franklin Library (U.S.), 1998 (signed, limited edition) £35
ditto, Hamish Hamilton, 1998 . . . . . £15/£5

Bech at Bay: A Quasi-Novel, Knopf (U.S.), 1999 . . . . £10/£5
ditto, Easton Press (U.S.), 1999 (1,100 signed, numbered copies) £75
ditto, Hamish Hamilton, 1999 . . . . . £15/£5
Gertrude and Claudius, Knopf (U.S.), 2000 . £10/£5
ditto, Franklin Library (U.S.), 2000 (signed, limited edition) £35
ditto, Hamish Hamilton, 2000 . . . . . £15/£5

Short Stories
The Same Door, Knopf (U.S.), 1959 . . £250/£30
ditto, Deutsch, 1962 . . . . £100/£20
Pigeon Feathers and Other Stories, Knopf (U.S.), 1962 . . . . £125/£20
ditto, Deutsch, 1962 . . . . £65/£15
Olinger Stories: A Selection, Vintage (U.S.), 1964 (wraps) £10
The Music School, Knopf (U.S.), 1966 (first issue with 'The state' on p. 46, line 15) . . . . £300/£250
ditto, Deutsch, 1967 . . . . £50/£15
Bech: A Book, Knopf (U.S.), 1970 . . . £20/£5
ditto, Knopf (U.S.), 1970 (500 signed copies, slipcase) . . . . £100/£65
ditto, Deutsch, 1970 . . . . £15/£5
The Indian, Blue Cloud Quarterly, 1971 (wraps) £45
Museums and Women and Other Stories, Knopf (U.S.), 1972 . . . . £15/£5
ditto, Knopf (U.S.), 1972 (350 signed copies, slipcase) . . . . £75/£50
ditto, Deutsch, 1973 . . . . £15/£5
Warm Wine: An Idyll, Albondocani Press (U.S.), 1973 (26 signed, lettered copies) £200
ditto, Albondocani Press (U.S.), 1973 (250 signed, numbered copies, wraps) £100
Couples, Halty Ferguson, 1976 (26 signed, lettered copies of 276) £200
ditto, Halty Ferguson, 1976 (250 signed, numbered copies, wraps) £100
Problems and Other Stories, Knopf (U.S.), 1979 . . . . £15/£5
ditto, Knopf (U.S.), 1979 (350 signed copies, glassine d/w and slipcase). . . . . . . £100/£75
ditto, Deutsch, 1980 . . . . £10/£5
Too Far to Go: The Maples Stories, Fawcett (U.S.), 1979 (wraps) £15
ditto, as *Your Lover Just Called: Stories of Joan and Richard Maple*, Penguin, 1980 (wraps) . . . £5
The Beloved, Lord John Press (U.S.), 1982 (100 signed, numbered deluxe copies) . . . £125
ditto, Lord John Press (U.S.), 1982 (300 signed, numbered copies) £100
Going Abroad, Eurographica (Helsinki), 1988 (350 signed, numbered copies, wraps) £100
Trust Me, Knopf (U.S.), 1987 . . . . . £10/£5
ditto, Knopf (U.S.), 1987 (350 signed, numbered copies, slipcase, d/w) . . . . . £75/£50
ditto, Deutsch, 1987 . . . . £10/£5

More Stately Mansions, Nouveau (U.S.), 1987 (300 signed, numbered copies) £75
The Afterlife, Sixth Chamber Press, 1987 (26 signed, lettered copies, no d/w) £200
ditto, Sixth Chamber Press, 1987 (175 signed, numbered copies, no d/w) £100
Brother Grasshopper, Metacom Press (U.S.), 1990 (150 signed, numbered copies) . . . . £75/£45
The Afterlife and Other Stories, Knopf (U.S.), 1994 .
. . . . £10/£5
ditto, Hamish Hamilton, 1994 . . . . . £10/£5
Licks of Love, Knopf (U.S.), 2000 . . . . £10/£5
ditto, Easton Press (U.S.), 2000 (1,650 signed, numbered copies) £75
ditto, Hamish Hamilton, 2000 . . . . . £10/£5

Children's Titles
The Magic Flute, Knopf (U.S.), 1962 (cloth, in d/w) .
. . . . £600/£250
ditto, Knopf (U.S.), 1962 (pictorial boards, no d/w) .
. . . . £500
ditto, Deutsch & Ward, 1964 . . . . . £250/£40
A Child's Calendar, Knopf (U.S.), 1965 . £125/£40

Plays
Three Texts from Early Ipswich: A Pageant, 17th Century Day Committee (U.S.), 1968 (950 numbered copies, wraps) £45
ditto, 17th Century Day Committee (U.S.), 1968 (50 signed, numbered copies, wraps) £175
ditto, 17th Century Day Committee (U.S.), 1968 (26 signed, lettered copies, glassine d/w) . . £750/£650
Buchanan Dying, Knopf (U.S.), 1974 . . £25/£10
ditto, Deutsch, 1974 . . . . £20/£5

Others
The Ring, Knopf (U.S.), 1964 . . . . £150/£45
Assorted Prose, Knopf (U.S.), 1965 . . . £35/£10
ditto, Knopf (U.S.), 1965 (signed copies, unspecified number) . . . . £125/£100
ditto, Deutsch, 1965 . . . . £20/£5
Bottom's Dream: Adapted from William Shakespeare's 'A Midsummer Night's Dream', Knopf (U.S.), 1969 . . . . . . £100/£30
A Conversation With John Updike, Union College (U.S.), 1971 (wraps) £25
A Good Place, Aloe Editions (U.S.), 1973 (26 signed, lettered copies, wraps) £300
ditto, Aloe Editions (U.S.), 1973 (100 signed, numbered copies, wraps) £200
Picked-Up Pieces, Knopf (U.S.), 1975 . . . £20/£5
ditto, Knopf (U.S.), 1975 (250 signed, numbered copies, slipcase) . . . . £125/£100
ditto, Deutsch, 1976 . . . . £15/£5
Talk from the Fifties, Lord John Press (U.S.), 1979 (75 signed, numbered deluxe copies, boards, no d/w) . .
. . . . £150
ditto, Lord John Press (U.S.), 1979 (300 signed, numbered copies, boards, no d/w) £100

Three Illuminations in the Life of an American Author, Targ Editions (U.S.), 1979 (350 signed, numbered copies, glassine d/w) . . . £125/£100
The Chaste Planet, Metacom Press (U.S.), 1980 (300 signed, numbered copies, wraps) £100
ditto, Metacom Press (U.S.), 1980 (26 signed, lettered copies) £350
Ego and Art in Walt Whitman, Targ Editions (U.S.), 1980 (350 signed, numbered copies, glassine d/w) .
. . . . £125/£100
People One Knows: Interviews with Insufficiently Famous Americans, Lord John Press (U.S.), 1980 (300 signed, numbered copies, boards, slipcase) . .
. . . . £100/£75
ditto, Lord John Press (U.S.), 1980 (100 signed, numbered copies, leather spine, slipcase) . £150/£125
Hawthorne's Creed, Targ Editions (U.S.), 1981 (250 signed, numbered copies, glassine d/w) . £125/£100
Hugging the Shore, Knopf (U.S.), 1983 . . £15/£5
ditto, Deutsch, 1984 . . . . £15/£5
Emersonianism, Bits Press (U.S.), 1984 (200 signed, numbered copies, no d/w) £65
Impressions, Sylvester & Orphanos (U.S.), 1985 (300 signed, numbered copies) £150
Self-Consciousness: Memoirs, Knopf (U.S.), 1989 .
. . . . £15/£5
ditto, Deutsch, 1989 . . . . £10/£5
Just Looking: Essays on Art, Knopf (U.S.), 1989 . .
. . . . £20/£5
ditto, Deutsch, 1989 . . . . £20/£5
Odd Jobs: Essays and Criticism, Knopf (U.S.), 1991 .
. . . . £10/£5
ditto, Deutsch, 1991 . . . . £10/£5
Memories of the Ford Administration, Knopf (U.S.), 1992 . . . . £10/£5
ditto, Hamish Hamilton, 1992 . . . . . £10/£5
Golf Dreams, Knopf (U.S.), 1996 . . . . £10/£5
ditto, Knopf (U.S.), 1996 (500 signed, large print copies) . . . . £45/£25
ditto, Hamish Hamilton, 1997 . . . . . £10/£5
More Matter: Essays and Criticism, Knopf (U.S.), 2000 . . . . £10/£5

FLORENCE UPTON
(b.1873 d.1922)

Born in New York, Florence Upton moved to England in her twenties. She illustrated the 'Golliwogg' stories (in verse and prose) written by her mother, Bertha Upton. Thus started a whole 'Golliwogg' craze.

The Adventures of Two Dutch Dolls and a Golliwogg, Longmans, [1895] £500
The Golliwogg's Bicycle Club, Longmans, [1896]. . .
. . . . £400
Little Hearts, Routledge, 1897 . . . . . £400

The Vege-Men's Revenge, Longmans, [1897] . £400
The Golliwogg at the Sea-side, Longmans, 1898 £400
The Golliwogg in War!, Longmans, 1899 . . £400
The Golliwogg's Polar Adventures, Longmans, [1900]
. . . . £450
The Golliwogg's 'Auto-Go-Cart', Longmans, [1901] .
. . . . £400
The Golliwogg's Air-Ship, Longmans, [1902] . £400
The Golliwogg's Circus, Longmans, [1903] . £400
The Golliwogg in Holland, Longmans. [1904] . £400
The Golliwogg's Fox-Hunt, Longmans, [1905] £400
The Golliwogg's Desert Island, Longmans, [1906] .
. . . . £400
The Golliwogg's Christmas, Longmans, 1907 . £400
*The Adventures of Borbee and the Wisp: The Story of
a Sophisticated Little Girl and an Unsophisticated
Little Boy*, Longmans, 1908. . . . . . £350
Golliwogg in the African Jungle, Longmans, 1909 .
. . . . £450

ALISON UTTLEY
(b.1884 d.1976)

An author of children's books which are not unlike
those of Beatrix Potter, Uttley also wrote many
volumes of essays and memoirs.

'Grey Rabbit' Books
The Squirrel, the Hare and the Little Grey Rabbit,
Heinemann, 1929 . . . . . . £150/£35
How Little Grey Rabbit Got Back Her Tail,
Heinemann, 1930 . . . . . . £125/£25
The Great Adventure of Hare, Heinemann, 1931 . .
. . . . £125/£25
The Story of Fuzzypeg the Hedgehog, Heinemann,
1932 . . . . £125/£25
Squirrel Goes Skating, Collins, 1934 . . £125/£25
Wise Owl's Story, Collins, 1935 . . . . £125/£25
Little Grey Rabbit's Party, Collins, 1936 . £125/£25
The Knot Squirrel Tied, Collins, 1937 . . £100/£20
Fuzzypeg Goes to School, Collins, 1938 . £75/£20
Little Grey Rabbit's Christmas, Collins, 1939 £75/£20
My Little Grey Rabbit Painting Book, Collins, 1940 .
. . . . £75/£20
Moldy Warp The Mole, Collins, 1940 . . £75/£20
Hare Joins the Home Guard, Collins, 1942 £75/£20
Little Grey Rabbit's Washing Day, Collins, 1942 . .
. . . . £65/£15
Water-Rat's Picnic, Collins, 1943 . . . £65/£15
Little Grey Rabbit's Birthday, Collins, [1944] £65/£15
The Speckledy Hen, Collins, [1945]. . . £60/£15
Little Grey Rabbit to the Rescue, Collins, 1946 . .
. . . . £45/£15
Little Grey Rabbit and the Weasels, Collins, 1947 . .
. . . . £45/£15
Grey Rabbit and the Wandering Hedgehog, Collins,
1948 . . . . £45/£15

Little Grey Rabbit Makes Lace, Collins, 1950 £45/£15
Hare and the Easter Eggs, Collins, 1952 . £45/£15
Little Grey Rabbit's Valentine, Collins, 1953 £45/£15
Little Grey Rabbit Goes to the Sea, Collins, 1954 . .
. . . . £45/£15
Hare and Guy Fawkes, Collins, 1956 . . £45/£15
Little Grey Rabbit's Paint-Box, Collins, [1958] . .
. . . . £45/£15
Grey Rabbit Finds a Shoe, Collins, [1960] . £45/£15
Grey Rabbit and the Circus, Collins, [1961] £45/£15
Three Little Grey Rabbit Plays, Heinemann, 1961 . .
. . . . £45/£15
Grey Rabbit's May Day, Collins, [1963] . £45/£15
Hare Goes Shopping, Collins, 1965 . . . £45/£15
Little Grey Rabbit's Pancake Day, Collins, 1967 . .
. . . . £45/£15
Little Grey Rabbit Goes to the North Pole, Collins,
1970 . . . . £45/£15
Fuzzypeg's Brother, Heinemann, 1971 . . £45/£15
Little Grey Rabbit's Spring Cleaning Party, Collins,
1972 . . . . £45/£15
Little Grey Rabbit and the Snow-Baby, Collins, 1973 .
. . . . £45/£15
Hare and the Rainbow, Collins, 1975 . . £45/£15

Other Children's Books
Moonshine and Magic, Faber, 1932. . . £100/£35
The Advenures of Peter and Judy in Bunnyland,
Collins, [1935] . . . . £100/£35
Candlelight Tales, Faber, 1936 . . . . £75/£25
The Adventures of No Ordinary Rabbit, Faber, 1937 .
. . . . £75/£25
High Meadows, Faber, 1938 . . . . . £45/£15
Mustard, Pepper and Salt, Faber, 1938 . . £75/£25
A Traveller in Time, Faber, 1939 . . . £75/£25
Tales of the Four Pigs and Brock the Badger, Faber,
1939 . . . . £45/£15
The Adventures of Sam Pig, Faber, 1940 . £45/£15
Sam Pig Goes to Market, Faber, 1941 . . £45/£15
Six Tales of Brock The Badger, Faber, 1941 £45/£15
Six Tales of Sam Pig, Faber, 1941 . . . £45/£15
Six Tales of the Four Pigs, Faber, 1941. . £45/£15
Ten Tales of Tim Rabbit, Faber, 1941 . . £50/£15
Nine Starlight Tales, Faber, 1942 . . . £35/£10
Sam Pig and Sally, Faber, 1942 . . . . £45/£15
Ten Candlelight Tales, Faber, 1942 . . . £35/£10
Cuckoo Cherry-Tree, Faber, 1943 . . . £35/£10
Sam Pig at the Circus, Faber, 1943 . . . £45/£15
Mrs Nimble and Mr Bumble, James, 1944 . £50/£15
The Spice Woman's Basket and Other Tales, Faber,
1944 . . . . £40/£15
Adventures of Tim Rabbit, Faber, 1945 . . £45/£15
Some Moonshine Tales, Faber, 1945 . . . £30/£5
The Weather Cock and Other Stories, Faber, 1945 .
. . . . £35/£10
When All Is Done, Faber, 1945 . . . . £35/£10
John Barleycorn: Twelve Tales of Fairy and Magic,
Faber, 1948 . . . . £45/£15
Sam Pig in Trouble, Faber, 1948 . . . £45/£15

Snug and Serena Meet a Queen, Heinemann, 1950 .
. . . . £65/£20
Snug and Serena Pick Cowslips, Heinemann, 1950 .
. . . . £65/£20
The Cobbler's Shop and Other Tales, Faber, 1950 .
. . . . £35/£10
Going to the Fair, Heinemann, 1951 . . £45/£15
Toad's Castle, Heinemann, 1951. . . . £45/£15
Yours Ever, Sam Pig, Faber, 1951 . . . £45/£15
Christmas at the Rose and Crown, Heinemann, 1952 .
. . . . £45/£15
Mrs Mouse Spring Cleans, Heinemann, 1952 £45/£15
Snug and the Chimney-Sweeper, Heinemann, 1953 · .
. . . . £45/£15
The Gypsy Hedgehogs, Heinemann, 1953 . £45/£15
Little Red Fox and the Wicked Uncle, Heinemann,
1954 . . . . £75/£35
Sam Pig and the Singing Gate, Faber, 1955 £45/£15
The Flower Show, Heinemann, 1955 . . £45/£15
The Mouse Telegrams, Heinemann, 1955 . £45/£15
Little Red Fox and Cinderella, Heinemann, 1956 . .
. . . . £75/£35
Magic in My Pocket: A Selection of Tales, Puffin,
1957 (wraps). £5
Mr Stoat Walks In, Heinemann, 1957 . . £40/£10
Snug and the Silver Spoon, Heinemann, 1957 £40/£10
Little Red Fox and the Magic Moon, Heinemann,
1958 . . . . £75/£35
Snug and Serena Count Twelve, Heinemann, 1959 .
. . . . £40/£10
Tim Rabbit and Company, Faber, 1959 . £40/£10
John at the Old Farm, Heinemann, 1960 . £50/£15
Sam Pig Goes to the Seaside, Faber, 1960 . £45/£10
Snug and Serena go to Town, Heinemann, 1961 . .
. . . . £35/£10
Little Red Fox and the Unicorn, Heinemann, 1962 .
. . . . £75/£30
*The Little Knife Who Did All The Work: Twelve Tales
of Magic*, Faber, 1962 . . . . . £25/£10
Tim Rabbit's Dozen, Faber, 1964 . . . £35/£10
The Sam Pig Storybook, Faber, 1965 . . £45/£15
Enchantment, Heinemann, 1966. . . . . £25/£5
The Mouse, The Rabbit and the Little White Hen,
Heinemann, 1966 . . . . £25/£5
Little Red Fox and the Big Tree, Heinemann, 1968 .
. . . . £75/£30
Lavender Shoes: Eight Tales of Enchantment, Faber,
1970 . . . . £20/£5
*The Brown Mouse Book, Magical Tales of Two Little
Mice*, Heinemann, 1971. . . . . . £30/£5
Fairy Tales, Faber, 1975 . . . . . . £20/£5
Stories for Christmas, Faber, 1977 . . . £20/£5
From Spring to Spring: Stories of the Four Seasons,
Faber, 1978 . . . . £20/£5
Foxglove Tales, Faber, 1984 . . . . . £20/£5

Others
The Country Child, Faber, 1931. . . . £100/£30
Ambush of Young Days, Faber, 1937 . . £50/£20
The Farm on the Hill, Faber, 1941 . . . £35/£10

Country Hoard, Faber, 1943 . . . . . £45/£15
*The Washerwoman's Child: A Play on the Life and
Stories of Hans Christian Andersen*, Faber, 1946 .
. . . . £40/£15
Country Things, Faber, 1946. . . . . £45/£15
Carts and Candlesticks, Faber, 1946 . . £45/£15
Buckinghamshire, Hale, 1950 . . . . . £35/£10
Macduff, Faber, 1950 . . . . £35/£10
Plowmen's Clocks, Faber, 1952 . . . . £45/£15
The Stuff of Dreams, Faber, 1953 . . . £35/£10
Here's a New Day, Faber, 1956 . . . . £35/£10
A Year in the Country, Faber, 1957 . . . £35/£10
The Swan's Fly Over, Faber, 1959 . . . £45/£15
Something for Nothing, Faber, 1960 . . £45/£15
Wild Honey, Faber, 1962 . . . . . . £45/£15
Cuckoo in June, Faber, 1964. . . . . £45/£15
Recipes from an Old Farmhouse, Faber, 1966 . .
. . . . £25/£10
A Peck of Gold, Faber, 1966 . . . . . £45/£15
The Button-Box and Other Essays, Faber, 1968 . .
. . . . £45/£15
A Ten O'clock Scholar and Other Essays, Faber, 1970
. . . . £45/£15
Secret Places and Other Essays, Faber, 1972 £50/£20
Country World: Memoirs of Childhood, Faber, 1984 .
. . . . £15/£5

LAURENS VAN DER POST
(b.1906 d.1996)

Sir Laurens Van der Post was a South African author,
explorer, anthropologist, linguist and philosopher. An
opponent of apartheid, in 1925 he helped found
Voorslag, an anti-apartheid magazine, and was forced
to leave South Africa because of his involvement with
it.

Novels
In a Province, Hogarth Press, 1934 . . £2,000/£200
ditto, Coward-McCann (U.S.), 1934 . . £1,250/£125
The Face Beside the Fire, Hogarth Press, 1953 . .
. . . . £100/£10
ditto, Morrow (U.S.), 1953 . . . . . £65/£10
A Bar of Shadow, Hogarth Press, 1954 . . . £20/£5
ditto, Morrow (U.S.), 1956 . . . . . £15/£5
Flamingo Feather, Hogarth Press, 1955 . . £15/£5
ditto, Morrow (U.S.), 1955 . . . . . £15/£5
The Seed and the Sower, Hogarth Press, 1963 . £15/£5
ditto, Morrow (U.S.), 1963 . . . . . £15/£5
The Hunter and the Whale, Hogarth Press, 1967 . .
. . . . £15/£5
ditto, Morrow (U.S.), 1967 . . . . . £15/£5
A Story Like the Wind, Hogarth Press, 1972 . £15/£5
ditto, Morrow (U.S.), 1972 . . . . . £15/£5
A Far-Off Place, Hogarth Press, 1974 . . £15/£5
ditto, Morrow (U.S.), 1974 . . . . . £15/£5
A Mantis Carol, Hogarth Press, 1975 . . £15/£5
ditto, Morrow (U.S.), 1975 . . . . . £15/£5

Non Fiction

Venture to the Interior, Morrow (U.S.), 1951 £65/£15
ditto, Hogarth Press, 1952 . . . . . £45/£10
The Dark Eye In Africa, Hogarth Press, 1955 £35/£10
ditto, Morrow (U.S.), 1955 . . . . . £25/£10
The Lost World of the Kalahari, Hogarth Press, 1958 .
. . . . £25/£5
ditto, Morrow (U.S.), 1958 . . . . . £20/£5
The Heart of the Hunter, Hogarth Press, 1961 . £20/£5
ditto, Morrow (U.S.), 1961 . . . . . £15/£5
Patterns of Renewal, Pendel Hill Pamphlets (U.S.),
1962 (wraps) £10
Journey Into Russia, Hogarth Press, 1964 . . £20/£5
ditto, as *A View of All the Russians*, Morrow (U.S.),
1967 . . . . £15/£5
A Portrait of All The Russias, Hogarth Press, 1967 .
. . . . £15/£5
ditto, Morrow (U.S.), 1967 . . . . . £15/£5
A Portrait of Japan, Hogarth Press, 1968 . £15/£5
ditto, Morrow (U.S.), 1968 . . . . . £15/£5
The Night of the New Moon: August 6 1945 . .
Hiroshima, Hogarth Press, 1970 . . . £15/£5
ditto, as *The Prisoner and the Bomb*, Morrow (U.S.),
1971 . . . . £15/£5
*Jung and the Story of Our Time: A Personal
Experience*, Pantheon Books (U.S.), 1975 . £15/£5
ditto, Hogarth Press, 1976 . . . . . £15/£5
First Catch Your Eland: A Taste of Africa, Hogarth
Press, 1977 . . . . £15/£5
ditto, Morrow (U.S.), 1977 . . . . . £15/£5
Yet Being Someone Other, Hogarth Press, 1982 £15/£5
ditto, Morrow (U.S.), 1982 . . . . . £15/£5
Testament To The Bushmen, Viking, 1984 (with Jane
Taylor) . . . . £25/£5
ditto, Viking (U.S.), 1984 . . . . . £25/£5
*A Walk With A White Bushman: Laurens Van Der
Post In Conversation*, Chatto & Windus, 1986 £15/£5
ditto, Morrow (U.S.), 1986 . . . . . £15/£5
About Blady, A Pattern Out of Time, Chatto &
Windus, 1991 . . . . £15/£5
ditto, Morrow (U.S.), 1991 . . . . . £15/£5
The Voice of the Thunder, Chatto & Windus, 1993 .
. . . . £15/£5
ditto, Morrow (U.S.), 1994 . . . . . £15/£5
The Admiral's Baby, Murray, 1996 . . . . £10/£5
ditto, Morrow (U.S.), 1996 . . . . . £15/£5

JULES VERNE
(b.1828 d.1905)

Born in Nantes, France, Verne studied law in Paris
and began his literary career while working at the
Stock Exchange. Famous for his escapist adventure
novels and short stories, Verne also wrote opera
libretti and plays.

Fiction

Five Weeks in a Balloon, Appleton and Co. (U.S.),
1869 . . . . £4,000
ditto, Chapman & Hall, 1870 . . . . . £3,500
A Journey to the Centre of the Earth, Griffith &
Farran, 1872 [1871] £4,000
ditto, Scribner's, Armstong & Co. (U.S.), 1874 [1873]
(with no address under publisher's imprint or ads) .
. . . . £3,000
ditto, Scribner's, Armstong & Co. (U.S.), 1874 [1873]
(with address and ads) £1,500
Twenty Thousand Leagues Under the Sea, Sampson
Low, 1873 [1872] £7,500
ditto, Osgood (U.S.), 1873 (10-15 copies only, with
central gilt vignette on the top board of a school of
jellyfish) £7,000
ditto, George Smith (U.S.), 1873 (with central gilt
vignette on the top board: the image of Nemo with
sextant) £3,500
*From the Earth to the Moon Direct in 97 Hours, 20
Minutes, and a Trip Round it*, Newark Publishing &
Printing Co. (U.S.), 1870 (wraps, first book only) .
. . . . £750
ditto, Sampson Low, 1873 (complete edition) . £1,250
ditto, Scribner's, Armstong & Co. (U.S.), 1874 . £1,000
*Meridiana: The Adventures of Three Englishmen and
Three Russians in South Africa*, Sampson Low, 1873
. . . . £1,250
ditto, Scribner's (U.S.), 1873 . . . . . £1,000
The Fur Country, Sampson Low, 1874 [1873] . £1,250
ditto, Osgood (U.S.), 1873 . . . . . £1,000
Around the World in Eighty Days, Osgood (U.S.),
1873 . . . . £7,500
ditto, Sampson Low, 1874 [1873] £7,500
In Search of the Castaways, Lippincott (U.S.), 1873 .
. . . . £1,250
ditto, as *A Voyage Round the World*, Routledge, 1876-
1877 (3 vols: *South America*, *Australia* and *New
Zealand*) £2,000
A Floating City, and The Blockade Runners, Sampson
Low, 1874 . . . . £1,250
ditto, Scribner's, Armstong & Co. (U.S.), 1874 ('1875'
also on some title pages) £1,000
Dr Ox's Experiment and Other Stories, Osgood
(U.S.), 1874 . . . . £750
ditto, Sampson Low, 1875 . . . . . £750
The Mysterious Island, Sampson Low, 1875 (3 vols:
Dropped from the Clouds, *Abandoned* and *The Secret
of the Island*) £2,000

ditto, Scribner's, Armstong & Co. (U.S.), 1875-1876 (3 vols) £2,000
The Adventures of Captain Hatteras: The English at the North Pole, Routledge, 1875 [1874] . . £500
ditto, Osgood (U.S.), 1875 [1874] (with *The Field of Ice*) £500
The Field of Ice, Routledge, 1876 . . . . £500
The Chancellor: The Survivors of the Chancellor, Sampson Low, 1875 . . . . £650
ditto, Osgood (U.S.), 1875 (with *Martin Paz*) . £650
Martin Paz, Sampson Low, 1876 . . . . £500
A Winter Amid the Ice and Other Stories, Sampson Low, 1876 . . . . £400
Michael Strogoff, Frank Leslie's Publishing House (U.S.), 1876 (wraps). £1,250
ditto, Sampson Low, 1877 [1876] £1,000
ditto, Scribner's (U.S.), 1877 . . . . . . £750
The Child of the Cavern, Munro (U.S.), 1877 (wraps). £1,000
ditto, Sampson Low, 1877 . . . . . £1,250
Hector Servadac, Travels and Adventures through the Solar System, Munro (U.S.), 1877 (wraps) . £1,000
ditto, Sampson Low, 1878 . . . . . £1,250
ditto, Claxton, Remsen & Haffelfinger (U.S.), 1877 . . . . £750
Dick Sands; or A Captain at Fifteen, Munro (U.S.), 1877 (wraps) £1,000
ditto, as *Dick Sands, The Boy Captain*, Sampson Low, 1879 [1878] £1,250
500 Millions of the Begum, Munro (U.S.), 1879 (wraps, does not include 'Mutineers of the Bounty) £1,000
ditto, as *The Begum's Fortune*, Sampson Low, 1880 [1879]. £1,250
ditto, Lipincott (U.S.), 1879 . . . . . £650
The Tribulations of a Chinaman, Sampson Low, 1880 . . . . £650
ditto, Lee & Shepherd (U.S.), 1880 . . . . £500
ditto, Dutton (U.S.), 1880 . . . . . . £600
The Steam House, Munro (U.S.), 1880-1881 (2 vols, wraps). £1,500
ditto, Sampson Low, 1881 (2 vols: *Demon of Cawnpore* and *Tigers and Traitors*) . . . £1,750
ditto, Scribner's (U.S.), 1881 (2 vols) . . . £1,250
The Giant Raft, Sampson Low, 1881 (2 vols: *Down the Amazon* and *The Cryptogram*) £1,000
ditto, Munro (U.S.), 1881-1882 (2 vols, wraps). £750
ditto, Scribner's (U.S.), 1881-1882 (2 vols). . £750
Godfrey Morgan, A Californian Mystery, Sampson Low, 1883 . . . . £1,000
ditto, as *Robinson's School*, Munro (U.S.), 1883 (wraps) £650
ditto, Scribner's (U.S.), 1883 . . . . . £650
The Green Ray, Sampson Low, 1883 . . . £750
ditto, Munro (U.S.), 1883 (wraps) . . . £650
ditto, Arco (U.S.), 1965 . . . . . . £50/£15
The Headstrong Turk, Munro (U.S.), 1883-1884 (2 vols: *The Captain of the Guidara* and *Scarpante the Spy*, wraps) £1,250

ditto, as *Keraban the Inflexible*, Sampson Low, 1884-5 (2 vols) £2,000
The Vanished Diamond, Sampson Low, 1885 . £1,250
ditto, as *The Southern Star or The Diamond Land*, Munro (U.S.), 1885 (wraps). £1,000
ditto, Arco (U.S.), 1966 . . . . . . £50/£15
The Archipelago on Fire, Munro (U.S.), 1885 (wraps) £1,000
ditto, Sampson Low, 1886 . . . . . £1,250
Mathias Sandorf, Munro (U.S.), 1885 (wraps) . £1,000
ditto, Sampson Low, 1886 . . . . . £1,250
The Clipper of the Clouds, Sampson Low, 1887 . . . . £1,250
ditto, as *Robur the Conqueror or A Trip Round the World in a Flying Machine*, Munro (U.S.), 1887 (wraps) £1,000
Ticket No 9672, Munro (U.S.), 1886 (2 vols, wraps) £1,250
ditto, as *The Lottery Ticket*, Sampson Low, 1887 . . . . £1,250
The Flight to France, Toronto National Publishing Co. (Canada), 1888 . . . . £1,000
ditto, Sampson Low, 1888 . . . . . £1,250
ditto, Lovell (U.S.), 1888 (wraps) . . . £1,000
Texan's Vengeance, or North Versus South, Munro (U.S.), 1887 (2 vols, wraps). £1,000
ditto, as *North Against South*, Sampson Low, 1888 . . . . £1,250
Adrift in the Pacific, Munro (U.S.), 1889 (wraps) £1,000
ditto, Sampson Low, 1889 . . . . . £1,250
ditto, Bromfield & Co. (U.S.), 1889 . . . . £750
A Family Without a Name, Lovell (U.S.), 1889 (wraps) £1,000
ditto, Sampson Low, 1891 [1890] . . . £1,250
The Purchase of the North Pole, Sampson Low, 1891 [1890]. £1,250
ditto, as *Topsy Turvy*, Ogilvie (U.S.), 1890 . £1,250
ditto, Ogilvie (U.S.), 1890 (wraps) . . . £1,000
Caesar Cascabel, Cassell (U.S.), 1890 . . £1,250
ditto, Sampson Low, 1891 . . . . . £1,250
Mistress Branican, Cassell (U.S.), 1891 . . £1,250
ditto, Sampson Low, 1892 . . . . . £1,250
The Castle of the Carpathians, Sampson Low, 1893 . . . . £1,250
ditto, Merrian (U.S.), 1894 . . . . . £1,250
Claudius Bombarnac, Sampson Low, 1894 . £1,250
ditto, as *The Special Correspondent, Or the Adventures of Claudius Bombarnac*, The U.S. Book Co. (U.S.), 1894 . . . . £1,250
Foundling Mick, Sampson Low, 1895 . . . £1,250
Captain Antifer, Sampson Low, 1895 . . . £2,000
ditto, Fenno (U.S.), 1895 (wraps) £1,000
ditto, Fenno (U.S.), 1895 . . . . . . £1,000
The Floating Island, Sampson Low, 1896 . £1,250
ditto, Allison (U.S.), 1897 . . . . . £1,250
Clovis Dardentor, Sampson Low, 1897 . . £2,000
Facing the Flag, Tennyson Neely (U.S.), 1897 £1,250
ditto, as *For the Flag*, Sampson Low, 1897. . £1,250

An Antarctic Mystery, Sampson Low, 1898 . £1,500
ditto, Lippincott (U.S.), 1898. . . . . . £1,450
The Will of an Eccentric, Sampson Low, 1900. £1,500
The Chase of the Golden Meteor, Grant Richards,
1909 . . . . £500
ditto, as *The Hunt for the Meteor*, Arco (U.S.), 1965 .
. . . . £50/£15
Master of the World, Parke & Co (U.S.), 1911 (as vol
14 of the 15 volume *Works of Jules Verne*) . £500
ditto, Sampson Low, [1914] £500
The Lighthouse at the End of the World, Sampson
Low, [1923] . . . .£500/£100
ditto, Watt (U.S.), 1924 . . . . . .£500/£100
Second Patrie: Their Island Home, Sampson Low,
[1923]. . . . . £500/£75
ditto, Watt (U.S.), 1924 . . . . . . £500/£75
The Castaways of the Flag, Sampson Low, [1923] .
. . . . £500/£75
The Barsac Mission: Into the Niger Bend, Arco
(simultaneous U.S. and U.K. editions), 1960 £50/£15
The City in the Sahara, Arco (U.S. and U.K.), 1960 .
. . . . £50/£15
The Survivors of the Jonathan: The Masterless Man,
Arco (U.S. and U.K.), 1962. . . . . £50/£15
The Unwilling Dictator, Arco (U.S. and U.K.), 1962 .
. . . . £50/£15
*The Golden Volcano: The Claim on Forty Mile
Creek*, Arco (U.S. and U.K.), 1962. . . £50/£15
Flood and Fame, Arco (U.S. and U.K.), 1962 £50/£15
The Secret of the Wilhelm Storitz, Arco (U.S. and
U.K.), 1964 . . . . £50/£15
The Village in the Treetops, Arco (U.S. and U.K.),
1964 . . . . £50/£15
Salvage from the 'Cynthia', Arco (U.S. and U.K.),
1964 . . . . £50/£15
Yesterday and Tomorrow, Arco (U.S. and U.K.), 1965
. . . . £50/£15
The Thompson Travel Agency: Package Holiday,
Arco (U.S. and U.K.), 1965 . . . . £50/£15
End of the Journey, Arco (U.S. and U.K.), 1965 . .
. . . . £50/£15
Drama in Livonia, Arco (U.S. and U.K.), 1967 . .
. . . . £50/£15
The Danube Pilot, Arco (U.S. and U.K.), 1967 . .
. . . . £50/£15
The Sea Serpent, Arco (U.S. and U.K.), 1967 £50/£15
Backwards to Britain, Chambers (U.S. and U.K.),
1992 . . . . £20/£5
Adventures of the Rat Family, O.U.P. (U.S. and U.K.),
1993 . . . . £20/£5
Paris in the 20th Century, Random House (U.S. and
U.K.), 1996 . . . . £20/£5

Non Fiction
The Exploration of the World (B.C. 505 - A.D. 1700),
Sampson Low, 1879 . . . . £200
ditto, as *Famous Travels and Travellers*, Scribner's
(U.S.), 1879 . . . . £200

The Great Navigators of the Eighteenth Century,
Sampson Low, 1880. . . . . . . £200
ditto, Scribner's (U.S.), 1880 . . . . . £200
The Great Explorers of the Nineteenth Century,
Sampson Low, 1881. . . . . . . £200
ditto, Scribner's (U.S.), 1881 . . . . . £200

GORE VIDAL
(b.1925)

An acclaimed U.S. novelist and essayist, Vidal offers
a sharp insight into contemporary American life.

Novels
Williwaw, Dutton (U.S.), 1946 . . . . £500/£50
ditto, Panther, 1965 (wraps) £10
ditto, Heinemann, 1970 . . . . . . £30/£10
In a Yellow Wood, Dutton (U.S.), 1947 . . £300/£35
ditto, New English Library, 1967 (wraps) . . £10
ditto, Heinemann, 1979 . . . . . . £25/£10
The City and The Pillar, Dutton (U.S.), 1948 £175/£20
ditto, Lehmann, 1949 . . . . . . £45/£10
ditto, Dutton (U.S.), 1965 (revised edition) . . £15/£5
ditto, Heinemann, 1965 (revised edition) . . £15/£5
The Season of Comfort, Dutton (U.S.), 1949 £125/£20
A Search for The King: A 12th Century Legend,
Dutton (U.S.), 1950 . . . . . . £125/£20
ditto, New English Library, 1967 (wraps) . . £10
Dark Green, Bright Red, Dutton (U.S.), 1950 . . .
. . . . £125/£20
ditto, Lehmann, 1950 . . . . . . £45/£10
ditto, Signet (U.S.), 1968 (revised edition, wraps) £10
ditto, New English Library, 1968 (wraps) . . £5
The Judgement of Paris, Dutton (U.S.), 1952 £75/£10
ditto, Heinemann, 1953 . . . . . £40/£10
Death in The Fifth Position, Dutton (U.S.), 1952
(pseud. 'Edgar Box') . . . . . £300/£35
ditto, Heinemann, 1954 . . . . . £65/£15
ditto, Ballantine (U.S.), 1961 (revised and abridged,
wraps). £5
ditto, Little, Brown (U.S.), 1961 (revised and abridged
edition) . . . . £10/£5
ditto, Heinemann, 1966 (revised and abridged edition)
. . . . £10/£5
Death Before Bedtime, Dutton (U.S.), 1953 (pseud.
'Edgar Box') . . . . £300/£35
ditto, Heinemann, 1954 . . . . . £65/£15
Death Likes It Hot, Dutton (U.S.), 1954 (pseud. 'Edgar
Box') . . . . £300/£35
ditto, Heinemann, 1955 . . . . . £65/£15
Messiah, Dutton (U.S.), 1954 . . . . £60/£15
ditto, Heinemann, 1955 . . . . . £50/£15
ditto, Little, Brown (U.S.), 1965 (revised and abridged
edition) . . . . £10/£5
ditto, Heinemann, 1968 (revised and abridged edition)
. . . . £10/£5
Three: Williwaw, A Thirsty Evil, Julian the Apostate,
Signet (U.S.), 1962 (wraps) £5

Julian, Little, Brown (U.S.), 1964 . . . £40/£15
ditto, Heinemann, 1964 . . . . . . £35/£10
Washington, D.C., Little, Brown (U.S.), 1967 . £30/£5
ditto, Heinemann, 1967 . . . . £25/£5
Myra Breckinridge, Little, Brown (U.S.), 1968 £30/£5
ditto, Blond, 1968 . . . . £25/£5
Two Sisters: A Memoir in the Form of a Novel, Little,
Brown (U.S.), 1970 . . . . £30/£5
ditto, Heinemann, 1970 . . . . . . £25/£5
Burr, Random House (U.S.), 1973 . . . . £30/£5
ditto, Heinemann, 1974 . . . . . . £25/£5
Myron, Random House (U.S.), 1974. . . . £25/£5
ditto, Heinemann, 1975 . . . . . . £20/£5
1876, Random House (U.S.), 1976 . . . . £25/£5
ditto, Random House (U.S.), 1976 (300 signed copies,
slipcase) . . . . £75/£50
ditto, Heinemann, 1976 . . . . . . £20/£5
Kalki, Random House (U.S.), 1978 . . . £20/£5
ditto, Franklin Library (U.S.), 1978 (signed limited
edition) £45
ditto, Heinemann, 1978 . . . . . . £20/£5
Creation, Random House (U.S.), 1981 . . . £20/£5
ditto, Random House (U.S.), 1981 (500 signed copies,
slipcase) . . . . £65/£50
ditto, Heinemann, 1981 . . . . . . £20/£5
Duluth, Random House (U.S.), 1983 . . £20/£5
ditto, Heinemann, 1983 . . . . . . £20/£5
Lincoln, Random House (U.S.), 1984 . . £20/£5
ditto, Random House (U.S.), 1984 (350 signed,
numbered copies, slipcase) . . . . £75/£50
ditto, Franklin Library (U.S.), 1984 (signed limited
edition) £45
ditto, Heinemann, 1984 . . . . . . £15/£5
Empire, Random House (U.S.), 1987 . . £15/£5
ditto, Random House (U.S.), 1987 (250 signed,
numbered copies, slipcase) . . . . £75/£50
ditto, Franklin Library (U.S.), 1987 (signed limited
edition) £45
ditto, Deutsch, 1987 . . . . £15/£5
Hollywood, Random House (U.S.), 1990 . £15/£5
ditto, Random House (U.S.), 1990 (200 signed,
numbered copies, slipcase) . . . . £75/£50
ditto, Deutsch, 1990 . . . . £15/£5
View from The Diner's Club, Random House (U.S.),
1991 . . . . £15/£5
ditto, Deutsch, 1991 . . . . £15/£5
Live from Golgotha, Random House (U.S.), 1992 . .
. . . . £15/£5
ditto, Deutsch, 1992 . . . . £15/£5
The Smithsonian Institute, Random House (U.S.),
1998 . . . . £15/£5
ditto, Franklin Library (U.S.), 1998 (signed limited
edition) £45
ditto, Little, Brown, 1998 . . . . . £15/£5
The Golden Age, Doubleday (U.S.), 2000 . £15/£5
ditto, Little, Brown, 2000 . . . . . . £15/£5

Short Stories
A Thirsty Evil: Seven Short Stories, Zero Press (U.S.),
1956 . . . . £125/£25

ditto, Heinemann, 1958 . . . . . . £45/£15
The Ladies in The Library and Other Stories,
Eurographica (Helsinki), 1985 (350 signed copies) .
. . . . £75

Plays
Visit to a Small Planet and Other Television Plays,
Little, Brown (U.S.), 1956 . . . . . £50/£10
The Best Man: A Play About Politics, Little, Brown
(U.S.), 1960 . . . . £40/£10
ditto, as *The Best Man*, Dramatists Play Service (U.S.),
1962 (revised edition, wraps) £10
Three Plays, Heinemann, 1962 . . . £35/£10
*Romulus, Adapted from a Play of Friedrich
Duerrenmatt: A New Comedy*, Dramatists Play
Service (U.S.), 1962 (wraps) £25
ditto, as *Romulus: The Broadway Adaptation*, Grove
(U.S.), 1966 . . . . £75/£10
Weekend: A Comedy in Two Acts, Dramatists Play
Service (U.S.), 1968 (wraps) £20
An Evening with Richard Nixon, Random House
(U.S.), 1972 . . . . £20/£5

Essays
Rocking The Boat, Little, Brown (U.S.), 1962 £50/£10
ditto, Heinemann, 1963 . . . . . . £35/£10
Sex, Death and Money, Bantam (U.S.), 1968 (wraps) .
. . . . £5
Reflections Upon a Sinking Ship, Little, Brown (U.S.),
1969 . . . . £30/£5
ditto, Heinemann, 1969 . . . . . . £25/£5
*Homage to Daniel Shays: Collected Essays 1952-
1972*, Random House (U.S.), 1972 . . . £20/£5
ditto, as *Collected Essays 1951-1972*, Heinemann,
1974 . . . . £15/£5
ditto, as *On Our Own Now*, Panther, 1976 (wraps). £5
Matters of Fact and Fiction: Essays, 1973-1976,
Random House (U.S.), 1977 . . . . £20/£5
ditto, Heinemann, 1977 . . . . . . £15/£5
The Second American Revolution and Other Essays,
Random House (U.S.), 1982 . . . . £15/£5
Armageddon? Essays 1985-1987, Deutsch, 1987 . .
. . . . £15/£5
ditto, as *At Home*, Random House (U.S.), 1988 £15/£5
United States: Essays, 1951-92, Deutsch, 1993 £15/£5
*Virgin Islands, A Dependancy of the United States:
Essays 1992-1997*, Deutsch, 1997 . . . £15/£5

Others
Great American Families, Norton (U.S.), 1977 (with
others). . . . . £15/£5
ditto, Times, 1977 . . . . £10/£5
Vidal in Venice, Weidenfeld, 1984 . . . £10/£5
ditto, Summit (U.S.), 1985 . . . . . £10/£5
Screening History, Harvard Univ. Press (U.S.), 1992 .
. . . . £10/£5
ditto, Deutsch, 1992 . . . . £10/£5
Palimpsest, Random House (U.S.), 1995 . £10/£5
ditto, Deutsch, 1995 . . . . £10/£5

KURT VONNEGUT, Jr.
(b.1922)

An American novelist, Vonnegut's experiences as a prisoner of war in Dresden during World War Two have influenced much of his writing.

Novels

Player Piano, Scribner's (U.S.), 1952 ('A' and publisher's seal on copyright page). . . £650/£75
ditto, Macmillan, 1953 . . . . . . £350/£50
The Sirens of Titan, Dell (U.S.), 1959 (wraps). £75
ditto, Houghton Mifflin (U.S.), 1961 . £1,000/£100
ditto, Gollancz, 1962 . . . . £500/£65
Mother Night, Fawcett (U.S.), 1962 (wraps) . £100
ditto, Harper & Row (U.S.), [1966] . . . £200/£30
ditto, Cape, 1968 . . . . £75/£15
Cat's Cradle, Holt Rinehart (U.S.), 1963 . £500/£65
ditto, Gollancz, 1963 . . . . £200/£35
God Bless You, Mr Rosewater or Pearls Before Swine, Holt Rinehart (U.S.), 1965 . . . . . £300/£45
ditto, Cape, 1965 . . . . £200/£35
Slaughterhouse-Five or The Children's Crusade: A Duty-Dance with Death, Delacorte (U.S.), 1969 . .
. . . . £500/£25
ditto, Cape, 1970 . . . . £150/£20
ditto, Franklin Library (U.S.), 1978 (signed limited edition) £65
Breakfast of Champions, Delacorte (U.S.), 1973 . .
. . . . £25/£5
ditto, Cape, 1973 . . . . £25/£5
Slapstick or Lonesome No More, Delacorte (U.S.), 1976 . . . . £25/£5
ditto, Delacorte (U.S.), 1976 (250 signed, numbered copies, slipcase) . . . . £200/£150
ditto, Franklin Library (U.S.), 1976 (signed limited edition) £35
ditto, Cape, 1976 . . . . £30/£5
Jailbird, Delacorte (U.S.), 1979 . . . . . £20/£5
ditto, Delacorte (U.S.), 1979 (500 signed copies, slipcase) . . . . £135/£100
ditto, Franklin Library (U.S.), 1979 (signed limited edition) £35
ditto, Cape, 1979 . . . . £20/£5
Deadeye Dick, Delacorte (U.S.), 1982 . . . £15/£5
ditto, Delacorte (U.S.), 1982 (350 signed copies, slipcase) . . . . £150/£125
ditto, Cape, 1983 . . . . £15/£5
Galapagos, Delacorte (U.S.), 1985 . . . . £15/£5
ditto, Delacorte (U.S.), 1985 (500 signed copies, slipcase) . . . . £150/£125
ditto, Franklin Library (U.S.), 1985 (signed limited edition) £40
ditto, Cape, 1985 . . . . £15/£5
Bluebeard, Delacorte (U.S.), 1987 . . . . £15/£5
ditto, Delacorte (U.S.), 1987 (500 signed copies, slipcase) . . . . £150/£125
ditto, Franklin Library (U.S.), 1987 (signed limited edition) £40

ditto, Cape, 1988 . . . . £15/£5
Hocus Pocus; Or, What's The Hurry Son?, Putnam (U.S.), 1990 . . . . £10/£5
ditto, Putnam (U.S.), 1990 (250 signed copies, slipcase)
. . . . £150/£125
ditto, Franklin Library (U.S.), 1990 (signed limited edition) £40
ditto, Cape, 1990 . . . . £10/£5
Timequake, Putnam (U.S.), 1997 . . . . £10/£5
ditto, Cape, 1997 . . . . £10/£5

Short Stories

Canary in a Cathouse, Fawcett (U.S.), 1961 (wraps) .
. . . . £65
Welcome to The Monkey House, Delacorte (U.S.), 1968 . . . . £300/£45
ditto, Cape, 1969 . . . . £125/£20
Bagombo Snuff Box: Uncollected Short Fiction, Putnam (U.S.), 1999. . . . . £10/£5
ditto, Putnam (U.S.), 1999 (175 signed, numbered copies, slipcase) . . . . . . £150/£100
ditto, Cape, 1999 . . . . £10/£5

Plays

Happy Birthday, Wanda June, Delacorte (U.S.), 1971 (price at top on front flap of d/w) . . . £600/£30
ditto, Cape, 1973 . . . . £150/£20
Between Time and Timbuctu or Prometheus-5, Delacorte (U.S.), 1972 . . . . . . £300/£65

Others

Wampeters, Foma, and Granfalloons (Opinions), Delacorte (U.S.), 1974 . . . . . £40/£10
ditto, Cape, 1975 . . . . £25/£10
Sun Moon, Star, Harper & Row (U.S.), 1980 (with Ivan Chermayeff) . . . . £15/£5
ditto, Hutchinson, 1980 . . . . . . £15/£5
Palm Sunday: An Autobiographical Collage, Delacorte (U.S.), 1981 . . . . . . £15/£5
ditto, Delacorte (U.S.), 1981 (500 signed copies, slipcase) . . . . £100/£75
ditto, Cape, 1981 . . . . £15/£5
Nothing is Lost Save Honor, Nouveau Press (U.S.), 1984 (300 signed copies, wraps) £100
ditto, Nouveau Press (U.S.), 1984 (40 signed deluxe copies, boards) £300
Fates Worse Than Death: An Autobiographical Collage of The 1980's, Putnam (U.S.), 1991 . £15/£5
ditto, Putnam (U.S.), 1991 (200 signed, numbered copies, slipcase) . . . . . . £150/£100
ditto, Cape, 1991 . . . . £10/£5

LOUIS WAIN
(b.1860 d.1939)

Highly successful British illustrator, well known for his drawings of cats.

Books Written and Illustrated by Louis Wain

Dreams by French Firesides, A. & C. Black, 1890 (pseud. 'Richard Leander') £400
Miss Lovemouse's Letters, Nelson, 1896 . . £400
Puppy Dogs' Tales, Nelson, 1896 . . . . £400
The Children's Tableaux: The Three Little Kittens, Nister, 1896 . . . . £400
The Dandy Lion, by Louis Wain and Clifton Bingham, Nister, [1900]. £600
Fun All The Way, Nister, 1900 . . . . . £200
Cats, Sands, [1901] (pseud. 'Grimalkin') . . £1,500
Fun For Everyone, Nister, 1902 . . . . . £200
Fun and Frolic, by Louis Wain and Clifton Bingham, Nister, [1902]. £1,000
Pa Cats, Ma Cats, and Their Kittens, Raphael Tuck, [1902] (pseud. 'Father Tuck') . . . £1,000
The Louis Wain Nursery Book, Clarke, [1902] £300
Louis Wain's Cats and Dogs, Raphael Tuck, 1902 . . . . £450
Big Dogs, Little Dogs, Cats and Kittens, Raphael Tuck, [1903] £1,500
Comic Annuals ABC, by Louis Wain, Collins, [1903]. £500
Louis Wain's Baby's Picture Book, Clarke, 1903 £400
Louis Wain's Dog Painting Book, Raphael Tuck, 1903 . . . . £400
Louis Wain's Cat Painting Book, Raphael Tuck, 1903 . . . . £400
Louis Wain's Summer Book, Hutchinson, 1903 £400
The Louis Wain Kitten Book, Treherne, [1903] (printed on one side of the page) £1,500
Funny Animals and Stories About Them, Clarke, 1904 . . . . £500
In Animal Land with Louis Wain, Partridge, [1904] £1,000
Kits and Cats, Raphael Tuck, 1904 . . . . £750
Louis Wain's Animal Show: With Stories in Prose and Verse, Clarke, 1905. . . . . . £350
Louis Wain's Summer Book for 1906, King, 1906 . . . . £350
Animal Playtime, Clarke, 1908 . . . . . £350
In Story Land with Louis Wain, Raphael Tuck, 1912 . . . . £1,000
Louis Wain's Painting Book, Shaw, 1912 . . £350
Louis Wain's Father Christmas, Shaw, 1912 . £350
Animal Happyland, Clarke, 1913 . . . . £350
Happy Hours with Louis Wain, Shaw, 1913 . £450
A Cat Alphabet and Picture Book for Little Folk, Blackie & Sons, [1914] £500
Animal Picture-Land, Clarke, 1914 . . . . £400
Daddy Cat, Blackie & Sons, [1915] . . . £750
Little Red Riding Hood and Other Tales, Gale & Poleden, [1917] £350

Cinderella and Other Fairy Tales, Gale & Poleden, 1917 . . . . £350
Cats at Play, Blackie, 1917 . . . . . . £750
The Story of Tabbykin Town in School and at Play, Faulkner, [1920] (pseud. 'Kittycat') . . . £1,000
Pussy Land, Geographia, [1920]. £450
The Kitten's House, Valentine, 1922 . . . £750
Charlie's Adventures, Valentine, 1922 . . . £750
Comical Kittens, Valentine, [1922] (painting book with paints and brush). £200
Louis Wain's Children's Book, Hutchinson, [1923] £350
Souvenir of Louis Wain's Work, Louis Wain Fund, 1925 . . . . £175
ditto, as *Animals 'Xtra' and Louis Wain's Annual 1925*, Louis Wain Fund, [1925]. £175
Louis Wain's Animal Book, Collins, 'Bumper Book', [1928]. £200
Louis Wain's Great Big Midget Book, Dean, 1934 . . . . £200

Annuals

Louis Wain's Annual, Treherne, 1901 . . £350
Louis Wain's Annual for 1902, Treherne, 1902 £350
Louis Wain's Annual 1903, Hutchinson, 1903 . £350
Louis Wain's Annual 1905, King, 1905 . £250
Louis Wain's Annual for 1906, Shaw, 1906 . £250
Louis Wain's Annual 1907, Bemrose, 1907 . £250
Louis Wain's Annual 1908, Bemrose, 1908 . £250
Louis Wain's Annual 1909-10, Allen, 1909 . £225
Louis Wain's Annual 1910-11, Allen, 1910 . £225
Louis Wain's Annual 1911, Shaw, 1911 . £225
Louis Wain's Annual 1911-12, Shaw, 1911 . £225
Louis Wain's Annual 1912, Shaw, 1912 . . £225
Louis Wain's Annual 1913, Shaw, 1913 . . £225
Louis Wain's Annual 1914, Shaw, 1914 . . £225
Louis Wain's Annual 1915, Shaw, 1915 . . £225
Louis Wain's Annual 1921, Hutchinson, 1921 . £225

Books Illustrated by Louis Wain

Madame Tabby's Establishment, by Kari, Macmillan, 1886 . . . . £1,500
Our Farm: The Trouble and Successes Thereof, by F.W. Pattenden, Clarke, 1888 . . . £400
Peter, A Cat O' One Tail: His Life and Adventures, by Charles Morley, Pall Mall Gazette Extras, 1892 £850
Old Rabbit, The Voodoo and Other Sorcerers, by M.A. Owen, Unwin, 1893 . . . . . . £250
More Jingles, Jokes and Funny Folks, by Clifton Bingham, Nister, 1898 . . . . £500
The Monkey That Would Not Kill, by Henry Drummond, Hodder & Stoughton, 1898 . . £125
Pussies and Puppies: With Verses and Tales by Various Writers, Partridge, [1899] £400
The Living Animals of The World, by C.J. Cornish, [1901]. £250
All Sorts of Comical Cats, by Clifton Bingham, Nister, 1902 . . . . £1,500

Ping-Pong Calendar for 1903, by Clifton Bingham, Raphael Tuck, [1903] £350
Kittenland, by Clifton Bingham, Collins, [1903] £1,500
With Louis Wain to Fairyland, by Nora Chesson, Raphael Tuck, [1904] £1,500
Funny Favourites, by Clifton Bingham, Nister, 1904 . . . . £750
Claws and Paws: Stories and Pictures from Kittenland and Puppyland, by C. Bingham, Nister, [1904] £1,450
Cat Tales, by W.L. Alden, Digby Long, 1905 . £750
The Adventures of Friskers and His Friends, by Marian Hurrell, Culley, 1907 . . . . . £750
Mephistopheles: The Autobiography and Adventures of a Tabby Cat, by C.Y. Stephens, Jarrold, 1907 £750
The Kings and The Cats: Munster Fairy Tales for Young and Old, by John Hannon, Burns & Oates, [1908]. £650
Cat's Cradle: A Picture Book for Little Folk, by May Clariss Byron, Blackie, [1908] £650
Full of Fun, by Clifton Bingham, Nister, [1908] £650
Holidays in Animal Land, by A.W. Ridler, Clarke, [1909]. £450
Two Cats at Large: A Book of Surprises, by S.C. Woodhouse, Routledge, [1910]. £750
The Merry Animal Picture Book, by A.W. Ridler, Clarke, [1910] £400
The Happy Family, by Edric Vredenburg, Raphael Tuck, 1910 . . . . £1,000
Such Fun with Louis Wain, by Norman Gale, Raphael Tuck, 1910 . . . . £450
To Nursery Land with Louis Wain, edited by Edric Vredenburg, Raphael Tuck, 1910 . . . . £350
Cats at School, by S.C. Woodhouse, Routledge, [1911] £750
Animals in Fun-Land, by A.W. Rider, Clarke, 1911 . . . . £400
Merry Times in Animal-Land, by A.W. Rider, Clarke, 1912 . . . . £400
The Cat Scouts: A Picture Book for Little Folk, by Jessie Pope, Blackie, [1912] £1,000
Louis Wain's Happy Land, by A.W. Ridler, Shaw, 1912 . . . . £300
Tinker, Tailor, by Eric Vredenburg, Raphael Tuck, 1914 . . . . £1,000
Animal Fancy-Land, by A.W. Rider, Clarke, 1915 . . . . £400
Little Soldiers, by May Crommelin, Hutchinson, [1915]. £300
Merry Times with Louis Wain, by Dorothy Black, Raphael Tuck, 1916 . . . . £750
The Tales of Little Priscilla Purr, by Cecily M. Rutley, Valentine, 1920 . . . . £600
The Tale of Naughty Kitty Cat, by Cecily M. Rutley, Valentine, 1920 . . . . £300
The Tale of Peter Pusskin, by Cecily M. Rutley, Valentine, 1920 . . . . £300

The Tale of The Tabby Twins, by Cecily M. Rutley, Valentine, 1920 . . . . £300
The Teddy Rocker: Naughty Teddy Bear, by Cecily M. Rutley, Valentine, 1921 (shape book) . . £325
The Pussy Rocker: Polly Puss, by Cecily M. Rutley, Valentine, 1921 (shape book) £325

ALFRED WAINWRIGHT
(d.1907 d.1991)

Wainwright was the author and illustrator of numerous guides to the fells of England and Scotland.

'A Pictorial Guide to the Lakeland Fells' Titles
The Eastern Fells, Henry Marshall, 1955 (in 'second impression' d/w) . . . . £200/£165
The Far Eastern Fells, Henry Marshall, 1957 . . . . £175/£75
The Central Fells, Henry Marshall, 1958 . £175/£75
The Southern Fells, Henry Marshall, 1960 . £175/£75
The Northern Fells, Henry Marshall, 1962 . £175/£75
The North-Western Fells, Westmorland Gazette, 1964 . . . . £175/£75
The Western Fells, Westmorland Gazette, 1966 . . . . £175/£75

'Lakeland Sketchbooks'
A Lakeland Sketchbook, Westmorland Gazette, 1969 . . . . £75/£25
A Second Lakeland Sketchbook, Westmorland Gazette, 1970. . . . . £50/£20
A Third Lakeland Sketchbook, Westmorland Gazette, 1971 . . . . £45/£15
A Fourth Lakeland Sketchbook, Westmorland Gazette, 1972. . . . . £45/£15
A Fifth Lakeland Sketchbook, Westmorland Gazette, 1973 . . . . £45/£15

Scottish Mountain Drawings
The Northern Highlands, Westmorland Gazette, 1974 . . . . £50/£20
The North-West Highlands, Westmorland Gazette, 1976 . . . . £40/£15
The Western Highlands, Westmorland Gazette, 1976 . . . . £40/£15
The Central Highlands, Westmorland Gazette, 1977 . . . . £40/£15
The Eastern Highlands, Westmorland Gazette, 1978 . . . . £40/£15
The Islands, Westmorland Gazette, 1979 . £40/£15

Others
Fellwanderer, The Story Behind the Guidebooks, Westmorland Gazette, 1966. . . . . £30/£10
Pennine Way Companion, Westmorland Gazette, 1968 . . . . £75/£25

Guide to First Edition Prices, 2004/5

Walks in Limestone Country, Westmorland Gazette, 1970 . . . . £50/£20
Walks on the Howgill Fells, Westmorland Gazette, 1972 . . . . £45/£15
A Coast to Coast Walk, St Bees Head to Robin Hood's Bay, Westmorland Gazette, 1973 . . . £45/£15
The Outlying Fells of Lakeland, Westmorland Gazette, 1974 . . . . £45/£15
Westmorland Heritage, Westmorland Gazette, 1974 (1,000 signed copies) . . . . . . £500/£200
ditto, Westmorland Gazette, 1988 . . . . £20/£5
A Dales Sketchbook, Westmorland Gazette, 1976 . . . . £45/£15
Kendal in the Nineteenth Century, Westmorland Gazette, 1977 . . . . £75/£15
A Second Dales Sketchbook, Westmorland Gazette, 1978 . . . . £40/£15
A Furness Sketchbook, Westmorland Gazette, 1978 . . . . £40/£15
Walks from Ratty, Ravenglass and Eskdale Railway Co, 1978 . . . . £40/£15
A Second Furness Sketchbook, Westmorland Gazette, 1979 . . . . £40/£15
Three Westmorland Rivers, Westmorland Gazette, 1979 . . . . £40/£15
A Lune Sketchbook, Westmorland Gazette, 1980 . . . . £40/£15
A Ribble Sketchbook, Westmorland Gazette, 1980 . . . . £40/£15
An Eden Sketchbook, Westmorland Gazette, 1980 . . . . £40/£15
Lakeland Mountain Drawings, Westmorland Gazette, 1980 (5 vols) . . . . . . £40/£15 each
Welsh Mountain Drawings, Westmorland Gazette, 1981 . . . . £40/£15
A Bowland Sketchbook, Westmorland Gazette, 1981 . . . . £40/£15
A North Wales Sketchbook, Westmorland Gazette, 1982 . . . . £40/£15
A Wyre Sketchbook, Westmorland Gazette, 1982 . . . . £40/£15
A South Wales Sketchbook, Westmorland Gazette, 1983 . . . . £40/£15
Wainwright in Lakeland, Abbott Hall Art Gallery, 1983 (1,000 signed copies) . . . . . £500/£200
A Peak District Sketchbook, Westmorland Gazette, 1984 . . . . £40/£15
Fellwalking with Wainwright, Joseph, 1984 (photographs by Derry Brabbs) . . . . . £20/£5
Old Roads of Eastern Lakeland, Westmorland Gazette, 1985 . . . . £15/£5
Wainwright on the Pennine Way, Joseph, 1985 (photographs by Derry Brabbs) . . . £15/£5
A Pennine Journey, Joseph, 1986 . . £15/£5
Wainwright's Coast to Coast Walk, Joseph, 1987 (photographs by Derry Brabbs) . . . £15/£5
Ex-Fellwanderer, Westmorland Gazette, 1987 . £15/£5
Wainwright in Scotland, Joseph, 1988 (photographs by Derry Brabbs) . . . . £15/£5

Fellwalking with a Camera, Westmorland Gazette, 1988 . . . . £15/£5
Wainwright on the Lakeland Mountain Passes, Joseph, 1989 (photographs by Derry Brabbs) . £15/£5
Wainwright in the Limestone Dales, Joseph, 1991 (photographs by Ed Geldard) . . . . . £10/£5
Wainwright's Favourite Lakeland Mountains, Joseph, 1991 (photographs by Derry Brabbs) . . . £10/£5
Wainwright in the Valleys of Lakeland, Joseph, 1992 (photographs by Derry Brabbs) . . . . . £10/£5
Memoirs of a Fellwanderer, Joseph, 1993 . . £10/£5
Wainwright: His Tour of the Lake District, Whitsuntide, 1931, Joseph, 1993 (photographs by Ed Geldard) . . . . £10/£5
The Walker's Log Book, Joseph, 1993 . . . £10/£5

Other Titles Illustrated by Wainwright
Inside the Real Lakeland, by A.H. Griffin, Guardian Press, 1961 . . . . £50/£15
Scratch and Co., by Molly Lefebure, Gollancz, 1968 . . . . £20/£5
The Hunting of Wilberforce Pike, by Molly Lefebure, Gollancz, 1970 . . . . . . £15/£5
The Plague Dogs, by Richard Adams, Allen Lane, 1977 . . . . £15/£5
Guide to the View from Scafel Pike, Chris Jesty Panoramas, 1978 . . . . £15/£5

A.E. WAITE
(b.1857 d.1942)

An occultist, poet, bohemian and mystic, Waite's contribution to occult literature is voluminous.

Principal Works
The Real History of The Rosicrucians, George Redway, 1887 . . . . £150
A Handbook of Cartomancy, George Redway, 1889 (pseud. 'Grand Orient') £125
The Interior Life from The Standpoint of The Mystics, 'Light', [1891] £200
The Occult Sciences, Kegan Paul, Trench, Trübner and Co., 1891 . . . . £150
Azoth: or The Star in The East, Theosophical Publishing Society, 1893 . . . . . . £200
Devil-Worship in France, George Redway, 1896 £125
The Book of Black Magic and Pacts, Redway, 1898 (500 copies) £250
The Life of Louis Claude de Saint-Martin, Philip Wellby, 1901 . . . . £150
The Doctrine and Literature of The Kabalah, Theosophical Publishing Society, 1902 . . £200
Studies in Mysticism, Hodder & Stoughton, 1906 £100
The Hidden Church of The Holy Graal, Rebman Ltd, 1909 . . . . £125
The Key to The Tarot, William Rider & Son Ltd, 1910 . . . . £75

ditto, 1920 (new edition) £75
The Pictorial Key to The Tarot, William Rider & Son Ltd, 1911 . . . . £75
The Book of Ceremonial Magic, William Rider and Son Ltd, 1911 . . . . £75
The Secret Tradition in Freemasonry, Rebman Ltd, 1911 . . . . £75
The Secret Doctrine in Israel, William Rider & Son Ltd, 1913 . . . . £100
The Way of Divine Union, William Rider & Son Ltd, 1915 . . . . £275
Deeper Aspects of Masonic Symbolism, privately printed, 1915 . . . . £65
New Encyclopaedia of Freemasonry, William Rider & Son Ltd, 1921 . . . . £125/£65
Robert Fludd and Freemasonry, offprint (1922) £45
Raymond Lully, William Rider & Son Ltd, 1922 . . . . £75/£45
Saint-Martin, William Rider & Son Ltd, 1922 . . . . £65/£35
Lamps of Western Mysticism, Kegan Paul, Trench, Trübner and Co., 1923 . . . . . £60/£35
The Brotherhood of The Rosy Cross, William Rider & Son Ltd, 1924 . . . . £75/£25
Emblematic Freemasonry, William Rider & Son Ltd, 1925 . . . . £65/£35
The Secret Tradition in Alchemy, Kegan Paul, Trench, Trübner and Co., 1926 . . . . . . £75/£35
The Holy Kabbalah, William & Norgate Ltd, 1929 . . . . £50/£30
The Holy Grail, William Rider & Son Ltd, 1933 . . . . £65/£35
The Secret Tradition in Freemasonry, Rider & Co., 1937 . . . . £65/£35
Shadows of Life and Thought, Selwyn & Blount, 1938 . . . . £65/£30

Poetry

An Ode to Astronomy and Other Poems, 1877?, (100 copies) £3,000
A Lyric of The Fairyland, Catty, 1879 . . £2,000
A Soul's Comedy, George Redway, 1887 . . £100
Lucastra, James Burns, [1890] £100
A Book of Mystery and Vision, Philip Wellby, 1902 . . . . £65
ditto, Philip Wellby, 1902 (10 signed copies on Japanese vellum) £350
Strange Houses of Sleep, Philip Wellby, 1906 (250 signed, numbered copies, with Arthur Machen) £125
The Collected Poems of Arthur Edward Waite, Rider, 1914 (2 vols) £65
The Book of The Holy Graal, J.M. Watkins, 1921 (500 copies) . . . . £75/£35
The Open Vision, Shakespeare Head Press, 1959 (500 copies) . . . . £30/£10

Fiction

Prince Starbeam, James Burns, 1889 . . . £100
The Golden Stairs, Theosophical Publishing Society, 1893 . . . . £100

Belle and The Dragon, James Elliot, 1894 . . £100
Steps to The Crown, Philip Wellby, 1906 . . £65
The Quest of The Golden Stairs, Theosophical Publishing House Ltd, [1927] . . . . £50/£25

Others

Israfel, Letters, Visions and Poems, E.W. Allen, 1886 . . . . £75
ditto, James Elliot & Co., 1894 (enlarged edition) £65
The House of The Hidden Light, privately printed, 1904 (with Arthur Machen, 3 copies) . £1,500
ditto, Tartarus/Ferret, 2003 . . . . . £30/£10
The Hermetic Text Society, Philip Wellby, 1907 £50

ALICE WALKER
(b.1944)

Novelist, poet, critic and essay-writer, Walker's third novel, *The Color Purple* secured her not only a Pulitzer Prize but a place as one of America's foremost living writers.

Novels

The Third Life of Grange Copeland, Harcourt, Brace, Jovanovich (U.S.), 1970 . . . . . £200/£25
ditto, Women's Press, 1985 . . . . . £35/£10
Meridian, Harcourt, Brace, Jovanovich (U.S.), 1976 . . . . £125/£15
ditto, Deutsch, 1976 . . . . £100/£15
The Color Purple, Harcourt, Brace, Jovanovich (U.S.), 1982 . . . . £300/£30
ditto, Women's Press, 1983 . . . . . £100/£20
The Temple of My Familiar, Harcourt, Brace, Jovanovich (U.S.), 1989 . . . . . . £15/£5
ditto, Harcourt, Brace, Jovanovich (U.S.), 1989 (500 signed, numbered copies, slipcase) . . . £100/£65
ditto, Women's Press, 1989 . . . . . £15/£5
Possessing the Secret of Joy, Harcourt Brace (U.S.), 1992 . . . . £15/£5
ditto, Harcourt, Brace, Jovanovich (U.S.), 1992 (250 signed, numbered copies, slipcase) . . . £100/£65
ditto, Cape, 1992 . . . . £15/£5
The Same River Twice, Scribner's (U.S.), 1996 £20/£5
ditto, Women's Press, 1996 . . . . . £25/£10
By the Light of My Father's Smile, Women's Press, 1998 . . . . £20/£5
ditto, Women's Press, 1998 . . . . . £15/£5

Short Stories

In Love and Trouble: Stories for Black Women, Harcourt, Brace, Jovanovich (U.S.), 1973 . £500/£45
ditto, Women's Press, 1984 . . . . . £100/£15
You Can't Keep a Good Woman Down, Harcourt, Brace, Jovanovich (U.S.), 1981. . . . £100/£15
ditto, Women's Press, 1982 . . . . . £45/£15

Poetry

Once, Harcourt, Brace & World (U.S.), 1968 £400/£45
Revolutionary Petunias and Other Poems, Harcourt, Brace, Jovanovich (U.S.), 1973. . . . . £200/£30
ditto, Women's Press, 1988 (wraps) £10
Good Night, Willie Lee, I'll See You in the Morning, Dial (U.S.), 1979. . . . . £100/£15
Horses Make a Landscape Look More Beautiful: Poems, Harcourt, Brace, Jovanovich (U.S.), 1984 .
. . . . £40/£10
ditto, Women's Press, 1985 . . . . . . £25/£5
Her Blue Body Everything We Know: Earthling Poems 1965-1990, Harcourt, Brace, Jovanovich (U.S.), 1991 . . . . £10/£5
ditto, Harcourt, Brace, Jovanovich (U.S.), 1991 (111 signed copies, slipcase) . . . . . . £125/£100
ditto, Women's Press, 1991 . . . . . . £25/£5

Children's Books

Langston Hughes, American Poet, Crowell (U.S.), 1974 . . . . £250/£45
To Hell With Dying, Harcourt, Brace, Jovanovich (U.S.), 1988 . . . . £20/£5
ditto, Hodder & Stoughton, 1988. . . . . £20/£5
Finding the Green Stone, Harcourt, Brace, Jovanovich (U.S.), 1991 . . . . £20/£5
ditto, Hodder & Stoughton, 1991. . . . . £15/£5

Others

In Search of Our Mothers' Garden: Womanist Prose, Harcourt, Brace, Jovanovich (U.S.), 1983 . £25/£10
ditto, Women's Press, 1984 . . . . . . £20/£5
Living by the Word: Selected Writings 1973-1987, Harcourt, Brace, Jovanovich (U.S.), 1988 . . £15/£5
Warrior Marks: Female Genital Mutilation and the Sexual Blinding of Women, Harcourt Brace (U.S.), 1993 (with Pratibha Parmar) . . . . . £15/£5

EDGAR WALLACE
(b.1875 d.1932)

Wallace's output of books was vast, and he made no attempt to disguise the fact that it was popular rather than critical success that he craved. In this ambition he was incredibly successful.

Novels

The Four Just Men, Tallis Press, 1905 (numbered competition slip) £125
ditto, Tallis Press, 1906 (includes chapter 12, a letter from Manfred as solution) £30
ditto, Tallis Press, 1911 (includes full chapter 12) £20
ditto, Small Maynard (U.S.), 1920 . . . £75/£20
Angel Esquire, Arrowsmith, 1908 . . . . £45
ditto, Holt (U.S.), 1908 . . . . £45
The Council of Justice, Ward Lock, 1908 . . £100
Captain Tatham of Tatham Island, Gale & Polden, 1909 . . . . £225

ditto, as *The Island of Galloping Gold*, Newnes, 1916
. . . . £25
ditto, as *Eve's Island*, Newnes, 1926 [wraps] . £35
The Duke in the Suburbs, Ward Lock, 1909 . £100
The Nine Bears, Ward Lock, 1910 . . . . £100
ditto, as *The Other Man*, Dodd, Mead (U.S.), 1911 £75
ditto, as *Silinski, Master Criminal*, World Syndicate, 1930 . . . . £30/£5
Private Selby, Ward Lock, 1912 . . . . . £85
Grey Timothy, Ward Lock, 1913. . . . . £75
ditto, as *Pallard the Punter*, Ward Lock, 1914 (wraps)
. . . . £75
The River of Stars, Ward Lock, 1913 . . . £75
The Fourth Plague, Ward Lock, 1913 . . . £75
ditto, Doubleday Doran (U.S.), 1930 . . £65/£15
The Melody of Death, Arrowsmith, 1915 . . £125
ditto, Dial (U.S.), 1927 . . . . . . £65/£25
1925: The Story of a Fatal Peace, Newnes, 1915 (wraps) £125
The Man Who Bought London, Ward Lock, 1915 £65
The Clue of the Twisted Candle, Small Maynard (U.S.), 1916 . . . . £75
ditto, Newnes, 1917 . . . . £65
A Debt Discharged, Ward Lock, 1916 . . . £65
The Tomb of Ts'in, Ward Lock, 1916 . . . £300
The Just Men of Cordova, Ward Lock, 1917 . £65
ditto, Doubleday Doran (U.S.), 1929 . . £65/£15
The Secret House, Ward Lock, 1917 . . . £65
ditto, Small Maynard (U.S.), 1919 . . . £65
Kate Plus Ten, Small Maynard (U.S.), 1917 . £100
ditto, Ward Lock, 1919 . . . . £100
Down Under Donovan, Ward Lock, 1918 . . £75
Those Folk of Bulboro, Ward Lock, 1918 . . £75
The Man Who Knew, Small Maynard (U.S.), 1918 £65
ditto, Newnes, 1919 . . . . £60
The Green Rust, Ward Lock, 1919 . . . . £75
ditto, Small Maynard (U.S.), 1920 . . . £200/£35
Jack O' Judgement, Ward Lock, 1920 . . £300/£65
ditto, Small Maynard (U.S.), 1921 . . . £200/£35
The Daffodil Mystery, Ward Lock, 1920 . £500/£125
ditto, as *The Daffodil Murder*, Small Maynard (U.S.), 1921. . . . . £300/£75
The Book of All Power, Ward Lock, 1921 . £250/£65
The Angel of Terror, Hodder & Stoughton, 1922 . .
. . . . £275/£75
ditto, Small Maynard (U.S.), 1922 . . . £225/£65
Sandi, The King-Maker, Ward Lock, 1922. £250/£50
Captains of Souls, Small Maynard (U.S.), 1922 . .
. . . . £250/£65
ditto, John Long, 1923 . . . . . . £300/£75
The Flying Fifty-Five, Hutchinson, 1922 . £600/£100
The Crimson Circle, Hodder & Stoughton, 1922 . .
. . . . £225/£65
ditto, Doubleday Doran (U.S.), 1929 . . £100/£20
Mr. Justice Maxell, Ward Lock, 1922 . . £500/£100
The Valley of Ghosts, Odhams, 1922 . . £400/£75
ditto, Small Maynard (U.S.), 1923 . . . £250/£65
The Clue of the New Pin, Hodder & Stoughton, 1923 .
. . . . £225/£45

ditto, Small Maynard (U.S.), 1923 . . . £175/£35
The Books of Bart, Ward Lock, 1923 . . £250/£50
The Green Archer, Hodder & Stoughton, 1923 . .
. . . . £225/£45
ditto, Small Maynard (U.S.), 1924 . . . £175/£35
Blue Hand, Small Maynard (U.S.), 1923 . £350/£100
ditto, Ward Lock, 1925 . . . . . . £250/£75
The Fellowship of the Frog, Small Maynard (U.S.), 1923 . . . . £300/£75
ditto, Ward Lock, 1925 . . . . . . £375/£100
The Missing Million, John Long, 1923 . . £350/£100
ditto, as **The Missing Millions**, Small Maynard (U.S.), 1925 . . . . £250/£65
The Dark Eyes of London, Ward Lock, 1924 £250/£65
ditto, Doubleday Doran (U.S.), 1929 . . £200/£45
The Sinister Man, Hodder & Stoughton, 1924 . . .
. . . . £150/£45
ditto, Small Maynard (U.S.), 1925. . . £100/£25
Room 13, John Long, 1924 . . . . . £350/£100
The Three Oak Mystery, Ward Lock, 1924 £350/£100
Double Dan, Hodder & Stoughton, 1924 . £150/£45
ditto, as **Diana of Kara-Kara**, Small Maynard (U.S.), 1924 . . . . £100/£25
The Face in the Night, John Long, 1924 . £250/£50
ditto, Doubleday Doran (U.S.), 1929 . . £175/£40
Flat 2, Garden City (U.S.), 1924 (wraps) . £65
ditto, John Long, 1927 . . . . . . £50/£15
The Strange Countess, Hodder & Stoughton, 1925 .
. . . . £75/£15
ditto, Small Maynard (U.S.), 1926 . . £50/£10
A King by Night, John Long, 1925 . . £250/£50
ditto, Doubleday Page (U.S.), 1926 . . . £175/£40
The Gaunt Stranger, Hodder & Stoughton, 1925 . .
. . . . £100/£30
ditto, as **The Ringer**, Doubleday Page (U.S.), 1926 .
. . . . £75/£20
The Three Just Men, Hodder & Stoughton, 1925 . .
. . . . £100/£15
ditto, Doubleday Doran (U.S.), 1929. . . £100/£15
The Man from Morocco, John Long, 1925 . £225/£45
ditto, as **The Black**, Doubleday Doran (U.S.), 1930 .
. . . . £75/£15
The Daughters of the Night, Newnes, 1925 (wraps) .
. . . . £100
The Hairy Arm, Small Maynard (U.S.), 1925 £150/£45
ditto, as **The Avenger**, John Long, 1926. . £225/£60
The Door with Seven Locks, Hodder & Stoughton, 1926 . . . . £40/£10
ditto, Doubleday Doran (U.S.), 1926 . . £40/£10
We Shall See, Hodder & Stoughton, 1926 . £65/£15
ditto, as **The Gaol-Breakers**, Doubleday Doran (U.S.), 1931 . . . . £45/£10
The Black Abbot, Hodder & Stoughton, 1926 £75/£15
ditto, Doubleday Page (U.S.), 1927 . . . £50/£10
The Terrible People, Hodder & Stoughton, 1926 . .
. . . . £45/£10
ditto, Doubleday Page (U.S.), 1926 . . . £45/£10
The Day of Uniting, Hodder & Stoughton, 1926 . .
. . . . £75/£15

ditto, Mystery League (U.S.), 1930 . . . £50/£10
Penelope of the Polyantha, Hodder & Stoughton, 1926
. . . . £65/£15
The Joker, Hodder & Stoughton, 1926 . . £45/£10
ditto, as **The Colossus**, Doubleday Doran (U.S.), 1932
. . . . £40/£10
The Square Emerald, Hodder & Stoughton, 1926 . .
. . . . £65/£15
ditto, as **The Girl from Scotland Yard**, Doubleday Doran (U.S.), 1927 . . . . . £65/£15
The Yellow Snake, Hodder & Stoughton, 1926. . . .
. . . . £45/£15
Barbara on Her Own, Newnes, [1926] . . £75/£15
The Million Dollar Story, Newnes, 1926 (wraps) £75
The Northing Tramp, Hodder & Stoughton, 1926 . .
. . . . £75/£15
ditto, Doubleday Doran (U.S.), 1929 . . £50/£10
The Hand of Power, John Long, 1926 . . £225/£75
ditto, Mystery League (U.S.), 1930 . . . £65/£15
The Traitor's Gate, Hodder & Stoughton, 1927 . . .
. . . . £65/£10
ditto, Doubleday Page (U.S.), 1927 . . . £50/£10
The Man Who Was Nobody, Ward Lock, 1927 . . .
. . . . £300/£75
The Feathered Serpent, Hodder & Stoughton, 1927 .
. . . . £100/£20
ditto, Doubleday Doran (U.S.), 1928 . . £65/£15
Terror Keep, Hodder & Stoughton, 1927 . £65/£10
ditto, Doubleday Page (U.S.), 1927 . . . £60/£10
Big Foot, John Long, 1927 . . . . . £100/£20
Number Six, Newnes, 1927 (wraps). . . . £75
The Squeaker, Hodder & Stoughton, 1927 . £65/£15
ditto, as **The Squealer**, Doubleday Doran (U.S.), 1928
. . . . £50/£10
The Forger, Hodder & Stoughton, 1927 . £100/£15
ditto, as **The Clever One**, Doubleday Doran (U.S.), 1928 . . . . £65/£10
The Double, Hodder & Stoughton, 1928 . £65/£10
ditto, Doubleday Doran (U.S.), 1928 . . £45/£10
The Thief in the Night, Readers Library, 1928 £35/£10
The Twister, John Long, 1928 . . . . £50/£10
ditto, Doubleday Page, 1929 . . . . . £40/£10
The Flying Squad, Hodder & Stoughton, 1928. . . .
. . . . £75/£10
ditto, Doubleday Doran (U.S.), 1928 . . £45/£10
The Gunner, Long, 1928 . . . . . . £50/£10
ditto, as **Gunman's Bluff**, Doubleday Doran (U.S.), 1929 . . . . £40/£10
Four Square Jane, Readers Library, 1929 . £45/£10
ditto, World Wide (U.S.), 1929 . . . . £35/£10
The India-Rubber Men, Hodder & Stoughton, 1929 .
. . . . £45/£10
ditto, Doubleday Doran, 1930 . . . . . £35/£5
The Terror, Collins, 1929 . . . . . £35/£10
The Golden Hades, Collins, 1929 . . . £65/£10
The Green Ribbon, Hutchinson, 1929 . . £300/£45
ditto, Doubleday Doran, 1930 . . . . £175/£25
Again the Ringer, Hodder & Stoughton, 1929 £45/£10

ditto, as *The Ringer Returns*, Doubleday Doran, 1931
. . . . £35/£10
White Face, Hodder & Stoughton, 1930 . £45/£10
ditto, Doubleday Doran (U.S.), 1931 . . £40/£10
The Calendar, Collins, 1930 . . . . . £100/£15
ditto, Doubleday Doran, 1931 . . . . £75/£10
The Clue of the Silver Key, Hodder & Stoughton, 1930
. . . . £45/£10
ditto, as *The Silver Key*, Doubleday Doran (U.S.), 1930
. . . . £40/£10
The Lady of Ascot, Hutchinson, 1930 . . £65/£15
The Devil Man, Collins, 1931 . . . . £125/£25
ditto, Doubleday Doran (U.S.), 1931 . . £100/£15
On the Spot, John Long, 1931 . . . £75/£15
ditto, Doubleday Doran (U.S.), 1931 . . £65/£10
The Man at the Carlton, Hodder & Stoughton, 1931 .
. . . . £45/£10
ditto, Doubleday Doran (U.S.), 1932 . £40/£10
The Coat of Arms, Hutchinson, 1931 . . £75/£10
ditto, as *The Arranways Mystery*, Doubleday Doran
(U.S.), 1932 . . . . £65/£10
When the Gangs Came to London, John Long, 1932 .
. . . . £325/£100
ditto, Doubleday Doran (U.S.), 1932 . . £250/£65
King Kong, Grosset & Dunlap (U.S.), 1932 (conceived
by Wallace and Merian C. Cooper, written by Delos
W. Lovelace) . . . . £3,500/£400
ditto, Corgi, 1966 (wraps) £5
The Frightened Lady, Hodder & Stoughton, 1932 . .
. . . . £45/£10
ditto, as *The Mystery of the Frightened Lady*,
Doubleday Doran (U.S.), 1933 . . . £40/£10
The Man Who Changed His Name, Hodder &
Stoughton, 1934 (with Robert Curtis) . . £250/£50
ditto, Doubleday Doran (U.S.), 1934 . £125/£25
The Mouthpiece, Hodder & Stoughton, 1935 (with
Robert Curtis) . . . . £250/£50
ditto, Dodge (U.S.), 1936 . . . . . £75/£15
Smoky Cell, Hodder & Stoughton, 1935 (with Robert
Curtis) . . . . £250/£50
The Table, Hodder & Stoughton, 1936 (with Robert
Curtis) . . . . £500/£150
The Sanctuary Island, Hutchinson, 1936 (with Robert
Curtis) . . . . £300/£75
The Road to London, Kimber, 1986 . . . £10/£5

Short Stories

Smithy, Tallis Press, 1905 (card covers) . . £300
Smithy Abroad, Hulton, 1909 (card covers) . £350
Sanders of the River, Ward Lock, 1911 . . £100
ditto, Doubleday Doran (U.S.), 1930 . . £45/£10
The People of the River, Ward Lock, 1912 . . £75
Smithy's Friend Nobby, Town Topics, 1914 . £300
ditto, as *Nobby*, Newnes, [1916] £25
The Admirable Carfew, Ward Lock, 1914 . . £65
Bosambo of the River, Ward Lock, 1914 . . £75
Bones, Ward Lock, 1915 . . . . £65
Smithy and the Hun, Pearson, 1915 (card covers) £450
*Smithy, Not to Mention Nobby Clark and Spud
Murphy*, Newnes, 1915 (card covers) . . . £125

The Keepers of the King's Peace, Ward Lock, 1917 £65
Lieutenant Bones, Ward Lock, 1918 . . . £65
Tam of the Scouts, Newnes, 1918 . . . . £65
ditto, as *Tam O' the Scoots*, Small Maynard (U.S.),
1919 . . . . £50
The Fighting Scouts, Pearson, 1919 . . . £50
The Adventures of Heine, Ward Lock, 1919 . £75
Bones in London, Ward Lock, 1921 . . £300/£75
Law of the Four Just Men, Hodder & Stoughton, 1921
. . . . £300/£75
ditto, as *Again the Three Just Men*, Doubleday Doran
(U.S.), 1933 . . . . £100/£25
Chick, Ward Lock, 1923 . . . . £300/£65
Bones of the River, Newnes, [1923] . . . £75/£10
Educated Evans, Webster, [1924] . . . £75/£10
The Mind of Mr. J.G. Reeder, Hodder & Stoughton,
1925 . . . . £75/£10
ditto, as *The Murder Book of Mr. J.G. Reeder*,
Doubleday Doran (U.S.), 1929 . . . . £65/£10
More Educated Evans, Webster, [1926] . £75/£10
Sanders, Hodder and Stoughton, 1926 . . £75/£10
ditto, as *Mr. Commissioner Sanders*, Doubleday Doran
(U.S.), 1930 . . . . £50/£10
The Brigand, Hodder & Stoughton, 1927 . £35/£10
The Mixer, John Long, 1927 . . . . . £45/£10
Good Evans, Webster, [1927] . . . . £75/£15
Again the Three Just Men, Hodder & Stoughton, 1928
. . . . £35/£10
ditto, as *The Law of the 3 Just Men*, Doubleday Doran
(U.S.), 1931 . . . . £30/£10
Again Sanders, Hodder & Stoughton, [1928] £75/£15
ditto, Doubleday Doran (U.S.), 1929 . . £50/£10
The Orator, Hutchinson, 1928 . . . . £125/£25
Elegant Edward, Readers Library, [1928] . £35/£10
Forty Eight Short Stories, Newnes, 1929 . £35/£10
Planetoid 127 and The Sweizer Pump, Readers
Library, 1929 . . . . £45/£10
The Cat Burglar, Newnes, 1929 (wraps) . . £25
Circumstantial Evidence, Newnes, 1929 (wraps) £25
ditto, as *Circumstantial Evidence and Other Stories*,
World Syndicate, 1934 . . . . . . £30/£5
Fighting Snub Reilly, Newnes, 1929 (wraps) . £25
ditto, as *Fighting Snub Reilly and Other Stories*,
World Syndicate (U.S.), 1933 . . . . £30/£5
*The Ghost of Down Hill, and The Queen of Sheba's
Belt*, Readers Library, 1929 . . . . £35/£10
The Little Green Man, Newnes, 1929 (wraps) . £25
The Prison-Breakers, Newnes, 1929 (wraps) . £25
Red Aces, Being Three Cases of Mr. Reeder, Hodder
& Stoughton, 1929 . . . . . . £75/£15
ditto, Doubleday Doran (U.S.), 1930 . . £50/£10
The Lone House Mystery, Collins, 1929 . £75/£15
The Black, Readers Library, 1929 . . . £35/£10
ditto, Digit Books, 1962 (wraps) £5
For Information Received, Newnes, 1929 (wraps) .
. . . . £125
The Governor of Chi-Foo, Newnes, 1929 (wraps) £25
ditto, as *The Governor of Chi-Foo and Other Stories*,
World Syndicate (U.S.), 1933 . . . . £30/£5

The Lady of Little Hell, Newnes, 1929 (wraps)   £125
The Reporter, Readers Library, 1929   .   .   £35/£10
The Big Four, Readers Library, 1929   .   .   £35/£10
The Iron Grip, Readers Library, 1929   .   .   £35/£10
Killer Kay, Newnes, 1930 (wraps) £125
The Lady Called Nita, Newnes, 1930 (wraps)   .   £150
Mrs William Jones and Bill, Newnes, 1930 (wraps)   .
.   .   .   .   £125
The Guv'nor and Other Stories, Collins, 1932 .   .   .
.   .   .   .   £100/£20
ditto, as Mr. Reeder Returns, Doubleday Doran (U.S.),
1932   .   .   .   .   £75/£15
Sergeant Sir Peter, Chapman & Hall, 1932 .   £175/£35
ditto, Doubleday Doran (U.S.), 1933   .   .   £150/£30
The Steward, Collins, 1932   .   .   .   .   .   £100/£20
Mr. J.G. Reeder Returns, Collins, 1934.   .   £25/£10
The Last Adventure, Hutchinson, 1934 .   .   £250/£35
The Woman from the East and Other Stories,
Hutchinson, 1934   .   .   .   .   .   .   £250/£35
The Undisclosed Client, Digit, 1963 (wraps)   .   .   £5
The Man Who Married His Cook, White Lion, 1976 .
.   .   .   .   £20/£5
The Sooper and Others, Dent, 1984 .   .   .   .   .   £10/£5
The Death Room: Strange and Startling Stories,
Kimber, 1986.   .   .   .   .   £10/£5

Poetry
The Mission that Failed, T. Maskew Miller, 1898
(wraps) £350
Nicholson's Nek, Eastern Press, 1900   .   .   .   £200
War and Other Poems, Eastern Press, 1900   .   £200
Writ in the Barracks, Methuen, 1900   .   .   .   £250

Others
Unofficial Dispatches, Hutchinson, [1901] .   .   £40
Famous Scottish Regiments, Newnes, 1914 (wraps)   .
.   .   .   .   £125
Field Marshal Sir John French and His Campaigns,
Newnes, 1914 (wraps) £125
Heroes All, Gallant Deeds of the War, Newnes, 1914 .
.   .   .   .   £40
My Life, Long, 1914 (pseud. 'Evelyn Thaw')   .   £125
The Standard History of the War, Newnes, [1914-15]
(4 vols) £45
Kitchener's Army and the Territorial Forces: The
Full Story of a Great Achievement, Newnes, 1915 (6
vols, wraps) £75
War of the Nations, Newnes, 1915-17 (12 vols, wraps)
.   .   .   .   £75
The Real Shell-Man, John Waddington, 1919 (wraps)
.   .   .   .   £50
The Black Avons, George Gill, 1925 (4 paperbacks)   .
.   .   .   .   £75
People: A Short Autobiography, Hodder & Stoughton,
1926   .   .   .   .   £65/£15
ditto, Doubleday Doran (U.S.), 1929   .   .   £50/£10
This England, Hodder & Stoughton, [1927]   £40/£10
My Hollywood Diary, Hutchinson, [1932]   .   £65/£15

HORACE WALPOLE
(b.1717 d.1797)

Although considered the greatest letter-writer of the
eighteenth century, Walpole will probably be
remembered for his ground-breaking *The Castle of
Otranto*, the first gothic horror novel.

Aedes Walpoliane, or A Description of the
Collection of Pictures at Houghton Hall, privately
printed, 1747 [1748] (100 copies) £1,500
ditto, Dodsley, 1752   .   .   .   .   £1,500
A Letter from Xo Ho, A Chinese Philosopher at
London, To His Friend Lien Chi at Peking,
Middleton, 1757 .   .   .   .   £500
A Catalogue of Royal and Noble Authors of England,
Scotland and Ireland, Strawberry Hill, 1758 (2 vols)
.   .   .   .   £350 the set
ditto, Strawberry Hill, 1759 (2 vols)   .   .   £150 the set
Fugitive Pieces in Verse and Prose, Strawberry Hill,
1758 .   .   .   .   £750
Catalogue of Pictures and Drawings in the Holbein
Chamber, Strawberry Hill, 1760   .   .   .   .   £300
Anecdotes of Painting in England, Strawberry Hill,
1762-1771 [1780] (4 vols) .   .   .   .   £500 the set
A Catalogue of Engravers Who Have Been Born or
Resided in England, Strawberry Hill, 1763   .   £150
The Castle of Otranto, Lownds, 1765 [1764]   £10,000
ditto, Bathoe/Lownds, 1765   .   .   .   .   .   .   £3,000
Historic Doubts on the Life and Reign of King
Richard the Third, Dodsley, 1768 .   .   .   .   £150
The Mysterious Mother: A Tragedy, Strawberry Hill,
1768 (50 copies) £3,000
ditto, Strawberry Hill, 1781 .   .   .   .   .   £450
A Description of the Villa at Strawberry Hill, Near
Twickenham, Middlesex, Strawberry Hill, 1774 £450
Description of Strawberry Hill, Strawberry Hill, 1784.
.   .   .   .   £350
Essay on Modern Gardening, Strawberry Hill, 1785 .
.   .   .   .   £500
Hieroglyphic Tales, Strawberry Hill, 1785 (7 copies) .
.   .   .   .   £10,000
ditto, Elkin Mathews, 1926 (250 copies)   .   .   £100
The Works of Horatio Walpole, Earl of Orford,
Robinson/Edwards, 1798 (5 vols)   .   .   £500 the set
ditto, Robinson/Edwards, 1798 (large paper edition, 5
vols)   .   .   .   .   £650 the set
Reminiscences, Richard Taylor, 1805 (25 copies)   .   .
.   .   .   .   £750 the set
Memories in the Last Ten Years of the Reign of
George the Second, Murray, 1822 (2 vols)   .   .   .
.   .   .   .   £200 the set
Memoirs of the Reign of King George the Third,
Richard Bentley, 1845 (4 vols) .   .   .   £250 the set
Journal of the Reign of King George the Third, from
the Year 1771 to 1783, Richard Bentley, 1859 (2
vols)   .   .   .   .   £250 the set
Journal of the Printing Office at Strawberry Hill,
Constable, 1923 (650 copies) £60

ditto, Houghton Mifflin Co (U.S.), 1923 (650 copies) .
. . . . £120
**Reminiscences, Written in 1788 for the Amusement of
Miss Mary and Miss Agnes Berry**, Milford/O.U.P.,
1925 (500 copies) . . . . . . £65/£30
**Strawberry Hill Accounts: A Record of Expenditure
in Building, Furnishing, etc, from 1747 to 1795**,
O.U.P., 1927 (500 copies) . . . . £65/£30
Fugitive Verses, O.U.P., 1931 . . . . . £50
ditto, O.U.P. (U.S.), 1923 (500 numbered copies) £50
Memoirs and Portraits, Batsford, 1963 . . . £20/£5

Letters
**Letters from the Hon Horace Walpole to George
Montagu, esq., From the Year 1736 to the Year
1770**, Rodwell & Martin/Henry Colburn, 1818 £125
**Letters from the Hon Horace Walpole to the Rev
William Cole, and Others, From the Year 1745 to
the Year 1782**, Rodwell & Martin/Henry Colburn,
1818 . . . . £125
**Letters from the Hon Horace Walpole to the Earl of
Hertford, During His Lordship's Embassy in Paris**,
Charles Knight, 1825 . . . . . . £100
**Private Correspondence of Horace Walpole, Earl of
Orford, Now First Collected**, Rodwell & Martin/
Henry Colburn, 1820 (4 vols) . . £150 the set
**Letters to Sir Horace Mann, British Envoy at the
Court of Tuscany**, Richard Bentley, 1833 (3 vols) .
. . . . £150 the set
Letters to Sir Horace Mann, Concluding Series,
Richard Bentley, 1843-44 (4 vols) . . £150 the set
The Letters of Horace Walpole, Earl of Orford,
Richard Bentley, 1840 (6 vols) . . £200 the set
**Letters Addressed to the Countess of Ossory, From the
Year 1769 to 1797**, Richard Bentley, 1848 (2 vols) .
. . . . £125 the set
**Correspondence of Horace Walpole and William
Mason**, Richard Bentley, 1851 (2 vols) £125 the set
**The Letters of Horace Walpole, Now First
Chronologically Arranged**, Richard Bentley, 1857-59
(9 vols) . . . . £200 the set
ditto, Richard Bentley, 1891 . . . . . £125
**Horace Walpole and His World, Selected Passages
from His Letters**, Seeley Jackson, 1884 . . £35
Letters of Sir Horace Walpole, T. Fisher Unwin, 1890
(2 vols) . . . . £30 the set
Some Unpublished Letters, Longmans, 1902 . £20
**The Letters of Sir Horace Walpole, Fourth Earl of
Orford, Chronologically Arranged**, Clarendon Press,
1903-5, 1919, 1925 (16 vols plus 3 supplementary
vols) . . . . £150/£75
ditto, Clarendon Press, 1903-5, 1919, 1925 (19 vols,
India Paper Edition) . . . . . £100 the set
ditto, Clarendon Press, 1903-5, 1919, 1925 (19 vols,
260 sets signed by the editor) . . . £300/£200
Selected Letters, Dent, Everyman's Library, 1926 . .
. . . . £15/£5
A Selection of Letters, O.U.P., 1927 (two vols) . .
. . . . £50/£25

Horace Walpole's Correspondence, Yale Univ. Press
(U.S.), 1937-83 (43 vols, plus 5 vols of indices) . .
. . . . £2,000/£1,500 the set

HUGH WALPOLE
(b.1884 d.1941)

Walpole was a popular and critical success in his day,
and his 'Herries' books are still in print. However, his
posthumous reputation was blighted by Somerset
Maugham's devastating portrayal of him in *Cakes
and Ale*. Walpole's short stories are appreciated by
aficionados of supernatural fiction.

Novels
The Wooden Horse, Smith Elder, 1909 . . . £150
Marradick at Forty, Smith Elder, 1910 . . . £45
Mr Perrin and Mr Traill, Mills & Boon, 1911 . £45
ditto, Doran (U.S.), 1911 . . . . . . £25
The Prelude to Adventure, Mills & Boon, 1912 £25
ditto, Century (U.S.), 1912 . . . . . . £25
Fortitude, Secker, 1913 . . . . £25
ditto, Doran (U.S.), 1913 . . . . . . £25
The Duchess of Wrexe, Secker, 1914 . . . £25
ditto, Doran (U.S.), 1914 . . . . . . £25
The Dark Forest, Secker, 1918 . . . . . £25
ditto, Doran (U.S.), 1916 . . . . . . £25
The Green Mirror, Macmillan, 1918 . . . £25
ditto, Doran (U.S.), 1918 . . . . . . £25
The Secret City, Macmillan, 1919 . . . £25
ditto, Doran (U.S.), 1919 . . . . . . £25
Jeremy, Cassell, 1919 . . . . £25
ditto, Doran (U.S.), 1919 . . . . . . £25
The Captives, Macmillan, 1920 . . . . £65/£25
ditto, Doran (U.S.), 1920 . . . . . . £65/£25
The Young Enchanted, Macmillan, 1921 . £65/£20
ditto, Macmillan, 1921 (250 signed copies) . . £40
The Cathedral, Macmillan, 1922 . . . £65/£20
ditto, Macmillan, 1922 (250 signed copies) . . £40
ditto, Doran (U.S.), 1922 . . . . . . £65/£20
ditto, Doran (U.S.), 1922 (500 numbered copies) £35
Jeremy and Hamlet, Cassell, 1923 . . . £50/£20
ditto, Doran (U.S.), 1923 . . . . . . £50/£20
The Old Ladies, Macmillan, 1924 . . . £50/£20
ditto, Macmillan, 1924 (250 signed copies) . . £40
ditto, Doran (U.S.), 1924 . . . . . . £50/£20
Portrait of a Man with Red Hair, Macmillan, 1925 .
. . . . £50/£20
ditto, Macmillan, 1925 (250 signed copies) . . £40
ditto, Doran (U.S.), 1925 . . . . . . £50/£20
ditto, Doran (U.S.), 1925 (250 numbered copies) £35
Harmer John, Macmillan, 1926 . . . . £40/£15
ditto, Macmillan, 1926 (250 signed copies) . . £35
ditto, Doran (U.S.), 1926 . . . . . . £40/£15
Jeremy at Crale, Cassell, 1927 . . . . £35/£15
ditto, Doran (U.S.), 1927 . . . . . . £35/£15
Wintersmoon, Macmillan, 1928 . . . . £35/£15

ditto, Macmillan, 1928 (175 signed copies) . .   £35
ditto, Doubleday Doran (U.S.), 1928   . . £35/£15
Farthing Hall, Macmillan, 1929 (with J.B. Priestley) .
. . . .   £35/£15
ditto, Doubleday Doran (U.S.), 1929   .   £35/£15
Hans Frost, Macmillan, 1929   . . . .   £35/£15
ditto, Macmillan, 1929 (175 signed copies) . .   £35
ditto, Doubleday Doran (U.S.), 1929   . .   £35/£15
Rogue Herries, Macmillan, 1930   . . .   £30/£10
ditto, Macmillan, 1930 (200 signed copies) . .   £35
ditto, Doubleday Doran (U.S.), 1930   . .   £30/£10
Above the Dark Circus, Macmillan, 1931   .   £30/£10
ditto, Macmillan, 1931 (200 signed copies) . .   £35
ditto, as *Above the Dark Tumult*, Doubleday Doran
(U.S.), 1930   . . . .   £25/£10
Judith Paris, Macmillan, 1931   . . . .   £30/£10
ditto, Macmillan, 1931 (350 signed copies) . .   £30
ditto, Doubleday Doran (U.S.), 1931   . .   £30/£10
The Fortress, Macmillan, 1932   . . . .   £30/£10
ditto, Macmillan, 1932 (310 signed copies) . .   £30
ditto, Doubleday Doran (U.S.), 1932   . .   £30/£10
Vanessa, Macmillan, 1933   . . . . .   £30/£10
ditto, Macmillan, 1933 (315 signed copies) . .   £30
Captain Nicholas, Macmillan, 1934 .   . .   £30/£10
ditto, Macmillan, 1934 (275 signed copies) . .   £30
ditto, Doubleday Doran (U.S.), 1934   . .   £30/£10
The Inquisitor, Macmillan, 1935   . . .   £30/£10
ditto, Macmillan, 1935 (250 signed copies) . .   £30
ditto, Doubleday Doran (U.S.), 1935   . .   £30/£10
A Prayer for My Son, Macmillan, 1936 . .   £30/£10
ditto, Macmillan, 1936 (200 signed copies) . .   £30
ditto, Doubleday Doran (U.S.), 1936   . .   £30/£10
John Cornelius, Macmillan, 1937   . . .   £30/£10
ditto, Macmillan, 1937 (175 signed copies) . .   £30
ditto, Doubleday Doran (U.S.), 1937   . .   £30/£10
The Joyful Delaneys, Macmillan, 1938 .   .   £30/£10
ditto, Macmillan, 1938 (180 signed copies) . .   £30
ditto, Doubleday Doran (U.S.), 1938   . .   £30/£10
The Sea Tower, Macmillan, 1939   . .   £30/£10
ditto, Doubleday Doran (U.S.), 1939   . .   £30/£10
The Bright Pavilions, Macmillan, 1940 .   .   £30/£10
ditto, Doubleday Doran (U.S.), 1940   . .   £30/£10
The Blind Man's House, Macmillan, 1941 .   £30/£10
ditto, Doubleday Doran (U.S.), 1941   . .   £30/£10
The Killer and the Slain, Macmillan, 1942 .   £30/£10
ditto, Doubleday Doran (U.S.), 1942   . .   £30/£10
Katherine Christian, Macmillan, 1944   .   £30/£10
ditto, Doubleday Doran (U.S.), 1944   . .   £30/£10

Short Stories
The Golden Scarecrow, Cassell, 1915   . .   £100/£35
ditto, Doran (U.S.), 1915   . . . . .   £100/£35
The Thirteen Travellers, Hutchinson, 1921.   £100/£35
ditto, Doubleday Doran (U.S.), 1921   . .   £100/£35
The Silver Thorn, Macmillan, 1928 .   . .   £100/£35
ditto, Macmillan, 1928 (175 signed copies) .   .   £30
ditto, Doubleday Doran (U.S.), 1921   . .   £100/£35
All Soul's Night, Macmillan, 1933   . .   £150/£50
ditto, Doubleday Doran (U.S.), 1921   . .   £150/£50

Head in Green Bronze, Macmillan, 1938   .   £75/£15
ditto, Doubleday Doran (U.S.), 1938   . .   £150/£50
Mr Huffam, Macmillan, 1948   . . . .   £75/£15
Tarnhelm, Tartarus Press, 2003   . . . .   £35/£10

Plays
The Cathedral, Macmillan, 1937   . . . .   £20/£5
The Haxtons, Deane, 1939   . . . . . .   £20/£5

Miscellaneous
Joseph Conrad, A Critical Study, Nisbet, 1916   £25
A Hugh Walpole Anthology, Dent, 1921   .   £35/£10
The Crystal Box, Glasgow Univ. Press, 1924 (150
signed, numbered copies) £65
The English Novel: The Rede Lecture, C.U.P., 1925   .
. . . .   £35/£10
Reading: An Essay, Jarrold, 1928   . . .   £25/£10
ditto, Harpers (U.S.), 1926   . . . . .   £25/£10
Anthony Trollope: A Study, Macmillan, 1928 £35/£10
ditto, Macmillan (U.S.), 1928   . . . .   £35/£10
My Religious Experience, Ernest Benn, 1928   . £15/£5
A Letter to a Modern Novelist, Hogarth Press, 1932   .
. . . .   £25/£10
The Waverley Pageant: An Anthology, Eyre &
Spottiswoode, 1932 . . . .   £25/£10
The Apple Trees, Golden Cockerel Press, 1932 (500
signed copies) £40
Extracts from a Diary, privately printed, 1934 £35/£10
Roman Fountain, Macmillan, 1940 .   . .   £25/£10
ditto, Doubleday Doran (U.S.), 1940   . .   £25/£10
Open Letter of an Optimist, Macmillan, 1941   . £20/£5

MINETTE WALTERS
(b.1949)

A contemporary crime writer, Minette Walters owes
much of her popularity to highly successful television
adaptations of her books.

Novels
The Ice House, Macmillan, 1992   . . .   £650/£45
ditto, Macmillan, 1992 (variant jacket, two heads under
the ice) . . . .   £1,250/£45
ditto, St Martin's Press (U.S.), 1992 .   .   £200/£25
The Sculptress, Macmillan, 1993   . . .   £60/£10
ditto, St Martin's Press (U.S.), 1992 .   . .   £45/£5
The Scold's Bridle, Macmillan, 1994   . .   £30/£5
ditto, Scorpion Press, 1994 (75 signed copies)   . £100
ditto, Scorpion Press, 1994 (15 lettered copies) .   £300
ditto, St Martin's Press (U.S.), 1994 . . .   £25/£5
The Dark Room, Macmillan, 1995   . . .   £15/£5
ditto, Putnam's (U.S.), 1996   . . . . .   £15/£5
The Echo, Macmillan, 1997   . . . . .   £15/£5
ditto, Putnam's (U.S.), 1997 . . . . .   £10/£5
The Breaker, Macmillan, 1998   . . . . .   £15/£5
ditto, Putnam's (U.S.), 1999   . . . . .   £10/£5
Shape of Snakes Macmillan, 2000   . . . .   £15/£5

ditto, Macmillan, 2000 (600 signed copies of second printing, slipcase) . . . . £50/£40
ditto, Putnam's (U.S.), 2000 . . . . . £10/£5
Acid Row Macmillan, 2001 . . . . . £15/£5
ditto, Putnam's (U.S.), 2002 . . . . . £10/£5
Fox Evil Macmillan, 2002 . . . . . £15/£5
ditto, Putnam's (U.S.), 2003 . . . . . £10/£5

REX WARNER
(b.1905 d.1986)

A poet, novelist and translator, Warner is perhaps best known for his Kafkaesque *The Aerodrome*.

Fiction
The Wild Goose Chase, Boriswood, 1937 . £75/£20
ditto, Knopf (U.S.), 1938 . . . . . . £35/£10
The Professor, Boriswood, 1938. . . . £45/£10
ditto, Knopf (U.S.), 1939 . . . . . . £25/£10
The Aerodrome, John Lane, 1941 . . £150/£30
ditto, Lippincott (U.S.), 1946 . . . . £25/£10
Why Was I Killed? A Dramatic Dialogue, John Lane, 1943 . . . . £25/£5
ditto, as *Return of the Traveller*, Lippincott (U.S.), 1944 . . . . £15/£5
Men of Stones: A Melodrama, Bodley Head, 1949 .
. . . . £15/£5
ditto, Lippincott (U.S.), 1950. . . . . £15/£5
Escapade: A Tale of Average, Bodley Head, 1953 . .
. . . . £15/£5
The Young Caesar, Collins, 1958 . . . £10/£5
ditto, Little, Brown (U.S.), 1958 . . . . £10/£5
Imperial Caesar, Collins, 1960 . . . . £10/£5
ditto, Little, Brown (U.S.), 1960 . . . . £10/£5
Pericles the Athenian, Collins, 1963 . . £10/£5
ditto, Little, Brown (U.S.), 1963 . . . . £10/£5
The Converts, John Lane, 1967 . . . . £10/£5
ditto, Little, Brown (U.S.), 1967 . . . . £10/£5

Poetry
Poems, Boriswood, 1937 . . . . . . £75/£25
ditto, Knopf (U.S.), 1938 . . . . . . £35/£10
ditto, as *Poems and Contradictions*, John Lane, 1945 .
. . . . £25/£10

Others
The Kite, Blackwell, 1936 . . . . . £100/£35
ditto, Hamish Hamilton, 1963 (revised edition). . .
. . . . £25/£10
English Public Schools, Collins, 1945 . . £15/£5
The Cult of Power: Essays, John Lane, 1946 £25/£10
ditto, Lippincott (U.S.), 1947. . . . . £25/£10
John Milton, Parrish, 1949 . . . . . £15/£5
ditto, Chanticleer Press (U.S.), 1950. . . £10/£5
Views of Attica and Its Surroundings, Lehmann, 1950
. . . . £15/£5
E.M. Forster, Longmans, 1950 (wraps) . . . £10

ditto, Longmans, 1960 (revised edition, wraps). . £5
Men and Gods, MacGibbon & Kee, 1950 . . £20/£5
ditto, Fararr Straus, Giroux (U.S.), 1959. . . £15/£5
Ashes to Ashes: A Post-Mortem on the 1950-51 Tests, MacGibbon & Kee, 1951 (with Lyle Blair) . £15/£5
Greeks and Trojans, MacGibbon & Kee, 1951 £10/£5
Eternal Greece, Thames & Hudson, 1953 (photographs by Martin Hurlimann) . . . . . . £30/£10
The Vengeance of the Gods, MacGibbon & Kee, 1954
. . . . £10/£5
ditto, Michigan State (U.S.), 1955 . . . . £10/£5
Athens, Thames & Hudson, 1956 . . . . £10/£5
The Greek Philosophers, Michigan State (U.S.), 1958
. . . . £10/£5
Athens at War: Retold from Thucydides History of the Pelopennesian War, Bodley Head, 1970 . . £10/£5
ditto, Dutton (U.S.), 1971 . . . . . . £10/£5
Men of Athens, Bodley Head, 1972 . . . . £10/£5
ditto, Viking (U.S.), 1972 . . . . . . £10/£5
The Stories of the Greeks, Fararr Straus, Giroux (U.S.), 1967 (includes *Men and Gods*, *Greeks and Trojans*, *The Vengeance of the Gods*) . . . £10/£5

Translations
The Medea of Euripides, John Lane, 1944 . . £15/£5
ditto, Univ. of Chicago Press (U.S.), 1955 (with *Euripides Alcestis*, translated by Lattimore, *The Heracleidae* translated by Ralph Gladstone, *Hippolytus* translated by David Grene, etc.) . £10/£5
Prometheus Bound, by Aeschylus, Bodley Head, 1947
. . . . £15/£5
The Persian Expedition, by Xenophon, Penguin, 1949
. . . . £5
Hippolytus, by Euripides, Bodley Head, 1949 . £15/£5
Helen, by Euripides, Bodley Head, 1951 . . £50/£5
The Peloponnesian War, by Thucydides, Penguin, 1954 . . . . £5
Fall of the Roman Republic. Martus, Sulla, Crassus, Pompey, Caesar, Cicero: Six Lives, by Plutarch, Penguin, 1958 . . . . £5
ditto, Penguin, 1972 (revised edition) £5
Three Great Plays, New American Library, 1958 (contains *Medea*, *Hippolytus* and *Helen*) . £10/£5
Poems of George Seferis, 1960 . . . . . £10/£5
War Commentaries of Caesar, New American Library, 1960 . . . . £10/£5
Confessions of St Augustine, New American Library, 1963 . . . . £10/£5
On the Greek Style: Selected Essays in Poetry and Hellenism, by George Seferis, Little, Brown (U.S.), 1966 (with Th. D. Frangopoulos) . . . . £10/£5
ditto, Bodley Head, 1967 . . . . . . £10/£5
History of My Times, by Xenophon, Penguin, 1966 £5
Moral Essays, by Plutarch, Penguin, 1971 . . . £5

SYLVIA TOWNSEND WARNER
(b.1893 d.1978)

A talented novelist, poet and short story writer, Warner's concerns are often with the ordinary and overlooked members of society. By examining the detail of their lives she shows what extraordinary people they often are.

Poetry
The Espalier, Chatto & Windus, 1925 . . £200/£65
ditto, Dial Press (U.S.), 1925 . . . . . £150/£45
Time Importuned, Chatto & Windus, 1928 . £200/£65
ditto, Viking Press (U.S.), 1928 . . . . £150/£45
Opus 7, Chatto & Windus, 1931 . . . . £30/£10
ditto, Chatto & Windus, 1931 (110 signed, numbered copies, glassine d/w and slipcase) . . . £150/£125
ditto, Viking Press (U.S.), 1931 . . . . £25/£10
Rainbow, Borzoi (U.S.), 1932 (wraps, in envelope) .
. . . . £125/£100
Whether a Dove or Seagull, Viking Press (U.S.), 1933
(with Valentine Ackland) . . . . . £125/£40
ditto, Chatto & Windus, 1934 . . . . £125/£45
Boxwood, Monotype Corporation, 1957 (500 copies, withdrawn) £75
ditto, Monotype Corporation, 1958 (500 copies). £75
ditto, Chatto & Windus, 1960 (enlarged edition) . .
. . . . £45/£15
King Duffus, privately printed, 1968 (wraps) . £125
Twelve Poems, privately circulated booklet, 1977 (duplicated sheets, stapled) £175
ditto, as *Azrael*, Libanus Press, 1978 (200 copies, wraps). £95
ditto, as *Twelve Poems*, Chatto & Windus, 1980 (reissue) . . . . £15/£5
Collected Poems, Carcanet Press/Viking Press (U.S.), 1982 . . . . £40/£20
Selected Poems, Carcanet Press, 1985 (wraps) . £10

Novels
Lolly Willowes, Chatto & Windus, 1926 . £125/£20
ditto, Viking Press (U.S.), 1926 . . . £125/£20
Mr Fortune's Maggot, Chatto & Windus, 1927 . .
. . . . £100/£20
ditto, Viking Press (U.S.), 1927 . . . . £100/£15
The True Heart, Chatto & Windus, 1929 . £75/£15
ditto, Viking Press (U.S.), 1929 . . . . £75/£15
Summer Will Show, Chatto & Windus, 1936 £45/£15
ditto, Viking Press (U.S.), 1936 . . . . £35/£10
After The Death of Don Juan, Chatto & Windus, 1938
. . . . £45/£10
ditto, Viking Press (U.S.), 1938 . . . . £35/£10
The Corner that Held Them, Chatto & Windus, 1948 .
. . . . £25/£10
ditto, Viking Press (U.S.), 1948 . . . . £25/£10
The Flint Anchor, Chatto & Windus, 1954 . £30/£10
ditto, Viking Press (U.S.), 1954 . . . . £25/£10

Short Stories
The Maze, Fleuron, 1928 (signed, wraps) . . £125
Some World Far From Ours and 'Stay Corydon, Thou Swain', Mathews & Marrot, 1929 (531 numbered, signed copies) . . . . . £45/£30
Elinor Barley, Cresset Press, 1930 (350 numbered, signed copies on mould-made paper, slipcase) . .
. . . . £125/£100
ditto, Cresset Press, 1930 (30 numbered and signed copies on handmade paper, extra set of engravings, slipcase) . . . . £600/£500
A Moral Ending, W. Jackson, 1930 (550 numbered, signed copies, glassine d/w with paper flaps) £75/£45
The Salutation, Chatto & Windus, 1932 . £75/£35
ditto, Viking Press (U.S.), 1932 . . . . £75/£35
More Joy in Heaven, Cresset Press, 1935 . £125/£50
The Cat's Cradle Book, Viking Press (U.S.), 1940. .
. . . . £75/£20
ditto, Chatto & Windus, 1960 . . . . £35/£10
A Garland of Straw, Chatto & Windus, 1943 £45/£15
ditto, Viking Press, 1943 . . . . . . £30/£15
The Museum of Cheats, Chatto & Windus, 1947 . .
. . . . £30/£10
ditto, Viking Press (U.S.), 1947 . . . . £25/£10
Winter in The Air Chatto & Windus, 1955 . £30/£10
ditto, Viking Press (U.S.), 1956 . . . . . £25/£5
A Spirit Rises, Chatto & Windus, 1962 . . £25/£10
ditto, Viking Press (U.S.), 1962 . . . . . £20/£5
Sketches from Nature, privately printed, 1963 (wraps)
. . . . £125
A Stranger with a Bag, Chatto & Windus, 1966 . .
. . . . £25/£10
ditto, as *Swans on an Autumn River*, Viking Press (U.S.), 1966 . . . . £20/£5
Two Conversation Pieces, privately printed, 1967 (wraps) £125
The Innocent and The Guilty, Chatto & Windus, 1971
. . . . £15/£5
ditto, Viking Press (U.S.), 1971 . . . . £15/£5
Kingdoms of Elfin, Chatto & Windus, 1977 . £15/£5
ditto, Viking Press (U.S.), 1977 . . . . £15/£5
Scenes of Childhood, Chatto & Windus, 1981 . £10/£5
ditto, Viking Press (U.S.), 1981 . . . . £10/£5
One Thing Leading to Another, Chatto & Windus, 1984 . . . . £10/£5
ditto, Viking Press (U.S.), 1984 . . . . £10/£5
Selected Stories, Chatto & Windus, 1989 . £15/£5
ditto, Viking Press (U.S.), 1989 . . . . £15/£5
The Music at Long Verney, Counterpoint (U.S.), 2001
. . . . £15/£5

Translations
By Way of Saint-Beuve, by Marcel Proust, Chatto & Windus, 1958. . . . . £40/£20
A Place of Shipwreck, by Jean Rene Huquenin, Chatto & Windus, 1963 . . . . £40/£15

Other Works
Somerset, Paul Elek, 1949 (withdrawn) . . £45/£20
Jane Austen, Longmans Green, 1941 (wraps) . £10

T.H. White, A Biography, Cape, 1967 . . £25/£10
ditto, Viking Press (U.S.), 1968 . . . . £25/£10
Letters, Chatto & Windus, 1982 . . . . £25/£10
The Diaries of Sylvia Townsend Warner, Chatto &
Windus, 1994. . . . . £20/£10
Sylvia and David, Sinclair Stevenson, 1994. . £15/£5
I'll Stand by You, Pimlico, 1998 (wraps) . . . £5
*The Element of Lavishness: Letters of Sylvia
Townsend Warner and William Maxwell, 1938-
1978*, Counterpoint (U.S.), 2001 . . . . £15/£5

EVELYN WAUGH
(b.1903 d.1966)

Waugh is best known for his humorous, satirical
novels. He also wrote a number of travel books.

Poetry
The World to Come: A Poem in Three Cantos,
privately printed, 1916 . . . . . . £12,000

Novels
Decline and Fall, An Illustrated Novelette, Chapman
& Hall, 1928 . . . . £6,000/£400
ditto, Doubleday (U.S.), 1929 . . . £1,000/£100
ditto, Farrar (U.S.), 1929 . . . . . £500/£50
ditto, Chapman & Hall, 1937 (12 copies) . . £3,000
Vile Bodies, Chapman & Hall, 1930. . £6,000/£300
ditto, Farrar (U.S.), 1930 . . . . . £500/£50
ditto, Chapman & Hall, 1937 (12 copies) . . £3,000
Black Mischief, Chapman & Hall, 1932. £1,500/£150
ditto, Chapman & Hall, 1932 (250 signed copies) . .
. . . . £2,000/£1,000
ditto, Farrar (U.S.), 1932 . . . . . £500/£50
ditto, Chapman & Hall, 1937 (12 copies) . . £3,000
A Handful of Dust, Chapman & Hall, 1934 . . .
. . . . £1,500/£150
ditto, Farrar (U.S.), 1934 . . . . . £400/£75
ditto, Chapman & Hall, 1937 (12 copies) . . £3,000
Scoop: A Novel about Journalists, Chapman & Hall,
1938 . . . . £1,000/£100
ditto, Little, Brown (U.S.), 1938 . . . £250/£45
Put Out More Flags, Chapman & Hall, 1942 £400/£50
ditto, Little, Brown (U.S.), 1942 . . . £125/£30
Work Suspended, Chapman & Hall, 1942 (unfinished
novel, 500 copies) . . . . . £1,000/£200
*Brideshead Revisited: The Sacred & Profane
Memories of Capt Charles Ryder*, privately printed
for the author, 1945 [1944] (50 copies, wraps) . .
. . . . £8,000
ditto, Chapman & Hall, 1945 . . . £1,000/£125
ditto, Little, Brown (U.S.), 1945 (600 copies) . .
. . . . £500/£150
ditto, Little, Brown (U.S.), 1946 . . . £125/£25
Scott-King's Modern Europe, Chapman & Hall, 1947
. . . . £50/£15
ditto, Little, Brown (U.S.), 1949 . . . £45/£10

The Loved One: An Anglo-American Tragedy,
Chapman & Hall, 1948 . . . . . . £75/£25
ditto, Chapman & Hall, 1948 (250 signed, numbered
copies, glassine d/w). . . . . . £750/£650
ditto, Little, Brown (U.S.), 1948 . . . £35/£10
Helena, Chapman & Hall, 1950 . . . . £35/£10
ditto, Chapman & Hall, 1950 (50 deluxe copies for
presentation) £1,750
ditto, Little, Brown (U.S.), 1950 . . . £25/£10
Men at Arms, Chapman & Hall, 1952 . . £100/£20
ditto, Little, Brown (U.S.), 1952 . . . £40/£10
Love Among The Ruins, Chapman & Hall, 1953 . .
. . . . £40/£10
ditto, Chapman & Hall, 1953 (350 signed copies,
glassine d/w) . . . . £400/£275
Officers and Gentlemen, Chapman & Hall, 1955 . .
. . . . £100/£20
ditto, Little, Brown (U.S.), 1955 . . . £40/£10
The Ordeal of Gilbert Pinfold: A Conversation Piece,
Chapman & Hall, 1957 . . . . . . £35/£10
ditto, Chapman & Hall, 1957 (50 large copies for
presentation) £1,500
ditto, Little, Brown (U.S.), 1957 . . . £25/£10
Unconditional Surrender, Chapman & Hall, 1961. .
. . . . £45/£10
ditto, as *The End of The Battle*, Little, Brown (U.S.),
1961 . . . . £25/£5
Basil Seal Rides Again, Chapman & Hall, 1963 (750
signed copies, glassine d/w). . . . £250/£100
ditto, Chapman & Hall, 1963. . . . . £45/£15
ditto, Little, Brown (U.S.), 1963 . . . £45/£15
ditto, Little, Brown (U.S.), 1963 (1,000 signed copies,
glassine d/w) . . . . £250/£225
Sword of Honour, Chapman & Hall, 1965 (comprises
Men at Arms, Officers and Gentlemen and
Unconditional Surrender) . . . . . £40/£10

Short Stories
Mr Loveday's Little Outing and Other Sad Stories,
Chapman & Hall, 1936 . . . . . £1,000/£100
ditto, Little, Brown (U.S.), 1936 . . . £450/£45
Tactical Exercise, Little, Brown, 1954 . £75/£20
Charles Ryder's Schooldays and Other Stories, Little,
Brown (U.S.), 1982 . . . . £15/£5
The Complete Short Stories, Everyman's Library,
1998 . . . . £10/£5

Essays
PRB: An Essay on The Pre-Raphaelite Brotherhood,
privately printed, 1926 (no d/w) £4,000
The Holy Places, Queen Anne Press, 1952 (50 signed
copies) . . . . £1,000/£750
ditto, Queen Anne Press, 1952 (900 copies) £200/£100
ditto, Queen Anne Press/British Book Centre (U.S.),
1952 (900 copies) . . . . £100/£65
ditto, Queen Anne Press/British Book Centre (U.S.),
1952 (50 signed copies) . . . . . . £500/£300

Travel
Labels, Duckworth, 1930 . . . . . £1,250/£125
ditto, Duckworth, 1930 (110 signed copies, page of manuscript laid in) £1,750
ditto, as *A Bachelor Abroad*, Farrar (U.S.), 1932 . .
. . . . £200/£30
Remote People, Duckworth, 1931 . . £1,250/£125
ditto, as *They Were Still Dancing*, Farrar (U.S.), 1932.
. . . . £200/£30
Ninety-Two Days, Duckworth, 1934. . £1,000/£100
ditto, Farrar (U.S.), 1934 . . . . . £200/£30
Waugh in Abyssinia, Longman, 1936 . . £750/£100
ditto, Farrar (U.S.), 1936 . . . . . £200/£25
Robbery Under Law, Chapman & Hall, 1939 £650/£75
ditto, as *Mexico: An Object Lesson*, Little, Brown
(U.S.), 1939 . . . . £200/£35
When The Going Was Good, Duckworth, 1946 . .
. . . . £350/£100
ditto, Little, Brown (U.S.), 1947 . . . £75/£20
A Tourist in Africa, Chapman & Hall, 1960 £125/£25
ditto, Little, Brown (U.S.), 1960 . . . . £65/£15

Biography
Rossetti: His Life and Work, Duckworth, 1928 . .
. . . . £1,000/£250
ditto, Dodd (U.S.), 1928 . . . . . . £450/£100
Edmund Campion, Longman, 1935 . . . £350/£75
ditto, Longman, 1935 (50 signed copies) . . £1,500
ditto, Sheed (U.S.), 1935 . . . . . £125/£35
The Life of the Right Reverend Ronald Knox,
Chapman & Hall, 1959 . . . . £35/£5
ditto, Little, Brown (U.S.), 1960 . . . . £30/£5

Others
An Open Letter to his Eminence the Cardinal Archbishop of Westminster, privately printed, 1933 .
. . . . £5,000
Wine in Peace and War, Saccone & Speed, [1947] .
. . . . £200/£150
ditto, Saccone & Speed, [1947] (100 signed copies) .
. . . . £1,000
A Little Learning: The First Volume of an Autobiography, Chapman & Hall, 1964 . £45/£10
ditto, Little, Brown (U.S.), 1964 . . . . £35/£10
Diaries, Weidenfeld, 1976 . . . . . £30/£10
ditto, Little, Brown (U.S.), 1976 . . . £30/£10
A Little Order: A Selection from his Journalism,
Methuen, 1977 . . . . £20/£5
ditto, Little, Brown (U.S.), 1981 . . . £15/£5
The Letters of Evelyn Waugh, Weidenfeld, 1980 . .
. . . . £20/£5
ditto, Ticknor & Fields (U.S.), 1980 . . . £20/£5
The Essays, Articles and Reviews of Evelyn Waugh,
Methuen, 1983 . . . . £20/£5
ditto, Little, Brown (U.S.), 1984 . . . . £20/£5

MARY WEBB
(b.1881 d.1927)

Webb only found success as a novelist after being championed by Stanley Baldwin, then Prime Minister. Her books are Hardyesque, with nature powerfully and beautifully described, and peopled by characters who battle grimly against fate.

Novels
The Golden Arrow, Constable, 1916 . . . £150
ditto, Dutton (U.S.), 1918. . . . . . £60
Gone to Earth, Constable, 1917 (dark red cloth) £100
ditto, Dutton (U.S.), 1917. . . . . . £40
The House in Dormer Forest, Hutchinson, [1920]. .
. . . . £125/£35
ditto, Doran (U.S.), 1921 . . . . . . £125/£30
Seven For A Secret, Hutchinson, 1922 . . £125/£30
ditto, Doran (U.S.), 1923 . . . . . . £125/£30
Precious Bane, Cape, 1924 . . . . £250/£100
ditto, Modern Library (U.S.), 1926 . . . £30/£10
Armour Wherein He Trusted, Cape, 1929 . £45/£15
ditto, Dutton (U.S.), 1929. . . . . . £35/£10

Short Stories
The Chinese Lion, Rota, 1937 (350 copies, glassine d/w and slipcase). . . . . £50/£35

Poetry
Poems and The Spring of Joy, Cape, 1928 £45/£15
ditto, Dutton (U.S.), 1929. . . . . . £35/£10
Fifty-One Poems, Cape, 1946 . . . . £25/£5
ditto, Dutton (U.S.), 1946. . . . . . £20/£5

Others
Spring of Joy: A Little Book of Healing, J.M. Dent & Sons, 1917 . . . . £65
A Mary Webb Anthology, Cape, 1935 (illustrated by Rowland Hilder and Norman Hepple) . . £20/£5
ditto, Dutton (U.S.), 1940. . . . . . £20/£5
The Essential Mary Webb, Cape, 1949 . . £15/£5

DENTON WELCH
(b.1915 d.1948)

Welch studied painting at Goldsmiths' School of Art, London, until a bicycle accident in 1935 severed his spine and left him temporarily paralysed and permanently ill. He took up writing as a career, producing three highly autobiographical books and numerous fragments.

Novels
Maiden Voyage, Routledge, 1943 . . . £200/£50
ditto, Fischer (U.S.), 1945 . . . . . £75/£20
In Youth is Pleasure, Routledge, 1944 [1945] £75/£25
ditto, Fischer (U.S.), 1946 . . . . . £65/£20

A Voice Through a Cloud, John Lehmann, 1950 . .
. . . . £50/£15
ditto, Dutton/Obelisk (U.S.), 1966 (wraps) . . £5

Short Stories/Miscellaneous
Brave and Cruel and Other Stories, Hamish Hamilton,
1948 [1949] . . . . £165/£35
A Last Sheaf, John Lehmann, 1951 . . . £100/£25
The Denton Welch Journals, Hamish Hamilton, 1952
(edited by Jocelyn Brooke) . . . . . £45/£15
I Left My Grandfather's House, James Campbell,
1958 (150 copies) £50
ditto, The Lion & Unicorn Press, 1958 (20 deluxe
copies of 200) £400
ditto, The Lion & Unicorn Press, 1958 (180 ordinary
copies of 200) £250
ditto, Allison & Busby, 1984 . . . . . £20/£5
ditto, Allison & Busby, 1984 (wraps) £5
Dumb Instrument, Enitharmon Press, 1976 (60
specially bound copies on blue paper of 600) . £250
ditto, Enitharmon Press, 1976 (540 copies of 600) . .
. . . . £100/£45
The Journals of Denton Welch, Allison & Busby,
1984 (edited by Michael De-la-Noy) . . £25/£10
ditto, Dutton (U.S.), 1984 . . . . . £15/£5
The Stories of Denton Welch, Dutton (U.S.), 1985 .
. . . . £10/£5
*Fragments of a Life Story: the Collected Short
Writings of Denton Welch*, Penguin, 1987 (edited
and with an introduction by Michael De-la-Noy) £10
A Lunch Appointment, Elysium Press (U.S.), 1993
(150 copies, bound in black silk) £100
ditto, Elysium Press (U.S.), 1993 (20 copies, bound in
black silk), signed by Edmund White, with an extra
signed etching by Le-Tan) £450

FAY WELDON
(b.1933)

A novelist and writer for television drama, Weldon's
popular success was *The Life and Loves of a She
Devil*.

Novels
The Fat Woman's Joke, MacGibbon & Kee, 1967 .
. . . . £100/£25
ditto, as *... and the Wife Ran Away*, McKay (U.S.),
1968 . . . . £50/£15
Down Among the Women, Heinemann, 1971 . £25/£5
ditto, St Martin's Press (U.S.), 1972 . . . . £15/£5
Female Friends, St Martin's Press (U.S.), 1974 £15/£5
ditto, Heinemann, 1975 . . . . . . £25/£5
Remember Me, Hodder & Stoughton, 1976 . . £20/£5
ditto, Random House (U.S.), 1976 . . . £15/£5
Words of Advice, Random House (U.S.), 1977 . £20/£5
ditto, as *Little Sisters*, Hodder & Stoughton, 1977 . .
. . . . £20/£5

Praxis, Hodder & Stoughton, 1978 . . . . £15/£5
ditto, Summit (U.S.), 1978 . . . . . . £15/£5
Puffball, Hodder & Stoughton, 1980 . . . £15/£5
ditto, Summit (U.S.), 1980 . . . . . . £15/£5
The President's Child, Hodder & Stoughton, 1982 .
. . . . £15/£5
ditto, Doubleday (U.S.), 1983 . . . . . £15/£5
The Life and Loves of a She Devil, Hodder &
Stoughton, 1983 . . . . £25/£5
ditto, Pantheon (U.S.), 1984 . . . . . £15/£5
The Shrapnel Academy, Hodder & Stoughton, 1986 .
. . . . £10/£5
ditto, Viking (U.S.), 1987 . . . . . . £10/£5
The Heart of the Country, Century Hutchinson, 1987 .
. . . . £10/£5
ditto, Viking (U.S.), 1988 . . . . . . £10/£5
The Hearts and Lives of Men, Heinemann, 1987 . .
. . . . £10/£5
ditto, Viking (U.S.), 1988 . . . . . . £10/£5
The Rules of Life, Century Hutchinson, 1987 . £10/£5
ditto, Harper & Row (U.S.), 1987 . . . . £10/£5
Leader of the Band, Hodder & Stoughton, 1988 . .
. . . . £10/£5
ditto, Viking (U.S.), 1989 . . . . . . £10/£5
The Cloning of Joanna May, Collins, 1989 . £10/£5
ditto, Viking (U.S.), 1990 . . . . . . £10/£5
Darcy's Utopia, Collins, 1990 . . . . . £10/£5
ditto, Viking (U.S.), 1991 . . . . . . £10/£5
Growing Rich, HarperCollins, 1992 . . . . £10/£5
Life Force, HarperCollins, 1992 . . . . . £10/£5
ditto, Viking (U.S.), 1992 . . . . . . £10/£5
Natural Love, HarperCollins, 1993 . . . . £10/£5
Trouble, Viking (U.S.), 1993 . . . . . £10/£5
ditto, as *Affliction*, Harper Collins, 1994 . £10/£5
Splitting, HarperCollins, 1995 . . . . . £10/£5
ditto, Atlantic Monthly Press (U.S.), 1995 . £10/£5
Worst Fears, HarperCollins, 1996 . . . . £10/£5
ditto, Atlantic Monthly Press (U.S.), 1996 . £10/£5
Big Women, HarperCollins, 1997 . . . . £10/£5
ditto, as *Big Girls Don't Cry*, Atlantic Monthly Press
(U.S.), 1997 . . . . £10/£5
Rhode Island Blues, Flamingo, 2000 . . £10/£5
ditto, Atlantic Monthly Press (U.S.), 2000 . . £10/£5
The Bulgari Connection, Flamingo, 2001 . . £10/£5
ditto, Atlantic Monthly Press (U.S.), 2001 . . £10/£5

Short Stories
Watching Me Watching You, Hodder & Stoughton,
1981 . . . . £15/£5
ditto, Summit (U.S.), 1981 . . . . . £10/£5
Polaris, Hodder & Stoughton, 1985 . . . £10/£5
ditto, Penguin (U.S.), 1989 (wraps) £5
Moon Over Minneapolis, Collins, 1991 . . £10/£5
A Question of Timing, Colophon Press, 1992 (125
unsigned, numbered copies of 231, wraps) . £20
ditto, Colophon Press, 1992 (100 signed, numbered
copies of 231, wraps) £35
ditto, Colophon Press, 1992 (6 signed, numbered
copies of 231, wraps) £150

Angel, All Innocence and Other Stories, Bloomsbury, 1995 (wraps) £5
Wicked Women, HarperCollins, 1995 . . . £10/£5
ditto, Atlantic Monthly Press (U.S.), 1997 . . £10/£5
A Hard Time To Be A Father, HarperCollins, 1998 . . . . £10/£5
ditto, Bloomsbury (U.S.), 1999 . . . . . £10/£5
Nothing to Wear & Nowhere to Hide, Flamingo, 2002 . . . . £10/£5

Children's Books
Wolf The Mechanical Dog, Collins, 1988 . . £25/£5
Party Puddle, Collins, 1989 . . . . . . £25/£5
Nobody Likes Me, Bodley Head, 1997 . . . £15/£5

Others
Letters to Alice, Joseph/Rainbird Books, 1984 . £15/£5
ditto, Taplinger (U.S.), 1985 . . . . . . £15/£5
Rebecca West, Penguin, 1985 (wraps) £5
Sacred Cows, Chatto & Windus, 1989 (wraps) . . £5
Godless in Eden: Essays, Flamingo, 1999 . . £10/£5
Auto Da Fay: A Memoir, Flamingo, 2002 . . £10/£5

H.G. WELLS
(b.1886 d.1946)

A versatile novelist whose work ranges from innovative science fiction through to social realism, Wells was also the author of works on politics, society and history.

Novels
The Time Machine, Henry Holt (U.S.), 1895 ('H.S. Wells' on title page) £20,000
ditto, Henry Holt (U.S.), 1895 (red cloth) . . £2,000
ditto, Heinemann, 1895 ('H.S. Wells' on title page) £20,000
ditto, Heinemann, 1895 (grey cloth) . . . £1,500
ditto, Heinemann, 1895 (red cloth) £500
ditto, Heinemann, 1895 (wrappers) . . . £1,000
The Wonderful Visit, Dent, 1895 (front board blank) £400
ditto, Dent, 1895 (front board stamped with gilt angel by Arthur Rackham). £350
ditto, Macmillan (U.S.), 1895 . . . . . £200
The Island of Doctor Moreau, Heinemann, 1896 (monogram blind-stamped on back board). . £750
ditto, Heinemann, 1896 (no monogram). . . £450
ditto, Stone & Kimball (U.S.), 1896 (black cloth) £225
The Wheels of Chance, Dent, 1896 . . . . £150
ditto, Macmillan (U.S.), 1896 . . . . . £75
The Red Room, Stone & Kimball (U.S.), 1896 (12 copies only) £10,000
The Invisible Man, Pearson, 1897 . . . £1,250
ditto, Arnold (U.S.), 1897. . . . . . . £750
The War of The Worlds, Heinemann, 1898 (16 pages of ads). £1,000
ditto, Heinemann, 1898 (32 pages of ads) . . £750

ditto, Harper (U.S.), 1898 (15 illustrations by Warwick Goble, frontispiece by Cosmo Rowe) . . . £400
When The Sleeper Wakes, Harpers, 1899 . . £200
ditto, Harper (U.S.), 1899. . . . . . . £175
ditto, Thomas Nelson, 1910 (revised edition) . £30
Love and Mr Lewisham, Harpers, 1900. . . £65
ditto, Stokes (U.S.), 1900. . . . . . . £45
The First Men in The Moon, Bowen-Merrill (U.S.), 1901 . . . . £650
ditto, Newnes, 1901 (first issue in dark blue cloth, black endpapers). £750
ditto, Newnes, 1901 (second issue in dark blue cloth, white endpapers). £650
ditto, Newnes, 1901 (third issue in light blue cloth) £500
ditto, Newnes, 1901 (fourth issue in blue/green cloth) £400
The Sea Lady: A Tissue of Moonshine, Methuen, 1902 . . . . £300
ditto, Appleton (U.S.), 1902 . . . . . . £150
The Food of The Gods, Macmillan, 1904 . . £300
ditto, Scribner's (U.S.), 1904 . . . . . . £200
A Modern Utopia, Chapman & Hall, 1905 . . £165
ditto, Scribner's (U.S.), 1905 . . . . . . £125
Kipps, Macmillan, 1905 . . . . £100
ditto, Scribner's (U.S.), 1905 . . . . . . £65
In The Days of The Comet, Macmillan, 1906 . £175
ditto, Century (U.S.), 1906 . . . . . . £125
The War in The Air, George Bell, 1908 (first issue, blue cloth with lettering and decorations in gilt) £400
ditto, George Bell, 1908 (second issue with blue cloth blindstamped) £200
ditto, Macmillan (U.S.), 1908 . . . . . £200
Tono-Bungay, Macmillan, 1909 (with ads dated '1.09'). £200
ditto, Macmillan, 1909 (with ads dated '2.09') . £75
ditto, Duffield (U.S.), 1909 . . . . . . £100
Ann Veronica, T. Fisher Unwin, 1909 . . . £75
ditto, Harper (U.S.), 1909. . . . . . . £50
The History of Mr Polly, Thomas Nelson, 1910 £75
ditto, Duffield (U.S.), 1910 . . . . . . £50
The New Machiavelli, Duffield (U.S.), 1910 (first issue with integral title page that does not have quotes by Lewes and James) £100
ditto, Duffield (U.S.), 1910 (second issue with cancel title page with quotes) £45
ditto, John Lane/Bodley Head, 1911. . . . £45
Marriage, Macmillan, 1912 . . . . . . £45
ditto, Duffield (U.S.), 1912 . . . . . . £25
The Passionate Friends, Macmillan, 1913 . . £45
ditto, Harper (U.S.), 1913. . . . . . . £45
The World Set Free, Macmillan, 1914 . . . £35
ditto, Dutton (U.S.), 1914. . . . . . . £30
The Wife of Sir Isaac Harman, Macmillan, 1914 £35
ditto, Macmillan (U.S.), 1914 . . . . . £30
Boon, T. Fisher Unwin, 1915. . . . . . £25
ditto, Doran (U.S.), 1915 . . . . £25
Bealby, Methuen, 1915 . . . . £20
ditto, Macmillan (U.S.), 1915 . . . . . £20

The Research Magnificent, Macmillan, 1915 . £20
ditto, Macmillan (U.S.), 1915 . . . . . £20
Mr Britling Sees It Through, Cassell, 1916. . £20
ditto, Macmillan (U.S.), 1916 . . . . . £20
The Soul of a Bishop, Cassell, 1917. . . . £15
ditto, Macmillan (U.S.), 1917 . . . . . £15
Joan and Peter, Cassell, 1918 . . . . . £15
ditto, Macmillan (U.S.), 1918 . . . . . £15
The Undying Fire, Cassell, 1919 . . . . £15
ditto, Macmillan (U.S.), 1919 . . . . . £15
The Secret Places of The Heart, Cassell, 1922 . . .
. . . . £100/£20
ditto, Macmillan (U.S.), 1922 . . . . £100/£20
Men Like Gods, Cassell, 1923 . . . . £150/£20
ditto, Macmillan (U.S.), 1923 . . . . £150/£20
The Dream, Cape, 1924 . . . . . . £100/£20
ditto, Macmillan (U.S.), 1924 . . . . £100/£20
Christina Alberta's Father, Cape, 1925. . £100/£15
ditto, Macmillan (U.S.), 1925 . . . . £100/£15
The World of William Clissold, Ernest Benn, 1926 (3 vols) . . . . £125/£35
ditto, Ernest Benn, 1926 (218 deluxe signed copies, 3 vols, slipcase) . . . . £350/£300
ditto, Doran (U.S.), 1926 (2 vols, slipcase) . £100/£20
Meanwhile, Ernest Benn, 1927 . . . . £100/£15
ditto, Doran (U.S.), 1927 . . . . . . £75/£15
Mr Blettsworthy on Rampole Island, Ernest Benn, 1928 . . . . £65/£15
ditto, Doubleday Doran (U.S.), 1928 . £65/£15
The King Who Was a King, The book of a film, Ernest Benn, 1929 . . . . £65/£15
ditto, Doubleday Doran (U.S.), 1929 . £65/£15
The Autocracy of Mr Parham, Heinemann, 1930 . .
. . . . £50/£15
ditto, Doubleday Doran (U.S.), 1930 . . £50/£15
The Bulpington of Blup, Hutchinson, 1932. £40/£15
ditto, Macmillan (U.S.), 1933 . . . . £40/£15
The Shape of Things to Come, The Ultimate Revolution, Hutchinson, 1933 . . . . £200/£35
ditto, Macmillan (U.S.), 1933 . . . . £200/£30
ditto, as Things to Come: A Film Story, Cresset Press, 1935 . . . . £65/£15
The Croquet Player, Chatto & Windus, 1936 £50/£15
ditto, Viking (U.S.), 1937. . . . . . £50/£15
Man Who Could Work Miracles: A Film Story, Cresset Press, 1936 . . . . . . £45/£15
ditto, Macmillan (U.S.), 1936 . . . . £45/£15
Star Begotten, Chatto & Windus, 1937 . . £50/£20
ditto, Viking (U.S.), 1937. . . . . . £50/£20
Brynhild, Methuen, 1937 . . . . . . £45/£15
ditto, Scribner's (U.S.), 1937 . . . . . £45/£15
The Camford Visitation, Methuen, 1937 . £45/£15
The Brothers, Chatto & Windus, 1938 . . £45/£15
ditto, Viking (U.S.), 1938. . . . . . £45/£15
Apropos of Dolores, Cape, 1938 . . . . £45/£15
ditto, Scribner's (U.S.), 1938 . . . . . £45/£15
The Holy Terror, Joseph, 1939 . . . . £45/£15
ditto, Simon & Schuster, (U.S.), 1939 . . £45/£15
The Final Men, Phantagraph Press, 1940 (wraps) £50

Babes in The Darkling Wood, Secker & Warburg, 1940 . . . . £45/£15
ditto, Alliance Book Corp. (U.S.), 1940 . . £45/£15
All Aboard for Ararat, Secker & Warburg, 1940 . .
. . . . £45/£15
ditto, Alliance Book Corp. (U.S.), 1941 . . £45/£15
You Can't Be Too Careful, Secker & Warburg, 1941 .
. . . . £40/£15

Omnibus Editions
Three Prophetic Novels of H.G. Wells, Dover, 1960 (wraps) £10

Short Stories
Select Conversations with an Uncle, Lane, 1895 £250
ditto, Merriam (U.S.), 1895 . . . . . £200
The Stolen Bacillus and Other Incidents, Methuen, 1895 . . . . £650
The Plattner Story and Others, Methuen, 1897 £200
Thirty Strange Stories, Edward Arnold (U.S.), 1897 .
. . . . £500
Tales of Space and Time, Harpers, 1900 [1899] £300
ditto, Doubleday (U.S.), 1899 . . . . . £250
Twelve Stories and a Dream, Macmillan, 1903 £250
ditto, Scribner's (U.S.), 1905 . . . . . £150
The Country of The Blind, and Other Stories, Nelson, 1911 . . . . £125
ditto, privately printed, (U.S.), 1915 . . . . £125
ditto, Golden Cockerel Press, 1939 (30 signed copies) .
. . . . £1,000
ditto, Golden Cockerel Press, 1939 (280 signed copies)
. . . . £300
The Door in The Wall and Other Stories, Mitchell Kennerley (U.S.), 1911 (240 copies with full set of plates by Coburn) £200
ditto, Mitchell Kennerley (U.S.), 1915 (300 copies with reduced set of plates) £100
ditto, Grant Richards, 1915 (60 signed copies with full set of plates) £2,000
The Short Stories of H.G. Wells, Ernest Benn, 1927 .
. . . . £50/£20
H.G. Wells: Short Stories, Folio Society, 1990 (with slipcase) . . . . £20/£10

Children's Titles
Floor Games, Palmer, 1911 . . . . . £200
ditto, Small, Maynard (U.S.), 1912 . . . £175
Little Wars, Palmer, 1913. . . . . . £200
ditto, Small, Maynard (U.S.), 1913 . . . £200
The Adventures of Tommy, Harrap, 1929 . £125/£25
ditto, Amalgamated Press, 1929 (numbered copies for private circulation) £400
ditto, Stokes (U.S.), 1929 . . . . . £125/£25

Others
Text-Book of Biology, W.B. Clive, 1893 (2 vols, with 47 two-page plates, first binding dark green cloth) .
. . . . £750

ditto, W.B. Clive, 1893 (2 vols, second binding brown cloth) £500
ditto, W.B. Clive, 1894 (revised edition of Part 1) £35
ditto, as *Text-Book of Zoology*, W.B. Clive, 1898 (revised edition) £25
Honours Physiography, Joseph Hughes, 1893 (with R.A. Gregory) £250
Certain Personal Matters, Lawrence & Bullen, 1898 [1897]. £100
Anticipations, Chapman & Hall, 1902 [1901] . £75
ditto, Harper (U.S.), 1902. . . . . . £75
Mankind in The Making, Chapman & Hall, 1903 £30
ditto, Scribner's (U.S.), 1904 . . . . . £25
The Future in America, Chapman & Hall, 1906 £35
ditto, Harpers (U.S.), 1906 . . . . . £25
Faults of The Fabian, Edward R. Pease, 1906 . £30
Socialism and The Family, Fifield, 1906 (hard covers) £30
ditto, Fifield, 1906 (paper covers) £30
Reconstruction of The Fabian Society, privately printed, 1906 . . . . £35
The So-Called Science of Sociology, Macmillan, 1907 . . . . £35
The Misery of Boots, The Fabian Society, 1907 £30
Will Socialism Destroy The Home?, Independent Labour Party, 1907 . . . . £35
New Worlds for Old, Constable, 1908 . . . £45
ditto, Macmillan (U.S.), 1908 . . . . £40
First and Last Things, Constable, 1908. . . £40
ditto, Putnams (U.S.), 1908 . . . . . £35
The Labour Unrest, Daily Mail, 1912 . . £25
War and Common Sense, Daily Mail, 1913 . £25
Liberalism and It's Party, Good, 1913 . . . £25
An Englishman Looks at The World, Cassell, 1914 . . . . £25
The War That Will End War, Palmer, 1914 (wraps) £75
The Peace of The World, Daily Chronicle, 1915 (wraps) £35
What is Coming: A Forecast of Things after The War, Cassell, 1916 . . . . £30
ditto, Macmillan (U.S.), 1916 . . . . £25
The Elements of Reconstruction, Nisbet, 1916. £25
War and The Future, Cassell, 1917 . . . £25
God The Invisible King, Cassell, 1917 . . . £25
ditto, Macmillan (U.S.), 1917 . . . . £20
In The Fourth Year: Anticipations of a World Peace, Chatto & Windus, 1918 . . . . . . £25
History is One, Ginn (U.S.), 1919 (pamphlet) . £30
The Outline of History, Newnes, [1919-1920] (24 parts, wraps) £100
ditto, Newnes, [1920] (2 vols) £45
Russia in The Shadows, Hodder & Stoughton, [1920]. . . . . £100/£30
The Salvaging of Civilisation, Cassell, 1921 £75/£25
ditto, Macmillan (U.S.), 1921 . . . . £50/£15
University of London Election: An Electoral Letter, H. Finer, 1922 (wraps) £20

The Story of a Great Schoolmaster, Chatto & Windus, 1924 . . . . £60/£20
ditto, Macmillan (U.S.), 1924 . . . . £50/£15
A Year of Prophesying, T. Fisher Unwin, 1924 £45
Mr Belloc Objects to 'The Outline of History', Watts, 1926 . . . . £40/£15
ditto, Doran (U.S.), 1926 . . . . . . £40/£15
Democracy Under Revision, Hogarth Press, 1927 . . . . £75/£25
The Way The World is Going, Ernest Benn, 1928 . . . . £100/£25
ditto, Doran (U.S.), 1929 . . . . . . £75/£20
The Open Conspiracy, Gollancz, 1928 . . £65/£20
The Common Sense of World Peace, Hogarth Press, 1929 . . . . £75/£30
The Science of Life, Amalgamated Press, [1930] (with Julian Huxley and G.P. Wells, 3 vols) . . £125/£50
ditto, Cassell, 1931 (1 vol.) . . . . . £50/£15
ditto, Doubleday Doran (U.S.), 1931 (750 signed copies, 4 vols) £250
ditto, Doubleday Doran (U.S.), 1931 (2 vols) . £250
The Problems of The Troublesome Collaborator, privately printed, 1930 (175 copies) . . . £125
Settlement of The Trouble Between Mr Thring and Mr Wells, A Footnote to The Problems of The Troublesome Collaborator, privately printed, 1930 (225 copies) £75
The Work, Wealth and Happiness of Mankind, Doubleday Doran (U.S.), 1931 (250 signed copies, 2 vols) £150
ditto, Heinemann, 1932 (1 vol.) . . . . £45/£20
After Democracy, Watts, 1932 . . . . £50/£15
Experiment in Autobiography, Gollancz & Cresset Press, 1936 (2 vols) . . . . £75/£30
ditto, Macmillan (U.S.), 1934 (1 vol.) . . . £50/£15
The New America: The New World, Cresset Press, 1935 . . . . £50/£15
ditto, Macmillan (U.S.), 1935 . . . . £50/£15
The Idea of a World Encyclopaedia, Hogarth Press, 1936 (wraps) £45
The Anatomy of Frustration, Cresset Press, 1936 . . . . £40/£10
ditto, Macmillan (U.S.), 1936 . . . . £40/£10
World Brain, Methuen, 1938 . . . . . £45/£10
Travels of a Republican Radical in Search of Hot Water, Penguin Special, 1939 (wrapper has title *In Search of Hot Water*) £20
The Fate of Homo Sapiens, Secker & Warburg, 1939. . . . . £50/£15
The New World Order, Secker & Warburg, 1940 . . . . £45/£15
ditto, Knopf (U.S.), 1940 . . . . . . £45/£15
The Rights of Man, or What Are We Fighting For? Penguin Special, 1940 . . . . . . £15
The Common Sense of War and Peace, Penguin, 1940 . . . . £15
Guide to The New World, Gollancz, 1941 . £35/£15
The Outlook for Homo Sapiens, Secker & Warburg, 1942 . . . . £30/£10

Phoenix, Secker & Warburg, 1942 . . . £40/£10
A Thesis on The Quality of Illusion, privately printed,
Watts, 1942 (wraps) £40
Crux Ansata, Penguin Special, 1943 (wraps) . . £5
'42 to '44, Secker & Warburg, 1944 . . . £45/£10
Mind at The End of it's Tether and The Happy
Turning, Heinemann, 1945 . . . . . £40/£10
ditto, Didier (U.S.), 1946 . . . . . . £35/£10

PATRICIA WENTWORTH
(b.1878 d.1961)

'Patricia Wentworth' was the pseudonym of Dora
Amy Elles, who began her career as a romantic
novelist but is remembered, through her creation of
'Miss Silver' and 'Benbow Smith', as one of the
writers of 'Golden Age' detective fiction.

'Miss Silver' Books
Grey Mask, Hodder & Stoughton, [1928] . £750/£75
ditto, Lippincott (U.S.), 1929 . . . . . £250/£50
The Case is Closed, Hodder & Stoughton, 1937 . .
. . . . £400/£50
ditto, Lippincott (U.S.), 1937 . . . . . £125/£25
Lonesome Road, Hodder & Stoughton, 1939 £300/£50
ditto, Lippincott (U.S.), 1939 . . . . £100/£25
In The Balance, Lippincott (U.S.), 1941 . £150/£35
ditto, as Danger Point, Hodder & Stoughton, 1942 .
. . . . £125/£25
The Chinese Shawl, Hodder & Stoughton, 1943 . .
. . . . £125/£35
ditto, Lippincott (U.S.), 1943 . . . . £50/£20
Miss Silver Deals With Death, Lippincott (U.S.), 1943
. . . . £150/£35
ditto, as Miss Silver Intervenes, Hodder & Stoughton,
1944 . . . . £75/£20
The Clock Strikes Twelve, Lippincott (U.S.), 1944. .
. . . . £150/£35
ditto, Hodder & Stoughton, 1945. . . . £75/£20
The Key, Lippincott (U.S.), 1944 . . £150/£35
ditto, Hodder & Stoughton, 1946. . . . £75/£20
She Came Back, Lippincott (U.S.), 1945 . £75/£25
ditto, as The Traveller Returns, Hodder & Stoughton,
1948 . . . . £50/£20
Pilgrim's Rest, Lippincott (U.S.), 1946 . £45/£20
ditto, Hodder & Stoughton, 1948. . . . £25/£10
ditto, as The Dark Threat, Popular Library (U.S.),
1961 . . . . £50/£20
Latter End, Lippincott (U.S.), 1947 . . . £40/£15
ditto, Hodder & Stoughton, 1949. . . . £30/£10
Wicked Uncle, Lippincott (U.S.), 1947 . . £35/£10
ditto, as Spotlight, Hodder & Stoughton, 1949 £25/£10
Eternity Ring, Lippincott (U.S.), 1948 . . £35/£15
ditto, Hodder & Stoughton, 1950. . . . £30/£10
The Case of William Smith, Lippincott (U.S.), 1948 .
. . . . £35/£15
ditto, Hodder & Stoughton, 1950. . . . £25/£10

Miss Silver Comes To Stay, Lippincott (U.S.), 1949 .
. . . . £35/£15
ditto, Hodder & Stoughton, 1951. . . . £25/£10
The Catherine Wheel, Lippincott (U.S.), 1949 £35/£15
ditto, Hodder & Stoughton, 1951. . . . £25/£10
The Brading Collection, Lippincott (U.S.), 1950 . .
. . . . £35/£15
ditto, Hodder & Stoughton, 1952. . . . £25/£10
ditto, as Mr Brading's Collection, Severn House, 1987
. . . . £10/£5
Through The Wall, Lippincott (U.S.), 1950 £35/£15
ditto, Hodder & Stoughton, 1952. . . . £25/£10
The Ivory Dagger, Lippincott (U.S.), 1951 . £35/£15
ditto, Hodder & Stoughton, 1953. . . . £25/£10
Anna, Where Are You?, Lippincott (U.S.), 1951 . .
. . . . £35/£15
ditto, Hodder & Stoughton, 1953. . . . £25/£10
ditto, as Death at the Deep End, Pyramid (U.S.), 1953
(wraps) £5
The Watersplash, Lippincott (U.S.), 1951 . £30/£10
ditto, Hodder & Stoughton, 1954. . . . £25/£10
Ladies' Bane, Lippincott (U.S.), 1952 . . £30/£10
ditto, Hodder & Stoughton, 1954. . . . £25/£10
Out of the Past, Lippincott (U.S.), 1953. . £25/£10
ditto, Hodder & Stoughton, 1955. . . . £25/£10
Vanishing Point, Lippincott (U.S.), 1953 . £25/£10
ditto, Hodder & Stoughton, 1955. . . . £25/£10
The Silent Pool, Lippincott (U.S.), 1954 . £25/£10
ditto, Hodder & Stoughton, 1956. . . . £25/£10
The Benevent Treasure, Lippincott (U.S.), 1954 . .
. . . . £25/£10
ditto, Hodder & Stoughton, 1956. . . . £25/£10
Poison In The Pen, Lippincott (U.S.), 1955 £25/£10
ditto, Hodder & Stoughton, 1957. . . . £25/£10
The Listening Eye, Lippincott (U.S.), 1955. £25/£10
ditto, Hodder & Stoughton, 1957. . . . £25/£10
The Gazebo, Lippincott (U.S.), 1956 . . £25/£10
ditto, Hodder & Stoughton, 1958. . . . £25/£10
ditto, as The Summerhouse, Pyramid (U.S.), 1967
(wraps) £5
The Fingerprint, Lippincott (U.S.), 1956 . £25/£10
ditto, Hodder & Stoughton, 1959. . . . £25/£10
The Alington Inheritance, Lippincott (U.S.), 1958 .
. . . . £25/£10
ditto, Hodder & Stoughton, 1960. . . . £25/£10
The Girl in the Cellar, Hodder & Stoughton, 1961. .
. . . . £25/£10

Others
The Astonishing Adventure of Jane Smith, Melrose,
1923 . . . . £2,500/£150
ditto, Small Maynard (U.S.), 1923 . . £1,250/£125
The Red Lacquer Case, Melrose, 1924 . . £600/£100
ditto, Small Maynard (U.S.), 1925 . . . £200/£100
The Annam Jewel, Melrose, 1924 . . . £500/£75
ditto, Small Maynard (U.S.), 1925 . . . £200/£75
The Dower House Mystery, Hodder & Stoughton,
[1925] . . . . £500/£75
ditto, Small Maynard (U.S.), 1926 . . . £200/£75

The Black Cabinet, Hodder & Stoughton, [1925] . .
. . . . £500/£75
ditto, Small Maynard (U.S.), 1926 . . . £150/£50
The Amazing Chance, Hodder & Stoughton, [1925] .
. . . . £500/£75
ditto, Small Maynard (U.S.), 1926 . . . £150/£50
Hue and Cry, Hodder & Stoughton, [1927]. £400/£75
ditto, Lippincott (U.S.), 1927. . . . . £125/£45
Anne Belinda, Hodder & Stoughton, [1927] £400/£75
ditto, Lippincott (U.S.), 1928. . . . . £125/£45
Will O' The Wisp, Hodder & Stoughton, [1928] . .
. . . . £400/£75
ditto, Lippincott (U.S.), 1928. . . . . £125/£45
Fool Errant, Hodder & Stoughton, [1929] . £400/£75
ditto, Lippincott (U.S.), 1929. . . . . £125/£45
The Coldstone, Hodder & Stoughton, [1930] £350/£50
ditto, Lippincott (U.S.), 1930. . . . . £100/£45
Beggar's Choice, Hodder & Stoughton, [1930] . .
. . . . £350/£50
ditto, Lippincott (U.S.), 1931. . . . . £100/£45
Kingdom Lost, Lippincott (U.S.), 1930 . . £350/£50
ditto, Hodder & Stoughton, [1931] . . . £350/£50
Danger Calling, Hodder & Stoughton, [1931] . . .
. . . . £350/£50
ditto, Lippincott (U.S.), 1931. . . . . £100/£40
Nothing Venture, Cassell, 1932 . . . . £350/£50
ditto, Lippincott (U.S.), 1932. . . . . £100/£45
Red Danger, Cassell, 1932 . . . . . £350/£50
ditto, as *Red Shadow*, Lippincott (U.S.), 1932 . .
. . . . £100/£45
Seven Green Stones, Cassell, 1933 . . . £300/£45
ditto, as *Outrageous Fortune*, Lippincott (U.S.), 1933.
. . . . £100/£45
Walk With Care, Cassell, 1933 . . . . £300/£45
ditto, Lippincott (U.S.), 1933. . . . . £100/£35
Fear By Night, Hodder & Stoughton, 1934. £300/£45
ditto, Lippincott (U.S.), 1934. . . . . £100/£35
Devil-In-The-Dark, Hodder & Stoughton, 1934 . .
. . . . £300/£45
ditto, as *Touch And Go*, Lippincott (U.S.), 1934 . .
. . . . £100/£35
Red Stefan, Hodder & Stoughton, 1935. . £300/£45
ditto, Lippincott (U.S.), 1935. . . . . £100/£35
Blindfold, Hodder & Stoughton, 1935 . . £300/£45
ditto, Lippincott (U.S.), 1935. . . . . £100/£35
Dead Or Alive, Hodder & Stoughton, 1936. £300/£45
ditto, Lippincott (U.S.), 1936. . . . . £100/£35
Hole And Corner, Hodder & Stoughton, 1936 . . .
. . . . £300/£45
ditto, Lippincott (U.S.), 1936. . . . . £100/£35
Down Under, Hodder & Stoughton, 1937 . £250/£45
ditto, Lippincott (U.S.), 1937. . . . . £75/£25
Run, Hodder & Stoughton, 1938. . . . £300/£45
ditto, Lippincott (U.S.), 1938. . . . . £100/£35
Mr Zero, Hodder & Stoughton, 1938 . . £300/£45
ditto, Lippincott (U.S.), 1938. . . . . £100/£35
The Blind Side, Hodder & Stoughton, 1939 £300/£45
ditto, Lippincott (U.S.), 1939. . . . . £100/£35
Rolling Stone, Hodder & Stoughton, 1940 . £250/£35

ditto, Lippincott (U.S.), 1940. . . . . £50/£20
Who Pays The Piper?, Hodder & Stoughton, 1940 .
. . . . £250/£35
ditto, as *Account Rendered*, Lippincott (U.S.), 1940 .
. . . . £50/£20
Unlawful Occasions, Hodder & Stoughton, 1941 . .
. . . . £200/£25
ditto, as *Weekend With Death*, Lippincott (U.S.), 1941
. . . . £50/£20
Pursuit of a Parcel, Hodder & Stoughton, 1942 . .
. . . . £150/£35
ditto, Lippincott (U.S.), 1942. . . . . £50/£20
Silence in Court, Lippincott (U.S.), 1945 . £50/£20
ditto, Hodder & Stoughton, 1947. . . . £50/£20

Historical Fiction
A Marriage Under The Terror, Melrose, 1910. £250
ditto, Putnam (U.S.), 1910 . . . . . . £125
A Little More Than Kin, Melrose, 1911. . . £200
ditto, as *More Than Kin*, Putnam (U.S.), 1911 . £100
The Devil's Wind, Melrose, 1912 . . . . £200
ditto, Putnam (U.S.), 1912 . . . . . . £100
The Fire Within, Melrose, 1913 . . . . . £200
ditto, Putnam (U.S.), 1913 . . . . . . £100
Simon Heriot, Melrose, 1914 . . . . . £150
Queen Anne Is Dead, Melrose, 1915 . . . £150

Poetry
A Child's Rhyme Book, Melrose, 1910 . . . £75
Beneath the Hunter's Moon, Hodder & Stoughton,
1945 . . . . £45/£10
The Pool of Dreams, Hodder & Stoughton, 1953 . .
. . . . £45/£10
ditto, Lippincott (U.S.), 1954. . . . . £40/£10

Others
Earl or Chieftan? The Romance of Hugh O'Neill,
Catholic Truth Society of Ireland (Dublin), 1919 £45

MARY WESLEY
(b.1912 d.2002)

Interest in Mary Wesley's novels was increased with
their adaptation for television in the 1990s.

Novels for Adults
Jumping The Queue, Macmillan, 1983 . . £45/£10
ditto, Penguin (U.S.), 1988 . . . . . . £10/£5
The Camomile Lawn, Macmillan, 1984. . £60/£10
ditto, Summit (U.S.), 1985 . . . . . . £20/£5
Harnessing Peacocks, Macmillan, 1985 . . £30/£5
ditto, Scribner's (U.S.), 1986 . . . . . £15/£5
The Vacillations of Poppy Carew, Macmillan, 1986 .
. . . . £30/£5
ditto, Penguin (U.S.), 1988 . . . . . . £10/£5
Not That Sort of Girl, Macmillan, 1987. . £20/£5
ditto, Viking (U.S.), 1988. . . . . . . £10/£5
Second Fiddle, Macmillan, 1988. . . . . £15/£5

ditto, Viking (U.S.), 1989. . . . . . . £10/£5
A Sensible Life, Bantam, 1990 . . . . . £10/£5
ditto, Viking (U.S.), 1990. . . . . . . £10/£5
A Dubious Legacy, Bantam, 1992 . . . £10/£5
ditto, Viking (U.S.), 1992. . . . . . . £10/£5
The Mary Wesley Omnibus, Macmillan, 1992 . £10/£5
An Imaginative Experience, Bantam, 1994. . £10/£5
ditto, Viking (U.S.), 1995. . . . . . . £10/£5
Part of the Furniture, Bantam, 1997 . . £10/£5
ditto, Viking (U.S.), 1997. . . . . . . £10/£5

Novels for Children

The Sixth Seal, Macdonald, 1969 . . . £75/£15
ditto, Stein & Day (U.S.), 1971 . . . . £45/£10
Speaking Terms, Faber, 1969 . . . . . £25/£5
ditto, Gambit (U.S.), 1971 . . . . . £15/£5
Haphazard House, Dent, 1983 . . . . . £25/£5
Magic Landscapes: A Mary Wesley Omnibus, Dent,
1991 . . . . £15/£5

Others

Part of the Scenery, Bantam Press, 2001 (photographs
by Kim Sayer) . . . . £10/£5

REBECCA WEST

(b.1892 d.1983)

Throughout her many and diverse writings, West was preoccupied with the idea of original sin. She was made a Dame in 1959.

Novels

The Return of the Soldier, Century Publishing (U.S.),
1918 . . . . £65
ditto, Nisbet, 1918. . . . . £45
The Judge, Hutchinson, 1922 . . . . £150/£65
ditto, Doran (U.S.), 1922 . . . . . . £100/£25
Harriet Hume, A London Fantasy, Hutchinson, 1929.
. . . . £100/£20
ditto, Doran (U.S.), 1929 . . . . . . £75/£10
War Nurse, Cosmopolitan Book Co. (U.S.), 1930
(anonymous) . . . . £125/£30
The Harsh Voice: Four Short Novels, Cape, 1935. .
. . . . £25/£10
ditto, Doubleday (U.S.), 1935 . . . . £25/£10
The Thinking Reed, Viking Press (U.S.), 1936. . .
. . . . £30/£10
ditto, Hutchinson, [1936] . . . . . £30/£10
The Fountain Overflows, Viking (U.S.), 1956 . £15/£5
ditto, Macmillan, 1957 . . . . £15/£5
The Birds Fall Down, Macmillan, 1966. . . £10/£5
ditto, Viking (U.S.), 1966. . . . . . . £15/£5
This Real Night, Macmillan, 1984 . . . £15/£5
ditto, Viking (U.S.), 1985. . . . . . . £10/£5
Cousin Rosamund, Macmillan, 1985 . . £10/£5
ditto, Viking (U.S.), 1986. . . . . . . £10/£5
Sunflower, Virago, 1986 . . . . £10/£5
ditto, Viking (U.S.), 1987. . . . . . . £10/£5

Others

Henry James, Nisbet, 1916 . . . . . . £45
ditto, Holt (U.S.), 1916 . . . . £25
The Strange Necessity, Cape, 1928 . . . £35/£10
ditto, Doran (U.S.), 1928 . . . . . . £30/£10
Lions and Lambs, Cape, 1928 . . . . £45/£15
ditto, Harcourt Brace (U.S.), 1928 . . . £45/£15
D.H. Lawrence, Secker, 1930 . . . . £40/£15
ditto, as *Elegy*, Phoenix (U.S.), 1930 (250 signed
copies, glassine d/w). . . . . . . £75/£50
Ending in Earnest: A Literary Log, Doubleday Doran
(U.S.), 1931 . . . . £60/£20
Arnold Bennett Himself, John Day (U.S.), 1931
(wraps) £15
St Augustine, Appleton (U.S.), 1933 . . £35/£10
ditto, Davies, 1933 . . . . £35/£10
A Letter to Grandfather, Hogarth Press, 1933 (wraps).
. . . . £25
The Modern 'Rake's Progress', Hutchinson, 1934 .
. . . . £75/£35
ditto, Hutchinson, 1934 (250 signed copies) . £175
Black Lamb and Grey Falcon, Viking Press (U.S.),
1941 (2 vols) . . . . £75/£35
ditto, Macmillan, 1942 (2 vols) . . . £75/£35
The Meaning of Treason, Viking Press (U.S.), 1947 .
. . . . £25/£5
ditto, Macmillan, 1949 . . . . £20/£5
ditto, Macmillan, 1952 (enlarged and revised) . £10/£5
A Train of Powder, Macmillan, 1955 . . £20/£5
ditto, Viking (U.S.), 1955. . . . . . . £20/£5
The Court and the Castle, Yale Univ. Press (U.S.),
1957 . . . . £20/£5
ditto, Macmillan, 1958 . . . . £20/£5
The Vassal Affair, Sunday Telegraph, 1963 (wraps) .
. . . . £10
McLuhan and the Future of Literature, The English
Association, 1969 (wraps) £25
Rebecca West, A Celebration, Macmillan, 1977 £10/£5
ditto, Viking (U.S.), 1977. . . . . . . £10/£5
1900, Weidenfeld & Nicolson, 1982. . . . £10/£5
ditto, Viking (U.S.), 1982. . . . . . . £10/£5
The Young Rebecca, Virago, 1982 . . . £10/£5
ditto, Viking (U.S.), 1982. . . . . . . £10/£5
Family Memories, Virago, 1987. . . . . £10/£5
ditto, Viking (U.S.), 1988. . . . . . . £10/£5
The Only Poet and Short Stories, Virago, 1992 £10/£5
Selected Letters of Rebecca West, Yale Univ. Press
(U.S.), 2000 . . . . £10/£5

EDITH WHARTON
(b.1862 d.1937)

An American novelist and short story writer, with *The Age of Innocence* she became the first woman to be awarded the Pulitzer Prize.

Novels and Novellas

The Touchstone, Scribner's (U.S.), 1900 . . £175
ditto, as *A Gift from The Grave*, Murray, 1900 . £150
The Valley of Decision, Scribner's (U.S.), 1902 (2 vols) £150
ditto, Murray, 1902 . . . . £100
Sanctuary, Scribner's (U.S.), 1903 . . . . £125
ditto, Macmillan, 1903 . . . . . . £75
The House of Mirth, Scribner's (U.S.), 1905 . £100
ditto, Macmillan, 1905 . . . . £75
Madame de Treymes, Scribner's (U.S.), 1907 . £50
ditto, Macmillan, 1907 . . . . £50
The Fruit of The Tree, Scribner's (U.S.), 1907. £65
ditto, Macmillan, 1907 . . . . £50
Ethan Frome, Scribner's (U.S.), 1911 (first issue with top edge gilt and perfect type in last line of p.135) .
. . . . £450
ditto, Scribner's (U.S.), 1911 (second issue without gilt top edge, and with broken type in last line of p.135) .
. . . . £75
ditto, Macmillan, 1911 . . . . . . £125
ditto, Scribner's (U.S.), 1922 (2,000 copies, new introduction, slipcase) . . . . . £75/£50
ditto, Limited Editions Club (U.S.), 1939 (1,500 copies signed by illustrator Henry Varnum Poor, slipcase) .
. . . . £50/£40
The Reef, Appleton & Co. (U.S.), 1912 . . . £40
ditto, Macmillan, 1912 . . . . . . £35
The Custom of The Country, Scribner's (U.S.), 1913 .
. . . . £40
ditto, Macmillan, 1913 . . . . . . £35
Summer, Appleton & Co. (U.S.), 1917 . . £45
ditto, Macmillan, 1917 . . . . . . £35
The Marne, Appleton & Co. (U.S.), 1918 . . £35
ditto, as *The Marne: A Tale of The War*, Macmillan, 1918 . . . . £25
The Age of Innocence, Appleton & Co. (U.S. and U.K.), 1920 (first issue: 'burial', p.186, no mention of Pulitzer Prize on d/w) . . . £4,000/£1,000
The Glimpses of The Moon, Appleton & Co. (U.S. and U.K.), 1922 . . . . £300/£40
A Son at The Front, Scribner's (U.S.), 1923 £175/£35
ditto, Macmillan, 1923 . . . . . £150/£25
Old New York, Appleton & Co. (U.S. and U.K.), 1924 (4 vols in d/ws and slipcase) . . . . £650/£150
The Mother's Recompense, Appleton & Co. (U.S. and U.K.), 1925 . . . . £200/£25
Twilight Sleep, Appleton & Co. (U.S. and U.K.), 1927
. . . . £150/£25
The Children, Appleton & Co. (U.S. and U.K.), 1928 .
. . . . £150/£25
ditto, as *The Marriage Playground*, Grosset & Dunlap (U.S.), 1928 . . . . £125/£30

Hudson River Bracketed, Appleton & Co. (U.S. and U.K.), 1929 . . . . £150/£25
The Gods Arrive, Appleton & Co. (U.S. and U.K.), 1932 . . . . £150/£25
The Buccaneers, Appleton-Century (U.S. and U.K.), 1938 . . . . £150/£25

Short Stories

The Greater Inclination, Scribner's (U.S.), 1899 (first issue: 'Wharton' only on spine). £300
ditto, John Lane, 1899. . . . . . . £150
Crucial Instances, Scribner's (U.S.), 1901 . . £125
ditto, Murray, 1901 . . . . £75
The Descent of Man and Other Stories, Scribner's (U.S.), 1904 . . . . £100
ditto, Macmillan, 1904 . . . . . . £75
The Hermit and The Wild Woman, and Other Stories, Scribner's (U.S.), 1908 . . . . . . £100
ditto, Macmillan, 1908 . . . . . . £75
Les Metteurs en Scène, Plon Nourrit (Paris), 1909 (in French) £50
Tales of Men and Ghosts, Scribner's (U.S.), 1910 . .
. . . . £150
ditto, Macmillan, 1910 . . . . . . £100
Xingu and Other Stories, Scribner's (U.S.), 1916 £150
ditto, Macmillan, 1916 . . . . . . £100
Here and Beyond, Appleton & Co. (U.S. and U.K.), 1926 . . . . £200/£35
Certain People, Appleton & Co (U.S. and U.K.), 1930
. . . . £150/£25
Human Nature, Appleton & Co. (U.S. and U.K.), 1933
. . . . £150/£25
The World Over, Appleton-Century (U.S. and U.K.), 1936 . . . . £150/£25
Ghosts, Appleton-Century (U.S. and U.K.), 1937 . .
. . . . £200/£35
Best Short Stories of Edith Wharton, Scribner's (U.S.), 1958 . . . . £45/£15
The Collected Short Stories of Edith Wharton, Scribner's (U.S.), 1968 (2 vols). . . . £45/£15
Quartet: Four Stories, Allen Press (U.S.), 1975 (140 copies) £300
The Ghost Stories of Edith Wharton, Scribner's, 1973
. . . . £25/£10
ditto, Constable, 1975 . . . . . . £25/£10
The Stories of Edith Wharton, Simon & Schuster, 1988 (selected by Anita Brookner) . . . £30/£10
The Ghost Feeler: Stories of Terror and Supernatural, Peter Owen, 1996 . . . . . £10/£5

Poetry

Verses, privately printed (U.S.), 1878 (wraps; pseud. 'Edith Newbold Jones') £25,000
Artemis to Actaeon and Other Verses, Scribner's (U.S.), 1909 . . . . £300
ditto, Macmillan, 1909 . . . . . . £250
Twelve Poems, The Medici Society, 1926 (130 signed copies) . . . . . . £2,000/£1,250

Others

The Decoration of Houses, Scribner's (U.S.), 1897
(with Ogden Codman Jr.) £650
ditto, Batsford, 1898 . . . . £500
Italian Villas and Their Gardens, Century (U.S.),
1904 . . . . £450
ditto, John Lane, 1904. . . . . £400
Italian Backgrounds, Scribner's (U.S.), 1905 . £150
ditto, Macmillan, 1905 . . . . £125
A Motor-Flight through France, Scribner's (U.S.),
1908 . . . . £75
ditto, Macmillan, 1908 . . . . £65
Fighting France: From Dunkerque to Belfort,
Scribner's (U.S.), 1915 . . . . £75
ditto, Macmillan, 1915 . . . . £65
The Book of the Homeless, Scribner's (U.S.), 1916
(edited by Wharton). £75
ditto, Scribner's (U.S.), 1916 (125 copies, glassine d/w,
slipcase) . . . . £2,000/£1,500
ditto, Scribner's (U.S.), 1916 (50 copies, glassine d/w,
slipcase) . . . . £2,500/£2,000
ditto, Macmillan, 1916 . . . . £50
French Ways and Their Meaning, Appleton & Co.
(U.S.), 1919 . . . . £65
ditto, Macmillan, 1919 . . . . . . £45
In Morocco, Scribner's (U.S.), 1920. . £125/£35
ditto, Macmillan, 1920 . . . . . £125/£30
The Writing of Fiction, Scribner's (U.S. and U.K.),
1925 . . . . £125/£20
A Backward Glance, Appleton-Century (U.S. and
U.K.), 1934 . . . . £125/£20
An Edith Wharton Treasury, Appleton-Century-Crofts
(U.S.), 1950 . . . . £25/£10
The Edith Wharton Reader, Scribner's (U.S.), 1965 .
. . . . £20/£5
The Letters of Edith Wharton, Simon & Schuster,
1988 . . . . £20/£5
Henry James and Edith Wharton Letters 1900-1915,
Scribner's (U.S.), 1990 . . . . £10/£5

DENNIS WHEATLEY
(b.1897 d.1977)

Wheatley's headstone describes him as the 'Prince of
Thriller Writers', and with worldwide sales of more
than 45 million copies few would argue with the
claim.

'Duke de Richleau' Titles
The Forbidden Territory, Hutchinson, [1933] . . .
. . . . £750/£75
The Devil Rides Out, Hutchinson, [1934] . £750/£75
The Golden Spaniard, Hutchinson, [1938] . £150/£15
Three Inquisitive People, Hutchinson, [1940] £50/£10
Strange Conflict, Hutchinson, [1941] . . £175/£20
Codeword - Golden Fleece, Hutchinson, [1946] £50/£5
The Second Seal, Hutchinson, 1950. . . . £20/£5

The Prisoner in The Mask, Hutchinson, 1957 . £10/£5
Vendetta in Spain, Hutchinson, 1961 . . . £10/£5
Dangerous Inheritance, Hutchinson, 1965 . . £10/£5
Gateway to Hell, Hutchinson, 1970 . . . . £10/£5

'Gregory Sallust' Titles
Black August, Hutchinson, [1934] . . . £275/£25
Contraband, Hutchinson, [1936]. . . . £100/£10
The Scarlet Impostor, Hutchinson, [1940] . £100/£10
Faked Passports, Hutchinson, [1940] . . £100/£10
The Black Baroness, Hutchinson, [1940] . £100/£10
'V' for Vengeance, Hutchinson, [1942] . . £65/£5
Come into my Parlour, Hutchinson, [1946]. . £45/£5
The Island Where Time Stands Still, Hutchinson, 1954
. . . . £20/£5
Traitor's Gate, Hutchinson, 1958 . . . £15/£5
The Used Dark Forces, Hutchinson, 1964 . £10/£5
The White Witch of The South Seas, Hutchinson,
1968 . . . . £10/£5

'Julian Day' Titles
The Quest of Julian Day, Hutchinson, [1939] . . .
. . . . £125/£10
The Sword of Fate, Hutchinson, [1941]. . £100/£10
The Bill for The Use of a Body, Hutchinson, 1964. .
. . . . £10/£5

'Roger Brook' Titles
The Launching of Roger Brook, Hutchinson, [1947] .
. . . . £35/£5
The Shadow of Tyburn Tree, Hutchinson, [1948] . .
. . . . £30/£5
The Rising Storm, Hutchinson, [1949] . . £25/£5
The Man Who Killed The King, Hutchinson, 1951 .
. . . . £20/£5
The Dark Secret of Josephine, Hutchinson, 1955 . .
. . . . £20/£5
The Rape of Venice, Hutchinson, 1959 . . £15/£5
The Sultan's Daughter, Hutchinson, 1963 . £10/£5
The Wanton Princess, Hutchinson, 1966 . £10/£5
Evil in a Mask, Hutchinson, 1969 . . . £10/£5
The Ravishing of Lady Mary Ware, Hutchinson, 1971
. . . . £10/£5
Desperate Measures, Hutchinson, 1974. . . £10/£5

Other Titles
Such Power is Dangerous, Hutchinson, [1933] . .
. . . . £275/£25
The Fabulous Valley, Hutchinson, [1934] . £275/£25
The Eunuch of Stamboul, Hutchinson, [1935]. . .
. . . . £100/£10
They Found Atlantis, Hutchinson, [1936] . £100/£10
The Secret War, Hutchinson, [1937] . . £100/£10
Uncharted Seas, Hutchinson, [1938] . . £125/£10
Sixty Days to Live, Hutchinson, [1939] . . £225/£25
The Man Who Missed The War, Hutchinson, [1945] .
. . . . £30/£5
The Haunting of Toby Jug, Hutchinson, [1948] . .
. . . . £35/£5

Star of Ill-Omen, Hutchinson, 1952 . . . . £20/£5
To The Devil - A Daughter, Hutchinson, 1953 . £25/£5
Curtain of Fear, Hutchinson, 1953 . . . . £20/£5
The Ka of Gifford Hillary, Hutchinson, 1956 . £20/£5
The Satanist, Hutchinson, 1960 . . . . . £20/£5
Mayhem in Greece, Hutchinson, 1962 . . . £10/£5
Unholy Crusade, Hutchinson, 1967 . . . . £10/£5
The Strange Story of Linda Lee, Hutchinson, 1972 .
. . . . £10/£5
The Irish Witch, Hutchinson, 1973 . . . . £10/£5
The Deception Planners: My Secret War, Hutchinson,
1980 . . . . £10/£5

Short Stories
Mediterranean Nights, Hutchinson, [1942]. . £65/£5
Gunmen, Gallants and Ghosts, Hutchinson, [1943] .
. . . . £100/£10

Non Fiction
Old Rowley: A Private Life of Charles II, Hutchinson,
1933 . . . . £100/£10
Red Eagle: A Life of Marshal Voroshilov, Hutchinson,
1937 . . . . £100/£10
Total War, Hutchinson, [1941] (wraps) . . £10
The Seven Ages of Justerini's, Riddle Books, 1949 (no
d/w) £5
ditto, as *1749-1965: The Eight Ages of Justerini's*,
Dolphin, 1965 . . . . £10/£5
Stranger than Fiction, Hutchinson, 1959 . . £25/£5
*Saturdays with Bricks and Other Days Under Shell-
Fire*, Hutchinson, 1961 . . . . . . £30/£5
The Devil and All His Works, Hutchinson, 1971 . .
. . . . £20/£5

Autobiography
The Young Man Said: 1897-1914, Hutchinson, 1977 .
. . . . £20/£5
Officer and Temporary Gentleman: 1914-1919,
Hutchinson, 1978 . . . . £20/£5
Drink and Ink: 1919-1977, Hutchinson, 1979 . £20/£5
The Time Has Come, Arrow, 1981 (wraps). . . £5
Crime Dossiers
Murder Off Miami, Hutchinson, [1936] (with J.G.
Links, sealed copy) £100
ditto, Hutchinson, [1936] (opened copy) . . £35
Who Killed Robert Prentice?, Hutchinson, [1937]
(with J.G. Links, sealed copy) £100
ditto, Hutchinson, [1937] (with J.G. Links, opened
copy) £35
The Malinsay Massacre, Hutchinson, [1938] (with
J.G. Links, sealed copy) £100
ditto, Hutchinson, [1938] (opened copy) . . £35
Herewith The Clues!, Hutchinson, [1939] (with J.G.
Links, sealed copy) £100
ditto, Hutchinson, [1939] (opened copy) . . £35

E.B. WHITE
(b.1899 d.1985)

Best known as the author of the children's books
Charlotte's Web and *Stuart Little*, White was for
many years a columnist on *The New Yorker*.

Children's Novels
Stuart Little, Harper (U.S.), 1945 . . . £300/£45
ditto, Hamish Hamilton, 1946 . . . . £50/£10
Charlotte's Web, Harper (U.S.), 1952 . . £300/£45
ditto, Hamish Hamilton, 1952 . . . . £50/£10
The Trumpet of the Swan, Harper (U.S.), 1970 . .
. . . . £25/£10
ditto, Hamish Hamilton, 1970 . . . . . £20/£5

Humour
*Is Sex Necessary? Or Why Do You Feel the Way You
Do?*, Harper (U.S.), 1929 (with James Thurber) . .
. . . . £1,000/£200
ditto, Heinemann, 1930 . . . . . £500/£100
Ho-Hum: Newsbreaks from 'The New Yorker', Farrar
& Rinehart (U.S.), 1931. . . . . . . £15/£5
*Another Ho-Hum: More Newsbreaks from 'The New
Yorker'*, Farrar & Rinehart (U.S.), 1932 . £15/£5

Poetry
The Lady Is Cold, Harper (U.S.), 1929 . . . £20/£5
The Fox of Peapack and Other Poems, Harper (U.S.),
1938 . . . . £10/£5
Poems and Sketches of E.B. White, Harper (U.S.),
1981 . . . . £10/£5

Others
Alice Through the Cellophane, John Day (U.S.), 1933
. . . . £15/£5
Every Day Is Saturday, Harper (U.S.), 1934 £25/£10
Farewell to Model T, Putnam (U.S.), 1936 . £15/£5
Quo Vadimus? Or The Case For The Bicycle, Harper
(U.S.), 1939 . . . . £15/£5
One Man's Meat, Harper (U.S.), 1942 . . £15/£5
ditto, Gollancz, 1943 . . . . £15/£5
*World Government and Peace: Selected Notes and
Comment, 1943-1945*, F.R. Publishing (U.S.), 1945 .
. . . . £10/£5
The Wild Flag, Houghton Mifflin (U.S.), 1946. £10/£5
Here Is New York, Harper (U.S.), 1949 . . £15/£5
ditto, Hamish Hamilton, 1950 . . . . £10/£5
The Second Tree From the Corner, Harper (U.S.),
1954 . . . . £10/£5
ditto, Hamish Hamilton, 1954 . . . . £10/£5
The Elements of Style, Macmillan (U.S.), 1959 (with
William Strunk Jr, wraps) £10
The Points of My Compass, Harper (U.S.), 1962 . .
. . . . £10/£5
ditto, Hamish Hamilton, 1963 . . . . £10/£5
An E.B. White Reader, Harper (U.S.), 1966 . £10/£5
Topics: Our New Countrymen At The U.N., Congres-
sional Press (U.S.), 1968 (wraps) £5

Letters of E.B. White, Harper (U.S.), 1976 . . £10/£5
Essays of E.B. White, Harper (U.S.), 1977 . . £10/£5
Writings From The New Yorker, 1925-1976, Harper
(U.S.), 1990 . . . . £10/£5

ETHEL LINA WHITE
(b.1876 d.1944)

The authoress of crime and macabre fiction, White's
The Wheel Spins was filmed by Alfred Hitchcock as
The Lady Vanishes.

Novels

The Wish-Bone, Ward Lock, 1927 . . . £200/£15
'Twill Soon Be Dark, Ward Lock, 1929. . £200/£15
The Eternal Journey, Ward Lock, 1930 . £200/£15
Put Out The Light, Ward Lock, 1931 . . £450/£30
ditto, Harper (U.S.), 1933. . . . . £200/£20
Fear Stalks the Village, Ward Lock, 1932 . £450/£30
ditto, Harper (U.S.), 1942. . . . . £200/£20
Some Must Watch, Ward Lock, 1933 . . £450/£30
ditto, Harper (U.S.), 1941. . . . . £200/£20
ditto, as *The Spiral Staircase*, World (U.S.), 1946 . .
. . . . £35/£10
Wax, Collins, 1935 . . . . . . £350/£30
ditto, Doubleday (U.S.), 1935 . . . £175/£20
The First Time He Died, Collins, 1935 . . £350/£30
The Wheel Spins, Collins Crime Club, 1936 £450/£45
ditto, Harper (U.S.), 1936. . . . . £250/£20
ditto, as *The Lady Vanishes*, Fontana, 1962 (wraps) £5
ditto, as *The Lady Vanishes*, Paperback Library (U.S.),
1966 (wraps) £10
The Third Eye, Collins Crime Club, 1937 . £300/£25
ditto, Harper (U.S.), 1937. . . . . £125/£15
The Elephant Never Forgets, Collins Crime Club,
1937 . . . . £300/£25
ditto, Harper (U.S.), 1938. . . . . £125/£15
Step in the Dark, Collins Crime Club, 1938 £300/£25
ditto, Harper (U.S.), 1939. . . . . £125/£15
While She Sleeps, Collins Crime Club, 1940 £250/£25
ditto, Harper (U.S.), 1940. . . . . £125/£15
She Faded Into Air, Collins Crime Club, 1941 . . .
. . . . £200/£20
ditto, Harper (U.S.), 1941. . . . . £100/£15
Midnight House, Collins Crime Club, 1942 £75/£10
ditto, as *Her Heart in Her Throat*, Harper (U.S.), 1942
. . . . £45/£10
The Man Who Loved Lions, Collins Crime Club, 1943
. . . . £75/£10
ditto, as *The Man Who Was Not There*, Harper (U.S.),
1943 . . . . £45/£10
They See In Darkness, Collins Crime Club, 1944 . .
. . . . £75/£10

PATRICK WHITE
(b.1912 d.1990)

An Australian novelist, short story writer and
dramatist, White won the Nobel Prize for Literature in
1973.

Novels

Happy Valley, Harrap, 1939 . . . . £2,000/£250
ditto, Viking (U.S.), 1940. . . . . £1,250/£200
The Living and the Dead, Viking (U.S.), 1941 . .
. . . . £600/£75
ditto, Routledge, 1941. . . . . . £500/£75
The Aunt's Story, Routledge, 1948 . . . £500/£75
ditto, Viking (U.S.), 1948. . . . . £250/£45
The Tree of Man, Viking (U.S.), 1955 . . £75/£20
ditto, Eyre & Spottiswoode, 1956 . . . £50/£10
Voss, Viking (U.S.), 1957. . . . . £40/£10
ditto, Eyre & Spottiswoode, 1957 . . . £40/£10
Riders in the Chariot, Viking (U.S.), 1961 . £35/£10
ditto, Eyre & Spottiswoode, 1961 . . . £35/£10
The Solid Mandala, Eyre & Spottiswoode, 1966 . .
. . . . £25/£10
ditto, Viking (U.S.), 1966. . . . . £25/£10
The Vivisector, Cape, 1970 . . . . £20/£5
ditto, Viking (U.S.), 1970. . . . . £20/£5
The Eye of the Storm, Cape, 1973 . . . £20/£5
ditto, Viking (U.S.), 1974. . . . . £20/£5
A Fringe of Leaves, Cape, 1976 . . . £20/£5
ditto, Viking (U.S.), 1976. . . . . £20/£5
The Twyborn Affair, Cape, 1979 . . . £20/£5
ditto, Viking (U.S.), 1980. . . . . £20/£5
Memoirs of Many in One, Cape, 1986 . . £15/£5
ditto, Viking (U.S.), 1986. . . . . £15/£5

Short Stories

The Burnt Ones, Eyre & Spottiswoode, 1964 £35/£10
ditto, Viking (U.S.), 1964. . . . . £25/£5
The Cockatoos, Cape, 1974 . . . . £20/£5
ditto, Viking (U.S.), 1975. . . . . £20/£5
Three Uneasy Pieces, Pascoe (Australia), 1987 (wraps)
. . . . £10
ditto, Cape, 1988 . . . . £15/£5
ditto, Viking (U.S.), 1988. . . . . £15/£5

Poetry

Thirteen Poems, privately printed, 1930 (wraps) . .
. . . . £3,000
The Ploughman and Other Poems, Beacon Press
(Australia), 1935 (200 copies) . . £3,000/£1,000

Plays

Four Plays, Eyre & Spottiswoode, 1965 . £35/£10
ditto, Viking (U.S.), 1966. . . . . £30/£10
The Night of the Prowler, Penguin/Cape, 1978 (wraps)
. . . . £10
Big Toys, Currency Press (Australia), 1978 (wraps) .
. . . . £10
Netherwood, Currency Press (Australia), 1983 (wraps)
. . . . £10

Signal Driver, Currency Press (Australia), 1983
(wraps) £10

Others
Flaws in the Glass, Cape, 1981 . . . . . £20/£5
ditto, Viking (U.S.), 1982. . . . . . £15/£5
Patrick White Speaks, Primavera Press (Australia),
1989 . . . . £15/£5
ditto, Cape, 1990 . . . . £15/£5

T.H. WHITE
(b.1906 d.1964)

A novelist and children's writer, White's major
success was the re-telling of the Arthurian legends in
a series of novels which began with *The Sword in the
Stone*.

Novels
Dead Mr Nixon, Cassell, 1931 (with R. McNair Scott)
. . . . £750/£200
Darkness at Pemberley, Gollancz, 1932 . £600/£150
ditto, Century (U.S.), 1933 . . . . . £400/£100
They Winter Abroad, Gollancz, 1932 (pseud. 'James
Aston') . . . . £500/£125
ditto, Viking (U.S.), 1932. . . . . . £300/£75
First Lesson, Gollancz, 1932 (pseud. 'James Aston') .
. . . . £500/£100
ditto, Knopf (U.S.), 1933 . . . . . £300/£75
Farewell Victoria, Collins, 1933 . . . . £250/£35
ditto, Smith & Haas (U.S.), 1934. . . . £125/£20
Earth Stopped, Or Mr Marx's Sporting Tour, Collins,
1934 . . . . £275/£65
ditto, Putnam (U.S.), 1935 . . . . . £165/£40
Gone to Ground, Collins, 1935 . . . . £250/£50
ditto, Putnam (U.S.), 1935 . . . . . £150/£35
The Elephant and The Kangaroo, Putnam (U.S.),
1947 . . . . £60/£15
ditto, Cape, 1948 . . . . £60/£15

Children's Titles
The Sword in The Stone, Collins, 1938 . . £600/£50
ditto, Putnam (U.S.), 1939 . . . . . £150/£25
The Witch in The Wood, Putnam (U.S.), 1939 . . .
. . . . £350/£40
ditto, Collins, 1940 . . . . £500/£65
The Ill-Made Knight, Putnam (U.S.), 1940 . £350/£40
ditto, Collins, 1941 . . . . £500/£65
Mistress Masham's Repose, Putnam (U.S.), 1946 . .
. . . . £65/£15
ditto, Cape, 1947 . . . . £65/£15
The Master, An Adventure Story, Cape, 1957 £50/£10
ditto, Putnam (U.S.), 1957 . . . . . £45/£10
The Once and Future King, Collins, 1958 . £150/£25
ditto, Putnam (U.S.), 1958 . . . . . £125/£20
The Book of Merlyn, Univ. of Texas Press (U.S.),
1977 . . . . £20/£5
ditto, Collins, 1978 . . . . £15/£5

The Maharajah and Other Stories, Putnam (U.S.),
1981 . . . . £15/£5
ditto, MacDonald, 1981 . . . . . . £15/£5

Poetry
*The Green Bay Tree, or The Wicked Man Touches
Wood*, Songs for Sixpence, No. 3, Heffer, 1929
(wraps) £300
Cambridge Poetry, No. 8, Hogarth Living Poets,
Hogarth Press, 1929 . . . . £250
Loved Helen and Other Poems, Chatto & Windus,
1929 . . . . £250/£50
ditto, Viking (U.S.), 1929. . . . . £250/£50
Verses, Shenval Press, 1962 (100 numbered copies) .
. . . . £750
A Joy Proposed, Bertram Rota, 1980 (500 numbered
copies) . . . . £25/£10
ditto, Univ. of Georgia Press (U.S.), 1983 . . £20/£5

Non Fiction
England Have My Bones, Collins, 1936 . £250/£35
ditto, Macmillan (U.S.), 1936 . . . . £150/£25
*Burke's Steerage, Or The Amateur Gentleman's
Introduction to Noble Sports and Pastimes*, Collins,
1938 . . . . £100/£20
ditto, Putnam (U.S.), 1939 . . . . . £75/£15
*The Age of Scandal: An Excursion Through a Minor
Period*, Cape, 1950 . . . . £45/£10
ditto, Putnam (U.S.), 1950 . . . . . £30/£10
The Goshawk, Cape, 1951 . . . . . £65/£15
ditto, Putnam (U.S.), 1952 . . . . . £45/£10
The Scandalmonger, Cape, 1952 . . . £30/£10
ditto, Putnam (U.S.), 1952 . . . . . £20/£5
The Godstone and The Blackymor, Cape, 1959
(illustrated by Ardizzone) . . . . . £40/£15
ditto, Putnam (U.S.), 1959 . . . . . £35/£10
*America At Last, The American Journal of T.H.
White*, Putnam (U.S.), 1965. . . . . . £20/£5
The White/Garnett Letters, Cape, 1968 . . . £20/£5
ditto, Viking (U.S.), 1968. . . . . . £20/£5
*Letters to a Friend, The Correspondence Between
T.H. White and L.J. Potts*, Putnam (U.S.), 1982 . .
. . . . £20/£5
ditto, Alan Sutton, 1984 (enlarged edition) . . £20/£5

WALT WHITMAN
(b.1819 d.1892)

Whitman was not an immediate success in America. It
was not until he was taken up by Rossetti, Swinburne
and others in England that his importance was widely
recognised.

Poetry
*Franklin Evans, or The Inebriate: A Tale of the
Times*, Winchester (U.S.), 1842 (original printed
brown, wraps) £10,000

ditto, Winchester (U.S.), 1842 (rebound) . . £2,500
Leaves of Grass, no publisher (U.S.), 1855 (anon., first issue without adverts or reviews, with marbled endpapers, both front and back covers with triple gilt-stamped line, and frontis portrait on plain paper) . .
. . . . £30,000
ditto, no publisher (U.S.), 1855 (second binding with both front and back covers with blind-stamped triple line) £25,000
ditto, no publisher (U.S.), 1855 (third binding, copies with light yellowish-green or pink wrappers) £25,000
ditto, Horsell, 1855 (as above but label pasted above Brooklyn imprint) £20,000
ditto, no publisher (U.S.), 1856 (second edition with 20 additional poems) £6,500
Drum-Taps, Peter Eckler (U.S.), 1865 . . . £1,500
Poems, Camden Hotten, 1868 (edited by W.M. Rossetti, first issue with no price on spine) . £275
Memoranda. Democratic Vistas, Redfield (U.S.), 1871 (first issue without author on title-page, wraps) £500
ditto, Walter Scott, 1888 . . . . £100
After All, Not To Create Only, Pearson (U.S.), 1871 (11 folio sheets printed on one side only) . £1,750
ditto, Roberts Bros. (U.S.), 1871 . . . . . £500
ditto, Roberts Bros. (U.S.), 1871 (wraps) . £350
Memoranda. During the War, published by Whitman (U.S.), 1875-6 (first issue with first page printed 'Remembrance Copy' and signed by Whitman below)
. . . . £2,000
ditto, published by Whitman (U.S.), 1875-6 (second issue lacks portraits and the 'Remembrance Copy' leaf) £500
As a Strong Bird on Pinions Free & Other Poems, published by Whitman (U.S.), 1872 . . . £1,000
Two Rivulets, published by Whitman (U.S.), 1876 (100 copies, signed frontispiece) £4,000
ditto, published by Whitman (U.S.), 1876 (650 copies)
. . . . £500
Specimen Days and Collect, Rees, Welsh (U.S.), 1882-3 (cloth) £200
ditto, Rees, Welsh (U.S.), 1882-3 (wraps) . . £300
ditto, David McKay (U.S.), 1883. . . . . £125
ditto, Wilson and McCormick, 1883 . . . . £125
ditto, as ***Specimen Days in America***, Walter Scott, 1887 . . . . £50
November Boughs, David McKay (U.S.), 1888 £200
ditto, David McKay (U.S.), 1888 (copies on large paper) £500
Complete Poems and Prose of Walt Whitman, Ferguson (U.S.), 1888-89 (600 signed copies) £3,500
Leaves of Grass with ***Sands at Seventy***, Ferguson Bros (U.S.), 1889 (300 signed copies) . . . £3,500
Good-bye My Fancy, David McKay (U.S.), 1891 £250
ditto, David McKay (U.S.), 1891 (copies on large paper) £300
Complete Prose Works, David McKay (U.S.), 1892 .
. . . . £300
ditto, David McKay (U.S.), 1892 (60 numbered copies)
. . . . £100

Selected Poems, Webster, 1892 . . . . . £75
Autobiographica, Webster (U.S.), 1892. . . £100
In Re Walt Whitman, David McKay (U.S.), 1893 £125
Poems, Chatto & Windus, 1895 . . . . . £65
Calamus, Laurens Maynard (U.S.), 1897. . . £250
ditto, Laurens Maynard (U.S.), 1897 (35 numbered large paper copies) £500
ditto, Putnam, 1897 . . . . £150
Walt Whitman at Home, Critic Pamphlet No.2 (U.S.), 1898 (wraps) £75
The Wound Dresser, Small, Maynard (U.S.), 1898 .
. . . . £150
ditto, Small, Maynard (U.S.), 1898 (60 large paper copies) £500
Notes and Fragments, Talbot & Co (U.S.), 1899 (250 copies) £200
When Lilacs Last in the Dooryard Bloomed, Essex House Press, 1900 (125 copies). £750
Letters ... To His Mother, Putnam (U.S.), 1902 (5 copies, wraps) £3,000
ditto, Goldsmith (U.S.), 1936 (325 copies) . . £125
The Complete Writings, Putnam (U.S.), 1902 (500 numbered sets, 10 vols) £400
Walt Whitman's Diary in Canada, Small, Maynard (U.S), 1904 (500 copies) £75
An American Primer, Small & Maynard (U.S), 1904 (500 copies) £75
The Gathering of the Forces, Knickerbocker Press (U.S.), 1920 (2 vols, 1250 sets). . . . £200
The Uncollected Poetry and Prose of Walt Whitman, Doubleday (U.S.), 1921 (2 vols) £200
Pictures: An Unpublished Poem, Faber/The June House, 1927 (700 copies) £65
The Half-Breed and Other Stories, Columbia Univ. Press (U.S.), 1927 (155 copies) £100
ditto, Columbia Univ. Press (U.S.), 1927 (30 copies) .
. . . . £250
Rivulets of Prose, Greenberg (U.S.), 1928 (499 copies)
. . . . £100

OSCAR WILDE
(b.1854 d.1900)

Known principally as a playwright, Wilde was also a fine essayist, poet and novelist. Even today his public persona often overshadows his considerable literary achievements.

Poetry
Ravenna, Thomas Shrimpton, 1878 (wraps) . £1,000
Poems, David Bogue, 1881 (750 copies printed and issued as 3 editions) £2,500
ditto, Roberts Bros. (U.S.), 1881 . . . . £250
ditto, Mathews and Lane, 1892 (220 signed copies) .
. . . . £3,000
The Sphinx, Mathews & Lane, 1894 (200 copies) . .
. . . . £6,000

ditto, Mathews & Lane, 1894 (25 large paper copies) .
. . . . £10,000
ditto, John Lane/Bodley Head, 1910 (cheap edition) .
. . . . £30
ditto, John Lane, 1920 (1,000 copies, 10 illustrations
by Alastair) £400
The Ballad of Reading Gaol, Leonard Smithers, 1898
(pseud. 'C.3.3.' [800 copies]) £1,250
ditto, Leonard Smithers, 1898 (30 numbered copies) .
. . . . £6,000
ditto, Leonard Smithers, 1898 (third edition, 99 signed
copies) £4,500
ditto, Alfred Bartlett (U.S.), 1902 (550 copies) . £150

Short Stories
The Happy Prince and Other Tales, David Nutt, 1888
. . . . £1,500
ditto, David Nutt, 1888 (75 signed copies, large hand
made paper edition) £6,000
ditto, Roberts Bros. (U.S.), 1888 . . . . . £400
ditto, Duckworth, 1913 (illustrated by Charles
Robinson). £75
ditto, Duckworth, 1913 (250 copies signed by artist, in
slipcase) . . . . £600/£500
ditto, Putnam's (U.S.), 1913 (illustrated by Charles
Robinson). £75
Lord Arthur Saville's Crime and Other Stories,
Osgood, McIlvaine & Co., 1891 . . . . £650
ditto, Dodd, Mead (U.S.), 1891 . . . . £500
A House of Pomegranates, Osgood, McIlvaine & Co.,
1891 . . . . £1,000
L'Anniversaire de L'Enfant, Black Sun Press (Paris),
1928 (9 illustrations by Alastair) £250
The Birthday of the Infanta, Black Sun Press (Paris),
1928 (100 copies, as above but text in English, 9
illustrations, slipcase) . . . . £1,250/£1,000

Plays
Vera, or The Nihilists Ranken & Co., 1880 (grey
wraps). £15,000
ditto, privately printed (U.S.), 1882 (wraps). £10,000
The Duchess of Padua, privately printed (U.S.), 1883
(20 copies printed as manuscript) . . . £12,500
ditto, Methuen, 1908 . . . . £500
Salome, Drama en un Acte, Librairie de L'art
Independant/Elkin Mathews et John Lane, 1893 £500
ditto, Librairie de L'art Independant/Elkin Mathews et
John Lane, 1893 (50 tall copies on hand made paper)
. . . . £1,500
Lady Windermere's Fan, Elkin Mathews & John Lane,
1893 . . . . £1,000
ditto, Elkin Mathews & John Lane, 1893 (50 deluxe
copies on hand made paper). £2,500
Salome, Elkin Mathews & John Lane, 1894 (775
copies, illustrated by Beardsley) £2,000
ditto, Lane & Mathews, 1894 (125 copies, on Japan
vellum, large paper issue) £10,000
ditto, Melmoth & Co., 1904 (250 numbered copies) .
. . . . £350

ditto, Melmoth & Co., 1904 (50 numbered copies). .
. . . . £500
ditto, G. Crès (Paris), 1922 (9 illustrations by Alastair)
. . . . £75
ditto, G. Crès (Paris), 1922 (100 copies on Imperial
Japon paper, 9 illustrations). £500
A Woman of No Importance, John Lane, 1894. £1,000
ditto, John Lane, 1894 (50 deluxe copies on hand made
paper). £1,500
The Importance of Being Earnest, Smithers, 1899 (by
the 'Author of Lady Windermere's Fan') . . £1,000
ditto, Smithers, 1899 (12 copies on Japanese vellum) .
. . . . £7,500
ditto, Smithers, 1899 (100 signed, deluxe copies) . .
. . . . £7,500
ditto, [Methuen], 1910 (1,200 copies) . . . £75
An Ideal Husband, Smithers, 1899 (by the 'Author of
Lady Windermere's Fan') £1,000
ditto, Smithers, 1899 (12 copies on Japanese vellum) .
. . . . £10,000
ditto, Smithers, 1899 (100 signed, deluxe copies) . .
. . . . £7,500

Novel
The Picture of Dorian Gray, Ward, Lock, 1891 . .
. . . . £1,500
ditto, Ward, Lock, 1891 (250 signed, numbered, large
paper copies) £10,000

Essays
Intentions, Osgood, McIlvaine & Co., 1891 . £350
ditto, Dodd, Mead (U.S.), 1891 . . . . . £200
The Soul of Man Under Socialism, Humphreys, 1895
(50 copies, brown paper wraps). £450
ditto, Luce (U.S.), 1910 . . . . . . £100
The Portrait of Mr W.H., Smithers, 1904 (200 copies)
. . . . £400
ditto, Mitchell Kennerley (U.S.), 1921 . . . £75
Essays, Criticisms and Reviews, Wright & Jones, 1901
(300 numbered copies) £125
De Profundis, Methuen, [1905] (with ads dated
February) £150
ditto, Methuen, [1905] (with ads dated March) . £100
ditto, Methuen, [1905] (200 copies on hand-made
paper). £750
ditto, Methuen, [1905] (50 copies on Japanese vellum)
. . . . £3,000
ditto, Putnams (U.S.), 1905 . . . . . £125
The Suppressed Portions of De Profundis, Paul
Reynolds (U.S.), 1913 (15 copies) . . . £1,500
De Profundis: A Facsimilie, British Library, 2000
(495 numbered copies) £45
ditto, British Library, 2000 (95 numbered copies signed
by Merlin Holland) £75

Letters
Four Letters, privately printed, 1906 (wraps) . £250

After Reading, Letters of Oscar Wilde to Robert Ross,
Beaumont Press, 1921 (75 numbered copies on Japan
vellum of 475) £250
ditto, Beaumont Press, 1921 (400 numbered copies of
475) £75
After Berneval, Letters of Oscar Wilde to Robert Ross,
Beaumont Press, 1922 (75 copies on Japan vellum of
475) £200
ditto, Beaumont Press, 1922 (400 numbered copies of
475) £75
Some Letters from Oscar Wilde to Alfred Douglas,
1892-1897, privately printed (U.S.), 1924 (225
copies, slipcase) . . . . £250/£200
Sixteen Letters from Oscar Wilde, Faber, 1930 (550
numbered copies) £75
ditto, Coward-McCann (U.S.), 1930 . . . . £65
The Letters of Oscar Wilde, Hart-Davis, 1962 £75/£25
ditto, Harcourt Brace (U.S.), 1962 . . . £75/£25
The Complete Letters of Oscar Wilde, Fourth Estate,
2000 . . . . £25/£10
ditto, Holt (U.S.), 2000 . . . . . . £25/£10

Others
Phrases and Philosophies for The Use of The Young,
privately printed, A. Cooper, 1894 (wraps) . £250
Oscariana, privately printed by Humphreys, 1895 (50
copies in buff paper wraps) £200
ditto, Humphreys, 1910 (200 copies in Japanese vellum
wrappers) £250
ditto, Humphreys, 1910 (50 copies on Japanese vellum)
. . . . £300
Children in Prison and Other Cruelties of Prison Life,
Murdoch & Co., [1898] (wraps) £1,000
Poems in Prose, Carrington, 1905 (50 copies on
Imperial Japanese vellum) £250
ditto, Carrington, 1905 (50 copies on Japanese vellum)
. . . . £250
*Wilde and Whistler: An Acrimonious Correspondence
in Art*, Smithers, 1906 (400 copies, wraps) . £200
Sebastian Melmoth, Humphries, 1904 . . . £75

CHARLES WILLIAMS
(b.1886 d.1945)

The author of many books on theological subjects,
Williams also wrote a number of supernatural thrillers
dealing with the conflict between good and evil.

Poetry
The Silver Stair, Herbert & Daniel, [1912] . . £300
Poems of Conformity, O.U.P., 1917 . . . . £125
Divorce, O.U.P., 1920 . . . . . . £200/£65
Windows of Night, O.U.P., 1925 . . . . £200/£65
Heroes and Kings, Sylvan Press, 1930 (300 copies) .
. . . . £200
Taliessin Through Logres, O.U.P., 1938 . £125/£30

The Region of The Summer Stars, Editions Poetry,
1944 . . . . £75/£25

Novels
War in Heaven, Gollancz, 1930 . . . . £250/£75
ditto, Pellegrini & Cudahy (U.S.), 1949 . . £60/£15
Many Dimensions, Gollancz, 1931 . . . £200/£60
ditto, Pellegrini & Cudahy (U.S.), 1949 . . £60/£15
The Place of The Lion, Gollancz, 1931 . . £200/£45
ditto, Gollancz, 1931 (wraps) £65
ditto, Norton (U.S.), 1932 . . . . . £125/£30
The Greater Trumps, Gollancz, 1932 . . £150/£45
ditto, Pellegrini & Cudahy (U.S.), 1950 . . £60/£15
Shadows of Ecstasy, Gollancz, 1933 . . £150/£35
ditto, Pellegrini & Cudahy (U.S.), 1950 . . £60/£15
Descent into Hell, Faber, 1937 . . . . £150/£40
ditto, Pellegrini & Cudahy (U.S.), 1949 . . £60/£15
All Hallows Eve, Faber, 1945 . . . . £125/£35
ditto, Pellegrini & Cudahy (U.S.), 1948 . . £60/£15

Drama
The Masque of The Manuscript, privately printed,
1927 (100 copies, wraps) £300
A Myth of Shakespeare, O.U.P., 1928 . . £200/£75
The Masque of Perusal, privately printed, 1929 (100
copies, wraps) £300
Three Plays, O.U.P., 1931 (red glassine d/w with paper
flaps) . . . . £200/£125
Thomas Cranmer of Canterbury, H.J. Goulden, 1936
(wraps) £45
ditto, O.U.P., 1936 . . . . £75/£25
Judgement at Chelmsford, O.U.P., 1939 (wraps) £50
The House of The Octopus, Edinburgh House, 1945 .
. . . . £50/£15
Seed of Adam and Other Plays, O.U.P., 1948 £30/£10
Collected Plays, O.U.P., 1963 . . . . £25/£10

Biography
Bacon, Barker, 1933 . . . . . . £125/£25
James I, Barker, 1934 . . . . . . £125/£25
Rochester, Barker, 1935 . . . . . £125/£25
Queen Elizabeth, Duckworth, 1936 . . . £100/£20
Henry VII, Barker, 1937 . . . . . £100/£20
Flecker of Dean Close, Canterbury Press, 1946 . .
. . . . £50/£10

Theology
He Came Down from Heaven, Heinemann, 1938 . .
. . . . £45/£10
The Descent of The Dove, Longmans, Green, 1939 .
. . . . £40/£10
Witchcraft, Faber, 1941 . . . . . £75/£20
The Forgiveness of Sins, Bles, 1942 . . £35/£10

Criticism
Poetry at Present, Clarendon Press, 1930 . £65/£20
The English Poetic Mind, Clarendon Press, 1932 . .
. . . . £65/£20
Reason and Beauty in The Poetic Mind, Clarendon
Press, 1933 . . . . £65/£20

Religion and Love in Dante, Dacre Press, [1941]
(wraps) £25
The Figure of Beatrice, Faber, 1943 . . £75/£20
Arthurian Torso, O.U.P., 1948 (with C.S. Lewis) . .
. . . . £75/£35
ditto, O.U.P. (U.S.), 1948 . . . . . £75/£35
The Image of The City, O.U.P., 1958 . . £50/£10

TENNESSEE WILLIAMS
(b.1911 d.1983)

An American playwright, many of whose works have
been filmed. Most of Williams' plays show a
sympathy with lost, lonely and self-punishing
characters.

Plays
Battle of Angels, Pharos (U.S.), 1945 (wraps) . £400
The Glass Menagerie, Random House (U.S.), 1945 .
. . . .£650/£100
ditto, Lehmann, 1948 . . . . . . £75/£20
You Touched Me! A Romantic Comedy, French
(U.S.), 1947 (with Donald Windham) . . £350/£35
ditto, French (U.S.), 1947 (grey wraps) . . . £100
A Streetcar Named Desire, New Directions (U.S.),
1947 . . . . £1,250/£100
ditto, Lehmann, 1949 . . . . £100/£25
American Blues, Dramatists Play Services (U.S.), 1948
(author's name misspelled on front cover: 'Tennesse',
wraps). £200
Summer and Smoke, New Directions (U.S.), 1948
(first issue d/w lists three plays by Williams on inside
back flap). . . . . £175/£15
ditto, Lehmann, 1952 . . . . . . £65/£15
The Rose Tattoo, New Directions (U.S.), 1951 (first
binding rose cloth) . . . . . . £200/£75
ditto, New Directions (U.S.), 1951 (second binding tan
cloth) . . . . £100/£15
ditto, Secker & Warburg, 1954 [1955] . £60/£15
*I Rise in Flame, Cried the Phoenix, A Play about
D.H. Lawrence*, New Directions (U.S.), 1951 (300
signed copies) . . . .£750/£700
ditto, New Directions (U.S.), 1951 (10 signed copies,
slipcase) . . . . £2,000/£1,750
Camino Real, New Directions (U.S.), 1953 . £75/£15
ditto, Secker & Warburg, 1958 . . . . £50/£10
Cat on a Hot Tin Roof, New Directions (U.S.), 1955 .
. . . . £300/£45
ditto, Secker & Warburg, 1956 . . . £200/£35
Suddenly Last Summer, New Directions (U.S.), 1958 .
. . . . £125/£25
A Perfect Analysis Given by a Parrot, Dramatic Play
Services (U.S.), [1958] (wraps). £40
Orpheus Descending/Battle of Angels, New Directions
(U.S.), 1958 . . . . £100/£20
Orpheus Descending, New Directions (U.S.), 1959 .
. . . . £75/£15
ditto, Secker & Warburg, 1958 . . . . £75/£15

Garden District, Secker & Warburg, 1959 . £75/£15
Sweet Bird of Youth, New Directions (U.S.), 1959. .
. . . . £65/£15
ditto, Secker & Warburg, 1961 . . . . £40/£10
*Period of Adjustment/High Point over a Cavern/A
Serious Comedy*, New Directions (U.S.), 1960 . .
. . . . £50/£10
ditto, Secker & Warburg, 1961 . . . . £35/£10
The Night of the Iguana, New Directions (U.S.), 1961
. . . . £75/£15
ditto, Secker & Warburg, 1963 . . . . £60/£10
The Milk Train Doesn't Stop Here Anymore, New
Directions (U.S.), 1964 (first issue, with pp.19-22
integral and scene 2 starting at p.22) . . £200/£100
ditto, New Directions (U.S.), 1964 (second issue, with
pp.19-22 tipped in and scene 2 starting at p.21) . .
. . . . £50/£15
ditto, New Directions (U.S.), 1964 (third issue, with
pp.19-22 bound in) . . . . . . £30/£10
ditto, Secker & Warburg, 1964 . . . . £45/£10
The Mutilated, Dramatists Play Service (U.S.), 1967
(wraps) £25
The Gnädiges Fräulein, Dramatists Play Service
(U.S.), 1967 (wraps). £25
Kingdom of Earth: The Seven Descents of Myrtle,
New Directions (U.S.), 1968 . . . . £35/£10
ditto, as *The Kingdom of Earth: The Seven Descents
of Myrtle*, Dramatists Play Service (U.S.), 1969
(wraps) £15
The Two-Character Play, New Directions (U.S.), 1969
. . . . £25/£5
In The Bar of a Tokyo Hotel, Dramatists Play Service
(U.S.), 1969 (wraps) £20
Small Craft Warnings, New Directions (U.S.), 1972 .
. . . . £25/£5
Vieux Carre, New Directions (U.S.), 1979 . £20/£5
A Lovely Sunday for Creve Coeur, New Directions
(U.S.), 1980 . . . . £15/£5
Steps Must Be Gentle, Targ (U.S.), 1980 (350 signed
copies, with plain d/w) . . . . . £150/£100
Clothes for a Summer Hotel, A Ghost Play, Dramatists
Play Service (U.S.), 1981 (wraps) £10
It Happened the Day the Sun Rose, Sylvester &
Orphanos (U.S.), 1981 (330 signed copies) . £200
The Remarkable Rooming-House of Mme Le Monde,
Albondocani Press (U.S.), 1984 (26 of 176 copies) .
. . . . £100
ditto, Albondocani Press (U.S.), 1984 (150 of 176
copies, wraps) £50
The Red Devil Battery Sign, New Directions (U.S.),
1988 . . . . £25/£5
Not About Nightingales, Methuen, 1998 (wraps) . £5

Novels
The Roman Spring of Mrs Stone, New Directions
(U.S.), 1950 . . . . £75/£15
ditto, New Directions (U.S.), 1950 (500 signed copies
in slipcase) . . . . £300/£250
ditto, Lehmann, 1950 . . . . . . £45/£15

Moise and the World of Reason, Simon & Schuster (U.S.), 1975 . . . . £45/£10
ditto, Simon & Schuster (U.S.), 1975 (350 signed copies) £200

Short Stories
One Arm and Other Stories, New Directions (U.S.), 1948 . . . . £50/£15
ditto, New Directions (U.S.), 1948 (50 signed copies, slipcase) . . . . £1,500/£1,300
ditto, New Directions (U.S.), 1948 (1,500 copies, slipcase) . . . . £150/£125
Hard Candy, A Book of Stories, New Directions (U.S.), 1954 . . . . £40/£15
ditto, New Directions (U.S.), 1954 (1,500 copies on laid paper, slipcase) . . . . . . £150/£125
Man Brings This Up Road, Street & Smith (U.S.), 1959 . . . . £35/£10
Three Players of a Summer Game and Other Stories, Secker & Warburg, 1960 . . . . £65/£15
Grand, House of Books (U.S.), 1964 (26 signed lettered copies, tissue d/w) . . . . . £650/£600
ditto, House of Books (U.S.), 1964 (300 signed copies, tissue d/w) . . . . £300/£275
The Knightly Quest, A Novella and Four Short Stories, New Directions (U.S.), 1967 . . £35/£10
Eight Mortal Ladies Possessed, A Book of Stories, New Directions (U.S.), 1974 . . . £25/£10
ditto, Secker & Warburg, 1975 . . . . £20/£5
Collected Stories, New Directions (U.S.), 1985. £15/£5

Screenplays
Baby Doll, The Script for a Film, New Directions (U.S.), 1956 . . . . £175/£50
ditto, Secker & Warburg, 1957 . . . . £150/£45
The Fugitive Kind, Signet (U.S.), 1960 (wraps) £10
Stopped Rocking and Other Screenplays, New Directions (U.S.), 1984 . . . . . . £15/£5

Poetry
In The Winter of Cities, New Directions (U.S.), 1956 .
. . . . £125/£25
ditto, New Directions (U.S.), 1956 (500 signed copies, slipcase) . . . . £750/£600
Androgyne, Mon Amour, New Directions (U.S.), 1977
. . . . £25/£5
ditto, New Directions (U.S.), 1956 (200 signed copies, slipcase) . . . . £250/£200

Other Titles
Lord Byron's Love Letter, An Opera in One Act, Ricordi (U.S.), [1955] . . . . . £45/£10
Memoirs, Doubleday (U.S.), 1975 . . . £35/£15
ditto, Doubleday (U.S.), 1975 (400 signed copies in slipcase) . . . . £250/£200
ditto, W.H. Allen, 1976 . . . . . . £25/£5
Tennessee Williams' Letters to Donald Windham, 1940-1965, Verona, 1976 . . . . . £25/£5
ditto, Holt (U.S.), 1977 . . . . . . £25/£5

Where I Live, Selected Essays, New Directions (U.S.), 1976 . . . . £25/£5
Conversations with Tennessee Williams, Univ. Press of Mississippi (U.S.), 1986 . . . . . £20/£5
Five O'Clock Angel: Letters of Tennessee Williams to Maria St. Just, 1948-1982, Knopf (U.S.), 1990 . .
. . . . £20/£5
The Selected Letters of Tennessee Williams, Volume I, 1920-1945, New Directions (U.S.), 2000 . £20/£5
ditto, Oberon, 2001. . . . . £20/£5

HENRY WILLIAMSON
(b.1895 d.1977)

Williamson's most successful writings are considered to be his nature novels, such as *Tarka the Otter* and *Salar the Salmon*. It is generally acknowledged that these owe a debt to the 19th century naturalist Richard Jefferies. Williamson's right-wing political sympathies during the 1930s did much to damage his reputation.

'A Chronicle of Ancient Sunlight' Titles
The Dark Lantern, Macdonald, 1951 . . £75/£10
Donkey Boy, Macdonald, 1952 . . . . £75/£10
Young Phillip Maddison, Macdonald, 1953 £75/£10
How Dear is Life, Macdonald, 1954 . . . £75/£10
A Fox Under My Cloak, Macdonald, 1955 . £75/£15
The Golden Virgin, Macdonald, 1957 . . £65/£10
Love and The Loveless: A Soldiers Tale, Macdonald, 1958 . . . . £50/£10
A Test To Destruction, Macdonald, 1960 . £40/£10
The Innocent Moon, Macdonald, 1961 . . £40/£10
It Was The Nightingale, Macdonald, 1962 . £40/£10
The Power of The Dead, Macdonald, 1963 . £40/£10
The Phoenix Generation, Macdonald, 1965 £35/£10
A Solitary War, Macdonald, 1966 . . . £35/£10
Lucifer Before Sunrise, Macdonald, 1967 . £35/£10
The Gale of The World, Macdonald, 1969 . £60/£15

Other Fiction
The Beautiful Years, Collins, 1921 . . . £400/£150
ditto, Faber, 1929 (revised edition) . . . £65/£15
ditto, Faber, 1929 (200 signed copies, revised edition).
. . . . £200
ditto, Dutton, 1929 (revised edition) . . . £65/£15
Dandelion Days, Collins, 1922 . . . . £125/£20
ditto, Faber, 1930 (revised edition) . . . £35/£10
ditto, Faber, 1930 (200 signed copies, revised edition).
. . . . £200
ditto, Dutton, 1930 (revised edition) . . . £35/£10
The Dream of Fair Women, Collins, 1924 . £75/£15
ditto, Faber, 1931 (revised edition) . . . £35/£10
ditto, Faber, 1931 (200 signed copies, revised edition).
. . . . £200
ditto, Dutton, 1931 (revised edition) . . . £35/£10

The Peregrin's Saga, Collins, 1923 (600 copies, no
d/w) £100
ditto, as *Sun Brothers*, Dutton (U.S.), 1925 (no d/w) .
. . . . £75
The Old Stag, Putnam, 1926 . . . . . £100/£25
ditto, Dutton (U.S.), 1927 . . . . . £40/£15
Tarka The Otter, Putnams, 1927 (100 signed copies,
privately printed for subscribers) £850
ditto, Putnam, 1927 (1,000 copies) £200
ditto, Dutton (U.S.), 1928 . . . . . £175/£30
The Pathway, Cape, 1928 . . . . £65/£10
ditto, Faber, 1931 (200 signed copies) . . . £150
ditto, Dutton (U.S.), 1929 . . . . . £50/£10
The Linhay on The Downs and The Firing Gatherer,
Woburn Press, 1929 (530 copies) . . . £55/£35
ditto, Cape, 1934 (revised and enlarged edition) . .
. . . . £35/£10
The Patriot's Progress, Bles, 1930 . . . £40/£10
ditto, Bles, [1930] (350 signed copies, slipcase) . .
. . . . £200/£150
ditto, Dutton (U.S.), 1930 . . . . . £35/£10
The Star Born, Faber, 1933 . . . . £40/£10
ditto, Faber, 1933 (70 signed copies) . . . £300
ditto, Faber, 1948 (revised edition) . . . £20/£5
The Gold Falcon or The Haggard of Love, Faber,
1933 (anonymous) . . . . . . £65/£25
ditto, Smith & Haas (U.S.), 1933 . . . £50/£15
ditto, Faber, 1947 (revised edition) . . . £20/£5
Salar The Salmon, Faber, 1935 . . . . £125/£20
ditto, Faber, 1935 (13 numbered copies signed and
corrected by the author) £1,500
ditto, Little, Brown (U.S.), 1936 . . . £65/£15
The Sun in The Sands, Faber, 1945 . . £25/£10
The Phasian Bird, Faber, 1948 . . . £25/£10
ditto, Little, Brown (U.S.), 1950 . . . £25/£10
Tales of Moorland and Estuary, Macdonald, 1953 .
. . . . £25/£10
Collected Nature Stories, Macdonald, 1970 . £10/£5
The Scandaroon, Macdonald, 1972 . . . . £20/£5
ditto, Macdonald, 1972 (250 signed copies, slipcase) .
. . . . £75/£50
ditto, Saturday Review Press (U.S.), 1973 . £20/£5

Omnibus Editions
The Flax of Dream, Faber, 1936 . . . £25/£10
ditto, Faber, 1936 (200 copies) £150

Children's Title
Scribbing Lark, Faber, 1948 . . . . £25/£10

Non Fiction
The Lone Swallows, Collins, 1922 (500 copies) £65
ditto, Dutton (U.S.), 1926 . . . . . £150/£35
ditto, Collins, 1928 (revised edition) . . £35/£10
The Wet Flanders Plain, Beaumont Press, 1929 (80 of
320 signed copies on handmade parchment vellum) .
. . . . £400
ditto, Beaumont Press, 1929 (240 of 320 copies,
numbered, on handmade paper) £150

ditto, Faber, 1929 (revised edition) . . . £65/£20
ditto, Dutton (U.S.), 1929 . . . . . £50/£15
The Ackymals, Windsor Press (U.S.), 1929 (225 signed
copies, slipcase) . . . . £150/£125
The Village Book, Cape, 1930 . . . . £35/£10
ditto, Cape, 1930 (504 signed copies) . . . £175
ditto, Dutton (U.S.), 1930 . . . . . £35/£10
The Wild Red Deer of Exmoor, Faber, 1931 (75
copies) £150
ditto, Faber, 1931 . . . . £45/£15
The Labouring Life, Cape, 1932 . . . £50/£15
ditto, Cape, 1932 (122 signed copies, acetate d/w) . .
. . . . £250/£175
ditto, as *As The Sun Shines*, Dutton, 1933 . £30/£10
On Foot in Devon, Maclehose, 1933 . . £50/£15
Devon Holiday, Cape, 1935 . . . . £40/£15
Goodbye West Country, Putnam, 1937 . . £40/£15
ditto, Little, Brown (U.S.), 1938 . . . . £40/£10
The Children of Shallowford, Faber, 1939 . £70/£15
ditto, Faber, 1959 (revised edition) . . . £15/£5
The Story of a Norfolk Farm, Faber, 1941 . £35/£10
Genius of Friendship - T.E. Lawrence, Faber, 1941 .
. . . . £75/£25
Norfolk Life, Faber, 1943 (with Lilias Rider Haggard)
. . . . £30/£10
Life in a Devon Village, Faber, 1945 . . £20/£5
Tales of a Devon Village, Faber, 1945 . . £20/£5
A Clear Water Stream, Faber, 1958 . . . £20/£5
ditto, Ives Washburn (U.S.), 1958 . . . £20/£5
In The Woods, St Albert's Press, 1960 (50 numbered
and signed copies, wraps) £75
ditto, St Albert's Press, 1960 (950 numbered copies,
wraps) £35

A.N. WILSON
(b.1950)

A prolific writer, Wilson is at his best in his tragi-
comic novels.

Novels
The Sweets of Pimlico, Secker & Warburg, 1977 . .
. . . . £200/£25
Unguarded Hours, Secker & Warburg, 1978 £100/£15
Kindly Light, Secker & Warburg, 1979 . . £50/£10
The Healing Art, Secker & Warburg, 1980 . £45/£5
Who Was Oswald Fish?, Secker & Warburg, 1981 .
. . . . £30/£5
Wise Virgin, Secker & Warburg, 1982 . . £20/£5
ditto, Viking (U.S.), 1983 . . . . . £15/£5
Scandal, Hamish Hamilton, 1983 . . . £15/£5
ditto, Viking (U.S.), 1984 . . . . . £15/£5
Gentlemen in England, Hamish Hamilton, 1985
£10/£5
ditto, Viking (U.S.), 1986 . . . . . £10/£5
Love Unknown, Hamish Hamilton, 1986 . £10/£5
ditto, Viking (U.S.), 1987 . . . . . £10/£5

Incline Our Hearts, Hamish Hamilton, 1988 . £10/£5
ditto, Viking (U.S.), 1989. . . . . . . £10/£5
A Bottle in The Smoke, Sinclair-Stevenson, 1990 . .
. . . . £10/£5
ditto, Viking (U.S.), 1990. . . . . . . £10/£5
Daughters of Albion, Sinclair-Stevenson, 1991 £10/£5
ditto, Viking (U.S.), 1991. . . . . . . £10/£5
Vicar of Sorrows, Sinclair-Stevenson, 1993 . £10/£5
ditto, Norton (U.S.), 1994. . . . . . . £10/£5
Hearing Voices, Sinclair-Stevenson, 1995 . . £10/£5
ditto, Norton (U.S.), 1996. . . . . . . £10/£5
A Watch in the Night, Sinclair-Stevenson, 1996 £10/£5
ditto, Norton (U.S.), 1996. . . . . . . £10/£5
Dream Children, Murray, 1998 . . . . . £10/£5
ditto, Norton (U.S.), 1998. . . . . . . £10/£5

Biography
The Laird of Abbottsford: A View of Walter Scott,
O.U.P., 1980 . . . . £25/£5
The Life of John Milton, O.U.P., 1983 . . . £15/£5
Hilaire Belloc, Hamish Hamilton, 1984 . . . £15/£5
ditto, Atheneum (U.S.), 1984. . . . . . £15/£5
Tolstoy: A Biography, Hamish Hamilton, 1988 £15/£5
ditto, Norton (U.S.), 1988. . . . . . . £15/£5
Eminent Victorians, BBC, 1989 . . . . . £20/£5
ditto, Norton (U.S.), 1990. . . . . . . £15/£5
C. S. Lewis; A Biography, Collins, 1990 . . £15/£5
ditto, Norton (U.S.), 1990. . . . . . . £15/£5
Jesus, Sinclair-Stevenson, 1992 . . . . . £15/£5
ditto, Norton (U.S.), 1992. . . . . . . £15/£5
The Rise and Fall of the House of Windsor, Sinclair-
Stevenson, 1993 . . . . £20/£5
ditto, Norton (U.S.), 1993. . . . . . . £15/£5
Paul: The Mind of the Apostle, Sinclair-Stevenson,
1997 . . . . £10/£5
ditto, Norton (U.S.), 1997. . . . . . . £10/£5

Poetry
*Lilibet: An Account in Verse of The Early Years of
The Queen Until The Time of Her Accession*, Blond
& Briggs, 1984 (wraps) £10

Essays
*How Can We Know? An Essay on The Christian
Religion*, Hamish Hamilton, 1985 . . . . £10/£5
ditto, Atheneum (U.S.), 1985. . . . . . £10/£5
The Church in Crisis, Hodder & Stoughton, 1986
(with Charles Moore and Gavin Stamp, wraps) . £5
*Penfriends from Porlock: Essay and Reviews, 1977-
1986*, Hamish Hamilton, 1988 . . . . . £10/£5
ditto, Norton (U.S.), 1989. . . . . . . £10/£5
Against Religion: Why we should try to live without it,
Chatto & Windus, 1990 (wraps) £5

Children's Titles
Stray, Walker Books, 1987 . . . . . . £15/£5
ditto, Orchard (U.S.), 1989 . . . . . . £10/£5
The Tabitha Stories, Walker Books, 1988 . . £15/£5
ditto, as *Tabitha*, Orchard (U.S.), 1989 . . £10/£5
Hazel The Guinea-pig, Walker Books, 1989 . £10/£5

Others
Landscape in France, Elm Tree, 1987 . . . £10/£5
ditto, St Martin's Press (U.S.), 1988 . . . . £10/£5
God's Funeral, Murray, 1999 . . . . . £10/£5
ditto, Norton (U.S.), 1999. . . . . . . £10/£5
The Victorians, Hutchinson, 2002 . . . . £20/£5
ditto, Norton (U.S.), 2003. . . . . . . £15/£5

ANGUS WILSON
(b.1913 d.1991)

A novelist and short story writer, Wilson's critical
writings are highly regarded, particularly his studies
of Zola and Dickens.

Novels
Hemlock and After, Secker & Warburg, 1952 . £30/£5
ditto, Viking (U.S.), 1952. . . . . . . £20/£5
Anglo-Saxon Attitudes, Secker & Warburg, 1956 . .
. . . . £75/£10
ditto, Viking (U.S.), 1956. . . . . . . £25/£5
The Middle Age of Mrs Eliot, Secker & Warburg,
1958 . . . . £30/£5
ditto, Viking (U.S.), 1959. . . . . . . £15/£5
The Old Men at The Zoo, Secker & Warburg, 1961 .
. . . . £30/£5
ditto, Viking (U.S.), 1961. . . . . . . £10/£5
Late Call, Secker & Warburg, 1964 . . . . £20/£5
ditto, Viking (U.S.), 1965. . . . . . . £10/£5
No Laughing Matter, Secker & Warburg, 1967 £15/£5
ditto, Viking (U.S.), 1967. . . . . . . £10/£5
As if by Magic, Secker & Warburg, 1973 . . £15/£5
ditto, Viking (U.S.), 1973. . . . . . . £10/£5
Setting The World on Fire, Secker & Warburg, 1980 .
. . . . £10/£5
ditto, Viking (U.S.), 1980. . . . . . . £10/£5

Stories
The Wrong Set and Other Stories, Secker & Warburg,
1949 . . . . £75/£20
ditto, Morrow (U.S.), 1950 . . . . . £35/£10
Such Darling Dodos and Other Stories, Secker &
Warburg, 1950 . . . . £35/£20
ditto, Morrow (U.S.), 1951 . . . . . £25/£10
A Bit Off The Map and Other Stories, Secker &
Warburg, 1957 . . . . £15/£5
ditto, Viking (U.S.), 1957. . . . . . . £10/£5
Death Dance: 25 Stories, Viking (U.S.), 1969 . £15/£5
Collected Stories, Secker & Warburg, 1987. . £10/£5
ditto, Viking (U.S.), 1987. . . . . . . £10/£5

Plays
The Mulberry Bush: A Play in 3 Acts, Secker &
Warburg, 1956 . . . . £30/£10

Others
Emile Zola, Secker & Warburg, 1952 . . £45/£15
ditto, Morrow (U.S.), 1952 . . . . . £25/£10

For Whom The Cloche Tolls, Methuen, 1953 (with
Philippe Jullian) . . . . £45/£10
ditto, Curtis Books (U.S.), 1953 (wraps). . . . £5
The Wild Garden: or, Speaking of Writing, Univ. of
California Press (U.S.), 1963 . . . . . £15/£5
ditto, Secker & Warburg, 1963 . . . . . £15/£5
Tempo: The Impact of Television on The Arts, Studio
Vista, 1964 . . . . £20/£5
ditto, Dufour (U.S.), 1966 . . . . . . £15/£5
The World of Charles Dickens, Secker & Warburg,
1970 . . . . £10/£5
ditto, Viking (U.S.), 1970. . . . . . . £10/£5
ditto, Arcadia Press, 1970 (265 signed copies) . £300
The Naughty Nineties, Methuen, 1976 . . . £15/£5
**The Strange Ride of Rudyard Kipling: His Life and
Works**, Secker & Warburg, 1977 . . . . £15/£5
ditto, Viking (U.S.), 1978. . . . . . . £10/£5
**Diversity and Depth in Fiction: Selected Critical
Writings**, Secker & Warburg, 1983. . . . £10/£5
ditto, Viking (U.S.), 1983. . . . . . . £10/£5
Reflections in a Writer's Eye, Secker & Warburg,
1986 . . . . £10/£5
ditto, Viking (U.S.), 1986. . . . . . . £10/£5

R.D. WINGFIELD

Wingfield' 'Inspector Jack Frost' is an unconventional
policeman who nevertheless manages to solve several
crimes per book.

Frost at Christmas, Paperjacks (Canada), 1984 (wraps)
. . . . £250
ditto, Paperjacks (U.S.), 1987 (wraps) . . . £50
ditto, Constable, 1989 . . . . £150/£20
A Touch of Frost, Paperjacks (U.S.), 1987 (wraps) .
. . . . £200
ditto, Constable, 1990 . . . . . £2,000/£200
ditto, Post Mortem Books, 1998 (350 signed copies) .
. . . . £35
Night Frost, Constable, 1992. . . . . £250/£45
Hard Frost, Scorpion Press, 1995 (85 signed copies,
acetate d/w) . . . . £75/£65
ditto, Constable, 1995. . . . . . . £35/£5
Winter Frost, Constable, 1999 . . . . £20/£5

JEANETTE WINTERSON
(b.1959)

A winner of numerous awards, Winterson's first
book, *Oranges Are Not The Only Fruit*, remains the
classic.

Novels
Oranges Are Not The Only Fruit, Pandora Press, 1985
(wraps) £300

ditto, Atlantic Monthly Press (U.S.), 1987 (price of
$6.95, wraps). £30
ditto, Guild, 1990 . . . . £75/£10
Boating for Beginners, Methuen, 1985 . . £300/£35
ditto, Methuen, 1985 (wraps). £35
The Passion, Bloomsbury, 1987 . . . . £75/£20
ditto, Atlantic Monthly Press (U.S.), 1988 . . £35/£5
Sexing The Cherry, Bloomsbury, 1989 . . . £25/£5
ditto, Atlantic Monthly Press (U.S.), 1990 . . £15/£5
Written on The Body, Cape, 1992 . . . £15/£5
ditto, Knopf (U.S.), 1993 . . . . . . £15/£5
Art and Lies, Knopf (U.S.), 1993 . . . £10/£5
ditto, Cape, 1994 . . . . £10/£5
Gut Symmetries, Granta, 1996 . . . . £10/£5
ditto, Knopf (U.S.), 1997 . . . . . . £10/£5
The PowerBook, Cape, 2000. . . . . . £10/£5
ditto, Knopf (U.S.), 2000 . . . . . . £10/£5

Short Stories
The World and Other Places, Cape, 1998 . . £10/£5
ditto, Knopf (U.S.), 1998 . . . . . . £10/£5
The Dreaming Place, Ulysses, 1998 (150 signed
copies) £65

Others
Fit for the Future, Pandora Press, 1986. . £150/£30
ditto, Pandora Press, 1986 (wraps) £75
Art Objects: Ecstasy and Effrontery, Cape, 1995 . .
. . . . £20/£5
ditto, Knopf (U.S.), 1996 . . . . . . £15/£5

WISDEN CRICKETERS'
ALMANACKS

The first editions of *Wisden*, the cricketers' bible,
were published in paper wrappers, with the first
hardback edition appearing in 1896. From 1938 the
limp edition was published in linen rather than paper.
The first dustjackets appeared on the hardback in
1965.

1864-1895, paper wraps

1864	. . . . £10,000
1865	. . . . £5,000
1866	. . . . £4,000
1867	. . . . £4,000
1868	. . . . £4,000
1869	. . . . £4,000
1870	. . . . £1,500
1871	. . . . £1,500
1872	. . . . £1,500
1873	. . . . £1,250
1874	. . . . £1,250
1875	. . . . £2,000
1876	. . . . £750
1877	. . . . £750
1878	. . . . £400

1879 . . . . £500	
1880 . . . . £400	
1881-1889 . . . . £300	
1890-1895 . . . . £250	

1896-1964
First value hardback (no d/w), sSecond value paper wraps (linen from 1938)

1896 . . . . £5,000/£125
1897 . . . . £3,500/£125
1898-1901 . . . . £2,500/£125
1902-3 . . . . £2,000/£100
1904-05. . . . . £1,000/£100
1906-07. . . . .£750/£100
1908-15. . . . .£500/£100
1916 . . . . £3,500/£750
1917-19. . . . . £1,500/£250
1920-33. . . . .£300/£100
1934 . . . .£400/£150
1935-37. . . . .£300/£150
1938-39. . . . .£400/£100
1940 . . . .£600/£250
1941 . . . .£600/£350
1942 . . . .£500/£350
1943-45. . . . .£300/£175
1946 . . . .£175/£100
1947-48. . . . .£125/£100
1949 . . . . £75/£25
1950-64. . . . . £45/£25

1965 to date
First value hardback with d/w, second value linen wraps

1965-76. . . . . £60/£30
1977 to present . . . . . . £20/£10

P.G. WODEHOUSE
(b.1881 d.1975)

A prolific comic author, Wodehouse's world is light, smart, superficial, and if you enjoy his humour, highly addictive.

'Jeeves and Wooster' Novels
Thank You, Jeeves, Jenkins, 1934 . . . £850/£100
ditto, Little, Brown (U.S.), 1934 . . . . £350/£45
Right Ho, Jeeves, Jenkins, 1934 . . . . £850/£75
ditto, as **Brinkley Manor**, Little, Brown (U.S.), 1934 .
. . . . £350/£45
The Code of The Woosters, Jenkins, 1938 . £700/£45
ditto, Doubleday (U.S.), 1938 . . . . £325/£45
Joy in The Morning, Doubleday (U.S.), 1946 . . .
. . . . £150/£30
ditto, Jenkins, 1947 . . . . £150/£25
The Mating Season, Jenkins, 1949 . . . £125/£20
ditto, Didier (U.S.), 1949 . . . . . . £100/£20
Ring for Jeeves, Jenkins, 1953 . . . . £125/£20
ditto, as **The Return of Jeeves**, Doubleday (U.S.), 1953
. . . . £100/£20
Jeeves and The Feudal Spirit, Jenkins, 1954 £125/£25

ditto, as **Bertie Wooster Sees It Through**, Simon & Schuster (U.S.), 1955 . . . . . . £100/£20
Jeeves in The Offing, Jenkins, 1960. . . £100/£15
ditto, as **How Right You Are, Jeeves**, Simon & Schuster (U.S.), 1960 . . . . . . £75/£15
Stiff Upper Lip, Jeeves, Jenkins, 1963 . . £75/£15
ditto, Simon & Schuster (U.S.), 1963 . . £65/£15
Much Obliged, Jeeves, Barrie & Jenkins, 1971. . .
. . . . £35/£10
ditto, as **Jeeves and The Tie that Binds**, Simon & Schuster (U.S.), 1971. . . . . . . £35/£10
Aunts Aren't Gentlemen, Barrie & Jenkins, 1974 . .
. . . . £35/£10
ditto, as **The Cat-Nappers**, Simon & Schuster (U.S.), 1974 . . . . £35/£10

'Jeeves and Wooster' Short Stories
The Man With Two Left Feet, Methuen, 1917 . £1,750
ditto, Burt (U.S.), 1933 . . . . . £500/£75
My Man Jeeves, Newnes, 1919 (first printing by Butler & Tanner). £500
The Inimitable Jeeves, Jenkins, 1923 . £2,000/£75
ditto, as **Jeeves**, Doran (U.S.), 1923 . . £2,000/£75
Carry On Jeeves, Jenkins, 1925 . . . . £850/£75
ditto, Doran (U.S.), 1927 . . . . . £750/£50
Very Good, Jeeves, Jenkins, 1930 . . . £750/£75
ditto, Doubleday (U.S.), 1930 . . . . £600/£50
A Few Quick Ones, Jenkins, 1959 . . . £100/£15
ditto, Simon & Schuster (U.S.), 1959 . £75/£15
Plum Pie, Jenkins, 1966 . . . . . . £75/£15
ditto, Simon & Schuster (U.S.), 1967 . . £75/£10

'Jeeves and Wooster' Omnibus Editions
Jeeves Omnibus, Jenkins, 1931 . . . . £600/£60
The World of Jeeves, Jenkins, 1967 . . . £100/£30

'Blandings' Novels
Something New, Appleton (U.S.), 1915. . . £750
ditto, as **Something Fresh**, Methuen, 1915 . . £2,000
Leave it to PSmith, Jenkins, 1923 . . £1,250/£200
ditto, Doran (U.S.), 1923 . . . . £1,000/£200
Summer Lightning, Jenkins, 1929 . . . £750/£125
ditto, as **Fish Preferred**, Doubleday, 1929 . £500/£100
Heavy Weather, Jenkins, 1933 . . . . £650/£125
ditto, Little, Brown (U.S.), 1933 . . . . £500/£125
Uncle Fred in The Springtime, Jenkins, 1939 . . .
. . . . £500/£65
ditto, Doubleday (U.S.), 1939 . . . . £250/£45
Full Moon, Jenkins, 1947 . . . . . £100/£25
ditto, Doubleday (U.S.), 1947 . . . . £100/£25
Pigs Have Wings, Jenkins, 1952 . . . . £75/£15
ditto, Doubleday (U.S.), 1952 . . . . £75/£15
Service with a Smile, Simon & Schuster (U.S.), 1961 .
. . . . £50/£10
ditto, Jenkins, 1962 . . . . £45/£10
Galahad at Blandings, Jenkins, 1965 . . £50/£10
ditto, as **The Brinkmanship of Galahad Threepwood**, Simon & Schuster (U.S.), 1967. . . . £40/£10

A Pelican at Blandings, Jenkins, 1969 . . £45/£10
ditto, as *No Nudes is Good Nudes*, Simon & Schuster
(U.S.), 1970 . . . . £35/£10
Sunset at Blandings, Chatto & Windus, 1977
(unfinished novel, finished by Richard Usborne) . .
. . . . £40/£10
ditto, Simon & Schuster (U.S.), 1977 . . £35/£10

'Blandings' Short Stories
Blandings Castle and Elsewhere, Jenkins, 1935 . .
. . . . £700/£75
ditto, Doubleday (U.S.), 1935 . . . . £450/£65
Lord Emsworth and Others, Jenkins, 1937 . £700/£75
ditto, as *Crime Wave at Blandings*, Doubleday (U.S.),
1937 . . . . £450/£50
Nothing Serious, Jenkins, 1950 . . . . £200/£35
ditto, Doubleday (U.S.), 1951 . . . £125/£25

'Blandings' Omnibus
The World of Blandings, Barrie & Jenkins, 1975 . .
. . . . £40/£10

Other Novels
The Pothunters, Black, 1902 (first binding with silver
loving cup on front board and spine, no ads) . £3,000
ditto, Black, 1902 (secondary binding with frontis
illustration on front cover, 8pps of ads) . £750
ditto, Macmillan (U.S.), 1924 . . . £1,000/£100
A Prefect's Uncle, Black, 1903 (first issue, no adverts)
. . . . £2,000
ditto, Black, 1903 (second issue with 8pps of ads.). .
. . . . £1,000
ditto, Macmillan (U.S.), 1924 . . . £650/£75
The Gold Bat, Black, 1904 . . . . . £1,250
ditto, Macmillan (U.S.), 1923 . . . £600/£75
William Tell Told Again, A. & C. Black, 1904 (first
issue, off-white cloth lettered in gilt on spine and
front cover, top edge gilt, publisher's monogram on
title page, 2pps of ads) £1,000
ditto, A. & C. Black, 1904 (second issue with 12pps of
ads) £500
ditto, A. & C. Black, 1904 (third issue, tan/brown
cloth, gilt lettering on spine only, 2pps of ads, gilt on
cover). £350
ditto, A. & C. Black, 1904 (variant issue, buff cloth,
black lettering) £250
The Head of Kay's, A. & C. Black, 1905 . . £750
ditto, Macmillan (U.S.), 1922 . . . . £600/£75
Love Among The Chickens, Newnes, 1906. . £3,000
ditto, Circle Publishing Co. (U.S.), 1909 . . £750
The White Feather, A. & C. Black, 1907 . £2,000
ditto, Macmillan (U.S.), 1922 . . . . £600/£75
Not George Washington, Cassell, 1907 (written with
H. Westbrook, 'Cassell & Company' on spine) .
. . . . £2,500
ditto, Cassell, 1907 ('Cassell' only on spine) . £750
ditto, Continuum (U.S.), 1980 . . . . £25/£10
The Swoop, Alston Rivers, 1909 (wraps) . . £2,500
Mike, A. & C. Black, 1909 . . . . . £2,000

ditto, Macmillan (U.S.), 1924 . . . . £600/£75
ditto, as *Enter PSmith*, Black, 1935 (re-issue of second
part of *Mike*). . . . . £500/£65
ditto, as *Mike at Wrykyn*, Jenkins, 1953, and *Mike and
PSmith*, Jenkins, 1953 (2 vol. re-issue, novel revised)
. . . . £250/£35
A Gentleman of Leisure, Alston Rivers, 1910 . £1,000
ditto, as *The Intrusion of Jimmy*, Watt (U.S.), 1910 .
. . . . £400
PSmith in The City, A. & C. Black, 1910 . . £1,250
The Prince and Betty, Mills and Boon, 1912 . £1,250
The Prince and Betty, Watt (U.S.), 1912 (different
from above) £600
ditto, as *PSmith Journalist*, A. & C. Black, 1915 . .
. . . . £1,000
The Little Nugget, Methuen, 1913 . . . . £1,000
ditto, Watt (U.S.), 1914 . . . . . . £300
Uneasy Money, Appleton (U.S.), 1916 . . . £300
ditto, Methuen, 1917 . . . . £1,750
Piccadilly Jim, Dodd, Mead (U.S.), 1917 . . £300
ditto, Jenkins, 1918 . . . . £750
A Damsel in Distress, Doran (U.S.), 1919 . . £250
ditto, Jenkins, 1919 . . . . £650
Their Mutual Child, Boni & Liveright (U.S.), 1919 .
. . . . £250
ditto, as *The Coming of Bill*, Jenkins, 1920. . . .
. . . . £1,250/£150
The Little Warrior, Doran (U.S.), 1920 . . £850/£200
ditto, as *Jill The Reckless*, Jenkins, 1921 . £1,500/£350
The Girl on The Boat, Jenkins, 1922 . £1,500/£300
ditto, as *Three Men and a Maid*, Doran, 1922 (revised
version) . . . . £650/£125
The Adventures of Sally, Jenkins, 1922. £1,250/£250
ditto, as *Mostly Sally*, Doran (U.S.), 1923 . £650/£125
Bill The Conqueror, Jenkins, 1924 . £1,000/£200
ditto, Doran (U.S.), 1925 . . . . . . £450/£100
Sam The Sudden, Methuen, 1925 . . . £750/£125
ditto, as *Sam in The Suburbs*, Doran (U.S.), 1925 . .
. . . . £300/£50
The Small Bachelor, Methuen, 1927 . . £750/£125
ditto, Doran (U.S.), 1927 . . . . . . £300/£50
Money for Nothing, Jenkins, 1928 . . . £750/£125
ditto, Doran (U.S.), 1928 . . . . . £300/£50
Big Money, Doubleday (U.S.), 1931. . . £300/£50
ditto, Jenkins, 1931 . . . . £750/£100
If I Were You, Doubleday (U.S.), 1931 . . £300/£100
ditto, Jenkins, 1931 . . . . £500/£100
Doctor Sally, Methuen, 1932. . . . . £450/£100
Hot Water, Jenkins, 1932. . . . . . £450/£100
ditto, Doubleday (U.S.), 1932 . . . . £300/£50
The Luck of The Bodkins, Jenkins, 1935 . £300/£45
ditto, Little, Brown (U.S.), 1935 . . . . £250/£50
Laughing Gas, Jenkins, 1936 . . . . £400/£100
ditto, Doubleday (U.S.), 1936 . . . . £300/£50
Summer Moonshine, Doubleday (U.S.), 1937 . .
. . . . £200/£45
ditto, Jenkins, 1938 . . . . £400/£100
Quick Service, Jenkins, 1940. . . . . £150/£25
ditto, Doubleday (U.S.), 1940 . . . . £125/£20

Money in The Bank, Doubleday (U.S.), 1942 . . .
. . . . £200/£25
ditto, Jenkins, 1946 . . . . £100/£20
Spring Fever, Doubleday (U.S.), 1948 . . £100/£25
ditto, Jenkins, 1948 . . . . £100/£25
Uncle Dynamite, Jenkins, 1948 . . . . £100/£25
ditto, Didier (U.S.), 1948 . . . . . . £100/£25
The Old Reliable, Jenkins, 1951 . . . . £75/£15
ditto, Doubleday (U.S.), 1951 . . . . £75/£15
Barmy in Wonderland, Jenkins, 1952 . . £75/£15
ditto, as *Angel Cake*, Doubleday (U.S.), 1952 £75/£15
French Leave, Jenkins, 1956 . . . . . £50/£15
ditto, Simon & Schuster, 1959 . . . . £50/£15
Something Fishy, Jenkins, 1957 . . . . £50/£15
ditto, as *The Butler Did It*, Simon & Schuster (U.S.),
1957 . . . . £50/£15
Cocktail Time, Jenkins, 1958 . . . . £50/£15
ditto, Simon & Schuster (U.S.), 1958 . . £50/£15
The Ice in The Bedroom, Simon & Schuster (U.S.),
1961 . . . . £50/£15
ditto, as *Ice in The Bedroom*, Jenkins, 1961 £50/£15
Biffen's Millions, Simon & Schuster (U.S.), 1964 . .
. . . . £45/£10
ditto, as *Frozen Assets*, Jenkins, 1964 . . £45/£10
The Purloined Paperweight, Simon & Schuster (U.S.),
1967 . . . . £50/£15
ditto, as *Company for Henry*, Jenkins, 1967 £65/£20
Do Butlers Burgle Banks?, Simon & Schuster (U.S.),
1968 . . . . £65/£20
ditto, Jenkins, 1968 . . . . £75/£20
The Girl in Blue, Barrie & Jenkins, 1970 . £25/£10
ditto, Simon & Schuster (U.S.), 1971 . . £25/£10
Pearls, Girls and Monty Bodkin, Barrie & Jenkins,
1972 . . . . £25/£10
ditto, as *The Plot That Thickened*, Simon & Schuster
(U.S.), 1973 . . . . £25/£10
Bachelors Anonymous, Barrie & Jenkins, 1973 . .
. . . . £25/£10
ditto, Simon & Schuster (U.S.), 1974 . . £25/£10
Sir Agravaine, Blandford, 1984 . . . . £25/£10

Other Short Stories
Tales of St Austin's, Black, 1903 . . . . £750
ditto, Macmillan (U.S.), 1923 . . . . £650/£50
The Man Upstairs, Methuen, 1914 . . . £1,500
Indiscretions of Archie, Jenkins, 1921 . £,1750/£125
ditto, Doran (U.S.), 1921 . . . . . £1,250/£65
The Clicking of Cuthbert, Jenkins, 1922 £1,500/£100
ditto, as *Golf Without Tears*, Doran (U.S.), 1924 . .
. . . . £750/£50
Ukridge, Jenkins, 1924 . . . . . £1,500/£75
ditto, as *He Rather Enjoyed It*, Doran (U.S.), 1926 .
. . . . £750/£50
The Heart of a Goof, Jenkins, 1926 . . £1,500/£75
ditto, as *Divots*, Doran (U.S.), 1927 . . £1,000/£50
Meet Mr Mulliner, Jenkins, 1927 . . . £750/£35
ditto, Doran (U.S.), 1928 . . . . . . £450/£35
Mr Mulliner Speaking, Jenkins, 1929 . . £750/£35
ditto, Doubleday (U.S.), 1930 . . . . £450/£35

Mulliner Nights, Jenkins, 1933 . . . . £750/£50
ditto, Doubleday (U.S.), 1933 . . . . £450/£45
Young Men in Spats, Jenkins, 1936 . . . £600/£50
ditto, Doubleday (U.S.), 1936 . . . . £350/£45
Eggs, Beans and Crumpets, Jenkins, 1940 . £400/£50
ditto, Doubleday (U.S.), 1940 . . . . £200/£30

Other Omnibus Editions
Nothing but Wodehouse, Doubleday (U.S.), 1932 . .
. . . . £250/£40
Mulliner Omnibus, Jenkins, 1935 . . . £400/£65
Weekend Wodehouse, Jenkins, 1939 . . £400/£65
ditto, Doubleday (U.S.), 1939 . . . . £300/£25
Wodehouse on Golf, Doubleday (U.S.), 1940 £300/£65
The World of Mr Mulliner, Barrie & Jenkins, 1972 .
. . . . £20/£5
ditto, Taplinger (U.S.), 1974 . . . . . £15/£5
The Golf Omnibus, Barrie & Jenkins, 1973 . £20/£5
ditto, Simon & Schuster (U.S.), 1974 . . £20/£5
The World of PSmith, Barrie & Jenkins, 1974 . £20/£5
The World of Ukridge, Barrie & Jenkins, 1975 . £20/£5
The Uncollected Wodehouse, Seabury Press (U.S.),
1976 . . . . £30/£5
Vintage Wodehouse, Barrie & Jenkins, 1977 . £15/£5
Tales from The Drones Club, Hutchinson, 1982 . .
. . . . £15/£5
Wodehouse Nuggets, Hutchinson, 1983 . . £15/£5
The World of Uncle Fred, Hutchinson, 1983 . £10/£5
The World of Wodehouse Clergy, Hutchinson, 1984 .
. . . . £10/£5
The Hollywood Omnibus, Hutchinson, 1985 . £10/£5
Wodehouse on Cricket, Hutchinson, 1987 . . £15/£5
The Aunts Omnibus, Hutchinson, 1989 . . £10/£5

Autobiography
Performing Flea, Jenkins, 1953 . . . . £75/£20
ditto, as *Author! Author!*, Simon & Schuster (U.S.),
1962 . . . . £50/£15
Bring on The Girls, Simon & Schuster (U.S.), 1953
(with Guy Bolton) . . . . £50/£15
ditto, Jenkins, 1954 (differences from above) £50/£15
America I Like You, Simon & Schuster (U.S.), 1956 .
. . . . £50/£15
ditto, as *Over Seventy*, Jenkins, 1957 (revised) £50/£15

Others
The Globe By The Way Book, Globe, 1907 (written
with H. Westbrook, wraps) £6,000
Louder and Funnier, Faber, 1932 . . . £600/£150
The Parrot and Other Poems, Hutchinson, 1988 . .
. . . . £10/£5
Yours, Plum, Hutchinson, 1990 . . . . £10/£5

TOM WOLFE
(b.1930)

An American novelist and journalist, Wolfe developed a 'new journalism', reporting hard facts with a spectacular and emotional graphic style.

Essays
The Kandy-Kolored Tangerine Flake, Farrar Straus (U.S.), 1965 . . . . £150/£25
ditto, as *Streamline Baby*, Cape, 1966 . . £100/£15
The Electric Kool-Aid Acid Test, Farrar Straus (U.S.), 1968 . . . . £175/£25
ditto, Weidenfeld & Nicolson, 1969 . . . £100/£20
The Pump House Gang, Farrar Straus (U.S.), 1968 . . . . £30/£10
ditto, as *The Mid-Atlantic Man and Other New Breeds in England*, Weidenfeld & Nicolson, 1969 £30/£10
Mauve Gloves and Madmen, Clutter and Vine and Other Stories, Farrar Straus (U.S.), 1976 . . £25/£5
In Our Time, Farrar Straus (U.S.), 1980 . £10/£5
ditto, Picador, 1980 (wraps) £5

Journalism and Others
Radical Chic and Mau-Mauing The Flak Catchers, Farrar Straus (U.S.), 1970 . . . . . £25/£5
ditto, Joseph, 1971. . . . . £25/£5
The Painted Word, Farrar Straus (U.S.), 1975 . £20/£5
The Right Stuff, Farrar Straus (U.S.), 1979 . £20/£5
ditto, Cape, 1979 . . . . £20/£5
From Bauhaus to Our House, Farrar Straus (U.S.), 1981 . . . . £20/£5
ditto, Farrar Straus (U.S.), 1981 (350 signed, numbered copies, slipcase) . . . . £150/£125
ditto, Cape, 1982 . . . . £15/£5
A Man in Full, Farrar Straus (U.S.), 1998 . £10/£5
ditto, Farrar Straus (U.S.), 1998 (250 signed, numbered copies, slipcase) . . . . . . £150/£125
ditto, Franklin Library (U.S.), 1998 (signed, limited edition) £75
ditto, Cape, 1998 . . . . £10/£5
Hooking Up, Farrar Straus (U.S.), 2000 . £10/£5
ditto, Franklin Library (U.S.), 2000 (signed, limited edition) £75

Fiction
The Purple Decades, Farrar Straus (U.S.), 1982 . . . . £20/£10
ditto, Farrar Straus (U.S.), 1982 (450 signed copies, slipcase) . . . . £75/£50
ditto, Cape, 1983 . . . . £15/£5
The Bonfire of The Vanities, Farrar Straus (U.S.), 1987 . . . . £35/£10
ditto, Farrar Straus (U.S.), 1987 (250 signed, numbered copies, slipcase) . . . . . . £200/£150
ditto, Franklin Library (U.S.), 1987 (signed, limited edition) £100
ditto, Cape, 1988 . . . . £25/£5

VIRGINIA WOOLF
(b.1882 d.1941)

Woolf's London home became the centre of the Bloomsbury Group. *To the Lighthouse* and *The Waves*, with their innovative stream-of-consciousness style, brought her to the forefront of Modernism.

Novels
The Voyage Out, Duckworth, 1915 . . . . £1,450
ditto, Doran (U.S.), 1920 (revised text) . £2,500/£200
ditto, Duckworth, 1920 (revised text) . £2,000/£150
Night and Day, Duckworth, 1919 . . . . £500
ditto, Doran (U.S.), 1920 . . . . . £2,250/£250
Jacob's Room, Hogarth Press, 1922 . . £25,000/£600
ditto, Hogarth Press, 1922 (40 copies with tipped-in slip) . . . . £25,000/£7,500
ditto, Harcourt Brace (U.S.), 1923 . £7,000/£250
Mrs Dalloway, Hogarth Press, 1925 . £15,000/£750
ditto, Harcourt Brace (U.S.), 1925 . £1,500/£100
To The Lighthouse, Hogarth Press, 1927 . . . . £12,500/£1,000
ditto, Harcourt Brace (U.S.), 1927 . £1,500/£150
Orlando: A Biography, Crosby Gaige (U.S.), 1928 (861 numbered, signed copies) £1,500
ditto, Hogarth Press, 1928 . . . . £2,500/£150
The Waves, Hogarth Press, 1931 . . £1,250/£100
ditto, Harcourt Brace (U.S.), 1931 . . £200/£35
The Years, Hogarth Press, 1937 . . . . £750/£50
ditto, Harcourt Brace (U.S.), 1937 . . £250/£30
Between The Acts, Hogarth Press, 1941 . £500/£45
ditto, Harcourt Brace (U.S.), 1941 . . £200/£25

Short Stories
Two Stories, Hogarth Press, 1917 (150 copies, wraps or paper-backed cloth, one story by Virginia and the other by Leonard Woolf) £10,000
Kew Gardens, Hogarth Press, 1919 (150 copies, in wraps.) £8,000
Monday or Tuesday, Hogarth Press, 1921 (1,000 copies) £1,500
ditto, Harcourt Brace (U.S.), 1921 (cloth and boards) . . . . £750/£100
ditto, Harcourt Brace (U.S.), 1921 (full cloth) . . . . £1,250/£125
A Haunted House, Hogarth Press, 1943. . £250/£25
ditto, Harcourt Brace (U.S.), 1944 . . £75/£15
Nurse Lugton's Golden Thimble, Hogarth Press, 1966 (glassine d/w). . . . . £75/£65
Mrs Dalloway's Party, Hogarth Press, 1973 £30/£10
The Pargiters, Hogarth Press, 1977 . . . . £20/£5
ditto, Harcourt Brace (U.S.), 1977 . . . . £15/£5

Essays
Mr Bennett and Mrs Brown, Hogarth Press, 1924 (wraps) £250
The Common Reader, Hogarth Press, 1925. . . . . £1,500/£200
ditto, Harcourt Brace (U.S.), 1925 . . . £350/£75

A Room of One's Own, Fountain Press (U.S.)/Hogarth
Press, 1929 (492 signed copies) . £3,000/£2,000
ditto, Hogarth Press, 1929 . . . . £1,500/£75
ditto, Harcourt Brace (U.S.), 1929 . . . £650/£35
Street Haunting, Westgate Press (U.S.), 1930 (500
signed copies, slipcase) . . . . . £1,000/£750
On Being Ill, Hogarth Press, 1930 (250 signed copies)
. . . . £2,500/£1,500
Beau Brummell, Rimington & Hooper (U.S.),
1930(550 signed copies, glassine d/w, slipcase) .
. . . . £1,250/£750
A Letter to A Young Poet, Hogarth Press, 1932 (wraps)
. . . . £65
The Common Reader: Second Series, Hogarth Press,
1932 . . . . £400/£50
ditto, Harcourt Brace (U.S.), 1932 . . . £125/£35
Walter Sickert: A Conversation, Hogarth Press, 1934
(wraps) £60
The Roger Fry Memorial Exhibition, Bristol, 1935
(125 copies) £500
Three Guineas, Hogarth Press, 1938 . . £300/£65
ditto, Harcourt Brace (U.S.), 1938 . . . £200/£40
Reviewing, Hogarth Press, 1939 (wraps) . . £40
The Death of The Moth, Hogarth Press, 1942 . . .
. . . . £175/£25
ditto, Harcourt Brace (U.S.), 1942 . . . £75/£15
The Moment and Other Essays, Hogarth Press, 1947 .
. . . . £150/£20
ditto, Harcourt Brace (U.S.), 1948 . . . £65/£15
The Captain's Death Bed, Harcourt Brace (U.S.), 1950
. . . . £150/£20
ditto, Hogarth Press, 1950 . . . . . £65/£15
Granite and Rainbow, Hogarth Press, 1958 £165/£20
ditto, Harcourt Brace (U.S.), 1958 . . . £50/£15
Contemporary Writers, Hogarth Press, 1965 £45/£10
ditto, Harcourt Brace (U.S.), 1966 . . . . £25/£5
Collected Essays, Volume 1-4, Harcourt Brace (U.S.),
1967 . . . . £40/£5
Books and Portraits, Hogarth Press, 1977 . . £25/£5
ditto, Harcourt Brace (U.S.), 1977 . . . . £15/£5
The London Scene, Hogarth Press, 1982 . . £15/£5
ditto, Random House (U.S.), 1982 . . . . £10/£5
The Essays of Virginia Woolf, Volume I, Chatto &
Windus, 1986. . . . . £30/£10
ditto, Volume II, Chatto & Windus, 1987 . £30/£10
ditto, Volume III, Chatto & Windus, 1988 . £30/£10
ditto, Volume IV, Chatto & Windus, 1994 . £30/£10

Biography
Flush: A Biography, Hogarth Press, 1933 . £350/£45
ditto, Harcourt Brace (U.S.), 1933 . . . £150/£25
Roger Fry: A Biography, Hogarth Press, 1940 . . .
. . . . £350/£45
ditto, Harcourt Brace (U.S.), 1940 . . . £225/£35

Autobiography
Moments of Being, Sussex Univ. Press, 1976 £25/£10
ditto, Harcourt Brace (U.S.), 1976 . . . £25/£10

Play
Freshwater, Hogarth Press, 1976 . . . . £25/£5
ditto, Harcourt Brace (U.S.), 1976 . . . . £25/£5

Letters
Virginia Woolf and Lytton Strachey: Letters, Hogarth
Press, 1956 . . . . £125/£25
ditto, Harcourt (U.S.), 1956 . . . . . £45/£15
*The Flight of The Mind: The Letters of Virginia
Woolf, 1888-1912*, Hogarth Press, 1975 . . £25/£5
*ditto, as The Letters of Virginia Woolf, Volume I:
1888-1912*, Harcourt Brace Jovanovich(U.S.), 1975 .
. . . . £25/£5
*The Question of Things Happening: The Letters of
Virginia Woolf, 1912-1922*, Hogarth Press, 1976. .
. . . . £25/£5
*ditto, as The Letters of Virginia Woolf, Volume II:
1912-1922*, Harcourt Brace Jovanovich(U.S.), 1976 .
. . . . £25/£5
*A Change of Perspective: The Letters of Virginia
Woolf, 1923-1928*, Hogarth Press, 1977 . . £20/£5
*ditto, as The Letters of Virginia Woolf, Volume III:
1923-1928*, Harcourt Brace Jovanovich(U.S.), 1978 .
. . . . £25/£5
*A Reflection of The Other Person: The Letters of
Virginia Woolf, 1929-1931*, Hogarth Press, 1978. .
. . . . £20/£5
*ditto, as The Letters of Virginia Woolf, Volume IV:
1929-1931*, Harcourt Brace Jovanovich(U.S.), 1979 .
. . . . £25/£5
*The Sickle Side of The Moon: The Letters of Virginia
Woolf, 1931-1935*, Hogarth Press, 1979 . . £20/£5
*ditto, as The Letters of Virginia Woolf, Volume V:
1931-1935*, Harcourt Brace Jovanovich(U.S.), 1979 .
. . . . £25/£5
*Leave The Letters Till We're Dead: The Letters of
Virginia Woolf, 1936-1941*, Hogarth Press, 1980 . .
. . . . £15/£5
*ditto, as The Letters of Virginia Woolf, Volume VI:
1936-1941*, Harcourt Brace Jovanovich(U.S.), 1980 .
. . . . £25/£5
Paper Darts: The Illustrated Letters, Collins & Brown,
1992 . . . . £15/£5

Diaries
A Writer's Diary, Hogarth Press, 1953 . . £250/£45
ditto, Harcourt Brace (U.S.), 1954 . . . £125/£25
The Diary of Virginia Woolf, Volume 1, 1915-1919,
Hogarth Press, 1977 . . . . £20/£5
ditto, Harcourt Brace (U.S.), 1977 . . . . £20/£5
The Diary of Virginia Woolf, Volume II, 1920-1924,
Hogarth Press, 1978 . . . . £20/£5
ditto, Harcourt Brace (U.S.), 1978 . . . . £20/£5
The Diary of Virginia Woolf, Volume III, 1925-1930,
Hogarth Press, 1980 . . . . £15/£5
ditto, Harcourt Brace (U.S.), 1980 . . . . £15/£5
The Diary of Virginia Woolf, Volume IV, 1931-1935,
Hogarth Press, 1982 . . . . £15/£5
ditto, Harcourt Brace (U.S.), 1982 . . . . £15/£5

The Diary of Virginia Woolf, Volume V, 1936-1941, Chatto & Windus, 1984 . . . . £15/£5
ditto, Harcourt Brace (U.S.), 1984 . . . £15/£5

CORNELL WOOLRICH
(b.1903 d.1968)

An American author of *noir* suspense fiction, Woolrich's story 'It Had to Be Murder', collected in *After-Dinner Story*, has been filmed as *Rear Window*, initially by Hitchcock.

Novels

Cover Charge, Boni & Liveright (U.S.), 1926 . . .
. . . . £2,000/£200
Children of the Ritz, Boni & Liveright (U.S.), 1927 .
. . . . £1,500/£200
Times Square, Boni & Liveright (U.S.), 1929 . . .
. . . . £1,500/£200
A Young Man's Heart, Mason (U.S.), 1930 . . .
. . . . £1,000/£150
The Time of Her Life, Boni & Liveright (U.S.), 1931 .
. . . . £1,000/£150
Manhattan Love Song, Godwin (U.S.), 1932 . . .
. . . . £1,000/£150
The Bride Wore Black, Simon & Schuster (U.S.), 1940
. . . . £1,500/£200
ditto, Hale, 1942 . . . . £250/£75
ditto, as *Beware the Lady*, Pyramid (U.S.), 1953
(wraps) £25
The Black Curtain, Simon & Schuster (U.S.), 1941 .
. . . . £1,000/£250
Black Alibi, Simon & Schuster (U.S.), 1942 . . .
. . . . £750/£150
ditto, Hale, 1951 . . . . £250/£75
The Black Angel, Doubleday (U.S.), 1943 . £500/£150
ditto, Hale, 1949 . . . . £250/£75
The Black Path of Fear, Doubleday (U.S.), 1944 . .
. . . . £600/£200
Rendezvous in Black, Rinehart (U.S.), 1948 £200/£75
ditto, Hodder & Stoughton, 1950. . . . £150/£35
Savage Bride, Fawcett Gold Medal, 1950 (U.S.), 1950
(wraps) £35
Death Is My Dancing Partner, Pyramid (U.S.), 1959
(wraps) £35
The Doom Stone, Avon, 1960 (U.S.), 1950 (wraps) .
. . . . £35
Into the Night, Mysterious Press (U.S.), 1967
(completed by Lawrence Block) . . . £25/£10
ditto, Simon & Schuster, 1988. . . . . . £20/£5

Short Stories

Nightmare, Dodd Mead (U.S.), 1956 . . £150/£50
Violence, Dodd Mead (U.S.), 1958 . . . £150/£50
Hotel Room, Random House (U.S.), 1958 . £125/£45
Beyond the Night, Avon (U.S.), 1959 (wraps) . £25

The Ten Faces of Cornell Woolrich, Simon & Schuster (U.S.), 1965 . . . . . £75/£25
ditto, Boardman, 1966. . . . . . . £25/£10
The Dark Side of Love, Walker (U.S.), 1965 £125/£40
Nightwebs, Harper (U.S.), 1971 . . . . £75/£25
ditto, Gollancz, 1973 . . . . £20/£5
Angels of Darkness, Mysterious Press (U.S.), 1979 .
. . . . £30/£10
ditto, Mysterious Press (U.S.), 1979 (250 numbered copies) £75
ditto, Mysterious Press (U.S.), 1979 (lettered copies) .
. . . . £75
The Fantastic Stories of Colonel Woolrich, Southern Illinois Univ. Press (U.S.), 1981 . . . £75/£25
Rear Window and Four Short Novels, Ballantine (U.S.), 1984 (wraps) £10
Darkness At Dawn, Southern Illinois Univ. Press (U.S.), 1985 . . . . £35/£10
ditto, Xanadu, 1988 . . . . £20/£5
Blind Date With Death, Carroll & Graf (U.S.), 1985
(wraps) £10
Vampire's Honeymoon, Carroll & Graf (U.S.), 1985
(wraps) £10

Novels Written as 'William Irish'

Phantom Lady, Lippincott (U.S.), 1942. . £750/£200
ditto, Hale, 1945 . . . . £250/£75
Deadline at Dawn, Lippincott (U.S.), 1944 . £450/£125
ditto, Hutchinson, 1947 . . . . . . £200/£50
Waltz into Darkness, Lippincott (U.S.), 1947 . . .
. . . . £350/£100
ditto, Hutchinson, 1948 . . . . . . £200/£50
I Married a Dead Man, Lippincott (U.S.), 1948 . .
. . . . £350/£100
ditto, Hutchinson, 1950 . . . . . . £200/£50
Strangler's Serenade, Rinehart (U.S.), 1951 £250/£75
ditto, Hale, 1952 . . . . £250/£75

Short Stories Written as 'William Irish'

I Wouldn't Be In Your Shoes, Lippincott (U.S.), 1943
. . . . £500/£150
ditto, Hutchinson, 1946 . . . . . £250/£75
ditto, as *And So To Death*, Spivak (U.S.), 1947 (wraps)
. . . . £30
ditto, as *Nightmare*, Spivak (U.S.), 1950 (wraps) £30
After-Dinner Story, Lippincott (U.S.), 1944 £400/£125
ditto, Hutchinson, 1947 . . . . . £250/£75
ditto, as *Six Times Death*, Popular Library (U.S.), 1948
(wraps) £25
If I Should Die Before I Wake, Avon Murder Mystery Monthly No.31 (U.S.), 1945 (wraps) . . . £75
The Dancing Detective, Lippincott (U.S.), 1946 . .
. . . . £275/£75
ditto, Hutchinson, 1946 . . . . . £75/£25
Borrowed Crime, Avon Murder Mystery Monthly No.42, 1946 (wraps). £125
Dead Man's Blues, Lippincott (U.S.), 1948 £275/£75
ditto, Hutchinson, 1950 . . . . . . £75/£25
The Blue Ribbon, Lippincott (U.S.), 1949 . £275/£75

ditto, as *Dilemma of the Dead Lady*, Graphic (U.S.),
1950 (wraps) £30
ditto, Hutchinson, 1951 . . . . . £75/£25
Somebody on the Phone, Lippincott (U.S.), 1950 . .
. . . . £750/£125
ditto, as *Deadly Night Call*, Graphic (U.S.), 1951
(wraps) £30
ditto, as *The Night I Died*, Hutchinson, 1951 £125/£35
Six Nights of Mystery, Popular Library (U.S.), 1950
(wraps) £40
Marihuana, Dell (U.S.), 1951 (wraps) . . . £100
You'll Never See Me Again, Dell (U.S.), 1951 (wraps)
. . . . £75
Eyes That Watch You, Rinehart (U.S.), 1952 £275/£75
Bluebeard's Seventh Wife, Popular Library (U.S.),
1952 (wraps) £30

Novels Written as 'George Hopley'
The Night Has a Thousand Eyes, Farrar & Rinehart
(U.S.), 1945 . . . . £275/£100
ditto, Penguin, 1949 (wraps) £10
Fright, Rinehart (U.S.), 1950. . . . . £300/£100
ditto, Foulsham, 1952 . . . . . . £75/£25

Collected Editions
The Best of William Irish, Lippincott (U.S.), 1960 .
. . . . £45/£15
Four Thrillers, Zomba Books, 1983 . . . £25/£10
Cornell Woolrich Omnibus, Penguin, 1998 (wraps) £5

Non Fiction
Blues of a Lifetime, Popular Press (U.S.), 1991 . .
. . . . £35/£10

S. FOWLER WRIGHT
(b.1874 d.1965)

One of the key authors of science fiction in the U.K.,
Wright paid for the publication of his earliest books,
but soon found himself a bestseller with *Deluge*.

Poetry
Scenes from the Morte d'Arthur, Erskine Macdonald,
1919 (pseud. 'Alan Seymour') £45
Some Songs of Bilitis, Poetry, [1921] . . £125/£45
The Song of Songs and Other Poems, Merton Press,
[1925]. . . . . £125/£45
ditto, Cosmopolitan Book Corp. (U.S.), 1929 £100/£30
The Ballad of Elaine, Merton Press, 1926 . £100/£45
The Riding of Lancelot: A Narrative Poem, Fowler
Wright, 1929 . . . . £100/£45

Novels
The Amphibians, Swan Press, 1925 . . £1,500/£450
ditto, Merton Press, 1925 . . . . . £250/£45
Deluge, Fowler Wright, 1927 . . . £175/£35
ditto, Cosmopolitan Book Corp. (U.S.), 1929 £75/£20

The Island of Captain Sparrow, Gollancz, 1928 . .
. . . . £200/£25
ditto, Cosmopolitan Book Corp. (U.S.), 1928 £45/£15
The World Below, Collins, 1929 . . . . £200/£35
ditto, Longmans, Green & Co (U.S.), 1930. £200/£45
ditto, Shasta (U.S.), 1949 . . . . . £25/£10
ditto, Shasta (U.S.), 1949 (500 signed copies) £75/£45
Dawn, Cosmopolitan Book Corp. (U.S.), 1929 . . .
. . . . £100/£30
ditto, Harrap, 1930 . . . . . . £100/£30
Elfwin, Harrap, 1930 . . . . . . £100/£25
ditto, Longmans, Green & Co. (U.S.), 1930. £75/£25
Dream; or, The Simian Maid, Harrap, 1931 . . .
. . . . £100/£25
Seven Thousand in Israel, Jarrolds, 1931 . £100/£25
Red Ike, Hutchinson, [1931] (with J.M. Denwood) .
. . . . £45/£10
Beyond the Rim, Jarrolds, 1932 . . . . £100/£25
Lord's Right in Languedoc, Jarrolds, 1933 . £75/£20
Power, Jarrolds, 1933 . . . . . . £75/£20
David, Butterworth, 1934 . . . . . £45/£10
Prelude in Prague: A Story of the War in 1938,
Newnes, 1935 . . . . £45/£10
ditto, as *The War of 1938*, Putnam's (U.S.), 1936 . .
. . . . £45/£10
Four Days War, Hale, 1936 . . . . £200/£45
Megiddo's Ridge, Hale, 1937 . . . . £200/£45
The Screaming Lake, Hale, [1937] . . £200/£45
The Adventure of Wyndham Smith, Jenkins, 1938 .
. . . . £250/£65
The Hidden Tribe, Hale, 1938 . . . £200/£45
Ordeal of Barrata, Jenkins, 1939 . . . £45/£10
The Siege of Malta, Muller, 1942 (2 vols) . £60/£20
The Throne of Saturn, Heinemann, 1951 . £45/£10
ditto, Arkham House (U.S.), 1949 . . . £40/£10
Spider's War, Abelard Press (U.S.), 1954 . £30/£10

Short Stories
The New Gods Lead, Jarrolds, 1932 . . . £100/£25
The Witchfinder, Books of Today, 1946 . £40/£10

Novels written as 'Sidney Fowler'
The King Against Anne Bickerton, Harrap, 1930 . .
. . . . £75/£20
The Bell Street Murders, Harrap, 1931 . . £75/£20
ditto, Macaulay (U.S.), 1931 . . . . . £75/£20
By Saturday, Lane, 1931 . . . . . . £75/£20
The Hanging of Constance Hillier, Jarrolds, 1931. .
. . . . £75/£20
The Hand-Print Mystery, Jarrolds, 1932 . £75/£20
ditto, as *Crime and Co*, Macaulay (U.S.), 1931. . .
. . . . £75/£20
Arresting Delia, Jarrolds, 1933 . . . . £75/£20
ditto, Macaulay (U.S.), 1933 . . . . . £75/£20
The Secret of the Screen, Jarrolds, 1933 . £75/£20
Who Else But She?, Jarrolds, 1934 . . . £75/£20
Three Witnesses, Butterworth, 1935 . . . £75/£20
Vengeance of Gwa, Butterworth, 1935 (pseud.
'Anthony Wingrave'). . . . . . £75/£20

ditto, as *The Vengeance of Gwa*, Books of Today, 1945 (by S. Fowler Wright) . . . . £75/£20
The Attic Murders, Temple, 1936 . . . £75/£20
Was Murder Done?, Butterworth, 1936. . £75/£20
Post-Mortem Evidence, Butterworth, 1936 . £75/£20
Four Callers in Razor Street, Temple, 1937 £75/£20
The Jordan's Murder, Jenkins, 1938 . . £75/£20
The Murder in Bethnal Square, Jenkins, 1938 . . .
. . . . £75/£20
The Wills of Jane Kantwhistle, Jenkins, 1939 £75/£20
A Bout with the Mildew Gang, Eyre & Spottiswoode, 1941 . . . . £75/£20
The Rissole Mystery, Rich & Cowan, 1941 . £75/£20
A Second Bout with the Mildew Gang, Eyre & Spottiswoode, 1942 . . . . £75/£20
Dinner in New York, Eyre & Spottiswoode, 1943 . .
. . . . £75/£20
The End of the Mildew Gang, Eyre & Spottiswoode, 1944 . . . . £75/£20
The Adventure of the Blue Room, Rich & Cowan, 1945 . . . . £75/£20
Too Much for Mr Jellipot, Eyre & Spotiswoode, 1945
. . . . £75/£20
Who Murdered Reynard?, Rich & Cowan, 1947 . .
. . . . £75/£20
With Cause Enough?, Harvill, 1954 . . £75/£20

Non Fiction
Police and Public: A Political Pamphlet, Fowler Wright, 1929 . . . . £20
The Life of Sir Walter Scott: A Biography, Poetry League, [1932] . . . . £35/£15
Should We Surrender Colonies?, Readers Library Publishing Co., [1939] £15

Translation
The Inferno From the Divine Comedy of Dante Alighieri, Fowler Wright, 1928 . . . . £100/£45

JOHN WYNDHAM
(b.1903 d.1969)

'Wyndham' is the pen name used by John Wyndham Parkes Lucas Beynon Harris, and he has written under several other variations of his name. He is best known for his peculiarly British science fiction novels.

Novels
The Secret People, Newnes, [1935] (pseud. 'John Beynon') . . . . £300/£75
ditto, Lancer (U.S.), 1964 (pseud. 'John Beynon Harris', wraps) £10
Foul Play Suspected, Newnes, [1935] (pseud. 'John Beynon') . . . . £300/£75
Planet Plane, Newnes, [1936] (pseud. 'John Beynon')
. . . . £250/£45
ditto, as *Stowaway to Mars*, Nova, 1953 (wraps) £45

The Day of The Triffids, Doubleday (U.S.), 1951 . .
. . . . £300/£35
ditto, Joseph, 1951. . . . . £600/£45
The Kraken Wakes, Joseph, 1953 . . . £175/£25
ditto, Ballantine (U.S.), 1953 (cloth). . . £150/£35
ditto, Ballantine (U.S.), 1953 (wraps) . . £20
Re-Birth, Ballantine (U.S.), 1955 (cloth) . £200/£35
ditto, Ballantine (U.S.), 1955 (wraps) . . £20
ditto, as *The Chrysalids*, Joseph, 1955 . £150/£20
The Midwich Cuckoos, Joseph, 1957 . . £200/£25
ditto, Ballantine (U.S.), 1957 . . . . . £75/£15
Trouble with Lichen, Joseph, 1960 . . . £75/£15
ditto, Ballantine (U.S.), 1960 (wraps) . . . £10
A John Wyndham Omnibus, Joseph, 1964 (*The Day of the Triffids, The Kraken Wakes, The Chrysalids*) . .
. . . . £35/£10
ditto, Simon & Schuster (U.S.), 1966 . . £35/£10
Chocky, Joseph, 1968 . . . . . . £35/£10
ditto, Ballantine (U.S.), 1968 (wraps) . . £10
Web, Joseph, 1979. . . . . . . £35/£10

Short Stories
Jizzle, Dennis Dobson, 1954 . . . . . £250/£30
Seeds of Time, Joseph, 1956 . . . . . £150/£20
Tales of Gooseflesh and Laughter, Ballantine (U.S.), 1956 (wraps) £10
The Outward Urge, Joseph, 1959 (with 'Lucas Parkes') . . . . £75/£15
ditto, Science Fiction Books Club, 1959 (1 extra story)
. . . . £30/£10
ditto, Ballantine (U.S.), 1959 (wraps) . . . £10
Consider Her Ways, Joseph, 1961 . . £35/£10
The Infinite Moment, Ballantine (U.S.), 1961 (wraps)
. . . . £10
The Best of John Wyndham, Sphere, 1973 (wraps) £5
ditto, as *The Man from Beyond*, Joseph, 1975 . £15/£5
Wanderers of Time, Coronet, 1973 (wraps). . . £5
ditto, Severn House, 1980. . . . . . £10/£5
Sleepers of Mars, Coronet, 1973 (wraps) . . £5
ditto, Severn House, 1980. . . . . . £10/£5
Exiles on Asperus, Coronet, 1979 (wraps) . . . £5
ditto, Severn House, 1979. . . . . . £10/£5

Others
Love in Time, Utopian Publications, 1946 (pseud. 'Johnson Harris', wraps) £50

W.B. YEATS
(b.1865 d.1939)

Irish poet and dramatist who was associated in his early career with the decadent movement of the 1890s.

Poetry
Mosada, A Dramatic Poem, printed by Sealy, Bryers and Walker, 1886 (wraps) £50,000

ditto, Cuala Press (Dublin), 1943 (50 copies, wraps in d/w) . . . . £1,500/£1,250

The Wanderings of Oisin and Other Poems, Kegan, Paul, Trench & Co., 1889 (500 copies, first binding in dark blue cloth) £2,000

ditto, Kegan, Paul, Trench & Co., 1889 (500 copies, later binding) £1,500

The Countess Kathleen, T. Fisher Unwin, 1892 (500 of 530 copies) £500

ditto, T. Fisher Unwin, 1892 (30 copies on vellum of 530) £3,000

The Land of Heart's Desire, T. Fisher Unwin, 1894 (500 copies, wraps, design by Aubrey Beardsley, presumed first state without two fleurons after 'Desire' on front cover) £1,000

ditto, T. Fisher Unwin, 1894 (presumed second state with two fleurons) £500

ditto, Stone & Kimball (U.S.), [1894] (450 copies in glazed boards, date incorrect on title-page as 1814, frontispiece by Aubrey Beardsley) £500

ditto, Mosher (U.S.), 1903 . . . . . £100

ditto, Mosher (U.S.), 1903 (100 copies on Japan paper) £1,000

ditto, Mosher (U.S.), 1903 (10 copies on vellum) £2,000

Poems, Unwin, 1895 (725 of 750 copies) . . £500

ditto, Unwin, 1895 (25 signed copies on Japan vellum) £5,000

ditto, Copeland & Day (U.S.), 1895 . . . . £500

The Wind Among the Reeds, Elkin Mathews, 1899 . . . . £450

ditto, Bodley Head (U.S.), 1899 . . . . . £300

The Shadowy Waters, Hodder & Stoughton, 1900 . . . . £175

ditto, Dodd, Mead (U.S.), 1901 . . . . . £150

In the Seven Woods, Dun Emer Press (Dundrum), 1903 (325 copies) £700

ditto, Macmillan (U.S.), 1903 . . . . £75

Poems, 1899-1905, Bullen, 1906. . . . . £250

The Golden Helmet, John Quinn (U.S.), 1908 (50 copies) £2,500

The Green Helmet, Cuala Press (Dundrum), 1910 (400 copies) £300

ditto, Macmillan (U.S.), 1912 . . . . . £50

Selections from the Love Poetry of William Butler Yeats, 1890-1911, Cuala Press (Dundrum), 1913 (300 copies) £125

Poems Written in Discouragement, Cuala Press (Dundrum), 1913 (100 copies) £3,000

Responsibilities: Poems and a Play, Cuala Press (Dundrum), 1914 (400 copies) £300

Easter, 1916, Clement Shorter, 1916 (25 copies signed by Shorter, wraps fastened by a silk cord) . . £150

Eight Poems, Morland Press, [1916] (8 copies on Dutch hand-made paper, wraps) £1,000

ditto, Morland Press, [1916] (70 copies on Japan vellum, wraps) £500

ditto, Morland Press, [1916] (170 copies on Italian hand-made paper, wraps) £350

The Wild Swans at Coole, Cuala Press (Dundrum), 1917 (400 copies) £300

ditto, Macmillan (U.S.), 1919 . . . . . £75

ditto, Macmillan, 1919 . . . . . . £75

Nine Poems, Clement Shorter, 1918 (25 copies, wraps) £150

Later Poems, Macmillan, 1922 . . . . £100/£50

ditto, Macmillan (U.S.), 1922 (250 signed copies) . . . . £1,000/£500

Seven Poems and a Fragment, (Dundrum), 1922 (500 copies) . . . . £300/£200

The Cat and the Moon and Certain Poems, Cuala Press (Dublin), 1924 (500 copies, no d/w) . £200

Early Poems and Stories, Macmillan, 1925. £200/£75

ditto, Macmillan (U.S.), 1925 . . . . £150/£100

ditto, Macmillan (U.S.), 1925 (250 signed copies) £500

October Blast, Cuala Press (Dublin), 1926 (350 copies) £250

The Tower, Macmillan, 1928. . . . . £1,000/£200

ditto, Macmillan (U.S.), 1928 . . . . £500/£100

Selected Poems, Lyrical and Narrative, Macmillan, 1929 . . . . £100/£35

Three Things, Faber, 1929 ('Ariel Poems', wraps) £75

ditto, Faber, 1929 (500 signed copies) . . £125

The Winding Stair, Fountain Press (U.S.), 1929 (642 signed copies) . . . . £650/£400

ditto, as *The Winding Stair And Other Poems*, Macmillan, 1933 . . . . £400/£200

The Collected Poems, Macmillan, 1933. . £75/£30

ditto, Macmillan (U.S.), 1933 . . . . £75/£30

The King of the Great Clock Tower, Cuala Press (Dublin), 1934 (400 copies). . . . . £375/£300

ditto, Macmillan (U.S.), 1935 . . . . £75/£25

A Full Moon in March, Macmillan, 1935 . £200/£75

New Poems, Cuala Press (Dublin), 1938 (450 copies) £200

Last Poems and Plays, Macmillan, 1940 . £75/£25

ditto, Macmillan, 1940 . . . . . £75/£25

Drama

Cathleen Ni Houlihan, Caradoc Press for A.H. Bullen, 1902 (300 of 308 copies) £750

ditto, Caradoc Press for A.H. Bullen, 1902 (8 copies on vellum of 308) £5,000

Where There Is Nothing: Being Volume One of Plays for an Irish Theatre, John Lane, 1902 (15 copies, wraps) £3,500

ditto, [John Lane], 1902 (30 numbered copies) . £3,000

ditto, Bullen, 1903. . . . . £100

ditto, Macmillan (U.S.), 1902 . . . . . £100

The Hour-Glass, Heinemann, 1903 (12 copies, the title-page serves as front cover). . . . £4,000

ditto, privately printed [Cuala Press] (Dublin), 1914 (50 copies, wraps) £1,000

The Hour-Glass, Cathleen Ni Houlihan, The Pot of Broth: Being Volume Two of Plays for an Irish Theatre, Bullen, 1904 . . . . £75

The King's Threshold, privately printed (U.S.), 1904 (100 copies, boards, glassine d/w, slipcase) . £1,000

ditto, privately printed (U.S.), 1904 (signed copies of
the 100, boards, glassine d/w, slipcase)   .   . £2,000
The King's Threshold: And on Baile's Strand: Being
Volume Three of Plays for an Irish Theatre, Bullen,
1904   .   .   .   .   £100
ditto, John Quinn (U.S.), 1904   .   .   .   .   £100
Deidre: Being Volume Five of Plays for an Irish
Theatre, Bullen, 1907 (first issue with printers'
imprint p.48) £100
ditto, Bullen, 1907 (second issue without printers'
imprint p.48) £50
The Unicorn from the Stars, Macmillan (U.S.), 1908
(with Lady Gregory). £100
Two Plays for Dancers, The Cuala Press (Dublin),
1919 (400 copies) £200
Michael Robartes and the Dancer, The Cuala Press
(Dundrum), 1920 (400 copies) £200
Four Plays for Dancers, Macmillan, 1921 (illustrated
by Dulac)   .   .   .   . £200/£125
ditto, Macmillan (U.S.), 1921   .   .   .   . £200/£125
The Player Queen, Macmillan, 1922 (wraps)   . £100
Plays in Prose and Verse, etc., Macmillan, 1922   .   .
.   .   .   . £100/£45
ditto, Macmillan (U.S.), 1924 (250 signed copies)   .   .
.   .   .   . £1,000/£500
ditto, Macmillan (U.S.), 1924   .   .   .   . £100/£45
Plays and Controversies, Macmillan, 1923 . £300/£100
ditto, Macmillan (U.S.), 1924 (250 signed copies,
slipcase)   .   .   .   . £600/£500
The Collected Plays, Macmillan, 1934   .   £75/£30
ditto, Macmillan (U.S.), 1935   .   .   .   £75/£30
Wheels and Butterflies, New Plays, Macmillan, 1934 .
.   .   .   . £75/£25
Nine One-Act Plays, Macmillan, 1937   .   . £75/£25

Novels
John Sherman and Dhoya, T. Fisher Unwin, 1891
(356 copies in boards) £1,500
ditto, T. Fisher Unwin, 1891 (wraps)   .   . . £1,500
The Speckled Bird, Cuala Press (Dublin), 1973-74 (2
vols, 500 numbered copies). £300

Short Stories
The Secret Rose, Lawrence and Bullen, 1897
(illustrated by Jack B. Yeats) £300
ditto, Dodd, Mead & Company (U.S.), 1897 (English
sheets). £250
The Tables of the Law, privately printed [Lawrence
and Bullen], 1897 (110 copies) £1,000
ditto, Elkin Mathews, 1904 (blue-grey boards) .   £200
ditto, Elkin Mathews, 1904 (green cloth)   .   . £175
ditto, Elkin Mathews, 1904 (wraps)   .   .   . £175
ditto, Shakespeare Head Press, 1904 (510 copies) £100
Stories of Red Hanrahan, Dun Emer Press (Dundrum),
1904 (500 copies) £200
Stories of Red Hanrahan: The Secret Rose: Rose
Alchemica, Bullen, 1913   .   .   .   .   . £125
ditto, Macmillan (U.S.), 1914   .   .   .   . £125

Essays
The Celtic Twilight, Lawrence and Bullen, 1893
(illustrated by Jack B. Yeats, first binding with the
name of the publishers on the spine in upper case)   .
.   .   .   .   £500
ditto, Lawrence and Bullen, 1893 (second binding with
the name of the publishers in lower case)   .   . £200
Ideas of Good and Evil, Bullen, 1903   .   .   . £100
Discoveries; a Volume of Essays, Dun Emer Press
(Dundrum), 1907 (200 copies) £350
Poetry and Ireland: Essays. Cuala Press (Dundrum),
1908 (250 copies) £400
The Cutting of an Agate, Macmillan (U.S.), 1912 £200
ditto, Macmillan, 1919   .   .   .   .   .   .   £75
Per Amica Silentia Lunae, Macmillan, 1918   . £100
ditto, Macmillan (U.S.), 1918   .   .   .   .   £100
Essays, Macmillan, 1924 .   .   .   .   . £250/£75
ditto, Macmillan (U.S.), 1924 (250 signed copies)   .   .
.   .   .   . £600
If I Were Four and Twenty, Cuala Press (Dublin),
1940 (450 copies) £300

Autobiography
Reveries Over Childhood and Youth, Cuala Press
(Dundrum), 1915 (425 copies, 2 vols including
portfolio). £400
ditto, Macmillan (U.S.), 1916 (1 vol, no portfolio) £75
ditto, Macmillan, 1916 (1 vol, no portfolio).   .   £75
Four Years, The Cuala Press (Dundrum), 1921 (400
copies)   .   .   .   . £300/£200
The Trembling of the Veil, T. Werner Laurie, 1922
(1,000 signed copies)   .   .   .   .   . £900/£500
ditto, Macmillan (U.S.), 1922   .   .   .   . £100/£45
ditto, Macmillan (U.S.), 1924 (250 signed copies)   .   .
.   .   .   . £1,000/£500
A Vision, Macmillan, 1925 (600 signed copies)   .   .
.   .   .   . £400/£250
ditto, Macmillan, 1937   .   .   .   .   . £150/£75
Autobiographies: Reveries Over Childhood and Youth
and The Trembling of the Veil, Macmillan, 1926   .
.   .   .   . £100/£45
ditto, Macmillan (U.S.), 1927 (250 signed copies) £500
ditto, Macmillan, 1927   .   .   .   .   . £100/£45
Dramatis Personae, Cuala Press (Dublin), 1935 (400
copies) £300
ditto, Macmillan (U.S.), 1936   .   .   .   . £75/£25
ditto, Macmillan, 1936   .   .   .   .   . £75/£25

Miscellaneous
Is the Order of R.R. & A.C. to Remain a Magical
Order?, [privately printed for the Order Rubidae
Rosae & Aureae Crucis, a section of the Order of the
Golden Dawn], 1901 (wraps) £5,000
Collected Works in Prose and Verse, Shakespeare
Head Press, 1908 (8 vols, 1,060 copies, half vellum
and cloth). £1,250
ditto, Shakespeare Head Press, 1908 (remainder
binding cloth and boards) £500

Synge and the Ireland of His Time, Cuala Press (Dundrum), 1911 (350 copies) £350
The Bounty of Sweden, Cuala Press (Dublin), 1925 (400 copies, glassine d/w) . . . . . £200/£150
Estrangement, Cuala Press (Dublin), 1926 (300 copies) £250
The Death of Synge and Other Passages from an Old Diary, Cuala Press (Dublin), 1928 (400 copies) . . . . £250/£175
A Packet for Ezra Pound, Cuala Press (Dublin), 1929 (425 copies, glassine d/w) . . . . . £400/£350
On the Boiler, Cuala Press (Dublin), 1939 (all but four copies of the first edition destroyed so second edition considered, wraps) £150
Letters on Poetry from W.B. Yeats to Dorothy Wellesley, O.U.P., 1940 . . . . . . £125/£35
Pages from a Diary Written in Nineteen Hundred and Thirty, Cuala Press (Dublin), 1944 (280 copies) £200
The Letters, Hart-Davis, 1954 . . . . £30/£10

Edited by Yeats

Fairy and Folk Tales of the Irish Peasantry, Walter Scott, 1888 . . . . £300
Irish Fairy Tales, Fisher Unwin, 1892 (illustrated by Jack B. Yeats) £300
ditto, Cassell (U.S.), 1892. . . . . . . £200
The Poems of William Blake, Lawrence & Bullen, 1893 . . . . £200
ditto, Scribner's (U.S.), 1893 . . . . . . £200

THE YELLOW BOOK

A literary and art periodical considered to be outrageous and decadent in its day. Many contributors went on to become major literary figures. It was Aubrey Beardsley's distinctive artwork that upset most commentators.

Volume 1, Matthews & Lane, April, 1894 . . £50
Volume 2, Matthews & Lane, July, 1894 . . £45
Volume 3, Lane/Bodley Head, October, 1894 . £45
Volume 4, Lane/Bodley Head, January, 1895 . £45
Volume 5, Lane/Bodley Head, April, 1895 . . £25
Volume 6, Lane/Bodley Head, July, 1895 . . £25
Volume 7, Lane/Bodley Head, October, 1895 . £25
Volume 8, Lane/Bodley Head, January, 1896 . £25
Volume 9, Lane/Bodley Head, April, 1896 . . £25
Volume 10, Lane/Bodley Head, July, 1896 . . £25
Volume 11, Lane/Bodley Head, October, 1896 . £25
Volume 12, Lane/Bodley Head, January, 1897 . £25
Volume 13, Lane/Bodley Head, April, 1897 . £25
Complete set (evenly coloured spines) . . . £850

APPENDIX I
SINGLE TITLE ENTRIES

EDWARD ABBEY (b.1927 d.1989)
The Brave Cowboy: An Old Tale in a New Time,
Dodd, Mead & Co. (U.S.), 1956 . . £3,000/£350
ditto, Eyre and Spottiswoode, 1957 . . £600/£60

CHINUA ACHEBE (b.1930)
Things Fall Apart, Heinemann, 1958 . . £150/£45
ditto, Obolensky (U.S.), 1959 . . . . £100/£20

W. HARRISON AINSWORTH (b.1805 d.1882)
The Tower of London, Bentley, 1840 (13 parts in 12,
wraps). £650
ditto, Bentley, 1840 . . . . £450
ditto, Lea & Blanchard (U.S.), 1841 . . . . £200

EDWARD ALBEE (b.1928)
Who's Afraid of Virginia Woolf?, Atheneum (U.S.),
1962 . . . . £300/£35
ditto, Cape, 1964 . . . . £100/£10

LOUISA MAY ALCOTT (b.1832 d.1888)
Little Women, Roberts Bros (U.S.), 1868 . . £6,000
ditto, Sampson Low, 1868 . . . . . £300
Little Women Part 2, Roberts Bros (U.S.), 1869 £4,500
ditto, as *Good Wives*, Sampson Low, 1869 . . £200

NELSON ALGREN (b.1908 d.1981)
Never Come Morning, Harper's (U.S.), 1942 £250/£30
ditto, Spearman, 1958. . . . . . . £65/£10

JAMES BALDWIN (b.1924 d.1987)
Go Tell It On The Mountain, Knopf (U.S.), 1953 . .
. . . . £2,000/£200
ditto, Joseph, 1954. . . . . £200/£25

RICHARD HARRIS BARHAM (b.1788 d.1845)
The Ingoldsby Legends, Bentley, 1840, 1842, 1847 (3
vols) £750

STAN BARSTOW (b.1928)
A Kind of Loving, Joseph, 1960 . . . . £35/£10
ditto, Doubleday (U.S.), 1961. . . . . . £15/£5

WILLIAM BECKFORD (b.1759 d.1844)
An Arabian Tale, Johnson, 1786 (a.k.a. *Vathek*,
anonymous) £1,000

THOMAS BEWICK (b.1753 d.1828)
A General History of Quadrupeds, Bewick, Beilby &
Hodgson, 1790 . . . . £650

R.D. BLACKMORE (b.1825 d.1900)
Lorna Doone, Sampson Low & Marston, 1869 (3 vols)
. . . . £3,000

WILLIAM BLAKE (b.1757 d.1827)
Songs of Innocence and Experience, 1789 . £200,000

ROLF BOLDREWOOD (b.1826 d.1915)
Robbery Under Arms, Remington, 1888 (3 vols) . .
. . . . £1,500

GEORGE BORROW (b.1803 d.1881)
Wild Wales, Murray, 1862 (3 vols) £300

JAMES BOSWELL (b.1740 d.1795)
The Life of Samuel Johnson, Baldwin, Dilly, 1791 (2
vols with 'gve' on p.235 of first volume) . . £4,000

E.R. BRAITHWAITE (b.1922)
To Sir, With Love, Bodley Head, 1959 . . £75/£10
ditto, Prentice-Hall (U.S.), 1959 . . . . £75/£10

RICHARD BRAUTIGAN (b.1935 d.1984)
The Return of the Rivers, Inferno Press (U.S.), 1958
(wraps) £1,500

PEARL BUCK (b.1892 d.1973)
East Wind, West Wind, John Day (U.S.), 1930. . .
. . . . £100/£15
ditto, Methuen, 1931 . . . . . . £75/£10

EDWARD BULWER LYTTON (b.1803 d.1873)
The Last Days of Pompeii, Bentley, 1834 (anonymous,
3 vols) £750
ditto, Harper's (U.S), 1834 . . . . . . £300

JOHN BUNYAN (b.1628 d.1688)
The Pilgrim's Progress, Nath. Ponder, Peacock, 1678.
. . . . £100,000

W.R. BURNETT (b.1899 d.1982)
Little Caesar, Dial Press (U.S.), 1929 . £750/£150

FANNY BURNEY (b.1752 d.1840)
Evelina, or A Young Lady's Entrance into the World,
Lowndes, 1778 (anonymous, 3 vols) . . . £6,000
Cecilia, or Memoires of an Heiress, Payne & Cadell,
1782 ('By the Author of Evelina', 5 vols) . . £1,000

SAMUEL BUTLER (b.1835 d.1902)
Erewhon or Over the Range, Trubner & Co, 1872
(anonymous) £250
The Way of All Flesh, Grant Richards, 1903 . £200

JAMES M. CAIN (b.1892 d.1977)
The Postman Always Rings Twice, Knopf (U.S.), 1934
. . . . £2,000/£200
ditto, Cape, 1934 . . . . . . £1,000/£10
Mildred Pierce, Knopf (U.S.), 1941 . . . £400/£40
ditto, Hale, 1943 . . . . £45/£10

ERSKINE CALDWELL (b.1903 d.1987)
Tobacco Road, Scribner's (U.S.), 1932 . £1,000/£100
ditto, Cresset Press, 1933 . . . . . . £125/£20

LOUIS-FERDINAND CÉLINE (b.1894 d.1961)
Journey to the End of the Night, Chatto & Windus,
1934 (translated by John Marks) . . . £250/£30
ditto, Little, Brown (U.S.), 1934 . . . . £200/£25

ERSKINE CHILDERS (b.1870 d.1922)
The Riddle of the Sands, Smith Elder, 1903 . £4,000
ditto, Dodd Mead (U.S.), 1915 . . . . . £250

SAMUEL TAYLOR COLERIDGE (b.1772
d.1834)
Lyrical Ballads, Longman, 1798 . . . . £12,500

RICHARD CONDON (b.1915 d.1996)
The Manchurian Candidate, McGraw-Hill (U.S.),
1959 . . . . £150/£25
ditto, Joseph, 1960 . . . . £35/£10

WILLIAM CONGREVE (b.1670 d.1729)
The Way of the World, Tonson, 1700 . . . £2,000

PAT CONROY (b.1946)
The Boo, McClure Press (U.S.), 1970 . £2,000/£50

STEPHEN CRANE (b.1871 d.1900)
The Red Badge of Courage, Appleton (U.S.), 1895 .
. . . . £2,000
ditto, Heinemann, 1896 . . . . £500

W. H. DAVIES (b.1871 d.1940)
The Autobiography of a Super-Tramp, Fifield, 1908 .
. . . . £100

THOMAS DE QUINCEY (b.1785 d.1859)
Confessions of an English Opium Eater, Taylor &
Hessey, 1822 . . . . £1,500

JOHN DOS PASSOS (b.1896 d.1970)
The Three Soldiers, Doran (U.S.), 1921. £2,000/£200

CHARLES M. DOUGHTY (b.1843 d.1926)
Travels in Arabia Deserta, C.U.P., 1888 (2 vols) . .
. . . . £1,750

RALPH ELLISON (b.1914 d.1994)
Invisible Man, Random House (U.S.), 1952 . . .
. . . . £1,500/£350
ditto, Gollancz, 1953 . . . . £400/£50

EDWARD FITZGERALD (b.1809 d.1883)
Rubáiyát of Omar Khayyám, Quaritch, 1859 £20,000

JOHN GAY (b.1685 d.1732)
The Beggar's Opera, Watts, 1728 . . . . £750

OLIVER GOLDSMITH (b.1730 d.1774)
The Vicar of Wakefield, Newbery, 1766 (2 vols,
anonymous) £2,500
ditto, Mentz (U.S), 1772 . . . . £1,250

NADINE GORDIMER (b.1923)
Face to Face, Silver Leaf Books (Johannesburg), 1949
. . . . £500/£50

GÜNTER GRASS (b.1927)
Die Blechtrommel, Luchterland (Germany), 1958 . .
. . . . £400/£40
ditto, as *The Tin Drum*, Secker & Warburg, 1962
(translated by Ralph Manheim) . . . . £40/£10
ditto, Pantheon Books, 1962 . . . . . £40/£10

JOHN GRAY (b.1866 d.1934)
Silverpoints, Elkin Mathews & John Lane, 1893 (250
numbered copies) £1,500

ZANE GREY (b.1872 d.1939)
Betty Zane, Charles Francis Press (U.S.), 1903 . £1,500
The Last of the Plainsmen, The Outing Publishing
Company (U.S.), 1908 . . . . £300

SUSAN HILL (b.1942)
The Enclosure, Hutchinson, 1961 . . . £125/£25
Do Me a Favour, Hutchinson, 1963 . . . £125/£25

TONY HILLERMAN (b.1925)
The Blessing Way, Harper & Row (U.S.), 1970 . .
. . . . £600/£50

E. T. A. HOFFMANN (b.1776 d.1822)
The Devil's Elixir, Blackwood & Cadell, 1824 (2 vols)
. . . . £350
Hoffmann's Strange Stories from the German,
Burnham Brothers (U.S.), 1855 . . . . £350
Hoffmann's Fairy Tales, Burnham Brothers (U.S.),
1857 . . . . £350

HEINRICH HOFFMANN (b.1809 d.1894)
*The English Struwwelpeter, or Pretty Stories and
Funny Pictures for Little Children*, Leipzig, 1848
(first English edition) £4,000

ANTHONY HOPE (b.1863 d.1933)
The Prisoner of Zenda, Arrowsmith, 1894 (first issue
with 16 titles advertised in the 3/6 list at rear of book)
. . . . £250

L. RON HUBBARD (b.1911 d.1986)
Buckskin Brigade, Macauley (U.S.), 1937 £2,000/£500
ditto, Wright & Brown, [1938] . . . £1,250/£200

W.H. HUDSON (b.1841 d.1922)
The Purple Land, Sampson Low, 1885 (2 vols) . .
. . . . £1,000

LANGSTON HUGHES (b.1902 d.1967)
The Weary Blues, Knopf (U.S.), 1926 (first issue d/w
without blurb for *Fine Clothes to the Jew*) . . .
. . . . £3,500/£200
ditto, Knopf (U.S.), 1926 (second issue d/w with blurb)
. . . . £2,000/£200

THOMAS HUGHES (b.1822 d.1896)
Tom Brown's Schooldays, Macmillan, 1857 . £750

SHIRLEY JACKSON (b.1916 d.1965)
The Haunting of Hill House, Viking (U.S.), 1959. .
. . . . £500/£50
ditto, Joseph, 1960. . . . . £200/£30

LIONEL JOHNSON (b.1867 d.1902)
Poems, Elkin Mathews/Copeland & Day, 1895 (25
signed copies) £4,000
ditto, Elkin Mathews/Copeland & Day, 1895 (750
copies) £500

SAMUEL JOHNSON (b.1709 d.1784)
A Dictionary of the English Language, various
publishers, 1755 (2 vols) £10,000

BEN JONSON (b.1572 d.1637)
The Workes of Benjamin Jonson, [first volume], Will
Stansby, 1616 . . . . £3,500
ditto, [second volume], Richard Meighen, 1640 £1,500

NIKOS KAZANTZAKIS (b.1885 d.1957)
Zorba the Greek, Lehman, 1952 . . . . £200/£25
ditto, Simon & Schuster (U.S.), 1953 . . £125/£15

CHARLES KINGSLEY (b.1819 d.1875)
The Water Babies, Macmillan, 1863 (first issue,
containing 'L'Envoi') £750

CHARLES LAMB (b.1775 d.1834)
Tales From Shakespeare, Hodgkins, 1807 (2 vols) .
. . . . £2,000

MATTHEW GREGORY LEWIS (b.1775
d.1818)
The Monk, Bell, [March] 1796 (first issue with 'In
Three Volumes' *above* quotation on title page, 3 vols)
. . . . £3,000
ditto, Bell, [April] 1796 (second issue with 'In Three
Volumes' *below* quotation on title page, 3 vols) . .
. . . . £1,750

SINCLAIR LEWIS (b.1885 d.1951)
Main Street: The Story of Carol Kennicott, Harcourt,
Brace and Howe (U.S.), 1920 . . . £1,500/£200

ANITA LOOS (b.1893 d.1981)
Gentlemen Prefer Blondes, Boni & Liveright (U.S.),
1925 (first issue with 'Divine' for 'Devine' on
contents page) . . . . £250/£65
ditto, Brentano's, 1926 . . . . . . £40/£15
ditto, Brentano's, 1926 (1,000 signed copies) . £125

RICHARD MARSH (b.1857 d.1915)
The Beetle, Skeffington, 1897 . . . . . £500

Rev. C.R. MATURIN (b.1782 d.1824)
Melmoth the Wanderer, Constable, 1820 (4 vols) . .
. . . . £1,750

HERMAN MELVILLE (b.1819 d.1891)
The Whale, Bentley, 1851 (3 vols) . . . £75,000
ditto, as *Moby Dick*, Harper (U.S.), 1851 . £15,000

JAMES A MICHENER (b.1907 d.1997)
Tales of the South Pacific, Macmillan (U.S.), 1947 .
. . . . £750/£100

JOHN MILTON (b.1608 d.1674)
Paradise Lost, Parker, 1667 . . . . . £30,000
Paradise Regain'd, Starkey, 1671 . . . . £1,500

BILL NAUGHTON (b.1910 d.1992)
Alfie, MacGibbon & Kee, 1966 . . . . £75/£10

TIM O'BRIEN (b.1946)
If I Die In A Combat Zone, Delacorte (U.S.), 1973 .
. . . . £1,500/£200
ditto, Calder & Boyars, 1973 . . . . . £200/£25

BARONESS ORCZY (b.1865 d.1947)
The Scarlet Pimpernel, Greening, 1905 . . . £600

WALKER PERCY (b.1916 d.1990)
The Moviegoer, Knopf (U.S.), 1961 . . . £750/£100
ditto, Eyre & Spottiswoode, 1963 . . . £300/£35

JOHN POLIDORI (b.1795 d.1821)
The Vampyre, Sherwood, Neely & Jones, 1819 . .
. . . . £2,500

ALEXANDER POPE (b.1688 d.1744)
The Rape of the Lock, Lintott, 1714 (wraps) . £5,000

COLE PORTER (b.1893 d.1964)
Red Hot and Blue, Random House (U.S.), 1936 (300
signed deluxe copies) . . . . £2,000/£1,000

ELEANOR H. PORTER (b.1868 d.1920)
Pollyanna, Page (U.S.), 1913 . . . . . £350
ditto, Pitman, 1913 . . . . £150

MARIO PUZO (b.1920)
The Godfather, Putnam (U.S.), 1969 . . £750/£75
ditto, Heinemann, 1969 . . . . . £45/£15

THOMAS PYNCHON (b.1937)
V, Lippincott (U.S.), 1963 (first issue d/w without
reviews) . . . . £1,250/£200
ditto, Cape, 1963 . . . . £250/£30

AYN RAND (b.1905 d.1982)
We The Living, Macmillan (U.S.), 1936 £2,000/£250
ditto, Cassell, 1936 . . . . . . £1,750/£150

CHARLES READE (b.1814 d.1884)
The Cloister and the Hearth, Trubner, 1861 (4 vols) .
. . . . £1,250

SAMUEL RICHARDSON (b.1689 d.1761)
Pamela, Rivington, 1741-1742 (4 vols) . . . £5,000

CHRISTINA ROSSETTI (b.1830 d.1894)
Goblin Market, Macmillan, 1862 . . . . £1,250

DANTE GABRIEL ROSSETTI (b.1828 d.1882)
Poems, privately printed, 1869 (wraps) . . . £2,000
ditto, Ellis, 1870 . . . . £450

HENRY ROTH (b.1906 d.1995)
Call It Sleep, Ballou (U.S.), 1934 . . £4,000/£600
ditto, Joseph, 1963. . . . . £250/£30

PHILIP ROTH (b.1933)
Goodbye, Columbus and *Five Short Stories*, Houghton
Mifflin (U.S.), 1959 . . . . . . £500/£75
ditto, Deutsch, 1959 . . . . . . £150/£25

ANTOINE DE SAINT-EXUPÉRY (b.1900
d.1944)
The Little Prince, Reynel & Hitchcock (U.S.), 1943 .
. . . . £400/£75
ditto, Reynel & Hitchcock (U.S.), 1943 (500 copies) .
. . . . £1,500/£750
ditto, Heinemann, 1945 . . . . . £300/£65

SIR WALTER SCOTT (b.1771 d.1832)
Ivanhoe, Constable, 1820 (3 vols) £500

RONALD SEARLE (b.1920)
Hurrah for St Trinian's!, Macdonald, 1948 £50/£10
ditto, Macdonald (U.S.), 1948 . . . . £35/£10

DR SEUSS (b.1904 d.1991)
The Cat in the Hat, Random House (U.S.), 1957 with
'200/200' printed on inner flap of d/w, unglazed
boards) . . . . £750/£125
ditto, Hutchinson, 1957 . . . . . £125/£35

PETER SHAFFER (b.1926 d.2001)
Equus, Deutsch, 1973. . . . . . . £75/£15
ditto, Atheneum (U.S.), 1974. . . . . £45/£10

PERCY BYSSHE SHELLEY (b.1792 d.1822)
Queen Mab, privately printed, 1812 (with title page) .
. . . . £20,000
ditto, privately printed, 1812 (without title page) .
. . . . £1,000
Poetical Works, Kelmscott Press (1894-1895) (250
copies, 3 vols) £2,000

EDMUND SPENSER (b.1552 d.1599)
The Faerie Queen, Ponsonbie, 1590-1596 (2 vols) .
. . . . £20,000

WALLACE STEVENS (b.1879 d.1955)
Harmonium, Knopf (U.S.), 1923 (first binding in
chequered boards) . . . . . . £3,000/£600
ditto, Knopf (U.S.), 1923 (second binding in striped
boards) . . . . £2,000/£250
ditto, Knopf (U.S.), 1923 (third binding in blue cloth) .
. . . . £1,250/£100
Ideas of Order, Alcestis (U.S.), 1935 (135 signed
copies, glassine d/w, slipcase) . . £2,000/£1,000
ditto, Knopf (U.S.), 1936 . . . . . £750/£75

REX STOUT (b.1886 d.1975)
Fer-de-Lance, Farrar & Rinehart (U.S.), 1934 . . .
. . . . £5,000/£600
ditto, Cassell, 1935 . . . . . . £2,000/£250

HARRIET BEECHER STOWE (b.1811 d.1896)
Uncle Tom's Cabin, Jewett (U.S.), 1852 (2 vols,
wraps). £7,500
ditto, Cassell, 1852 . . . . £1,250

WILLIAM STYRON (b.1925)
Lie Down in Darkness, Bobbs-Merrill (U.S.), 1951 .
. . . . £200/£30

PATRICK SUSKIND (b.1949)
Perfume: The Story of a Murderer, Hamilton, 1986
(translated by John E. Woods.) . . . . £45/£15
ditto, Knopf (U.S.), 1986 . . . . . £45/£15

ELIZABETH TAYLOR (b.1912 d.1976)
At Mrs Lippincote's, Davies, 1945 . . . £200/£25
ditto, Knopf (U.S.), 1946 . . . . . £100/£15

B. TRAVEN (b.1882 d.1969)
The Treasure of the Sierra Madre, Chatto & Windus,
1934 . . . . £2,000/£200
ditto, Knopf (U.S.), 1935 . . . . . £1,000/£75

ANNE TYLER (b.1941)
If Morning Ever Comes, Knopf (U.S.), 1964 . . .
. . . . £1,000/£75
ditto, Chatto & Windus, 1965 . . . . £250/£30

S.S. VAN DINE (b.1880 d.1939)
The Benson Murder Case, Scribner's (U.S.), 1926 .
. . . . £3,000/£200

ROBERT PENN WARREN (b.1905 d.1989)
All The King's Men, Harcourt, Brace & Co. (U.S.),
1946 . . . . £1,250/£100

NATHANIEL WEST (b.1903 d.1940)
Miss Lonelyhearts, Liveright (U.S.), 1933 £4,000/£450

GILBERT WHITE (b.1720 d.1793)
The Natural History and Antiquities of Selbourne,
Bensley/White, 1789. . . . . £2,000

LAURA INGALLS WILDER (b.1867 d.1957)
The Little House on the Prairie, Harper (U.S.), 1935 .
. . . . £350/£75
ditto, Methuen, 1957 . . . . £150/£20

COLIN WILSON (b.1931)
The Outsider, Gollancz, 1956 . . . . £100/£15
ditto, Houghton Mifflin (U.S.), 1956 . . £75/£15

LEONARD WOOLF (b.1880 d.1969)
The Village in the Jungle, Arnold (U.S.), 1913 . .
. . . . £250/£25
ditto, Harcourt Brace (U.S.), 1926 . . . £50/£10

APPENDIX II
REFERENCES

Although the author-specific bibliographies represent the best sources of information on particular authors and their work, the following general reference works were also used in the compilation of this Guide.

Ahearn, Allen and Patricia, *Collected Books, A Guide to their Values, 2002 Edition*, Putnam's, 2001.
Bédé, Jean-Albert, and Edgerton, William B., eds., *Columbia Dictionary of Modern European Literature*, Columbia Univ. Press, 1980.
Breese, Martin, *Breese's Guide to Modern First Editions, 2000 Edition*, Breese Books, 1999.
Browning, D.C. (ed.), *Everyman's Dictionary of Literary Biography*, Everyman, 1970.
Bruccoli, Matthew J. et al., *First Printings of American Authors, Vols 1-5*, Gale Research, 1977-1987.
Cole, Michael (ed.), *Annual Register of Book Values, Modern First Editions*, The Clique (various editions).
Connolly, Joseph, *Modern First Editions*, Little, Brown, 1993.
Cooper, John, and Pike, B.A., *Detective Fiction: The Collector's Guide*, Scolar Press, 1994 (second edition).
Currey, Lloyd, *Science Fiction and Fantasy Authors, A Bibliography of First Printings of Their Fiction*, G.K. Hall, 1979. Updated by Rb Publishing, 2002 (cd rom).
Cutler and Stiles, *Modern British Authors, Their First Editions*, Allen & Unwin, 1930.
Foord, Peter and Williams, Richard, *Collins Crime Club: A Checklist of the First Editions*, Dragonby Press, 1999 (second edition).
Hamer, Martin, *The Hamer Comic Annual Guide*, Hamer 20th Century Books, 2000. Also *Comic Annual Supplement* No.2, 2002.
Hubin, Allen J., *The Bibliography of Crime Fiction, 1749-1975*, Publisher's Inc., 1979.
Jackson, Crispin (ed.), *The Book and Magazine Collector*, Diamond Publishing, various issues.
Jackson, Crispin (ed.), *Collecting Children's Books*, Book and Magazine Collector, 1995.
McBride, Bill and Arledge, Amy A., *Points of Issue: A Compendium of Points of Issue of Books by 19th-20th Century Authors*, McBride, 1996 (third edition, wraps).
Nehr, Ellen, *Doubleday Crime Club Compendium, 1928-1991*, Offspring Press, 1992.
Ousby, Ian (ed.), *The Cambridge Guide to Literature in English*, Guild Publishing, 1989.
Smiley, Kathryn (ed.), *Firsts: The Book Collector's Magazine*, Firsts (various issues).
Ward, K. Anthony, *First Editions, A Field Guide*, Scolar Press, 1994.
Woodcock, George, *20th-Century Fiction*, Macmillan, 1983.

On-line Resources
Abebooks: www.Abebooks.com
Bodhran Books: www.Bodhranbooks.com
British Library Public Catalogue: www.blpc.bl.uk
Fantastic Fiction: www.fantasticfiction.co.uk
The Library of Congress: www.loc.gov

Individual Author Bibliographies

ANTHONY ABBOT
Detective Fiction: The Collector's Guide, by John Cooper and B.A. Pike, Scolar Press, 1994, pps13-14.
PETER ABRAHAMS
Peter Abrahams, by Michael Wade, Evans Brothers, 1972.
20th-Century Fiction, by George Woodcock, Macmillan, 1983.
J.R. ACKERLEY
Ackerley - A Life of J.R. Ackerley, by Peter Parker, Constable, 1994.
'J.R.Ackerley, Author and Editor', by Colin Wiles, *Book and Magazine Collector*, No. 152, November 1996, pps.28-36.
PETER ACKROYD
'Peter Ackroyd', by Crispin Jackson, *Book and Magazine Collector*, No.97, April 1992, pps.49-55.
DOUGLAS ADAMS
Don't Panic: Douglas Adams and the Hitch-Hiker's Guide to the Galaxy, by Neil Gaiman, Titan, 1993.
RICHARD ADAMS
'Richard Adams', by June Hopper, *Book and Magazine Collector*, No.187, October 1999, pps.16-27.
CHAS ADDAMS
'Chas Addams', by Richard Dalby, *Book and Magazine Collector*, No.103, October 1992, pps.65-73.
JAMES AGEE
James Agee, by Victor A. Kramer, Twayne/Gale, 1975.
ROBERT AICKMAN
Robert Aickman: An Introduction, by Gary William Crawford, Gothic Press, 2003.
CONRAD AIKEN
Conrad Aiken: A Bibliography, (1902-1978), by F.W. and F.C. Bonnell, Huntington Library, 1982.
JOAN AIKEN
'The Children's Books of Joan Aiken', by Daphne Stroud, *Book and Magazine Collector*, No.102, September 1992, pps.37-45.
ALAIN-FOURNIER
Alain-Fournier: A Brief Life, by David Arkell, Carcanet, 1996.
'Alain-Fournier', by Martin Spence, *Book and Magazine Collector*, No.149, August 1996, pps.65-73.
ALASTAIR
Alastair, by Victor Arwas, Thames and Hudson, 1979.

CECIL ALDIN
Cecil Aldin, The Story of a Sporting Artist, by Roy
Heron, Webb & Bowe, 1981.
RICHARD ALDINGTON
*A Bibliography of the Works of Richard Aldington
from 1915 to 1948*, by Alister Kershaw, The
Quadrant Press, 1950.
BRIAN ALDISS
Brian Aldiss, A Bibliography, 1954-62, by Margaret
Manson, Dryden Press, 1962.
MARGERY ALLINGHAM
*Ink in Her Blood: The Life & Crime Fiction of
Margery Allingham*, by Richard Martin, U.M.I.
Research Press, 1988.
ERIC AMBLER
Eric Ambler, by Peter Lewis, Continuum, [n.d.,
c.1990.]
'Heroes Among Us: Eric Ambler's Novels of
Intrigue', by Katherine Kominis, *Firsts: The Book
Collector's Magazine*, June 1993, Vol.3, No.6,
pps.24-19.
KINGSLEY AMIS
Kingsley Amis, A Checklist, by Jack Benoit Gohn,
Kent State Univ. Press, 1976.
MARTIN AMIS
*Bruce Chatwin, Martin Amis, Julian Barnes, A
Bibliography of their First Editions*, by David Rees,
Colophon Press, 1992.
SHERWOOD ANDERSON
Sherwood Anderson: A Bibliography, by Eugene
Sheehy and Kenneth Lohf, The Talisman Press, 1960.
MAYA ANGELOU
bodhranbooks.com
EDWARD ARDIZZONE
*Edward Ardizzone, a preliminary hand-list of His
Illustrated Books (1929-1970)*, by Brian Alderson,
The Private Library, second series, Vol.5, No.1,
Spring 1972.
MICHAEL ARLEN
Michael Arlen, by Henry Keyishian, Twayne, 1975.
DAISY ASHFORD
Daisy Ashford - Her Life, by R.M. Malcomson,
Chatto & Windus/Hogarth Press, 1984.
ISAAC ASIMOV
*Science Fiction and Fantasy Authors, A
Bibliography of First Printings of Their Fiction*, by
Lloyd Currey, Rb Publishing, 2002 (cd rom.)
MABEL LUCIE ATTWELL
Mabel Lucie Attwell, by Chris Beetles, Joseph, 1988.
MARGARET ATWOOD
'A Preliminary Checklist of Writings by and About
Margaret Atwood', by Alan J. Horne, *Malahat
Review*, No.41, Univ. of Victoria, 1977.
W.H. AUDEN
W.H. Auden: A Bibliography 1924-69, by B.C.
Bloomfield and Edward Mendelson, Univ. of Virginia
Press, 1973.

JANE AUSTEN
Jane Austen: A Bibliography by Geoffrey Keynes,
Nonesuch Press, 1929.
REV. W. AWDRY & CHRISTOPHER AWDRY
The Thomas the Tank Engine Man, by Brian Sibley,
Heinemann, 1995.
ALAN AYCKBOURN
*Twenty Modern British Playwrights: A
Bibliography, 1956-1976*, by Kimball King, Garland,
1977.
Alan Ayckbourn, Grinning at the Edge, by Paul
Allen, Methuen, 2001.
'BB'
BB: A Celebration, by Tom Quinn (ed.), including a
Bibliography by Tim Scott, Wharncliffe Publishing,
1993.
H.C. BAILEY
Detective Fiction: The Collector's Guide, by John
Cooper and B.A. Pike, Scolar Press, 1994, pps.21-23.
BERYL BAINBRIDGE
'Beryl Bainbridge', by Martin Spence, *Book and
Magazine Collector*, No.134, May 1995, pps.18-26.
R.M. BALLANTYNE
R.M. Ballantyne, A Bibliography of First Editions,
by Eric Quayle, Dawsons of Pall Mall, 1968.
J. G. BALLARD
*Science Fiction and Fantasy Authors, A
Bibliography of First Printings of Their Fiction*, by
Lloyd Currey, Rb Publishing, 2002 (cd rom.)
IAIN BANKS
'Ian Banks', by David Howard, *Book and Magazine
Collector*, No.148, July 1996, pps.76-85.
HELEN BANNERMAN
Sambo Sahib, The Story of Helen Bannerman, by
Elizabeth Hay, Paul Harris, 1981.
JOHN BANVILLE
bodhranbooks.com
CLIVE BARKER
Shadows in Eden, by Clive Barker and Stephen
Jones, Underwood, 1991.
PAT BARKER
'Pat Barker', by Jane Roscoe, *Book and Magazine
Collector*, No.176, November 1998, pps.86-94.
ROBERT BARNARD
Detective Fiction: The Collector's Guide, by John
Cooper and B.A. Pike, Scolar Press, 1994, pps.23-25.
DJUNA BARNES
Djuna Barnes: A Bibliography, by Douglas Messeri,
David Lewis, 1975.
JULIAN BARNES
*Bruce Chatwin, Martin Amis, Julian Barnes, A
Bibliography of their First Editions*, David Rees,
Colophon Press, 1992.
J.M. BARRIE
Sir James M. Barrie: A Bibliography, by B.D.
Cutler, Franklin, 1931.
H.E. BATES
A Bibliographical Study, by Peter Eades, St Paul's
Bibliographies, 1990.

L. FRANK BAUM
Bibliographia Oziana, by Douglas G. Greene and Peter Hanff, The International Wizard of Oz Club, 1988.

THE BEANO
The Hamer Comic Annual Guide, No.1, by Martin Hamer, Hamer 20th Century Books, 2000.

AUBREY BEARDSLEY
Aubrey Beardsley, Catalogue of Drawings and Bibliography, by A.E. Gallatin, Appel [n.d.].

SAMUEL BECKETT
No Symbols Where None Intended, Carlton Lake, Humanities Research Center, 1984.

FRANCIS BEEDING
'Hilary Saunders and Francis Beeding', by A.R. James, *Book and Magazine Collector*, No.152, November 1996, pps.52-62.

MAX BEERBOHM
A Bibliography of the Works of Max Beerbohm, by A.E. Gallatin and L.M. Oliver, Hart-Davis, 1952.

BRENDAN BEHAN
Brendan, by Ulick O'Connor, Prentice Hall, 1971.

HILLAIRE BELLOC
The English First Editions of Hillaire Belloc, by Patrick Cahill, published in London, 1953.

SAUL BELLOW
Bellow: A Comprehensive Bibliography, by B.A. Sokoloff and Mark E. Posner, Folcroft Library Editions, 1974.

LUDWIG BEMELMANS
Ludwig Bemelmans: A Bibliography, by Murray Pomerance, Heinemann, 1993.

ALAN BENNETT
'Alan Bennett', by Colin Wiles, *Book and Magazine Collector*, No.157, April 1997, pps.50-60.

ARNOLD BENNETT
Bennett, A Bibliography, by Norman Emery, Central Library, Stoke-on-Trent, 1967.

E.F. BENSON
The Life of E.F. Benson, by Brian Masters, Chatto & Windus, 1991.

E.C.BENTLEY
Detective Fiction: The Collector's Guide, by John Cooper and B.A. Pike, Scolar Press, 1994, pps.28-30.

LORD BERNERS
'Lord Berners: Author and Eccentic', by Mark Valentine, *Book and Magazine Collector*, No.170, May 1998, pps.58-67.

JOHN BETJEMAN
Sir John Betjeman: A Bibliography of Writings By and About Him, by Margaret L. Stapleton, Scarecrow Press, 1974.

ALGERNON BLACKWOOD
Algernon Blackwood, A Bio-Bibliography, by Mike Ashley, Greenwood Press, 1987.

NICHOLAS BLAKE *see C. Day Lewis*

ROBERT BLOCH
The Complete Robert Bloch, by Randall D. Larson, Fandom Unlimited, 1977.

EDMUND BLUNDEN
A Bibliography of Edmund Blunden, by B.J. Kirkpatrick, Clarendon Press, 1989.

ENID BLYTON
A Comprehensive Bibliography of the Books of Enid Blyton 1922-1970, by Tony Summerfield, 1997.

LUCY M. BOSTON
'Lucy M. Boston', by Daphne Stroud, *Book and Magazine Collector*, No.104, November 1992, pps.16-22.

ELIZABETH BOWEN
Elizabeth Bowen, by Jocelyn Brooke, Longmans, 1952.

PAUL BOWLES
Paul Bowles: A Descriptive Bibliography, by Jeffrey Miller, Black Sparrow Press, 1986.

WILLIAM BOYD
'The Novels of William Boyd', by David Howard, *Book and Magazine Collector*, No.81, December 1990, pps.18-22.

KAY BOYLE
Kay Boyle: A Bibliography, by Clark Chambers, Oak Knoll Press, 2001.

MALCOLM BRADBURY
bodhranbooks.com

RAY BRADBURY
The Ray Bradbury Companion by William F. Nolan, Bruccoli Clark/Gale Research, 1975.

JOHN BRAINE
'John Braine', by Kenneth Fields, *Book and Magazine Collector*, No.86, May 1991, pps.28-35.

ERNEST BRAMAH
'Ernest Bramah', by Mark Valentine, *Book and Magazine Collector*, No.160, July 1997, pps.40-49.

ANGELA BRAZIL
'The Schoolgirl Stories of Angela Brazil', by Katharine Gunn, *Book and Magazine Collector*, No.74, May 1990, pps.23-30.

ELINOR BRENT-DYER
Behind the Chalet School, by Helen McClelland, Bettany Press, 1996.

ANNE, CHARLOTTE & EMILY BRONTË
A Bibliography of the Writings of the Brönte Family, by Thomas J. Wise, Dawsons of Pall Mall, 1917.

JOCELYN BROOKE
'Jocelyn Brooke', by Colin Scott-Sutherland, *Book and Magazine Collector*, No.176, November 1998, pps.64-75.

RUPERT BROOKE
A Bibliography of the Works of Rupert Brooke, by Geoffrey Keynes, Hart-Davis, 1964.

ANITA BROOKNER
bodhranbooks.com

FREDRIC BROWN
A Key to Fredric Brown's Wonderland, by Newton Baird, Talisman Press, 1981.

JEAN de BRUNHOFF
The Art of Babar: the Work of Jean and Laurent de Brunhoff, Abrams, by Nicholas Fox Weber, 1999.

JOHN BUCHAN
The First Editions of John Buchan, by Robert Blanchard, Archon, 1981.

ANTHONY BUCKERIDGE
The Jennings Companion, by David Bathurst, Summersdale, 1995.

ANTHONY BURGESS
Anthony Burgess: A Bibliography, by Paul W. Boytinck, West, 1978.

JAMES LEE BURKE
'Collecting James Lee Burke', by Robin H. Smiley, *Firsts: The Book Collector's Magazine*, July 1991, Vol.1, No.7, pps.16-19.

W.J. BURLEY
Detective Fiction: The Collector's Guide, by John Cooper and B.A. Pike, Scolar Press, 1994, pps.55-56.

FRANCES HODGSON BURNETT
Frances Hodgson Burnett, by Phyllis Bixler, Twayne, 1984.

ROBERT BURNS
A Bibliography of Robert Burns, by J.W. Egerer, Oliver & Boyd, 1965.

EDGAR RICE BURROUGHS
A Golden Anniversary Bibliography of Edgar Rice Burroughs, by Henry Hardy Heins, Donald Grant, 1964.
Edgar Rice Burroughs: The Exhaustive Scholar's and Collector's Descriptive Bibliography of American Periodical, Hardcover, Paperback and Reprint Editions, by Robert B. Zeuschner, McFarland, 1996.

WILLIAM S. BURROUGHS
William S. Burroughs: A Bibliography 1953-1973, by Joe Maynard and Barry Miles, Univ. Press of Virginia, 1978.

A.S. BYATT
A.S.Byatt, by Kathleen Coyne Kelly, Twayne, 1996.

RANDOLPH CALDECOTT
'Randolph Caldecott', by William H.P. Crewdson, *Antiquarian Book Monthly*, May 2000, pps32-36.

ALBERT CAMUS
Camus: A Bibliography, edited by Robert F. Roeming, Univ. of Wisconsin Press, 1968.

TRUMAN CAPOTE
Truman Capote, A Checklist, by Kenneth Starosciak, Starosciak, 1974.

PETER CAREY
'Peter Carey', by David Howard, *Book and Magazine Collector*, No.169, April 1998, pps.30-39.

JOHN DICKSON CARR
Detective Fiction: The Collector's Guide, by John Cooper and B.A. Pike, Scolar Press, 1994, pps.65-74.

LEWIS CARROLL
A Bibliography of the Writings of Lewis Carroll, by Sidney Herbert Williams, Bookman's Journal, 1924.

ANGELA CARTER
Angela Carter, by Allison Lee, Twayne, 1997.

RAYMOND CARVER
'Collecting Raymond Carver', by Charles Michaud, *Firsts: The Book Collector's Magazine*, June 2002, Vol.12, No.6, pps.26-33.

JOYCE CARY
Joyce Cary: A Descriptive Bibliography, by Merja Makinen, Mansell, 1989.

WILLA CATHER
Willa Cather: A Bibliography, by Joan Crane, Univ. of Nebraska Press, 1982

RAYMOND CHANDLER
Raymond Chandler: A Descriptive Bibliography, by Matthew J. Bruccoli, Univ. of Pittsburg Press, 1979.

LESLIE CHARTERIS
The Saint and Leslie Charteris, by W.O.G. Lofts and Derek Adey, Baker, 1970.

BRUCE CHATWIN
Bruce Chatwin, Martin Amis, Julian Barnes, A Bibliography of their First Editions, David Rees, Colophon Press, 1992.

GEOFFREY CHAUCER
Chaucer, A Bibliographical Manual, by E.P. Hammond, Peter Smith, 1933.

JOHN CHEEVER
'John Cheever: A Bibliographical Checklist', *American Book Collector*, Vol.7, No.8, New Series, August 1986.

G.K. CHESTERTON
G.K. Chesterton: A Bibliography, by John Sullivan, Univ. of London Press, 1958.

PETER CHEYNEY
The Bibliography of Crime Fiction, 1749-1975, by Allen J. Hubin, 1979, pps.78-79.

AGATHA CHRISTIE
A Talent to Deceive: An Appreciation of Agatha Christie, by Robert Barnard, Collins, 1980.

TOM CLANCY
The Tom Clancy Companion, by Tom Clancy and Martin H. Greenberg, Fontana, 1992.

JOHN CLARE
'Nature Poet, John Clare', by F.N. Crack, *Book and Magazine Collector*, No.113, August 1993, pps.50-57.

ARTHUR C. CLARKE
Science Fiction and Fantasy Authors, A Bibliography of First Printings of Their Fiction, by Lloyd Currey, Rb Publishing, 2002 (cd rom.)

HARRY CLARKE
A Bibliographical Checklist of the work of Harry Clarke, by M. Steenson, Books & Things, London 2003.

WILLIAM COBBETT
William Cobbett: A Bibliographical Account of His Life and Times, by M.L. Pearl, O.U.P., 1953.

LIZA CODY
'Liza Cody', by David Howard, *Book and Magazine Collector*, No.166, January 1998, pps.58-67.

JOHN COLLIER
Science Fiction and Fantasy Authors, A Bibliography of First Printings of Their Fiction, by Lloyd Currey, Rb Publishing, 2002 (cd rom.)

WILKIE COLLINS
Wilkie Collins: An Annotated Bibliography, 1889-1976, by Kirk H. Beetz, Scarecrow Press, 1978.

IVY COMPTON-BURNETT
Secrets of a Woman's Heart, by Hilary Spurling, Hodder and Stoughton, 1984.

CYRIL CONNOLLY
'Cyril Connolly, Critic and Novelist', by Kevin Nudd, *Book and Magazine Collector*, No.85, April 1991, pps.39-46.

JOSEPH CONRAD
A Bibliography of the Writings of Joseph Conrad 1895-1921, by Thomas J. Wise, Dawsons of Pall Mall, 1972.

A.E. COPPARD
The First Editions of A.E. Coppard, A.P Herbert and Charles Morgan, by Gilbert H. Fabes, Myers, 1933.

BERNARD CORNWELL
'A Bernard Cornwell Checklist', by Elizabeth Wessels and Jennifer Busick, *Firsts: The Book Collector's Magazine*, March 1999, Vol.9, No.3, pps.56-57.

PATRICIA CORNWELL
'Patricia Cornwell', *Breese's Guide to Modern First Editions*, Martin Breese, Breese Books, 1999, pps.247-249.

HUBERT CRACKANTHORPE
bodhranbooks.com

WALTER CRANE
A Bibliography of the First Editions of Books Illustrated by Walter Crane, by Gertrude C.E. Masse, published in London, 1933.

JOHN CREASEY
John Creasey In Print, Hodder & Stoughton, 1969.

MICHAEL CRICHTON
'Michael Crichton', by Richard Dalby, *Book and Magazine Collector*, No.114, September 1993, pps.22-30.

EDMUND CRISPIN
Detective Fiction: The Collector's Guide, by John Cooper and B.A. Pike, Scolar Press, 1994, pps.97-98.

FREEMAN WILLS CROFTS
Detective Fiction: The Collector's Guide, by John Cooper and B.A. Pike, Scolar Press, 1994, pps.98-101.

RICHMAL CROMPTON
'Richmal Crompton', *Breese's Guide to Modern First Editions*, Martin Breese, Breese Books, 1999, pps.41-47.

HARRY CROSBY
Black Sun, The Brief Transit and Violent Eclipse of Harry Crosby, Geoffrey Wolff, Hamish Hamilton, 1976.
A Bibliography of the Black Sun Press, by George Robert Minkoff, Minkoff, 1970.

ALEISTER CROWLEY
Bibliography of the Published Works of Aleister Crowley, by Gerald Yorke, Black Cat Books, 2002.

E.E. CUMMINGS
E.E. Cummings, A Bibliography, George J. Firmage, Wesleyan Univ. Press, 1960.

ROALD DAHL
'Roald Dahl', *Breese's Guide to Modern First Editions*, Martin Breese, Breese Books, 1999, pps.48-53.

THE DANDY
The Hamer Comic Annual Guide, No.1, by Martin Hamer, Hamer 20th Century Books, 2000.

LINDSEY DAVIS
'Lindsey Davis', *Breese's Guide to Modern First Editions*, Martin Breese, Breese Books, 1999, pps.271-273

C. DAY LEWIS
C. Day Lewis, the Poet Laureate: A Bibliography by Geoffrey Handley-Taylor and Timothy d'Arch Smith, St. James Press, 1968.
Detective Fiction: The Collector's Guide, by John Cooper and B.A. Pike, Scolar Press, 1994, pps.33-35.

LOUIS DE BERNIÈRES
'Louis de Bernières', by David Howard, *Book and Magazine Collector*, No.207, June 2001, pps.71-80.

DANIEL DEFOE
A Checklist of the Writings of Daniel Defoe, by J.R. Moore, Archon Books, 1971 (second edition.)

LEN DEIGHTON
Len Deighton: An Annotated Bibliography 1954-1985, by Edward Milward-Oliver, Sammler Press, 1985.
The Len Deighton Companion, by Edward Milford-Oliver, Grafton, 1987.

WALTER DE LA MARE
Walter de la Mare: A Checklist Prepared on the Occasion of an Exhibition of His Books . . . , National Book League, 1956.

MAURICE AND EDWARD DETMOLD
The Fantastic Creatures of Edward Julius Detmold, edited by David Larkin, Peacock Press/Bantam Books, 1976.

COLIN DEXTER
'Colin Dexter and Peter Lovesey', *Breese's Guide to Modern First Editions*, Martin Breese, Breese Books, 1999, pps.54-60.

MICHAEL DIBDIN
'The Detective Fiction of Michael Dibdin', by David Howard, *Book and Magazine Collector*, No.150, September 1996, pps.60-67.

PHILIP K. DICK
PKD: A Philip K. Dick Bibliography by Daniel J.H. Levack, Underwood/Miller, 1981.

CHARLES DICKENS
The First Editions of the Writings of Charles Dickens, by John C. Eckel, published in Folkestone, 1993.

Charles Dickens in the Original Cloth: A Bibliographical Catalogue, Part I and II, by Walter E. Smith, Heritage Book Shop, 1982.

ISAK DINESEN
Isak Dinesen: A Bibliography, by Liselotte Henriksen, Gydendal, 1977.

BENJAMIN DISRAELI
Excursions in Victorian Bibliography, by M. Sadleir, Chaundy & Cox, 1922.

J.P. DONLEAVY
'J.P. Donleavy', by Colin Overall, *Book and Magazine Collector,* No.205, April 2001, pps.55-64.

LORD ALFRED DOUGLAS
'The Poetry of Lord Alfred Douglas', by John Stratford, *Book and Magazine Collector,* No.133, April 1995, pps.66-77.

NORMAN DOUGLAS
A Bibliography of the Writings of Norman Douglas, by Edward D. McDonald, Centaur Book Shop, 1927.

ERNEST DOWSON
Modern British Authors, Their First Editions, Cutler and Stiles, Allen & Unwin, 1930.

SIR ARTHUR CONAN DOYLE
A Bibliographical Catalogue of the Writings of Sir Arthur Conan Doyle 1879-1928, by H. Locke, published in London, 1929.

A Bibliography of A. Conan Doyle, by Richard Lancelyn Green and John Michael Gibson, Clarendon Press, 1983.

RODDY DOYLE
'Roddy Doyle', by David Howard, *Book and Magazine Collector,* No.225, December 2002, pps.66-76.

MARGARET DRABBLE
Margaret Drabble:An Annotated Bibliography, by Joan Garret Packer, Garland, 1988.

THEODORE DREISER
A Bibliography of the Writings of Theodore Dreiser, by Edward D. McDonald, Burt Franklin, 1968.

EDMUND DULAC
Edmund Dulac: His Book Illustrations: A Bibliography, by Anne Connolly Hughey, Buttonwood Press, 1995.

DAPHNE DU MAURIER
'The Early Books of Daphne du Maurier', by Tim Scott, *Book and Magazine Collector,* No.71, February 1990, pps.5-13.

'The Post-War Books of Daphne du Maurier', by Tim Scott, *Book and Magazine Collector,* No.90, September 1991, pps.34-44.

GEORGE DU MAURIER
'George du Maurier', by Brian Jones, *Book and Magazine Collector,* No.85, April 1991, pps.48-57.

DOUGLAS DUNN
bodhranbooks.com

LORD DUNSANY
Lord Dunsany: A Bibliography, by S.T. Joshi and Darrell Schweitzer, Scarecrow Press, 1993.

FRANCIS DURBRIDGE
The Bibliography of Crime Fiction, 1749-1975, by Allen J. Hubin, Publisher's Inc., 1979.

GERALD DURRELL
'Gerald Durrell', by Tim Scott, *Book and Magazine Collector,* No.68, November 1998, pps.45-52.

LAWRENCE DURRELL
Lawrence Durrell, A Study, by G.S.Fraser and Alan G Thomas, Faber, 1968.

UMBERTO ECO
bodhranbooks.com

BERESFORD EGAN
Beresford Egan: An Introduction to His Work, by Paul Allen, Scorpion Press, 1966.

GEORGE ELIOT
George Eliot in Original Cloth: A Bibliographical Catalogue, by Brian Lake and Janet Nassau, Jarndyce Antiquarian Books, 1988.

T.S. ELIOT
T.S. Eliot: A Bibliography, by Donald Gallup, Faber, 1969.

ALICE THOMAS ELLIS
bodhranbooks.com

BRET EASTON ELLIS
bodhranbooks.com

JOHN MEADE FALKNER
'John Meade Falkner', by Mark Valentine and Richard Dalby, *Book and Magazine Collector,* No.141, December 1995, pps.68-77.

G.E. FARROW
'G.E. Farrow', by Colin Scott-Sutherland, *Book and Magazine Collector,* No.146, May 1996, pps.58-68.

WILLIAM FAULKNER
Each in Its Ordered Place: A Faulkner Collector's Notebook, by Carl Petersen, Ardis, 1975.

SEBASTIAN FAULKS
'Sebastian Faulks', by David Howard, *Book and Magazine Collector,* No.216, March 2002, pps.64-74.

HENRY FIELDING
Henry Fielding: An Annotated Bibliography, by George H. Hahn, Scarecrow Press, 1979.

RONALD FIRBANK
A Bibliography of Ronald Firbank, by Miriam J. Benkowitz, Hart-Davis, 1963.

Supplement to a Bibliography of Ronald Firbank, by Miriam J. Benkowitz, Enitharmon Press, 1980.

F. SCOTT FITZGERALD
Scott Fitzgerald: A Descriptive Bibliography, by Judith S. Baughman and Matthew J. Bruccoli, Gale, 1999.

PENELOPE FITZGERALD
'Penelope Fitzgerald', by David Howard, *Book and Magazine Collector,* No.153, December 1996, pps.70-78.

JAMES ELROY FLECKER
Modern British Authors, Their First Editions, Cutler and Stiles, Allen & Unwin, 1930.

IAN FLEMING
'The James Bond Books of Ian Fleming: A Descriptive Bibliography', by Lee Biondi and James M. Pickard, *Firsts: The Book Collector's Magazine*, November 1998, Vol.8, No.11, pps.38-51.

W. RUSSELL FLINT
More Than Shadows: A Biography of W.Russell Flint, by Arnold Palmer, The Studio, 1943.

FORD MADOX FORD
Ford Madox Ford, 1873-1939, by David Dow Harvey, Gordian Press, 1972.

C.S. FORESTER
C.S. Forester, by Allen and Patricia Ahearn, Quill & Brush, 1995.

E.M. FORSTER
A Bibliography of E.M. Forster, by B.J. Kirkpatrick, Clarendon Press, 1985.

FREDERICK FORSYTH
'Frederick Forsyth', by Craig Cabell, *Book and Magazine Collector*, No.203, February 2001, pps.4-12.

DION FORTUNE
'Dion Fortune: Mystic and Novelist', by Mark Valentine, *Book and Magazine Collector*, No.142, January 1996, pps.40-47.

JOHN FOWLES
'John Fowles', *Breese's Guide to Modern First Editions*, Martin Breese, Breese Books, 1999, pps.70-74.

DICK FRANCIS
'Collecting Dick Francis', by Sheldon McArthur, *Firsts: The Book Collector's Magazine*, July/August 1993, Vol.3, No.7/8, pps.24-29.

GEORGE MACDONALD FRASER
'Collecting George MacDonald Fraser', by Kathryn Smiley, *Firsts: The Book Collector's Magazine*, February 1992, Vol.2, No.2, pps.20-25.

R. AUSTIN FREEMAN
Detective Fiction: The Collector's Guide, by John Cooper and B.A. Pike, Scolar Press, 1994, pps.137-141.

ROBERT FROST
Robert Frost: A Bibliography, by W.B.S. Clymer and C.R. Green, published in Amherst, 1937.

GABRIEL GARCÍA MÁRQUEZ
'Collecting Gabriel García Márquez', by Don Klein, *Firsts: The Book Collector's Magazine*, February 1993, Vol.3, No.2, pps.24-30.

ALAN GARNER
A Fine Anger: A Critical Introduction to the Work of Alan Garner, by Neil Philip, Collins, 1981.

DAVID GARNETT
'David Garnett', by George Jefferson, *Book and Magazine Collector*, No.97, April 1992, pps.24-32.

EVE GARNETT
'Eve Garnett', by June Hopper, *Book and Magazine Collector*, No.162, September 1997, pps.48-58.

JONATHAN GASH
'The "Lovejoy" Novels of Jonathan Gash', by David Howard, *Book and Magazine Collector*, No.95, February 1992, pps.40-47.

ELIZABETH GASKELL
Elizabeth C. Gaskell: A Bibliographical Catalogue of First and Early Editions 1848-1866, by Walter E. Smith, Heritage Book Shop, 1998.

LEWIS GRASSIC GIBBON
'Lewis Grassic Gibbon', by Mark Valentine, *Book and Magazine Collector*, No.203, February 2001, pps.40-50.

STELLA GIBBONS
'Stella Gibbons', by Crispin Jackson, *Book and Magazine Collector*, No.130, January 1995, pps.18-26.

GILES' ANNUALS
'Giles Annuals', *Book and Magazine Collector*, No.65, August 1989, pps.14-19.

WARWICK GOBLE
'The Illustrations of Warwick Goble', by Richard Dalby, *Book and Magazine Collector*, No.47, February 1988, pps.58-65.

SIR WILLIAM GOLDING
William Golding: A Bibliography, by R.A. Gekoski and David Hughes, Deutsch, 1991.

SUE GRAFTON
Detective Fiction: The Collector's Guide, by John Cooper and B.A. Pike, Scolar Press, 1994, pps.154-155.

KENNETH GRAHAME
Beyond the Wild Wood; the World of Kenneth Grahame, by Peter Green, Webb & Bower, 1982.

ROBERT GRAVES
Robert Graves: A Bibliography, by Fred H. Higginson and William P. Williams, St Paul's Bibliographies, 1987.

ALASDAIR GRAY
Brian Moore, Alasdair Gray, John McGahern, A Bibliography of their First Editions, David Rees, Colophon Press, 1991.

HENRY GREEN
Romancing, The Life and Work of Henry Green, by Jeremy Trelown, Faber, 2000.

KATE GREENAWAY
Printed Kate Greenaway: A Catalogue Raisonne, by Thomas Schuster and Rodney Engen, T.E. Schuster, 1986.

GRAHAM GREENE
Graham Greene: A Bibliography and Guide to Research, by R.A. Woobe/Wobbe, Garland, 1979.
Graham Greene: An Annotated Bibliography, by A.F. Cassis, Scarecrow Press, 1981.

JOHN GRISHAM
bodhranbooks.com

THOM GUNN
Thom Gunn: A Bibliography 1940-1978, by Jack W. C. Hagstrom and George Bixby, Bertram Rota, 1979.

H. RIDER HAGGARD
Bibliography of the Works of Sir Henry Rider Haggard 1856-1925, by J.E. Scott, Elkin Mathews, 1947.

KATHLEEN HALE
'Kathleen Hale', by Kevin Nudd, *Book and Magazine Collector*, No.170, May 1998, pps.49-57.

RADCLYFFE HALL
'Radclyffe Hall', by Katharine Gunn, *Book and Magazine Collector*, No.160, July 1997, pps.59-67.

PATRICK HAMILTON
'The Novels and Plays of Patrick Hamilton', by Martin Loughlin, *Book and Magazine Collector*, No.93, December 1991, pps.30-37.

DASHIELL HAMMETT
Dashiel Hammett: A Descriptive Bibliography, by Richard Layman, Univ. of Pittsburgh Press, 1997.

THOMAS HARDY
Thomas Hardy: A Bibliographical Study, by R.L. Purdy, Oxford Univ. Press, 1968.
A Bibliography of the Works of Thomas Hardy, by A.P. Webb, Burt Franklin, 1968.

CYRIL HARE
Detective Fiction: The Collector's Guide, John Cooper and B.A. Pike, Scolar Press, 1994, pps.162-164.
The Bibliography of Crime Fiction, 1749-1975, Allen J. Hubin, Publisher's Inc., 1979.

ROBERT HARRIS
bodhranbooks.com

THOMAS HARRIS
'Thomas Harris', by David Whitehead, *Book and Magazine Collector*, No.204, March 2001, pps.18-24.

L.P. HARTLEY
L.P. Hartley, by Edward T. Jones, Twayne, 1978.
L.P. Hartley, by Paul Bloomfield, Longmans, Green & Co., 1970.

NATHANIEL HAWTHORNE
Nathaniel Hawthorne: A Descriptive Bibliography, by C.E. Frazer Clark Jr., Univ. of Pittsburgh Press, 1978.

SEAMUS HEANEY
Seamus Heaney, by Thomas C. Foster, The O'Brien Press, 1989.

ROBERT A. HEINLEIN
Robert A. Heinlein: A Bibliography, by Mark Owings, Croatan House, 1973.

JOSEPH HELLER
Three Contemporary Novelists: An Annotated Bibliography, by Robert M. Scotto, Garland, 1977.

ERNEST HEMINGWAY
Ernest Hemingway: A Comprehensive Bibliography, by André Hanneman, Princeton Univ. Press, 1967 and 1975 (supplement).

G.A. HENTY
G.A. Henty: A Bibliography, by Robert L. Dartt, John Sherratt, 1971.

JAMES HERBERT
'Collecting James Herbert', by Craig Cabell, *Book and Magazine Collector*, No.128, November 1994, pps.23-31.

EDWARD HERON-ALLEN
'Edward Heron-Allen and Christopher Blayre', by R.B. Russell, *Antiquarian Book Monthly*, May 2000, pps.18-23.

HERMANN HESSE
Hermann Hesse: Biography and Bibliography, Joseph Mileck, Calif. Univ. Press, 1977 (2 vols).

PATRICIA HIGHSMITH
Patricia Highsmith, by Russell Harrison, Twayne, 1997.

REGINALD HILL
Detective Fiction: The Collector's Guide, by John Cooper and B.A. Pike, Scolar Press, 1994, pps.168-170.

WILLIAM HOPE HODGSON
Science Fiction and Fantasy Authors, A Bibliography of First Printings of Their Fiction, by Lloyd Currey, Rb Publishing, 2002 (cd rom.)

NICK HORNBY
'Nick Hornby', by Kevin Nudd, *Book and Magazine Collector*, No.227, February 2003, pps.102-111.

GEOFFREY HOUSEHOLD
'Geoffrey Household', by D.C. Hogg, *Book and Magazine Collector*, No.58, November 1989, pps.52-58.

A. E. HOUSMAN
A.E. Housman: A Bibliography, by John Carter and John Sparrow, St Paul Bibliographies, 1982.

ELIZABETH JANE HOWARD
'Elizabeth Jane Howard', by David Howard, *Book and Magazine Collector*, No.65, August 1989, pps.66-71.

ROBERT E. HOWARD
'Collecting Robert E. Howard', by Don Herron, *Firsts: The Book Collector's Magazine*, July/August 2000, Vol.10, No.7/8, pps.26-41.

L. RON HUBBARD
Science Fiction and Fantasy Authors, A Bibliography of First Printings of Their Fiction, by Lloyd Currey, Rb Publishing, 2002 (cd rom.)

RICHARD HUGHES
Richard Hughes: Novelist, by Richard Poole, Poetry Wales Press, 1987.

TED HUGHES
Ted Hughes, A Bibliography, 1946-1980, by Keith Sagar and Stephen Tabor, Mansell, 1983.

ALDOUS HUXLEY
Aldous Huxley: A Bibiography 1916-1959, by Claire John Eschelbach and Joyce Lee Shober, Univ. of California Press, 1961.

J. K. HUYSMANS
J.K. Huysmans: A Reference Guide, by G. Cevasco, Hall, 1980.

HAMMOND INNES
'The Novels of Hammond Innes', by David Whitehead, *Book and Magazine Collector*, No.102, September 1992, pps.14-21.

MICHAEL INNES
Detective Fiction: The Collector's Guide, by John Cooper and B.A. Pike, Scolar Press, 1994, pps.174-176.

CHRISTOPHER ISHERWOOD
Chrsitopher Isherwood: A Bibliography, by Selmer Westby and Clayton M. Brown, California State College, 1968.

KAZUO ISHIGURO
'Kazuo Ishiguro: A Checklist of First Editions', by Robin H. Smiley, *Firsts: The Book Collector's Magazine*, March 2001, Vol.11, No.3, p 30.

HENRY JAMES
A Bibliography of Henry James, by Leon Edel and Dan H. Laurence, O.U.P., 1982.

M.R. JAMES
Science Fiction and Fantasy Authors, A Bibliography of First Printings of Their Fiction, by Lloyd Currey, Rb Publishing, 2002 (cd rom.)

P.D. JAMES
'Collecting P.D. James', by Kathryn Smiley, *Firsts: The Book Collector's Magazine*, June 1997, Vol.7, No.6, pps.38-48.

RICHARD JEFFERIES
The Forward Life of Richard Jefferies: A Chronological Study, by H. Matthews and P. Treitel, Petton Books, 1994.

JEROME K. JEROME
Jerome K Jerome, by Ruth Marie Faurot, Twayne, 1974.

RUTH PRAWER JHABVALA
Ruth Prawer Jhabvala, by Ralph J. Crane, Twayne, 1992.

CAPTAIN W.E. JOHNS
Biggles: The Life Story of W.E. Johns; Creator of Biggles, Worrals, Gimlet & Steeley, by Berresford Ellis and Jennifer Schofield, Comet, 1985.

B.S. JOHNSON
B.S. Johnson: A Critical Reading, by Philip Tew, Manchester Univ. Press, 2001.

JAMES JOYCE
A Bibliography of James Joyce 1882-1941, John Slocum and Herbery Cahoon, Rupert Hart-Davis, 1953.

FRANZ KAFKA
A Kafka Bibliography 1908-1976, by Angel Flores, Gordian Press, 1976.

ERICH KÄSTNER
'Erich Kästner', by Martin Spence, *Book and Magazine Collector*, No.108, March 1993, pps.30-37.

JOHN KEATS
Keats: A Bibliography and Reference Guide with an Essay on Keats' Reputation, by J.R. MacGillivray, Univ. of Toronto Press, 1949.

THOMAS KENEALLY
Australian Melodramas: Thomas Keneally's Fiction, by Peter Pierce, Univ. of Queensland Press, 1965.

JACK KEROUAC
A Bibliography of Works by Jack Kerouac 1939-1967, by Ann Charters, Phoenix Bookshop, 1975.

KEN KESEY
Ken Kesey, by Allen and Patricia Ahearn, Quill & Brush, 1995.

KEYNOTES
bodhranbooks.com

FRANCIS KILVERT
'William Plomer & Kilvert's "Diary"', by Andrew Thomas, *Book and Magazine Collector*, No.220, July 2002, pps.84-97.

C. DALY KING
Detective Fiction: The Collector's Guide, by John Cooper and B.A. Pike, Scolar Press, 1994, pps.184-186.

STEPHEN KING
Science Fiction and Fantasy Authors, A Bibliography of First Printings of Their Fiction, by Lloyd Currey, Rb Publishing, 2002 (cd rom.)

RUDYARD KIPLING
A Bibliography of the Works of Rudyard Kipling, by Flora V. Livingstone, Burt Franklin, 1968.
Rudyard Kipling: A Bibliographical Catalogue, by J. McG. Stewart, O.U.P., 1959.

C.H.B. KITCHIN
'The Novels of C.H.B. Kitchen', by David Whitehead, *Book and Magazine Collector*, No.139, October 1995, pps.62-69.

ARTHUR KOESTLER
Arthur Koestler: An International Bibliography, by Reed Merrill and Thomas Frazier, Ardis, 1979.

DEAN KOONTZ
A Checklist of Dean R. Koontz, by Christopher P. Stephens, Ultramarine Publishing Co., 1987.

PHILIP LARKIN
Philip Larkin: A Bibliography 1933-76 by B.C. Blomfield, Faber, 1979.

D.H. LAWRENCE
A Bibliography of D.H. Lawrence, by Warren Roberts, C.U.P., 1982.

T.E. LAWRENCE
T.E. Lawrence: A Bibliography, by Philip O'Brien, St Paul's Bibliographies, 1988.

EDWARD LEAR
Edward Lear, 1812-1888, by Vivien Noakes, Royal Academy of Arts, 1985.

JOHN LE CARRÉ
'John Le Carré and Len Deighton', *Breese's Guide to Modern First Editions*, Martin Breese, Breese Books, 1999, pps.111-118.

LAURIE LEE
Laurie Lee, The Well-loved Stranger, by Valerie Grove, Viking/Penguin, 1999.

J. SHERIDAN LE FANU
J. Sheridan Le Fanu: A Bio-Bibliography, by Gary William Crawford, Greenwood Press, 1995.

RICHARD LE GALLIENNE
Modern British Authors, Their First Editions, Cutler and Stiles, Allen & Unwin, 1930.

URSULA LE GUIN
Ursula K. LeGuin: A Primary and Secondary Bibliography, by Elizabeth Cummins Cogell, Hall, 1983.

ROSAMOND LEHMANN
'Lehmann: A Bibliography' by M.T. Gustafson, in *Twentieth Century Literature 4*, 1959.

ELMORE LEONARD
A Checklist of Elmore Leonard, by Christopher P. Stephens, Ultramarine, 1991.

GASTON LEROUX
'Gaston Leroux', by Richard Dalby, *Book and Magazine Collector*, No.38, May 1987, pps.14-22.

DORIS LESSING
Doris Lessing: A Bibliography of Her First Editions, by Eric T. Brueck, Metropolis, 1984

C.S. LEWIS
C.S. Lewis: An Annotated Checklist of Writings About Him and His Works, by Joe R. Christopher and Joan K. Ostling, Kent State Univ. Press, [n.d.].

NORMAN LEWIS
'Norman Lewis', by David Howard, *Book and Magazine Collector*, No.125, August 1994, pps.30-37.

WYNDHAM LEWIS
A Bibliography of the Writings of Wyndham Lewis, by Bradford Morrow and Bernard LaFourcade, Black Sparrow Press, 1978.

DAVID LINDSAY
Science Fiction and Fantasy Authors, A Bibliography of First Printings of Their Fiction, by Lloyd Currey, Rb Publishing, 2002 (cd rom.)

DAVID LODGE
David Lodge, by Bruce K. Martin, Gale, 1999 (Twayne's English Authors Series.)

JACK LONDON
The Fiction of Jack London: A Chronological Bibliography, by Dale L. Walker and James E. Sisson III, Texas Western Press, 1972.
Jack London First Editions, by James E. Sisson III and Robert W. Martens, Star Rover House, 1979.

E.C.R. LORAC
Detective Fiction: The Collector's Guide, by John Cooper and B.A. Pike, Scolar Press, 1994, pps.193-196.

H.P. LOVECRAFT
The Revised H.P. Lovecraft Bibliography, by Mark Owings and Jach L. Chalker, Mirage Press, 1973.

PETER LOVESEY
'Colin Dexter and Peter Lovesey', *Breese's Guide to Modern First Editions*, Martin Breese, Breese Books, 1999, pps.54-60.

MALCOLM LOWRY
Malcolm Lowry: A Bibliography, by J. Howard Woolmer, Woolmer/Brotherson, 1983.

ROSE MACAULAY
Rose Macaulay, by Alice R. Bensen, Twayne, 1969.

GEORGE MACDONALD
George Macdonald: A Bibliographical Study, by Raphael B. Shaberman, St Paul's Bibliographies, 1990.

PHILIP MACDONALD
Detective Fiction: The Collector's Guide, by John Cooper and B.A. Pike, Scolar Press, 1994, pps.199-201.

ROSS MACDONALD
Ross Macdonald/Kenneth Millar: A Descriptive Bibliography, by Matthew J. Bruccoli, Univ. of Pittsbergh Press, 1983.

IAN McEWAN
Muriel Spark, William Trevor, Ian McEwan, A Bibliography of their First Editions, David Rees, Colophon Press, 1992.

JOHN McGAHERN
Brian Moore, Alasdair Gray, John McGahern, A Bibliography of their First Editions, David Rees, Colophon Press, 1991.

ARTHUR MACHEN
A Bibliography of Arthur Machen, by Adrian Goldstone and Wesley Sweetser, Haskell House, 1973.

COLIN MACINNES
bodhranbooks.com

ALISTAIR MACLEAN
'Alistair Maclean', by David Whitehead, *Book and Magazine Collector*, No.157, April 1997, pps.16-26.

LOUIS MACNEICE
A Bibliography of the Works of Louis MacNeice, by Christopher Armitage and Neil Clark, Kaye & Ward, 1973.

NORMAN MAILER
Norman Mailer: A Comprehensive Bibliography, by Laura Adams, Scarecrow Press, 1974.

THOMAS MANN
Thomas Mann, by Andrew White, Grove Press, 1965.

KATHERINE MANSFIELD
The Critical Bibliography of Katherine Mansfield, by Ruth E. Mantz, published in New York, 1931.

CAPTAIN FREDERICK MARRYAT
Captain Frederick Marryat: Sea-Officer, Novelist, Country Squire: A Bio-Bibliographical Essay to Accompany an Exhibition . . . , by Alan Buster, Univ. of California Press, 1980.

NGAIO MARSH
Ngaio Marsh: A Bibliography of English Language Publications in Hardback and Paperback, by by Rowan Gibbs and Richard Williams, Dragonby Press, 1990.

W. SOMERSET MAUGHAM
A Bibliography of the Works of W. Somerset Maugham, by Raymond Toole Stott, Univ. of Alberta Press, 1973.

ABRAHAM MERRITT
Science Fiction and Fantasy Authors, A Bibliography of First Printings of Their Fiction, by Lloyd Currey, Rb Publishing, 2002 (cd rom.)

ARTHUR MILLER
Arthur Miller: A Checklist of his Published Works, by Tetsumaro Hayashi, Kent, 1967.

HENRY MILLER
A Bibliography of Henry Miller 1945-1961, by Maxine Renken, Swallow, 1962.

A.A. MILNE
Modern British Authors, Their First Editions, Cutler and Stiles, Allen & Unwin, 1930.

GLADYS MITCHELL
Detective Fiction: The Collector's Guide, by John Cooper and B.A. Pike, Scolar Press, 1994, pps.214-218.

MARGARET MITCHELL
'Margaret Mitchell's "Gone With the Wind"', by Brian Jones, *Book and Magazine Collector*, No.130, January 1995, pps.28-37.

NAOMI MITCHISON
The Nine Lives of Naomi Mitchison, by Jenni Calder, Virago, 1997.

MARY RUSSELL MITFORD
First Editions, A Field Guide, by K. Anthony Ward, Scolar Press, 1994, pps.249-250.

NANCY MITFORD
Nancy Mitford: A Biography, by Selina Hastings, Dutton, 1986.

NICHOLAS MONSARRAT
'Nicholas Monsarrat', by David Whitehead, *Book and Magazine Collector*, No.203, February 2001, pps.14-25.

MICHAEL MOORCOCK
Michael Moorcock: A Reader's Guide, by John Davey, Jayde Design, 2000.

BRIAN MOORE
Brian Moore, Alasdair Gray, John McGahern, A Bibliography of their First Editions, David Rees, Colophon Press, 1991.

WILLIAM MORRIS
The Books of William Morris by H.B. Forman, Holland Press, 1967.

TONI MORRISON
Toni Morrison: An Annotated Bibliography, by David L. Middleton, Garland, 1987.

JOHN MORTIMER
'John Mortimer', by Dee Taylor, *Book and Magazine Collector*, No.100, July 1992, pps.50-57.

IRIS MURDOCH
Iris Murdoch & Muriel Spark: A Bibliography, by Thomas A. Tominaga and Wilma Schneidermeyer, Scarecrow Press, 1976.

Iris Murdoch: A Descriptive Primary and Annotated Secondary Bibliography, by John Fletcher and Cheryl Bove, Garland, 1994.

VLADIMIR NABOKOV
Nabokov: A Bibliography, by Andrew Field, McGraw-Hill, 1974.
Vladimir Nabokov: A Descriptive Bibliography, by Michael Juliar, Garland, 1986.

SHIVA NAIPAUL
bodhranbooks.com

V.S. NAIPAUL
'V.S. Naipaul', by David Howard, *Book and Magazine Collector*, No.64, July 1989, pps.26-32.

VIOLET NEEDHAM
The Password is Fortitude: An evaluation of some children's books by Violet Needham, by Judith Crabb, Hermit Press, 1992.

KAY NIELSEN
'The Illustrated Books of Kay Nielsen', by Richard Dalby, *Book and Magazine Collector*, No.30, September 1986, pps.28-37.

PATRICK O'BRIAN
Patrick O'Brian: Critical Appreciations and a Bibliography, by A.E. Cunningham, British Library, 1994.

EDNA O'BRIEN
'Edna O'Brien', by Kenneth Fields, *Book and Magazine Collector*, No.94, January 1992, pps.22-28.

FLANN O'BRIEN
'The Novels and Journalism of Flann O'Brien', by Crispin Jackson, *Book and Magazine Collector*, No.92, November 1991, pps.15-24.

LIAM O'FLAHERTY
Liam O'Flaherty: An Annotated Bibliography, by Paul A. Doyle, Whitston, 1972.
Liam O'Flaherty: A Descriptive Bibliography of His Works, by George Jefferson, Wolfhound Press, 1993.

JOHN O'HARA
John O'Hara: A Descriptive Bibliography, by Matthew J. Bruccoli, Univ. of Pittsburg Press, 1978.

EUGENE O'NEILL
Eugene O'Neill: A Descriptive Bibliography, by Jennifer McCabe Atkinson, Univ. of Pittsburgh Press, 1974.

JOE ORTON
Twenty Modern British Playwrights: A Bibliography, 1956-1976, by Kimball King, Garland, 1977.

GEORGE ORWELL
George Orwell: A Selected Bibliography, by Z.G. Zeke and W. White, published in Boston, 1962.

JOHN OSBORNE
John Osborne, by Simon Trussler, Longmans Green, 1969.

WILFRED OWEN
Wilfred Owen (1893-1918): A Bibliography, by William White, Kent State Univ. Press, 1967.

DOROTHY PARKER
'Dorothy Parker.' by Val Tongue, *Book and Magazine Collector*, No.86, May 1991, pps.47-53.

THOMAS LOVE PEACOCK
'Thomas Love Peacock', by Martin Spence, *Book and Magazine Collector*, No.168, March 1998, pps.54-62.

MERVYN PEAKE
Mervyn Peake, by John Watney, St Martin's Press, 1976.

ELLIS PETERS
'Collecting Edith Pargeter/Ellis Peters', by Barbara G. Peters, *Firsts: The Book Collector's Magazine*, November 1995, Vol.5, No.11, pps.32-41.

HAROLD PINTER
Twenty Modern British Playwrights: A Bibliography, 1956-1976, by Kimball King, Garland, 1977.

SYLVIA PLATH
Sylvia Plath: A Bibliography, by Gary Lane and Maria Stevens, Scarecrow Press, 1978.

EDGAR ALLAN POE
Bibliography of the Writings of Edgar A. Poe, by John W. Robertson, Kraus Reprint, 1969.

WILLY POGÁNY
'Willy Pogány', by Richard Dalby, *Book and Magazine Collector*, No.93, December 1991, pps.62-76.

BEATRIX POTTER
Beatrix Potter: A Bibliographical Checklist, by Jane Quinby, Sawyer, 1954.
A History of the Writings of Beatrix Potter, by Leslie Linder, Frederick Warne, 1971.

EZRA POUND
A Bibliography of Ezra Pound, by Donald Gallup, Univ. of Virginia Press, 1983.

ANTHONY POWELL
Anthony Powell-A Bibliography, by George Lilley, St Paul's, 1993.

JOHN COWPER POWYS
A Bibliography of the Writings of John Cowper Powys 1872-1963, by Dante Thomas, Paul P. Appel, 1975.

LLEWELYN POWYS
The Life of Llewelyn Powys, by Malcolm Elwin, Bodley Head, 1946.

T.F. POWYS
A Bibliography of T.F. Powys, by Peter Riley, Brimmell, 1967.

TERRY PRATCHETT
A Checklist of Terry Pratchett's Novels, Shorter Writings and Related Publications, Colin Smythe, privately printed by Colin Smythe, 2001.

ANTHONY PRICE
'Anthony Price', by David Howard, *Book and Magazine Collector*, No.161, August 1997, pps.50-59.

J.B. PRIESTLEY
J.B. Priestley, An Annotated Bibliography, by Alan Edwin Day, Hodgkins and Co., 1980.

V. S. PRITCHETT
V.S. Pritchett, by Dean R. Baldwin, Twayne, 1987.

MARCEL PROUST
The Magic Lantern of Marcel Proust, by Howard Moss, Faber, 1963.

PHILIP PULLMAN
'Philip Pullman', by Barbara Richardson, *Book and Magazine Collector*, No.218, May 2002, pps.20-34.

BARBARA PYM
Barbara Pym: A Reference Guide, by Dale Salwak, G.K. Hall, 1991.

ELLERY QUEEN
Royal Bloodline: Ellery Queen, by Francis M. Nevins, Jr., Bowling Green Univ. Press, 1974.

JONATHAN RABAN
'Jonathan Raban', by David Howard, *Book and Magazine Collector*, No.89, August 1991, pps.14-20.

ARTHUR RACKHAM
Arthur Rackham, A New Bibliography, Richard Riall, Louise Ross and Co., 1994.

ANN RADCLIFFE
Ann Radcliffe: A Bio-Bibliography, by Deborah P. Rogers, Greenwood, 1996.

IAN RANKIN
Detective Fiction: The Collector's Guide, by John Cooper and B.A. Pike, Scolar Press, 1994, pps.251-252.

ARTHUR RANSOME
Arthur Ransome: A Bibliography, by Wayne G. Hammond, Oak Knoll Press, 2000.

FORREST REID
Forrest Reid: A Portrait and Study, by Russell Burlingham, Faber, 1953.

RUTH RENDELL
'Ruth Rendell', *Breese's Guide to Modern First Editions*, Martin Breese, Breese Books, 1999, pps.142-148.

JEAN RHYS
Jean Rhys: A Descriptive and Annotated Bibliography of Works and Criticism, by Elgin W. Mellown, Garland, 1984.

ANNE RICE
The Unauthorized Anne Rice Companion, by George Beahm, Andrews and McMeel, 1996.

FRANK RICHARDS
'Frank Richards', *Breese's Guide to Modern First Editions*, Martin Breese, Breese Books, 1999, pps.149-155.

W. HEATH ROBINSON
William Heath Robinson, by James Hamilton, Pavilion Books, 1992.

SAX ROHMER
Masters of Villainy, by Cay Van Ash and Elizabeth Sax Rohmer, Bowling Green Univ. Popular Press, 1972.

FREDERICK ROLFE (BARON CORVO)
A Bibliography of Frederick Rolfe Baron Corvo, by Cecil Woolfe, Rupert Hart-Davis, 1957.

J.K. ROWLING
'J.K. Rowling's "Harry Potter" Books', by Barbara Richardson, *Book and Magazine Collector*, No.196, July 2000, pps.4-17.

RUPERT see Mary Tourtel

SALMAN RUSHDIE
Contemporary World Writers: Salman Rushdie, by Catherine Cundy, Manchester Univ. Press, 1996.

VITA SACKVILLE-WEST
Vita Sackville West: A Bibliography, by Robert Cross and Ann Ravenscroft-Hulme, St Paul's Bibliographies, 1999.

SAKI
'Saki, A Life of Irony', by Jesse F. Knight, *Firsts: The Book Collector's Magazine*, September 1999, Vol.9, No.9, pps.50-57.

J.D. SALINGER
J.D. Salinger: A Thirty-Year Bibliography, 1938-1968, by Kenneth Starosciak, [no publisher, n.d.].

SAPPER
The Bulldog Drummond Encyclopedia, by Lawrence P. Treadwell Jr., McFarland, 2001.

SARBAN
'Brief Bibliography', by Mark Valentine, *The Doll Maker*, by Sarban, Tartarus press, 1999, p.227.

SIEGFRIED SASSOON
A Bibliography of Siegfried Sassoon, by Geoffrey Keynes, Hart-Davis, 1962.

HILARY SAUNDERS see Francis Beeding

THE SAVOY
Publisher to the Decadents, by James G. Nelson, Rivendale Press, 2000.

DOROTHY L. SAYERS
A Bibliography of the Works of Dorothy L. Sayers, by Colleen B. Gilbert, Archon Books, 1978.

JACK SCHAEFER
'Collecting Jack Schaefer', by Larry Dingman and Robin H. Smiley, *Firsts: The Book Collector's Magazine*, May 1993, Vol.3, No.5, pps.24-29.

PAUL SCOTT
'Paul Scott', by Jeremy Parrott, *Book and Magazine Collector*, No.163, October 1997, pps.29-39.

ANNA SEWELL
Anna Sewell and Black Beauty, by Margaret J. Baker, Longmans, Green & Company, 1957.

TOM SHARPE
'The Comic Novels of Tom Sharpe', by David Howard, *Book and Magazine Collector*, No.41, August 1987, pps.15-22.

GEORGE BERNARD SHAW
Bernard Shaw: A Bibliography, Dan H. Laurence, O.U.P., 1983.

MARY SHELLEY
Mary Shelley: An Annotated Bibliography, by W.H. Lyles, Garland, 1975.

M.P. SHIEL
The Works of M.P. Shiel, by A. Reynolds Morse, Fantasy Publishing Co., 1948.

NEVIL SHUTE
Nevil Shute, by Julain Smith, Twayne, 1976.

ALAN SILLITOE
Alan Sillitoe: A Bibliography, by David E. Gerard, Mansell, 1988.

GEORGES SIMENON
Georges Simenon: A Bibliography of the British First Editions . . . and of the Principal French and American Editions, by Peter Foord, Richard Williams and Sally Swan, Dragonby Press, 1988.

EDITH, OSBERT and SACHEVERELL SITWELL
A Bibliography of Edith, Osbert and Sacheverell Sitwell by Robert Fifoot, Hart-Davis/O.U.P., 1971.

CLARK ASHTON SMITH
Emperor of Dreams, A Clark Ashton-Smith Bibliography, by Donald Sidney-Fryer, Grant, 1978.

STEVIE SMITH
Stevie Smith: A Bibliography, by Jack Barbera et al., Mansell, 1987.

C.P. SNOW
The World of Snow, by Robert Greacen, Scorpion Press, 1962.

ALEXANDER SOLZHENITSYN
Alexander Solzhenitsyn: An International Bibliography of Writings By and About Him, by Donald M Fiene, Ardis, 1973.

MURIEL SPARK
Muriel Spark, William Trevor, Ian McEwan, A Bibliography of their First Editions, David Rees, Colophon Press, 1992.
Iris Murdoch & Muriel Spark: A Bibliography, by Thomas A. Tominaga and Wilma Schneidermeyer, Scarecrow Press, 1976.

STEPHEN SPENDER
Stephen Spender Works and Criticism: An Annotated Bibliography, by H.B. Kulkarni, Garland, 1976.

MICKEY SPILLANE
'Collecting Micket Spillane', by Laurence Miller, *Firsts: The Book Collector's Magazine*, June 1996, Vol.6, No.6, pps.36-43.

GERTRUDE STEIN
Gertrude Stein: A Bibliography, by Robert A. Wilson, Quill & Brush, 1994.

JOHN STEINBECK
John Steinbeck: A Biographical Catalogue of the Adrian H. Goldstone Collection, by Adrian H. Goldstone and John R. Payne, Univ. of Texas Press, 1974.

COUNT ERIC STENBOCK
'A Bibliography of Count Stenbock' by Timothy d'Arch Smith, *Stenbock Yeats and the Nineties*, by John Adlard, Woolf, 1969, pps.95-102.

LAURENCE STERNE
Laurence Sterne, by William Piper, Twayne, 1965.

ROBERT LOUIS STEVENSON
A Bibliography of the Works of Robert Louis Stevenson by Colonel W.F. Prideaux, Burt Franklin, 1968.

BRAM STOKER
Bram Stoker, A Bibliography of First Editions, by Richard Dalby, Dracula Press, 1983.

TOM STOPPARD
Twenty Modern British Playwrights: A Bibliography, 1956-1976, by Kimball King, Garland, 1977.

DAVID STOREY
bodhranbooks.com

GILES LYTTON STRACHEY
'Lytton Strachey', by Helen Macleod, *Book and Magazine Collector*, No.35, February 1987, pps.53-61.

MONTAGUE SUMMERS
A Bibliography of the Works of Montague Summers, by Timothy d'Arch Smith, Aquarian, 1983.

R.S. SURTEES
R.S. Surtees, by Leonard Cooper, Arthur Barker Ltd., 1952.
The Sporting World of R.S. Surtees, by John Welcome, O.U.P., 1982.

GRAHAM SWIFT
'The Novels of Graham Swift', by David Howard, *Book and Magazine Collector*, No.92, November 1991, pps.62-67.

A.J.A. SYMONS
'A.J.A. Symons', by Richard Dalby, *Book and Magazine Collector*, No.119, February 1994, pps.74-84.

JULIAN SYMONS
Julian Symons: A Bibliography, by John J. Walsdorf, Oak Knoll Press/St Paul's Bibliographies, 1996.

JOSEPHINE TEY
Detective Fiction: The Collector's Guide, John Cooper and B.A. Pike, Scolar Press, 1994, pps.287-288.
The Bibliography of Crime Fiction, 1749-1975, Allen J. Hubin, Publisher's Inc., 1979.

W.M. THACKERAY
A Thackeray Library by Henry Sayre Van Duzer, Burt Franklin, 1971.

PAUL THEROUX
Paul Theroux, by Allen and Patricia Ahearn, Quill & Brush, 1995.

DYLAN THOMAS
Dylan Thomas: A Bibliography, by J. Alexander Rolph, Dent, 1956.
ditto, New Directions, 1956.
Dylan Thomas in Print: A Bibliographical History, by Ralph Maud, Dent, 1970.
ditto, Univ. of Pittsburgh Press, 1970.

EDWARD THOMAS
Edward Thomas, A Biography and a Bibliography, by Robert P. Eckert, Dent, 1937.

FLORA THOMPSON
'Flora Thompson', by Paul Robinson, *Book and Magazine Collector*, No.158, May 1997, pps.14-24.

HENRY DAVID THOREAU
'Collecting Henry David Thoreau', by Kevin MacDonnell, *Firsts: The Book Collector's Magazine*, September 1999, Vol.9, No.9, pps.22-55.

COLIN THUBRON
'Travel Writer and Novelist: Colin Thubron', by David Howard, *Book and Magazine Collector*, No.119, February 1994, pps.64-71.

JAMES THURBER
James Thurber: A Bibliography, by Edwin T. Bowden, Ohio State Univ. Press, 1968.

WILLIAM M. TIMLIN
'William Timlin: Author-Artist Extraordinary', by Richard Dalby, *Book and Magazine Collector*, No.99, June 1992, pps.58-63.

J. R. R. TOLKIEN
J.R.R. Tolkien: A Descriptive Bibliography, by Wayne G. Hammond and Douglas Anderson, Oak Knoll Press/St Paul's Bibliographies, 1993.

MARY TOURTEL
The New Rupert Index, by John Beck, privately printed, 1991.

WILLIAM TREVOR
Muriel Spark, William Trevor, Ian McEwan, A Bibliography of their First Editions, David Rees, Colophon Press, 1992.

ANTHONY TROLLOPE
Trollope: A Bibliography by Michael Sadleir, Dawson, 1977.

MARK TWAIN
A Bibliography of the Works of Mark Twain, by Merle Johnson, Harper & Brothers, 1935.

BARRY UNSWORTH
bodhranbooks.com

JOHN UPDIKE
John Updike: A Bibliography, by C. Clarke Taylor, Kent State Univ. Press, 1968.

FLORENCE UPTON
A Lark Ascends, Florence Kate Upton, Artist and Illustrator, by Norma S. Davis, Scarecrow Press, 1992.

ALISON UTTLEY
Alison Uttley: The Life of a Country Child (1884-1976), by Denis Judd, Joseph, 1986.

LAURENS VAN DER POST
Laurens Van Der Post, by Frederic I. Carpenter, Twayne, 1969.

JULES VERNE
Jules Verne: A Bibliography, by Edward and Judith Myers, Country Lane Books, 1989.

GORE VIDAL
Gore Vidal: A Primary and Secondary Bibliography by Robert J. Stanton, Hall, 1978.

KURT VONNEGUT
Kurt Vonnegut Jr.: A Descriptive Bibliography and Annotated Secondary Checklist, by Asa B. Pieratt Jr. and Jerome Klinkowitz, Archon Books, 1974.
Kurt Vonnegut: A Comprehensive Bibliography, by Asa B. Pieratt Jr. et al., Archon Books, 1974.

LOUIS WAIN
Louis Wain: The Man Who Drew Cats, by Rodney Dale, William Kimber, 1968.

ALFRED WAINWRIGHT
Wainwright: The Biography, by Hunter Davies, Joseph, 1995.

A.E. WAITE
A.E. Waite A Bibliography, by R.A. Gilbert, Aquarian Press, 1983.

ALICE WALKER
'An Addiction to Joy: Collecting Alice Walker', by Kathryn Smiley and Jerry Weinstein, *Firsts: The Book Collector's Magazine*, February 1995, Vol.5, No.2, pps.28-33.

EDGAR WALLACE
The British Bibliography of Edgar Wallace, by W.O.G. Lofts and Derek Adley, Howard Baker, 1969.
A Guide to the First Editions of Edgar Wallace, by Charles Kiddle, The Ivory Head Press, 1981.

HORACE WALPOLE
A Bibliography of Horace Walpole, A.T. Hazen, Yale Univ. Press, 1948.

HUGH WALPOLE
Hugh Walpole: A Biography, by Rupert Hart-Davis, Macmillan, 1952.

MINETTE WALTERS
'Minette Walters', *Breese's Guide to Modern First Editions*, Martin Breese, Breese Books, 1999, pps.282-283.

REX WARNER
'Rex Warner', by Mark Valentine, *Book and Magazine Collector*, No.207, June 2001, pps.100-109.

SYLVIA TOWNSEND WARNER
A Bibliography, by R.B. Russell and J. Lawrence Mitchell, Tartarus Press [unpublished].

EVELYN WAUGH
A Bibliography of Evelyn Waugh, by Robert Murray Davis et al., Whitston, 1986.

MARY WEBB
Mary Webb, by Gladys Mary Coles, Seren Books/ Poetry Wales Press, 1990.

DENTON WELCH
Denton Welch: Writer and Artist, by James Methuen-Campbell, Tartarus Press, 2002.

FAY WELDON
Fay Weldon, by Lana Faulks, Gale, 1998 (Twayne's English Authors Series).

H. G. WELLS
Comprehensive Bibliography of H.G. Wells, by M. Katanka, Katanka Ltd., 1968.

PATRICIA WENTWORTH
Detective Fiction: The Collector's Guide, by John Cooper and B.A. Pike, Scolar Press, 1994, pps.306-310.

MARY WESLEY
'Mary Wesley', by David Howard, *Book and Magazine Collector*, No.156, March 1997, pps.14-22.

REBECCA WEST
Rebecca West, by Carl Rollyson, Scribner, 1995.

EDITH WHARTON
A Bibliography of the Writings of Edith Wharton, by Lavinia Davis, Southworth Press, 1933.
Edith Wharton: A Descriptive Bibliography, by Stephen Garrison, Univ. of Pittsburgh Press, 1990.

DENNIS WHEATLEY
'The Historical and Adventure Novels of Dennis Wheatley', by Mike Stotter, *Book and Magazine Collector*, No.119, February 1994, pps.4-14.

E.B. WHITE
E.B. White: A Bibliographical Catalogue of Printed Materials in the Department of Rare Books, Cornell Univ. Library, Garland, 1979.

ETHEL LINA WHITE
The Bibliography of Crime Fiction, 1749-1975, Allen J. Hubin, Publisher's Inc., 1979.

PATRICK WHITE
Patrick White, by Alan Lawson, O.U.P. Australia, 1974.

T.H. WHITE
T.H. White: An Annotated Bibliography, by François Gallix, Garland, 1986.

WALT WHITMAN
The Bibliography of Walt Whitman, by Frank Shay, Friedmans, 1920.

OSCAR WILDE
Bibliography of Oscar Wilde, Stuart Mason (pseud. of Christopher Millard), Bertram Rota, 1967.

CHARLES WILLIAMS
Charles W.S. Williams, A Checklist, by Lois Glenn, Kent State Univ. Press, 1975.

TENNESSEE WILLIAMS
Tennessee Williams: A Bibliography, by Drewey Wayne Gunn, Scarecrow Press, 1980.

HENRY WILLIAMSON
A Bibliography and a Critical Survey of the Works of Williamson, by I. Waveney Girvan, Alcuin Press, 1931.

A.N. WILSON
bodhranbooks.com

ANGUS WILSON
Angus Wilson, by K.W. Gransden, Longmans, Green & Co., 1969.

R.D. WINGFIELD
Detective Fiction: The Collector's Guide, by John Cooper and B.A. Pike, Scolar Press, 1994, pps.311-312.

JEANETTE WINTERSON
British Writers, Supplement IV, Eric Ambler to Jeanette Winterson, by George Stade and Carol Howard, Scribner's, 1997.

WISDEN CRICKETERS'ALMANACKS
'Collecting Wisden Cricketers' Almanacks', by Deryk Brown, *Book and Magazine Collector*, No.111, June 1993, pps.74-83.

P.G. WODEHOUSE
A Bibliography and Reader's Guide to the First Editions of P.G. Wodehouse, by David A. Jasen, Greenhill Books, 1970.

P.G. Wodehouse: A Comprehensive Bibliography and Checklist, by Eileen McIlvaine and James H. Heineman, Heineman, 1991.

TOM WOLFE
Tom Wolfe, by William McKeen, Twayne, 1995.

VIRGINIA WOOLF
A Bibliography of Virginia Woolf, by B.J. Kirkpatrick, Clarendon Press, 1989.

CORNELL WOOLRICH
Cornell Woolrich: A Descriptive Bibliography and Price Guide, by Otto Penzler, Mysterious Bookshop, 1999.

S. FOWLER WRIGHT
Science Fiction and Fantasy Authors, A Bibliography of First Printings of Their Fiction, by Lloyd Currey, Rb Publishing, 2002 (cd rom.)

JOHN WYNDHAM
Science Fiction and Fantasy Authors, A Bibliography of First Printings of Their Fiction, by Lloyd Currey, Rb Publishing, 2002, (cd rom.)

WILLIAM BUTLER YEATS
A Bibliography of the Writings of W.B. Yeats, by Allan Wade, Ruper Hart-Davis, 1958.

THE YELLOW BOOK
The Yellow Book: A Checklist and Index, by Mark Samuels Lasner, The Eighteen Nineties Society, 1998.

APPENDIX III
PSEUDONYMS

This is an aid to identifying some of the alternative names which writers sometimes use.

Alternative Name	Usual Name
352087 A/C Ross	T.E. Lawrence
A Lady of Fashion	Djuna Barnes
Abhavananda	Aleister Crowley
Andrezei, Pierre	Isak Dinesen
Ashdown, Clifford	R. Austin Freeman
Ashe, Gordon	John Creasey
Aston, James	T.H. White
Axton, David	Dean Koontz
Bachman, Richard	Stephen King
Bassetto	George Bernard Shaw
Francis Beeding	Hilary Saunders
Barum Browne	Hilary Saunders
Brust, Howard	Peter Cheyney
Bell, Acton	Anne Brontë
Bell, Currer	Charlotte Brontë
Bell, Ellis	Emily Brontë
Beynon, John	John Wyndham
Bishop, George Archibald	Aleister Crowley
Blake, Nicholas	C. Day Lewis
Blayre, Christopher	E. Heron-Allen
Blixen, Karen	Isak Dinesen
Box, Edgar	Gore Vidal
Boz	Charles Dickens
Bryan, Michael	Brian Moore
Burke, Leda	David Garnett
C.3.3.	Oscar Wilde
Camberg, Muriel	Muriel Spark
Carnac, Carol	E.C.R. Lorac
Carr, H.D.	Aleister Crowley
Carr, Jolyon	Ellis Peters
Catherall, Arthur	'BB'
Chaucer, Daniel	Ford Maddox Ford
Cherry	Benjamin Disraeli
Clerk, N.W.	C.S. Lewis
Clifford, Martin	Frank Richards
Coffey, Brian	Dean Koontz
Cornelius Coffyn	Hilary Saunders
Comte de Fénix	Aleister Crowley
Comus	R.M. Ballantyne
Cooke, M.E.	John Creasey
Cooke, Margaret	John Creasey
Cousins, Sheila	Graham Greene (with Ronald Matthews)
Coyle, William	Thomas Keneally
Credo	John Creasey
Crosby, Henry Grew	Harry Crosby
Daviot, Gordon	Josephine Tey
Davison, Lawrence H.	D.H. Lawrence
Deane, Norman	John Creasey
Derry Down Derry	Edward Lear
Dixon, Carter	John Dickson Carr
Douglas, Michael	Michael Crichton
Douglass, G. Norman	Norman Douglas
Doyle, John	Robert Graves
Dwyer, Deanna	Dean Koontz
Dwyer, K.R.	Dean Koontz
Dwyer, K.R.	Dean Koontz
Earle, William	Captain W.E. Johns
Early, Jon	Captain W.E. Johns
Eastway, Edward	Edward Thomas
Fairbairn, Roger	John Dickson Carr
Farran, Richard M.	John Betjeman
Father Tuck	Louis Wain
Felcamps, Elise	John Creasey
Firth, Violet M.	Dion Fortune
Flying Officer 'X'	H.E. Bates
Frazer, Robert Caine	John Creasey
French, Paul	Isaac Asimov
Furey, Michael	Sax Rohmer
Gaunt, Graham	Jonathan Gash
Gaunt, Jonathan	Jonathan Gash
Gentleman of the University Of Cambridge, A	Aleister Crowley
Gill, Patrick	John Creasey
Grand Orient	A.E. Waite
Grimalkin	Louis Wain
H.B.	Hillaire Belloc
Halliday, Michael	John Creasey
Hamilton, Clive	C.S. Lewis
Hammond, Ralph	Hammond Innes
Harris, John Beynon	John Wyndham
Harris, Johnson	John Wyndham
Haycraft, Anna	Alice Thomas Ellis
Hill, John	Dean Koontz
Hockaby, Stephen	Gladys Mitchell
Hogarth, Charles	John Creasey
Hope, Brian	John Creasey
Hopley, Heorge	Cornell Woolrich
Hudson, Jeffery	Michael Crichton
Hueffer, Ford Maddox	Ford Maddox Ford
Hueffer, H. Ford	Ford Maddox Ford
Hughes, Colin	John Creasey
Hunt, Kyle	John Creasey
Irish, William	Cornell Woolrich
Jones, Edith	Edith Wharton
Kell, Joseph	Anthony Burgess
Kerouac, John	Jack Kerouac
Khan, Khaled	Aleister Crowley
Kittycat	Louis Wain
Leander, Richard	Louis Wain
Lear, Peter	Peter Lovesey
Lee, William (Willy)	William S. Burroughs
Lincoln, Geoffrey	John Mortimer
Lucas, Victoria	Sylvia Plath
Lutiy, the late Major Lutiy	Aleister Crowley
Macdonald, John Ross	Ross Macdonald
Macdonald, John	Ross Macdonald
Mahatma Guru Sri Parahamsa Shivaji	Aleister Crowley
Mallowan, A.C.	Agatha Christie

Malone, Louis	Louis Macniece	Westmacott, Mary	Agatha Christie
Mann, James	John Harvey	Wilson, John Burgess	Anthony Burgess
Manton, Peter	John Creasey	Wingrave, Anthony	S. Fowler Wright
Mara, Bernard	Brian Moore	Wolfe, Aaron	Dean Koontz
March, Maxwell	Margery Allingham	York, Jeremy	John Creasey
Markham, Robert	Kingsley Amis	Young, Collier	Robert Bloch
Marric, J.J.	John Creasey		
Marsden, James	John Creasey		
Master Therion	Aleister Crowley		
Mattheson, Rodney	John Creasey		
McClure, S.S.	Willa Cather		
Millar, Kenneth	Ross Macdonald		
Mitchell, James Leslie	Lewis Grassic Gibbon		
Moorland, Dick	Reginald Hill		
Morgan, Claire	Patricia Highsmith		
Morton, Anthony	John Creasey		
Myles na gCopaleen	Flann O'Brien		
Nabokoff-Sirin, Vladamir	Vladimir Nabokov		
Nichols, Leigh	Dean Koontz		
Norden, Charles	Lawrence Durrell		
Normyx	Norman Douglas		
North, Anthony	Dean Koontz		
O'Casey, Brenda	Alice Thomas Ellis		
Paige, Richard	Dean Koontz		
Palinurus	Cyril Connolly		
Pargeter, Edith	Ellis Peters		
Peeslake, Gaffer	Lawrence Durrell		
Perdurabo, Frater	Aleister Crowley		
Pilgrim, David	Hilary Saunders		
Pollock, Mary	Enid Blyton		
Ramal, Walter	Walter de la Mare		
Ranger, Ken	John Creasey		
Redfern, John	Ellis Peters		
Reed, Eliot	Eric Ambler		
Reid, Desmond	Michael Moorcock		
Reilly, William K.	John Creasey		
Rich, Barbara	Robert Graves (with Laura Riding)		
Richards, Hilda	Frank Richards		
Riley, Tex	John Creasey		
Ruell, Patrick	Reginald Hill		
Seymour, Alan	S. Fowler Wright		
Siluriensis, Leolinus	Arthur Machen		
Somers, Jane	Doris Lessing		
Sparks, Timothy	Charles Dickens		
St John Cooper, Henry	John Creasey		
St. E. A. of M. & S	Aleister Crowley		
Steele, V.M.	Dion Fortune		
Stuart, Ian	Alistair Maclean		
Tanner, Lt-Col., William	Kingsley Amis		
Temple, Paul	Francis Durbridge		
Titmarsh Mr M.A.	W.M. Thackeray		
Torre, Malcolm	Gladys Mitchell		
Traherne, Michael	'BB'		
Underhill, Charles	Reginald Hill		
Verey, Rev. C.	Aleister Crowley		
Vine, Barbara	Ruth Rendell		
Warddel, Nora Helen	E. Heron-Allen		
West, Owen	Dean Koontz		

APPENDIX IV
100 CLASSIC FIRST EDITIONS
OF THE 20th CENTURY

The following list is a personal selection of the 100 most collectable books of the 20th century. It is not a list of the most valuable books, nor is it a list, *per se*, of the literary giants. However, if you managed to acquire all of these you'd have a representative cross section of the most desirable books imaginable!

Amis, Kingsley, *Lucky Jim*
Barrie, J.M., *Peter Pan in Kensington Gardens* (illustrated by Arthur Rackham)
Baum, L. Frank, *The Wonderful Wizard of Oz*
Beckett, Samuel, *En Attendant Godot*
Blyton, Enid, *Five on a Treasure Island: An Adventure Story*
Borges, Jorge Luis, *Fictions*
Bradbury, Ray, *Dark Carnival*
Brooke, Rupert, *1914 and Other Poems*
Burgess, Anthony, *A Clockwork Orange*
Burroughs, Edgar Rice, *Tarzan of the Apes*
Burroughs, William, *The Naked Lunch*
Chandler, Raymond, *The Big Sleep*
Christie, Agatha, *The Mysterious Affair at Styles*
Clarke, Arthur C., *2001 - A Space Odyssey*
Conrad, Joseph, *Heart of Darkness* (in *Youth*)
Louis de Bernières, *Captain Corelli's Mandolin*
Dexter, Colin, *Last Bus to Woodstock*
Doyle, Arthur Conan, *The Hound of the Baskervilles*
Du Maurier, Daphne, *Rebecca*
Durrell, Lawrence, *The Alexandria Quartet*
Eliot, T.S., *Four Quartets*
Eliot, T.S., *The Waste Land*
Ellison, Ralph, *Invisible Man*
Faulkner, William, *The Sound and the Fury*
Fitzgerald, F. Scott, *The Great Gatsby*
Fleming, Ian, *Casino Royale*
Forester, C.S., *The African Queen*
Forster, E.M., *A Passage to India*
Fowles, John, *The Magus*
Francis, Dick, *Dead Cert*
Garcia Marquez, Gabriel, *One Hundred Years of Solitude*
Golding, William, *Lord of the Flies*
Grahame, Kenneth, *The Wind in the Willows*
Grass, Gunter, *The Tin Drum*
Graves, Robert, *I, Claudius*
Greene, Graham, *Brighton Rock*
Hammett, Dashiel, *The Maltese Falcon*
Hartley, L.P., *The Go Between*
Heller, Joseph, *Catch 22*
Hemingway, Ernest, *A Farewell to Arms*
Herbert, Frank, *Dune*
Huxley, Aldous, *Brave New World*
Isherwood, Christopher, *Goodbye to Berlin*
James, Henry, *The Wings of the Dove*
James, M.R., *Ghost Stories of an Antiquary*

James, P.D. *Cover Her Face*
Joyce, James, *Portrait of the Artist as a Young Man*
Joyce, James, *Ulysses*
Kafka, Franz, *The Trial*
Keneally, Thomas, *Schindler's Ark*
Kerouac, Jack, *On the Road*
Kesey, Ken, *One Flew Over the Cuckoo's Nest*
King, Stephen, *Carrie*
Kipling, Rudyard, *Kim*
Koestler, Arthur, *Darkness at Noon*
Lawrence, D.H., *Lady Chatterley's Lover*
Lawrence, D.H., *Sons and Lovers*
Lawrence, T.E., *The Seven Pillars of Wisdom*
Lee, Harper, *To Kill a Mocking Bird*
Lewis, C.S., *The Lion, the Witch and the Wardrobe*
Lovecraft, H.P., *The Outsider*
Lowry, Malcolm, *Under the Volcano*
Madox Ford, Ford, *The Good Soldier*
Miller, Arthur, *Death of a Salesman*
Miller, Henry, *The Tropic of Cancer*
Milne, A.A., *Winnie the Pooh*
Mitchell, Margaret, *Gone With the Wind*
Nabokov, Vladimir, *Lolita*
Nesbit, Edith, *The Railway Children*
Orwell, George, *1984*
Orwell, George, *Animal Farm*
Owen, Wilfred, *Poems*
Peters, Ellis, *A Morbid Taste for Bones*
Plath, Sylvia, *The Bell Jar*
Potter, Beatrix, *The Tale of Peter Rabbit*
Pound, Ezra, *Thirty Cantos*
Pratchett, Terry, *The Colour of Magic*
Proust, Marcel, *A la Recherche du Temps Perdu* (*Remembrance of Things Past*)
Remarque, Erich Maria, *All Quiet on the Western Front*
Rendell, Ruth, *From Doon With Death*
Rowling, J.K., *Harry Potter and the Philosopher's Stone*
Rushdie, Salman, *Midnight's Children*
Salinger, J.D., *The Catcher in the Rye*
Sassoon, Siegfried, *The War Poems*
Seuss, Dr, *The Cat in the Hat*
Solzhenitsyn, Alexander, *A Day in the Life of Ivan Denisovich*
Solzhenitsyn, Alexander, *The Gulag Archipelago*
Spender, Stephen, *Nine Experiments*
Steinbeck, John, *The Grapes of Wrath*
Thomas, Dylan, *Under Milk Wood*
Tolkein, J.R.R., *The Lord of the Rings*
Vonnegut, Kurt, *Slaughterhouse Five*
Walker, Alice, *The Color Purple*
Waugh, Evelyn, *Brideshead Revisited*
White, E.B., *Charlotte's Web*
Williams, Tenessee, *A Streetcar Named Desire*
Wodehouse, P.G., *The Inimitable Jeeves*
Wolfe, Tom, *The Bonfire of the Vanities*
Woolf, Virginia, *To the Lighthouse*

APPENDIX V
THE NOBEL PRIZE FOR LITERATURE

Alfred Nobel stipulated in his will that prizes for Literature should be given to those who, during the preceding year, 'shall have conferred the greatest benefit on mankind' and who 'shall have produced in the field of literature the most outstanding work in an ideal direction'. The Nobel Prize for Literature is therefore awarded to an author rather than a book.

2002 Imre Kertész, Hungary
2001 V.S. Naipaul, United Kingdom
2000 Gao Xingjian, China
1999 Gunter Grass, Germany
1998 Jose Saramago, Portugal
1997 Dario Fo, Italy
1996 Wislawa Szymborska, Poland
1995 Seamus Heaney, Ireland
1994 Kenzaburo Oe, Japan
1993 Toni Morrison, U.S
1992 Derek Walcott, The Antilles/US
1991 Nadine Gordimer, South Africa
1990 Octavio Paz, Mexico
1989 Camilo Jose Cela, Spain
1988 Naguib Mahfouz, Egypt
1987 Joseph Brodsky, U.S.
1986 Wole Soyinka, Nigeria
1985 Claude Simon, France
1984 Jaroslav Seifert, Czechoslovakia
1983 William Golding, England
1982 Gabriel Garcia Marquez, Colombia
1981 Elias Canetti, Bulgaria
1980 Czeslaw Milosz, U.S.
1979 Odysseus Elytis, Greece
1978 Isaac Bashevis Singer, U.S.
1977 Vicente Aleixandre, Spain
1976 Saul Bellow, U.S.
1975 Eugenio Montale, Italy
1974 Henry Martinson, Sweden
1974 Eyvind Johnson, Sweden
1973 Patrick White, Australia
1972 Heinrich Boll, Germany
1971 Pablo Neruda, Chile
1970 Aleksandr Solzhenitsyn, U.S.S.R.
1969 Samuel Beckett, France
1968 Yasunari Kawabata, Japan
1967 Miguel Angel Asturias, Guatemala
1966 Shmuel Yosef Agnon, Israel
1966 Nelly Sachs, Sweden
1965 Mikhail Sholokov, U.S.S.R.
1964 Jean-Paul Sartre, France
1963 Giorgios Seferis, Greece
1962 John Steinbeck, U.S.
1961 Ivo Andric, Yugoslavia
1960 St.-John Perse, France
1959 Salvatore Quasimodo, Italy
1958 Boris Pasternak, U.S.S.R.

1957 Albert Camus, France
1956 Juan Ramon Jimenez, Spain
1955 Halldor Kiljan Laxness, Iceland
1954 Ernest Hemingway, U.S.
1953 Winston Churchill, England
1952 Francois Mauriac, France
1951 Par Lagerkvist, Sweden
1950 Bertrand Russell, England
1949 William Faulkner, U.S.
1948 T.S. Eliot, England
1947 Andre Gide, France
1946 Hermann Hesse, Switzerland
1945 Gabriela Mistral, Chile
1944 Johannes V. Jensen, Denmark
1943 No award given
1942 No award given
1941 No award given
1940 No award given
1939 Frans Eemil Sillanpaa, Finland
1938 Pearl S. Buck, U.S.
1937 Roger Martin Du Gard, France
1936 Eugene O'Neill, U.S.
1935 No award given
1934 Luigi Pirandello, Italy
1933 Ivan Bunin, Russia
1932 John Galsworthy, England
1931 Erik Karlfeldt, Sweden
1930 Sinclair Lewis, U.S.
1929 Thomas Mann, Germany
1928 Sigrid Undset, Norway
1927 Henri Bergson, France
1926 Grazia Deledda, Italy
1925 George Bernard Shaw, England
1924 Wladyslaw Reymont, Poland
1923 William Butler Yeats, Ireland
1922 Jacinto Benavente, Spain
1921 Anatole France, France
1920 Knut Hamsun, Norway
1919 Carl Spitteler, Switzerland
1918 No award given
1917 Karl Gjeilerup, Denmark
1917 Henrik Pontoppidan, Denmark
1916 Verner Von Heidenstam, Sweden
1915 Romain Rolland, France
1914 No award given
1913 Rabindranath Tagore, India
1912 Gerhart Hauptmann, Germany
1911 Maurice Maeterlinck, Belgium
1910 Paul Von Heyse, Germany
1909 Selma Lagerlof, Sweden
1908 Rudolf Eucken, Germany
1907 Rudyard Kipling, England
1906 Giosue Carducci, Italy
1905 Henryk Sienkiewicz, Poland
1904 Jose Echegaray, Spain
1904 Frederic Mistral, France
1903 Bjornstjerne Bjornson, Norway
1902 Theodor Mommsen, Germany
1901 Rene F.A.S. Prudhomme, France

APPENDIX VI
THE BOOKER PRIZE

The Booker Prize for Fiction is perhaps the world's most famous and prestigious literary prize. It is awarded for the best novel of the year written by a citizen of the U.K., British Commonwealth, Eire, Pakistan or South Africa.

2002 *Life of Pi* by Yann Martel
2001 *True History of the Kelly Gang* by Peter Carey
2000 *The Blind Assassin* by Margaret Atwood
1999 *Disgrace* by J.M. Coetzee
1998 *Amsterdam* by Ian McEwan
1997 *The God of Small Things* by Arundhati Roy
1996 *Last Orders* by Graham Swift
1995 *The Ghost Road* by Pat Barker
1994 *How Late It Was, How Late* by James Kelman
1993 *Paddy Clarke Ha Ha Ha* by Roddy Doyle
1992 *The English Patient* by Michael Ondaatje/
　　 Sacred Hunger by Barry Unsworth
1991 *The Famished Road* by Ben Okri
1990 *Possession* by A.S. Byatt
1989 *The Remains of the Day* by Kazuo Ishiguro
1988 *Oscar and Lucinda* by Peter Carey
1987 *Moon Tiger* by Penelope Lively
1986 *The Old Devils* by Kingsley Amis
1985 *The Bone People* by Keri Hulme
1984 *Hotel du Lac* by Anita Brookner
1983 *Life and Times of Michael K* by J.M. Coetzee
1982 *Schindler's Ark* by Thomas Keneally
1981 *Midnight's Children* by Salman Rushdie
1980 *Rites of Passage* by William Golding
1979 *Offshore* by Penelope Fitzgerald
1978 *The Sea, The Sea* by Iris Murdoch
1977 *Staying On* by Paul Scott
1976 *Saville* by David Storey
1975 *Heat and Dust* by Ruth Prawer Jhabvala
1974 *The Conservationist* by Nadine Gordimer
1973 *The Siege of Krishnapur* by J.G. Farrell
1972 *G* by John Berger
1971 *In a Free State* by V.S. Naipaul
1970 *The Elected Member* by Bernice Rubens
1969 *Something to Answer For* by P.H. Newby

APPENDIX VII
THE PULITZER PRIZE

The Pulitzer Prize is named after Hungarian newspaper publisher Joseph Pulitzer. It honours books that depict the positive and negative aspects of the human condition, giving preference to those which portray American life.

2002 *Empire Falls* by Richard Russo
2001 *The Amazing Adventures of Kavalier and Clay* by Michael Chabon
2000 *Interpreter of Maladies* by Jhumpa Lahiri

1999 *The Hours* by Michael Cunningham
1998 *American Pastoral* by Philip Roth
1997 *Martin Dressler: The Tale of an American Dreamer* by Stephen Millhauser
1996 *Independence Day* by Richard Ford
1995 *The Stone Diaries* by Carol Shields
1994 *The Shipping News* by E. Annie Proulx
1993 *A Good Scent from a Strange Mountain* by Robert Olen Butler
1992 *A Thousand Acres* by Jane Smiley
1991 *Rabbit at Rest* by John Updike
1990 *The Mambo Kings Play Songs of Love* by Oscar Hijuelos
1989 *Breathing Lessons* by Anne Tyler
1988 *Beloved* by Toni Morrison
1987 *A Summons to Memphis* by Peter Taylor
1986 *Lonesome Dove* by Larry McMurtry
1985 *Foreign Affairs* by Alison Lurie
1984 *Ironweed* by William Kennedy
1983 *The Color Purple* by Alice Walker
1982 *Rabbit is Rich* by John Updike
1981 *Confederacy of Dunces* by John Kennedy Toole
1980 *The Executioner's Song* by Norman Mailer
1979 *The Stories of John Cheever* by John Cheever
1978 *Elbow Room* by James Alan McPherson
1977 No Award
1976 *Humboldt's Gift* by Saul Bellow
1975 *The Killer Angels* by Michael Shaara
1974 No Award
1973 *The Optimist's Daughter* by Eudora Welty
1972 *Angle of Repose* by Wallace Stegner
1971 No Award
1970 *Collected Stories* by Jean Stafford
1969 *House Made of Dawn* by N. Scott Momaday
1968 *Confessions of Nat Turner* by William Styron
1967 *The Fixer* by Bernard Malamud
1966 *The Collected Stories of Katherine Anne Porter* by Katherine Anne Porter
1965 *The Keepers of the House* by Shirley Ann Grau
1964 No Award
1963 *The Reivers* by William Faulkner
1962 *The Edge of Sadness* by Edwin O'Connor
1961 *To Kill a Mockingbird* by Harper Lee
1960 *Advise and Consent* by Allen Drury
1959 *The Travels of Jaimie McPheeters* by Robert Lewis Taylor
1958 *A Death in the Family* by James Agee
1957 No Award
1956 *Andersonville* by MacKinlay Kantor
1955 *A Fable* by William Faulkner
1954 No Award
1953 *The Old Man and the Sea* by Ernest Hemingway
1952 *The Caine Mutiny* by Herman Wouk
1951 *The Town* by Conrad Richter
1950 *The Way West* by A.B. Guthrie, Jr.
1949 *Guard of Honor* by James Gould Cozzens
1948 *Tales of the South Pacific* by James A. Michener